GUIDE
to
RECORDED
OPERA

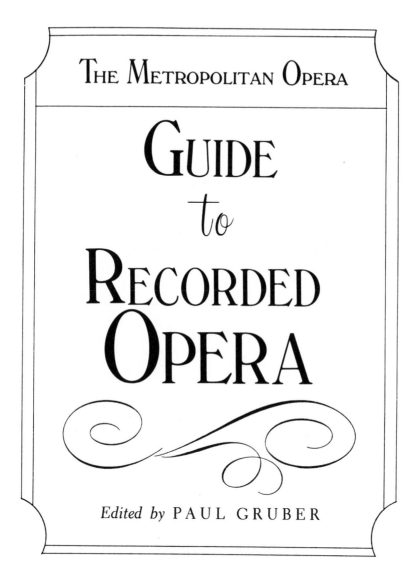

THE METROPOLITAN OPERA

GUIDE to RECORDED OPERA

Edited by PAUL GRUBER

THE METROPOLITAN OPERA GUILD

W·W·NORTON & COMPANY·NEW YORK·LONDON

Printed in the United States of America

The text of this book is composed in Electra with the display set in Windsor. Composition and Manufacturing by the Maple-Vail Book Manufacturing Group. Book design by Antonina Krass, adapted by Jack Meserole.

Library of Congress Cataloging-in-Publication Data
The Metropolitan Opera guide to recorded opera / edited by Paul Gruber.
p.   cm.
Includes index.
1. Operas—Discography.   2. Sound recordings—Reviews.
I. Gruber, Paul.   II. Metropolitan Opera Guild.
ML156.4.O46M5   1993
016.7821'026'6—dc20   92-32618

ISBN 0-393-03444-5

W. W. Norton & Company, Inc., 500 Fifth Avenue, New York, N.Y. 10110
W. W. Norton & Company Ltd., 10 Coptic Street, London WC1A 1PU

2 3 4 5 6 7 8 9 0

Contents

CONTENTS BY OPERA TITLES

PREFACE

The genesis of *The Metropolitan Opera Guide to Recorded Opera* goes back to the mid-1980s, when Roland Gelatt, then an editor for the publishers Thames & Hudson, first told me his idea of a Met guide to opera recordings. Roland himself had written *The Fabulous Phonograph*, which is still the definitive history of the art of recording, and envisioned this project as a series of three books, covering the repertory alphabetically. At the time, we were in the throes of producing *The Metropolitan Opera Encyclopedia*, a book Roland conceived and, sadly, one he did not live to see published.

After Roland's death, I was still eager to pursue this project. With the compact disc revolution in full swing, there seemed to be a real need for an easy-to-use consumers' guide to opera recordings. The record companies were embarking on CD reissue programs that promised future life to virtually all the opera recordings of the past, and opera lovers rebuilding their recording libraries with this new, more expensive format were avid for advice on selecting "the best" *Tristan*, *Aida*, *Gioconda*, or *Turandot*. Other record guides had been published, but even the most complete ones were not easy to use if you were looking for commentary on a specific recording. Most of these guides seemed written for an audience already knowledgeable enough not to need them.

One of the Guild's most successful books had been John W. Freeman's *Stories of the Great Operas*, which we published with W. W. Norton in 1984, and a recording guide seemed a logical companion volume. By the end of 1987, Norton's music editor Claire Brook and I had concocted a plan for a sibling to the Freeman book, which would cover every complete recording made of the 150 operas whose stories John told. (We immediately ran into the first hitch: one of the works, Carlisle Floyd's *Susannah*, had never been commercially recorded. To keep the number of operas even, we added Janáček's *The Cunning Little Vixen*.)

Both Claire and I felt that no single writer would ever live long enough to write such a book, and we liked the idea of having the different points of view of several leading opera critics. Writers were fairly quick to sign on for this project, and most were also quick to realize that what looked like an easy assignment involved grueling detective work (rare recordings had to be *found* before they could be evaluated), endless listening, and finally, arduous writing. Most of the writers admitted that while they had not planned to re-listen to every note of every recording, that level of scrutiny became necessary as they got into the specifics of comparing performances. Years passed, and as some writers got closer to completing their original assignments (while others departed screaming), we began to experience a sort of "sorcerer's apprentice" effect: no sooner would a chapter be completed, when two or three new recordings of the opera would be released, and the process would begin all over again.

The resulting book, while somewhat longer than anticipated, follows a fairly simple format, some of which mirrors that of *The Stories of the Great Operas*. The operas are arranged alphabetically by composer, and chronologically within composer. (There's also an alphabetical table of contents if you can't remember if *Rigoletto* was written before or after *Il Trovatore*.) The rendering of opera and character names also follows that of the Freeman book, in which the original language is generally used; exceptions are those in Slavic languages, where the most familiar English equivalent is given, and two Verdi operas, *I Vespri Siciliani* and *Don Carlo*, both performed most frequently in their Italian editions.

Chapters open with a key to the headings used for each recording, assigning a **letter** and **voice type** for each major cast member from sopranos through basses [e.g., A: Gilda (s); B: Maddalena (ms); D: Duke (t); D: Rigoletto (bar); E: Sparafucile (bs)]. This is followed by an introduction in which important issues are discussed, such as textual differences from recording to recording, cuts, etc.

After this, the recordings are reviewed chronologically, each headed by a recording date and the name of the record label. Assigning dates and labels has been a tricky business. We can't claim to be authoritative as to recording dates—they are the most accurate dates we could find, and are there only as guideposts. When we know a date to be a year of publication rather than recording, we note it with a "p."

The names of international record companies and their labels have changed so often that it is often impossible to list all the labels on which a specific recording has appeared. We have tried to name the label on which the recording is most likely to be found, and in the case of four companies (Decca/London, EMI/Angel, RCA/BMG, and CBS/Sony) have simplified corporate history by combining names. If a review sends you to second-hand record stores in search of an out-of-print 78 or LP, you can use the label as a guide, but should probably search by cast and conductor.

Further codes in the headings are: (M) Mono, (S) Stereo, (D) Digital, and (P) Live performance. A pictogram (CD) indicates that, as of the date this book went to press, a compact disc has appeared. Be advised, however: this does not necessarily mean it is still available on CD, and the absence of the symbol cannot guarantee

that, somewhere in the world, a CD issue does not exist.

The headings serve a graphic purpose as well in that they visually separate one recording from another. The book can be used in either of two ways: each chapter can be read complete, or the critiques of specific recordings can be easily found for a quick answer to "What did they think of . . . ?"

At the conclusion of each complete set of reviews for each opera, the writer has attempted to recommend one particular recording. This has often proved to be an insurmountable problem, for, in more cases than not, there is no single "best" recording of an opera. (This is a fact, and can be demonstrated by locking any three opera experts in a hot room and explaining that they will never again eat or drink until they agree on the best recording of *La Traviata*.) After the recommendation comes a list of the recordings which we were not able to find, as well as any released too late for us to include.

This leads to the next question: which recordings have been included, and which left on the shelves? Basically, there were three rules for inclusion. The first was that the recordings had to represent the complete opera, and while some abridged performances have been countenanced, highlight recordings are not covered. The second rule was that the recording be in the original language of the opera's composition, or in English. This was basically to keep the book from becoming too unwieldy. And while we recognize the existence of recordings of *Tosca* in French, *Carmen* in German, and *Lohengrin* in Italian (not to mention all those wonderful Bulgarian translations), most of these are of interest only to connoisseurs of the arcane, or fans of specific singers. We broke this rule in a few cases, such as the aforementioned *I Vespri Siciliani* and *Don Carlo*, and *Médée* and *La Favorite*, which are rarely heard in their original French.

The final rule will probably bring us a few letters from readers. We banned pirated recordings, unless, as with some of the recent EMI issues or the Met Historic Broadcasts, we were sure that they were issued with the permission of the participants. There were many reasons for this: it was another attempt to control the size of the book, and since many of these recordings are of poor sound quality, they are of little interest to all but aficionados. Perhaps most important is the fact that the Metropolitan Opera perceives the sale of all unauthorized recordings of its performances as infringements on its copyrights and trademark. The Guild can hardly recommend recordings that cannot legally be sold in the United States, and furthermore, cannot imply that recordings of Met performances should receive more legal protection than those of performances from other theaters.

Of course, it is not as easy to spot a pirated recording as it once was. Before CDs, a pirated record was usually pretty obvious: it came in an un- (or badly) marked box, and could be purchased only by mail or in certain stores, which were never found west of the Hudson River or east of the Rockies. But with international compact disc distribution many CDs have come out that at best could be described as borderline; they look like commercial CDs, and offer well-recorded souvenirs of live performances, and if they have been issued with or without the agreement of the artists, only the record company and artists know for sure. A few of these performances have probably found their way into the book, even though we've tried to be diligent.

As an added feature, scattered throughout the book is a series of "Ten Favorite Opera Recordings" lists, which were contributed by intendants of opera houses and celebrities who happen to love opera. (These lists do sometimes include highlight recordings, or pirate recordings, or recordings in unusual languages, but it's hard to tell a celebrity that his favorite recording should not be a pirate.)

Of course, this book would not have been possible without the hard work of the twenty writers who are represented in it, several of whom took on additional assignments after their original work was completed. The contributions of these critics are self-evident, but there are a few additional people whose help would remain unacknowledged if I did not recognize them here. Besides writing several chapters, David Hamilton voluntarily put together the initial list of recordings, which was a starting point for the book. That list was refined, and many recording dates on it confirmed or changed, by John W. N. Francis. Besides David Hamilton, several other collectors generously loaned rare recordings, including Peter G. Davis and Dorle Soria. Among those at the record companies who helped us find recordings were Nancy Zannini of PolyGram Classics, Alison Ames of Deutsche Grammophon, Jack Pfeiffer of BMG Music, and Tony Locantro of EMI.

Above all, I must thank Claire Brook of W. W. Norton for her patience and fortitude. She believed in the book from the beginning and nursed it through many a dark hour, much of the time exclaiming, "This thing is a *monster!*" Thanks to her, the monster has now been let loose on the public.

PAUL GRUBER

GUIDE
to
RECORDED
OPERA

DOMINICK ARGENTO

POSTCARD FROM MOROCCO (1971)

A: Mirror Lady (s); B: Cake Lady (s); C: Foreign Singer (ms); D: First Puppet (t); E: Mr. Owen (t); F: Second Puppet (bar); G: Cornet Man (bs)

orn in Pennsylvania in 1927 of Italian immigrant parents, Dominick Argento has proved one of the most versatile and prolific of United States opera composers. His music, while readily incorporating techniques from the more adventurous contemporary schools, remains traditionally lyrical in its vocal writing. Argento studied with a variety of distinguished teachers—Nicolas Nabokov, Henry Cowell, Hugo Weisgall, Bernard Rogers, Alan Hovhaness, Howard Hanson, Luigi Dallapiccola—and appears to have been inspired by the operas of Benjamin Britten, though his own display greater emotional candor.

Postcard from Morocco, an early, shorter work, shows an experimental bent. Its libretto, by John Donahue, treats puppets as people and vice versa. Setting a stage within a stage, it plays upon the relationship of fantasy and reality. The scene is the waiting room of a railway station in Morocco or some other strange, exotic place in 1914.

p. 1972 DESTO (S) CD

Sarita Roche (A), Barbara Brandt (B), Janis Hardy (C), Yale Marshall (D), Vern Sutton (E), Barry Busse (F), Edward Foreman (G), Center Opera of Minnesota—Philip Brunelle

Desto's recording is based on the premiere production. Four of the roles are doubled; one is tripled. The chamber orchestra consists of only nine players. Because Argento tailored his score for these performers and this cast, the performance is organic and authoritative, creating the work's tenuous atmosphere. Like one of Joseph Cornell's sculpture boxes, *Postcard from Morocco* is a time capsule of nostalgic, mysterious associations. The players are primarily a group of travelers, each idiosyncratic and isolated. The personality of each—a fragile tissue of symbol and illusion contained in his or her suitcase—cannot be shared with the others, who seem embarrassed by intimacy. In the end, Mr. Owen, who is supposed to while away the long wait by painting a postcard portrait of the group, has his paintbox knocked open and shown to be empty. As the others drift away, he embarks on an imaginary odyssey, a childhood fantasy he described earlier.

There is a Mirror Lady, her coloratura glitter dispensed by Sarita Roche; a Foreign Singer (like Daisy Doody in *Aniara*), done by Janis Hardy; an Old Luggage Man, plaintively sung by Yale Marshall. At one point the onstage band plays a pastiche of Wagner themes. There are dull stretches, as when the Cake Lady (Barbara Brandt) tells about her imaginary lover and nothing happens, either in her part or in the orchestra. But then there is a nice dialogue between the Hat Lady (Miss Hardy) and Mr. Owen (Vern Sutton), the voice parts dovetailing antiphonally over guitar accompaniment. Mr. Owen, whose solo has a hard unaccompanied start, eventually makes it to where he's going— off on his flight of fancy.

Despite its desultory pace and patchwork

1

materials, *Postcard from Morocco* weaves a certain spell. Argento's feeling for opera is strong enough to pull the closing scenes together into something that moves, in both senses of the word. And he cannot bring himself to write other than musically for the singing voice. One does not look for stars in such an opera: this is an ensemble performance, and the excellent Minnesota company under Philip Brunelle is itself the star. But many of the vignette portraits are drawn with artful touches by the individual members.

JOHN W. FREEMAN

SAMUEL BARBER

VANESSA (1958)

A: Vanessa (s); B: Erika (ms); C: Old Baroness (ms);
D: Anatol (t); E: Old Doctor (bs)

Given its world premiere by the Metropolitan Opera on January 15, 1958, *Vanessa* continues to be produced with some frequency, in this country at least. From today's perspective, the work now looks like one of the last attempts by an American composer to write an opera in the grand Strauss-Puccini tradition. And for all its derivative, slightly decadent flavor, it remains one of the most stageworthy. Both Gian Carlo Menotti's melodramatic libretto and Barber's lush, neoromantic score were designed with singers and audiences in mind, and a good performance can be as devilishly effective as *Tosca* or *Salome*.

1958 RCA / BMG (S) CD

Eleanor Steber (A), Rosalind Elias (B), Regina Resnik (C), Nicolai Gedda (D), Giorgio Tozzi (E), Metropolitan Opera Chorus and Orchestra—Dimitri Mitropoulos

Recorded soon after the opera's Met premiere, RCA's *Vanessa* has by now acquired the patina of a historic document, and rightly so. It is valuable not only to have this memento of how the first cast performed the piece, but also to hear how the opera was originally conceived, before the composer revised the score into its present three-act form. The title role might have been written for Eleanor Steber, although the part became hers only after Maria Callas and Sena Jurinac turned it down. By the late fifties, Steber's soprano had ripened into its luscious maturity: a full-bodied, richly textured instrument over which she exercised total control, soaring gloriously over Barber's throbbing orchestra and effortlessly negotiating the lacy figurations of Vanessa's tricky Skating Aria. Beyond that, the generously committed spirit of her singing is irresistible, giving dramatic life—even credibility—to a character some may find rather improbable.

While it might be too much to say that *Vanessa* made a star out of Rosalind Elias, the young mezzo-soprano did create enough of a stir for some critics to suggest that the opera might well have been named *Erika*. Certainly she found a part that flattered what was then a fresh, vulnerable vocal presence, and her most appealing qualities come across vividly on these discs. Nicolai Gedda's chameleon-like tenor could be tailored to suit most any operatic style, and here his honeyed cosmopolitan sound and suave vocal manners seem exactly right for that enigmatic seducer Anatol. The subsidiary characters only hover on the periphery of this triangle, but Giorgio Tozzi is endearing as the befuddled Old Doctor, and Regina Resnik's ramrod delivery of the stern Old Baroness's few lines conveys the proper chill. Mitropoulos is the fiery conductor, and the intricate, colorful orchestral score—perhaps *Vanessa's* most impressive ingredient—makes a passionate statement under his hands.

It seems unlikely that this original-cast *Vanessa* will ever have a rival, so anyone interested in American opera should grab the album while it remains available.

PETER G. DAVIS

BÉLA BARTÓK

DUKE BLUEBEARD'S CASTLE (1918)

A: Judith (ms); B: Bluebeard (bs)

Bartók's only opera has exerted an influence on twentieth-century music out of all proportion to its currency as a stage piece. Because the dramatic action is slight, and because the score so vividly depicts what is behind each of the doors in Bluebeard's castle—the clash of armaments, the flash of jewels, the moaning of a lake of tears—this singular one-act dialogue comes across ideally in recordings. Despite its nodding kinship with the Central European expressionism that also begat Strauss's *Elektra*, Bartók's work is more closely aligned with the predominantly French movements of symbolism and impressionism. *Bluebeard's Castle* takes place within man's psyche. Like a theme with variations, it explores the various recesses of personality. It also has been called an allegory of the loneliness of the artist. The two characters, Bluebeard and his latest bride, lack real-life definition, yet they express vivid, credible emotions and must be etched with growing intensity. The orchestral palette, with its trenchant originality of texture, draws as much on Hungarian folk melody and rhythm as on Debussy's *Pelléas et Mélisande*. Therefore the conductor is a partner rather than an accompanist to the singers.

p.1955 BARTÓK (M)

Judith Hellwig (A), Endre Koreh (B), New Symphony of London—Walter Susskind

This landmark recording, engineered by the composer's younger son, Peter Bartók, introduced *Bluebeard's Castle* to its first wide audi-

ence. Like many such pioneering efforts, it lacks that measure of assurance that comes with greater familiarity, but it remains a classic reading—rather careful and understated, adding to the score's dignity and mystery. To the problematic role of Judith, which combines a mezzo's lower range with strong high notes, Hellwig brings a dramatic-soprano voice and a sense of drama, making Judith's fear and determination real. As her enigmatic spouse, Koreh shows a depth of humanity and a linguistic nuance that remain exemplary. Susskind leads an atmospheric, respectful reading. The mono sound, though good for its period, is a bit constricted in detailing and dynamic range.

1956 HUNGAROTON (M) CD

Klára Palánkay (A), Mihály Székely (B), Budapest Philharmonic—János Ferencsik

This "historic performance" recording was made at a concert or broadcast reading under Ferencsik, a Bartók specialist. There are some rough edges here and there due to minor memory lapses by the soloists, but the singing and orchestral playing have a dramatic verisimilitude and fervor less evident in studio-recorded versions. Palánkay, who does not even attempt the high C at the start of the fifth-door episode, shows a strong lower register; hers is not a luscious but a strong, firm tone, capable of registering awe and reaction. Székely's big, loose voice, though more than somewhat wobbly, conveys authority; to avoid sustained high passages, he uses lower alternates, said to have

4

been devised or sanctioned for him by the composer. Both singers deliver their lines with natural syncopation, dictated more by the language than by the printed notes. The orchestra, while not a virtuoso ensemble, attacks sharply and plays with energy. Ferencsik takes aggressive tempos in the fast parts, giving the score more tension than most readings (including his own later one). Recorded sound, however, suffers from lackluster imaging and restricted spatial range.

1962 CBS / SONY (In English) (S)

Rosalind Elias (A), Jerome Hines (B), Philadelphia Orchestra—Eugene Ormandy

Hearing this opera in English, one gains a comprehension of the text but loses the accentuation of the original language, which helps to shape and propel the singers' phrases. This, along with the solidly professional but not highly profiled personalities of soloists and conductor, may account for the relative blandness of the CBS reading. Elias and Hines sing handsomely and enunciate clearly, creating figures credible to an English-speaking listener. Ormandy details the score carefully, taking advantage of the rich sonority of the Philadelphia Orchestra, but there is little sweep or impulse.

1962 MERCURY / PHILIPS (S) CD

Olga Szönyi (A), Mihály Székely (B), London Symphony Orchestra—Antal Dorati

Though Mercury recordings were noted in their time for high engineering fidelity, this disc, originally from 35mm. film, sounds unremarkable today, and in fact the big final climax seems repressed. Three Hungarian interpreters collaborate on a temperamentally close-geared performance. Dorati, a champion of Bartók's music, has an instinct for its style and plays it impulsively, subordinating many details to the larger importance of narrative surge. Szönyi sings with stylistic grasp but unsteady, woolly, edgy tone. Székely, who coached his role with Bartók in the late 1920s, has lost some of his power but little of his majesty; in one high-lying section, he uses alternate lines supplied by the composer. Both singers read the syncopations of the first-syllable-accented text with greater freedom of note values than most of their opposite numbers in other recordings.

1965 DECCA / LONDON (S) CD

Christa Ludwig (A), Walter Berry (B), London Symphony Orchestra—István Kertész

Both Ludwig and Berry sing expressively and with attractive tone, though one might ask a shade more subtlety from the former, a more chilling sense of mystery and alienation from the latter. Carefully coached in Hungarian, the singers enunciate it for the most part correctly and effectively. Though a conductor of temperament, Kertész opts for clarity and sensitivity rather than overt dramatics, bringing out the radiance and sadness of the score, shading its emotional and intellectual chiaroscuro. The LP version was criticized for shortness of bass, a problem overcome with the CD transfer.

1973 WESTMINSTER (In Russian) (S)

Nina Poliakova (A), Yevgeny Kibkalo (B), Bolshoi Theater Orchestra—Gennady Rozhdestvensky

Both singers offer exciting timbre, sensitive dynamics, steady tone, and dramatic flair—but in Russian, which is likely to interest only those conversant with the language. Rozhdestvensky's conducting, somewhat short on atmosphere, emphasizes tension and color, though the engineers have not fully captured the climaxes. There are half a dozen brief cuts, hard to justify musically; perhaps the aim was to fit the work on two LP sides, but other versions show this can be done without cutting.

1976 CBS / SONY (S)

Tatiana Troyanos (A), Siegmund Nimsgern (B), BBC Symphony Orchestra—Pierre Boulez

Like Ludwig, Troyanos sings Judith with dramatic intensity, and her fine points of interpretation show even more polish. Nimsgern, a baritone Bluebeard in a bass-baritone role, suggests its noble remoteness if not its dark coloration. Boulez's meticulous balances and textures do not always make up for his less than urgent approach; this is a score of continually shifting pace, and both his leadership and the orchestra's response betray a certain lack of sheer involvement. Highly resonant recording also damps the clarity of his reading.

1979 DECCA / LONDON (S) CD

Sylvia Sass (A), Kolos Kováts (B), London Philharmonic Orchestra—Georg Solti

Sass, an interesting dramatic-coloratura sofjprano in the Callas / Sutherland tradition, uses a less veiled sound here than in some of her other recordings. Though she suggests an in-depth characterization of Judith, her singing remains curiously recessive, to the point of sometimes being covered by the orchestra. Kováts, not a very firm or imposing Bluebeard, starts out with spread tone but does well by the eloquent, moving final scene, in which he describes how he found his wives. Solti too does his best work here, climaxing an otherwise often un-Solti-like performance: neither driven, tensile, nor especially clearly pointed, it takes its time, notably during the Lake of Tears episode, which Solti reads as truly mournful. In general, if lacking the *slancio* of Dorati and Kertész, Solti's *Bluebeard* is quite gripping in its own way. Minor defects of the recording are its resonance around Kováts's voice and the lack of prominence it gives the flute, some of whose detail is lost. As a curiosity, the spoken introduction by a Bard—usually omitted—is included here.

1979 DEUTSCHE GRAMMOPHON (S) CD

Julia Varady (A), Dietrich Fischer-Dieskau (B), Bavarian State Orchestra—Wolfgang Sawallisch

Varady makes a great deal of the gradual development in Judith's character, from a frightened start to an almost exalted climax as she succeeds in opening one door after another of Bluebeard's gloomy castle. Vulnerable and mysterious, she profits from a secure lower register. Fischer-Dieskau, however, presents too gentle and smooth a Bluebeard, and as a baritone he is handicapped by the wrong vocal color: his first line takes him to a bottom F-sharp, which he can only fake, and the general lack of weight makes him a less threatening figure than Varady's hesitancy implies. Sawallisch's well-balanced reading integrates the score's variegated elements without making capital of its contrasts and dramatic drive.

1981 HUNGAROTON (S) CD

Elena Obraztsova (A), Yevgeny Nesterenko (B), Hungarian State Opera Orchestra—János Ferencsik

Ferencsik recorded Bartók's opera several times: this is his final one, with Russian soloists singing in Hungarian. Obraztsova's sumptuous timbre suits the ripe, sunset coloration of the scoring, but her diction is covered and mealy-mouthed, muzzling the music's raw power in such a way as to subdue its dramatic thrust. Nesterenko, gifted with authoritative bass tone, renders some of the unwritten syncopations that are implicit in the language, usually lost in any translated performance. Ferencsik, steeped in the score, leads an atmospheric account. His orchestra may lack such sheer flash as one finds in the Kertész or Solti versions, but an instinct for the folk-based style (in turns by the solo clarinet, for example) gives this reading a special authenticity.

1987 CBS / SONY (S,D) CD

Eva Marton (A), Samuel Ramey (B), Hungarian State Orchestra—Adam Fischer

Most Judiths, mezzo or otherwise, tend to waver in the first half of *Bluebeard*, which lays the heaviest demands on them; by the time they are settled in the role, its requirements lighten. Eva Marton, a strong soprano, is no exception. She does not find the lower reaches especially congenial, but the brightness of her tone, as it unfolds upward, illuminates where others sometimes labor. The title role is easier, in that the bass can warm up at a natural pace, but it too can be taxing, as in the passage "Lásd ez az én birodalmam" (Now behold my spacious kingdom), where Bluebeard's domain is strewn with high Es. Ramey, sounding well coached in Hungarian, rises to the occasion here. His Achilles' heel is the lure of a big, expansive tone, but in portraying Bluebeard's gradual transformation from laconic to grandiloquent he achieves thrilling effect without undue pressure. Fischer elicits warmth and spirited playing from the orchestra. If his reading is a little tame in comparison with the more tensile Dorati or Kertész, its tendency toward restraint is not unwelcome, and big moments, such as the climax near the end, are given full pedal.

Dorati's is the most impassioned and dramatically alive reading. Kertész, Ferencsik, and Solti achieve intensity with somewhat less impulse. A pairing of the best Judith (Troyanos, Ludwig, or Varady) with the best Bluebeard (Székely or Ramey) cannot be found. Yet in no version is the casting really substandard, and one cannot go wrong with any of these recordings. For the hi-fi enthusiast, Fischer's digital *Bluebeard* is a sonic trip into Bartók's multi-faceted score.

JOHN W. FREEMAN

Unavailable for review:
1970 HUNGAROTON

PETER HEMMINGS
General Director,
Los Angeles Music Center Opera

1. **Gershwin,** *Porgy and Bess*: Mitchell, Quivar, Hendricks, Conrad, Clemmons, White, Thompson, Boatwright—Maazel. DECCA / LONDON

2. **Handel,** *Alcina*: Augér, Hickox. EMI / ANGEL

3. **Musgrave,** *Mary, Queen of Scots*: Putnam, Garrison, Busse, Gardner, Bell, Soriano—Mark. MOSS MUSIC GROUP

4. **Offenbach,** *Orpheus in the Underworld*: Bronhill, Miller, Shilling, Crofoot—Faris. EMI / ANGEL

5. **Berlioz,** *Les Troyens* (Final Scene): Baker—Gibson. EMI/ANGEL

6. **Puccini,** *Madama Butterfly* (Love Duet): Ricciarelli, Carreras—Gardelli. PHILIPS

7. **Strauss,** *Der Rosenkavalier* (excerpts): Dernesch, Howells, Cahill, Langdon—Gibson. EMI / ANGEL

8. **Verdi,** *Il Trovatore* (excerpts): Fretwell, Johnson, Craig, Glossop, McIntyre—Moore. EMI / ANGEL

9. **Verdi,** *Otello*: Plowright, Squires, Craig, Bottone, Howlett—Elder. EMI / ANGEL

10. **Wagner,** *Tristan und Isolde*: Price, Fassbaender, Kollo, Fischer-Dieskau, Moll—Kleiber. DEUTSCHE GRAMMOPHON

LUDWIG VAN BEETHOVEN

FIDELIO
(1805; revised 1806 and 1814)

A: Leonore (s); B: Marzelline (s); C: Florestan (t); D: Jacquino (t);
E: Don Pizarro (bar); F: Rocco (bs); G: Don Fernando (bs)

*B*eethoven wanted to call his opera *Leonore*, but was persuaded to change the title to *Fidelio* to avoid confusion with an opera on the same subject by Ferdinand Paer. Today we use the title *Leonore* to distinguish the original 1805 version of the opera from the definitive 1814 rewrite. There is one commercial studio recording of *Leonore*, which will be discussed below. All of the other recordings of the opera use the 1814 text.

The musical numbers of *Fidelio* are never cut to any significant extent in modern performances, and all of the recordings are complete in this respect (the exception is the Toscanini set, in which a literal repeat, which all the other conductors dutifully observe, is dropped).

A recording of *Fidelio*, to be taken seriously, must include at least a modicum of the spoken dialogue that connects and sets up the musical numbers. The RCA/Toscanini and EMI/Furtwängler recordings present the score in "concert" form (i.e., as a succession of musical numbers, without any dialogue); as fine as they are, neither can be recommended as a collector's only version of the opera.

Regarding the dialogue, two further points should be made. All of the recordings that do include dialogue abridge it to a greater or lesser extent. No recording, for example, includes the little exchange that should provide a breathing space between the end of the Act I trio ("Gut, Söhnchen, gut") and the subsequent march. I

would agree that we do not need to hear every word of the original dialogue. However, some of the traditionally omitted material has a realism that is interesting from the dramatic standpoint. The fairly matter-of-fact conversation between husband and wife after "O namenlose Freude" is a good example: in performance, this is almost always either reduced to a bare minimum or rewritten.

Another *Fidelio* performance tradition is the practice, apparently begun by Mahler in Vienna, of interpolating the Overture we now refer to as *Leonore* No. 3 into Act II, as a sort of symphonic intermezzo before the opera's final scene. All of the recordings of the 1814 score respect Beethoven's final decision by prefacing the opera with the *Fidelio* Overture. Eight of the recordings discussed below also include *Leonore* No. 3; as a general rule, the older the recording, the more likely it is to contain this bonus.

1943 VOX (M,P)

Hilde Konetzni (A), Irmgard Seefried (B), Torsten Ralf (C), Peter Klein (D), Paul Schöffler (E), Herbert Alsen (F), Tomislav Neralic (G), Vienna State Opera Chorus and Orchestra—Karl Böhm

I heard a worn pressing of the Artia edition, which is in artificial stereo. The sound was atrocious, but I am reliably informed that the Vox version, in undoctored mono, is no better.

This is a shame, for the performance is obviously a fine one. Although derived from a concert performance, the recording includes enough of the dialogue to provide dramatic continuity between the musical numbers; *Leonore* No. 3 is inserted before the final scene.

Karl Böhm paces the music well, phrasing the lyrical sections with great warmth and building steadily to rousing climaxes. His orchestra and chorus are proficient, however shoddily reproduced.

Two members of the cast are disappointing. Hilde Konetzni's large, warm voice is a good match for Leonore, and she sings musically and with temperament. But the instrument is under imperfect control, and goes wild at the top. Anything above G tends to be either cautious or desperate-sounding, and "Abscheulicher!" (the whole scene, not just the opening recitative) is a mess. Herbert Alsen is a dull Rocco, and sounds more like a baritone than a bass in weight and timbre.

The rest of the cast, however, is a prize crew. Torsten Ralf displays a healthy tenor with some ring at the top, and manages to make Florestan sound both heroic and vulnerable. He has a worthy adversary in the Pizarro of Paul Schöffler, whose dark, velvety bass-baritone is almost too beautiful for the role; as singing, though, Schöffler's performance is impeccable. The young Irmgard Seefried is a ravishing Marzelline, well partnered by Peter Klein's alert Jacquino. Tomislav Neralic is a superior Don Fernando; one wishes he had been given the larger role of Rocco instead.

1944 RCA / BMG (M,P) CD

Rose Bampton (A), Eleanor Steber (B), Jan Peerce (C), Joseph Laderoute (D), Herbert Janssen (E), Sidor Belarsky (F), Nicola Moscona (G), NBC Symphony Chorus and Orchestra—Arturo Toscanini

This famous recording, drawn from NBC broadcasts of December 10 and 17, 1944, has two serious liabilities: all of the spoken dialogue is eliminated, except for the Act II melodrama; even Jacquino's interruption of the subsequent quartet is missing, so that "Es schlägt der Rache Stunde" follows hard upon the second trumpet call. The other major problem is the dry, boxy sound, which drains both voices and instruments of color, and hardly does justice to the superior playing by the NBC Symphony (especially the winds and horns).

Arturo Toscanini rushes through the Overture and the Jacquino / Marzelline scene as though he is eager to get to the more dramatic episodes. Other numbers that seem "too fast" at first acquaintance (e.g., the Leonore / Marzelline / Rocco trio) may be legitimately exciting after repeated hearings, and the Act I finale has a fine, suspenseful tension. Toscanini, incidentally, cuts the repeat of the march in Act I. Act II (which presumably stems from the second broadcast) is paced just about perfectly (and Toscanini sings up a storm all through it). For the LP edition, an intense performance of *Leonore* No. 3 (from a later broadcast) is inserted in the traditional place; the CD includes *Leonore* No. 3 from the concert.

Both sopranos are good. Rose Bampton is a dignified Leonore, her rather compact, well-focused sound tracing the heroine's music with unusual accuracy and incisiveness. Eleanor Steber's bright, poised Marzelline is a further asset—Toscanini must have been pleased by her ability to hit all her notes, not only accurately but expressively, at his very fast speeds.

Jan Peerce never sang Florestan onstage, but learned the role at Toscanini's insistence. He is altogether excellent. His vowel formation and legato are superior to many of his German counterparts ("In des Lebens Frühlingstagen" is a good place to make comparisons), and his fervent, unaffected delivery is most welcome.

Despite his reputation, Herbert Janssen strikes me as a dull, clumsy Pizarro. "Ha! welch' ein Augenblick!" falls flat—despite the magnificent support given the soloist by Toscanini and the superb male chorus—and so does the subsequent duet with Rocco. In the latter role, Sidor Belarsky has good intentions, but his actual vocalism is weak and muffled.

1953 EMI / ANGEL (M) CD

Martha Mödl (A), Sena Jurinac (B), Wolfgang Windgassen (C), Rudolf Schock (D), Otto Edelmann (E), Gottlob Frick (F), Alfred Poell (G), Vienna State Opera Chorus, Vienna Philharmonic Orchestra—Wilhelm Furtwängler

As on the Toscanini set, most of the spoken dialogue is eliminated, except for the Act II melodrama and the Jacquino / Rocco exchange during the subsequent quartet. *Leonore* No. 3 once again precedes the final scene, but this slow, sluggish performance of the Overture makes it seem like even more of a dramatic intrusion than usual.

The Vienna Philharmonic does not entirely live up to its reputation here: there are a surprising number of moments of ragged ensemble, and the horns make a poor showing in "Komm, Hoffnung."

Wilhelm Furtwängler, not surprisingly, takes a rather stately approach to much of the score. The performance seems to get slower as it goes along. The Prisoners' Chorus (with an excessively lugubrious-sounding chorus and two dull soloists) is the first number that seems to be drawn out too long for its own good. Sometimes, of course, the deliberate pacing is beneficial: in this laid-back rendition of the Act II quartet, every word and note can for once be clearly articulated, and Martha Mödl, in particular, is able to play her registers against each other to good effect, in lines that often sound awkward when rushed.

The cast is uneven. Sena Jurinac has a larger, warmer voice than most Marzellines on records; as sheer sound, her singing is lovely, but many of her words are hard to catch—in part because of her strong Viennese accent. By contrast, Rudolf Schock, the Jacquino, is verbally clear and incisive, with a more powerful voice than most tenors cast in the role.

Otto Edelmann, though a true bass, has no difficulty with the high tessitura of Pizarro's music, but he is entirely too gentle of temperament—many key lines, such as "Ein Stoss . . . und er verstummt," are virtually thrown away. The Rocco of Gottlob Frick provides an instructive contrast: Frick hardly possesses the most beautiful bass voice imaginable (and, in fact, is below par here, often sounding both nasal and tubby), but he sings with unfailing dramatic involvement.

The heroic couple is problematic. Mödl's voice betrays its mezzo-soprano origins: the sound is powerful but often hooty in timbre, and the tonal production is strained throughout—she seems to be squeezing out the high notes by sheer will power. She is highly musical and a resourceful interpreter, but the vocalism is too effortful for comfort. Wolfgang Windgassen's Florestan offers an uneasy compromise: he does not possess the weight or resonance of a true dramatic tenor, but he doesn't have much sweetness of tone or phrase very lyrically, either. Nor does he do anything extraordinary with the role from an interpretive standpoint.

1957 DEUTSCHE GRAMMOPHON (S) ℗

Leonie Rysanek (A), Irmgard Seefried (B), Ernst Häfliger (C), Friedrich Lenz (D), Dietrich Fischer-Dieskau (E), Gottlob Frick (F), Kieth Engen (G), Bavarian State Opera Chorus and Orchestra—Ferenc Fricsay

Ferenc Fricsay's *Fidelio*, as heard here, is taut and unsentimental, but also somewhat literal, hard-driven, and lacking in warmth and expressivity. The performance is more efficient than beautiful, and not particularly dramatic, either—fast tempos, firm rhythms, and sharp accents do not automatically create theatrical excitement. The orchestral playing is loud and uninflected, and the choral singing has more vigor than polish.

Leonie Rysanek has some vocally untidy moments (the notoriously difficult runs and leaps in "Ich folg' dem innern Triebe" defeat her), but she is an impulsive, undeniably exciting Leonore.

Seefried, her voice noticeably darker in timbre and more carefully produced than it was on the Vox / Böhm set, is still a distinguished Marzelline. Frick is once again a fine Rocco, although he got more eloquence out of the part at Furtwängler's more expansive tempos.

Ernst Häfliger's voice is on the light side for Florestan, but he uses his lyric instrument with great skill. He suffers the most from Fricsay's insensitive conducting.

Dietrich Fischer-Dieskau's lyric baritone is too lightweight for Pizarro. He hits the downbeats hard, snarls in the recitatives, and shouts the high notes, all in a futile attempt to compensate for the tonal resources that are not his to command. The result is a performance that is overwrought and comes dangerously close to being vulgar.

The dialogue is not only heavily abridged and spoken by a separate cast of actors; it is recorded in a different acoustic than the music. The solo voices are too closely miked for comfort; otherwise, the stereo sound is good for its date. *Leonore* No. 3 is omitted.

p.1957 NONESUCH (S)

Gladys Kuchta (A), Melitta Muszely (B), Julius Patzak (C), Helmut Kretschmar (D), Heinz Rehfuss (E), Karl Kümmel (F), Erich Wenk (G), North German Radio Chorus and Orchestra—Carl Bamberger

When it was first released domestically by Nonesuch, in the mid-sixties, this recording filled a gap: a stereo *Fidelio*, with dialogue, available at a very low price. Today, however, the gap no longer exists, and one tends to judge the Nonesuch production more harshly. It's the kind of performance that might make for an enjoyable evening if you found yourself in a small town in Germany and decided to check out the local opera house, but is hardly distinguished enough to stand up to the test of repeated hearings back home.

Carl Bamberger, in fact, conducts the score neatly and with some feeling, and the orchestral and choral work is solidly professional, if short on nuance.

There is one major-league vocal performance: Heinz Rehfuss brings a dark-timbred, rock-solid bass-baritone and plenty of malevolence to Pizarro.

Julius Patzak, though a great tenor, is probably too light of voice for Florestan to begin with, and was recorded well past his prime. He pulls himself together for some reasonably good vocalism during "In des Lebens Frühlingstagen" and "Euch werde Lohn," but runs into serious trouble in the quartet, the duet with Leonore, and the Act II finale.

Gladys Kuchta, the Leonore, may not be a very accurate or subtle singer, but she is loud. Melitta Muszely's Marzelline is thin, shrill, and tremulous. The Jacquino, Rocco, and Don Fernando are barely adequate, the sound (at least on Nonesuch's LP pressings) mediocre. *Leonore* No. 3 is not included.

1961 WESTMINSTER / MCA (S) CD

Sena Jurinac (A), Maria Stader (B), Jan Peerce (C), Murray Dickie (D), Gustav Neidlinger (E), Dezsö Ernster (F), Frederick Guthrie (G), Bavarian State Opera Chorus and Orchestra—Hans Knappertsbusch

The original Westminster LP set included *Leonore* No. 3; the MCA reissue, on two bargain-priced CDs, omits it.

Hans Knappertsbusch's tempos are consistently slower than any other conductor's—even Furtwängler and Klemperer seem impatient by comparison. The result is inevitably a stately, abstract performance of the score, more oratorio than opera, often fascinating to hear but difficult to recommend as one's only recording of the opera. The Munich orchestra and chorus turn in superior work (they sound much better than they did under Fricsay, despite some of the obvious difficulties imposed on them by Knappertsbusch's slow-motion pacing).

There is an oddly assorted cast. Peerce is even better than he was on the RCA / Toscanini set: his voice is noticeably darker and more mature in timbre (an advantage, in this role), and he uses it just as stylishly.

Jurinac, Furtwängler's Marzelline, attempts Leonore here. Her voice is still lovely in timbre, and used with great skill; but it is definitely on the light side for the music, and the big moments tax her. Once again, her strong Viennese accent (with "ich" shortened to "i' " most of the time) is distracting.

Maria Stader, although a fine singer, is really too mature in timbre and impersonal in manner for Marzelline.

There are interesting contributions from Murray Dickie, a shrewd Jacquino, and Dezsö Ernster, a remarkably saturnine Rocco. Gustav Neidlinger is an uncommonly malevolent-sounding Pizarro, but his actual singing is rough-edged and strained.

The early stereo sound is good. At least some of the dialogue seems to have been assigned to a separate cast of actors; in his memoirs Peerce states that it is his voice on the finished recording. The production uses some amusingly literal-minded sound effects (e.g., rattling chains): the creak of the dungeon door is straight out of *Tales from the Crypt*.

1962 EMI / ANGEL (S) CD

Christa Ludwig (A), Ingeborg Hallstein (B), Jon Vickers (C), Gerhard Unger (D), Walter Berry (E), Gottlob Frick (F), Franz Crass (G), Philharmonia Chorus and Orchestra—Otto Klemperer

From the time of its initial release, this recording has been considered something quite special. Otto Klemperer's conducting is uniquely magisterial: although his tempo choices are by no means invariably slow, the reading has compelling weight and grandeur, and the conductor sustains tension even in the most static moments. The orchestral playing is wonderfully alert, with every detail in the instrumental writing falling naturally into place. (*Leonore No. 3* is not included.)

Christa Ludwig, although a mezzo-soprano, hits some high Bs that would be the envy of many a dramatic soprano, and of course brings an uncommon richness of timbre to the bottom octave, where a great deal of Leonore's music lies ("Komm, Hoffnung" is a typical example). Naturally, though, there is not much sense of real ease or float in the upper fifth of the range. Dramatically, she is strong—more heroic than vulnerable, which seems to suit Klemperer's conception.

Jon Vickers brings unique intensity to Florestan's music (and to the spoken dialogue), although his voice does not have the kind of warmth and roundness that would be ideal for the role, and he sometimes fails to sustain the line as he should. A great performance, nonetheless. This larger-than-life Florestan and Leonore are well matched against Walter Berry's Pizarro: Berry has a more attractive voice than we usually hear in the role, and manages to convey nastiness without sacrificing musical accuracy.

Frick's third recorded Rocco is, on balance, his best: a very warm and human portrayal, handsomely sung.

Ingeborg Hallstein and Gerhard Unger are effective as the young lovers, although neither possesses much sensuality of timbre. Franz Crass, with his dark, smooth bass, would be hard to improve upon as Don Fernando.

The LP edition of this recording still sounds fine, and the transfer to CD is impressively clear, detailed, and impactive in sound.

1964 DECCA / LONDON (S)

Birgit Nilsson (A), Graziella Sciutti (B), James McCracken (C), Donald Grobe (D), Tom Krause (E), Kurt Böhme (F), Hermann Prey (G), Vienna State Opera Chorus, Vienna Philharmonic Orchestra—Lorin Maazel

Lorin Maazel's tempos are often insanely fast—this is certainly the speediest *Fidelio* on records—and he indulges in some violent dynamic contrasts and accents that strike me as crude (rather than "dramatic," which was presumably the intention). His more recent operatic work suggests that he would conduct this score quite differently today.

Maazel reduces the number of strings in the more intimate numbers—an interesting idea in theory, although the effect is hard to judge here because of all the sonic manipulation going on. The orchestral work is expert for the most part (some of the Viennese wind chording is rather thick in sound), and the chorus is outstanding.

Birgit Nilsson, of course, is a true dramatic soprano (as opposed to a merely loud one), capable of suggesting both heroic resolve and womanly vulnerability through vocal coloration alone. She seems to thrive on Maazel's tempos, and is always rhythmically on the mark. This is one of her best recorded performances.

Partnering Nilsson with James McCracken probably made sense on paper, since he was one of the few tenors around in 1964 who matched Nilsson in vocal caliber. But the voice is under constant pressure, and never really sounds relaxed or lyrical. In addition, some of his attempts at dramatic inflection sound self-conscious.

Tom Krause, a relatively small-scaled Pizarro, sensibly plays to the microphone instead of trying to make his voice sound bigger than it really is; he also steers clear of some of the traditional ranting and raving.

Kurt Böhme brings a good deal of common sense and earthy humor to his portrayal of Rocco, and sings the music handsomely with his large, "black" bass. Graziella Sciutti sings prettily and with a girlish charm; as so often with this artist, though, a critical listener might be bothered by her habit of pecking away at individual notes instead of really sustaining the line. She is well matched by Donald Grobe's slender-voiced, convincingly boyish-sounding Jacquino. Hermann Prey is luxurious casting as Don Fernando.

The fast tempos and the omission of *Leonore* No. 3 make it possible for the performance to fit onto two LPs without strain. The sound is typical of Decca's mid-sixties work: rich and detailed, yet with certain artificialities. It's obvious that, because Krause's voice isn't as large or as powerful as Nilsson's or McCracken's, the engineers are boosting his volume to match theirs. The use of an echo chamber to suggest Florestan's dungeon is another sonic blot.

1969 DEUTSCHE GRAMMOPHON (S)

Gwyneth Jones (A), Edith Mathis (B), James King (C), Peter Schreier (D), Theo Adam (E), Franz Crass (F), Martti Talvela (G), Leipzig Radio Choir, Dresden State Opera Chorus, Dresden State Orchestra—Karl Böhm

1970 was the two-hundredth anniversary of Beethoven's birth, and this *Fidelio* was one of many recordings planned specifically in honor of the bicentennial. Böhm's conducting is masterful, combining dramatic tension with lyric warmth in ideal proportions. I can't pigeonhole the approach as fast or slow, or heavy as opposed to lightweight—it all just sounds like Beethoven. This is the kind of recording that stands up well to the test of repeated playing. The performance is beautifully executed by the Dresden orchestra; the combined Leipzig and Dresden choruses are also superb.

The cast is without serious weaknesses.

Gwyneth Jones manages to sound both dignified and impulsive in the title role. She resembles Rysanek in many respects: the same warm, rich, womanly vocal quality; the same soaring top; the same fearless approach to the technical hurdles. Jones has a few hooty and edgy moments, but, for the most part, she is one of the most satisfying Leonores on the complete sets.

James King has more of an Italianate ring to his voice than most Florestans, and approaches the role in a straightforward, mature manner that is refreshingly devoid of histrionics.

Edith Mathis brings a warm lyric soprano and great charm to Marzelline, and Peter Schreier is typically incisive as Jacquino. Theo Adam does not possess the most sensuous timbre imaginable, but Pizarro does not really need vocal beauty, and Adam gives him power and intensity.

From the purely vocal point of view, Franz Crass (Klemperer's Don Fernando) is the best Rocco on any of the complete recordings, singing as smoothly, richly, and securely as one could desire. Interpretively, too, he is strong. Martti Talvela's Don Fernando, weighty and very distinctive in timbre, easily dominates the final scene.

Leonore No. 3 is included. The sound of this recording is excellent.

1970 EMI / ANGEL (S) (D

Helga Dernesch (A), Helen Donath (B), Jon Vickers (C), Horst Laubenthal (D), Zoltan Kélémen (E), Karl Ridderbusch (F), José van Dam (G), Chorus of the Deutsche Oper, Berlin, Berlin Philharmonic Orchestra—Herbert von Karajan

Like so many of Herbert von Karajan's opera recordings, his *Fidelio* is very beautifully executed, but a little mannered and lacking in spontaneity at times. The opening pages of the overture are typical of Karajan's predilection for violent tempo and dynamic contrasts: the four bars of dotted figurations (marked *allegro* and *forte*) are hammered out with almost brutal force, and they are followed by eight bars for horns and clarinets (marked *adagio* and *p, dolce*), played here very slowly indeed and with a rapt, mysterious tonal quality worthy of the Grail episodes in *Parsifal*. There are similar exaggerations all through the performance.

In fairness to Karajan, he is one of the few conductors who convey Beethoven's elegance and sophistication. Often, too, in this *Fidelio*, conductor, orchestra, and singers work together to capture a dramatic color with extraordinary specificity—the glacial chill of the gravedigging duet is a good example.

Heard with the benefit of hindsight, Helga Dernesch's Leonore clearly shows why she subsequently abandoned the dramatic-soprano repertory and restructured her voice as a mezzo; the sound is as warm and lustrous as one could desire until she must sing above G: there, the notes, whether loud or soft, emerge pinched, colorless, and strained. Despite her occasional upper-register difficulties, Dernesch is a resourceful and sympathetic artist who has many lovely moments.

Vickers repeats his Florestan from the Klemperer set. Karajan encourages him to do a great deal of very soft singing, and as a result the two performances are quite different in effect.

Helen Donath is a fresh-voiced, charming Marzelline, Horst Laubenthal an above-average Jacquino. Karl Ridderbusch sings very smoothly and suavely as Rocco, as does José van Dam as Don Fernando. Zoltan Kélémen, by contrast, is often harsh of tone as Pizarro (his baritone is on the light side for the role), but undeniably forceful.

Leonore No. 3 is not included. The engineering, like the conducting, is full of quirks (e.g., the prominence given to Kelemen's voice in the Act I finale), but the CD reissue is superior in sound to the original Angel LP pressings.

1976 EMI / ANGEL (S)

Edda Moser (A), Helen Donath (B), Richard Cassilly (C), Eberhard Büchner (D), Theo Adam (E), Karl Ridderbusch (F), Hermann-Christian Pollster (G), Leipzig Radio Chorus, Dresden State Orchestra—Herbert Blomstedt

What is performed here is not *Fidelio* as we know it, but *Leonore*—the original 1805 version of the opera, at least to the extent that it can be reconstructed. For example, the 1805 version of the prison scene's melodrama has not survived, and the number was cut altogether in 1806; as a result, Herbert Blomstedt is forced to perform the familiar 1814 version of the melodrama—even though it includes a quotation, by the solo oboe, of a melody that Florestan sings in his aria only in the 1814 score.

The differences between the 1805 and 1814 scores are many. It would scarcely be an exaggeration to say that Beethoven altered every page of the score, for even where he retained a musical number, he changed melodies, harmonies, vocal lines, and instrumentation. Briefly, however: *Leonore* is an opera in three, rather than two, acts; its overture is the one we now call *Leonore* No. 2. Three numbers heard here— a Marzelline / Jacquino / Rocco trio, a duet for Marzelline and Leonore, and a second aria with chorus for Pizarro—were dropped in the course of the revision. Leonore's and Florestan's solo scenes were extensively rewritten; so were their duet and the opera's final scene. In general, the original score is more expansive in scale and more elaborate in detail—the vocal writing is even more demanding than it is in the familiar 1814 score (Leonore's music, in particular, is higher and more florid), and the introduction to the prison scene has a dense instrumental layout worthy of Richard Strauss.

The EMI performance, as the only one of *Leonore* available on commercial discs, is somewhat of a take-it-or-leave-it proposition. But Herbert Blomstedt seems to have the score well in hand; all that is missing (as it is on most such made-from-scratch studio recordings of operatic rarities) is the kind of firm shaping and refinement that could probably come only after repeated performances in the theater. The Dresden orchestra and Leipzig chorus perform extremely well for him, as they did for Böhm on the 1969 DG set.

The cast is good, on the whole. Edda Moser has some shrill, edgy moments, but is a passionate Leonore, and she has the agility to cope with the extra coloratura demands of this version. Richard Cassilly is a sturdy, unsubtle Florestan, who at least brings some basic vocal heft to the part; he is rather good in the dialogue. Eberhard Büchner is an uncommonly big-voiced Jacquino.

This recording offers more of the dialogue than most other sets; however, since the 1814 revisions encompassed the dialogue as well as the musical numbers, what we hear spoken in this performance is often unfamiliar. *Leonore* No. 3 is not inserted into the last act—nor can it be, because in the 1805 version there is no scene change at this point: the opera's finale takes place down in the dungeon.

1978 DEUTSCHE GRAMMOPHON (S) CD

Gundula Janowitz (A), Lucia Popp (B), René Kollo (C), Adolf Dallapozza (D), Hans Sotin (E), Manfred Jungwirth (F), Dietrich Fischer-Dieskau (G), Vienna State Opera Chorus, Vienna Philharmonic Orchestra—Leonard Bernstein

Like most of Leonard Bernstein's opera recordings, this one is based on a theater production, with essentially the same cast. In an interview printed in the accompanying booklet, Bernstein discusses some of his interpretive decisions. Pointing out that the original score is almost devoid of dynamic indications for the vocal parts, he has supplied them in abundance. He also follows Maazel's example by reducing the strings in the less "heroic" portions of the score. The conductor does make one unfortunate textual choice: he includes *Leonore* No. 3, but cuts its opening bar and dovetails its second bar into the final chord of the postlude to "O namenlose Freude!" As a result, the overture cannot be excised cleanly during playback, even on the CD edition of the recording. The dialogue is severely compressed.

Bernstein's reading is generally on the slow side, with a great deal of rhythmic flexibility and some highly personal inflections. I find this kind of subjective response to the music refreshing after the dour literalism of some conductors. Other listeners may dismiss the Bernstein performance as self-indulgent (those who accuse Furtwängler of taking unauthorized *ritards* in this music will be scandalized by some of the liberties Bernstein takes). The reading is well

executed by the Vienna orchestra and chorus and well recorded by the DG engineers.

I admire Gundula Janowitz's Leonore. She sings with a combination of instrumental accuracy and technical command, sculpting the music with classical restraint rather than extroverted passion. Although probably the wrong *kind* of soprano for Bernstein's intensely dramatic concept of the opera (he needs a big-voiced, extroverted soprano like Nilsson or Jones), she and the conductor work beautifully together.

René Kollo is superb in the dialogue, and his musical intentions are obviously good, but his actual singing is hard-toned and strained too much of the time.

Lucia Popp, bright-toned and full of girlish enthusiasm and innocence, is an ideal Marzelline. Although Adolf Dallapozza is not quite in the same vocal class, he is more than adequate as Jacquino.

It seems strange that Hans Sotin—a deep, smooth bass—should be cast as Pizarro rather than as Rocco. Sotin reaches the high notes, but there is no leeway whatsoever, and the adjustments he must make to handle the tessitura seem to have a deleterious effect on his singing. Perversely enough, Manfred Jungwirth's Rocco seems rather lightweight and baritonal in timbre by comparison. Jungwirth brings a good deal of individuality to the character, though, including a pronounced Viennese accent.

Dietrich Fischer-Dieskau makes a predictably vivid cameo appearance as Don Fernando, his incisive delivery of the words compensating to a great degree for his lack of sheer vocal heft.

1979 DECCA / LONDON (S,D) CD

Hildegard Behrens (A), Sona Ghazarian (B), Peter Hofmann (C), David Kuebler (D), Theo Adam (E), Hans Sotin (F), Gwynne Howell (G), Chicago Symphony Chorus and Orchestra—Georg Solti

Made in conjunction with concert performances, this set is noteworthy as the first digitally recorded opera. A decade later, the sound still seems unusually clear and detailed, and this is one of the few recent opera recordings in which the solo singers are not too closely miked.

Sir Georg Solti elicits exceptional playing from the Chicago Symphony Orchestra, and the chorus is most impressive—these American choristers yield nothing to their German and Austrian counterparts in terms of enunciation and dramatic involvement. Yet for some reason I cannot put my finger on, I find Solti's reading less satisfying than Klemperer's, Böhm's, Karajan's, or (see below) Masur's. The problem may be one common to many latter-day opera recordings: everyone involved is so preoccupied with surface precision and polish—with "getting the notes right"—that there is no room left for spontaneity or theatrical flair.

On the whole, the singing is disappointing. The best of the soloists is Hildegard Behrens, an exciting Leonore. Operating with a voice that is really no more suitable for the music than Janowitz's (and is actually less evenly produced and less beautiful in timbre), Behrens throws herself into the role, and does everything she can with verbal inflection and careful shading of her one basic vocal color.

She deserves a better Florestan than Peter Hofmann, who is blandly matter-of-fact as an interpreter and always very careful in his approach to the top (when he must let his voice out, the sound is tense and unpleasant). It is also alarming to hear such a young tenor singing with a pronounced quaver on sustained tones.

Hans Sotin confirms my suspicion that Rocco is a much more suitable role for him than Pizarro. Unfortunately, Adam, in his third recording of the latter role, is in serious vocal trouble: wobbly, dry of timbre, and approximate in pitch.

Sona Ghazarian is a bright, accurate Marzelline, David Kuebler a rather small-scaled, tight-voiced Jacquino. Neither possesses much individuality: in their opening duet, for example, they seem to be carefully following Solti's instructions rather than recreating their characters. Gwynne Howell, however, brings a nice paternal quality to Don Fernando's pronouncements.

Leonore No. 3 is not included. An oddity of the production is the elimination of all of the dialogue between Leonore's aria and the Pris-

oners' Chorus (as a result, it is not made clear that Rocco is breaking the rules by allowing the prisoners to come out into the courtyard); on both the LP and CD sets, a side-break occurs at this point—apparently in a deliberate attempt to disguise the lapse in dramatic continuity.

1981 EURODISC (S,D) CD

Jeannine Altmeyer (A), Carola Nossek (B), Siegfried Jerusalem (C), Rüdiger Wohlers (D), Siegmund Nimsgern (E), Peter Meven (F), Theo Adam (G), Leipzig Radio Chorus, Male Chorus of the Berlin Radio, Leipzig Gewandhaus Orchestra—Kurt Masur

This is a seriously undervalued set. For one thing, Kurt Masur conducts the opera as well as anyone on records. It is a beautifully proportioned reading, rivaling Böhm's or Klemperer's in its clarity and logic; it is also intensely dramatic, and yet it sounds like a performance of an opera written in 1814—nothing is inflated to late-romantic dimensions, and there is a *bel canto* quality to the phrasing that is revelatory. The entire performance is filled with insights (listen to the balancing of the solo voices in either act finale: every note seems to fall naturally and inevitably into place, resulting in an unusually accurate *and* spontaneous-sounding rendition of the sequence).

Masur's orchestra is a fine one, and—for better or worse—it is thoroughly "German" in sound: on the one hand, wonderfully rich, open-air horns; on the other, a solo oboist who seems to be duck-calling at times. The quicksilver string execution is nothing short of phenomenal.

The cast may not be ideal, but it is good enough to realize Masur's conception. Jeannine Altmeyer is another lightweight, bright-toned Leonore. Her voice is a little shallow at the bottom, and a little thin at the top, but she uses it with great skill, and is a direct, touching interpreter.

The Florestan, Siegfried Jerusalem, and Pizarro, Siegmund Nimsgern, both have comparatively small, tightly focused voices; both men, however, manage to turn this to their advantage, relying upon nuance and incisiveness rather than bluster. Peter Meven is an above-average Rocco, with a soft, round tone and gentle, understated approach to the role.

Carola Nossek is a pert yet sensual Marzelline, and Rüdiger Wohlers is one of the few Jacquinos on records who actually sounds like a highly sexed, macho young man. In each case, the vocal quality is not absolutely first class, but the singer's intelligence compensates.

The dialogue is exceptionally well performed on this recording.

My copy of the original Eurodisc release is a three-CD set, with *Leonore* No. 3 (a riveting performance, by the way) included as an appendix, *after* the finale—an eminently sensible procedure. The digital sound, clear and ungimmicky, is outstanding.

1989 PHILIPS (S,D) CD

Jessye Norman (A), Pamela Coburn (B), Reiner Goldberg (C), Hans Peter Blochwitz (D), Ekkehard Wlaschiha (E), Kurt Moll (F), Andreas Schmidt (G), Dresden State Opera Chorus, Dresden State Orchestra—Bernard Haitink

This recording shows every sign of careful preparation, and has a great deal to commend it. There is one truly great performance: the Leonore of Jessye Norman. Here, at last, is a recorded Leonore who has *everything*: a glorious voice, combining a beautiful timbre with power, delicacy, *and* agility; womanly vulnerability *and* heroic resolve; a monumental quality *and* great dramatic intensity. I don't think Norman has done anything quite this extraordinary on records.

She easily dominates the performance, but in fact the production has other major strengths. Chief among them is the conducting of Bernard Haitink. His tempo choices tend to be on the deliberate side, but he keeps everything moving and extremely well defined from the rhythmic standpoint. The instrumental textures are unusually subtle and transparent, rivaling the Karajan performance in this respect. The Dres-

den orchestra and chorus once again provide magnificent support.

If only Philips had been able to find a young Jon Vickers for Norman's Leonore to rescue, and a young Paul Schöffler for her to hurl defiance at! The Florestan here, Reiner Goldberg, sings neatly, but rather carefully, especially in the upper register—an inoffensive performance, but hardly an exciting one. Ekkehard Wlaschiha, on the other hand, is an undeniably incisive Pizarro, although his high, tightly focused baritone can develop a raspy edge under pressure, and is relatively weak at the bottom of its range.

Kurt Moll misses some of the earthy humor that Rocco can have, but sings the part exceptionally well. Pamela Coburn's Marzelline is pleasant, though a little subdued in manner; Hans Peter Blochwitz, however, is a lively Jacquino.

Philips includes the usual condensed dialogue—exceptionally well handled by this cast. Like the Eurodisc set, this one includes *Leonore* No. 3 as an appendix, *after* the opera's final scene—a sensible procedure. The recorded sound is unobtrusively state of the art.

So many of the complete recordings of *Fidelio* are distinguished that choice is once again largely a question of individual taste.

To me, the best versions of the opera are the DG / Böhm and the Eurodisc / Masur. Both are exceptionally well conducted, in a style that does justice to the score without letting personal interpretive idiosyncrasies get in the way. Both of these sets are also well sung, on the whole, and well recorded.

Finally, the EMI / Blomstedt recording of *Leonore* is required listening for anyone who is seriously interested in Beethoven's first thoughts on the opera.

ROLAND GRAEME

Unavailable for review:
1950 OCEANIC
1992 DECCA / LONDON

VINCENZO BELLINI

LA SONNAMBULA (1831)

A: Amina (s); B: Elvino (t); C: Rodolfo (bs)

The seventh of Bellini's nine operas, *La Sonnambula* had its premiere at the Teatro Carcano in Milan in 1831, four years before the composer's death. It was composed between *I Capuleti e i Montecchi* and *Beatrice di Tenda*—both tragedies. As Bellini's only attempt at lyric comedy, *La Sonnambula* poses unique interpretive problems. The three principal roles demand the utmost in *bel canto* virtuosity, and since the heroine is called upon to portray pathos rather than heavy drama, her balance is as precarious on the vocal line as it is on the footbridge she is supposed to cross while sleepwalking. Given imperceptive nuances or a gloss of the music, *La Sonnambula* is apt to sound like a poor imitation of Gilbert and Sullivan. Its deceptive simplicity has led more than one critic astray, but audiences of the *bel canto* era appear to have been unanimous in succumbing to its spell when charismatic singers like Giuditta Pasta or Maria Malibran (in a mezzo-soprano adaptation) played the title role. Giovanni Battista Rubini, the first Elvino, was likewise an artist of exceptional accomplishments. Elvino's music, written in an extremely high tessitura, is usually transposed down and simplified for modern performance, though some recent tenors have cultivated an aptitude for florid coloratura flourishes. The bass role of Rodolfo, appreciably shorter and simpler, calls for a mellow, sustained *legato* and affable personality rather than the more usual bass characteristics of stern authority and imposing utterance. The conductor's role is scarcely less difficult, as he must sustain the elasticity of repetitive accompaniment figures and support the lines shaped by the singers. Lack of character in any of these assignments will be exposed mercilessly by the clear texture of the music.

1953 CETRA (M)

Lina Pagliughi (A), Ferruccio Tagliavini (B), Cesare Siepi (C), Italian Radio Chorus and Orchestra—Franco Capuana

Born in Brooklyn to Italian immigrant parents, Lina Pagliughi became a protégée of Luisa Tetrazzini. Her Amina in *La Sonnambula*, though recorded relatively late in her career, shows the lyric charm and expressive phrasing at which she excelled. It also reveals her occasional tendency to stray a little from true pitch in coloratura passagework. The timbre of her voice, with its exceptional purity and poignancy, lends itself ideally to the role, and she spins out Bellini's lines poetically. Comparable in lightness and smoothness is Ferruccio Tagliavini as Elvino, though in florid nimbleness he is no match for his partner. In spite of this limitation, plus a tendency to coarsen his interpretation with sobs, Tagliavini remains one of the few tenors of his generation who cultivated the art of singing softly, and his agility surpasses that of most of his contemporaries. As a result, he is able to convey quite a bit of what Bellini must have wanted—a gentle, vulnerable, rustic character whose lack of experience leads him readily to misunderstand his fiancée's behavior. Once wounded, Elvino treats Amina harshly, and for this a somewhat more dramatic address than Tagliavini's would be an asset. Cesare Siepi, one of the finest basses of the period, has the nobility required for Count Rodolfo, but his rich timbre and dignified delivery do not prevent a modicum of humor and geniality. Franco Capuana's leadership, if it brings out no great distinction in the score, shapes it with an idiomatic, seasoned touch.

1957 EMI / ANGEL (M) CD

Maria Callas (A), Nicola Monti (B), Nicola Zaccaria (C), La Scala Chorus and Orchestra—Antonino Votto

Although she sang roles from the classical and *verismo* repertory, Maria Callas reached her greatest refinement in the *bel canto* operas—particularly those of Bellini, whose long melodic lines and expressive *fioriture* called forth the soprano's most intense concentration. Of several extant recordings of her Amina in *La Sonnambula* (the others being broadcast or stage-performance transcriptions), this studio version typifies her most stable and even work. The recitatives are handled expressively, while the familiar obstacles—the duets and especially the closing arias—find Callas both poised and volatile. There are certain drawbacks to the recording as well. For one thing, the opera is rather stringently cut. For another, its conductor, Antonino Votto, though well grounded, lacks the individuality and brio that would be ideal. And of course the role of Elvino, even in simplified form, presents problems to Nicola Monti, who is relatively adept in the florid style. Not an especially refined stylist, he does match Callas well in the duets, since his lyric voice has a robust enough timbre. The Rodolfo of Nicola Zaccaria typifies the high level of La Scala casting during the 1950s.

1962 DECCA / LONDON (S)

Joan Sutherland (A), Nicola Monti (B), Fernando Corena (C), Chorus and Orchestra of the Maggio Musicale Fiorentino—Richard Bonynge

In lighter roles, such as Marie in *La Fille du Régiment*, Joan Sutherland has shown a more animated side to her interpretive personality. Though Amina is not a comic role, it is more delicate than any of Bellini's other heroines, and the bucolic setting encourages a lighter approach. In general this *Sonnambula* is vintage Sutherland, showing the agility and brightness of the soprano's best work. Though never especially adept either at clarifying the words or at sustaining a drawn-out melodic line, she handles ornamentation and rapid-fire flights with assurance, expressive shading, and a certain indefinable grasp of what the *bel canto* period was all about. If her personal point of view—an indispensable ingredient to a full interpretation of this music—is not strongly defined, neither is the role, and her sense of pathos never oversteps the borderline separating *comédie larmoyante* from melodrama. Monti, repeating his Elvino five years after the Callas recording, shows the same degree of security in it, which is to say he cannot go all the way with what Bellini has written but does deliver the adapted version convincingly. Fernando Corena, like Salvatore Baccaloni before him, started out in standard bass roles calling for *legato* and smooth tone, but years of specializing in exaggerated readings of *basso-buffo* roles eventually took their toll. Though he could suggest the genial, worldly-wise side of Rodolfo in *La Sonnambula*, the flow and shaping of Bellini's lines were no longer within his purview at this point. Richard Bonynge, whose elastic meters suggest the considerate keyboard accompanist, also has the ballet conductor's sense of rhythmic buoyancy that helps this music no end.

1980 DECCA / LONDON (S,D) CD

Joan Sutherland (A), Luciano Pavarotti (B), Nicolai Ghiaurov (C), London Opera Chorus, National Philharmonic—Richard Bonynge

There are various reasons for rerecording an opera with one or more of the same soloists, but this *Sonnambula* remake exemplifies only one of them—the commercial motive. There is no stepping around the fact that Luciano Pavarotti is a more marketable name than the competent but little-known Nicola Monti; though not especially adept at this type of music, Nicolai Ghiaurov also enjoyed an important reputation in Decca's stable of regular singers. To the credit of the new album, Sutherland sounds like her old self; Pavarotti is at his most persuasive; Richard Bonynge maintains a lively hand at the controls; and digital sound makes everything a little clearer and crisper.

Although Elvino is not the perfect role for Pavarotti, he can still lighten his voice and keep it flowing with honeyed smoothness. The duets and tenor arias are transposed down a whole tone from the first published version—a standard practice in this opera—except for "Ah! perchè non posso odiarti," which is taken down a third. The results are not always optimal: Bellini would not have intended his first soprano-tenor duet to be in the same key as the bass aria that follows, nor would he have written a cavatina in a different key from its cabaletta (Elvino's "Tutto è sciolto" and "Ah! perchè non posso odiarti"). Without these compromises, however, *La Sonnambula* would no longer be performable. It is a pleasure, in "Come per me sereno," to hear Sutherland start a trill as a secure alternation between two defined tones and gradually accelerate its beat. Whenever a top E-flat is called for, she delivers, but the soprano sounds less happy in the lower keys she is obliged to take in the duets. The characterizations are all rather bland. Though soprano Isobel Buchanan's Lisa sounds mischievous enough to have left her handkerchief in the room of Count Rodolfo, one wonders, hearing Ghiaurov's phlegmatic portrayal, why she would want to.

1986 OPUS (S,D) CD

Jana Valášková (A), Jozef Kundlák (B), Peter Mikuláš (C), Slovak Philharmonic Chorus, Bratislava Radio Orchestra—Ondrej Lenárd

While one might be happy to encounter such a performance onstage in a city outside the international circuit, the Opus set offers little competition to older versions. It does offer crisp, lively conducting and orchestral sound. In fact, the Bratislava wind players are more adept and secure than the singers. In the title role, Jana Valášková treads carefully, generating little melting sweetness or sunny innocence. Her lower tones are of adequate strength, the top piercing when loud, the use of *portamento* self-conscious rather than natural. Never quite on top of the role, Valášková sounds uncertain of pitch during transitions and modulations, and the closing "Ah! non giunge" is too much for her. The Elvino, Jozef Kundlák, has more of an Italianate style and an agreeable lightness of timbre; "Prendi, l'anel ti dono" is sustained with purity and suave *legato*. The Rodolfo of Peter Mikuláš tends toward a draggy line, though his velvety tone lends itself to smooth continuity.

———

The style of Bellini's day must remain in large part a matter of conjecture. We know the tuning pitch was somewhat lower than ours, but this is a complex subject, because tuning standards varied from one city to another and were subject to change. Bellini evidently wanted an expressive soprano with dramatic potential, operating at half-throttle, for the role of Amina. Callas and Sutherland both qualify with nimble technique and soulful accents; the choice is one of taste, between an intense, pointed reading and a softer, less focused one. Tenors Monti and Pavarotti also sing with more than enough grace, smoothness, and flexibility; Monti's is the lighter, more appropriate timbre, but Pavarotti's lightening of his voice is expert. As for textual authenticity, Bonynge leads the most complete accounts of the score.

J OHN W. F REEMAN

Unavailable for review:
1970 FABBRI

VINCENZO BELLINI

NORMA (1831)

A: Norma (s); B: Adalgisa (s or ms); C: Pollione (t); D: Oroveso (bs)

*B*eginning in the 78-rpm era, record companies seem to have acknowledged the fact that *Norma* cannot be treated like just another opera. As beautiful and powerful as the score is, it will not quite play itself (compare *Norma* to an opera like *Lucia di Lammermoor*, which can scarcely fail to make an effect in performance, no matter how wretchedly executed). All four leading roles present formidable vocal and dramatic challenges to their interpreters.

Furthermore, *Norma* has never been a truly popular, crowd-pleasing opera, either in the theater or on records. Because of all these factors, there have been relatively few complete recorded versions, and most of them show signs of careful preparation. Even the least successful of the sets discussed below contain individual performances of distinction, and thus can be said to illuminate some facet of the work.

Norma presents some interesting textual problems. We badly need a critical edition of this opera. In the meantime, the Ricordi vocal and miniature scores need to be supplemented by reference to reprints (by Boosey & Hawkes, Kalmus, Novello, et al.) of older vocal scores. Bellini's autograph survives, but it is ambiguous and even self-contradictory in many passages. The string accompaniment to Oroveso's Act II aria "Ah! del Tebro," for example, is marked to be played with the bows, with *legato* slurs over the triplet phrases; but the slurs are crossed out, and *pizzicato* is written in, in the composer's handwriting. It looks as though he tried the

passage out both ways in rehearsal, but did not make his final decision clear.

Two numbers are commonly transposed down in performance. "Casta Diva" is written in G in the autograph, and is printed in that key in some vocal scores (e.g., the Boosey & Hawkes); but the now-standard transposition to F was introduced by Giuditta Pasta, the creator of the role, presumably with the composer's consent. The Act II Norma / Adalgisa duet is usually transposed down a tone in order to accommodate a mezzo-soprano Adalgisa.

It would be a strange record collector who chose his *Norma* solely on the basis of these and other textual questions; for most of us, the singing is more important. The complete sets discussed below certainly offer us hours of fascinating vocalism to study, to compare, and to start arguments about.

1936 CETRA (M) CD

Gina Cigna (A), Ebe Stignani (B), Giovanni Breviario (C), Tancredi Pasero (D), Italian Radio Chorus and Orchestra, Turin—Vittorio Gui

As one might expect, there are a few cuts in this performance—but really very few, considering its date. In Act I, the cabalettas of Pollione ("Me protegge, me difende") and Norma ("Ah! bello a me ritorna") are shorn of their repeats; there is a small cut (12 bars of transitional material) in the "Vieni in Roma" section of the Adalgisa / Pollione duet; and so on. Act II is substantially complete.

The orchestration has definitely been touched up at a few points, with some discreet wind and string doublings that are heard on none of the subsequent recordings. In Act I, the trumpets and gong are, properly, offstage; but there is no stage band: its music is distributed among the "pit" instruments.

Vittorio Gui's tempos are almost invariably slower than those of other conductors, but his beat—well defined, yet infinitely elastic—sustains the musical line at all times. As a result, the performance has a genuine *bel canto* quality. The orchestra and chorus are excellent.

Gina Cigna was a famous Norma; we might expect more from an interpreter of the part today. On the recording, Cigna is a well-schooled, hard-working soprano, who reminds us of how difficult the role is. Her voice can be beautiful, and she has a good instinct for *legato* phrasing. She declaims the words with clarity and force. When the emotional temperature rises, she tends to tense up and belt out the notes, sounding more querulous than indignant.

Ebe Stignani, if not necessarily the best Adalgisa on records, is still pretty extraordinary. Although her voice is basically light and youthful-sounding, she has the power, timbral richness, and authority of a true dramatic mezzo-soprano at her ready command. Her molding of the phrases and delivery of the text are wonderfully incisive, yet the performance seems spontaneous. And if Stignani doesn't exactly toss off the coloratura all of the time, she faces up to the technical demands in an honest and resourceful way.

Giovanni Breviario's Pollione seems to me to be well above the recorded average. The voice is attractive and not too heavy; the singing is accurate, the manner direct and ardent. Breviario does not always connect his notes with as much *legato* as one might like, but he has figured out a way to negotiate the florid writing without conspicuous compromise. Not a great performance, perhaps, but a worthy one.

Tancredi Pasero is a surprisingly understated Oroveso: the bass sings gently and lyrically most of the time, and in the final scene I was disappointed by his rather casual approach to the dramatic situation—a line like "Oh! mio dolor!" is virtually thrown away.

The recording has been reissued on CD by Pearl and by Nuova Era, both of which manage to fit the performance onto two discs; I heard the Pearl CDs. The company does not believe in using extensive filtering or other techniques on such historical material. As a result, the surface noise is strong and persistent, but the music comes through with startling vividness.

1954 EMI / ANGEL (M) CD

Maria Callas (A), Ebe Stignani (B), Mario Filippeschi (C), Nicola Rossi-Lemeni (D), La Scala Chorus and Orchestra—Tullio Serafin

The same basic textual choices were made for this recording as in the Cetra set: the Act I cabalettas lack their repeats, "Casta Diva" is in F, and the Act II Norma / Adalgisa duet is transposed down. EMI provides a stage band, however (as do all subsequent recordings), and the orchestration is mostly Bellini's. The accompaniment to "Ah! del Tebro" is bowed rather than *pizzicato*.

Tullio Serafin's conducting is more energetic than Gui's, but has the same combination of suppleness and imposing weight. One odd exception is his handling of the "Guerra, guerra!" chorus in Act II: Bellini, it is true, asks for *allegro feroce* here, but Serafin hammers the number out at a breathless *prestissimo*. As a result, the chorus can barely get the words out. Still, Serafin's is a great reading of the score, and La Scala's orchestra and chorus live up to their reputation.

The cast is dominated by Maria Callas, which is not to imply that her colleagues are inadequate; it's just that they are up against the soprano in her youthful prime, in her most famous role. With two studio recordings and at least five "pirates" in circulation, Callas's Norma is well documented. Her singing here reminds us that she began her career as a dramatic soprano: the sound is powerful and dark in timbre in the lower and middle registers, and rather steely on top; when she lightens up in the moments of tenderness and introspection, the change almost takes the listener by surprise.

There are moments of tonal harshness and unsteadiness that cannot be ignored; there are also moments of transcendent beauty and insight that are altogether disarming.

Stignani's voice is even lighter and more girlish in quality than on her earlier recording. She has to work hard for effects that came easily to her before; but despite some huffing and puffing, she delivers the goods, and is still an Adalgisa to be reckoned with.

Mario Filippeschi, an underrated singer, becomes decidedly lachrymose in the opera's final scene, but sings honestly and well.

Nicola Rossi-Lemeni phrases and declaims with authority, but it's difficult to overlook the fact that his voice wobbles all over the place. Not once is the tone truly steady.

EMI's CD transfer is a vast improvement upon the cramped, shallow sound of the Seraphim LP set.

1960 EMI / ANGEL (S) CD

Maria Callas (A), Christa Ludwig (B), Franco Corelli (C), Nicola Zaccaria (D), La Scala Chorus and Orchestra—Tullio Serafin

In many ways, this remake of the 1954 EMI set is an improvement upon the original. Serafin, if anything, molds the music even more eloquently than before. He now plays the accompaniment to "Ah! del Tebro" *pizzicato*, but once again tears through "Guerra, guerra!" as though determined to prove that he has the energy of a man half his age. The orchestra and chorus are once again excellent, and the fact that they have been recorded in good stereo sound enables us to hear them more clearly.

Callas's performance is now a triumph over waning vocal resources. The voice quality is rougher under pressure than before, and much of the soft singing is curiously drained of color. There are some excruciating wobbles, and not just on exposed high notes. But once a listener learns to distinguish between the actual sound of the voice and what is being done with it, the performance seems infinitely more varied and subtle than before.

Franco Corelli's Pollione is one of his best recorded performances: although he doesn't

project the elegance that some of the Proconsul's music should have, he works hard to achieve lightness and good *legato* flow, and his vocal security allows him to bring off many thrilling effects. When he and Callas pass their low-lying phrases back and forth during "In mia man," for example, the listener feels for once that soprano and tenor are equally matched, vocally as well as temperamentally.

Christa Ludwig, in one of her rare forays into Italian opera on records, partners Callas and Corelli well in their respective duets, but somehow just doesn't sound like an Italian dramatic mezzo. In addition, she is not in her best vocal form here; her timbre, so soft and velvety in the lower and middle registers, can turn unpleasantly bright and edgy higher up.

Nicola Zaccaria is an impressive Oroveso, recalling Pasero in his calm dignity.

1964 DECCA / LONDON (S) CD

Joan Sutherland (A), Marilyn Horne (B), John Alexander (C), Richard Cross (D), London Symphony Chorus and Orchestra—Richard Bonynge

Richard Bonynge is the first conductor who seems to have made a serious effort to consult the autograph score and other sources in order to compile a more authoritative performance edition. Most of the cuts made on previous versions are opened: John Alexander sings all of "Me protegge," for example—a first on records. Joan Sutherland sings "Casta Diva" in the autograph key, G. She takes the repeat of the cabaletta (omitting only 7 bars of the "Ah, riedi ancora" reprise), and her effective embellishments include some beautiful soft high Cs.

The final scene of Act I includes two valuable restorations from the autograph. This performance of the first Norma / Adalgisa duet includes, before the final cadenza, 25 bars that can be heard on no other recording to date. In this passage, the two ladies toss a descending figuration back and forth, then trill upward in thirds, before embarking upon an elaborate repeat of the "Ah! si, fa core" melody. The extreme difficulty of the sequence no doubt explains why it was cut early on in the opera's performance history, and why it is not even printed in most scores, but once it has been heard, the duet seems incomplete without it. Bonynge also performs the subsequent Norma / Adalgisa / Pollione trio in an augmented version.

Sutherland's vocalism is as full, beautiful, and flexible as one could desire. Interpretively, she is especially good at conveying the character's wounded pride and resignation. Rage does not come so easily to her, although she takes a good stab at such moments as "Tremi tu?" and "Troppo il fellon presume."

This Adalgisa may be, on balance, Marilyn Horne's best recording of a complete role. Certainly, few of her recorded performances demonstrate her protean vocal qualities quite so strikingly: she sounds like a genuine contralto one moment, like a lyric soprano the next. She phrases like a great cellist, with a seamless *legato* and an apparently inexhaustible supply of breath. She and Sutherland set a formidable standard in their duets.

John Alexander and Richard Cross are both disappointing. The tenor, a fine artist, just doesn't sound like an Italian tenor: there is little warmth to his timbre, and no ring to his high notes. The bass is very musical but lightweight for Oroveso.

Unfortunately, Bonynge's conducting—at least at this stage in his career—is less impressive than his scholarship. He shapes the lyric portions of the score beautifully, but even these episodes would benefit from sharper rhythm and more varied articulation. Much of the performance is simply too quick and bouncy for my taste.

1967 DECCA / LONDON (S)

Elena Souliotis (A), Fiorenza Cossotto (B), Mario del Monaco (C), Carlo Cava (D), Chorus and Orchestra of the Accademia di Santa Cecilia, Rome—Silvio Varviso

One scarcely knows where to begin in cataloguing the deficiencies of this version. It is the sort of release that can ruin a record company's reputation.

In order to fit the performance onto four LP sides, the opera is massacred, with the role of Oroveso all but edited out of the opera.

There are all sorts of other cuts. It would be tedious to list them all, but they include dropping many repeats and development sections, as well as compression of the recitatives.

The one redeeming feature is the Adalgisa of Fiorenza Cossotto—a dignified, securely sung portrayal, very much in the Stignani tradition. Even she is handicapped at times by the insensitive conducting and by the cuts. Fortunately, Cossotto recorded the role a second time under much more favorable conditions (see below).

Elena Souliotis's Norma is easily characterized: imitation Callas without the genius. The two sopranos' voices are often eerily similar in timbre, but next to Callas's supple phrasing, Souliotis seems stiff and amateurish. In addition, her dark, mezzo-like sound thins out drastically in the upper register ("Casta Diva" is, predictably, in F; the Act II duet with Cossotto is also transposed down). Souliotis has some moments of undeniable excitement—the sheer recklessness of her vocalism carries her through Norma's angry and vindictive responses—but her career should be a warning to all overambitious young sopranos.

Unlike Souliotis, who burned out early, Mario del Monaco was a survivor. But his contribution to this recording is appalling—and I speak as a fan. Del Monaco gave some fine performances of Pollione in the fifties. By 1967, the tenor was reduced to blaring and bleating, which is exacerbated by Decca's very close miking. He brings a certain stoicism and virility to some of the declamatory passages, but most of his singing on this set is painful to hear.

In what is left of his role, Carlo Cava sings in a dignified manner, but with woolly, unfocused tone (a feature of almost all of his recordings—he is simply not a particularly phonogenic artist).

Silvio Varviso rushes through the score as though he is embarrassed by the cuts and the substandard vocalism. An exception is "Meco all'altar," where Varviso slows down drastically every time del Monaco wants to hold on to a high note. Even modest Gs above the staff seem to qualify for this treatment!

The orchestra and chorus display more energy

than refinement, but no doubt earned their pay checks. Decca's engineers, for once, did not: the sound is excessively reverberant, with crude balances and perspectives.

1972 RCA / BMG (S) CD

Montserrat Caballé (A), Fiorenza Cossotto (B), Plácido Domingo (C), Ruggero Raimondi (D), Ambrosian Opera Chorus, London Philharmonic Orchestra—Carlo Felice Cillario

This could have been a great recording of the opera: all four of the principal singers carry the right basic vocal credentials. Unfortunately, it is, on the whole, just another opera set off the assembly line.

I am inclined to place much of the blame on the conductor. Carlo Felice Cillario is competent but unimaginative. He lacks energy, variety, and flexibility, and he does not sound involved in the opera's emotional events.

The orchestra plays well but suffers from this lack of true musical guidance. The musically precise chorus betrays its British identity with some slovenly Italian pronunciation.

Caballé comes so close to meeting the demands of the title role that one is inclined to be rather hard on her. Her voice is gorgeous except at the extreme top (where it tightens) and extreme bottom (where the sound can turn guttural). She is dignified yet womanly in the declamatory sections, and phrases the gentler music exquisitely; in fact, whenever tenderness or introspection is called for, her Norma is uniquely satisfying. But she is not completely comfortable with the coloratura: she smears the runs, renders some of the rapid *staccatos* imprecisely, and her trill at the end of "Casta Diva" is a strange little stutter on one note (some of the subsequent indicated trills are simply omitted).

As on her earlier recording, Cossotto is firm, clear, and incisive—a highly satisfying portrayal, if not exactly subtle (she doesn't even begin to suggest the character's vulnerability or indecision).

The male roles suffer, to some extent, from "name" casting. Both Plácido Domingo and Ruggero Raimondi sound as though they are sight-reading. The tenor makes consistently pleasing sounds, but there is no dynamic shading, no finish to the phrasing, and thus no characterization of Pollione—only a sincere-sounding gentleman who sings well. Raimondi is monotonously loud in both of his solo scenes, and his tonal production is far from being ideally smooth or beautiful; in addition, his voice is on the light, baritonal side for this music.

The recorded sound is clear but a little dull on top, shallow in terms of bass response, and the climaxes are not very exciting.

1973 EMI / ANGEL (S)

Beverly Sills (A), Shirley Verrett (B), Enrico di Giuseppe (C), Paul Plishka (D), John Alldis Choir, New Philharmonia Orchestra—James Levine

James Levine, in his recording debut, goes all-out for intensity and excitement: this is a fast, tense, hard-driven reading of the score, with some stunning orchestral work. It's effective enough on its own terms, but it's not *Norma* (the Act I trio sounds positively cheerful). This is also the noisiest of all the opera's recordings. The edition is once again basically Ricordi. "Casta Diva" is in G and the Act II duet for the two women is also "up," but none of the extra music heard on the Bonynge set is included.

Singing Norma, Beverly Sills is at a double disadvantage. Her voice is simply too light in weight and limited in color for the role; her undeniable intelligence and musicianship cannot really compensate for her limitations. Furthermore, she is not in good form here, frequently sounding both shrill and tremulous (each of the sustained tones in "Casta Diva" has a distinct beat). Even some of her coloratura is ragged and breathy.

Shirley Verrett is a powerful and lustrous Adalgisa, despite some huskiness in the bottom octave of her range. She sings with great poise, and does not commit the common error (in this role) of "coming on too strong"—she always sounds like a gentle young woman. Unfortunately, her voice does not blend with Sills's at all in the duets; the two instruments, so very different in weight and color, remain as distinct as oil and water.

As Pollione, Enrico di Giuseppe reveals a pleasant enough voice, but one that is light for the role and monochromatic in timbre. He is taxed both by the florid writing and by the high tessitura.

Paul Plishka turns in a competent Oroveso, neither sumptuous in sound nor imposing in manner.

The original ABC Audio Treasury LP set is a notoriously poor engineering and production job: the sound, too reverberant to begin with, is further compromised by pre- and post-echo on the actual records.

1979 CBS / SONY (S)

Renata Scotto (A), Tatiana Troyanos (B), Giuseppe Giacomini (C), Paul Plishka (D), Ambrosian Opera Chorus, National Philharmonic Orchestra—James Levine

This recording is quite good, on the whole. Levine has mellowed considerably and shapes much of the music with greater sensitivity than before. He still seems reluctant, though, to trust his singers to set the pace in passages where the solo voice should dominate. The textual choices are virtually the same as on the earlier recording (although Scotto takes a far more austere approach to embellishment than Sills).

Scotto is, surprisingly, the only native Italian Norma on any of these sets (Cigna was French by birth). None of her rivals—not even Callas—makes so much of the text. Her weighting and pacing of the recitatives is exemplary; she colors the voice with sensitivity; one can almost hear her determination to make the coloratura expressive of specific emotions. Her voice is beautiful throughout most of its range.

The problem is a rebellious upper register: the high notes are steady and on pitch, but most of them—whether loud or soft—take on an unpleasantly *squillante* quality. "Casta Diva" (in F) goes well until the ascents to the repeated As, which are painfully strident: in fact, the aria is by far the least persuasive part of Scotto's performance.

Tatiana Troyanos is another superb Adalgisa: sensual-sounding and undaunted by the role's

technical demands (the Act II duet is once again sung in the higher keys). The only possible criticism is that her smoky mezzo, with its warm vibrato, is comparatively unvaried in color. Giuseppe Giacomini's voice is a nicely focused *spinto* tenor, not particularly beautiful in timbre or refulgent up top, but used with great skill and sensitivity. He works well with Scotto and Troyanos in their scenes together. Plishka repeats his solid Oroveso from the EMI/Angel set: his singing is a little more animated and varied in delivery than before, and CBS has recorded his voice more flatteringly.

The analogue recording is good, although the original CBS LP pressings are no more than adequate in quality.

1984 DECCA / LONDON (S,D) (D

Joan Sutherland (A), Montserrat Caballé (B), Luciano Pavarotti (C), Samuel Ramey (D), Welsh National Opera Chorus and Orchestra—Richard Bonynge

This glamorously cast remake of the 1964 Decca recording of the opera is an impressive achievement, on the whole. As on the earlier recording, Richard Bonynge has prepared his own performing edition of the opera, consulting Bellini's autograph score as well as other sources. (The booklet, I am sorry to report, does not contain a word of information about Bonynge's textual choices.)

As a conductor, Bonynge shows impressive signs of artistic growth. This reading is far superior to his work on the 1964 set. In many episodes, the execution is much sharper—the rapid trumpet figurations in the Overture are an early example. It's almost as though Bonynge were determined to fight his reputation for rhythmic slackness.

One mild surprise is the pace at which some of the music is taken. "Dell'aura tua profetica" is fast, as it was in 1964, and so is the Druid March. Many of the lyrical numbers, which Bonynge was tempted to linger over before, move more urgently. In a couple of places, I'm not sure I like the new approach (during Adalgisa's "Solo, furtiva, al tempio," for example).

Bonynge is helped by the fact that the Welsh National Opera orchestra is a fine ensemble, with bold, noble-toned horns; the chorus is also good, especially the men in Act II, Scene 2 ("Non parti?," etc.). Unlike some complete-opera recordings made in London, this one suggests a real performance, not just a highly professional first run-through of the score by competent musicians.

Sutherland, inevitably, does not sound as fresh and fluent as before. The voice has clearly suffered a reduction in its basic power; Decca's close miking and careful balancing allow Sutherland to sing the entire role without venturing above a basic level of *mezzo forte* more than once or twice. Except for a couple of slightly cautious runs, her agility remains unimpaired; and, as though to confound the nay-sayers, she once again hurls out a sustained top D at the end of the Act I trio.

Whether all of this adds up to a great Norma is certainly open to question. The basic vocal "stance" is dignified and womanly. There is not a wide variety of vocal color, and that is probably a question as much of temperament as of actual vocal estate. However, even at this late stage in her career, Sutherland shows herself capable of artistic growth.

For the first time in a studio recording of the opera, we hear a soprano Adalgisa, with no hint of mezzo-soprano in her timbre or registration. Just as we have always been told, this does make a difference—for once, Adalgisa sounds like a vulnerable young girl, and audibly less mature than the Norma of the performance.

Fortunately, Caballé turns out to have been an inspired choice for the role, and gives an unusually interesting performance. Her opening soliloquy ("Sgombra e la sacra selva") is delivered in rapt, delicate tones, but with careful attention to verbal values (later on, at a couple of difficult spots, she indulges in her old bad habit of simply omitting the consonants). There is a really great moment: the phrase "Io l'obbliai," where she not only observes the indicated *messa di voce assai lungo* on the initial A above the staff but rounds off the rest of the phrase very beautifully, in a tender, nostalgic

tone color—all in a single, seemingly inexhaustible breath.

Luciano Pavarotti is on his best behavior, and the role of Pollione lies well for him; except for some breathiness at the bottom, he is in secure, expressive voice. In the reprise of the cabaletta he essays some "embellishment," consisting mostly of taking isolated notes and phrases up an octave; this sort of token decoration is really not much of an improvement upon *come scritto* purism.

Samuel Ramey—firm, smooth, dark in timbre—is very good. Unlike many Orovesos, Ramey conveys a real sense of frustration at "E fino a quando oppressi ne vorrai tu?" and in the recitative before "Ah! del Tebro."

The recording, provided one can accept the fact that the star soloists sound larger than life, is first-rate.

1986 MELODIYA (S) CD

M. Bieshu (A), L. Nem (B), G. Grigoryan (C), G. Seleznev (D), U.S.S.R. Ministry of Culture State Chamber Chorus, Bolshoi Theater Orchestra—Mark Ermler

This set is of little more than curiosity value. The performance is virtually uncut; once again, though, the textual basis would appear to be straight Ricordi.

Mark Ermler secures a big, massive sound from the orchestra, and musters some excitement in the martial episodes. The more restrained, lyrical portions of the score—which, of course, predominate—suffer from sluggish tempos and rhythmic sponginess. The orchestral playing is rich but tends to be monotonously loud and uninflected. The choral singing is lusty.

The British label Olympia, which has transferred this Melodiya recording to CD, perpetuates the quaint old Soviet habit of identifying the soloists only by their first initials and surnames. Most of the singing might politely be described as extroverted in manner, bringing to mind the hoary old *bel canto / can belto* pun. The Italian pronunciation is often surprisingly good, though, with few obtrusive Slavic accents.

Soprano M. Bieshu is obviously Russia's answer to Souliotis—a powerful voice with a tough chest register and a steely top, a makeshift technique, reasonable agility, and plenty of temperament. She is oddly paired with the Adalgisa of L. Nem, whose mezzo-soprano combines a shallow timbre with a fierce vibrato, and who handles the coloratura in a gingerly and imprecise manner.

The Pollione, G. Grigoryan, seems to have taken Corelli and (especially) del Monaco as his models, offering firm, virile tone, stiff phrasing, and not much in the way of dynamic variety.

The best performance on the set is the Oroveso of G. Seleznev, who is majestic as only a Russian bass can be.

The (analogue) engineering is mediocre: a harsh, boomy acoustic, with the solo voices grotesquely overmiked. When Bieshu goes after a loud high C (e.g., at "Ah, trema, fellon, per me!") the listener expects plaster to fall from the ceiling.

———————————

I believe that every collector should own one of the Callas recordings—probably the second, for the sake of its stereo sound, its strong supporting cast, and because the soprano herself gives such a fascinating (though vocally uneven) performance. But I also believe that every collector should own one of the Sutherland recordings. The first set makes the more interesting textual decisions, and Sutherland is in better vocal form; the second is in some ways a stronger overall production.

Those who are new to the opera should probably start with the 1964 set, which is less expensive—at least in its CD format—than the 1984 digital remake. The latter, however, is definitely the *Norma* for audiophiles.

ROLAND GRAEME

VINCENZO BELLINI

I PURITANI (1835)

A: Elvira (s); B: Enrichetta (ms); C: Arturo (t);
D: Riccardo (bar); E: Giorgio (bs)

*L*ike the last works of so many musical geniuses, even those who die young, *I Puritani* seems both a consolidation and a fulfillment. Had he lived, Bellini would certainly have gone on to explore new expressive and formal techniques, but this opera, if a sadly premature conclusion, crowns his accomplishments in the form. The tragic nobility of *Norma* is here, along with the delicate sentimental pathos of *La Sonnambula*, the sweeping melodrama of *Il Pirata*, and even some of the compositional experiments Bellini tried out in his earliest operas before consciously simplifying his style. *I Puritani* never really vanished from the repertory after its first performance in 1835 at the Théâtre Italien in Paris—the score contained too much beauty and dramatic force to be completely ignored. Like so many *bel canto* works of the period, though, it became mainly a vehicle for light coloratura sopranos, the score was often brutally abridged, and the power of the overall conception severely compromised. Although Elvira clearly dominates, the opera is still essentially an ensemble work, thanks to the careful symmetries of Bellini's design and his deep commitment to each character in the drama.

1953 EMI / ANGEL (M) CD

Maria Callas (A), Aurora Cattelani (B), Giuseppe di Stefano (C), Rolando Panerai (D), Nicola Rossi-Lemeni (E), La Scala Chorus and Orchestra—Tullio Serafin

This famous first recording of the opera was, for most people, an introduction to both *I Puritani* and a young soprano named Maria Callas—a potent combination. As she did with so many *bel canto* heroines, Callas discovered undreamed-of emotional depths in Elvira's dilemma in addition to singing the role with magisterial musicianship and sovereign technique. Elvira's mad scene is the glorious central arch of the opera and of Callas's interpretation. The fascinating burnt-walnut quality of her voice, the pristine clarity of her coloratura singing (the downward chromatic scales in the cabaletta are breathtakingly articulate), the immaculately sculptured phrases, and each poignantly weighted syllable of the text—this is great singing by anyone's standards, a superb memento of Callas in her all too brief and comparatively untroubled prime.

As he often did in their long partnership, di Stefano tended to sound rather plebeian next to this aristocratic vocal spirit, but here the youthful freshness and ringing ardor of his voice as he fearlessly tackles the role's stratospheric tessitura are hard to resist. Panerai handles Riccardo's music with fair agility and considerable dignity, while Rossi-Lemeni's Giorgio convinces more as a sympathetic character portrait than a piece of firm singing. Both baritone and bass, in fact, are a shade too tremulous and pitch-shy for comfort.

Serafin accommodates the cast with a considerate orchestral backdrop of extraordinary plasticity, yet one that still effectively underscores the opera's atmosphere and dramatic tension— a masterly demonstration of *bel canto* accompaniment, now apparently a lost art. The score is trimmed in ways that were traditional at the time—in those days, apparently, literal repetition in Italian opera was deemed a liability rather than a structural strength—and there are the usual slew of awkwardly prepared climactic top notes. No matter. This is a great recording, and none of its successors more searchingly explores the dark elegiac spirit of Bellini's swan song.

1963 DECCA / LONDON (S)

Joan Sutherland (A), Margreta Elkins (B), Pierre Duval (C), Renato Capecchi (D), Ezio Flagello (E), Chorus and Orchestra of the Maggio Musicale Fiorentino—Richard Bonynge

As if in response to some natural law, Joan Sutherland appeared in the late 1950s to sing the rediscovered *bel canto* repertory as an antipode to the demonic genius of Callas: with a healthy voice of flawless tonal purity and technical precision coupled with a basically lyrical, sometimes maddeningly placid, temperament. Heard in her youthful prime in this performance, Sutherland will take your breath away with a sound that is incomparable in its ripe amplitude, easy agility, and shining clarity. Progress in stylistic matters is also evident in the soprano's tasteful ornaments, cadenzas, and decorated reprises, all of which Callas eschews. On the other hand, Sutherland does very little to explain who Elvira may be or why she finds herself in such a dreadful predicament except to suggest a generalized droopy moodiness. Even so, perhaps no soprano past or present has ever sung this music in quite such a meltingly beautiful fashion.

Otherwise, there is not much here to praise. Bonynge gives us more of the opera than Serafin—including Elvira's concluding cabaletta drawn from manuscript sources, now a permanent addition to the score—although there are still many damaging interior cuts and the conducting as a whole is rather lackadaisical. A passable Arturo, Duval rivals di Stefano in terms of security and crude vigor but not for tonal

splendor or sheer animal excitement, while Capecchi and Flagello offer sturdy, unexceptional accounts of their roles.

1973 EMI / ANGEL (S)

Beverly Sills (A), Heather Begg (B), Nicolai Gedda (C), Louis Quilico (D), Paul Plishka (E), Ambrosian Chorus, London Philharmonic Orchestra—Julius Rudel

Like its predecessors, this recording was clearly planned as a showcase for the prima donna, Beverly Sills, who may be fairly said to combine the dramatic accents of a Callas with the purely lyrical approach of a Sutherland, but unfortunately her performance never coheres and only fitfully convinces. Despite thoughtful musicianship, intelligent characterization, and stylish ornamentation, the voice is simply not up to the job. Narrowly focused and afflicted with a small but persistent quaver, Sills's soprano mostly sounds worn and overextended, compromising most of her good intentions—no wonder this set never circulated outside of the United States. Future historians will have to look for reasons other than her disappointing recordings to explain this singer's remarkable, if brief, superstar career at home.

One might have hoped for better things from Gedda. For all his astonishing versatility, this refined tenor never seemed entirely comfortable in the Italian repertory, and as Arturo he was apparently caught on a bad day, sounding tired and hard-pressed. Quilico's burly baritone shapes Riccardo's elegant phrases with little finesse, Plishka gives a dependably secure but plodding account of Giorgio's music, and Rudel conducts like an efficient bandmaster. The fact that the opera has at last been recorded uncut—at least as published in the standard Ricordi score—almost seems irrelevant.

1974 DECCA / LONDON (S) CD

Joan Sutherland (A), Anita Caminada (B), Luciano Pavarotti (C), Piero Cappuccilli (D), Nicolai Ghiaurov (E), Chorus of the Royal Opera House, Covent Garden, London Symphony Orchestra—Richard Bonynge

A vast improvement over its predecessor, London's second recording is the first to treat the opera as a genuine ensemble piece rather than a soprano vehicle. The fabled singers of the world premiere—Giulia Grisi, Giovanni Battista Rubini, Antonio Tamburini, and Luigi Lablache—were not dubbed the *Puritani* Quartet for nothing, and to have four important voices on hand as we do here, all at the peak of their powers, makes a great difference. The two lower-pitched roles gain the most from such luxury casting. Cappuccilli and Ghiaurov may not be paradigms of *bel canto* grace and expressive subtlety, but the sheer quality and solidity of their voices count for much, especially in the rousing patriotic duet that ends Act II. Pavarotti is gloriously in his element, producing sweet, ringing tones and an affectionate caress for every phrase. Like Gedda, he attempts the high F in the finale, although in both cases listeners will have to make up their own minds about the controversial results. Sutherland is the same vocal marvel as before, now with a slightly darker vocal coloration and a bit more bite in her diction—all to the good.

A decade's experience on the podium tells in Bonynge's increased confidence with the orchestra, although the rhythmic pulse still tends to be too slack and the big finales never quite build into the imposing edifices that the score indicates. This time, though, the conductor gives us a full text, including the *andante* section of the Elvira / Arturo duet in Act III, cut by Bellini after the 1835 premiere. Overall, as a finely realized and unified statement of the opera, this recording of *I Puritani* is still the most satisfying to date.

1979 EMI / ANGEL (S) CD

Montserrat Caballé (A), Julia Hamari (B), Alfredo Kraus (C), Matteo Manuguerra (D), Agostino Ferrin (E), Ambrosian Opera Chorus, Philharmonic Orchestra—Riccardo Muti

It seems a bit perverse to use the conductor's name to identify a recording of a Bellini opera, but there's no mistaking this performance as anything but the Muti *Puritani*. In some respects, it is stimulating to hear a strong-willed conduc-

tor, especially an Italian versed in the idiom, treat the score with the care and reverence usually reserved for Beethoven. Muti's fastidious observation of accents and dynamics, the tautly sprung rhythms, superbly blended instrumental sonorities, and the imposing architectural strength of his reading clearly reveal that Bellini knew exactly what he was doing when he devised such a deceptively simple orchestral backdrop, one that so precisely and skillfully serves his expressive needs.

The singers are also kept on a very tight leash—interpolated top notes are not allowed and ornamentation is minimal in this strict *come scritto* conception—and they tend to remain somewhat in the background, surely more so than the composer either intended or expected. At least Caballé, perhaps cowed by having such a disciplinarian on the podium, gives a remarkably conscientious, alert performance compared to the casual surface-coasting she often settles for. Kraus is a predictably elegant Arturo, although the characteristically *secco* tonal quality of his tenor may sound a trifle tight and parched to ears accustomed to the open-throated generosity of Pavarotti. Manuguerra is a smoothly faceless Riccardo and Ferrin a decent but decidedly provincial Giorgio. On the whole, the performance sounds more like a brilliantly conducted experiment than a real performance.

1986 CETRA (S,P) CD

Katia Ricciarelli (A), Eleonora Jankovic (B), Chris Merritt (C), Juan Luque Carmona (D), Roberto Scandiuzzi (E), Coro Ente Artistico Teatro Petruzzelli, Orchestra Sinfonica Siciliana—Gabriele Ferro

This curious recording adds an intriguing musicological footnote to the *I Puritani* discography. Shortly after the world premiere in Paris, on January 25, 1835, Bellini prepared a new version of the score for Maria Malibran, who was to perform the opera later that year in Naples. That meant many drastic downward transpositions of Elvira's music—the exact nature of Malibran's voice is still subject to debate, but she obviously did not command the high options of Giulia Grisi, who had sung the role in Paris.

Apparently there was no baritone readily available in Naples at the time, so Riccardo was recast for tenor. Either for that reason or because Bellini wished to spotlight Elvira even more prominently, the baritone-bass duet "Suoni la tromba" was eliminated, although several interesting passages deleted during the Paris performances were restored, and Acts II and III are now joined into a single unit.

The production never took place, however, and less than a year later both Bellini and Malibran were dead. Although the existence of the Naples *I Puritani* had never been a secret, the score was not heard until 1986 in Bari, the performance preserved on these discs. It is unlikely to displace the familiar version—a more balanced, coherently organized, and satisfying piece than this rather lopsided reworking—but lyric sopranos with agile techniques may wish to revive it occasionally, and of course scholars will be grateful to have this flawed but useful reference recording. Even in these lower keys, Ricciarelli often moves awkwardly over the notes, although the pretty pastel timbre of her soprano retains much of its delicate appeal and she is definitely involved. The other singers are at least competent, but the orchestral playing is ragged and undernourished.

The Callas recording, despite cuts and variable singing from others in the cast, will always remain special for the soprano's remarkable insights into this *bel canto* masterpiece. For a more vocally consistent view of the opera, as well as a more complete text, London's 1974 recording continues to lead the field.

PETER G. DAVIS

ALBAN BERG

WOZZECK (1925)

A: Marie (s); B: Drum Major (t); C: Andres (t);
D: Captain (t); E: Wozzeck (bar); F: Doctor (bs)

*B*erg remarked, in a famous lecture in 1928, that to bring about a revolution in opera was the last thing on his mind when he wrote *Wozzeck*. Despite the disclaimer, however, *Wozzeck* has been seen as a revolutionary work in every way since its premiere in 1925—revolutionary in its musical language and design, in its declamatory style, in its unheard-of vocal and instrumental difficulty, even in its political message. Above all, *Wozzeck* has no precedent as music for the stage, Berg having realized with uncanny certainty that the new conception of theatrical tragedy represented by Büchner's play demanded a new kind of operatic language as well.

Six decades of performances all over the world have demonstrated conclusively that the effectiveness of "the opera" depends above all on accurate realization of a tremendously difficult score. The exaggerated instrumental writing, the constant changes of tempo, and the precise correlation of details of staging with the music present special problems for the conductor; but the special problems faced by the singers in maintaining accurate pitch in a work whose musical language is mostly atonal are seldom fully solved even today. Additionally, there is the problem of the *Sprechstimme* (speech-song), which Berg adopted from Schoenberg, though he was no more successful in stating clearly what he wanted, let alone notating it. Listening to all the different recordings with score in hand, one is constantly impressed by the different ways in which singers, faced with these notational difficulties, have responded to them, intelligently as well as intuitively.

Berg's greatest achievement in this opera is the remarkable communication of the human message of the play. The opera requires very little staging and almost no scenery; the story and music are everything, even in a radically new kind of dramaturgy with an unprecedentedly complex and unfamiliar musical idiom. When the opera was first produced it was praised by only a few critics, but was an instantaneous success with the public, and has remained so wherever it has been performed since.

1951 CBS / SONY (M,P)

Eileen Farrell (A), Frederick Jagel (B), David Lloyd (C), Joseph Mordino (D), Mack Harrell (E), Ralph Herbert (F), Choruses of the High School of Music and Art and the Schola Cantorum, New York Philharmonic Orchestra—Dimitri Mitropoulos

The first recording ever of *Wozzeck* is a tribute not only to Mitropoulos's superlative skill but also to his courage in bringing to American audiences a work that in 1951 was still considered very controversial. Despite technical defects almost beyond counting, after nearly forty years this live concert recording remains, in its remarkable expressive and dramatic qualities, the standard against which all subsequent recordings must be measured.

The recorded sound is generally very good, with audience noise noticeable only at the beginning of each act. The chief musical problems are in the accuracy of the sung pitches. Harrell and Lloyd are the most consistently accurate, although Harrell's precision fails at some critical moments, such as the murder scene. Farrell's pitch is sometimes off as far as a fourth for considerable stretches and Mordino appears much of the time to have given up on even attempting to sing the right notes. Yet all of these singers—Harrell's desperate and browbeaten Wozzeck, Farrell's alternately tender and fierce Marie, Mordino's wonderfully crazy, gibbering Captain—project an intensity of characterization that has hardly been surpassed by others.

Notwithstanding a number of minor errors, the orchestral performance is heroic, even dazzling, and Mitropoulos brings out a richness of sound and color that seems almost unbelievable for its time. Although all the later recordings are certainly more orchestrally precise, no other conductor on records seems to have naturally understood this music so well.

1965 DEUTSCHE GRAMMOPHON (S) CD

Evelyn Lear (A), Helmut Melchert (B), Fritz Wunderlich (C), Gerhard Stolze (D), Dietrich Fischer-Dieskau (E), Karl Christian Kohn (F), Chorus and Orchestra of the Deutsche Oper, Berlin—Karl Böhm

The first studio recording of *Wozzeck* shows the considerable improvement in sound quality obtainable after thirteen years of developing technology. Both the orchestral and vocal sound are more precise and immediate, and the rich detail of the orchestration is much more easily discernible, even when, as occasionally happens, the balance has been adjusted too much to the singers' advantage. Karl Böhm's conducting is well controlled, even restrained, but at the price of a certain heaviness resulting from tempos that are often too slow. Nevertheless, his overall conception of the opera is well unified and attentive to the drama.

Dietrich Fischer-Dieskau, in the title role, can hardly be faulted for accuracy, but paradoxically his sound is too richly dramatic for this opera, and one is left with the impression that

Fischer-Dieskau overacts vocally in what is essentially a lyric role. The same is true, though to a lesser extent, of Evelyn Lear, who brings to Marie's role a greater range of expression than we need to hear, when the totality of the music has so much expressivity already built into the score. Yet these criticisms may seem like carping when the performances are so intelligent and sensitive as to sustain the drama so fully. Of the other singers, Gerhard Stolze comes across as a memorably nasty Captain, and Karl Christian Kohn is excellent as the Doctor; it is well to remember how much raving there is in both these roles, and how careful the singers must be not to overdo it.

1966 CBS / SONY (S)

Isabel Strauss (A), Fritz Uhl (B), Richard Van Vrooman (C), Albert Weikenmeier (D), Walter Berry (E), Karl Dönch (F), Paris Opéra Chorus and Orchestra—Pierre Boulez

For a recording that displays such excellent orchestral performance, with Boulez's precise attention to tempos and dynamics, this version shows a remarkably free attitude toward the sung pitches, an attitude that must be regarded as frank experimentalism. Time and again one hears excellent, full-toned singing, precisely on pitch, juxtaposed only a few measures later by a complete abandonment of accurate pitch in favor of an exaggerated *parlando* style, whether Berg calls for it or not. Karl Dönch, who made a splendid career as Wagner's Beckmesser, is the worst offender in this regard, and in any case his voice is nothing like the *buffo* bass that the Doctor's role demands. Walter Berry is more controlled, and his sound is wonderful, but like Fischer-Dieskau's, his vocal acting is too exaggerated to be as convincing as, for instance, Harrell's relatively plain lyricism. Isabel Strauss, as Marie, also has a superb sound and a fine understanding of the role, but a number of her vocal gestures seem to depend on Farrell's example. As in most of the recordings, the quality and conviction of the *Sprechstimme* vary widely in this version. All of this eclectic approach to Berg's vocal writing gives an uneven impression, and one wonders why

Boulez, who demanded and got forty orchestral rehearsals when he conducted this opera in Paris in 1964, did not insist on a comparable level of fidelity for the singers.

1974 ETERNA (S,P)

Gisela Schröter (A), Reiner Goldberg (B), Helmuth Klotz (C), Horst Hiestermann (D), Theo Adam (E), Konrad Rupf (F), Dresden Children's Chorus, Leipzig Radio Chorus and Radio Symphony Orchestra—Herbert Kegel

For those listeners with absolute pitch, this recording suffers from a catastrophic flaw: it is consistently a semitone too high. That difficulty aside, this East German recording is an excellent performance, which ought to be more widely available and better known.

Like the original *Wozzeck* recording, this one was made at a concert performance, a further testimony to the adaptability of *Wozzeck* to the concert hall, where it can make a big impact with minimal or no staging, and proof positive that audience noise and stage noises can be kept to a minimum. In many ways the listener is reminded of the best qualities of the Mitropoulos recording, especially in specific gestures of the vocal acting. Theo Adam's Wozzeck is well acted, with restraint and even a general coolness which does not impede his passion where needed, as in the confrontation scene; his vocal quality is quite comparable to Mack Harrell's. Gisela Schröter is a fine Marie, with a full range of unexaggerated expression, less pungent than Eileen Farrell's; yet her grasp of pitch is too often imprecise, especially in vocally excited passages, and she tends to interpret Berg's *parlando* instructions as merely singing with a light voice. Reiner Goldberg is possibly the best Drum Major on any of these recordings; he projects a stolid, oafish vocal sound that is just right. Horst Hiestermann, as the Captain, aims for the same qualities of squealing querulousness that Joseph Mordino brings off so well in the original recording, even when that means going wildly off the mark in accuracy of pitch.

There are some flaws in the tone of the trumpets and trombones, but otherwise the orchestra plays with superb understanding of the music, and Herbert Kegel's control of both ensemble and changes of tempo is excellent, even if some of his tempos are a bit rushed. Kegel's final interlude begins more softly than any other recording, bringing to this summarizing episode a hushed sense of tragedy completely overlooked by other conductors. Perhaps the most remarkable performance in this recording is that of the engineers, who have managed to capture so much of the rich complexity of the orchestration without ever interfering with the intelligibility of the singers. All in all, this recording maintains a very high standard in all of its dimensions, particularly for a live concert performance.

1979 DECCA / LONDON (S,D) CD

Anja Silja (A), Hermann Winkler (B), Horst Laubenthal (C), Heinz Zednik (D), Eberhard Wächter (E), Alexander Malta (F), Vienna State Opera Chorus, Vienna Philharmonic Orchestra—Christoph von Dohnányi

This is in every way an excellent performance by all forces, with Anja Silja's fine lyric characterization of Marie being particularly outstanding. All singers have obviously made a special effort to maintain accuracy of pitch, which is superior here to all the other recordings; not even Mitropoulos's so consistently approaches Berg's indicated tempos and dynamics. Technical flaws are few and unobtrusive, and the drama is well sustained and communicated from beginning to end.

Like the Eterna recording, this one is particularly well engineered; coupled with Dohnányi's superlative handling of the orchestra, this makes for a well-balanced sound which is lucid and rich in detail, but never overpowers the singers.

1987 DEUTSCHE GRAMMOPHON (S,D,P) CD

Hildegard Behrens (A), Walter Raffeiner (B), Philip Langridge (C), Heinz Zednik (D), Franz Grundheber (E), Aage Haugland (F), Vienna Boys' Choir, Vienna State Opera Chorus, Vienna Philharmonic Orchestra—Claudio Abbado

The newest recording of *Wozzeck* comes from the Vienna State Opera's production of June 1987. The live recording doesn't eliminate a certain amount of audience noise and unexplained sounds on stage (one can even hear the curtain rising in some scenes—and not at the precisely notated speed that Berg asks for in the score), but it provides an immediacy of sound that is lacking in the other versions. Unfortunately, the engineering is sometimes wildly wrong, so that the voices are occasionally drowned out by improbably loud instruments, and at other times important details (like the toad calls in the drowning scene) are hardly audible.

The vocal performances are generally very good, and pitches are in most instances quite precise. Franz Grundheber's Wozzeck stands out with an unadorned naturalness that is refreshing. Hildegard Behrens, who has sung the role in several other productions, has a richer vocal sound than one might like for Marie, but her understanding of the role is thorough, and her idea of *Sprechstimme*, particularly in the Bible scene, is more convincing than anyone else's in any of these recordings. Aage Haugland is a vocally effective Doctor, though lacking the element of furious megalomania that usually marks this role.

Claudio Abbado's handling of the orchestra is fully in keeping with the fine understanding of Berg's music for which he has long been noted. Some details in the orchestral performance stand out with exemplary precision, and the control of tempos and dynamics is good throughout (except the beginning of Act II, which is too slow).

All recordings of *Wozzeck* are complete, without any cuts. Among the newer recordings the Dohnányi version, by a narrow margin, is superior by virtue of better singing, with the Kegel and Abbado versions close behind; but the serious student of *Wozzeck* should not fail to know the old Mitropoulos recording for its many moments of unmatched poignancy and drama.

MARK DEVOTO

ALBAN BERG

LULU

A: Lulu (s); B: Geschwitz (ms); C: Alwa (t); D: Painter (t); E: Schön (bar);
F: Animal Trainer / Athlete (bar); G: Schigolch (bs)

*J*n *Wozzeck* Berg owed a significant portion of his success to the human poignancy of Büchner's play, which, whatever its psychological complexities, is dramatically a relatively simple message to carry off in the theater. In putting together his libretto for *Lulu* by carefully rebuilding two long plays by Frank Wedekind, Berg had to deal with a drama of a very different type. Except perhaps in the German-speaking world, where they would be readily understood as belonging to a particular time and place, Wedekind's Lulu plays could hardly hold the stage today on their own terms, for the character types are period figures when they are not caricatures; the one exception to this is Lulu herself, whom Wedekind endowed with mythic dimensions, as an innocent symbol of the eternal temptress, the incarnation of feminine sexuality.

The dramatic challenge which Berg set for himself in composing Wedekind's text occupied him intensively during the last seven years of his life, as his own personal life underwent much change and stress, and as the world he lived in began to collapse with the advent of Nazism. When he died in 1935 at the age of fifty, he had sketched *Lulu* completely in all its essential details, and orchestrated the first two acts and about one-third of the last act.

The subsequent history of *Lulu* in publication and performance is complex and fascinating and will only be given in outline here. In 1936 Berg's widow, Helene, asked her late husband's closest professional and personal friends, the composers Arnold Schoenberg and Anton von Webern, if they thought that the unorchestrated remainder could be finished; each did think so, but declined to do it himself. The first two acts of *Lulu*, and fragments of the third which had been orchestrated by Berg for concert performance, were produced in Zurich in 1937; the next year, the incorporation of Austria into the Third Reich effectively stopped all performances of Berg's music in Europe. Not until after World War II, in 1949, was *Lulu* staged again, and by that time Helene Berg had taken the position that no attempt should be made to complete the orchestral score of the third act. The result was that for some thirty years the opera was usually staged as a torso, with a makeshift scene substituting for the third act. This consisted of an orchestral prelude (the Variations in the *Lulu-Symphonie*, Berg's concert suite) and a pantomimed murder scene (the Adagio) in which Jack the Ripper appears in a silent role. After Helene Berg's death in 1976, Universal Edition, which had, after all, contracted with Berg for a three-act opera, let it be known that the Austrian composer Friedrich Cerha had been secretly commissioned some years before to prepare a performing score of the third act. The three-act *Lulu* with the Cerha score was triumphantly produced for the first time on February 24, 1979, at the Paris Opéra under the direction of Pierre Boulez. The performance was recognized everywhere as one of the most significant operatic events in decades, despite the intense controversy generated by the

Patrice Chéreau staging, which departed radically from Berg's specific stipulations.

It is well to remember that while the opera is no longer a torso, it still must be considered unfinished, for there is every evidence that Berg would have subjected the entire opera to a careful retouching and polishing of details. Nevertheless, the scrupulousness of Cerha's performing version has stood up to the severest scrutiny of Berg scholars for over a decade, and it is unlikely that there will ever be another version of Act III that will more authentically represent Berg's intentions.

1949 CBS / SONY (M)

Ilona Steingruber (A), Maria Cerny (B), Hans Libert (C), Waldemar Kmentt (D), Otto Wiener (E), Karl Loida (F), Emil Siegert (G), Vienna Symphony Orchestra—Herbert Häfner

This first recorded *Lulu* is testimony to the interest in Berg's music that became so quickly revitalized after World War II. This was the *Lulu* recording that taught the opera to a generation of listeners; it remained in print for many years, despite its unprepossessing appearance, its crudely printed libretto, and its almost nonexistent liner notes. Another annoyance is the variability of recording speed, which puts sides 1 and 6 a half step too high, and sides 2, 3, and 5 almost that.

The performance, on the other hand, is generally very good, with a sound which is well engineered for its time. Ilona Steingruber sets an excellent standard for a light voice in the title role, with accurate pitch and great style; one can only imagine what her task must have been in mastering such a difficult role for which there were practically no precedents. Sometimes she reaches the high Ds with graceful ease, and other times she prefers Berg's *ossia*, for which nobody could blame her. Maria Cerny's Countess Geschwitz is well sung, although her vocal sound is a bit too light for this role. One has a feeling that Hans Libert's voice is more of a baritone than is appropriate for Alwa, and that Otto Wiener's baritone comes across more as a tenor, but both singers do very well dramatically as well as vocally. Herbert Häfner's

leadership of the Vienna Symphony is particularly good, with rich sound and good tempos, and fine orchestral playing.

1968 EMI / ANGEL (S)

Anneliese Rothenberger (A), Kerstin Meyer (B), Gerhard Unger (C), Erwin Wohlfahrt (D), Toni Blankenheim (E), Benno Kusche (F), Kim Borg (G), Hamburg State Philharmonic Orchestra—Leopold Ludwig

Much of the operatic critical press in the late 1960s was occupied with the controversial production of the Hamburg Opera staged by Günther Rennert, which went on tour as far as New York. This live EMI recording, on just two discs, followed from that production. The only controversial aspect, and a serious one, is the constant tampering with Berg's libretto, ranging from a few changes of text early in the opera to many abridgments and changes in the spoken dialogue.

Musically the performance is generally good. One can take issue with Leopold Ludwig's tempos, which are sometimes inflexible and often rather slow (although the "Hymne," at the end of Act II, is faster than most other conductors'), but these are not serious weaknesses. Anneliese Rothenberger's Lulu has the richest vocal sound of all these recordings, and her technique, after a somewhat sluggish start, warms up to magnificent virtuosity throughout the rest of the opera. Rothenberger and Gerhard Unger, a fine light tenor who knows no fear in music of this kind, consistently have the most accurate pitch of all the singers in this recording; Kerstin Meyer, as Geschwitz, is also very good. Toni Blankenheim is dramatically expressive as Dr. Schön, but his voice projects more aged weariness than seems warranted, and the accuracy of his pitch is sometimes faulty; nevertheless, he brings off this very difficult role convincingly, especially in Act II. Benno Kusche is the least accurate of any of the singers, although he projects his characters very well through his exaggerated vocal gestures. Kim Borg is a wonderful Schigolch, singing mostly *parlando*, wheezing and creaking in every measure to good effect.

The hazards of recording a live staged performance are nowhere better illustrated than in this recording. The volume level in the mastering was not set properly until after the beginning of Act I, Scene 2, and thereafter one is constantly aware of every extraneous noise; and there are noises aplenty. The rising and lowering curtain sounds like a strange kind of maraca; people running or things falling onstage sound thunderous; and there is altogether too much audience noise. And somebody didn't get the message backstage at the end of Act I, when the electric doorbell rings continuously. On the positive side, the offstage jazz band sounds very clearly, which is welcome when one hears, probably for the first time, that Berg really did understand this kind of sound.

1968 DEUTSCHE GRAMMOPHON (S,P) CD

Evelyn Lear (A), Patricia Johnson (B), Donald Grobe (C), Loren Driscoll (D), Dietrich Fischer-Dieskau (E), Gerd Feldhoff (F), Josef Greindl (G), Orchestra of the Deutsche Oper, Berlin—Karl Böhm

This live recording was made during the new production of the Berlin Opera in 1968, staged by Gustav Rudolf Sellner. Extraneous noises are well controlled, although one can hear the audience laughing in Act II when Schigolch coughs. Three of the principals—Lulu, Dr. Schön, and the conductor—were also part of the 1965 DG recording of *Wozzeck*. By the time of this recording, Evelyn Lear had already made Lulu a specialty, and her strong and full-toned voice is certainly very good in this recording even though she does not always have the highest notes, relying on Berg's *ossias*. Fischer-Dieskau, better suited for this role than for *Wozzeck*, is a powerful and even imperious Schön, sometimes almost too fierce. Gerd Feldhoff's Animal Trainer is very good, but his Athlete tends to be noisy and often inaccurate in pitch; Patricia Johnson has some problems with accuracy also, but her Geschwitz is well acted.

The orchestra is at its weakest in the Act III makeshift, where the brass in the Variations have a generally poor tone, and the overall dynamics get out of hand in the Adagio. Not-

withstanding the inevitable small flaws in a live performance, the orchestra in the rest of this recording plays very well, and Böhm's masterly direction keeps ensemble and balance well controlled.

1976 DECCA / LONDON (S) CD

Anja Silja (A), Brigitte Fassbaender (B), Josef Hopferwieser (C), Horst Laubenthal (D), Walter Berry (E), Kurt Moll / Manfred Schenk (F), Hans Hotter (G), Vienna Philharmonic Orchestra—Christoph von Dohnányi

Anja Silja had made a specialty of the title role for at least ten years before this recording was made. Her Lulu is marked by a bright and clear vocal quality that combines seemingly effortless lightness with unshakable strength, projecting a quality of innocence that both Wedekind and Berg strove for. If one could imagine a Lulu singing Schubert, it would be this one; yet Silja's lyric vocal quality in no way weakens her dramatic power. The vocal accuracy of all the singers in this recording is generally excellent, with very few missed pitches, but Silja's control is particularly outstanding. Of the others, it can be said that Walter Berry as Dr. Schön lacks the kind of expressive desperation that this character needs; yet musically he makes up for this with a flawless performance. Brigitte Fassbaender as Geschwitz sometimes wanders off pitch, but her understanding of the role is intelligent and sympathetic. For some reason, the doubled role stipulated by Berg for the Athlete (in Act II) and the Animal Trainer (Prologue) is given here to two singers, both of them good. A real delight is the fine performance of Schigolch by Hans Hotter, the great Wotan at Bayreuth in the 1950s and 1960s; he was seventy-seven years old when this recording was made.

As with his recording of *Wozzeck*, Christoph von Dohnányi delivers a consummate performance with the Vienna Philharmonic. Certainly this recording surpasses all others, even Boulez's, in the sheer beauty of its orchestral sound, which is supported by excellent recording engineering to assure a good balance with the singers. One is constantly aware of Dohnányi's scrupulous attention to details of tempo and dynamics, and to the continuity of expression generally.

1979 DEUTSCHE GRAMMOPHON (S) CD

Teresa Stratas (A), Yvonne Minton (B), Kenneth Riegel (C), Robert Tear (D), Franz Mazura (E), Gerd Nienstedt (F), Toni Blankenheim (G), Paris Opéra Orchestra—Pierre Boulez

If the 1967–68 Hamburg Opera production of *Lulu* was deemed controversial because of the liberties taken with Berg's libretto and explicit stage directions, then the 1979 world premiere of the complete three-act opera was certainly much more so. Perhaps the most notorious of Patrice Chéreau's willful departures from Berg's wishes was the final scene in Act III, which Berg, following Wedekind, set in a dismal attic which he described and depicted in meticulous detail; Chéreau decided, for inscrutable reasons of his own, that Lulu's last scene should be set in a public toilet in the Paris Métro, and enlivened the audience's interest in Lulu's first client by bringing in a dwarf. Fortunately, the libretto included with the recording preserves Berg's directions, not those of the Paris production, although some idea of the latter can be seen in the accompanying photographs.

From a musical standpoint, this recording is of historic importance not only as the first complete *Lulu* but as an example of just how good a recorded performance can get, of an opera that in every way must be one of the most difficult in the entire repertory. The orchestra of the Paris Opéra is not a world-class ensemble like the Vienna Philharmonic, but Boulez managed, in this recording, to extract from it a sound that fully meets the demands of the music. There are any number of places in this recording where one can point to the excellence of the orchestral playing, to the acute attention paid to every aspect of accent, dynamics, balance, and continuity of details. If there is a certain lack of flexibility in the control of *rubato*, which is definitely not Boulez's forte, the extraordinary clarity of the orchestral performance more than compensates for this.

Teresa Stratas worked on the title role with great intensity, and her performance is so strong and so technically brilliant that one can easily hear why she has been identified with the role of Lulu for more than a decade. Stratas's Lulu, just in its sound quality, has an undercurrent of quiet menace that is entirely absent from Silja's, made all the more powerful by its bigger vibrato. All of the other singers give excellent performances as well, especially Franz Mazura and Kenneth Riegel; Gerd Nienstedt, as the Animal Trainer and the Athlete, has more trouble with accuracy of pitch than the others, but he comes across very well as the dull brute Berg called for; Toni Blankenheim, who sounded too old for Schön in 1968, sounds not quite old enough for Schigolch, but his mastery of the role is evident all the same.

The 1976 London recording is the best version of the truncated score. The Boulez set is to be preferred to all others, not only as the one complete version available so far but also because of the outstanding clarity, expression, and accuracy of the performance.

MARK DeVOTO

Unavailable for review:
1991 EMI/ANGEL

HECTOR BERLIOZ

LES TROYENS (1863)

A: Cassandre (s); B: Didon (ms); C: Anna (a); D: Énée (t);
E: Iopas (t); F: Hylas (t); G: Chorèbe (bar); H: Narbal (bs)

es Troyens is Berlioz's unique fusion of Gluckian classicism, Shakespearean variety, and Meyerbeerian spectacle, set to music that embraces both classical serenity and romantic passion. The latter, more conventionally associated with this composer, has been the easier of the two for interpreters to grasp, along with the expected inventiveness of orchestral color. Yet if the solemnity and amplitude of the ritual scenes—or, equally, the lyricism and humor of the genre scenes—are sacrificed, the balance and proportions are upset. (Judicious cutting may not be amiss in the theater, especially in the ballet music, the Second-Empire elegance of which may surprise some listeners.) And the vocal writing calls for classical French declamation—spacious, forceful, linguistically focused—as well as appreciation of the music's dimensions.

Although *Les Troyens* is no longer than several of the Wagner operas, Berlioz was forced to bisect it even before the first performance, which included only the last three acts, as *Les Troyens à Carthage*; for this occasion, he composed an impressive Prelude (which Colin Davis has recorded separately for Philips). Not until after the composer's death were the first two acts (*La Prise de Troie*) performed, and subsequent revivals generally retained the division into two operas (and the mutilations of the Carthaginian part practiced during the initial run), if for no better reason than that the only available performing materials did so. Hugh MacDonald's critical edition made possible the first performances ever of *Les Troyens* as Berlioz wrote it, in 1969 at Covent Garden under Colin Davis, on which the Philips recording was based.

1951 SELMER / WESTMINSTER
(*Les Troyens à Carthage* only) (M,P)

Arda Mandikian (B), Jeannine Collard (C), Jean Giraudeau (D), André Dran (E), Bernard Gallet (F), Xavier Depraz (H), Paris Vocal Ensemble, Paris Conservatory Orchestra—Hermann Scherchen

This French radio performance took place on May 10, 1952, at the Palais de Chaillot. Except for a cut in Hylas's song, the text is complete, including the Prelude Berlioz composed to introduce the 1863 performances (though not the spoken narrative and the playing of the Trojan March, which were to fill in the story line of the missing two acts); the Royal Hunt and Storm is in its proper place, before rather than after the love duet, where an inauthentic "tradition" long placed it. Alas, the recorded sound is dull and boxy, though clear enough to reveal much evidence of insufficient rehearsal.

Scherchen relates well to the music's tempestuous moments, its bounding syncopated surges of energy, but the classical aspect is shortchanged. The Didon / Anna and Anna / Narbal duets lack both line and variety, the ballet music is wayward rather than dancelike, the love duet never achieves an effortless flow. Messy choral and orchestral work undermines the effectiveness of the ceremonial passages, and the lack of rehearsal badly mars tricky scenes such as the duet for two sentries in the last act. Thereafter the atmosphere warms pretty steadily, thanks to Scherchen's intense tempos and to the temperament of the Didon, Arda Mandikian, who improves after a shaky start. The Énée, Jean Giraudeau, is a lyric tenor, which pays dividends in the role's quieter passages; to the bigger scenes, he can offer verbal commitment but little tonal bite, and he evades the high C in the last-act aria. The others have language on their side, but not much voice; Collard flats a lot, Depraz has authority in recitative but wobbles on longer notes, the Iopas is drily heady, and the Hylas sweeter but uncertain in tempo (Giraudeau would have been perfect in either role).

Deserving mention is a two-LP "highlights" package recorded by French EMI in 1965, centered on the Cassandre and Didon of Régine Crespin, with Paris Opéra forces under Georges Prêtre. Both the abridgments and the conductor's gusty approach offset the opera's scale, and Crespin does not sing subtly, though her commitment and idiomatic delivery are not lightly dismissed. As a reference point of French style in the work, this set suggests something of what is missing in the Davis recording.

1969 PHILIPS (S) CD

Berit Lindholm (A), Josephine Veasey (B), Heather Begg (C), Jon Vickers (D), Ian Partridge (E), Ryland Davies (F), Peter Glossop (G), Roger Soyer (H), Wandsworth School Boys' Choir, Chorus and Orchestra of the Royal Opera House, Covent Garden—Colin Davis

Not merely the absence of significant competition makes this recording indispensable. It is shot through with conviction about—and understanding of—the opera's special nature; both the classical breadth and the romantic passion coexist in vivid realization. Davis is never afraid to take his time (and the steadiness

of his beat makes the spaciousness work), yet the continuity and excitement rarely flag; no doubt the proximity of performances and recording sessions contributed to this sense of total immersion in Berlioz's world and musical language, as well as to the assurance of the choral and orchestral performances, the wealth of finely realized detail.

Roger Soyer's performance is about the only real manifestation of French style to be heard here (and a source of vocal strength as well). Even the cast's most admirable singer, Jon Vickers, convinces through voice and intensity of expression rather than through projection of the words; whether rousing his compatriots, confiding his son to Didon's care, or regretting the demands of fate, his Énée is always emotionally specific and involving. In the final section of his last-act aria, Vickers devours the notes with a tigerish appetite. Berit Lindholm, too, relies on commitment and urgency to bring Cassandre to life; her heavy voice, with its slow vibrato and weak chest register, is hardly the ideal instrument for the role. Josephine Veasey's mezzo is more appropriate for Didon, despite a vibrato that occasionally clouds the pitch. Peter Glossop, sturdy of voice, embodies perhaps too well Chorèbe's stolidity, and Heather Begg is a clumsy Anna, whose duet with Didon is the only point where the performance comes close to sinking. The two light tenors do well by their evocative solos. The recording has breadth and range; the ghosts that visit Énée are presented in close-up, rather than in theatrical perspective. (Deplorably, the editors of the CD package have failed to provide a proper cast list.)

Despite defects of detail, the Davis performance makes a powerful case for *Les Troyens* and the world it embodies. We can be almost certain, however, that the next recording, whatever its virtues, will be still further from the vanishing French operatic style.

DAVID HAMILTON

GEORGES BIZET

LES PÊCHEURS DE PERLES (1863)

A: Léila (s); B: Nadir (t); C: Zurga (bar); D: Nourabad (bs)

*A*lthough the engaging one-act *Le Docteur Miracle* had been produced when he was only 19, *Les Pêcheurs de Perles* was Bizet's first successful opera, a product of his twenty-fourth year. It shows few signs of the dramatic cogency of *Carmen*, which came only a dozen years later, but the score is nonetheless a cornucopia of memorable tunes. Its popularity is perhaps also due to the musical spell the composer seems to cast over his lovers, a kind of erotic hypnosis felt most powerfully (but not exclusively) in the tenor's first-act aria and in his duets with Zurga and Léila. It pervades the score and is an extraordinary achievement for so young a musician.

In spite of critical praise from Berlioz, during Bizet's lifetime the opera made little headway with the public, but a rehashed (and unauthorized) edition appeared after his death, and it is in this version that it has until recently been heard. It involves a "revised" ending to the great tenor-baritone duet of Act I (the contrasted F-major final section replaced by a return to the main theme), and in Act III cuts in the scene for Léila and Zurga, as well as a recomposed finale (music by Benjamin Godard). All but two of the complete recordings follow the "corrupt" score, and in French sets there are additional small cuts evolved over the years at the Opéra-Comique. As a further complication, the opera belongs to a period when singers were accustomed to transpose for vocal comfort, with the result that, even in one of the complete sets, the tenor's great solo, "Je crois entendre encore," may be heard not in the original A minor but transposed either by a semitone or even a tone. This gives the tenor the possibility of an effective high B (or B-flat) in an interpolated but by now familiar cadence; the transposition can reduce the effect of Nadir being possessed by a higher power, which is a feature of his music.

The tampering is, of course, to be deplored, the cuts are better opened, and Godard's Act III finale is inferior even to Bizet's unsatisfactory solution. All the same, second thoughts have prompted conductors to prefer the reprise of the big opening E-flat tune—one of the sources of the opera's popularity—in the tenor-baritone duet, and a recent commentator has suggested the reprise represents Bizet's own second thoughts. Plasson in his complete recording appears to take this point of view but as a postscript adds the original version with its quicker F-major finale.

p.1952 PERIOD (M)

Mattiwilda Dobbs (A), Enzo Seri (B), Jean Borthayre (C), Lucien Mars (D), Paris Philharmonic Chorus and Orchestra—René Leibowitz

Idiomatic conducting by René Leibowitz (Schoenberg's pupil and known for his work in contemporary music) distinguishes a set which makes the cuts habitual at the Opéra-Comique. In theory the performance sounds like a typical product of that institution—the French horns very French in sound—but in fact only the admirable Zurga belonged there, having made his debut in this role a year before the recording

43

was made. His singing is robust and forthright, his third-act aria passionate and committed, but unfortunately the same cannot be said of his male colleague Enzo Seri, who, in spite of some affecting soft singing, particularly in "Je crois entendre encore" (which he transposes by a semitone), frequently sounds uncomfortable in a role which demands the acme of French style. Mattiwilda Dobbs, early in her career, sings with charm and fresh vocal quality, the floated top notes and good trill at the end of Act I being particular assets. Even though she was once Pierre Bernac's pupil, her French is less than immaculate, but her basically light voice copes well with the music's demands, and there is pleasure to be had from her innocent musicality.

1953 PHILIPS (M) CD

Pierrette Alarie (A), Léopold Simoneau (B), René Bianco (C), Xavier Depraz (D), Lamoureux Orchestra—Jean Fournet

Six years before he sang Nadir onstage (if his biography is correct), Léopold Simoneau recorded the role with such beauty of tone, clarity of diction, and rhythmic point as to make most other singers pale at the comparison. The high tessitura presents no problems, and the listener is left to decide whether to admire most the poise and beauty at the start of the duet with Zurga or the sense of wonder and total involvement the singer produces, or in the aria the delicacy of the line or the attack in mixed voice on the high As and B-natural. Whether in recitative or the great numbers, he is nothing short of ideal. Bianco's Zurga is no more than decently sung, but Alarie produces knowledgeable, neat singing, and, in spite of a voice light for the role, she makes the most of her gifts of precision and accuracy. Cuts are as expected, but Fournet conducts a mostly ardent, only occasionally four-square performance. Orchestra and chorus are good, and the recording is admirable for its period. I should not want to be without it for the sake of Simoneau's rare qualities.

1955 EMI / ANGEL (M)

Martha Angelici (A), Henri Legay (B), Michel Dens (C), Louis Noguéra (D), Chorus and Orchestra of the Opéra-Comique—André Cluytens

If Léopold Simoneau's singing of Nadir's music is the most distinguished on records (as I am convinced), André Cluytens's direction of his Opéra-Comique forces shows him to be the score's strongest recorded interpreter. It is a performance without exaggeration, balanced and well controlled, which with a stronger cast could have been ideal. The singers succeed in making a convincing case for what was then a customary French virtue—a natural delivery of text combined with music—and their work is not without style, but only Michel Dens has vocal attributes of the sort that rewards repeated gramophone listening.

1959 CHANT DU MONDE (M) CD

Janine Micheau (A), Alain Vanzo (B), Gabriel Bacquier (C), Lucien Lovano (D), Chorus and Orchestre National de la RTF, Paris—Manuel Rosenthal

Issued under the now defunct "double mono" system, this in many ways admirable recording has the entire opera on a single disc and requires the left- and right-hand channels to be used *independently*; it is unplayable on a machine whose channels cannot operate in such a way. It has the advantages and disadvantages of a public performance (in this case radio, perhaps with audience present), in that the singers sound free from studio inhibition, but neither chorus nor orchestra exhibits the precision available with re-takes. Manuel Rosenthal knows when to give his fine cast their heads, contrasts the languorous start with elegantly played dances to follow, whips up the drama in the third-act duet for Léila and Zurga, and generally shapes the score with musicianly finesse and the knowledge which comes from the best kind of routine. The singers are admirable, and Janine Micheau, singing confidently from the start, shows (possibly for the only time on records) why she was so highly regarded at the time. The voice is of ideal weight for the role, heavier than recorded competitors, the tone round and limpid, and, with good trills and thrilling top notes, she has the vocal poise to do the music full justice. This is a different artist from the inhibited, studio-bound performer of a year later. Vanzo's voice has the brilliance of a leading singer in mid-career, and he is the only tenor in a complete set to rival Simoneau. In the aria he adopts a light tone which allows for soft high notes to grow out of a seamless *legato*, and he starts the love duet in Act II with an elegance and ecstasy reminiscent of de Lucia in a not-to-be-forgotten recording of nearly ninety years ago. This is splendid singing. Gabriel Bacquier exhibits authority from the outset, the sound is attractively firm, his narrative of the approach of Léila in Act I the most interesting on records, and he makes a great dramatic *scena* of Zurga's aria. For the period, the recording is good, apart from a complete absence of distancing in Nadir's beautiful offstage serenade in Act II. Cuts are normal, but additional losses (not specially damaging, I found) are the recitative and reprise of the dance after Nadir's entrance; the play-out for Léila's exit in Act I (before the tenor aria); orchestra and chorus at the start of Act II (and the same chorus after the scene of Léila and Nourabad); and internal cuts in the finales of Acts II and III.

1960 EMI / ANGEL (S) CD

Janine Micheau (A), Nicolai Gedda (B), Ernest Blanc (C), Jacques Mars (D), Chorus and Orchestra of the Opéra-Comique—Pierre Dervaux

What should have been an ideal cast turns out something of a disappointment. Janine Micheau was the leading French soprano of her generation: the voice is of ideal weight for the role, heavier than competitors in complete sets, the tone limpid, and there is occasionally some attractive singing from her. Yet she never

sounds truly comfortable in this music; perhaps she never did herself justice in the studio as opposed to the theater. Nicolai Gedda, a stylist in any repertory and usually a star in French music, provides ringing tone throughout but, in spite of a very fine aria, demonstrates less consistency—and evokes less magic—than one could hope for. When recorded, Ernest Blanc was among the finest baritones in Europe, an international star yet wholly French in vocal color and style, and he more than his colleagues does himself justice in a recording which somehow suggests too hasty assembly, or maybe just an ill-starred day in the studio. (Forty-five minutes of excerpts from Bizet's opera *Ivan IV* make a valuable, because otherwise unavailable, filler).

1970 CARILLON (S)

Adriana Maliponte (A), Alfredo Kraus (B), Sesto Bruscantini (C), Antonio Campò (D), Chorus and Orchestra of Gran Liceo, Barcelona—Carlo Felice Cillario

Two Italian and two Spanish singers may not sound like definitive ingredients for an opera which for all its international success remains very French, but the conducting as well as the singing is good, and no complete opera recording featuring Alfredo Kraus can be dismissed too summarily. The voice itself is outstanding, the singing as confident as it is accomplished, and only the style, however experienced in French music he may be, is a little wanting. In a word, he remains an Italianate performer. But he works the magic in "De mon amie," and any disc is worth having which contains such a performance of Nadir's aria, with a delicate line, poised as if hallucinating as he conjures up the memory of Léila, then—to prove memory can become reality—rising to top C in the interpolated cadence. Nor is he alone, as Bruscantini sings Zurga's aria touchingly, and Maliponte, a soprano once resident in France, sings "O dieu Brahma" at the end of the first act very well indeed (better in fact than she does "Comme autrefois").

1977 EMI / ANGEL (S) CD

Ileana Cotrubas (A), Alain Vanzo (B), Guillermo Sarabia (C), Roger Soyer (D), Paris Opéra Chorus and Orchestra—Georges Prêtre

Prêtre in 1977 led a strong cast in an uncut performance with Bizet's original ending. Vanzo remains a supreme French stylist and, though one may regret some explosive recitative (a disadvantage of his otherwise immaculate singing late in his career) and an over-reliance on *mezza voce* verging on falsetto, this is a performance of authority and grace. Cotrubas uses the French language much better than most singers not born in France, and her artistry (as well as her inability to steer clear of contrivance) shows in the way she colors tone and shapes a phrase. She is at her best in the duets: catching the innocence and casting the spell in the love duet with Vanzo; making the uncut "Je frémis, je chancelle" with Sarabia into a highlight of the score. In spite of all-purpose French and an element of rich "international" veneer in the voice, Sarabia makes a powerful Zurga and brings a fine frenzy to the last act. Chorus and orchestra are excellent, and Prêtre for the most part avoids any risk of sentimentality and moves the music along at a good pace. Recording is fine.

1989 EMI / ANGEL (S,D) CD

Barbara Hendricks (A), John Aler (B), Gino Quilico (C), Jean-Philippe Courtis (D), Chorus and Orchestra of the Théâtre du Capitole, Toulouse—Michel Plasson

This is a serious attempt to solve the opera's problems: there are no cuts, no Godard, although Plasson does make the reprise in "Au fond du temple saint." However, the effect is marred by two factors: the inadequacy of two of the singers, and the sluggish tempos adopted by the conductor. Recognition of the score's need to hypnotize, which helps the love duet, seems to have lead to ultra-slow speeds in the duet for Nadir and Zurga, for instance, a main factor in establishing the opera's prevailing mood. Barbara Hendricks makes some gloriously full sounds as Léila and her aria is one of the best (even though the engineers, unlike the microphones, seem not to have noticed some extraneous hammering). On a lower level are Gino Quilico, a splendid singer in the theater but on this evidence short of authority in the recording studio, and John Aler, a lightweight tenor whose good intentions are mostly nullified by a significant lack of color in the voice.

1990 NUOVA ERA (S,P,D) CD

Alessandra Ruffini (A), Giuseppe Morino (B), Bruno Praticò (C), Eduardo Abumradi (D), Slovak Philharmonic Chorus of Bratislava, Orchestra Internazionale d'Italia—Carlos Piantini

French opera recorded live by non-French singers at a summer festival with a conductor from the Dominican Republic—even though the concert was highly praised at the time—seems a curious enterprise. Obvious snags intrude: the generally good recording captures some excellent orchestral playing and choral singing, but it sounds as if it had been a windy night; and, in spite of good intentions, the French pronunciation has strong Italian overtones, an Italian "e" tending to overwhelm French "le" and "je" syllables. Nevertheless, the performance is well conducted, with plenty of panache and yet a generous and subtle *rubato* so that good committed singing brings out the magic of the score. Alessandra Ruffini is outstanding, the voice bright, full, and under complete control, and her soft high singing an invariable source of pleasure. She sings the aria with distinction, a proper spell is cast in the love duet, and, some unidiomatic French apart, there is no more attractive Léila in any of these sets. Giuseppe Morino is an Italian tenor, but he attempts valiantly to sing softly, and in the aria succeeds additionally in capturing the essential sense of rapture. Praticò's is clear, straightforward, serious singing, and he and Ruffini make something of a climax, in the last act, of "Je frémis, je chancelle," which starts with one of Bizet's melodic inspirations but in performance tends to lose its way before the end; perhaps the singers are helped here because the conductor opens one (sadly not both) of the customary Opéra-Comique cuts. Not perhaps a definitive recording, but undoubtedly one to enjoy.

———————

The choice between several sets is not simple. Probably Prêtre's is the safest recommendation, in a "correct" version and with good singing all through, but I cannot hide my conviction that Simoneau's is the most definitive individual performance in any set, and that Micheau and Vanzo made stronger contributions in 1959 than in later sets (and led the strongest cast). Many listeners will think of this as (in the old-fashioned sense) a singers' opera and choose accordingly.

LORD HAREWOOD

GEORGES BIZET

CARMEN (1875)

A: Carmen (s or ms); B: Micaela (s); C: Don José (t); D: Escamillo (bar)

When *Carmen* had its premiere at the Opéra-Comique in 1875, the critics found it obscene, Wagnerian, or both. Shortly afterward, Bizet died at thirty-seven of heart disease, and for the first performance in Vienna later in the year his friend Ernest Guiraud composed recitatives to replace the original passages of dialogue. In that form *Carmen* was usually played throughout the rest of the world for ninety years and from 1908 onward was repeatedly recorded more or less complete. Then in 1964 the musicologist Fritz Oeser published a very controversial new edition of the score restoring not only the dialogue but also about fifteen minutes of music cut in rehearsal before the original performance. Since that time, no two recordings have used precisely the same text. The changes may seem trifling, but they are not; the musical restorations involve some key passages, among them the knife fight between Don José and Escamillo, the close of Act III, and the death scene itself. Every critic, it seems, has written passionately on his or her choices. I myself have an unswerving preference for the longer version of the fight scene but also for the traditional and dramatically more forceful conclusions of Acts III and IV.

Ultimately, though, one's choice among *Carmen* recordings may depend as much on the depth and direction of the portrayals as on the version used. One can think of no opera but *Don Giovanni* which offers such a fascinating variety of approaches. The Carmen of Merimée's 1845 novella is inscrutable, sensual, wolf-eyed—and is seen through the eyes of Don José, himself painted as a heroic bandit of almost legendary stature. Onstage these characters, like Hamlet, take on the illusions of the eras and regions in which they are enacted. French Carmens, especially those in the *opéra comique* tradition, tend to remain cool and lightly but pungently satiric. Italian Carmens are more brutally passionate and the Spanish elegantly spicy. Americans, generally singing in French, have taken something from each of these styles. In Moscow, as far back as 1925, Carmen was played as a Polish Jew stabbed to death after her fiery panegyric on Communism. In these days of conductorial hegemony and directorial experiment, we are as far from consensus as ever. *Carmen*, though, remains inimitable: no other French opera has absorbed so many performing styles with such striking effect.

1928 EMI / ANGEL (M)

Raymonde Visconti (A), Marthe Nespoulous (B), Georges Thill (C), Louis Guénot (D), Chorus of the Opéra-Comique, unidentified orchestra—Elie Cohen

Cuts abound in this early performance: they include the Act I finale, many transitional passages, a second verse or two, and several choral sections—about forty minutes of music. The set's central interest is Georges Thill, the Paris Opéra's leading lyric tenor from the twenties through World War II. Any five minutes of his rich *legato* explains his fame, though his dramatic vision of Don José is simpler than Bizet's.

His Flower Song, for example, is more publicly reflective than privately anguished, and the portrayal as a whole lacks something in both rapture and agonized humiliation, though it is smoothly phrased. His Carmen, Raymonde Visconti, has a promising lyric mezzo which she uses, however, with the faceless inefficiency of a new telephone operator. The Habanera verses are all hammered out alike, and the Seguidilla has nothing of insinuation in it: finally the listener is alienated without being aroused. As Micaela, Marthe Nespoulous is coldly fragile and occasionally harsh—Don José's woodpecker friend. Her aria is taken fast, and there is certainly little sense of a private conversation with God. Louis Guénot's Escamillo introduces a note of drollery when singing of Carmen's discarded lover, but elsewhere he provides bluster and some unsteadiness rather than charm. In contrast, the Frasquita and Mercédès, André Vayon and Andrée Bernadet, are as pleasant as any on records, and the chorus is spirited, if rough. Conductor Elie Cohen plows ahead industriously with what sounds like a reduced orchestra.

1928 EMI / ANGEL (M)

Lucy Perelli (A), Yvonne Brothier (B), José de Trévi (C), Louis Musy (D), Chorus of the Opéra-Comique, unidentified orchestra—Piero Coppola

Only Acts III and IV of this relatively complete recording were available for review. The memorable singer here is José de Trévi, of the Brussels Monnaie Opera. At once distraught and heroic, he sweeps through phrases to create a mythic bandit not in the least tearful or vulgar. The voice is light and gritty; one imagines that much singing like this would destroy it, but the performance is more exhilarating than some that are better sung. The Opéra-Comique's Lucy Perelli is a lively Carmen, though without shadows, as it were; she rushes the Card Song (which lies low for her), flats on a high note or two, and brays in the finale. Yvonne Brothier, like Marthe Nespoulous in the Cohen set, was a well-known Mélisande. The voice is both lyric and hard, the effect neat but indifferent. As

Escamillo, Louis Musy has firm top tones and some sense of line but little charm. Coppola's orchestra is eager but the Opéra-Comique chorus is rough.

1937 MET (M,P)

Rosa Ponselle (A), Hilda Burke (B), René Maison (C), Julius Huehn (D), Metropolitan Opera Chorus and Orchestra—Gennaro Papi

This notorious performance is a 1937 Metropolitan Opera live broadcast from Cleveland. It heralded the stormy close of Rosa Ponselle's career. Her Carmen was from the first a bitterly controversial achievement, marked by pugnacious allure and strewn with muttering and growls. The Habanera is rough and dirty, she baits Zuniga with vicious contempt, and her Seguidilla exploits register changes violently, while the Card Song is baleful and the finale raucous. On the other hand, her reading of the *épinglette* scene in Act I has infectious good humor, and her later recall of the Habanera is easy and inviting, tapering off enticingly at the close. In all, she plays something of a young Azucena: compulsive, totally self-absorbed, often repellent. For the intimacy of a recording it is all matchlessly crude—the Cleveland house seated 9,000—and yet in a few passages just matchless. Opposite her is René Maison, a Belgian known in Europe primarily for his work in Wagner. He sang for eight seasons at the Metropolitan, where one of his successes was Florestan, opposite Flagstad. Almost alone among Don Josés recorded complete, he has an authentic French sound, heroic and sometimes sweet, but he frequently forces his voice, so that some of the climaxes are agonizingly under pitch. At one point he claws his way up to a top tone, flats, works at it, gets it right, and then strangles the beast with a grunt. But the yearning is there and the tears are sometimes in abeyance: a portrayal deeply flawed and yet often absorbing.

The others are of less interest. Hilda Burke is an industrious but dull Micaela, with some forced and some flat high notes. Julius Huehn's burly, raw Escamillo has a certain baseball-player charm but no irony, French or otherwise. The quintet is a big-time, slam-bang performance of the music, but Thelma Votipka, the Met's most enduring *comprimaria*, stands out, with a voice pretty in itself and yet fleet and clear enough to balance with the others. Leading the attack is Gennaro Papi, who spent a career of twenty-five seasons as repertory conductor at the Metropolitan and Chicago Operas. The stars are here encouraged to hack out dramatic statements, sometimes to the detriment of their singing, but there are many moments of visceral excitement and some of subtlety and perfume, too. It's a performance of several kinds of fascination.

1950 EMI / ANGEL (M)

Solange Michel (A), Martha Angelici (B), Raoul Jobin (C), Michel Dens (D), Chorus and Orchestra of the Opéra-Comique—André Cluytens

This was the first commercial recording of the original *opéra comique* version, with spoken dialogue rather than the customary recitatives composed by Guiraud for the Viennese premiere after Bizet's death. The difference is more than technical. The recitatives provide less information about the characters but invite a more theatrical performance, whereas the *opéra comique* score suggests in its central figure an emotional objectivity in itself implacable enough to drive the tenor to murder. Charismatic Carmens, no matter what the version used, have combined aspects of both approaches. This ambiguity is reflected in the variety of singers who have taken the role: everyone from erstwhile Juliettes (Farrar) to Erdas (Schumann-Heink). The view here is singularly objective. André Cluytens, regular conductor for the Opéra and Opéra-Comique for twenty years, leads a quick and genial performance. His Carmen, Solange Michel, is accurate, amused, and, for those who respond, infuriating. Her Habanera teases, with little variation in vocal color, and much of the rest of her performance is satirically remote: attractive in its lyricism. What she lacks, for me, is thrust, command, and tragic stature. Faced with this enigmatic heroine, Raoul Jobin

offers a Don José whose tone at least suggests the heroic, with a full-voiced, graceful Flower Song (far better than his earlier American version) and a committed manner throughout. Martha Angelici sings "Parle-moi de ma mère" prettily and is elsewhere dramatically dutiful but without a compelling sense of Micaela's courage and conviction. As Escamillo, Michel Dens has some buoyant grace and a sunny upper register, though the rest of his voice lacks glamour and depth. The Gypsies sing with hearty gentility, and their detention of Zuniga at the end of Act II has considerable charm. The chorus is accurate and yet sounds convincingly like a city crowd. Altogether, this is a painless and sometimes provocative performance.

1951 DECCA / LONDON (M)

Suzanne Juyol (A), Janine Micheau (B), Libero De Luca (C), Julien Giovannetti (D), Chorus and Orchestra of the Opéra-Comique—Albert Wolff

This was Decca's first entry in the *Carmen* competition, recorded in the year following the EMI performance mentioned above, with the same orchestra and chorus but a new conductor and cast. The Guiraud recitatives are used. Wolff's work is lively but sometimes inexact. The major problem is the cast of principals, all of whom have vocal difficulties. The best of them is Janine Micheau, who made her debut at the Opéra-Comique in 1933 and sang for many years there and at the Opéra. She is pleasant enough but motherly. Julien Giovannetti sings Escamillo with some seductive drollery, though he is insecure above and below the staff. As Don José, the Swiss tenor Libero De Luca has conviction but a voice of limited color, which betrays him into whining and wobbling at moments of stress. Most problematic is Suzanne Juyol, whose voice has a cutting edge which served her well in Wagner. Here, though, her manner is about as seductive and insinuating as Ethel Merman's, without the good humor. The Seguidilla scene is tough rather than impudent, the Card Song is noisy, and in the finale she plays a slattern to De Luca's whining José: an unfortunate coupling. The psychology of Carmen's character remains unexplored.

1951 RCA / BMG (M) CD

Risë Stevens (A), Licia Albanese (B), Jan Peerce (C), Robert Merrill (D), Robert Shaw Chorale, RCA Victor Orchestra—Fritz Reiner

Here we have an international-style performance, with four Metropolitan stars dominated by a German conductor who leads with a superb but charmless control suggesting Beethoven more than Bizet. It is quite beautifully played, without eccentricity but without much seductive spontaneity, either. That limits, to an extent, its famous Carmen. Risë Stevens was often a galvanic figure onstage. Here she is both earthy and elegant, but not as impetuous as her broadcasts and earlier recordings demonstrate. The voice is at its peak—a dark lyric mezzo admirably used; only one or two top notes lack authority. Despite the conductor's gravity she really does try to enjoy her little dance for Don José in Act II, and her Card Song is brooding, though Reiner understates the accompaniment. In such a setting she is more successful with anger than charm, and at her strongest in much of the final duet.

Jan Peerce is always better at noble outrage than dalliance. Here his voice is powerful and focused, without sensual languor but reflecting plenty of compulsive anxiety and despair. The Flower Song has characteristically luscious tone, though it is sung too fast and loudly to be the intimate and heartrending thing it can be. Like Stevens, he is sometimes more impassioned than the orchestra, as at the close of Act III. In the final scene he exemplifies the tragic. Licia Albanese is certainly the most moving Micaela on records. The lower voice is not always smooth and the vocal method is Italianate, but the top voice is brilliant and full of yearning, and the characterization is complete. In Act I she colors her voice for both infatuation and propriety, and later for the terrorized faith that has brought her to the Gypsy camp at dawn. In her final

confrontation with Don José she is one of the few recorded Micaelas to take command: innocent and purposeful at once—a portrayal of distinction.

Robert Merrill's Toreador, very smoothly vocalized, lacks the character's jaunty intractability, but so does practically every other Escamillo on records. The others form a typical Metropolitan cast of the time. The chorus sings with energy and precision. Altogether this is a bracing and well-recorded performance of great historical interest, distinguished for some fine vocalism and an outstanding Micaela.

1957 PATHÉ (M)

Jean Madeira (A), Janette Vivalda (B), Nicola Filacuridi (C), Michel Roux (D), Choeurs du Conservatoire, Concerts Pasdeloup Orchestra—Pierre Dervaux

This recording commemorates an Aix-en-Provence Festival production of orchestral grace and spirit: all the instrumental—and choral—passages are done with panache. Of the soloists, only Jean Madeira is notable: her lustrous contralto and forthright manner make for a strong, conventionally outspoken Carmen. There are occasional breath-control problems and some of the elephantine chirping typical of this species of Carmen, but her Habanera is surprisingly offhand and the Seguidilla rhythmically alert. Her Card Song might have been overwhelming; here it lacks the seamless *legato* and expansive phrasing for a fully developed tragic realization. She does the heroics of the death scene well. Nicola Filacuridi is a Don José of desperate conviction but ugly tone. The conclusions of Acts III and IV are at least forthright, but all his lyric moments are gritty and pressured. Michel Roux has some charm of manner if not tone, but Janette Vivalda is a brassy Micaela without either the sweet reserve for Act I or the sense of terrorized faith for Act III. Of the others, Daniel Marty is a pleasant, spirited Morales. Altogether, Dervaux's rhythmic vitality and orchestral balance and Madeira's tone quality—and occasional humor—are the attractive elements here.

1958/59 EMI/ANGEL (S) CD

Victoria de los Angeles (A), Janine Micheau (B), Nicolai Gedda (C), Ernest Blanc (D), Chorus and Orchestre National de la RTF—Thomas Beecham

This renowned recording is distinctive for both its conductor and its heroine. Both perform with a languorous but not languid grace which for many critics defines the difference between Bizet's opera and the tempestuous and exotic novella on which it is based. Certainly Beecham and his French chorus and orchestra respond with a charm and grave delight found in none of the other sets, and Victoria de los Angeles, with her silvery, sometimes dusky tone and her fine phrasing, is bewitching. The performance has elegance, command, sweetness, and even grit at the close—each of them qualities the soprano also demonstrated, apparently, during the difficult year or more that it took to complete the recording. But where, in this portrayal, is the danger? Is this the woman who stabs someone in a factory brawl? Is hers the scorn that rouses Don José to his most poignant moment of lyricism? Even with this reservation, de los Angeles enchants, and the conception is clear, alluring, and cherishable.

Opposite her, Nicolai Gedda, a fine musician, supplies a lyrical voice thick enough to qualify him for some of the heroic aspects of the role. He lacks something of the murderous temper that has forced Don José into the army before the opening curtain, and his Flower Song is perhaps more the retreat into a dream than an effort to persuade Carmen of his passion. In the final duet, he works up considerable tension, but there his frenzied pleas are sometimes overpowered by the orchestra. Janine Micheau's second recorded Micaela has, like her first, a warmth of tone that distinguishes her from most French lyric sopranos, but again the voice is a trifle unsteady and the emotional temperature low. Under Beecham, the Toreador Song goes with panache, but Ernest Blanc's Escamillo, like many others, fails to smile; the detached amusement of Act III eludes him—precisely the element that attracts Carmen. Nevertheless, the set (the first in stereo) is one of the most attractive on records and well worth study.

1963 DECCA/LONDON (S) CD

Regina Resnik (A), Joan Sutherland (B), Mario del Monaco (C), Tom Krause (D), Geneva Grand Théâtre Chorus, Orchestre de la Suisse Romande—Thomas Schippers

A bizarre performance. It has an energetic conductor, a brilliantly artful Carmen, an accomplished group of *comprimarios*, and a plausible chorus—the boys' group is particularly convincing. To offset these, it also presents some egregious sound effects and crowd noises, some breathlessly fast tempos, and del Monaco and Sutherland at their most willful. Regina Resnik's Carmen is consistently fascinating, even if now and then coarsely vocalized. In the Habanera she muses, and in the Seguidilla she manages both insouciance and maturity—one of the subtlest of modern performances. "Non, tu ne m'aimes pas" in Act II is at the same time alienating and inviting: certainly the effect that Bizet sought. The Card Song is restrained but freighted with baleful subtext, and the end of Act III insultingly matter-of-fact. Her last moments are also effective, but there she is finally done in by her monomaniacal tenor, Mario del Monaco—commanding in tone but immutably brash and angry in manner. His Act I scene with Sutherland is a travesty; he nags and she droops. He saws through the Flower Song quickly: a pity, since the sound of the voice, aside from his use of it, really evokes Merimée's iconoclastic outlaw.

As noted, Sutherland is lugubrious, though her high B in the aria is a memorably chilling tone. Tom Krause is efficient and spirited as the Toreador, but despite his efforts at grace he and del Monaco sound in Act III like two unpleasant thugs scrapping over a harlot. In charge of this menagerie is Thomas Schippers, who conducts the Guiraud version with impulsiveness and color. He accelerates distractingly from time to time, but in the Flower Song del Monaco rushes *him*—a new exemplification of "fast." The album is valuable for the Resnik interpretation and for the distinctive Morales and Zuniga under a vigorous conductor.

1963 RCA / BMG (S) CD

Leontyne Price (A), Mirella Freni (B), Franco Corelli (C), Robert Merrill (D), Vienna State Opera Chorus, Vienna Philharmonic Orchestra—Herbert von Karajan

Of course, this performance is dominated by its conductor, Herbert von Karajan. His prelude leads us to expect a dashing production, the ideas tumbling over one another in a passionate exposition of the Guiraud version, but once the curtain is up, the show stops. Even when the score's orchestral transparency has been exquisitely revealed, the opera emerges as a heavily academic study of nonchalance, and not as a drama. The boys' chorus is but one example. They sing very well, but with Prussian exactitude, like military midgets. The chief victims of this humorless approach, however, are the soloists, all of them outstanding singers and none of them, here, subtle or interesting actors.

The voice of Leontyne Price is like a big, deep-colored cassia flower. There is seduction in the tone itself and she is often a marvelous vocalist. Act I begins promisingly with offhand charm, but almost immediately in the Habanera she is announcing Carnality for the Millions. The Seguidilla is delightful, but elsewhere Karajan conducts such a melodramatically lumbering performance that his Carmen appears forced to overact to fill in the spaces. The Card Song suggests intergalactic doom, and the close of the final scene is growled. To play that scene exclusively for anger, rather than as an indomitable quest for freedom, trivializes it. Franco Corelli, as nearly always on records, is grandiose in tone, at once labored and prodigal, though the Flower Song is more restrained than one would expect. Elsewhere he roars and bawls magnificently, and in the final scene he gives the impression of playing both the bull and Don José at the same time, a concept which some enterprising director will no doubt soon foist upon us. Once again, Robert Merrill is splendidly solid and stolid. Mirella Freni, in one of her earliest recordings, demonstrates a rich and warm sound but little dramatic tension, so that the third-act prayer is both lovely and somewhat inert. There is, in sum, much gorgeous playing and vocalizing in this set: the sort of recording from which one prefers, in the end, to hear only an annihilatingly beautiful excerpt or two.

1964 EMI / ANGEL (S) CD

Maria Callas (A), Andrea Guiot (B), Nicolai Gedda (C), Robert Massard (D), René Duclos Chorus, Paris Opéra Orchestra—Georges Prêtre

Maria Callas recorded Carmen toward the close of her career, in 1964. She never sang this, or indeed any other role in French, onstage. In writing of another Callas characterization, that of Norma, Andrew Porter alluded to its comprehensiveness as well as its individuality; he was forced to go back to Lilli Lehmann for a parallel exhibition of what is in the score. I find myself with a similar view of Callas's Carmen, despite her practical inexperience with the role. Certainly some of its qualities can be found elsewhere. Emma Calvé's records reveal feline grace, Emmy Destinn's impetuousness, Mary Garden's brooding lyric power, and Conchita Supervia's wit and sexual mystery—to name only a few singers from an earlier age. With Callas's Carmen, one gets *all* of these elements, not as a mélange but as individual aspects of a single powerful vision. Strangely, they glitter and fade as one listens again and again; the impression is never quite the same, although of course the recording remains *exactly* the same.

There is a Gypsy quality of mind in her portrayal. For once, we do not have to take the power of this haunting figure on faith; it is as if Callas's Carmen is saying, "I have experienced, in my own special way, everything: why do we live, if not to do so?" Her Carmen is such a Gypsy: mythical, if you will—subtle, adventurous, full of emotional and even intellectual byplay, inviting, and intensely alive beneath the veneer of seductive grace. Even her contempt is bewitching, so that she mocks and magnetizes at the same time. She enlarges Don José as she turns him into a tragic figure.

With all this, her performance is remarkably intimate. The Seguidilla is almost murmured, and the Card Song manages to imply the universal in a reading of special quietude. In the final scene she has dignity and tremendous purpose: to express her own truth. One may cavil here; the animal cry is effective—no one does it better—but is it really expressive of such a Carmen's overwhelming candor? In all, Callas's is a Carmen that for once has the heroine's own charisma.

The portrayal has a respectable setting. Nicolai Gedda is a committed if not, in this context, a heroic Don José. As Escamillo, Robert Massard is at least pleasant, and Andrea Guiot is a bright Micaela, less complacent than any of her French competitors. As conductor, Georges Prêtre is sometimes eccentric in tempo but also exhilarating. He deals well with his leading lady, and that is, for once, enough.

c.1964 ELECTRECORD (S)

Alexandrina Milcheva (A), Lilyana Vassileva (B), Nikola Nikolov (C), Nicola Ghiuselev (D), Chorus and Orchestra of the Sofia National Opera—Ivan Marinov

This Bulgarian view adds little to one's understanding of Gypsies or Carmen. Marinov's orchestra is continually slow; there is nothing of Bizet's superb balance of charm and fatality here, though the opening of Act IV has a certain proletarian force. The quintet is at least energetic, and some of the interludes have a touching melancholy. Alexandrina Milcheva, the best of the vocalists, has a stunningly rich, if marginally unsteady, tone. Her effect, though, is industrious rather than mercurial or shocking: the Card Song is her most powerful moment. Bass Nicola Ghiuselev turns up as Escamillo, bonking through the Toreador Song like Varlaam. In Act III he shows some authority, but under Marinov he and Milcheva sound in Act IV like an old married couple by the fireside. Nikola Nikolov has the basic lyric-heroic voice for Don José, but his vocal uncertainty and effort kill off the character almost immediately. Lilyana Vassileva has a large, cutting soprano with little control over dynamics, vibrato, and color: no Micaela. The other women are harsh, the men guttural, and most of the French is—

well—amusing. The album serves only as a souvenir of Milcheva's rich, Slavic sound.

1969–70 EMI / ANGEL (S) CD

Grace Bumbry (A), Mirella Freni (B), Jon Vickers (C), Kostas Paskalis (D), Chorus and Orchestra of the Théâtre National de l'Opéra—Rafael Frühbeck de Burgos

About this production there are several points of special interest—the version used, the conducting, and especially the cast—but as a whole the set is almost continually frustrating. It offers an early *opéra comique* version of the score, with an unfamiliar sequence for Morales, an extension of the third-act fight scene which adds something to the psychological stature of Don José and Escamillo, and much enlightening dialogue. This, however, is delivered by a largely separate cast in a different spatial ambience, so that dramatic illusion is completely destroyed.

Rafael Frühbeck de Burgos, for twenty years chief conductor of symphony orchestras in Bilbao and Madrid, is little known on opera recordings. His performance of the opening is very vivid, but later some sentimental or grandiose ideas of tempo deprive the score of shape and also worry the singers. The Cigarette Chorus, for a single example, seems to be taking place in an opium den.

The cast looks provocative. Grace Bumbry has a voice of impact and on the stage is often a figure of dramatic power, but here vocal insecurities, tempo changes, and an aggressive but unsubtle approach deprive her Carmen of depth and irony. As always, Mirella Freni's voice is quite beautiful, but the aria has neither fear nor excitement in it, and unsteady tempos further reduce its interest. Kostas Paskalis, not often recorded, has a big, glamorous sound and a hearty high register, but he destroys the *legato* and thus much of the charm of the Toreador Song. In the extended version of Act III, though, his dark voice admirably suggests both presence and will.

The profound characterization here is Jon Vickers's Don José, though that, too, is at times undone by mannerisms of tone and attack and the conductor's shifting tempos. At that, this

Don José is a heroic figure of extraordinary dimension. Full of intimate feeling from the start, he is already unhinged during the Seguidilla, when his intensity, together with the characteristic Vickers resonance, suggests paranoia. In the Flower Song he savors the words with a yearning seldom experienced. The aria ends, for once, with a fully expressive *pianissimo*: a wonderful accomplishment, though, brilliant as it is, it loses, through unsteady tempo, something in continuity and cumulative impact. Here is an individual performance of great insight, partly undone by its setting.

1970 EURODISC (S)

Anna Moffo (A), Helen Donath (B), Franco Corelli (C), Piero Cappuccilli (D), Chorus and Orchestra of the Deutsche Oper, Berlin—Lorin Maazel

This was the first recording to be based on Fritz Oeser's 1964 edition of the score. For what is left of the dialogue the set uses a separate cast recorded in a different acoustic: a self-defeating solution to the problem of singers as straight actors. The Oeser emendations used here all weaken the power of the familiar score and the cast is ludicrously mismatched and largely inappropriate in style, so that all of the disadvantages of modern scholarship, technology, and artistic policy are gloriously combined. Conductor Lorin Maazel is in a wayward mood: the performance is alternately militant and sluggish, and some of the discontinuities are bizarre.

Even on paper the casting looks nonsensical: the Merry Widow as Carmen, Sophie as Micaela, Turridu as Don José, and Macbeth as Escamillo. Individually some of these types might be plausible, but here they are snuggling very uncomfortably together, as on one of those old *Stories from the Opera* book covers. The idea of Anna Moffo as Carmen is intriguing: a dark lyric voice which might be convincing in a little hall. Here, though, she is vanquished by style, conductor, acoustics, and her partners. The Habanera tells it all. The singer slides about, the conductor distorts the time, the immense chorus sounds as if recorded in another room, and there is a ghastly pause before each choral

entry: a parody of the scene. The Card Song is rushed to the point of triviality and the death scene full of melodramatic distortions and grunts. Surprisingly, even her top range is pallid.

With such a Carmen, Corelli's outsized crudity is even more embarrassing than in his previous recording. They both scoop: he at *mezzo forte* and she at *mezzo piano*. "Dût-il m'en coûter la vie," toward the close of Act III, suits him better than anything earlier, but the conclusion of the act has been altered to allow him yet another anguished high note. In the final scene he makes the glorious Corelli noises, full of tears, *portamenti*, and self-pity. Piero Cappuccilli's Escamillo has the top tones, but he, too, smears and shouts: a brutal performance. The best of the soloists is Helen Donath. She is a fine *Rosenkavalier* Sophie: the tradition goes back to Minnie Nast, the premiere Sophie and also the Micaela on Emmy Destinn's 1908 recording of *Carmen* in German. Donath's tone is fresh but frankly too blond for the impassioned aria. The Berlin Opera Orchestra plays very efficiently, but the tempo distortions remain more arresting than convincing.

1972 DEUTSCHE GRAMMOPHON (S) CD

Marilyn Horne (A), Adriana Maliponte (B), James McCracken (C), Tom Krause (D), Manhattan Opera Chorus, Metropolitan Opera Orchestra—Leonard Bernstein

This recording commemorates what was to have been Goeran Gentele's opening night as General Manager of the Metropolitan. It uses an Oeser-based version, nearly all of the emendations of which are destructive to the coherence and cumulative force of the familiar score. The extension of the Cigarette Chorus, for example, is theatrically dull; Frasquita's introduction of Escamillo seems academic; the cuts surrounding Micaela's aria isolate her dramatically; and the additions to the death scene rob it of raw impact. Compounding this, the shifts from music to dialogue (unconvincingly spoken) are clumsily handled here, breaking the mood every time.

The cast is large-voiced and international.

Marilyn Horne is a great singer. In Bizet, as in Rossini, though, she does defiance better than seduction and joy better than either. There is no duplicity in that wonderful voice. The Seguidilla, for example, is very thoroughly worked out, every syllable measured for its teasing quality, but that warm, generous sound transforms the aria into something quite innocent, so that we have the spectacle of a Don José driven mad by a jovial, strong Carmen with an essentially good heart. The Card Song is given the amphitheater treatment, but the top does not ring out in quite the way she wants. In the death scene, she is suddenly snarling and screaming; it is fast and furious at the end but lacking in tragic magnitude.

Her Don José, James McCracken, has certainly tried to tame that violent voice to the subtleties of the role. The Flower Song, for example, is quite restrained: a real effort at lyric ecstasy. Underneath it all, of course, remains a savage element. One applauds the intelligence that went into creating this enactment, even if the result sometimes has more bulk than stature. Tom Krause's Escamillo has determination but a blunt voice more useful in Act III than elsewhere. Adriana Maliponte, not often recorded, possesses a rich individual timbre which in itself suggests peasant drama, but the textual cutting and Bernstein's leaden tempo in Micaela's aria curtail its effect. There are fine moments in this set, but it is more interesting as a souvenir than as an operatic statement.

1974 ERATO (S) CD

Régine Crespin (A), Jeannette Pilou (B), Gilbert Py (C), José van Dam (D), Opéra du Rhin Chorus, Strasbourg Philharmonic Orchestra—Alain Lombard

With what is nearly an all-French cast, headed by the most distinguished of recent French sopranos, this set promises to be of special interest. What it offers, though, is amiable and sometimes stylish but extremely uneven: an urbane performance often short of compelling dramatic impulse. Carmen is largely a series of impassioned confrontations between the lovers. There are no moments of shared rapture in it,

and the closest approximation of a love scene is the tepid little passage in Act IV for Carmen and Escamillo. For combat, though, Alain Lombard substitutes a rather leaden grace. The Overture is spirited and sinewy, but other passages intended as seductive emerge as a trifle sleepy and disaffecting. The riot in Act I sounds more like a romp, the Intermezzos are suave but underpowered, and the finale is slow.

These qualities extend to most of his cast, too. Régine Crespin presents a full, sunny soprano, a little ungainly throughout its range. The Habanera and Seguidilla are amusing, although there is no devil in the voice and she has not quite the tonal command for the final scene. Jeannette Pilou presents Micaela as a competent, careful young lady, plausible but unenlightening. Gilbert Py, on the other hand, is dramatically varied but vocally unsteady, with a baritonal lower range and suspect pitch above. The Flower Song demonstrates all of these elements: every phrase is inflected, the total engaging but unsure. José van Dam, however, is the only really stylish Escamillo on complete recordings. The Toreador Song is smooth, powerful, and charming to a degree, and in Act IV his fine line and creamy tone make something rather touching of the duet. This is, incidentally, the one modern cast that could have handled the dialogue of Bizet's *opéra comique* effectively, but they perform instead the traditional Guiraud version with sung recitatives.

1975 DECCA / LONDON (S) CD

Tatiana Troyanos (A), Kiri Te Kanawa (B), Plácido Domingo (C), José van Dam (D), John Alldis Choir, London Philharmonic Orchestra—Georg Solti

Sir Georg Solti here presents an effective fusion of the traditional and Oeser editions. His choices have been made on the basis of musical interest and dramatic relevance, and include the longer version of the Cigarette Chorus and the traditional versions of the close of Acts III and IV, together with the extended fight scene in Act III and some other atmospheric changes. His own contribution is dashingly accurate and extrovert, though without much sense of dalliance or drollery. His cast is vocally gorgeous but surprisingly inert dramatically. Tatiana Troyanos is in glittering voice. She has the richness of Risë Stevens and a suggestion of Conchita Supervia's unforgettable vibrancy, and handles the dialogue with great vivacity. Why, then, is the singing so neutral in effect? Acts I and II are smooth and intimate, but lack variety, edge, and irony; her outspoken moments are as plainly earnest as Don José's. The Card Song is plaintive and the final scene anonymously accurate: a puzzling performance, as it was on the stage, since she is normally an ebullient actress and can do anything she wants with her voice.

Plácido Domingo gives a generously emotional characterization with fine tone. Kiri Te Kanawa is in ravishingly beautiful voice, of precisely the right weight, color, and vibrancy for the virginal charm of Act I. The aria is sumptuously sung but unimpassioned; after the first hearing, it's lovely background music for some more meaningful activity. José van Dam is again the best of Escamillos but not so suave here as with Lombard. Of the others, Thomas Allen is a strong, amiable Morales, and the Gypsies include Michel Roux and Michel Sénéchal, distinguished veterans who sound that way. In all, this is a resounding production of a plausible edition which, despite the exceptional cast and energetic conductor, fails to intrigue.

1977–78 DEUTSCHE GRAMMOPHON (S) CD

Teresa Berganza (A), Ileana Cotrubas (B), Plácido Domingo (C), Sherrill Milnes (D), Ambrosian Singers, London Symphony Orchestra—Claudio Abbado

As one might expect, the Abbado treatment of *Carmen* is brilliantly dynamic and the London Symphony plays with exemplary spirit and sensuality. There are some arbitrary and inorganic tempo changes, but generally the conductor's work is enlivening and persuasive. The edition used is intriguing, if not my own favorite. There is much dialogue, nearly all of it informative. We are given the extended Cigarette Chorus, the shortened fight scene in Act

III, and an unappealing Oeser addition to the finale.

Abbado's cast is vital. Teresa Berganza may on occasion be too intimate for her vast surroundings, but there is ravishing youth in her Habanera together with a mocking tone that invites: so often one is repelled by this piece. Her Seguidilla has a rare and attractive repose, and willfulness, too. The Card Song may lack a sense of fate's cold edge and the death scene an element of contained desperation, but this is an individual and dramatically focused performance, beautifully vocalized. Plácido Domingo sings the richest of modern Don Josés and projects indomitable commitment. He is one of the few to sing equally well with both his Carmen and his Micaela; harder voices have found a greater note of desperation in the role, but often at the expense of the lyric passages. Ileana Cotrubas is a magnetic ingenue, charming in Act I and both delicate and vibrant in Act III. As Escamillo, Sherrill Milnes sings strongly, without quite the easy flexibility or humor that some ideal baritone of the mind might bring to the role, though he really tries to make the Toreador Song a captivating narrative. Without providing quite the knife thrust of tragedy, this is a charming set.

1982 ERATO (S,D) CD

Julia Migenes Johnson (A), Faith Esham (B), Plácido Domingo (C), Ruggero Raimondi (D), RTF Chorus, Orchestre National de France—Lorin Maazel

This album is derived from the soundtrack for the extraordinary Francesco Rosi film, which is dominated by some fine photography and the superb physical assumption of Carmen by Julia Migenes Johnson. It is an *opéra comique* edition with some bits of Oeser added, among them the uncut Cigarette Chorus and a revision of the death scene. On screen, Migenes Johnson is a breezy, matter-of-fact seductress. The soprano has mastered the art of operatic film acting; she has utter believability, spontaneity, and mythic charisma all at once. On the sound track alone she is much less effective. She has the same vocal fluidity and imagination, but the lack of body and color in this lyric-soprano voice cannot be talked away, although with some intimate miking she tries to do just that. What is deeply involving on film often seems far more fragile—merely insouciant—on the recording. The Card Song is a single example. It is tellingly acted (this Carmen seems rendered almost insensible by fate), but the voice remains a light, bright soprano, not quite the vehicle for Migenes Johnson's complex conception. Again, in the final act she has plenty of imagination and seldom roughens the voice for effect, but there is insufficient color for a really authentic vocal presentation of what she has in mind.

Of the others, Plácido Domingo is for the third time a full-voiced and impassioned Don José. This time in the Flower Song he ascends to a rather nasal *pianissimo* top note: the effort, at least, is commendable. As Micaela, Faith Esham has a voice of bright warmth but sings with such eviscerating care that she sounds emotionally alienated throughout. Ruggero Raimondi, with a rich top voice, introduces, unlike almost any other modern Escamillo, a playful spirit into the Toreador Song and a light touch into the fourth-act duet with Carmen: welcome additions both. Lorin Maazel's conducting is disjointed partly by miking, sound effects, and theatrical pauses but also by eccentric tempo choices.

1982 DEUTSCHE GRAMMOPHON (S,D) CD

Agnes Baltsa (A), Katia Ricciarelli (B), José Carreras (C), José van Dam (D), Paris Opéra Chorus, Berlin Philharmonic Orchestra—Herbert von Karajan

Hearing this recording is like examining a Degas with a magnifying glass: one is forced to forget about the whole when overcome by the details. There is superb orchestral clarity here, together with that ponderous Karajan elegance that overwhelms not only the singers but also the excellent cast of actors assembled, in a more intimate setting, to play the dialogue. The effect is sometimes nightmarish: half the time the characters are talking at normal speed in a living room and the other half singing in slow motion

to a stadium. Each musical moment is played as an ultimate, and the whole is certainly less than the sum of its expertly engineered parts. The intermezzos are among the most convincing sequences in the set. The version includes several Oeser additions.

Ah, yes: there are also the singers. Agnes Baltsa has a focused, vibrant mezzo that can be quite effective as Carmen, but here she is sometimes betrayed into a performance so overdrawn as to verge on caricature. The Habanera is slow, the Seguidilla halting, the Card Song overplayed, and the death scene full of eccentric tempos. The other singers fare even less well. José Carreras's occasional unsteadiness is exacerbated by the leaden pace. The Flower Song, though, is a nice reverie, with a welcome soft ending, and in Act IV (his best scene) the desperation is dramatically legitimate. Katia Ricciarelli is even less steady than her tenor, and seems to be sleepwalking dramatically. The admirable José van Dam, in his third recording of Escamillo, is asked to beat the Toreador Song to death in a display of virile energy. He is, however, smooth and suggestive in Act III, providing just the right sort of deadly vocal smirk. As a whole, though, the performance is devitalized and dejected, and the singers occasionally sound less like human beings than inexpertly played instruments in the Berlin Philharmonic. With all its grandiosity, the set made me yearn for the hopelessly anachronistic but lively Emmy Destinn performance in German, recorded in 1908 in what sounds like a broom closet.

1989 PHILIPS (S,D) CD

Jessye Norman (A), Mirella Freni (B), Neil Shicoff (C), Simon Estes (D), RTF Chorus, Orchestre National de France—Seiji Ozawa

The talents involved in this performance arouse considerable expectation. Ozawa is a master of orchestral color with success in Berlioz; Norman, with her richness and extended range, has an ideal Carmen voice; Freni has been singing Micaela for thirty years; and Shicoff is at his best a strong lyric tenor of some dramatic force. These discrete qualities—and little more—are precisely what one gets in the recording. A generally reasonable version of Oeser is used, though few of the singers handle the dialogue with credibility. Ozawa's view is "symphonic," with very little atmospheric brashness, humor, or sense of spontaneity. There *are* passing pleasures: the Changing of the Guard and Children's Chorus are both breezily handled, the Cigarette Chorus is elegantly—too elegantly—sung, and the orchestra throughout has extraordinary polish. Otherwise the general conception is disappointingly heavy. The opening scene has little fun in it. Later passages—the Seguidilla, for instance—have been worked to death for sensuousness, and the Gypsy Song refined beyond the point of dramatic return (where are those "frenzied guitars" of which the text speaks?). The natural flow of the opera from one mode to another—one of its distinctive qualities—is continually interrupted by such exaggerations.

Jessye Norman does have a fine Carmen voice: full, bright, rich, and mobile, but she is a victim of Ozawa's hesitancy and her own inexperience, and still seems to be demonstrating to herself some possibilities in the role rather than playing it. What she needs is a run of performances (concert or otherwise) to integrate and proportion all of the elements she has in mind. The others are an ill-assorted group. Shicoff, light-voiced for his Carmen, resorts to orations and tears almost immediately, leaving the character diminished and with no further dramatic destination. Freni's Micaela is nicely sung but lacks dramatic profile. Simon Estes is desperately miscast. His French is embarrassing, his voice dark and pressured, his manner charmless. None of these singers seems to be inhabiting the same stylistic or dramatic world.

A final choice among complete performances is impossible, given the variety of approaches to the major characters and the many different editions of the work. The one Carmen I would not want to be without is Callas, though de los Angeles sings beautifully and the Ponselle version, with all of its excesses, is historically fascinating, as is the richly cast Stevens performance. Among Don Josés, Vickers and Domingo (Abbado) are probably the most satisfying. Albanese and Cotrubas are the compelling Micaelas and van Dam the ranking Escamillo. Of the later sets, the Berganza-Abbado is probably the most satisfactory.

LONDON GREEN

Unavailable for review:
1912 PATHÉ
1959 GUILDE INTERNATIONALE DU DISQUE

Marc Blitzstein

Regina (1949)

A: Regina (s); B: Birdie (s); C: Alexandra (s); D: Addie (c); E: Leo (t);
F: Ben (bar); G: Oscar (bar); H: Cal (bar); I: Horace (bs)

Blitzstein's musicalization of Lillian Hellman's *The Little Foxes* is an exploration of the "crossover" territory between opera and the American musical, about which there is now plenty of talk but which, back in the 1940s and 1950s, was actually the focus of some solid professional composing and performing. The piece is full of the stylistic unease inherent in its form. It moves from straight dialogue to underscored declamation to full song and back, in an only partially successful effort to meet the problem that has defeated most American composers trying to work in our mainstream theater tradition: how to convey plot (and this play is more plot than anything else) through music while maintaining some level of reality. Blitzstein's libretto is a fairly straightforward setting of the play, with some cuts, some additions (mostly drawn from the play's "prequel," *Another Part of the Forest*, and intended to give the title character more depth), and a few bits of operaizing. Some of these last are clever and useful (weaving Leo's theft of the bonds, the first Horace / Regina quarrel, and party preparations into a finale for Act II, Scene 1), and others not. Nonetheless, much of the writing has genuine interest. Several of the lyrical solos and ensembles for the sympathetic characters are affecting; a couple of Regina's pieces have force and point, if not much emotional complexity, and there is edge and wit to the presentation of the boys of the clan. Throughout, there is pungency of musical thought, theatrical professionalism of craft, and a determined effort at a lifelike texture. These, with the strong backbone of the play's central conflict, lend *Regina* a continuing legitimacy.

1958 CBS / SONY (M)

Brenda Lewis (A), Elisabeth Carron (B), Helen Strine (C), Carol Brice (D), Loren Driscoll (E), George S. Irving (F), Emile Renan (G), Andrew Frierson (H), Joshua Hecht (I), Chorus and Orchestra of the New York City Opera—Samuel Krachmalnick

The City Opera's recording is a gutsy ensemble production that recalls the excitement of the company's erstwhile American opera campaigns. The chief difficulty is simply stated: few singers are good straight actors, and even good straight actors can have trouble playing scenes with some naturalness and nuance while contending with the problems of timing and acoustics posed by under-scoring, which is extensive here. The most complete solutions are offered by Driscoll and Brice, and the latter's deep, true contralto in her plea to Birdie contributes the set's richest singing. Irving, a protean performer, is convincing as Ben. Most of the others have dialogue troubles, ranging from the overwrought to the stiff. But Carron's pretty lyric soprano is musically handled in Birdie's laments, and though Hecht is in terrible voice in his opening scene, he recovers to do some powerful singing. Helen Strine, doubtless picked for type and / or acting skills for Zan, has an underdeveloped lyric soprano that washes out in the part's more demanding pages. Brenda Lewis presents Regina as an obvious vulgarian—a decision by no means discouraged by the vocal writing and the *mélodrame* scenes. Not the most interesting possible choice, this still might be the most playable one in the operatic context. She is consistent with it and committed to it, and within its bounds, her work has strength and clarity. Her singing is commanding but not often beautiful or shapely; the score's requirement for cutting edge in the middle range is particularly inconsiderate in this part. Orchestra and chorus are solid, and Krachmalnick's leadership has a good snap.

1991 DECCA / LONDON (S,D) CD

Katherine Ciesinski (A), Sheri Greenawald (B), Angelina Réaux (C), Theresa Merritt (D), David Kuebler (E), Timothy Noble (F), James Maddalena (G), Bruce Hubbard (H), Samuel Ramey (I), Scottish Opera Chorus and Orchestra— John Mauceri

Of interest here is material cut from previous productions and the earlier recording. Most of this involves the servants, Cal and Addie, and an additional black character, Jazz, with his "Angel Band"—but there are other restorations, too. Hellman and Blitzstein fought over these cuts. The composer wanted the sparky popular element in his score, some outsider commentary in his libretto, and set-up for his social-realist / triumphalist interpretation of the play's end. The playwright saw much of this as sentimental and false, and wanted to keep a tighter focus.

Both were right. Blitzstein clearly enjoyed the Dixieland, blues, and gospel idioms, and wrote entertainingly in them. The Act II party scene gains considerable theatrical interest in the original, its fine opening choral sequence far more effective in completed form. On the other hand, the original embraces even more of the problematic underscored dialogue, encourages a villains-and-victims view of the drama, and throws into sharper relief Blitzstein's rela-

tive failure to cope convincingly with the play's central conflict.

The performance benefits from lush, cushioned orchestral playing and a full choral sound. Mauceri does empathetic, careful work that doesn't always drive the dramatic points quite home. Indeed, dramatic points are left untallied pretty much across the board. Even dialogue left in the clear by the scoring sounds like timed recitation. Only Merritt and Tim Johnson, who does Jazz, have consistent life or naturalness, and with Ciesinski and Ramey the farthest at sea, the play's spine turns to rubber.

Ciesinski's singing offers a round, soft-textured middle range and intelligent musicianship. But the role's demands with respect to tessitura, verbal clarity, rhythmic bone, and dramatic imagination are often a little beyond her reach, and the theoretical advantage of this version's mezzo options goes largely unrealized. And though Réaux has a far more developed voice than Strine, its very pleasing mid-range inclines toward a breathy thinness at the top. Greenawald is an emotionally committed Birdie whose vocalism is an unpredictable mixture of the firm and full with the scrappy and edgy; she has a couple of knockout high *pianissimos*. Merritt is a fine Addie: not an exceptional voice, but beautifully controlled line and a touching *Innigkeit*.

Ramey, Noble, and Maddalena have more important voices than their CBS counterparts, but none actually gives a more persuasive performance; considering Ben's strangely limited opportunities, Noble is probably the most successful of them. The dynamic range of the recording is a real problem, with stretches of laid-back dialogue punctuated by bursts of penetrating choral / orchestral utterance.

Collectors who value completeness, contemporary sonics, and / or a more polished musical surface will want the Mauceri. But the earlier effort has a bit more punch and flavor.

CONRAD L. OSBORNE

ARRIGO BOITO

MEFISTOFELE (1868)

A: Margherita (s); B: Elena (s); C: Faust (t); D: Mefistofele (bs)

Of Italian operas written in the half century between *Don Pasquale* (1843) and *Cavalleria Rusticana* (1890), Boito's *Mefistofele* is one of only two non-Verdian works to survive on today's international operatic stage. (The other is Ponchielli's *La Gioconda*, for which Boito, incidentally, was the librettist.) At that, its hold has been tenuous. With typical audacity, Boito tried to encompass both the emotional and philosophical aspects of his source, Goethe's *Faust*. As a result, the premiere performance (La Scala, 1868, conducted by the 26-year-old composer himself) was six hours long, and a failure. For its revival in Bologna in 1875, Boito made Faust a tenor instead of a baritone; removed, among other elements, several of Faust's philosophical disquisitions; revised the final scene; and added "Lontano, lontano" and "Spunta l'aurora pallida," two of the most moving moments in the score. With further revision for Venice, *Mefistofele* then played throughout Italy and elsewhere with success. Feodor Chaliapin, Nazzareno de Angelis, Ezio Pinza, and Tancredi Pasero all sang in spectacular productions. In the United States its most famous recent revival was two decades ago with Norman Treigle at the New York City Opera, although there was also a series of notable performances in 1952–53 in San Francisco with Nicola Rossi-Lemeni and such singers as Ferruccio Tagliavini, Jan Peerce, Bidú Sayão, and Licia Albanese in alternating casts.

The problems in successfully recording *Mefistofele* are formidable: the work can easily degenerate into the merely grandiose. The choral and conducting requirements are very exacting, the title role demands a bass of dramatic command and prismatic vocal color, and the role of Faust needs a voice of great beauty trained for both lyric and heroic singing. Even the short role of Helen of Troy demands a soprano of Aida-like range and tone for satisfaction.

1931 EMI / ANGEL (M)

Mafalda Favero (A), Giannina Arangi-Lombardi (B), Antonio Melandri (C), Nazzareno de Angelis (D), La Scala Chorus and Orchestra—Lorenzo Molajoli

For its scenes in heaven, the Brocken, and ancient Greece, *Mefistofele* depends more on sonic grandeur than almost any other Italian opera. However, this aurally restricted 1930 recording is not unlistenable; it has dramatic energy and features three notable singers whose work is otherwise not widely available. Mafalda Favero was for nearly a quarter century a distinguished La Scala lyric soprano. Her Margherita is both artful and passionate, full of piercing lyricism. Like Tassinari and Olivero, she always presents a touchingly detailed and lovingly executed dramatic picture. As Helen of Troy, Giannina Arangi-Lombardi discloses a firm and beautiful dramatic soprano, equalized throughout its range and triumphant at the top. In phrasing she suggests the eternal and in sound the movingly temporal: a classic performance.

In the decade before recording it, Nazzareno

de Angelis sang Mefistofele with great success throughout Italy. Boito's music for the role has often been disparaged, but to me it dramatizes with curious brilliance not only the devil's brutal wit but also his eternal sense of insignificance in the face of God: the music of cosmic frustration. De Angelis's voice is clamorous, earthy, and magisterial. Even with pitch and control problems, he remains more challenging in the part than anyone on records but Chaliapin, Pasero, and Treigle: full of bluster, evasion, and even pain. As Faust, Antonio Melandri has a sound suggesting heroism, but also a sentimental style and an incomplete technique which trivialize the character. Lorenzo Molajoli conducts his unruly La Scala forces with a briskness that can rob Puccini and Verdi of grace but in the windy expanse of Boito is bracing.

1952 URANIA (M) CD

Rosetta Noli (A), Simone dall'Argine (B), Gianni Poggi (C), Giulio Neri (D), Milan Opera Chorus and Orchestra—Franco Capuana

This performance is massive but not often rousing. None of the four leads creates a convincing character or sings with much technical command. Giulio Neri, with his big, black, immobile, and slightly unsteady voice, is initially impressive but thereafter charmless as the monolithic protagonist, and without the variety of color and attack to sustain interest. Gianni Poggi is, for a change, not always at his worst. "Giunto sul passo estremo," Faust's final vision of a world at peace, is a considerable piece of singing. Earlier, though, "Forma ideal," Faust's reverent address to Helen of Troy, is a catalogue of the singer's mannerisms: scooping, throaty sound, flatness, and lack of line. Simone dall'Argine, who also recorded Tosca, has a dark lyric voice with a brilliant top, but also an effortful manner which robs her scene of Attic repose. Rosetta Noli makes a pretty lyric moment of "L'altra notte": she wants only the passion to make a mildly touching performance moving. Franco Capuana conducts portentously. Though the chorus is industrious, there are occasional ensemble difficulties. The sound is both reverberant and boxy.

1954 CETRA (M)

Marcella Pobbe (A), Disma de Cecco (B), Ferruccio Tagliavini (C), Giulio Neri (D), Italian Radio-Television Chorus and Orchestra, Turin—Angelo Questa

Angelo Questa is no more successful than Franco Capuana in projecting the force and charm of this score; the performance is often leaden or sentimental. The heavenly choruses are diffuse, the earthly ones lumbering without being amusing, the hellish ones grandiose: a dull universe. Neri is again powerful in voice, limited in color. Disma de Cecco and her Pantalis, Ede Marietta Gandolfo, are both tremulous—a couple of fishing matrons poaching in Faust's classical paradise. Marcella Pobbe has at least a pretty tone of lyric warmth, but she is also marginally unsteady and unequal to the simplest passagework. Ferruccio Tagliavini's voice is uniquely beautiful, though his conception, as might be expected, is tinged with pomposity and self-pity. He, though, is the attraction in this performance.

1955 EMI / ANGEL (M)

Orietta Moscucci (A), [B not present], Giacinto Prandelli (C), Boris Christoff (D), Rome Opera Chorus and Orchestra—Vittorio Gui

It is the singers and conductor who are of prime interest here, for the set has major cuts, including some choral work, the Faust-Wagner scene in Act I, and all of the Helen of Troy sequence. Christoff has, as always, energy, command, and a serrated vocal edge. In Margherita's garden, though, he lacks insinuating charm, and elsewhere variety of approach. The satiric elements of "Ecco il mondo," for example, are in this performance hammered into a simpler configuration of massive contempt. One admires the effort but wearies of the oration. As Faust, Giacinto Prandelli phrases musically—important in an opera in which the recitative melodies are not always ideally expressive. His light voice, however, cannot provide the heroic rapture that gives the character philosophical significance.

As so often, the Margherita is the most

absorbing member of the cast. Orietta Moscuc-ci's voice is also light and occasionally dry, but she knows how to color her tone and inflect the music without playing the tragedy queen. She shapes Margherita's penultimate moment, "Spunta l'aurora pallida" (one of the loveliest in the score), very touchingly; only the brief climax is disappointing. Vittorio Gui elicits from his orchestra and chorus a sense of both spiritual yearning and strength. Occasionally the mood becomes ponderous or the execution inexact.

1958 DECCA / LONDON (S)

Renata Tebaldi (A), Floriana Cavalli (B), Mario del Monaco (C), Cesare Siepi (D), Chorus and Orchestra of the Accademia di Santa Cecilia, Rome—Tullio Serafin

Mefistofele is a role demanding the expression of shattered grandeur, satiric malevolence, and cosmic frustration. Wit, terror, and yearning must all move through his outbursts if he is not to wear out his theatrical welcome; the singer must charm and enrage with diabolic ease. On other recordings, Boris Christoff focuses on the stabbing evil and Giulio Neri simply flattens the role with his steamroller of a voice. Cesare Siepi attempts something more varied, but his is essentially a benevolent bass, soft in contour and elegant in operas such as *Faust* and *Don Giovanni*. Even in the present assignment he offers some admirable singing when the voice is not pushed to instability.

On the other hand, Faust is a figure with moral imagination and ideals of beauty and serenity. Mario del Monaco's manner scarcely suggests such a visionary. He has a moment of intimacy in "Lontano, lontano," but elsewhere he offers what sounds like a military proclamation of spring, yells at the devil, and appears to get drunk with Helen of Troy: a combination here of cadmium tone and insensitivity. Renata Tebaldi, however, is in her loveliest voice and phrases with art, though her self-possession sometimes suggests Helen more than Marghe-rita. As Helen, Floriana Cavalli shows wonderful potential, but the actual sound is rather

driven and tremulous; if the role is to make philosophic sense, her voice must be an eroge-nous zone of ideal proportion. So we have some jeweled voices here, but most of them are in an inappropriate setting. Serafin surrounds his singers with stately sensibility and power, and the sound is quite full.

1973 EMI / ANGEL (S) CD

Montserrat Caballé (A), Josella Ligi (B), Plácido Domingo (C), Norman Treigle (D), Ambrosian Opera Chorus, London Symphony Orchestra—Julius Rudel

If this opera is to succeed as a tragedy of cosmic forces, it needs a protagonist of vocal pungency, strong rhythmic sense, wit, and theatrical authority. The creature who renounces a world which nevertheless haunts him fascinated Boito, who also devised Barnaba for Ponchielli, reworked Shakespeare's Iago for Verdi, and composed his own *Nerone*. Norman Treigle creates such a figure. His approach is broad but varied and imaginative, and his voice refulgent, penetrating, and focused, if light at the bottom. It is both sinewy and sinuous, with an occasional overtone of mystery in the sound, and the characterization is alternately wry, vicious, and grand. Its theatricality has come in for criticism, but Treigle's remains for me the most successful portrayal since Chaliapin's excerpts, recorded live at Covent Garden in 1926.

As Faust, Plácido Domingo sings with rich *legato* and tasteful enough tenor histrionics. There may be the suggestion of a tear behind his view of world peace, but the voice is sweet and healthy. Montserrat Caballé is a magnifi-cently pensive Margherita. That quality under-cuts the playfulness of the garden sequence, but she is superb in the prison scene, which she invests with a touchingly mad intimacy. Her trill suggests the flutter of a bird's wing, and "Spunta l'aurora pallida" is a perfect vehicle for her famous *pianissimo*. Josella Ligi, as Helen of Troy, has a full and free voice, unsteady at the top. Thomas Allen, then at the start of his career, makes Wagner sound like Faust's intellectual colleague and not, for once, like an aged pander.

Conducting this provocative ensemble is Julius Rudel, who sometimes settles for mere grandeur where there can be brilliance. That works fairly well in the Prologue in Heaven, but the garden sequence (always a problem) seems here more halting than comic or flirtatious, and some of the Brocken scene lacks thrust. The sound is superb, and the finale is quite eloquently performed.

1980 / 82 DECCA / LONDON (S,D) CD

Mirella Freni (A), Montserrat Caballé (B), Luciano Pavarotti (C), Nicolai Ghiaurov (D), London Opera Chorus, National Philharmonic Orchestra—Oliviero de Fabritiis

In performance, Boito's Faust can and generally does degenerate into just another operatic tenor, bereft of his intellect. In this matter, the current set triumphs over its competition, for Luciano Pavarotti's is, rather surprisingly, the most profound of all recorded portrayals. His concentrated and luminous tone suggests to a remarkable degree a Faust of consuming intellectual passion. The contemplative moments hint at a certain mystic vibrance: the aspiring man in aspiring voice. His garden scene may be rather sober, but elsewhere the artistry of his "Dai campi, dai prati" and the elation of his "Elena, Elena" are quite moving. Like other Fausts, he sings of his vision of Margherita in chains without a note of horror in the voice, but, in all, this is the only Faust among complete recordings to suggest the ardent philosopher.

Mirella Freni offers a careful, lovely performance of Margherita, with a striking climax in "L'altra notte" and graphic terror at the sight of Mefistofele. As Helen of Troy this time, Montserrat Caballé begins with a tone of unique purity and sensuousness, though by the time she envisions the burning Troy there is a slight beat in the voice. Even at that, her only real competition is the classic interpretation of Giannina Arangi-Lombardi in the 1931 set. As Mefistofele, Nicolai Ghiaurov is disappointing.

He has here the potent remains of a powerful voice and a blockbuster manner, but the tone diminishes at both the top and the bottom. Moreover, he sings the music of damnation blandly, sounding rather more like a big bass schoolteacher than the spirit that denies. His "Ecco il mondo," for example, is really neither satiric nor contemptuous, and the climax is hollow and slightly wobbly: a hardworking devil. Oliviero de Fabritiis offers spacious grandeur but his forces lack consistent dramatic conviction. Even Act III seems earthbound and Act IV a little lackadaisical, though the Prologue and finale are quite eloquent. The sound, incidentally, is magnificent.

1988 SONY (S,D) CD

Eva Marton (A), Eva Marton (B), Plácido Domingo (C), Samuel Ramey (D), Hungaroton Opera Chorus, Hungarian State Orchestra—Giuseppe Patanè

This set, dedicated to the memory of its conductor, has several technical and artistic strengths, and one important failing (see below). The sound is full and spacious, as it is in the Treigle and Ghiaurov recordings. Patanè's conducting is lively and proportionate, though he (or chorus master Piergiorgio Morandi) does not contrast the timbres of the choirs of angels, cherubim, penitents, and townspeople as dramatically as he might. The Brocken scene is suitably frenzied and the rest has a welcome vitality and rhythmic articulation. As Faust, Plácido Domingo may lack some of the poetry of peace in "Dai campi, dai prati," but his voice is filled with yearning in "Se tu mi doni" (his opening duet with Mefistofele) and "Forma ideal,"and properly contemplative for "Giunto sul passo estremo"—a moving, mature performance of the role. Samuel Ramey has a voice of great beauty and considerable expressive range. In truth, Mefistofele demands a vocal and dramatic daring associated with such singers as Michael Bohnen and, of course, Chaliapin.

The practice of giving both soprano roles to one singer seems to rob each of its individuality. The real problem in this recording is that Eva

Marton suggests neither the agonized fraility of Margherita nor the classical passion of Elena. The voice is dark and inflexible for Margherita's prison scene and tremulous for Elena's Night of the Classical Sabbath. Her natural gustiness is a little less unsuitable for the passage on the burning of Troy. All this is an important consideration, since Margherita, at least, sings much of the most haunting music in the score. Meanwhile, Patanè is persuasive, Ramey at least suave, and Domingo powerful, though his work can be found also in the superior set with Treigle and Montserrat Caballé.

Several of the recordings mentioned offer star singers in typical form. The 1980–82 album on Decca provides an especially fine performance of Faust by Pavarotti, and the 1958 Decca gives us Tebaldi in glorious voice. For all its very restricted sound, the 1931 EMI offers energetic conducting, a very moving Margherita (in a style almost lost to us) by Mafalda Favero, and the finest of all Helens of Troy by Giannina Arangi-Lombardi. The most satisfying of the modern sets is the 1973 EMI, with a rousing Mefistofele in Norman Treigle, Montserrat Caballé at her best as Margherita, and Plácido Domingo.

LONDON GREEN

TONY RANDALL
Actor, Producer

1. **Rossini,** *Il Barbiere di Siviglia*: Capsir, Borgioli, Stracciari, Bettoni, Baccaloni—Molajoli. EMI / ANGEL

2. **Verdi,** *Rigoletto*: Capsir, Bassi, Borgioli, Stracciari, Dominici—Molajoli. EMI / ANGEL

3. **Wagner,** *Der Ring des Nibelungen*: Nilsson, Crespin, Flagstad, Ludwig, King, Windgassen, Fischer-Dieskau, London, Hotter, Neidlinger, Frick—Solti. DECCA / LONDON

4. **Mozart,** *Don Giovanni*: Souez, Helletsgrüber, Mildmay, von Pataky, Brownlee, Henderson, Baccaloni, Franklin—Busch. EMI / ANGEL

5. **Verdi,** *La Traviata*: Albanese, Peerce, Merrill—Toscanini. RCA / BMG

6. **Puccini,** *La Bohème*: De los Angeles, Amara, Bjoerling, Merrill, Reardon, Tozzi—Beecham. EMI / ANGEL

7. **Puccini,** *Madama Butterfly*: Freni, Ludwig, Pavarotti, Kerns—Karajan. DECCA / LONDON

8. **Verdi,** *Simon Boccanegra*: Rethberg, Martinelli, Tibbett, Pinza, Warren—Panizza. MET

ALEXANDER BORODIN

PRINCE IGOR (1890)

A: Yaroslavna (s); B: Konchakovna (ms); C: Vladimir (t);
D: Igor (bar); E: Galitsky (bs); F: Konchak (bs)

As *Prince Igor* is generally heard today, and as it is heard on all of its recordings, it is an opera made by three pairs of hands with a great many problems. Borodin (for whom scientific work took precedence over musical composition) labored sporadically on the opera from 1869 until his death in 1887, and it was Rimsky-Korsakov and Glazunov who finally pieced the work together into the form by which it is commonly known. While nearly all the music was written by Borodin, about half of the opera was orchestrated by Rimsky; the Overture was composed by Glazunov (based, he claimed, upon Borodin's plan for it); substantial parts of the third act were either finished by or actually composed by Glazunov, and this act is frequently omitted in performance and recording. The result is a rambling, grand, nationalist epic, rather than a dramatically concise stagework. But if Borodin is sometimes criticized for not revealing the profound depth of character found in that other great nineteenth-century ramshackle Russian epic opera, *Boris Godunov*, he nevertheless proved inspired in his ability to capture, in wonderfully atmospheric orchestral writing and compelling vocal melodies, an unerring sense of the time, place, and people of twelfth-century Russia. Being among the most Russian of all operas, *Prince Igor* asks for rich Slavic voices and no less than two deep Russian bassos (shared by the same singer on two of the recordings). Thus far the work has been recorded only in Moscow, Sofia, and Belgrade.

1951 MELODIYA (M)

Evgenia Smolenskaya (A) , Vera Borisenko (B), Sergei Lemeshev (C), Andrei Ivanov (D), Pirogov (E), Mark Reizen (F), Bolshoi Theater Chorus and Orchestra—Alexander Melik-Pashayev

From the first bars of the Overture there is little question about the kind of rough-and-ready enthusiasm to be found at the postwar Bolshoi. There is almost a comic-book theatricality to the performance, and it is heard right from the start in the way Melik-Pashayev slows down or speeds up. Throughout one has the sense that everyone involved really wanted to tell a story as gregariously as possible. Perhaps a symptom of the Stalinist era, the performance proves both the crudest and most alive in the Polovtsian scenes. The Polovtsian dances are unrestrained, as lurid and frenzied as to be found anywhere, and similar dramatic eagerness is felt in the singing. Borisenko is a sexy, breathy Polovtsian princess, while Reizen is just as spectacularly big-voiced as Konchak. Neither is an especially accurate singer, but Borisenko, so eager that she regularly anticipates the beat, is effective in stimulating Lemeshev's prissy-sounding Vladimir into a frenzied passion. The same is true for Reizen in his duet with Ivanov, a dignified, lyric Igor. Smolenskaya's husky Yaroslavna, Igor's upstanding wife, is less malleable, but she too is a nice foil for Pirogov's boorish Galitsky, whose tendency is to sink into laughable melodrama. The chorus, like the orchestra, is always enthusiastic-sounding, no matter how sloppy the first-act maidens or squeaky the slave women are. The third act is omitted, and there are a small number of trims throughout.

1955 DECCA / LONDON (M)

Valeria Heybalova (A), Melanie Bugarinovich (B), Noni Zhunetz (C), Dushan Popovich (D), Zharko Tzveych (E,F), Chorus and Orchestra of the National Opera, Belgrade—Oscar Danon

This Bulgarian performance, the first complete *Igor* on disc, is the opposite of the Bolshoi recording of three years earlier. Whereas the Russians sang with almost too much character, here is a stolidly efficient reading that robs the score of much of its essential character, color, and drama. Danon's conducting, is blandly deliberate, careful in the letter, but casual in the more important spirit, of each phrase. Yet even for an efficient performance, it is a failure. The orchestra is ineffectual—the tiny solo oboe, for instance, becomes downright annoying as it takes away from any mystery in Konchakovna's cavatina. None of the singers is particularly appealing either. Popovich is a healthy-sounding baritone, firm enough in the upper register to milk high notes, but he makes a pompous Igor. Tzveych, taking on both the basso roles of Galitsky and Konchak, is also vocally apt, but there is little in his wooden phrasing to differentiate two very different roles. The women are all seriously hampered by leaden tempos—especially the thick-voiced Zhunetz. The orchestra and chorus are questionable at best. Nor does Danon make a convincing case for the inclusion of the third act. Important as it may be for advancing the plot and for revealing the origin of important themes in the Overture, the conductor mainly emphasizes Glazunov's dully prosaic musical contributions.

1966 EMI / ANGEL (S) CD

Julia Wiener (A), Reni Penkova (B), Todor Todorov (C), Constantin Cherkerliiski (D), Boris Christoff (E,F), Chorus and Orchestra of the National Opera Theater, Sofia—Jerzy Semkow

There is only one really compelling performer here, but he comes as close as a single basso can to carrying the entire show. Of course, it helps that Christoff sings both bass roles. A celebrated Boris Godunov, Christoff brings a regal sound (and a priceless wicked laugh) to Galitsky, making the sleazy Russian prince seem all the more dangerous. As Konchak, Christoff simply luxuriates in his voice—particularly striking in the booming low F in Konchak's aria—making the enigmatic Polovtsian leader seem more scandalous and again more dangerous than usual. Otherwise, this Bulgarian performance has little else to recommend it. Not only is it lacking the third act, but it is greatly cut throughout, so much so at points that the opera sounds downright perfunctory, especially in the last act. Christoff manages well under Semkow's slow and weighty direction, since such tempos offer him space to find interpretive nuance. But the other singers sound overwhelmed by such an overblown approach: Wiener's vocally unsteady Yaroslavna turns hysterical under pressure; Cherkerliiski, a warm Verdian baritone and an unusually smooth Igor, languishes into a stolid and uninteresting interpretation; Todorov and Penkova are a curious pair of lovers—a tight, vibrating, androgynous-sounding tenor oddly matched with a deep, dark, masculine mezzo. The orchestra and chorus are acceptable but unexceptional.

1969 MELODIYA (S)

Tatiana Tugarinova (A), Elena Obraztsova (B), Vladimir Atlantov (C), Ivan Petrov (D), Artur Eizen (E), Alexander Vedernikov (F), Bolshoi Theater Chorus and Orchestra—Mark Ermler

The comparison of this *Igor* with the Bolshoi performance of nearly forty years earlier is noteworthy. Unlike the earlier Bolshoi version, here is a complete, well-played, well-sung account, a performance with no real weaknesses. Yet it is also an *Igor* with almost none of the character and little of the dramatic fire of that earlier one. The most exciting performance is that of Vedernikov's particularly wicked Konchak. For sheer consistency, phrase to phrase, Petrov is the most reliable Igor on record, but his well-rounded phrases too easily turn into the expression of hollow platitudes. Next to him, Obraztsova sounds a bit too young and light as Yaroslavna, and she is reduced occasionally to pushing. Eizen, another rich Russian basso, again offers vital sound but not vitality to Galitsky. The most impressive singing comes from Atlantov's heroic, ringing Vladimir—maybe the only non-wimp Vladimir on records—and the equally grand but far from seductive Konchakovna. Ermler's conducting is capable but not poetic. He moves the performance along when the need exists, and he is responsive to impassioned outbursts, but like all else here, his seems an approach more calculated than motivated by the theatrical moment. Even his slight tendency to rush along the drama now and then rarely displays theatrical urgency. The orchestra and chorus are decent, but the recorded sound is blunt, and some audible tape splices only add to the pervading studio feeling of the performance.

1990 SONY (S,D) CD

Stefka Evstatieva (A), Alexandrina Milcheva-Nonova (B), Kaludi Kaludov (C), Boris Martinovich (D), Nicola Ghiuselev (E), Nicolai Ghiaurov (F), Sofia National Opera Chorus and Festival Orchestra—Emil Tchakarov

Here is the most polished *Igor*, and by far the best recorded, if hardly the most finely sung or characterful. And since much of what is stirring in the opera is its sheer grandeur of sound and its engaging melody, such qualities can go a long way. Still, good taste frequently gets in the way. The most intriguing aspect of the performance lies in Ghiaurov's peculiarly warm, and hence mysterious, Konchak. However, Ghiaurov's is the only interesting psychological portrait in the performance, the other singers ranging from agreeably even-tempered to just plain dull. Martinovich is a hollow Igor; Evstatieva, a secure and unobjectionable Yaroslavna; Kaludov, a careful, passionless Vladimir; and Milcheva-Nonova, a square Konchakovna. Tchakarov, too, offers little drive, let alone any ferocity. Throughout it is a workmanlike performance, highlighted by a good chorus and efficient orchestra. Like the later Bolshoi effort, this is an uncut four-act version, but, also like the other, it makes little case for its length.

Prince Igor has yet to be ideally—or even well—served on records. The most pressing decision about the opera—whether or not to include Glazunov's journeyman third act, with its important musical thematic material—remains unresolved when the three recordings in which it is included are all bland performances that make the act seem tiresome and the opera overlong. Of the two far more idiomatic but incomplete recordings, the 1951 Bolshoi effort, while wonderfully vital, is dated in its crude recorded sound. It is only through Boris Christoff's inspired work that the 1966 version successfully reveals an inkling of the score's true personality.

MARK SWED

Unavailable for review:
c.1935 MELODIYA

BENJAMIN BRITTEN

PETER GRIMES (1945)

A: Ellen Orford (s); B: Mrs. Sedley (ms); C: Auntie (c);
D: Peter Grimes (t); E: Balstrode (bar)

eter Grimes can be argued to have been the greatest international operatic success of the postwar period. It had its premiere at Sadler's Wells in London in 1945 and has since played with some regularity throughout Europe, the United States, and elsewhere. Its alienated and yet touching hero prefigured those of John Osborne, Harold Pinter, and even Samuel Beckett, and, to a greater extent than is sometimes realized, helped to form a major movement in postwar British theater. Grimes's moral guilt can never be either proven or disproven, even though we witness some of the relevant circumstances during the course of the opera. In that damning latency and, of course, in Britten's continually evocative and individual score lie the power of the work. His music calls up not only the atmosphere of an English fishing village a century and a half ago but the specter of implacable fate itself. For what end do we possess all our capacities and civilized psychological weaponry? In dramatizing that question, the opera takes on something of the universality of Sophocles. The two recordings discussed document wonderful if quite different performances; it bespeaks the profundity of the work that it can exhaust both approaches and perhaps half a dozen others as well.

1958 DECCA / LONDON (S) CD

Claire Watson (A), Lauris Elms (B), Jean Watson (C), Peter Pears (D), James Pease (E), Chorus and Orchestra of the Royal Opera House, Covent Garden—Benjamin Britten

This is, of course, the composer's own version, and the recording through which many of us got to know the work. He makes of the opera a moving tone poem, evocative and interior, vibrant and unforgettable in its melancholy. His approach is somewhat sparer than others. The sea interludes are peerlessly shaped. At the center of this conception is the Grimes of Peter Pears, for whom the work was written. His performance is tensile but frail, always distinctive vocally, and especially gripping in the final scene, where his voice takes on the shifting colors of madness. Odd as it may seem, that voice at times reminds me in its concentration of tone and line of Giovanni Martinelli's, though of course Pears's is much lighter.

Claire Watson, often a distinguished soprano in Mozart, is a lyrical Ellen, touching but perhaps less suggestive of spiritual yearning than either the later Ellen, Heather Harper, or the original, Joan Cross, who projected a greater compulsion and sense of life experience than her successors. James Pease, with his fresh but slightly grizzled baritone, makes a splendid Balstrode, and Owen Brannigan is a very fine Swallow, grave, clear, and convincing. Raymond Nilsson as Bob Boles is the definitive zealot, and Geraint Evans is superb as Ned Keene, his diction very clear without being fussy. The orchestra and sound are fine and the chorus strongly in character, if not so polished as Davis's.

1978 PHILIPS (S) CD

Heather Harper (A), Patricia Payne (B), Elizabeth Bainbridge (C), Jon Vickers (D), Jonathan Summers (E), Chorus and Orchestra of the Royal Opera House, Covent Garden—Colin Davis

Colin Davis conducts a performance commensurate with the work's genius. He is a master of that grave lyricism which in my mind yokes Britten with Berlioz, and yet the performance is full of hard wit and wryness, too. A single passionate vision illuminates Davis's work, so that the sea interludes, for example, seem to well up out of the opera and flood the scene with subconscious images. The same sense of tragic structure obsesses his soloists. Jon Vickers's Grimes is unique in its pained strength. The character seems forever on the edge of desperate discovery: a rough, lonely, unaware, intuitive poet—a shaman dishonored. Vickers's extraordinary *legato* becomes the vehicle for a desperate questing energy. In "Now the great bear," the hut scene, and the finale, he shifts from reality into nightmare vision with the utmost ease, and makes the character almost mythical in both his power and his fragility. Grimes's entry in the last scene is very forcefully realized; here is quiet agony, bare of artifice and yet epic in stature.

Heather Harper is a touching, dignified, and wholly believable Ellen, sympathetic and yet with something of the cold sea in her voice. Like Vickers, she echoes heroic fragility at the close of the Prologue, and she captures exactly the private, rather sensuous mood of the Embroidery Aria. Forbes Robinson is a Swallow of precision and vigor who in the opening scene provides a fine contrast to Vickers's superb line and abstracted mood. Patricia Payne offers a voice of authority for Mrs. Sedley, who can verge on caricature, and Jonathan Summers presents a well-sung Balstrode, perhaps a little lacking in salt. The others are strong, and the chorus is superb. Under Davis, one or two passages, such as Ellen's "Let her among you," may be a bit fast, but the performance is a profound one, with grandeur, spontaneity, and significance.

A choice between the two recordings is as difficult as between two great recordings of *Otello* or *Traviata*. Both supporting casts are fine, though the Philips is perhaps a little stronger in that respect. Britten's conception is more interior, but Davis's has a robust force that does not eliminate its poignancy. Peter Pears is a poet whose distinctive voice will probably always be associated with this role; Vickers is, however, the rugged and visionary seaman to the life. As a pendant to these, I would also recommend the excerpts recorded in 1948 by Pears, in gleaming voice, and Joan Cross, still the most passionate and touching of Ellens, under the fiery direction of Reginald Goodall, the original conductor.

LONDON GREEN

Unavailable for review:
1992 EMI / ANGEL

BENJAMIN BRITTEN

ALBERT HERRING (1947)

A: Lady Billows (s); B: Nancy (ms); C: Mrs. Herring (ms);
D: Albert (t); E: Sid (bar)

Commentators long ago noticed that *Albert Herring* is the comic counterpart to *Peter Grimes*—both operas depict an outsider at odds with his community. The music sparkles with wit and fun, but there is also a touch of melancholy and a coiled intensity that suggests the darker side of a small town's zeal in bringing nonconformists like Albert to heel. It's all there in the score, especially in the ingeniously textured chamber instrumentation and the cunningly plotted vocal lines, both of which tell us more about the characters' true nature than perhaps even Britten himself realized.

1963 DECCA / LONDON (S) CD

Sylvia Fisher (A), Catherine Wilson (B), Sheila Rex (C), Peter Pears (D), Joseph Ward (E), English Chamber Orchestra—Benjamin Britten

This composer-directed recording brings out both the opera's light and its shadow in a masterly fashion. Britten asks for no more than what is written on the page, and the fifteen virtuosos from the English Chamber Orchestra give the conductor everything the composer could possibly want. All the musicians are members of the composer's large musical "family" as it was constituted in the early 1960s—the singers and instrumentalists who worked closely with him at the Aldeburgh Festival and in so many of his recording projects—and Peter Pears sings yet another of the Britten roles specifically tailored for his voice and extraordinary technique. By 1963 the tenor may have been too old to perform young Albert credibly on the stage, but he sounds as fresh as ever on these discs, and we are lucky to have his interpretation preserved. And anyone looking for further evidence of the *Grimes / Herring* parallels need only compare Pears in Peter's mad scene and Albert's drunk scene: two compelling moments of truth for the sorely beset heroes, ravishingly sung by the tenor who created them both.

It was perhaps more sentiment than sense to have Sylvia Fisher recreate her formidable Lady Billows this late in the day—the soprano sounds too squally and strained for comfort, although there is no question that we are dealing with a dragon of Wagnerian dimensions. All else is well, however. Loxford's leading citizens are sharply characterized, and Catherine Wilson and Joseph Ward excel as the free young spirits who help Albert cut Mum's apron strings. Best of all, there is Britten on the podium, inspiring everyone and invariably getting superb results. The performance is remarkable for its precision, clarity, and grace, as well as for an expressive urgency that goes directly to the heart of the matter. Alternate versions of *Albert Herring* are bound to appear on disc eventually, and they will be welcome, but this authoritative recording is likely to remain in a class of its own.

PETER G. DAVIS

BENJAMIN BRITTEN

BILLY BUDD (1951)

A: Vere (t); B: Billy (bar); C: Claggart (bs)

Since its premiere in 1951, *Billy Budd* has gradually secured a firm spot in the international repertory; among Britten's large-scale operas, only *Peter Grimes* is performed more frequently. Considering the fact that the work calls for an all-male cast, precluding such sure-fire operatic conventions as passionate love scenes and squabbling jealous rivals, not to mention the vocal contrast that women's voices provide, *Billy Budd*'s success with audiences is even more remarkable. The clashing, compassionately observed personalities who make up the tense floating society on board the British man-of-war *Indomitable* gave Britten ample opportunity to create living characters and musical variety with his typically brilliant command of instrumental color and sonority. The opera was originally in four acts, but the composer devised a two-act version in 1961, while making some minor revisions in the score. This is now the universally accepted edition, and the one Britten conducts on the Decca recording.

1967 DECCA / LONDON (S) CD

Peter Pears (A), Peter Glossop (B), Michael Langdon (C), Ambrosian Opera Chorus, London Symphony Orchestra—Benjamin Britten

No one is likely to have any serious complaints about this valuable composer-directed performance, although *Billy Budd* is now familiar enough to warrant an alternate recorded view. Ideally, one might want a Billy with a freer, more lyrical instrument than Glossop's rather rough-edged baritone, even though his direct, open-hearted approach to the role is right on the mark. More reservations arise over Langdon's Claggart, much too obvious a villain with a bass voice that often sounds smeared and puffy. On the other hand, there is Pears's incomparable Captain Vere, a riveting vocal presence, whether elegantly quoting Plutarch, vigorously preparing his men for the attack, or agonizing in conflict with his conscience.

What makes this performance indispensable, aside from being the only recorded version of the opera at the moment, are the sterling contributions of so many distinguished Britten specialists in smaller roles: John Shirley-Quirk, a warmly human Mr. Flint; Owen Brannigan, a gruff but lovable Dansker; Robert Tear as the tormented Novice; and Benjamin Luxon as his concerned friend. And of course there is Britten himself on the podium. Other conductors will certainly discover different qualities to emphasize in this prismatic score, but it would be hard to imagine a reading with greater clarity of design, rhythmic vitality, or sonorous beauty.

PETER G. DAVIS

BENJAMIN BRITTEN

THE TURN OF THE SCREW (1954)

A: Governess (s); B: Mrs. Grose (s); C: Miss Jessel (s);
D: Flora (s); E: Miles (treb); F: Quint (t)

To many opera goers, *The Turn of the Screw* seems more and more like Britten's operatic masterpiece. As a statement of his lifelong preoccupation with the theme of innocence corrupted, nothing he wrote has quite such a crushing impact. As a musical construction, the score is ingenious: sixteen scenes laid out as a theme and variations that mirror and intensify each harrowing twist in Henry James's classic ghost story. Yet as the opera unfolds, listeners are never consciously aware of the compositional craft, so cunningly does the composer conjure up the atmosphere of unspeakable evil that surrounds and eventually overwhelms the unhappy inhabitants of the house at Bly. It is an amazing tour de force that seldom fails to make a powerful effect onstage, even though much depends on the often risky vocal and acting skills of a small boy. This does not appear to have hampered the opera's progress, however. Over the past thirty-five years there have been many amazingly accomplished performers of Miles—a juicy role coveted by boy sopranos as much as coloraturas yearn to sing Lucia.

the cast that gave the world premiere in 1954 in Venice. Seldom can a new opera have been more auspiciously launched, and this performance definitely stands as a paradigm for all others. A brilliant and versatile singer who never had the international career she deserved, Jennifer Vyvyan is the ideal embodiment of James's ambiguous Governess, quietly but frighteningly communicating the character's repressed hysteria while singing the notes with a clarity, precision, and tonal beauty that take the breath away. Quint, of course, was written for Peter Pears's voice, never more bewitchingly seductive than when spinning out those dangerous *bel canto melismas* that lure Miles to his doom. Miles, too, must have been conceived for the special vocal qualities of David Hemmings, who created several important Britten treble parts before he grew up to become a film star. Even listeners allergic to boy sopranos should respond to a performance so musicianly and dramatically involved. If not quite on the same exalted plane as their colleagues, the other three singers are always positively in the picture. Needless to say, the chamber ensemble realizes the bejeweled score with stunning virtuosity under Britten's meticulous direction.

1955 DECCA / LONDON (M) CD

Jennifer Vyvyan (A), Joan Cross (B), Arda Mandikian (C), Olive Dyer (D), David Hemmings (E), Peter Pears (F), English Opera Group Orchestra—Benjamin Britten

This was the first Britten opera to be recorded complete under the composer's direction, with

1981 PHILIPS (S,D)

Helen Donath (A), Ava June (B), Heather Harper (C), Lillian Watson (D), Michael Ginn (E), Robert Tear (F), Members of the Orchestra of the Royal Opera House, Covent Garden—Colin Davis

For those who know the Britten recording well, Colin Davis's very different realization of the instrumental score will be especially intriguing. The composer tends to be more coolly objective, putting a premium on crisply articulated sonorities and smart rhythmic definition without discouraging individual expression. Davis, on the other hand, takes an almost impressionistic view of the opera, blending his colors, lingering over the most beautiful bits, and warming to the music's lyrical content. The music responds equally well to either approach, each is superbly brought off, and we are lucky to have them both.

The excellent Philips cast is clearly absorbed by the opera, although their opposite numbers on the Decca recording manage to project just that extra measure of vocal flair, dramatic conviction, and ensemble spirit to make a difference. Even so, Donath's vulnerable but determined Governess, Tear's menacing Quint, and Ginn's dulcet Miles are very effective while we listen to them, and the sopranos of Harper, June, and Watson nicely personalize their respective characters. This recording, by the way, also serves as the soundtrack for an imaginative and striking film of the opera directed by Petr Weigl, commercially released on video disc. The actors are Czech, but the dubbing, expertly done, is in no way distracting.

If pressed for a choice, there is only one: the composer-led version is certainly one of the classic recordings of twentieth-century opera.

Peter G. Davis

GUSTAVE CHARPENTIER

LOUISE (1900)

A: Louise (s); B: The Mother (ms); C: Julien (t); D: The Night
Prowler and King of the Fools (t); E: The Father (bar)

Charpentier, who was nearly forty at the time of the premiere of *Louise* in February 1900, had by then acquired some of the musical elegance of his teacher Massenet, plainly admired Berlioz and Wagner, and in this anecdotal tale of ordinary Parisian life found a theme perfectly suited to his socially aware, rebellious nature and his lyrical gift. For it, he drew unashamedly on music written during his sojourn in Italy as winner of the Prix de Rome (1887–90), and, for the not wholly relevant scene of the crowning of the Muse of Montmartre, on a cantata written in 1898. After the first night, the composer Paul Dukas pronounced a verdict: "The first and last acts are those of a master; the other two are those of an artist; the whole is the work of a man."

Charpentier called *Louise* a "roman musical"—a musical novel—and in it as in a novel mixes realism (*verismo*, we might say) and symbolism with extraordinary success. Realism rules the outer acts and the famous scene of the dressmakers in the atelier where Louise works; symbolism takes over with the figures of the Night Prowler, who stands for the evils of Paris and free love, and the King of the Fools, who presides over its glamour and leads the crowning of the Muse of Montmartre. The two ingredients mingle easily enough when street criers and workers crawl out in the morning and the mixture they make emerges half actual, half allegorical. The achievement is that, with his idiomatic depiction of ordinary conversation and the skillfully worked atmosphere of the orchestral preludes to individual scenes, Charpentier has succeeded in writing a hymn to Paris, with its pervading sense of freedom and pleasure, and its lurking background of struggle for survival, even degradation and misery.

Louise was an immediate success, as much because of its emancipated story as for the music, but when now you hear the whirl of the waltz that stands for the pleasures of Paris, it is easy to see how the theme caught the imagination of a whole generation. Here was the pull of the forbidden at its most seductive, and it still holds today.

Some cuts are marked in the vocal score as customary at the Opéra-Comique or elsewhere. None of the sets is complete. All omit the Divertissement in Act III, Scene 2, together with the introduction by the King of the Fools and the comment by the old Bohemian after it; all shorten the duet for Louise and Julien in Act III, Scene 1 (but in different degrees), and all but one remove a verse of Julien's serenade in Act II, Scene 2. Maybe some of these cuts were sanctioned by Charpentier himself, but it is impossible to accept from Fournet and Cambreling the dropping in the last act of "Voir naître un enfant," one of the Father's most eloquent monologues. Other snips are less damaging.

p. 1956 PHILIPS (M)

Berthe Monmart (A), Solange Michel (B), André Laroze (C), Louis Rialland / Pierre Giannotti

(D), Louis Musy (E), Chorus and Orchestra of the Opéra-Comique—Jean Fournet

What might be a French cast on an above-average day at the Opéra-Comique more than a generation ago does something like justice to the score, in spite of a considerable number of small cuts and two much more damaging: the Mother's plea to Julien in Act III, Scene 4 and "Voir naître un enfant" in Act IV. Fournet is a less than inspiring conductor, but Monmart's Louise is full of good moments ("Depuis le jour" unfortunately not among them). Laroze's tenor has a bright ring to it at the start, is well up to the weight of the love duet, and he shows himself a singer able to enunciate words with clarity while maintaining an expressive singing line. When the Opéra-Comique celebrated fifty years of *Louise*, Louis Musy not only directed the new production with sets by Utrillo but also sang the role of the Father. His is not grand vocalism but his strong, burly baritone is well suited to homely philosophy, the singing always expressive, and there is nothing insubstantial about his top G in the monologue early in Act IV. Solange Michel sings decently what is left of her role, and the small parts are competently done, with Giannotti better as the King of the Fools than Rialland as the Night Prowler (the roles are, unusually, divided).

1976 CBS / SONY (S) CD

Ileana Cotrubas (A), Jane Berbié (B), Plácido Domingo (C), Michel Sénéchal (D), Gabriel Bacquier (E), Ambrosian Singers, New Philharmonia Orchestra—Georges Prêtre

Strong casting and, apart from the usual, only a single cut—in the scene for Louise and her Father in Act I—and a very positive and convincing view of the score from the conductor contribute to a highly acceptable set. Prêtre is throughout lively with a strong sense of climax, yet coaxes playing of the utmost delicacy at, for instance, the long, sustained string theme of the Father's entry. It is hard to imagine the opera better done. The cast is dominated by Bacquier's magnificent performance of the Father, forthright and poetic, with strong diction which

never threatens the musical line, ringing top notes balanced by easy lower register, and a feeling of total involvement.

The singing is at the same time grand and simple, gruff and infinitely touching; even the bitterness of "Les pauvres gens, peuvent-ils être heureux?" hardly prepares the listener for that terrible last cry of "Oh, Paris!," to which no other recorded baritone brings so powerful an anguish. Cotrubas's brand of innocence, touching in its vulnerability yet at the same time knowing, makes of Louise an adorable heroine, the voice full of color, the performance of subtle, delicate touches. Berbié cannot impose herself by voice alone as the Mother, but her personality jumps from the disc and she makes full use of music in the first and third acts cut from the earlier set. Sénéchal's sharpness is as always wholly appropriate and the greater tenorial glory but lesser French style of Domingo suffers a little in comparison. The Spaniard produces brilliance of sound (occasional hardness as well), but one is grateful for those sustained climaxes which result from such luxury casting.

1977 EMI / ANGEL (S)

Beverly Sills (A), Mignon Dunn (B), Nicolai Gedda (C), Martyn Hill (D), Jośe van Dam (E), Paris Opéra Chorus and Orchestra—Julius Rudel

Cuts are more or less as in the previous set, and Rudel secures an idiomatic performance from orchestra and chorus, although the Coronation of the Muse at his tempo risks stagnation. Both Beverly Sills and Nicolai Gedda have strong affinities to their roles, the latter with his easy French style and fluent, reverberant singing, the former with her vocal knowledge and musical resource to back it up. There can have been few roles better suited at this stage of Sills's career to her very considerable vocal and dramatic talents than Louise, even though her voice is no longer quite ideal for "Depuis le jour" (she was still singing it onstage in the year of this recording). Sills and her tenor show such tenderness toward each other in the opening scene as to go a long way toward absolving Julien from accusations of being on the make at the start and later on dealing coldly with Louise's family. Here he is impulsive and involved. Mignon Dunn is arguably of too grand a vocal caliber for her role, or at least insufficiently incisive, but makes an impressive thing of the plea to Julien in Act III, Scene 4. There remains José van Dam's Father, magnificent—perhaps too magnificent—of voice, wholly appropriate of timbre, and yet somehow cast slightly beside the point. He does not find it easy to suggest an older man, and his tenderness lacks the whole-hearted conviction of Bacquier's; the listener could be forgiven for admiring the vocalism more than the characterization. Small parts are good.

1983 ERATO (S,D)

Felicity Lott (A), Rita Gorr (B), Jerome Pruett (C), Christian Jean (D), Ernest Blanc (E), Chorus and Orchestra of Théâtre de la Monnaie, Brussels—Sylvain Cambreling

Recorded in January 1983 from the stage of La Monnaie, this performance is accurate but full of coughs, stage noises, and things that go bump in the night. That is perhaps a lesser drawback than the curious and very numerous cuts the conductor imposes, none more harmful than that of "Voir naître un enfant" in Act IV and in the Prelude to Act II. These would be easier to forgive had he maintained the liveliness he shows at the start, but good street cries and seamstresses and energy in the Montmartre Crowning are counterbalanced by some sluggishness in lyrical music, and he seems to lack the ability to maintain momentum while doing justice to slower music. With the Opéra-Comique in abeyance during Rolf Lieberman's administration, Louise was probably no longer in the Paris repertory while he was studying, and it shows.

More's the pity since Felicity Lott sings Louise admirably, pleading touchingly with her Mother, making a great thing of "Depuis le jour" with its floated high notes, and singing the emblematic "Tout être a le droit d'être libre!" in Act IV with as much simplicity and conviction as she later brings to her outburst of love and defiance. Jerome Pruett cannot quite match her, but the voice is sturdy if a little short of contrast and color. Ernest Blanc is not quite at ease in a role of bass-baritone tessitura (though many baritones have sung it before him), and in Act I he sounds petulant and misses the confidence of the old paterfamilias, which is what Louise cannot stand up to. He is powerful in Act IV (in spite of the heinous cut), but less effective than another veteran, the authoritative Rita Gorr. If Gorr's pleading in Act III, Scene 4 is not quite as moving as history suggests was that of Deschamps-Jéhin, the role's creator, this is only a comment on singing distinguished for granite tone and brilliantly incisive diction.

Each of these sets has its virtues, both of cast and style, but in the end CBS's must gain the vote because of consistently fine singing, the unmatched performance of Bacquier, and the admirable conducting. Ingredients like this turn any surmise that Louise may be one of the twentieth-century's operatic masterpieces into certainty.

LORD HAREWOOD

LUIGI CHERUBINI

MÉDÉE (1797)

A: Médée (s); B: Néris (c); C: Jason (t); D: Créon (bs)

Cherubini's terrifying masterpiece, a late eighteenth-century classical tragedy poised on the edge of the nineteenth century and peering far into the romantic distance, has not yet been recorded. This may seem a startling opening statement for a *Médée* chapter in a book of this kind; but it needs to be made clear that what commonly goes under the name of Cherubini's *Medea* in the world's opera houses, as well as on the three recordings discussed here, is a drastic dilution of Cherubini's work. The 1797 original is an *opéra comique* consisting of spoken dialogue and sung numbers in carefully weighted alternation. In the history of opera, speech and song have generally been considered uncomfortable bedfellows; certainly, this opera gained a wider popularity after 1855, when the German composer Franz Lachner replaced the dialogue with recitatives to make up a completely sung-through version. For the first La Scala performance in 1909, the Lachner edition was translated and became the basis for the Ricordi score on which the three recordings depend. The Lachner *Medea* recitatives, impressive in themselves, jar badly with Cherubini's fiery post-classical mode; worse, cuts have to be made in Cherubini's own music to accommodate the long-winded recitative linkage. As the Serafin-Ricordi set shows, later conductors have cut into the original numbers, altering the ratio of Cherubini to non-Cherubini still further. The recitative version is essentially a counterfeit; without a soprano of genius in the title role it is all too easy for the opera to

drag, and for its dramatic vision to become badly clouded.

1957 EMI / ANGEL (In Italian) (S) CD

Maria Callas (A), Miriam Pirazzini (B), Mirto Picchi (C), Giuseppe Modesti (D), La Scala Chorus and Orchestra—Tullio Serafin

The first of the studio recordings has a soprano of genius in the title role—it is this that sets it apart from the others, and validates the version used. Callas's Medea is one of the most celebrated operatic portrayals in the history of the medium; even via records, one catches more than a glimpse of its barbaric splendor. The singer's comprehension of music and drama, and the way each informs the other, is simply overwhelming, and the command of classical style, the ability to etch detail while preserving line, the art of making recitative continuously vivid, renders Cherubini-Lachner as stylistically "whole" as it is ever likely to get. This was, of course, one of Callas's three most famous roles (Norma and Violetta the other two), and the documentation on pirate records of the various *Medea* productions in which she took part is complete. Examining the best of these side by side with this commercial recording, it soon becomes doubly, and sadly, clear that she was vocally off form while working in the Milan recording studios. High notes in Act I are thin, not so much wobbly as cautious: the tone lacks fiber. Later in the opera she gets into her stride, in time to produce some awesomely grand, chilling phrases in Act III, and even "thin" Callas is precious beyond compare. The other leading members of the cast—the underrated tenor Picchi, the delightfully fresh young Renata Scotto (Dircé, or Glauce, as she is called in Italian)—inevitably remain in her shadow. But a greater shadow over the opera is cast by the great but aged conductor Serafin, whose command of the work lacks force and forward motion. It is a joy, in such numbers as Dircé's Beethovenian C-major aria, to hear the vocally inspired interplay of solo singer and instruments (even when ensemble is untidy, as it quite often is); but the pacing, notably in Act I, is too often becalmed (the slowing down of Néris's *andantino* aria to *adagio affetuoso* is traditional but unfortunate, and particularly unhelpful to the rather coarse mezzo, Pirazzini). The cuts are distressing—well beyond those already built into the Ricordi-Lachner score—and the recorded sound (in spite of its early-stereo dimension) is dry. This Callas *Medea* is both essential and disappointing.

1967 DECCA / LONDON (In Italian) (S)

Gwyneth Jones (A), Fiorenza Cossotto (B), Bruno Prevedi (C), Justino Díaz (D), Chorus and Orchestra of the Accademia di Santa Cecilia, Rome—Lamberto Gardelli

Gwyneth Jones's Medea—a role she never played in the theater—was recorded when the voice was still uninvaded by the wobbles and vibrations that became commonplace later in her career. There are big, broad, shining sounds here. Even in 1967, however, the uneven technique and the weak low register interfere with her unfolding of the music, and, perhaps because of this, she seems to have not much to say about the role, other than to address it with unstinted energy and power. In this version above all, recitative is the giveaway: Jones's Italian is thick-tongued, and verbal light and shade play little part in its utterance. In the earlier of Gardelli's two *Medea* recordings, the text is fuller than Serafin's, less full than Gardelli-Hungaroton, but this is less of an advantage than it might have been, because of the mediocre quality of the orchestral playing and choral singing. A

neutral impression is left by the strong-voiced Prevedi (a fine singer who never did himself justice on records) and Díaz. Cossotto's Néris is firm, not particularly tender (but Gardelli strikes at least the correct *andantino* tempo for her aria); greatest pleasure comes from Pilar Lorengar's singing of Dircé's aria, not perhaps ideally classical in style but vibrantly appealing and wonderfully free at the top. Anyone who requires proof of how difficult it is to bring this *Medea* edition to life will find here handy long stretches of demonstration material.

1977 HUNGAROTON (In Italian) (S)

Sylvia Sass (A), Klara Takács (B), Veriano Luchetti (C), Kolos Kováts (D), Hungarian Radio and Television Chorus, Budapest Symphony Orchestra—Lamberto Gardelli

Gardelli's second Medea starts with certain advantages—a version that contains more of *echt*-Cherubini than any other (including, for instance, those dramatically poignant bars of instrumental introduction to Néris's aria normally pruned); a decent orchestra and chorus; a genuinely kingly, dignified (if at moments slightly woolly-toned) Créon in Kováts; and an impassioned, attractively Italianate Jason in Luchetti (the other principals are capable but somewhat pale). But the conductor, always competent, rarely strikes fire from Cherubini's rhythmically charged figuration: the articulation tends to be of the automatic-pilot variety. More important, Sylvia Sass simply fails to carry the weight placed on her by the tremendous title role. Her whole performance is obviously modeled on Callas's: the plunges into darkened chest register or *subito piano* for dramatic emphasis particularly betray the influence. But Sass's very peculiar Italian (harsh, guttural consonants and closed Magyar vowels) robs the recitative of Callas's classical clarity; more important, the vocal technique is insufficiently finished to allow her to do more than scratch the surface of the role's immense emotional range. This is a melodramatic, and thus a one-dimensional, Medea—something that can never be said of Callas's. There are many touching moments, and the shaping of Medea's marvelous Act III aria "Du trouble affreux" (Del fiero duol), in which Gluck, Mozart, and Beethoven seem to meet, is lyrical and affecting. As a whole, however, Hungaroton's leading soprano must be deemed insufficient, if not actually inadequate.

It must be clear from the foregoing that (in the opinion of the present writer, at least) the absence of an original-language, original-version Médée leaves one of the most substantial holes in the opera-record catalogue. Meanwhile, the three commercial recordings in existence demonstrate three different aspects of the Italianized Cherubini-Lachner Medea problems. But Callas's, for all its failings, is at least more than a stopgap.

MAX LOPPERT

FRANCESCO CILEA

ADRIANA LECOUVREUR (1902)

A: Adriana (s); B: Princess (ms); C: Maurizio (t); D: Michonnet (bar)

*A*driana Lecouvreur owes its hold on the repertory in large part to prima donnas attracted by the opportunity to portray a noted eighteenth-century stage actress—a mixed blessing given that the title role (and not just the title role) also seems to provide an almost irresistible temptation for hammy overacting in the name of Thespian art. The opera was premiered at La Scala on November 6, 1902, with Caruso as Maurizio, and within less than a month the tenor recorded "No, più nobile," from Act II, in a rendition fraught with exaggerated emotion (along with spellbindingly intense fervor). But this, the first of Cilea's two operas, happens to be a remarkable, maybe even unique, example of a delicate *verismo* opera. Indeed, its finest qualities lie not in deeply developed characters—these are the usual jealous and hyper-emotional veristic bunch, resulting in the poisoning of Adriana by the wicked Princess, jealous of Adriana's love for the heroic Maurizio—but in Cilea's carefully crafted score, with its colorful evocation of the bustle of eighteenth-century French theatrical life. So for modern tastes, the challenge of any performance is to find a convincing balance between the raw passions of the characters and the delicate flavor of the period setting.

1949 COLOSSEUM (M)

Mafalda Favero (A), Elena Nicolai (B), Nicola Filacuridi (C), Luigi Borgonovo (D), Chorus and Orchestra of the Opera Italiana—Federico Del Cupolo

By the time this first complete recording of *Adriana* was made, the opera had accumulated any number of bad performance precedents, and this, at times, wildly melodramatic version is practically a catalogue of them. Favero and Filacuridi, for instance, compete not with high notes but with the tasteless exaggeration of their sobs in Adriana's prolonged death scene. Yet when not succumbing to sentimental extravagances, Favero displays a proud theatrical temperament, her singing generally secure, impassioned, and noble, and her second-act confrontation with Nicolai's particularly vituperative Princess is a hair-raising spitting match. The men, however, reduce the drama to trivial soap opera. Filacuridi, a tenor who continually forces when the pitch goes above the staff, loves to end a phrase with his voice breaking with emotion, and does it so often that it begins to sound like an annoying and meaningless tick. Borgonovo makes a weepy, maudlin, self-pitying Michonnet. Cupolo's conducting plays into the singers' worst instincts, one moment allowing slurping strings to wring every last bit of pathos, the next suddenly shifting to wildly melodramatic outbursts. Nor is ensemble precision, so important to this opera, a noticeable priority here, which means that little of Cilea's atmospheric subtlety is retained. But Cupolo, like his ladies, does respond without inhibition to the moments of real drama, and at those moments the temperature runs higher than in any other recorded performance, with Favero as the most theatrical Adriana on disc. The transfers from 78-rpm discs are as uneven and distorted, at least on the Italian RCA LP version, as is the performance.

1950 CETRA (M)

Carla Gavazzi (A), Miti Truccato Pace (B), Giacinto Prandelli (C), Saturno Meletti (D), Italian Radio Orchestra—Alfredo Simonetto

Although another rough-and-ready Italian performance from the early 1950s, this one takes a far more cautious approach, lacking both the extremes of tastelessness and of electricity that the Colosseum recording displays. Gavazzi—a reliable but not particularly characterful singer—makes all the obvious points, her Adriana generally poised but capable of rising to moments of passion. Prandelli is an altogether sweeter and more reserved tenor than Filacuridi, but he is a less heroic Maurizio as well. Pace is another careful singer, her woolly mezzo not having that dynamically abrasive edge of Nicolai's Princess. Only Meletti's overly fretful Michonnet, his voice always quavering with emotion, sinks into the kind of sappy melodrama found on the Colosseum set. The ensemble work is tidier, too, since Simonetto seems more concerned with keeping everything together than making the music sparkle or strain. He does occasionally drive his singers into climaxes, forcing them beyond their capacities, but those climaxes sound more like dramatic desperation than well-considered drama, and the result is sloppiness. The secondary singers are anonymous, none standing out or hurting the effort. The sound, like all else here, is more reliable than the Colosseum effort, but the overall result is more dramatically boring.

1961 DECCA / LONDON (S) CD

Renata Tebaldi (A), Giulietta Simionato (B), Mario del Monaco (C), Giulio Fioravanti (D), Chorus and Orchestra of the Accademia di Santa Cecilia, Rome—Franco Capuana

If the first two recordings of *Adriana* personify the gritty 1950s, this one from a decade later is a typical glamour product of its age. It is an *Adriana* that seems to exemplify the spirit of soft, rounded furniture, of fat luxury cars, of Montovanni background music, and of coy stardom. Nevertheless, Tebaldi's stands out as the finest sung Adriana on disc. She clearly knows something of Adriana's stagy glamour, and she projects a haughty allure. But beyond that, there is little dramatic conviction to her singing, and certainly less fire than most of her competition. Del Monaco makes a narcissistic, cardboard Maurizio—his absurdly long-held high B in Maurizio's third-act martial aria, for instance, sounds too calculated and processed to have even the force of vulgarity. Fioravanti's Michonnet is so unremarkably sung as to be hardly a factor in the drama at all, and the same can be said of the secondary characters. That leaves only Simionato's Princess as a richly developed character. But what robs the performance of any theatricality (both Tebaldi and del Monaco were far more effective onstage in the roles than they are here) is Capuana's slow, soft-edged, uninflected conducting, which replaces the score's all-important atmosphere with a kind of generic mood-music personality. Under such circumstances the weepy ending, lacking any dramatic conviction preceding it, sounds entirely false. The recorded sound has an innocuous romantic plushness that suits the performance.

1977 CBS / SONY (S) CD

Renata Scotto (A), Elena Obraztsova (B), Plácido Domingo (C), Sherrill Milnes (D), Ambrosian Chorus and Philharmonia Orchestra—James Levine

In comparison with the recordings described above, Levine's *Adriana*—and it really is the conductor who dominates the performance—is downright revelatory. From the scurrying opening, Levine creates the sense that every bar is music about something, that it sets a scene, motivates characters, or reveals a vital aspect of what they are thinking or feeling. He enforces precision, showing Cilea's score to have far more substance than might be imagined from any other recording, yet he never slights strong dramatic urgency—and the combination is one of almost constant musical urgency. Best of all, Levine seems to draw his singers inside the music and their characters. That is particularly welcome with Scotto, who is not as vocally distinguished as Tebaldi nor as dramatically arresting as Favero, her voice showing signs of strain in her biggest climaxes. Even so, she distinguishes herself by offering a surprisingly nuanced characterization of an actress more vulnerable and less hammy than that conveyed by any of the other sopranos. Domingo's Maurizio is sung with a firm and handsome tone, and again he offers, by far, the most nuanced and complex of Maurizios on disc. Milnes is an unusually masculine Michonnet, making his unrequited love for and devotion to Adriana more touching than it is in any other recorded performance. Obraztsova's Princess is a showy affair, but Levine keeps her dramatically focused and she makes an exciting sound. Typical of *Adriana* recordings, not much effort is made with the secondary parts, but all are competent. The sound, like the performance, is bright and compelling.

1990 DECCA / LONDON (S, D) CD

Joan Sutherland (A), Cleopatra Ciurca (B), Carlo Bergonzi (C), Leo Nucci (D), Welsh National Opera Chorus and Orchestra—Richard Bonynge

In her prime, Joan Sutherland was a vocally resplendent Adriana, so resplendent, in fact, that it could be easily overlooked that hers was never the theatrical presence that lies at the heart of the role. In her recording, however, that lack of theatricality is glaring. Waiting until her sixty-second year to record Adriana, Sutherland exhibits an extreme unsteadiness of pitch and a thick, mealy sound that wavers precipitously at top. Moreover, the sheer effort involved in hitting pitches denies her the freedom for whatever little dramatic involvement with the

role she once might have brought to it. Bergonzi, two years older than Sutherland, boasts a better preserved voice, and his famous elegance of phrase is still in evidence, but the ringing tone of a hero is not. And like Sutherland, he too sounds as if he has to take great care with the placement of every pitch. In comparison, Nucci seems particularly healthy-sounding; indeed, his is the most suave of Michonnets but also the blandest. That leaves only Ciurca, a rather sour Princess, to supply what little vocal flair the performance can muster, and Michel Sénéchal's wonderfully slimy Abbé the only character with any real character at all. Bonynge generally makes a bad situation worse with disastrously indulgent conducting, which may necessarily support his aging singers but does so at the cost of dramatic propulsion. Tempos are often so slow that they only exaggerate the vocal exertions of Sutherland and Bergonzi while placing a Wagnerian weight on the music that it cannot possibly withstand.

Levine's animated, nuanced, colorful performance is the only one that treats the opera as refined music theater, although Favero is the most exciting of the recorded Adrianas while Tebaldi is the most vocally resplendent. Levine's cast offers, in every instance (including Scotto), the richest characterizations; and Levine alone achieves the refinement of ensemble that is one of the opera's greatest charms and necessary for producing its special atmosphere. The Colosseum set surely has more raw passion but at the price of awful overindulgences and pitiful ensemble. The other recordings are all badly conducted and have only blandness or mawkishness to recommend them.

MARK SWED

Domenico Cimarosa

Il Matrimonio Segreto (1792)

A: Elisetta (s or ms); B: Carolina (s); C: Fidalma (ms or c);
D: Paolino (t); E: Geronimo (bs); F: Count Robinson (bs)

The most famous of Cimarosa's sixty-five operas, *Il Matrimonio Segreto* had a triumphant premiere in Vienna in 1792: the emperor enjoyed the work so much that he ordered a lavish supper for the performers, after which the entire opera was repeated. Unlike many eighteenth-century comic operas, *The Secret Marriage* held the stage throughout the nineteenth century. In recent years, however, its popularity seems to have slipped considerably.

There are at least three reasons for the neglect of this masterpiece. First, it's an intimate opera—six singers, a small orchestra, no chorus—that would be lost in a large auditorium. Second, the libretto's humor is of the subtle, verbal sort, with little room for sight gags or boisterousness. Finally, the opera is a true ensemble piece: the vocal writing, though both demanding and rewarding, does not offer the opportunities for solo display that we encounter in Haydn's or Mozart's operas, to say nothing of Rossini's.

There have been only three commercial recordings, none of them note-complete. Both mono versions observe once-standard stage cuts, and even the stereo DG recording, though by far the most complete, abridges the recitatives. A further peculiarity is that none of these recordings offers anything significant in the way of vocal embellishment—all of the singers seem to make a point of sticking to the printed notes. Although Cimarosa's melodies are effective enough when sung as written, he surely expected performers to insert cadenzas at appropriate

points; and, at the very least, the literal repeats in the arias could only benefit from the addition of tasteful and stylish embellishments.

1950 CETRA (M)

Ornella Rovero (A), Alda Noni (B), Giulietta Simionato (C), Cesare Valletti (D), Sesto Bruscantini (E), Antonio Cassinelli (F), Orchestra of the Maggio Musicale Fiorentino—Manno Wolf-Ferrari

This recording, though spread over six LP sides (as are the others), is heavily cut. Whole pages of recitative are eliminated; and there is a great deal of unfortunate internal abridgment of musical numbers, so that in some cases the original shape is no longer discernible. Furthermore, several fine numbers are dropped altogether. Paolino loses both his Act I aria ("Brillar mi sento il core") and his subsequent duet with the Count ("Signor, deh! concede"). In Act II, we lose the delightful aria "Son lunatico, bilioso." Later on, Elisetta's aria "Se son vendicata" is omitted, and so is her encounter with the Count (comprising eight pages of vocal score) that should begin the finale.

Wolf-Ferrari's conducting, though lively, has more energy than elegance. The orchestral playing is monotonously loud and often ragged in ensemble.

Only half the cast is really satisfactory. Rovero is an ordinary mezzo, dull of timbre, often suspect in intonation. Noni's good intentions as Carolina are compromised by wiry, acidulous tone. Cassinelli sings acceptably, but is monochromatic, making little of the Count's contradictory character.

Bruscantini would rather be hammy than dull, which is a step in the right direction: his Geronimo is enjoyable enough despite the stereotyped *buffo* effects. Valletti sings what is left of his role with ardor and fresh, beautiful tone. Simionato has almost the perfect voice and temperament for Fidalma: the recitative scene between her and Valletti, in which Fidalma declares her intention to marry Paolino and he faints, is a tiny masterpiece of comic timing and inflection.

On a reissue, Everest's rechanneling into artificial stereo has created a strident, over-reverberant acoustic sound, obliterating any virtues the original mono sound may have had.

1956 EMI / ANGEL (M)

Eugenia Ratti (A), Graziella Sciutti (B), Ebe Stignani (C), Luigi Alva (D), Carlo Badioli (E), Franco Calabrese (F), La Scala Orchestra—Nino Sanzogno

EMI also makes cuts in the recitatives and in the musical numbers—although more discreetly, on the whole, than Cetra. At least once (in the Act II quintet "Deh, lasciate ch'io respiri") a melody is "developed" without having been heard in its original form, as a result of these cuts.

Paolino's "Brillar mi sento il core," the Count's "Son lunatico," and Elisetta's "Se son vendicata" are once again missing, but "Signor, deh! concedete" and the beginning of the Act II finale have been restored.

Sanzogno conducts in a relaxed, elegant way that is most attractive; some listeners may prefer a crisper, more sparkling approach, but this is a poised, aristocratic reading. The small orchestra plays exquisitely.

Ratti has just enough of an edge to her timbre to suggest the waspish side of Elisetta's personality: this is arguably her best recording of a complete operatic role. In order to enjoy Sciutti's artistry, one must accept her fragile-sounding, breathy tone and her tendency to peck at high notes. Stignani, recorded near the end of her career, sometimes sounds huffy and effortful, but she certainly knows how to put this kind of music across.

Alva, sounding exceptionally suave and spontaneous, is the best Paolino on the three sets. Badioli is a genuinely funny, unexaggerated Geronimo, Calabrese an appropriately worldly Count; both sing well.

The undoctored mono sound, complete with some convincing distance effects, holds up well.

1975–76 DEUTSCHE GRAMMOPHON (S) CD

Julia Varady (A), Arleen Augér (B), Julia Hamari (C), Ryland Davies (D), Dietrich Fischer-Dieskau (E), Alberto Rinaldi (F), English Chamber Orchestra—Daniel Barenboim

Despite some unnaturally close miking of the voices, the stereo sound is excellent, making more of the score audible than on either of the two earlier recordings.

All of the musical numbers are included, for the first time on disc, and without internal cuts; there are still some extensive cuts in the recitatives (ironically, some exchanges performed on the two older recordings are omitted here).

Barenboim's conducting resembles Sanzogno's in its steady, understated approach. One might prefer sharper attacks and a livelier range of tempos, but not at the expense of the elegance Barenboim brings to the music. The English Chamber Orchestra plays extremely well.

DG's cast is strongest where Cetra's is weakest: both sisters are superb. Varady is an ideal Elisetta, combining beautiful tone with incisive attack, and suggesting the vulnerability that underlies the character's bitchiness. She is well partnered by Augér, who outsings both Noni and Sciutti while fully matching the latter's charm.

Hamari sings Fidalma smoothly and securely, but could have more fun with the part; Stignani and Simionato are preferable, but it's no disgrace for a mezzo to place third against such formidable competition.

Davies is a superior Paolino, if not quite on Alva's level, and Rinaldi is an interestingly sensual, ironic Count.

Unfortunately, Fischer-Dieskau is by no stretch of the imagination the true bass needed for Geronimo's music, and in addition he is often dry of timbre and effortful. He overinflects the text, becoming downright manic in some of the recitatives. He is too intelligent and musical to disfigure the performance, but he is still miscast.

———————

With none of these recordings readily available, the situation is obviously unsatisfactory. We must hope for CD reissues of the EMI and DG sets.

ROLAND GRAEME

CLAUDE DEBUSSY

PELLÉAS ET MÉLISANDE (1893–1902)

A: Mélisande (s); B: Geneviève (ms); C: Pelléas (t or bar);
D: Golaud (bar); E: Arkel (bs)

Pelléas already lands us in difficulties in the attempt simply to assign it a date. Although the opera was substantially complete by 1895, Debussy continued to revise it while it awaited performance, and even after the 1902 premiere never stopped tinkering with it.

Most of the revisions are subtle adjustments, reflecting Debussy's preoccupation with detail. The payoff for this preoccupation is, perhaps paradoxically for such a "difficult" opera, an unexpected clarity and simplicity, as well as strength, of expression. This underlying clarity goes a long way toward explaining the surprisingly successful run of recordings.

It's true that, as with such operas in the "difficult" group as *Parsifal* and *Ariadne*, the very singularity of the piece tends to screen out—or at least *used* to screen out—performers who aren't in some basic way tuned in. Not that there is anything resembling a "standard" or "correct" interpretation. In fact, one of the nicest things about the *Pelléas* discography is its diversity. You could buy two or three well-chosen recordings and wind up effectively with two or three different operas, each drawing on the depth and complexity with which the mysterious doings of the characters have been imagined.

On a technical note, the arrival of stereo might seem a lesser issue for *Pelléas*, with its relatively light, transparent scoring, than for, say, Wagner's textural extravaganzas. The reality is that the mono recordings of *Pelléas* are at

a *greater* disadvantage. Which isn't fair, since these recordings, different as they are, as a group have a general interpretive distinction that I attribute to their still more active grappling with the substance of the opera. They deserve a hearing, but there's no denying that the sound makes them harder to appreciate.

The only significant textual variant is the small restoration in 1988 Disques Verany.

1941 EMI / ANGEL (M) CD

Irène Joachim (A), Germaine Cernay (B), Jacques Jansen (C), (Henri) Etcheverry (D), Paul Cabanel (E), Yvonne Gouverné Chorus, Symphony orchestra—Roger Désormière

Hearing how effectively the principals and the conductor work together, you can appreciate Jacques Jansen's emphasis, in his 1984 reminiscence included in the CD booklet, on the fact that they *were* a team, from their performances together at the Opéra-Comique—not to mention what seem to have been fairly intense piano rehearsals before each recording session.

Irène Joachim is a successful representation of what we might call the Mélisande soprano: a voice that isn't really ample or wide-ranging enough to make much impact in normal repertory but is unforcedly attractive in the midrange and better able than most standard sopranos to trace the role's idiosyncratic intricacies. (Far from random example: her first lines, the repetitions of "Ne me touchez pas!") And Jansen, in the first of three recordings, brings to Pelléas about as much youthful freshness of sound as one may expect from a baritone in the role.

Etcheverry, whose voice isn't exceptionally beautiful and falters at the upper end, is a dignified, strong-voiced Golaud. Golaud might have also been an interesting role for Paul Cabanel, but as Arkel he is a wonderful baritone holding his own in a bass role.

While Germaine Cernay's mezzo is also on the high and light side for Geneviève, whose writing in the letter scene is anchored down around the break, she is such a lovely and alert singer that the overall result is strongly positive.

1952 DECCA / LONDON (M)

Suzanne Danco (A), Hélène Bouvier (B), Pierre Mollet (C), Heinz Rehfuss (D), André Vessières (E), Chorus and Orchestre de la Suisse Romande—Ernest Ansermet

Ernest Ansermet's first Pelléas has plausible texture and weight, but streams onward carrying the singers forlornly along. And the cast *looks* promising. Of course, these aren't exactly vocally overpowering singers, so it's hard to know whether their reticence was intended or merely happened. But here, for example, we have Suzanne Danco, a lovely singer whose range shouldn't be overtaxed by Mélisande, and a generally winning, sympathetic performer. Yet although the straight singing passages are pretty enough, for the most part she just seems to be trailing along.

Then, here is Heinz Rehfuss, another singer from whom one customarily expects some empathic personal projection, even if the prospect of Golaud sets off alarm signals—first, because his warm bass-baritone doesn't afford much force at the top, where the character's violence is released, and second, because he's not an artist from whom one easily imagines violence. And indeed, while the singing is often exceptionally lovely, it's only the civilized side of the character that comes to life. The penitent Golaud of the opening of Act V ("J'ai tué sans raison") is heartbreaking; left alone with Mélisande, however, he launches the final duet ("Mélisande, as-tu pitié de moi") as if it were a lullaby, and he never does get from there to the inner torment that drives him into one last act of savagery.

And again: Pierre Mollet, although a vocally forthright and, except in the highest reaches, rather attractive baritone Pelléas, tends to blend into the background. André Vessières, whose warmly plangent bass would seem just about perfectly suited to Arkel, is unfortunately in generally insecure voice for most of the opera. Fortunately he's in much better shape in Act IV, and he achieves real eloquence in the haunting *arioso* before Mélisande dies.

The veteran Hélène Bouvier, now sounding quite distressed, is a weak Geneviève.

1953 PHILIPS (M) CD

Janine Micheau (A), Rita Gorr (B), Camille Maurane (C), Michel Roux (D), Xavier Depraz (E), Elizabeth Brasseur Choir, Lamoureux Orchestra—Jean Fournet

This recording takes a markedly different approach from that of any of the earlier ones, and it really hasn't been quite duplicated since. Jean Fournet plays the opening bars slowly and essentially without inflection: flat, plain, stark. And his reading follows through on this unprettified beginning, responding to the score's dark, primitive, and mysterious dimension. When Arkel announces the news of the recovery of Pelléas's father in Act IV, normally one of the opera's sunniest moments, it sounds here almost ominous, as if in these parts good news is perceived as the harbinger of bad—which certainly fits this case. Similarly, Mélisande's Tower Song at the start of Act III rises from a distinctly ominous-sounding orchestral introduction.

Two factors give this performance its considerable staying power. First, Fournet's choices are drawn from the score, rather than imposed on it. He doesn't stifle the lyricism of the orchestral interludes, or undercut the playfulness of the music for Pelléas and Mélisande in Acts II and III. In fact, as a result of his attention to the score's dark elements, the lighter ones can achieve sharper contrast with less effort. And so this performance, without slighting the gentle consolation that can always be heard in the gorgeous orchestral introduction to Act V, which places Mélisande on her deathbed, at the same time powerfully intimates disaster.

The second factor is the role of the singers, who are allowed to shoulder the burden of the pursuit of their characters' needs. They may not be completely successful, but the reality is that however much help the conductor may provide, in the end the singers are the only ones who can do their job.

And it's a rather good cast. Janine Micheau's lyric soprano isn't as well focused as I would expect, but she does some fine singing when the writing allows her to set properly for it. At her best she is a fine partner for Camille Maurane, the most smoothly integrated and lyrically free of the baritone Pelléases.

Michel Roux is a strong, serious Golaud. The bass part of his bass-baritone is just right for the role, combining power and beauty. Where I have a problem is in the baritone part, which tapers into a characteristically French, rather nasal sound that lends itself more to a prissy kind of control than to the uninhibited outpourings of Golaud.

We certainly can't complain about the vocal weight or range of the Arkel and Geneviève. Xavier Depraz's bass isn't terribly attractive, though, which doesn't make for a very sympathetic Arkel, but he's unquestionably a presence. And so is Rita Gorr, even if her full-bodied mezzo is already subject to the excessive vibrato that prematurely disabled this fine voice. Of course, if you've gotten into the rather dour spirit of the performance, the fact that these aren't pretty voices seems right in character.

Annik Simon is a rather good Yniold.

1956 EMI / ANGEL (M)

Victoria de los Angeles (A), Jeannine Collard (B), Jacques Jansen (C), Gérard Souzay (D), Pierre Froumenty (E), Raymond St-Paul Chorus, Orchestre National de la RTF—André Cluytens

Like 1953 Philips, this performance is in no hurry, but it makes strikingly different use of the space gained. In contrast to Fournet's textually literal-minded austerity, André Cluytens shows a great deal of interest in the score's atmospheric and coloristic possibilities, while

allowing room for unselfconsciously full articulation of the words (a general characteristic of the mono recordings, actually). This isn't a lush performance exactly, but it has both a sweetness and a luxuriant mysteriousness that can be quite winning, at least in moderate doses.

This can be a powerfully frustrating performance, with a tendency to bog down, not from heaviness but from a simple lack of momentum. When Geneviève finishes reading the letter, note the lumbering quality of the phrase handed from the basses to the cellos; or in the last scene of Act I, note how Pelléas, responding to his mother's greeting, seems to be counting out the eighth notes in his entrance line, "Oui, je venais du côté de la mer."

And while the cast *seems* well chosen, in terms of vocal weight (light to medium) and temperament (ditto) for this kind of performance, I think what you in fact need are singers who will to an extent *counteract* its inclination to sluggishness. Victoria de los Angeles, for example, does some lovely singing, but when her already edge-prone soprano is stretched out as it is here, it tends to become *all* edge. Nor is this an optimal environment for Jacques Jansen.

Gérard Souzay's lyric baritone, though still in quite good shape, seems an odd choice for Golaud, especially opposite a baritone Pelléas, but within this framework I have come to admire this performance. Given the limitation of the vocal resources, this is necessarily an awfully civil Golaud (the opening scene sounds more like a Fauré *chanson* about evening in the forest than a hunter coping with the realization that he is lost). But no one except José van Dam generates more lyric intensity, and of course his voice *does* have a top, even if it's not classically Golaud-esque. He deals surprisingly successfully with the problematic scene with Mélisande after he has been thrown from his horse, and while there isn't much he can do to make Golaud's rages believable, the impassive calm he affects ("Vous ferez comme il vous plaira, voyez-vous!") in his Act IV scene with Arkel is impressively cool and steely.

Both Pierre Froumenty (Arkel) and Jeannine Collard (Geneviève) have voices of appropriate size and weight, but their lack of steadiness is italicized by the moderate pacing.

Unexpectedly, given EMI's conservative engineering philosophy of the period, the Pelléas-Golaud scene in the underground vault is bathed in echo. Why not?

1962 DISQUES MONTAIGNE (S,P) CD

Micheline Granchet (A), Solange Michel (B), Jacques Jansen (C), Michel Roux (D), André Vessières (E), Chorale Lyrique and Orchestre National de la RTF—D.-E. Inghelbrecht

This may be the best single performance of *Pelléas* I've heard. It falls almost at the end of the series of twenty-plus annual concert performances of *Pelléas* that Désiré-Emile Inghelbrecht gave with his Orchestre National (eight of which are reportedly preserved in the official archives). Although the performance gathers plenty of weight when needed, it's in general fleeter, and lither and subtler in the shaping of lines than any of the commercial recordings that preceded it. While its interpretive solutions are in no way definitive, it is remarkable in having plausible solutions for everything in the score. It progresses with aptness and urgency, striking an uncanny balance between filling out individual moments and compelling attention to what happens next.

Revealed in this performance is Inghelbrecht's ability to draw the best out of both the principals and the orchestra—the National here throws caution to the winds and, despite some imprecision of ensemble and pitch, sounds like a world-class virtuoso ensemble. The orchestral interludes achieve a level of intensity that's all the more impressive for the absence of Karajan-style "look what I discovered" italicizings.

The surprise of the performance is the Pelléas of Jacques Jansen, then over fifty years old. Yes, if you listen for it, there is some strain in his voice, but on the whole it is in considerably better shape than in 1956 EMI, and I haven't heard any Pelléas communicate this active a struggle with his own sense of awareness in the final duet. Micheline Granchet, a classic "Mélisande soprano" (a nice sound in the mid-range when not under pressure; not much top or

bottom), although the weakest of the principals, is still quite adequate.

Michel Roux's Golaud offers basically the same strengths-with-qualifications as in 1953 Philips, in more concentrated and intense form. The initial appeal to Mélisande in the last act has remarkable vocal and emotional focus. André Vessières, in full and vibrant voice, is flat-out the best Arkel on records. And Solange Michel is also the best Geneviève. The voice, in excellent shape, has some real depth, and she, Vessières, and Inghelbrecht do wonderful things with the letter scene.

One note of caution concerning Disques Montaigne's richly annotated and handsome booklet: except for a single-page English "abstract," it's all in French.

1963 ORTF (S,P)

Micheline Granchet (A), Marie Luce Bellary (B), Camille Maurane (C), Jacques Mars (D), André Vessières (E), Chorus and Orchestre National de l'ORTF—D.-E. Inghelbrecht

For once, the performance that *is* available is actually the one to have. In outline, this *Pelléas* resembles the 1962 one, but it doesn't have the same level of cohesion and intensity, the cast is less impressive, and for some reason the sound is cooler and more distant—the two performances were after all recorded in the same auditorium by the same producer.

Of the cast holdovers, Granchet is again an adequate if unspectacular Mélisande (the down side is perhaps more noticeable in these less inspired surroundings), while Vessières is in less good voice, though as in 1952 Decca / London the last act is somewhat better. Of the others, Camille Maurane once again sings a sturdy Pelléas but, unlike Jansen, doesn't seem stimulated by Inghelbrecht (check out 1964 Decca / London, though); Jacques Mars, whom one might expect to encounter as Arkel, predictably brings some welcome vocal weight and solidity to Golaud, and predictably gets into trouble when the writing demands mobility (this wasn't the most agile of basses) or strength on top; Marie Luce Bellary, although a vocally steady, sensible Geneviève in her own right, is no match for Michel.

1964 DECCA / LONDON (S) CD

Erna Spoorenberg (A), Josephine Veasey (B), Camille Maurane (C), George London (D), Guus Hoekman (E), Chorus of the Grand Théâtre, Geneva, Orchestre de la Suisse Romande—Ernest Ansermet

It's possible that the difference in sound exaggerates the difference between the two Ansermet recordings: the rich, warm stereo version is to my taste the best-sounding *Pelléas* we've had. But the two performances do seem to me quite different; indeed, none of my complaints about the first applies to the second, which is sung and played with irresistible vividness and immediacy. The playing of the Suisse Romande here is so colorful and vibrant that the occasional Gallic tuning and ensemble lapses aren't intrusive. The performance has points of similarity to the 1962 Inghelbrecht. Again, there is a strong sense of energetic forward movement, with perhaps a richer as well as darker and weightier range of orchestral color and body, although also with a slight letdown in the climactic scenes of Act IV (*not* the case in the 1952 Ansermet version).

The heavily "international" cast, which may look questionable in prospect, comes through extremely well, and even manages the French text with considerable assurance. Erna Spoorenberg is one of my favorite Mélisandes, and perhaps the most touchingly vulnerable. Her lyric soprano remains full and attractive throughout its range, and handles the intricacies of the writing well. Camille Maurane's Pelléas is less secure vocally than in 1953 Philips, but this performance seems to me noticeably more alive dramatically, with a distinctive introspective quality.

Some listeners will be put off by the increasingly gravelly sound of George London's bass-baritone. For those who can adjust to it, however, this is an ideal Golaud voice, and a nearly ideal Golaud temperament—London can scale the voice down to achieve a virile simplicity and dignity, and has the reserve power that so many

Golauds don't. And Guus Hoekman is, apart from André Vessières in 1962 Disques Montaigne, the only fully satisfactory Arkel on records. Within the relatively limited range required by the role (up around middle C, you can hear that he doesn't have much more to give), the voice is strikingly full and authoritative, and he's unfailingly committed and humane.

Josephine Veasey is also a superior Geneviève of the higher-and-lighter-than-ideal variety.

1969 CBS / SONY (S) CD

Elisabeth Söderström (A), Yvonne Minton (B), George Shirley (C), Donald McIntyre (D), David Ward (E), Chorus and Orchestra of the Royal Opera House, Covent Garden—Pierre Boulez

Pierre Boulez's performance sounds as if it means to investigate the inward dimension of the score; only it doesn't really. It just executes, with admirable sensitivity to notated values, including some real delicacy, but with what sounds like a willful refusal to look for anything beyond the literal value of the notes.

This remains an accomplished reading, however, with a good cast headed by an outstanding Pelléas and Mélisande. There is that slight droopy quality to Elisabeth Söderström's soprano, but she's otherwise the most ample-voiced of the recorded Mélisandes, and she also creates the most fully dimensional character. George Shirley is a strong candidate for the best of the Pelléases. The strength of his lower range makes the role available to him as a tenor, and he can then manage its upper reaches without the strain and artificiality of most of the baritones. His full-voiced restlessness in the early scenes sets up a memorable final duet.

Yvonne Minton is an excellent lightweight Geneviève, and then there's a falloff. Donald McIntyre and David Ward aren't actively unpleasant, and can even be plausible enough when light vocal handling suffices. But when the music insists on full voice, neither has much fullness to offer.

A word of caution concerning the CD edition: the sound at first seems impressively fuller than on LP, but this puffed-up quality as applied to the voices recalls the era of Everest stereo rechannelings.

1978 EURODISC (S) CD

Michèle Command (A), Jocelyne Taillon (B), Claude Dormoy (C), Gabriel Bacquier (D), Roger Soyer (E), Ensemble Vocal of Burgundy, Orchestra of Lyons—Serge Baudo

Like 1953 Philips, this performance may not grab you immediately, but it repays continued attention. Although not as austere, it's also a dark performance, and perhaps because the recorded sound (in what sounds like a fairly resonant space) is so much better, it's a more ominous one. And the somberness of the castle and its surroundings, which once made such a strong impression on Geneviève and now so oppresses Mélisande, is part of the given circumstances. What's more, the performance really *plays*. It has a consistent sense of purposeful movement.

And it carries along a cast that's more workmanlike than distinguished. Michèle Command's pretty enough "Mélisande soprano" and Claude Dormoy's earnest baritone just barely fill out their roles. Gabriel Bacquier is an intelligent Golaud, but the voice is now merely functional. Roger Soyer's now rather monochromatic bass isn't actively unpleasant, but he doesn't create much of an Arkel; it's tantalizing to imagine the full, vibrant sound of the sensational Doctor, Xavier Tamalet, applied to the role. Jocelyne Taillon's ample mezzo is well suited to Geneviève.

1978 EMI / ANGEL (S) CD

Frederica von Stade (A), Nadine Denize (B), Richard Stilwell (C), José van Dam (D), Ruggero Raimondi (E), Chorus of the Deutsche Oper Berlin, Berlin Philharmonic Orchestra—Herbert von Karajan

Every time I think I know how I feel about this performance, it confounds me. It's executed with a great deal of orchestral fullness, and with considerable vocal polish—all under tight conductorial control. Practically speaking, the kind of control Karajan exercises here seems to me self-defeating: only the singers themselves can make the characters real and meaningful to us; anything coming from anywhere else falls under the heading of commentary.

And even as a commentary on *Pelléas* I have a problem with Karajan. So much of what he so carefully lays out as Profound Insight isn't new or original. Before he superheated the orchestral interludes to this degree, for example, any number of conductors had found plenty of intensity in them, and found it in the context of a dramatic presentation. Still, much of this recording is remarkably beautiful, and José van Dam in particular realizes Golaud's writing more completely than anyone else I've heard—as long as we accept that it's a reading rather than a performance of the role.

Frederica von Stade and Richard Stilwell also sing attractively. There's just very little to respond to. Ruggero Raimondi's rather slithery Arkel isn't much to my taste, but Nadine Denize is a firmly assured Geneviève and Christine Barbaux one of the best Yniolds.

1979 ERATO (S) CD

Rachel Yakar (A), Jocelyne Taillon (B), Eric Tappy (C), Philippe Huttenlocher (D), François Loup (E), Monte Carlo Opera Chorus and Orchestra—Armin Jordan

Armin Jordan's ability to strike through to the basic sense of a phrase has made such "difficult" works as *Parsifal*, the Ravel operas, and Haydn's *Seasons* sound almost easy, and the *Pelléas* too is an outstanding piece of work. In spirit, it most closely resembles the fluid and flexible Inghelbrecht and Ansermet performances, though it's leaner and more concentrated in tone and accenting than the Ansermet.

Rachel Yakar and Eric Tappy rank with the best recorded interpreters of the title roles. The bright, clear focus of Yakar's light but full-range soprano gives an endearing radiance to much of Mélisande's music, while Tappy, like 1969 CBS's George Shirley, enjoys the automatic advantages of a tenor who can truly *sing* Pelléas. His singing is smoother-textured and more "French"-sounding, perhaps more closely attuned to the curves of the phrases, than Shirley's—it's not "better," it's an interesting alternative.

Philippe Huttenlocher's baritone doesn't have the range or weight for Golaud, but because he is a sensible singer, and because he gets such sensible help from Jordan, he doesn't let the performance down. François Loup does, even though his tonally sufficient bass should have an Arkel in it; something in his vocal production works against fully articulated and smoothly bound lines, a real problem in this role. Colette Alliot-Lugaz is an excellent Yniold, Michel Brodard a fine Doctor.

1988 DISQUES PIERRE VERANY (S,D) CD

Éliane Manchet (A), Carol Yahr (B), Malcolm Walker (C), Vincent Le Texier (D), Peter Meven (E), Nice Opera Chorus, Nice Philharmonic Orchestra—John Carewe

It would be hard not to admire the thorough preparation of this performance, or the solidity and honesty of its execution. It's full-bodied in sound, yet texturally nuanced. (The recording job is unspectacularly first-rate.) It moves unforcedly but steadily. It is clearly built on deep respect for and sophisticated understanding of the score. I *like* it.

I don't *love* it, though. There are cast problems, which we'll come to in a moment. But there is also something too settled about the performance. It has conscientiously arrived at sensible and often interesting answers to all its questions about the score, but there is a sense that in the actual performance there is no longer anything to be discovered—the performance knows too well what's coming.

As an example, if I hadn't been tipped, I might well have missed the tiny textual restoration near the end of the scene in which Golaud forces Yniold to spy on his stepmother and uncle. Originally Golaud got an answer to his question "Are they near one another?" (no), and the music came to a halt as he asked whether they were near the bed, but Yniold couldn't *see* the bed. To appease the censor, Debussy cut the passage—late enough that it appears in the first published vocal score. But it's hardly an issue; the scene hardly needs another instance of Golaud's irrationality. What interested me is

that several times through the scene I managed to miss the passage, even listening for it, because the scene didn't hold my attention. And this even though Vincent Le Texier is singing a sturdy Golaud, making a solid, pleasing sound with some depth.

Otherwise the cast is spotty. Eliane Manchet displays some spunk as Mélisande but is vocally unsteady. Malcolm Walker's baritone is seriously overextended by Pelléas. Peter Meven as Arkel doesn't seem able to focus his good bass into phrases in Acts I and IV but gets it together nicely in Act V. Carol Yahr's Geneviève is beset by a persistent beat.

In the booklet, the notes are translated into English, but the libretto is in French only.

1990 DECCA / LONDON (S,D) CD

Colette Alliot-Lugaz (A), Claudine Carlson (B), Didier Henry (C), Gilles Cachemaille (D), Pierre Thau (E), Chorus and Symphony Orchestra of Montreal—Charles Dutoit

In its way, this is an attractive performance. The problem is that its way—sleek and mobile (or, if you don't cotton to it, slick and quick)—excludes an awful lot of the potential expressive range of the opera. The orchestra plays very fluently, and with a good deal of snazzy color, but the performance is almost devoid of bite, weight, or depth. Even when it does get loud, as at the end of Act III and the start of Act IV, the sound is simply piled on—it still doesn't have much real force.

The cast doesn't make a terribly strong impression either, but it's hard to suppress the feeling that the singers might have more to bring to the opera in a less surfacey, disengaged environment. Mélisande, for example, shouldn't be an impossible stretch for Colette Alliot-Lugaz, but the transition is only moderately successful. Yes, the voice is light, but voices no weightier have registered positively in the role. There just isn't much going on. Similarly, Didier Henry, while in fact fairly well endowed for a baritone tackling Pelléas, doesn't demonstrate much sense of why he wants to sing the role *except* that he can. Gilles Cachemaille's decent but rather undistinguished medium-weight baritone isn't an ideal Golaud instrument, but again, you have to feel that under other circumstances he could get closer to the role.

Pierre Thau's Arkel is a somewhat different case. His bass was never exactly beautiful, but it had presence, and it still does, even with the tone now deteriorated to something like a vigorous shudder. His scenes at least communicate the sense that something is *happening*. And Claudine Carlson has some appropriate vocal weight for Geneviève, if not the ultimate in steadiness.

The performances to which I most eagerly return are 1962 Disques Montaigne and 1964 Decca / London, which by happy coincidence have the good Arkels. A plausible alternative, though it *doesn't* have a good Arkel, is 1979 Erato, which is not only available but attractively priced and accompanied by full texts.

I would also need a contrasting performance like 1978 Eurodisc—and perhaps, for their special qualities, 1969 CBS and 1941 EMI. And then the individual claims of half a dozen other recordings still demand consideration.

KENNETH FURIE

Unavailable for review:
1990 DEUTSCHE GRAMMOPHON

LÉO DELIBES

LAKMÉ (1883)

A: Lakmé (s); B: Mallika (ms); C: Gérald (t);
D: Frédéric (bar); E: Nilakantha (bs-bar)

akmé, a nosegay of 1883, is hardly a neglected masterpiece by modern standards, offering neither the melodic richness nor the emotional intensity nor the musical characterization found in the popular Italian *bel canto* repertory. Léo Delibes, an animated and sometimes inspired ballet composer, wrote with only intermittent felicity for the voice. For his formal models he harked back to the *opéra comique* of Auber and Adam, the *Mignon* of Thomas, applying spurious "local color" as innocently as if *Carmen* or even *Der Barbier von Bagdad* had never been written. The Bell Song, for which *Lakmé* is remembered, is atypical of the work as a whole—one of few flights of flashy coloratura in a basically lyric score, characterized by charm and grace.

1952 DECCA / LONDON (M)

Mado Robin (A), Agnès Disney (B), Libéro De Luca (C), Jacques Jansen (D), Jean Borthayre (E), Chorus and Orchestra of the Opéra-Comique—Georges Sebastian

Mado Robin (1918–60) has passed into history as a high soprano in the Lily Pons tradition. Her stylish singing can serve as a yardstick to judge more recent recordings. Robin's "Dans la forêt près de nous," for example, is a classic of poised, limpid tone, and her timbre—slightly acid yet soft—suits the music to perfection. This performance is not just a star turn, however, for Robin's colleagues are uniformly excellent, both

individually and as a well-routined ensemble upholding the best Opéra-Comique tradition. Robin's opening barcarole duet with Agnès Disney is beautifully light and floating, without unduly milking the implicit ripeness of the music. Claudine Collart as Ellen, Gérald's fiancée, resembles Robin in style and timbre, while Jane Perriat portrays the most amusing Mrs. Bentson (her easily flustered governess) on records. De Luca's Gérald deploys a firmly grounded, penetrating lyric voice; though he takes his high notes quite loudly, there is no sign of forcing. Jacques Jansen plays an elegant, expressive Frédéric rather than a shallow stock character, and the stern Nilakantha of Borthayre strikes the right balance between paternal tenderness and fanaticism. Sebastian, not usually a strong conductor in more demanding music, shapes the score with a smoothly practiced hand. There are standard brief cuts of repeated material, and sung recitative, added when *Lakmé* went on from the Comique to other theaters, replaces the original spoken dialogue. Like all other *Lakmé* recordings, this one omits the trio shortly before the end.

1955 RODOLPHE (M,P)

Mado Robin (A), Agnès Disney (B), Charles Richard (C), Unknown (D), Pierre Savignol (E), Chorus and Orchestre National de la RTF—Gressier

This radio performance, a few years after the Decca studio recording, reproduces Robin's

Lakmé on about the same level. Again her farewell ("Tu m'as donné le plus doux rêve") is touchingly traced, with exquisitely modeled *legato* and no mawkish sentiment. Her Mallika is the same as in the Decca set. Charles Richard as Gérald and Pierre Savignol as Nilakantha add to the sense of atmospheric togetherness, and this is the only *Lakmé* taken from a live performance, which generates a mood comparable to that of a stage event.

1967 DECCA / LONDON (S) CD

Joan Sutherland (A), Jane Berbié (B), Alain Vanzo (C), Claude Calès (D), Gabriel Bacquier (E), Monte Carlo Opera Chorus and Orchestra—Richard Bonynge

Given a two-dimensional doll to play, Joan Sutherland breathes into the role a warm languor that grows in appropriateness as the plot advances, phrasing her limpid coloratura with gentle piquancy rather than the often-encountered twittering or brassy shrillness. Her customary covered tone and vague diction, however, deprive Lakmé of the bell-like clarity Delibes intended for the Bell Song, which is softened further by transposition a half-tone down. Gérald's lines in the Act II finale are similarly transposed. Alain Vanzo's reedy light-lyric tenor, managed with admirable sweetness, conveys an image of Gérald as a likable dreamer, while Gabriel Bacquier's sinister Nilakantha sounds like the zealot he is supposed to be. Jane Berbié also proves to be an expert French stylist, though her role of Mallika offers less scope; in exchanges with Lakmé, her more forward word-pointing offers a telling contrast to the indistinct Sutherland delivery. Richard Bonynge shapes the score with understanding patience and flexibility. The score as recorded differs from the Heugel published version in replacing the Act III trio with another version of the scene, also in reinstating fairly extensive dialogues that were later set to music as recitative. A pair of phrases for Lakmé at the end of her duet "Dans la forêt près de nous" with Gérald are omitted too. The recorded sound, like the singing, is notable for ease and naturalness.

1970 EMI / ANGEL (S) CD

Mady Mesplé (A), Danièle Millet (B), Charles Burles (C), Jean-Christophe Benoit (D), Roger Soyer (E), Chorus and Orchestra of the Opéra-Comique—Alain Lombard

In her first important recording to be issued in the United States, Mady Mesplé upholds the stylistic and vocal standards of her illustrious predecessor Mado Robin. Neither saccharine nor shrill, Mesplé's tone has a freshness like spring water, and she uses it throughout with penetrating intelligence as well as calm interpretive warmth. What animates Mesplé's Lakmé is rhythmic precision and prompt attack, though her phrasing and tone are so smooth that one never has a sense of machinery at work. Despite her clarity, Mesplé can generate vaporous mystery in the barcarole she sings with Mallika, or in "Pourquoi dans les grands bois." The Bell Song has never sounded lovelier or more musical. It would be too much to ask anyone to make Lakmé real, but Mesplé gives as much contour and shading as possible within so soft a charcoal sketch of a character.

As Gérald, a sort of gentler British Pinkerton, Charles Burles offers matching line and sonority, faltering only (and slightly) when his air "Ah! viens, dans la forêt profonde" calls for a couple of awkward shifts from head range to lower-middle voice. (At this point one realizes why De Luca, in the 1952 Decca set, avoids head tones altogether.) The others of Gérald's English set are less convincingly suggested, though Jean-Christophe Benoit as Frédéric brings out some of their superciliousness. Alain Lombard's pacing, in a rare moment of weakness, denies Bernadette Antoine the support she needs for "Nous sommes conquises avec moins d'éclat!" in the otherwise charming quintet. Roger Soyer sings Nilakantha handsomely, stressing fatherly concern rather than heavy dramatics; his pleasant upper voice serves him well, and his Act II cavatine, "Lakmé, ton doux regard," is exemplary. Such voices ought not to be recorded with too much resonance, and they are not.

The last-act trio is omitted, as are the spoken dialogues: though this, like Decca's of 1952, is an Opéra-Comique performance, recitative is substituted. Except for ten bars in one duet and eight in another, there are no further cuts.

———————

In sum, all these recordings rate high. Because of its mid-1950s radio sonics, however, the 1955 Robin *Lakmé* on Rodolphe is a souvenir rather than a competitive version. The soprano's earlier Decca set, though mono, remains an extraordinary achievement. The Sutherland will appeal primarily to devotees of its diva, with Vanzo's Gérald and the completeness of Bonynge's edition as added attractions. Mesplé's Lakmé ranks as a phonograph classic. Though the soprano has recorded in Italian and German, these show less character than her French, in which linguistic idiosyncrasy is transfigured into a personal, singular musical style.

JOHN W. FREEMAN

GAETANO DONIZETTI

ANNA BOLENA (1830)

A: Anna (s); B: Giovanna Seymour (s); C: Smeton (c);
D: Percy (t); E: Enrico VIII (bs); F: Rochefort (bs)

It is of more than passing historical interest that Donizetti wrote the title role of *Anna Bolena* for Giuditta Pasta, and that the work's revival in this century is due primarily to Maria Callas. By all accounts the two had a lot in common—namely, a powerful theatrical temperament and formidable powers of musical-dramatic expression, allied to an imperfectly trained and unruly but shrewdly managed voice. Not only did Donizetti write the role for Pasta, but he was staying in her villa on Lake Como in 1830 as he was composing the work on a commission for the Teatro Carcano in Milan; it can be taken for granted that he had plenty of advice from the soprano on what did and did not suit her voice. In the event, the role is not exceptionally demanding in vocal range (at some points in duets, the second soprano line lies a third higher), and the written vocal embellishments are less elaborate than some he wrote in other operas and for other voices; but they are always put to dramatic purpose. In any case, the principal problem posed in recording *Anna Bolena* probably comes in confronting the demands of the title role by sopranos whose qualities, however great, are not the same as Pasta's. Purely vocal considerations aside, this is the opera that put Donizetti on the map. Within a year of its premiere at the Carcano on December 26, 1830, it had become the first of the composer's works produced in London and Paris. Although he borrowed extensively from his earlier operas, it is a superbly integrated work, solidly and elaborately structured, full of original solutions to traditional problems, replete with intensely dramatic recitative and dialogue, and rich in complex extended finales. Blessed with a superior libretto from Felice Romani, it became a model of the lyric tragedy for decades, with high politics and high drama leading to a dénouement that was not vitiated by a happy ending. Although, with more than three hours of music in its two acts and six scenes, it is frequently cut in stage revivals, the three recordings here are virtually complete, or close enough to make no difference.

1968–69 DECCA / LONDON (S)

Elena Suliotis (A), Marilyn Horne (B), Janet Coster (C), John Alexander (D), Nicolai Ghiaurov (E), Stafford Dean (F), Vienna State Opera Chorus and Orchestra—Silvio Varviso

The glory of this recording, and by the same token an element that unbalances it, is the performance of Marilyn Horne in the second soprano part. It might as well be renamed *Giovanna Seymour* for the occasion. Horne sails through the role with supreme assurance, resplendent tone, and dramatic intensity, and her vocal embellishments, written or not, are thrown off with authority and aptness. This is one modern singer who understands the dramatic uses of florid song and executes it with an aplomb reinforced by experience in the music of earlier epochs. As Anna, Elena Suliotis is a curious case. The strongly, even vehemently produced voice suggests some of the problems of a Pasta / Callas variety without the compensations. The notes are there, but not the style. There is very little sign of easy agility and, for instance, the famous series of ascending trills in the final scene comes out merely as an ascending scale. Nor is there much sign of a dramatic profile in what is, after all, a great tragic role. For all her effort, the effect is bland. John Alexander, as Percy, does an honest job in an assignment for which he is essentially unsuited. He has no problem with the tessitura, but he does not bother with the embellishments. On the other hand, the somewhat baritonal quality of his voice gives Percy a certain weight in confrontations with Enrico VIII, all the more so since Nicolai Ghiaurov delivers a smooth and soft-edged portrayal of the devious and dangerous monarch. Janet Coster and Stafford Dean are excellent as Smeton and Rochefort, and the veteran Piero de Palma is notable in the minor but frequent interventions of Hervey, the king's deputy and official announcer of bad news. Silvio Varviso conducts a straightforward performance, the most literal of these recordings, greatly aided by the luscious sound of the orchestra (alias the Vienna Philharmonic) and the fullness of the State Opera chorus. Both are given relative prominence in the balance of this recording.

1972 EMI / ANGEL (S)

Beverly Sills (A), Shirley Verrett (B), Patricia Kern (C), Stuart Burrows (D), Paul Plishka (E), Robert Lloyd (F), John Alldis Chorus, London Symphony Orchestra—Julius Rudel

This is a splendid record of Beverly Sills as one in her trilogy of English queens that graced the repertory of the New York City Opera a couple of decades ago. Sills achieves a superbly convincing dramatic realization through impeccable vocal control. Her silvery soprano is in prime state here, the trills and other written embellishments are eloquently handled, and the unwritten ones—in which she is far more adventurous than her rivals—are dramatically convincing as well as evidential of robust vocal health. Yet she also delivers the ravishingly

unadorned lines of the Bellini-esque "Al dolce guidami" to similar effect—in all, madness and a tragic fate conveyed by the art of song. Shirley Verrett's Giovanna, more soprano than mezzo in quality here, is a worthy partner, strong in her confrontations with the king and affecting in her remorse before the queen. Stuart Burrows as Percy has the vocal weight and suavity of a *tenore di grazia*, but not really the technique for the music's more florid aspects. Paul Plishka is a robust, heavyweight Enrico, Robert Lloyd a sonorous Rochefort, Patricia Kern a stylish Smeton, and Robert Tear a bit of luxury casting as Hervey. The recorded sound is excellent, and there is one effective introduction of background crowd noises in the final scene as Anna is snapped back to reality by the celebration of Enrico's unseemly rush into his third marriage. Julius Rudel presses constantly forward with brisk tempos—the *vivace* sections really zip along—and he is solidly abetted by the London Symphony and the John Alldis Chorus.

1987 DECCA / LONDON (S,D) CD

Joan Sutherland (A), Susanne Mentzer (B), Bernadette Manca di Nissa (C), Jerry Hadley (D), Samuel Ramey (E), Giorgio Surian (F), Welsh National Opera Chorus and Orchestra—Richard Bonynge

It is possible to regret that Joan Sutherland waited so long to record *Anna Bolena* and still be glad she made it when she did. True, time has taken a toll. Sustained notes and *cantilena* reveal a vibrato that often becomes a distinct wobble, and the tone thins out at the top, but rapid passagework and the decorations are handled with something close to the erstwhile authority. And one detects a greater attention to words and enunciation and more of an effort at dramatic phrasing, as if to compensate for the loss of pure vocal splendor. In any case, nothing is shirked as a great soprano leaves a worthy record of one of her great roles. She is handsomely supported by the rest of the cast. Samuel Ramey's Enrico is a bundle of malevolent aggression, perhaps a bit unrelentingly so, but triumphantly on top of all the notes. Jerry

Hadley's Percy is far ahead of the competition in the role, even if the tone is sometimes hard-edged and his phrasing not unfailingly elegant. Susanne Mentzer delivers an impeccably sung, youthfully fresh-sounding Giovanna, while Bernadette Manca di Nissa's warm and flexible contralto makes her a convincing Smeton. Giorgio Surian is an adequate Rochefort, no more. Richard Bonynge paces the performance expertly with his usual solicitude for the singers, and gets solid support from the forces of the Welsh National Opera. The singers are well forward in this version. The effect is a bit like being in the front row of a small theater.

A choice among these recordings is very much a personal one, although on balance Bonynge-Sutherland and company, a strong supporting cast, and digital sound have more to offer over-all. But Sills and Verrett make a strong case, and Horne's performance makes it hard to write off the earlier London version.

DAVID STEVENS

GAETANO DONIZETTI

L'ELISIR D'AMORE (1832)

A: Adina (s); B: Nemorino (t); C: Belcore (bar); D: Dulcamara (bs)

The number of recordings testify to the continuing popularity of Donizetti's *melodramma* in two acts, which rivals *Don Pasquale* among his comic operas and is often rated the better on account of its superior libretto by Felice Romani. Full recordings began in 1952 and therefore span the LP era through stereo and digital recording to compact disc. Almost all are successful to some extent, especially those conceived as ensemble performances rather than vehicles for star singers (though the Decca Bonynge album with Joan Sutherland and Luciano Pavarotti has particular distinction in being the only version without cuts of some sort).

In recordings before this a variety of "traditional" cuts were usually taken, of which the most common are *stretta* passages in Act I at the ends of Belcore's entry aria, "Come Paride vezzoso," of the Adina-Nemorino duet "Chiedi all'aura lusinghieri" and of their second duet, "Esulti pur la barbara," and some scraps of recitative. In Act II the usual cuts are the quartet "Dell'elisir mirabile" in whole or in part, the second verse of the cabaletta to Adina's "Prendi, per me se libero," and the middle verse of Dulcamara's finale, again with some lines of recitative and occasionally of choruses. Of all these only the loss of the Act II quartet seriously disturbs the content, and this does not happen in the later recordings after Bonynge, which are all much fuller than those preceding it.

1952 CETRA (M)

Alda Noni (A), Cesare Valletti (B), Afro Poli (C), Sesto Bruscantini (D), Italian Radio Chorus and Orchestra—Gianandrea Gavazzeni

A characteristically Italian performance of its time, such as might have been heard in any of a dozen theaters there during a carnival season, transferred to the studio and straightforwardly recorded. The radio orchestra sometimes sounds vinegary in tone, with Gavazzeni feeling it necessary to belabor the rhythm, putting emphatic accents on downbeats and the like and having a piano for *secco* recitative. Most of the traditional cuts occur; those involving the heavy-footed chorus are no loss.

Noni sings a bright, poised Adina; one can imagine a vivacious stage character, very sure of herself, and ready to launch into scintillating vocal embellishment, as in the high-flying *fioriture* she adds in "Prendi, per me" in Act II, making one wish she had included the triple-time cabaletta with its fast eighth-note runs. Valletti offers the conventionally lachrymose Nemorino, not so much by sobs in the voice as by pulling phrases about and making a vocal meal of any florid writing, but he sustains a good line for "Una furtiva lagrima."

What little sense of comedy emerges is less from the music than from the two lower voices, with Poli a swaggering Belcore and Bruscantini, in particular, relishing the humor of Dulcamara without overdoing it. Of all the principals he is the most musical in phrasing and contributes much to the overall performance character.

1952 EMI / ANGEL (M)

Margherita Carosio (A), Nicola Monti (B), Tito Gobbi (C), Melchiorre Luise (D), Rome Opera Chorus and Orchestra—Gabriele Santini

Santini's conducting generates ebullient spirit and sense of comedy without extravagance. Historically the album is of interest in having Gobbi as Belcore, conveying an acceptably self-important character with a ready chuckle in the voice. At times the character is allowed to get over-indulgent, aided by relatively close microphone placing. He is at his best in the scenes with Carosio, who often sang with him in this work in the leading Italian opera houses of the time, including La Scala. She has a bright, fresh gleam in her tone, and much feeling for the expressive phrase as well as agility in always clean, polished *fioriture*.

Monti's admirable *tenore leggiero* brings unexpected charm to Nemorino, with a fine-spun "Una furtiva lagrima" that is as elegant as you are likely to hear. He creates a winning sense of character that makes Adina's deeper feeling for him the more credible. Luise is a dry-voiced Dulcamara, the timbre light and baritonal, making a good deal of the verbal comedy and with a crisp line in patter, not least in duet with Adina. The voices of all the principals blend well and the chorus singing is acceptable.

No doubt to help contain the original recording on four LP sides instead of six, the performance is peppered with cuts. Most serious is the loss of the entire Act II quartet, not just the latter part of it. Other losses include *strettos* of arias and ensembles and some trimming of recitative.

1955 DECCA / LONDON (M) CD

Hilde Gueden (A), Giuseppe di Stefano (B), Renato Capecchi (C), Fernando Corena (D), Chorus and Orchestra of the Maggio Musicale Fiorentino—Francesco Molinari-Pradelli

The earlier of two Molinari-Pradelli recordings is also the first to have a non-Italian in the cast, as gramophone companies looked around for ways to exploit contract artists much as Hollywood did a couple of decades previously. Gueden by this time was a firm favorite at Vienna and elsewhere in the lyric-soprano roles of Mozart and the Strausses, and in other operetta, so an excursion into the Italian *leggiero* repertory must have been tempting. Adina consequently sounds soubrettish, not unduly coy but very consciously the minx-like "capricciosa" she calls herself. At least she includes some triple-time cabaletta to "Prendi, per me" in Act II.

Orchestra and chorus sound somewhat recessed in relation to principals brought well forward, which imparts a spread around the note-edges in di Stefano's Nemorino, almost a tendency to bray. He was closely associated with the role, but here lards it with self-conscious sentiment, not a few sobs and catches in the vocal line. "Una furtiva lagrima" is loud and artful to the extent of forcing awareness of the voice rather than the sentiments expressed. Capecchi and Corena fill out their characters, the former with plummy tone, the latter with too little variation of color in his harangues.

After being six-sided originally, the set was re-mastered for stereo on four sides in the late 1960s. Cuts are still numerous, and seem always to have left out the entire Act II quartet. Dulcamara simply leaves out a line or two in his following duet with Adina, "Quanto amore." Molinari-Pradelli favors broad tempos but gives a welcome lift to the rhythm at times. *Secco* recitative has what sounds like a harp instead of keyboard, and the orchestral playing is adequate.

1958 EMI / ANGEL (S)

Rosanna Carteri (A), Luigi Alva (B), Rolando Panerai (C), Giuseppe Taddei (D), La Scala Chorus and Orchestra—Tullio Serafin

Serafin is surprisingly pedestrian, with jog-trot rhythms and four-square approach diminishing the spirit that should gather up and carry the listener along. Only one of the principals generates this in enough abundance: Taddei. He sounds a dark-toned Dulcamara but suggests an absolutely credible old trickster well able to get the better of the "rustici." His diction for every line is exemplary, the rapid patter trips off his tongue in effortless syllabic flow, and he breathes a benign confidence in all he sings.

Others leave much to be desired. Carteri sounds a less capricious Adina than many, whose feeling for Nemorino is apparent early on and whose yearning phrases in *legato* music are beguiling. Her coloratura sounds more effortful, notably above the stave, and from time to time the intonation is at fault. Alva's Nemorino is a lovelorn adolescent, covering shyness with a clipped manner in exchanges and bringing vocal elegance to longer phrases, including his main aria sung very slowly indeed—too much for the context. Panerai is a blustery Belcore, less than comfortable in florid music. Serafin makes "traditional" cuts, and omits all the Act II quartet. The chorus comes across well enough and the orchestral playing is secure, but for such a diverting comedy the general effect is disappointingly charmless.

1966 EMI / ANGEL (S) CD

Mirella Freni (A), Nicolai Gedda (B), Mario Sereni (C), Renato Capecchi (D), Rome Opera Chorus and Orchestra—Francesco Molinari-Pradelli

The conductor's second recording for a rival label a decade after his previous album is slightly brisker in pacing but otherwise shares similar qualities of routine direction, mostly the same cuts in performance, and a noticeably inferior orchestra, rough in attack and ensemble. In addition, little of the singing either derives much spirit from that direction or imparts enough sparkle of its own.

Freni had not then learned how to match the visual charm of her big eyes and generous smile onstage to a comparable vocal quality of equivalent spirit. She is never less than secure, and affords Adina many a melting phrase of well-molded singing, but it mostly remains bland as well as accurate so that one takes little more than polite interest in what she sings. Gedda is also correspondingly uninvolved, singing smoothly and with constant intelligence, but drawing only an outline of character without the vocal charm or gaiety to fill it out. "Quanto è bella" seems overloud, but "Una furtiva lagrima" has more style.

Capecchi this time moved across from Belcore to sing a versatile Dulcamara, with many a touch of humor and relish for the verbal comedy, almost overloading it at times and lacking any finer shades of expression. Sereni's ladykiller sergeant swaggers confidently without finding more than surface effect in the character. The album suggests a blueprint for a performance in the making rather than a finished achievement.

1967 SUPRAPHON (S)

Fulvia Ciano (A), Ferruccio Tagliavini (B), Gianni Maffeo (C) Giuseppe Valdengo (D), Czech Philharmonic Chorus, Prague Chamber Orchestra—Ino Savini

Anybody who might encounter Tagliavini for the first time in this album would be justified to wonder how he came to be so greatly admired for his lyrical style in *bel canto*. In this recording, made in Prague some three years after he formally retired, the once-honeyed voice sounds drained of sweetness, strained at the top (painfully so when reaching for a B-flat or two), and with but a shadow of the expressive charm he once brought to Nemorino. Only some former elegance of phrasing still remains here and there and that is regrettably not enough.

Other principals seem to have been assembled around him to get a performance together while he lasted. Ciano's Adina is hard-voiced, clear and precise enough in negotiating *legato* and coloratura but effortful in doing so, and lacking any feeling or warmth of personality. Maffeo makes a stiffly correct, even solemn Belcore; Valdengo finds no humor at all in Dulcamara and sings everything in the same rough tone. Add a lack of feeling for Italian style in the playing of a Prague orchestra under a conductor who measures out each number without shaping it beyond the barest essentials, and the set has to remain just a historical curiosity.

1970 DECCA / LONDON (S) CD

Joan Sutherland (A), Luciano Pavarotti (B), Dominic Cossa (C), Spiro Malas (D), Ambrosian Opera Chorus, English Chamber Orchestra—Richard Bonynge

A new dimension was given to *L'Elisir* by this recording through the contributions of Sutherland and Pavarotti, but also because Bonynge, as in his other recorded operas, insisted on it being properly complete. Duration thereby extends to around two hours and twenty minutes, six sides in LP format. One departure from the score is made by replacing Adina's cabaletta to "Prendi, per me" in Act II with a florid waltz-time *allegro*, "Nel Dolce incanto de tal momento," written for Maria Malibran by her husband de Bériot and interpolated then, it is said, with Donizetti's consent.

The disconcerting effect at first hearing is perhaps justified by the sheer vitality Sutherland brings to its *fioriture*, an accumulation of runs, turns, trills, and glittering E-flats *in alt* which more sparingly embellish the earlier arias. Her performance is no mere vocal display: as a counter to the brilliant technique at her command she invests Adina with unusual seriousness of character. Instead of a provocative flirt, this is a woman aware of her feelings and her weaknesses and ready to express them honestly, whether in fine-spun line of arias and ariosos or in buoyant conversational exchanges.

Pavarotti is likewise adept at illuminating words in his recitatives and ensemble exchanges as much as in filling out his arias. "Quanto è bella" even loses some desirable *legato* for the sake of word pointing, but "Una furtiva lagrima" is sung with quiet introspection that adds to the honeyed charm of the vocal line. Whatever may have happened to him since, this is a Pavarotti ready and able to create a credible operatic character with simplicity, affection, and style in the musical context around him.

As if taking his cue from others, Cossa makes Belcore a younger, dangerous rival for Adina, replacing comic bluster with more direct confidence and swagger, while Malas is very much the foreigner from distant parts, not entirely at ease in Dulcamara's patter but fresh of voice and jubilantly good-natured. It is a general sense of jubilation that gives the cachet to Bonynge's performance. There is a spring in its step and an infectious exhilaration that comes through excellent orchestral playing. It is always held in good balance with the singing and poised ensemble, though the otherwise admirable chorus is recessed too much at the start.

1977 CBS / SONY (S) CD

Ileana Cotrubas (A), Plácido Domingo (B), Ingvar Wixell (C), Geraint Evans (D), Chorus and Orchestra of the Royal Opera House, Covent Garden—John Pritchard

By the time of this recording, Domingo had begun singing Otello, and if "Una furtiva lagrima" is here less winning than it would have been earlier, he maintains a resourceful flexibility. This comes out well in exchanges like the recruiting duet, "Venti scudi," with Wixell's self-preening, eye-flashing Belcore, colorfully drawn through the voice alone. Cotrubas as a winsome Adina will delight most admirers; others may be less attracted to the hard, sometimes whitened tone-quality and corresponding blandness in places where more feeling is desirable.

Evans is a little larger than life but communicates so much fun that he is consistently enjoyable; for a non-Italian the words trip off the tongue with that instinct for placing and stress that made him so renowned in the language. Pritchard finds the advantage of having worked with the stage production in the inspired spirit and tautness of ensemble he achieves with the Covent Garden orchestra. Some minimal cuts are made (at the end of "Venti scudi" and the last Adina-Nemorino scene). Pritchard sustains a good balance between comedy and sentiment but the chorus were encouraged to contribute "rent-a-crowd noises"—oohs and aahs and gasps and sighs—in simulation of stage performance, fun for some but possibly irritating with repetition.

1982 EURODISC (S,D) CD

Lucia Popp (A), Peter Dvorsky (B), Bernd Weikl (C), Yevgeny Nesterenko (D), Bavarian Radio Chorus and Orchestra—Heinz Wallberg

By comparison with the previous non-Italian cast on CBS, the Slovak, Viennese, and Russian assortment here is almost as effective in getting the right degree of vocal flexibility and expressive conviction into the Donizetti style. Popp is a virtually ideal Adina, always keenly phrased for the sense and purpose of her words in conversational scenes, drawing a well-rounded character from teasing charm to disarming candor, and with ample resources of vocal technique to sparkle vividly in all the coloratura: it would be a hard-hearted listener who did not respond.

Unfortunately, in relation to this captivating character Dvorsky begins as a disappointingly wimpish Nemorino, palely loitering around in Act I without even the lovelorn feeling to be expected in "Quanto è bella." His words in recitative sound stiff and bloodless, perhaps a deliberate calculation to bring about more vocal color after he has downed Dulcamara's elixir. Then he becomes more personable, achieving expressive style in "Una furtiva lagrima." Here, though, the orchestra is less than ideally supportive in response to Wallberg's competent, cheerful, but routine conducting.

Weikl is suitably forthcoming in Belcore's swagger and poise without caricature, and Nesterenko's dark-voiced Dulcamara gives generous weight of feeling to verbal comedy and vocal line. Small cuts involve nothing of major consequence and balance of voices to orchestra has spacious warmth of perspective, the singers less markedly forward than in some albums but no less ready than the Italians to add traditional cadenzas and top notes by way of acceptable embellishment.

1984 PHILIPS (S,D) CD

Katia Ricciarelli (A), José Carreras (B), Leo Nucci (C), Domenico Trimarchi (D), Italian Radio Chorus and Orchestra—Claudio Scimone

This recording represents a reversion to an almost wholly Italian cast. Carreras's Nemorino is vulnerable without being wimpish, beginning with a wonderfully heartfelt account of "Quanto è bella" before tugging at the heart with his pleas to Adina, summoning a cautious courage to approach the "doctor" for that love-potion of Isolde he has been hearing about, and expressing a youthful recklessness once he has dared sample it. "Una furtiva lagrima" later becomes a testament to feeling, not just an exercise in style.

Ricciarelli is a less individual personality than some of her competitors as Adina, somewhere in the center between minx-like provocation and Sutherland's seriousness, though without Popp's effervescence. Here and there the tone gets less ingratiating, but the performance has stylish musicality and likable spirit. She responds well to Nucci's Belcore, so intent on enjoying himself that never for a moment would even a village girl be deceived into thinking otherwise. Trimarchi is supremely confident in Dulcamara's humorous self-promotion, and has a distinctively smooth *legato* line as well as verbal skill in conversation and patter.

Scimone is a key factor in this album's success, occasionally a martinet in rhythmic accents and insistence on clean phrasing but obtaining verve and clarity from the Turin-based orchestra. Slight trimming is made from traditional cuts, and for the first time a closer period character is given to *secco* recitative by the tone of a fortepiano. Overall, it sounds an idiomatic Italian performance a generation further on, correspondingly more polished in musical manner and recording technique.

1986 DEUTSCHE GRAMMOPHON (S,D) CD

Barbara Bonney (A), Gösta Winbergh (B), Bernd Weikl (C), Rolando Panerai (D), Chorus and Orchestra of the Maggio Musicale Fiorentino—Gabriele Ferro

Adina is one of Bonney's first major roles, and shows her to rival the best of the *leggiero*-type singers previously. Her singing has attractive warmth and gaiety, teasing and flirtatious in the opening scenes and with a touching candor when she eventually persuades Nemorino of her love. The coloratura is lightly, fluently voiced, gleaming and bell-like in the highest register, and she has the vocal advantage over Winbergh from their "Chiedi all'aura lusinghieri" duet onward. The Swedish tenor here forces his tone too much and is little concerned about shading or style to avoid gracelessly overloading the vocal line.

Weikl is not a lot different in his second Belcore, a straightforward, assertive *buffo* soldier who suggests a practiced success with the opposite sex. Panerai, who was a vigorous, rather wild Belcore for Angel more than twenty-five years previously, now turns in an accomplished Dulcamara of ripe vocal experience, the voice still acceptable if inclined to lose pitch in places. He overdoes the Gondoliera Song by affecting a quavery nasal voice which could rapidly become tiresome in repeated hearing.

Ferro's conducting does not spring the rhythms as tautly as some, but communicates a sense of fun in the music, though chorus and orchestra alike sometimes slip into untidy ensemble almost as if caught in a stage performance instead of under studio control. A fortepiano is used in *secco* recitative and the recording is based on a "new critical edition" by Alberto Zedda; there are cuts at the end of the Act I Adina-Nemorino duet and in the cabaletta to her last aria; the quartet is given in full.

1989 DEUTSCHE GRAMMOPHON (S,D) CD

Kathleen Battle (A), Luciano Pavarotti (B), Leo Nucci (C), Enzo Dara (D), Metropolitan Opera Chorus and Orchestra—James Levine

No doubt the recording made in the wake of some highly successful Met performances will have its special appeal, and for a listener who did not hear those there is much enjoyment in the lively overall spirit generated by Levine, even in sanitized studio conditions at New York's Manhattan Center, removed from stage char-

acter. Orchestral playing is a prime virtue, polished and gleaming in tone and well balanced with the singing, but the recording acoustic has a closed-in character, without always enough air around the notes to give real zest to events supposedly taking place in the storytelling.

Besides several of the short "traditional" cuts the Act II quartet, "Dell'elisir mirabile" is shorn of the final part of its *stretta*, and at Adina's "Ah, come rapido" just before this, about 24 bars of tenor line that should join her ("le smanie, i palpiti," etc.) are simply left out. Pavarotti is otherwise an engaging Nemorino, twenty years on from his previous recording, of course, and to that extent sounding less impetuous or vocally exciting, but still with a fine *legato* line for "Una furtiva lagrima" and elsewhere, and making much of Nemorino's changing feelings to express character and incident through voice alone.

For all the beauty and (perhaps excessive) sweetness of Battle's singing, she does not give Adina the vital spark of personality to etch the character on a listener's imagination; it remains a voice of exquisite grace but little content. For vocal pleasure she is matched by Dawn Upshaw's delightful Giannetta. Dara is a good, straightforward Dulcamara, avoiding mannered delivery or caricature, verbally intelligent if without much feeling for humor. Nucci overcomes an unfortunate start (could it not have been redone?) to act up well as Belcore. Chirpy chorus singing includes suitable exclamations of surprise and the like to make exhilarating ensemble scenes.

Choice will depend to some extent on personal preference among individuals, such as Sutherland's unconventional Adina with Pavarotti in the fullest version, or Evans's personalized Dulcamara with Cotrubas and Domingo. Scimone conducts the most convincingly up-to-date Italianate performance, surpassing any individual interest among older albums.

NOËL GOODWIN

Unavailable for review:
1992 ERATO

GAETANO DONIZETTI

LUCREZIA BORGIA (1833)

A: Lucrezia (s); B: Orsini (c); C: Gennaro (t); D: Alfonso (bs)

*D*onizetti wrote four operas in 1833—
*Il Furioso all'Isola di San Domingo,
Parisina, Torquato Tasso,* and
Lucrezia Borgia. All of them are of
special interest, as each contains musical and
dramatic features in which Donizetti advanced
his mastery of the medium. In this case, last is
undoubtedly best. *Lucrezia* was one of the Donizetti operas occasionally revived even in the
long period when this composer's works had
fallen from popular favor, since it offers a title
part written with remarkable skill for a soprano
(Méric-Lalande) at a late stage in her career;
Lucrezia's scene-by-scene balance of tessitura
and vocal figuration provides models of tact,
practicality, and long-range conservation. Nowadays we recognize this opera as one of the
peaks of Italian early romanticism: rich in its
contrasts of dark and light, serio-comic and
melodramatic, wonderfully economical in its
delineation of atmosphere and character, for-
ward-looking in its design (this is one of the
most "Verdian" of Donizetti operas). It has
received only two commercial recordings, both
focused upon its prima donna. Neither is complete (Donizetti's forms and formulas, with their
internal repeats, are almost always trivialized by
the sort of snipping to which they are prey);
more important, and for different reasons, neither gives more than a fitful impression of the
work's energy and dramatic vigor.

1965 RCA / BMC (S) CD

Montserrat Caballé (A), Shirley Verrett (B),
Alfredo Kraus (C), Ezio Flagello (D), RCA
Italiana Chorus and Orchestra—Jonel Perlea

Lucrezia was the role in which Montserrat
Caballé achieved star status, in the now-fabled
1965 New York concert revival of the opera.
Perlea conducted those concerts, as he did the
subsequent RCA set; pirate recordings of the
live event exist to show how much of an "occasion" it had been, and how much of the excitement had been drained out by the time the
soprano and conductor reached the studios.
There is a serious shortage of rhythmic definition and "go"—the RCA Italiana chorus and
orchestra are of high (and, of course, idiomatic)
quality, as are the comprimarios (very important
in this opera), but dramatic tension is very
largely missing from their work. This was the
soprano's first full operatic assignment on records:
in it she introduces listeners to an all-purpose
expressivity, a soft-edged, dreamy delicacy of
manner that we have come to know well in
many subsequent albums. The florid singing is
sometimes marvelously fine-spun, sometimes
sketchy; only in "Era desso il mio figlio," the
flashy finale that Donizetti created for Méric-
Lalande, does she at last produce the temperament and brilliance that characterized her original performance. Shirley Verrett's Orsini scoops
in middle and low registers; the role lies too low
for her to capture its sparkle, though the sound
of the voice is fresh and appealing. Ezio Flagello's Duke is secure and unrelievedly dull: the

suave, glinting menace of Donizetti's character-ization is one of the opera's great strengths, but that could never be guessed here. The prime attraction—and, indeed, the real star—of the set is Alfredo Kraus, ideally stylish, clean-toned, elegant: the whole performance stirs to life at his every appearance.

1977 DECCA / LONDON (S) CD

Joan Sutherland (A), Marilyn Horne (B), Gia-como Aragall (C), Ingvar Wixell (D), London Opera Voices, National Philharmonic Orches-tra—Richard Bonynge

Joan Sutherland first sang Lucrezia at Van-couver in 1972, and thereafter made the role one of the mainstays of her career in its "mature" phase. It suited her voice; indeed, one of the main pleasures of the London set—and they are considerable—consists in hearing the large instrument cope so unflappably with Donizetti's more strenuous vocal demands. But little sense of theater attaches to the singing; words are either unclear or, when audible, inexpressively uttered, and whenever "feeling" is required the soprano overlays the lines with generalized lan-guor. Marilyn Horne lavishes much easy virtu-osity on Orsini, but as here recorded, the tone sounds puffed up, breathy; the impression is of a prima donna going through her paces in the recording studio, not a dashing young blade. Giacomo Aragall, well cast and in good voice (apart from a few passing patches of doubtful intonation), catches very well the youthful naiveté of Gennaro (as well he might, next to these

vocally heavyweight leading ladies!). Bonynge's edition includes, one after the other, the two endings devised by Donizetti—the original florid finale for Lucrezia, then (via an unconvincing modulation) the death scene for Gennaro, which the composer himself substituted and preferred, and which Aragall here makes the expressive high point of the performance. The gritty edge to Ingvar Wixell's baritone permits a suggestion of menace, but prevents any aristocratic suavity of vocal style. With the exception of Piero de Palma as Vitelozzo, Anglo-Saxon singers take the smaller parts, and vary from the just-accept-able to the painfully unidiomatic. Bonynge's conducting is energetic but not always adept at keeping the orchestra under control; its main aim seems to be to give each of the principals his or her chance to shine, not to shape a dramatic whole.

Neither of these two performances does much more than outline the opera. With this caveat in mind, either can be recommended according to the listener's prima donna preferences. *Lucrezia Borgia* is one of the Donizetti operas that Maria Callas should have taken up (even perhaps in the final stage of her career) and didn't; her recording of "Com'è bello," Lucre-zia's entrance aria, on a late EMI recital disc, is vocally frail and, in spite of that, absolutely magical—a performance to point up, and sup-plement, the qualities missed in both these complete recordings.

MAX LOPPERT

GAETANO DONIZETTI

MARIA STUARDA (1834; revised 1835)

A: Maria (s); B: Elisabetta (s); C: Leicester (t); D: Talbot (bar); E: Cecil (bs)

*I*nterest in *Maria Stuarda* was reawakened after its first modern revival at Bergamo (1958), and was fueled when Montserrat Caballé began to sing the title role in the next decade. Her Carnegie Hall performance for the American Opera Society (December 6, 1967) furnished the first of at least three "private" recordings of her in this role. It drew public attention to an opera not perhaps in the front rank of Donizetti but with some passages deservedly rated the equal of, if not superior to, the better-known *Anna Bolena,* not least the fictional confrontation between Mary Stuart, Queen of Scots, and Queen Elizabeth I of England in the opera's Act II.

A complex edition problem persists because there is no autograph score of the two known versions by Donizetti, the one for the Naples premiere in 1834 having been revised by him for Maria Malibran at La Scala, Milan, the following year. Performances depend mainly on the secondary source of a Paris edition by Gérard published in the 1850s, supplemented by some numbers from the "Malibran version," with a wider range and more elaborate writing for the prima donna, published by Ricordi. Of the singers in the following recordings, only Dame Joan Sutherland includes variants from the "Malibran version." All are otherwise derived from the Gérard score, with various transpositions, editing, and cuts.

1971 EMI / ANGEL (S)

Beverly Sills (A), Eileen Farrell (B), Stuart Burrows (C), Louis Quilico (D), Christian du Ples-

sis (E), John Alldis Choir, London Philharmonic Orchestra—Aldo Ceccato

The performance begins with the 1835 "Malibran" Overture, but is otherwise based on Gérard. At curtain-up there is a chatter of courtiers as if to simulate stage performance but this is not continued. Sills follows the Malibran example of extravagant vocal decoration, adding a cadenza over one and a half octaves on the word "gioia" in the first line of her entry recitative. She uses the music throughout as a means to fanciful embellishment, often splendidly achieved, and ends with a farewell aria, "Di un cor che muore," in which there are many more notes by Sills than can properly be ascribed to Donizetti.

Farrell, as the rival queen for the love of Leicester, personifies an almost wholly unsympathetic role with musicality and a strong use of chest register, as in her opening cavatina and much decorated cabaletta, but she begins to tire by her last contribution in Act III. Dramatically, the opera hinges on the confrontation between Mary and Elizabeth when the former, incensed, hurls the charge of "vil bastarda" at the English queen. Here it fails to acquire the necessary dramatic definition from the lack of specific character both singers bring to their roles.

Burrows here recorded his first Italian opera, giving ample pleasure in the style and accomplishment of his *legato* phrasing ("Leicester" is sung throughout in two syllables, not the "Lay-chest-air" usually favored in Italian performance). Quilico is an eloquent Talbot, to whom the Catholic Mary makes her confession, and du Plessis a competent Cecil. Microphone balance favors the orchestra at the expense of singers, who can sound over-recessed except when audibly spotlit, to the detriment of words and those of the otherwise firm chorus. Ceccato's conducting is idiomatic, the orchestra spirited, but to generalized purpose rather than affording the help weaker passages sometimes need.

1974–75 DECCA / LONDON (S) CD

Joan Sutherland (A), Huguette Tourangeau (B), Luciano Pavarotti (C), Roger Soyer (D), James Morris (E), Chorus and Orchestra of the Teatro Comunale, Bologna—Richard Bonynge

No overture here, but Bonynge has otherwise made his own amalgam of the Gérard and "Malibran" versions, using the latter to rewrite decoration into the soprano register for Sutherland while keeping Tourangeau in her lowest chest register, as if to underline the contrast between them. Both vocal lines are considerably rewritten to achieve this. Elizabeth's first aria and its cabaletta, for instance, are transposed down a semitone while the ensemble between is not, and in Mary's cabaletta, "Nella pace," Sutherland sings two verses of which the first is in B-flat, the second in D-flat. A number of cuts are applied to *strettas* in cabalettas and ensembles and, more regrettably, to over half the opening chorus.

Sutherland matches Sills in vocal skill of performance, as well as the agility of her coloratura. She adds to *legato* phrases more idiomatic trills and turns in keeping with the kind of period style Bonynge seems to aim at, also managing to express a stronger sense of identity with the character. The snarl on "vil bastarda" is more telling than Sills's slower articulation of the words. Tourangeau achieves a chilling effect in pronouncing sentence of death while taking her voice down to low B-flat, but sometimes distorts the line in the interests of character.

Pavarotti has the expected Italianate quality in generous degree, and characterizes Leicester as young and adoring in the best romantic manner. He throws in some splendid top notes of his own choice at the ends of arias and ensembles, including a resounding D-flat with Sutherland to finish their Act II duet. Morris and Soyer bring their roles forcefully to life and strengthen the ensembles. A cast recorded in their best form deserved more stylish choral singing and orchestral playing, but Bonynge's lively spirit covers occasional untidiness.

1982 EMI / ANGEL (In English) (S,D,P) CD

Janet Baker (A), Rosalind Plowright (B), David Rendall (C), Alan Opie (D), John Tomlinson (E), English National Opera Chorus and Orchestra—Charles Mackerras

A compilation from performances at the London Coliseum on four dates in April 1982, made possible by the Peter Moores Foundation and Shell UK Ltd. It preserves the memorable performance by Dame Janet Baker in the role she chose for her farewell to opera, singing an excellent English translation which sits well on the music and brings greater immediacy of character and situation for English-speaking listeners. It also has the tension implicit in live performance, as well as a certain amount of inescapable audience noise.

Mackerras conducts the Gérard edition, with cuts in *stretta* passages. Changing the vocal register for the two queens, with Mary the mezzo and Elizabeth the soprano (as it would have been at the Malibran performances), reinforces the music's tragic feeling. Baker is vibrant and deeply moving, not entirely clear in diction, but projecting the lines with a wealth of emotional expression, from quiet recitative to despairing outbursts like "Ah, what torture!" In contrast to the vocal displays of Sills and Sutherland, this is a performance of Shakespearean caliber, made more eloquent by Plowright's bold command as a younger Elizabeth of generous vocal resource and radiant tone.

Rendall is an ardent Leicester, more in the gentlemanly Burrows mold than the authentic Italian *spinto* of Pavarotti. Tomlinson, Bayreuth's Wotan in 1988, brings powerful tone if sometimes uneven phrasing to Talbot; Opie, Bayreuth's recent Beckmesser, endows Cecil with strong character. The chorus singing is competent though not entirely secure. Mackerras obtains alert, vivid playing from the ENO orchestra, imparting urgency and feeling, setting judicious tempos, and keeping an effective balance.

1989 PHILIPS (S,D) CD

Edita Gruberova (A), Agnes Baltsa (B), Francisco Araiza (C), Francesco Ellero d'Artegna (D), Simone Alaimo (E), Bavarian Radio Chorus, Munich Radio Orchestra—Giuseppe Patanè

A spirited performance again using the Gérard score, recorded in Munich only weeks before Patanè's death in May 1989. It should remain a tribute to his skill as conductor of opera, concentrating on feeling for drama through the music even where voices themselves are not as dramatically persuasive as one hopes. This is regrettably true of both queenly characters. Baltsa summons a better produced tone than might be expected for Elizabeth, though she sings only one verse of her cabaletta in Act I and is less attentive to changes of emotional mood and situation as the role develops. Even her formidable chest register is not heard to real dramatic advantage.

Gruberova makes the title role a more vivid personality, singing with exciting brilliance of tone and flexibility of phrase except only in that one crucial climax of the confrontation between the two queens. Her cry of "vil bastarda" sounds more like a complaint than the furious and direct insult which triggers the hinge of tragedy. Elsewhere she gives an affecting portrait of a woman trapped by political and emotional forces beyond her control, showing considerable depth of feeling to balance the display of coloratura technique.

Araiza is a lyrically persuasive Leicester, though less than careful over small details of phrasing, and manages to convey youthful ardor. D'Artegna is vocally firm and unbending for Talbot; Alaimo is adequate but no more as Cecil. The chorus plays a lively part in creating ambience as well as offering spirited singing character. Small cuts are made in several coda passages, and the Italianate structure in aria, cabaletta, and ensemble is shaped by Patanè with warm instrumental tone and rhythmic flexibility, in a well-balanced recording.

No clear recommendation emerges in relation to previous sets. Mackerras remains the most vivid in English-language dramatic character; each of the others has the particular attraction of individual voices according to personal preference.

NOËL GOODWIN

GAETANO DONIZETTI

LUCIA DI LAMMERMOOR (1835)

A: Lucia (s); B: Edgardo (t); C: Enrico (bar); D: Raimondo (bs)

When *Lucia di Lammermoor* premiered at the San Carlo opera house in Naples on September 26, 1835, it was a triumph. That triumph seemed preordained. The story of the opera was based on Sir Walter Scott's *The Bride of Lammermoor*, a novel then popular throughout Europe. Donizetti, known for the lyrical beauty and dramatic thrust of his operas, was at the peak of his powers. And the cast featured two prominent singers of the time: soprano Fanny Tacchinardi Persiani and the famous French tenor Gilbert Duprez. Both the tenor and soprano roles were considered important by the composer—in fact, the opera ends with a scene for the tenor. But since the title role requires a great deal of florid singing, *Lucia* soon became a showpiece for sopranos who were more interested in showing off their vocal agility than in bringing drama to life. That approach generally persisted until the *bel canto* revival of the 1950s, spearheaded by Maria Callas. Since then, the opera has been recognized for its dramatic validity as well as its musical strengths. Certain cuts have become traditional; i.e., portions of arias and ensembles and, more important, two scenes. The first is the Raimondo / Lucia scene which follows her confrontation with Edgardo in Act II, Scene 1. The second is the entire first scene of Act III, set in the tower at Wolf's Crag, in which Enrico challenges Edgardo to a duel. Although these scenes are necessary for the logic of the plot and the musical balance of the opera, they were deleted from early recordings and still are often cut in performance. Unless otherwise noted,

recordings up to 1960 contain traditional cuts. Recordings made after that year vie to present as complete and authentic a *Lucia* as possible. All four leading roles in this opera are challenging in that they require mastery of the principles of *bel canto*: beauty of tone, seamless *legatos*, expressivity, and a command of *fioritura*.

1929 OASI (M)

Mercédès Capsir (A), Enzo de Muro Lomanto (B), Enrico Molinari (C), Salvatore Baccaloni (D), La Scala Chorus and Orchestra—Lorenzo Molajoli

This first complete recording of *Lucia* is an exuberant one. Molajoli moves the opera along at a brisk pace and the recitatives are sung vigorously. As Lucia, Mercédès Capsir substitutes energy for emotion. In her squeezed, nasal voice, she tosses off *fioriture*, singing with remarkable assurance until the Mad Scene. Driven by Molajoli's fast tempos, she falls apart vocally with pitch problems, harsh high notes, and aspirated runs that verge on the ludicrous. Lomanto tends to be more comfortable in the lyrical passages than the declamatory. His final aria is sung with elegance, but his light voice is often pushed to its extreme and he tends to sharp, particularly in the recitatives. Molinari's Enrico is an imposing presence: the baritone sings with verve and commitment to the text. The surprise in this recording is Raimondo, sung by Salvatore Baccaloni, who would become one of the great *basso buffos* of his time. Despite the flutter in his voice, Baccaloni sings with compelling warmth. This early recording captures the lush sound of the La Scala strings particularly well.

1939 CETRA (M)

Lina Pagliughi (A), Giovanni Malipiero (B), Giuseppe Manacchini (C), Luciano Neroni (D), Italian Radio Chorus and Orchestra, Turin—Ugo Tansini

Lina Pagliughi gives a dazzling performance as Lucia. Her voice is clear, limpid, secure, and light, but not lightweight. The sound is full when the drama warrants it, and the coloratura is consistently precise and graceful. Her Lucia is real: wistful and gentle, touching rather than tragic. Gentleness also pervades Malipiero's characterization of Edgardo. Although his performance is frequently marred by a lack of precision, he sings with nuance. Manacchini's performance, on the other hand, tends to be monochromatic. In Raimondo's aria "Dalle stanze," one of the highlights of the recording, Neroni's heartfelt telling of the murder, resounds with sadness and compassion. His singing is fluid, his *legato*s seamless. Ugo Tansini seems content to accompany his singers, occasionally jolting them and the listener to attention with erratic changes of tempo. The chorus is poorly miked: it is either so close that individual sopranos can be heard, or so far as to disturb the balance of the ensembles.

1951 URANIA (M)

Dolores Wilson (A), Gianni Poggi (B), Anselmo Colzani (C), Silvio Maionica (D), Milan Chorus and Orchestra—Franco Capuana

Dolores Wilson's performance of the title role is amateurish; the *fioriture* are heavy-handed, the pitch often sharp, and the delivery devoid of style. Poggi's expressive singing is a welcome contrast to the soprano's, but he often shouts his high notes for dramatic effect. While Maionica turns in a bland performance as Raimondo, Anselmo Colzani's Enrico emerges as a volatile, believable character. The baritone's voice has an appealing resonance, particularly in the middle register. The chorus and orchestra are not always together, but then neither are the instrumentalists. Other than Colzani's perfor-

mance, the only redeeming feature of this recording is that it restores some of the traditional cuts, such as the complete second-act finale and the Wolf's Crag scene.

1953 EMI / ANGEL (M) CD

Maria Callas (A), Giuseppe di Stefano (B), Tito Gobbi (C), Raffaele Arié (D), Chorus and Orchestra of the Maggio Musicale Fiorentino—Tullio Serafin

In the hands of Maria Callas, Lucia becomes a tragic heroine, with all the depth and struggle and agony that those words imply. From the first line she sings, the very sound of her voice embodies a character who is young, delicate, melancholy, and vulnerable. Callas never exaggerates to achieve dramatic effect; she trusts in the power of the text and the music. *Legato*s are seamless; *fioriture* are treated as extensions of a phrase, of the feelings expressed in that phrase. In scene after scene, Callas communicates the depth of those feelings, imbuing the role with sadness and yearning. Gobbi matches Callas in expressivity and in the complexity of the character he creates. He is clearly all-villain. But for Gobbi, even villainy has many facets; he can be furious, menacing, conniving, and finally, in the sextet, remorseful. Gobbi sings into the words, snarling as he savors their meaning, and he is uncompromising when it comes to rhythmic precision. As a result, the taut rhythmic figures in Enrico's vocal line create the dramatic tension intended by the composer. Although di Stefano does not create a complex character, the velvety sound of his voice establishes Edgardo as a highly sympathetic hero. The beauty of that sound is sustained even in the heavily accented passages of the "Malcdetto." Di Stefano's heartfelt reading of the last aria is a model of *bel canto* singing: he caresses the words and sings a meltingly beautiful *legato*. Arie is not the master singer that his three colleagues are, but he delivers an expressive, secure performance. The dark color of his voice is particularly effective in his third-act aria. Serafin's choice of tempos and dynamics is so in keeping with the musical and dramatic values of the score as to seem inevitable. His performance is a study in equipoise, precision, and fluidity.

1954 CBS / SONY (M)

Lily Pons (A), Richard Tucker (B), Frank Guarrera (C), Norman Scott (D), Metropolitan Opera Chorus and Orchestra—Fausto Cleva

Lily Pons made her Metropolitan Opera debut as Lucia on January 3, 1931. Legendary in the role, she chose it for her Met farewell on April 12, 1958. Regrettably, this recording was made nearly a quarter of a century after her Met debut, and it cannot be considered representative of Pons's Lucia. There are still some lovely bell-like sounds in the voice and the coloratura passages can be exciting. But the voice wobbles, her pitch tends to flat, and she cuts short the last note of many phrases. Richard Tucker gives a first-rate performance both musically and dramatically. The voice is full and bright, the high notes solid, and he delivers an impassioned reading of the text. His Edgardo is a stalwart figure: haughty at his entrance in the betrothal scene, forceful in the "Maledetto." In the last scene, the simple "Ah" he sings when learning that Lucia is dying is touching, and the aria that follows exemplary in its beauty of tone and musicality. Frank Guarrera is capable of producing a rich sound, but the voice is often woolly and the pitch not always precise. His gruff portrayal of Enrico tends to be pedestrian. Norman Scott's bass, dry and throaty through most of this recording, improves in his third-act aria, where the voice has more substance. Instead of the usual thin-voiced tenor in the small role of Normanno, this recording opens with a full-bodied singer in the part. It is James McCracken, who, although he had not yet learned the rudiments of Italian pronunciation, was obviously headed for a major career. The chorus is poorly miked, and the cuts in this recording verge on the ruthless. Fausto Cleva conducts a brisk performance, highlighting orchestral details with sensitivity and grace.

1955 EMI / ANGEL (M,P) CD

Maria Callas (A), Giuseppe di Stefano (B), Rolando Panerai (C), Nicola Zaccaria (D), La Scala Chorus, RIAS Symphony Orchestra, Berlin—Herbert von Karajan

This performance, recorded live at the Berlin State Opera on September 29, 1955, throbs with passion without sacrificing nuance. Callas creates a more ardent heroine than in her 1953 studio recording. Her performance is filled with unforgettable details from the moment she appears onstage: her incredulity as she describes the apparition of the ghost, for example, and her delight in her own femininity as she sings of "estasi" in the cabaletta. She can spin an exquisite *pp* in the recitative and negotiate trills with breathtaking ease, but the music never seems to be sung. Callas is in such total command of voice and musical detail that singing becomes the natural way in which to "speak" the text. Her Mad Scene is emotionally shattering. The easy distractibility of the insane that is inherent in Donizetti's score comes to life with Callas. She sounds fragile as she begins, speaking Edgardo's name with profound desire, and assuming her "little girl" voice when she speaks of the chill she feels. Suddenly, the voice is imbued with terror as she sees the ghost; then, just as suddenly, it assumes an eerie young sound as she leads Edgardo to the altar. Vocally, this is the best of the Callas Lucias, as it is of di Stefano's Edgardos. His voice is brighter and fuller in this set than in the 1953 recording with Callas and the 1959 with Scotto. He sings with greater freedom and a greater variety of dynamics. In an outpouring of beautiful sound, di Stefano makes Edgardo a more passionate lover, a more volatile character. His fury in the betrothal scene is harrowing, his agony over the death of Lucia touching. Panerai's performance bristles with energy. Enrico's desperation is evident from his first scene when he seems wrenched by the news of Lucia's meetings with Edgardo. Zaccaria, whose voice is exceptionally warm, makes Raimondo both authoritative and compassionate. From the opening chords, Karajan establishes this as a highly intense performance. The orchestral introductions throughout are spacious and grand; the dramatic passages swirl with excitement. His approach to the sextet is masterly; in fact, the ensemble is encored. Technically, this set is less than ideal. Balances are often poor, and audience noises can be heard. But Lucia comes to life in this recording. There is not a trace of artifice here; everyone is immersed in the drama, and Callas gives the performance of a lifetime.

1957 RCA / BMG (S)

Roberta Peters (A), Jan Peerce (B), Philip Maero (C), Giorgio Tozzi (D), Rome Opera Chorus and Orchestra—Erich Leinsdorf

Youth, with all its sweetness and innocence, is the key to Roberta Peters's performance as Lucia. Vocally secure and absolutely precise, she displays total technical command of the role. Her perception of Lucia as a naive young girl comes through most successfully in the lyrical passages, where the singing is fresh and expressive. The coloratura, however, seems a thing apart, somewhat detached from the appealing character Peters has created. Jan Peerce presents a staunch Edgardo. Although he sings musically, his voice seems out of place in this opera, and it does not mesh with Peters's soprano in their duet. In the first act, Peerce sounds as though he is fighting a cold; by the final scene, however, the sound is much clearer. He comes into his own then with a tastefully sung "Fra poco a me ricovero," a tender recitative, and a truly poignant final aria. The expressive singing of Giorgio Tozzi makes Raimondo a strong presence in this recording. Tozzi's voice is luxuriant, and he shows commitment to the text. Philip Maero's singing is marred by a throaty sound and pitch problems. Leinsdorf's performance lacks verve, and the chorus, plagued by wobbly sopranos and poor intonation, often seems reluctant to follow the tempo set by the conductor.

1959 RICORDI (S) CD

Renata Scotto (A), Giuseppe di Stefano (B), Ettore Bastianini (C), Ivo Vinco (D), La Scala Chorus and Orchestra—Nino Sanzogno

Ettore Bastianini delivers an extraordinary performance in this set. His Enrico is imposing, proud, powerful, consistently elegant, even in his furious confrontation with Lucia. Bastianini's voice is dark and vibrant, his singing supple, his diction clear. He brings an exceptional sense of reality to Enrico, making him a complete character: nobleman, enemy, villain, and

brother. Scotto paints a refreshing portrait of Lucia. She is spunkier than most, with a boundless capacity for joy. There is no hint of melancholy in the character until Edgardo announces he is leaving; her agitation then is touching. In keeping with the personality Scotto has carefully established for Lucia, joy is uppermost in the first half of the Mad Scene as she fantasizes about her marriage to Edgardo. Then, totally crushed, she sinks into despair in the recitative that follows. Scotto sings musically and expressively throughout, but her studied performance lacks spontaneity. Given di Stefano's superb singing in the Callas sets, this Edgardo is disappointing. There are shades of his velvety tone, but the voice lacks fullness and support here. Ivo Vinco's voice sounds strained, and his Raimondo emerges as a two-dimensional character. The dynamic nuances in the choral passages are exceptionally effective. The orchestra, under Nino Sanzogno, is eloquent; the strings and woodwinds of the La Scala orchestra sing in this recording.

1959 EMI / ANGEL (S) CD

Maria Callas (A), Ferruccio Tagliavini (B), Piero Cappuccilli (C), Bernard Ladysz (D), Philharmonia Chorus and Orchestra—Tullio Serafin

Callas remains the epitome of the tragic heroine in this, the last of her three recordings of *Lucia*. Here, the character is more self-assured than the one she created in the first set, more mature and less ardent than in the 1955 live performance. As in the latter, the Mad Scene is a marvel of vocal color, with instant changes in color connoting the disjointed thinking of the insane Lucia. Vocally, her performance is uneven. She has difficulty with high notes and the wobble in her voice is sometimes distressing. Tagliavini excels in the lyrical passages, but he is past his prime here. There are remnants of his honeyed tenor, particularly in the "Verranno" duet and the last scene. There, Tagliavini floats high notes with ease and sings a superb *legato*. In highly dramatic moments, however, he resorts to shouting for emphasis. Cappuccilli's performance is more fully human in this set than in his 1970 recording with Sills.

This solid baritone depicts an Enrico who is agitated and distraught rather than evil. He sings expressively, and his remorse during the sextet provides one of the most touching moments in this set. Ladysz's voice is uneven, but the dark color of the lower register serves him well for Raimondo's third-act aria. Immersed in the text, the bass makes Raimondo's distress palpable. As in 1953, Serafin again brings an extraordinary sense of proportion and fluidity to the Donizetti score. The technical quality of this set is superior to the other Callas recordings.

1961 DECCA / LONDON (S) CD

Joan Sutherland (A), Renato Cioni (B), Robert Merrill (C), Cesare Siepi (D), Chorus and Orchestra of the Accademia di Santa Cecilia, Rome—John Pritchard

In Sir Walter Scott's novel, Edgar perceives Lucy Ashton as "an angel descended on earth, unallied to the coarser mortals among whom she deigned to dwell for a season." In Joan Sutherland's first recording of Donizetti's opera, that angelic quality is what the soprano brings to Lucia, the role that catapulted her to fame. In her opening aria, Sutherland floats the sound in a voice that is pure, fresh, limpid, ethereal. The trills and runs are crystal-clear, sung with astonishing delicacy and ease. The excitement of Sutherland's performance comes from virtuosity and beauty of tone, rather than color and expressivity. At this point in her career, she focused on sound with little regard for the power of language, and her middle voice tended to be hooty. Despite these drawbacks, this Mad Scene is worth hearing for her mesmerized description of the fantasized wedding, her near-whimper as she pleads "Non mi guardar si fiero" in the recitative, the total detachment from reality in the cabaletta, and the sheer effortlessness of the coloratura. Robert Merrill's performance is also centered in sound rather than text. His voice is warm, full, rounded, and evenly produced, and he sings expressively, yet he tends to sing about the words rather than into the words. Renato Cioni, a blustery Edgardo, strains vocally and relies on sobs and unrestrained emotionalism to carry him through the performance. His voice has a pleasing ring, but it pales vis-à-vis Suth-

erland and Merrill. Cesare Siepi is disappointing: the warmth of his voice is not enough to redeem his bland portrayal of Raimondo. Although the second-act finale is energetic, John Pritchard conducts a performance marked by gentility rather than dramatic tension. With this set, the traditional Lucia cuts no longer pertain. The Raimondo / Lucia and Wolf's Crag scenes are restored, as are many of the other conventional cuts in arias, recitatives, and ensembles.

1966 RCA / BMG (S) CD

Anna Moffo (A), Carlo Bergonzi (B), Mario Sereni (C), Ezio Flagello (D), RCA Italiana Opera Chorus and Orchestra—Georges Prêtre

The warmth of Moffo's voice makes her a pleasure to listen to, but the soprano is not convincing in this opera. Although she sings with feeling and shows an understanding of the text, the emotions emerge as those of a generic heroine rather than Lucia. The top voice is sometimes forced and Moffo exhibits little grasp of the bel canto style. The Mad Scene verges on the bland, but much of that might be due to the matter-of-fact conducting by Prêtre, whose performance lacks energy and cohesiveness. Bergonzi portrays an ardent hero. His voice has less body here than in his later recording with Sills. Yet, the golden sound of that voice, the legatos, the attention given to each word make his final scene memorable, and his duet with Sereni in the Wolf's Crag scene is a highlight of this set. There is a Verdian thrust to the duet as the two of them vigorously agree to a duel. Sereni, who depicts Enrico as a character motivated solely by vengeance, sings expressively, producing a wide spectrum of vocal colors. Ezio Flagello conveys Raimondo's compassion superbly in a voice of exceptional richness. In his third-act aria, he paints a vivid picture of the tragedy he has witnessed.

1970 EMI / ANGEL (S)

Beverly Sills (A), Carlo Bergonzi (B), Piero Cappuccilli (C), Justino Díaz (D), Ambrosian Opera Chorus, London Symphony Orchestra— Thomas Schippers

Donizetti originally used the glass harmonica, an instrument invented by Benjamin Franklin, in his scoring of the Mad Scene. Since no musician in Naples could play it at the time of the premiere, the composer substituted the flute. This is the only recording in which the glass harmonica is used, and the instrument transports the listener into the realm of the insane mind. The eerie atmosphere it creates is particularly appropriate for this set because a sense of madness permeates Beverly Sills's finely detailed, psychologically astute portrait of Lucia from the first lines she utters. She sounds skittish as she mentions the fountain; she verges on instability as she cries "Ah!" at the very thought of the ghost. Sills's musicianship is impeccable, and she tosses off the coloratura with remarkable flexibility. Her voice is not at its best in this recording, however, and the cabaletta of the Mad Scene in particular is marred by vocal fatigue. Bergonzi portrays a tender Edgardo. His voice is fuller and better focused here than in the set with Moffo, and he phrases his final arias with sensitivity. Cappuccilli's Enrico is Iagoesque, more conniving than in the 1959 Callas set. Though vocally uneven, Justino Díaz sings with feeling, creating a somber Raimondo. Schippers conducts a taut, focused performance, with close attention to orchestral detail.

1971 DECCA / LONDON (S) CD

Joan Sutherland (A), Luciano Pavarotti (B), Sherrill Milnes (C), Nicolai Ghiaurov (D), Chorus and Orchestra of the Royal Opera House, Covent Garden—Richard Bonynge

Sutherland's performance in this recording is far superior to the 1961 set, and she is surrounded by a first-rate cast. Her voice is warmer and more open than before, without losing any of its purity. The vitality of her Lucia still emanates primarily from her virtuosity and the very sound of her voice, but virtuosity is more at the service of the drama this time around. The coloratura is given more meaning, and the recitatives are freer and more expressive. Although Sutherland's characterization is not profound,

the soprano now creates a character more fully human. Pavarotti's full-bodied sound matches Sutherland's in its beauty. His *legatos* are extraordinary, his diction exemplary. His Edgardo is not only a tender, ardent lover but a man who carries with him the pain of his family history. The tenor's voice rings with fury in the "Maledetto" and takes on a heroic dimension in the Wolf's Crag confrontation. In Pavarotti's hands, the final scene becomes a drama in miniature. Edgardo's recitative is imbued with pathos, and his last aria is deeply poignant. Sherrill Milnes, in superb voice, gives a vivid portrayal of Enrico. The baritone seems to gnaw at the words, spewing them out in a variety of colors and a wide range of dynamics. The cavernous sound of Ghiaurov's voice gives Raimondo real stature, even grandeur. The Russian bass sings with grace and assurance, presenting a presbyter who can be compassionate with Lucia, yet imperious in his condemnation of Normanno. Richard Bonynge conducts a buoyant, superbly balanced performance, precise yet seemingly spontaneous, detailed yet fluid. He zeroes in on the mood of the moment and carefully builds each scene to its inexorable conclusion. The clarity of the solo instruments is a credit both to the conductor and to the engineers of this superbly recorded set.

1976 PHILIPS (S) CD

Montserrat Caballé (A), José Carreras (B), Vicente Sardinero (C), Samuel Ramey (D), Ambrosian Opera Chorus, New Philharmonia Orchestra—Jésus Lopez-Cobos

The liner notes for this set promise an authentic version of *Lucia*. Over one hundred discrepancies that exist between the original score and the one traditionally used have been corrected, and three scenes have been transposed up to those in the autograph score. The only exception is the glass harmonica, which is indicated in the autograph but is not used here. Although the singers of Donizetti's time were expected to provide ornamentation and cadenzas, this set presents the opera "as written, i.e., with minimal embellishments." This approach, contrary to the style and history of the piece, deprives the opera of much of its grace. In Caballé's case, however, the literal reading of the score is fortuitous because the soprano's *fioriture* tend to be labored and, surprisingly, top notes uncontrolled. In the lyrical passages, such as her exquisite "Soffriva nel pianto," her voice glows, yet her response to the text is generic rather than connected to this specific character. Flair, a sense of grandeur, and beautiful sounds are what this performance is about. These qualities also mark Carreras's performance, and the blend of his voice with Caballé's luminous soprano in the first-act duet is ravishing. The tenor's Edgardo is vulnerable, lacking the more turbulent aspects of the character that are inherent in the music. Although Carreras relies on lachrymose sounds too often in an effort to capture that vulnerability, he sings with genuine feeling. The Raimondo in this set is a master of beautiful sound. Ramey uses his full-bodied voice to portray a formidable presbyter who, in Act III, is shattered by the grisly scene in the bridal chamber. Vincente Sardinero, whose singing is assured and powerful, portrays a haughty Enrico. Lopez-Cobos is erratic. His reading of the Prelude is one of the most satisfying on these complete sets, and dramatic passages in the opera erupt with energy. But the more lyrical ones, such as the introduction to "Quando, rapito," lack elegance. Lopez-Cobos relies heavily on the timpani for effect and the orchestra occasionally overpowers the singers. Given these factors and the sparing use of coloratura, the overall performance tends to be ponderous.

1983 EMI / ANGEL (S,D) ℗

Edita Gruberova (A), Alfredo Kraus (B), Renato Bruson (C), Robert Lloyd (D), Ambrosian Opera Chorus, Royal Philharmonic Orchestra—Nicola Rescigno

The basic tenets of *bel canto* are alive and well in the person of Alfredo Kraus. The tenor, who brings a bright virile sound to his performance, creates a supremely confident Edgardo. In scene after scene, his sheer sense of presence

and the elegance of his delivery command the listener's attention. Kraus captures the irascibility inherent in much of Edgardo's vocal line, and knows how to use rhythmic precision to good dramatic effect. Edita Gruberova spins out stunning *pianissimo* high notes and capably negotiates the coloratura. She brings freshness to the role, creating a spirited Lucia who is capable of real passion. Renato Bruson makes an imposing Enrico, but his performance is uneven. The voice is dry and he is plagued by an annoying sibilance which grates on the ear. Although the problem is obviously his, more diligent engineering might have reduced it to a tolerable level. Robert Lloyd is a highly expressive performer. When Raimondo sees Lucia enter after she has killed Arturo, for example, the bass captures the tension of the moment in a single word, "Eccola," uttered in a hushed, haunted voice. Lloyd sings well in lyrical passages, but sounds hooty in more emotional ones. The chorus in this recording is truly involved in the text. The ebb and flow of the performance, under Rescigno's baton, is first-rate, with the orchestra providing an eloquent commentary on the drama.

A unique combination of artistry and visceral excitement places Callas's 1955 live performance above other recordings of this opera. Di Stefano is also at his peak in this set, and Karajan conducts a performance of passion and grandeur. Technically, the recording leaves a lot to be desired. But the musicality and dramatic truth of this legendary performance more than compensate for the technical shortcomings.

BRIDGET PAOLUCCI

Unavailable for review:
1951 REMINGTON
1958 ORPHEUS
1969 SUPRAPHON
1972 EURODISC
1991 TELDEC
1992 DEUTSCHE GRAMMOPHON

GAETANO DONIZETTI

ROBERTO DEVEREUX (1837)

A: Elisabetta (s); B: Sara (ms); C: Roberto (t); D: Nottingham (bar)

onizetti's 57th opera has gotten a new lease on life in the general revival of the composer's works in the last three or four decades. Written in 1837, at a time when Donizetti was grief-stricken by the death of his young wife and when Naples was in the grip of a cholera epidemic, it had its delayed but successful premiere at the Teatro San Carlo on October 29th of that year. Salvatore Cammarano supplied a solid libretto (derived in part from one that Felice Romani wrote for Meyerbeer on the same subject), with well-defined characters and clear-cut motivation. For his part, the composer produced the most complete and complex of his musical portraits of Queen Elizabeth, here a woman torn apart by her passions, hoping for love, enraged by jealousy and a sense of betrayal as a woman and a queen, and finally devastated by remorse. The role was written for the dramatic soprano Giuseppina Ronzi de Begnis, for whom Donizetti had already written several parts, and it is rich in technical and dramatic demands, with leaps and runs of almost two octaves as well as passages of radiant lyricism. There are also rewarding roles for the three other principal singers, an economical use of the chorus, and frequently an unconventional handling of operatic conventions—for instance, in Act II Donizetti pairs Elisabetta with one character (Raleigh) in a recitative, and with another (Nottingham) in the subsequent duet. The composer's command of the orchestra is evident in many passages, among them the introduction to Roberto's prison scene, evoca-

tive of the grimness of the Tower of London in a manner that remotely echoes Florestan's dungeon in *Fidelio*. After being widely performed for more than four decades, the opera disappeared from the boards until its revival in Naples in 1964 (for Leyla Gencer) launched it on a new career.

1969 EMI / ANGEL (S)

Beverly Sills (A), Beverly Wolff (B), Robert Ilosfalvy (C), Peter Glossop (D), Ambrosian Opera Chorus, Royal Philharmonic Orchestra—Charles Mackerras

This is by now something of a historic recording, preserving Beverly Sills's interpretation of Elisabetta in a studio recording made about a year before its staged presentation by the New York City Opera, where the work took its place in the celebrated Tudor trilogy with *Anna Bolena* and *Maria Stuarda*. Although her essentially lyric voice almost certainly does not have the dramatic thrust of a Ronzi, for whom Donizetti wrote the part, Sills is nevertheless in complete charge of the role. Her silvery clarity and technical agility are not surprising, and in the more flamboyantly dramatic passages her projection of the text is telling even where sheer vocal weight is not. She is undaunted even in the frequent descents to the neighborhood of middle C. The Hungarian tenor Robert Ilosfalvy is a reliable but unvarying Roberto, although he rouses himself for the splendid prison scene. Peter Glossop's thick baritone is vigorously employed in running Nottingham's gamut from nobility to rage, while Beverly Wolff as his duchess, Sara, sings with secure ease. Charles Mackerras is the firm and unhurried conductor. Some theatrical atmosphere has been added in spots with unobtrusive sound effects. The recording is just a few notes short of being complete.

David Stevens

LA FILLE DU RÉGIMENT (1840)

A: Marie (s); B: Tonio (t); C: Sulpice (bs)

Donizetti moved to Paris in the fall of 1838, after the death of his beloved 28-year-old wife, when he could no longer bear Italy with its painful reminders of his loss. Already known and admired for his *Lucia di Lammermoor* by Parisian opera goers, Donizetti conquered the French capital as early as 1840, a vintage year which saw premieres of three of his better works—a revision of *Poliuto* (written for Naples and scuttled by her censors, now entitled *Les Martyrs*), *La Favorita*, and *La Fille du Régiment*.

Fille's debut at the Opéra-Comique was not altogether successful, but subsequent audiences could not resist the emotional content which warmed the convential comedy of this frankly popular entertainment; the opera racked up 44 performances in its first year. Its title role became a favorite vehicle for lyric divas after Jenny Lind introduced it to London in 1847. The libretto for *Fille* was written by Vernoy de Saint-Georges and Jean François Bayard. Translated into Italian by none other than Donizetti himself, it was equally successful in Italy as *La Figlia del Reggimento*.

1950 CETRA (In Italian) (M)

Lina Pagliughi (A), Cesare Valletti (B), Sesto Bruscantini (C), Italian Radio Chorus and Orchestra—Mario Rossi

There are only three complete recordings of *La Fille du Régiment*: the first was sung in Italian and derives, like most of Cetra's output, from broadcast concert tapes. Judging by its ill-defined orchestral sound and tight focus on the singers, the recording is a few years older than its release date. The score is well paced and shaped by Mario Rossi. The critical flaw in the performance lies where one least expects it—in the title role. Pagliughi, one of the best Italian coloraturas of her day, seems miscast and perhaps past her best days, considering her struggle with intonation. She makes a good impression in "Convien partir," but in lighter moments (the majority of the role) she lacks spirit and personality. Valletti, who often gives pleasure, is not at his best either. His voice sounds unusually light and his delivery is wanting in brilliance. Bruscantini is a model Sulpice.

1967 DECCA / LONDON (S) CD

Joan Sutherland (A), Luciano Pavarotti (B), Spiro Malas (C), Chorus and Orchestra of the Royal Opera House, Covent Garden—Richard Bonynge

To his credit, Richard Bonynge employs the longer, original version in French rather than the Italian translation his cast might have found more comfortable. Although the performance has no more than a nodding acquaintance with French style, it has its own kind of merry enthusiasm. Bonynge presents the score with an affection and respect that make one lenient in judging his deficiencies in rhythmic pointing and ensemble housekeeping, and that of the cast in enunciating French. Joan Sutherland is temperamentally well suited to the role of Marie. She is a good-humored *vivandière* (not a wind-up doll), who sings with feeling and effortlessly deals with the most difficult vocal acrobatics. Pavarotti matches his partner's success, touching in his cavatina and dazzling in his number with the nine high Cs. Among his operatic roles on disc, Tonio, recorded somewhere near the tenor's vocal high noon, remains unsurpassed for brilliance, ease, and personal charm. Malas makes a spirited Sulpice. Monica Sinclair, lively if a bit heavy-handed as the Marchioness, seems, like the entire ensemble, to be having a wonderful time. The recording, which appears to have been made in London's excellent Kingsway Hall, offers sound that is rich, airy, resonant, and a trifle grainy.

1986 EMI / ANGEL (S,D,P) CD

June Anderson (A), Alfredo Kraus (B), Michel Trempont (C), Paris Opéra Chorus and Orchestra—Bruno Campanella

This issue is a conflation of two live performances heard at the Opéra-Comique (now called the Salle Favart) on May 14 and 19, 1986. The recording is impressively clean and a bit boxy, with less resonance than London's, so that the orchestral timbres are lighter and more characterful. There is lots of stage noise, but, gratefully, little from the audience excepting its applause, with which EMI has been altogether too generous. There is superfluity of dialogue; especially for listeners who do not speak French; the supplied libretto includes only text and translation for the musical numbers. June Anderson, an agreeable and good-humored Marie, displays, like Sutherland, a voice happily more ample than that usually associated with the part and a similar penchant for plenty of decoration and unwritten cadenzas. Its production is decidedly uneven, with frequent squally tones near the top and just above the soprano clef but usually brilliant on the highest notes. Breath support is inconsistent; some phrases are well shaped, others not. Anderson's rhythm needs tightening (she is too often behind the beat) and her diction is at least as fuzzy as Sutherland's. Alfredo Kraus copes bravely and artfully with a role which requires a more youthful sound. Nevertheless, the nine high Cs are tossed off in tune in his first-act aria, and his second-act Romance, even though achieved with palpable effort, has charm. The secondary parts are dispatched with spirit but are less secure vocally than those in the London set. The Opéra-Comique ensemble, though no better than decent, does offer the advantage of a French chorus singing in its own language. The conducting of Bruno Campanella wants greater control and more consistent sparkle.

———————————

The Sutherland / Pavarotti set represents them at their best, and is the preferred version.

C. J. LUTEN

GAETANO DONIZETTI

LA FAVORITE (1840)

A: Léonor (ms); B: Fernand (t); C: Alphonse (bar); D: Balthazar (bs)

*L*a Favorite has a complicated history: a French *grand opéra*, written for the Paris Opéra and first performed there in 1840, which has kept its position in the repertory in a later Italian translation. In the original the libretto is clear in motivation and sustained in tone, and it inspired music in Donizetti's noblest and (particularly in the fourth and final act) most elevated pre-Verdian manner; even though *La Favorite* was produced in haste, and assembled from both new and existent Donizettian musical material, the total is one of the composer's most "continuous" and consistent scores. For Italian performances, for reasons initially to do with nineteenth-century Italian censorship, changes were made in some of the characters' identities which resulted in a hopelessly muddled plot (just to take a single example, Balthazar, Superior of St. James of Compostela, becomes in the Italian version an impossible combination of monk and Fernand's father); in addition, many small alterations or excisions were practiced on the score which spoil its clarity of outline, and the fit of Italian syllables to vocal line is extremely clumsy. Most extant *Favorite* records use the standard Italian score (as do most *Favorite* revivals)—the principal arias, Léonor's "O mon Fernand" and Fernand's "Ange si pur," are all but unknown, while as "O mio Fernando" and "Spirto gentil" they are widely known. But it is important to emphasize the many textual differences between the two versions, particularly as the whole work is so often dismissed as second-rate when given in Italian.

1912 PATHÉ (M)

Ketty Lapeyrette (A), Robert Lassalle (B), Henri Albers (C), Marvini (D), Chorus and Orchestra—François Ruhlmann

The earliest of the *Favorite* sets is in many ways the essential one to have. If not absolutely complete, it is rather fuller in text than some of its successors in Italian translation, largely disfigured by "traditional cuts" beyond those already built into the Italian version. More to the point, it is in French, given by a cast of distinguished Paris Opéra and Opéra-Comique regulars of the period, under a conductor whose Opéra career lasted thirty-five years, and thus an exposition of Donizetti style miles removed from the heavyweight Italian *verismo*-influenced vocal manners to be encountered elsewhere. The Belgian Henri Albers, the best-known name among the singers, shapes Alphonse's music with warmth of tone, elegance of line, and weight (but no undue heftiness) at both ends of his compass. These attributes he shares with the mezzo Ketty Lapeyrette, not perhaps the most affecting heroine, but at once grandly stylish and passionate. The tenor Robert Lassalle (son of the baritone Jean) and the bass Marvini make a less distinct impression—as, for obvious reasons of recording technique, do chorus and orchestra. This is not the *Favorite* to display Donizetti's coloristic skills (which, as he was excited by the challenge of writing for the Opéra, were at their most resourceful); in addition, the pitching of the LP transfers—the original was recorded at speeds varying between 80 and 100 rpm—is not uniformly convincing. What it does do is to underline Donizetti's success at marrying Italianate lyricism and the French *grand opéra* form. The clean cut of the French text, and of the French singing style, is a revelation.

1955 DECCA / LONDON (In Italian) (S)

Giulietta Simionato (A), Gianni Poggi (B), Ettore Bastianini (C), Jerome Hines (D), Chorus and Orchestra of the Maggio Musicale Fiorentino—Alberto Erede

The first of the Italian sets is essential in exactly the opposite sense—the one which most fully demonstrates both the worst aspects of the Italian version and (not coincidentally) the worst features of the *verismo*-tainted singing style which, in the long decades before Donizetti was rediscovered, was too often deemed appropriate for the revival of all nineteenth-century Italian opera. For the insensitive orchestral and choral work under Erede (a long-experienced conductor prone to limp routine), and above all the blaring coarseness of the tenor, Gianni Poggi, the word "provincial" might have been invented—the special qualities of the opera and, in particular, of Fernand's characterization are all but effaced. Giulietta Simionato and Ettore Bastianini, two of the great Italian voices of the period, deal out lots of voice but little interpretive imagination (though the mezzo recovers a measure of her distinction in time for her Act IV death scene); as Balthazar the ample-voiced Jerome Hines is dignified but uninteresting. The early-stereo sound in which the set was later reissued is remarkably good for the date—just about the only feature that one can praise without reservation.

1956 CETRA (In Italian) (M)

Fedora Barbieri (A), Gianni Raimondi (B), Carlo Tagliabue (C), Giulio Neri (D), Italian Radio Chorus and Orchestra—Angelo Questa

Cetra's *Favorite*, roughly contemporary with Decca's (and similar in its "standard" cuts), is a much more attractive example of the 1950s approach to Donizetti. None of the singers commands the *sfumature*, the nuances and delicacies of tonal variation, or the smooth, supple phrasing ideally required, but the voices of the leading couple carry their own characteristically Italianate appeal—Fedora Barbieri's lush mezzo and Gianni Raimondi's lean, ringing tenor both sound in prime condition—and each manages to steer decently clear of any crudities of style. The baritone, Carlo Tagliabue, was well past his prime; the bass, Giulio Neri, both cavernous and ponderous; but Questa's conducting is "vocal" in its sympathy with the voices, as well as being alive to the color and detail of Donizetti's scoring, and to the importance of the minor roles (mostly well taken). This performance presents the more acceptable face of Italian *Favorite* "tradition."

1974–77 DECCA / LONDON (In Italian) (S) CD

Fiorenza Cossotto (A), Luciano Pavarotti (B), Gabriel Bacquier (C), Nicolai Ghiaurov (D), Chorus and Orchestra of the Teatro Comunale, Bologna—Richard Bonynge

By comparison with the previous two Italian-language sets, this represents at least an attempt to find some form of accommodation between the original score and its "traditional" Italian mutant. Richard Bonynge restored many of Donizetti's internal repeats, plus the tenor's *marziale* aria close to Act I (almost always cut elsewhere). But other unhappy Italian features (for instance, the bluntly truncated ending) are retained, and in general a sense of idiomatic Donizettian style is only fitfully imparted. The Bologna forces, under Bonynge's typically excitable but not always authoritative baton, seem middling-to-feeble, and though there are some big names in the cast, most of these bring disappointments. Nicolai Ghiaurov uses his splendid bass with a sore lack of light and shade; Gabriel Bacquier is the intelligent but rusty-toned baritone (the arias show his keen aware-ness of *bel canto* requirements, but also his incomplete technical means of fulfilling them); and Fiorenza Cossotto's normally firm mezzo is persistently flawed by spread high notes, uncer-tain intonation, and gusty phrasing—Léonor, whose mature, troubled womanliness is so beautifully characterized in the vocal line, emerges here in blowsy condition. There is, however, one good reason for exploring this recording—Luciano Pavarotti as Fernand. In 1974 he had not yet assumed the superstar status that would eventually leave its mark on his performance practices; the role lies very well for him: he addresses himself with complete com-mitment to its vocal and emotional contours, and though it is by no means the most honeyed, subtle Donizetti-tenor singing on records, Pava-rotti's clean-lined ardor regularly raises the tem-perature of the whole performance.

———————

The 1912 French-language *Favorite* is more than a "historical" item: it is both a badly needed Donizetti corrective and a genuinely affecting Donizetti performance. People unable to toler-ate its primitive recorded sound and uneven orchestral and choral execution are probably most conveniently directed to the later of the two Decca sets, with its compelling hero, though the Cetra gives a more rounded impression of the opera's other qualities.

MAX LOPPERT

PLATO KARAYANIS
General Director, The Dallas Opera

1. **Wagner**, *Die Walküre*: Nilsson, Crespin, Ludwig, King, Hotter, Frick—Solti. DECCA / LONDON

2. **Bellini**, *Norma*: Callas, Stignani, Filippeschi, Rossi-Lemeni—Serafin. EMI / ANGEL

3. **Verdi**, *Otello*: Freni, Malagù, Vickers, Bottion, Glossop—Karajan. EMI / ANGEL

4. **Strauss**, *Elektra*: Nilsson, Collier, Resnik, Stolze, Krause—Solti. DECCA / LONDON

5. **Verdi**, *Nabucco*: Dimitrova, Valentini Terrani, Domingo, Cappuccilli, Nesterenko—Sinopoli. DEUTSCHE GRAMMOPHON

6. **Puccini**, *La Bohème*: De los Angeles, Amara, Bjoerling, Merrill, Reardon, Tozzi—Beecham. EMI / ANGEL

7. **Puccini**, *Tosca*: Callas, di Stefano, Gobbi—de Sabata. EMI / ANGEL

8. **Sondheim**, *Sweeney Todd*: Lansbury, Rice, Garber, Cariou—Gemignani. RCA / BMG

9. **Donizetti**, *Lucia di Lammermoor*: Gruberova, Kraus, Bruson, Lloyd—Resigno. EMI / ANGEL

10. **Donizetti**, *Lucia di Lammermoor*: Callas, di Stefano, Gobbi, Arie—Serafin. EMI / ANGEL

GAETANO DONIZETTI

DON PASQUALE (1843)

A: Norina (s); B: Ernesto (t); C: Malatesta (b); D: Pasquale (bs)

This beautiful little opera, though it gives every sign of being eminently playable, suffers agonies in performance. It is difficult by its very nature: an old generation-gap comedy, at once cruel and sentimental, closely bonded to the social and political issues of its time, but drawn on an old-fashioned libretto full of ancient theatrical usages that are long since matters of antique artifice. The interesting tensions created by this mix have subsided into a conflict between the exhausted *buffo* tradition and a pretense that the humors and realities of the piece are the same as those of a sitcom. *Our buffo* traditions, exhausted from birth.

The recordings reflect the problems: taken collectively, they are rather unsatisfying. They fall chronologically into two coherent groups. In Group I are performances by Italian singers and conductors. Reflective of early- to mid-century performance practice, they all smack more of theater ensemble than of conductorial concept, and embrace the cuts once considered standard for the piece. In Group II (beginning with the 1965 Kertész), the personnel are predominantly non-Italian, conductors start to throw the hawkeye, and all the cuts are opened. These are the development and repeat sections of the arias for Pasquale and Norina and of the Ernesto / Pasquale and Norina / Malatesta duets; the entire second section of Ernesto's double aria at the opening of Act II; development and repeat in the finale; and some recitative. The only important exceptions are noted in the discussions of specific recordings.

1932 EMI / ANGEL (M) CD

Adelaide Saraceni (A), Tito Schipa (B), Afro Poli (C), Ernesto Badini (D), La Scala Chorus and Orchestra—Carlo Sabajno

This performance had a two-decade reign as the only "complete" *Pasquale*, and has remained a reference point for Schipa's Ernesto. Actually, it has other solid virtues. Sabajno knows how to play the piece in a theatrically clear manner—the Act II ensembles are very comfortable, and the major point of a section always emerges. The combination of his approach and the 1930s sonics makes the orchestra sound like a jolly Italian village band, likable and easy, though not brilliant and rich. Afro Poli is as close as we will come here to a distinguished Malatesta. We are constrained to observe from the outset that only a couple of the baritones on records can render the modest divisions and flourishes of the role with true bravura or polish, but Poli's warm, strong tone, smooth line, and confidence in the idiom are pleasurable. Finally, there *is* Schipa, his voice still in good trim in 1932, and the limits of its range of consequence only in the Garden Scene duet, where Saraceni must take the upper line and we lose the effect of the sixths. He is alert, fresh, and direct in his interpretation, while the expert control over *legato* and *mezza voce*, combined with free, ringing top As and B-flats, gives an expressive release to the music that is still unsurpassed.

The remaining elements (the two leads, unfortunately) are not as positive. Saraceni's singing is to be admired for its command: her soprano is large and well equalized with decent flexibility and dynamic control, and she is firm and decisive. The tone itself, however, is edgy and hard; this Norina is a tough old bird, tiring to hear for any length of time. Badini, at this stage very much an experienced pro who probably gave pleasure in the theater, discloses a stock approach to the part and a thin baritone voice that is perfectly secure but has little richness or beauty. The full Norina-Malatesta scene is retained.

1949 CETRA (M)

Alda Noni (A), Cesare Valletti (B), Mario Borriello (C), Sesto Bruscantini (D), Chorus and Orchestra of the RAI, Turin—Mario Rossi

This is a nicely cast performance. The men all have lovely voices, and everyone is familiar with the Italian comedic habits referred to above, into which they slip unquestioningly and comparatively unexaggeratedly. Some Norina trouble, though: Noni, whose voice sounds quite brilliant in recordings only a few years earlier, is wiry and scrappy here, and pushes her interpretation, as well. She's more resourceful than enjoyable.

Valletti, on the other hand, is wonderful. True, there are moments—especially on closed vowels above the break—when his voice thins and tightens under pressure. But no one, not even Schipa, tips in such exquisite coloring, expands into a swelling line with such an instinct for its arc and pulse, or so touchingly captures the lugubrious melancholy of the early scenes. Passages like "Sogno soave e casto" and the aria "Cercherò lontana terra" are given their most complete fulfillment on these records. Borriello has a nappy, tolerably smooth middleweight baritone, rather similar to Poli's. He manages the technical hurdles with more dignity than most, and tallies a majority of the traditional interpretive points. Bruscantini's sunny, plump light bass is in its youthful prime here: for sheer timbral beauty and ease of production, his is the best-sung Pasquale on records. He has plenty of expressive flair, too, but gets cute far too often. It's a hard role for a young man.

Rossi's instrumental and choral forces are

only so-so. He certainly knows where the accents are, has a nice feeling for the tempos and *rubato*s, and accompanies solo passages well. There is not much real pointing in his reading, though, and sometimes it's hard to know whether one is hearing slackness in the performance or just the dimness and distance of the sonics. (I comment on the Everest pressing—with most releases of this series, the Cetra-Soria originals were superior. Avoid, if possible, the reconstructed stereo.)

1952 URANIA (M)

Dora La Gatta (A), Agostino Lazzari (B), Afro Poli (C), Fernando Corena (D), Members of La Scala Chorus and Orchestra—Armando La Rosa Parodi

This is a respectable, idiomatic performance, better than provincial, solid enough in its orchestral and choral elements, under a knowledgeable theater conductor who tends to push too hard when the tempos quicken. The big, biting voice of Corena—the preeminent *basso buffo* of the 1950s and 1960s—is in fresher, more supple estate than the later Kertész recording finds it, and his expert but entirely stereotypical characterization (words like "droll and splenetic!" come to mind) still has some freshness in it. La Gatta is a perfectly competent soprano of whatever the "-ina" type can be called (lyric soubrette?). She gets around the music professionally with that slightly shrill, vixenish sort of sound the Italians seem to consider apt, and makes many small points with intelligence and wit. Like several other Norina / Pasquale couples, she and Corena do their best work in the Act III scene, where everyone seems to concede that it is all right to "become more human."

Lazzari has a voice of the accepted weight for Ernesto, and can sing the part without major problems. Both tonally and musically, though, his performance is extremely plain, and does not convey much beyond the notes. Poli, again the Malatesta, is still in fine voice and better recorded than in 1932. By this time, though, he is trusting himself and the music less, and trying a little too hard in the illustrative manner that will turn to grotesquerie in some later interpretations.

p. 1952 WESTMINSTER (M)

Lina Aimaro (A), Juan Oncina (B), Scipio Colombo (C), Melchiorre Luise (D), Vienna Chamber Chorus, Vienna State Opera Orchestra—Argeo Quadri

This is a highly pleasurable performance, and is by far the closest to a complete performance of those in Group I. Quadri has a tender, unforced way with the score. Most of his tempos are on the slow side, but the music never meanders, and both the players and the singers are able to expand into their moments, to make them beautiful and specific. There is plenty of pep where it's needed, but the pace never sounds pumped up—musical points are always rounded off, and the playing of the scene is never swamped by excitability. This sounds like a theater-tested ensemble: the pit-stage relationship is close, and the characters and situations are conveyed in a manner that is not only vivid but often charged with some actual wit and sophistication. True comedy's underlying dignity, which arises from the essential validity of the characters' conflicting desires, is never lost sight of. Choral and orchestral execution is very good, if not of the ultimate high-gloss variety, and shows every sign of care and affection—the tiny scene for the servants at the opening of Act III, for example, has brilliant life. Among the singers, Colombo must be mentioned first, for he is nothing less than masterful. Singing in a mellow, potent baritone that never loses its poise, he truly draws the line of the music, and invests every phrase with a grounded intent. He is alone among the Malatestas in making us feel some of the character's motive, his appetite, his maturity. At the same time, he tosses out the cadenza of his aria with a fluency that recalls classic models. This is a connoisseur's performance. Aimaro has a light, airy soprano, mobile and pretty, that can turn hard and chirpy on occasion. Luise's voice, also light for his role, is nonetheless pleasant, despite the normal ration of chortles and splutters. Oncina, very young here, bases nearly

everything on gradings of *mezza voce* touched with a hint of nasality—attractive, tasteful singing. All these artists contribute to a valid, chamber-theater rendition that fully conveys the nature of the piece.

p. 1953 PLYMOUTH (M)

Josephine Guido (A), Antonio Pirino (B), Walter Monachesi (C), Andrea Mongelli (D), Rome Opera Chorus and Orchestra—Luigi Ricci

An instance of well-merited obscurity, this recording. Ricci was a highly respected coach, and in the Prelude one can certainly detect stylistic ideas. But his players can barely wrap themselves around the notes, the chorus is pathetic, and the engineering has the earmarks of one of those ethnic field recordings.

Among the singers, Mongelli has a real voice, though of a strange sort for the part—a snarly heavyweight baritone, complete with low E and more top than Pasquale will ever need. No wit or comic spark, mind you, it's all quite wrong, though occasionally a touch of ferocity suggests something interesting. Pirino could be worse— the voice has a sweet enough quality, and he is not lethargic or musically uncaring—but the upper middle gives him intonation worries, and there is no retouching to disguise them. Monachesi was a second-line professional, useful in certain capacities. He shows life in recitative, but his technique balks at quieter dynamics and notes above E-flat. Guido is fondly remembered for her years with Brooklyn's Salmaggi Opera Company. An apologetic sigh escapes as we note that her Norina is, by any standard applicable here, pretty gruesome.

1955 PHILIPS (M)

Bruna Rizzoli (A), Petre Munteanu (B), Giuseppe Valdengo (C), Renato Capecchi (D), San Carlo Chorus and Orchestra, Naples—Francesco Molinari-Pradelli

There is much to enjoy in this version. The younger Molinari-Pradelli was a first-rate maestro in this repertory—the melodies dance and sing along, the ensembles are lively and pointed, and much of the accompanying is brilliant. The

Naples forces execute well, and there's a precision and sharpness of detail here quite above the average of these Italian renditions.

Capecchi gives a performance of enormous expertise. It is bursting with *buffo*-isms, but with this artist there is usually the sense of something genuine behind them, and even the overdone moments have a specificity. We always have a picture of what's being done and who's doing it, and his pleasing baritone is fresh and accurate. The Norina of Rizzoli is also an asset. There's just a touch of acid in her *leggiera* voice, but the prevailing tone is a light, floating one, faintly remniscent of Lily Pons. She snaps off crush-notes and trills with alacrity, and teases at the *rubato*s winningly.

The remaining singers have some limitations: Munteanu's light tenor hasn't the punch wanted for some of the vigorous moments, while Valdengo's lyric baritone is weak at the bottom, and its owner just tacks together the runs and triplets. The saving grace, though, is that both voices are truly beautiful and appropriate, and both singers know how to maintain line and make it say something.

No astonishing elements, perhaps, but these days a performance that is snappily conducted by a musician who knows and concedes a theatrical or vocal point when he sees one, and in which all concerned sing quite prettily and idiomatically, deserves a loving home.

1964 DEUTSCHE GRAMMOPHON (S)

Anna Maccianti (A), Ugo Benelli (B), Mario Basiola, Jr. (C), Alfredo Mariotti (D), Chorus and Orchestra of the Maggio Musicale Fiorentino—Ettore Gracis

This version has some elements that just pass muster, but its ensemble feeling is rather nice, and in its low-key fashion, it renders the piece. The best of the singers is Maccianti, who is a sporty Norina. As with most Italians of this vocal type, there is some edge on the tone toward the top. But this is only intermittently bothersome, and in all other respects she is first-class: no holes or bald patches, the singing firm and even dashing, a good trill, completely formed phrases. Ugo Benelli's little *tenorino* is given

everything it can handle by this music (this is *not*, by the way, an easy role to sing, even if we confine ourselves to the basics), but he copes, and at times projects some emotional vitality.

Basiola, son of the excellent like-named baritone of the 1920s and 1930s, has an instrument of the correct weight and reach, and sings a perfectly sensible Malatesta; unfortunately, there is a mealiness and a strange, buzzing undertone in much of his vocalism. Mariotti has only a bit more than an octave of solid, dark bass sound, but offers some discreet solutions for the rest, so he avoids sounding too strung-out. He makes an honorable stab at singing the part, and doesn't resort to gimmicks. His interpretation is extremely sober, but at least it's not the phogna bologna.

Gracis's conducting proves to be sensible, tidy, well balanced, and a little careful. The important ensembles come off well. The Maggio Musicale orchestra is one of the better Italian ones—still not a virtuoso ensemble, but acceptable. This set's basic sound is also the best of the Group I performances, though in the DG fashion of the time, the soloists are recorded very close.

1964 DECCA / LONDON (S) CD

Graziella Sciutti (A), Juan Oncina (B), Tom Krause (C), Fernando Corena (D), Vienna State Opera Chorus and Orchestra—István Kertész

We enter Group II, and since from this point forward all cuts are restored, these restorations merit a moment's consideration. On the page, none of the cuts is justifiable. It is absurd, for example, to reduce Pasquale's song to a snippet; to deprive Ernesto of the whole *moderato* of his double aria; to excise recitative that clarifies plot and enriches character; to leave duets and ensembles with no time to work themselves out. The writing is certainly strong enough to support its own structures. Yet it seems unlikely that these cuts originated in contempt for Donizetti or in a desire to harm performance of his opera. More likely they were made (and later endorsed, perhaps too unquestioningly) by experienced theater musicians who were trying to make the piece work—not on the page but in reality. Most of the cut sections elaborate and repeat material in a way that is simple and effective, but not overly fascinating from a purely musical standpoint. In performance, they can readily become tedious unless two questions are satisfactorily answered: 1. What is the actor playing while his voice repeats a statement? (E.g., what is Pasquale *doing* during the full length of his song—more *buffo* jackanapery? Or, what is happening to the characters' relationships during the repeat of a trio—more forced antics, or facing front and winking at the audience?) 2. How are the musicians treating the restorations, particularly the repeats? Are they embellishing, or finding other variants that will lead us to interesting new places not discovered the first time round? The cuts originated, one feels sure, with conductors who were smart enough to notice that neither they nor the performers had good answers to these questions—let alone the ability to make musical solutions that were answers to the dramatic questions, which is what one actually wants—and that audiences were bored. For the restorations to fulfill their promise, these problems must be solved.

This recording is a perfect, though by no means unique, case in point. Four talented singers of less than virtuosic standing dutifully and neatly say everything one more time, and we wait around longer for the structures to run their completely predictable courses. Kertész, a superior conductor of much romantic orchestral repertory, seems content with excellent playing and with a gentle, shapely reading that, after a lively but rather clipped Prelude, never takes off; the Act II ensembles, especially (the heart of the piece), just mope amiably along. It's all nice, and harmless, and a little *long*.

Sciutti, an excellent artist with modest vocal means, coaxes lightly at the music, shows intelligence and subtlety in her phrasing, and achieves all that can be achieved through clever understatement. But since her voice will withstand only the slightest pressure, she cannot really animate the more extroverted passages, and the tone turns fluttery and breathy when she tries. Corena was a most enjoyable big-house Pasquale, and his voice's heft and solidity are apparent here. His singing, though, never a

model of grace, is by this time pretty clumsy, the line barked and simplified, and the characterization is so busy and heavy-handed that its very real accomplishment goes by the wayside. The earlier Urania version represents him better.

Oncina's voice has strengthened in the thirteen years since the Quadri recording. But while he is never less than secure and musicianly, his voice has lost a measure of its beauty and freedom, and his intelligent playing of the part seems less interesting here. Krause's baritone is in fine youthful shape, satisfying to hear. But whenever the music moves (often), he chops and aspirates—runs and triplets are a mess. And he is completely outside the role, burying the music in flurries of literally arbitrary inflectional variations, overdone accents, and guttural fulminations. False life, in other words.

1978 EMI / ANGEL (S)

Beverly Sills (A), Alfredo Kraus (B), Alan Titus (C), Donald Gramm (D), Ambrosian Opera Chorus, London Symphony Orchestra—Sarah Caldwell

This is the American Pop version, with very much the flavor of a high-level American regional performance. It is also the Inverted Generations version—the young lovers give every evidence of a certain maturity, while Pasquale himself shoulders the cares of the thirties generation and Malatesta sounds all of eighteen. This is not an incidental peculiarity, but touches directly on credibility.

Caldwell's view of the score is not dissimilar to Kertész's. Her Prelude is brisk to the point of pushiness; then she settles into an uneventful, lilting approach that has almost no sense of moment, but a strange timidity where anything so vulgar as a climax might be in the offing. Orchestral and choral execution is excellent. The recording philosophy (again as with the Kertész) keeps the proceedings at a chaste distance.

Gramm and Titus purl along casually with their attractive voices, solid techniques, and unruffled musical manners. The former is the first Pasquale I have heard who sounds to be a gentleman of irreproachable taste and some sophistication. He eschews most of the standard *buffo* solutions (which is welcome), but doesn't offer much else beyond an occasional half-spoken "natural" inflection—an approach he shares with the other Americans in the cast. Sills goes far overboard with it, showing that she knows some sort of life is required but not what the sources of it might be. Her voice, though past its prime, is nonetheless pretty, and trips off the florid writing pertly enough. But she has no consistent control of tonal purity and movement in sustained singing or at any dynamic above *mezzo piano*.

Kraus sings an admirable Ernesto. Despite his years of service, his voice remains fresh and clear, the line of his singing firm and finely etched, the voice's reach capable of a beautifully controlled high ending to the serenade. Even he, though, is not truly involving—there is a commitment to singing *per se*, but nothing to disturb the overall feel of a performance that has no real conflict, and in which no one is ever in the slightest emotional danger.

1979 EURODISC (S)

Lucia Popp (A), Francisco Araiza (B), Bernd Weikl (C), Yevgeny Nesterenko (D), Chorus and Orchestra of the Bavarian State Radio—Heinz Wallberg

There is some fine singing on this set, but as with many modern performances, the whole somehow adds up to less than the sum of the parts. Wallberg plays the Prelude rather slowly, almost pedantically, and some interesting detail emerges. But when the singing starts, this proves to be not representative of the complete performance: he presses on through. My Act II notes read, ". . . a 'modern' reading—precise text, but no setting up of moments or shaping of events. No fun, despite efforts at 'liveliness.' " I'll let that stand.

Popp's voice occasionally betrays traces of the slightly garbled, tight sound so often developed by Central and Eastern European sopranos, but on the whole she is in good form, the voice a nice combination of lightness and flexibility with some body and bite. Interpretively, she

loses her way a bit after some intriguing moments in the aria and duet with Malatesta—the important scene with Pasquale in Act III is well sung but rattles on by. Araiza's strong lyric tenor is at its best here, its warmth and loveliness blooming in a congenial role, and the reserve range and power counting at several points, including the same interpolated D-flat eked out by Kraus. His phrasing is smooth and even supple but, like that of other recent singers, will sound square and plain to those who know Schipa or Valletti.

Nesterenko is also in good fettle. His is the most imposing voice recorded in this role; its balance, easy power, orotundity, and generally good line are balm to the *buffo*-wearied ear. He has life and wit, too, though at times he appliqués onto the music stratagems (e.g., a mock-Italian opening of vowels) that do not come naturally. Weikl's fine baritone is another first-rank instrument—one will seldom hear Malatesta's Fs and G-flats given such healthy licks. But they are atolls in a vasty ocean of nonsense: the objections noted with respect to Tom Krause's Malatesta must be repeated here, but with even greater force.

1982 EMI / ANGEL (S,D) CD

Mirella Freni (A), Gösta Winbergh (B), Leo Nucci (C), Sesto Bruscantini (D), Ambrosian Opera Chorus, Philharmonia Orchestra—Riccardo Muti

Muti here makes the best possible case for his kind of "conductor's opera." The Prelude is worrisome: brilliantly played but neither relaxed nor graceful, with the fast sections rammed almost savagely forward; it sets us up for yet another opera-as-military-drill exhibition. Then, however, the combination of this pre-Verdian, romantic-comic score with the presence of veteran star singers who know what they want to do seems to loosen the ferocious-old-man-Toscanini grip, and Muti leads with more accompanimental flexibility than one generally associates with him. With the singers only infrequently pressed and allowed to make most of their points, we are free to appreciate Muti's superior musical understanding, his ability to create a stylistic unity from disparate elements, and his knack for securing from his orchestra playing that is not only exact and beautiful but informed with dramatic intent. His puritanical ban on high notes is still in force and most discouraging—why on earth can't Pasquale end "Un foco insolito" with a nice, fat middle C, or join Malatesta in their duet with exhilarating top Fs?—but on the whole this is an uplifting reading.

Freni is an enjoyable, gratifying Norina. Her seniority is apparent from time to time in an effortful high note, an over-careful run, or a phrase that lacks balance or focus. But the voice's beauty, fullness, and native timbre are much in evidence, and her instinctive grasp of this repertory is now augmented by the survivor's savviness—we almost believe her Sofronia, and that seldom happens. Bruscantini, naturally, is operating here with a voice thinned and frayed by the thirty intervening years since the Rossi performance. Only the low notes have actually departed, though, and Bruscantini is shrewd with the rest. This is now an extremely elaborate interpretation: the entire *buffo* lexicon is recited several times through in its course. Recited by a master born to this manner, however, and (as with Capecchi's rendition) with a genuine sense of the character's predicament informing most of the choices.

Nucci is a vocally splendid Malatesta. His voice moves freely and colorfully at this weight level, and while he does not quite answer the question of who Malatesta is and exactly why he is doing all this, he is interpretively awake, and gives the part some interesting insinuation without losing dignity. Winbergh, regrettably, is lost. The middle of this sweet little voice is pleasing—one can hear it echoing plaintively through some Buxtehude in a North European chapel. But this part is full of top notes and strenuous proclamations; there is no substitute for a voice of appropriate range and resonance.

1983 HUNGAROTON (S,D) CD

Magda Kalmár (A), János Bándi (B), István Gáti (C), József Gregor (D), Hungarian Radio and Television Chorus, Hungarian State Orchestra—Ivan Fischer

This is a likable performance, one in which an affection for the work and an ease of ensemble playing come through despite execution that is only decent. This feeling is reinforced by the sixtyish stereo spread and by a warmth in the sound unusual for the digital process. Fischer conducts with a comfortable swing and with some patience about the proportions. The ensembles go well, and the finales are telling because the preceding tempos are logical and unforced.

The singers work together in a manner that is entirely conventional, but trustingly so, and often with at least a sense of theatrical situation (the dictation of the marriage contract, for instance, is not the usual bag of stock-company tricks). They *try* to set up effects and play moments, even if they don't always succeed. Kalmár has a lyrical, lightly tinted approach to the music and a voice that is relaxed and quite beautiful in the middle, though pinched unattractively at the top. Gregor sings in a light bass that is very pleasing except, again, for the high notes, which are raw and open. He's an engaging performer, though like most in this role pushes too hard at the affects, and is given to the same sort of underlining that afflicts Caldwell's singers—the sort of "expressive" reading one does to children, to make sure they understand.

Gáti's baritone is a nice, soft-textured one, and he gives a sort of lazy-August-day performance with it. After a lethargic "Bella siccome un angelo" and rather doleful Norina scene, he wakes up and sings out a bit. Bándi's is another tenor awash to the gunwales in Ernesto's music. He's fiery in the recitatives, and goes all-out to invest even the most trying phrases with feeling, but his technique is so constricted that the vocal struggle swallows his excellent intentions.

1988 NUOVA ERA (S,P,D) CD

Luciana Serra (A), Aldo Bertolo (B), Alessandro Corbelli (C), Enzo Dara (D), Chorus and Orchestra of the Teatro Regio, Turin—Bruno Campanella

A throwback to Group I, this live Italian performance is refreshing and a sign of life amid the ruins. While the best way to define its qualities is through discussion of conductorial choices, the exciting thing about the recording is that it sounds like the audible portion of a lively, fully played production in which conductor, director, and stage and pit performers have arrived at a way to sing, act, and play *Don Pasquale* with intelligence, sentiment, and an adult sense of humor.

Though his orchestra is less virtuosic than some, Campanella's work eclipses all competition in this piece. That is not because he is more talented or musical than several of the others, but because he is working on the right problem: how to impregnate first this moment with theatrical specificity and suspense, then the next, and then the next. In some operas, this would be only one important aspect of the story; in this one, it is virtually the whole story. The most obvious outcome of this is a nearly continuous succession of decisions about tempo and about rhythmic and dynamic flux that are unusual and surprising, especially to a contemporary ear. These decisions are theatrical, not structural—one type may serve as an example. The accompaniment is studded with interspersions—sometimes simple repeated braces of chords, sometimes little ascending flourishes like the ones before and after Pasquale's "Voi frattanto, signorino" in the "Prender moglie" duet—that are normally played with uninflected emphasis, like exclamation points. Campanella renders many of these with playful *decrescendos*, and the effect is the same as that of a fade-under in radio drama—to lead the ear, with some suspense, into the next line, as opposed to finishing off the previous one. Nearly every page of the score brings something similar, and the feel is unerring.

Of the singers, Bertolo and Corbelli are excellent. The tenor has an essentially light instrument, but it is one that can swell into the upper climaxes satisfyingly without losing its lovely quality, and his sense of phrase shaping and musico-dramatic pointing is the best since Valletti's. An occasionally overly open G and some moments of questionable intonation in "Com'e gentil" (offstage in live performance, after all) are the only worrisome moments in a fine performance. The baritone has a lean, warm voice, firm and in good balance. He sings with line, flexibility, and rhythmic snap, does interesting variations in the aria's cadenza, and brings a relish to the plotting that helps drive the action. Dara seems caught between something truly interesting and a stock *buffo* Pasquale. "Un foco insolito" isn't an auspicious start, with the grace notes omitted and the phrase endings cheated, but later he seems more drawn in, and does some committed work. His light bass-baritone, with its momentary touches of tremolo, has color and substance and is always pleasurable; further, he rises well to the challenge of Campanella's fleet tempos in the patter sections. A drawback for many listeners, unfortunately, will be Serra's Norina. She enters as willingly as the others into the playing of the piece and clearly knows what she is after interpretively, but the voice is hard in quality and not under consistent control; sustained *acuti* are close to screams. There's just enough audience presence here to lend some extra pulse, and the sound is exceptionally well balanced for a live recording.

1990 ERATO (S,D,P) CD

Barbara Hendricks (A), Luca Canonici (B), Gino Quilico (C), Gabriel Bacquier (D), Chorus and Orchestra of the Lyons Opera—Gabriele Ferro

This performance, based on a live production but executed in the studio, is thoroughly professional but of no special interest. Ferro's leadership is comfortable, sensible, fairly lively, reasonably relaxed. His orchestra plays well. Bacquier has more voice and vitality than his years entitle him to, but of course he cannot truly sustain much of a line. He gives a bangy, show-biz sort of performance, hitting those downbeats. It's admirable but rather wearing. Canonici sings a modest, clean Ernesto in a tenor that is of attractive quality without being distinctive. He avoids the extreme top throughout, but phrases musically and manages some nice *diminuendos*. Hendricks's voice is certainly pretty, but has the slackness and covered color of many contemporary sopranos. There's no bite in the tone or spring in the rhythm, no brightness or openness in her Italian. Interpretively, she seems concerned only to sing through the role gently and slowly. Quilico also offers a prevailing loveliness of tone, and little more. His "Bella siccome un angelo" has a certain oiliness that can be taken as apposite, but his performance soon reveals itself as yards of dreamy note-spinning of the late-night, easy-listening variety. If the Norina and Malatesta don't get things cooking, there's really no *Don Pasquale* to be played, and that is pretty much the case here.

———————

The Campanella takes pride of place, perhaps complemented by the Muti. The Quadri is a very respectable second choice, and the Molinari-Pradelli and Rossi performances are also possibilities, depending on one's priorities.

CONRAD L. OSBORNE

ANTONÍN DVOŘÁK

RUSALKA (1901)

A: Rusalka (s); B: Foreign Princess (s); C: Ježibaba (ms);
D: Prince (t); E: Spirit of the Lake (bs)

*D*vořák wrote as many operas as symphonies, and in Czechoslovakia, *Rusalka* is second in popularity only to Smetana's *The Bartered Bride*. Its appeal can be put down to an extraordinarily compelling vein of lyricism, directed by a practiced symphonist for whom the shaping of opera held no terrors.

The music is so passionately felt that the fairy tale emerges with the force of the fiercest human emotions. As contrast for the lovers' story, the composer disposes of the supernatural forebodings of the Water Spirit, the grotesqueries of the witch Ježibaba, the comedy of a pair of palace hangers-on, a ballroom scene, and the Rhine-maiden-like cavortings of three wood nymphs; it is even possible to sense a certain prolixity in the scenes for wood nymphs and the comedy of forester and kitchen boy even in the first Ježibaba scene, in all of which cuts are sometimes made.

Dvořák has no apparent difficulty with the built-in handicap of a heroine who can retain her human shape only at the price of silence in the presence of the hero, and his triumph lies not only in creating an adolescent female figure longing for first love but in conjuring up an atmosphere of gentle erotic expectancy in which that urge seems certain to find fruition.

Musing on *Lohengrin*, Ernest Newman once lamented that Wagner had not continued to write in that vein, and lovers of romantic opera might, with *Rusalka* in mind, feel the same when contemplating the nineteenth century's *Angst*-ridden attempts at improving the form.

1955 SUPRAPHON (M)

Lída Červinková (A), Marie Podvalová (B), Marta Krásová (C), Beno Blachut (D), Eduard Haken (E), Chorus and Orchestra of the Prague National Theater—Jaroslav Krombholc

Krombholc is one of the few under-hyped conductors of the postwar era, a committed Czech musician who spent most of his career conducting in his native Prague. His conducting of *Rusalka* is beyond praise, brilliantly rehearsed so that balance and unanimity are in evidence throughout; taking ample account of the score's romanticism and color; full of fire, so that it is a very brisk *allegro molto* we get before curtain rise with the introduction to the wood nymphs. Throughout, there is high expectancy, built on unerring choice of tempos for each new section.

The cast shows signs of a fallacious belief much in evidence in Prague at the time, that the most senior singers were most likely to deliver the goods. Style in plenty we get from this cast but most of them are past their best; witness a comparison with their earlier records. Červinková's voice was devoid of lyrical charm by this stage of her career, and she makes heavy weather of the top range of the role, while Podvalová's vocal material shows little vestige of the opulence of two decades earlier. Krásová still demonstrates true authority as Ježibaba, and Haken, never steady of voice, is notwithstanding a pillar of strength as the Water Spirit, paradoxically full of humanity in a role distinguished for its constant cries of "Beda!" (Woe!). For many Europeans, this music has become indissolubly associated with his voice and art. A little of the urgent brilliance of Blachut's excellent wartime recordings (*Dalibor*, etc.) still remains, and the singing is full of imaginative touches, yet the voice sounds shallow and too closely geared to the microphone.

Some of the cuts made are indicated in the score, or are concerned with what are effectively repeats (comics in second and third acts, Rusalka in her second-act outburst, Act III's Prelude), but there are also excisions in Ježibaba's Act I spell and in her scene with Rusalka in Act III, which I don't much like.

Krombholc tells you exactly how the music should sound; his cast knows too, but can no longer accurately impart the information.

1961–2 SUPRAPHON (S)

Milada Šubrtová (A), Alena Miková (B), Marie Ovčačiková (C), Ivo Žídek (D), Eduard Haken (E), Chorus and Orchestra of the Prague National Theater—Zdeněk Chalabala

What I have written above applies also to this set—but in reverse. Chalabala died in 1962 and his name was revered when I was first in Prague over twenty-five years ago. But he gives a barnstorming kind of performance of this subtle score, not without excitement, full of half-remembered truths (wood nymphs less precise than Krombholc's but more fun), and in the end short of authority. The orchestra plays well enough, but for Krombholc the same band seemed to be asserting nothing less than its country's continued existence.

Youth and color are in Šubrtová's voice, the top rings out bravely, and she sings the title role fluently, even if she is taxed by the outbursts of the second and third acts which turn a great lyrical role into a kind of junior Tosca for five minutes at a time. Žídek, one of the most powerfully musical tenors of his day, full of zest and power, lacks only vocal glamour to be an

ideal Prince, but Miková as the Foreign Princess sounds at full stretch most of the time with correspondingly raw tone. Ovčačiková is younger of voice than Krásová and makes an impressive Ježibaba, while Eduard Haken, sounding if possible even older than with Krombholc, nonetheless turns in an impeccable Water Spirit.

There are cuts in both scenes for the comic palace servants, in Rusalka's second-act outburst, and two in her third-act scene with Ježibaba; also a variant for the end of her third-act lament.

1982 SUPRAPHON (D) CD

Gabriela Beňačková (A), Drahomira Drobková (B), Věra Soukupová (C), Wieslaw Ochman (D), Richard Novák (E), Prague Philharmonic Chorus and Orchestra—Václav Neumann

It would seem that an effort was made at a definitive set: the Prague Philharmonic, a distinguished elder statesman among Czech conductors, a prime cast for whom no apology need be made, and no cuts. The result is not far off a bull's-eye. I don't find true insight in Neumann, but he nonetheless secures a strong performance from cast and orchestra alike, and, if he makes rather a mouthful of some *rits.*, under him the graceful Act II chorus emerges as one of the highlights of the set. Sound and balance are first-rate.

The cast is fine, with individually fresh voices to make a strong ensemble of wood nymphs, and a decent pair of comics (though casting a soprano rather than a mezzo introduces an acid note I think Dvořák did not intend). Drobková's strong, overbearing singing fits the Foreign Princess all too well and Soukupová, strongest at the top of her voice (surprising for a Bayreuth Erda), has the measure of Ježibaba. There is firm, sound singing from Novák as the Water Spirit, though he lacks the presence and imagination of Haken, and Ochman's athletic singing and slightly Russian timbre of voice is thoroughly satisfactory as the Prince.

The glory of the cast is Beňačková, the voice very warm and even over a wide compass. She is just as impressive flat-out as singing piano, possesses a magnificent top range, and seems to have all the time in the world to phrase the music to perfection. It is hard to imagine the lovely Song to the Moon better sung, the outbursts in second and third acts are mighty fine, and her lament early in Act III is one of the major pleasures of the set: ideal singing of a role which repays just Beňačková's qualities.

———————————

The most recent set is easy to recommend and only an old user of the gramophone con-scious of might-have-beens is left wishing that the Prince and Spirit of the Lake had been coached in the music's nuances by singers of an older generation, and that Krombholc had conducted this recording rather than the trailblazer of more than twenty-five years before. Then might the glorious score have had the definitive performance it deserves.

LORD HAREWOOD

FRIEDRICH VON FLOTOW

MARTHA (1847)

A: Lady Harriet (s); B: Nancy (ms); C: Lionel (t);
D: Plunkett (bs); E: Lord Tristan (bs)

*M*artha, a repertory staple through-out the second half of the nine-teenth century, now strikes most listeners as a faded period piece. When the Met revived the work (in English) during the Bing era, not even Victoria de los Angeles could save it.

The work should not be so lightly dismissed. Flotow's score is masterly, combining Schuber-tian lyricism for the more serious scenes with—in the lighter episodes—an Italianate verve wor-thy of Donizetti. The most famous numbers, and the only ones that have been recorded separately with any regularity, are both solos—Lionel's "Ach, so fromm" and Lady Harriet's "Letze Rose" (the latter, of course, is not an original melody, but Flotow's adaptation of an "Irisches Volkslied"). But the true strength of the score lies in its many duets and other ensembles, all of which not only are beautifully crafted but invariably advance the plot.

Only one of the recordings discussed here—the 1977 Eurodisc (now BMG), conducted by Heinz Wallberg—is truly complete. The others observe traditional stage cuts, consisting mostly of repeats, developmental sections, and the ensemble *strettos*. For example, in Act I, Scene 2 (the Fair scene) the opening chorus loses its middle section and its repeats; later on in the same episode, the busy ensemble based on the "Ich kann stricken" business is tightened up by the omission of its intriguing quasi-fugal sec-tions. Since the opera is neither long nor lack-ing in variety, and the omitted passages add up to no more than three or four minutes' worth of music, there seems to be no justification for any significant cutting.

c.1952 CETRA (In Italian) (M)

Elena Rizzieri (A), Pia Tassinari (B), Ferruccio Tagliavini (C), Carlo Tagliabue (D), Bruno Carmassi (E), Cetra Chorus, Italian Radio Symphony Orchestra, Turin—Francesco Mol-inari-Pradelli

This performance is sung in Italian, which renders it non-competitive, to a degree, with the German-language versions. Like most of the recordings in the Cetra / Everest series, it preserves a concert performance prepared spe-cifically for radio broadcast. *Martha* has a long and honorable performance history in Italian, but only an Italian chauvinist could prefer this set to the two stereo recordings discussed below.

The title role is seriously undercast. Rizzieri is a decent, uninteresting Italian lyric soprano, acidulous in timbre and charmless in manner.

The husband-and-wife team of Tagliavini and Tassinari brings a good deal of vocal individu-ality to Lionel and Nancy. The tenor seems to be doing a Gigli imitation at times, with much use of a heavily damped, crooning *mezza voce*, and a certain amount of sobbing in Acts III and IV. His instrument is basically an attractive one, though, and when the mannerisms do not intrude, his singing is secure and passionate. Tassinari had one of those ambiguous voices that is arguably either soprano or mezzo. Her

Nancy is least effective in Act I, Scene 1, where she negotiates the florid writing of the duet with Lady Harriet and the subsequent trio with Tristan rather cautiously. She improves in the later episodes, in which—despite some edgy moments—her large, handsome voice fills out the music well enough, and her delivery brings out the character's earthy humor in a way that none of her recorded rivals quite matches.

Tagliabue, a powerful Verdi baritone caught past his best years, does not sound comfortable in Plunkett's bass tessitura. In addition, his aggressive interpretation lacks humor: Plunkett may indeed be angry with Nancy at the beginning of Act III, but Tagliabue sounds as though he's ready to murder her.

Molinari-Pradelli, typically lenient toward his soloists, leads the performance with the right kind of spirit. The orchestra and chorus go about their business with vigor, if not always the ultimate in polish. Unfortunately, Everest's rechanneled sound—judged by a cassette made from a worn set of LPs—is unpleasant to listen to: approximately a semitone sharp throughout, and frequently distorted in loud passages.

1968 EMI / ANGEL (S) CD

Anneliese Rothenberger (A), Brigitte Fassbaender (B), Nicolai Gedda (C), Hermann Prey (D), Dieter Weller (E), Chorus and Orchestra of the Bavarian State Opera, Munich—Robert Heger

This, the first stereo recording of *Martha*, was well worth waiting for, and is still the most satisfactory complete version. Veteran conductor Heger not only understands this music thoroughly but obviously loves it: his warm, affectionate, carefully proportioned reading is close to ideal. There is excellent orchestral and choral work.

The cast, too, could hardly be improved upon. Rothenberger, so often typecast in soubrette roles, is a Lady Harriet to cherish. Her round, creamy lyric soprano, lovely to listen to in the arias and ensembles, meets the coloratura challenges with brilliance and assurance. Best of all, she sounds totally involved with the character. She has an ideal partner in Fassbaender's Nancy, which combines rich, rock-solid,

contraltoish tone with lively, pointed delivery.

Gedda is reliable rather than exciting. His voice does not have the round, beautiful quality that one longs to hear in Lionel's music, and his upper register can sound a bit cautious, but he sings with taste and imagination. Prey is altogether extraordinary: his warm lyric baritone encompasses the low notes with no trouble at all, and the characterization is vivid.

The original LP set has the opera on five sides, with the sixth devoted to a mini-recital by Rothenberger. This bonus material has been dropped from the mid-priced CD reissue, which includes the libretto in German only. By way of partial compensation, though, the digitally remastered sound of the CDs is absolutely superb.

1977 EURODISC (S) CD

Lucia Popp (A), Doris Soffel (B), Siegfried Jerusalem (C), Karl Ridderbusch (D), Siegmund Nimsgern (E), Chorus of the Bavarian Radio, Munich Radio Orchestra—Heinz Wallberg

Eurodisc's cast, though enjoyable, is not on quite the same level as EMI's. Popp, a wonderful artist, produces enough squeezed, pinched tones to prevent her Lady Harriet from matching Rothenberger's accomplishment in purely vocal terms. Soffel, though a good, solid lightweight mezzo, is less striking than Fassbaender in the role of Nancy. Jerusalem is conscientious and musical, makes a pleasant sound, and actually sings more smoothly and sweetly than Gedda much of the time, but it is Gedda who delivers the more memorable performance, on the whole.

Ridderbusch, however, sings at least as well as Prey, and seizes Plunkett's opportunities with equal relish: impossible to choose between them. Nimsgern is also luxurious casting as Tristan, and easily faces down his recorded competition.

Wallberg conducts with a lighter touch and a livelier range of tempos than Heger, stressing the score's Italianate qualities. He has the advantages of an uncut text, an excellent chorus, and extremely sharp orchestral execution. The sound is very clear and detailed.

Eurodisc's CD reissue—like EMI's, digitally remastered and offered at mid-price, on two discs—at least includes an English translation of the libretto, as well as the original German.

––––––––––

If I had to pick only one recording of the opera to live with, it would have to be the EMI set, because of its all-round excellence; the Eurodisc is a viable alternative, however, and may be the first choice of collectors who are attracted to Popp, the uncut score, the best recorded sound, or all three.

ROLAND GRAEME

Unavailable for review:
1944 ACANTA

PORGY AND BESS (1935)

A: Bess (s); B: Serena (s); C: Clara (s); D: Maria (c); E: Sporting Life (t);
F: Porgy (bs-bar); G: Jake (bar); H: Crown (bar)

In its relatively brief life, *Porgy and Bess* has accumulated a surprisingly knotty textual history. Its piano-vocal score, prepared prior to rehearsals in 1935, does not reflect the large and small cuts made under the composer's supervision to tighten the action and reduce running time. Still, with or without cuts, *Porgy* was at this point undeniably a through-composed opera in three acts. In a revival shortly after Gershwin's death it was essentially turned into a musical through rewriting and rescoring. The hugely popular two-act version that toured during the 1950s and 1960s continued to misrepresent *Porgy*'s genre and format, although more music was restored, often as dialogue underscoring. The London and RCA recordings took a new step by presenting the whole published score. With this text now established at Glyndebourne and the Met and for recordings, perhaps we have come full circle and it is time to reconsider the desirability of at least some of the composer's own cuts. There were important partial recordings. The 1942 revival preserved the interpretations of the original stars, Todd Duncan and Anne Brown. In 1963, RCA made a single disc of extended scenes with Leontyne Price and William Warfield, from the 1950s production.

1951 CBS / SONY (M)

Camilla Williams (A), Inez Matthews (B), June McMechen (C), Helen Dowdy (D), Avon Long (E), Lawrence Winters (F), Eddie Matthews (G), Warren Coleman (H), J. Rosamond Johnson Chorus, unidentified orchestra—Lehman Engel

At a time when a streamlined rewritten *Porgy* was sweeping the world, CBS took the brave and valuable step of returning to the original score. Cuts correspond in many though not all cases to those made in the original production (the larger ones include the Jasbo Brown piano music, Maria's spoken aria, "I ain't got no shame," and the prayer sextet; the Buzzard Song, omitted in 1935, is included here). Lehman Engel, an experienced theater conductor, leads a lively, dramatically involved performance that survives even the crude rechanneling of the last Odyssey reissue.

Preeminent among the cast is the Porgy of Lawrence Winters; his soaring baritone (most Porgys are bass-baritones) provides many thrilling moments, and he presents an unaffectedly personable character, the most complete and human on any of these recordings. His Bess, Camilla Williams, is less satisfying: intense, but inconsistent and a bit edgy, and without much expressive variety. Serena and Clara both contribute effective, rather muted performances, the former a fluttery lyric soprano unlike more recent Serenas, the latter capable but not quite magical. Sporting Life is in the hands of Avon Long, exactly the sort of tenorish vaudeville comedian for whom the role was written; with only a thread of voice and a surprisingly faithful rendition of the music, Long creates a fascinatingly insinuating character.

Survivors from the original cast include Crown, Jake, Frazier (who is also choral director), Nelson / Crab Man, and Lily / Strawberry Woman. Of these the last-named, the spirited Helen Dowdy, adding Maria to her original doubling, sounds relatively unaffected by the passing of sixteen years. The others have suffered some vocal erosion, though only with Warren Coleman's Crown, who resorts to speaking wherever he can, does this matter seriously. In general the casting enlists a greater variety of voice types (including untrained or popular-style voices) than we generally hear today, and the chorus stresses personal involvement over smooth blend. Though it's impossible not to miss some of the omitted music, this set still has something distinctive to offer.

1975 DECCA / LONDON (S) CD

Leona Mitchell (A), Florence Quivar (B), Barbara Hendricks (C), Barbara Conrad (D), François Clemmons (E), Willard White (F), Arthur Thompson (G), McHenry Boatwright (H), Cleveland Chorus, Children's Chorus, and Orchestra—Lorin Maazel

This production provided the first chance since the pre-rehearsal run-through of 1935 to hear every note of the published score. With some of the cast new to their roles, and some of the score new to everyone, it is hardly surprising that the performance sounds polite, even cautious at times (the effect compounded by the Cleveland Orchestra's excessive size and lushness). Lorin Maazel does not emphasize the popular stylistic elements, but he does not seem seriously out of touch with them either—except at rare moments when he intervenes and adds a gratuitous effect like the *rallentando* imposed on the end of Act II, Scene 1.

The cast, mostly new to records at the time, is an exceptionally talented group. The one holdover from a previous recording, McHenry Boatwright, is the least persuasive, sounding stiffer and less accurate than on the Price disc.

Willard White, more bass than baritone in timbre, succeeds remarkably well at freeing his performance from recording-studio constraint and bringing Porgy to life; his two solos in the last scene are especially moving. Leona Mitchell is somewhat less satisfactory—tonally attractive but impersonal in projection and pulling back from her high notes.

Two others make superlative contributions. Barbara Hendricks's glistening lyric soprano fits "Summertime" like a glove and gives it one of its most melting renditions ever. François Clemmons, clearly both a thoughtful musician and an assured actor, ingeniously reconciles his lyric tenor with Sporting Life's jazz-flavored music.

Florence Quivar fields a powerful mezzo as Serena, not intelligible enough in the higher phrases of "My man's gone now" but startlingly earthy and compelling in her prayer for Bess's healing. Arthur Thompson is a robust Jake, and Barbara Conrad a deliciously feisty Maria, who makes the most of her restored solo (she's a lovely Strawberry Woman, too).

The chorus, Cleveland's regular group, sounds attractive in a generalized way, occasionally too staid and oratorio-like. The prayer sextet, cast with singers of secondary roles, is a stunning success, staying in perfect synchronization while maintaining the improvisational feeling and fervent mood.

1976 RCA / BMG (S) CD

Clamma Dale (A), Wilma Shakesnider (B), Betty Lane (C), Carol Brice (D), Larry Marshall (E), Donnie Ray Albert (F), Alexander B. Smalls (G), Andrew Smith (H), Ensemble and Orchestra of the Houston Grand Opera—John DeMain

Recordings based on stage performances do not always provide the extra vitality that one hopes for, but this one (made during a successful Broadway run, and restoring its minor cuts) definitely does. Musically extremely sharp and confident, it also bursts with life. The assured characterfulness of the many small roles shows the advantage of the cast's shared stage work, with tricky scenes like the crap game playing effortlessly. John DeMain deserves enormous credit for this achievement: time and again a passage that has sounded stilted or ineffective in other recordings reveals its point here.

The cast is a strong one, with a phenomenal Bess in Clamma Dale, who with perfect balance between word and tone creates a characterization that makes Bess understandable in her vulnerability. The other stellar soloist in the cast is Carol Brice, who by force of voice (almost tenor in range by this time) and presence turns Maria into a pivotal character.

The others, good vocalists all, also have a sure sense of the dramatic possibilities and create a well-rounded and believable community. Some of Larry Marshall's musical liberties as Sporting Life might be questioned, but he is an expert showman and makes the character live. Clara sings her lullaby very prettily indeed; Serena puts her difficult role across both vocally and dramatically; Porgy commands the stage easily, especially memorable for the easy swing with which he sails through "I got plenty o' nuttin' "; Crown's vocal power makes him a potent presence despite momentary hints of formality in his demeanor; and Jake delivers "A woman is a sometime thing" with such offhand humor that one believes totally that he's making this up as he goes along. Chorus and orchestra are first-rate in every respect, and Dick Hyman, brought in especially for the Jasbo Brown piano music, is hard to beat. So is the whole recording.

1988 EMI / ANGEL (S) CD

Cynthia Haymon (A), Cynthia Clarey (B), Harolyn Blackwell (C), Marietta Simpson (D), Damon Evans (E), Willard White (F), Bruce Hubbard (G), Gregg Baker (H), Glyndebourne Chorus, London Philharmonic Orchestra—Simon Rattle

Recorded after a two-year run at Glyndebourne, this recording makes an appealing initial impression as one samples favorite excerpts, for the cast provides exceptional vocal allure, the orchestra sounds glorious, and Simon Rattle accompanies these set pieces lovingly if linger-ingly. Heard in continuity, the performance presents some thought-provoking problems, related to the impression that the performance is dictated in every detail by the conductor. Simon Rattle seems to think that *Porgy* needs special help: quite apart from his added orchestral effects, he insists on extremes. His fast tempos are the fastest ever (the prelude opens at breakneck speed, then accelerates into a ludicrously rushed piano blues), his slow tempos the slowest, his louds the loudest, and his cast must accommodate him. Whereas most *Porgys* offer the refreshing operatic experience of a stageful of singers who feel the idiom as their own and know how to create magic with it (just so, one feels, must Italian opera have been "owned" by its performers when new), this one subjugates the singers' prerogatives to the conductor's, and thereby drains away much of *Porgy*'s life.

This is a special pity, as the cast is in many ways the most consistently satisfying of all. Willard White repeats his Porgy from the Maazel set, just as vocally impressive as before and even more involved dramatically. As Bess, Cynthia Haymon impresses more in high-lying phrases than in her relatively pallid middle range, but she presents a touching characterization and copes ably with those very slow speeds.

Harolyn Blackwell is yet another in the seemingly inexhaustible line of gorgeous-sounding Claras, and Cynthia Clarey's top-to-bottom authority makes her a most imposing Serena. Damon Evans is more problematic: a sturdy voice, but a coarse manner that bespeaks the singer's self-indulgence rather than the character's. The other two male leading roles are in near-ideal hands, with both Gregg Baker and Bruce Hubbard not only singing beautifully and excitingly but projecting that indefinable star quality that makes one listen to their every utterance. There are no real weaknesses among the other roles or in the chorus; it's a shame that Rattle's iron control makes this matter so little.

_____

All four recordings boast memorable casts, with their strengths evenly distributed: CBS has the best Porgy, London the best Clara and Sporting Life, RCA the best Bess and Maria, Angel the best Jake and Crown, with honors even among the Serenas, but the differences are generally small and the overall quality very high. If only one set is to be chosen, it must be RCA for its musical insight and unforced live quality.

JON ALAN CONRAD

Alberto Ginastera

Bomarzo (1967)

A: Julia (s); B: Pantasilea (ms); C: Diana (c);
D: Pier Francesco Orsini (t); E: Silvio (b)

Ginastera's operas stirred things up for a few seasons in the 1960s. The first, *Don Rodrigo*, was chosen for the New York City Opera's premiere at the State Theater. Well produced and performed, it had a certain success and even subsequent revival. It wasn't recorded, however. *Bomarzo* was then commissioned by the Washington Opera Society and first performed there, though its production team and cast were from the New York City Opera, and subsequent performances took place there. The operatic Ginastera had the talent and skills of a grand romantic entertainer, unfortunately squeezed into the head of a mid-twentieth-century musical intellectual. He saddled himself with a Bergian method that has not demonstrated a broad dramatic applicability, and a harmonic language that seems always to lead to vocal writing of a parched quality; the musical meat has been pulled away from the dramatic bone, though why it also need be so rhythmically dogged is unclear. Yet intermixed with this there is Ginastera the orchestral colorist, something of a sensualist and unabashed titillator, evoking horror-show and soft-porn thrills with a palette that runs from Berlioz and Liszt to Ravel and Respighi. The effect of this is that each time we start to have some fun (principally in the introductions, interludes, and dances), along comes the singing to ruin it. The libretto of Manuel Mujica Láinez evinces a similar duality: it shows a shrewd, even sensationalist, eye for the theatrical possibilities of the story of the hunchback Orsini, with his garden of stone monsters and his mystical quest for immortality, but the insights are the sort that first-generation Freudians passed back at the first turn, and the dramatization tends toward the schematic. Still, most of these scenes register their main events, and the atmosphere of the piece cannot be denied.

1967 CBS / SONY (S)

Isabel Penagos (A), Joanna Simon (B), Claramae Turner (C), Salvador Novoa (D), Richard Torigi (E), Chorus and Orchestra of the Opera Society of Washington—Julius Rudel

The recording is in most respects an admirable one. The orchestra is fine, and the chorus is vocally and musically decent, though a few more voices wouldn't have hurt. The supporting roles are taken either by City Opera veterans (Torigi and Turner—both important members of the company in the fifties and sixties) or then-young singers who have since made substantial careers (Michael Devlin, Brent Ellis). They are all solid performers, and all scantily recorded, so it's good to have them here. In the lengthy, angular title role, the Mexican tenor Novoa does serious, committed work. His voice is clear, attractive, and strong most of the time. He shows good dynamic control, and even a fairly sophisticated command of the idiom. His tone thins out on the highest notes, and he is sometimes afflicted with a waver on sustained phrases around the top of the staff, but given the nature of the writing, one must be grateful that he copes so well. Isabel Penagos, the Julia, brings a beautiful, well-centered, and full lyric soprano to the role, and is musically and temperamentally alert. She and Novoa, simply by virtue of their linguistic nativity, are able to make the music simulate a natural line more closely than their American colleagues. As the courtesan Pantasilea, Joanna Simon is vocally and musically secure enough, though her upper voice hasn't quite the freedom to float her lines with the delicacy and voluptuousness wanted. The recording job is excellent, balanced and musical, with plenty of brightness and clarity.

CONRAD L. OSBORNE

UMBERTO GIORDANO

ANDREA CHÉNIER (1896)

A: Maddalena (s); B: Chénier (t); C: Gérard (bar)

Ever since its premiere at La Scala in 1896, *Andrea Chénier*, Giordano's only opera to have gained even a small foothold in the international repertory, has owed its popularity to tenors attracted by a title role that maximizes rapt ardor and heroic posturing. And it has been surely at their insistence that the opera has been so well represented on recordings. Yet *Chénier*, for all its kitsch spectacle of the French Revolution, happens to be among the most ambitious and expansive of early *verismo* operas. Its melodramatic love triangle—between the anti-poet Chénier, the aristocratic Maddalena, and the servant-turned-revolutionary leader Gérard, who attempts to use his power to force himself on Maddalena—anticipates *Tosca*, written four years later. But if Giordano's characters are less finely etched than Puccini's and his sentimentality quotient higher, he compensates with his larger portrait of the Revolution itself through a variety of telling smaller roles that prove excellent opportunities for character studies as well as grand crowd scenes. Indeed, the real quality of *Chénier* lies more in the sheer richness and theatricality of its setting, from the aristocratic ballrooms to the mean streets of the Bastille to the revolutionary tribunals. And ultimately the responsibility for *Chénier* to succeed on disc lies less in the title role than in the conductor, who must capture that sense of milieu and bring to life the fervor of the crowd scenes as well as tempting star tenors from vulgarity.

1931 EMI / ANGEL (M)

Lina Bruna Rasa (A), Luigi Marini (B), Carlo Galeffi (C), La Scala Chorus and Orchestra— Lorenzo Molajoli

A lot of bad habits had set in at La Scala by 1930, and so had routine, at least as far as casting is concerned; if this performance is to be taken as a typical *Andrea Chénier* of the company at the time. The principal singers are not only lacking in much vocal distinction but have a way of calling unwanted attention to themselves through their pronounced and increasingly predictable tendency to exaggerate emotion whenever possible. Luigi Marini is an excitable Chénier, whose nasal tenor becomes pinched by the high notes he seems to relish. Lina Bruna Rasa's strident, colorless Maddalena boasts only unhesitating ferocity in her favor. Carlo Galeffi is an overwrought, near-comical Gérard. Of the small parts, Salvatore Baccaloni, as an affable Mathieu, the bungling Revolutionary, alone stands out. Yet this performance as much as any proves that *Chénier* relies more on conveying a sense of theatricality than it does on riveting characterization. And the star of the effort is ultimately Molajoli, who—leading a fleet, poetic, and eminently sensible reading that rings true dramatically at all points—enforces a precision from orchestra and chorus that calls to mind the influence Toscanini asserted on the company at the time. Molajoli resists Giordano's tendency to sentimentalize and maintains a tight reign on his singers, usually managing to keep them in relative check until they sloppily explode at climax time. The recorded sound is quite decent for the period, although one is sorry not to have more detail from the orchestra, since what does come through there is splendid.

1941 EMI / ANGEL (M) CD

Maria Caniglia (A), Beniamino Gigli (B), Gino Bechi (C), La Scala Chorus and Orchestra— Oliviero de Fabritiis

Perhaps La Scala couldn't mount a very impressive *Chénier* cast for its 1930 recording, but things certainly had changed eleven years later. Thanks to Gigli, this is the most characterful Chénier on disc. One may miss some of the youthful glamour of Gigli's earlier recording of Chénier's opening Improvviso, "Un dì all'azzuro spazio," and the tenor's occasionally crude sobs can be tiresome. But the combination of his lyrical gift and a ringing heroic sound that he almost seems to pull out of a hat is just right for a character who must mouth massive platitudes and sound as if he means them. But ultimately Gigli may be just a little bit too good a singer for a character who never really develops beyond his ardent single dimension, and who consequently steals attention from the more interesting Gérard. Bechi, however, is a superb Gérard, balancing pent-up anger, power, and his passionate love for Maddalena with moving elegance. Caniglia is a girlish and believable Maddalena. And many of the smaller parts are lovingly cast here as well, often with young singers who would later become stars. Giulietta Simionato is an unusually robust-sounding Countess, Maddalena's mother; Giuseppe Taddei offers a suave Fléville and Fouquier-Tinville; Italo Tajo is a potent Roucher. Moreover, the whole performance seems to glow under Fabritiis, who approaches the opera with a Wagnerian scope and who offers deeply felt support to the singers. The Scala forces play lyrically, if not with the captivating precision they did under Molajoli. The sound, appropriately, flatters the voices.

1953 CETRA (M)

Renata Tebaldi (A), Jose Soler (B), Ugo Savarese (C), RAI Chorus and Symphony Orchestra, Turin—Arturo Basile

The attraction of this set is likely to be the young Tebaldi, and she does stand out, especially in contrast to the other provincial-sounding singers. The intensity and spectacular vocal control of her sentimental aria, "La mamma morta," is certainly finer than any of the singing in her later studio recordings. But little dramatic chemistry is possible when the Gérard of Savarese is revealed in a scooping and tremulous baritone, while Soler offers little of vocal merit in his competent but hardly stirring account of the title role. The smaller parts stand out not at all. And yet this is a performance with at least a modicum of vitality, sounding as if it has come from performers well used to performing onstage, and the whole, remarkably, seems more satisfying than any of its individual parts. Part of that comes from the absolute naturalness and lack of pretension found in Basile's conducting. But even that is undercut by the recorded sound that, at least on the Everest reissue, is hollow, constricted, and full of echoes.

1954 MET (M,P) CD

Zinka Milanov (A), Mario del Monaco (B), Leonard Warren (C), Metropolitan Opera Chorus and Orchestra—Fausto Cleva

This set is of historic value for collectors, since it captures two ideal interpreters for their roles: Milanov's fiery Maddalena and Warren's majestic Gérard. But its value lies also in the fact that this is a live performance. While not resistant to the studio, *Chénier* thrives less on note-perfect refinement than it does on bustling stage theatricality, on playing the raw individual passions against raucous crowd scenes, and this performance has an urgency that seems contagious. Being live, the performance is far from flawless, but even that works to its advantage. Warren starts out uninspired, but by his great monologue "Nemico della patria?" in which Gérard balances his burning love and social conscience, he has developed a Boris-like majesty and complexity that is all the more impressive for the degree to which he has risen. Milanov, a heroic Maddalena from the start, simply becomes more and more riveting as she goes along. Del Monaco is not an inspired Chénier, but he has plenty of ardor and all the ringing tone needed to create raw excitement. Much of the credit for the performance, however, goes to Cleva's conducting. More perhaps than any other conductor who has recorded *Chénier*, Cleva is able to convey the pictorial nature of Giordano's score. His aristocratic dance numbers have more grace than anyone else's, his tribunal scene, more of that scary interplay of pomp and meanness. He weights a chord and captures a rhythm just right. Best of all, he both accompanies and leads, allowing singers plenty of freedom and supplying character to all his baton touches. Small roles are surprisingly good for a live production, especially a young Rosalind Elias's spunky Bersa and Salvatore Baccaloni's resonant Mathieu. The sound is barely acceptable for its broadcast vintage.

1957 DECCA / LONDON (S) CD

Renata Tebaldi (A), Mario del Monaco (B), Ettore Bastianini (C), Chorus and Orchestra of the Accademia di Santa Cecilia, Rome—Gianandrea Gavazzeni

One only needs to compare del Monaco's contrived performance here with his dynamic one three years earlier on the Met stage to get a notion of the difference between a white-hot live performance and the kind of coolly calculated studio effort this recording represents. In fact, self-conscious calculation seems to be the controlling feature here, where every climax and every melodramatic sob sounds prepackaged. And the result, ironically, is a kind of polished sentimentality that seems less dramatically acceptable than outright vulgarity would be. The extravagant poetic outbursts of Chénier's "Un dì all'azzurro spazio," for instance, become downright crude when del Monaco delivers them with so little sense of spontaneity. And throughout, del Monaco seems concerned

mostly with just such attention-getting clarion calls. Tebaldi, too, is far less convincing here than she was under the theatrical if less classy surroundings of her Turin account on Cetra four years earlier—one can almost hear her gearing up for each sob in "La mamma morta," as if she had rehearsed her dramatic outburst to Gérard's advances many times over, instead of being taken by surprise. Even Bastianini's smooth phrases, as nicely sung as they are, are far too tame, too little threatening or tormented. This extreme studio approach is heard in all aspects of the production, such as Maria Teresa Mandalari's lackluster and unsteady Countess. In fact, the only real vocal highlights are found in Fiorenza Cossotto's feisty Bersa and Fernando Corena's mellifluous Mathieu. Clearly subservient to the singers, Gavazzeni functions mainly as a traffic cop, keeping the big vocal egos from colliding with each other; the orchestra is recessed, but what one does hear of it is mostly sloppy, as is the careless chorus. Any sense of atmosphere is entirely lacking.

1963 EMI / ANGEL (S) CD

Antonietta Stella (A), Franco Corelli (B), Mario Sereni (C), Rome Opera Chorus and Orchestra—Gabriele Santini

Chénier may not be the most dramatically interesting character in the opera, but his irrepressible ardor in the face of tragedy has a certain appeal, and no one is quite so irrepressible as Corelli. It always sounds a real strain when Corelli attempts a *piano* or even a *mezzo piano* dynamic, which here is seldom. In fact, he commits nearly every musical sin a singer could in this performance. He constantly attempts to outsing his rivals, which is how he seems to view the rest of the cast. He ignores dynamics; his rhythm can be his own; intonation is never as important to him as nice, slurpy swoop or a big fat sob. And yet there is nothing quite like this as a portrayal of the romantic notion of the heroic, self-obsessed poet. The other characters, however, are entirely subsumed by Corelli. Stella is reduced to unladylike forcing and fluttery tones in her attempt to match the tenor, although she gets a dubious revenge when her own failing intonation is usually enough to pull Corelli's intonation down with it. Their duets can sway in pitch like a ship in a storm. Sereni's Gérard is surprisingly intelligent and elegant under the circumstances, but unfortunately, there is little room for intelligence or elegance here, and he mostly sounds overwhelmed. Santini's conducting is never firm enough to keep Corelli in check or to assist anyone else; the singers are on their own.

1976 RCA / BMG (S) CD

Renata Scotto (A), Plácido Domingo (B), Sherrill Milnes (C), John Alldis Choir, National Philharmonic Orchestra of London—James Levine

Typical of all Italian opera recordings made in London studios each summer during the seventies by Domingo, Milnes, and Scotto, this performance has a slight cookie-cutter quality to it, all of the principals singing their roles with their familiar all-purpose dramatic interpretations. Yet with Levine as the driving force behind the performance, this often works to an advantage. Levine's conducting may lack some of the theatrical finesse or the subtlety of Cleva, but it captures the grand sweep of the Revolutionary drama more forcefully than any on records. It helps, of course, that he has the advantage of a better orchestra and modern recording techniques to convey the scope of the score. But Levine also boasts an irresistible youthful energy that seems to carry everything along with it. Domingo sounds familiarly Domingoian, bringing his usual hefty vigor, intelligence, and musical care to the role. Milnes is a properly mellifluous and somewhat gruff Gérard. Scotto is not in her prime, but she uses her voice with dramatic flair. The smaller parts are important and they are particularly well done here, especially the luminous Bersi from the young Maria Ewing and a really creepy L'Incredibile, the spy, by Michel Sénéchal.

1982 DECCA / LONDON (S,D) CD

Montserrat Caballé (A), Luciano Pavarotti (B), Leo Nucci (C), London Opera Chorus, National Philharmonia Orchestra—Riccardo Chailly

As it had in 1957, London once again assembled an all-star *Chénier* that is more an exercise in celebrity vocalizing than in musical drama. But a quarter-century later the emphasis had changed from the crude sensationalism of del Monaco and company to a celebration of tonal beauty. And this time the producers succeeded in achieving the most all-around beautifully sung *Chénier* on disc. What they are singing, though, seems to matter less than producing string after string of gorgeously polished and phrased utterances. Still, Pavarotti happily radiates such vocal health, and sings so accurately, that there is a certain élan to the interpretation. Floating her exquisite *pianissimos* every chance she gets, Caballé can hardly help but be an attractive Maddalena. Nucci makes little dramatic impact, but he produces lovingly rounded phrases. More characterful are the elaborately cast walk-on appearances by Christa Ludwig as the tearful old woman, Madelon, and Hugues Cuénod as Fléville. And there is the curiosity of Astrid Varnay, at seventy-four, returning to sing the Countess de Coigny with striking personality. Like the 1957 effort, this too is a rudderless performance, Chailly underscoring everything with rhythmically flabby, impressionistic conducting that emphasizes lushness over propulsion. And, fittingly, this is also the most beautifully recorded *Chénier*.

1987 CBS / SONY (S,D) CD

Eva Marton (A), José Carreras (B), Giorgio Zancanaro (C), Hungarian State Chorus and Orchestra—Giuseppe Patanè

Of the modern *Chénier* recordings, this is the most urgently dramatic. Carreras lacks the interpretive authority of Domingo or the vocal luster of Pavarotti, and he often sounds as if he is trying too hard to compete with their vocal power, causing him to seem an almost too eager Chénier. Since eagerness is perhaps the leading element in Chénier's character, this might have made him more believable than either Domingo or Pavarotti were it not for the presence of Marton. An aggressive and loudly impressive Maddalena, she simply overwhelms Carreras and nearly everyone else in the cast almost as much as Corelli did in his recording. Zancanaro, something of an understated Gérard with little that is personal in his interpretation, is no competition at all. All of which makes this the most curious recording of any, except perhaps a pirate Callas version—where Maddalena seems to be the dominating character. It doesn't particularly work; Marton is no Callas, but she does produce some vocal electricity in her big moments, especially as she keeps raising the ante with Carreras in their grand final duet, "Vicino a te." But even Marton is in some ways undercut by the Bersi of Klara Takács, who brings a surprising theatricality and fire to the small role of Maddelena's maid, standing out with every note she utters. Patanè seems to encourage the sheer wildness of the proceedings, leading the Hungarians in a performance that is inspiring in its verve and unpredictability. But he also lets it get out of hand, either sinking into slushy sentimentality or weirdly cutting off a climax here and there, just often enough to keep the performance from really taking off, despite all the raw energy of the Hungarian company.

———————

Less a tenor's opera than most tenors would have us believe, the most successful *Chénier* recordings have proven to be those with a broader sense of the drama as a whole and those that emphasize theatricality above interpretive niceties. Consequently, the 1954 Met performance, which doesn't have a particularly attractive Chénier, is the most exhilarating performance all around because it is so vivid (and because the other singers are also so fine). Likewise, Levine's 1976 account satisfies because of its strong conducting and dramatic scope, despite somewhat ordinary singing. As for Chénier, none matches Gigli for expressivity, Corelli for bluster, or Pavarotti for vocal splendor.

MARK SWED

Unavailable for review:
1920 EMI / ANGEL
1951 URANIA

Mikhail Glinka

Ruslan and Ludmila (1842)

A: Ludmila (s); B: Gorislava (s); C: Naina (ms); D: Ratmir (c);
E: Finn (t); F: Bayan (t); G: Ruslan (bs); H: Farlaf (bs)

Ruslan is a rich, exhilarating opera, one of a number from the Russian repertory that we in the West are much the poorer for not knowing better. The Pushkin-derived libretto is ambitious and complex, a legendary epic of Old Russia wherein lovers embark on their quest for one another against forces of enchantment that separate them, confuse their desires, or confound them with inappropriate suitors. The score lays itself out in a sprawling structure that reflects an infinite appetite for—or at least patience with—narration, description, prophecy, and ritual celebration. It is a fascinating combination of native usages (traditional Russian wedding choruses, romances, Oriental dances) with contemporaneous Western models (Italian double arias, pure French ballet). The forms are always fully elaborated, complete with introductions and perorations and, usually, repeats; this is not a piece for those short on attention span. But the writing has a remarkable melodic fecundity and rhythmic vitality, an orchestral texture that is particularly intriguing in the scoring for woodwinds and the numerous and extended solo *obbligato* passages. The virtuosic vocal setting shows a shrewd awareness of color and technical balance, and thus brings out the best in important voices of the romantic types.

1938 MELODIYA (M)

Valeria Barsova (A), Elena Slivinskaya (B), Ludmila Stavrovskaya (C), Elisaveta Antonova (D), Nikander Khanayev (E), Solomon Khromchenko (F), Mark Reizen (G), Vassily Lubenchov (H), Bolshoi Theater Chorus and Orchestra—Samuel Samosud

Two problems will disqualify this set for some listeners: engineering and cuts. The basic sound is thinner and more congested than that of most Western efforts of the same period, and there is enough distortion to seriously mar a few passages. Anyone familiar with the older Soviet recordings will have heard worse, but by Western standards this is roughly equivalent to an unreconstructed thirties broadcast pirate. The excisions are copious—structurally devastating in the finale, spirit-dampening in some fine solo and ensemble developments. On the other hand, the extensive instrumental dances and marches are note-complete, with all repeats. Odd priorities, and in this performance, what's missing truly matters because these people can flat out sing. Indeed, three of them are incomparable. Reizen is stupendous. His lush, voluminous *basso* rolls through the music unconstrainedly. It sits easily at the bottom, peals forth brilliant Fs and F-sharps at the top (and one hair-raising G), and in between displays flowing line and a *mezza voce* that rivals prime Pinza or Chaliapin. Ruslan's heroic fire and tenderness are there—it's a complete piece of work. Of equal stature is the Ratmir of Antonova. Her deep-set, full-throated voice is well mated with this true contralto tessitura. She has the relaxed balance, the easy blend in and out of chest, that are needed, as well as a light, sophisticated touch for the waltz section of her first aria and the flexibility for the *melismas* of the second. Beautiful timbre, sinuous line. And while the opening-scene songs of Bayan, with their persistent middle-ish tessitura and generous repetitions, can in some hands seem interesting only for their accompaniments, Solomon Khromchenko makes us wish he'd show up with a few more: he displays a lovely, strong lyric tenor, perfectly welded to the line, and a genuine polish and finish of phrase. We hang on his words, which is just the function the old minstrel must carry out. The Ludmila, Barsova, handles much of the music with classic coloratura command—a pretty, floating voice of sufficient fullness, and a real instinct for setting up and dashing off the flourishes. Once in a while, a squeaky phrase ending or scrappiness on repeated attacks will crop up. The other soprano, Slivinskaya, seems a fine Gorislava, rendering her lament with passion and control—"seems," because her substantial voice suffers the most from the recording's distortion. Khanayev is a strong, lively Finn. Lubentsov does only an ordinary job with Farlaf's patter song (the "rondo" made familiar in the West by Chaliapin's recording), but he and Stavrovskaya are sprightly and flavorful in their delightfully written scene. Samosud sets firm, sensible tempos, encourages incisive attacks, and gets some unashamed romantic *obbligatos* and cadenzas from his orchestral soloists. Both chorus and orchestra have moments that arouse suspicion, but a fair judgment is difficult under these technical conditions.

p.1955 MELODIYA (M)

Vera Firsova (A), N. Pokrovskaya (B), Elena Korneyeva (C), Elena Verbitskaya (D), Georgi Nelepp (E), Sergei Lemeshev (F), Ivan Petrov (G), Alexei Krivchenya (H), Bolshoi Theater Chorus and Orchestra—Kiril Kondrashin

This set has important strengths. It is uncut, so that the work's epic nature is fully realized. It has decent mono sound, not as full-ranged or well balanced as one could hope, but acceptable. In Kondrashin it has an admirably unwor-

ried conductor, one not afraid to take his time and completely render the moments; many sections (ensembles, in particular) receive their most caring treatment here. It also has first-class work in the two leading roles. Firsova, in fact, is pretty spectacular. Her firm, free high soprano has both roundness and bite, and the ductility to render the ornaments and runs with authority. The soulful Act IV aria is especially fine, but she's good with the spunky side of the writing, too. Petrov's handsome and sizable bass is in prime shape. He is commanding and spirited, and if he's not quite Reizen, it's only in the sense that Siepi is not quite Pinza. The third leading role, Ratmir, is less persuasively sung. Verbitskaya is a musicianly artist who has done some valuable work on records, but she hasn't much of the timbral richness or technical address wanted in the role. Both tenors are good: Lemeshev shows his blandishing lyric tenor and effects some fine *morendi*; Nelepp's sturdier instrument has a few patches of loosening or nasality, but he renders Finn with his customary confidence and intelligence. Krivchenya, always enjoyable and expressive despite some dryness of voice, is at his best, and projects a vivid Farlaf. The Gorislava, Pokrovskaya, approaches her music seriously and shirks nothing, but a characteristic Slavic squalliness intrudes too often to let us relax and enjoy her work. Korneyeva is a solid Naina.

1978 MELODIYA (M)

Bela Rudenko (A), N. Fomina (B), Galina Borisova (C), Tamara Sinyavskaya (D), Alexei Maslennikov (E), A. Arkhipov (F), Yevgeny Nesterenko (G), Boris Morozov (H), Bolshoi Theater Chorus and Orchestra—Yuri Simonov

Like so many of the more recent recordings, this *Ruslan* seems to offer all the necessary capabilities, but is not a convincing whole. The theoretical advantage of latter-day stereo engineering is squandered—the hard, close-up sound has a glassy glare, and in many of the massed sections the balances actually make more sense in the old mono versions. Simonov gives this redolent old score the terminator treatment— everything's shipshape and foursquare, the quicker tempos lashed to the edge of mania, the singers seldom allowed to relax or expand. Nesterenko is in fine form, a few slippery E-naturals notwithstanding, and does much smooth, impressive singing. But his work sounds casual compared with that of his predecessors. Rudenko is an able-bodied but rather charmless Ludmila; the top of her strong lyric soprano does not quite release when the combination of tempo and tessitura makes her scramble. Sinyavskaya is the best of the three leads, offering a Ratmir of welcome musical sensitivity—some delicacy, even—along with her round, rich mezzo. Maslennikov is a superb artist, but his voice is not quite right for Finn, whose writing needs the authority and ring of the more dramatic type of Russian tenor. The Bayan, Arkhipov, has a rather cloudy character tenor that can do only the basic things, and his songs are fairly heavy going. Borisova is an excellent Naina, partnered by the Farlaf of Morozov, who sings rather well but caricatures the comic elements. Fomina, the Gorislava, is a decent, typical lyric soprano of the Slavic sort. There are cuts here, not as extensive as those of the 1938 performance, but still serious in the later acts.

————

The Kondrashin must certainly be the basic choice (perhaps you can locate the old Westminster edition—good pressings, English-language libretto), supplemented if possible by the Samosud, for the great singing found thereon.

CONRAD L. OSBORNE

CHRISTOPH WILLIBALD VON GLUCK

ORFEO ED EURIDICE
(1762; revised 1769 and 1774)

A: Amor (s); B: Euridice (s); C: Orfeo (originally male c; also ms, ct, t, or bar)

*O*rfeo ed Euridice has been recorded often, but in a bewildering variety of "performance editions." The original opera, first performed in Vienna in 1762, was an unusually concise work (because it was intended to form only part of an evening's entertainment), sung in Italian.

In 1769 Gluck revised it for a Parma production. Most of the changes were adjustments to the role of Orfeo, so that it could be sung by the soprano castrato Giuseppe Millico.

In 1774 Gluck rewrote the opera completely for Paris. It became *Orphée et Eurydice*, with a French text and with Orphée sung by a *haute-contre* (high tenor). The composer rewrote all of the recitatives to fit the words of the new French libretto, and made significant alterations in some of the set pieces.

But Gluck also added a great deal of "new" music, much of which was actually adapted from his earlier works. Amor—now Amour—was given a second aria ("Si les doux accords") in Act I, and Orphée now ended the act with a display aria, "L'espoir renait."

The other Paris additions include a trio ("Tendre Amour"—adapted from *Paride ed Elena)* in the final scene, and a great deal of ballet music. Act II, Scene 1 now ends, rousingly, with a Dance of the Furies. In the following scene, set in the Elysian Fields, an anonymous *ballo* in F from the 1762 score becomes a Dance of the Blessed Spirits. Act III of the 1774 score ends with an extended sequence of danced numbers, culminating in the magnificent Chaconne.

The Vienna and Paris versions of the opera should really be treated as two distinct works, each with its own merits. But the tradition of tampering with Gluck's own score(s) began during the composer's lifetime, and continued through the nineteenth century.

Anyone who wants to perform the opera today thus has some tough decisions to make. Increasingly, the trend has been to revert to Gluck's original version of 1762. The part of Orfeo can be sung at its original pitch either by a female mezzo-soprano or by a countertenor—although many singers in both of these vocal categories find the tessitura too low for comfort at times.

Many conductors who use the 1762 score are tempted to insert at least two numbers from the 1774 Paris score—the Dance of the Furies and the Dance of the Blessed Spirits. Because these two dances, and Orfeo's Act III aria, are the most famous numbers in the opera (and deservedly so), the lapse from strict textual integrity is forgivable.

An 1859 adaptation by Hector Berlioz has recently been recorded (see the discussion of the Gardiner set, below). Most recordings of the opera, however, are conflations of the 1762 and 1774 scores, and are sung in Italian. Since many of these performances contain more music from the 1774 rewrite than from the 1762 original, the choice of language seems illogical—why sing music that Gluck wrote to a French text, or adapted to French words, in an inauthentic nineteenth-century Italian translation?

1951 EMI / ANGEL (M,P) CD

Nel Duval (A), Greet Koeman (B), Kathleen Ferrier (C), Netherlands Opera Chorus and Orchestra—Charles Bruck

During her tragically brief career, Kathleen Ferrier sang only two operatic roles in staged productions: Lucretia, in Britten's *The Rape of Lucretia*, and Gluck's Orfeo. This January 1951 broadcast tape at least allows us to hear her Orfeo in reasonably complete form. Ferrier's voice—one of the last true contraltos to appear on the international scene—was a magnificent instrument. She has some hooty moments here, as well as some harshness and wobble under pressure, but she also displays the kind of command that makes the passing flaws seem irrelevant. There is a cool majesty to her portrayal, and yet her vocalism is replete with human overtones.

Unfortunately, everything else about the performance is inadequate. The edition appears to be the 1889 Ricordi score, but with some cuts. Amor sings his 1774 entrance aria ("Se il dolce suon" in Italian) in Act I, but Orfeo's bravura aria ("Addio, o miei sospiri") is omitted, so that the act ends with the 1762 recitative and orchestral coda. Act II, Scene 2 (set in the Elysian Fields) is mostly Paris. So is Act III; the *Paride ed Elena* trio "Divo Amore" is included, but several of the ballet numbers are dropped.

Charles Bruck, a dependable enough *routinier* in other repertory, sounds bored by the music and gives it a brisk, impatient reading that is no improvement whatsoever upon the standard lugubrious approach. The orchestral playing is clumsy: lax in ensemble and intonation, and riddled with mistakes. The chorus sings in a bland, undramatic manner and its Italian vowels are impure.

Both sopranos are poor technicians, and their insecurity is all the more cruelly exposed when they are heard in conjunction with Ferrier. The contralto's performance is hardly in need of any

enhancement from the deficiencies of her colleagues, but next to Nel Duval's shrill Amor and Greet Koeman's feeble-toned, rhythmically sluggish Euridice, her Orfeo does indeed sound like a demigod.

Finally, the recorded sound on Verona's CD set is dim and distorted. The strong tape hiss almost drowns out the music in the quieter passages. It is obvious, though, that this recording can be recommended only to those who wish to study Ferrier's Orfeo.

1955 EMI / ANGEL (In French) (M)

Liliane Berton (A), Janine Micheau (B), Nicolai Gedda (C), Paris Conservatory Chorus and Orchestra—Louis Froment

This recording allows us to hear *Orphée et Eurydice*—i.e., the 1774 score, sung in French, with a tenor Orphée. Unfortunately, the performance is not very satisfactory. For one thing, either the conductor or the producer has decided to "improve upon" Gluck's own sequence of musical numbers. The third stanza of Orphée's Act I lament ("Objet de mon amour"), beginning with the words "Plein de troubles," is cut. Orphée's biggest challenge—the aria "L'espoir renaît"—is omitted completely. The Dance of the Furies, which should end Act II, Scene 1, is inserted at the start of the act. Act II ends, anticlimactically, with the B-flat *ballo* (a holdover from 1762) that originally preceded Orphée's final recitative. In Act III, the ballet sequence is abridged, and the vocal ensemble "L'Amour triomphe" is once again moved to the very end.

Louis Froment's conducting is dutiful but dull. His tempos—nearly always a shade too slow to begin with—have a tendency to lose impetus before a number reaches its end, and one section of the score does not lead logically to the next. The orchestral playing, persistently imprecise and soft-edged in attack, also suffers from excess vibrato.

The one redeeming feature of the recording is the stylish solo work. Nicolai Gedda sings the 1774 tenor part as written, without any hint of strain. The vocal security is welcome, but from the interpretive standpoint this is not one of Gedda's most interesting recorded efforts—his

Orphée is no more than a pleasant gentleman who sounds mildly distressed by his wife's death.

The Amour, Liliane Berton, though a little thin and brittle of timbre, is lively in manner. Janine Micheau sounds rather mature as Eurydice, but brings a certain grandeur to her phrases that is appropriate to this heroine of myth.

The sound on these pressings is artificial stereo, rather mushy and over-reverberant, with a constricted dynamic range—acceptable, but no more.

1956 PHILIPS (In French) (M)

Pierrette Alarie (A), Suzanne Danco (B), Léopold Simoneau (C), Roger Blanchard Vocal Ensemble, Lamoureux Concert Orchestra—Hans Rosbaud

Hans Rosbaud, like Froment, performs the 1774 score in French—but once again minus "L'espoir renait." In addition to evading this challenge, Léopold Simoneau resorts to some downward transpositions of Orphée's music, notably in the confrontation with the Furies in Act II, Scene 1. Nevertheless, Simoneau is revelatory in the part, phrasing with a cool, polished beauty but suggesting the emotional turbulence lying below this calm surface. This aristocratic singer, like Ferrier, really does make Orpheus sound as though he could be the son of Apollo and Calliope. Rosbaud supports him intelligently, providing a serene, unhurried reading of the score that turns out to be surprisingly dramatic in its cumulative impact, and is filled with subtle details (the dances are especially well realized). The orchestra and chorus are not always the last word in virtuosity, but are alert and idiomatic.

The two women, if not on Simoneau's level, are more than adequate. Pierrette Alarie brings plenty of personality to Amour, but her tone is shallow and fluttery. Suzanne Danco also displays a vibrato that some listeners may find excessive, particularly on sustained notes, but her Eurydice is vividly feminine. Both sopranos compensate for their purely vocal deficiencies with their ideally clear, forward enunciation of the text.

1957 RCA / BMG (M)

Roberta Peters (A), Lisa della Casa (B), Risë Stevens (C), Rome Opera Chorus and Orchestra—Pierre Monteux

This performance is quite painful to listen to. Pierre Monteux has a good general grasp of the requisite style, and phrases some of the music with suavity, but he has been sabotaged by his producers. The performance sounds unrehearsed. The orchestral execution—slack in attack, sour in intonation, and riddled with wrong notes—is inexcusably shoddy. The chorus sings lustily, as though it were doing just another *Cavalleria*.

Peters is the best of the soloists, combining musical accuracy with a direct, unaffected approach to her role. Risë Stevens simply waited too long to record Orfeo: her obviously good intentions are undermined by unsteadiness, shortness of breath, and pitch problems. Let us not remember her thus.

Lisa della Casa sings well (provided one can accept her quite regular habit of extracting the vibrato from her tone, and singing deliberately flat for "emphasis"); but her Euridice is cold and unemotional.

As though these shortcomings weren't enough, the mono engineering is crude, with the solo voices much too closely miked and the distantly positioned chorus blanketed in echo.

1963 RCA / BMG (S) CD

Judith Raskin (A), Anna Moffo (B), Shirley Verrett (C), Rome Polyphonic Choir, I Virtuosi di Roma and the Instrumental Ensemble of Collegium Musicum Italicum—Renato Fasano

This performance follows the 1889 Ricordi score quite closely; it includes virtually everything printed in that edition. Only "Addio, o miei sospiri" is omitted—somewhat perversely, for surely Shirley Verrett would have been able to sing the aria more than satisfactorily. All of the other Paris additions are played, and as a result this version is especially well endowed with dance numbers.

Renato Fasano's conducting is elegant and spirited. Although he can summon an imposing weight and richness of timbre where these qualities are appropriate, the performance never becomes ponderous. The orchestra and chorus (both of intimate, chamber proportions) are excellent—well above the recorded average.

All three soloists are good. Verrett's soft, round mezzo, with its intriguing mixture of bright and dark colorations, always falls gratefully upon the ear. There is seriousness and nobility in her singing, but the intensity she has brought to so many other of her roles is only hinted at here.

Anna Moffo also makes a warm and sympathetic sound. This writing does not expose her incipient vocal difficulties; only a certain breathy, unsupported quality in the lower and middle register is cause for concern.

Judith Raskin sings Amor's music in firm, clear tones and projects the words exceptionally well—a distinguished performance by an underrated, and under-recorded, singer.

BMG's CD reissue, on two well-filled discs, has been digitally remastered and offers warm, forward sound.

1966 BACH GUILD (S) (D

Hanny Steffek (A), Teresa Stich-Randall (B), Maureen Forrester (C), Vienna Academy Choir, Vienna State Opera Orchestra—Charles Mackerras

This recording represents a serious attempt to approximate eighteenth-century performance practice—at least, as it was understood a quarter century ago; if some elements of the performance now sound outdated, and even quaint, the obvious effort that went into the production is still commendable.

Sir Charles Mackerras, to his credit, does not subscribe to the theory that this opera is one long dirge. Tempos are lively, rhythms clearly defined, and dynamic levels vividly contrasted. On the other hand, some of the double-dotting is overdone, and the very prominent harpsichord *continuo* can be distracting.

Mackerras deserves a better orchestra and chorus. The instrumental playing is imprecise and ill-balanced much of the time; the choral singing often sags in pitch, with lazy-lipped Italian enunciation.

Unfortunately, Mackerras is also let down by his three famous soloists: one can hardly describe any of the vocalism as poor, but it does little to bring the opera to life.

Maureen Forrester sings beautifully and with unperturbed dignity, and unlike so many of her recorded rivals her voice sits comfortably in the contralto tessitura. The richness of Forrester's timbre is welcome, but the overall effect is on the monotonous, matronly side. She uses some of Guadagni's own embellishments, notably in "Che farò"; although these are, of course, interesting, I must confess that I find them a little fussy at times.

Teresa Stich-Randall is an impossibly mannered Euridice, her cold, vibrato-less soprano conveying no emotion whatsoever, and she pulls the music about with all sorts of exaggerated dynamic effects.

Hanny Steffek sounds rather sophisticated for Amor, and tends to peck at her notes, Viennese style.

None of these three ladies sings clear, open Italian vowels; in fact, Stich-Randall, with her heavily covered vocal production, scarcely seems to be singing Italian at all.

1966 EMI / ANGEL (S)

Ruth-Margret Pütz (A), Anneliese Rothenberger (B), Grace Bumbry (C), Leipzig Radio Chorus, Leipzig Gewandhaus Orchestra—Václav Neumann

A disappointing version, on the whole. Václav Neumann has proved his worth in other repertory (e.g., Dvořák), but his Gluck is ponderous and dull. The orchestra produces a thick, heavy sound; the solo oboe is pinched and nasal in timbre. Incongruously, a harpsichord tinkles away feebly, "reinforcing" this big, nineteenth-century style ensemble. The chorus, also too large, enunciates the Italian text poorly.

Grace Bumbry, with her strong, clear high mezzo, is a dignified yet passionate Orfeo. Some of the music lies too low for her, however, exposing the relatively breathy, unsupported sound of her lower register.

Anneliese Rothenberger and Ruth-Margret Pütz both sing accurately, but their style seems wrong for this opera—both sopranos sound like refugees from an operetta performance. Despite her warm, attractive timbre, Rothenberger lacks the tonal purity and calm *legato* line of an ideal Euridice. Pütz, with her puffy tone, her scooping up to high notes, and her tendency to sing marginally flat for "expressive" effect, is rather too soubrettish even for Amor.

1967 DEUTSCHE GRAMMOPHON (S)

Edda Moser (A), Gundula Janowitz (B), Dietrich Fischer-Dieskau (C), Munich Bach Choir and Orchestra—Karl Richter

Except for the presence of the Dance of the Furies, this version is almost all 1762; the final ballet sequence is slightly abridged, however. Karl Richter's conducting is taut, sharply profiled, and often exciting. The orchestra plays well. The chorus makes a beautifully balanced sound, with immaculate intonation, but seems dramatically uninvolved—these choristers are more convincing as Blessed Spirits than as mourners, Furies, or the celebrants in the final scene.

The casting of a baritone as Orfeo is a mixed blessing. The contrast between a deep male voice and the two sopranos is welcome in Acts I and III. Most of the time, though, Dietrich Fischer-Dieskau simply sings the original contralto line an octave lower; Richter is too much of a purist to adjust the harmonies or the orchestration, and as a result Fischer-Dieskau sometimes goes lower than the instrumental bass line that is supposedly accompanying him. Fischer-Dieskau is in good voice here, and does many interesting things with the character. He is not the kind of artist who is content to let his voice carry the burden unaided, even in passages that call for "straight singing," and as a result much of his singing can seem calculated and lacking in spontaneity.

Edda Moser has a more powerful voice than we usually hear in Amor's music; some of her loud high notes acquire an edge, but she is impressive in the coloratura. Her god of love sounds more mature and stern than the usual

boyish interpretation—although this may not have been the composer's intention.

Gundula Janowitz's pure, poised singing creates some striking effects in Act III—she is a lovely Euridice, if not the warmest or most impulsive imaginable.

1969 DECCA / LONDON (S) CD

Helen Donath (A), Pilar Lorengar (B), Marilyn Horne (C), Chorus and Orchestra of the Royal Opera House, Covent Garden—Georg Solti

Textually, this recording (based on a Covent Garden production, in which Yvonne Minton sang Orfeo) is somewhat of a jigsaw puzzle. It continually jumps back and forth between the Vienna and Paris scores, with a little Berlioz thrown in.

Marilyn Horne sings the Viardot-Garcia line when it suits her, and transposes some of the other music to exploit her own extraordinary range. She also embellishes her music. The variants in "Chiamo il mio ben così" strike me as excessive, disrupting the mood of the piece, but the decorations are effective enough elsewhere. This is the first Italian-language recording to include "Addio, o miei sospiri" at the end of Act I, and Horne sings the number excitingly, quite justifying its inclusion.

Provided the listener does not object to her characteristic rapid vibrato, Pilar Lorengar is an urgent, womanly Euridice. Everyone should enjoy Helen Donath's Amor: her flutelike voice fills out the music without a trace of shrillness or breathiness, and she makes a great success of her Act I arias.

Sir Georg Solti goes all-out for drama: he obtains a warm, solid sound from his excellent chorus and orchestra, and indulges in some dynamic contrasts that might be more suitable in Beethoven, or even Wagner. He makes *Orfeo ed Euridice* sound very much like a nineteenth-century opera; in fact, with Horne so imposing a presence, one almost regrets that Decca didn't go ahead and simply record the Berlioz edition, in French.

The sound is fine, both on the original LP set and the CD transfer.

p.1980 HUNGAROTON (S) CD

Maria Zempleni (A), Veronika Kincses (B), Julia Hamari (C), Hungarian State Opera Chamber Chorus, Hungarian State Opera Orchestra—Ervin Lukacs

Ervin Lukacs, unusually, performs the original 1762 score intact, resisting the temptation to insert any numbers from the 1774 Paris version. Unfortunately, although Lukacs has a good orchestra and chorus at his disposal, his ideas about the opera are conventional. Tempos are slow, rhythms uninflected, and contrasts ironed out. The recitatives sound like careful note-renderings rather than musical dialogues.

Julia Hamari's cool, even mezzo is the right *kind* of voice for Orfeo, but her understated interpretation is perhaps too restrained. Her "Che farò," however, is very beautifully sung.

Maria Zempleni is an appealing Amor, bright of tone and lively in manner. Veronika Kincses, however, is miscast as Euridice: her thin soprano turns shrill and tremulous under pressure, and her Italian pronunciation is most peculiar.

The recorded sound is surprisingly lackluster for its date.

1981 EMI / ANGEL (S,D) CD

Edita Gruberova (A), Margaret Marshall (B), Agnes Baltsa (C), Ambrosian Opera Chorus, Philharmonia Orchestra—Riccardo Muti

Riccardo Muti, like Lukacs, has chosen the puristic approach, recording the 1762 score without any interpolations from 1774. He makes no attempt to approximate eighteenth-century style; his chorus and orchestra, both numerically large, produce a correspondingly massive sound. Provided one can accept the somewhat anachronistic scale of the performance, much of the score is beautifully executed—this is no waxwork *Orfeo ed Euridice*, but a real drama.

Although Agnes Baltsa is yet another high mezzo who sounds marginally uncomfortable in the low-lying phrases written for Guadagni, she is a resourceful artist whose singing combines classical poise with intensity.

Edita Gruberova resembles Edda Moser (on the DG / Richter set) in that she, too, is a "coloratura" soprano, but one whose voice is powerful enough to make the masculine impersonation plausible. Margaret Marshall is a superior Euridice, womanly yet forceful in her delivery, with just enough vibrato to give her bright soprano an attractive shimmer.

EMI's digital sound is very fine.

p.1982 ACCENT (S) CD

Magdalena Falewicz (A), Marjanne Kweksilber (B), René Jacobs (C), Collegium Vocale, La Petite Bande—Sigiswald Kuijken

This is the first recording of the opera to employ an orchestra of period instruments—which turns out to be a significant advantage. One can hear the difference literally in the first bar of the overture, which has a slashing attack and a vibrancy of timbre unmatched by any other version. Sigiswald Kuijken (who, like Lukacs and Muti, performs the 1762 score without any interpolations from 1774) gives us brisk tempos, sharply defined rhythms, clean articulation, and very transparent instrumental textures (the original accompaniment to "Che puro ciel" is particularly otherworldly in timbre).

The small chorus produces a pure, delicate sound that still manages to be wonderfully expressive—the choruses in the Elysian Fields scene, "Vieni ai regni dell riposo" and "Torna, o bella, al tuo consorte," are more beautifully rendered than on any other recording.

René Jacobs, a fine musician, has absolute control over his voice; his singing is remarkable for its accuracy of intonation. But his instrument is a countertenor, often glassy or hooty in timbre, and some of the music lies uncomfortably low for him. There is emotion in his singing, but it is conveyed by careful attention to verbal values rather than by any change in the color of the voice, which tends to be monochromatic. Like Forrester, he uses Guadagni's embellishments in "Che farò."

Marjanne Kweksilber is in some ways the most interesting Euridice on records, bringing a stinging intensity to "Che fiero momento," an aria that can sound dull in performance (in the middle section, at the words "d'un placido oblio," she sings a sensational trill). This is no passive, submissive spouse, but a proud, passionate woman who demands that her husband respond to her entreaties.

Magdalena Falewicz's Amor is also far gutsier than the standard cutesy interpretation.

The recorded sound (analogue, despite the date) is superb.

1982 ERATO (S,D)

Elizabeth Gale (A), Elisabeth Speiser (B), Janet Baker (C), Glyndebourne Chorus, London Philharmonic Orchestra—Raymond Leppard

Like the Decca / Solti set, this version (based on a Glyndebourne Festival production) makes no pretense of textual integrity. We start out with the 1762 score, but Amor's entrance aria ("Se il dolce suon") from 1774 is included. Janet Baker, like Marilyn Horne, ends Act I with "Addio, o miei sospiri," and, also like Horne, she embellishes it to suit her own voice (elsewhere, she sticks more closely to the printed notes).

Raymond Leppard, as usual, goes after the spirit of the score rather than the letter—there seem to be some slight retouchings of the instrumentation, and in general the performance is robust, highly colored, and intensely dramatic. The orchestra cannot be faulted, and the choral work is especially good.

With her ringing, *spinto*-like head tones, Baker sounds more like a soprano than a mezzo; one suspects that she would be even more comfortable in the higher tessitura of the 1769 Parma version. She has a few moments of unsteadiness and dubious intonation, and there is not much real weight of tone in the bottom octave. Nevertheless, this uniquely satisfying artist does so many fine things with the role that one can single out only a few of them for special praise. Her soft singing is delicate and beautiful. Her pacing and inflection of the recitatives is exemplary. No other female Orfeo on records quite matches her awe in "Che puro ciel," or her desolation and suicidal despair after Euridice's death in Act III (she transposes the climax of the outburst directed at Amor—"E tu chi sei," etc.—up an octave, turning it into a veristic cry of rage).

Elizabeth Gale is a perky, very musical Amor. The Euridice, Elisabeth Speiser, is a perfectly competent singer, but one whose bleak, dull timbre gives the listener little sensual pleasure.

The recorded sound is fine.

1982 METRONOME (S,D)

Allan Bergius (A), Julia Conwell (B), Peter Hofmann (C), Dortmund Music Society Chorus, Cologne Philharmonic Orchestra—Heinz Panzer

This strange recording seems to have been conceived as a vehicle for *Heldentenor* Peter Hofmann, who, with his halo of blond curls, undeniably does look like a Greek god in the photo on the box front. The notes, for once, are candid about which version is performed: the basis is the score edited by Alfred Dörffel and published in Leipzig in 1866. Essentially, it's the Berlioz version, but with the 1774 instrumentation restored, an Italian-language libretto, and with "Addio, o miei sospiri" and most of the Act III ballet sequence omitted. Despite the use of modern instruments, a pair of chalumeaux is provided for the echo effects in "Chiamo il mio ben," as called for in the 1762 score, but not in any of the subsequent revisions.

Hofmann sings not the 1774 tenor part but Viardot-Garcia's contralto line—an octave lower, which carries him down into baritone territory much of the time (thus "Che farò" is in C, rather than in F)—and, of course, minus Viardot-Garcia's cadenzas and embellishments. His powerful voice gives his Orfeo a certain heroic stature, but there is no sweetness in his timbre, no elegance in his phrasing, and little variety in his sound.

A further novelty is the casting of a boy soprano, Allan Bergius, as Amor. Bergius is altogether extraordinary, combining a beautiful timbre and accurate intonation with good musical instincts. He is just a little cautious here, but holds his own quite nicely against the adult female competition.

Julia Conwell has a bright, attractive voice and does her best to bring some drama to the proceedings.

Heinz Panzer is another earnest, uninspired conductor, who seems to think that slow tempos and a massive orchestral sonority automatically add up to profundity in this music. His orchestra and chorus are good.

The digital sound is impressive.

1987 EURODISC (S,D) CD

Julie Kaufmann (A), Lucia Popp (B), Marjana Lipovšek (C), Bavarian Radio Chorus, Munich Radio Orchestra—Leopold Hager

Leopold Hager performs the 1762 score, and—like Richter—includes the Dance of the Furies (but—again like Richter—not the Dance of the Blessed Spirits). Hager is a solid musician who brings some excitement to Act II, Scene 1 and some buoyancy to the celebration at the end of Act III. Elsewhere, though, he is too polite—another maestro who obviously believes that Gluck's music is predominantly elegiac. Once again we hear a chorus and orchestra that are good on their own terms, but too large in numbers and heavy in sound for the music. There is a very elaborate harpsichord *continuo*, which only serves to underline the lack of Baroque style elsewhere.

All three soloists are good without quite matching the best of the recorded competition. Marjana Lipovšek has a powerful mezzo, which turns a little tense and steely on loud high notes. She is a forceful Orfeo, and takes the character's grief and despair seriously; her Italian enunciation could be clearer, though.

Lucia Popp, always a giving artist, works hard as Euridice. Her voice—with its bright, rather hard tone and its rapid vibrato—is not quite right for the music, though, and one suspects that she would have been more effectively cast as Amor. In the latter role, Julie Kaufmann sings pleasantly enough, but doesn't do anything extraordinary from either the musical or the dramatic standpoint.

1988 CAPRICCIO (S,D) CD

Christian Fliegner (A), Dagmar Schellenberger-Ernst (B), Jochen Kowalski (C), Berlin Radio Chorus, Carl Philipp Emanuel Bach Chamber Orchestra—Hartmut Haenchen

This version competes directly with the 1982 Accent / Kuijken set: it, too, offers the 1762 score, with a countertenor Orfeo and an orchestra of period instruments. The only textual oddity is the inclusion of some (not all) of the 1774 dance movements, as a series of appendices which fill out the second CD *after* the opera's conclusion.

Hartmut Haenchen's direction is not quite as lively as Kuijken's, and his fine chorus and orchestra are not always as transparent in texture as the Belgian forces heard on the Accent recording. Nevertheless, Haenchen's is a distinguished performance, on the whole: he brings more warmth and sensuality to the music than does Kuijken, and his approach is amply dramatic.

Jochen Kowalski is an interesting and often exciting singer. He has a larger, more powerful voice than most countertenors, and is almost unique among them in possessing a strong chest register—the sound he produces in the lower and middle registers is, in fact, startlingly similar to a female contralto's at times. Unfortunately, he switches, in the upper register, to a very open, non-vibrato vocal configuration that is much less pleasant to listen to. At least, Kowalski does not tiptoe through the music, but sings out boldly and with passion. He also embellishes his music freely.

The Euridice, Dagmar Schellenberger-Ernst, has a fresh and attractive voice and an urgent manner.

Haenchen, like Panzer on the 1982 Metronome set, casts a boy soprano as Amor—in fact, Christian Fliegner, like Allan Bergius, is a Bach specialist. Fliegner is acceptable in the part, but not as persuasive as Bergius; some of his low notes are hollow and unsupported to the point of inaudibility, and some of his coloratura is cautious.

1989 EMI / ANGEL (In French) (S,D) CD

Brigitte Fournier (A), Barbara Hendricks (B), Anne Sofie von Otter (C), Monteverdi Choir, Lyons Opera Orchestra—John Eliot Gardiner

In a sense, this recording is non-competitive with other versions: uniquely, it uses the 1859

Berlioz edition of the score. Berlioz, of course, was a great admirer of Gluck's music, and his emendations to the score are less extensive, and less drastic, than one might expect. He made some cuts—e.g., the third stanza of "Objet de mon amour," and the final ballet sequence. John Eliot Gardiner observes these cuts, but reinstates—without comment—two other numbers that Berlioz dropped: the Dance of the Furies and the trio "Tendre Amour." Berlioz ends the opera with a chorus, "Le Dieu de Paphos," borrowed from *Echo et Narcisse*.

Berlioz—assisted by none other than the young Camille Saint-Saëns—"modernized" some of Gluck's instrumentation, especially for the brasses. Most important, Berlioz adjusted the role of Orphée for Pauline Viardot-Garcia. She was a talented composer in her own right, and provided her own embellishments and cadenzas (which are sung on this recording).

Gardiner gives an extremely subtle account of the score: never either bland or heavy-handed, it has a restrained intensity and momentum that carry the listener from the beginning to the end of the opera in one powerful sweep. His orchestra (made up of modern instruments but reinforced by a couple of antiques, including a boxwood clarinet and a *cornet à piston*) plays beautifully. The choral work is also good.

Contemporary descriptions of Viardot-Garcia's voice, and the repertory she excelled in, suggest that she was a contralto who forced herself to sing high: her upward extension, though exciting, seems to have been unreliable. There is no reason to believe that Anne Sofie von Otter, with her soft-grained high mezzo, resembles her illustrious nineteenth-century predecessor in the slightest. Nevertheless, von Otter is altogether admirable on this recording. She brings a controlled agony to Orphée's grief that is very much in tune with Gardiner's concept of the work, and she is sensational in "Amour, viens rendre," making the technical challenges sound easy and expressive, rather than like a series of mere vocal stunts.

Brigitte Fournier sings Amour's music very attractively, and it is hardly her fault that she sounds utterly feminine. Barbara Hendricks is a

fine Eurydice, her pure, delicate soprano capable of a surprising urgency.

The recorded sound is pleasingly clear and natural.

Before choosing a complete recording of the opera, a collector must first decide what *kind* of performance is desired. If one's preference is for the 1762 score, a countertenor Orfeo, and period instruments, then the choice is between the Accent / Kuijken and the Capriccio / Haenchen sets. The former is the stronger performance, on the whole, but not by a wide margin. Those who would rather hear the 1762 version of the opera with a mezzo-soprano Orfeo and a modern orchestra should definitely acquire the EMI / Muti recording, which is much more satisfactory than its direct competitors (i.e., the EMI / Neumann and Hungaroton / Lukacs sets).

For the 1774 score, sung in French and with a tenor Orphée, our "choice" is between the EMI / Froment and Philips / Rosbaud recordings—both of which are incomplete, currently out of print, and last appeared in artificially rechanneled pseudo-stereo sound. I much prefer the Philips / Rosbaud performance.

The EMI / Gardiner is a strong production (being well sung, played, conducted, and engineered), and is interesting for its use of the Berlioz edition, but—precisely for that reason—it can hardly be recommended as one's only recording of the opera.

Those who can leave textual questions to scholars have a decided advantage: they can simply sit back and enjoy the individual merits of one or another of the "mixed" recordings, several of which are good. The RCA / Fasano, Decca / Solti, and Erato / Leppard sets are particularly impressive; I would suggest that a collector who possesses one or more of these versions need not look much farther, unless the specific lineup of singers on some other recording has a particular appeal.

ROLAND GRAEME

Unavailable for review:
1952 ACANTA

CHARLES GOUNOD

FAUST (1859)

A: Marguerite (s); B: Siébel (ms); C: Faust (t);
D: Valentin (bar); E: Méphistophélès (bs)

history of complete recordings of *Faust* begins with three from the early days of such enterprises. Besides the 1912 set conducted by François Ruhlmann (in French, but unavailable for review), there was one in Italian (Carlo Sabajno) and one in German (Bruno Seidler-Winkler). This last, recorded in Berlin in 1908, is well worth hearing for the singing of its protagonists, Emmy Destinn and Karl Jörn—voices of heroic calibre, deftly and lightly handled. An essential item is the 1947 Bolshoi performance in Russian, under Vassily Nebolsin. Its Valentin (Pavel Lisitsian, in glorious voice) is the standard by which to judge the others, while both its Marguerite (Elisaveta Shumskaya) and its Faust (Ivan Kozlovsky) must rank among the best, and its conductor understands that in this music, it is worth stretching with singers to create dramatic moments.

Faust is an opera that has often been subjected to cutting. Until quite recently, the Walpurgis Night tableaux of Act IV were omitted in most performances outside France, and the opening scene of Act III (the "real" Spinning Wheel Scene, with Marguerite's "Il ne revient pas" and Siébel's little loyalty song) was always cut everywhere. To this day, the latter is seldom encountered in the theater, but has practically become *de rigueur* on records; no recording before the 1966 Bonynge includes it, but almost all since then do. Walpurgis fragments (with no ballet music) crop up on the 1931 Büsser, but then we get nothing of the scene until the 1953

Cluytens, which embraces all of it, including all seven ballet numbers. This has been the rule ever since, though the Prêtre and Davis performances insert Faust's drinking song, "Doux nectar," and relegate the ballet to an appendix.

Several shorter cuts were once common in the theater. With one or two exceptions, they are made on the older recordings, then opened on the more recent ones. (Valentin's "Avant de quitter," formerly cut in France, is omitted from Beecham's French recording.)

There is not a thing wrong with the old standard-cut edition for repertory purposes. Those who contrived it showed perfectly good judgment and taste, and the result makes a nice, tight theater piece of considerable impact that can survive half-baked performances. The restorations unquestionably offer the potential for a richer, broader experience, but the promise would be kept only in a performance of exceptional qualities.

1929–30 EMI / ANGEL (In English) (M)

Miriam Licette (A), Doris Vane (B), Heddle Nash (C), Harold Williams (D), Robert Easton (E), BBC Choir and Orchestra—Thomas Beecham

One is not going to encounter this English-language set outside the archives, except in the form of a single disc of excerpts released in 1974, which concentrates on the music of Faust and Marguerite. The translation (mostly Chorley's with some changes that are none for the better) and the silent-movie musical manners of the singers lend the proceedings a palm-court atmosphere.

Palm courts can be pleasant places, though, and the better silent-movie romances can still entrance, if watched sympathetically. This is the case with Nash's singing. He brings to the music the ideal oratorio tenor—a strong one, not quite complete at the range extremes, but beautifully poised and lovely in quality everywhere else. He has a poetic sense of phrase and an instinct for the romantic moment; there is finish to both music and words. Beecham accompanies him in kind: his introduction to the aria, slow and grave, filled with suspense and anticipation and closing with a lingering *diminuendo*, shows what a sensitive musician can find in the score. Yet such moments are set in a basically brisk reading that shows the music's potential for excitement and passion.

Licette is much less interesting: a bright, capable voice, but not a special one, and an approach that remains fixed in period, sometimes amusingly so. There is nothing on this disc of Williams's Valentin, and just enough of Easton's Mephisto to disclose a genial, tremolo-ridden pub bass with some nice lower notes and no upper ones to speak of.

1930 EMI / ANGEL (M) CD

Mireille Berthon (A), Martha Coiffier (B), César Vezzani (C), Louis Musy (D), Marcel Journet (E), Paris Opéra Chorus and Orchestra—Henri Büsser

This was the first electrically recorded *Faust* in French. With its native cast that ranges from the solid to the truly outstanding, it still has powerful attractions. First among these must be Journet, the only Méphistophélès to be both a great singer and a Frenchman. Despite his age (mid-sixties in 1930), his plush, supple voice had lost none of its range and very little of its beauty and puissance. He husbands it shrewdly, and tries nothing fancy with the breath—but then French singers in general are not addicted to endless *legato* (it offends their understanding of recitational good sense). To be sure, he does not always avoid the clichés of his native tradi-

tion. But his treatment of the music has such ease and freedom, his delivery of the text such a natural mastery, that his performance remains in many ways the reference point for the role.

Vezzani's Faust is also an ear-opener from a contemporary perspective: a tenor with a clear, well-knit voice of the robust type, and a fiery temperament that doesn't preclude a well-controlled line. If we're in search of the utmost elegance or tonal sweetness, we turn elsewhere, but the strength and profile of this singing are welcome.

In Mireille Berthon we meet a representative, decent French lyric soprano. Her voice is strong and pungent to top A-flat or so; then it either thins or forces to an edge. Her phrasing is firm and musical without being particularly illuminating. Musy's baritone is another voice typical of the French school when there was one—clear and lean, slightly twangy, and a bit extended by the considerable reach of this role. He copes, and gives the part dignity. Coiffier is entirely competent, except for a B-flat that's gone south for "Victoire!" Büsser's orchestra and chorus lack the snap and sharpness of some of the more recent groups, and of course the combination of 78 side requirements and the relative dimness of the sound detract from our view of their work. Nevertheless, it is clear that Büsser was a master of accompaniment, and that he knew the music's stylistic grammar cold. This makes him worth a respectful listen.

1947–48 EMI / ANGEL (M)

Géori Boué (A), Huguette Saint-Arnaud (B), Georges Noré (C), Roger Bourdin (D), Roger Rico (E), Royal Philharmonic Chorus and Orchestra—Thomas Beecham

Beecham's second recording of *Faust* is in French, with some of the leading Parisian singers of World War II vintage. It makes great sense of the score in the lyrical sections. The reading is perhaps a shade less poetic than the earlier one—no doubt the Beecham of the 1920s seemed sentimental to the Beecham of the 1940s. But this is still a performance to study for its command of the arts of expanding and contracting within bars; of using *retards* not merely to slow the pace, but to make statements; of broadening at cadential points—in short, of French Romantic *rubato*. As before, Beecham establishes brisk tempos and incisive phrasing as the framework for these easements.

The finest individual performance on this set is Géori Boué's, and it is very good indeed. She represents the same vocal type as Berthon, but at a higher level: without losing the characteristic French point, her tone is rounder and the top releases and blooms more freely. She sings with delicacy and precision, the shapes of the line truly sculpted, and has plenty of amplitude and bite where required. Despite the presence of some glamorous voices on subsequent sets, Géori Boué's remains my favorite Marguerite: she retains the simplicity and center of one who speaks from within the artistic language.

Noré's Faust has some of the same virtues. He has a lovely lyric tenor with a compact, tingling top, and his presentation is straightforward and lucid. It's just that not much passion or imagination comes through; it sounds a little tame. Rico is the last of the French light basses to record the part of Mephisto. The voice is pleasing and appropriate, but there is little urgency, and the effect is finally too casual.

With his aria cut, Valentin is reduced to the status of a *comprimario* who dies. Bourdin just manages what's left of the role. The Siébel, Saint-Arnaud, brings a brightly reinforced light soprano to the part, and is fine.

1951 CBS / SONY (M)

Eleanor Steber (A), Margaret Roggero (B), Eugene Conley (C), Frank Guarrera (D), Cesare Siepi (E), Metropolitan Opera Chorus and Orchestra—Fausto Cleva

This set preserves one great performance: Siepi's Méphistophélès. The voice, here in its youthful prime, is the most beautiful and balanced to be heard in the role, and has a dark, velvety power. Siepi's French, while not native, has some flavor, and his interpretation more specificity than I had remembered. An aristocratic insinuation colors his work, not far removed from the ironic sophistication of the better French singers, and his taste protects him from the

forced nonsense that is reluctantly described below and below. But most of all: what wonderful singing!

For the rest, the performance represents a studio version of a second-line night at the Met, circa 1951—not a horrible night, just an ordinary one. While from our standpoint it is sobering to realize that the second- and third-choice artists of that roster present voices of better quality and more grand-opera thrust and vitality than most of today's first run, they nonetheless offer only the basics of this music, and a distinct whiff of American Provincial reaches the nostrils from time to time. Steber is a strong, commanding Marguerite whose voice is pretty and focused until it starts to spread at the top during the Church Scene and final trio. Conley's firm tenor is always reliable, and he has some stunning moments in the high range, along with some clumsy covering that often dulls the upper-middle notes. Guarrera's Valentin is macho: the voice has quality and force, though already a touch of grit; the French is *exécrable*. Roggero's mezzo, with its touch of sharpness and squareness, gives profile to Siébel's music. Cleva conducts a vigorous, theatrically knowledgeable performance that is not insensitive, but not insightful, either.

1953 EMI / ANGEL (M)

Victoria de los Angeles (A), Marthe Angelici (B), Nicolai Gedda (C), Jean Borthayre (D), Boris Christoff (E), Chorus and Orchestra of the Théâtre National de l'Opéra—André Cluytens

1958 EMI / ANGEL (S) CD

Victoria de los Angeles (A), Liliane Berton (B), Nicolai Gedda (C), Ernest Blanc (D), Boris Christoff (E), Chorus and Orchestra of the Théâtre National de l'Opéra—André Cluytens

These albums, so alike in most essentials (the second was a stereo remake of the first), are best considered together. Cluytens's way with the score—expansive, stately, unforced—is more successful in the 1958 version than in the 1953, where it is blameless but a touch boring, with a tendency to plod. I think it is partly that his work *is* a little more incisive, his forces' execution marginally livelier, the second time around, and partly that the spread and depth of the stereo engineering (of which this is a splendid early example) serve the reading particularly well. It is rich, warm and trusting, not without its moments of protest—the organ roars through the postlude to the Church Scene at full throttle, against all Gounod's indicated protestations, and the Horror of Church is powerfully conveyed.

De los Angeles has some marvelous things to offer with her Marguerite: the native beauty of her full lyric soprano, her cool, gentle temperament, her taste and thoughtfulness constitute fine credentials for the part. In the conversational passages and in monologue, her intent is always clear and alive, often lovably so. Her choices tend to be of the conservative, "sympathetic" sort, but they are readable and genuine. She is in freer voice on the earlier recording—by 1958, her habit of counteracting weight in the upper E-to-G area by squeezing and straightening the tone has already taken some spontaneity from an interpretation that had none to lose. It's still high-level singing, but in places it builds you up to let you down.

Gedda's is a matching Faust: expert, clean, musically shapely, interpretively thoughtful, the French beautifully formed, if just a tic self-conscious. The entire Garden Scene is as justly proportioned and balanced as you will ever hear it. It's almost a great Faust. Yet the final measure of tonal magic isn't quite there, nor is there any real emotional directness; we always hear his cerebral cortex. As with de los Angeles, Gedda's voice is warmer and freer, and his approach a little less sophisticated, on the earlier version.

If one wishes both these admirable singers would cut loose here and there, one cannot register such a complaint about Boris Christoff, who cuts loose here, there, and everywhere. But with what? With exhaustingly loud, raw tone, awful French, and a stomping Slavic bully-boy approach to the music. The singing is remarkably uninflected, and though the voice was then at its peak, and very welcome in the

Russian repertory, I find this performance just about unlistenable.

Both Valentins are vocally excellent, with solid, fat voices of importance. Borthayre's has more core and bite in the middle, Blanc's more sail and room at the top. Neither is a graphic actor, but both are satisfying singers. Of the two Siébels, I prefer Berton, a delightful light soprano with sufficient strength and point. Angelici was a good singer, but seems a trifle insecure here. Both Marthes, by the way, are exceptional: Rita Gorr with a major voice, Solange Michel with a fine one that is put to dramatically enlivening use.

1966 DECCA / LONDON (S) CD

Joan Sutherland (A), Margreta Elkins (B), Franco Corelli (C), Robert Massard (D), Nicolai Ghiaurov (E), Ambrosian Opera Chorus, London Symphony Orchestra—Richard Bonynge

There are important things to enjoy in this version, many of them having to do with a trio of superb voices, all reasonably near their peaks, in the leading roles. But some of the pleasures should be credited to Bonynge. It's true that the Prelude and opening scene of his reading are terribly slack and soft-textured, and that he and Sutherland between them manage to let the tension drop completely in certain passages. But I think Bonynge basically loves and understands the shapes and textures of the music, and in all the sections that provide their own rhythmic energy, he gives a crisp, fizzy account. The whole Kermesse scene is splendid, as is the ballet and such passages as the Soldiers' Chorus and final trio. There is also a tender lyricism to much of the Garden Scene.

The three great vocalists who head the cast are all wrong but wonderful. The trade-offs: Sutherland picks her way through the music too much, and falls into the trap of playing sadness and mooniness instead of desires; the character sounds passive. But the beauty, roundness, reach, and alacrity of the singing give great pleasure. She is by a good margin the most complete technician of any of these Marguerites. Corelli's French is poor, and he brings stylistically inappropriate kinds of expression to the music—sentimentalized Mediterranean passion, full of glides and sobs. At least it is *some* sort of passion, however, and while this writing does not give wide scope to the full-throated strength of his voice, there's a lot of exciting, rich singing. Ghiaurov makes a number of childish-sounding choices and persists in whitening the lower part of his range (always relatively weak) into what he hopes are snarls and sneers. It's not a very caring performance, and seldom subtle. But when he simply lets his powerful, pudding-smooth voice sing, the results are impressive and seductive.

Massard brings a serious approach to Valentin, but is hampered by a dry, nondescript timbre that will not carry much expressive weight. Elkins has a lovely mezzo of good amplitude, which she employs lightly and tastefully for Siébel.

Bonynge's version is the only one to restore any of the mass of material found only in the earliest performances but not incorporated into the score. The restorations are musically minor, but serve to bolster the lesser characters and clarify the continuity. The single exception is a fairly extended repeat and variation in the Prison Scene duet. Bonynge also places the Church Scene after the return and death of Valentin.

1976 ERATO (S) CD

Montserrat Caballé (A), Anita Terzian (B), Giacomo Aragall (C), Philippe Huttenlocher (D), Paul Plishka (E), Rhine Opera Chorus, Strasbourg Philharmonic Orchestra—Alain Lombard

Lombard's reading is, I believe, the slowest I've ever heard. I like much of it: the Prelude and first scene have real gravity, and the choral and ensemble episodes benefit from this expansive laying-out—each entrance, each rest is an event. Nor does Lombard let the bottom fall out of the extended solo passages, where his tempos are more normal.

Here, though, he must depend on his soloists to do more than cooperate, and the results are partial. Caballé begins well, capturing a dreamy,

introspective feeling in the "Roi de Thulé," and more life in the rest of the scene than I'd expected. Throughout, there is some vitality, and moments when the pellucid timbre of a phrase, the ring of a high note, will count. But the performance becomes more generalized as it moves on, the singing scrappier and increasingly disfigured by glottal clicks and clucks. All the equipment is there, but it's not always in top repair or used to purpose.

Aragall's Faust, too, starts promisingly, then seems to lose direction. He brings more to the opening monologue than most singers do, but is soon giving just another respectable, international-tenor performance. His excellent voice, strong and clear in the middle, isn't quite open in the upper reaches, and teeters on the intonational brink at odd moments. Plishka contributes his rock-solid, brave-sounding bass of the modern sort (big top, guttural bottom) to Mephisto. His devil is a bluff, hearty, blue-collar loudmouth who doesn't seem to command many strategies. To me, it's a less-than-plausible view, but the voice is decidedly capable.

Huttenlocher possesses a pleasant, innocuous light baritone, shaky under pressure, that is just no match for Valentin. You can't cheat on this role; it's too difficult. Terzian, on the other hand, is as close as you'll hear to a dramatic-mezzo Siébel—a big, nervy kid. I don't think it's right, but I found it refreshing.

1978 EMI / ANGEL (S) CD

Mirella Freni (A), Michèle Command (B), Plácido Domingo (C), Thomas Allen (D), Nicolai Ghiaurov (E), Paris Opéra Chorus and Orchestra—Georges Prêtre

I have often liked Prêtre, with his ear for color and his willingness to assume some responsibility for tempo and *rubato*. The former attribute can be heard here in the rich, if sometimes soupy, textures. As to the latter, the reading is, like Lombard's, slow. But in this case, the pacing combines with a smoothing of accent and a softening of attack that removes the starch and bite from lengthy sections that need them. It all represents a point of view, for sure, and at times draws good things from the soloists. But the consistency tends to be that of half-chewed caramel.

Marguerite has been a fine role for Freni. This occasion, though, finds her below form. There is still some round, substantial tone, but she is fighting balance problems in the voice, and securing a standoff at best. She rather belts her way through, and while there's some feeling in it, there's neither any particular profile to the character nor many illuminating moments. Domingo's Faust is musical, often thoughtful. His treatment of both language and music is serious and careful. On his personal one-to-ten scale, the voice is about seven and a half (some too-open vowels above the break, constriction on some top notes), which is certainly thoroughly sufficient.

By this time Ghiaurov's voice had suffered since his previous recording of this part: there's a dry, husky quality, and a loss of command in the upper range. Interpretively, though, his Mephisto is immeasurably improved—much more pulled-in and grown-up, at places even pointed. If we had the 1978 performance in the 1966 throat, we'd have *the* performance. Allen's Valentin offers a well-balanced, tightly focused high baritone, good French, smooth line, and some dash—it's easily the best on records since the Cluytens days. Command's solid mezzo is not ideally equalized, but she does have some punch, and makes dramatic efforts that deserve appreciation.

1988 PHILIPS (S,D) CD

Kiri Te Kanawa (A), Pamela Coburn (B), Francisco Araiza (C), Andreas Schmidt (D), Yevgeny Nesterenko (E), Bavarian Radio Chorus and Orchestra—Colin Davis

Davis is convincing in the Prelude and a few other orchestral or ensemble passages, and secures excellent execution throughout. But when the singing starts, he falls into lockstep in the deadliest contemporary fashion: the reading is so literal, so predictable in its patterns, that you soon know you can hit the kitchen for a beer just about any time and miss nothing. Davis is a fine musician, but I do not believe he has the

slightest temperamental affinity with this music.

Te Kanawa's voice still has that timbral shine except at the range extremes, where she draws back. But her Marguerite is a poor man's Sutherland—all the droopy enervation, little of the authority—white bread, as they say. Araiza, so far as I can judge through the buzzing bubble of reverb in which his voice is encased, sings every note of his role (including an absurd C howled at "Ah, fuyons!"—the one liberty Davis finds room for) with reasonable security and some vigor. A few lyrical spots have some sweetness; elsewhere, there's a pressurized darkness, as if he were mimicking an important voice through a megaphone some engineer has handed him.

The revels sink to grade-school Halloween-pageant level with the Méphistophélès of Nesterenko. This is surely the silliest performance of the role on records, and the voice, while still essentially equal to the part, is used with little sense of line. Schmidt is a lieder-ish Valentin: the light, high-open sort of baritone that (like Huttenlocher's) can be of use, but not in this role. Coburn has a pretty, soft-grained voice of the could-be-mezzo category; it is neither here nor there for Siébel.

1991 EMI / ANGEL (S,D) CD

Cheryl Studer (A), Martine Mahé (B), Richard Leech (C), Thomas Hampson (D), José van Dam (E), French Army Chorus, Chorus and Orchestra of the Capitole de Toulouse—Michel Plasson

This version squirms to life in the tableaux of Act IV and the Walpurgis Scene in Act V; there, Plasson provides some impetus and shape. Studer sings out solidly with her roundest, loveliest sound for "Il ne revient pas" and the Church Scene, Hampson works honestly to bring some sense to the Duel Trio and Valentin's Death, Leech delivers a good Drinking Song, and the assembled *poilus* are wonderful in the Soldiers' Chorus. Elsewhere, things just droop. No one seems to have any thought of locating dramatic purpose in the lyrical writing. Plasson conducts right on through all potential events, so that everything has the same (slight) importance.

The only real performance life in the first three acts comes from Mahé and Nadine Denize (as Marthe) in the Garden Scene, and from the end of the Kermesse, where there is a whiff of madness for two or three pages. Vocally, Leech is bright, firm, and square; Studer is full and often beautiful at *forte*, but slack in the softer passages, and without the trill or the attack on the runs for the Jewel Song. Van Dam's fine bass-baritone still hangs together, but is starting to sound dry and flat—he improves in the later scenes. Hampson's baritone, of the heady modern sort, hasn't the core one really wants, but shows at least more body and thrust than Schmidt's or Huttenlocher's. The restored sections—about fifteen minutes' worth—included in the appendix prove to be pale stuff. The ballet is here, too, in a sleepy rendition. The performance's problems are exacerbated by the fairly typical contemporary recording ambience, suggestive of no real place or familiar circumstance. It's our New Oz, this digital Never-Never Land. Does anyone enjoy being there?

I cannot bring myself to a recommendation. Blade at throat, I suppose I would gasp something like "Cluytens! With Bonynge for some of the vocalism and the extra music." But my real suggestion is to read the foregoing, then decide what's important to you.

CONRAD L. OSBORNE

Unavailable for review:
1912 PATHÉ
1957 GUILDE INTERNATIONALE DU
  DISQUE

TERRENCE McNALLY
Playwright

1. **Mozart,** *Don Giovanni*: Sutherland, Schwarzkopf, Sciutti, Alva, Wächter, Cappuccilli, Taddei, Frick—Giulini. EMI / ANGEL

2. **Beethoven,** *Fidelio*: Ludwig, Hallstein, Vickers, Unger, Berry, Frick, Crass—Klemperer. EMI / ANGEL

3. **Rossini,** *Il Barbiere di Siviglia*: De los Angeles, Alva, Bruscantini, Cava, Wallace—Gui. EMI / ANGEL

4. **Bellini,** *Norma*: Callas, Stignani, Filippeschi, Rossi-Lemeni—Serafin. EMI / ANGEL. Or Callas, Ludwig, Corelli, Zaccaria—Serafin. EMI / ANGEL

5. **Donizetti,** *Lucia di Lammermoor*: Callas, di Stefano, Panerai, Zaccaria—Karajan. EMI / ANGEL

6. **Verdi,** *Otello*: Nelli, Merriman, Vinay, Assandri, Valdengo—Toscanini. RCA / BMG

7. **Wagner,** *Tristan und Isolde*: Flagstad, Thebom, Suthaus, Fischer-Dieskau, Greindl—Furtwängler. EMI / ANGEL

8. **Bizet,** *Carmen*: De los Angeles, Micheau, Gedda, Blanc—Beecham. EMI / ANGEL

9. **Berlioz,** *Les Troyens*: Lindholm, Veasey, Begg, Vickers, Partridge, Davies, Glossop, Soyer—Davis. PHILIPS

10. **Britten,** *Peter Grimes*: C. Watson, Elms, J. Watson, Pears, Pease—Britten. DECCA / LONDON

CHARLES GOUNOD

ROMÉO ET JULIETTE (1867)

A: Juliette (s); B: Stéphano (s); C: Roméo (t); D: Mercutio (bar);
E: Frère Laurent (bs); F: Capulet (bs)

ounod's *Roméo et Juliette* was an international success from the beginning. It was composed mainly in the spring and summer of 1865 (six years after the premiere of *Faust*), though several early editions show score changes made in the years following. When the work was finally taken up by the Paris Opéra in 1888, the obligatory ballet was added. The libretto was adapted from Victor Hugo's translation of Shakespeare, with several scenes dropped for brevity and a few added for variety and spectacular effect. Thus we have the new character of Stéphano, Roméo's page, instigating the conflict which ends in the deaths of Mercutio and Tybalt, and a wedding scene (now usually cut) in which Juliette, having taken the sleeping potion, faints before Paris and the assembled crowd. The finale, inspired by David Garrick's eighteenth-century adaptation, has Juliette waking before Roméo dies, to allow for a final duet. From the earliest years there have been traditional stage cuts, including the potion scene and the aforementioned wedding of Juliette and Paris. Such cuts are generally observed on records, though the 1953 Decca includes the ballet music and the 1983 EMI version has almost everything *but* the ballet. These rarely heard sections are of some interest but inessential to enjoyment of the work as a whole.

The opera demands both elegance and eloquence, and was a very popular vehicle for the great stars of the late nineteenth and early twentieth centuries, among them Patti, Melba, Eames, Jean de Reszke, Clément, Farrar, and Ansseau. With the international decline of French operatic style and the coming of Italian *verismo* the opera became more difficult to cast, and the complete recordings under review reflect this difficulty. The earliest set recalls both the opera's popularity and some voice types seldom heard today. The later ones are few and largely undistinguished vocally, except for the one which features a Swede and a Brazilian in the leads—and that cast achieved only two performances at the Metropolitan.

1912 PATHÉ (M)

Yvonne Gall (A), Mlle. Champel (B), Agustarello Affre (C), Alexis Boyer (D), Marcel Journet (E), Henri Albers (F), Chorus and Orchestra of the Opéra-Comique—François Ruhlmann

This relatively complete recording is treasurable for the now-rare kinds of voice it preserves: the heroic French tenor, the elegant French baritone, and the French lyric soprano of some warmth. Yvonne Gall had a major career in Europe and the United States—*and* the sort of voice not well captured by the acoustical recording process. She is touching in the lyric moments but, as recorded, hard and relentlessly bright in higher reaches. She seems least confident and accurate in Juliette's enchanting first entrance, more efficient in the Waltz (accompanied on the LP transfer by the bongo drums of the original recording machine), and at her touching best in the later moments. Agustarello Affre recorded Roméo when he was about fifty-four, after a long career in heroic roles. His is something of an Otello voice, bound in brown leather and stolid but healthy except occasionally at the very top of the range. His style has elements of authenticity but is also somewhat graceless and earthbound. He and Gall do not complement one another ideally, but he is at his burnished *mezzo forte* best in the Act V monologue.

Alexis Boyer is a nimble Mercutio with a focused voice and style: a trifle heavy but better, perhaps, than anyone on complete recordings in the seventy-five years since. Henri Albers is a charming Capulet with a pleasant, forward bass-baritone: again a sort of voice we seldom hear today. The early recording process limits the dynamic variety he seems certain to have brought to the role in the theater.

On the other hand, the middling reputation that Marcel Journet had in the earlier part of his very long career may be partly explained in this recording. Scoops, slides, and pitch problems disfigure an already dull characterization of Frère Laurent, despite the natural beauty of Journet's voice and its free and open top register. There is a world of difference between this and the expertly managed Méphistophélès he recorded nearly twenty years later. François Ruhlmann conducts a prosaic performance, but then in 1912 sound restrictions placed great limits on what he could do. Few of the dynamic choral markings, for example, can be observed, so that the group sometimes sounds as relentless as something out of *Marat / Sade*.

1947 MET (M,P)

Bidú Sayão (A), Mimi Benzell (B), Jussi Bjoerling (C), John Brownlee (D), Nicola Moscona (E), Kenneth Schon (F), Metropolitan Opera Chorus and Orchestra—Emil Cooper

This live performance offers not only some spectacular singing but considerable orchestral vitality. Under Emil Cooper, the party scenes are bracing and the conversational exchanges fly past us just as they should. The chorus may at times lack polish but it has interest and

presence. In the cast are the best Roméo, Juliette, and Frère Laurent on records. Bidú Sayão may occasionally sound brittle in the acoustics of the old Met, but she is always shaping and coloring the melody to give it pulsation, spontaneity, and warmth. "Non! ce n'est pas le jour" is a measure of her art: she fills that light, clear voice with longing, and without shattering the music or roughening her delicate tone, in which there is amazing presence and dramatic range, too. The Waltz is both commanding and charming, and at the close of the final scene her very sound seems to die. Jussi Bjoerling is in magnificent voice: a rapturous presence who always speaks through the music. In this live performance, he may not always sing at the *piano* level indicated, but the dynamics are almost invariably proportionate. He and Sayão begin as sunny, youthful lovers who do not expect the tragedy that befalls them, so that their attitudes and vocal colors can change from scene to scene. Bjoerling's "Ah! Jour de deuil," sung after the Duke's order for banishment, has the sound of doom in it. In the moments following, the tenor does breathe, but he phrases so evenly that one is unaware of it. He rises to a glowing high C that for once is justified by the excitement of what has gone before. The soliloquy in Act V is likewise freighted with sorrow and yet beautiful simply as vocalization.

In addition, Nicola Moscona is the only interesting Frère Laurent I have ever heard: craggy, thoughtful, and decisive. Even the lovers' wedding scene is transformed by his conviction. As Mercutio, John Brownlee sings responsibly, but in those blunt tones there is almost nothing of mercurial fantasy. Mimi Benzell is spirited and accurate, though as Stéphano she seems to be singing below her best range much of the time. Of the others, Claramae Turner offers a rich-voiced nurse. The cuts are broader than usual: they include the quartet in which Juliette discovers she is to be married to Paris.

1953 DECCA / LONDON (M)

Janine Micheau (A), Claudine Collart (B), Raoul Jobin (C), Pierre Mollet (D), Heinz Rehfuss

(E), Charles Cambon (F), Paris Opéra Chorus and Orchestra—Alberto Erede

This is a relatively painless performance in acceptable sound. The ensemble is French, which means something in consistency of style. Alberto Erede conducts with considerable animation, though the romance is distinctly autumnal. As Juliette, Janine Micheau provides warm but sometimes irresolute tone; her technique is awkward enough to deprive the character of effortless charm. Raoul Jobin has at times grace and intensity, though the vision and voice are both a little mature in a role in which the illusion of youth is of the essence. Pierre Mollet's Mercutio is rather timid; he sings the Ballad of Queen Mab with some ease, if scant thrust or joy. His tenor sound robs the dueling scenes of vocal contrast. Heinz Rehfuss is a careful, focused Frère Laurent, with, however, a slender low voice and little dramatic imagination; and Charles Cambon is an incisive Capulet who nevertheless registers but meager delight in the party scene. At that, the performance as a whole is bettered on records only by the Metropolitan Opera live broadcast. Though the ballet music is provided, the other standard cuts are all observed.

1968 EMI / ANGEL (S)

Mirella Freni (A), Eliane Lublin (B), Franco Corelli (C), Henri Gui (D), Xavier Depraz (E), Claude Calès (F), Paris Opéra Chorus and Orchestra—Alain Lombard

This performance is infuriating, especially since the idea behind it seems sensible enough: get an internationally famous heroic voice for Roméo and a beloved lyric soprano for Juliette and stir in a French supporting cast and conductor. The difficulties are that the French singers are miscast and dull; the conductor is often slumbrous; the tenor (for all his naturally huge sound) gulps, cries, and shouts; and the soprano, trapped in this *No Exit* production, is simply uninteresting.

Franco Corelli has, of course, a magnificent voice and some notion of how to produce it, but his French and style are awful: boringly

tearful, inexact, and outsized. The few quiet moments are self-advertising effects; his singing is generally so loud and fierce that Roméo's eventual anger at Tybalt in Act III means nothing, since he has been shouting all through the opera. In "Ah! Jour de deuil" there is some grand tone but no *legato*: in effect he salivates all over the music. Mirella Freni's voice is warmer than Yvonne Gall's and fresher and steadier than Janine Micheau's: the Waltz, for example, is full-toned and accurate, but it is also without character. The rest is rich, bland, and often lacking in intimacy. What is one to do, with a partner like Corelli?

Of the others, Henri Gui is a light, nervous Mercutio. With Corelli shouting, he seems more like Roméo's comic servant than a noble colleague. Xavier Depraz is a dry Frère Laurent and Claude Calès a light Capulet. Neither is interesting. Robert Cardona is a character tenor; one can't take him seriously as the fiery young Tybalt. Eliane Lublin is a pale and rather melancholy Stéphano and Michèle Vilma tremulous as the nurse. Presiding over this is Alain Lombard, who begins decisively enough but is soon either hammering out the joyous passages or sentimentalizing the romantic ones. The cuts are generally standard. All of this is captured in full, modern sound.

1983 EMI / ANGEL (S,D) CD

Catherine Malfitano (A), Ann Murray (B), Alfredo Kraus (C), Gino Quilico (D), José van Dam (E), Gabriel Bacquier (F), Midi-Pyrénées Regional Chorus, Chorus and Orchestra of the Capitole de Toulouse—Michel Plasson

An advantage of this set is its relative completeness. Though the ballet music is cut, the performance does include the potion scene, nuptial procession, epithalamium, final scene of Act IV, and a few other little sections customarily dropped. The Roméo of Alfredo Kraus is a cultivated creation, thoughtful, intimate, and often elegant. The voice is a little dry and unsteady and the *legato* not always as smooth as one expects, but the top is generally firm. As Juliette, Catherine Malfitano is bright-voiced and efficient. Her manner sometimes lacks warmth, but she handles the potion scene well and is touchingly frail in the death scene. Gino Quilico is an accomplished Mercutio, though with less of a smile in the Mab scene and less power in Act III than one would like. José van Dam is dull but in handsome voice, and Gabriel Bacquier is the best of Capulets; he gets much of the good nature, gruffness, and heartbreak of the role. Though her sound is light for Stéphano, Ann Murray performs with both irony and control. Under Michel Plasson, the chorus and orchestra have greater vitality than some of the cast.

The 1912 Pathé set is historically fascinating, the 1953 Decca at least presents a French cast, and the 1983 EMI offers a score almost uncut, in stereo. It is, however, the 1947 live Metropolitan Opera version, with its cast of Sayāo, Bjoerling, and Moscona, under the vital direction of Emil Cooper, that is unforgettable.

LONDON GREEN

GEORGE FRIDERIC HANDEL

GIULIO CESARE (1724)

A: Cleopatra (s); B: Sesto (s); C: Giulio Cesare (c or bar);
D: Cornelia (c); E: Tolomeo (c or bs); F: Achille (bs)

lthough it is still among the most famous and most frequently performed of Handel's Italian operas, *Giulio Cesare* has had only a spotty representation on records. This continued neglect seems particularly ironic in light of the fact that several other once-obscure Handel operas and oratorios have recently been recorded with great success.

The opera presents numerous textual challenges to its performers. Handel did not leave the score in a definitive state. We cannot even describe any performance as complete or incomplete without qualification. Handel began the opera in 1723 and wrote most of the first act—for a soprano Cornelia, a contralto Sesto, and a tenor Tolomeo; when a different cast was assembled, the composer made many changes in both the libretto and the music before the first performance, in 1724. The opera was revived three times in Handel's lifetime (in 1725, 1730, and 1732), and for each of these productions he made further revisions—adding, deleting, and rewriting arias to suit the particular talents of individual singers. In 1725, for example, Sesto—originally sung by a female soprano—was assigned to a tenor; Handel revised two of the character's arias, replaced three more of them with completely new pieces, and cut Sesto's duet with Cornelia ("Son nata a lagrimar") altogether.

A conductor can attempt to reconstruct what Handel actually performed on a specific occasion, or an ideal version of the opera can be created, drawn from all the available source material.

But most problematic of all is the question of the vocal distribution. On the opening night in 1724, high voices dominated the vocal texture, as they did in most Baroque operas. In addition to Cleopatra (soprano) and Cornelia (contralto), Sesto, as has been previously mentioned, was a female soprano; Cesare, Tolomeo, and Nireno (a small part) were all alto castratos. Only Achille and Curio (the other supporting roles) were sung by basses.

Traditionally, ever since the first twentieth-century revivals of Handel's operas (in Germany, in the 1920s), the castrato parts have been transposed down an octave and assigned to baritones or basses. However, many Handelians have pointed out how this procedure alters the composer's vocal textures and does serious damage to the music.

Increasingly, the trend has been to cast women or countertenors in the castrato roles, in order to preserve the original pitch.

There are other matters that must be resolved before a recording can be made: e.g., whether, and how, to embellish and whether to employ period instruments.

1952 GUILDE INTERNATIONAL DU DISQUE (M)

Elisabeth Roon (A), Herbert Handt (B), Otto Wiener (C), Mira Kalin (D), Philip Curzon (E), Academy Chorus, Pro Musica Chamber Orchestra, Vienna—Hans Swarowsky

Although presented as a "complete recording," this set in fact offers extended excerpts. All of the *secco* recitative is eliminated, except for Cesare's brief comments before and during Cleopatra's aria "V'adoro, pupille." As a result, one *da capo* aria simply follows another, even though the dramatic situation may have changed quite drastically in the meantime. The role of Achille has been cut out altogether, and the remaining characters are deprived of several of their arias: Cleopatra, for example, loses "Non disperar" as well as "Venere bella."

In addition to the aforementioned scraps of recitative, the performance includes the Overture, the choruses, and the sinfonia before the final scene. Some old record catalogues state that baritone Alfred Poell sings the role of Achille on this set. All of this leads me to speculate that the original German release may have included Achille's arias as well as some connective recitative, but was reduced from three LPs to two for the American market.

Hans Swarowsky, whom one scarcely thinks of as a Handelian, in fact conducts quite firmly, with a good feel for the flow of the melodies. The orchestra has a warm, full, sweet sound, without any trace of either thinness or excess weight, that is attractive in itself and by no means inappropriate to the music. Not surprisingly, most of the arias sound as though they come from a Bach Passion rather than an Italian opera, but there is nothing desperately unstylish about the basic approach.

None of the singers attempts anything in the way of vocal embellishment, and none of them can trill. The Italian pronunciation tends to be correct rather than incisive or expressive.

Elisabeth Roon has a pretty lyric soprano, rather reedy and brittle in timbre; she phrases carefully, and lacks spontaneity. She takes a brave stab at "Dal tempeste," but without ever quickening the listener's pulse. Mira Kalin's heavy, fruity contralto is not a bad match for Cornelia's music, but she displays little in the way of musical or verbal imagination.

Tenor Herbert Handt sings Sesto's music in the original soprano version, transposing everything an octave down, without availing himself of any of the composer's own alternatives for tenor voice. He is the liveliest and most stylish of the soloists.

Neither of the other two men sings well

enough to justify the transposition of the castrato roles into the bass clef. Otto Wiener makes a sincere effort to adjust his dark, woolly bass to the demands of the title role, but vocally it's a compromise at best, and his delivery is monotonous. Baritone Philip Curzon—rusty of timbre, short on *legato*, and cautious in his one-note-at-a-time negotiation of the coloratura—sounds thoroughly uncomfortable in Tolomeo's music.

The mono sound is quite good for its age, with the solo voices nicely balanced against the orchestra, and a plausible placement of the offstage instrumental ensemble in "V'adoro, pupille." On the whole, though, this recording simply documents how far Baroque performance practice has progressed since the early LP era.

1967 RCA / BMG (S) CD

Beverly Sills (A), Beverly Wolff (B), Norman Treigle (C), Maureen Forrester (D), Spiro Malas (E), Dominic Cossa (F), New York City Opera Chorus and Orchestra—Julius Rudel

The New York City Opera's 1966 revival of *Giulio Cesare* was successful enough to inspire this studio recording, made the following year with the same cast, orchestra, and conductor.

No less an authority than Winton Dean has dismissed this recording as "a travesty." I would say that his judgment is too harsh: twenty-five years ago, many people thought that the New York City Opera was crazy to attempt a revival of any Handel opera in the first place, and the performance edition used was admittedly a compromise, designed to make the opera palatable to a modern audience unfamiliar with the Baroque idiom.

There are, of course, many cuts. Some arias are dropped altogether, and only a handful of those that remain are performed in truly complete form. Sometimes we hear only the A section, with the B section and *da capo* cut. The usual procedure, however, is to perform A and B intact (often with embellishments), followed by an abridged, elaborately ornamented reprise of A. Some of the vocal decoration does strike me as excessive: in the *da capo* of "Dal tempeste," for example, the melody is transformed almost beyond recognition.

Julius Rudel conducts the piece exactly as he would a nineteenth-century Italian opera, which is a step in the right direction: there is nothing tentative or "quainty-dainty" about the reading, and the contrasting moods of individual arias are vividly realized. The orchestra plays well.

The role of Cleopatra made Beverly Sills a star, and happily the recording suggests what all the excitement was about. She is the only Cleopatra on the complete sets who creates a three-dimensional character. She is extraordinarily vivid and spontaneous-sounding in the recitatives. The coloratura fireworks, including a truly birdlike trill and some startling (interpolated) excursions above high C, are exhilarating to listen to. But the most remarkable moments in the performance occur in her three slow, subdued arias: "Piangero la sorte mia," "V'adoro, pupille," and (especially) "Se pietà di me non senti." Here the delicate tonal quality, the purity of line, the sure grasp of Baroque style, and—above all—the directness of expression, the warmth and femininity, all set a formidable standard.

This is probably the best of Norman Treigle's all-too-few commercial recordings. His voice is a true bass-baritone, dark and imposing in quality, but not excessively weighty, and capable of a surprising lightness and lyricism. His Cesare has tremendous dignity—yet is convincing as a lover.

Maureen Forrester has a magnificent contralto, well suited to Cornelia's mournful arias. Her approach to the music is rather stately and abstract, and her Italian is poor. Still, the warm, velvety sound of the voice is right for the music, and hard to resist.

As Sesto, Beverly Wolff displays a big, hefty mezzo that sounds more like a Verdi than a Handel voice; she throws herself into the role, however, and is undeniably exciting.

The recording was originally issued on three LPs. The CD reissue is on two discs. A booklet note states that the sinfonia preceding the opera's final scene has been deleted in order to fit the performance on two CDs. But—at least on my copy of the CD set—the sinfonia is present. What has been deleted is the penultimate scene of the opera—a brief (as originally recorded)

sequence in which Sesto kills Tolomeo in front of Cornelia. (To add to the confusion, the text of the scene is printed in the CD booklet.)

1969 DEUTSCHE GRAMMOPHON (S)

Tatiana Troyanos (A), Peter Schreier (B), Dietrich Fischer-Dieskau (C), Julia Hamari (D), Franz Crass (E), Gerold Schramm (F), Munich Bach Chorus and Orchestra—Karl Richter

This recording is complete in the sense that it includes all the music printed in the complete-edition score. Several arias appear on records for the first time.

There is no vocal embellishment whatsoever: the *da capo* repeats are sung exactly the same way as they were the first time around. A solo double bass reinforces the harpsichord in the recitatives, and the sustained, uninflected pedal notes of the string player create a very monotonous effect.

The casting is peculiar. We have a mezzo-soprano Cleopatra and a tenor Sesto—who once again sings the original soprano part an octave down, ignoring the 1725 alternatives. Cesare is still a baritone, Tolomeo a bass; even Nireno, who is supposed to be Cleopatra's eunuch, is assigned to a bass (Michael Schopper)!

Karl Richter is a good, disciplined musician, but his Handel lacks elegance, variety, and warmth. One polite aria follows another, separated by long stretches of dutiful recitative, and the listener quickly becomes bored. The orchestra plays beautifully, but is held on too tight a rein by the conductor. The chorus sounds far too genteel in its brief contributions: although it is a mixed chorus, the women produce a cold, white, vibrato-less sound, and could easily be mistaken for boy sopranos and altos.

Although Cleopatra's music does not lie extraordinarily high as written, it is still something of a feat for a mezzo-soprano to sing it at all. Tatiana Troyanos is both regal and seductive in the role, but the weight and color of her voice seem wrong for the music. She would surely be better suited to Cornelia. In the latter role, however, Julia Hamari is outstanding, her firm, clear mezzo filling out the music with fine expressive effect, and avoiding any impression of heaviness.

If we must have a baritone Cesare, then Dietrich Fischer-Dieskau is a logical choice. This imaginative and resourceful artist has a fine conception of the role, but the execution is flawed. He can spin out a silken *legato* line, with subtle dynamic shadings, in the more lyric numbers; but his coloratura is rough and heavily aspirated throughout, his high notes often seem hard-pressed, and he occasionally sounds gruff and overemphatic in the recitatives.

Peter Schreier has the advantage of sounding boyish, but his dry, shallow tenor is simply not the kind of *bel canto* instrument required here.

Whatever reservations one may have about a bass Tolomeo vanish in the face of Franz Crass's performance: his very dark timbre is beautiful; his flexibility remarkable, considering the size of his voice; and he is always dramatically persuasive. The Achille, Gerold Schramm, has a less imposing bass, but uses it well.

The recording is exceptionally well engineered.

1984 EMI / ANGEL (In English) (S,D) CD

Valerie Masterson (A), Della Jones (B), Janet Baker (C), Sarah Walker (D), James Bowman (E), John Tomlinson (F), English National Opera Chorus and Orchestra—Charles Mackerras

This recording—another studio job documenting a stage production—is sung in English, which will automatically deter some prospective purchasers. The translation (by Brian Trowell) used here is an excellent one: it is sometimes free with the sense of the original text, but it is straightforward and dignified in tone, and it fits the music well.

The score is sensibly abridged. Ten arias are omitted altogether and three are heard in abridged form. Most of the numbers that are included are performed complete—the exceptions include Cesare's "Al lampo dell'armi," of which only the A section is sung, no doubt as a gesture toward dramatic verisimilitude. There is a good deal of vocal decoration, although it tends to be less extravagant than that heard on the RCA set.

Sir Charles Mackerras, an experienced Han-

delian, conducts stylishly and with a good theatrical sense, and he has a solidly professional orchestra and chorus at his disposal.

Although the casting avoids octave transposition of vocal parts, a certain monotony results—ironically enough—from the fact that Dame Janet Baker, Della Jones, and Sarah Walker all have very similar-sounding mezzo-soprano voices. All three are fine artists, however. Baker does not sound as fresh and free as she might have had she recorded Cesare a decade earlier, but she is vivid and authoritative. Jones is an impulsive Sesto. Walker suggests an unusually aggressive Cornelia, eager to avenge her husband's death and bitterly resentful of the way Tolomeo and Achille behave toward her.

Valerie Masterson's cool, flutey soprano gives her Cleopatra a certain well-bred reserve—next to the three high-intensity mezzos in the cast, she seems remarkably self-possessed.

A countertenor Tolomeo is a good idea in principle, but (as on most of his other recordings) James Bowman sings with a glassy, hooty timbre that is not particularly attractive or expressive. He's a musical performer, but it's hard to imagine such an androgynous-sounding pharaoh being much of a political or sexual threat to anyone.

John Tomlinson is a firm, nicely focused Achille, with above-average agility and pointed inflection of the words.

The digital sound is excellent.

1989 NUOVA ERA (S,D,P) CD

Patrizia Orciani (A), Josella Ligi (B), Martine Dupuy (C), Raquel Pierotti (D), Susanna Anselmi (E), Pietro Spagnoli (F), Pro Arte Orchestra of Bassano—Marcello Panni

This "live" recording is a compilation of three staged performances given during July 1989 at the fifteenth Festival della Valle d'Itri. The sound quality is, naturally, a cut below what might have been achieved under studio conditions. There is a good deal of stage noise (mostly footsteps), but applause is heard only at the end of each act, and the opera seems to have been performed with only one intermission; Acts II and III are combined into a continuous sequence.

There are extensive cuts in the recitatives, but most of the arias are retained (some of them in abridged form). Cleopatra is allowed all eight of her arias; oddly, her duet with Cesare in the final scene ("Più amabile belta") is omitted, although its text is printed in the booklet. The penultimate scene, in which Sesto kills Tolomeo, is eliminated completely.

All of the roles are sung at original pitch. Since Italian audiences have not yet embraced countertenors with any great enthusiasm, this means an abundance of sopranos and mezzos; even Nireno is sung by a mezzo (Sara Mingardo). Some listeners, of course, may find this casting as monotonous as the preponderance of low male voices on the DG/Richter set.

Da capo repeats are liberally embellished—sometimes to good effect, sometimes not. The harpsichord chords that punctuate the *secco* recitatives are reinforced by very short, violently accented jabs from a solo cello; after a couple of scenes have gone by, this mannerism becomes every bit as irritating as the double-bass drone on the DG/Richter set.

In general, though, conductor Marcello Panni has a good grasp of the style: he sets sensible tempos, supports his singers ably, and his reading combines lyricism with drama. The orchestra sounds small, which at least gives the performance an appropriately intimate scale, but some of the playing is insecure. The strings have their rough moments, and the horns are excruciating in their brief but exposed appearances. There is no chorus: the passages marked "coro" are sung by the soloists.

Most of the singing is good. Patrizia Orciani has a larger voice than we usually hear in this repertory. She phrases firmly, declaims the recitatives with bold, clear words, and floats some beautiful high, suspended *pianos*. She negotiates the coloraturas accurately enough, if without the kind of security and abandon that could make them really memorable.

The Cornelia, Raquel Pierotti, has a warm, full mezzo and good dramatic instincts. Josella Ligi, with her reedy soprano, is an appropriately boyish-sounding Sesto.

It is probably absurd to complain that neither Martine Dupuy, as Cesare, nor Susanna Anselmi, as Tolomeo, sounds even remotely masculine—Dupuy, in particular, is alluringly sensual and feminine in timbre.

1991 HARMONIA MUNDI (S,D) CD

Barbara Schlick (A), Marianne Rorholm (B), Jennifer Larmore (C), Bernarda Fink (D), Derek Lee Ragin (E), Furio Zanasi (F), Concerto Köln—René Jacobs

While this new *Giulio Cesare* may not be ideal, it serves the opera more faithfully than any previous recording.

Harmonia Mundi's first advantage is completeness. The textual question, unfortunately, is not addressed in the booklet accompanying the set; but it is obvious that Handel's full, original 1724 score is the basis. Some stretches of *secco* recitatives that the composer cut before the opera's opening night, or dropped in the course of its initial run, are restored. As a result, this performance runs for over four hours and contains more music than any previous version. Furthermore, many textual misreadings and other errors that have been perpetuated in the older printed scores and on previous recordings have been corrected.

Harmonia Mundi's second strength is the conducting of René Jacobs. He is never guilty of the common "authentic performance" fault of excessive haste, and yet the performance flows beautifully, with the individual mood of each aria captured, yet well integrated into the whole.

The Cologne ensemble is one of the oldest and most skillful period instrument groups; the playing is warm and technically confident, never tentative of attack or desiccated in tone. The singers embellish the *da capo* repeats; the ornamentation (much more restrained than that on the RCA/Rudel set) is generally effective.

It seems ungrateful to express reservations about the Cesare and the Cleopatra of this performance: both singers are resourceful technicians, and both are experienced Baroque stylists. But Jennifer Larmore's mezzo must be described as useful rather than beautiful; when her voice must move (as in "Al lampo dell'armi"), it acquires a colorless, bleached-out quality. Larmore, however, knows how to create the aural illusion of masculinity. She is impressive in Cesare's great monologues "Alma del gran Pompeo" and "Dall'ondoso periglio."

Barbara Schlick is an uncommonly youthful, vulnerable-sounding Cleopatra. There is not much sensuality or variety of color in her pure, virginal soprano, though. As a result, Schlick is superb in a light, teasing aria like "Non disperar," but one wants more narcissism and seduction in "V'adoro, pupille" and more tonal body and pathos in "Se pietà" and "Piangero."

The rest of this cast maintains a very high standard. Bernarda Fink is a warm, seductive-sounding Cornelia, and the spirited Marianne Rorholm is easily the best Sesto on any "complete" recording of the opera to date.

Both villains are also excellent. In Derek Lee Ragin, we at last have a high-voiced Tolomeo whom we can take seriously as a threat to the other characters. Ragin's countertenor, though cold and white in timbre, can take on a penetrating quality under pressure; he makes Tolomeo sound fierce as well as effete. Ragin also does some astonishing things with the coloratura.

The sound is unobtrusively first-rate.

The new Harmonia Mundi/Jacobs recording is by far the most desirable, and eclipses most of its competitors. Here, at last, is a truly complete, stylistically up-to-date, and well-prepared recording, featuring an orchestra of period instruments and conducted by an experienced Baroque specialist. All the roles are, properly, sung at original pitch: Cesare and Sesto by mezzo-sopranos, Tolomeo and Nireno by countertenors. Most important of all, this performance really does "play" as a drama, rather than as a succession of vocal-display pieces.

ROLAND GRAEME

PAUL HINDEMITH

MATHIS DER MALER (1938)

A: Ursula (s); B: Regina (s); C: Albrecht (t); D: Schwalb (t); E: Mathis (bar)

Based on incidents in the life of the sixteenth-century painter Matthias Grünewald, *Mathis der Maler* questions an artist's function and relevance in times of acute social, political, and religious crisis—a touchy topic in Germany of the 1930s—and Hindemith's answers were hardly calculated to please the Nazi regime. The opera takes place at the time of the Peasants' War of 1524, and scenes of book burning, mob hysteria, and individual oppression uncomfortably parallel contemporary events. Hindemith, who wrote his own libretto, contends that an artist's mission is to create according to his conscience, even when society dictates otherwise—a courageous message contained in the work itself, as well as in the composer's very act of making such a statement in dangerous times. And yet the opera is no didactic treatise: *Mathis* has flesh-and-blood characters, effective theatrical situations, and a text of literary distinction. There is much beautiful music as well, although its rather severe, objective tone will probably always limit the opera's appeal—a noble but demanding score, perhaps best reserved for festivals or contemplative listening, at home, on the phonograph.

1979 EMI / ANGEL (S)

Rose Wagemann (A), Urszula Koszut (B), James King (C), William Cochran (D), Dietrich Fischer-Dieskau (E), Bavarian Radio Chorus and Orchestra—Rafael Kubelik

Since this recording is unlikely to have a rival any time soon, *Mathis* fanciers have no choice but to hunt it down and make the best of a less than ideal performance. Kubelik's respect and affection for the score are always in evidence, but the music would surely not sound quite so gray if played with more passion and a more pronounced dynamic profile. Part of the problem may be the tape-to-disc transfer, at least as heard on Angel's made-in-America quadri-phonic pressings. The airless and excessively recessed ambience is especially disadvantageous to the orchestra, and remastering for compact discs might possibly open up the sonic perspective. Fischer-Dieskau was the Mathis in the opera's famous 1959 Berlin revival, and his experience with the part tells, as does his consummate musical intelligence and lieder-like inflection of the words. As recorded here, unfortunately, the voice sounds very tired. King is a dull Cardinal Albrecht, whose only apparent means of expressing emotion, when aroused, is to sing with an added touch of phlegm. Wagemann's pressured, uncomfortably pushed-up mezzo-soprano vitiates her stressful attempts to make Ursula's problems seem sympathetic, and Koszut's pallid Regina is only intermittently affecting. The supporting cast is adequate, no more.

About an hour's worth of excerpts conducted

by Leopold Ludwig and dating from the time of the Berlin production has been reissued by DG, coupled on a two-disc set with a complete performance of Hindemith's *Cardillac*. Fischer-Dieskau's Mathis is in much fresher voice, Pilar Lorengar sings the dying Regina with much poignancy, and Donald Grobe—inexplicably demoted to the smaller role of Sylvester on EMI's recording—turns Albrecht into a genuinely moving, three-dimensional character.

PETER G. DAVIS

ENGELBERT HUMPERDINCK

HÄNSEL UND GRETEL (1893)

A: Gretel (s); B: Hänsel (ms); C: Gertrude (ms);
D: Witch (ms); E: Peter (bar)

The confection that Humperdinck spun out of his incidental music for a children's play by his sister remains a delight for its fascinatingly detailed craftsmanship and its balance between sentiment and humor. On records it has attracted some distinguished interpreters who accord it greater care and subtlety than is common in live performance.

Humperdinck specifies some variants in the score, none of crucial importance. For instance, he allows the possibility of joining the first scene directly to the following interlude without pause; on these recordings only Suitner, Wallberg, and Solti make this elision. As for the easier alternatives provided for some of the Witch's highest notes, most Witches choose the higher lines, some have to create additional low options, and some interpret the score so freely that their pitch is indeterminate.

Most interesting is an area of flexibility not hinted at in the score: the freedom as to vocal type with which nearly all the opera's roles are commonly cast. (The listing above simply duplicates the score's specification.) Nominally mezzo-sopranos, both Hänsel and Gertrude are sometimes sung, often to fine effect, by sopranos. Peters cover the spectrum from Wagnerian bass-baritones to light Mozartians, and the Witch may be a high soprano, a deep mezzo, or even a male voice. About the only certainty is that Gretel will be a soprano—and even that practice is given a new twist on the EMI recording which casts brother, sister, Sandman, and Dew Fairy with children's voices.

The two recordings most obviously derived from stage productions both happen to be in English. Though uncredited (at least on recent reissues) and diverging slightly in detail, both texts clearly derive from the standard Constance Bache translation, a rather old-fashioned one for present-day taste.

1943 URANIA (M)

Erna Berger (A), Marie-Luise Schilp (B), Elisabeth Waldenau (C), Margarete Arndt-Ober (D), Hans Heinz Nissen (E), Berlin Mozart Children's Choir, Berlin Radio Symphony Orchestra—Artur Rother

The first recording of *Hänsel und Gretel* is in many ways an impressive one. Unfortunately, the sonic limitations curtail one's pleasure in the orchestral playing (the dream pantomime conveys little magic), which is nevertheless clearly in expert hands under Artur Rother. This is not at all an easy score to conduct, as several recordings by eminent maestros prove, but Rother's prevailingly lively tempos, his careful grading and balancing of the complex textural overlays, his alertness to variety and dramatic eventfulness in the extended dialogue accompaniments, and his zestful realization of the bouncier sections all combine to put him among the handful who have met the challenge on records.

In Erna Berger, the recording rejoices in a

Gretel born to the role, with a clear, sweet, unaffected sound that is also full of personality. (Unfortunately, Berger endures the only cut on any *Hänsel* recording: one stanza of her "Männlein" solo.) Hänsel, Marie-Luise Schilp, sounds more conventionally operatic, rich, and womanly—but steady in tone and agreeably straightforward in manner. Elisabeth Waldenau makes Gertrude grand and rather swoopy in style, but with a conviction that makes it work. Hans Heinz Nissen, too, employs a big voice to good effect, hearty and personable though tending to inaccuracy in detail. Hildegard Erdmann, the Sandman, resembles Schilp in voice type, a plummy mezzo—different from usual casting for the part and an interesting contrast to the strong, vibrant soprano of Gertrud Walter, the Dew Fairy.

Besides Berger, the most noteworthy name in the cast is the great contralto Margarete Arndt-Ober, in her only complete opera recording. Her age reveals itself in some fleeting unwieldiness and inflexibility, but she still has substantial tonal resources and dramatic vividness, as well as a sense of humor and a fine high B-flat. She makes a distinguished contribution to a set that would be recommendable were it not for the sonic dimness.

1947 CBS / SONY (In English) (M)

Nadine Conner (A), Risë Stevens (B), Claramae Turner (C), Thelma Votipka (D), John Brownlee (E), Metropolitan Opera Chorus and Orchestra—Max Rudolf

Originally released on 78s (which sometimes refuse to overlap properly in the transfer), this recording represents Metropolitan Opera performances of its time. It has curiously little theatrical life in its character interaction, but the cast's ostentatiously clear English enunciation (unabashedly American, except for Brownlee's British) suggests long experience putting the work across to large, somewhat inattentive audiences. Conductor Rudolf apparently regards the orchestral contribution as pure accompaniment once the curtain is up, and the instrumental subservience is exacerbated by a recording qual-

ity that manages to be both dry and murky (and is plagued by a persistent hum). Staging for records plays no part here; the offstage Peter is on mike from the start.

Nadine Conner exemplifies a good opera-house standard for Gretel: a light voice, used straightforwardly but not without imagination. Hänsel, Risë Stevens, was a noted interpreter of other trouser roles; in this one she remains oddly unconvincing, with overdone "Aren't we jolly?" inflections. The parents do honorable work but at no point rise to memorability, and Brownlee attains his higher notes only with some difficulty. Thelma Votipka, a beloved member of this company for years, often performed the part of the Witch—which indeed constitutes her principal recorded legacy. Her basically attractive lyric soprano is really heard to best advantage in her brief cameo as the Sandman. Some of the Witch's role she sings quite straightforwardly, sounding like a nice pleasant woman even after unmasking her true intentions; she only approximates the more ambitious musical requirements, and on occasion simply improvises in lieu of the written notes. A very adult chorus (unique among all recordings) sounds disappointingly wrong as the children and leaves a heavy-handed feeling at the end—which is in fact typical of the whole enterprise.

1953 EMI / ANGEL (M) CD

Elisabeth Schwarzkopf (A), Elisabeth Grümmer (B), Maria von Ilosvay (C), Else Schürhoff (D), Josef Metternich (E), Choirs of Leighton High School for Girls and Bancroft's School, Philharmonia Orchestra—Herbert von Karajan

This set has often been praised for the skill with which Herbert von Karajan realizes the orchestral score; indeed, he and the Philharmonia provide many marvelous moments—none more magical than the gathering dark and fear in the forest—but his realization of intricacies of orchestration no longer seems so unique, having been equaled (even surpassed?) on other recordings. In particular, his insistence on mellifluous sonority at all cost sacrifices too much rhythmic impulse. He is especially prone to unmarked slowdowns, losing momentum at crucial points where it should continue unchecked; one such is "Habt Dank" in the finale, where the rhythmic figuration is treated as decorative rather than propulsive.

The set benefits from an exceptional Hänsel, Elisabeth Grümmer, with a beautiful, perfectly even soprano and clear, straightforward ideas about the character. Elisabeth Schwarzkopf, on the other hand, knowing that her soprano sounds anything but childlike, tries to compensate in exactly the wrong way, with a careful series of little-girl mannerisms that call attention to themselves and make her performance a trial— more witchlike than the Witch. She sounds best in her nearly whispered "Männlein" solo.

Maria von Ilosvay makes a really exceptional Gertrude, full of feeling and dark velvet tone, unusually personal and sympathetic in her anger and subsequent prayer. She is well matched by Josef Metternich as a Peter on a Wagnerian scale. His voice sounds big, easy, and resonant, and he sends it sailing expressively through this role. Both benefit from Karajan's amazing clarification of the musical progress of their scene together, which here receives its most complete realization.

Both the spirits are sung by the usually excellent Anny Felbermayer as if she had been ordered to sound thin and breathy. The same problem seems to afflict the Witch: initially, her voice sounds embarrassingly worn out, with no volume or tonal center. Then for "Hocus, pocus, Holderbusch!" Else Schürhoff audibly transforms herself from a feeble old lady into a threatening sorceress, and the effect is absolutely hair-raising (I'd been fooled completely). Unfortunately, after the surprise wears off the real voice turns out to be only somewhat more imposing than the fake one; it's limited in volume and she has to invent optional low notes even where Humperdinck didn't write any. This is one of several respects in which later recordings have done better by Humperdinck.

p.1954 DEUTSCHE GRAMMOPHON (M)

Rita Streich (A), Gisela Litz (B), Marianne Schech (C), Res Fischer (D), Horst Günter (E), Wittelsbach Gymnasium Boys' Choir, Bavarian Radio Women's Chorus, Munich Philharmonic Orchestra—Fritz Lehmann

This is perhaps the least theatrical-sounding of all *Hänsel und Gretel* recordings (though the 1947 CBS runs it close). Competent in all departments, it hardly ever comes to life; hearing it, one pictures only singers and instrumentalists in a studio, determined to read their notes correctly.

The best-known name in the cast is Rita Streich, an exquisite high soprano of exactly the right type for Gretel. Yet, unlike her predecessor Erna Berger and her successor Helen Donath, both similarly endowed, Streich fails to capitalize on her natural advantages: her Gretel remains emotionless throughout and impresses only in the poised beauty of her reflective solos. Hänsel is Gisela Litz, a rather heavy mezzo with similar lack of success at characterization; lacking Streich's vocal prettiness, she emerges as blankly dull, and tends to hoot and fall shy of pitch when she must sing quietly.

The parents suffer from a similar lack of spark. Marianne Schech makes a fine strong impression vocally and is thereby preferable to a number of other Gertrudes. And Horst Günter brings the first hint of liveliness onstage with his opening song. Still, it remains only a hint, and the pair fails to make any memorable impression.

Res Fischer represents the aging-mezzo casting tradition for the Witch in quite impressive form. She declines most of the showier options (though she can knock out a good isolated B-flat when she has to) and is clearly happiest when the part stays low. Yet she executes the music carefully and with an imaginative ear for its dramatic effect, without overdoing things, and is all in all the most successful member of the cast. Elisabeth Lindermeier deserves mention for her dark-toned, elegant rendering of the Sandman, far superior to the wispy boy-soprano Dew Fairy.

Fritz Lehmann makes a fine initial impression for his musicality and carefulness but eventually becomes too exclusively focused on a purely musical accuracy. The preludes and interludes sound meticulously prepared, with a scrupulous (and rare) balance between atmosphere and energy, but the rest of the work needs more abandon and drama in the playing.

1963–64 EMI / ANGEL (S)

Anneliese Rothenberger (A), Irmgard Seefried (B), Grace Hoffman (C), Elisabeth Höngen (D), Walter Berry (E), Vienna Boys' Choir, Vienna Philharmonic Orchestra—André Cluytens

This first stereo *Hänsel* is especially disappointing as it has some promising elements. The main problem is the labored attitude toward phrasing and articulation evident in most of the connective passages, as if few of the participants had bothered to acquaint themselves with anything but the familiar set pieces. Much of the conversational underpinning of the first scene and the one with the Witch needs sure guidance from the conductor if it is to convey a coherent shape and line; here Cluytens fails to supply such leadership. In addition, he lets some disturbing orchestral intonation and blatant brass playing pass (the Vienna Philharmonic does not always sound its distinguished self here) and neglects to balance the more complex textures intelligibly. His best moments come in the evocations of mystery and magic (the Witch's Ride interlude and much of the following scene), which do convey appropriate mood. But much of it is unpleasant in articulation and dramatically inattentive.

The biggest asset in the cast is the Hänsel of Irmgard Seefried, not as impeccably vocalized as Grümmer but in a class of her own in terms of uttering each line as if she had just thought of it and couldn't wait to communicate it. Unlike some of her other recordings from this time, her soprano sounds poised and free, losing its clarity only at the very top. As Gretel, Anneliese Rothenberger sounds pretty and musical in a general way, but unspecific and uninteresting; in the prayer, her vocal quality proves too unlike Seefried's for a satisfying blend, and she cannot pull back to the very quiet dynamics called for.

The parents are exceptionally strong vocally but less so theatrically, Berry being the more communicative of the two. The Sandman and Dew Fairy are both in the capable hands of Liselotte Maikl, particularly good in the latter role, for which she evokes an uninhibited energy and sparkle. As the Witch, Elisabeth Höngen shows the attention to detail of the distinguished operatic veteran she was at the time, and finds some unique inflections for many moments. But the singing (despite decent high notes when they occur in isolation) is too spread and worn to provide pleasure on a recording, and she is not helped by Cluytens's unresponsive conducting. The Vienna Boys' Choir makes a polished contribution to the last scene, the set's chief asset besides Seefried.

1964 EMI / ANGEL (In English) (S)

Margaret Neville (A), Patricia Kern (B), Rita Hunter (C), Ann Howard (D), Raimund Herincx (E), Sadler's Wells Chorus and London Boy Singers, Sadler's Wells Orchestra—Mario Bernardi

This product of the Sadler's Wells company has much to recommend it, with especially fine conducting by Mario Bernardi. Second only to Kurt Eichhorn among recorded *Hänsel* conductors, he finds the right balance of liveliness and refinement, supporting his singers expertly, keeping the show moving, but not ignoring musical values. His most valuable asset is his skill at clarifying the theatrical import of a musical moment: he not only makes the most of changes of color or texture but makes them seem inevitable dramatic developments.

Margaret Neville is not one of nature's Gretels, for her soprano sounds unmistakably adult, and serviceable rather than beautiful. Nevertheless, she characterizes and inflects so well (without condescending to the idea of being a child) that she comes through successfully in the end. Patricia Kern, with a warm, solid mezzo and equally uncomplicated interpretation, makes a splendid partner. The two play together easily and (unlike the other recording in English) not on too broad a scale.

The portrayers of the adult characters all achieved considerable recognition a few years later when they starred in the company's Wagner productions, and already show their quality here. Rita Hunter, a Brünnhilde in the making, moves easily through Gertrude's difficult music, banishing all thoughts of the usual tiresome shrew and making one wish the role were longer. Raimund Herincx makes an equally authoritative Peter on a large scale, not subtle but very good to hear. And Ann Howard scores a coup by executing the standard Witch exaggerations in a way that is both genuinely funny and vocally imposing. Her strong dramatic mezzo allows her more contrast than usual between her cajoling and strident moments. Sandman and Dew Fairy are disappointments, as if both were trying to sound like children's weak voices, but the actual children's chorus is charming.

1970 TELEFUNKEN (S)

Renate Hoff (A), Ingeborg Springer (B), Gisela Schröter (C), Peter Schreier (D), Theo Adam (E), Dresden Cross Choir, Dresden State Orchestra—Otmar Suitner

If *Hänsel und Gretel* were an orchestral tone poem unencumbered by voices, this might well be the most desirable recording of all. It presents a great orchestra with a distinctive personality, the Dresden State Orchestra, recorded with a clarity unsurpassed in any other recording, under the direction of a conductor who must be at least partly responsible for the way each instrumental section makes the most of its opportunities. From the easily flowing counterpoint of the prelude, unmarred by excessive shifts of speed, through the domestic scenes, the gathering spell of the forest, the sighting of the gingerbread house, and the exuberant finale, the instrumental colors remain hypnotically ravishing. Since Humperdinck filled each scene with orchestral elaboration that goes by the boards in many performances, this virtuosity is a real strength.

Alas, *Hänsel und Gretel* is not a tone poem. An opera performance which becomes more enjoyable minus the singing has something amiss. This East German cast never falls below minimum acceptability, but few of its members really merit permanent preservation on a recording. Best, probably, are the two mezzo-

sopranos. Ingeborg Springer sounds as if she would be an asset to a live *Hänsel:* a solid voice, not distinctive in timbre but capable of executing everything required musically, with a vital sense of character. Gisela Schröter does nothing with the character of Gertrude, but at least brings a substantial instrument to the task.

As her husband, Theo Adam is livelier but also less musically gratifying, his good ideas undermined by persistent tremulousness. Renate Hoff's Gretel also has this problem, in addition to a difficulty in sustaining pitches accurately that makes for highly uncomfortable listening.

Stage productions often employ a male Witch, but this is the only recording to do so. Peter Schreier's performance has drawn sharply divided reactions: to those familiar with Schreier's usual persona, hearing him in this role is like seeing a favorite stuffy professor clowning for his colleagues in the university show—nobody thought the old boy had it in him. To my ears, Schreier's earnest efforts at broad humor are self-defeating; what's the point of a *travesti* Witch who isn't having a grand time with the part?

1971 EURODISC (S) CD

Helen Donath (A), Anna Moffo (B), Charlotte Berthold (C), Christa Ludwig (D), Dietrich Fischer-Dieskau (E), Tölz Boys' Choir, Bavarian Radio Symphony Orchestra—Kurt Eichhorn

This set (also available on RCA) contains at least four vocal performances that set a standard for their roles. But perhaps the real star of the show is Kurt Eichhorn, who conducts the work in a way that seems utterly simple and obvious, until one hears how many other conductors miss it. He succeeds better than any other conductor on records in balancing and clarifying the orchestral textures to bring out the constant variety and rhythmic impetus with which Humperdinck filled the work, and the Bavarian Radio Symphony plays beautifully for him. A special delight is his success at continuing the momentum of the Act III Prelude through the Dew Fairy's scene—the character simply explodes into life—and Lucia Popp seizes her opportunity in a zestful way that obliterates all other interpreters of the role.

Helen Donath has a vocal quality and personality that make her a natural Gretel; every phrase is realized to perfection in this irresistible portrayal. Dietrich Fischer-Dieskau, in his best voice and on his best behavior, honors all of the composer's musical instructions and unites them into a memorable, lovable portrayal of Peter the broom maker. But superb as all these are, the real treasure is Christa Ludwig's Witch; with the resources of her rich high mezzo, she sings every note and characterizes every line, and becomes genuinely funny by being truly frightening. She recently cited this as her favorite of all her recordings, and it's easy to hear why.

Alongside such memorable portrayals, Arleen Augér is merely a quite good Sandman. And the conscientious but ripely vibrating Hänsel of Anna Moffo and the shrill Gertrude of Charlotte Berthold assume less importance than they otherwise would. Perhaps one is simply determined not to let them matter, since everything else about the performance is so good.

1974 EMI / ANGEL (S) CD

Brigitte Lindner (A), Eugen Hug (B), Ilse Gramatzki (C), Edda Moser (D), Hermann Prey (E), Cologne Children's Choir, Cologne Gürzenich Orchestra—Heinz Wallberg

After enduring the heavy-handed impersonations of childhood deemed appropriate for live performances of *Hänsel und Gretel*, probably many an opera goer has wondered momentarily, "Why can't they just cast children?" We must be grateful to Heinz Wallberg and German EMI for a well-executed demonstration of why "they" can't.

It is especially valuable because Eugen Hug and Brigitte Lindner, both in their teens at the time, were remarkably mature musicians and interpreters (Lindner has gone on to an adult soprano career), and made as good a case for such casting as we are likely ever to hear. There are half a dozen unimportant alterations to their vocal lines (maybe some are simply mistakes), and some curtailment of phrase endings, but basically the children sing the parts as written.

They achieve a touching effect in some of the more subdued set pieces like the "Männlein" solo and the prayer, but in nine-tenths of the score their trebles are simply too thin for the job, even with Wallberg's considerate accompaniment and a healthy boost from the engineers. Additionally, Humperdinck (following universal operatic convention) composed the girl's part higher than the boy's, and it would appear that nature thinks otherwise; thus both performers are singing at the weak ends of their voices, with consequent strain. The other two child soloists have an easier time in their less extended roles (the use of a girl Sandman and a boy Dew Fairy tacitly acknowledges the disparity just mentioned).

The adult roles are in assured professional hands. Prey is his hearty and amiable self as Peter; Moser, a high-soprano Witch, takes the all-out caricature approach but digs into it with spirit and humor. The most pleasant surprise on the set is Ilse Gramatzki, who puts her attractive lyric mezzo to imaginative use as a young, unaggressive mother unlike any other on records; she is, of course, spared the usual challenge of singing opposite adults who are supposed to be her children. Wallberg's conducting is wonderful for orchestral detail, less satisfying in maintaining momentum; no doubt his choices were constrained by the unique circumstances.

1978 DECCA / LONDON (S) CD

Lucia Popp (A), Brigitte Fassbaender (B), Julia Hamari (C), Anny Schlemm (D), Walter Berry (E), Vienna Boys' Choir, Vienna Philharmonic Orchestra—Georg Solti

Georg Solti's Wagner recordings have benefited so sumptuously from Viennese orchestral and recorded sound that the prospect of a *Hänsel* recorded under similar circumstances seems enticing indeed. The very opening—those incomparable Vienna horns intoning the prayer—does embody a tonal ideal for those pages, and there are many similarly successful orchestral passages. But the performance as a whole is disappointing; Solti lays a heavy hand on tempo changes, and his undifferentiated textures leave details to sort themselves out and allow important orchestral lines to be swamped. The engineering, while perhaps playing its part in this, has the nearly unique merit of preserving a fairly natural balance between voices and orchestra (a startling effect after any of the other *Hänsels* save Telefunken's).

Lucia Popp's vocal quality, if not exactly childlike, is certainly lovely and free, and she has the sense to keep her characterization simple, resulting in a most pleasing Gretel. Her partnership with the equally straightforward and sensitive Brigitte Fassbaender (a deeper voice than most recorded Hänsels) provides many treasurable scenes, with the stylistic kinship to Richard Strauss clearer than in other recordings.

The parents are somewhat undercast, with Walter Berry vocally diminished since his earlier recording of Peter—incorporating some endearing personal touches, however—and Julia Hamari a fine light mezzo trying unsuccessfully to emulate a heavy one. (When she confronts her son, it sounds as if the two singers should have swapped roles.) As the Witch, Anny Schlemm goes all out for a shrieking, rasping ogress; she does it with some originality, and she gets her effects, but the approach and the noises it entails do not wear well.

The recorded tradition, begun by Eurodisc, of contrasted star casting for the two short roles gives us in this case a marvelously hypnotic Sandman (Norma Burrowes) and a rather fierce Dew Fairy (Edita Gruberova). The children in the final scene are embodied to perfection by the Vienna Boys' Choir—a strong final impression, but not enough so to make up for the disappointing nature of much that has gone before.

1978 CBS / SONY (S)

Ileana Cotrubas (A), Frederica von Stade (B), Christa Ludwig (C), Elisabeth Söderström (D), Siegmund Nimsgern (E), Cologne Opera Children's Choir, Cologne Gürzenich Orchestra—John Pritchard

The all-star cast that CBS assembled for this project promised better on paper than it turns out on disc. The Cologne orchestra, which achieved such beguiling results for Wallberg, fails to match its earlier standard here, John Pritchard settling for safe, stodgy pacing and haphazard balance and articulation.

Frederica von Stade has just the voice and manner for Hänsel, running very close to the Grümmer/Seefried standard. Ileana Cotrubas, alas, is nowhere near the same league; her only way of simulating an unaffected, childlike tone is to shut the voice down to a piping quasi-falsetto that won't admit expansion or nuance, and the result is small-scale and uninteresting. Another drawback is the disappointing Gertrude of Christa Ludwig, curiously edgy and ill at ease. On the positive side, Siegmund Nimsgern's sturdy bass-baritone makes for a solid Peter, if not a memorably personal one. Star casting for the forest creatures this time gives us an enticing Sandman (Kiri Te Kanawa) and a proficient if excessively cute Dew Fairy (Ruth Welting).

The most unexpected piece of casting is the Witch, Elisabeth Söderström. Her rather frail soprano might not sustain the role onstage, but she has come up with a unique and characteristically resourceful way of projecting it for a recording: as an artful flirt, beguiling the children with coquetry and endless arch nuances. In German this inevitably starts to turn into a Schwarzkopf spoof, and in certain moods I have found it sidesplitting. Söderström and von Stade are the best reasons to listen to this recording.

1989 EMI / ANGEL (S,D) CD

Barbara Bonney (A), Anne Sofie von Otter (B), Hanna Schwarz (C), Marjana Lipovšek (D), Andreas Schmidt (E), Tölz Boys' Choir, Bavarian Radio Orchestra—Jeffrey Tate

This *Hänsel* adds up as one of the best. First of all, it is in excellent conductorial hands: Jeffrey Tate has absorbed the score completely and can make every detail tell without losing line and mood. He secures a fluent singing quality from his orchestra, without neglecting the essential rhythmic bounce that conductors often miss. Even in the darkening-forest sequence, where most *Hänsel* conductors are good, Tate achieves something special and makes it genuinely frightening. Only in the two episodes of the children's otherworldly protectors do he and his singers let matters down: he makes an unwanted hiatus before the Sandman's solo, and this music never allows Barbara Hendricks access to her vocal trump card, her luscious high range. Tate also slows down for the Dew Fairy's entrance (so admittedly do most conductors), and Eva Lind's coarse-toned vocalism disappoints.

Otherwise, all is more than well. Barbara Bonney is right in the Berger/Donath tradition as Gretel, with a clear bell-like light soprano that needs no manipulation to sound childlike, and a pleasantly straightforward (if not quite individual) interpretation. (What syllables is she singing for "Tirelireli," though?) Anne Sofie von Otter is one of the few true mezzos to make a complete success of Hänsel on records (most of the best ones are soprano in timbre); stopping short of alto plumminess, her clean, quick-speaking tone makes a fine contrast with Bonney yet blends perfectly, and is put at the service of a spirited characterization. Their prayer is just about the loveliest on any recording; two steady, well-matched voices, helped by Tate's simple undragged pulse and eloquent shaping.

As the liner note points out, "Young children should have young parents," and that precept has been well carried out. Hanna Schwarz is vocally first-rate, solid top to bottom vocally and entirely convincing dramatically if not as personal as some Gertrudes. Andreas Schmidt provides a fine baritone as Peter, with a welcome absence of overdramatization. His important solos could use more nuance and coloristic variety, though; in fact, his narrative of the Witch is effective because of Tate's contribution more than his own.

The Witch herself presents a rather different individual than is heard on other recordings: a real monster with nothing funny about her. She benefits from the big dark mezzo (close to contralto) of Marjana Lipovšek, a major voice in its prime. Such a serious interpretation makes this recording a dubious proposition for children's listening, but adults will find that it reveals the real stature of Humperdinck's work as do few other versions.

———————

An ideal *Hänsel und Gretel* could be approximated by combining Donath (or Berger) as Gretel, Grümmer (or Seefried or von Stade or von Otter) as Hänsel, Ilosvay (or Gramatzki) as Gertrude, Fischer-Dieskau (or Metternich) as Peter, Ludwig (or Lipovšek) as the Witch, Te Kanawa (or Burrowes) as the Sandman, and Popp as the Dew Fairy; Kurt Eichhorn (or Mario Bernardi or Jeffrey Tate) would conduct the Dresden State Orchestra and Vienna Boys' Choir, recorded by Telefunken. Since the Eurodisc recording supplies five first choices for this composite, it earns top recommendation, with Tate a close second and Bernardi a very good alternative for those who prefer a performance in English.

JON ALAN CONRAD

LEOŠ JANÁČEK

JENŮFA (1904)

A: Jenůfa (s); B: Kostelnička (s); C: Laca (t); D: Števa (t)

or *Jenůfa*'s Prague premiere in 1916, twelve years after the first performance in Brno, the composer-conductor Kovařovic, who had delayed the Prague performances because Janáček had given him a bad press notice years before, insisted on "editing" the score. He made many small cuts and reorchestrated certain passages and these changes were universally accepted until 1981. Charles Mackerras, the Australian who has become Janáček's leading interpreter, conducted a painstakingly restored edition in Paris. He later pointed out the almost impossible difficulties which must have faced the original performers, partly because of poor orchestral material, partly because the music was so quirkily original—time has worked wonders in each area—and suggested Kovařovic's edition may perhaps be seen as no more permanently subversive than Rimsky-Korsakov's version of *Boris*.

Folk music, which by the time he wrote *Jenůfa* he tended to invent rather than to quote, and the inflections of everyday Moravian speech were Janáček's source materials. The musical language of his operas tends to swing between an intense lyricism and a sometimes harsh, ejaculatory style of vocal and orchestral writing, with much repetition of short phrases. To reconcile these contrasts and maintain the lyrical flow without sentimentalization are the performers' main problems; Janáček's writing moves urgently and, as with Verdi, there is something uncompromising and even hard about his textures and rhythms. To soften it is to falsify Janáček.

Of the four complete recordings, only one is pure Janáček.

1952 SUPRAPHON (M)

Štepanka Jelínková (A), Marta Krásová (B), Beno Blachut (C), Ivo Žídek (D), Prague National Theater Chorus and Orchestra —Jaroslav Vogel

Jaroslav Vogel is the author of the standard work on Janáček and an authority on the composer. His performance is forthright and firmly pulsed from the outset, and fairly bristles with integrity. He sets an invigorating tempo for Act I's recruits, zips into Števa's dance, and without insistence or pressing throughout preserves an intense mood.

This early LP is decently recorded for the period, and the cast is strong, with a rather senior soprano for the title role who is often touching and is a scrupulous observer of the written notes. Both Blachut and Žídek are first-rate in the tenor roles, the former individual of voice, the latter also sustaining the high tessitura well and suggesting less the confident braggart of tradition, more a young man of intelligence living on his nerves.

Small parts are admirably done, but the classical performance is Krásová as Kostelnička, chilling at her entrance through sheer vocal presence. She is heartrending in her plea to Števa, nerves ajangle in the subsequent scene with Laca, and rising to great tragic heights as she decides to do away with the baby. Though often sung by a mezzo, Kostelnička's is truly a soprano part, comparable in range and tessitura to Ortrud, and it is amazing that a mezzo, however famed in the role (which Krásová was), should have tackled it on records for the first time when she was over fifty and brought it off so triumphantly.

1969 SUPRAPHON (also EMI / ANGEL) (S)

Libuše Domanínská (A), Naděžda Kniplová (B), Vilém Přibyl (C), Ivo Žídek (D), Prague National Theater Chorus and Orchestra—Bohumil Gregor

Gregor takes a more lyrical view of the score than Vogel and, in spite of the conductor's renown in this music, I find the softer approach not quite so appropriate for this idiomatic composer. Again, a good cast does justice to the score. Domanínská, a major interpreter of Czech music, is appropriately urgent and forthright, but by this stage of her career not ideally steady of voice and is stretched in the final duet, making heavy weather of top C-flats. Přibyl and Žídek are the equal of Blachut and Žídek, Přibyl in particular distinguishing himself with some virile and direct singing, more brilliance in the voice than in Blachut's and a comparable sweetness of tone. The ecstatic quality of the high B-flat as he greets Jenůfa in Act II would convince anyone of the musico-dramatic validity of a tenor's top notes. So aptly does Kniplová's dramatic soprano fit Kostelnička's music and so overwhelming is her singing at its best that it may seem like caviling to suggest that she is a bit self-conscious in her approach and tends to sail through portentously rather than to dominate effortlessly.

With the slight reservations mentioned, this is a fine and representative set with generally good sound and much more detail audible than in the recording of seventeen years before.

1977–78 SUPRAPHON (S) ℗

Gabriela Beňačková (A), Naděžda Kniplová (B), Vilém Přibyl (C), Vladimír Krejčík (D), Brno Janáček Opera—František Jílek

Jenůfa started life in Brno and the orchestra and its chief conductor, František Jílek, plainly know the score very well indeed; in fact, they

need fear no comparison with their Prague colleagues (the same is true of the small-part singers). Jílek takes a relatively light-handed view of the score, quick and airy in the opening scenes where the accent is on narrative action, later on sometimes over-reacting to passages of heavier sentiment. On the other hand, there is no denying the tenderness of his view of Jenůfa when she is alone in Act II or in her scene with Kostelnička, and this compassion is one of the composer's salient characteristics.

Přibyl sings with even more authority than eight years before and his voice shows no diminution of quality, which at well over age fifty is no mean feat for a tenor. Krejčík, in contrast, sounds throaty and his petulantly plaintive approach to the role seems at odds with the character. The veteran Karel Berman is here an outstanding Miller, rough and matter of fact, the voice of sanity in this context.

Kniplová has authority in plenty, but as a performer by this date she seems to have moved into the category of the *monstre sacré*; the voice has deteriorated sadly over eight years, developing a massive Slav wobble under pressure. Pleasure from the recording therefore largely disappears, which is the more disappointing since Beňačková sings the title role outstandingly well. The voice is glorious, her diction perfect, and she has a sense of the music's beauty which is wholly admirable. To re-hear her voicing of the Act II prayer, and the infinite sadness she conveys as she learns of her little son's death, would make the set valuable, but Kniplová's singing in a recording is a major handicap.

1982 DECCA / LONDON (S,D) ℗

Elisabeth Söderström (A), Eva Randová (B), Wieslaw Ochman (C), Peter Dvorsky (D), Vienna State Opera Chorus, Vienna Philharmonic Orchestra—Charles Mackerras

Some of Kovařovic's changes were concerned with idiom—he removed a number of repeats of one- and two-bar phrases (a process, his defenders argue, the composer himself had already started), but the reorchestration undoubtedly affects some of the character of the original. Mackerras restores Janáček's final thoughts (1908) but allows himself one piece of editorial license, reinstating Kostelnička's substantial Act I monologue which Janáček himself had cut. As postscripts, Mackerras gives us the final duet in Kovařovic's version, followed by a cracking performance of the fascinating *Jealousy* prelude, an overture written for the opera but apparently never before 1959 performed in connection with a stage production.

At the opera's start comes a surprise—the eerie xylophone motif played an octave lower than we are used to. Mackerras's conducting, if a little less uncompromising than Vogel's, is more urgent than others on disc, his attack confident and bold, the whole performance rhythmically alert, with that sense of inevitability only a master brings to performance.

The cast has no weakness, founded on artists like Lucia Popp, Věra Soukupová, and Václav Zítek in short roles. Dvorsky's beautiful voice is the operatic equivalent of Števa's good looks, and he manages additionally to suggest an empty-headed braggart; Ochman is fine if not very

individual as Laca. Randová makes a thoroughly sound Kostelnička, singing the notes of her Act II scene clearly and accurately, but the role requires a star and she has neither the presence nor the vocal amplitude. Söderström, on the other hand, with no particular built-in vocal magic, sings the title role with great artistry, tingling with nervous excitement throughout and touching in monologue and prayer in Act II.

The four sets have particular virtues: Vogel's exemplary conducting and Krásová's Kostelnička in the earliest; Gregor's controlled, middle-of-the-road conducting of the second; Beňačková's brilliant singing of the title role in the Brno album; Mackerras's fine performance of his own reconstruction of the original version in the fourth—which must be the choice for anyone looking for the best all-round version. But I shall not want to part with Vogel's.

LORD HAREWOOD

LEOŠ JANÁČEK

KÁŤA KABANOVÁ (1921)

A: Káťa Kabanová (s); B: Varvara (ms); C: Kabanicha (ms); D: Boris
Grigorjevič (t); E: Tichon (t); F: Váňa Kudrjáš (t); G: Dikoj (bs)

With *Káťa*, Janáček may be said to have entered a new operatic phase, adding an extraordinary musical compression to his other characteristics: the entire scene of Káťa's suicide, from her jump until the body is laid out, lasts about as long as a child can hold its breath! Signs of the move forward could already be found in *Osud*, *Jenůfa*'s unjustly neglected successor, where the ability to compress and to pass rapidly from situation to situation had already reached new levels.

In *Káťa*, it is the conductor who faces a real problem. From the outset, there developed inside Czechoslovakia two schools of Janáček performance, the smoother "Prague style," evolved by the great conductor Václav Talich, and the tougher "Brno style," from the composer's home town, where his orchestration was adhered to without compromise. In a note to his recording, Charles Mackerras describes his surprise when studying with Talich in 1947–48 to find that the orchestration of *Káťa* had been retouched and "beautified" by Talich, and that it sounded quite different in Brno, where what he perceptively calls the "rough, often primitive, muscle" of the music was much more in evidence. A reconciliation of this toughness with the score's extraordinary lyricism, and—even harder—with the polish a modern audience expects from an orchestra, poses a real challenge.

1959 SUPRAPHON (S)

Drahomíra Tikalová (A), Ivana Mixová (B), Ludmila Komancová (C), Beno Blachut (D), Bolemír Vích (E), Viktor Kočí (F), Zdeněk Kroupa (G), Prague National Theater Chorus and Orchestra—Jaroslav Krombholc

Krombholc conducted the opera regularly with roughly these forces in Prague and in 1964 at the Edinburgh Festival. Unfortunately, the recording is not clear enough to allow dynamic contrasts, vital in this score, to be brought out, and, though Krombholc catches the music's tenderness as well as its nerves, the result seems less than the understanding product of years of performance. It embodies small textual changes (made presumably by Talich), which even allow, perhaps for clarity, one voice to succeed another instead of sounding together as written—clearly, Prague rather than Brno style.

Casting is strong, with a Kabanicha lacking only the vocal imagination to chill the blood at the end of Act II, Scene 1; a vigorous, bullying Dikoj; and a Varvara who manages the awkward tessitura with skill. The three tenors, led by the authoritative and vocally fluent Beno Blachut, are well contrasted, with Vích incisive as Tichon and Viktor Kočí fresh of voice and idiomatic as Váňa. Tikalová sings her opening phrases with pure rounded sound but, whatever her skill with the high-lying writing of much of the role, there is more raw, shallow tone than allows for consistent pleasure.

1976–78 DECCA/LONDON (S) CD

Elisabeth Söderström (A), Libuše Márová (B), Naděžda Kniplová (C), Peter Dvorsky (D), Vladimír Krejčík (E), Zdeněk Švehla (F), Dalibor Jedlička (G), Vienna Philharmonic Orchestra—Charles Mackerras

When Decca resolved to record the main Janáček operas with Charles Mackerras and with Elisabeth Söderström in leading soprano roles, they took a risk. This, the first of the group, triumphantly vindicates their decision. Right from her entry Söderström's singing is sympathetic, with a strong sense of character, and no Slav acid or wobble. (Think of castigating in such terms a breed that has produced singers like Destinn, Jeritza, Milanov, and Beňačková!) The narrative in Act I, Scene 2—an early intimation of mental instability—produces beautifully poised singing which at the same time never denies the music's distraught nature, and the voice itself is well up to those phrases of near-heroic weight which Janáček slips in from time to time. But then this is a singer, if not a voice, of never less than heroic stature.

Dvorsky provides more beauty than individuality of sound, but he contrasts well with the rather elderly-sounding Krejčík as Tichon, and the outstandingly good Zdeněk Švehla as Váňa. Márová has some problems with tessitura, Jedlička is perhaps an insufficiently bass-sounding Dikoj, but Kniplová is marvelously right as Kabanicha, vocally ripe, domineering, explosive; in spite of her soprano career, voice and manner are perfect for the role.

Mackerras spent years trying to bring Janáček's scoring into a performing edition and the result is to be heard here. Muscle the Vienna Philharmonic Orchestra may lay claim to, but no one would describe their performing characteristic as primitive, and indeed more polished playing of this music, greater (and never obtrusive) orchestral detail, would be hard to imagine. Recording quality is first-rate and clarity is the order of the day. Mackerras allows himself certain glosses. Seduced more by the name than its soft tone quality, Janáček writes for *viola d'amore* and Decca's engineers make it possible to record in the studio what would be inaudible in the theater. To suit the scene changes of a 1928 Brno production, the composer wrote two new interludes here recorded: between the scenes of Act I, a beautiful elaboration of the first scene's music, and in Act II a jaunty "play-out" march for Dikoj and Kabanicha, rather in the manner of *From the House of the Dead*, on which he was then working.

It is hard to know whether most to admire the unsurpassed tenderness which Mackerras brings to, for instance, the reunion of Káťa with Boris in the last scene or the controlled urgency of the same act's introduction, the fine balance of the great double duet in Act II or the manic progress of the confession scene. From any standpoint, it is a performance of rare quality, and I don't mind admitting I was haunted by the beauty of the score for days after listening to it.

The Mackerras recording is much recommended.

LORD HAREWOOD

LEOŠ JANÁČEK

THE CUNNING LITTLE VIXEN (1924)

A: Sharp-Ears (s); B: Goldenstripe (s); C: Lápak (ms); D: Schoolmaster (t);
E: Forester (bs); F: Priest / Badger (bs)

This nature fable is a favorite of many Janáček admirers, less because of its Walt Disney setting than because it speaks, as all of Janáček does, of the spark of the divine in everything—animal, human, and inanimate. Though the world the composer pictures is anthropomorphic, it is not prettified, and its center is not the character of the Vixen but that of the Forester, who subsumes the world of nature into himself in his last, moving scene, and in addition stresses the ongoing inexorability of nature from generation to generation. The Vixen may be transformed into a human being in Act I (with a theme that returns, triumphantly, in the last pages of the opera), but she is very much an animal, who cannot resist killing chickens, even when such activity—she must know—will lead to her death. But Janáček makes little of that death—preferring to concentrate on the transcendence of nature, both in the surroundings of orchestral interludes which, as it were, cradle the text and in the final moments—one of the most powerful closes of any opera.

Four of the recordings of *Vixen* show a great degree of homogeneity of performance, since the basis for all of them is a group of Czech artists who have performed the roles a number of times, and who are entirely comfortable in the style.

1959 SUPRAPHON (M)

Hana Bohmová (A), Libuše Domanìnská (B), Ludmila Hanzaliková (C), Antonin Votavá (D), Rudolf Asmus (E), Vaclav Halir (F), Prague National Theater Chorus and Orchestra—Václav Neumann

This performance, in the typical boxy mono of the period, with close-miked voices dominating, has nonetheless a sense of theater. Neumann keeps the work constantly forward-moving and alive, and his cast is strong, led by the extraordinary humanity of Rudolf Asmus as the relaxed Forester.

1972 SUPRAPHON (S)

Helena Tattermuschová (A), Eva Zikmundová (B), Libuše Márová (C), Jan Hlavsa (D), Zdeněk Kroupa (E), Dalibor Jedlička (F), Prague National Theater Chorus and Orchestra—Bohumil Gregor

Gregor's reading of the score is more expansive and lyrical than Neumann's, and the Vixen, unlike any other, is here a very young, frisky voice, which gives the opera a fresh perspective. The early stereo sound uses a lot of speaker separation.

1980 SUPRAPHON (S) CD

Magdaléna Hajossyová (A), Gabriela Beňačková (B), Jarmila Svobodová-Zilkova (C), Miroslav Frydlewicz (D), Richard Novák (E), Karel Provsa (F), Czech Philharmonic Chorus and Orchestra—Václav Neumann

The main interest in this remake will be Beňačková's appearance in the short role of the

Vixen's mate. The performance is quite strong; Hajossyová as the Vixen is slightly shrill, while the recorded sound has little depth.

1981 DECCA / LONDON (S,D) CD

Lucia Popp (A), Eva Randová (B), Libuše Márová (C), Vladimír Krejčík (D), Dalibor Jedlička (E), Richard Novák (F), Vienna State Opera Chorus, Vienna Philharmonic Orchestra— Charles Mackerras

As part of Charles Mackerras's cycle of Janáček recordings, this performance is both unified and propulsive. Though Mackerras benefits by a fine ensemble cast, it is the orchestra that is at the center, and the recording highlights orchestral detail, making it the protagonist of the opera. Jedlička is more a hearty than an introverted Forester, Popp is at her finest in the evocative love duet, and Mackerras—as is usual with him—is not afraid to emphasize the harshness in Janáček's writing, at times almost at the expense of its innate humanity.

1991 EMI / ANGEL (In English) (S,D) CD

Lillian Watson (A), Diana Montague (B), Karen Shelby (C), Robert Tear (D), Thomas Allen (E), Gwynne Howell (F), Chorus and Orchestra of the Royal Opera House, Covent Garden— Simon Rattle

This recent encapsulation of the 1990 Covent Garden production has as its chief strength the exuberant, vital conducting of Simon Rattle, and the singing of Lillian Watson and Thomas Allen. The performance, however, must be considered an alternate recommendation, since it is sung in the English translation of Yveta Synek Graff and Robert T. Jones. As a bonus, the recording includes a passionate reading of Janáček's orchestral rhapsody *Taras Bulba*, with Rattle leading the Philharmonia Orchestra.

––––––––––––––––––

The London-Mackerras recording is the choice. Those who wish a fully Czech-flavored performance should choose the second Neumann version.

PATRICK J. SMITH

Unavailable for review:
1970 SUPRAPHON

Leoš Janáček

The Makropoulos Case (1926)

A: Emilia Marty (s); B: Krista (ms); C: Albert Gregor (t); D: Hauk-Šendorf (t);
E: Vitek (t); F: Janek (t); G: Jaroslav Prus (bar); H: Dr. Kolenatý (bs-bar)

*J*anáček's next-to-last opera is, perhaps, not his most accessible because it is closely based on a rather talky play of Karel Čapek. In fact, Janáček's music, combined with the central theme of a 337-year-old heroine who finally comes to terms with her mortality, contrives to build what could be a bloodless work into a moving and ultimately transcendent drama, as well as a vehicle for a great singing actress.

The later twentieth century has provided few such operatic vehicles, and the nearest in spirit is Alban Berg's *Lulu*. But, while both Lulu and Emilia Marty-Elina Makropoulos are *femmes fatales* who effortlessly ensnare those around them, Janáček's heroine remains a creature of the nineteenth century when she surmounts mundane concerns to rise to a diva's final *scena* worthy of Lucia, while Lulu disappears into the cloaca of twentieth-century anonymity.

It is this echo of an earlier time, wrapped in the world of the 1920s, that gives *The Makropoulos Case* its resonance—that, and Janáček's mature, assured score, which everywhere reflects his motto (given for his last opera, *From the House of the Dead*): "In every creature, a spark of the divine."

1965 SUPRAPHON (S)

Libuše Prylová (A), Helena Tattermuschová (B), Ivo Žídek (C), Milan Karpisek (D), Rudolf Vonásek (E), Viktor Koci (F), Premsyl Kočí (G),

Karel Berman (H), Prague National Theater Chorus and Orchestra—Bohumil Gregor

Both of the recordings of *The Makropoulos Case* suffer from the same deficiency: a weakness at the center. But the deficiency is far graver with this earlier, Czech recording. Libuše Prylová, as Emilia Marty, may be effective onstage, but on disc she is shrill and one-dimensional. At the end of her first-act scene with Gregor, when she is supposed to suggest anxiety and impatience, the voice comes across like that of an agitated fishwife, thus losing sympathy for the character and—worse—making her into a minor figure instead of the fulcrum of events.

More's the pity, one is tempted to add, because the rest of the cast is fine, and obviously well acquainted with the opera and their roles. Bohumil Gregor's conducting, moreover, is well attuned to their strengths, and fully responsive to the drama, particularly in the final pages. Ivo Žídek, as Albert Gregor, carries much of the first act, and is effective in his scene with Marty; Premsyl Kočí, as Jaroslav Prus, uses his voice to create a character that sounds younger than the normal operatic Prus. *His* scene with Marty, in Act II, is the highlight of the recording, as his sly insinuations of knowledge are underpinned by Bohumil Gregor's equally knowledgeable conducting.

The recording is in decent, forward sound, and "concert style" in that, although there is stereo movement, it is without stage sound effects.

1978 DECCA / LONDON (S) CD

Elisabeth Söderström (A), Anna Czaková (B), Peter Dvorsky (C), Beno Blachut (D), Vladimír Krejčík (E), Zdeněk Švehla (F), Václav Zítek (G), Dalibor Jedlička (H), Chorus of the Vienna State Opera, Vienna Philharmonic Orchestra—Charles Mackerras

The Mackerras / London recording is in quite good stereo sound, with more than a suggestion of depth and good miking of the orchestral detail—to its advantage, since Mackerras brings out individual moments in the scoring, and conducts a generally more rhythmically brash and grainy reading than does his Czech colleague.

Elisabeth Söderström was probably, at one time in her vocal career, close to an ideal Emilia Marty, but unfortunately this recording came about a decade too late to catch the voice in its full bloom. One can—as with the Wotan of Hans Hotter on the Solti *Walküre* record-ing—infer what is no longer present, and one does have the guiding intelligence and instant response of a major acting singer, which is hardly negligible, especially for the crucial last scene. But Söderström's lack of firmness of pitch and the thinning-out of the voice in fast passages count against total vocal effectiveness.

It's a pleasure to have such a strong lyric tenor as Peter Dvorsky as Albert Gregor, though the voice fades above the staff, and Václav Zítek is an urbane Prus. The rest of the cast is quite good, but the casting gem is that of the great Czech tenor Beno Blachut as Hauk-Sendorf. It is imperative that his scenes with Marty not be played as farce, but as tender reminiscence, for it is only here—at least, until the end of the opera—that the near-immortal heroine evinces any compassionate humanity: Blachut's still-vibrant voice strengthens the scenes.

The vocal and histrionic deficiencies of Prylová largely eliminate the Epic version; the London recording remains the clear choice.

PATRICK J. SMITH

SCOTT JOPLIN

TREEMONISHA (1915)

A: Treemonisha (s); B: Monisha (s); C: Remus (t);
D: Zodzetrick (t); E: Luddud (bar); F: Ned (bs-bar)

*C*omposed soon after Joplin moved from Sedalia, Missouri, to New York in 1907, *Treemonisha* was printed in piano-vocal score in 1911 at his own expense because no publisher would take it. The score of a previous opera, A *Guest of Honor* (1903), was lost, and the production of *Treemonisha* became an obsession with Joplin who, in 1915, hired a Harlem hall for a single runthrough performance with himself as pianist. The lack of success hastened his mental decline (he died two years later), and no more was heard of *Treemonisha* until Joplin's collected works were published in 1971, giving rise to semi-professional productions the next year at Morehouse College, Atlanta, and Wolf Trap Farm Park. A version orchestrated by Gunther Schuller was given its professional premiere by the Houston Grand Opera in 1975 and thence went to Broadway, when this studio recording was made.

Treemonisha is in some respects a forerunner to *Porgy and Bess* as an American folk opera, but in spite of Joplin's ragtime fame, his surviving opera suffers from his inability to extend basically melodic technique to larger forms, and also from his own libretto, written in rhyming couplets which are less than well set on the voices. The best writing is for chorus (Joplin wrote some of his earliest compositions for a male vocal octet with whom he toured in 1895–96). They are given three exhilarating song-and-dance numbers in ragtime: No. 4, "We're goin' around," and the finales to Acts II and III:

No. 18, "Aunt Dinah has blowed de horn," and No. 27, "A real slow drag." The solo writing is more like nineteenth-century balladeering, with academic harmonies and some religious feeling. In spite of the lack of dramatic and musical tension, the work's very limitations are part of its interest.

1975 DEUTSCHE GRAMMOPHON (S) CD

Carmen Balthrop (A), Betty Allen (B), Curtis Rayam (C), Ben Harney (D), Dorceal Duckens (E), Willard White (F), Chorus and Orchestra—Gunther Schuller

An "original cast" album derived from the Houston Grand Opera / Broadway production is given the benefit of first-class predigital stereo, with bright and clear placing of singers and orchestra. They perform with serious commitment and evident concern to show the work to as much advantage as possible, in its conflict between right and wrong in terms of education versus superstition. Schuller's orchestration is for about 35 players: wind and reduced strings with piano and drums, much as would have been available to Joplin had it been possible at the time. The effect is of ragtime / ballad character in a fuller dimension than Schuller's well-known versions of Joplin's individual rags.

Balthrop is a light but clear-voiced heroine with an appreciable personality, and even at this time White could convey the forceful vocal portrait of a role limited in scope. Allen and

Rayam are effectively heard as the heroine's adopted mother and her rescuer respectively, and credit is due to the unidentified chorus for creating a sense of context and character for the succession of events. Schuller's conducting imparts overall enthusiasm and vitality to the performance.

NOËL GOODWIN

ERICH WOLFGANG KORNGOLD

DIE TOTE STADT (1920)

A: Marietta (s); B: Paul (t); C: Fritz (bar); D: Frank (bar)

The young Erich Wolfgang Korngold displayed an awesome compositional facility in this, his best-remembered opera. He already commanded the strengths that would serve him so well as a film composer in later years: fertility in invention of striking musical gestures and timbral combinations, ability to conjure a place or mood instantly, varied textural and rhythmic ideas. He put these gifts to fascinating use in this story (after a novel and play by Georges Rodenbach) of obsession, dreams, and death in a "dead" city, Bruges. The librettist, Paul Schott, was revealed in 1975 to be a pseudonym for Korngold and his father, Julius.

The opera's need for glamorous, large-scale vocal personalities in the two leading roles was fulfilled to perfection in the 1924 recording of Marietta's Lute Song: Lotte Lehmann and Richard Tauber, with George Szell conducting—still probably the most beguiling guide into the world of *Die Tote Stadt*.

A number of brief cuts are marked in the score. They have probably been made in nearly all live performances, as they ease the demands of the taxing leading roles, but the RCA recording is complete. It does, however, contain some vocal variants that suggest a textual source other than the published vocal score.

1975 RCA / BMG (S) CD

Carol Neblett (A), René Kollo (B), Hermann Prey (C), Benjamin Luxon (D), Bavarian Radio Chorus, Tölz Boys' Choir, Munich Radio Orchestra—Erich Leinsdorf

As RCA had provided excellent recordings of Korngold's film music in the 1970s, it was a logical choice to give us *Die Tote Stadt* on records for the first time. This version starts with the important advantage of discerning and idiomatic orchestral direction by Erich Leinsdorf. Leinsdorf thoroughly understands and conveys the score's continuity, equally in command whether festive brilliance or surging passion is called for. Only in the last ounce of Viennese *Schlag* does Leinsdorf fall short, as with his shortchanging of Korngold's characteristic (and explicitly marked) lingering upbeats. But it is surely to the conductor's credit that the orchestral contribution is so satisfying. The supporting cast is well chosen too, with a strong piece of work from Rose Wagemann as Brigitte, the housekeeper, getting the opera off to a convincing start. Benjamin Luxon reminds us of the silky quality of his lyric baritone in these years; only the most extroverted moments tempt him into unpitched bluster.

Paul and Marietta call for vocal splendor, also idiomatic ease with the dense conversational material; here we have a pair each of whom commands a different one of these qualities. René Kollo reads his lines persuasively, but his tenor sounds hard and intractable. Though he executes all the notes and is careful to sing softly when asked to, the vocal quality is so uningratiating that all opportunities for passion or charm go unrealized. Carol Neblett handles her role ably from the latter point of view; she can set her soprano soaring or floating, and it has a rich quality that matches the orchestration well. But it is all rather "international opera" in manner, unmodified by any verbal flavor or delicacy. The two of them thus fail to realize the potential of the big duet scenes, and we must concentrate on the orchestra to hear the real action. Hermann Prey, in what is admittedly a much shorter role built around one aria, shows how the two necessary qualities can be combined to Korngold's advantage. In his waltz, almost unbearably nostalgic for days gone by, Prey's schmaltzy teasing of the words and the musical line suggests the sort of star quality that might make the whole opera continuously hypnotic.

This recording, while not ideal, at least gives us a vivid realization of the orchestral fabric and partially successful attempts at the leading roles.

JON ALAN CONRAD

FRANZ LEHÁR

DIE LUSTIGE WITWE (1905)

A: Hanna (s); B: Valencienne (s); C: Camille (t); D: Danilo (t or bar)

his most popular Viennese operetta was given a new lease on life when, in 1953, Walter Legge made the first of two recordings with his wife, Elisabeth Schwarzkopf, as Hanna. It demonstrated how much an operetta of this quality can gain when singers, orchestra, and conductor represent the best in their respective professions. There are some who think otherwise—that operetta needs actors who sing rather than singers who act—but whatever the merits this may have in theater terms, most record listeners want the music and singing to be paramount.

Cuts are applied in almost every recording; only one, Eurodisc / Stolz, is almost complete. Most regrettable is the frequent loss of No. 5, "Zauber der Häuslichkeit," dropped because it is thought to hold up the story en route to the Act I finale. One vexing question persists: what voice should sing Danilo? Lehár, it is known, preferred a tenor, though the score has places where he wrote alternative vocal lines and indicated a preference for the lower one. What is certainly needed is a voice to encompass either line without transposing it. Again, in the following recordings, different solutions have been chosen.

1953 EMI / ANGEL (M) CD

Elisabeth Schwarzkopf (A), Emmy Loose (B), Nicolai Gedda (C), Erich Kunz (D), Philharmonia Chorus and Orchestra—Otto Ackermann

There is still much that is magical about this performance, especially in its 1978 reprocessing for stereo, which improved the general acoustic quality. When the recording was made, Schwarzkopf was in her thirties and more spontaneous in phrasing than she was in subsequent years. She establishes a winning, glamorous personality with her entry song, and although "Vilja" is perhaps too slow, it sounds right for her wonderfully pure tone and expressive poise. Her spoken lines are also perfectly inflected. Would that Gedda had been Danilo instead of Kunz, whose baritone transposes his praise of Maxim's down a full third, and who sounds unduly mature and submissive for a supposedly raffish man-about-town.

Then a newcomer, Gedda makes Camille lyrically seductive as well as elegant, and is admirably matched with Loose, whose delightful Valencienne is not entirely at home among the grisettes in Act III. It is sad not to have their "Zauber der Häuslichkeit" duet in Act I, one of the many cuts which also include the non-vocal dance scenes in Acts II and III. Enough spoken dialogue is included to set up an atmosphere and make sense of the story, in which Anton Niessner is an excellent Baron Zeta, both speaking and singing (Valencienne and Cascada are given speaking-voice doubles). Ackermann obtains orchestral playing of sensuous charm and lilt, but does not make an adequate case for prefacing the work with the long, revised Overture that Lehár himself arranged in 1940 for concert performance: here it simply sounds top-heavy for what follows.

1958 DECCA / LONDON (S)

Hilde Gueden (A), Emmy Loose (B), Waldemar Kmentt (C), Per Grundén (D), Vienna State Opera Chorus and Orchestra—Robert Stolz

When Stolz died in 1975, a few weeks short of his ninety-fifth birthday, a direct link with the original *Merry Widow* was broken: he had been Lehár's musical assistant in preparing the Vienna premiere at the Theater an der Wien, and he conducted some of the performances in the initial season. That he was not in Lehár's league as a composer is evident from his own heavy-handed arrangement, labeled "Overture" on this recording, but thereafter the performance catches the right style and exuberance and is more complete than any other.

It shares the same Valencienne as the earlier EMI / Ackermann set, and Loose again sings with much charm and presence of character. Gueden's flirtatiousness suggests a widow whose first marriage must have been one of convenience and conveniently short at that: she has vocal sex appeal, and engaging sweetness for "Vilja." Grundén, a tenor Danilo, was for some years a principal at the Vienna Volksoper and sings with more artfulness than style. He does not sound likely to take readily to domesticity as a husband, while the dry-voiced Kmentt would probably find it a relief not to have to sing any more for his supper.

The recording manages to suggest a party in progress at all the right moments without overdoing the extraneous chatter. Voices in the "Weiber, Weiber" septet in Act I are clearly placed and Valencienne's entry with the grisettes in Act III is effectively managed. In an otherwise uncut performance Stolz was given his head once too often when, a few bars before the end, he crudely brings back the Merry Widow Waltz theme for one more hearing and has everybody singing it.

1962 EMI / ANGEL (S) CD

Elisabeth Schwarzkopf (A), Hanny Steffek (B), Nicolai Gedda (C), Eberhard Wächter (D), Philharmonia Chorus and Orchestra—Lovro von Matačic

Nine years after their first album, Schwarzkopf recorded her second Hanna with husband-producer Walter Legge, this time taking advantage of stereo to the great benefit of all. Detailed comparisons will favor the later recording in almost every respect, except for those listeners who find Schwarzkopf's performance a bit more mannered and studied, though still beautiful in tone and expression, and "Vilja" taken a fraction less slowly. Perhaps the difference in her character can best be compared to a young woman who, previously reveling in her freedom, now becomes a lady more circumspectly aware of her position.

She again succumbs to a baritone Danilo, though Wächter has a wider range than Kunz and can sing the notes. Unfortunately, he has a tendency to "sing-speak" too much, not only justifiably in the Act II ballad but in his earlier references to Maxim's, where proper singing is needed. Gedda is again a stylish Camille, often reminiscent of Tauber, especially in the beautifully sung "Pavillon" duet with Steffek. Her light and creamy-toned Valencienne is sometimes disconcertingly similar to Schwarzkopf, as if the latter had a younger sister; she greatly enjoys herself among the grisettes. That number and the "Weiber, Weiber" septet for the men testify to capable casting throughout.

Legge obviously had second thoughts about the Overture, and reverts here to the original, also restoring some of the previous cuts but not, regrettably, the "Häuslichkeit" duet or the Cakewalk music before the grisettes' entry. He improved the dance music in Act II by including something like *tamburizzas* instead of relying only on orchestral strings and percussion. Matačic achieves enough Viennese lilt to sustain high spirits and a good presence, in addition to subtle shading in the excellent orchestral playing.

1966 EURODISC (S)

Margit Schramm (A), Dorothea Chryst (B), Jerry J. Jennings (C), Rudolf Schock (D), Deutsche Oper Chorus, Berlin Symphony Orchestra—Robert Stolz

By the time Stolz conducted this recording, he had passed his eighty-sixth birthday. His advanced age is manifest in a general lack of vitality, though the spirit is still evident in the brisk pace he sets for some numbers, like the "Weiber, Weiber" septet. The famous waltz theme is phrased with an instinct for its finest quality. So too is the "Häuslichkeit" duet, the inclusion of which makes this one of the more complete performances in which only the entr'acte music before Act III is omitted.

Each act is prefaced by a gong stroke for no apparent reason, and an attempt is made to emulate a live performance by including background chatter throughout the recording. *Tamburizzas* are properly heard in the dance music at the start of Act II, where Schramm sings "Vilja" with a kind of chrome-plated tone that is polished on the surface but lacks body and feeling. Indeed, she communicates a worldly, sophisticated character whom neither situation nor emotion will throw off-balance as she sails on.

Schock, a tenor Danilo, is an experienced singer of some style who is here inclined to press his voice and become over-assertive to the detriment of tone quality. A young-sounding Chryst, bright and eager of voice, and the very accomplished Jennings make an acceptable Valencienne and Camille, not least in the "Häuslichkeit" duet and in their later scenes.

1972–73 DEUTSCHE GRAMMOPHON (S) CD

Elizabeth Harwood (A), Teresa Stratas (B), Werner Hollweg (C), René Kollo (D), Deutsche Oper Chorus, Berlin Philharmonic Orchestra—Herbert von Karajan

To hear the orchestral introduction is to be instantly caught up in a whirl of gaiety and high spirits that promises an infectious performance. But in this performance the effect is immediately dispelled when the voices enter from a kind of middle distance, the tempo drops sharply, and all too soon it becomes another example of Karajan's familiar preference for lush orchestral sound over verbal character, a tone poem with voices. That is not to deny its many musical

merits, but to question whether an approach that has achieved wonders with Wagner is right for Lehár.

The singers have to adjust accordingly, as if their roles embraced weighty matters of life and death from some other opera. Harwood, an English soprano who often worked with Karajan at Salzburg and was much admired, is an ideal Hanna for this context in the spun silk of her tone and considerable charm of character within the predominantly slow speeds set for her. Kollo, a tenor Danilo, sounds almost too youthful; his voice is finely threaded into the fabric without establishing quite enough character. Stratas and Hollweg are good-natured if sometimes strenuous as the second pair; yet again they are deprived of the "Häuslichkeit" duet, which is all the sadder when the rest is played in full.

About the actual sound of the orchestral playing there can be no reservations, full and sensuous as it is, with a lovely sheen on the strings. So that voices "interfere" as little as possible, we are not even given the spoken exchanges over music in the Hanna-Danilo dance scene in Act II, thereby detracting from its purpose; there is enough other dialogue to tell the story without making too much of it.

1979 EMI / ANGEL (S)

Edda Moser (A), Helen Donath (B), Siegfried Jerusalem (C), Hermann Prey (D), Bavarian Radio Chorus, Munich Radio Orchestra—Heinz Wallberg

Most of the right ingredients combine to make this a satisfactory performance, if not a memorably distinctive one, though it may be said that renewed acquaintance discloses some virtues not altogether acknowledged at the time it was issued. This applies to the lilt of Wallberg's conducting and the bright colors of the orchestral playing as much as to Moser, whose singing is always beguiling and whose character is convincingly merry. She needed to work harder, though, to entice Prey's baritone Danilo—a rather self-centered reprobate, only too ready to bask in female adoration.

As in some other versions the second couple is musically more alluring, especially as they are given all three duets: Donath an appealing Valencienne, who makes much of the character as well as the vocal line, and Jerusalem, then still almost new to records, a firm and elegantly sung Camille. The lesser roles are all well enough taken to keep the listener entertained. Wallberg takes no liberties, apart from substituting what could be a cimbalom for the *tamburizzas* in the Act II dance music, and he fashions the performance with buoyant rhythm and much orchestral polish. Only the entr'acte before Act III is omitted.

1982 DENON (S,D,P) CD

Mirjana Irosch (A), Dagmar Koller (B), Ryszard Karczykowski (C), Peter Minich (D), Vienna Volksoper Chorus and Orchestra—Rudolf Bibl

This is a theater performance recorded on June 17, 1982, at the Tokyo Bunka Kaikan, where the Vienna Volksoper company was on tour. For those with memories of the production, here or elsewhere, it would be an acceptable souvenir of what the accompanying booklet calls "state of the art quality (digital technique) conveying the feeling of a live and lively evening at the theater"—here including instant audience applause breaking in, encores (one refrain of "Vilja," two of "Weiber, Weiber"), laughter at what are presumably sight-gags, and so on.

Volksoper director Karl Dönch mentions this as the first available recording of his company, and on this evidence the singing is entirely professional but variable in individual quality.

Irosch was then a company singer for twenty years or so and gives Hanna an attractive vocal focus of personality, with Minich an experienced though dry-voiced Danilo. Koller is a twittery Valencienne with overmuch vibrato, and Karczykowski an ardent Camille often bleached of tone. Others play up to their parts in a performance no more and no less than what is claimed for it.

Bibl's conducting keeps a lively pace, too much so in the hurried finale to Act II, but we are told he has "3/4 time pulsating in his vains" [*sic*]. Hanna's first entry is brought forward before the Valencienne-Camille duet (the usual No. 2); the latter's "Häuslichkeit" duet is cut, as is the entr'acte before Act III and the introduction music following this. Instead, there is extra unidentified dance music at the start of both Act II and Act III, and the grisettes' number is supplemented by the can-can from Offenbach's *Orphée aux enfers*, replete with girlish squeals and dancing noise.

The 1968 EMI / Matačic performance is still a potent choice for its overall musical and vocal charm in spite of a blustery Danilo; EMI / Wallberg from 1980 would be an adequate alternative, as would DG / Karajan for those who like voices woven into a lush orchestral fabric, but a definitive uncut digital recording is still awaited.

NOËL GOODWIN

Unavailable for review:
1907 EMI / ANGEL

RUGGERO LEONCAVALLO

PAGLIACCI (1892)

A: Nedda (s); B: Beppe (t); (C): Canio (t); D: Tonio (bar); E: Silvio (bar)

Pagliacci, now a hundred years old, is indestructible—in the sense that this music cannot fail to make at least some effect in performance, no matter how wretchedly executed. The opera has been accorded greater respect on records than it usually receives in the theater (where productions often all but announce their contempt for the work's conventions and aesthetic ambitions).

Pagliacci presents few textual difficulties; I will discuss some of them in detail in connection with the 1979 EMI / Muti set, which claims to be based on the composer's autograph score and other "authentic" sources. Leoncavallo was a practical man of the theater (he gives the soprano permission to omit the two bars of trills before Nedda's Ballatella, for instance), and he does not seem to have objected to emendations that became common practice during his lifetime.

The only "standard" cut in this score is a particularly frustrating one: 42 bars of the Nedda / Silvio duet. The omitted passage is essentially a reprise of Nedda's "Non mi tentar" (not a literal repeat; the melody is quite beautifully varied). Silvio is given a contrapuntal line, and the writing for the two voices builds logically and effectively to a climax—which breaks off for Silvio's "No, più non m'ami!" (the point at which cut performances resume).

Once you have heard the duet sung complete, abridged performances of the scene sound strangely incomplete, and yet *all* of the recordings made prior to 1967 observe the cut. The duet is performed complete on the pioneering 1967 Decca / Gardelli set, and on four of the five subsequent studio recordings (the exception is the 1983 Philips / Prêtre set).

1907 EMI / ANGEL (M)

Giuseppina Huguet (A), Gaetano Pini-Corsi (B), Antonio Paoli (C), Francesco Cigada (D), Ernesto Badini (E), La Scala Chorus and Orchestra—Carlo Sabajno

This recording, the opera's first, is a bit of a jigsaw puzzle. The notes accompanying Opal's LP reissue claim that it was transferred from the only complete set of 78s known to exist (in the possession of the Yale Collection of Historical Sound Recordings); furthermore, that the original recordings were never issued as a complete package in any one country—i.e., collectors back in 1907 had to assemble as much of the opera as they wanted themselves. The sides containing Canio's music were made in two distinct versions: one featuring Antonio Paoli, the other Augusto Barbaini.

Opal has made no effort to join the sides together, claiming that "mechanical problems inherent in the original 1907 recording equipment have caused pitch fluctuations between the beginnings and ends of the sides." Surely this could be corrected with modern technology? In any event, the stop-and-start nature of the proceedings, with the music coming to an abrupt halt every few minutes, gives those of us who were born in the LP era a vivid idea of what listening to a complete opera on 78s must have been like. (Some of the sides come to full stops, complete with "concert endings"—did Leoncavallo "compose" these, or was the job entrusted to some hack?)

The sound is, of course, primitive, with fierce surface noise throughout. Voices and instruments sometimes emerge with startling clarity, sometimes recede into the murk.

For the first time we encounter what old record labels grandly describe as the "Professori d'Orchestra e l'interno Corpo Corale del Teatro alla Scala di Milano"—the all-time *Pagliacci* champs, with at least nine studio versions to their credit. They are drastically reduced in numbers and crowded around the acoustical horn, making it unfair to try to judge their contribution; one can, however, hear much sweet, singing string tone, with graceful *portamento* phrasing. The *ragazzi* sound like female sopranos to me.

Sabajno does not seem to have been under much pressure to speed up the music to fit the individual sides. It is interesting that this performance, taking place only fifteen years after the opera's premiere, already features some of the "traditional" performance practices supposedly not authorized by the score (e.g., the broadening of tempo for the final section of Nedda's Ballatella—very pronounced here: the pulse is reduced by half). It's entirely possible that Leoncavallo, who supervised this recording, not only tolerated them, but liked them and encouraged them.

Paoli displays a firm, penetrating instrument, and knows how to generate dramatic intensity without sacrificing musical values. Cigada's Tonio is suitably forceful without sacrificing vocal control.

I think it is safe to assume that the acoustical recording process does not do full justice to Giuseppina Huguet, stripping her light, silvery voice of some of its overtones. She is an expert technician and has many lovely, delicate moments. Interpretively, she makes an improbably genteel adulteress, and the taunts hurled at Tonio might as well be an invitation to tea. She is at her best as Colombina, sophisticated and teasing. Ernesto Badini, a lyric baritone with an ingratiating manner, partners her well in the duet.

1929–30 EMI / ANGEL (M)

Adelaide Saraceni (A), Nello Palai (B), Alessandro Valente (C), Apollo Granforte (D), Leonildo Basi (E), La Scala Chorus and Orchestra—Carlo Sabajno

I have heard only OASI's LP reissue of the original pressing: the sound is shallow and cramped, but seems to be correctly pitched throughout. It's apparent, though, that recording technology has made considerable progress in the two decades since the 1907 set, and Sabajno's conducting now comes into focus: everything is warm and atmospheric, if not always the last word in sharpness of attack. The Scala forces, now at full strength, play and sing well. The expressive wind timbres fall pleasantly on the ear. Once again, the listener notes the seemingly instinctual use of *portamento* effects by the instrumentalists. The singers use them, too: the Nedda sings "Sei la? Credea che te ne fosti andato!" with a pronounced downward slide connecting her last two notes, and the Tonio echoes this in his response ("È colpa del tuo canto").

The cast contains one truly great singer: Apollo Granforte sings the Prologue with such elegance that it's a bit of shock when he proves equally adept at conveying the nastiness of Tonio's character.

Alessandro Valente's Canio must be accounted a failure: his voice sounds terribly weak in the lower and middle registers, and afflicted with a rattly vibrato; he lunges desperately at the high notes; his ideas about the character are banal and uncertainly projected.

Adelaide Saraceni's thin, acidulous soprano is definitely an acquired taste, and she turns screechy in the climaxes. Leonildo Basi is a dull Silvio—he and Saraceni make little effect in their duet.

1930 EMI / ANGEL (M)

Rosetta Pampanini (A), Giuseppe Nessi (B), Francesco Merli (C), Carlo Galeffi (D), Gino

Vanelli (E), La Scala Chorus and Orchestra—Lorenzo Molajoli

This represents a big improvement over the 1929 set. I would suggest, in fact, that here is the first recording of the opera that can still be enjoyed as a performance rather than as a historical curiosity, with little need to make allowances for shortcomings of execution or sound quality.

Lorenzo Molajoli's conducting has the same virtues as Sabajno's, but is much more disciplined and specific in its interpretive intent. The orchestra and chorus are superb. Even the recorded sound is marginally cleaner and fuller when compared to that of the 1929 set.

Francesco Merli brings a steely tone, a short top, and some explosive attacks to Canio's music; he projects Canio's jealousy and bitterness, but he isn't exactly subtle or suave.

Rosetta Pampanini's lyric soprano is a little thin and brittle in quality, but she is a resourceful singer and her Nedda sounds appropriately young, impulsive, and sensual.

Carlo Galeffi has a beautiful voice and (on this occasion, at least) some strange interpretive ideas—he sounds tearful and sniveling throughout the scene with Nedda (punctuating "M'ha vinto l'amor" with an awful Gigli-like sob), and his protracted bursts of demented laughter after "Nedda, lo giuro, me la pagherai!" are the sort of thing one associates with the mad scientist's deformed assistant in a Grade-B horror film. Gino Vanelli, by contrast, uses his attractive baritone in a straightforward, unaffected manner; he and Pampanini make quite a success of their duet.

Giuseppe Nessi is a classy Beppe, offering an unusually witty and sophisticated impersonation of Arlecchino.

1934 EMI / ANGEL (M) (D

Iva Pacetti (A), Giuseppe Nessi (B), Beniamino Gigli (C), Mario Basiola (D), Leone Paci (E), La Scala Chorus and Orchestra—Franco Ghione

This performance is dominated by Beniamino Gigli's Canio—a role the tenor recorded before he actually sang it onstage. Gigli's familiar honeyed tone and warm, expansive phrasing are very much in evidence. But, for better or worse, the striking thing about his Canio is the uninhibited way he throws himself into the part. This Canio seems to be having the time of his life as he banters with the villagers in the opera's opening scene. Gigli punctuates "Vesti la giubba" with sobs (and sets a bad precedent by blubbering his way all through the aria's orchestral postlude), and works himself into a frenzy during the final scene. Love the man or despise him—boring, he's not.

His colleagues are not among the era's superstars, but they know their business. Mario Basiola, for example, rides roughshod over some of the music's fine detail, but he is eminently forceful as Tonio. It's good to hear Nessi as Beppe again, doing the part at least as well as he did four years previously.

Iva Pacetti has a bigger voice than most Neddas; along with the imposing weight and the capacity for dramatic colorations, though, comes a certain amount of heaviness throughout the range and a lack of floating ease in the upper register. Interpretively, though, she is effective. Leone Paci's Silvio is undistinguished—neither bad enough to hurt the performance nor good enough to raise his contribution above a routine level.

The Scala ensemble is once again impressive, but Franco Ghione's conducting is strictly routine, lacking the consistent lift and forward momentum heard on the Molajoli performance.

1951 CBS / SONY (M)

Lucine Amara (A), Thomas Hayward (B), Richard Tucker (C), Giuseppe Valdengo (D), Clifford Harvuot (E), Metropolitan Opera Chorus and Orchestra—Fausto Cleva

A drab affair, on the whole. Fausto Cleva pushes the music a bit hard—a crisp, no-nonsense reading, with little sense of expansiveness or warmth. The orchestral playing is quite poor; the chorus does rather better.

The outstanding performance here is Richard

Tucker's Canio: his voice has an impressive weight and solidity, and he manages to be more authentically Italian in style than some of the native Italian tenors on records. (The "authenticity" extends to some gulps and sobs, apparently inspired by the Gigli recording.)

Lucine Amara sings well, despite some weakness in the lower register; her ideas about the character are conventional, not very individual.

The two baritones are capable professionals, but decidedly short on tonal warmth and plushness of timbre: they are outclassed, with room to spare, by many of their recorded rivals. The Beppe, Thomas Hayward, has a lyric tenor that is uncommonly fresh and attractive in quality.

The recorded sound is mediocre even by 1951 standards: closely miked solo voices, and no attempt at all to suggest distance effects.

1951 CETRA (M, P)

Carla Gavazzi (A), Salvatore di Tommaso (B), Carlo Bergonzi (C), Carlo Tagliabue (D), Marcello Rossi (E), Italian Radio Chorus and Orchestra, Turin—Alfredo Simonetto

Like so many of the operas in this Cetra / Everest series, this is an idiomatic but undistinguished performance, prepared specially for radio broadcast. The orchestra and chorus sound willing enough, but would probably have benefited from more rehearsal. The conductor is content to beat time for the most part, but lets his soloists get away with murder—some of the distending of phrases in order to linger on high notes (or get ready for them) is really amazing.

Carlo Bergonzi recorded this Canio shortly after making the transition from baritone to tenor: his singing here retains some of the weight and dark coloration of his former range, and the upper register is not yet under complete control, often sounding raw and effortful. It's an exciting performance, though, and an interesting souvenir of the artist. (Bergonzi's mature thoughts on Canio are preserved on the 1965 DG / Karajan recording discussed below.)

It's too bad that posterity may judge Carlo Tagliabue by his performances on these Cetra operas; most of them were made when his voice was past its prime. His upper register is unreliable, and he has moments of unsteadiness and dubious intonation. Still, he is a good artist who knows what he wants to do with Tonio.

The Nedda, Carla Gavazzi, has plenty of temperament, but her singing is unpleasantly squally. Her Silvio, Marcello Rossi, is a mediocre singer; this account of the Nedda / Silvio duet is decidedly short on sensuality and ardor.

The fake-stereo sound of later pressings is mediocre at best, and close to intolerable during some of the loud choral passages, where distortion sets in.

1952 DECCA / LONDON (M)

Clara Petrella (A), Piero de Palma (B), Mario del Monaco (C), Afro Poli (D), Aldo Protti (E), Chorus and Orchestra of the Accademia di Santa Cecilia, Rome—Alberto Erede

Textual curiosity: the Prologue isn't sung by Tonio. On the first edition of this set, it was performed by the Canio, Mario del Monaco—in the original baritone keys, without benefit of transposition. Del Monaco's Prologue (a solid rendition, not just a stunt) was later transferred to a recital LP, and subsequent editions of the complete set feature Aldo Protti, the Silvio, in the Prologue.

Alberto Erede takes a leisurely stroll through the score, often slowing down further to admire something along the way. The Roman orchestra and chorus do their job, but would probably make a better impression under more dynamic leadership.

Luckily, Erede has some aggressive singers in his cast. The brazen-voiced del Monaco makes Canio's frustration and rage terrifyingly real. If we compare his performance to Bjoerling's (see below), we would have to admit that del Monaco's vocalism is unpolished, and even vulgar at times. It's also undeniably exciting.

After a relatively cautious negotiation of the Ballatella, Clara Petrella turns into a sensational Nedda, lashing out at Tonio with sadistic relish and throwing herself at Silvio in a way that suggests that this woman's lovemaking could be both violent and debilitating.

Protti handles the Prologue rather well, and is smooth, if bland, in the duet with Nedda.

It's painfully obvious why Afro Poli wasn't allowed to sing the Prologue: his sound is rough and insecure in the extreme, and his deviations from the indicated pitches in the scene with Nedda must be heard to be believed. Even with his voice in such poor shape, he manages to make an effect in the role, but it's just not good singing. (Any reservations one may have about del Monaco fade to insignificance whenever the two men have a scene together.)

The mono engineering still sounds agreeable.

1953 EMI / ANGEL (M) CD

Victoria de los Angeles (A), Paul Franke (B), Jussi Bjoerling (C), Leonard Warren (D), Robert Merrill (E), Robert Shaw Chorale, Columbia Boys' Choir, RCA Victor Orchestra—Renato Cellini

The big surprise here is the work of conductor Renato Cellini, who is hardly a cult figure. He really knows how this score ought to go, though: his reading is on the quick side, with plenty of dramatic thrust, but Cellini is flexible enough to help his soloists make the most of their vocal opportunities. The pickup orchestra is excellent—lively, colorful playing. Less of a surprise is the solid contribution of the chorus, which shows the benefits of Robert Shaw's training and coaching: we hear idiomatic Italian and dramatic involvement, even from the *ragazzi*.

This is arguably the most smoothly and richly sung *Pagliacci* on records. Most of these singers are not "great vocal actors" (in the sense that we use the phrase to praise a Callas or a Gobbi), but they don't *just* sing: they all know what the opera is about.

Of all the tenors who have recorded Canio complete, Jussi Bjoerling probably has the most beautiful voice. The instrument is really on the light side (in terms of both weight and color) for some of the music; furthermore, Bjoerling's Italian has more than a trace of an accent, and he is awfully phlegmatic from an interpretive standpoint. But the vocalism is hard to resist, and the restraint is, at least, a welcome corrective to the self-indulgence of some other tenors: this Canio sounds like a pleasant gentleman to whom violence does not come naturally, or

easily—making the outcome of the action all the more shocking.

Victoria de los Angeles's Nedda, like her recorded Carmen with Sir Thomas Beecham, represents a successful case of casting against type. De los Angeles sings so sweetly, projects such a warm, lovable personality, and has so much obvious class that it's difficult to imagine her Nedda going beyond hand-holding with Silvio—or belonging to Canio's troupe in the first place. Still, she manages to make her performance work on its own refined, dignified terms.

Leonard Warren's idea of characterization is to permit a bit of a rough edge to creep into his tone during Tonio's nastier moments; as singing, though, his contribution is magnificent. Robert Merrill is a first-rate Silvio, touching all of the vocal and dramatic bases with easy assurance.

This performance makes all of the standard cuts, including the Nedda / Silvio exchange at the start of Act II. Interestingly, Warren sings the opera's final line.

EMI's CD transfer is a one-disc job with outstandingly good remastered sound.

1954 EMI / ANGEL (M) CD

Maria Callas (A), Nicola Monti (B), Giuseppe di Stefano (C), Tito Gobbi (D), Rolando Panerai (E), La Scala Chorus and Orchestra—Tullio Serafin

Tullio Serafin's conducting is a little slow and heavy even for my taste, but his deliberation brings an imposing weight to several episodes and unearths instrumental details that tend to get lost in brisker performances. The Milanese chorus and orchestra continue to maintain a high standard.

The main attraction of this set is, of course, the Nedda of Maria Callas. In fine form, Callas does full justice to musical as well as dramatic values. Perhaps none of her other studio recordings illustrates so vividly her ability to change the color of her voice to reflect a changing dramatic situation. A classic example occurs after her tongue-lashing of Tonio (her voice dripping sadistic glee and loathing), when, at

Silvio's unexpected appearance, she melts before our ears and becomes all delicate femininity. It comes as no surprise when Callas, as Colombina, really sounds like an *actress* going through a well-rehearsed routine. Her final defiance of Canio rings absolutely true; there is no sense that we are listening to a passive victim.

Giuseppe di Stefano sounds a bit young and lightweight for Canio, and the reckless abandon of his assaults on the upper register hint at his subsequent vocal problems. But this is an exciting, committed performance, full of ardor and anger.

Tito Gobbi is a singer with some obvious shortcomings: a dry timbre, a limited top (he doesn't take the traditional A-flat in the Prologue), a tendency to alternate between a raw, wide-open full voice and an exaggerated croon. But as a vocal actor, he is a class by himself. The Prologue sounds poignant and very human (even when the actual phrasing isn't all that smooth), and his Tonio is a terrifying creation, in the grip of a "bestial delirium," indeed.

The Silvio of Rolando Panerai is first-rate: Panerai sings with an incisiveness, variety of tone color, and dramatic insight that make him a worthy partner for Callas in their duet.

1958 PHILIPS (S)

Aureliana Beltrami (A), Alfredo Nobili (B), Gianni Poggi (C), Aldo Protti (D), Walter Monachesi (E), Chorus and Orchestra of the San Carlo Opera, Naples—Ugo Rapalo

With all the good will in the world, this just won't do. Ugo Rapalo has ideas about the score, but both the orchestral playing and the choral singing are on the soggy side.

The Nedda, Aureliana Beltrami, sounds game, but both her voice and her technique are undeveloped. She is up against some formidable recorded competition, and I'm afraid she must be ranked near the bottom of the list. Gianni Poggi emits sounds that are unpleasantly constricted in quality and unpleasantly inaccurate in pitch; he has a yowl where other singers have a vibrato. His ideas about the character are juvenile.

Next to this pair, the two baritones almost seem like reincarnations of Mattia Battistini.

Protti now sings Tonio rather than Silvio and is reasonably effective in the role. The Silvio, Walter Monachesi, sounds more like a bass than a baritone: despite some cautious approaches to high notes, his work is acceptable.

The sound is poor, with the solo voices too closely miked.

1959 DECCA / LONDON (S) CD

Gabriella Tucci (A), Piero de Palma (B), Mario del Monaco (C), Cornell MacNeil (D), Renato Capecchi (E), Chorus and Orchestra of the Accademia di Santa Cecilia, Rome—Francesco Molinari-Pradelli

Del Monaco and de Palma repeat their roles from the Decca / Erede recording; both gentlemen are in good form. Del Monaco's vocal production is noticeably heavier and more nasalized than before, but it's interesting to hear his obvious awareness of the problem—he works hard to keep things light, equalized, and flowing. Dramatically, he is once again wholly convincing, as is de Palma.

Gabriella Tucci's warm, lyric soprano develops a bit of flutter on sustained tones, but it is an attractive instrument, used with skill. Her Nedda is lively, and more tender and womanly than some. It seems strange that such a good soprano made so few commercial recordings.

The two baritones are well contrasted. Renato Capecchi's Silvio sounds young, fresh, and ardent—a distinct asset to the performance. Cornell MacNeil, operating with a much darker, richer timbre than Capecchi's and a seemingly limitless top, sings Tonio's music magnificently. Interpretively, he is rather bland, but his conservative choices are preferable to some other baritones' histrionics.

Francesco Molinari-Pradelli is another laid-back conductor, consistently relaxed in tempo and lazy in attack; he doesn't do anything to prevent the performance from happening, though. The orchestra and chorus are impressive, as is the recorded sound.

1960 EMI / ANGEL (S) CD

Lucine Amara (A), Mario Spina (B), Franco Corelli (C), Tito Gobbi (D), Mario Zanasi (E),

La Scala Chorus and Orchestra—Lovro von Matačic

Lovro von Matačic gives a taut, fast-paced, colorful account of the score, one that fairly crackles with theatrical excitement. The La Scala chorus and orchestra once again demonstrate their chameleon-like ability to adapt to a conductor's concept of the opera. Every choral and instrumental phrase is sharply profiled and yet falls naturally into place, doing its part to guide the action forward.

The success of the performance as a whole more than compensates for any weaknesses in the cast. Gobbi is in rougher voice than he was on the EMI / Serafin set. Ironically, this time he attempts the interpolated A-flat at "Al pari di voi" in the Prologue, which he avoided on the previous recording—and doesn't sustain it very well. His Tonio is still a vivid portrayal. Unfortunately, he no longer has Callas to play against: Amara is also in rather uneasy vocal condition, compared to her earlier effort (the CBS / Cleva set), sounding weak at the bottom and a little hard of tone and tremulous up top. Some of her attempts at vocal acting (e.g., the taunts hurled at Tonio and her subsequent defiance of Canio) seem forced and artificial.

This Canio is one of Franco Corelli's best recordings: he pours out a flood tide of refulgent tone, but also displays good *legato* and a command of quiet dynamic levels. Corelli's Canio seems *hurt* by Nedda's betrayal, not just enraged. If only he didn't break up the musical line of "No, Pagliaccio non son" with gulps and sobs (the Gigli syndrome again), his performance could be admired without reservation.

Mario Zanasi brings a gorgeous, velvety tone and great intensity to Silvio's music; of his recorded rivals, only Panerai makes as much of an effect in the part.

The stereo sound is still impressive after thirty years.

1965 DEUTSCHE GRAMMOPHON (S) (D)

Joan Carlyle (A), Ugo Benelli (B), Carlo Bergonzi (C), Giuseppe Taddei (D), Rolando Panerai (E), La Scala Chorus and Orchestra—Herbert von Karajan

This *Pagliacci* is one of Herbert von Karajan's greatest opera recordings. No other performance of the opera on records makes so much of the score sound so beautiful and musically sophisticated. Paradoxically, though, the drama is not slighted. Right at the start of the action, Karajan's handling of the opening chorus perfectly conjures up the hot, humid August afternoon and the crowd's mood of holiday expectancy. Listening to the Nedda / Silvio duet (in which Karajan, regrettably, observes the traditional cut) is almost indecent: we really seem to be eavesdropping on a couple during a moment of intimacy and crisis. Canio's jealous rages build to terrifying climaxes.

The Scala orchestra surpasses itself: no other orchestra on records (not even La Scala's, on other occasions) plays the score with this combination of transparency, tonal balance, and refinement of phrasing. The chorus is predictably fine.

Karajan has assembled one of the most distinguished casts on records. The big surprise is the Nedda of Joan Carlyle: her light lyric soprano is unvaryingly bright in timbre and lacks a strong chest register, but she sings exquisitely (a ravishing account of the Ballatella) and manages to sound either tough or sensual as the dramatic situation requires.

Bergonzi is heard at his very best. His singing rivals Bjoerling's in tonal beauty and smoothness of line, and his Canio is much more interpretively specific than the Swedish tenor's. Bergonzi's "Un tal gioco" is typical of his work here: it is a beautiful piece of vocalism, but under the surface polish there is a lurking menace.

Both baritones are splendid. In the Prologue, Giuseppe Taddei seems to be experimenting (no doubt at the conductor's suggestion, or insistence) with all sorts of fussy *mezza voce* and *parlando* effects; the results are rather lacking in spontaneity. In the opera itself, however, Taddei is tremendous—almost as intense as Gobbi, while vocalizing much more smoothly and beautifully. Panerai is even better here than he is on the EMI / Serafin recording: utterly secure singing, full of warmth and color and dynamic variety. No other Silvio on records conveys the man's *need* for Nedda—the idea that it's not just the woman he wants, but all that she represents—quite so poignantly.

The engineering, like the performance, is luxurious.

1967 DECCA / LONDON (S)

Pilar Lorengar (A), Ugo Benelli (B), James McCracken (C), Robert Merrill (D), Tom Krause (E), Chorus and Orchestra of the Accademia di Santa Cecilia, Rome—Lamberto Gardelli

This is the first truly complete recording of the opera—the important restoration, of course, being the opening of the previously inevitable cut in the Nedda / Silvio duet.

Lamberto Gardelli, usually a reliable maestro, seems to have been off-form on this occasion. His reading is slow and languid, with insufficient rhythmic definition or contrast. Crucial passages like Canio's futile pursuit of Silvio, and Nedda's subsequent defiance of her husband, are not cued tightly enough to make their full dramatic effect. The Roman orchestra and chorus turn in dutiful, uninspired performances, not always the last word in crispness of ensemble or tonal refinement.

James McCracken has the right weight of voice for Canio, but his singing is technically crude. His tonal production sounds strained, in general; he cannot produce a smooth *legato*; and when he tries to ease up and sing softly, the singing position changes so drastically as to suggest crooning. Worse, McCracken seems determined to "act out" the role, instead of singing it—everything from Canio's discovery of the lovers on is lost in a welter of hysteria (another sob-wracked "Vesti la giubba"), and the outbursts just before the murders are slasher-movie stuff.

Merrill here abandons Silvio, his usual role, in favor of Tonio, and makes quite a good effect. His voice is still full, beautiful, and well balanced; and, although he is hardly in Gobbi's class as an interpreter, his restraint can seem like a virtue when contrasted to McCracken's exaggerations.

Pilar Lorengar makes a bright, attractive sound. Some listeners may object to her characteristic wide vibrato, and she is another in a succession of rather ladylike Neddas on disc. As Silvio, Tom Krause displays a strikingly dark baritone timbre, but also some mushy, accented Italian.

The sound is on the artificial side: the singers often do not seem to be in the same space as their colleagues, let alone the chorus and orchestra; and there are all sorts of Ping-Pong stereo staging effects, most of which are simply distracting.

1971 RCA / BMG (S) CD

Montserrat Caballé (A), Leo Goeke (B), Plácido Domingo (C), Sherrill Milnes (D), Barry McDaniel (E), John Alldis Choir, London Symphony Orchestra—Nello Santi

This version must be accounted a failure—though an honorable one. The idea seems to have been to play the score strictly for musical values, and to restore a certain *bel canto* elegance and refinement to the vocalism.

Nello Santi's conducting is just plain dull: there is not an incisive attack or a hint of dramatic contrast in the entire 80 minutes (as on the Decca / Gardelli set, all of the cuts are dutifully opened, and this time the opera seems to go on forever). The London Symphony Orchestra is wasted, because the players have not been asked to do anything beyond accurate note-rendering. The choral singing is limp, and these choristers do not seem to have been told what they are supposed to be singing about—the words go for little. The children, impersonating tough Italian street urchins, sound like meek choirboys.

Plácido Domingo, oddly enough, sounds vocally ill at ease in parts of Canio's music. Despite his dark, almost baritonal timbre, "Un tal gioco" seems to lie too low for him. He also attacks some of his high notes gingerly. Nor does Domingo present us with a fully rounded character. After "Vesti la giubba," he emulates Gigli by loudly boo-hooing his way through the postlude—an embarrassing moment.

Montserrat Caballé makes some lovely sounds, especially when she is floating her trademark *pianissimo*. When she must let her voice out at full volume, though, it develops an abrasive edge and a beat. She underplays Nedda's earthy qualities, and is at her best as Colombina, where her arch inflections suggest that Nedda is enjoying herself in front of the audience.

Sherrill Milnes does some good singing, warm and rich in tone at full volume, but his use of shaky *mezza voce* and *piano* effects in an attempt to sound sinister quickly becomes monotonous.

Barry McDaniel has an attractive lyric baritone, but his singing as Silvio is small-scaled and colorless.

1977 DECCA/LONDON (S) CD

Mirella Freni (A), Vincenzo Bello (B), Luciano Pavarotti (C), Ingvar Wixell (D), Lorenzo Saccomani (E), London Opera Chorus, Finchley Children's Music Group, National Philharmonic Orchestra—Giuseppe Patanè

Here is a near-total disaster. Giuseppe Patanè's conducting—slow, slack, and fragmented—makes Santi's sound good by comparison. The orchestra and chorus, both professional groups that are probably capable of giving a real performance of the opera, are clearly helpless in the face of the lack of any real direction from the podium, and just go through the motions. This is opera-by-the-numbers.

It's conceivable that another conductor could have pulled this cast together and minimized its problems, but in actuality most of the singing is disillusioning. Luciano Pavarotti, recording Canio without the benefit of stage experience, makes appropriate interpretive gestures, but never penetrates below the surface of the character. He is not in very confident voice on this occasion: Decca's close miking exposes some uneasy high notes, some unsteadiness on sustained tones, and some imbalances between the registers.

Mirella Freni displays exactly the same set of vocal problems as Pavarotti, and her Nedda is a bland, generalized portrayal—a real disappointment, coming from this usually reliable artist.

Neither baritone manages to suggest more than basic competency. Ingvar Wixell, an intelligent artist, is handicapped by his constricted tone, pronounced vibrato, and uneasy top. Lorenzo Saccomani sounds willing, but is taxed by the high tessitura of Silvio's music.

The engineering has a claustrophobic quality, as though all the air has been sucked out of the studio; voices and orchestra occupy two distinct acoustical spaces.

1979 EMI/ANGEL (S) CD

Renata Scotto (A), Ugo Benelli (B), José Carreras (C), Kari Nurmela (D), Thomas Allen (E), Ambrosian Opera Chorus, Southend Boys' Choir, Philharmonia Orchestra—Riccardo Muti

The selling point of this set is that the conductor and producer have gone back to the composer's manuscript, correcting errors that have crept into the printed scores over the years—and atoning for the sins of generations of performers.

All of those nasty, impure, unwritten high notes and upward octave transpositions are banished—proving, I must admit, that while some of the traditional emendations can serve a useful purpose, there's nothing musically wrong with these phrases as they were originally conceived.

The album notes claim that in about sixty places in the score, discrepancies exist between Leoncavallo's autograph and the printed scores concerning tempo indications, dynamic markings, accents, expression, etc., and that in each case the recorded performance reverts to the composer's first thoughts. Frankly, unless you are following the recording with an uncorrected full score in hand, few of these changes are likely to leap out at you.

But the notes also claim that "taken as a whole, these markings reveal that Leoncavallo wished for a lighter, cleaner performance, certainly one less weighed down with quick operatic effects and rhetoric." You *can* hear this change in emphasis in Riccardo Muti's conducting: his reading is fast, tense, clear, and sharply pointed (so much so that it sounds breathless at times), and it is quite brilliantly played by the excellent London orchestra.

Unfortunately, only two of his singers can be called satisfactory. Thomas Allen handles Silvio's music firmly and idiomatically, and would probably be even more effective in the role if Muti did not keep him so rhythmically straitjacketed. Benelli is an expert Beppe, although his voice has dried out in timbre and lost much of its elasticity.

Renata Scotto's Nedda is painful to hear: she obviously has good ideas about the music and the character, but is too vocally insecure to realize all of her intentions. Scotto's soft singing is still beautiful, but the moment the slightest pressure is applied, her tone becomes tense and edgy, and her loud high notes are strident and wobbly.

The Tonio of Kari Nurmela is downright bad: the vocalism is harsh and labored, with insufficient security in the upper register even for those high notes that Leoncavallo *did* write. His delivery of the text is curiously neutral, as though he is sight-reading the part.

José Carerras sounds too young for Canio; if his voice were operating with balance and precision, he could be an ideal Beppe. But he is in poor vocal shape here: weak in the lower register, unsteady and strained on top.

1983 EURODISC (S,D) CD

Lucia Popp (A), Alexandr Ionita (B), Vladimir Atlantov (C), Bernd Weikl (D), Wolfgang Brendel (E), Tölz Boys' Choir, Munich Radio Chorus and Orchestra—Lamberto Gardelli

Gardelli's conducting is livelier than his previous effort, but his reading is still too soft-edged and relaxed in attack for my taste. The Munich orchestra plays well, but the chorus betrays its nationality with some indistinct Italian enunciation. For that matter, the producer has allowed Vladimir Atlantov to get away with some blatant mispronunciations (e.g., "uhbeeta" for "abbietta"), while Lucia Popp's characteristic squeezed tone seems to prevent her from producing clear, open Italian vowels.

Atlantov is a genuine *tenore di forza*, but he is a mannered singer who squanders this basic vocal advantage. He persistently skimps note values and jumps Gardelli's beat, as though he were short of breath and anxious to reach the ends of his phrases; he scoops up to his high notes, makes strange little *crescendo*s on them, and releases them with a sort of sputter. He is uninteresting from the dramatic standpoint, and gives a brusque, prosaic account of "Vesti la giubba."

Popp, by contrast, has good ideas about what kind of a woman Nedda is. Her voice is light for the music, though, and lacks the warmth and sensuality of a topflight Italianate soprano.

Bernd Weikl seems to be doing a Fischer-Dieskau imitation in the Prologue—note his self-conscious applications of a soft, purring head voice. In the opera proper, however, he sings out strongly and is dramatically effective; as Taddeo, he spares us a lot of the traditional comic exaggerations. Wolfgang Brendel's voice is so similar to Weikl's in weight and timbre—even in technique and style—that an unwary listener could be forgiven for assuming that the same singer is doing both parts on this set. On its own merits, though, Brendel's Silvio is effective enough.

The sound is low-level and dull, not at all up to the German record industry's usual high standards.

1983 PHILIPS (S,D) CD

Teresa Stratas (A), Florindo Andreolli (B), Plácido Domingo (C), Juan Pons (D), Alberto Rinaldi (E), La Scala Chorus and Orchestra—Georges Prêtre

This dismal affair is the soundtrack of a Franco Zeffirelli film. The film is at least pretty to look at much of the time. The recording, in cruel contrast, is unpleasant to listen to throughout.

Georges Prêtre gives a tired-sounding account of the score, one that is quite lacking in rhythmic definition or animation of any kind. The chorus and orchestra sound bored and listless—proving that even these experienced musicians are only as good as whoever is wielding the baton. The lack of ensemble between solo voices and the orchestra is frequently disastrous, with singers lagging behind the beat or lurching ahead of it with alarming regularity. Could the soloists be synchronizing their performances to a pre-recorded instrumental track?

Interpretively, Domingo improves on his performance (the RCA / Santi set): much more intensity and variety, a greater sense of maturity. But he is not very successful in disguising the fact that he was going through a bad vocal patch at the time of these sessions: his tone is often rough and unsteady, with uncertain negotiation of register breaks and even some lapses from pitch.

Teresa Stratas is fascinating to watch in the film, but on records, without her intense acting to distract us, we can't help noticing that her voice is threadbare throughout its range and that the upper register is precarious in the extreme.

Juan Pons is a decent, uninteresting Tonio, Alberto Rinaldi a decent, uninteresting Silvio.

———————————

Two of the best performances—the EMI / Serafin and the DG / Karajan—are unfortunately the most expensive.

The CD collector on a budget should give serious consideration to the EMI / Cellini reissue—one disc with good mono sound. Of the stereo alternatives, the Decca / Molinari-Pradelli and the EMI / Matačic sets are both good bargains—in each case *Pagliacci* is paired with *Cavalleria* on a two-disc set with excellent sound.

ROLAND GRAEME

Unavailable for review:
1917 EMI / ANGEL
1927 EMI / ANGEL (In English)
1954 ROYALE
1963 CETRA
1966 ELECTRECORD
1992 PHILIPS

PIETRO MASCAGNI

CAVALLERIA RUSTICANA (1890)

A: Santuzza (s or ms); B: Lola (ms); C: Mamma Lucia (c or ms);
D: Turiddu (t); E: Alfio (bar)

Cavalleria has been recorded in complete form many times, and the list of versions that were unavailable for review is a long one. The opera has also been issued on records, over the years, in performances sung in English, French, German, and Hungarian; I have not attempted to track down these "wrong language" versions, although they may be of interest to specialist collectors.

Cavalleria is often paired with Leoncavallo's *Pagliacci*—not only in the opera house but on records. Most of the major-label recordings of the opera have already been reissued on compact disc—ready proof of the work's great popularity.

This opera presents very few textual problems. The only cut ever made in *Cavalleria* is a tiny one: 15 bars of quasi-fugal writing for the soloist and chorus near the end of Alfio's entrance song ("Il cavallo scalpita"). About a third of the recordings discussed below observe this cut. (I honestly cannot imagine anyone selecting a recording on the basis of whether or not these 15 bars are performed, so I will note only exceptions to this rule.)

Two production notes: First, it's astonishing how many of the Alfios on records continue whipping their poor horses long after the cart has supposedly come to rest. Second, what has been described as "the brief but electrifying role of A Woman"—the one who screams out "Ah! hanno ammazzato compare Turiddu!" twice at the opera's end—is usually assigned to a member of the chorus. Record companies almost never identify her by name. But over the years a succession of uninhibited ladies have placed their vocal cords at risk in order to scare the hell out of us at this point in the opera's action, and there is scarcely one whose "interpretation" is poorly conceived or less than thrillingly executed. I salute them here.

1929–30 EMI / ANGEL (M)

Delia Sanzio (A), Mimma Pantaleoni (B), Olga de Franco (C), Giovanni Breviario (D), Piero Basini (E), La Scala Chorus and Orchestra—Carlo Sabajno

This recording has a certain curiosity value. It gives us a fair idea of what the average Italian repertory performance c. 1929 might have sounded like on a night when none of the era's superstars was available.

The orchestra and chorus are superb, and from the first page of the Prelude on, one notices a style of string playing—sweet-toned, and enriched with unabashed *portamento* phrasing—that simply vanished from the international musical scene during the forties. Carlo Sabajno's conducting is snappy, but all too often he seems to be rushing the music in order to fit it onto the 78 sides: Alfio's entrance song, the Easter hymn, and the Brindisi all make a brusque impression.

The soloists share one stylistic peculiarity: they all wobble to a greater or lesser extent, in stark contrast to the steady tones produced by the choristers and instrumentalists. Giovanni

Breviario is the most satisfactory performer. Despite a steely top and a strong vibrato, he utilizes a wide variety of tonal colors, phrases with elegance, and displays considerable temperament.

Delia Sanzio produces a reasonably attractive sound in the lower and middle registers, but her high notes are painfully thin and strident. She is not a very imaginative artist, and her Santuzza does a lot of whining; when Turiddu responds to her entreaties with "Non tediarmi," he has our full sympathy. Baritone Piero Basini has a wobble wide enough to drive Alfio's cart through; when he and Sanzio really get going in their duet, the results are almost unbearable.

The sound is good for its date. There is one interesting "staging effect," unique to this version: Breviario begins the Siciliana from a distance, then moves gradually closer.

1930 EMI / ANGEL (M) (D

Giannina Arangi-Lombardi (A), Maria Castagna (B), Ida Mannarini (C), Antonio Melandri (D), Gino Lulli (E), Unidentified chorus, Milan Symphony Orchestra—Lorenzo Molajoli

I enjoyed listening to this version. Even though the engineers attempt nothing in the way of distant effects, this set of 78s doesn't sound like a mere runthrough in the studio, but creates the illusion of a theatrical performance. Lorenzo Molajoli deserves much of the credit. After a slightly nervous, impatient Prelude, he—unlike Sabajno—does not seem to have been under any pressure to speed up the music to fit the 78 sides: the opera unfolds naturally, with tempos subtly modified to help the singers make their effects. Once again one admires that beautiful *portamento* phrasing, by the string section in particular but also by the solo winds. (The chorus and orchestra are, in all probability, those of La Scala, but for some reason they are not identified as such on the original record labels.)

The cast is built around one star: dramatic soprano Giannina Arangi-Lombardi. The sheer responsiveness of her voice is a pleasure in itself—there is never any suggestion of hesitation in her attack; her tones are always steady and accurately pitched; she commands a wide variety of dynamics. Her full-bodied soft singing is sumptuous. I suppose that some of her emoting, particularly in "Voi lo sapete," is old-fashioned—rather the equivalent of silent-film acting styles—but she is a great Santuzza.

Antonio Melandri displays a classic case of "goat bleat" vibrato, which will automatically turn off some listeners. He also gets into serious technical trouble at the end of the Siciliana, where the upward intervals of thirds and fourths on "Ah!," which must be more difficult to sing than they look on paper, emerge as atonal squawks. After this shaky start, he develops into an interesting Turiddu, handling the music at least capably, and building a direct, manly characterization. He is among the few tenors on any of these complete sets who make a gesture toward cutting short the final "Addio," the way the composer indicates in the score.

The Alfio, Gino Lulli, stumbles over the text a couple of times during his entrance song (which is performed complete, by the way), but is firm and forceful enough, on the whole.

Standing Room Only's CD transfer utilizes a rather worn set of 78s; the Preiser CD offers much better sound. Neither label provides a libretto. Preiser, a bit misleadingly, has a photo of Caruso, in costume as Turiddu, on its box!

1940 EMI / ANGEL (M) (D

Lina Bruna Rasa (A), Maria Marcucci (B), Giulietta Simionato (C), Beniamino Gigli (D), Gino Bechi (E), La Scala Chorus and Orchestra—Pietro Mascagni

Maestro Mascagni's tempos are among the slowest I have ever heard in the work—with a total running time of 83 minutes, this is easily the longest performance of the opera on records. He takes *ritards* at places that aren't so marked; in virtually every case, I would say that the expressive end justifies the means.

On the other hand, his performance isn't invariably slow: the *stringendo . . . crescendo e stringendo . . . sempre stringendo molto* indication as the Easter hymn builds to its climax is very sharply emphasized—almost violently so, in fact.

Occasionally, Mascagni ignores his own markings: the strings are supposed to begin the "big tune" in the Intermezzo *pp*, then swell it in a gradual *crescendo*; but the La Scala players attack the first chord at a healthy *forte*, and even with a hint of a *sforzando*.

But what is really interesting and surprising about this performance is its high level of musical discipline. Despite the generally slow range of tempos, there is nothing rhythmically slack or melodramatically self-indulgent about the reading.

La Scala's orchestra and chorus once again live up to their reputation. For the last time in a performance of this opera on records, we hear a lavish, apparently instinctive use of string *portamento*.

From the interpretive standpoint, Gigli is the most obnoxious Turiddu on any of the complete sets—and I hope everybody understands that I mean that as a compliment. The "here we go again" boredom and irritability with which he begins the encounter with Santuzza; the embarrassment in front of Lola; the shock and guilt and fear during the scene with Alfio—it is all vividly projected, without ever disrupting the flow of smooth, beautiful vocalism. Admittedly, he becomes rather lachrymose in the final scene, but no more so than is justified by the dramatic situation.

Gino Bechi's tough, snarling baritone, with its hint of peasant crudeness, is the almost perfect voice for Alfio, and he is every bit as spontaneous, as responsive to the dramatic situation, as Gigli—a tremendous performance.

The Santuzza, Lina Bruna Rasa, was only thirty-three years old in 1940, but already near the end of her career—and I am afraid she sounds it. She displays both dignity and temperament; her actual singing, though, must be described as honest and efficient, rather than beautiful. The chest voice is hollow, and the top, though steady and on pitch, is hard and unpliant in timbre. She also seems reluctant to risk much truly soft singing. She sustains the course, but there is simply not much sense of reserve or expansiveness behind her vocalism.

No one who is interested in the performance will be deterred by the slightly dry acoustic, or by the occasional patches of groove noise that remind us the recording is a transfer from 78s. I recommend the recent CD transfer.

1950 CETRA-SORIA (M)

Giulietta Simionato (A), Fernanda Cadoni (B), Liliana Pellegrino (C), Achille Braschi (D), Carlo Tagliabue (E), Lyric Chorus and Orchestra of Cetra, Turin—Arturo Basile

This performance is slightly more polished than the average Cetra production of the early fifties. The orchestra and chorus are good, but Arturo Basile seems to be asking little of them except for accuracy and tidy ensemble.

Giulietta Simionato's Santuzza is a classic portrayal (and, with two studio recordings and at least three "live performance" tapings in existence, it is certainly well documented). This Santuzza is dignified and deeply wounded, nursing her grief. Simionato's firm, clear mezzo has absolutely no trouble with the high notes of the part, and she sculpts her phrases with great eloquence.

She deserves a better Turiddu than Achille Braschi, whose vocalism is painfully raw-toned and callow, and whose ideas about the character are limited to the standard clichés.

Carlo Tagliabue, caught past his best singing days, blusters a bit as Alfio, but his is still a major voice, well suited to the role.

I heard a copy of the original Cetra set—with the opera, somewhat unusually for a major-label production, spread over four LP sides; the sound was surprisingly good.

1951 REMINGTON (M)

Vassilka Petrova (A), Rina Benucci (B), Lidia Malani (C), Edward Ruhl (D), Ivan Petrov (E), Chorus and Orchestra of the Maggio Musicale Fiorentino—Erasmo Ghiglia

For a brief period in the early fifties, Remington tried to corner the market for opera on LP by issuing all sorts of second- and third-rate Italian performances of standard repertory works. This *Cavalleria* is typical of the label's product.

The orchestra and chorus are ordinary, and Erasmo Ghiglia's conducting is limp.

The three principals are a trial to listen to. Vassilka Petrova displays a hefty soprano, along with some wow and flutter. Her Italian is poor. The Turiddu, Edward Ruhl, conducts himself in a reasonably professional manner, but his tone is terribly constricted, and more than one energetic assault on a high note falls short of the required pitch. Baritone Ivan Petrov shouts his way through Alfio's music—crude, pushy vocalism, not redeemed by any insight into the character or the drama.

The reproduction, like the performance, is harsh and unpleasant to listen to.

1953 RCA / BMG (M) CD

Zinka Milanov (A), Carol Smith (B), Margaret Roggero (C), Jussi Bjoerling (D), Robert Merrill (E), RCA Chorus and Orchestra—Renato Cellini

This version, though undeniably idiomatic, is on the bland side. Renato Cellini sets sensible tempos, and his orchestra and chorus are entirely professional. In general, though, the rough edges of the music are smoothed away—this Brindisi, for example, comes across as a polite social gathering.

Zinka Milanov's Santuzza is mature and stately, very much the diva. She has a few moments of gusty attack and dubious intonation during the Easter hymn (one gets the impression that this recording was made on a tight schedule, and that retakes were considered a luxury), but is entirely in command elsewhere.

Jussi Bjoerling's Turiddu is in a class by itself. His singing is unfailingly smooth, beautiful, and poised—a sensuous listening experience (in fact, the way Bjoerling caresses the end of the Siciliana—the same phrases that gave poor Melandri so much trouble, back in 1930—is almost indecent). But Bjoerling is also splendid from the interpretive standpoint: his Turiddu is a selfish, thoughtless young man, hedonistic throughout the action, until his final moments of introspection and remorse.

Robert Merrill, as Alfio, sings with richness

and security, but seems no more than mildly annoyed by his wife's infidelity.

The Victrola LP reissue is in the standard two-disc format, with the fourth side containing Milanov recordings made in 1945 and 1946. The recent CD reissue, on a single mid-priced disc, naturally omits this bonus material, but boasts superior sound.

1953 CBS / SONY (M)

Margaret Harshaw (A), Mildred Miller (B), Thelma Votipka (C), Richard Tucker (D), Frank Guarrera (E), Metropolitan Opera Chorus and Orchestra—Fausto Cleva

Fausto Cleva's conducting is shapely and idiomatic, but the Metropolitan Opera Chorus and Orchestra fail to distinguish themselves—there are minor lapses in ensemble, intonation, and tonal quality throughout.

Richard Tucker, a fine Turiddu, beats the Italian tenors at their own game, offering plangent tone and direct, unaffected emoting.

Margaret Harshaw displays a healthy voice and technique, but little temperamental affinity for Santuzza—she does a decent, basic hit-the-notes job, but no more. Frank Guarrera, by contrast, is dramatically effective as Alfio, but his actual vocalism isn't particularly warm or ingratiating in tone.

The sound is poor by 1953 standards, with the solo voices too far forward and virtually nothing in the way of distance effects. This Easter Mass is an *al fresco* affair: Lola's "E voi sentite le funzioni in piazza?," which is supposed to be ironic, becomes a rhetorical question in this context.

1953 EMI / ANGEL (M) CD

Maria Callas (A), Anna Maria Canali (B), Ebe Ticozzi (C), Giuseppe di Stefano (D), Rolando Panerai (E), La Scala Chorus and Orchestra—Tullio Serafin

Despite some high-voltage vocalism from three famous singers, the main attraction of this album, for me, has always been the conducting of Tullio Serafin. He is somewhat deliberate in tempo (though never as consistently slow as

Mascagni himself), and the basic approach might be described as laid back—climaxes are carefully prepared· and allowed to sink in; there is none of the nervous energy and superficial excitement that some other conductors bring to the score.

Maria Callas, Giuseppe di Stefano, and Rolando Panerai are as strong a team as has ever been assembled for a recording of this work. Callas sings with her typical incisiveness, paying careful attention to details (e.g., dynamic markings and accents) that some other sopranos skate over, and "burning in" phrase after phrase with memorable intensity.

Di Stefano's vocalism is not a model of smoothness or elegance, but it is full of passion and energy. Panerai is an unusually sympathetic Alfio—and his enunciation should be a model for other singers.

The sound, even on the digitally remastered CD reissue, is a little cramped and shallow—not quite up to EMI's usual high standard.

1954 DECCA / LONDON (M)

Elena Nicolai (A), Laura Didier (B), Anna Maria Anelli (C), Mario del Monaco (D), Aldo Protti (E), Unidentified chorus and orchestra, Milan—Franco Ghione

This performance exemplifies the good Italian routine of its era, and still has a fair amount of life about it. Unusually for Decca, the ensemble is not identified—all we are told, on the box and on the record labels, is "orchestra and chorus (Milan)." They are presumably pick-up groups, perhaps even drawing upon the prestigious La Scala forces. In any event, they play and sing well. Franco Ghione is not exactly a ball of fire on the podium, but he keeps the performance moving, and gives the lyrical passages a nice, old-fashioned *cantabile* quality.

Mario del Monaco, in the first of his three studio recordings of the opera (all for Decca), displays the power and abandon for which he was famous—or notorious. The voice is a true *tenore di forza*, remarkable for its solidity up and down the range. Del Monaco was a singer with obvious limitations—e.g., his inability (or refusal) to sing softly, or to phrase with true

legato flow—but in his prime he also had undeniable strengths: verbal immediacy, masculine swagger, fervor. The role of Turiddu, at least on this early outing, brings out the best in him.

The Santuzza, Elena Nicolai, is very much a mezzo—a powerful, dark-hued instrument. Her chest register is exciting to listen to, as is her confident way of attacking the high notes. But there is little vulnerability or tenderness in her portrayal: hers is a tough, aggressive Santuzza, who would be likely to pull a knife on Turiddu (or on Lola!) herself.

Aldo Protti is a dull Alfio, who tends to be cavalier (and at times downright rustic) about pitch and rhythm.

The mono sound is quite good for its age.

1957 DECCA / LONDON (S) CD

Renata Tebaldi (A), Lucia Danieli (B), Rina Corsi (C), Jussi Bjoerling (D), Ettore Bastianini (E), Chorus and Orchestra of the Maggio Musicale Fiorentino—Alberto Erede

This recording reminds us that the good old days weren't always all that great. Three superstar singers are on hand, and they live up to their reputations. But nearly everything else about the performance is unsatisfactory.

Conductor Alberto Erede is inoffensive whenever he confines himself to beating time, or passively allows the soloists to set the pace. Elsewhere, he lurches from climax to climax in a crude, spasmodic manner—the Prelude is almost comical. The orchestral playing is scandalously bad. So is the choral singing. The Easter hymn is given one of its worst performances on any of these complete sets: leaden pace, flabby rhythm, wheezy organ tone, out-of-tune choruses (those inside the church seem to be in a different key than those outside), bleating muted trumpets—you name it, this excruciating rendition has it. But then Renata Tebaldi calmly takes charge, floating "Inneggiamo, il Signor non è morto" over her inadequate colleagues, and the heavens open.

Tebaldi is one of the recording's biggest strengths. Her voice is in exceptionally full, easy, beautiful shape here, and anyone who believes that she was not an imaginative vocal actress will be surprised by the intensity of her portrayal. I only question whether "Battimi, insultami" should sound quite so ecstatic—as though Santuzza were, literally, a masochist.

Bjoerling sings just as beautifully as he did on his previous recording, and reveals a bit more animation and variety of delivery at certain key points.

Ettore Bastianini seems more interested in displaying his voice than in telling us what kind of a man Alfio is; the voice is the genuine article, though, and the baritone's uninhibited use of it is undeniably exciting.

1958 PHILIPS (S)

Caterina Mancini (A), Adriana Lazzarini (B), Aurora Cattelani (C), Gianni Poggi (D), Aldo Protti (E), San Carlo Chorus and Orchestra, Naples—Ugo Rapalo

Released in the United States a decade after it was recorded, this version has been out of print for some time, and is no great loss. The performance is on a provincial level. If you found yourself in Naples with an evening to kill, such a *Cavalleria* might provide a modicum of enjoyment—especially if you were fortified with the local food and wine beforehand.

Ugo Rapalo's conducting is rhythmically slack. The orchestral and choral work are adequate, but hardly worthy of an opera house with the San Carlo's illustrious history.

Caterina Mancini has temperament and knows what she wants to do with Santuzza's music, but whenever the emotional temperature, pitch, or volume rises, her singing becomes unruly and strident. Gianni Poggi indulges in querulous caterwauling that suggests a cruel parody of an operatic tenor: his Turiddu must be accounted a near-total loss. Protti, his tone worn at full volume and frequently unsteady, is no better than he was on the Decca / Ghione set.

The sound is poor, with the solo voices much too closely miked.

1960 DECCA / LONDON (S) CD

Giulietta Simionato (A), Ana Raquel Satre (B), Anna di Stasio (C), Mario del Monaco (D), Cornell MacNeil (E), Chorus and Orchestra of the Accademia di Santa Cecilia, Rome—Tullio Serafin

Serafin's pacing is even broader and more relaxed than it was on the 1953 EMI set, and the overall effect may be too luxuriant and lingering for the opera's good. Once again, though, the maestro has a responsive orchestra and chorus to work with.

Simionato's Santuzza (rather like Serafin's conducting) is more studied, less spontaneous, than before. Her voice is in impressively secure shape, though.

By contrast, del Monaco now shouts a little, and his vocal condition in general is less free and balanced than it was on his first recording, but his Turiddu is still a male in uninhibited rut.

Cornell MacNeil's warm, fat baritone sails easily through Alfio's music, amply compensating for his relative lack of interpretive specificity.

1962 EMI / ANGEL (S) CD

Victoria de los Angeles (A), Adriana Lazzarini (B), Corinna Vozza (C), Franco Corelli (D), Mario Sereni (E), Rome Opera Chorus and Orchestra—Gabriele Santini

Gabriele Santini's conducting has old-fashioned virtues and shortcomings. His tempo choices are almost invariably on the slow side, and he phrases the music freely, with an affectionate *col canto* quality. This approach yields beautiful results and is unarguably right in such numbers as the Prelude and the Easter hymn. The big dramatic confrontations—Santuzza / Turiddu, Santuzza / Alfio, Turiddu / Alfio—do lack muscle and forward impetus, though. The orchestra and chorus, never less than pleasant to listen to, are not exactly models of razor-sharp precision—sluggish attacks abound, and ensemble is less than unanimous on more than one occasion.

All three principals are good, though only Mario Sereni's Alfio can be enjoyed without reservation: his voice is warm and full, his manner thoughtful but unfussy.

Franco Corelli, like del Monaco, is a true *tenore di forza* whose voice easily encompasses the music. His singing has ample energy, and is more varied in color and dynamic level than one might expect. On this occasion, though, Corelli is not a very specific vocal actor: his Turiddu doesn't seem to be paying attention to what Santuzza is saying in their scene together (a legitimate way of playing the role in theory, perhaps, but rather limiting in practice), and he relies on an all-purpose plaintive vocal mode in the scenes with Alfio and Lucia.

Victoria de los Angeles's Santuzza is problematic. Except for a little cautiousness at the top, her voice is in warm, lovely condition, and she shapes the music most expressively. But she definitely seems too passive, even bland. Furthermore, because of their vocal and stylistic differences, she and Corelli don't seem to be participating in the same opera—one wishes that she could have recorded the work with a tenor like Bjoerling or Bergonzi.

1965 DEUTSCHE GRAMMOPHON (S) CD

Fiorenza Cossotto (A), Adriane Martino (B), Maria Gracia Allegri (C), Carlo Bergonzi (D), Giangiacomo Guelfi (E), La Scala Chorus and Orchestra—Herbert von Karajan

Based on a famous stage production, this is, hands down, the most sensuously beautiful performance of the opera on records. The Scala orchestra has played this score well for other conductors, but Herbert von Karajan makes it sound like a major symphonic ensemble. One need go no farther than the start of the Prelude, where this magical realization of the violins' high, exposed lines leaves all other recorded performances in the dust.

Karajan's ideas about the opera may be too stately and lingering for some listeners' tastes. Certainly the Santuzza / Turiddu scene, taken very deliberately and beautifully sung, sounds more like an abstract musical form than a violent dramatic confrontation. There are typical Karajan mannerisms—the "A casa, a casa, amici" chorus (immediately after the Intermezzo) is done in a conspiratorial *sotto voce*, as though the villagers were afraid of being overheard.

Fortunately, the La Scala chorus (in superb form) is on hand, and so is an excellent all-Italian cast—the idiomatic vocalism prevents the performance from becoming too rarefied for its own good.

All five soloists are in fact first-rate. Fiorenza Cossotto sets the standard with one of the best-sung Santuzzas on records. Like Simionato, Cossotto is a high mezzo, whose secure upper register would be the envy of many a dramatic soprano. Her *legato* is flawless, her shrewd applications of dark and light timbres enormously expressive. Best of all, her portrayal has true tragic grandeur—it is intense and anguished, but always dignified.

The only criticism that can be made of Carlo Bergonzi's Turiddu is that he is too gentlemanly for the character. But this is aristocratic singing, as beautiful as Bjoerling's, and actually more consistently Italianate in style.

Giangiacomo Guelfi's tightly focused high baritone drives through Alfio's music with an elemental, penetrating quality—and yet Karajan makes sure that Guelfi pays careful attention to purely musical values. This is the best performance that I have ever heard Guelfi give on a recording, commercial or otherwise.

DG's sound is splendidly weighty, clear, and detailed. Some of the distance effects do seem a bit extreme—the offstage chorus is very far away during the Easter hymn (suggesting that this particular Sicilian village boasts a piazza and a church the size of St. Peter's Basilica in Rome).

1966 DECCA / LONDON (S)

Elena Souliotis (A), Stefania Malagù (B), Anna di Stasio (C), Mario del Monaco (D), Tito Gobbi (E), Chorus and Orchestra of Rome—Silvio Varviso

If there were a prize for the Worst Recording of a Standard Repertory Opera by a Major Record Company, then this nightmarish rendition of *Cavalleria* would be a strong contender.

The "Orchestra e Coro di Roma" are presumably pick-up groups, perhaps drawn from the opera house and the Academy of Santa Cecilia. The playing and the choral singing are not all that bad—but they do sound under-rehearsed.

Silvio Varviso's conducting is fast, crude, and clumsy.

A recording of this opera is in big trouble when the only satisfactory solo performances are given by the Lola and the Lucia. Those two experienced and reliable mezzos, Stefania Malagù and Anna di Stasio, have the good sense to ignore the fiasco that is going on around them; they just sing their parts, with their usual professionalism. In fact, it's too bad that Malagù wasn't given a crack at Santuzza.

Two of the three principals are well past their vocal primes and are particularly distressing to hear. Del Monaco has plenty of volume left, but the sounds he emits are harsh, constricted, and ugly. He blares away heartily, though, and hangs onto his raw, wide-open high notes as though they were the most ravishing tones ever to emerge from a human throat.

It is unfortunate that Tito Gobbi was not given a chance to record Alfio in the fifties, when he might have done himself justice in the role. Here, he manages some appropriate line readings in the final confrontation with Turiddu, but is reduced to yelling during his entrance song and the duet with Santuzza.

Elena Souliotis, handicapped by a coarse chest register and a squally top, sounds almost amateurish in Santuzza's music. This is stiff, unschooled, and thoroughly unpleasant vocalism.

Decca's typically aggressive recorded sound is too reverberant and too multi-miked. In the climaxes, the trombones, timpani, bass drum, and cymbals overwhelm the rest of the ensemble, and there are boomy echoes after each of these outbursts.

1976 DECCA / LONDON (S) CD

Julia Varady (A), Carmen Gonzales (B), Ida Bormida (C), Luciano Pavarotti (D), Piero Cappuccilli (E), London Opera Chorus, National Philharmonic Orchestra—Gianandrea Gavazzeni

The veteran conductor Gianandrea Gavazzeni gives a distinguished reading of the score, songful and flowing, and well executed by the thoroughly professional London pick-up ensemble. Tempos seem neither fast nor slow, but exactly right.

The cast could be stronger. The best of the principals is Julia Varady: her warm lyric soprano is distinctive in timbre and capable of mournful colorations, she phrases with considerable expertise, and she has a good sense of the character's combination of guilt, resentment, and passion.

Luciano Pavarotti has not sung Turiddu on stage; although he makes appropriate interpretive gestures, he has some distance to go before he can rival Gigli, Bjoerling, or Bergonzi in the role. His phrasing is stiff, and many of his high notes do not sound comfortably produced or sustained.

Piero Cappuccilli, with his rather soft-grained baritone, is lightweight casting for Alfio, and he does not seem to be temperamentally well suited to the role—bland stretches alternate with sudden, unmotivated bursts of energy.

Decca's sound is highly artificial—the solo voices are much too closely miked, and there are strange balances that are clearly the result of mixing at the console after the fact.

1978 RCA / BMG (S) CD

Renata Scotto (A), Isola Jones (B), Jean Kraft (C), Plácido Domingo (D), Pablo Elvira (E), Ambrosian Opera Chorus, National Philharmonic Orchestra—James Levine

James Levine's concept of the opera is slow and weighty, rather like Serafin's. The London pick-up orchestra makes a rich, lush sound. This is a particularly beautiful account of the Intermezzo, with the organ chords saturating the warm, vibrant string sonorities.

Renata Scotto's intense, three-dimensional Santuzza is one of the most interesting on records. Her singing is consistently beautiful (provided one doesn't object to the slight edge on high notes). Like Callas, Scotto believes in every marking the composer wrote, and always turns this accuracy to expressive effect. A typical example is her handling of the first statement of "Turiddu mi tolse l'onore"; it is sung very softly, as though Santuzza is so ashamed by what she is saying that she can barely bring herself to utter the words out loud.

Plácido Domingo has recorded Turiddu three times. On this first outing, he makes a splendid sound—warm and velvety, yet virile—and, if his portrayal is a bit generalized, it is not careless.

Pablo Elvira is a bit lightweight for Alfio, but very musical.

Back in 1978, RCA broke new technical ground by fitting this leisurely-paced performance onto a single LP, with no discernible compromise in the sound quality. (Levine, surprisingly, makes the cut in Alfio's song, which saves a few seconds.) The CD reissue, on which groove spacing is not a problem, also sounds fine.

1979 EMI / ANGEL (S) CD

Montserrat Caballé (A), Julia Hamari (B), Astrid Varnay (C), José Carreras (D), Matteo Manuguerra (E), Ambrosian Opera Chorus, Philharmonia Orchestra—Riccardo Muti

This production serves as further proof, if any is needed, that an impressive line-up of names is not necessarily the same thing as a good cast, and does not guarantee a good performance.

I like a great deal of what Riccardo Muti does here. He does not go along with the trend toward exaggeratedly slow tempos; his reading flows easily, has a sharp rhythmic profile, and is cleanly executed by the excellent choral and orchestral forces. There is often a pleasing lyrical quality to the more introverted sections of the score (e.g., the beginning and end of the Prelude). For some reason, though, all of this doesn't quite add up to *Cavalleria*: the performance has the abstract, sanitized quality that has become all too typical of studio-recorded opera.

The only satisfactory vocal performance here is Matteo Manuguerra's robust Alfio—not the most intense or exciting portrayal imaginable, perhaps, but firmly and honestly vocalized.

Turiddu ought to be a good role for José Carreras, but his singing here is curiously small-scaled, tentative in attack, and neutral in delivery. (No doubt at Muti's insistence, though,

Carreras's final "Addio" is not only *tronca* but *tronca assai*.)

Muti's firm beat prevents Montserrat Caballé from languishing too much; the soprano's extraordinary breath control and her ability to reduce her sound to a disembodied *pianissimo* enable her to bring off many striking musical effects. On the negative side, her voice turns harsh and unsteady at full volume, and she resorts too often to gulpy attacks, glottal stops, and a hard chest tone in her attempts to sound "dramatic."

1981 EURODISC (S) CD

Martina Arroyo (A), Livia Budai (B), Juliana Falk (C), Franco Bonisolli (D), Bernd Weikl (E), Bavarian Radio Chorus, Munich Radio Orchestra—Lamberto Gardelli

This performance has serious problems. Lamberto Gardelli keeps the music moving most of the time, but does not seem to have demanded much more than competence from the good German chorus and orchestra.

Franco Bonisolli's Turiddu is a qualified success: the voice is basically a good one, used with abandon, and Bonisolli has a firm grasp on the young man's character. But Gardelli should not have indulged the tenor's insistence on stretching so many of his phrases for "expressive" effect—this must be the slowest account of the Siciliana on records, for example; and there are other places where Bonisolli loiters on his high notes until the musical line falls apart. This is not the kind of controlled flexibility of tempo and rhythm heard on the older recordings of the opera: it's just a singer on an ego trip.

If her voice were functioning with balance and precision, Martina Arroyo might be an interesting Santuzza; unfortunately, she seems to be going through a bad vocal patch here. The middle of her voice is still beautiful (though a little too soft-grained in timbre to be ideal for the role), but the bottom is weak and the top turns both tight and wobbly under pressure—she encounters real difficulties in the duet with Alfio. After a subdued start, she shows some animation in the scene with Turiddu.

Bernd Weikl sings handsomely as Alfio, but

doesn't do anything extraordinary with the part. Some of the Italian baritones who have recorded the role are more individual, and (almost inevitably) sound more idiomatic.

The sound (stereo, but apparently not digital) is dull, with the solo voices too far forward for comfort.

1985 PHILIPS (S,D) CD

Elena Obraztsova (A), Axelle Gall (B), Fedora Barbieri (C), Plácido Domingo (D), Renato Bruson (E), La Scala Chorus and Orchestra—Georges Prêtre

This recording is the soundtrack of Franco Zeffirelli's film of the opera—which explains some rather strange sonic perspectives and balances, as well as a plethora of "sound effects," few of which are convincing. The film (available on both videotape and laser disc) is glossy and overblown, in typical Zeffirelli fashion, but is certainly worth seeing. Without the visual element, the performance makes a feeble impression.

Georges Prêtre's tempos are erratic, and one section of the score does not lead logically to the next. The Scala forces sound under-rehearsed—one would never guess that this is the same ensemble that performed so magnificently for Serafin and Karajan.

Renato Bruson (who does by far the best acting in the film) is a restrained, sinister Alfio. His colleagues are, without exception, miscast, vocally below par, or both.

Domingo sounds vocally tired, in general, and does not equal his achievement on the RCA / Levine version. Elena Obraztsova is a heavy, lugubrious Santuzza: her big, tough mezzo, with its exaggerated chest tones, wide vibrato, and insecure upper register, plows its way through the music with an undeniable visceral impact, but also with little refinement.

The single-disc CD includes the libretto in Italian only.

1989 DEUTSCHE GRAMMOPHON (S,D) CD

Agnes Baltsa (A), Susanne Mentzer (B), Vera Baniewicz (C), Plácido Domingo (D), Juan Pons (E), Chorus of the Royal Opera House, Covent Garden, Philharmonia Orchestra—Giuseppe Sinopoli

Despite a line-up of talent that looks promising on paper, this is a dull performance, on the whole. Giuseppe Sinopoli's tempos are broad, and he favors weighty emphases. The orchestral playing is expert, with all sorts of fine instrumental detail coaxed out into the open—a process abetted by DG's truly sensational sound (which boasts a huge dynamic range, and the kind of solidity in the bass response that turns timpani and bass drum rolls into detonations). Despite the obvious care that has gone into the performance, the overall effect is curiously abstract—the opera sounds more like a Mahlerian symphonic poem, with vocal *obbligatos* of distinctly secondary importance.

The singers often seem constrained, as though they are dutifully dropping their lines into place to suit the conductor's preconception. Domingo is in much better form than on the Philips / Prêtre set, although his voice has become very dark in timbre and sluggish in attack at times.

Agnes Baltsa does not always seem comfortable with Sinopoli's slow tempos, nor is her handsome high mezzo voice in its best condition—the high notes sound tight, and her soft singing can be curiously colorless. Juan Pons is a sturdy, rather unimaginative Alfio.

1990 PHILIPS (S,D) CD

Jessye Norman (A), Martha Senn (B), Rosa Laghezza (C), Giuseppe Giacomini (D), Dmitri Hvorostovsky (E), Chorus and Orchestre de Paris—Semyon Bychkov

This *Cavalleria*, Semyon Bychkov's first recording of a complete opera, is a disappointment. Bychkov is a talented musician, and one can hear what he is aiming at: this is a gentle, lyrical, understated reading of the score. It rivals Karajan's in refinement, but is even less Italianate. Of gutsy *verismo* drama there is no trace.

The Paris orchestra is not a front-line ensemble: the violins' tone thins out in the upper reaches, the brasses are soft-grained and reticent, and the solo bassoon has a curiously weak, colorless timbre. The chorus is accurate, but betrays its nationality with some mushy Italian enunciation.

Giuseppe Giacomini, an intelligent tenor who has made few commercial records, is a strong, forthright Turiddu—even though his voice, with its hard, metallic timbre, must be described as useful rather than beautiful.

Vocally, Jessye Norman's Santuzza gives us the best of both worlds, for she has a mezzo's dark coloration and plushness of timbre in the lower and middle range, but combines this with a full-bodied, soaring dramatic-soprano top. She sings with her customary generosity and intensity; over the long run, however, her Santuzza (like Milanov's) retains too much of the studied quality of the diva.

Dmitri Hvorostovsky is an impressive Alfio. His voice is beautiful and his Italian expressive. He doesn't dig into the role the way singers like Bechi and Panerai do, but he touches all of the interpretive bases, and his restraint is welcome.

The sound is good, but the engineers have miscalculated the offstage effects. Giacomini seems to be a mile away from the microphone during the Siciliana, as though he really *were* in Francofonte. Lola's voice is also too distant at the start of her Stornello, making it implausible that her singing would interrupt Santuzza and Turiddu's argument.

If money is no object, I urge every collector to acquire either the EMI / Serafin or the DG / Karajan set, or both. These are distinguished realizations of the opera (but very different in stylistic approach and emotional impact, which helps to justify the duplication); in each case, an equally fine version of *Pagliacci* is part of the package. If you want *Cavalleria* by itself, then the RCA / Levine recording is a good alternative.

The CD collector on a tight budget should give serious consideration to the Decca / Serafin and EMI / Santini recordings. In each case, solid, idiomatic performances of both *Caval-*

leria and *Pagliacci* are available as a mid-priced two-CD set, in excellent stereo sound.

ROLAND GRAEME

Unavailable for review:
1915 EMI / ANGEL
1928 EMI / ANGEL (in English)
c. 1950 FIDELIO
1954 REMINGTON
1966 ELECTRECORD
1969 FABBRI

DAVID GOCKLEY
General Director,
Houston Grand Opera

1. **Wagner,** *Tristan und Isolde*: Flagstad, Thebom, Suthaus, Fischer-Dieskau, Greindl—Furtwängler. EMI / ANGEL

2. **Puccini,** *Madama Butterfly*: Scotto, di Stasio, Bergonzi, Panerai—Barbirolli. EMI / ANGEL

3. **Gershwin,** *Porgy and Bess*: Dale, Shakesnider, Lane, Brice, Marshall, Albert, Smalls, Smith—DeMain. RCA / BMG

4. **Puccini,** *Tosca*: Callas, di Stefano, Gobbi—de Sabata. EMI / ANGEL

5. **Verdi,** *Otello*: Scotto, Kraft, Domingo, Little, Milnes—Levine. RCA / BMG

6. **Strauss,** *Ariadne auf Naxos*: Schwarzkopf, Streich, Seefried, Schock, Prey, Dönch—Karajan. EMI / ANGEL

7. **Mozart,** *Don Giovanni*: Sutherland, Schwarzkopf, Sciutti, Alva, Wächter, Cappuccilli, Taddei, Frick—Giulini. EMI / ANGEL

8. **Wagner,** *Lohengrin*: Grümmer, Ludwig, Thomas, Fischer-Dieskau, Frick—Kempe. EMI / ANGEL

9. **Strauss,** *Der Rosenkavalier*: Stich-Randall, Schwarzkopf, Ludwig, Wächter, Edelmann—Karajan. EMI / ANGEL

10. **Britten,** *Peter Grimes*: Harper, Payne, Bainbridge, Vickers, Summers—Davis. PHILIPS

L'AMICO FRITZ (1891)

A: Suzel (s); B: Beppe (ms); C: Fritz (t); D: Rabbi David (bar)

L'Amico Fritz was the second of Mascagni's operas. Based on the popular pastoral novel of the previous generation by Émile Erckmann and Alexandre Chatrian, it was first performed in 1891, the year after his success with *Cavalleria Rusticana*. After the violence of *Cavalleria*, Mascagni sought to show his versatility by writing this gentle romance of a reluctant landowner and his steward's daughter brought together by blossoming cherry trees, benevolent instinct, and a matchmaking rabbi. It was first produced in Rome at the Costanzi Theater, which had brought out *Cavalleria*, and featured Emma Calvé and Fernando di Lucia, both of whom then sang it in London and at the Met. Verdi thought the libretto idiotic, but George Bernard Shaw, moderately enthusiastic, found the work "fresh, freehanded, bouncing, rather obstreperous." He also thought Calvé, whom he was seeing for the first time, "affecting in the simple grace and naive musical feeling which exhaust the scope of the part of Suzel," an interesting comment for the light it sheds on what is required for successful performance of the opera. Lucrezia Bori and Miguel Fleta sang it at the Met revival in 1923, and two generations of lyric singers had success with it in Italy, among them Gilda dalla Rizza, Giuseppina Baldassare-Tedeschi (Licia Albanese's teacher), Adelaide Saraceni, Albanese, Pia Tassinari, Beniamino Gigli, and Ferruccio Tagliavini. From some of these singers there are cherishable recordings, among them the first complete set described below.

1942 CETRA (M)

Pia Tassinari (A), Amalia Pini (B), Ferruccio Tagliavini (C), Saturno Meletti (D), EIAR Chorus and Symphony Orchestra—Pietro Mascagni

L'Amico Fritz can be a delightful experience if singers and audience know just what to expect. The opera needs as specific a sense of its style as, for example, *Pelléas et Mélisande* does. Without delicately shifting tonal colors and word pointing it is banal; with them it is a charming revelation of both the characters and the singers. Pia Tassinari and Ferruccio Tagliavini never seem more themselves than here. She, particularly, shades her lovely voice at will for shyness, propriety, and yearning, turning all those tempo changes (about which Verdi complained) into a conversational flow of feelings. In the great Puccini recordings there are numerous examples of this sort of singing, but it is fascinating to see just how fully such detailed work enlivens the frailer melodic idiom of Mascagni. Tagliavini also offers some of this skill. Most of the time, and particularly in Acts II and III, his tone is incomparably dulcet. Even in 1942, early in his career, he was occasionally huffing and puffing, breaking the *legato* line and hardening the top tones, but these are mannerisms of the singer, not the music. In general, the little arias and duets of these two singers are among the most engaging on records.

In addition, Saturno Meletti is a capital David, his vibrant voice possessing an insistent character which suits the role well. Amalia Pini has an interesting vibrato that suggests the Gypsy boy she plays. Anyone who has heard Ebe Stignani in some of this music, though, will not be fully satisfied. Conducting his own score in this fiftieth-anniversary performance, Mascagni is both loving and animated. The orchestra and sound are at least tolerable. One devastating reminder of the time in which this recording was made: the word "rabbino" (rabbi) is changed to "dottore" (doctor) throughout.

1968 EMI / ANGEL (S) CD

Mirella Freni (A), Laura Didier Gambaradella (B), Luciano Pavarotti (C), Vincenzo Sardinero (D), Chorus and Orchestra of the Royal Opera House, Covent Garden—Gianandrea Gavazzeni

Certainly the recording here is clearer and the orchestra of better quality than in Mascagni's set: advantages for an opera in which instrumental timbre is so evocative of atmosphere. It can also be argued that these singers are in many respects as cultivated as their predecessors. Luciano Pavarotti is in particularly beautiful voice and generally sings with superb breath control. In the earlier set, though, Ferruccio Tagliavini has a ravishing sweetness of tone that I find irresistible despite his occasional mannerisms. Mirella Freni sings with care, but the sound is a little cold and dark, the palette not nearly so varied as that of Pia Tassinari, who sings with unflagging charm and warmth. Vincenzo Sardinero is a pleasant David, but Saturno Meletti presents a fuller character. With her wobbly mezzo and difficult high notes, Laura Didier Gambaradella scarcely suggests a beardless youth. Gianandrea Gavazzeni's conducting is affectionate but needs proportion and playfulness; some of the more intriguing passages drag.

The newer recording has better sound and Luciano Pavarotti in fine form, but Mascagni's own effort has an irresistible flavor, with Ferruccio Tagliavini generally at his most eloquent, Pia Tassinari superb as Suzel, and more convincing support from Saturno Meletti and Amalia Pini.

LONDON GREEN

JULES MASSENET

MANON (1884)

A: Manon (s); B: Pousette (s); C: Javotte (s); D: Rosette (ms);
E: Chevalier des Grieux (t); F: Guillot de Morfontaine (t);
G: Lescaut (bar); H: de Brétigny (bar); I: Count des Grieux (bs)

*M*anon is Jules Massenet's most successful work in the *opéra comique* genre, and for many it represents the culmination of this style of French lyric theater. The work received its premiere at the Opéra-Comique in Paris in January 1884, and it was immediately acclaimed a great success, although some critics accused the composer of the sin of "excessive Wagnerism."

Essentially, in *Manon* Massenet revitalized the old-fashioned *opéra comique* form, which involved sung set-pieces separated by stretches of spoken dialogue. With superb craftsmanship, he adapted the form by blending song and speech into a continuous musical texture, with the dialogue passages mostly spoken over the music, in the style of melodrama.

In addition to arias, duets, sung recitatives, and ensembles, Massenet employed such antique forms as the minuet, gavotte, and Rameau-like ballet entrées in order to recreate the eighteenth-century atmosphere of the Abbé Prévost's novel. Consequently, a lightness of tone pervades the opera, interrupted only by the religiosity and sensuality of the St. Sulpice scene, and by the overt brutality of the gambling scene at the Hôtel de Transylvanie.

Any review of the recorded history of *Manon* must raise the issue of French vocal style, one of the great national traditions lost in the internationalization of opera in recent times. Historically, the greatest interpreters of French operatic singing have tended to share certain basic traits. Of utmost importance is clarity of diction and an innate feeling for the French language which, unlike Italian, does not offer open vowels on which to base roundness of tone or purity of *legato*. Great French singers have tended to favor a very forward pronunciation of the words, facilitated by a vocal placement "in the mask." For lyrical roles, this usually means voices of somewhat slender tone, with a bit of nasality, and with an even but rapid vibrato. The rich plumminess of Italianate voices, with throbbing vibratos and slower verbal articulation, works against the clarity and precision of French style.

At the same time, the singer of Massenet's music must combine ardency with elegance, freshness with immediacy, and atmosphere with accent. Intonation must be above suspicion. Fortunately, the recorded history of *Manon*, from the earliest days to the recent present, contains a wealth of singers who meet these requirements.

Interestingly enough, for a work so prominent in the international operatic repertory, there have been relatively few complete recordings of *Manon*, and only two have been produced in the last thirty-five years. Of the six complete recordings, which chronologically span the years from 1923 to 1982, the four earliest all derive from the Paris Opéra-Comique itself, mapping the history of *Manon*'s performance traditions at its birthplace. In these, standard theater cuts abound, usually involving choruses, ballet music in the Cours la Reine Scene, second verses of Lescaut's and Count des Grieux's arias, and byplay among Guillot, de Brétigny, and the three actresses Pousette, Javotte, and Rosette.

1923 PATHÉ (M)

Fanny Heldy (A), Marthe Coiffier (B), Madeleine Sibille (C), Lucienne Estève (D), Jean Marny (E), Louis Mesmaecker (F), Léon Ponzio (G), Maurice Sauvageot (H), Pierre Dupré (I), Orchestra and Chorus of the Opéra-Comique—Henri Büsser

This earliest recording of *Manon* was recorded in Paris by Pathé using the forces of the Opéra-Comique, and was originally released on 48 sides. An excellent LP transcription was released by Bourg in 1984.

The performance essentially captures the third generation of famous *Manon* interpreters and it is a highly valuable document of the style and musical intent of the period. Henri Büsser, a reputable musicologist, conductor, composer, and later director of the Opéra-Comique, leads what is audibly a French orchestra. The pungency and nasality of the winds are particularly noticeable, along with the sharpness of tone and use of *portamento* by the undernourished string section. Rhythms tend to be swiftly articulated, though some of the tempos are stiff and square. There are a few hiccups and bumps charmingly retained by the old recording process, whereby a side would have to be completely remade to correct such errors.

The title role is taken by Fanny Heldy, who, although she was in fact Belgian, was the most internationally renowned "French" soprano of the interwar years. Heldy's voice is that of a typical Gallic soprano, a high, light, forwardly placed, focused sound with narrow tone and girlish timbre. She possesses a bit of a cutting edge, which undoubtedly allowed her to undertake heavier parts in the theater, and may have sounded more pleasing there than it does on records. Her top notes tend to be pinched and, when pressed, not always squarely on pitch. Sweetness and purity of tone are sacrificed for dramatic impact and presence. Her entrance aria in Act I, "Je suis encore tout étourdie," is

sung straightforwardly, without much light and shade and with little dynamic variety, as if to first establish the character's wide-eyed naiveté. Later in this act, after the reprimand from Lescaut, her "Voyons, Manon, plus de chimères" exhibits more interesting phrasing, with ravishing *pianissimos* and an expressive weighting of the words. Her Act II "Adieu, notre petite table" is preceded by a passionate and feverish recitative, although the farewell itself is somewhat dry-eyed. Clearly, Heldy has carefully thought through her choices so as to heighten our awareness of Manon's character development in the course of the opera, which she handles with subtlety.

Heldy's des Grieux is the aristocratic Jean Marny. Though less well known than his illustrious partner, his tenor is clear, fresh, forward, not too nasal, with a quick, unobtrusive vibrato and a good line. He speaks the dialogue lines with great emotion, and his singing is similarly vibrant and youthful. The Act I duet with Manon, "Nous vivrons à Paris," is ardent, with each grace note in place and fluent use of *pianissimos* and *voix mixte* (a French-style blend of head voice approaching—but not quite—a falsetto sound). Marny's Act II dream aria, "En fermant les yeux," displays beautiful *legato*, with exquisite use of dynamics and *mezza voce* effects.

The Lescaut of this performance is Léon Ponzio, a light baritone with good flexibility, excellent top notes, and a vibrato which occasionally widens on sustained tones.

Pierre Dupré's Count des Grieux provides a good example of another vocal type which is almost extinct, the low-baritonal French bass. Traditionally, French basses have possessed a lighter, drier sound than their Italian or Russian counterparts, and have emphasized a clarity of articulation over voluptuousness of tone. Nevertheless, Dupré sings with great feeling.

1928–29 EMI / ANGEL (M) CD

Germaine Féraldy (A), André Vayon (B), Mes. Rambert and Ravery (C), Andrée Bernadet / Marinette Fenoyer (D), Joseph Rogatchewsky

(E), Émile de Creus (F), Georges Villier (G), André Gaudin / Jean Vieuille (H), Louis Guénot (I), Chorus and Orchestra of the Opéra-Comique—Elie Cohen

This time around, the Opéra-Comique orchestra and chorus are led by Elie Cohen, in what was to be the first of EMI's four recordings of the opera.

This performance shares certain aspects—positive and negative—with its predecessor. As in 1923, the overall pacing is fairly swift, the strings are again undernourished, and the chorus again sounds meager and scrappy. The ballet sequences are played with clarity and verve. Cohen, like Büsser, makes the traditional theater cuts, including choruses and a number of transitional passages. On the positive side, the characterizations are specific and well thought through, and the spoken dialogue is again flavorful. The supporting cast maintains the Opéra-Comique tradition of liveliness, and the feeling for the work is thoroughly authentic, with the flair of a real theater performance. Most important, the new electric recording process results in a much richer and more full-bodied sound than the acoustic process of 1923, and is amazingly detailed for its age.

As Manon, Germaine Féraldy offers a strong lyric soprano with good line and flexible articulation. Her voice is somewhat more substantial than that of the typical light French soprano, although this greater weight does not prevent her from being effective in the high coloratura passages. She can float *pianissimo* notes, although she chooses not to do so at every available opportunity. Her characterization is charming and unaffected in nature. The "petite table" farewell is taken at a fast clip, which minimizes the sentimentality of this number. Féraldy's spoken French is evocative and particularly beautiful, rounding out a charming, innocent concept of the role.

An interesting textual variant included in an appendix following the opera proper is Féraldy's 1928 recording of the so-called Fabliau Scene—literally a short recitation in verse but essentially a lengthy accompanied recitative leading to a coloratura showpiece. Massenet wrote this alternative aria in the early 1890s for the soprano Georgette Bréjean-Silver as a replacement for the gavotte in the Cours la Reine. Féraldy executes the *fioratura* fireworks and roulades required in this scene with spirit and delight.

The Ukrainian tenor Joseph Rogatchewsky sings the role of des Grieux. Although he brings much plangency and attractive middle-register richness to his singing, his tonal production becomes unsteady in the upper-middle range as the voice moves through the *passaggio*, and his top notes are often strained. At full voice he reveals some awkwardness of phrasing and is sometimes careless with note values. In addition, his French is noticeably accented. Despite these flaws, he brings a passionate Italianate approach to the role which some may find compelling enough as to overlook the lack of French style and subtlety.

Georges Villier, as Lescaut, possesses the good French qualities of clear diction and forwardness of tone, but also the less-good ones of extreme nasality and dryness of tone. He has a tendency to push on top notes and becomes overemphatic in expression. In his reprimand of Manon he is suitably pompous, and quite characterful at the Cours la Reine.

Louis Guénot, the Count des Grieux, specialized in the "noble father" roles. His smooth basso is somewhat weightier than Dupré in 1923, and he displays more power in his singing.

1951 DECCA / LONDON (M)

Janine Micheau (A), Claudine Collart (B), Jacqueline Cauchard (C), Agnès Disney (D), Libero de Luca (E), Jean-Christophe Benoit (F), Roger Bourdin (G), Guy Godin (H), Julien Giovannetti (I), Chorus and Orchestra of the Opéra-Comique—Albert Wolff

In January 1952, Manon received its two-thousandth performance at the Opéra-Comique. Six months earlier, in June 1951, after a gap of twenty-two years, the Opéra-Comique company had again entered the recording studio, this time under the aegis of Decca, with many of the same cast members.

The recording that resulted is an oddity in at

least two significant ways. The producer, Max de Rieux, attempted to present the opera through the eyes of the novel's author, the Abbé Prévost, by means of a spoken narration. The narrator, Roland Bourdin, sets each scene and describes the action of the plot, all, of course, in French. Almost all of the dialogue spoken over orchestral accompaniment is eliminated in favor of the running commentary. In addition to the standard chorus cuts, second verses of Lescaut's and Comte des Grieux's arias are eliminated, as well as most of the byplay among the minor characters. The ballet is reduced to only the first entrée and introduction to the second.

The other curiosity is that this is the only *Manon* recording to omit the gavotte at the Cours la Reine entirely, in favor of the more highly decorative fabliau.

Narration aside, the performance has much to recommend it, and is never less than perfectly competent. Under the experienced, idiomatic direction of Albert Wolff, it has spirit and verve. Ensembles are propulsive but cleanly articulated. The orchestral textures are bright, stringy, and heavily weighted toward the treble instruments. The chorus is sizable, youthful-sounding, and precise—a vast improvement over the 1923 and 1928–29 groups.

Janine Micheau, the Manon, was the most important French lyric coloratura of her generation. Her voice is solid and bright, with some tartness in the upper register. Despite her habit of scooping into notes in the upper-middle part of her voice, she excels at expressive word coloring and mood shifts. She captures the wistful feeling of the "petite table" farewell to perfection, while in the Cours la Reine Scene she sings the fabliau exceedingly well, with splendid coloratura and delightful expression. In the final act she is at her best, singing with even more tonal richness.

The Swiss tenor Libero de Luca is the des Grieux of this performance. His instrument is of medium weight, with good *legato* and an attractive sound. But he employs little dynamic or expressive variety, colors his voice very little, and therefore his performance tends toward monotony. His St. Sulpice aria, "Ah! fuyez, douce image," is not at all strong on French

style: the vowels are too Italianate and open, the vibrato is too wide, and the pitch is not consistently accurate. The result hardly conjures up the vision of Manon's "douce image," though the character certainly sounds desperate enough.

Roger Bourdin, an Opéra-Comique veteran of more than thirty years, offers another strong performance as Lescaut. He is lively and characterful, and possesses a solid baritone of good range. Julien Giovannetti's Comte des Grieux possesses a firm, if somewhat oily, bass. He too is vivid in his St. Sulpice aria, "Épouse quelque brave fille," where he presents a stern, extremely serious-sounding father. The performers of the minor roles all do honor to the Opéra-Comique tradition of ensemble excellence.

1955 EMI / ANGEL (M) CD

Victoria de los Angeles (A), Liliane Berton (B), Raymonde Notti (C), Marthe Serres (D), Henri Legay (E), René Hérent (F), Michel Dens (G), Jean Vieuille (H), Jean Borthayre (I), Chorus and Orchestra of the Opéra-Comique—Pierre Monteux

As with the two recordings from the 1920s, only a few years separate this recording from its predecessor. Here, the house forces of the Opéra-Comique under the direction of Pierre Monteux turn in a performance that is truly inspired.

The orchestra sounds full and fresh, the music shaped with passion yet precision. The choral work, like that of the orchestra, is sparkling. The sound of the compact disc reissue is gorgeous, bringing forth all the elegance of the performance. As with all great maestros, Monteux's approach has a rightness about it which seems perfectly natural.

In Victoria de los Angeles, Monteux has a Manon of distinction. In the first act, she begins with a wonderfully pure and girlish tone, and an endearing coquettish inflection in her entrance aria, "Je suis encore tout étourdie." Through her flawless pronunciation of French and the enchanting giggle in her voice, she exhibits oodles of personality. In "Voyons, Manon, plus de chimères" she colors the words beautifully and creates a charming effect. This is a portrayal of richness and total commitment, with all the vocal expressiveness and interpretive insight of a superb singing actress.

Henri Legay is a light-voiced des Grieux, but he is never less than an ardent one. He possesses excellent command of dynamics, a caressing *legato*, and an excellent line. What Legay's performance lacks in vocal weight it more than makes up for in freshness, imagination, and poise.

Michel Dens's Lescaut is a solid performance, somewhat vocally overblown. He uses his juicy tone to good effect, blustering appropriately when called for, but he is also attentive to dynamics and rhythmic subtleties under Monteux's guidance.

Jean Borthayre's Count des Grieux is authoritative, in the French light-bass tradition. His voice is resonant and steady, and he sings his aria "Épouse quelque brave fille" with dignity and warmth. As with Jean-Christophe Benoit in 1951, René Hérent's Guillot has a light touch and solid vocal resources. The standard cuts are observed in what is otherwise a gem of a performance.

1970 EMI / ANGEL (S) ⓒ

Beverly Sills (A), Michèle Raynaud (B), Helia T'Hezan (C), Patricia Kern (D), Nicolai Gedda (E), Nico Castel (F), Gérard Souzay (G), Michel Trempont (H), Gabriel Bacquier (I), Ambrosian Opera Chorus, New Philharmonic Orchestra—Julius Rudel

This is the first recording of the work complete without theater cuts. In addition, it is the first recording which does not involve the forces of the Opéra-Comique, and is thereby somewhat "international" in style and approach.

Julius Rudel conducts with full-blooded passion and sweep; his orchestra and chorus are quite large-scaled. The recording's sonics are grand and reverberant, and the overall feeling is propulsive and emphatic, but ultimately short on refinement and traditional French grace and delicacy. The effect is exciting but generalized, without Monteux's specificity and musical shapeliness. The sound of the compact disc reissue is an improvement over the congested-sounding LP version.

The Manon of Beverly Sills is a complete portrayal in both voice and persona. Many consider Manon to have been the diva's very best role, as the French language tended to bring out the best qualities in her voice. Reportedly, Sills was not in her best voice during the recording sessions, but aside from an occasional wiry or unsteady sustained note, it is hard to find evidence of any vocal deficiencies whatsoever. With her shimmering, girlish timbre and her scintillating *fioriture*, Sills establishes Manon's innocence immediately. Later in the first act, she becomes more yearning, as if poised on the precipice of a life of pleasure, but not quite able to take the plunge. Her second-act farewell is supremely expressive in every phrase, and the voice quivers with emotion on the final "adieux." Such individual insights abound in Sills's performance. Although many of the European critics never really warmed to Sills's accomplishments, this recording reminds us of what she was capable of achieving at her best.

Nicolai Gedda's des Grieux is passionate from the outset. His command of high notes, and the ease with which he can perform *diminuendos* on them, complements his forceful portrayal. After the delicacy and grace of Legay in 1955, Gedda may seem too forceful and extrovert, but he makes a compelling case for this concept of the role.

The distinguished recitalist Gérard Souzay as Lescaut is luxuriant casting, although not totally successful. His pronunciation of the language is elegant, but the voice itself sounds grayish and dry. At the Cours la Reine, the tone is more flexible, with good dynamic control and a decent trill, but overall Souzay comes across as an aged roué rather than a young *bon vivant*.

Gabriel Bacquier is another bit of distinguished casting as Comte des Grieux, and he is more successful with his role than Souzay. He brings weight and conviction to the concerned father, and inflects the music in a determined fashion. Among the smaller roles, Nico Castel is a put-upon, comical Guillot, somewhat dry but exceedingly detailed, with each and every phrase given meaning. As in the 1928–29 EMI recording, the fabliau, "Oui, dans les bois," is included as a supplement after the opera proper.

Sills's performance of this coloratura showpiece is sparkling, with lots of gaiety and personality.

1982 EMI / ANGEL (S,D) CD

Ileana Cotrubas (A), Ghyslaine Raphanael (B), Colette Alliot-Lugaz (C), Martine Mahé (D), Alfredo Kraus (E), Charles Burles (F), Gino Quilico (G), Jean-Marie Frémeau (H), José van Dam (I), Chorus and Orchestra of the Capitole de Toulouse—Michel Plasson

This performance is stylish and atmospheric, like others in EMI's series of French operas led by Michel Plasson with the forces of the Capitole of Toulouse. Tempos are fast and bouncy, and the pacing is theatrical. The chorus, a medium-sized group, sings with a light touch and good ensemble.

Ileana Cotrubas is an endearing Manon. Her lyrical, naturally girlish timbre is perfect for the character and her French pronunciation is good. In the course of the first act, she has already grown from a naive waif, and her sense of wonderment at her thoughts of Paris is engaging. Her "petite table" farewell is very feminine and yearning. Although she may lack the ultimate pathos of de los Angeles or the incandescence of Sills, Cotrubas's portrayal is a success due to her tenderness and natural charm.

Alfredo Kraus's des Grieux is excellent in French stylistics, if not quite so in French pronunciation. His basic sound is no longer youthful, and his naturally nasal and dry voice is not at its freshest here. He also displays a tendency to scoop. Nevertheless, Kraus can be a picture of elegance in his beautiful and insightful phrasing. He is especially tender in the final scene with Manon, and throughout he brings many wonderful touches to his characterization.

The Lescaut of Gino Quilico is a real treat, the best since Bourdin in 1951. His vocal placement is forward and very French, with vibrant tone and beautiful *legato*, if a little short at the bottom end of the range. His reprimand "Ne bronchez pas" is forceful, to the point, and with excellent dynamic subtleties. At the Cours la

Reine, his singing of "A quoi bon l'économie" is flavorful and performed with verve. He is certainly the only Lescaut on disc to bring a youthful sexiness and charisma to the role, and thereby presents a much more interesting character than most.

José van Dam is an inspired choice for Count des Grieux. His deluxe voice, beautiful line, and knowing expression also bring this character to life more vividly than most. At St. Sulpice he is kind, loving, concerned, yet imposing, and he sings with more tonal splendor and nobility than usually heard in this role. His expressive nuances and his rich timbre combine to make this a memorable assumption.

The smaller roles in this recording are mostly cast with major voices. The Guillot of Charles Burles is sweet-voiced and elegant, while Jean-Marie Frémeau brings an important-sounding baritone to de Brétigny.

The selection of a single *Manon* is a rather difficult choice to make, due to the generally fine quality of many of the opera's recordings, as well as the excellence of many individual performances. The primitive sound of the 1923 Pathé will eliminate it from consideration for most, although the 1928–29 EMI in better sound may be of interest for those with a special devotion to older recordings and authentic performance style. The narration and disfiguring cuts of the 1951 Decca are not compensated by the quality of the performance. While the 1982 EMI presents a well-conducted performance with deluxe casting in many of the major and minor roles, the choice for most listeners will come down to de los Angeles versus Sills. Both are highly recommendable, with the de los Angeles given the palm due to the stylish and characterful conducting of Pierre Monteux and the elegance of the supporting cast. Neither set will disappoint the devotee looking for a basic *Manon*.

STEWART PEARCE

Unavailable for review:
1966 MONDIOPHONIE

JULES MASSENET

WERTHER (1892)

A: Sophie (s); B: Charlotte (ms); C: Werther (t); D: Albert (bar)

*M*assenet's talent and aim was to please. He judged to perfection the tastes of the French public, but at the time of his death in 1912 his star was on the wane and for over fifty years could be observed mainly in French skies. *Manon* clung on in the repertory, but by the 1970s, productions of *Werther* had again become frequent and there were successful revivals of other operas: *Cendrillon, Le Cid, Hérodiade, Thaïs, Don Quichotte,* even the extravagant *Esclarmonde.* The critics of thirty years before began to eat their words and the public continued to be pleased.

If *Manon* remains Massenet's most immediately attractive score, *Werther,* with its musical nuance and illumination of inner feelings, its ability to pin down half-truths, fears, deceits, its greater intensity and even sharper focus, is possibly his best. As with *Manon,* it is not only in the great moments of heightened expression that Massenet excels (though there are plenty of those), but in the conversational scenes, where subtleties are sought out, human beings shown fencing with each other, and hidden motives revealed.

All this is done with scrupulous respect for the French language, which Massenet sets with the precision of Rameau, Bizet, or indeed Debussy, and one of the curious comments on international opera as practiced today is that the French singer, even the French specialist, has become almost extinct, to the great impoverishment of the operatic scene. Of these seven complete recordings, the first three are cast with specialists, but thereafter, on records as in the opera house, the language becomes less integral a part of the performance, a state of affairs due less to the inadequacy of singers than to impresarios who don't care and to recording companies who you might charitably suppose don't know any better.

1931 EMI / ANGEL (M) CD

Germaine Féraldy (A), Ninon Vallin (B), Georges Thill (C), Marcel Roque (D), Opéra-Comique Orchestra, Paris—Elie Cohen

This ancient set remains a candidate for the best recording of the music and stands as a rampart against opinion which denigrates French standards, then high partly because the opportunities on which standards thrive were available to French singers. Orchestral sounds, particularly strings, are less sumptuous than in modern recordings, but not less communicative, and the recording is, for the period, excellent, the transfer well engineered. Cohen never exaggerates the music's expressive qualities with stressed *rall.* or *rit.,* and the music is allowed to speak for itself. There is a tiny cut (Johann and Schmidt) in Act II, and two of some 20 bars each in the orchestral passage linking Acts III and IV.

If you want to be reminded how the French language can be sung expressively while the performers maintain a grand singing line, listen to Thill and Vallin—his enunciation of the line "O spectacle idéal d'amour et d'innocence" is in itself a shot fired across the bows of those who maltreat it. Thill added two Wagnerian roles to his repertory during the season he recorded *Werther*, but *piano* phrases and notes at the top of the range are managed without difficulty, and his breath control rivals that of a Martinelli or Domingo. The sound is virile, and a forthright "J'aurais sur ma poitrine"—a composer's afterthought which provided one of the highlights of the French tenor's repertory— suggests no languishing young man, rather someone "perplex'd in the extreme." A tiny bubble in the second climactic A-sharp in "Pourquoi me réveiller" should not have passed the engineer's scrutiny, but Thill's gently modulated singing of the death scene packs more punch than more overt histrionics ever could.

Vallin's performance is cast in the same classical mold, with immaculate articulation of music and text, and an arm's-length attitude to the drama which I would describe as dispassionately involved—no bad thing where Charlotte is concerned. Some may prefer a mezzo heroine, but Vallin's light, unemphatic singing compensates in conversational sections for the warmer mezzo sound, and the voice is intrinsically attractive, the singing a model of clarity. Féraldy sings the innocent adolescent Sophie as easily as the more sophisticated Manon in another (less successful) complete recording, and the supporting singers are fine.

p. 1953 URANIA (M)

Agnes Léger (A), Suzanne Juyol (B), Charles Richard (C), Roger Bourdin (D), Opéra-Comique Orchestra, Paris—Georges Sebastian

A prosaic performance based on the Opéra-Comique production has a fine dramatic mezzo, Suzanne Juyol, too straightforward in a role full of dissembling, and Charles Richard, in spite of good vocal material a matter-of-fact Werther. Bourdin sings a strongly felt Albert, but there is little vocal freshness thirty years after his Paris debut, and only Agnes Léger as Sophie and the admirable Michael Roux, understated in the small role of the Magistrate, make the case for postwar French standards.

1964 ADÈS (M)

Mady Mesplé (A), Rita Gorr (B), Albert Lance (C), Gabriel Bacquier (D), Chorus and Orchestra of the ORTF, Paris—Jesus Etcheverry

Gorr and Lance, who often sang the opera together, demonstrate similar qualities: beautiful voices in prime condition, used with more sense of vocal than musical style, but with a strong feel for theatrical values. Lance sings the music with glorious tone and limitless breadth of phrase, but one could wish for more nuance of delivery. Nonetheless, the performance represents something of a peak in recordings of French opera by French singers.

1968–69 EMI / ANGEL (S) CD

Mady Mesplé (A), Victoria de los Angeles (B), Nicolai Gedda (C), Roger Soyer (D), Orchestre de Paris—Georges Prêtre

An excellent set dominated by the supersensitive Charlotte of Victoria de los Angeles, a marriage of role and artist undoubtedly made in heaven. Never was charm less cloying, never beauty of tone better adapted to music, never the shift from conversational mood (as in her sudden awareness in the middle of the "Clair de lune" that she can never be Werther's) to heightened perception (as in the white vocal sound in the reading of the letters) more subtly achieved. Gedda's French is more idiomatic than hers, although I find her slight accent wholly beguiling, but his dynamic variations are extreme, which after a bit sound mannered and detract from an otherwise stylish performance. Good support from Mesplé and Soyer, though some may find the latter a little grand of manner for the essentially domestic Albert. Prêtre is for my taste liable to overreact to the music's moods, but few on records apart from Cohen and Davis wholly avoid this trap.

1979 EMI / ANGEL (S) CD

Christine Barbaux (A), Tatiana Troyanos (B), Alfredo Kraus (C), Matteo Manuguerra (D),

London Philharmonic Orchestra—Michel Plasson

This very impressive performance goes some of the way toward vindicating international standards, with both major principals non-French speaking—Kraus may well be fluent, but with him "ce" tends to come out "ces" and "sincère" nearer to "sancerre," a drawback in French opera. Troyanos has a naturally quick vibrato, but with her dark, plangent voice makes a distinguished Charlotte, short only in variety of vocal coloring. A very attractive quality of voice and aristocratic style have made Alfredo Kraus the most renowned Werther of the postwar period, but he was over fifty when he recorded the role and one might wonder how suited he still was to a hero whose behavior is excusable only in the very young. Nevertheless, he suggests the vulnerability beneath the surface and rises magnificently to the vocal challenge of Act II, which, with its animadversions to the subject of suicide, is the reason why so many French Werthers have also sung Lohengrin.

Barbaux is an ingénue of true vocal sweetness, Manuguerra (a Tunisian with perfect French) subdues a voice used to thundering as Barnaba to float an expressive line. Jules Bastin is unpretentiously idiomatic, and Philip Langridge and Jean-Philippe Lafont make the repetitions of "Vivat Bacchus" go with appropriate swing. Plasson is inclined to milk such things as the beautiful "Clair de lune" interlude but generally conducts with balance and a sense of the music's beauty.

1979 DEUTSCHE GRAMMOPHON (S) ⓒ

Arleen Augér (A), Elena Obraztsova (B), Plácido Domingo (C), Franz Grundheber (D), West German Radio Orchestra—Riccardo Chailly

Domingo came to record Werther rather late in the day; the music often sounds a little high for him, and however skillfully he may modulate his Otello voice (he had been singing that role for some years), the conversational mood which underlies so much of the score often

eludes him. There are many moments of tenderness and subtlety which show what he feels about the role, but his performance remains inescapably (though sometimes enjoyably) Italianate. Few such enjoyments from the Delilah-like Charlotte of Obraztsova, baleful of voice, unvarying in color, and in context bloated. Phrase after phrase goes by with no response from her except perhaps an extra application of her powerful vibrato, and only the low-lying "Air des larmes" brings out the qualities which, presumably, caused her acceptance in the international hierarchy. Her French diction is poor, but then, in spite of Domingo's flawed fluency in the language, so is that of most of the cast. The exception to this rule is Arleen Augér, who sings Sophie with charm and sensitivity. Not a set for lovers of French opera, though essential for anyone who (understandably) wants Domingo in all his roles.

1980 PHILIPS (S) ⓒ

Isobel Buchanan (A), Frederica von Stade (B), José Carreras (C), Thomas Allen (D), Orchestra of the Royal Opera, Covent Garden—Colin Davis

Colin Davis leads an excellent cast, of whom all but Thomas Allen took part in a Covent Garden revival in the year of the recording. Davis's is a strongly felt performance, responsive to every nuance, with lovely sounds from the orchestra and fine shaping of the letter scene of Act III. I don't know who conducts the music so well on disc, unless it be Elie Cohen. Another crucial influence on the performance is Janine Reiss, named as "musical and language counsellor," to whose efforts must be partly due the consistently good French diction (good, though perhaps, apart from von Stade, not as good as if they had actually *been* French).

The delicacy of von Stade's singing of Charlotte's music is a source of acute pleasure, and not even de los Angeles shows more imagination in coloring the voice, whether as she appears almost drugged with new-found love at the start of "Clair de lune," or agonized at "Nous somme fous! Rentrons" a moment later. No one better demonstrates longing as well as the infinite sadness of the letter scene, and she must be nearly unique in that the pathos she brings to the music almost runs away with the death scene. There is poise in the singing, a tear in the voice; she has the vulnerability and the responsiveness of de los Angeles, with a voice that is fresher and in better shape. Beside her, Carreras's characterization must seem a little generalized—you feel his contemplation of the natural world induces bonhomie rather than romantic rapture. Verbal magic is absent, but if his singing is seldom imaginative, it is invariably youthful; and that is a good quality in *Werther*. Isobel Buchanan is ideally light and fresh as Sophie, and Thomas Allen's beautiful singing of the ariette and sinuous phrasing of all his

music makes him a very plausible suitor for Charlotte.

———————

I doubt if Carreras's singing is sufficiently idiomatic for the word "ideal" to be pinned to the Philips set, which might otherwise qualify for it. There is much to be said for the combination of de los Angeles and Gedda, to say nothing of Kraus, Troyanos, and Plasson; and only a little less for Lance and Gorr. Personal preference will go to individual singers, but anyone who wants to hear classical French singing will go to the oldest performance with Thill and Vallin under the almost forgotten Elie Cohen.

LORD HAREWOOD

JULES MASSENET

THAÏS (1894)

A: Thaïs (s); B: Nicias (t); C: Athanaël (bar)

When Vincent d'Indy wrote of the discreet and semi-religious eroticism of Massenet's music, it was *Thaïs* he had particularly in mind, but the *bon mot* obscures the power of the opera's central relationship between Thaïs and Athanaël, the courtesan-turned-nun and the monk drawn toward the worldly life he thought he despised. Anatole France's book takes a more ambivalent view of Paphnuce / Athanaël, whom he mocks more than he pities, but in the opera Athanaël provides the pivotal figure, a fine creation, torn between his over-confident urge to denounce the sinner and the irresistible attraction of the beauty his young manhood cannot ignore. Thaïs is fully drawn in opera and novel, graceful, teasing, tempted by fear of losing her beauty into looking for another center to her existence. The conflict stimulates two splendid central roles and the music which surrounds them is graceful for Nicias and his friends, direct and austere for the Cenobites, and evocative for the desert. (The Oasis scene, which became the score's central episode, was added during the opera's first run; orchestrally, it is full of the shimmering heat and destructive sun which constitutes Thaïs's first penance.)

There are five so-called complete recordings, of which only two truly satisfy the description. Four include the ballet music, which is service-able rather than distinguished, but the episode called La Charmeuse (far from its worst feature) is dropped from the three sets made in France.

Another cut is the second scene of Act III, when Athanaël returns from the desert to his Cenobi-tic community. There he is tormented by visions of Thaïs's beauty—a scene crucial to the drama, of which Athanaël is the center, and it has the additional advantage of providing a breathing space between the Oasis scene and Thaïs's death.

1952 URANIA (M)

Géori Boué (A), Jean Giraudeau (B), Roger Bourdin (C), Chorus and Orchestra of the Paris Opéra—Georges Sebastian

The Hungarian-born, French-based Sebas-tian gives due weight to a score that was at the center of French repertory at the time he recorded it, and the leading French exponent of the title role, qualified physically as well as vocally, leads the cast. Géori Boué has the kind of typically French voice many people find very unpleasant. The sound is clear, the music approached cleanly, and a few gentle phrases suggest the artist I remember from stage perfor-mance. But she sounds uninvolved, the voice is hard and brittle, and a beautiful start to "L'amour est une vertu rare," one of Massenet's lyrical inspirations, cannot hide the fact that too much of the singing is loud. Roger Bourdin makes an impassioned Athanaël, but his voice is worn and light for the role. There are internal cuts in the ballet and in the finale to Act II, and the role of the servant before Athanaël's famous denunciation of Alexandria is eliminated.

1959 LE CHANT DU MONDE (M,P) CD

Andrée Esposito (A), Jean Mollien (B), Robert Massard (C), Chorus and Orchestra of Radio-Lyrique, Paris—Albert Wolff

Wolff and the orchestra earn nothing but praise for their performance, though the same cannot always be said for the clarity of the sound, in spite of a transfer of decent quality for its date (the tape comes from French Radio archives). But more serious drawbacks than a dated recording come from snips in the score (made presumably to shorten it for radio), in addition, of course, to the loss of ballet, La Charmeuse, and Act III, Scene 2; also from a sudden intrusion of narrative over the orchestra during the first scene when a vision of Thaïs appears to Athanaël. All this is the more regrettable since Andrée Esposito, with fresh, beautiful, youthful sound, clear words, and easy technique, comes nearer than anyone else in a complete recording to doing justice to Thaïs. Perhaps it was early in her career for her to record an exacting role she first sang only months before, but at her best she is very good and sings the Oasis Scene and the death with exquisite poise and control. Massard sings smoothly but has little of Bourdin's commitment, and Thaïs with an uninvolved Athanaël is not easy to bring off.

1961 VEGA (S)

Renée Doria (A), Michel Sénéchal (B), Robert Massard (C), Chorus and Orchestra—Jesus Etcheverry

Etcheverry provides a workmanlike account of the score, without the extra cuts of the earlier recordings and with a cast just as distinctly French. Text and music are meaningfully enunciated, but there is little vocal beauty. Style is in better supply: Doria with her quick vibrato on high notes has the measure of the role and is in fresher voice than Boué; Sénéchal, always stylish, is properly elegant as Nicias; Massard still sings well but with no more involvement than before.

1974 RCA / BMG (S)

Anna Moffo (A), José Carreras (B), Gabriel Bacquier (C), Ambrosian Opera Chorus, New Philharmonia Orchestra—Julius Rudel

If nothing else, the idiomatic urging of Julius Rudel would recommend this set. Even the uncut ballet music goes with more verve than elsewhere, and only a rather sentimental Meditation detracts from his account of the score. There is, in addition, the magnificent Athanaël of Bacquier—no young Cenobite, it is true, but with all the intensity of Bourdin in the 1952 set and, in spite of some worn vocal patches, infinitely greater vocal means with which to express his conviction. His debut at the Paris Opéra took place after Thaïs left the repertory, but here his singing is full of contrasts of color and phrases are shaped with ease as well as with fire. Just to hear him sing "O Seigneur, je remets mon âme entre tes mains" is to know his quality, and the whole performance takes fire from him. Well, perhaps not quite the whole, because the Thaïs of Anna Moffo is an almost total liability. It is hard to believe that, in such dire vocal shape, she would not have been better advised to cancel the sessions. As it is, the music is crooned, top notes are either screeched or barely indicated, and sustained phrases end with that unsupported quaver and drop from the written pitch, which is an accepted mannerism in many jazz singers but impossible in this context. That the title role is hardly sung at all makes for too big a reservation over this set, which has otherwise much going for it: a superb Athanaël, good support in smaller roles (the golden voice of Carreras flatters the ear and reminds one that Nicias was the debut role of the great Georges Thill), excellent conducting; but Thaïs without a Thaïs was hardly what Massenet had in mind.

1976 EMI / ANGEL (S)

Beverly Sills (A), Nicolai Gedda (B), Sherrill Milnes (C), John Alldis Choir, New Philharmonia Orchestra—Lorin Maazel

Apart from an uncut score, including La Charmeuse in the ballet (charmingly sung by

Norma Burrowes), there is little reason to re-commend this set. Maazel shows no positive sympathy for the score; he also misguidedly plays the Meditation himself. I miss the way native French casts have with text—this must always weigh heavily in a search for the idio-matic performance of French opera—and in addition Sills was recording this role too late in her career for ideal ease of projection, floating of high notes, virtuosity in a virtuoso role. By 1976 the voice as recorded had a strong beat and it is rare that her artistic instincts overcome her weakening physical means. Milnes provides torrents of sound but less commitment than his role requires, and the normally reliable Gedda totally misses Nicias, the most laid-back playboy in all opera.

None of these five sets is even close to ideal. Either you take the cut and not particularly distinguished version with Renée Doria and Massard, or the even more butchered but in other respects slightly preferable performance with Esposito and Massard, or the uncut RCA with Rudel and Bacquier and accept that you have to imagine how the role of Thaïs should go. It is a palpable gap in the recorded repertory.

LORD HAREWOOD

JULES MASSENET

CENDRILLON (1899)

A: Cendrillon (s); B: Fairy (s); C: Noémie (s); D: Dorothée (ms); E: Mme.
de la Haltière (c); F: Prince (s or t); G: King (bar); H: Pandolfe (bs)

*M*any long-neglected Massenet operas have been revived in recent times, but none seems more likely to recapture a place in the repertory than *Cendrillon*, a great success when first lavishly produced at the Paris Opéra-Comique in 1900. Unlike Rossini's down-to-earth, *opera buffa* treatment of the familiar legend, Massenet's approach is an irresistible combination of human sentiment and fairy-tale fantasy. Why it disappeared in the first place is hard to understand. Perhaps its gossamer magic and confectionery charm struck a generation brought up on the weightier messages of Wagner and Verdi as trivial and unworthy of attention. Or perhaps the singers who understood the composer's intentions, appreciated his immaculate craftsmanship, and could do justice to his graceful vocal writing have vanished from the stage. Luckily, we now have artists who find Massenet congenial, as well as audiences eager to savor the delicate traceries and lyrical beauties of his operas. And so, for the moment at least, Cinderella has become a princess once again.

1978 CBS / SONY (S) CD

Frederica von Stade (A), Ruth Welting (B), Teresa Cahill (C), Elizabeth Bainbridge (D), Jane Berbié (E), Nicolai Gedda (F), Claude Méloni (G), Jules Bastin (H), Ambrosian Opera Chorus, Philharmonia Orchestra—Julius Rudel

It is just possible that without von Stade *Cendrillon* would never have been revived at all. Others have performed the title role with success, but she was the first to bring the opera back to international attention, no doubt because some wise impresario had the wit to realize that the perfect singer and the perfect part were just waiting to discover each other. Von Stade's heart-tugging, tear-in-the-voice appeal is captured here in its first youthful freshness and vulnerability—all the infectious vocal charm one remembers from her live performances, and exactly what the phonograph was invented to preserve.

The other star of this recording is Rudel—Vienna-born but an unexpected master of French style, and a sympathetic, graciously knowledgeable, expert Massenet conductor. All the vocal and instrumental elements in this delicious treat fit smoothly into place, with one unfortunate exception. Cinderella's adolescent Prince Charming was specifically designed to be sung by a soprano or high mezzo, and a male voice in the role is tantamount to the ghastly prospect of a tenor Cherubino or Octavian. For all his customary elegance and musical refinement, Gedda can scarcely help but sound miscast.

PETER G. DAVIS

GIAN CARLO MENOTTI

THE MEDIUM (1946)

A: Monica (s); B: Mrs. Gobineau (s); C: Mrs. Nolan (ms); D: Mme.
Flora (Baba) (c); E: Mr. Gobineau (bar); F: Toby (mute)

The Medium is the work that catapulted Gian Carlo Menotti to fame and firmly established his reputation in America as an opera composer. The idea first occurred to him while he was attending a séance with friends in 1936. During the course of the séance, Menotti's initial skepticism was transformed into something more troubling to him as it became clear that his hosts—in their pathetic desire to believe in the powers of the supernatural—actually saw and heard their deceased daughter Doodly (a name retained in the opera for Mrs. Nolan's child). The power of their faith and conviction led Menotti to examine his own cynicism and to wonder at the multiple textures of reality.

In 1945, Menotti received a commission for *The Medium* from Columbia University, where it received its first performance on May 8, 1946, with the composer directing. The conductor was Otto Luening, Mme. Flora was sung by Claramae Turner, and Monica was Evelyn Keller. Shortly thereafter, Menotti interested Lincoln Kirstein in the work. Kirstein was organizing an evening of short operas for Ballet Society and *The Medium* was presented on February 18, 1947, with Menotti's *The Telephone* as a curtain raiser. The performances were conducted by Leon Barzin and Emanuel Balaban. In response to critical praise, the production moved to Broadway, where it began its run on May 1, 1947. Although Menotti had hoped to retain the original cast, Claramae Turner decided not to risk the transfer to Broad-

way, and Marie Powers was hired for the title role. Despite another enthusiastic reaction from the press, theater-going audiences did not flock to the Barrymore Theater until Arturo Toscanini attended the production three times within a few days. An eight-month Broadway run resulted from the ensuing publicity.

1947 CBS / SONY (M)

Evelyn Keller (A), Beverly Dame (B), Catherine Mastice (C), Marie Powers (D), Frank Rogier (E), Unidentified orchestra—Emanuel Balaban

The Broadway run of *The Medium* resulted in what is essentially an "original cast" album. The success of the production brought stardom to the eccentric Marie Powers, who continued to appear in the title role in countless revivals of the work. Her extraordinary performance of Mme. Flora forms the centerpiece of this recording. She exhibits a formidable contralto voice, secure across a range of two octaves, with a full top and a strong chest register. Though the role is largely declamatory, she employs a large number of expressive vocal devices, including glottal attacks, luxuriant *portamento*, and vocal coloration. She is totally immersed in the role of the desperate medium driven to madness by her own fear, and the recording captures her gripping, primal performance.

Evelyn Keller displays a fresh soprano in the role of Monica, Mme. Flora's daughter. She combines sweetness of tone with good diction to produce a touching portrait of the naive but loving girl. She is most effective in the long, arching phrases of the "Black Swan" lullaby "The sun has fallen" and in the folklike "Monica, Monica, dance the waltz."

The remaining cast members—Beverly Dame, Frank Rogier, and Catherine Mastice—are all effective as Mme. Flora's believing clients, with fine voices and good sense of the drama. The conducting of Emanuel Balaban is dramatic and precise, with clear contrapuntal woodwinds and pungent string tone.

1950 MERCURY / PHILIPS (M)

Anna Maria Alberghetti (A), Beverly Dame (B), Belva Kibler (C), Marie Powers (D), Donald Morgan (E), Symphony Orchestra of Rome Italian Radio—Thomas Schippers

In 1950 *The Medium* was adapted for film. It was shot in Rome and starred Marie Powers and a young newcomer, Anna Maria Alberghetti. Although a great deal of the film action was improvised, Menotti felt hampered by having the inflexible framework of a prerecorded soundtrack, which was released separately as an album in 1951. Menotti also underwent a number of tribulations involving Marie Powers, who by this point had become quite a prima donna, claiming the success of *The Medium* for herself. The film received mixed notices; many felt that although it was a visual success, it nevertheless added little to the opera itself. Menotti expanded the score for the film version with a scene at Mrs. Nolan's house after the séance and a nightmarish search sequence for Monica and Toby at a carnival, as well as an offstage chorus in the introduction and some connective material at other points in the score.

The recording of the film soundtrack has much to recommend it, even if it represents an *Urtext*-plus version of the opera. Thomas Schippers's conducting of the Rome Radio Italiana Orchestra is passionate and extremely characterful, although it is accompanied by a rude assortment of distracting film noises, including bangs, crashes, moans, and shouts.

Marie Powers's Mme. Flora, with several years of performance experience, is if anything even more gripping than in the 1947 recording.

Her resonant sound, grand style, and frightening emotional extremes are fully captured as if during an actual stage performance, and she is in marginally better voice than in 1947.

The Monica of Anna Maria Alberghetti is the set's major disappointment. The young Italian actress achieves much in creating a high-spirited, impish portrait, more playful than naive. Her voice, however, turns shrill and pinched in its top range, and her heavily accented English pronunciation is incongruous. At its best, her singing is sprightly but thin-voiced. A coloratura cadenza is interpolated at the end of "Monica, Monica, dance the waltz," producing another odd effect, while her "Black Swan" is aggressive and too emphatic in expression, not at all the calming lullaby.

Beverly Dame's second recording of Mrs. Gobineau is sung in a fresh soprano, with good diction and impassioned expression. Belva Kibler's Mrs. Nolan employs a rich contralto to create a somewhat morose characterization, and her added scene is effective. Donald Morgan brings a dry baritone to Mr. Gobineau, somewhat wobbly and stilted.

1968 CBS / SONY (S) CD

Judith Blegen (A), Emily Derr (B), Claudine Carlson (C), Regina Resnik (D), Julian Patrick (E), Chorus and Orchestra of the Opera Society of Washington—Jorge Mester

This recording—although now almost a quarter of a century old—provides a modern view of the opera: clear, sleek, vigorous, and ironic in approach. The forces of the Opera Society of Washington are led by Menotti specialist Jorge Mester, whose conducting is brisk and bouncy, but not without atmosphere. Although the string playing is a bit raw, the chamber-sized orchestra phrases with point and expressiveness, albeit in a style owing more to German expressionism than Italian *verismo*.

The dramatic mezzo-soprano Regina Resnik brings considerable intensity—and volume—to the role of Mme. Flora. In fine voice with a throbbing vibrato, she brings her renowned skills as a vocal actress to the role, shaping every phrase with meaning and subtlety. She carries her highly developed chest register quite high, intentionally using her register break to convey venom and insinuation. Her half-spoken declamation is blood-curdling, down to her final words to the corpse of Toby, "Was it you?" Hers is a towering performance with tremendous emotional impact.

The young Judith Blegen sings Monica in a full-throated lyric soprano, with much charm and a smile in the voice. Her characterization is both spunky and innocent, and she sings the "Black Swan" lullaby with gorgeous, almost voluptuous, tone. Her "Monica, Monica, dance the waltz" is bright-voiced and delightful, but with poignant underpinnings. Although the soprano was to go on to many more successes in her career as a lyric soubrette, her portrayal here is more ardent and multifaceted than one would expect.

Julian Patrick—a future Alberich—sings a rich-voiced and solid Mr. Gobineau. Emily Derr's Mrs. Gobineau is a strong-voiced, clear soprano, while Claudine Carlson brings a plummy and expressive contralto to Mrs. Nolan. All three are first-rate.

Overall, if a single recording of *The Medium* is to be recommended, it would be the 1968 CBS, for its terrifying performance by Regina Resnik, its endearing one by Judith Blegen, and its superior grouping of supporting cast. The devotee of Menotti's work, however, would not want to be without a souvenir of Marie Powers's portrayal; the earlier recording is to be preferred due to the better supporting cast and the more authentic edition of the score.

STEWART PEARCE

GIAN CARLO MENOTTI

AMAHL AND THE NIGHT VISITORS (1951)

A: Amahl (treble); B: His Mother (ms or s); C: King Kaspar (t); D: King Melchior (bar); E: The Page (bar); F: King Balthazar (bs)

Commissioned in 1951 by NBC producer Samuel Chotzinoff, *Amahl and the Night Visitors* was the first opera written specifically for television. Although conceived for a young audience, its popularity with audiences of all ages and its small cast ensure its place as one of the most successful operas in the United States, with hundreds of performances each year by professional opera companies, conservatories, universities, and community groups. A fixture at Christmas, its harmonic simplicity, melodic clarity, and touching story of hope and healing make *Amahl* Menotti's most beloved work.

The original production was televised live by NBC on December 24, 1951, with Menotti himself directing and Kirk Browning as television director. Other distinguished participants were Eugene Berman, who designed the sets and costumes, and the young Thomas Schippers conducting, with dancers Melissa Hayden and Glen Tetley. Taped performances continued to be shown on NBC until 1964, when Menotti ended his relationship with the network.

Stylistically, Menotti's music is rooted in nineteenth-century Italian operatic tradition. Often accused by critics of being too "Puccini-esque," Menotti considered the most personal aspect of his musical language to be his style of recitative—a melodic *parlar cantando* both evocative in itself and directed toward achieving dramatic effects, without elaborate orchestral accompaniment.

1952 RCA / BMG (M) CD

Chet Allen (A), Rosemary Kuhlmann (B), Andrew McKinley (C), David Aiken (D), Frank Monachino (E), Leon Lishner (F), Unidentified chorus and orchestra—Thomas Schippers

In early January 1952, a few weeks after *Amahl*'s Christmas Eve premiere, the original cast of the NBC television production committed the opera to disc "under the personal direction of Mr. Menotti."

This first recording of *Amahl* captures the creators' performances fresh from the triumph of the first telecast, under the sanction of the perfectionist composer. Interestingly enough, for a work of chamber dimensions written for the confines of the television studio, the recorded performance reflects a deeply felt, grand approach, with warmth, passion, and lyricism from all participants.

Schippers's orchestra is full-bodied, almost plush, and his conducting has the sweep and scope suitable to a much larger work. The chorus likewise sings with a large, rich sound and much dynamic variety. This is a performance that captures the passionate emotions of the work, albeit somewhat at the expense of precision and clarity.

Rosemary Kuhlmann brings a velvety, rich dramatic mezzo-soprano to the role of the mother. Absolutely steady in tonal production at both extremes of its range, her voice is expressively employed, with a variety of color, passionate declamation, and high *pianissimos*. Her ensemble with the three kings ("Have you seen a Child?") is the musical and dramatic climax of an altogether gripping performance.

Chet Allen's Amahl provides an unsophisticated, natural approach to the role. His voice is a fairly gentle one, clear and easily produced, although his diction is a bit stilted (rolled "r's" and the like). His performance is touching, if a bit bland.

The three kings' vocal blend is excellent, particularly in the "open" harmonies of their entrance, "From far away we come." Individually, weaknesses are noticeable, however. McKinley's Kaspar is a Mozartian tenor with a not easily produced top, while Aiken's Melchior is nasal and limited in color and range. But Lishner's Balthazar is a rich basso, with good diction and roundness of tone. He is the only one of the three to provide any real *legato* and tonal beauty.

1963 RCA / BMG (S)

Kurt Yaghjian (A), Martha King (B), John McCollum (C), Richard Cross (D), Julian Patrick (E), Willis Patterson (F), Unidentified chorus and orchestra—Herbert Grossman

Like its predecessor, this recording is another product of an NBC telecast, utilizing the cast of the NBC Opera Company television production of December 1963. Again, the orchestra and choral forces are sizable, with rich, firm sound. Under conductor Herbert Grossman, the strings respond with poignancy, and the musical performance is fervent.

There are many fine aspects to Martha King's performance of the Mother. Her voice is a *spinto* soprano, but with a quick, tight vibrato that is used expressively to heighten the character's desperation. Her use of the text is biting, with excellent pointed diction and vivid dramatic insights. Overall, her performance is not so monumental as that of the role's creator, but rather more human and vulnerable. Kurt Yaghjian's voice is that of a typical boy soprano, with an underdeveloped, flutey sound and not much tonal solidity. His undernourished voice is poignant but lacking in variety and dimen-

sion, limiting his ability to elicit much sympathy from the listener.

The kings all possess beautiful, well-schooled voices. Kaspar's "This is my box" may lack the ultimate wit that this comedic turn can supply, but on the whole these kings provide the most dramatically developed and best sung performances of all *Amahl* recordings.

1986 MCA (D) ℗

James Rainbird (A), Lorna Haywood (B), John Dobson (C), Donald Maxwell (D), Christopher Painter (E), Curtis Watson (F). Chorus and Orchestra of the Royal Opera House, Covent Garden—David Syrus

This most recent recording provides a totally different approach to the work. Recorded in conjunction with a Covent Garden staging at the Sadler's Wells Theater, the musical style is altogether more intimate. David Syrus conducts in a lively chamber-music style, with a snappy Prokofiev-like entrance of the kings and pungent wind playing during the shepherds' dance. The choral work is well tuned and rhythmically precise, like a small group of Christmas carolers or madrigal singers.

Lorna Haywood's soprano is strong, but with a wide—and at times wild—vibrato. She colors words well and makes the most of the text, but the basic unsteadiness of her vocal production at climactic moments is troubling.

James Rainbird, on the other hand, provides the best Amahl on records. He has a plaintive, solid voice, with clear diction and an exceptionally well-supported top. His "Look, Mother, I can dance" is only one of many spirited and delightful moments in a fully characterized, imaginative performance.

Of the kings, John Dobson's Kaspar is a comic *tenorino* with little *legato* but much wit and incisiveness. Donald Maxwell's Mechior is solid with some vocal beauty, but Curtis Watson's Balthazar is indifferent. The kings' vocal blend is raw and out of tune.

Generally, this recording provides a valid alternative approach to the piece, less grand and Italianate and more related to the British early-music performance style in its intimacy.

Each *Amahl* recording has significant points to recommend it. The 1952 RCA offers the creators' performances, led by Rosemary Kuhlmann's towering portrait of the Mother, with vocal resources to match her dramatic insights. The 1963 RCA has Martha King's more human performance, with the best grouping of kings. The 1986 MCA provides James Rainbird's Amahl, the best sung and most vividly characterized. If one recording is to be recommended over the others, it would be the 1952 RCA for its historic importance and fervor.

STEWART PEARCE

GIACOMO MEYERBEER

LES HUGUENOTS (1836)

A: Marguerite (s); B: Valentine (s); C: Urbain (ms); D: Raoul (t);
E: Saint-Bris (bar); F: Nevers (bar); G: Marcel (bs)

*B*erlioz's famous remark that *Les Huguenots* had enough in it for ten operas can be taken two ways, and both would be accurate. The opera, all four-hours-plus of it, is packed full of the kind of theatrical spectacle, historical pageantry, and musical invention that defined French grand opera. Moreover, it contains unprecedented opportunities for florid and dramatic singing for a whole parade of opera stars (*Les Huguenots* called for nothing less than seven of the best singers in the world). But it was also an opera intended to satisfy the nineteenth-century Parisian appetite for sheer extravagance. Such requirements alone have made it hard for *Huguenots* to maintain a hold on the modern repertory. And, of course, Meyerbeer's stylistic eclecticism and his penchant for irrational brilliant effects do seem naive today. Nonetheless, *Huguenots* is not entirely unsuited to a postmodern age, and its atmospheric writing still sounds vivid.

1969 DECCA / LONDON (S) CD

Joan Sutherland (A), Martina Arroyo (B), Huguette Tourangeau (C), Anastasios Vrenios (D), Gabriel Bacquier (E), Dominic Cossa (F), Nicola Ghiuselev (G), Ambrosian Opera Chorus, New Philharmonia Orchestra—Richard Bonynge

This recording of *Les Huguenots* proved something of a mixed success; it was good enough to help create new interest in the opera, but not so startling as to return the work to many stages, or to generate more recordings. The project was clearly a labor of love for Bonynge and a suitable showpiece for Sutherland, whose singing is supple and silvery. But Marguerite is a limited role, and no single singer, however winning, can carry this opera. Tourangeau's oboe-like mezzo, with its plumb low notes and roller-coaster changes of register, makes for a dazzling Urbain, but from there on the singing ranges from acceptable to weak. Most disappointing is Vrenios, who can handle Raoul's lyric lines with a certain finesse, but whose mousy sound is especially bothersome for a part in which Meyerbeer called for a real lyric tenor who could also turn powerfully heroic. But as the voices become lower they grow in ability to command: Bacquier offers a distinctively French Saint-Bris; Cossa supplies a measure of swagger for the playboy Nevers with a heart of gold; Ghiuselev rolls deep for the opera's most amusing and appealing character, the crusty old Protestant, Marcel. Where the performance runs into its greatest difficulties is with Bonynge's conducting. Meyerbeer loves tricky changes of phrases and meters in the Berlioz manner, and every one seems to catch the conductor by surprise. Otherwise he superficially floats along, often running into difficulty keeping ensemble together and bringing too little character to Meyerbeer's extravagant orchestration. The performance is nearly complete, but there are occasional trims of a repetitive bar or two in finales, nothing that is likely to be missed.

MARK SWED

GIACOMO MEYERBEER

LE PROPHÈTE (1849)

A: Berthe (s); B: Fidès (ms); C: Jean (t); D: Oberthal (bar)

The most consistently satisfying of all Meyerbeer's operas, *Le Prophète* is also one of the most successful examples of French grand opera. It is practically as grand as its predecessor, *Les Huguenots*, but without the impractical extravagance; it is not nearly so kitschy as Meyerbeer's last opera, *L'Africaine*. Indeed, *Prophète* manages to convey, with a theatrical cogency rare to grand opera, how historical forces—in this case the Anabaptist uprising in sixteenth-century Holland—influence behavior. Typically, Meyerbeer offers a full pageant of characters and scenic grandeur, but with telling dramatic innovations. The main drama—the assumption of a peasant, Jean de Leyde, as prophet of the Anabaptists in order to avenge the abduction of Berthe, his betrothed, by the Count Oberthal, and Jean's eventual corruption through power—is reflected in two of Meyerbeer's most intriguing dramatic creations. One is the representation of the Anabaptists through a trio of bass-baritones with a collective personality. The other is the character of Fidès, Jean's mother, one of Meyerbeer's richest characters and finest musical portraits, a plum role for a dramatic mezzo-soprano, one that has attracted the likes of Ernestine Schumann-Heink and Louise Homer. *Prophète* has been revived in modern stagings and been given its single recording thanks mainly to Marilyn Horne's advocacy.

p. 1976 CBS / SONY (S) CD

Renata Scotto (A), Marilyn Horne (B), James McCracken (C), Jules Bastin (D), Ambrosian Opera Chorus, Royal Philharmonic Orchestra—Henry Lewis

This only complete recording of *Le Prophète* documents the cast and conductor responsible for the Met's 1977 revival of it, although the recording itself is a British studio effort. Clearly the impetus behind the entire project is Marilyn Horne, and Fidès—the mother torn between her love for her son and her horror at the overzealous, barbarous Anabaptist prophet he becomes—proves one of her great roles. Throughout, Horne handles Meyerbeer's excessive technical demands with a thrilling accuracy and ease, while always finding a noble and expressive core to every phrase she sings. Horne also seems to inspire all who surround her. McCracken and Scotto tend to bluster their way through in the early acts, but in later duets with Horne, they invariably shape their own responses to Fidès with far greater sensitivity, which gives the overall impression of this obscure mother really shaping history. Vocally, McCracken sounds pressed much of the time, but he can strike appropriately heroic attitudes; Scotto handles generic rage capably but has decidedly too little voice in the earlier portion of the opera. Jules Bastin is appropriately suave and nasty as the one-dimensional villainous Count Oberthal, and he also supplies a French grace that is lacking in McCracken and Scotto. Jerome Hines, Jean Dupouy, and Christian du Plessis are just right for the three dark-voiced Anabaptists. Henry Lewis, though, consistently lets down. Meyerbeer's wonderful sense of orchestral detailing, which at its best can almost rival Berlioz and which had an influence on Wagner, rarely is brought out with telling purpose; the ballets, over which Meyerbeer took such care, are flaccid and ordinary-sounding; the glorious massed moments that had such an effect on Verdi are boisterous, lacking an exciting, driving tension. Also a drawback, especially on compact disc, are bright, glaring sonics, lacking in the richness and sense of spaciousness necessary for so grand an operatic spectacle. The performance is essentially complete, with only an occasional shortening of a number or trims of a few transitional bars.

MARK SWED

L'AMORE DEI TRE RE (1913)

A: Fiora (s); B: Avito (t); C: Manfredo (bar); D: Archibaldo (bs)

L'Amore dei Tre Re used to be a repertory piece at the Metropolitan, chalking up a respectable 49 performances between 1914 and 1949. The opera subsequently vanished from the Met stage, however, and performances elsewhere have been scarce in recent times. One reason could be the *bel canto* revival, which made early twentieth-century Italian opera, Puccini excepted, a low priority for opera companies. A more likely explanation is the fact that the powerful singers and stage personalities who feel comfortable performing these highly charged, stressful *verismo* melodramas have all but disappeared. This is a shame, for Montemezzi's urgent response to Sem Benelli's poetic tragedy resulted in one of the era's most concise, gripping, and consistently eloquent scores, combining lush post-Wagnerian harmonies and instrumental colors with typically full-throated Italian lyricism. If the right singers should ever appear again, vocally and temperamentally equipped to bring the operas of Montemezzi's generation back into vogue, *L'Amore dei Tre Re* will surely be a prime candidate for revival.

scratchy and disheveled: the strings invariably come to grief over the syncopated *pizzicato* chords that describe blind Archibaldo's faltering steps, and the dead, boxed-in studio acoustics scarcely help matters. The singing is pretty raw, too, but the performers are clearly committed to the piece and they generate an edge-of-the-ledge excitement unlikely to be encountered nowadays. An impassioned Fiora with a soprano of cutting steel, Petrella obviously has just one thing on her mind: here is definitely a woman prepared to sacrifice all for love. Capecchi also projects a ferocious sensual obsession with tremendous conviction and at full voice; small wonder that he soon wore out his lovely baritone and turned to the bass *buffo* repertory. Ironically, Bruscantini went in the other direction and later experimented with baritone roles. His voice seems much too light and undernourished for Archibaldo, although that hardly prevents him from extracting every ounce of melodrama from the role. Even Berdini, a reliable tenor of no special tonal or interpretive distinction, seems completely caught up in this go-for-broke performance.

1950 CETRA (M)

Clara Petrella (A), Amedeo Berdini (B), Renato Capecchi (C), Sesto Bruscantini (D), Italian Radio Chorus and Orchestra—Arturo Basile

Like most of the old Cetra opera sets, this is a rough-and-ready affair that almost sounds thrown together on the spur of the moment— and probably was. The orchestra is especially

p.1969 DELPHI (S)

Luisa Malagrida (A), Pierre Duval (B), Enzo Sordello (C), Ezio Flagello (D), Coro Accademia Filarmonica and Orchestra Sinfonica di Roma—Richard Karp

This strange recording was apparently intended to showcase Ezio Flagello, the performance's only real point of interest. Although he never quite made it to the top ranks, Flagello had a rich, roomy bass voice of real quality, and he sounds in grand form here. Unfortunately, his Archibaldo is not very specific, more generalized bluster than a three-dimensional portrait of the vengeful, half-demented blind monarch. The other three singers are truly dreary. Malagrida's gummy soprano, Duval's opaque tenor, and Sordello's characterless baritone might possibly be borne on an average evening in a small Italian house, but this is not the sort of performance one wants to hear more than once. With clumsy tape splices at every turn, the recording seems put together by scissors and paste. The strings are in the left speaker, the winds come from the right, and the brass is centered in the middle, all in a dry, constricted ambience; the singers, on the other hand, seem to be performing in a completely different studio, cavernous and reverberant. Under the circumstances, it's hardly surprising that the orchestra under Karp's direction often sounds incoherent.

1976 RCA / BMG (S)

Anna Moffo (A), Plácido Domingo (B), Pablo Elvira (C), Cesare Siepi (D), Ambrosian Opera Chorus and London Symphony Orchestra— Nello Santi

Although far from perfect, this set will at least give listeners a fair idea of the score's musical quality, especially Montemezzi's colorful instrumentation. Santi's conducting has little individual character, but he clearly understands how the opera has been put together, and the orchestra plays well for him. After a long absence from the recording studio, Siepi returned to sing this swan song, a patrician performance of genuine vocal distinction. His Archibaldo may not be an impersonation of overwhelming dramatic power, but he never rants or distorts the line as he ranges easily over two octaves, shaping one noble phrase after another with a velvety bass that seems untouched by time.

The other three principals sing their parts dependably but blandly, making only a tentative connection with the idiom. After those disastrous RCA discs of the early 1970s, Moffo temporarily managed to regain enough technique to sound respectable, although her light lyric soprano still seems several sizes too small for the role. In fine voice, Domingo gives another of his tasteful but essentially faceless recitals of notes, and Elvira uses his appealing baritone to turn in a blunt, straightforward piece of work.

All three recordings leave a great deal to be desired, but while waiting for the appearance of a definitive version—an unlikely prospect any time in the near future—the RCA edition will have to do.

PETER G. DAVIS

CLAUDIO MONTEVERDI

ORFEO (1607)

A: Euridice (s); B: La Musica (s); C: Proserpina (s); D: La Messaggera (a); E: Speranza (s or a); F: Orfeo (t or bar); G: Apollo (t or bar); H: Plutone (bs); I: Caronte (bs)

Universally regarded as the first masterpiece in the history of opera, Monteverdi's *Orfeo* went unheard for nearly three centuries between its initial hearings in 1607 and its first modern revival (Paris, 1904, under Vincent d'Indy). It challenges modern performers on two levels. The first is textual: the surviving sources are two printed editions (occasionally at variance with each other), incorporating frequent but not unequivocal instrumental indications, as well as other ambiguities of notation and interpretation; in particular, realization of the recitative accompaniments is very much at the discretion of the modern performer and / or editor. Though differing in decisions about repeats in dance movements, etc., most recordings are substantially complete; significant deviations are noted below.

Far more central to the effect of a modern performance are the basic (if once essentially unconsidered) assumptions about vocal and instrumental style, and a half-century's worth of recordings vividly documents the development of a historically self-conscious approach to *Orfeo*. Under any conditions, the role of the protagonist is crucial; from his appearance at the start of Act II, he is onstage almost continuously. Not only must he be able to project Monteverdian recitative in a natural, vocally convincing way; as the embodiment of mythology's greatest singer, he must realize the set pieces—notably "Possente spirto," his plea to Charon—with

credible virtuosity. If he fails, so does the opera. By comparison, the other solo roles are "cameos," though some (La Musica in the Prologue, the Messaggera who reports Euridice's death) occupy theatrical cruxes. Substantial choral pieces underline the legend's moral lessons; along with the lighter dancelike numbers of the pastoral opening, they call for a mastery of madrigal style not normally at the command of opera-house choruses. (Not considered here, and definitely to be avoided, is the 1975 Acanta recording under Kurt Eichhorn of Carl Orff's very arbitrary, very abridged, very hyped-up edition.)

1939 EMI / ANGEL (M)

Ginevra Vivante (A,B), Vittoria Palombini (C,E), Elena Nicolai (D), Enrico de Franceschi (F), Giuseppe Manacchini (G), Albino Marone (H,I), Chorus and orchestra—Ferruccio Calusio

The personnel of the first recorded *Orfeo* represents the second string of prewar Italian theatrical practice. Avid collectors will recognize some of these singers from recordings of standard Italian literature (the exception is Ginevra Vivante, who specialized in both early and modern music); they sing in the full-throated style of the day. The Argentinian conductor Ferruccio Calusio, active at La Scala in 1930–31, was briefly on the Met roster (1940–41). By the standards of the *verismo* era, the tessitura of Monteverdi's roles is low, and they are here cast primarily with mezzos and baritones. To modern ears, all these well-upholstered voices with their plangent, rounded tones, plummy vibratos, and fervently emotional styles generate an effect lugubrious in the extreme. (That EMI Italiana's LP reissue was pitched too low didn't exactly ameliorate the problem.)

Yet these people are clearly dealing with the music as best they can in terms of their training, their vocal adjustments and limitations. (Vivante, whose Supervia-like vibrance implies more fluency than her colleagues own, is something of an exception, as her imaginative treatment of Musica's final stanza immediately tells us.) Because Enrico de Franceschi has to aspirate even the most rudimentary embellishment, we are relieved when he elects the undecorated form of "Possente spirto" in Act III. Occasionally, as in his response ("Ahi, sventurato amante") to Caronte's second speech, where expressive climax and high tessitura correspond, he briefly connects with his normal line of work and achieves a convincing utterance—only to prove totally at a loss in the lengthy fifth-act soliloquy (which may explain why the editor decked it out with a remarkably active harp counterpoint). The pervasive rhythmic rigidity is oppressive, but unavoidable given the time and place; it would take a generation or more to unlearn. Improvised cadential ornamentation was not yet thought of.

Another, more conscious impulse is detectable: to make *Orfeo* sound like a Masterpiece by the lights of Rome, *c.* 1940. In this cause, a self-conscious solemnity is imposed on the ingrained habits of late-*verismo* singing. *Parlando* and shouting are avoided (they will enter the *Orfeo* discography with Nikolaus Harnoncourt's Zurich version). Perhaps because most "early music" then in the repertory was sacred, the recitative is generally delivered in the stately manner associated with religious music. Besides receiving a patina of string tone appropriate to Respighi's Baroque transcriptions, some of the measured pieces are taken extraordinarily slowly: for example, Musica's *ritornello* creeps at an elegiac quarter-note = 40. Other tempos are livelier; the Hades sinfonias fall within the range of modern performances, and the choruses are

downright vigorous, if also rough in intonation and ensemble. The collective passages for shepherds at the ends of the first two acts are assigned to small choruses rather than to soloists. The forms of expressivity that manage to assert themselves rarely coincide with the opera's strengths; instead of asking the score to define its ways of working, these performers are making it respond to a preexisting image of significance and sanctity.

Sadly, this remains to date the only substantial encounter in the *Orfeo* discography between Italian voices and the first great Italian opera. These surely aren't the right singers for the job, yet one wants to believe that, in a more historically aware context, the classic native qualities of liquid sound and enunciation and of firmly bound *legato* would be at home in this music and could render it service.

p.1950 DISCOPHILES FRANÇAIS (M)

Elfriede Trötschel (A), Eva Fleischer (B), Gerda Lammers (C,D,E), Max Meili (F), Helmut Krebs (G), Friedrich Härtel (H,I), Berlin Radio Vocal Ensemble and Chamber Orchestra— Helmut Koch

The first postwar *Orfeo* recordings stem from a quite different vocal and stylistic tradition, traceable to sources north of the Alps, notably the Schola Cantorum Basiliensis, established in 1933 for the study and performance of early music. Its founders included the Swiss tenor Max Meili, protagonist in the first postwar *Orfeo* (a Berlin Radio tape from the late forties), and the cellist and gamba player August Wenzinger, director of the 1955 DG (based on performances at that summer's Hitzacker Festival). In marked contrast to the chesty orientation of Calusio's Italians, these Germans and Swiss prefer a distinctly lighter, headier production, and the principal roles tend to be cast with sopranos and tenors, yielding a less ponderous overall color. Koch is still in the grip of the Masterpiece Syndrome, though a northern variant thereof. The orchestra phrases romantically, and the choral numbers boast a grand and solid sound— along with plodding tempos: "Nulla impresa per uom" is altogether turned to stone. Though other set numbers are generally faster than under Calusio (Musica's *ritornello* now goes at 64), the prevalent attitude is reverential rather than dramatic—a characteristic underlined by frequently imprecise Italian diction, peppered with "kvesto," "kvello," and the like.

Although an exception to the latter stricture, Meili doesn't place the language on his tone in a truly idiomatic way. Like most recorded Orfeos, he belongs to the *Fach* we think of as "Bach tenors," implying a range topping out around A, facility with *fioritura*, eloquent diction (at least in German), and (perhaps unfairly) an unglamorous sound. Forty years ago, his handling of the ornamentation must have been a considerable achievement; today his cautious negotiation of the florid version of "Possente spirto" seems clumsy and tedious. At his best, he shapes the recitatives well, and the fifth-act soliloquy is paced with some art, gently accumulating tempo and metrical rigor. Aside from him, little in this performance rewards repeated attention.

1955 DEUTSCHE GRAMMOPHON ARCHIV (M)

Hanni Mack-Cosack (A), Margot Guilleaume (B,C), Jeanne Deroubaix (D,E), Helmut Krebs (F), Fritz Wunderlich (G), Horst Günter (H), Peter Roth-Ehrang (I), Chorus of the Hamburg Hochschule für Musik, Orchestra of the Hitzacker Summer Music Festival 1955—August Wenzinger

Wenzinger's recording constitutes a step forward. Period instruments are used; though the intonation of the brass sinfonias renders them nearly unlistenable and the string technique remains essentially modern, a start has been made. By now, the refreshing breeze of postwar eighteenth-century performance practice has blown into earlier music, and tempos are lively. As the Messaggera, Jeanne Deroubaix's narration is persuasive with tonal and verbal color, and that whole scene has the direct urgency of conversation. The Orfeo, Helmut Krebs, graduating from small parts for Koch, is a "Bach tenor" of unusual liquidity, who can also muster a touch of metal; not exactly Italianate, he

brings to the role some desirable vocal glamour. A small treat is the presence of 25-year-old Fritz Wunderlich as a Shepherd and Apollo, in the year of his professional debut. (Regrettably, cuts are made in Acts IV and V, presumably in order not to exceed two LPs.)

1968 ERATO (S) CD

Magali Schwartz (A), Wally Stämpfli (B), Juliette Bise (C), Laura Sarti (D), Margrit Conrad (E), Eric Tappy (F), Theo Altmeyer (G), Jakob Stämpfli (H), François Loup (I), Vocal Ensemble of Lausanne, Tarr Brass Ensemble, instrumental ensemble—Michel Corboz

A dozen years later, Michel Corboz's first Erato set, made in Lausanne, improves on Wenzinger's achievement only in details: more secure cornetti, easier projection of choral cross-rhythms, etc. It does boast a noble Orfeo, the Swiss tenor Eric Tappy, who, despite a voice dryer than Krebs's, audibly "tastes" the Italian words, singing them with snap and elegance to vary the stanzas of "Vi ricorda, o bosch'ombrosi"; "Possente spirto" is scanned in long phrases with clean divisions. When Caronte sleeps, Tappy sings softly so as not to disturb him, and makes vivid Orfeo's grasp of the situation's urgency. Although his rhythm is still fairly strict, one feels, more than in earlier recordings, that the singer is setting the pace and not simply fitting his lines to a conductor's beat—important progress toward an appropriate ecology of Monteverdi practice. The other singers are ordinary.

1968 TELDEC (S) CD

Rotraud Hansmann (A,B), Eiko Katanosaka (C), Cathy Berberian (D,E), Lajos Kozma (F), Max van Egmond (G), Jacques Villisech (H), Nikolaus Simkowsky (I), Munich Capella Antiqua, Vienna Concentus Musicus—Nikolaus Harnoncourt

The next impulse brought to bear upon *Orfeo* was the new (and decisive) wave of period-instrument advocacy stemming from Nikolaus Harnoncourt's work with the Vienna Concentus Musicus in the 1960s. After a principal initial focus on Bach, Harnoncourt recorded for Telefunken an *Orfeo* of startling originality. To begin with, the instrumental execution is leagues ahead of Wenzinger's; if details of the sometimes fussy scoring are debatable, the playing is undeniably professional. So, for that matter, is the choral singing by the Munich Capella Antiqua, which blends with the cholesterol-free instrumental tone to yield a refreshing transparency. Tempos are definitely up: nearly everything is as fast as or faster than in any previous set. (Musica's *ritornello* goes at 16o!) In his liner notes, Harnoncourt expresses reservations about the effectiveness of improvised ornamentation when it has been rendered unchangeable by recording, but this does not prevent his cast from essaying quite a bit, to good effect.

In that cast, Harnoncourt reached beyond his customary Bach roster. His Orfeo is the Hungarian tenor Lajos Kozma, whose Roman training gives him an Italianate placement and warmth; while missing the heroic posture of Tappy (he falls into crooning à la Tagliavini when abandoned by Speranza and into choppy aspirates in "Possente spirto"), Kozma hints at the appropriateness of the best Italian vocal manners to this music. Another successful departure is the casting of contemporary specialist Cathy Berberian as both Messaggera and Speranza, producing utterances of vivid, instinctive conviction and spontaneity, as well as a plausible realization of the single-note Baroque *trillo*. Rotraud Hansmann is a clear, bright Musica and Euridice, bass Max van Egmond an older, more somber Apollo than most; Caronte has an edge of scorn, but Plutone is the conventional heavy.

1973 DEUTSCHE GRAMMOPHON ARCHIV (S)

Emilia Petrescu (A,B), Anna Reynolds (C,D), James Bowman (E), Nigel Rogers (F), Ian Partridge (G), Stafford Dean (H), Alexander Malta (I), Hamburg Monteverdi Chorus, Hamburg Camerata Academica and Early Music Wind Circle—Jürgen Jürgens

Like Krebs before him, the English tenor Nigel Rogers moved up from *comprimario* (in 1968 Teldec) to protagonist of this recording, which combines primarily British soloists with Hamburg forces under Jürgen Jürgens. More conventional in approach than Harnoncourt's, this performance has less profile, except that conveyed by the rather dry and raspy singing of the men (in striking contrast to Anna Reynolds's overripe, pitch-beclouded Messaggera and Proserpina). In "Possente spirto," Rogers deploys an unconventional sort of yodeling technique that articulates the *fioritura* quickly and without aspirates, enabling him to traverse the phrases tautly and expressively; he will, however, later surpass this effort. Alongside admirable features (including an arresting initial Toccata), Jürgens offers such puzzling details as the ill-informed substitution of "Parnasso" for "Permesso" in La Musica's opening line. The Musica / Euridice pitches cleanly, Speranza is a good countertenor, and the other men sing well if blandly.

1980 TELDEC (S) CD

Rachel Yakar (A), Trudeliese Schmidt (B,E), Glenys Linos (C,D), Philippe Huttenlocher (F), Roland Hermann (G), Werner Gröschel (H), Hans Franzen (I), Zurich Opera Monteverdi Ensemble—Nikolaus Harnoncourt

"Startling" and "extravagant" are possible descriptions for Harnoncourt's second *Orfeo*, derived from the soundtrack for the TV film of his and Jean-Pierre Ponnelle's Zurich production of the opera; few "remakes" in such violent contrast to their predecessors can be found in the history of recorded opera. Several roles are cast with heavier voices than before; Orfeo is now a baritone with limited coloratura fluency, Musica and Messaggera invoke chesty mezzo emphases, Apollo is also a baritone, and nearly everyone sings with *verismo* vehemence, accented by very close miking. The net effect is to make the opera more ordinary, less distinctive and subtle in its variety.

One textual oddity: the final Moresca is inserted between Orfeo's fifth-act soliloquy and the descent of Apollo. This may represent a bow to the original printed libretto, in the final scene of which the distraught Orfeo is tormented by Bacchantes rather than transmuted to the heavens by Apollo—probably an early version that was found unsuitable for the celebratory occasions of the first performances and for which no music survives.

1980 JUBILATE (S)

Melinda Liebermann (A), Rosemarie Bühler (B,E), Rochelle Travis (C), Heidi Blanke-Roeser (D), Joachim Seipp (F), Cornelius Hauptmann (G,H), Uwe Bliesch (I), Frankfurt Madrigal Ensemble, Chorus and Orchestra of the Bad Hersfeld Festival 1980—Siegfried Heinrich

The single distinctive aspect of Siegfried Heinrich's 1980 Bad Hersfeld production and recording is the editor / conductor's attempt to incorporate something of the aforementioned original ending. Very little, actually: a single refrain of the Bacchantes is fitted to two brief numbers from Monteverdi's 1619 ballet *Tirsi e Clori* (the final choral dance, "Balliam e giriamo," and the earlier duet, "Già Clori gentile"), after which the opera proceeds as usual with Apollo's intervention. In most respects, Heinrich follows in the footsteps of Harnoncourt's first version, though the undistinguished, predominantly German cast (who don't always avoid Teutonic Italian) features an unfluent baritone Orfeo.

1983 EMI / ANGEL (S,D)

Patrizia Kwella (A), Emma Kirkby (B), Jennifer Smith (C), Guillemette Laurens (D), Catherine Denley (E), Nigel Rogers (F), Mario Bolognesi (G), Stephen Varcoe (H), David Thomas (I), Chiaroscuro—Nigel Rogers; London Baroque—Charles Medlam; London Cornett & Sackbut Ensemble

In the latest recordings, we encounter a substantially fresh generation of singers, international in origin and many of them specialists in early music. The first of two recent versions from Britain, made in 1983 for EMI's Reflexe series, combines Nigel Rogers's Chiaroscuro vocal ensemble with Charles Medlam's London Baroque instrumental group and the London Cornett & Sackbut Ensemble. Rogers now sings the title role more magisterially than in 1973;

his voice will never have the allure of Gigli's, but in a decade his *legato*, range of color, mastery of florid work, and response to Monteverdi's harmonic movement have all ripened tangibly, and are put to impressively concentrated ends. One spot misfires: the fourth-act *ritornello* aria "Qual onor di te fia degno" is taken just enough faster than before that the vowels don't have time to develop between the consonants, and the effect is choppy instead of brave.

I'm less enthusiastic about some other singers, such as the white-toned Musica (Emma Kirkby, with fussy Italian) and Euridice (Patrizia Kwella). For a change, Plutone is not a growling replay of Caronte (indeed, they are often assigned to the same singer), but a gentler baritone (Stephen Varcoe) whom we can relate to Proserpina's tenderness. The pace of the action is well considered, aptly tense at such points as the arrival of the Messaggera (the vibrant Guillemette Laurens), and clearly governed by the singers; few of the tempos for the set numbers are as extreme as Harnoncourt's (our bellwether, Musica's *ritornello*, is taken at 124).

1985 ERATO (S,D)

Audrey Michael (A,E), Colette Alliot-Lugaz (B), Danielle Borst (C), Carolyn Watkinson (D), Gino Quilico (F), Eric Tappy (G), Frangiskos Voutsinos (H,I), Vocal Ensemble of the Chapelle Royale, Orchestra of the Lyons Opera—Michel Corboz

Corboz's second Erato recording, based on a 1985 Aix Festival production, includes several British singers, and its Orfeo is the Canadian baritone Gino Quilico. He proves we've come a long way from de Franceschi; it's a lighter, headier voice, and his excellent Italian is well placed on the tone—if only he had the virtuosity to make "Possente spirto" convincing! The presence of Tappy as Apollo is a nice touch; the voice is slightly tremulous, the authority still palpable. In spite of its theatrical run, this is an unfocused affair, with a good deal of perfunctory, mushy *continuo* work, and no consistent point of view; Corboz has been outflanked by the onward march of early-music performance.

1985 DEUTSCHE GRAMMOPHON ARCHIV (S,D) CD

Julianne Baird (A), Lynne Dawson (B), Diana Montague (C), Anne Sofie von Otter (D), Mary Nichols (E), Anthony Rolfe Johnson (F), Nigel Robson (G), Willard White (H), John Tomlinson (I), Monteverdi Choir, English Baroque Soloists, His Majesties Sagbutts & Cornetts—John Eliot Gardiner

Some of 1983 EMI's instrumental personnel (but no singers) overlap onto John Eliot Gardiner's set (the third to come from Archiv), taped two years later. The protagonist, tenor Anthony Rolfe Johnson, has smooth tone, good Italian, reasonable command of the *fioritura*, and earnest expressivity, yet he fails to reach the Rogers level of concentration and expertise.

Gardiner's cast includes its share of "early music" voices, and again I resist an etiolated Musica (Lynne Dawson), whose consonants are barely audible: if this music isn't about words, then none ever was! The Euridice (Julianne Baird) does better, and makes certain we feel the harmonic bite of her final speech. The whitish keening of Anne Sofie von Otter's Messaggera is a severe trial. On the other hand, the low male voices are both good; Plutone (Willard White) is a bass, but a gentler one than usual, and we may hope that this sensible reconsideration of the character will now become standard. Especially in the instrumental pieces, Gardiner's is possibly the most lavishly ornamented version of the opera on records. More important, it sounds entirely spontaneous, as does the relation between singers and *continuo*. Tempos tend to be slightly slower than with Rogers and Medlam.

In the recent British sets, as in Harnoncourt's first version, one could easily quibble with details of realization—particularly matters of scoring (where a variety of criteria can be brought into play: interpretation of Monteverdi's incomplete and occasionally confusing rubrics, instrumental symbolism, considerations of symmetry) and of tempo relationships. The choices in these performances obviously stem from thorough knowledge of the work and reverence for its unique qualities, and they deserve respect; that they differ should not alarm us, for such questions have no definitive answers (though doubtless some wrong ones). On balance, 1968 Teldec and 1983 EMI are probably the pick of the lot to date, but the modern rediscovery of *Orfeo* is surely not yet over. In these and other recent performances, the right questions have been asked, and musically, dramatically eloquent results are forthcoming.

DAVID HAMILTON

Unavailable for review:
1991 L'OISEAU-LYRE

CLAUDIO MONTEVERDI

L'INCORONAZIONE DI POPPEA (1642)

A: Poppea (s); B: Drusilla (s); C: Nerone (originally male s; also s, ms, or t);
D: Ottone (originally male c; also ct or bar); E: Ottavia (ms); F: Seneca (bs)

L'Incoronazione di Poppea has traditionally been described as a product
of Monteverdi's old age, and the
crowning glory of his career. Now,
some musicologists have put forth
the theory that parts of the score—including the
famous final duet, "Pur ti miro"—are the work
of other composers, and that the entire opera
may in fact be a collaborative work, put together
under Monteverdi's supervision. The question
of authorship is intriguing, but hardly impairs
our enjoyment of the music. Even if it could be
proven that Monteverdi had nothing to do with
the opera at all, the curtain rises and falls on an
undisputed masterpiece.

As we might expect, a survey of the recordings of the opera allows us to follow the progress
of two ongoing performance trends: a striving
for greater textual authenticity, along with an
attempt to recapture a convincing seventeenth-
century performance style. But before the opera
can be performed at all, its interpreters have
many crucial decisions to make.

Neither of the two surviving manuscripts (one
from Naples, the other from Venice) even
remotely resembles a full score in the sense we
use the term today: both manuscripts show the
vocal parts, supported by a single bass line,
with—infrequently—additional parts for the
instrumental *ritornellos* lightly sketched in.
Contrapuntal lines (if desired), harmonies, and
instrumentation must all be provided before a
performance can take place.

Next, there is the question of the vocal distribution. Originally, Nerone was a male soprano,
Ottone a male alto; the roles of the Page (Val-
etto) and Amore were presumably sung by female
sopranos. Arnalta's music is written in the tenor
clef, leading many to believe that it, too, may
have been treated as a travesty role.

The earliest twentieth-century revivals of
Poppea predictably transposed the parts of Nerone and the Page for tenor voices, and assigned
Ottone to a baritone or bass. Arnalta was sung
by a woman.

For a long time, it was taken for granted that
a nonspecialist audience would not accept a
female singer in the role of Nerone. Elisabeth
Söderström's brilliant performance, on the 1975
Teldec / Harnoncourt recording, shattered that
prejudice once and for all, and set a precedent
that has been followed on two subsequent
recordings (and in the theater as well).

A countertenor Ottone has also become the
norm, thanks in part to the precedent set in
several recordings. It has also become common
to have Arnalta sung by a man.

p.1963 VOX (S)

Ursula Buckel (A), Genia Wilhelmi (B), Hans-
Ulrich Mielsch (C), Grayson Burgess (D),
Eugenia Zareska (E), Eduard Wollitz (F), San-
tini Chamber Orchestra—Rudolf Ewerhart

Although this set, the first stereo recording of
the opera, occupies three LPs, the cuts are

considerable. The Prologue is omitted, and, in the opera itself, the characters of Ottavia's Nurse, the Page, the Lady-in-Waiting (Damigella), Pallas, Mercury, and Lucano are eliminated entirely.

Rudolf Ewerhart's realization of the score is on the conservative side. The full instrumental ensemble is used only in the sinfonias and *ritornellos*; the voices are accompanied only by a variety of *continuo* instruments, including harpsichord, organ, harp, lute, theorbo, viola da gamba, cello, and contrabass gamba.

Ewerhart favors rather deliberate tempos: the scenes between Nerone and Poppea, for example, have a grave, formal beauty rather than suggesting erotic urgency. Nevertheless, the performance proves that the opera can be made to work in this way.

The singers are mostly German, and several of them enunciate the Italian less than idiomatically, with impure vowels. All of the soloists work hard to bring their characters to life, though, and such features of the vocal style as the *trillo* (essentially, a stutter on one pitch) are dutifully observed. Nerone is a tenor, Ottone a countertenor, Arnalta a contralto (Sonia Karamanian), and Amore a soprano (Antonia Fahberg).

Hans-Ulrich Mielsch, the Nerone, has an attractive tenor voice. The Poppea, Ursula Buckel, has a larger soprano, darker in timbre, than most of her successors on disc. If not the most incandescent pair of lovers imaginable, both sing well.

Grayson Burgess, unfortunately, does not make a very convincing case for assigning Ottone to a countertenor. Despite his obvious intelligence and musicianship, Burgess's voice is small and colorless, and he ascends into the upper register with a deadening caution. Genia Wilhelmi is a little tight and shrill as Drusilla, but certainly adequate.

The best of the soloists are Eugenia Zareska, a rich-voiced, dignified Ottavia, and Eduard Wollitz, who is somewhat rusty of timbre and ponderous of manner, but manages to suggest that these qualities are not inappropriate to Seneca's character.

The recording is in good stereo sound.

1964 EMI / ANGEL (S)

Magda Laszlo (A), Lydia Marimpietri (B), Richard Lewis (C), Walter Alberti (D), Frances Bible (E), Carlo Cava (F), Glyndebourne Festival Chorus, Royal Philharmonic Orchestra—John Pritchard

This set is a souvenir of a Glyndebourne Festival production, first performed in 1962. Raymond Leppard's revivals of Monteverdi and Cavalli operas, both in the theater and on records, did a great deal to bring this music to the attention of the general public. It is ironic that Leppard's performing editions of these works now seem decidedly old-fashioned.

The recording is brutally cut: the two LPs, with a total playing time of 98 minutes, contain only about half the score, and should really be billed as "Highlights from *Poppea*." The Prologue is once again missing. To detail all of the other cuts would be tedious: suffice it to say that Ottavia's Nurse is once again absent from the cast list; that Ottone agrees to kill Poppea the moment Ottavia suggests that he do so, without protest or coercion; and that Drusilla does not ask to accompany Ottone into exile.

Leppard's lush instrumentation, with five-part string writing and newly composed wind parts competing with the voices almost throughout, tends to weigh the opera down. The elaborate organ figurations and chromatic harp swirls are especially distracting, and suggest a late nineteenth-century pastiche of Baroque style. John Pritchard conducts ably, and the orchestra produces the rich, heavy sound, with generous string vibrato, that the arranger apparently wants.

Although a disappointing realization of Monteverdi's score, this recording cannot be dismissed without regret, because it has a fine cast. The women are especially good. Magda Laszlo is a superb Poppea—sensuous, amoral, provocative—and sings beautifully with a full, round soprano voice. Mezzo Frances Bible, by contrast, is all wounded pride and bitter vindictiveness as Ottavia. A further contrast is provided by the Drusilla of Lydia Marimpietri, with her bright lyric soprano and vivid words.

. Richard Lewis is a dignified Nerone—perhaps too much so, for the sinister side of the character is underplayed. Transposing Ottone's music downward for a baritone undeniably does some harm to the music but also lends the character some much needed virility; Walter Alberti handles the rather ungrateful assignment capably. Carlo Cava is an appropriately stern Seneca, although his dark bass voice is not always ideally steady.

Once again, the stereo sound is outstanding.

1966 CAMBRIDGE (S)

Carole Bogard (A), Judith Nelson (B), Charles Bressler (C), John Thomas (D), Sharon Hayes (E), Herbert Beattie (F), Berkeley Instrumental Ensemble—Alan Curtis

Alan Curtis, who directs the performance from one of the two harpsichords, is also responsible for the performing edition—a careful conflation of the Venice and Naples manuscripts, with Nerone and the Page once again transposed down for tenor voices. (Arnalta is sung by a female contralto, Louise Parker.) The Prologue is performed for the first time on records. Elsewhere, there are only a few small cuts, notably in the Act III trial scene; as a result, the recording fills four LPs.

One is grateful for the near-completeness, but unfortunately the performance is somewhat of a bore. The instrumentation is extremely austere: for long stretches, the voices are accompanied only by one of the harpsichords or a chitarrone, reinforced by solo cello or bassoon. Curtis encourages his singers to adopt a rather deliberate, rhetorical approach to the recitatives, and as a result the performance lacks spontaneity. Another closely related problem is the assignment of so many of the smaller parts to young American singers, presumably students: some of them have good voices, but virtually all of them sound as though they are reading the Italian off a Teleprompter.

Among the leads, Carole Bogard, the Poppea, and Judith Nelson, the Drusilla, are both outstanding, with pure lyric soprano voices and a sure grasp of the stylistic requirements.

Tenor Charles Bressler has a lighter, more flexible voice than either Mielsch or Lewis, and

works hard to draw Nerone's character for us.

Regrettably, the Ottone, Ottavia, and Seneca are all disappointing. Countertenor John Thomas sounds vocally undernourished and makes even less of a dramatic impression than Burgess. Mezzo Sharon Hayes and Herbert Beattie (who sounds more like a baritone than a true bass) both lack authority.

The stereo engineering places one harpsichord in each channel, resulting in some distracting Ping-Pong effects.

p.1974 TELDEC (S) CD

Helen Donath (A), Rotraud Hansmann (B), Elisabeth Söderström (C), Paul Esswood (D), Cathy Berberian (E), Giancarlo Lucciardi (F), Concentus Musicus, Vienna—Nikolaus Harnoncourt

This set is going to drain me of superlatives, for it is one of the most satisfying recordings of a seventeenth-century opera in the catalogue. It is also the most expensive set of *Poppea*, filling four CDs, but it's worth every penny.

The opera is performed without cuts, for the first time on records (once again both manuscripts are consulted, with Venice as the primary source). Furthermore, all of the vocal parts are sung at the original pitch. There is a boy soprano Amore (an anonymous member of the Vienna Choir Boys). Carlo Gaifa, though a tenor, sings Arnalta's music in the original keys, resorting to falsetto for the lullaby ("Oblivion soave").

Nikolaus Harnoncourt's realization strikes a good balance between purism and the expectations of a modern listener. Different *continuo* instruments—harpsichord, virginals, chitarrone, lute, harp, organ—are associated with the various characters. A small string ensemble discreetly fills out the arias and ariosos. Recorders, oboes, and even trumpets appear from time to time.

Elisabeth Söderström's Nerone is one of a handful of recorded operatic performances that can truly be described as revelatory. Through careful coloring of her voice and inflection of the words, this quintessentially feminine soprano creates a convincing aural portrait of a ruthless, impetuous young man.

She is ideally partnered by Helen Donath's Poppea. Like Söderström, Donath has a beautiful and distinctive lyric soprano voice. She, too, is a resourceful vocal actress, creating a willful yet basically sympathetic young woman.

Paul Esswood sings Ottone's music more securely than either of his countertenor predecessors on disc, and is admirable from the dramatic standpoint. Cathy Berberian, operating with a warm, soft mezzo-soprano, is an uncommonly three-dimensional Ottavia—vulnerable, yet with flashes of ruthlessness.

In the major roles, only Giancarlo Lucciardi, the Seneca, is slightly disappointing: a fine voice, but rather lugubrious in his delivery of the stoic's pronouncements.

Teldec's CD transfer of the original analogue recording is outstandingly clear and detailed.

1981 TELDEC (S)

Rachel Yakar (A), Janet Perry (B), Eric Tappy (C), Paul Esswood (D), Trudeliese Schmidt (E), Matti Salminen (F), Monteverdi Ensemble of the Zurich Opera House—Nikolaus Harnoncourt

This recording—the soundtrack of a television production—represents a step backward, in many respects, from the high standard set by the earlier Teldec version. Harnoncourt now makes some cuts. The instrumental playing is less polished than before, and the whole production simply seems less well prepared, less "right."

Tenor Eric Tappy and soprano Rachel Yakar are thoroughly professional singers, but no match for Söderström and Donath in their roles. Esswood, in marginally less good voice than before, is still a fine Ottone. Janet Perry's Drusilla is pert and appealing, but does not convey the character's growth in Act III. Trudeliese Schmidt at least brings a stinging intensity to Ottavia, and Matti Salminen is an impressively dark-voiced Seneca.

The other roles are indifferently taken, on the whole. Alexander Oliver makes little impression as Arnalta; and it seems strange to cast Philippe Huttenlocher—a baritone of limited flexibility—as Lucano when that fine Rossini tenor Francisco Araiza is on hand, in the bit part of the Lictor.

1985 CBS / SONY (S,D) CD

Catherine Malfitano (A), Colette Alliot-Lugaz (B), John Elwes (C), Gerard Lesne (D), Zehava Gal (E), Gregory Reinhart (F), La Grande Ecurie et la Chambre du Roy—Jean-Claude Malgoire

Against the strong competition, this set must be described as an also-ran. I fear that the blame must be laid at the feet of the conductor. Jean-Claude Malgoire favors very slow tempos, and his leadership is deficient in rhythmic definition. He also uses an austere instrumentation: for long stretches, the singers are accompanied by nothing but one or two *continuo* instruments. The playing, like the conducting, tends to be rather soft-edged and lacking in energy.

In Malgoire's favor, he gives us the first complete recording of the Neapolitan manuscript, with no readings borrowed from the Venetian version—a legitimate textual choice. As a result, some music (e.g., an Act III episode in which Amore boasts to Venus that he has made Poppea's coronation possible) is recorded for the first time. (It is included on both of the subsequent recordings.)

The CBS recording cannot be readily dismissed, however, because it features another fine cast. Catherine Malfitano, with her bright yet sensuous soprano, is another compelling Poppea—more aggressive than Donath, for example. John Elwes, a tenor Nerone, sings sweetly and accurately, but is particularly good at conveying the emperor's petulance and ruthlessness. Zehava Gal has a beautiful soft-grained mezzo; her dignified, vulnerable Ottavia is obviously no match for these two schemers.

The Ottone, Gerard Lesne, possesses an unusually full-bodied countertenor, and brings a great deal of passion to the role—it's impossible to choose between him and Esswood. Gregory Reinhart has a magnificent bass voice: firm and clear throughout its wide range, never unwieldy, with immaculate intonation and Italian diction. Although his performance is dragged down a bit by Malgoire's ponderous tempos, he is a magnificent Seneca.

The performance has been recorded in good digital sound. Like the two sets discussed below, it has been accommodated on three CDs.

1989 VIRGIN (S, D) CD

Arleen Augér (A), Sarah Leonard (B), Della Jones (C), James Bowman (D), Linda Hirst (E), Gregory Reinhart (F), City of London Baroque Sinfonia—Richard Hickox

This studio recording was made in conjunction with a series of staged performances, with the same cast. Richard Hickox has interesting ideas about the score. He bases his (uncut) performing text primarily on the Venetian manuscript, but (in a booklet note) states his conviction that editorial additions should be kept to a minimum. His realization of the *continuo* is thus more austere than anyone else's; often, we hear only a solo voice and one instrument. Hickox also eschews the little instrumental flourishes that most of the other conductors insert to mark the beginnings and ends of individual episodes; as a result, changes of scene are left to the listener's imagination, as in a radio play. In general, Hickox paces the music more swiftly than Harnoncourt, and a listener who is not fluent in Italian may find some of the rapid-fire dialogue exchanges difficult to follow.

The performance has uncommon dramatic conviction, thanks to the presence of a true ensemble of gifted vocal actors. Arleen Augér, a consistently satisfying artist who seems incapable of making a poor record, is a predictably fine Poppea—an exquisitely sung performance, filled with subtle nuances.

Della Jones, always an exciting performer, sometimes presses her handsome mezzo a bit hard in an effort to suggest Nerone's vehemence. Her duets with Augér are remarkable examples of true ensemble singing, however, with the two very different voices perfectly blended. "Pur ti miro," in particular, is ravishing—the most beautiful rendition of this number on any of these recordings, and the unforgettable climax of this performance.

Reinhart repeats his Seneca from the CBS set, and benefits enormously from Hickox's firmer support; despite the strong competition, this is the best performance of the role on disc.

Countertenor James Bowman gives one of his best recorded performances: his voice is warmer, rounder, and much less hooty in timbre than it has often sounded in the past, and the interpretation is direct and honest. Sarah Leonard has a larger, more sensuous voice than most of the recorded Drusillas, which is all to the good.

Linda Hirst, though billed as a mezzo, sounds like a lyric soprano with a light, clear timbre. Although there is no reason why Ottavia should sound matronly (the historical Octavia was still a fairly young woman when Nero divorced her), somehow the dark colorations of a true mezzo seem more appropriate in her music. This reservation aside, Hirst is eloquent enough.

Superb recorded sound.

1990 HARMONIA MUNDI (S,D) CD

Danielle Borst (A), Lena Lootens (B), Guillemette Laurens (C), Axel Köhler (D), Jennifer Larmore (E), Michael Schopper (F), Concerto Vocale—René Jacobs

Here is another studio recording that has clearly benefited from having been preceded by a theater production (in Montpellier, France). Countertenor René Jacobs is responsible for the edition of the score recorded here, and directs the performance, but (regrettably) does not participate as a singer. Jacobs takes some bold liberties (described at length in his excellent notes) with the surviving performance material. He makes a number of small cuts in passages that he considers repetitive or dramatically expendable; although I object to this in principle, I must admit that most of these cuts work very well in practice. Jacobs inserts brief sinfonias, adapted from pieces by other seventeenth-century composers, to indicate scene changes or the entrances of characters. He transposes some of the vocal lines to suit the capabilities of his cast, and even rewrites two sections of recitative in which he believes the word setting to be faulty as a result of copyists' mistakes. His instrumentation is varied and colorful, yet never distracts the listener's attention from the singers.

This cast—to a greater extent than any previous group on records—succeeds in bringing a truly conversational, improvisatory quality to the recitatives.

We have another exciting female Nerone—mezzo-soprano Guillemette Laurens, whose portrayal is less neurotic than Söderström's, more smoothly vocalized than Jones's. In the duet with Lucano (the excellent Guy de Mey) Laurens displays a dizzying command of the coloratura writing; in the slow section, no previous Nerone on records has made the exclamations of "Ahi!" sound more orgasmic.

Danielle Borst has an attractive lyric-soprano voice, and her approach to Poppea is unique: Borst suggests an innocent (!) young girl, desperately infatuated with the emperor, and almost frightened by the violence with which he responds to her love.

Axel Köhler is another good countertenor Ottone, not as passionate as Esswood or Lesne, but secure and often beautiful of voice. Jacobs has a first-rate Drusilla in Lena Lootens, who is flighty and passionate by turns. Christina Högman is the best Page on records, capturing a real Cherubino / Octavian flavor in her scenes.

Michael Schopper sings well, and his Seneca is interesting—more human than most, with moments of arrogance and impatience as well as noble resignation.

The digital engineering is once again admirable.

———————

My firm recommendation is the 1974 Teldec / Harnoncourt set—a performance of great distinction, with generally superb vocal and instrumental work. It's also extremely well recorded, holding its own quite well against the more up-to-date sonics of the three digitally engineered sets. (The 1981 Teldec / Harnoncourt remake simply can't compare, and is out of the running.)

If one wants an alternative to the Harnoncourt set, or a supplemental version to put beside it, the difficult choice is between the Virgin/Hickox and Harmonia Mundi / Jacobs sets. The Hickox has the greater degree of textual integrity; the Jacobs performance has extraordinary dramatic conviction. Both are superb productions.

ROLAND GRAEME

Unavailable for review:
1952 GUILDE INTERNATIONAL DU DISQUE
1980 FONIT-CETRA

THE BALLAD OF BABY DOE (1956)

A: Baby Doe (s); B: Augusta (ms); C: Horace (bar); D: Bryan (bs-bar)

*M*usical sophisticates crinkle their noses at *Baby Doe*, and not without some cause. The strengths and weaknesses of Moore's score and John Latouche's libretto are parallel. Both men wrote engagingly and warmly, in a homey populist-poet style, for song-and-chorus set pieces and lyric monologues. And both were stumped by any passages in which the song element could not dominate: plot scenes or dramatic confrontations. Here, Latouche produced clean, functional prose that reads like sensible radio-script writing, and Moore—evidently determined to through-compose—set the words in that awkward, dogged manner that discloses an honest lack of dramatic imagination. For these reasons, the score thins rather desperately in the middle, and the important character of Augusta has little life, save in her introspective final monologue. Nevertheless, audiences do not leave *Ballad* unmoved. The relationship of Horace and his Baby is simple but deep—we truly care about them, and their legend confers that kind of confirmation that is the mark of history-turned-folk-myth. Fortunately, the writing attains its best sustained level in the final scenes, and *Ballad* at last rises above its limitations.

1959 DEUTSCHE GRAMMOPHON (S)

Beverly Sills (A), Frances Bible (B), Walter Cassel (C), Joshua Hecht (D), New York City Opera Chorus and Orchestra—Emerson Buckley

In this work's only recording to date, the principals are strong enough to pull us home against the powerful undertow of the abominable engineering and some shaky support elements. The young Sills did some of her best singing as Baby Doe. Her fresh soprano sails and floats through the role's considerable demands—it has the reach and quickness for the display side of the writing, and the warmth and body wanted for the touching "Leadville *Liebestod*." Expressively, she is unaffected and heartfelt. Walter Cassel originated the role of Horace Tabor and, short of Lawrence Tibbett, it's hard to imagine a better choice. His weighty, pemmican baritone and bluff musical temperament are exactly on target.

Frances Bible, a pillar of the City Opera roster for many years, sings powerfully and sensitively as Augusta, though one can imagine a less covered, fruity elocution coming a bit closer to humanizing this difficult character. Hecht's dark, sometimes throaty bass is at its best in the oration of William Jennings Bryan, and there's good work in important secondary roles by Beatrice Krebs and Chester Ludgin.

Buckley's leadership is lively, and the orchestra plays decently. The chorus is scrappy, though, and the entire ensemble has a thin sound—they are too few in number, and don't seem to have been accorded much in the way of either rehearsal or retakes. Some of the bit parts, too, are excruciating to hear: there are problems inherent in attempting to set Broadway character voices in a more or less classical frame, but they can be solved better than this.

The recording flatters no one. It is edgy, shallow, and over-reverberant. Despite all this, the leading singers bring us the essentials of *Baby Doe*, and that will be enough for those of us susceptible to this cherishable opera.

CONRAD L. OSBORNE

IDOMENEO, RÈ DI CRETA (1781)

A: Ilia (s); B: Elettra (s); C: Idamante (s or t); D: Idomeneo (t); E: Arbace (t)

ozart's first mature opera, *Idomeneo* is drawn on a grand scale, in a Mannheim-Munich tradition that leavened the Italian *opera seria*'s concentration on the solo voice with a French emphasis on chorus and ballet. Scenically elaborate and musically prodigal, with daring harmonies and finely detailed orchestral textures, it is more continuous in fabric than the usual *opera seria*, yet needs to be paced differently from the later Mozart works; much of the action unfolds in recitative rather than ensembles. Its recorded history documents a significant shift from altering the opera to discovering how it works on its own terms.

Idomeneo had to be abridged even before its 1781 Munich premiere—mostly for reasons of length, but also because of the limitations of some of the singers. The opera was heard only once more in Mozart's lifetime, a private performance in Vienna in 1786, for which the composer wrote two fresh numbers and adjusted the castrato role of Idamante for tenor. This history has bequeathed to modern editors and performers a profusion of alternatives: no two recordings have the same content. The bravura tenor aria "Fuor del mar" (No. 12) exists in a shorter, easier form as well as a more florid original. At the Munich performances, in addition to recitative cuts, several entire numbers were omitted from the last act: Idamante's "No, la morte" (No. 27a), Elettra's "D'Oreste, d'Ajace" (No. 28a), and Idomeneo's "Torna la pace" (No. 30a); Mozart also made four different versions of Neptune's oracle. In Vienna, Arbace's

first aria (No. 10a) was replaced by "Non temer, amato bene" (No. 10b), an aria for Idamante with violin *obbligato*, and "S'io non moro" (No. 20a), the original duet for Ilia and the castrato Idamante (No. 20a), gave way to "Spiegarti non poss'io" (No. 20b). The extensive concluding ballet music is omitted from most recordings.

As early as the 1840s, *Idomeneo* was being "adapted for the modern stage," as the pace and conventions of *opera seria* were found increasingly old-fashioned. Even in the opera's sesquicentenary year, 1931, major productions in Vienna and Munich introduced arrangements by, respectively, Richard Strauss and Ermanno Wolf-Ferrari; sung in German, both involved extensive cuts and plot alterations, as well as new composition, to conform the opera to current ideas of musical drama.

1950 HAYDN SOCIETY (M)

Gertrud Hopf (A), Gertrude Grob-Prandl (B), Greta Menzel (C), Horst Taubmann (D), Herbert Handt (E), Vienna State Opera Chorus, Vienna Symphony Orchestra—Meinhard von Zallinger

More an act of piety than a real performance, this was at least a serious attempt to record Mozart's opera in something like its original form. The text is a plausible one: the Munich alternatives are used, with Nos. 27a, 28a, and 30a in place; Arbace's second aria is omitted, and the recitatives are abbreviated, often awkwardly (among the missing pages is Idomeneo's public naming of Idamante as the required sacrificial victim).

Unfortunately, once past the Overture, the conductor seems to be feeling his way, often choosing tempos wide of the mark—usually on the sluggish side. Except for Handt, the cast deals unidiomatically with Italian, and the recitatives are generally ponderous. However musical, Hopf is not always in tune; Grob-Prandl, with an imposing instrument, gets no assistance from Zallinger in her rage arias; Menzel is fluent and slightly shrill, Taubmann throaty and stressed by the florid writing. Both chorus and orchestra have scrappy moments, and the inclusion of the ballet music is neutralized by Zallinger's many wrong-headed tempos.

1956 EMI / ANGEL ℗

Sena Jurinac (A), Lucille Udovick (B), Léopold Simoneau (C), Richard Lewis (D), James Milligan (E), Glyndebourne Festival Chorus and Orchestra—John Pritchard

Idomeneo's resurrection received major impetus from its first production at Glyndebourne, under Fritz Busch, in 1951. That year, EMI recorded excerpts, and in 1956 ventured a "complete" version under Pritchard, who had succeeded Busch on the podium. Outright omissions are limited to the two Arbace arias, and, with a tenor Idamante, No. 20b is preferred (No. 10b is omitted); a curious composite is made of Nos. 12a and 12b, and all the last-act arias are included. However, drastic internal cuts are made in many set numbers, as well as in the recitatives (comparison of parallel passages in the 1951 and 1956 recordings suggests that this text probably represents Busch's editorial choices).

The 1956 set is distinguished by the presence of two of the best Mozart singers of mid-century, Jurinac and Simoneau. The soprano's sense of line and commitment is exemplary; her voice was steadier in the 1951 excerpts (her three solos from which are on her EMI recital CD), but in 1956 the recitatives are more vividly spoken—perhaps a consequence of her marriage, in the intervening years, to an Italian, Sesto Bruscantini. Simoneau is the most melli-

fluous and expressive of tenor Idamantes. An earnest, workmanlike Idomeneo, Lewis lacks the incisiveness of tone and attack that would bring the music to life rhythmically and verbally. Udovick is a capable, slightly edgy Elettra. Pritchard paces well, but shapes and textures lack the focus achieved by Busch—in fact, this "complete" version seems more dispensable than the highlights set.

For some reason, EMI's CD edition is mono, although the Seraphim LP incarnation was in quite reasonable stereo that registered the orchestra with greater fullness and clarity. The CD libretto includes Italian text but no translation.

1968 PHILIPS (S) ℗

Margherita Rinaldi (A), Pauline Tinsley (B), Ryland Davies (C), George Shirley (D), Robert Tear (E), BBC Chorus and Symphony Orchestra—Colin Davis

Colin Davis belongs to a younger generation than Busch or Zallinger (or the conductors of the next two recordings of *Idomeneo*), and his way of dealing with the work is different: he clearly isn't worried that the music's scale will risk boredom, and his cuts (no doubt partly conditioned by a commercial mandate not to exceed three LPs) follow the lines along which Mozart himself dealt with the opera's extravagant length: omitting entire numbers and abridging *secco* recitative, rather than taking niggling tucks within the numbers. Again both Arbace arias are omitted, also No. 10b and Idamante's No. 27a; oddly—considering the use of a tenor Idamante—No. 20a is preferred. The long version of No. 12 is used.

Davis has forceful and precise ideas about tempo and expressivity, and gets superior work from the BBC forces—lots of zinging articulation from the strings, lucent tone from the winds, full-throated, well-balanced choral sound. Leading a strong cast, Shirley has the metal and bite to convince as a man passionate enough to curse the gods themselves; he's not a truly fluent florid singer and loses the pitch now and then, yet the extended "Fuor del mar" is drawn on a broad canvas, with nobility and spirit. His recitatives are lively and expressive, his final aria slightly whiny in tone, his dynamics somewhat unvaried. The latter is true also of Davies, whose more flexible instrument is otherwise well used. Tear overdoes the emotion in Arbace's recitatives—but then, without arias, he hasn't much else to work with.

Rinaldi, not as luminous as Jurinac, is a lovely Ilia; an overbright patch in the voice around the top of the staff is rarely troublesome, and she phrases with sensitivity to harmonies as well as melodic shapes. Like most Elettras, Tinsley has the force and edge in the voice for the first and last arias (which really crackle in the orchestra, Davis's tempos underscoring the manic abruptness of the dynamic and harmonic shifts), but is ill at ease in the second-act music. (Davis's one problematic tempo is the sluggish andante for her "Idol mio.") *Appoggiaturas* are widely if not always wisely employed, *fermatas* are ornamented, and some rather plain cadenzas introduced. Well recorded, with good contrast of the double chorus in Act I, this has the feel of a continuous, integrated performance, marked by the zeal of advocacy.

1971 EMI / ANGEL (S) CD

Anneliese Rothenberger (A), Edda Moser (B), Adolf Dallapozza (C), Nicolai Gedda (D), Peter Schreier (E), Leipzig Radio Chorus, Dresden State Orchestra—Hans Schmidt-Isserstedt

Schmidt-Isserstedt presides competently over this still more comprehensive recording, but without Davis's involvement; the expressivity is generic rather than specific. For the first time, every single number is present in some form or other; Nos. 10a, 12b, and 20b are preferred to the alternatives, only No. 27a undergoes a small internal cut, and the recitatives are trimmed somewhat. This inclusiveness would have counted for more with a stronger feeling for shape and scale, and a stronger cast. Rothenberger is a plain, not-quite-steady Ilia, with a tone that never opens up. Moser gets her teeth into the rage arias, but is surprisingly thick-toned and scoopy in the second act. Gedda ought to be an interesting Idomeneo, but he seems not

really "into" the part, with little fire in the crises, little exaltation upon their resolution; his timbre contrasts well with that of the nasal Dallapozza in their dialogues. Schreier is a dry but fluent Arbace. The Italian diction is often Teutonic and little attention has been paid to niceties of period performance practice. Absent the conviction that this music is truly dramatic, a "concert performance" results, which comes to life most often in the choral episodes.

1977 DEUTSCHE GRAMMOPHON (S) CD

Edith Mathis (A), Julia Varady (B), Peter Schreier (C), Wieslaw Ochman (D), Hermann Winkler (E), Leipzig Radio Chorus, Dresden State Orchestra—Karl Böhm

Though Böhm's recording claims to be based on Daniel Heartz's critical edition, it reverts to the bad old tradition of internal cutting. With a tenor Idamante, not only is No. 20b preferred, but also the concertlike 10b. Two of the third-act pieces eliminated in Munich, Nos. 27a and 30a, are dropped, but Elettra's No. 28a is retained, seriously unbalancing the opera's ending: after this enormous and vivid chunk of angry princess, Idomeneo's accompanied recitative (trimmed by a third, to boot) is hardly sufficient to establish the requisite atmosphere of resolution and orderly succession. Nine other set numbers are mangled; in "Fuor del mar" (the short version), some musical material is "recapitulated" without ever having been heard in the exposition!

In any case, this is another "concert performance," with sleepy tempos, stiff recitatives, underarticulated and occasionally scrappy playing. Mathis distinguishes herself with a smoothly sung Ilia, and Ochman, who has little flexibility for the florid writing, does make something impressive out of the third-act invocation to Neptune (a passage that eludes both Shirley and Gedda). Schreier's Idamante is characteristically musical, short on tonal glamour and sweetness; he was better suited to Arbace—and was a better Arbace than Winkler. Varady, smoother than most Elettras in Act II, is still not truly at ease.

1981 TELDEC (S,D) CD

Rachel Yakar (A), Felicity Palmer (B), Trudeliese Schmidt (C), Werner Hollweg (D), Kurt Equiluz (E), Zurich Opera Chorus and Mozart Orchestra—Nikolaus Harnoncourt

Harnoncourt comes to this opera from extensive experience with Baroque music and period instruments. Though the latter are not used here, metal strings, plastic mutes, and soft timpani sticks are banished, and the entire sonic image is rougher, less blended than on earlier recordings; the insistence of trumpets and drums occasionally grows wearing. Particularly effective is the intensely expressive treatment of recitatives, rhythmically free and highly inflected in the manner of speech, as many sources of the period attest was appropriate. Tempos are vigorous and well judged, and, as with Davis, the opera's carefully ordered continuity never flags.

The text chosen is essentially that used at the Munich premiere, with the longer "Fuor del mar" and the ballet music. For the first time, we can hear how the end of the opera works in this form, minus Nos. 27a, 28a, and 30a—undeniably less impressive when you know the alternative, but still clearly effective (Elettra retains a chunk of spiteful accompanied recitative for her departure); the elaborate ballet adds compensating weight (and also makes interesting motivic references to the opera itself). The LP edition was followed by a supplementary single disc including the omitted pieces, the two new pieces for Vienna (Francisco Araiza is the tenor Idamante), and a gavotte whose proper placement in the score is not known (its tune was recycled in the finale to the Piano Concerto in C, K. 467). Too bad that this was not incorporated into the CD version so that listeners could restore or substitute the missing pieces at the appropriate places.

Harnoncourt's voices are generally less opulent than those on earlier recordings. Both Yakar and Palmer tend to whiteness and registral unevenness, and Schmidt has some trouble with intonation. Hollweg is admirably fluent, and though "Vedrommi intorno" lies low for him, he makes its spectral imagery very vivid. Equiluz, eloquent in Arbace's recitatives, is clearly overparted. Simon Estes is the most impressive Voice of Neptune in any recording. Probably not for vocal connoisseurs, this recording embodies a view of *Idomeneo* different from any other, and a remarkably stimulating one.

1983 DECCA / LONDON (S,D) CD

Lucia Popp (A), Edita Gruberova (B), Agnes Baltsa (C), Luciano Pavarotti (D), Leo Nucci (E), Vienna State Opera Chorus, Vienna Philharmonic Orchestra—John Pritchard

Pritchard here offers a much fuller text than twenty-seven years earlier: essentially the Munich version, but restoring the third-act pieces (mostly) and some of Mozart's last-minute recitative cuts (though other tucks are taken in the *secco*). Small cuts (evidently to avoid cadenzas) are taken in Arbace's arias, and larger ones that really degut Idomeneo's final accompanied recitative and aria. That's a shame, for this is music of impressive dignity, and there would have been ample room for it.

The performance has virtues. Gruberova is a surprisingly effective Elettra, the only one to be completely convincing in Act II. Popp's Ilia is accomplished, especially in "Zeffiretti lusinghieri," where a certain tightness at the top of the staff is less evident than elsewhere. A more proficient mezzo Idamante than Baltsa would be hard to imagine, but she's a curiously faceless singer, rarely expressive. Pavarotti has a fine instrument for the title role (though the tone has little sweetness left), and he deals idiomatically with the words; his traversal of the shorter "Fuor del mar" is commanding, while the invocation to Neptune is a couple of stages too loud for the appropriate mood. The decision to cast a baritone as Arbace (defensible in some earlier sets where the arias were omitted) courts outright disaster, for the arias lie too high for Nucci and he spends most of No. 22 sliding upward, loudly and stressfully, into the notes. Chorus and orchestra are excellent, but much of the performance is short on life and projection—

best in the choral episodes, often static in the slower arias.

1990 DEUTSCHE GRAMMOPHON ARCHIV (S,D,P) CD

Sylvia McNair (A), Hillevi Martinpelto (B), Anne Sofie von Otter (C), Anthony Rolfe Johnson (D), Nigel Robson (E), Monteverdi Choir, English Baroque Soloists—John Eliot Gardiner

Recorded at three concert performances in London, this set goes beyond Harnoncourt in historicism to the use of period instruments and the inclusion of virtually "all the surviving music Mozart composed for Munich in 1781" except some *secco* recitative, the shorter "Fuor del mar," and the least interesting of the four Neptunic oracles. The main sequence includes all the set numbers, plus the recitatives as in Harnoncourt; alternate versions of several passages are included in appendices at the ends of the apposite CD sides.

Always proficient and musical, Gardiner's performance is at its best in the choral numbers, the dance-like pieces, the energetic music—strengths one might expect from his background in choral literature and the French operatic tradition that influenced *Idomeneo*. Elettra's rages are well realized in the orchestra. The end of Act II, with its contrasts as terror turns to flight, is particularly striking. Overture and ballet are splendidly played, the trumpets and drums a shade raucous but not outwearing their welcome as in Harnoncourt. Less successful are the contemplative episodes, for example Idomeneo's "Vedrommi intorno," Ilia's "Se il padre perdei" and "Zeffiretti," Arbace's "Se colà ne' fati," which lack a firm rhythmic line to keep them moving forward—they just amble on. And the recitatives, though flexible, lack the vividness of Harnoncourt's.

Perhaps the singers are in part responsible. McNair's sweet soprano is also monochromatic, without much sensuous warmth, and Martinpelto, with a brighter tone, is plain and angular in her singing; even in "D'Oreste, d'Ajace" she seems curiously restrained. Von Otter has more color but not much more personality. Robson is fluent, a bit thin at the top, and also bland.

The exception is Rolfe Johnson: his voice contains both sweetness and metal, his strong florid technique eschews aspirates, he has dignity as well as passion, though his work has less tension here than at his Met debut in 1991. For all its strengths and textual interest, Gardiner's performance doesn't consistently take fire as both Davis's (1968) and Harnoncourt's do.

1991 PHILIPS (S,D) CD

Barbara Hendricks (A), Roberta Alexander (B), Susanne Mentzer (C), Francisco Araiza (D), Uwe Heilmann (E), Bavarian Radio Chorus and Symphony Orchestra—Colin Davis

Presumably because the Philips "Complete Mozart Edition" required a more integral text than was used in Davis's 1968 recording, a remake was undertaken. As with Harnoncourt and Pritchard, the basic text is what was actually performed in Munich, though here Nos. 28a and 30a are restored to the main text, while the two Arbace arias and the ballet music, along with No. 27a, are relegated to an appendix at the end of the last CD. A cut is also taken in the accompanied recitative No. 27, and, contrary to the booklet listing, the longer version of No. 12 is sung, though ending with the modulating conclusion that Mozart added for the shorter version; Davis continues to prefer No. 20a—this time a defensible practice, for he now uses a mezzo Idamante. The libretto neglects to specify where the appendix items should be inserted, and the placement of the appendix precludes easy inclusion of the Arbace arias via CD programming facilities. The main sequence is, however, a viable one.

The Overture begins well, laying to rest fears that the zeal of Davis's earlier advocacy might have been tempered by time. As the performance progresses, however, it becomes clear that neither orchestra nor chorus is quite first-rate when it comes to unanimity of ensemble and intonation, and that the crucial lead oboist is a particularly trying exemplar of the old and quacky German school; as a result, such passages as the striking chromatics leading into Elettra's "Tutto nel cor vi sento" (No. 4) fail to register with full musical impact, and music that should be liquescent (the wind writing in the invocation to Neptune) is sometimes anything but.

Much of the cast is strong enough to make such incidental imperfections tolerable. Hendricks, whose pearly soprano has an attractive shimmer, phrases beautifully and engages more vividly with the words than McNair. Mentzer, occasionally under the note at the top of her range, is a vigorous singer in the set pieces (don't miss No. 27a in the appendix, which she sings with real fire) but tends to drag out the pathos in recitative. Except for a frayed top A, Alexander commands all of Elettra's music, the sensual side as well as the aggressive; the voice has more substance and thrust than Gruberova's, more color than Martinpelto's. Heilmann's Arbace is plain, a tad throaty; only if you stick around for the appendix will you discover that he's reasonably fluent in the arias, though skimping on the tiny ornaments at the beginning of No. 22. A slightly hoarser Hollweg turns up as a forceful High Priest. *Appoggiaturas* are sung frequently, though not in all applicable places, and cadenzas (more elaborate than those in the earlier Davis recording) are inserted where appropriate.

The good report on the cast does not extend, alas, to the central figure: Araiza, a lyric tenor, resorts to a puffed-up, darkened tone that turns whiny (and is often under the pitch) whenever the music moves quickly, shouty whenever it becomes impassioned. The vigor and aptness of his textual delivery (not only in the recitatives, but also in "Vedrommi, intorno," for example) is welcome, but the big moments, such as the final recitative and aria, are woefully devoid of breadth and authority—not even a better orchestra than this could make the music effective with such weak singing. The sound is acceptable, though the singers are close enough to mask a good deal of interesting instrumental detail.

Textually, 1990 DG offers the most satisfactory solution, 1968 Philips the greatest musical and dramatic conviction. 1981 Teldec makes a stimulating alternative, especially if the supplementary disc reappears—it would be a shame to do without the missing pieces; 1991 Philips fulfills the same function, though it certainly does not supersede the first Davis set.

DAVID HAMILTON

ARDIS KRAINIK
General Director,
Lyric Opera of Chicago

1. **Puccini, *Tosca*:** Callas, di Stefano, Gobbi—de Sabata. EMI / ANGEL

2. **Bizet, *Carmen*:** Migenes Johnson, Esham, Domingo, Raimondi—Maazel. ERATO

3. **Verdi, *Requiem*:** Caniglia, Stignani, Gigli, Pinza—Serafin. EMI / ANGEL

4. **Wagner, *Der Ring des Nibelungen*:** Nilsson, Crespin, Flagstad, Ludwig, King, Windgassen, Fischer-Dieskau, London, Hotter, Neidlinger, Frick—Solti. DECCA / LONDON

5. **Bellini, *I Puritani*:** Callas, Cattelani, di Stefano, Panerai, Rossi-Lemeni—Serafin. EMI / ANGEL

6. **Britten, *Peter Grimes*:** Harper, Payne, Bainbridge, Vickers, Summers—Davis. PHILIPS

7. **Mozart, *Le Nozze di Figaro*:** Te Kanawa, Popp, von Stade, Berbié, Kenny, Tear, Allen, Ramey, Moll—Solti. DECCA / LONDON

8. **Giordano, *Andrea Chénier*:** Tebaldi, del Monaco, Bastianini—Gavazzeni. DECCA / LONDON

9. **Donizetti, *Lucia di Lammermoor*:** Sutherland, Pavarotti, Milnes, Ghiaurov—Bonynge. DECCA / LONDON

10. **Strauss, *Der Rosenkavalier*:** Stich-Randall, Schwarzkopf, Ludwig, Wächter, Edelmann—Karajan. EMI / ANGEL

11. ***A Memorable Evening at the Lyric Opera of Chicago***

WOLFGANG AMADEUS MOZART

DIE ENTFÜHRUNG AUS DEM SERAIL (1782)

A: Constanze (s); B: Blonde [Blondchen] (s); C: Belmonte (t);
D: Pedrillo (t); E: Osmin (bs)

We need to try to imagine Mozart at the time of the creation of *Idomeneo* and *Entführung*. He's desperate to prove himself an operatic big-leaguer, but he doesn't yet know his own strength. And so, as he strains with all his compositional might, he's a menace to everyone and everything in his path. It's *all too much*—too much in terms of executant difficulties, and too much in terms of compositional scale. Arias and ensembles extend beyond their readily sustainable length by half again, or even double. Mozart will acknowledge this himself on some level as he slightly trims and simplifies numbers in both operas (five in *Entführung*).

Where *Idomeneo* seems to me a hopeless cause, in *Entführung*, with all the obstacles and frustrations (and we will see shortly how extreme they are), Mozart's operatic voice for the first time explodes beyond the confines of the immediate situation. Who else would have heard in this conventional harem-rescue story such cosmic resonances? The composer's fascination with the inner workings of the human spirit even makes of Osmin far more than a stock comic villain. (All it takes is the depth, resonance, and fluency of, say, Alexander Kipnis's 1931 recording of the brooding entrance song.)

The older recorded editions reflect attempts to tame the structural unwieldiness of *Entführung*—the second act in particular. Belmonte's gorgeous "Wenn der Freude Tränen fliessen," written for the moment when he and Constanze are finally reunited, used to be routinely relo-cated to the start of Act III, in place of the hard-to-bring-off "Ich baue ganz." Sir Thomas Beecham went further, breaking up Constanze's Act II aria logjam by moving "Martern aller Arten" to Act III. (Another approach, taken by 1954 GID, is simply to omit "Traurigkeit.") The modern-day passion for textual inclusiveness has made musically complete versions common, and brought more-than-complete ones as well: 1985 Teldec and 1990 Oiseau-Lyre restore Mozart's own cuts.

As with *The Magic Flute*, the spoken dialogue is heavily (sometimes extremely heavily) edited, but here not much of substance is lost. The all-speaking role of Pasha Selim pretty much disappears from our discussion, I'm afraid. There *are* differences among the recorded interpreters, but there isn't much to say about them.

1950 DECCA / LONDON (M)

Wilma Lipp (A), Emmy Loose (B), Walther Ludwig (C), Peter Klein (D), Endre Koreh (E), Vienna State Opera Chorus, Vienna Philharmonic Orchestra—Josef Krips

You make a set of defensible casting choices, you have on hand the best possible Mozart orchestra and an outstanding Mozart conductor, and what do you get? As it turns out, not all that much. Nobody said life is fair.

By unhappy chance, the opening scene casts the performance in an especially unfavorable light. The Overture is fine, up to the segue into Belmonte's opening aria. As Josef Krips demonstrates throughout the performance, he has a special feeling for the shape of a Mozartian phrase, building in tremendous physical strength and weight that actually propels rather than impedes the flow of the line—note the vitality and momentum of such different kinds of music as the introduction to Belmonte's "Wenn der Freude Tränen fliessen" and the zany Pedrillo-Osmin drinking duet "Vivat Bacchus!"

However, as soon as Belmonte begins to sing, we're in trouble. We have to listen to Belmonte and Osmin sing pretty much uninterruptedly for some twenty minutes, and while both Walther Ludwig and Endre Koreh were singers with undeniable qualities, this music cruelly highlights their shortcomings. Ludwig had made a fair number of pleasant if technically worrisome recordings (including two of Belmonte's arias) in the early thirties, but by 1950s, sensible as his interpretive instincts are, he's not fun to listen to. The voice warms up a bit in Act II, but that doesn't help us here, and Koreh's voluminous but tonally unappealing bass isn't much fun to listen to either.

Wilma Lipp represents the classic Constanze compromise: she can hit the notes, but do we want to hear them? Her thin soprano isn't aggressively unpleasant when it's not under pressure, but when isn't she under pressure in this role? Blondchen also takes a toll on Emmy Loose, who was often capable of giving pleasure in light roles but here almost always sounds strained. Her Pedrillo, Peter Klein, certainly makes an impression with that baritonal gargling sound he produces in the mid-range, but the voice here has no upper range whatever—he has to resort to a limp falsetto.

The spoken dialogue is moderately well done (note: by the singers themselves), in a stagey comic-opera-ish way. The musical text is complete except for the shift of Belmonte's "Wenn der Freude Tränen fliessen" to Act III in place of "Ich baue ganz."

1954 GUILDE INTERNATIONAL DU DISQUE (M)

Marilyn Tyler (A), Helene Petrich (B), John van Kesteren (C), Karl Schiebener (D), August Griebel (E), Cologne Opera Chorus, Cologne Gürzenich Orchestra—Otto Ackermann

This recording is our sleeper. It shouldn't be all that surprising that Otto Ackermann accomplishes what so many better-known conductors didn't; he was, after all, a fine conductor. But he does it with a cast at which we would hardly think to give a second look.

The first thing Ackermann brings to the score, however he came by it, is an almost unmatched dramatic empathy. Guided by it, he accommodates his cast by creating a musical framework that is lightweight tonally but not emotionally, thereby giving his singers opportunities that could hardly exist otherwise.

At the center are a dominating performance by John van Kesteren and an uncommonly persuasive one by Marilyn Tyler. Van Kesteren is operating with the merest slip of a tenor, but it's an attractive slip, spun into lines of lyrical elegance and inquiring innocence. Although he has no extra vocal weight to give, he can create those special glowing emphases of *Belmonte* (e.g., the Act I aria "O wie *ängstlich*, o wie *feurig*") through intensity. As for Tyler, her pleasant light lyric soprano isn't all that remarkable in itself, but more than any other recorded Constanze she finds an expressive need for all the vocal torture tests Mozart bequeathed her. I find myself for once, instead of reflexively dreading her impending solos, actually looking forward to them. Her Blondchen, Helene Petrich, with a somewhat less attractive instrument, finds much the same kind of identification with the writing.

There's nothing special about Karl Schiebener's Pedrillo or August Griebel's Osmin; the latter often sounds more like a baritone than a bass. But they don't let down the show.

The Discophilia LP reissue (in its seventies Ackermann edition) has, in addition to some not very discreet stereo rechanneling, a pervasively peculiar acoustic for the spoken dialogue, with an echo that becomes so pronounced that Pedrillo seems to have taken Osmin to Fafner's cave for their drinking session. One hopes this isn't traceable to the original materials; a good reissue would be welcome.

p.1954 DEUTSCHE GRAMMOPHON (M)

Maria Stader (A), Rita Streich (B), Ernst Häfliger (C), Martin Vantin (D), Josef Greindl (D), RIAS Chamber Chorus and Symphony Orchestra (Berlin)—Ferenc Fricsay

In contrast to 1950 Decca / London, where phrases are lovingly shaped Viennese style, here they are Berlin-molded for maximum strength and handling capacity at advanced speeds. Fricsay leads a dynamic and zestful performance that doesn't exactly solve the opera's difficulties but more or less sweeps them aside. With one of the better-balanced casts, this recording is a strong contender.

The most successful individual contribution is Ernst Häfliger's. This is a straight lyric tenor, but it is used with such fluency and grace as to place this Belmonte at the top of the second group—i.e., those for whom the commanding stature of Wunderlich's performance isn't possible. Maria Stader, although uneven vocally, is such a winning singer that she emerges as one of the most likable Constanzes, and it's nice to have a Blondchen who is more a "different" soprano than a "second" soprano. Rita Streich, too, is occasionally overstressed by the demands of the writing but is still arguably the most spirited Blondchen on records.

Streich and Josef Greindl, the Osmin, speak their own dialogue (all the others have speaking doubles), and Greindl in fact turns in one of the better Osmins on records, even though his vibrato-less bass is no joy to hear. He sings full-out, and applies the same unstinting intelligence that he does to his Wagner roles (an admittedly slowly and painfully acquired taste). It won't do for Sarastro, but for Osmin, well, perhaps. Martin Vantin also has a voice of no real attractiveness, but through energy and determination fulfills at least the basic requirements of Pedrillo.

The sound is a bit muffled even by 1954 standards, but no more so in the not-hard-to-find American Decca LP issue than in the German DG edition.

1956 EMI / ANGEL (S) CD

Lois Marshall (A), Ilse Hollweg (B), Léopold Simoneau (C), Gerhard Unger (D), Gottlob Frick (E), Beecham Choral Society, Royal Philharmonic Orchestra—Thomas Beecham

There are two indispensable performances here: Gottlob Frick's robustly sung Osmin would stand unchallenged until Kurt Moll's quite different effort in 1973 DG, while Gerhard Unger's Pedrillo wasn't matched until Robert Gambill's in 1991 Sony.

As Frick's live performances show, he was capable of letting his tough-timbred bass ooze all over the place, but here he has it under good control, producing a full, directed sound with an appropriate tinge of malevolence imparted by his basic timbre. Unlike so many other basses who also try to *sing* this music, Frick is able to wrap his voice around it; note the tonal ripeness he musters, even at this fairly quick tempo, in the uncomprehending apostrophe to those incomprehensible women-coddling Englishmen ("O Engländer . . .") in the Act II duet with Blondchen. Unger simply sings Pedrillo's music better than anybody else—well, not so "simply," since it's his free, appealing vocalism plus the gusto with which he seizes his vocal opportunities that enable him to create such a diverting, personable character.

Léopold Simoneau certainly brings an attractive lyric tenor to his much admired Belmonte, but I don't get much sense of the character. The Constanze, Lois Marshall, sings on the whole attractively, if ever so carefully—an honest effort at a role that sneers at mere honest efforts. Ilse Hollweg is a competent, somewhat frumpy-sounding Blondchen.

Sir Thomas's *Entführung* strategy seems to be to make the most of every note—the "Turkish" orchestral battery clatters merrily, the strings bounce up a storm in the introduction to Belmonte's "Wenn der Freude," etc. This high-profile conducting might achieve success in operas where the significance of all those notes is more self-evident; in *Entführung*, it achieves a certain generalized energy plus incidental effects. It's no help that a separate cast speaks the (minimal) dialogue, although the voices are tolerably well matched.

As noted in the introduction, Constanze's "Martern aller Arten" is transposed to Act III, following Osmin's "O wie will ich triumphieren," with no dialogue lead-in—no Pasha Selim, no threat of "tortures of all kinds."

1962 ETERNA (S)

Jutta Vulpius (A), Rosemarie Rönisch (B), Rolf Apreck (C), Jürgen Förster (D), Arnold van Mill (E), Dresden State Opera Chorus, Dresden State Orchestra—Otmar Suitner

What is there to say? We have a very good Mozart orchestra under an honorable conductor; fortunately the orchestra will get a real crack at *Entführung* in 1973 DG. The one major singer in the cast, Arnold van Mill, is disappointing—he just can't consistently load the voice into the writing. The others don't disgrace themselves (though the standout performance is probably that of the Pasha, naturally unidentified in the Turnabout LP edition), but you're unlikely to want to hear them more than once.

1965 DEUTSCHE GRAMMOPHON (S)

Erika Köth (A), Lotte Schädle (B), Fritz Wunderlich (C), Friedrich Lenz (D), Kurt Böhme (E), Bavarian State Opera Chorus and Orchestra—Eugen Jochum

The cast for this first uncut *Entführung* undoubtedly wasn't Jochum's dream assemblage, but he doesn't fret over it. He concentrates on getting the best performance he can out of the people at hand, and what he gets is, I think, the best single *Entführung* on records. The performance responds more adroitly than any other to immediate situations. It can be broad and full-bodied (Jochum makes choices as big as Beecham's, but he and his people justify them); it can sustain the gentlest melodic line.

Jochum takes full advantage of the one great singer at his disposal. In the Overture, he phrases the minor-key "B" section expansively, knowing how gorgeously his Belmonte can match this

phrasing when the repetition of "B" not only turns into the major but turns into Belmonte's opening aria. This is probably Wunderlich's most important recording, in that it does so much to define the possibilities of such an important role. With the unflagging ease and ring of the sound, backed up by explosions of color for moments like "O wie ängstlich," and with the singer's generous performing disposition, he takes charge of the opera in a most appealing way. The reinstatement of "Ich baue ganz" is a real gain.

But Jochum is also getting superior performances from his less generously endowed singers. Although you might sooner think of the wiry-toned Erika Köth for Blondchen than for Constanze, she in fact gives a performance of great conviction and sympathy. Kurt Böhme, vocally even less attractive and less limber than 1954 DG's Josef Greindl, also gives a superior performance. In the opening scene, he has found the inner world in which Osmin lives, so that he is truly intruded on by Belmonte and Pedrillo, and an important part of the battle is won. Lotte Schädle and Friedrich Lenz are similarly more alive than many vocally better-endowed Blondchens and Pedrillos.

The singers, rather than obligatorily discharging the spoken dialogue, have found in it enlivening sources for their musical performances.

1966 EMI / ANGEL (S) CD

Anneliese Rothenberger (A), Lucia Popp (B), Nicolai Gedda (C), Gerhard Unger (D), Gottlob Frick (E), Vienna State Opera Chorus, Vienna Philharmonic Orchestra—Josef Krips

Krips's performance, not surprisingly, bears a strong resemblance to his earlier one (1950 Decca / London), though from the orchestral standpoint the earlier is in some ways preferable. The Krips of 1966 is a bit less expansive in his phrasing, perhaps in part because, although he seems determined not to speed up his tempos, a certain pressure can be felt to keep the recording within the confines of four LP sides. In addition, EMI in 1966 was enjoying a rare crack at the Vienna Philharmonic and just didn't get from it the richness of sound that Decca / London was getting even back in 1950.

The cast, however, is a vast improvement over 1950's—it's probably the best balanced of any. The Beecham veterans Unger and Frick, although both reduced of voice after ten years, remain strong competitors. Anneliese Rothenberger generally keeps her attractive lyric soprano in good working order through Constanze's vocal rigors, and Lucia Popp is a vocally poised and dramatically dashing Blondchen. Nicolai Gedda is a fairly effective Belmonte—not quite as commanding as his Ottavio and Tamino with Klemperer, but assertive enough to avoid the role's fatal trap of passivity. (Note that this is the last recording to omit "Ich baue ganz.")

If the performance as a whole doesn't catch fire, its overall competence level warrants consideration. Within the limits suggested above, it sounds fine in the CD edition (better, certainly, than on the old Seraphim LPs).

1967–68 EMI / ANGEL (In English) (S)

Mattiwilda Dobbs (A), Jennifer Eddy (B), Nicolai Gedda (C), John Fryatt (D), Noel Mangin (E), Ambrosian Singers, Bath Festival Orchestra—Yehudi Menuhin

If you particularly want *Entführung* in English, the present translation is workable and the performance is competitive. For all Menuhin's inexperience as an opera conductor, he's hardly alone in not finding what makes this opera tick, and he leads a tidy, stylish performance.

After a discouraging Act I aria, Mattiwilda Dobbs settles in for a nicely sung Constanze. Gedda sings Belmonte well enough but sounds marginally less assured than in 1966; his fans will of course need both, since he didn't get to sing "Ich baue ganz" in the earlier recording. Noel Mangin is another almost-Osmin—he sings reasonably well, but not well enough really to get control of the music. Jennifer Eddy and John Fryatt are a serviceable Blondchen and Pedrillo.

In the dialogue, it's fun to hear a very English Blondchen (who *is* English) harangue Osmin concerning the delicate treatment accorded women in England. But then, Pasha Selim sounds just as English, and our other Turk, Osmin, as well as Pedrillo the Spaniard also sound mightily British, whereas our remaining Spaniards—the American Constanze and the Swedish Belmonte—don't.

1973 DEUTSCHE GRAMMOPHON (S) CD

Arleen Augér (A), Reri Grist (B), Peter Schreier (C), Harald Neukirch (D), Kurt Moll (E), Leipzig Radio Chorus, Dresden State Orchestra—Karl Böhm

Here's another conductor who gets it. The richness of Böhm's phrasing recalls Krips's in 1950 Decca / London, but with a darker and more pensive tinge. His old Dresden cohorts play beautifully for him, and the performance as a whole has a reassuring air of confidence.

The standout performance is Kurt Moll's Osmin, sung with an unforced richness and fullness of sound (and even a suggestion of a trill) that places him very much in the Kipnis class. I used to regret that he is so straitlaced here, since he has performed the role with considerable swagger, but re-encountering the performance I'm glad that we have at least this one wholly unfaked, cliché-free Osmin, which fits nicely with the tone of comic gravity Böhm is working for.

Against expectation, Peter Schreier is also a first-class Belmonte. Given the voice's basic limitations of color, thrust, and upward extension, this is a Belmonte more in the van Kesteren than in the Wunderlich mold, but it's sung with surprising confidence and dash— Schreier even finds his own charming solution for the arduous "Ich baue ganz."

Arleen Augér is another attractive lyric soprano who is overmatched by Constanze but refuses to be overwhelmed, and emerges with relative honor. Reri Grist is a pleasant Blondchen, Harald Neukirch a feisty Pedrillo.

A separate speaking cast is used.

1978 PHILIPS (S) CD

Christiane Eda-Pierre (A), Norma Burrowes (B), Stuart Burrows (C), Robert Tear (D), Robert Lloyd (E), John Alldis Choir, Academy of St. Martin in the Fields—Colin Davis

Almost everything goes wrong here. For one thing, Colin Davis seems truly mystified, and this in an opera where, more than most, the singers must have help from the conductor. Number after number is disassembled for inspection and not put back together.

And the cast has possibilities. Maybe Stuart Burrows couldn't by this date have matched the fine Tamino he had sung some years earlier in Solti's *Magic Flute*, but was he really capable of nothing more than this strained, disorganized runthrough? Robert Tear brings more voice to Pedrillo than anyone else on records, and on other occasions he has done incisive character-tenor work, but this Pedrillo is tentative and uninteresting. Robert Lloyd's excellent sonorous Wagner recordings (Fasolt, Gurnemanz) suggest suitable qualifications for Osmin, but he's never in the picture vocally.

Despite some early tentativeness, Christiane Eda-Pierre sings Constanze quite attractively, although the lightness of the voice allows for little variety. And Norma Burrowes is vocally as assured as any Blondchen on records. Yet neither performance adds up to . . . well, a performance.

The singing and speaking casts are so defiantly mismatched as to suggest deliberate intent.

1978 EURODISC (S) CD

Edita Gruberova (A), Gudrun Ebel (B), Francisco Araiza (C), Norbert Orth (D), Roland Bracht (E), Bavarian Radio Chorus, Munich Radio Orchestra—Heinz Wallberg

The tone is established by the conductor. Wallberg is a conscientious, eyes-front musician who sets plausible, mobile tempos and secures alert, well-balanced orchestral playing, and who has thereby produced perfectly satisfactory accounts of more straightforward operas, but who doesn't seem to notice that *Entführung* doesn't work this way.

And it is certainly not, under normal circumstances, a vehicle for talented but vocally incomplete singers. Edita Gruberova, for one, has passages of heartening fearlessness, but in general, while she is sometimes capable of substantial technical fluency and sometimes capa-

ble of generating personal warmth, she is rarely capable of both, and Constanze insists on both. Roland Bracht, for another, possesses what sounds like a potentially important bass, and he does score some points in Acts II and III, but the voice isn't produced with the rolling freedom to create the impact that he (and we) would clearly like. And Francisco Araiza, for yet another, while he doesn't sing at all badly—better, in fact, than he has often sung since attaining stardom—can't or doesn't do anything about the vocal thickness that limits his mobility. (Wallberg, however, delivers the zippiest accompaniment to "Ich baue ganz" that I've heard.)

Gudrun Ebel is an earnest Blondchen. Norbert Orth, the Pedrillo, has a beefy chest voice, which he tries to complete by shouting up and over the break.

The (extensive) spoken dialogue is performed by a separate cast almost as brazenly mismatched as that of 1978 Philips. Ebel in particular is saddled with a sort of German Hermione Gingold.

p.1985 TELDEC (S,D) CD

Yvonne Kenny (A), Lillian Watson (B), Peter Schreier (C), Wilfried Gahmlich (D), Matti Salminen (E), Zurich Opera House Chorus and Mozart Orchestra—Nikolaus Harnoncourt

This is a tough call. The performance has attractive qualities but once again hasn't quite located the opera in there trying to get out.

Harnoncourt was at this point just poised to break free of his Pedantic Period; he still felt obliged to justify everything he did with reference to some book he had read. Here, some of his research produces interesting results. He has come up with the most gloriously clangorous Turkish battery I've heard, and his restoration of the original piccolo part—generally an octave higher—adds a delightfully piquant flavor. Less productive is his discovery of numerous indicated tempo fluctuations, which leads him to play the fluctuations rather than find the inner need for either the "before" or the "after" tempo. As a whole, however, setting theory aside, the performance has a solid, durable lyric flow that

I sometimes find quite wholesomely pleasing, at least for a while. But again, neither the conductor nor the singers have tapped into the opera's underlying flow.

Under the circumstances, the opening of Mozart's cuts in both of Blondchen's arias, Constanze's "Martern aller Arten," and Belmonte's "Wenn der Freude" and "Ich baue ganz" is of primarily archival interest. (There are distinctive twists in all the excised chunks.) Note that four of these arias are in Act II, which is thus performed at its full original length, and at generally moderate pace to boot. It helps you understand why so many custodians of the score, beginning with the composer, have sought to bring this act down to more manageable size.

We have yet another pair of very nice sopranos who cause no pain while they're singing but who leave no impression in the imagination. Schreier is okay but closer to expectation than in 1973 DG: vocally less secure, dramatically less focused. Wilfried Gahmlich is a game but unremarkable Pedrillo. Matti Salminen produces a stream of impressive bass sound, but his yawny mode of articulation seems to me especially problematic for Osmin.

The singers speak their own dialogue.

1984–85 DECCA/LONDON (S,D) CD

Edita Gruberova (A), Kathleen Battle (B), Gösta Winbergh (C), Heinz Zednik (D), Martti Talvela (E), Vienna State Opera Chorus, Vienna Philharmonic Orchestra—Georg Solti

Anyone who knows and loves *Entführung* will marvel at Solti's adroitness. He makes big choices (nobody plays the *sinfonia concertante* introduction to "Martern aller Arten" more beautifully) but carefully avoids the opera's pitfalls, never pushing or stretching more than the music will bear, however enticing the immediate temptations. Unfortunately, the result is a performance that tends to be constantly *not* doing things, and this is not a cast equipped or inclined to take action on its own.

Gruberova's Constanze is more of a piece than in 1978 Eurodisc, but this means that the more attractively assertive moments are flattened out. Gösta Winbergh is another Belmonte

who doesn't rise to the crucial challenges of the opening scene, where he sounds stiff and labored. Later the voice sounds better—"Wenn der Freude" is quite nice.

Martti Talvela is a lumbering Osmin, Kathleen Battle a perky Blondchen—if you enjoy that sort of thing. Heinz Zednik can sing Pedrillo, and does so without indulging in standard shtick, but much as we may applaud the eschewal of bad clichés, this ought not to be confused with the making of creative choices.

The singers speak their own dialogue.

1990 L'OISEAU-LYRE (S,D) CD

Lynne Dawson (A), Marianne Hirsti (B), Uwe Heilmann (C), Wilfried Gahmlich (D), Günter von Kannen (E), Academy of Ancient Music Chorus and Orchestra—Christopher Hogwood

There is one powerful attraction here: the Belmonte of Uwe Heilmann. The voice isn't as robust as Wunderlich's, but it has some magic of its own. He produces a beautiful flowing line with some real command of dynamics—a lovely piece of singing.

Unfortunately, during Belmonte's long absence in Act II, further lengthened here by the restoration of Mozart's cuts, I find myself mostly reflecting on what a really long time it has been since we heard that nice Belmonte fellow. The other singers aren't that awful, and the music isn't amateurishly enervated as it so often is in Hogwood performances. But no audible effort has been made to deal with the real musical problems of this score. Of course the use of period instruments provides a built-in excuse for drab, inexpressive playing (1985 Teldec is a better place to hear the piccolo part and some unholy clatter for the Turkish battery). Strangely, this quality seems almost deliberately to have been carried over into the singing.

As Constanze, Lynne Dawson, with what sounds like it could be a useful light soprano, manages so consistently—despite the hugely varied conditions of the role—to produce the same blank, inexpressive sound that she appears deliberately to have chosen to sing this way. Marianne Hirsti, making a somewhat blunter sound, is otherwise distinctly similar. One performance does stick out, but the plainness of his colleagues may be responsible: on rechecking, Wilfried Gahmlich's Pedrillo turns out to be very much the same as in 1985 Teldec ("game but unremarkable"). Günter von Kannen has a bass of some size and weight but doesn't get much singing quality out of it.

Once again, these aren't the people one wants to hear sing the longer versions of the arias abridged by Mozart; even Heilmann is done no favor by the restorations. Hogwood also includes a zany little march (included in the Neue Mozart Ausgabe edition) for the entrance of Pasha Selim in Act I. It's charmingly goofy, but its leisurely character belies the urgency with which Pedrillo has hustled Belmonte off, and it makes the ensuing Janissaries' chorus, which has always worked perfectly well as the entrance music, seem redundant. (The "little" march is also *longer* than the chorus.)

1991 SONY (S,D) CD

Cheryl Studer (A), Elzbieta Szmytka (B), Kurt Streit (C), Robert Gambill (D), Günther Missenhardt (E), Vienna State Opera Chorus, Vienna Symphony Orchestra—Bruno Weil

Pay no attention to the billing: CHERYL STUDER andsomeotherpeople. Studer is in fact just swell, but it's the generally high quality of the cast, combined with the vigor and general coherence of the conducting, that makes this recording a strong contender.

Bruno Weil is known for his work with period instruments but fortunately isn't using them here, because there's no way he could have achieved the bold, buoyant, richly textured wind playing he gets from the Vienna Symphony. His approach is generally outgoing and forward-driving, which isn't a bad idea. Like Fricsay, he doesn't allow the proceedings to bog down, and he does it with a more supple touch.

In the cast, the American contingent makes a strong showing. Studer slurs the higher *fioritura* a bit, but even there she is actually singing

the notes, and the performance as a whole is impressively sung and has spirit. Kurt Streit's Belmonte is better than his very likable *Così* Ferrando with Barenboim. Not only is the voice a pleasure to listen to, but it proves capable of some real firmness of line. This is one of the best Belmontes on records. And Robert Gambill as Pedrillo sings better than many of the Belmontes. The high As in "Frisch zum Kampfe" are a reach, but he and Weil do a bang-up job with it, and the Act III serenade pulses with color.

Elzbieta Szmytka's Polish accent is a nice stand-in for Blondchen's English one, and she completes the lovers' quartet fairly well. Although she's caught short a bit in "Welche Wonne" by rapid-fire phrases from the mid-range up, the voice in general has a distinctive color and some useful bite. The one disappointment is Günther Missenhardt's Osmin. There's decent vocal material here, and he holds up his end of the show, but you wouldn't guess the role's true vocal and dramatic importance.

A nice touch: separate track cues are consistently provided for spoken dialogue and musical numbers.

The arrival of 1991 Sony alters and simplifies the *Entführung* picture. You could get remarkably comprehensive coverage by combining its boldly extroverted approach and strong soprano-tenor quartet with the more introspective 1973 DG and its strong Osmin. My own all-around favorite recording is probably still 1965 DG, with nods to 1954 GID and 1954 DG. Which still leaves 1966 EMI for its balanced cast, and 1956 EMI for Frick and Unger. And then there's 1985 Teldec for its special qualities, and 1990 Oiseau-Lyre for its special quality (the Belmonte).

KENNETH FURIE

Unavailable for review:
1991 DEUTSCHE GRAMMOPHON ARCHIVE

WOLFGANG AMADEUS MOZART

LE NOZZE DI FIGARO (1786)

A: Countess Almaviva (s); B: Susanna (s); C: Cherubino (s or ms); D: Marcellina (s or ms); E: Barbarina (s); F: Basilio (t); G: Count Almaviva (bar); H: Figaro (bar or bs); I: Bartolo (bs)

Throughout the nineteenth century and well into the twentieth, *Le Nozze di Figaro* was seldom performed outside German-speaking countries. Stendhal called it "a sublime mixture of wit and melancholy, which has no equal"; but the romantic age was not listening, for it had little interest in Mozart apart from *Don Giovanni*. The long shadow cast by that age almost eclipsed the sweet humanity of the rationalistic *Figaro* until the 1930s. During the reign of Gatti-Casazza at the Metropolitan Opera, for example, *Figaro* was mounted for Gustav Mahler in 1908–09, revived in 1916–17 for two seasons under Artur Bodanzky, and was not heard again until Edward Johnson gave it a new production in 1940. *Figaro* has earned popular international success in just a little over fifty years, and is regarded by many as the most perfect opera ever composed.

1934–35 EMI / ANGEL (M)

Aulikki Rautavaara (A), Audrey Mildmay (B), Luise Helletsgruber (C), Constance Willis (D), Winifred Radford (E), Heddle Nash (F), Roy Henderson (G), Willi Domgraf-Fassbänder (H), Norman Allin / Italo Tajo (I), Glyndebourne Festival Chorus and Orchestra—Fritz Busch

A major influence on the Met—and on several European companies during the thirties—to return *Figaro* to repertory was the enormous success of the opera at the first Glyndebourne Festival in 1934, followed by the worldwide currency of the critically acclaimed recording by HMV. Anticipating small sales, HMV recorded a cut version of the opera and sold the result by subscription via the Mozart Opera Society, dividing the records into three albums to make it easier for a depression-pinched public to consider purchase. The recording turned out to be a steady seller, has seldom been out of print, and it is still available on two Pearl CDs. Its sound, warm and agreeably balanced though quite restricted in range, conveys well enough the high spirits and musicality of an impressively rehearsed ensemble animated by Fritz Busch's energy, style, and tempos. Some of the roles seem under-characterized by today's standards, some want vocal enrichment; and there is hardly a suggestion of revolutionary menace. It has no value as one of two or three desert-island *Figaro*s; but, once heard, one does not easily forget the ebullient charm and wit of Willi Domgraf-Fassbänder's Figaro, the *demi-sourire* of Heddle Nash's Basilio, or the rhythmic vitality and lively inflection of line that Luise Helletsgruber brings to Cherubino's music.

1940 MET (M,P)

Elisabeth Rethberg (A), Licia Albanese (B), Jarmila Novotna (C), Irra Petina (D), Marita Farell (E), Alessio de Paolis (F), John Brownlee (G), Ezio Pinza (H), Salvatore Baccaloni (I), Metropolitan Opera Chorus and Orchestra—Ettore Panizza

Bracingly robust and exuberant, this performance reflects the taste of Ettore Panizza for light textures, rhythmic snap, prompt attack, and lithe delivery of words and music that characterized the Met production throughout its honorable life, not withstanding subsequent changes of cast and musical leadership. There are some cuts, most of them in the last act—Marcellina-Figaro and Barbarina recitatives, the arias of Marcellina and Basilio.

The cast is strong and typical, except for its Susanna. For all her good will and usual commitment, Licia Albanese is uncomfortable in Mozart. In lightening her voice to negotiate the rapid passages, she pinches her tone, sounds unnatural, and is sometimes approximate in pitch. She is nonetheless free of coyness and vocal faking, and gives a cunningly shaded account of her aria. Now past her prime (note the loosened vibrato and struggle with pitch at her entrance), Elisabeth Rethberg still conveys a noble Countess with the grandeur of her recitative and aria "Dove sono," passionately projected with no self-pity, begun magically *piano* and concluded with determined resolve. Jarmila Novotna, an endearingly impulsive page, ever musical, rhythmically alive, offers a particularly fresh and radiant "Voi che sapete," gracefully supported by Panizza. Irra Petina is the perfect Marcellina, deliciously malicious in conflict; her changes in mood during the sextet, as she discovers that Figaro is her long-lost son, are masterstrokes of comic timing. The male singers, however, are the glory of this set, above all Ezio Pinza. His rich and flexible *basso cantante*, verbal clarity, and dramatic penetration—wit, irony, guile, stubbornness, manly charm in equipoise—are matchless when measured against his recorded competitors. John Brownlee, aristocratic, frustrated, testy, alert in recitative as in song, was the Met's Almaviva during much of the life of this production. A stalwart veteran of Glyndebourne, he is an admirable Mozart singer. A little less than amorous in the garden scene perhaps, he is dramatically apt elsewhere, especially telling in his solo in the third act (hear the bite in "servo mio") despite some vocal insecurity near its end. This performance documents the Met debut of

Salvatore Baccaloni, the possessor of a velvety bass, impeccable diction, and a *buffo* personality greatly admired by his public. He is a Bartolo with humanity and bluster who relishes every word of his part. This off-the-air product, though flat in perspective, is almost always clear in sound—at its best in the garden scene, elsewhere slightly deficient in bass and sometimes harsh in the high frequencies.

1950 EMI / ANGEL (M) CD

Elisabeth Schwarzkopf (A), Irmgard Seefried (B), Sena Jurinac (C), Elisabeth Höngen (D), Rosl Schwaiger (E), Erich Majkut (F), George London (G), Erich Kunz (H), Marjan Rus (I), Vienna State Opera Chorus and Vienna Philharmonic Orchestra—Herbert von Karajan

One had expected more from EMI. Herbert von Karajan, who leads the Viennese forces, strives for brilliant effect with overly fast tempos, many of which are uncomfortable for his starry cast of singers. A number of passages in the great finales to Acts II and IV are afflicted with mannered dynamics and tempos, some so quick the ensemble must scramble to keep together and words become unintelligible. The delightfully bitchy duet involving Susanna and Marcellina and the trio "Susanna, or via sortite" are also races without winners. One such number followed directly by another without intervening recitative destroys any feeling of dramatic action.

Another irritant is the bad old Viennese habit of pecking at rather than singing the notes, displayed in master-class fashion by Irmgard Seefried, the Susanna, and to lesser extent by Elisabeth Schwarzkopf, in the pink of vocal health as the Countess, with a memorable last half of "Porgi amor" and a mostly appealing "Dove sono." Both ladies are occasionally overcome by a rash of the "cutes" as their arch account of the letter duet attests. Seefried, in recompense, is convincingly seductive in "Crudel! perchè finora" and quite charming in her aria, once she has skipped through its recitative. In the context of this recording, happy memories of Erich Kunz's lovable Figaro in the theater are apt to slip a bit out of focus. His presence is most palpable in the last act, perhaps the high point of the performance. As Cherubino, Sena Jurinac offers a nice helping of her vocal cream to offset her still callow Mozartian manners. The young George London is the Almaviva—fierce, impassioned, but insufficiently libidinous, somewhat blustery, and, in the end, more proletarian than aristocrat.

1951 CETRA (M)

Gabriella Gatti (A), Alda Noni (B), Jolanda Gardino (C), Miti Truccato Pace (D), Graziella Sciutti (E), Angelo Mercuriali (F), Sesto Bruscantini (G), Italo Tajo (H), Fernando Corena (I), Italian Radio Chorus and Orchestra, Rome— Fernando Previtali

The Cetra set's sound is not so well balanced as EMI's, nor is the performance as good. One suspects the reason it was issued at all (it disappeared quickly) was its inclusion of some of the *secco* recitatives. Previtali's conducting is innocent of anything one could call Mozartian and deficient in expression. The Cherubino, Marcellina, and Basilio are poor. The attractive voices of Gabriella Gatti and Alda Noni, the strong characterization of Sesto Bruscantini (an Almaviva barbarously deprived of his aria), Italo Tajo as a servant to be taken seriously, Fernando Corena's Bartolo, and a glimpse of the very young Graziella Sciutti as Barbarina might appear to be sufficient compensation for this recording's defects. They are not.

1955 EMI / ANGEL (M) CD

Sena Jurinac (A), Graziella Sciutti (B), Risë Stevens (C), Monica Sinclair (D), Jeannette Sinclair (E), Hugues Cuénod (F), Franco Calabrese (G), Sesto Bruscantini (H), Ian Wallace (I), Glyndebourne Festival Chorus and Orchestra—Vittorio Gui

EMI returned to Glyndebourne in 1955 for its first *Figaro* recorded on tape. A presiding Italian conductor, Vittorio Gui, and three Italian singers in the cast promise a care for the words almost always honored. The musical preparation and ensemble are what one would expect, considering the source. And yet, the performance, effective in individual numbers

here and there, does not inscribe a firm musical arch nor maintain a rising dramatic trajectory. Gui seems to skate over the second-act finale, for example.

Sena Jurinac, new to the role of the Countess, is ravishing in tone but without the consistent vitality in recitative or the grandeur she later achieved in her two arias. A high bass rather than the baritone appropriate to the Count, Franco Calabrese struggles with the upper reaches of his part and omits the high F-sharp in his aria. His dark voice is attractive, his portrayal ardent and aristocratic, but his "Contessa, perdono" is begun too loudly. The servant lovers are Graziella Sciutti and Sesto Bruscantini, both spirited with a smile in their voices. One quickly understands why Sciutti was the dominant Susanna in smaller theaters for twenty years. Bruscantini is a little light in the lower tonal fundamentals for Figaro and misses the irony and rage implicit in his last-act aria. Cherubino is taken by a Glyndebourne veteran (class of 1939), who was the first page of the 1940 Met production, Risë Stevens. By this time, her rich mezzo is a bit heavier, a little less flexible than is ideal for the part, and she is not always scrupulous about dynamics; but she is still dramatically persuasive. Most memorable of all is Hugues Cuénod, the quintessential dirty old man, a Basilio so outstanding he is rewarded with his usually omitted aria. The supporting cast is good, and the warm recording favors the voices.

1955 EMI / ANGEL (M,P) CD

Teresa Stich-Randall (A), Rita Streich (B), Pilar Lorengar (C), Christiane Gayraud (D), Madeleine Ignal (E), Hugues Cuénod (F), Heinz Rehfuss (G), Rolando Panerai (H), Marcello Cortis (I), Aix-en-Provence Festival Chorus and Orchestra—Hans Rosbaud

This recording, live from the festival at Aix-en-Provence, has bleak and steely sound. Recitatives are accompanied by piano rather than harpsichord, and there is nary a vocal ornament to be heard. The conductor is Hans Rosbaud, cool, stingy in expression, but impressively analytical.

Rolando Panerai, lively as a cricket as Figaro, offers a most impressive "Aprite un po' quegl' occhi." Charming in a less mature way, without the spunkiness all great Susannas possess, Rita Streich, though pleasing in her two arias and musically secure in ensemble, is inadequate. The voice of Heinz Rehfuss, with its darkness and weight closer to the requirements of Figaro than Almaviva (he, too, ducks the high note in his aria), does suggest the menace and force if not the elegance of the nobleman. A much admired Mozartian in her day (especially in middle Europe), Teresa Stich-Randall, an American, was brought to the attention of a large public via Toscanini's broadcast performances of *Aida* and *Falstaff*. On this particular evening, she was inconsistent. Her musicality, her phrasing and pointed rhythm are often arresting and she is splendid in ensemble, but there are some aspirates in her opening aria and a couple of trouble spots in her second. The young Pilar Lorengar as Cherubino provides a welcome warmth of expression with her fresh, vivid soprano, secure except for a hint of flutter in "Voi che sapete." Hugues Cuénod is on hand again for another masterful Basilio, this time without his aria.

1955 DECCA / LONDON (S) CD

Lisa della Casa (A), Hilde Gueden (B), Suzanne Danco (C), Hilde Rössl-Majdan (D), Anny Felbermayer (E), Murray Dickie (F), Alfred Poell (G), Cesare Siepi (H), Fernando Corena (I), Vienna State Opera Chorus and Vienna Philharmonic Orchestra—Erich Kleiber

From Vienna at the dawn of stereo came a *Figaro*—the first to be presented complete—that remains to this day one of the most authoritative, persuasive, and lovable accounts on records. Despite a consistent hum (mostly eliminated in its CD transfer), somewhat bass-heavy sonics, and restricted dynamic range, the engineering conjures up the sweet sound of the Vienna Philharmonic's strings and winds and uses the stereo sound stage to enhance the theatrical energy of this magically flowing performance inspired by its conductor, Erich Kleiber, everywhere vital, Olympian, serene.

As it should be, the drama is sprung by the servants. Charming, resourceful, never at a loss even when desperate, this Susanna, really sung by Hilde Gueden, makes things happen. She is as forceful in recitative as in her arias and alive in ensemble. Cesare Siepi is the Figaro, a worthy successor to Pinza, his bass lightened and forward, easy in *legato*. His "Se vuol ballare" bites rather than barks. The aristocrats may not be ideal, but neither do they let anyone down. Lisa della Casa, a bit languid from time to time, sings with beauty of tone (what a lovely, full-throated letter duet with Gueden), but there is scarcely a touch of anguish in her "Dove sono." Her Countess gives much satisfaction, but she goes beyond that in the RCA recording four years later. A distressing German accent is Alfred Poell's burden, but he wins his audience in the end by virtue of his admirable vocal quality, musicality, and ensemble spirit. Suzanne Danco's crystalline soprano does not leap to mind when contemplating the required voice for Cherubino. Nevertheless, she almost succeeds by dint of her impressive musical style and gift for portraiture. Neither the enthusiasm of the recitative to her first aria nor her sweetly sung "Voi che sapete" is easily forgotten. The remainder of the cast is best basic Vienna for its day: Hilde Rössl-Majdan, the Marcellina, wrongly deprived of her aria (which is inexplicably allotted to Gueden), Fernando Corena, about to become the world's most famous *buffo* (with good reason), Murray Dickie, a sly Basilio (a little strained in his aria), and Anny Felbermayer as Barbarina, singing her brief number to Kleiber's bewitching, nocturnal F-minor accompaniment.

1956 PHILIPS (M)

Sena Jurinac (A), Rita Streich (B), Christa Ludwig (C), Ira Malaniuk (D), Rosl Schwaiger (E), Erich Majkut (F), Paul Schöffler (G), Walter Berry (H), Vienna State Opera Chorus and Vienna Symphony Orchestra—Karl Böhm

With Karl Böhm's first commercial recording of *Figaro* we come to the last of the monophonic issues in this survey. Taped in Vienna's Brahmssaal, the sound has a rather flat perspective through most of the first half of the opera. Commencing with "Susanna, via sortite," a new setup appears to have been employed that yields more hall ambience and a greater sense of presence. The performance seems afflicted with a heaviness of thought that begins with the conducting, resulting in sustained periods of theatrical blackout (e.g., from the Count's entrance through the end of the first act, from the beginning of the second-act finale up to Antonio's appearance with his broken pot of carnations). There is not much fun in the sextet, and lovely singing in the letter duet is vitiated by stodgy rhythm. At this time Böhm is not the capable Mozartian one hears in his 1967 recording of the same opera for Deutsche Grammophon.

Outstanding in this cast is Sena Jurinac, delighting with her steady tone shaped into more subtly inflected phrases and her livelier approach to the recitatives. Rita Streich is heard to better advantage in her second Susanna—if not very witty, at least not coy, with a memorable recitative to her last-act aria most pleasingly rendered. A youthful and appealing Christa Ludwig is ever so romantic as Cherubino; hear her sigh "un desio" in her first number. Walter Berry provides a well-sung, good-natured Figaro. Trying to cope with a tessitura uncomfortably high, Paul Schöffler, his *Heldenbariton* still handsome in its middle register, offers a nobleman *d'un certain âge*, too reserved to create a proper sense of opposition but able to impress here and there.

1959 RCA / BMG (S)

Lisa della Casa (A), Roberta Peters (B), Rosalind Elias (C), Sandra Warfield (D), Anny Felbermayer (E), Gabor Carelli (F), George London (G), Giorgio Tozzi (H), Fernando Corena (I), Vienna State Opera Chorus and Orchestra—Erich Leinsdorf

The RCA sonics are quite compelling—open, airy, well balanced with theatrical atmosphere. The conducting is brisk, shipshape, and often superficial in thoughtful soliloquy and in most of the deeply expressive passages. The singing is

uncommonly good, but more than a few comic points are permitted to be driven home with a sledgehammer, particularly by Sandra Warfield (Marcellina) and Fernando Corena (Bartolo). A lively Susanna—a bit brassy here and there—excellently sung by Roberta Peters, is probably this artist's most cherishable recorded souvenir. The same may be said of Rosalind Elias, whose art and dusky mezzo are most appealing in a generously communicative Cherubino, as effective in recitative as in her beautifully sung arias. Lisa della Casa, a more characterful Countess than before, sings "Porgi amor" with special radiance. "Dove sono" and the letter duet, almost as well sung, are diminished by glib accompaniment. There is a smile in Giorgio Tozzi's rich, fluent bass difficult to resist, but one wants more from a Figaro. Nine years after his first recorded Count, George London is much more effective in recitative. He has learned to lighten his voice, minimizing its tendency to thickness. His aria boils with rage, but he still begins "Contessa perdono" too loudly. Fernando Corena offers a ripely sung "Vendetta" that reveals the face of Bartolo himself. Gabor Carelli doubles in the roles of Don Basilio and Don Curzio, the former poisonous, both impressively inflected.

1959 EMI / ANGEL (S) CD

Elisabeth Schwarzkopf (A), Anna Moffo (B), Fiorenza Cossotto (C), Dora Gatta (D), Elisabetta Fusco (E), Renato Ercolani (F), Eberhard Wächter (G), Giuseppe Taddei (H), Ivo Vinco (I), Philharmonia Chorus and Orchestra—Carlo Maria Giulini

For vocal splendor and textual clarity, the 1959 Angel cast is probably the best of all competing versions. (And it is expertly recorded with separation that suggests movement onstage.) Certainly all three of the leading ladies are heard at something near high noon in their careers. Elisabeth Schwarzkopf has become regal, effortless in seamless delivery of the long phrases in her arias, proud and lively, yet vulnerable—without a trace of anything wimpish, soppy, or masochistic. Such a magisterial portrayal runs the risk of overshadowing the Susanna. Not to worry. Anna Moffo, her shining soprano at its smoothest and sweetest, her musical manners, her spunk and charm conquering all vicissitudes, is a peerless Susanna, Mozart's irrepressible, lovable survivor. The young Fiorenza Cossotto is a deliciously impulsive Cherubino. Vivacious in recitative and song, she seems to taste the words of her first aria, and for once "Voi che sapete" is really sexy. The men are almost of equal excellence. With his dark, mature baritone (his lowest notes are a little weak) and personal sparkle, Giuseppe Taddei is cheeky enough to let us know the Count is overmatched. Brilliantly acid in his aria about the untrustworthiness of women, he is just as effective in reconciliation ("Pace, pace, mio dolce tesoro"). Eberhard Wächter uses his bright, manly baritone to convey an Almaviva appropriately febrile, scheming, and lusting. In an unusually well-shaded performance, he even manages to sound tender in "Crudel! perchè finora." Ivo Vinco, with his dark, handsome bass and forceful approach, proclaims his Bartolo as someone not to be underestimated. As both Don Basilio and Don Curzio, Renato Ercolani is quiet, making of everything a conspiracy. Dora Gatta is a smooth and able Marcellina.

Giulini has prepared his forces with care and intelligence. His tempos are sensible and supportive. He is attentive to dynamic considerations; rhythms are well pointed. His care with orchestral chording discloses harmonic splendors too often glossed over. He favors a richer sound palette than some will find ideal. Such fastidiousness is always welcome. It helps to obscure this stony reality: Giulini's conducting is mostly sober and joyless. One can only dream about the *Figaro* one might have had with this cast under Erich Kleiber's direction.

1960 DEUTSCHE GRAMMOPHON (S) CD

Maria Stader (A), Irmgard Seefried (B), Hertha Töpper (C), Lilian Benningsen (D), Rösl Schwaiger (E), Paul Kuen (F), Dietrich Fischer-Dieskau (G), Renato Capecchi (H), Ivan Sardi (I), RIAS Chamber Choir and Berlin Radio Symphony Orchestra—Ferenc Fricsay

Ferenc Fricsay, with a number of good recordings to his credit, including a first-rate *Entführung aus dem Serail*, was selected by DG to lead its first *Figaro*. In an effort to inject theatrical life into its recording, the producers, intending that no listener should miss a dramatic point, encouraged excursions into the land of ham. The worst offenders were, of course, the three singers with the most imagination: Renato Capecchi, Dietrich Fischer-Dieskau, and Irmgard Seefried. One of the better party arias is Capecchi's "Non più andrai," a riot of smirks, giggles, and rolled Rs. Seefried, in very good voice this late in her career, pokes and pecks at the recitatives and exaggerates whenever possible elsewhere. Fischer-Dieskau is a caricature of himself; he blusters, whispers, and proves that he can be king of the explosive phrase. That the Count ultimately became one of his most celebrated roles in the theater is a matter of record; just compare this one and his next (for DG under Böhm) eight years later. The remainder of the cast is bland. The veteran Hertha Töpper's overripe sound is too mature and feminine for Cherubino, her *portamento* excessive, her rhythm sometimes loose. The brilliant, forward tone of Maria Stader, as attractive as ever, is deployed in an instrumental manner, leaving the listener with a lifeless Countess. Fricsay actually has his moments, with harmonies relished and inner parts revealed. The Berlin Radio Symphony plays well enough, and DG's recording has the solidity, balance, and luster that made the company famous during the sixties. The score is presented complete except for the Marcellina and Basilio arias.

1968 DEUTSCHE GRAMMOPHON (S) CD

Gundula Janowitz (A), Edith Mathis (B), Tatiana Troyanos (C), Patricia Johnson (D), Barbara Vogel (E), Erwin Wohlfahrt (F), Dietrich Fischer-Dieskau (G), Hermann Prey (H), Peter Lagger (I), Deutsche Oper Chorus and Orchestra, Berlin—Karl Böhm

Karl Böhm's second recording of *Figaro* in 1968, abetted by the ensemble of the Deutsche Oper in Berlin, is better paced and pointed than before, altogether lighter and more vivacious. DG's engineering produces clear, crisp sonics. Outstanding in an international cast is the Swiss soprano Edith Mathis as Susanna, animated, alluring, in the bloom of vocal health. Gundula Janowitz, with whom Mathis sings an especially winning letter duet, displays beauty of tone, exemplary attack, and lively musical response. She brings to the Countess a becoming patrician quality, despite some softness in enunciation. Hermann Prey, sweet-toned, zestful, bright, and friendly, a Figaro threatening to none, has the best Italian diction among the predominantly German-speaking players. Fischer-Dieskau, in top voice, gives the listener a full-length portrait of the Count, keeping bluster at bay except at the end of his aria. He alone among the cast draws attention to the social tensions of the play. Tatiana Troyanos has the right dramatic ideas but not the tight, youthful spin on the voice that suits Cherubino best. A great Mime, but a too-Teutonic Basilio, Erwin Wohlfahrt is disappointing except in his aria. Patricia Johnson, a lively Marcellina, excellent in florid passages, gives a sterling account of hers. The Bartolo, Peter Lagger, phrases well enough but brays whenever he reaches E.

1970 EMI / ANGEL (S) CD

Elisabeth Söderström (A), Reri Grist (B), Teresa Berganza (C), Annelies Burmeister (D), Margaret Price (E), Werner Hollweg (F), Gabriel Bacquier (G), Geraint Evans (H), Michael Langdon (I), John Alldis Choir and Philharmonia Orchestra—Otto Klemperer

Otto Klemperer, finally a gramophone star in the late autumn of his career, is the conductor of this EMI version. At once captivating and perverse, his tempos produce the slowest of all recorded *Figaros* and devitalize many an energetic number, not least the nervous and intense second-act finale. On the other hand, assisted by superb recording, he digs deep into the score, exposing detail often smudged or obscured in routine renditions. Klemperer's reaction to this wonderful score is that of a clockmaker. He takes the clock apart for his audience, puts it back together, lovingly, with care. His unhurried demonstration fascinates, but when it is over, the clock does not keep the right time.

The art, ebullience, and theatrical savvy of Geraint Evans (Figaro) and Gabriel Bacquier (Count) tend to compensate for the absence of youthful vocal quality. Reri Grist is eloquent in song and convincing in her ingratiating impersonation of Susanna. Humane, warm, intense, and musical, Elisabeth Söderström touches the heart as the Countess, even though long-breathed phrases are effortful. Teresa Berganza, her femininity thinly disguised, is in luscious voice as Cherubino. Michael Langdon is a sonorous Bartolo, strained by Klemperer's tempo for his aria, *allegretto* at best instead of the required *allegro con spirito*. Annelies Burmeister (Marcellina) and Werner Hollweg (Basilio), able enough, get to sing their arias. Two sopranos in small parts foreshadow future glory: Margaret Price as Barbarina and Kiri Te Kanawa as one of the two peasant girls.

1971 PHILIPS (S) CD

Jessye Norman (A), Mirella Freni (B), Yvonne Minton (C), Maria Casula (D), Lillian Watson (E), Robert Tear (F), Ingvar Wixell (G), Wladimiro Ganzarolli (H), Clifford Grant (I), BBC Symphony Chorus and Orchestra—Colin Davis

The Philips set, magnificently conducted by Colin Davis, is hardly the most satisfying recording of *Le Nozze di Figaro* in terms of vocal achievement, but dramatically it is fascinating and unique. Presented complete, the usual order of numbers in the third act has been altered. Based on the belief that Bartolo and Antonio were performed by the same singer in Mozart's day, the brief Barbarina / Cherubino dialogue and the grand recitative and aria for the Countess precede the sextet. The recording, which favors the orchestra, is odd. A living sound stage is the producer's aim; players can be followed—left, right, down- and upstage— but there is a sacrifice: the voices are sometimes off mike; when they are, they lose body, sound hollow and out of focus, and can be irritating.

In no other competing recording is one so aware of the conflict between master and servants. Attentive preparation is apparent in the Overture, scrupulously clean in reading and in execution. Susanna and Figaro inhabit a dangerous, grown-up world, as their first two duets attest. There is nothing jolly about "Se a caso madama." The predominant feeling is apprehension: looking over the shoulder, taking the trouble to be quiet; the edge of fear is being overheard. Wladimiro Ganzarolli sounds older than the Figaros one is apt to encounter—his bass rather dry and short at the top—and Mirella Freni, a little off mike, sounds worn. All the same, Ganzarolli is never less than passionate and precise in expression and Freni improves as the opera continues, becoming the dominant presence in the drama. Her arias go far beyond vocalise, her "Deh vieni, non tardar" amorally sensuous. Jessye Norman, direct, dignified, and rich of voice, is an affecting Countess who avoids cheap effects. She is not always even on pitch, and is sometimes breathy, but she always gives a good idea of the role's tensions. Ingvar Wixell's baritone, not elegant and satiny as one would like, often imperfectly focused, nevertheless tells us a good part of what one needs to know about the Count; it oozes rage and frustration. Yvonne Minton makes little impression as Cherubino, but perhaps the role slips through the cracks in a production emphasizing class conflict. The remaining characters are well taken by Clifford Grant, a serious Bartolo, Maria Casula, a squally but effective Marcellina, and Robert Tear, a convincing Basilio. The harpsichordist John Constable, who provides such witty *continuo*, must not go unnoticed.

1976 EMI / ANGEL (S) ℗

Heather Harper (A), Judith Blegen (B), Teresa Berganza (C), Birgit Finnila (D), Elizabeth Gale (E), John Fryatt (F), Dietrich Fischer-Dieskau (G), Geraint Evans (H), William McCue (I), John Alldis Choir and English Chamber Orchestra—Daniel Barenboim

EMI's issue of 1976 with an ensemble led with sensitivity by Daniel Barenboim has the confidence and polish that comes from performances onstage at the Edinburgh Festival. Unfortunately, its vocal drawbacks outweigh its enthusiastic teamwork. Geraint Evans, the Figaro, has a bad case of the wobbles, the gray patches in his voice evidence of the march of time. Fischer-Dieskau adds little to the role of the Count undisclosed in his two previous recordings, and the nap on his baritone begins to show wear. Experience has helped Teresa Berganza's Cherubino: she is now more acceptable as a page boy and very much the young romantic in her rapturously sung arias. Judith Blegen, always agreeable and perky, offers an immature, honestly sung Susanna. Birgit Finnila camps up Marcellina. The remainder of the cast is lively. The recording is spacious and well lit.

1978 DECCA / LONDON (S) ℗

Anna Tomowa-Sintow (A), Ileana Cotrubas (B), Frederica von Stade (C), Jane Berbié (D), Christine Barbaux (E), Heinz Zednik (F), Tom Krause (G), José van Dam (H), Jules Bastin (I), Vienna State Opera Chorus and Vienna Philharmonic—Herbert von Karajan

Herbert von Karajan's second *Figaro* is more relaxed, less breathless than before, but rhythmically buffed, often to blandness. Ultimately, the result is almost as superficial as the first, except for the cumulative momentum now achieved in the large spans of the two finales. As in the Philips set, "Dove sono" is heard before the sextet. The aggravating recording offers a plushy surface without a texture of distinct, individual strands; the sound seems to have been manufactured in a blender. There is too much bass and balances are not natural.

Veterans of Karajan *Figaros* at Salzburg, the cast—at least its leading players—are curiously muted, except for Frederica von Stade, who earns the right to be dubbed the phonograph's peerless Cherubino, and the redoubtable José van Dam, probably the best Figaro in the theater since Pinza, whose vital presence is somewhat diminished in this context. Ileana Cotrubas is a warm and intelligent Susanna, with tone no longer consistently compact. Tom Krause, a tough and threatening Count, barks too much, often obscuring pitch in the process. Most unworthy of all is Anna Tomowa-Sintow, whose voice is so unstable in tone and pitch, that she continually has difficulty shaping consecutive, firmly outlined phrases. The shorter roles leave mixed impressions. To counterbalance a poor Bartolo and Antonio, one gets deliciously spicy portrayals of Marcellina (Jane Berbié) and Don Basilio (Heinz Zednik), each filled out by exemplary renditions of their arias in the last act.

1981 DECCA / LONDON (S,D) CD

Kiri Te Kanawa (A), Lucia Popp (B), Frederica von Stade (C), Jane Berbié (D), Yvonne Kenny (E), Robert Tear (F), Thomas Allen (G), Samuel Ramey (H), Kurt Moll (I), London Opera Chorus and London Philharmonic Orchestra—Georg Solti

London introduced Figaro and his bride to the age of digital recording in 1981. A most felicitous meeting, it ranks with the best the phonograph has to offer. The sonics are Kingsway Hall deluxe, crystal clear in detail, well defined in space, and, of course, absolutely quiet—no tape hiss. The conductor, Georg Solti, has been praised for his interpretation of *Figaro* ever since 1973, when he launched the Rolf Liebermann administration of the Paris Opéra with two magical performances in the palace theater at Versailles. This recorded souvenir (little decorated, but complete with all arias) has not lost its edge. Although Solti favors highly contrasting tempos, the excellent London Philharmonic and an alert vocal team are responsive and relaxed. The result has a welcome ease, grace, and warmth—not altogether characteristic of the majority of Solti's operatic recordings—and few shortcomings. Lucia Popp, the Susanna, tends to squeeze her vowels, mostly in the first half of the opera, and Samuel Ramey, a model *basso cantante* who does sing out, is a sincere Figaro, sixties style, who clearly believes in making love, not war. Their first duets are strangely faceless. With the arrival of Kurt Moll (Bartolo) and Jane Berbié (Marcellina), the performance ignites, sparked by a uniquely powerful rendition of the "Vendetta" aria and then by a deliciously witty account of the ensuing duet.

Each successive entrance heightens the drama, building to a steady, sustained theatrical blaze. First, the irrepressible Cherubino of Frederica von Stade, unsurpassed, whether sighing "E se non ho chi m'oda" to himself and to Susanna or drafting the poised, elegant line that reveals the beauty of "Voi che sapete." Then, the ever musical Thomas Allen, brilliant in song and portraiture as Almaviva, aristocratic even when embarrassed (rage, persistence, lust, and contrition kept in convincing balance), rhythmically accurate even in the florid conclusion of his aria, and touching in "Contessa perdono." Finally, Kiri Te Kanawa is the vocal glory of this performance. The Countess is the role that brought her renown; one feels she knows it and loves it as no other. Her entrance aria—a perfect partnership with Solti—is a model of what is necessary to convey private melancholy with spacious grandeur. "Dove sono" is also compelling, with the words appropriately colored and the voice floated enchantingly. Always alive to situation in recitative and ensemble, she, along with Schwarzkopf, heads the list of Countesses. Te Kanawa will be preferred by many for spontaneity and the art that conceals art. Last, but surely not least, is the buoyant support of Jeffrey Tate's *continuo*.

1986 PHILIPS (S,D) CD

Lucia Popp (A), Barbara Hendricks (B), Agnes Baltsa (C), Felicity Palmer (D), Cathryn Pope (E), Aldo Baldin (F), Ruggero Raimondi (G), José van Dam (H), Robert Lloyd (I), Ambrosian Opera Chorus and Academy of St. Martin in the Fields—Neville Marriner

Philips's digital entry employs the orchestra of St. Martin in the Fields, an ensemble smaller than most of the competition and closer to the size heard in Mozart's day, conducted by the energetic, facile Neville Marriner—too fast in some numbers, e.g., "Crudel! perchè finora" and the start of the second-act finale, some others insufficiently differentiated. Agreeably lightweight (even in *tuttis*), quick and easy in execution, the winds delightfully forward, the strings a bit undernourished, the instrumental web is easy to penetrate. The score is performed complete. The twin pivots of this rendition are its Figaro (José van Dam), thoughtful, ironic, almost sassy, and its Almaviva (Ruggero Raimondi), fiery and bitter with dissatisfaction. Their conflict would be more sharply realized if their baritones were better differentiated. Barbara Hendricks's characterization of Susanna is just a little bland, but her light soprano is sweet and true. "Venite" is gay and sparkling, "Deh vieni" winsome with its interpolated cadenza. Agnes Baltsa is generally overly tempestuous— "Non so più" almost hysterical and rushed—but more continent in a quite nicely sung "Voi che sapete." Lucia Popp, now graduated to the Countess, lacks amplitude for the role, even though she brings understanding to the recitatives; she gives a good, small-scaled account of "Dove sono" and, with Hendricks, of the letter duet. Aldo Baldin is a routine Basilio; but Felicity Palmer offers a sharply observed Marcellina, Robert Lloyd a forceful Bartolo, no one's buffoon, and Cathryn Pope a credible Barbarina, who sings her cavatina better than most.

1987 EMI / ANGEL (S,D) CD

Margaret Price (A), Kathleen Battle (B), Ann Murray (C), Mariana Nicolesco (D), Patrizia Pace (E), Alejandro Ramirez (F), Jorma Hynninen (G), Thomas Allen (H), Kurt Rydl (I), Vienna State Opera Chorus and Vienna Philharmonic Orchestra—Riccardo Muti

Angel's high-gloss, big-sound, made-in-Vienna *Figaro*, conducted by Riccardo Muti, is emotionally undernourished. Its engineering is another problem, proving that the placement of the mikes and the noodling of the master tapes (less is better) is just as critical in the digital age as it was before. The ambience, more that of a ballroom than of the theater, is over-resonant and places an annoying emphasis on thé upper middles of the female voices. The small voice of Kathleen Battle, which would benefit from sympathetic recording cosmetics, suffers most from this acoustical frame, heard to little effect before a sweetly sung and deliciously accompanied "Deh vieni, non tardar." A slightly different setup—with less sonic glare—seems to have

been employed for "Non più andrai" and some other later numbers. Muti's direction, typically meticulous, exacting in dynamics, rhythm, and insistence on adequate period decoration, appears almost impatient, without the ease that inspires singers to verbal intensity and detailed portrayal.

Once the Count supreme, Thomas Allen, now a very sober Figaro, is the sadly all-too-typical baritone miscast in a role which belongs to basses, his recitative and aria in the garden his only moment of comfortable, spontaneous grace. The estimable Finnish baritone Jorma Hynninen is below par as an angry, one-dimensional Count, momentous only in an incendiary account of his aria. Ann Murray (Cherubino) is gifted in portraiture, less so vocally; one wants more tone. Ditto Mariana Nicolesco as Marcellina. Lovely, cool, silvery tone is what one gets from Margaret Price, a too often detached Countess with not enough vivid moments like her recitative to "Dove sono." Kurt Rydl tends to rush, throwing away the recitative to his aria. Alejandro Ramirez has an unbecoming flutter in his voice but gets through Basilio's aria honorably.

1988 EMI / ANGEL (S,D) CD

Felicity Lott (A), Gianna Rolandi (B), Faith Esham (C), Anne Mason (D), Anne Dawson (E), Ugo Benelli (F), Richard Stilwell (G), Claudio Desderi (H), Artur Korn (I), Glyndebourne Chorus and London Philharmonic— Bernard Haitink

The cast of this Glyndebourne production, predominantly youthful, without a single star name, typifies those usually encountered at the festival in Sussex. Total respect for an opera and thorough rehearsal often produces an ensemble, such as this one, which radiates pleasure in its task, and is, at its best, more enjoyable than many others with more expensive, less committed singers. The leader of this merry and talented team is Bernard Haitink, conducting with a sweetness, a purity of style—without any excentricity—and richness of detail perfectly mirrored by engineering skills and resource unmatched in previous recordings of *Figaro*. The sound is both luscious and impressively analytical, the seductive woodwinds audible in an appropriately intimate orchestral framework. The London Philharmonic Orchestra may not have the rich patina of the Vienna Philharmonic, but it is everywhere alert and sings at Haitink's bidding.

So, also, do the singers, who are encouraged to use their *legato* skills. Right away, in the first two duets following the Overture, one is aware of uncommon attention to lyric opportunity by Claudio Desderi and Gianna Rolandi, the servant couple. Although a baritone, Desderi seems comfortable with the tessitura while offering a penetrating portrait notable for exceptional verbal and musical shading. Rolandi's vibrant soprano is not always in sharp focus under pressure, but her characterization always is. She punctuates her recitatives, refuses to glide blandly through them. Her singing is most pleasing in Susanna's second-act aria, many an ensemble, and in the letter duet with Felicity Lott, the Countess. Lott is one of those intelligent artists who satisfy without a lot of vocal glamour. She is quite musical and acts well with her voice, even though from time to time she is irritating with her tendency toward white attack. Richard Stilwell, not quite so subtle as Thomas Allen in the Solti set, has personality and sustained force as Almaviva. His ample baritone is pleasing, his technique equal to all of Mozart's hurdles, even the end of his aria. Faith Esham, vocally a trifle weak in her lowest notes, may not present the most multifaceted Cherubino, but she has an attractive, all-purpose youthful charm and sings a very nice "Voi che sapete." Anne Mason is a convincing Marcellina, except in her aria, ever troublesome because its tessitura is higher than the rest of the role. Artur Korn, a well-schooled bass, is one of the serious Bartolos, as his direct and forceful manner attests. Ugo Benelli is good and characterful and makes something of Basilio's aria.

1988 L'OISEAU-LYRE (S,D) CD

Arleen Augér (A), Barbara Bonney (B), Alicia Nafé (C), Della Jones (D), Nancy Argenta (E), Eduardo Gimenez (F), Håkan Hagegård (G), Petteri Salomaa (H), Carlos Feller (I), Drottningholm Court Theater Chorus and Orchestra—Arnold Östman

This *Figaro*, the first to be recorded with period instruments, gives the opera a newly minted sound. Every instrument is at least subtly different from today's counterpart. The gut-stringed instruments are cleaner, less brilliant, more easily articulated in rapid passages. The winds, each with a very distinctive timbre, do not have to play all out to balance with strings, and the natural hand-stopped horns are more vivid but less weighty than those of today. The pacing is livelier, particularly in numbers marked *andante* (the eighteenth century took *andante* to mean a walking speed). Such an orchestra and more animated tempos encourage an intimacy of expression that changes the way one has perceived Mozart's operas. The grosser aspects of grand opera are replaced by the human scale observed at close range. Under Arnold Östman, this performance is as exhilarating as one might expect, conveyed with state-of-the-art digital recording technique. The excellently prepared vocal cast has been welded into a strong ensemble that achieves the naturalness and quick give and take of a performance in the spoken theater. Petteri Salomaa, a resourceful, convincing baritone Figaro who never forgets he is a servant, has smooth vocal quality, musicality, and ease. As Susanna, the young American Barbara Bonney employs her clear and flexible soprano with good taste and dramatic awareness. The high baritone of Håkan Hagegård, perfectly suited to the role of Almaviva, is particularly impressive in the duet with Susanna—intimate, tender, and full of sighs. The style of this *Figaro* tends to undercut the nobility of the Countess. Her two arias, taken very briskly ("Porgi amor" goes *andante*, not at Mozart's *larghetto*), become merely reflective without the accents of dignified pathos one usually looks for. In any event, Arleen Augér offers a well-sung, small-scaled Countess, who pays close attention to the other characters and whose response to the Count's apology in the finale touches the heart. Alicia Nafé, sometimes tonally breathy and explosive in phrasing as Cherubino, is nevertheless convincing. Della Jones sounds as if she were born to sing Marcellina's aria: it fits her like a glove; no one on records sings it better. Accordingly, the rest of the part lies a bit low for her. Carlos Feller is a delightful blustering Bartolo. Eduardo

Gimenez's Basilio is a bit unsteady vocally early on, but his boring aria goes just about as well as it can.

Yes, this splendid recording of *Figaro* is complete—and then some. It includes a half-dozen variants, most of them probably by Mozart, used in the Prague premiere in late 1786 and the Vienna revival in 1789. None of these is without interest, but none seems as effective as what it replaced.

1990 DEUTSCHE GRAMMOPHON (S,D) CD

Kiri Te Kanawa (A), Dawn Upshaw (B), Anne Sofie von Otter (C), Tatiana Troyanos (D), Heidi Grant (E), Anthony Laciura (F), Thomas Hampson (G), Ferruccio Furlanetto (H), Paul Plishka (I), Metropolitan Opera Chorus and Orchestra—James Levine

This is a big-opera-house *Figaro*, sonically a bit overrich and less intimate than some will like, but beautifully prepared and confidently performed with an ensemble finish that comes only from frequent teamwork. Although the spacious recording suggests a sizable, quite resonant venue, its sound is well focused, with a pleasing balance between voices and instrumental forces larger than one encounters in most relatively recent sets of *Figaro*.

One would be grateful to encounter such a performance in the theater, but on disc, in competition with so many worthy *Figaros*, it just misses inclusion among the preferred sets. It allows the music only fitful smiles and sometimes shortchanges its ebullience. After a mostly brusque first act, Levine settles down, conducting with ever greater sensitivity, except for an occasional episode that is rushed and insufficiently inflected.

The cast is uneven as well. Lovely sound is all Te Kanawa has to offer; although she was an involved Countess under Solti in the London set, here she is unaccountably vague. Had Furlanetto a more compact sound, he might make a more incisive, energetic Figaro. Upshaw, tonally thin at times (but not in her marvelously realized arias), is a believable Susanna, for once one neither coy nor overly cute. Troyanos and Plishka, Figaro's parents, are well-routined art-

ists, but they struggle with their arias. Awards for the most persuasive vocal quality and acting go to Thomas Hampson, an aristocrat conniving, angry, and infatuated by turns; von Otter, throbbingly youthful, in love with love; and Laciura, a reticent but vivid Basilio who actually makes something of his ungrateful aria. By its responsiveness, tonal refinement, and exemplary execution, the Metropolitan Opera Orchestra proves yet again it is second to none among the world's pit ensembles.

1991 ERATO (S,D) CD

Lella Cuberli (A), Joan Rodgers (B), Cecilia Bartoli (C), Phyllis Pancella (D), Hilde Leidland (E), Graham Clark (F), Andreas Schmidt (G), John Tomlinson (H), Gunter von Kannen (I), RIAS Chamber Chorus and Berlin Philharmonic—Daniel Barenboim

Daniel Barenboim has led *Figaro* for a second time and it is as uncompetitive as his first. He has not kept the Berlin Philharmonic from sounding overrich, a critical error in conducting this opera; and the Jesus-Christus Church, the recording venue, is so resonant it exacerbates Barenboim's inability to lighten sonorities, with a consequent loss of much orchestral detail. The mostly well-paced performance of the complete score, except for a few overdeliberate tempos, is warm and flowing but wants finer pointing and crisper rhythm.

Regrettably, this is not the suave, stylish vocal ensemble that might have drawn attention from Barenboim's shortcomings. An international cast without a sustained point of view and a variety of Italian accents, its principal redeeming feature is its eagerness to breathe dramatic life into the characters. John Tomlinson makes Figaro's points with a hammer rather than a rapier. Joan Rodgers, a light and sparky Susanna, is better in recitative than in song. The Almavivas are not aristocratic. Andreas Schmidt has an imperfect *legato* and barks too much. When she is comfortable with her role's vocal demands, Lella Cuberli provides some noble phrasing and her soprano has a lovely spin on it, but her "Dove sono" is insufficiently secure in line and the letter duet is decidedly prosaic. Young Cecilia Bartoli is as lively as a cricket, a deliciously impulsive Cherubino, especially in her first aria, although not yet in full vocal control of the role. Graham Clark is a waspish Basilio, consistently satisfying until he runs into the most difficult phrases in his last-act aria. The Marcellina and Bartolo are either gusty, woolly in tone, or both.

1991 RCA / BMG (S,D) CD

Julia Varady (A), Helen Donath (B), Marilyn Schmiege (C), Cornelia Kallisch (D), Ingrid Kertesi (E), Heinz Zednik (F), Ferruccio Furlanetto (G), Alan Titus (H), Siegmund Nimsgern (I), Bavarian Radio Chorus and Symphony Orchestra—Colin Davis

This recording is cause for celebration. Although Davis made greatly admired recordings of this repertory around twenty years ago, time has not dimmed his enthusiasm for Mozart's music or his feeling for appropriate tempo, rhythmic accuracy, and faithful dynamics. Davis has galvanized a cast the equal of any of its competitors in expressive shading—into an ensemble that honors both Mozart and da Ponte. This is the liveliest recording of *Figaro* since that led by Georg Solti and, overall, one of the three or four best around. The clear, resonant sound, balanced well enough (the strings are a bit recessed), favors the voices and allows one to hear the care taken to make words tell in recitative, aria, or ensemble.

Davis's latest view of the opera is not so dark as his first. Not that he slights the conflict between aristocrats and servants. This time, however, there is not such a climate of fear in the castle. The Count is determinedly amorous, but when he loses the upper hand in one situation after another, is inclined more to angry impatience and bluster than to menacing threat.

Here the servants are not running scared. Alan Titus as Figaro (some of his low notes are weak) and Helen Donath as Susanna (some of her high notes are shrill) are energetic, wily, and completely believable. Julia Varady is an intensely expressive Countess—dignified in lament and a dedicated recruit in conspiracy. Her purity of line and tone in "Porgi amor" is uncommonly affecting.

For her first appearance in recorded opera, Marilyn Schmiege is a passionate and involved Cherubino. The opera is performed complete; happily, the Marcellina (Cornelia Kallisch) and the Basilio (Heinz Zednik) are sufficiently artful to animate their normally boring arias. Siegmund Nimsgern, serious and combative, is a resonant, no-nonsense Bartolo.

The responsiveness of the Bavarian orchestra and chorus to Davis's leadership is everywhere impressive.

Selection among twenty-odd *Figaros* recorded over a half-century span is impossible, but if forced to flee a burning building with only two, I would cling to two of the London sets—Kleiber's and Solti's.

C. J. LUTEN

WOLFGANG AMADEUS MOZART

DON GIOVANNI

A: Donna Anna (s); B: Donna Elvira (s); C: Zerlina (s); D: Ottavio (t);
E: Don Giovanni (bar or bs); F: Masetto (bar or bs); G: Leporello (bs);
H: Commendatore (bs)

*M*ozart's *Don Giovanni* had its premiere in Prague in 1787, soon after *Le Nozze di Figaro* had been successful there. For its subsequent Vienna opening, the arias "Dalla sua pace" and "Mi tradi" were composed, and later a farcical little scene for Zerlina and Leporello was inserted. The standard performing edition includes everything but this last, and even that has been recorded in some of the newer complete sets, as noted below.

The central question for performers and listeners is the spirit in which the work is to be approached. The opera concludes with divine retribution for sin, but it also involves the subtlest musical exploration of the comic and tragic motivations for compassion and moral indifference. Who is the most profoundly realized character: Leporello? Donna Elvira? the Commendatore? And what are we to make of Don Giovanni himself? Is he simply a faceless libertine whose real significance is in what other more concretely realized characters see in him, or is he in some way a tragic protagonist defending his genius against complacent practicality? Or is he an animal rendered obsolescent by civilization? A medieval Vice figure, Marlowe's Faustus, Brecht's Baal? Mozart suggests all of these possibilities, and sometimes simultaneously. Is the viewpoint human or divine? He has created in this opera a work in which the comic, the compassionate, and the tragic are profound and deathless aspects of one another.

In considering the recordings of *Don Giovanni*, there are, of course, the questions of who sings or plays well or badly and what stylistic conventions are to be observed. But beyond those inquiries, there is the question of what approach reveals the opera most completely to each of us. Listening to all of these recordings only increases one's wonder at the work's synoptic insight.

1936 EMI / ANGEL (M) CD

Ina Souez (A), Luise Helletsgruber (B), Audrey Mildmay (C), Koloman von Pataky (D), John Brownlee (E), Roy Henderson (F), Salvatore Baccaloni (G), David Franklin (H), Glyndebourne Festival Chorus and Orchestra—Fritz Busch

This famous set preserves the Glyndebourne production of 1936. Busch, who had previously headed the Dresden Opera for a decade, leads a performance distinguished for its geniality and swift grace. Its classic portrayal is Baccaloni's Leporello, played for comic charm and considerable sympathy. His voice at thirty-six is superb—forward, natural, and round—and he never betrays the music. His "Madamina" is alternately grand, sly, overbearing, and insinuating, but always dexterous: a brilliant characterization. Brownlee's Don Giovanni is energetic but blunt in tone and manner; he sounds, rather amusingly, more like Macheath in *The Beggar's Opera* than an oily cavalier. When Baccaloni's

Leporello pretends to be the Don, he sounds so much more seductive than his master that an unintentionally subversive point is made. Audrey Mildmay's Zerlina (how difficult to cast this role well!) is both coy and cold in tone, and David Franklin and Roy Henderson sound like very proper Englishmen indeed, though Henderson is responsible for the funniest and most convincing beating scene on records. They are all buoyed up by the lively pace.

Luise Helletsgruber has drive and a charmingly feminine approach to Elvira, though some moments lack either dramatic conviction or musical exactitude. Ina Souez, a Canadian who studied in Denver and Milan, sings an Anna of power, warmth, and efficient technique. She and Busch both play sorrow a little more convincingly than vengeance. Pataky's Ottavio is sweetly sung but bland. As a whole, the performance is still quite delightful. Nearly all the participants have something intriguing to contribute under the warm, disciplined leadership of the conductor.

1950 HAYDN SOCIETY (M)

Gertrude Grob-Prandl (A), Hilde Konetzni (B), Hedda Heusser (C), Herbert Handt (D), Mariano Stabile (E), Alfred Poell (F), Alois Pernerstorfer (G), Oskar von Czerwenka (H), Vienna State Opera Chorus, Vienna Symphony—Hans Swarowsky

This is in general a dreadfully sung and aimlessly conducted *Don Giovanni*, notable only for the presence of its leading baritone. Mariano Stabile was a singing actor renowned throughout Europe more for the finish of his characterizations than for his power and beauty of voice. He was famous in this role, and also sang Falstaff for forty years under such conductors as Toscanini, Ettore Panizza, and Victor de Sabata. At the time of this recording he was sixty-two. The voice is dry and unsteady, but his command of recitative is a considerable stimulation. Despite his grace, though, he seems no more dangerous than Santa Claus; one has little sense that he is mired in temptations that are about to damn him.

The supporting cast is ill equipped to deal with the music, style, or language. Pernerstorfer is accurate, though hard-voiced, humorless, and oddly sentimental in "O statua gentilissima." Poell is a brutish Masetto and Czerwenka, just twenty-five at the time, unsteady as the Commendatore. Handt is graceful in Don Ottavio's arias, if not technically accomplished or forceful. He and Grob-Prandl, an erstwhile Wagnerian, make a ludicrous pair. Her singing is passionless and often sharp; "Non mi dir" is particularly ghastly. For all her fame, Hilde Konetzni is here very disappointing. She cannot attack a note cleanly, sustain it steadily, or release it surely. Hedda Heusser sounds like a boy soprano; "Batti, batti" is rushed and "Vedrai, carino" lifeless. Leading this unpleasant crew is Hans Swarowsky, who is occasionally forceful and pointed, as in the final ensemble, but mostly ambling and ineffective. "Dalla sua pace" sleeps and "Non mi dir" is a disaster at such a slow tempo. The edition is odd. The original pressing used the Prague version, with "Dalla sua pace" and "Mi tradi" in separate bands at the end. In my set, the tenor aria is back in place but "Mi tradi" is gone: probably just as well.

1953 CETRA (M)

Mary Curtis-Verna (A), Carla Gavazzi (B), Elda Ribetti (C), Cesare Valletti (D), Giuseppe Taddei (E), Vito Susca (F), Italo Tajo (G), Antonio Zerbini (H), Italian Radio-Television Chorus and Orchestra, Turin—Max Rudolf

Max Rudolf provides a performance of earthy energy, sometimes too fast for expressivity (as in "Ho capito" and "Batti, batti") and at other times suggesting a certain exhilarating Mozartian madness. For once, because there is so much life force in it, the hero's philandering does not seem simply trivial. The three leading men are exceptionally persuasive. Giuseppe Taddei is a healthy lecher with a beautiful voice, all appetite in private and all dulcet seduction elsewhere. He provides just the amorous tone that Anna remembers with horror, and later imitates his Leporello's very distinctive voice with delightful results. The Champagne Aria is exceptionally graceful, and he faces death first with courage and then rage and terror. Italo Tajo complements him with a crafty, vibrant young Leporello. His dialogue is beautifully modulated, building to climaxes which in themselves suggest music. "Madamina" is mercurial and "Ah, pietà," with its nimble changes of color, a brilliant piece of singing. All through his performance, fear, resentment, and perception are intriguingly integrated. Cesare Valletti, with his slightly grainy tone, is nevertheless a passionately committed Don Ottavio: when he sings "Lo giuro," he means it. "Dalla sua pace" has its moments of conviction as well as reverie, and "Il mio tesoro" is full of dramatic intent. Antonio Zerbini, by the way, contributes well to a touching trio just before the Commendatore's death.

The women are much less satisfactory. Mary Curtis-Verna has some radiance of tone and demonstrates conviction and vulnerability but lacks the technique for most of the role. Carla Gavazzi is a passionate but raw and inaccurate Elvira. She begins to sound insane just at the moment when Anna comments on her rationality, and by the end her vocalism has become a trial. Elda Ribetti is a nervous Zerlina, lacking *legato* and in "Vedrai, carino" suggesting the stiffness of *Hoffman*'s Olympia. Nevertheless, this is in some ways a very interesting set, in which the three leading men are outstanding for vocalism and dramatic interest.

1954 EMI / ANGEL (M,P) CD

Elisabeth Grümmer (A), Elisabeth Schwarzkopf (B), Erna Berger (C), Anton Dermota (D), Cesare Siepi (E), Walter Berry (F), Otto Edelmann (G), Dezsö Ernster (H), Vienna State Opera Chorus, Vienna Philharmonic Orchestra—Wilhelm Furtwängler

This live performance from the 1954 Salzburg Festival is dominated by its conductor, Wilhelm Furtwängler, whose conception projects a crushing sense of fate. The humor is largely lost but not the thrust: the Overture, for example, is an experience of mystical power, its *moderato* section played with tremendous decision. The tempos are in general slow, though

proportionate. One senses the long lines of climax, as in the conductor's Wagner. On the other hand, such passages as the graveyard scene and the final confrontation seem to make their points interminably.

Some of the vocalists handle this approach very well indeed, while others are overwhelmed by it. Cesare Siepi, in his handsomest voice, is dramatically spicier than in his two studio recordings, though to me a bass voice often seems too sensible and daunting in this mercurial role. At this tempo, the Champagne Aria is done with finish (though it ends with a charmless laugh), and the Serenade, heavy with ritards, is vocally beautiful. His death screams are among the most anguished on records. And what of his alter ego? Together, Otto Edelmann and Furtwängler crush the humor out of Leporello, who is here purposely graceless and rough—unseductive even in caricature. In "Madamina" the nasty message is all that is left, and at the slow speed the repetitions go for almost nothing. Dezsö Ernster's Commendatore is, in the Act I trio, steadier than expected, but later he demonstrates only the wreck of a voice which cannot command as the final scene requires. As Masetto, the 24-year-old Walter Berry is a genial presence who in "Ho capito" suggests both ironic servility and anger: a nascent Figaro. In his two very slowly sung arias, Anton Dermota demonstrates more technical control than beauty of voice or emotional illumination.

The women are all remarkable. As Donna Anna, Elisabeth Grümmer, with her lovely, blond sound, is romantic, aristocratic, and engaging all at once: how seldom that happens! Furtwängler sets a very leisurely tempo for "Non mi dir," but even so Grümmer manages to make its reprise ravishingly tender and beguiling. At fifty-five, Erna Berger is still a superb Zerlina, in fresh voice. "Batti, batti" is a stream of fine tone, and she handles the slow tempo of "Vedrai, carino" by tasting the words: the lines retain all their shape and *legato*. As for Elisabeth Schwarzkopf, she uses the demanding tempos to increase the panache and dramatic focus of Elvira's music. "Non ti fidar" is both melancholy and commanding without being coercive, and "Mi tradi" remains intimate but bristling with yearning and dynamic variety. All told, this is a recording for a lover of the opera who wants to dwell on its tragic aspects and to enjoy some of the era's great singers, characteristically disciplined even in live performance.

1955 PHILIPS (M)

Hilde Zadek (A), Sena Jurinac (B), Graziella Sciutti (C), Léopold Simoneau (D), George London (E), Eberhard Wächter (F), Walter Berry (G), Ludwig Weber (H), Vienna Chamber Chorus, Vienna Symphony Orchestra—Rudolf Moralt

Rudolf Moralt and his interesting cast bring us a performance of suppressed violence, commanding in the first act but, like so many of this kind, less effective in the second. The Overture tells us what to expect: it is alternately martial, murky, and gossamer, and full of dramatic conflict. George London, aggressive and thick-voiced, is a lustful Don Giovanni who uses his rather weighty charm to feed his appetites. The Champagne Aria is rushed at the expense of natural joy, and the Serenade is heavy at first but more delicate later on. By the end, his vocal toughness has grown a little wearisome. He and his Leporello are confrontational figures. Walter Berry's portrayal is hearty and sometimes unpleasant, but firm in line and not disfigured with vulgarities. Ludwig Weber sings the graveyard scene in a magnificently steady ghostly whisper and at the finale is effectively craggy. To this powerful trio, Hilde Zadek adds a flaming voice. Her opening scene is a violent one, and she later describes the Don's attack with real horror and delivers "Or sai, chi l'onore" with raging fury. The lyrical moments are clumsier: "Non mi dir" is not nearly so compelling.

Luckily she is working with a brilliantly involved Ottavio. Léopold Simoneau is outraged but also tender, and sings an elegant, dramatically shaped "Dalla sua pace," though "Il mio tesoro" is less finished. Eberhard Wächter's Masetto is at first warm and later a young firebrand, suggestive of his later recording of the title role. In the midst of all this aggression, Sena Jurinac as Elvira is at first uneven, but

often lovely and vulnerable. The melting darkness of her voice goes well with George London's, and "Non ti fidar" is beautiful and "Mi tradì" moving. As Zerlina, Graziella Sciutti is lively and delicate, but "Batti, batti" is a little rushed, and neither there nor in "Vedrai, carino" does she expand into lyrical warmth. In sum, this set offers a combative and sometimes gripping performance, less convincing in some of its lyrical moments but notable for the conviction of a few of its rather rarely recorded soloists.

1955 DECCA / LONDON (S) CD

Suzanne Danco (A), Lisa della Casa (B), Hilde Gueden (C), Anton Dermota (D), Cesare Siepi (E), Walter Berry (F), Fernando Corena (G), Kurt Böhme (H), Vienna State Opera Chorus, Vienna Philharmonic Orchestra—Josef Krips

This is a luxuriously cast and amiably conducted album, but, surprisingly, only its Anna and Masetto provide much more than pleasant vocalism. Though there are stretches of lovely sound, the performance is oddly forgettable. To begin, Josef Krips's Overture is lugubrious and sometimes wheedling, and the rest is rich but often unshaped. Cesare Siepi's Don is here comfortable, cultivated, and seductive but also monochromatic; one misses the slyness, the real anger, and the manic joy that make the character fascinating. Corena is likewise stylish but only hints at the complexities of Leporello. There is just the suggestion of a beat in his highest notes. Lisa della Casa's Elvira is attractively distraught in some of the recitative and touching in "Non ti fidar," but her "Mi tradì" is at most an agreeable romp, the voice almost toneless at the very bottom and the roulades neither particularly exciting nor dramatically rousing.

On the other hand, Suzanne Danco delivers a passionate Anna, in which her tonal clarity and vibrancy compensate for the lack of vocal weight. She hasn't quite the depth of sound to make "Non mi dir" definitively comforting or the arresting technique to make the most of the cadenza, but it's a devoted piece of work, even though she is working with an inert Ottavio.

Hilde Gueden is a glossy and pouting Zerlina, glittering in tone but a little unsteady at the end of "Vedrai, carino." Walter Berry's Masetto is as lively as in the Furtwängler set. Considering the réclame of the cast, this is a disappointing performance, though nicely recorded in stereo.

1956 EMI / ANGEL (M) CD

Teresa Stich-Randall (A), Suzanne Danco (B), Anna Moffo (C), Nicolai Gedda (D), Antonio Campò (E), André Vessières (F), Marcello Cortis (G), Raffaele Arié (H), Aix-en-Provence Festival Chorus, Orchestra of the Société des Concerts du Conservatoire—Hans Rosbaud

This recording arose from the Aix-en-Provence Festival production of 1956, and, though a studio product, it has the conviction of a live event. With a distinctive cast, Hans Rosbaud provides continuity and a point of view; the confrontations are often riveting and the drive toward damnation inescapable. Typical is the Anna of Teresa Stich-Randall. At twenty-seven she has a light, sometimes cutting voice and great rhythmical and dramatic vitality. The opening scene and "Or sai, chi l'onore" show horror, passion, and weakness at once, and, with Nicolai Gedda a committed Ottavio, the vengeance duet is full of certainty. "Non mi dir" is mannered but tenderly phrased: it has the effect of a sophisticated lullaby. To this kind of conviction, Gedda adds an affection of his own. His "Dalla sua pace" is a statement of love, and "Il mio tesoro" verges on the technically spectacular. Here singing Elvira, Suzanne Danco is riveting in her dialogue and distinguished in the music, though "Mi tradi" is not quite so dramatic as expected. Her vocal method is interesting; it seems to mix the Italian (vibrant tone) and the German (forward placement). Marcello Cortis as Leporello has a healthy sound and an extroverted approach. There are some dreadful giggles at the end of "Madamina," but generally this young man is satirical rather than vulgar.

At the center of all this is the Don Giovanni of Antonio Campò, with a voice dark in color but light in weight and of no particular glamour. It has an old-fashioned vibrato reminiscent of Andreas de Segurola, who made many records in the first part of the century. Campò is, though, a Don of some flavor, responsive to the energy of those around him, and in fact he sings one of the most graceful of Champagne Arias. As Masetto, André Vessières sounds a little like a cabaret baritone, bright enough and obviously in love with his Zerlina, Anna Moffo. Her two arias are rushed but tonally lovely. Raffaele Arié is a generally impressive Commendatore, with a focused voice exotically Eastern in quality. The trio preceding his death is exceptionally touching. In this set, then, we have a less than perfect cast which nevertheless has great energy and individuality and is generally well used by a lively conductor.

1956 DEUTSCHE GRAMMOPHON (S) CD

Sena Jurinac (A), Maria Stader (B), Irmgard Seefried (C), Ernst Häfliger (D), Dietrich Fischer-Dieskau (E), Ivan Sardi (F), Karl Kohn (G), Walter Kreppel (H), RIAS Chamber Chorus, Berlin Radio Symphony Orchestra—Ferenc Fricsay

This is a middle-European *Don Giovanni*, Germanic in accent and fateful in outlook. Under Ferenc Fricsay, nothing lags, the orchestral timbres are clear, and the entire production has a theatricality which is galvanizing even when charmless. The world of this lecher may be threatening, but it is seldom dull. Dietrich Fischer-Dieskau plays a driven genius of a Don Juan, compulsive and cruel, enjoying manipulation as much as conquest, and damned before he kills the Commendatore. The portrait is fascinating even in its excess. "Là ci darem la mano," for example, is dulcet in tone, but the singer cannot leave it so: he worries it with special effects, minor pre-seductions, hints of command. He takes the Champagne Aria by the neck and wrings it. This Don is too manic to be joyous; there is something of *Lulu*'s Dr. Schoen in him. As Leporello, Karl Kohn is unpleasant, humorless except for an occasional smirk, impatient, and jealous of his master. "Madamina" is a lecture about a monster: direct, realistic, and dirty.

Maria Stader, as Elvira, has all sorts of vocal

mannerisms and a heavy German accent, but is often commanding anyway. In "Ah! fuggi il traditor," she is a termagant, and even in "Non ti fidar" much more forthright than some Elviras. "In quali eccessi" is, by contrast, tender and pearly in tone. The effect is schizophrenic but the performance nearly always compelling. Sena Jurinac, singing Donna Anna this time, gives us a glamorous voice and considerable dramatic focus. "Or sai, chi l'onore" is less varied and effective than her opening scene, but "Non mi dir" is generous, warm, and radiant. Ernst Häfliger as Ottavio offers drama at first but is oddly spineless in the arias. Irmgard Seefried, pretty in tone, plays a shallow, self-interested Zerlina. Ivan Sardi's Masetto has considerable dramatic variety. As the Commendatore, Walter Kreppel is moving in the trio but insufficiently powerful in Act II. This is a *Don Giovanni* dominated by damnation, with precision from its conductor and brilliant if mannered work from its leading baritone.

1959 DECCA / LONDON (S)

Birgit Nilsson (A), Leontyne Price (B), Eugenia Ratti (C), Cesare Valletti (D), Cesare Siepi (E), Heinz Blankenburg (F), Fernando Corena (G), Arnold van Mill (H), Vienna State Opera Chorus, Vienna Philharmonic Orchestra—Erich Leinsdorf

This recording, like the 1955 Decca set under Josef Krips, features Cesare Siepi, Fernando Corena, and the Vienna Philharmonic Orchestra. The advantages here are in Leinsdorf (more incisive than Krips) and in completeness. For the first time the comic scene in which Zerlina threatens Leporello with a razor is included, and nicely performed. The spoken passages are livelier and the musical pacing sometimes swifter than under Krips, but the relative merits of the sets are otherwise debatable. There are some vocal mismatches here (Siepi-Ratti and Nilsson-Valletti) and some stylistic discontinuities, too. Eugenia Ratti is, despite a small, rather dry voice, a winning Zerlina, and Heinz Blankenburg a vital Masetto. As Donna Anna, Birgit Nilsson has peerless top notes and works for delicacy, but caution, insecurity, and approxi-

mate pitch deaden the effects she seeks. Cesare Valletti, as in the 1953 Cetra set, is a passionate and accomplished Ottavio. Leontyne Price has glorious tone and remarkable technique, but the voice has not the natural mobility for some of Elvira's music, and Price's warm sound cannot quite capture the vindictive element in the character she plays. Cesare Siepi is again suave and Corena stylish. Neither characterizes very provocatively, though, and both are marginally more worn than in the earlier performance.

1959 EMI / ANGEL (S) CD

Joan Sutherland (A), Elisabeth Schwarzkopf (B), Graziella Sciutti (C), Luigi Alva (D), Eberhard Wächter (E), Piero Cappuccilli (F), Giuseppe Taddei (G), Gottlob Frick (H), Philharmonia Chorus and Orchestra—Carlo Maria Giulini

This set is a revelatory theatrical experience. Not only is it brilliantly cast and stunningly conducted, but it exposes in a breathlessly exciting performance the profundity of a legend often taken as merely melodramatic, amusing, and safely outdated. We have here Don Giovanni as a tragically compulsive, almost mad figure, Anna as earnestly outraged, Elvira as noble yet faintly ridiculous, Leporello as a craven satirist, the Commendatore as inexorable fate, and Zerlina and Masetto as, perhaps, simple youth. For once the *dramma giocoso* evokes the spectrum of reactions attributed to it by critics so often in the 200 years since it was written. Its several levels here compete in vitality. Wit and depth nourish each other.

Carlo Maria Giulini directs a superb ensemble. The rhythms are strong, the textures clear, the pacing alert. One often has the sense of a lifetime's feelings reflected in a moment, and yet there are continuity and proportion. The forms *contain* the force without repressing it. At the center is the Don Giovanni of Eberhard Wächter, scheming, full of demonic energy, and just at the point in life when satiety becomes damnation. At his side is Giuseppe Taddei's Leporello, a cunning servant in the *commedia* tradition, with a different face for every situation and yet unified as a character: ironic, disgruntled, and terrified in turn. It is all done with a deft hand, too. The Catalogue Aria, for example, goes like the wind, almost weightless and yet forceful at once. As Donna Anna, Joan Sutherland is not only in magnificent voice but dramatically vital as well. "Don Ottavio, son morta!," the passage in which she describes Don Giovanni's attack, is taken at terrific speed and is full of specific histrionic intention. The diction becomes a little cloudy in "Non mi dir," but the aria is treated as a very private moment, full of love, and the *fioriture* are fabulous. Luigi Alva provides an Ottavio both tender and commanding. "Dalla sua pace" has form and grace even at its rather slow tempo, and "Il mio tesoro" is a miracle of breath control. Gottlob Frick is among the best Commendatores, firm and forward in the first scene, inescapable in the graveyard, and hair-raising at the end. Graziella Sciutti as Zerlina has charm and expert control of a small voice, and Piero Cappuccilli is first-rate as Masetto.

To close, Elisabeth Schwarzkopf is a classic Elvira, outraged and loving, grand and a little absurd all at once. She is brilliant in the recitatives and vivid, exact, and inimitable in the music. There are other fine *Don Giovanni*s, but this well-recorded performance gives us a profound and absorbing view of its dramatic and musical riches.

1966 EMI / ANGEL (S) CD

Claire Watson (A), Christa Ludwig (B), Mirella Freni (C), Nicolai Gedda (D), Nicolai Ghiaurov (E), Paolo Montarsolo (F), Walter Berry (G), Franz Crass (H), New Philharmonia Chorus and Orchestra—Otto Klemperer

In this 1966 recording, both the opera and many of the cast are overwhelmed by the monumental conception of the conductor, Otto Klemperer. The power and articulation of the Overture are beyond dispute, but the performance itself frequently lacks both wit and impetuosity, and without these the drama becomes less penetrating. Certain passages, such as the Catalogue Aria, retain some of their playfulness, but others become either chilly or bland, and several fine singers are sacrificed, as is that miraculous balance of comedy and trag-

edy, of the temporal and eternal, that remains at the heart of this opera.

In 1966 Nicolai Ghiaurov had one of the most beautiful bass voices in the world. The problem is that, though he does much to characterize the role (in "Là ci darem la mano" and "Metà di voi," for example), he sounds more like a force for morality and faith than like a rake; in that voice there is simply nothing suggesting damnable appetite. The three women are also very accomplished singers, but in this setting none of them retains the complexity and variety of Mozart's characters. Claire Watson's Anna provides lovely sound but does not project much outrage or desperation. What is left in Act I is an appealingly lost quality. Later, at such a leisurely tempo, "Non mi dir" seems more indifferent than contained. Mirella Freni's Zerlina offers uncommonly pretty tone and apt phrasing, but there is neither joy nor innocent flirtation in what she does. As Elvira, Christa Ludwig sings with command and acts with compulsion, but the tempos and the dark voice together suggest only a matron with a rather absurd infatuation. That is less interesting than what Mozart offers.

Walter Berry again presents a firmly sung, serious Leporello. Alone among the cast, Paolo Montarsolo seems capable of some joy, but even at this early stage in his career he seems to be playing some Rossini roué, with his tricks and variations. Nicolai Gedda survives with tenderness and heroism intact, but even he is forced to snatch breaths in this slow "Il mio tesoro." Klemperer's view has moments of undeniable force, but often the tension between his conception and his singers' capacity supersedes the *dramatic* tension of Mozart's opera.

1967 DEUTSCHE GRAMMOPHON (S) CD

Birgit Nilsson (A), Martina Arroyo (B), Reri Grist (C), Peter Schreier (D), Dietrich Fischer-Dieskau (E), Alfredo Mariotti (F), Ezio Flagello (G), Martti Talvela (H), Prague Czech Choir, Prague National Theater Orchestra—Karl Böhm

Karl Böhm's interpretation of the score is forceful but heavy, a point made even clearer by the contrasting speed of some of the dialogue. His cast, moreover, is ill matched in vocal weight and dramatic impulse. Birgit Nilsson is even less reliable here than in the Leinsdorf set of seven years before. At this slow speed, "Non mi dir" is aimless, tentative, and endless. Ezio Flagello has the most beautiful bass voice of any of the Leporellos, but except in the scenes with Dietrich Fischer-Dieskau, where he takes on some spirit, his singing is monochromatic. Martti Talvela's Commendatore has striking power, though little in his performance suggests the style and attack necessary to Mozart. Amongst these vocal giants, Fischer-Dieskau, Reri Grist, and, to an extent, Peter Schreier sound like beings from another, more intimate, world. Fischer-Dieskau is more genial than in his recording with Fricsay. Many moments are dulcet, but several are fussy, and he has almost no one to play against dramatically. Grist is a delightful singer with a diminutive voice. Given the slow tempo, "Batti, batti" is a trifle awkward at the end, though "Vedrai, carino" is charming. With her, Alfredo Mariotti sounds more like an elderly, querulous Don Pasquale than Masetto. Peter Schreier sings respectably but is unimaginative in his treatment of the text. These ill-assorted voices and temperaments make heavy weather of some of the ensembles.

1968 DECCA / LONDON (S)

Joan Sutherland (A), Pilar Lorengar (B), Marilyn Horne (C), Werner Krenn (D), Gabriel Bacquier (E), Leonardo Monreale (F), Donald Gramm (G), Clifford Grant (H), Ambrosian Singers, English Chamber Orchestra—Richard Bonynge

With this album, one hardly knows where to begin. The idea of a restudied *Don Giovanni*, textually complete and with vocal elaborations, sounds appealing, in that it suggests stylistic unity and at the same time affirms the thought that memorable performances are, after all, a volatile combination of what is in the score and the particular characteristics of an accomplished cast. The use of a chamber orchestra likewise implies that the opera will be reduced to human size, so that the singers can concentrate on

points of character rather than sheer grandeur of sound.

Alas, none of this happens. The reading is sentimentalized beyond belief, the dialogue is tedious, and most of the aria performances lack spine and proportion. This approach might be thought to indulge the singers, but if anything it highlights their dependence on the conductor; they are simply left there hanging. The idea of ornamentation is theoretically interesting but pointless in practice unless it rises out of heightened dramatic response. The chamber orchestra is pleasant, but Richard Bonynge's direction reduces much of its work to insipidity.

Gabriel Bacquier is a singer of accomplishment and an actor of resource. As Don Giovanni, though, he sounds more like a middle-aged host fancying glamour than a glamorous figure himself. There is no cruelty in that voice, and little that seems to call for damnation. If his Don Giovanni is a reasonable but self-indulgent older man, Donald Gramm's Leporello is a reasonable younger one: it's a bright reading, lacking sufficient irony, greed, envy, and humor. In "Madamina," the added decorations matter not a whit if the characterization has not been worked out to give inescapable rise to them.

Joan Sutherland, so rousing in the 1959 set with Giulini, does the *fioriture* with her accustomed expertise but is elsewhere throaty and dull. The narrative sections are shapeless and in "Non mi dir" the diction obscured. The piece sounds, in fact, a little lost, like a mad scene. Pilar Lorengar, as Elvira, enters primly rather than passionately. Her upper voice can glint like a scimitar, but the slow tempos and vibrato together destroy the impact of much of her music.

Marilyn Horne's contribution as Zerlina is a little more interesting. She works hard for buoyancy and performs the added comic scene with Leporello and the razor expertly; it has just the sort of hearty practical humor that she handles so well in Rossini. She and Bacquier have fun together, but they suggest Falstaff and Mistress Quickly more readily than Don Giovanni and Zerlina. Her dark vocal color tends to neutralize the ensembles: the voice does not come as the ray of light that is often wanted. As Masetto, Leonardo Monreale has a nice sound, but he sometimes substitutes tears and whining for anger. Clifford Grant is an inappropriately benevolent and restrained Commendatore. Werner Krenn's Ottavio begins prosaically, but "Il mio tesoro" gains some conviction. This aria and the added scene for Zerlina can be counted among the set's few successes.

1973 PHILIPS (S) CD

Martina Arroyo (A), Kiri Te Kanawa (B), Mirella Freni (C), Stuart Burrows (D), Ingvar Wixell (E), Richard Van Allan (F), Wladimiro Ganzarolli (G), Luigi Roni (H), Chorus and Orchestra of the Royal Opera House, Covent Garden—Colin Davis

The great success of this album can be attributed largely to Colin Davis. In several cases he has coaxed committed dramatic performances from fine singers less effective as actors in other contexts. The set has a powerful, specific, and yet varied theatrical focus matched only in the Giulini album, among previous issues. Davis's view is clear, vital, and worldly; spiritual significance seems to rise almost unbidden from the intensely examined lives he and Mozart set before us. He never lets his singers flounder, and he shapes scenes and builds climaxes well. As Donna Anna this time, Martina Arroyo is in beautiful voice and, under the conductor's taut direction, more aware dramatically at the start than in any of her other recordings. The arias may be less specifically motivated, but they do not languish. Likewise, Kiri Te Kanawa is in lovely voice and performs here with tremendous rhythmic fervor. Later there are occasional moments of blandness, but much of the role retains its sting and the cadenzas are often glorious. In the final scene she is almost laughably distracted: a profound blend of comedy and tragedy. Mirella Freni is in fine voice, and her sobriety, which in the Klemperer set seems merely congenial, is here given greater dramatic motivation. Just before "Vedrai, carino," for example, the beating of Masetto has been vicious, and the aria emerges as one of

genuine comfort, neither farcical nor sentimental.

Ingvar Wixell is a driven, determined Don Giovanni, compulsive about his next conquest. His voice is sometimes grainy, but it has focus, color, and character. When wooing Zerlina, for example, he integrates, at a jaunty tempo, the longing and the persuasion. The Champagne Aria is speedy but well articulated and the Serenade graceful but neither epicene nor sentimentalized. Wladimiro Ganzarolli is a lively Leporello. The voice is unremarkable, but he sings lightly and well, for example, in the Catalogue Aria: "Isn't it ridiculous to be concerned about being seduced by such a man?," he seems to be asking. The leering at the aria's end may be unnecessary, but his performance throughout is adroit, and well supported by Davis. Stuart Burrows's Ottavio is excitingly responsive: panicked, tender, and decisive. The swearing scene has a muscular assertiveness that reminds one of early Verdi. He is equally firm in the arias, which are technically marvelous, displaying his free and vibrant voice to advantage. Richard Van Allan is a rather dark and leathery Masetto, but Luigi Roni, a lyric bass, is vibrant in the graveyard scene and effectively recorded in the finale. The ensemble as a whole is brilliantly directed and the set can be strongly recommended.

1973–74 EMI / ANGEL (S) CD

Antigone Sgourda (A), Heather Harper (B), Helen Donath (C), Luigi Alva (D), Roger Soyer (E), Alberto Rinaldi (F), Geraint Evans (G), Peter Lagger (H), Scottish Opera Chorus, English Chamber Orchestra—Daniel Barenboim

This performance is more interesting to speculate on than to hear. Several of its singers are not widely known in America, and the idea of a Barenboim *Don* sounds provocative. The Prague version is used, with the Vienna additions (including the seldom performed Zerlina / Leporello scene) done at the end. The performance begins powerfully, with granitic weight and a sense of purpose, but conviction and interest flag with ambling and unsteady tempos, restricted characterization, and increasingly unsure singing. For Don Giovanni, Roger Soyer shows a polished and beautiful light bass voice, seductive in the duet with Zerlina and in the Serenade, but he makes little dramatically of the final scenes. Geraint Evans sings a lively, disgruntled Leporello, lacking some of the charm that he projected onstage but possessing great animation in a performance which needs it. Antigone Sgourda's Anna seems at first an exception: she shows vitality and brilliant promise in parts of Act I, but then her "Non mi dir" drags, lacking both accuracy and confidence. As Elvira, Heather Harper has a powerful but matronly sound, emphasized by Barenboim's increasingly leaden approach. At "Non ti fidar" she gets a more forward "Viennese" tone which begins to suggest aristocratic charm, but it soon disappears. Nor has Helen Donath quite the warmth or security to sustain the conductor's lingering approach to Zerlina's arias. Alberto Rinaldi is a colorful, self-righteous Masetto. As the Commendatore, Peter Lagger, like others, begins with authority, but later he sounds more comforting than chilling and hasn't the top voice needed for the finale. Luigi Alva also starts with energy, but the slow tempo of both of Ottavio's arias is a merciless exposition of his technical shortcomings. The makings of a convincing *Don Giovanni* are here, but the performance disintegrates as the challenges grow more subtle.

1977 DEUTSCHE GRAMMOPHON (S,P)

Anna Tomowa-Sintow (A), Teresa Zylis-Gara (B), Edith Mathis (C), Peter Schreier (D), Sherrill Milnes (E), Dale Duesing (F), Walter Berry (G), John Macurdy (H), Vienna State Opera Chorus, Vienna Philharmonic Orchestra—Karl Böhm

Like his first recording, Böhm's live Salzburg performance has a bias toward the massive and the violent, but this one is more appropriately cast and splendidly played. His view differs from Kubelik's graceful one and Karajan's encyclopedic attempt to include both the courtly and the universal; Böhm's is a drama of cruel

appetites and damnation. Milnes takes charge of his fate as few other recorded Giovannis have. The courtliness is a mask to get what he needs. The Champagne Aria and Serenade may go a little heavily, but one certainly has a sense of his engorging appetite, and his interplay with Walter Berry's Leporello is generally brilliant. The final scene has a ruthless grandeur beyond most other recordings. Berry is again a knowing servant, full of appetite himself and terror-struck at the end, and his conception has its best setting in this recording. Tomowa-Sintow's Anna is both passionate and accurate in Act I, and she sings "Non mi dir" with delicacy and finish, laboring only toward the end. As Zerlina, Edith Mathis is fresher than in the Kubelik set, and her sobriety fits in rather well with Böhm's view. Dale Duesing characterizes "Ho capito" sharply, but Masetto lies at the bottom of his range. In his second Ottavio, Peter Schreier has a new conviction: he can hardly wait to hear the next detail of Anna's narrative, and how that energy helps the scene! In "Dalla sua pace," the tone may not be outstandingly beautiful, but he controls it very well. As for Teresa Zylis-Gara, she is in sable-and-diamonds voice, though dramatic motivation is sometimes vague. John Macurdy's Commendatore is brooding but small-voiced for Böhm's overpowering conception of the finale. Of its muscular kind this is, all told, an outstanding release, well recorded and convincingly played.

1978 CBS / SONY (S) CD

Edda Moser (A), Kiri Te Kanawa (B), Teresa Berganza (C), Kenneth Riegel (D), Ruggero Raimondi (E), Malcolm King (F), José van Dam (G), John Macurdy (H), Paris Opéra Chorus and Orchestra—Lorin Maazel

This recording served as the soundtrack for the Joseph Losey film. The performance is interestingly cast, but after a decisive and exciting opening it sometimes loses dramatic direction. Several passages seem too slow for the singers, and in Act II one senses little tightening of the springs, scant movement toward real tragedy. The recorded sound is also distractingly blurred. Of the performances, José van Dam's Leporello is the most intriguing. This is a young man full of his own sexual energy, clever, and both perceptive and jealous of his master, while going along for the fascinating ride. These elements, however, are obscured in the second act; slyness, fear, and self-interest are insufficiently reflected in the voice. Ruggero Raimondi is glamorous and active in the first act, if not possessed of that grudging self-knowledge that can rescue the story from triviality. In Act II he seems more efficiently practical than deeply ironic and angry. As Anna, Edda Moser opens with great dramatic intensity and vocal thrust: an attractive and vital older woman. "Non mi dir," however, is hobbled by its slow tempo, and the character loses momentum. Kiri Te Kanawa is again a ravishing (and accurate) Elvira, though "Mi tradi" and some other passages become progressively less compelling under Maazel's direction. As Ottavio, Kenneth Riegel is respectable in his first aria and just insecure enough to be charmless in the second. Teresa Berganza, a mezzo Zerlina, is cultivated in "Batti, batti," and in "Vedrai, carino" has particularly gleaming tone. Malcolm King is her appealing Masetto. Some of the vocalism and characterization is striking in this issue, though the erratic conducting and recording are distinct disadvantages.

1978 DECCA / LONDON (S) CD

Margaret Price (A), Sylvia Sass (B), Lucia Popp (C), Stuart Burrows (D), Bernd Weikl (E), Alfred Sramek (F), Gabriel Bacquier (G), Kurt Moll (H), London Opera Chorus, London Philharmonic Orchestra—Georg Solti

This is an interesting album, but not for the usual reasons. Here we have a major conductor and an international cast of important voices, and what appears to be a catalogue of competing national vocal manners, too. Bacquier's sophistication, Weikl's exaggeration, Sass's closed tone, Price's coolness, Popp's coyness; one thinks of models like Fugère, Domgraf-Fassbänder, Hilde Gueden, and half a hundred others. Sir Georg, meanwhile, is in a moderate mood if not a poetic one: tempos and attack are lively and only the party scenes are demonic. Under him, though, the singers are encouraged to exploit the music for special theatrical effects. Bernd Weikl has a blunt sound for Don Giovanni but plays the compulsive and especially the seductive aspects beyond the point of credibility. As Leporello, Gabriel Bacquier tends to do everything with the role but sing it. His Catalogue Aria is a master class on character devices, quite brilliant but not quite satisfying. It emerges as slightly self-congratulatory, as if cleverness were the dramatic aim. He might be an analytical bystander: da Ponte himself, perhaps. Lucia Popp is among the most cultivated vocalists alive. She can do anything she wants with this music, and seems to have opted for coyness. Like the others, Alfred Sramek as Masetto is so busy with effects (outrage in "Ho capito," for example) that we hardly get a singing line.

Sylvia Sass is one of the world's most exasperating singers. She has a strikingly beautiful voice but often seems more bent on making an effect than giving a performance, so that her roles tend to emerge as both melodramatic and cold, as here. With the opaque vowel sounds, the weak bottom range, and the occasionally witch-like approach to Elvira, she loses the vulnerability and charm. "Mi tradi" is disappointing both technically and dramatically. On the other hand, Margaret Price, as Anna, sings surpassingly well, though the magnificent recitative to "Or sai, chi l'onore" is so slow under Sir Georg that it falls apart dramatically. The aria itself is distinguished, if a little cool, but "Non mi dir" is superb. Stuart Burrows sings quite tenderly but is not in his best voice. Kurt Moll is impressive as the Commendatore; there seems a halo of resonance in the sound itself. Despite its absolute completeness and its several virtues, though, the set can't really be recommended except as a fascinating anthology of conflicting statements about Mozart.

1984 EMI / ANGEL (S) CD

Carol Vaness (A), Maria Ewing (B), Elizabeth Gale (C), Keith Lewis (D), Thomas Allen (E),

John Rawnsley (F), Richard Van Allan (G), Dimitri Kavrakos (H), Glyndebourne Chorus, London Philharmonic Orchestra—Bernard Haitink

This cast performed the work at Glyndebourne under the stage direction of Peter Hall. The performance is more intimate though not more restrained emotionally than some others, and marked by the exceptional dramatic responsiveness of its singers. Bernard Haitink's orchestra plays neatly and sometimes with gossamer lightness. Each member of the cast projects a controlling vision of character which makes for provocative confrontation even when the vocalism is more respectable than brilliant. Immediately absorbing are the Elvira and Anna, Maria Ewing and Carol Vaness. Ewing's vocal vibrancy, aplomb, and dramatic commitment suggest a passion and propriety that seem indubitably Spanish, youthful, and aristocratic. It's a whip of a voice; the top glitters, the bottom is dusky, and she flings herself through the cadenzas with extraordinary purpose, signaling at once the vulnerability and tenacity of the character. For a brief sample, one should hear what she does with the recitative of vengeance, often cut, which follows Leporello's Catalogue Aria. Its anguish and eloquence are unique. To Anna, Carol Vaness initially brings similar commitment and a fiery, firm soprano. There may not always be total finish in "Or sai, chi l'onore," and Haitink's tempo variations sometimes emphasize details at the expense of design, but this is exciting singing. "Non mi dir" is a little more detached.

As Don Giovanni, Thomas Allen is a vivacious actor who has fine control of a voice essentially amiable in color. He alternates between irony, anger, and seductive sweetness; at other moments the natural pleasantness of his tone takes over. The final scene projects a rare agony.

The other singers are stylish and intelligent, but less striking vocally. Richard Van Allan has a snarl ready in the voice for Leporello and plays his recitatives with swift conviction. Elizabeth Gale is a rather hard-toned but affectionate Zerlina, Keith Lewis a gentle Ottavio, Dimitri

Kavrakos a light but firm Commendatore, and John Rawnsley a knowing Masetto: "Ho capito" lies a little low for him. The set is bracing for the intimate conviction of its cast and conductor, the dramatic range of its Don Giovanni, the vocalism of its Anna, and particularly its strikingly complex Elvira.

p. 1985 EURODISC (S,D) CD

Julia Varady (A), Arleen Augér (B), Edith Mathis (C), Thomas Moser (D), Alan Titus (E), Rainer Scholtze (F), Rolando Panerai (G), Jan-Hendrik Rootering (H), Bavarian Radio Chorus and Symphony Orchestra—Rafael Kubelik

Rafael Kubelik and his cast offer an aristocratic entertainment of grace and spirit. The characters sometimes lose dramatic impetus as the opera continues, but the singing is accomplished and almost all quite lovely. Alan Titus enacts a sinuous and attractive Don Giovanni, especially persuasive in the recitatives. Just before Anna's "Don Ottavio, son morta!," for example, he delivers such a seductive exit line that we know exactly the tone that has revealed his identity to her. Some of the lyric moments don't have quite this elegance or conviction, but it's a dexterously sung performance. His partner, Rolando Panerai, sings very beautifully as Leporello. In the Catalogue Aria there are both a delicate ironic edge and a suggestion of savagery, although, surprisingly from him, much of Act II seems underplayed, and the terror, when it comes, is quite subdued. Likewise, Julia Varady offers a strongly sung Anna, with considerable drive at the start but later vague at times in its dramatic message. Arleen Augér is in pretty voice and at her best enacting Elvira's plaintive concern and fragility; in the more active or vengeful moments she can be tentative. Edith Mathis, with her dark lyric voice, is not a playful Zerlina but is warm and comforting in "Vedrai, carino." Thomas Moser's Ottavio is rich enough in sound but a little breathless and unsteady, and dramatically a blank. Though the damnation scene is not the overwhelming thing it can be, Kubelik's pacing and the spirit of the whole are knowing and consistent. On that account and the vocalism of an interesting cast, the set is one of the half-dozen best.

1985 DEUTSCHE GRAMMOPHON (S,D) CD

Anna Tomowa-Sintow (A), Agnes Baltsa (B), Kathleen Battle (C), Gösta Winbergh (D), Samuel Ramey (E), Alexander Malta (F), Ferruccio Furlanetto (G), Paata Burchuladze (H), Berlin Opera Chorus, Berlin Philharmonic Orchestra—Herbert von Karajan

This is a beautifully played, well paced, and finely recorded set with a strong cast of dramatically aware singers. Herbert von Karajan sees the *dramma giocoso* as the basis for the interplay of philosophic forces, so that the performance has both verve and profundity: an attempt to realize several layers of the work. In the title role, Samuel Ramey is suave, rich-voiced, and technically adroit. The final scene may lack something in ultimate dramatic commitment, but this is a performance of theatrical spirit and surpassing vocal beauty. Around him are some equally lively singing actors. Ferruccio Furlanetto may be exceeded in richness of tone by several recorded Leporellos, but his work is marked by great dynamic variety. The recitatives are vibrantly delivered, he imitates Ramey amusingly, and his terror is quite convincing. On the videotape of this Salzburg production a further dimension was evident. With his handsome presence, he and his master seemed often like two aspects of the same appetite. The aural impression alone is more conventionally comic.

Tomowa-Sintow is in Act I a very outspoken Anna, sometimes rather coarse in tone but so vivid in her depiction of horror, outrage, and moral strength that one is convinced. "Non mi dir" also goes well, though the pace is slow enough and the method so painstaking that one may pay more attention to the technique displayed than to the comfort expressed. Gösta Winbergh is her Don Ottavio, a little light-voiced for her but romantic in feeling and musically distinguished. Both arias are sung with complete control and are rhythmically vital, too. Agnes Baltsa is an accomplished Elvira, and less single-minded than some oth-

ers; she sometimes cannot get to the end of an expression of outrage without falling in love with Don Giovanni all over again. Kathleen Battle's Zerlina is a little light vocally, but she is charming in "Batti, batti" and bewitching in "Vedrai, carino," delivered in something of a hush and meant for Masetto alone. In that role Alexander Malta is mature-sounding but vital. Paata Burchuladze provides the vocal presence for a striking Commendatore. One of the memorable moments is the trio just before his death. For the balance of its conductor's conception and the beauty and commitment of its vocal work, this is certainly among the most satisfying recent recordings.

1988 TELDEC (S,D) CD

Edita Gruberova (A), Roberta Alexander (B), Barbara Bonney (C), Hans Peter Blochwitz (D), Thomas Hampson (E), Anton Scharinger (F), László Polgár (G), Robert Holl (H), Netherlands Opera Chorus, Royal Concertgebouw Orchestra—Nikolaus Harnoncourt

This is a performance full of challenging ideas. Nikolaus Harnoncourt and his cast seem to want to have it all: the energy and the lyricism, the carnality and the courtliness, the comic illusion of freedom and the tragedy of fate. The recitatives are excitingly delivered and much of the performance is refreshingly specific in dramatic intention, though some of it is a little overstated. "Giovinette" (too fast), "Là ci darem la mano" (precious), "Don Ottavio, son morta!" (disjointed), and "Dalla sua pace" (too slow)—all suffer in this way. The singers are nearly all strong actors and musicians, though only Alexander and Bonney are outstanding vocalists in this score. Gruberova is a splendidly responsive performer, though her voice is uneven and her tone acidulous enough to disturb the music. Blochwitz is an occasionally insecure Ottavio, irresolute rather than romantic. Alexander brings a glittering darkness of tone and formidable technique to Elvira, though her expertly managed "Mi tradi" lacks the fury which would seem her natural gift in this music. Scharinger is an apt Masetto, youthful in tone. Bonney reveals a lovely lyric voice as Zerlina;

occasionally she has been asked to coo rather than sing. Polgár sings efficiently but misses, vocally at least, a point of view toward Leporello: where are the irony and terror? Hampson is a fiery, articulate Don—perhaps he lacks only that final vocal charisma to suggest a special genius for seduction. The ensemble work is generally brilliant. With all the caveats, the conception is continually provocative. For its aims as well as its accomplishments, this is one of the most intriguing recordings in a very large field.

1990 EMI / ANGEL (S,D,P) CD

Cheryl Studer (A), Carol Vaness (B), Susanne Mentzer (C), Frank Lopardo (D), William Shimell (E), Natale De Carolis (F), Samuel Ramey (G), Jan-Hendrik Rootering (H), Vienna State Opera Chorus, Vienna Philharmonic Orchestra—Riccardo Muti

Riccardo Muti shapes this performance with extraordinary energy and rhythmic clarity. The ensemble scenes nearly all have panache, variety, and dramatic focus even at the conductor's sometimes frenetic tempos. His speed does not eliminate grace either: "Il mio tesoro" is a charming example. He also has an exceptionally able cast. Cheryl Studer is both appealing and impassioned as Donna Anna. Her forward vocal production and attention to words remind one of an older tradition, though an occasionally excessive attempt at refinement results in unsteadiness. Similarly, Muti has roused Carol Vaness to surprising dramatic commitment, and her ruby-colored voice is at its best; only the lowest notes are pallid.

Samuel Ramey sings Leporello so beautifully as to disarm criticism: the voice is rich, varied, focused, and accurate in pitch, rhythm, and attack. He is, in fact, more elegant than his master, but there is great pleasure and indeed revelation in hearing the music so well sung. Jan-Hendrik Rootering provides the Commendatore with a fresh and free sound. He does not overwhelm in the final scene, where the very top is a trifle constricted, but his voice is a delight in a role in which everything is often sacrificed to weight and age. Frank Lopardo's

Ottavio is of exceptional interest. The thickness of his voice qualifies him for the heroic aspects of the role and yet does not limit his flexibility or accuracy. His technique and thoughtful conception give "Dalla sua pace" unusual dramatic focus, and as noted he and Muti achieve a virile grace unique in "Il mio tesoro." Natale De Carolis has a younger and more focused baritone sound than most Masettos and he is theatrically quite lively—all to the good, although the beating scene is not convincingly realized. Susanne Mentzer is no more than promising as Zerlina, and better in the ensembles than in "Batti, batti," which is labored, and "Vedrai, carino," where she sounds both consciously genteel and uncomfortably maternal: an easy trap.

At the center of all of this is William Shimell's Don, an aristocrat with a rough edge. The voice is weighty and sometimes insufficiently seductive, but he is an imaginative singer with a useful technique and dramatic vision; this is a ruthless Don with the trappings of style. Altogether the performance has one of the most provocative of recent casts and is led, if with ferocity, also with dramatic sophistication by Muti.

1990 ERATO (S,D) CD

Lella Cuberli (A), Waltraud Meier (B), Joan Rodgers (C), Uwe Heilmann (D), Ferruccio Furlanetto (E), Michele Pertusi (F), John Tomlinson (G), Matti Salminen (H), RIAS Chamber Chorus, Berlin Philharmonic Orchestra—Daniel Barenboim

Daniel Barenboim's second *Don Giovanni* is little more convincing than his first. The conception and performance are again weighty but listless and the singing is almost equally problematic. As Donna Anna, the striking Lella Cuberli is accurate but shrewish in tone: certainly not the appealing figure implied in "Dalla sua pace." By unfortunate contrast, Uwe Heilmann is a light Ottavio, rather callow in sound, though he phrases well and would doubtless arouse more enthusiasm in a better-balanced cast. Waltraud Meier, so moving in Wagner, has a fresh mezzo tone, but it is a little bulky and awkward for Mozart; the effect is to make Elvira maternal and uncertain—far from the distraught beauty of Schwarzkopf or the beguiling confusion of, say, Zylis-Gara. Joan Rodgers begins unpersuasively as Zerlina but warms to the lyricism of her two arias. John Tomlinson and Matti Salminen as Leporello and the Commendatore are earnest and serviceable, and Michele Pertusi is an apt Masetto. But for Rodgers and Heilmann, they are all largely charmless, though. Likewise, Ferruccio Furlanetto, though lively and commanding, is neither seductive nor particularly smooth in voice; he is a performer who must be seen. There is much talent here, but ultimately the performance lacks shape and a point of view.

1990 L'OISEAU-LYRE (S,D) CD

Arleen Augér (A), Della Jones (B), Barbara Bonney (C), Nico van der Meel (D), Håkan Hagegård (E), Bryn Terfel (F), Gilles Cachemaille (G), Kristinn Sigmundsson (H), Drottningholm Court Theater Chorus and Orchestra—Arnold Östman

This elegantly comic performance derives from a recent Drottningholm production. The conductor, Arnold Östman, has said that he sees Mozart's *dramma giocoso* as a specifically Shakespearean complex of farce and tragedy—a traditional enough view but interesting here in that the performance he elicits is the most courtly and amiable in the catalogue: closer to Molière, in my view, than to the Renaissance. From the first it is swift, light, and a little sentimental. Orchestral timbres are clear, ambience and projection intimate, recitatives quick and pointed, and dramatic responses more often comically temperate than envenomed. Thus the first confrontation between Giovanni and Anna is speedy but not savage, her reaction more amazed than outraged, and her father's interruption full of modest alarm; the element of terror is missing. Gilles Cachemaille's Leporello is pleasantly ironic, but there is little sense of his degradation. As Don Giovanni, Håkan Hagegård is both fresh-voiced and sensual but, it would seem, more high-spirited than damned

by lustful self-interest. He offers a dulcet "Là ci darem la mano" (punctuated, it is true, by a surprisingly coercive "Vieni!") and what must be the most intimate Serenade on records. That is all: both God and Hell seem to be missing.

The rest of the singing is entirely in line with this approach. Arleen Augér sings a concerned but contained "Or sai, chi l'onore," and her "Non mi dir" is sweet and delicate, not the impressive formal statement of personal sacrifice that others have made it. Della Jones as Elvira dispenses with the classical *legato* of which she is eminently capable. With this kind of soft humility such sublime moments as "Non ti fidar" lose the grand poignancy toward which virtually all other Elviras have worked, and "Ah, che mi dice mai" sheds most of its fury. Barbara Bonney, a lively Zerlina in the Harnoncourt performance, here pecks a little more at her vocal line: pretty but hardly as mesmerizing. All of this makes for an interesting view of *Don Giovanni*, and the interpretation is consistent to an extent not reached by many other recorded versions. Your view of it may depend on just how much of the pain inherent in the opera you wish to accept at a given moment. The Prague version is performed, though the Vienna additions are all included as an appendix.

1990 PHILIPS (S,D) CD

Sharon Sweet (A), Karita Mattila (B), Marie McLaughlin (C), Francisco Araiza (D), Thomas Allen (E), Claudio Otelli (F), Simone Alaimo (G), Robert Lloyd (H), Ambrosian Opera Chorus, Academy of St. Martin in the Fields—Neville Marriner

Sir Neville Marriner's performance is a miraculous integration of grace and compulsion. The articulation of the score is exceptional and its shaping always tempered by the drama. Further, the recitatives are built as surely as the music for mood and climax: swift, natural, theatrical, and intimate all at once. The singers—even those with vocal problems—all find sources of vitality in their roles, and we get masterful characterizations from Thomas Allen, Simone Alaimo, and Francisco Araiza. This last is of special interest, for few Ottavios have found the energy, gallantry, and heroism that the character needs. Here we have all three: the most impassioned Ottavio on records, and one of the most intimate and touching. "Dalla sua pace," for example, has an element of the mystic, well sustained by Araiza's very accomplished vocalism. Alaimo's baritone Leporello is equally striking: a nascent Figaro with a minor element of burlesque. He points the text for wit and plays brilliantly with Allen's Giovanni. Alaimo may not have the vocal weight or range to make the usual effect in "O statua gentilissima" and a few other moments in Act II, but his dramatization elsewhere is delightful. In other performances, the Don often appears prettier but duller than his servant, but not here. Allen's Giovanni has not only appetite but attractive cunning. His voice is not as commanding as some, but his technique is complete (for once a Champagne Aria of some charm) and his mastery of recitative—so important in this role—is an unending stimulation. If any moment is less persuasive, it may be his final scene, which Alaimo and Allen play strikingly but which needs a darker tone to make its overwhelming effect fully. Of the others, Robert Lloyd has, for once, the vocal stature requisite to the Commendatore, and Claudio Otelli is an attractive Masetto.

The women are less satisfying, although they share in Marriner's urgent vision. Sharon Sweet is a promising Anna, though she occasionally fails in attack and steadiness in this impassioned role. Karita Mattila's Elvira is full of determination; pitch and technique, however, are approximate, which disturbs some of the ensembles. As Zerlina, Marie McLaughlin does some of the recitatives charmingly—the arias remain a little ungainly despite her obvious intent. To sum up, the dramatic and musical revelations of the production as a whole certainly outweigh certain specific problems. The performance is magnetic and highly recommended.

———————

Among the two dozen or so recordings of this inexhaustible work, there are many unforgettable characterizations; the names of Baccaloni, Taddei, Tajo, Ramey, Sutherland (Giulini), Schwarzkopf, Berger, Grümmer, Te Kanawa, Ewing, Burrows, Winbergh, and Valletti are just a few of those that stand out. What you find satisfying will depend upon your view of the work. Busch offers a pleasurable and Furtwängler a sometimes compelling historical perspective. The Böhm (1977) and Fricsay recordings stress in their different ways the drive toward damnation, and the Karajan is richly played and beautifully sung. The Harnoncourt performance takes a complex view and is performed with great vitality, as is the Muti. The Östman is courtly, and the Marriner has compelling musical and dramatic wit and brilliant characterizations among the men. Perhaps the most durable and satisfying of all is the Giulini performance, which offers several classic portrayals in a reading of great depth and driving theatrical excitement.

LONDON GREEN

Unavailable for review:
1974 GUILDE INTERNATIONAL DU DISQUE
1980 FONIT-CETRA
1991 CHANDOS

Wolfgang Amadeus Mozart

Così Fan Tutte (1790)

A: Fiordiligi (s); B: Despina (s); C: Dorabella (ms); D: Ferrando (t);
E: Guglielmo (bs-bar); F: Don Alfonso (bs-bar)

An "ensemble opera": that's what we're always told Così is, and there are legitimate reasons: no other repertory opera has so symmetrically balanced a set of characters—all principals—and a major portion of the action takes the form of musical ensembles. But of which Mozart opera is this *not* true?

There *is* something different about Così, though: some way in which the individual characters' identities are concealed within group identities. We think of Fiordiligi and Dorabella as "the sisters," of Ferrando and Guglielmo as "the men," of the four collectively as "the lovers." It's not that da Ponte and Mozart didn't give them strong individual identities. The ensembles, for example, are special even by Mozart's standards; individual vocal lines generally have a distinctiveness and radiance that other operatic ensembles are happy to achieve in the "melody" line.

What's difficult is really searching out those individual identities within the outwardly symmetrical framework. To the extent that performers think of an ensemble piece as one in which only the group matters, rather than one in which each individual is defined largely through interaction with the others, Così, the "ensemble opera," is at best half alive.

Textually, although there are now a number of uncut recordings, it is still fairly standard to omit the little Ferrando-Guglielmo duet "Al fato dan legge," which provides either a breather or an unwelcome interruption—depending on your point of view—between the two great quintets of Act I and Ferrando's frenetic Act II aria "Ah! lo veggio." The duet is no great loss, and neither, practically speaking, is the aria—it's awfully tough to make work. It is, however, what drives Fiordiligi to "Per pietà." These two cuts, possibly along with some recitative, are described herein as "standard" cuts.

Extended standard cuts are, in addition, Dorabella's Act II aria "È amore un ladroncello" and Ferrando's other Act II aria, "Tradito, schernito." Such performances may be assumed to abridge the recitative and the Act I military music as well (usually eliding the initial orchestral statement). From here we move into the madcap world of free-lance cuts, with Act II especially vulnerable. There seems to be a fatigue factor at work: if it's too hard to make all that music work, why not make a little less music?

One final dangling musical number: Guglielmo's original Act I aria, "Rivolgete a lui lo sguardo," which Mozart replaced with the simpler and more effective "Non siate ritrosi," is included in some recordings, either as an appendix or in its original place.

1935 EMI / ANGEL (M) ℂ𝔻

Ina Souez (A), Irene Eisinger (B), Luise Helletsgruber (C), Heddle Nash (D), Willi Domgraf-Fassbänder (E), John Brownlee (F), Glyndebourne Festival Chorus and Orchestra—Fritz Busch

The very absence of a performing tradition for *Così*—relative to *Figaro* and *Don Giovanni*—may have worked in this Glyndebourne production's favor. At least on the musical side, the performance depended on the good sense of that most sensible conductor Fritz Busch. The questions of tone and content that would bedevil later recordings basically don't come up here. The performance moves with assurance, with ample wit and rich appreciation of the score's lyric beauty.

The drawbacks? First, Busch's level of comfort with the score would eventually be reached by other conductors, who would benefit from engineering that does fuller justice to the opera's range of tone colors and its diverse musical strands. Also, the cast as a whole doesn't hold up well to extended scrutiny.

The obvious exception is the prodigious Fiordiligi of Ina Souez, perhaps the role's least daunted recorded exponent: vocally shiny and forceful through amazingly near the full range required. Luise Helletsgruber, a light-soprano Dorabella, is surprisingly pleasant-sounding but is overshadowed. Irene Eisinger brings hardly any voice to Despina.

Heddle Nash gets off to a good start as Ferrando—the early scenes have a fair amount of focus. But when faced with more extended lyric obligations, he is beset with that familiar oddly curdled sound in the upper mid-range and top. Brownlee is a fairly smooth, sensible Alfonso who ought to be a strong exemplar of the baritone-Alfonso option, except that the performance somehow doesn't develop.

Willi Domgraf-Fassbänder's ringing baritone can be heard to good effect in recorded excerpts ranging from Papageno to Wolfram, but he's somehow out of place here. Not only does he succumb to the overemphases common to singing baritones in the role, but he sings unidiomatically in Italian. His German-language Figaro, after all, also has a smug quality that we associate with German Mozart.

In addition to abridged recitative and extended standard cuts, there are trims in both finales and the Fiordiligi-Ferrando duet "Fra gli amplessi."

1952 CBS / SONY (In English) (M)

Eleanor Steber (A), Roberta Peters (B), Blanche Thebom (C), Richard Tucker (D), Frank Guarrera (E), Lorenzo Alvary (F), Metropolitan Opera Chorus and Orchestra—Fritz Stiedry

A decent performance could probably have been put together from these ingredients, but the production it's based on is crippled by a tone built into the Ruth and Thomas Martin translation, which manages to be simultaneously patronizing, hard to sing, and hideously unfunny. (My favorite example: the transformation of Ferrando and Guglielmo's simple recitative response "Bravissimo, Signor Don Alfonsetto" into "Bravissimo, you connoisseur of women.")

When performers aren't launching elbows at our ribs, they don't seem to know what to do. Important chunks of the score consequently shuffle tentatively, making them even less satisfactory than the bumptious "comical" numbers.

Although the fine quality of the young Roberta Peters's soprano occasionally shines through, her Despina is mostly vocal edge. Frank Guarrera's baritone still has some lyric quality in it, but he doesn't make much use of it. Most regrettably, Richard Tucker, whose hefty tenor could have been a sensational Ferrando instrument, and who does a fair amount of strong singing, gets all too readily into the bumptious spirit of things. By contrast, Lorenzo Alvary's chalky bass and mealy delivery, not to mention his strangely accented English, suit the performance all too well. (Although the voice at this time still had some usable lower notes, it's a sound that jangles my nervous system.)

Eleanor Steber as Fiordiligi escapes most of the tomfoolery, and her forceful, wide-ranging vocalism, with its iron-willed mechanical underpinning, might almost make this recording worth hearing if the climate weren't so inhospitable to serious work. This remains a considerable piece of singing by any standard, but again, what one wants to hear is a no-holds-barred crack at the role. Blanche Thebom also suffers from the performance's lack of direction for real work, which leaves her fair-size mezzo sounding rather ungainly. It's sobering to remember that only the following month she recorded such a durable Brangäne in Furtwängler's *Tristan*.

Cuts are "extended standard" plus some trimming in the finales and in various Act II numbers, and of course in the recitative.

1954 EMI / ANGEL (M) CD

Elisabeth Schwarzkopf (A), Lisa Otto (B), Nan Merriman (C), Léopold Simoneau (D), Rolando Panerai (E), Sesto Bruscantini (F), Philharmonia Chorus and Orchestra—Herbert von Karajan

Because this recording, like producer Walter Legge's 1962 stereo remake, has an exalted reputation, you'll probably need to check it out for yourself. To my hearing, both recordings are not only unsatisfactory but in some ways disastrous.

In both cases, an interesting-looking cast was assembled and then not asked, or perhaps allowed, to do much of anything. In the case of 1954 EMI, it's not so much that the performers make bad choices as that they mostly avoid making choices at all. The performance has a certain low-gloss surface polish that mustn't be scuffed, even if it means reining in singers of such demonstrated temperament and vocal presence as Nan Merriman, Rolando Panerai, Sesto Bruscantini, and Léopold Simoneau.

While this restraint may protect Merriman and Panerai from the vibrato overload to which their voices are prone, restraint is hardly a quality for which we turn to these distinctive artists. If you want a shock, compare this pale Dorabella with the vivid Mahler songs she recorded about this time, or with her vivacious Dorabella in 1962–63 DG.

Where Panerai is concerned, and Simoneau as well, this is really two performances. At the point, not quite halfway through Act II, when Guglielmo reveals to Ferrando his success in wooing Dorabella, the men finally begin to sing as if what's happening actually means something to them. This could be defended as an Interpretive Concept—for example, "At this point the previously larky shenanigans turn all too devastatingly real. . . ." Except what perverse kind of Concept consigns the first three-quarters of the opera to an exhibition of arch rococo tedium?

Nobody sounds especially good. There is enough outside documentation of the vocally strong and incisive work of the young Bruscantini, still singing mostly as a bass, to make this generally bland and fussy Alfonso a jolt, and hardly any of the charm and light-soprano competence of which Lisa Otto was demonstrably capable is evidenced in this Despina. As for Elisabeth Schwarzkopf, it's hard to believe that the little pufflets of sound she puts out here give pleasure even to her ardent admirers.

The only musical numbers omitted are "Al fato dan legge" and "Ah! lo veggio." The recitatives, though, are considerably trimmed.

1955 DECCA / LONDON (S) CD

Lisa della Casa (A), Emmy Loose (B), Christa Ludwig (C), Anton Dermota (D), Erich Kunz (E), Paul Schöffler (F), Vienna State Opera Chorus, Vienna Philharmonic Orchestra—Karl Böhm

This is a beautiful performance, but there's no getting around the infamous cuts. Beyond the omission of the four "extended standard" numbers, there's the snipping, and on occasion hacking, within numbers: in Act I, the "Sento, o Dio" quintet, Dorabella's "Smanie implacabili," and the finale; in Act II, almost every number.

The fact remains that Karl Böhm, the conductor most closely identified with *Così*, customarily made liberal cuts, as documented by live performances from Geneva and from various Salzburg Festivals. In this company, the more inclusive 1962 is clearly the aberration. The uncut-text movement, it should be recalled, was of little interest to Dr. Böhm, possibly a pernicious effect of his formative association with old Dr. Strauss, who didn't fuss even when his own operas were cut.

What did concern the good doctors was what

they could perform effectively. And when the first statement of musical material is as clear and forceful as it almost invariably is in this recording, the cuts just don't seem to me to matter that much—especially now that we have so many alternative sources for the missing music.

The general pace of the performance is unhurried, with a concern for the dramatic function of Mozart's musical structures matched on records only by the temperamentally very different Klemperer recording (1971 EMI). The fine early stereo sound puts in excellent perspective the lively, beautifully balanced collaboration of Böhm and the Vienna Philharmonic.

The cast comes through with a lovely ensemble performance. Shocking as it is to contemplate the abridgment of the "Sento, o Dio" quintet, these performers make its musical and dramatic points far more completely than almost any of their no-cut competitors. The same is true of the young Christa Ludwig's melting and heroic, albeit brief, "Smanie implacabili": which Dorabella has made as much of this aria at full length? Ludwig is heard here in the warmer, brighter coloration of those years, and sings so winningly that one does regret the quantity of music the character has lost.

The other standout performance in this set is Emmy Loose's Despina, from an all-around standpoint my favorite on records: a beautiful piece of singing allied to a first-rate piece of lively, believable characterization. Of course, a cast that includes Lisa della Casa is going to contain a measure of radiant singing, the only problem being that Fiordiligi is unquestionably a stretch for her—the little snip at the end of "Per pietà," at minimal sacrifice, protects her from spoiling what came before.

The men, as noted, contribute effectively to the ensembles, but are less striking individually. While the fullness and general attractiveness of Anton Dermota's tenor are excellent tools for Ferrando, there is a fair amount of strained production. Erich Kunz as Guglielmo does perhaps the most disciplined work I've heard from him, but the voice is more a character baritone than a legitimate singing baritone. Paul Schöff-

ler, although somewhat dry and shaky of voice, is a solid Alfonso.

1955 PHILIPS (M)

Teresa Stich-Randall (A), Graziella Sciutti (B), Ira Malaniuk (C), Waldemar Kmentt (D), Walter Berry (E), Dezsö Ernster (F), Vienna State Opera Chorus, Vienna Symphony Orchestra—Rudolf Moralt

No, this isn't a performance worth searching out, but it's not completely without interest. Conductor Rudolf Moralt, usually a deadening force, while still no dynamo, isn't entirely unsympathetic. The performance has some pleasant lyric flow, so that even if it never builds up much momentum, neither does it neuter the score in the manner of 1954 EMI.

The cast, of necessity assembled from the ranks of singers unaffiliated with the major opera-producing record companies, is about as peculiar an assortment as one can imagine: a pair of piercing, slender-toned sopranos, a mezzo and bass recruited from the Wagner wars, a tenor and baritone actually plausibly matched to their roles but linguistically hobbled.

Teresa Stich-Randall isn't in good form, and this is a voice—narrow and white-toned—that under the best of circumstances is a special taste. But the special concentration and technical sweep of which the singer was capable, qualities that made Fiordiligi a showpiece role for her, aren't much in evidence here. Interested listeners are directed to the 1957 Aix performance conducted by Hans Rosbaud, where she needs time to warm up but, when she gets there, does some spectacular singing.

Ira Malaniuk isn't exactly a fluent Mozartian, but the voice does have a bit of presence, which is welcome for Dorabella. Graziella Sciutti's Despina is steeped in the attitudes of Comic Opera, but within this framework she performs adroitly—her Doctor and Notary caricatures are even moderately amusing. Dezsö Ernster's bass is a strong impact instrument, in rather ragged shape here but still a sound that commands attention without resort to gimmickry.

Waldemar Kmentt's tenor, on the plus side,

is more robust than the average Ferrando, and there are many places where the weight and ring are much to the point. On the minus side, this was never an especially malleable voice—and certainly not one we want to hear tackle the restored "Ah! lo veggio." Its handling difficulties make for some fairly fierce tone production, and the situation isn't improved by his limited facility singing in Italian. Walter Berry isn't a smooth Italian stylist either, but Guglielmo seems to me vocally and temperamentally a better match for him than Alfonso (1962 EMI).

The text is surprisingly inclusive. Only Dorabella's "È amore un ladroncello" is omitted entirely, though there are brief trims in the finales and in the recitative.

1962 EMI / ANGEL (S) CD

Elisabeth Schwarzkopf (A), Hanny Steffek (B), Christa Ludwig (C), Alfredo Kraus (D), Giuseppe Taddei (E), Walter Berry (F), Philharmonia Chorus and Orchestra—Karl Böhm

For what it's worth, this is a better performance than 1954 EMI. If you listen in an abstract way, here at least you'll hear actual phrase shapes and textures, such as might be employed in an actual performance of Così.

These phrase-forms appear to delimit the contribution of Karl Böhm, who seems to have functioned essentially in the manner of a decorator bearing books of fabric and color samples. The sample phrases are merely displayed; nothing progresses or develops. Compare the monotonous repetitiveness of the string and woodwind figurations in the Overture with the spirited flow of all Böhm's other performances of it.

The prevailing dourness of the sample phrases used is surprising set alongside 1955 Decca / London and 1974 DG. But there is some precedent in Böhm's early-sixties Salzburg performances, except that there these choices form a deadpan contrast to the fairly broad humor. Note that apart from Elisabeth Schwarzkopf and Christa Ludwig, no one else in this cast had ever done Così with Böhm, and indeed none of the men had ever sung his role.

Schwarzkopf is at least *singing* Fiordiligi now,

more or less. And there are phrase-segments of striking beauty. But then there's all that fussing and whimpering and meowing, which surely nobody would mistake for interpretation. Ludwig's Dorabella, in the darker-toned format of her mature voice and with all the music she lost in 1955 Decca / London restored, gives the most serious performance in the set. But she's left having to work on her own, and the performance consequently isn't all that interesting.

Alfredo Kraus hasn't absorbed much of Ferrando's music into his idiosyncratic tenor, with its usable but tonally pressed upper range. Some of the tougher passagework, in fact, is plain garbled. Giuseppe Taddei, similarly, can often be heard simply shoving out notes as he does when a role stumps him, as for some reason all his recorded Mozart roles largely did. Creepy coincidence: at Guglielmo's "Donne miei" and Ferrando's "Tradito, schernito," Taddei and Kraus suddenly show what they can do. This is the exact point at which a performance began to happen in 1954 EMI.

Alfonso not only leaves Walter Berry a bit thick-toned but brings out some of his annoyingly boorish notions of characterization. Guglielmo took better advantage of the dark tinge of his bass-baritone, especially if he'd have worked on his Italian singing. As Despina, Hanny Steffek seems to have wandered in from the Viennese Operetta Maids' Guild.

Except for "Al fato dan legge" and "Ah! lo veggio," the performance is complete.

1962–63 DEUTSCHE GRAMMOPHON (S)

Irmgard Seefried (A), Erika Köth (B), Nan Merriman (C), Ernst Häfliger (D), Hermann Prey (E), Dietrich Fischer-Dieskau (F), RIAS Chamber Chorus, Berlin Philharmonic Orchestra—Eugen Jochum

There are conductors who are plugged into the way this astonishingly beautiful score is put together; there are others who are plugged into its built-in forward momentum. (There are conductors who are pretty much unplugged, but we're not concerned with them just now.) The conductor who plugs into both, and better than anybody else, is Eugen Jochum.

The cast doesn't look all that promising, and indeed none of the six principals would number among my favorites in their roles—although Ernst Häfliger's winningly lyric Ferrando and Nan Merriman's authoritative Dorabella (a big improvement over 1954 EMI) would finish strongly in the second group, and Hermann Prey's Guglielmo is a major surprise.

Nevertheless, this is by a secure margin my favorite *Così*. The Berlin Philharmonic is splendid. No other orchestra plays with such balanced beauty and clarity—albeit with a certain tonal coolness or reserve, which establishes an objective framework for the performance—and with such a sure sense of forward movement.

And the cast performs almost entirely from its strengths rather than its weaknesses. Irmgard Seefried is clearly underequipped for Fiordiligi in availability of range extremes and in tonal freedom and flexibility. And Seefried, Prey, and Dietrich Fischer-Dieskau have all been known to "personalize" by displaying attitude rather than finding the content of the music.

Yet somehow the performance manages to align these habits with the areas of their lives about which the characters themselves are ignorant, and which become the subject of their Act II voyage of discovery. Seefried is a persuasive Fiordiligi, Fischer-Dieskau a plausible Alfonso, and Prey—eschewing all gimmickry—one of the most successful of an admittedly underwhelming lot of Guglielmos.

Except for "Al fato dan legge" and "Ah! lo veggio," the text is complete.

1967 RCA / BMG (S) CD

Leontyne Price (A), Judith Raskin (B), Tatiana Troyanos (C), George Shirley (D), Sherrill Milnes (E), Ezio Flagello (F), Ambrosian Opera Chorus, New Philharmonia Orchestra—Erich Leinsdorf

For some reason, listeners who don't know this recording are frequently surprised to discover how good it is. Is there perhaps some feeling that a Mostly American Mozart production can't be competitive? (Conductor Erich Leinsdorf qualifies as American by adoption. The participation of a British orchestra and chorus is a mere technicality.)

In fact, the cast—allowing for mixed results in the lower-male regions, which are hardly unique to this endeavor—is as strong as there is on records. And more than any other recording, this one insists on treating Mozart on a full operatic scale, allowing the characters the full scope of their dramatic circumstances.

Leontyne Price and Tatiana Troyanos would certainly be my favorite Fiordiligi-Dorabella pairing. Price did some of her most treasurable work with Mozart, and despite the hoarse lower range and the somewhat smudgy passagework, the richness and fullness of the sound and the unstinting emotional commitment make this performance irresistible. Troyanos's bright, thrusting, lean, and agile mezzo makes a perfect complement, and she sings with the life-or-death intensity characteristic of these early years of her international career.

Mozart was also a good composer for George Shirley; it's a shame he never got to record Ottavio and Tamino. His Ferrando seems to me the best on records: a voice at the fullest end of the lyric-tenor spectrum, handled with tremendous grace and ardor. Mozart, on the other hand, has not been a happy match for Sherrill Milnes, who needs a different kind of musical coatrack on which to hang his manner of vocal emphases, and a different kind of musical platform from which to launch his vocal rockets. He leaps into the traps Guglielmo sets for big-time singing baritones. It's not awful, and it doesn't disfigure the overall performance, but it's not what you'd call an attraction either.

Ezio Flagello sings well enough, but can't make much impact, in the way that pretty much all of the bass Alfonsos can't make much impact. Judith Raskin, a lovely artist, is in general a very nice Despina, though I wonder whether she would have remained so committed to some of her comic ideas—e.g., the clichéd Doctor impersonation—if she'd had sympathetic and enlightened directorial collaboration.

Some of which could, of course, have come from the conductor, but this isn't Leinsdorf's strong suit. Credit him with the scale and drive of the performance, and then take off perhaps a few points for a slightly general quality. But a framework is created in which the singers can do their job, and they do. This first uncut recording remains a strong contender among the textually complete sets—and, for that matter, among the general competition.

1969 ETERNA (S)

Celestina Casapietra (A), Sylvia Geszty (B), Annelies Burmeister (C), Peter Schreier (D), Günther Leib (E), Theo Adam (F), Berlin State Opera Chorus, Berlin State Orchestra—Otmar Suitner

The muffled acoustic obscures what sounds like highly cultivated playing by the Berlin State Orchestra under Otmar Suitner's agreeably light but steady hand. Unfortunately, while this isn't a cast one wants to hear in X-ray close-up, the distant sound calls undue attention to the singers by forcing the listener to listen too hard.

Some perfectly honorable, if un-Italianate and sometimes overcareful, work wilts under this scrutiny. Despite Annelies Burmeister's characterless mezzo and Günther Leib's decent but unremarkable baritone, they make a presentable Dorabella and Guglielmo. Despite the basic sourness of Peter Schreier's tenor, and the aggressive mode in which he attacks Ferrando in both his recordings, he's earnest and hard-working. Theo Adam's dry, shuddery bass-baritone isn't prime Alfonso material, but he's sober and reliable.

In this company, Sylvia Geszty as Despina sounds like a major singer: notes cleanly attacked, phrases more or less sustained with singing tone. Of course, it's still the rather acidic tone familiar from her brief period of international coloratura celebrity. Regrettably, there is nothing kind to say about Celestina Casapietra's Fiordiligi. As heard here, the voice is a rather pale, unfocused sound gliding forlornly around pitches.

Under the circumstances, it's hard to complain about the unprecedented omission of Fiordiligi's "Per pietà," along with Ferrando's

"Ah! Io veggio." (Yes, "Al fato dan legge" is included!)

1971 EMI / ANGEL (S) CD

Margaret Price (A), Lucia Popp (B), Yvonne Minton (C), Luigi Alva (D), Geraint Evans (E), Hans Sotin (F), John Alldis Choir, New Philharmonia Orchestra—Otto Klemperer

Like his other Mozart operas, Klemperer's Così isn't for all tastes. Yes, it's slow, and it makes extraordinary demands on the singers. And Klemperer's kind of slow isn't luxuriant or embellished. It's austere, and obsessed with the function of the musical structures as vehicles for the pursuit of character needs. In contrast to the recent spate of "sensitive" performances, which amble in exploratory mode, this one is stubbornly decisive.

The performances that pop out on reacquaintance are Lucia Popp's and Hans Sotin's. Perhaps neither offers an especially studied piece of interpretation, but both sing exceptionally well—these are, in fact, probably the best-sung Despina and Alfonso on records. Popp doesn't even do fake voices for Despina's impersonations—she sings fluidly and alertly, and even sounds fairly comfortable in Italian. Sotin is the one thoroughly satisfactory bass Alfonso; just listen to him launch the sextet ("Alla bella Despinetta"). Considering how much these two characters have to do with the reasons the events of the opera take place, strong casting gives this performance a solid foundation.

The women are also fine, especially considering the difficulty of filling out their music at Klemperer's tempos. Margaret Price is an exceptional Fiordiligi: the voice lovely and wide-ranging, with everything taken touchingly personally. Yvonne Minton holds up her end nicely, no easy feat in this context.

Luigi Alva, never the sweetest-voiced tenor, remains at this relatively late date a reliable singer, and again it's all the more impressive that he is able to fill out Klemperer's broad structures. Geraint Evans might have seemed better cast as Alfonso, but in this case, too, at the sacrifice of real tonal pleasure we do get a steady, crafty artist.

Standard cuts ("Al fato dan legge" and "Ah! lo veggio") plus some recitative abridgment.

1973–74 DECCA / LONDON (S) CD

Pilar Lorengar (A), Jane Berbié (B), Teresa Berganza (C), Ryland Davies (D), Tom Krause (E), Gabriel Bacquier (F), Chorus of the Royal Opera House, Covent Garden, London Philharmonic Orchestra—Georg Solti

Solti's *Così* recording may not be as clear-cut a triumph as his *Magic Flutes*, but perhaps the intimacy and subtlety of the score don't lend themselves to clear-cut triumphs. All the same, this is a warm, caring, sane performance that may not transcend the limitations of the singers but certainly makes good use of their strengths.

The men deserve first consideration. Ryland Davies here gets everything there is to be gotten out of his pleasing rather than remarkable tenor, and he allows himself to be guided by the music's wild swings and truly nutty behavioral realities—he earns a place in the upper group of Ferrandos. He and Tom Krause form the best Ferrando-Guglielmo team on records, and Krause may in fact be the best of the (admittedly underwhelming) Guglielmos.

Since Krause is most familiarly heard attempting to slot his light-to-medium-weight baritone into troublesome roles that better-endowed baritones have the luxury of bypassing, it's startling to hear him connecting with this one, which has given the more glamorous baritones such grief. He understands that even when the music rises into the territory where the Big Guys expect to be able to make the Big Impression, the music doesn't respond to such treatment. And since he's not overproducing up there, he has an easier time keeping the lower-lying writing in scale.

Gabriel Bacquier as Alfonso puts us in the two-baritone configuration, which has generally produced the best results. At this point he's making a rather husky sound, but it's at the service of a superior performing intelligence. Jane Berbié is also vocally less than ideal as

Despina but does a satisfactory job.

The text is complete.

1974 PHILIPS (S) CD

Montserrat Caballé (A), Ileana Cotrubas (B), Janet Baker (C), Nicolai Gedda (D), Wladimiro Ganzarolli (E), Richard Van Allan (F), Chorus and Orchestra of the Royal Opera House, Covent Garden—Colin Davis

It can't be fun for hugely talented people, always having their accomplishments measured against their "potential." Why we hold them to that standard is suggested by the pleasure of hearing a Caballé really connect—and in such unexpected roles as Salome and Fiordiligi.

The mechanical difficulties of the latter role might not seem such a great stretch for Caballé, though in truth the mechanics are no more glitch-free here than in her *bel canto* roles. But the voice is powerful, vibrant, and wide-ranging: ample at the bottom, reaching up with melting delicacy on top—viz. the gentle ascent on "Sempre ascoso" in "Per pietà." And the role is sung full-out, giving full, real-life weight to the character's desperate stakes—without the pitter-patter commenting that often passes for "stylish" Mozart singing. Even more than the other Spanish Fiordiligis, she has built-in vocal access to a stark, touching vulnerability.

The bad news is that apart from Caballé this *Così* is honorable but rather plain. Janet Baker produces a small patch of pleasant sound in the middle of the voice; the rest isn't much more than a light tracing. Ileana Cotrubas's pretty but perilously under-supported sound sets me on edge, and interpretively her Despina is a subdued version of the obvious cute clichés.

Nicolai Gedda is heard in his sour-toned late estate. Goodness knows, there's no lack of energy in his Ferrando, and he holds his own in the large ensembles. But there's no getting around the unpleasantness of the sound, and he gets scant help from his conductor—"Ah! lo veggio" is taken just quickly enough to leave him gasping behind. Wladimiro Ganzarolli's bass-baritone doesn't have much color, but he's not bad, and he might have had some interest as a low-voice Guglielmo, except that Alfonso has been cast with a bass, and a distressed one at that. When the recording was released, I speculated that Richard Van Allan was trying to make himself sound old; now it seems to me that the voice is simply in disastrous shape.

Where is Colin Davis in all of this? Leading a tidy, symmetrical performance that to my ears doesn't go anywhere. The text is complete.

1974 GUILDE INTERNATIONAL DU DISQUE (S)

Enriquetta Tarrés (A), Rotraud Hansmann (B), Kari Lövaas (C), Erik Geisen (D), Philippe Huttenlocher (E), Klaus Hirte (F), Chorus of the Théâtre National de l'Opéra, Monte Carlo National Opera Orchestra—Pierre Colombo

An unassuming but in its way pleasant performance. The pace here is on the unhurried side, allowing leisure to savor the score and maximizing contrast with inherently more diverse music like the military choruses. (The chorus itself sounds rather feeble, however. Was it dubbed in?) The orchestral ensemble isn't gleamingly polished, and the reedy French-style winds don't blend quite euphoniously, but even these qualities lend the performance a certain friendly personality.

The cast is presentable. The characteristic Spanish edge to Enriquetta Tarrés's soprano lends itself to a vulnerability appropriate for Fiordiligi. The somewhat darker coloration of Kari Lövaas's soprano (and of course the lower lie of the writing) provides a measure of contrast for Dorabella, but the voice's less than ideal tonal focus doesn't help her cope with the mezzo range. Rotraud Hansmann deploys her light soprano for all it is worth, producing a certain amount of sparkle without cuteness— one of the nicest of the Despinas.

Erik Geisen is a pleasantly sweet, light-toned Ferrando, and the amiable Philippe Huttenlocher is a satisfactory light-toned Guglielmo. Maybe it's the German accent, but Klaus Hirte's tolerably well-sung Alfonso has a distinctly schoolmasterish cast.

The text omits "Al fato dan legge" and Ferrando's "Ah! lo veggio" and "Tradito, scher-nito." There's also a fair amount of internal cutting, as well as abridgment of recitative.

1974 DEUTSCHE GRAMMOPHON (S,P) CD

Gundula Janowitz (A), Reri Grist (B), Brigitte Fassbaender (C), Peter Schreier (D), Hermann Prey (E), Rolando Panerai (F), Vienna State Opera Chorus, Vienna Philharmonic Orchestra—Karl Böhm

The comedy is on the broad side, but this performance, taped on Karl Böhm's eightieth birthday (an excellent live-performance recording), happily recovers the warm, outgoing spirit of 1955 Decca / London, thanks in part to the renewal of the conductor's collaboration with the Vienna Philharmonic. The package of cuts is also reminiscent of 1955 Decca / London. At least "Smanie implacabili" is spared this time.

Gundula Janowitz's Fiordiligi seems to me one of the most impressive on records, all the more so for having been recorded live. She does tend to under-articulate words in Italian, but her hauntingly pure tone and sensitive phrasing leave no doubt about her dramatic intentions. The unusually dark-toned Dorabella of Brigitte Fassbaender makes an excellent contrast, and Fassbaender also makes some interesting character points—once again Böhm has a top-quality Dorabella, causing one to regret the loss of her second aria.

Peter Schreier's voice is not in good condition here—it's hoarse and barely functional in the upper range. Whether or not this is the reason, he gives a fairly bumptious performance. In this case, the lost music is no loss. Hermann Prey, however, substantially repeats his fine Guglielmo from 1962–63 DG, resisting the temptation to clowning, which one suspects the production may have encouraged.

Roland Panerai might have made the case for a baritone Alfonso if he had been in better voice, but when this instrument goes out of whack it's best to duck for cover. Reri Grist's soprano comes in a single, *very* bright color, which fortunately is plausible for Despina, and she gives an enjoyable performance.

1977 ERATO (S) CD

Kiri Te Kanawa (A), Teresa Stratas (B), Frederica von Stade (C), David Rendall (D), Philippe Huttenlocher (E), Jules Bastin (F), Rhine Opera Chorus, Strasbourg Philharmonic Orchestra—Alain Lombard

Within certain limits, this is an attractive and enjoyable presentation. Alain Lombard's conducting is a bit general, and this generality is magnified by the extremely resonant acoustic. But in compensation, the performance has an engaging decisiveness and a fullness of scale.

Even at this stage of her career, Kiri Te Kanawa was stretched by Fiordiligi, for whose range extremes she never had an especially workable alternative solution. But while the character does tend to fade when the music emphasizes the range extremes ("Per pietà," for example, isn't a high point), much of her singing does have the special personal attractiveness of her best work. And she is well partnered by Frederica von Stade as Dorabella: the voice full and creamy, the temperament heading toward an appropriate impulsiveness.

David Rendall sings agreeably, though his somewhat odd upper-range tone formation undercuts his basically attractive light tenor. Philippe Huttenlocher, as in 1974 GID, is an agreeable if unmemorable Guglielmo. Jules Bastin produces some strikingly potent phrases but suffers both from his own vocally uneven production and from the limitations of a true bass as Alfonso. Teresa Stratas might have been a dream Despina, and some of her singing is bold and alive, but some of the humor is forced-funny.

"Al fato dan legge" and "Ah! lo veggio" are omitted and the recitative somewhat trimmed.

1982 EMI / ANGEL (S,P) CD

Margaret Marshall (A), Kathleen Battle (B), Agnes Baltsa (C), Francisco Araiza (D), James Morris (E), José van Dam (F), Vienna State Opera Chorus, Vienna Philharmonic Orchestra—Riccardo Muti

While this isn't a terribly personal performance, it's lively and entertaining, brisk and bracing without being manic. Riccardo Muti's customary phraseological squareness, with its predictable emphases, would seem a deadening prospect for Mozart, and yet I've often found him more at home in the eighteenth and early nineteenth centuries than in his favored romantic repertory.

Agnes Baltsa's strong-willed Dorabella is the most interesting performance in the set. But Margaret Marshall is a reasonably appealing if vocally overtaxed Fiordiligi; Francisco Araiza, despite some constriction in his singing, is a presentable Ferrando; and José van Dam displays the makings of a fine Alfonso, though the performance doesn't quite come together.

Because of the basic gravelly texture of James Morris's voice, which hardly allows for the formation of a clean, limber Mozartian phrase, this unfortunately doesn't provide a fair test of the possibilities of a bass Guglielmo. (And, note, he's paired with a bass-baritone Alfonso.) Nor am I wild about the brittle perkiness of Kathleen Battle's Despina.

Some listeners have been put off by the recorded sound, which for once actually sounds like a live performance, with a measure of opera-house distance that I find a refreshing change of pace. The text has standard cuts.

1984 L'OISEAU-LYRE (S,D) CD

Rachel Yakar (A), Georgine Resick (B), Alicia Nafé (C), Gösta Winbergh (D), Tom Krause (E), Carlos Feller (F), Chorus and Orchestra of the Drottningholm Court Theater—Arnold Östman

This is what happens when you perform a theory instead of an opera. Original instruments are used, which is okay, but the performance work still has to get done. Someone has to notice, for example, that all three of the women are in over their heads.

Instead, the performance devotes the first half-hour or more to establishing that no silly-fast tempo will be considered too preposterous, beginning with the double-time introduction to the Overture. But even this doesn't seem to represent any real belief about the piece: even while demolition is under way on the musical numbers of the first two scenes (including the two great quintets), the recitative is being taken at a perfectly sensible pace, and after a while even the musical numbers cease being cockeyed demonstration points.

There's not much to say about the women, except that all three *might* have been able to do something with these roles under the most favorable circumstances. What we have here are something like the least favorable circumstances. The original-instrument orchestra may produce a lighter sound, but that doesn't by itself change the nature of the vocal demands of the writing, and these singers are approaching from the lightest possible point of entry.

Tom Krause knows how to sing Guglielmo, and goes ahead and does it. Carlos Feller as Alfonso puts us in two-baritone configuration, and again it works out well. Feller is terrific: a full, buzzy sound and a tremendously inventive characterization, within the limits possible in this performance. Gösta Winbergh has good moments as Ferrando, but again, the role is vocally problematic enough for him that, in addition to work on those specific problems, he needs help from his conductor.

The text is complete, with Guglielmo's original Act I aria, "Rivolgete a lui lo sguardo," appended at the end of the first CD, where it can be programmed in place of its replacement, "Non siate ritrosi."

1986 EMI / ANGEL (S,D) CD

Carol Vaness (A), Lillian Watson (B), Delores Ziegler (C), John Aler (D), Dale Duesing (E), Claudio Desderi (F), Glyndebourne Festival Chorus, London Philharmonic Orchestra—Bernard Haitink

Bernard Haitink approaches *Così* with a measure of humility, which no composer rewards more generously than Mozart. This is a sane and balanced performance that reveals a generous measure of the score's beauties. One remarkable circumstance: those orphaned numbers, the standardly cut "Al fato dan legge" and "Ah! lo veggio," not only are restored but are high points of the performance.

This may be due in part to the beneficial influence of a stage director. (The recording, although studio-made, is based on Peter Hall's Glyndebourne production.) This influence must surely have something to do with the unusual life in the recitative.

The drawbacks? First, the exploratory process that Haitink has undertaken *is* a process, and the performers haven't quite come out the other end. There are conductors—although, granted, not many—who have made many of the same discoveries, and even a couple (Jochum, Barenboim) who have bound those discoveries into a somewhat compelling performance.

Second, there is the cast, which is on the whole adequate but not exactly compelling. There is one terrific performance, Claudio Desderi's Alfonso, and another highly likable one, John Aler's Ferrando. Desderi sings with a good deal of tonal fullness, verbal and musical wit, and a sense of his stake in engineering the plot. Aler is a Ferrando of what we might call "school of Häfliger": a lightweight lyric tenor, but a full-voiced specimen, who sings with gracious, unforced lyricism. As noted, nobody on records makes better sense of "Ah! lo veggio."

Delores Ziegler is a perfectly satisfactory Dorabella, and Dale Duesing a rather colorless but satisfactory Guglielmo. Lillian Watson has a pleasing soprano and some interesting notions for Despina, but there's not much follow-through. Which leaves the Fiordiligi of Carol Vaness: certainly a creditable piece of singing, and less sharp-edgedly mechanistic than it has been in the past, but still a performance that winds up being *about* the mechanics, whether successful or not.

The text is complete.

1988 DEUTSCHE GRAMMOPHON (S,D) CD

Kiri Te Kanawa (A), Marie McLaughlin (B), Ann Murray (C), Hans Peter Blochwitz (D), Thomas Hampson (E), Ferruccio Furlanetto (F), Vienna State Opera Chorus, Vienna Philharmonic Orchestra—James Levine

This is another of those performances that sounds all right listened to casually. But closer attention induces a queasy mixture of nitpicking, strange wonderment, and ennui.

To begin with the wonderment, what on earth is the idea in the recitatives? From the cascading cocktail-fortepiano *continuo*, one might guess that someone forgot to shut the door to the adjoining bowling-alley lounge. But then what's the deal with the reinforcement by what sounds like the entire Vienna cello and bass sections?

The performance as a whole mixes occasional bursts of aggression with a prevailing neat, balanced, uneventful expanse of notes—lots and lots of notes. And the singers seem to be pretty much on their own.

In a role that was problematic for her even in her vocally stronger years (see 1977 Erato), Kiri Te Kanawa seems now impelled to rein everything in. As a result, much of what was appealing in the earlier performance comes out rather matter-of-fact here. Ann Murray is a sensible singer, but the voice isn't terribly substantial, and it's hard to make much of an impression as Dorabella under those circumstances.

Hans Peter Blochwitz is clearly not vocally at ease singing in Italian, and his Ferrando is decent but unmemorable. Thomas Hampson is another star baritone sandbagged by Guglielmo—there's this pool of bright sound being pushed out too far up in the voice to make much sense of this writing's lower center of gravity. What's more, the performance substitutes the original aria, "Rivolgete a lui lo sguardo," a bass aria, for its replacement, "Non siate ritrosi," which is consigned to an appendix.

Ferruccio Furlanetto has now been heard as both Don Giovanni and Leporello, Figaro and the Count, and Guglielmo and Alfonso, which might seem a mark of versatility but which might also represent a search for one among these roles that truly suits him. Words and tone are thick and immobile. The potential bright light in the cast is Marie McLaughlin, with plenty of voice and spirit for Despina, but without much idea of where to channel them, and seemingly without useful outside guidance.

The text, as noted, is complete-plus.

1988–89 PHILIPS (S,D) CD

Karita Mattila (A), Elzbieta Szmytka (B), Anne Sofie von Otter (C), Francisco Araiza (D), Thomas Allen (E), José van Dam (F), Ambrosian Opera Chorus, Academy of St. Martin in the Fields—Neville Marriner

This is another recording whose attractions, while real enough, fade a bit under close scrutiny or set against some of the competition. It recalls 1986 EMI in its unhurried, exploratory attention to the beauties of the score, but has on the whole even less forward drive. At times it seems almost as expansive as 1971 EMI, though in a soft-grained, contemplative mode worlds removed from that of Klemperer. And then there will be moments like the military music, with drums banging wildly: quite exciting, but it sort of pops out of nowhere.

And the cast, while certainly not painful, commands even less attention than that of 1986 EMI. Sometimes Karita Mattila sounds as if she has a Fiordiligi in her, and sometimes she doesn't—there's good vocal material there, but it's not reliably under control. Almost the same thing happens, on a lighter scale, with Elzbieta Szmytka's Despina. Instead of listening for the character, we're listening to hear whether the voice will be there or not. Anne Sofie von Otter is certainly a more finished singer, but the finished product—smooth, polite, small-scaled—is rather meager for Dorabella, who, as we have noted, can so easily fade from sight.

Francisco Araiza (Ferrando) and José van Dam (Alfonso) are reunited from 1982 EMI. Araiza, while still not singing with complete lyric ease, is in somewhat better voice here. Van Dam, however, who seemed on the way to a fine Alfonso before, and still sings well enough, appears to have lost the thread. The performance is scatter-shot, rather like the performance as a whole: almost watching itself, disinterestedly curious to hear what happens next. Thomas Allen as Guglielmo has passages where his good baritone makes a lovely effect, and others where the voice hardly works at all.

The text is complete.

1989 ERATO (S,D) CD

Lella Cuberli (A), Joan Rodgers (B), Cecilia Bartoli (C), Kurt Streit (D), Ferruccio Furlanetto (E), John Tomlinson (F), RIAS Chamber Chorus, Berlin Philharmonic Orchestra—Daniel Barenboim

If it sounds suspicious to you, it was wholly unexpected to me. Suddenly, after twenty-five-plus years, along comes a recording that at long last has much of the same combination of physical beauty and effortless, from-the-inside forward momentum as 1962–63 DG, and it happens to feature the same orchestra and chorus!

Over that period of time, is it possible that the two recordings have enough personnel in common to make possible some actual aural recall? Or are Daniel Barenboim's goals—consciously or not—that closely aligned with Jochum's? It doesn't matter. The fact remains that this recording gives a kind of satisfaction unattainable elsewhere and, unlike 1962–63 DG, it's available.

And the cast, at least down through the tenor level, is quite good. Bravura isn't Lella Cuberli's strong point, which is too bad for Fiordiligi, but she has a lovely instrument with a distinctive, sympathetic quality—a likableness that is invaluable for the role. Cecilia Bartoli's Dorabella is fluent, pointed, and impulsive—one of the best. And Joan Rodgers's Despina is handsomely sung and unexaggeratedly believable.

Kurt Streit's lovely lyric tenor recalls (of all people!) Ernst Häfliger's—and Streit too sings an unassumingly charming Ferrando. But the pair of basses is less successful. Ferruccio Furlanetto does score some points as a bass Guglielmo, but in general the voice's lack of mobility takes its toll in this role as it does in Alfonso (1988 DG). John Tomlinson's bass is a good instrument, but it's a bit dull-sounding in Italian, and of course it *is* a bass, a handicap in the role which on records only Hans Sotin (1971 EMI) has fully overcome.

Except for "Al fato dan legge" and "Ah! lo veggio," the text is complete.

1990 ORFEO (S,D,P) CD

Anna Caterina Antonacci (A), Laura Cherici (B), Monica Bacelli (C), Richard Decker (D), Albert Dohmen (E), Sesto Bruscantini (F), Coro Lirico Marchigiano "Vincenzo Bellini," Orchestra Filarmonica Marchigiana—Gustav Kuhn

Although I have gotten a good deal of enjoyment from this performance, I'm not sure how often I would want to hear it, which makes general recommendation problematic.

The strengths and weaknesses are hard to separate. The performance was recorded live at the first Macerata Festival, and the orchestral standard stops short of the highest level of international polish. On the other hand, an unusually extensive rehearsal schedule was apparently made available for conductor-director Gustav Kuhn, who in my experience is a conductor of considerable sensitivity.

It's not surprising, then, that the performance has a beautiful, unforced flow, with balances and shapes discovered and savored rather than mechanically regurgitated. The music generally has the freshness of creation in real time. And with the conductor serving as director as well, there is no question of the performers being caught between interpretive imperatives.

Judging from the tiny production photos in the booklet, we are perhaps fortunate not to be concerned with the production itself, which updates the action to a tale of yuppified beach-front condominium dwellers. But indirectly we *are* concerned, since the casting places such a premium on physical appearance for all roles except Alfonso, in which the veteran Sesto Bruscantini mostly rasps authoritatively. (It is, all the same, a more interesting performance than his Alfonso in 1954 EMI.)

Not that the cast, when heard and not seen, is vocally that much below the present-day norm. Monica Bacelli (Dorabella), Albert Dohmen (Guglielmo), and Laura Cherici (Despina) in fact are all quite presentable. And Anna Caterina Antonacci (Fiordiligi) and Richard Decker (Ferrando), while vocally overmatched by their assignments, still cope well enough to hold up their ends. Antonacci musters an altogether honorable "Per pietà."

For a live performance, the text is remarkably complete—only "Al fato dan legge" is omitted.

1990 NAXOS (S,D) CD

Joanna Borowska (A), Priti Coles (B), Rohangiz Yachmi (C), John Dickie (D), Andrea Martin (E), Peter Mikuláš (F), Slovak Philharmonic Chorus, Capella Istropolitana—Johannes Wildner

Even as an uncut *Così*, this set has to contend with the likes of 1967 RCA and 1973–74 Decca /

London, both of which come with Italian-English texts (Naxos provides notes in English, but an Italian-only libretto). That said, I've grown fond of it. There's an engaging, intimate, unforced flow in which many good things can happen; few performances realize the "Alla bella Despinetta" sextet on this full a scale, which, like Klemperer's, not only supports but almost demands a bass Alfonso.

And Peter Mikuláš, the only native Slovak in the cast, does the home team proud. His distinctively textured bass provides a solid underpinning. There's also an above-average Despina. The British soprano Priti Coles sometimes has an acidic edge in the voice and sometimes doesn't; if she's using it as a character choice, I wish she wouldn't. Most of her singing, however, including both arias (especially "In uomini"), is fresh, firm, and lovely.

The Polish soprano Joanna Borowska, with a pronounced vibrato that recalls the Spanish Fiordiligis, in fact also calls to mind the dignified warmth and vulnerability of Pilar Lorengar, except that her voice is under better control than Lorengar's in her recording—a highly likable performance.

The others are working hard, and are plausible in ensemble. The Iranian mezzo Rohangiz Yachmi's voice has some welcome weight, but it's also rather wobbly and ungainly. The English tenor John Dickie produces a generally forced sound at and above the break, but through earnestness of effort he manages the arias credibly. Andrea Martin's baritone isn't long on ease or color, and strains audibly in even modest upward reaches.

1991 TELDEC (S,D) CD

Charlotte Margiono (A), Anna Steiger (B), Delores Ziegler (C), Deon van der Walt (D), Gilles Cachemaille (E), Thomas Hampson (F), Netherlands Opera Chorus, Royal Concertgebouw Orchestra—Nikolaus Harnoncourt

What is there to say about this peculiarly uninteresting, uncut performance? There isn't even much pleasure to be had in the playing of the Concertgebouw, perhaps because of the odd articulation modes Harnoncourt has concocted

in his search for new phrase shapes for *Così*. Especially in Act I, he seems to favor either blunt attacks with abrupt releases or unsupported glide-ins. Even when the performance isn't eccentric, it hardly ever just "plays."

If you turn to the booklet, you find that Harnoncourt has done lots of interesting thinking about the opera (and some fairly loopy thinking), and that many of the most peculiar choices—the immobile farewell quintet, for example—are numbers that he has thought hardest about. Hasn't he noticed, though, that none of the thinking is translated into believable or involving musical action? Not that the cast is well equipped to do so.

There's one unquestionably major singer: Deon van der Walt's lovely liquid tenor is just unsettled enough here, especially when he tries to scale it down, to fall short in the major lyric challenges like "Un aura amorosa," where one expects a payoff from such a fine instrument. Charlotte Margiono is a tonally veiled, barely noticeable Fiordiligi. Delores Ziegler is a decent but not very appealing Dorabella. Anna Steiger substitutes some sort of imagined cleverness for singing. Gilles Cachemaille, whose baritone doesn't have much flexibility, gets off some solid phrases, but is all too often the victim of Harnoncourt's innovations. Thomas Hampson does nothing to advance the cause of a baritone Alfonso; his singing makes hardly any impact—all that attracts notice is the nasty hectoring.

If you can find a copy of 1962–63 DG, get it! In its absence, 1989 Erato is a plausible substitute. The uncut 1967 RCA and 1973–74 Decca / London are worthy contenders, with honorable mention to 1986 EMI.

For their special qualities, attention is directed to the recordings conducted by Otto Klemperer (1971 EMI) and Karl Böhm (1955 Decca / London or, if need be, 1974 DG). Easy to overlook is the no-frills 1982 EMI, and the Alfonso of Carlos Feller in the 1984 L'Oiseau-Lyre.

KENNETH FURIE

Unavailable for review:
1951 PERIOD

WOLFGANG AMADEUS MOZART

LA CLEMENZA DI TITO (1791)

A: Vitellia (s); B: Servilia (s); C: Sesto (ms); D: Annio (ms); E: Tito (t)

Die Zauberflöte and *La Clemenza di Tito*, written concurrently, were Mozart's last two operas, utterly different in character—one a German *Singspiel*, the other a classical *opera seria*. It has been stated many times that the ailing composer really did not want to write in the old-fashioned *opera seria* form and did so only because he needed the commission. The fact is, however, that Mozart always felt at home with *opera seria*, and one of his favorite works, *Idomeneo*, shows how imaginatively he treated it, stretching the traditional boundaries of its set-piece style to incorporate his own innovations. *La Clemenza di Tito*, popular for some decades after his death, has lain in neglect since. The reasons— its less personal tone and static subject, attributes of *opera seria*—seem less important today than the power, conciseness, and beauty of the score. Modern revivals, if not plentiful, have served to restore *Tito* to public favor, a restoration in which recordings certainly have played an important part.

1951 PERIOD (M)

Käthe Nentwig (A), Unknown (B), Hetty Plümacher (C), Unknown (D), Albert Weikenmeier (E), Württemberg State Opera Chorus and Orchestra—Gustav Lund

In this first complete recording of *La Clemenza di Tito*, the *secco* recitatives, believed to be the work of Mozart's pupil Franz Xaver Süssmayr, are omitted. Perhaps the most noteworthy singing is that of soprano Hetty Plü-macher as Sesto, a role originally meant for castrato; both technically and interpretively, Plümacher makes the most of the character and serves the music well. The wide-ranging dramatic part of Vitellia places too many demands on Käthe Nentwig, though she is a well-schooled singer within her limits. In the title role, Albert Weikenmeier typifies the rather muscular, inflexible German dramatic tenor. The secondary couple, Annio and Servilia, are played in soubrette manner, with pert, attractive vocalism but little more. The recorded sound is harsh even for its period, but the suitably modest-sized orchestra plays well under the controlled if not inspired leadership of Gustav Lund.

1967 DECCA / LONDON (S) CD

Maria Casula (A), Lucia Popp (B), Teresa Berganza (C), Brigitte Fassbaender (D), Werner Krenn (E), Vienna State Opera Chorus and Orchestra—István Kertész

This recording enlists strong soloists and captures them in clear, vivid sonic profile. István Kertész's elegant, lively, elastic conducting carries the day. In addition, the recitatives, though somewhat cut, are included. Maria Casula's singing may be a bit uneven, but she encompasses the tessitura of Vitellia (including its top D in the trio) while combining expressive line with dramatic thrust; in short, she characterizes the part. Lucia Popp brings pristine tone and sweet phrasing to the short but exposed role of Servilia, while Teresa Berganza (Sesto) and Brigitte Fassbaender (Annio) cope admirably with music meant for male trebles. Werner Krenn has the poise, agility, and vocal lightness for the title role. We are reminded that there is at least one advantage in neglecting a masterpiece: it can be approached afresh.

1976 PHILIPS (S) CD

Janet Baker (A), Lucia Popp (B), Yvonne Minton (C), Frederica von Stade (D), Stuart Burrows (E), Chorus and Orchestra of the Royal Opera, Covent Garden—Colin Davis

This performance, less cut in the recitatives than Decca's, is rather slow getting under way, with Colin Davis taking the Overture at a stately pace, but after a while things hit their stride. Yvonne Minton (Sesto) hits hers in the aria "Parto, parto," its agility expressive if a bit breathy toward the end, and in her fiery scene of repentance for disloyal intentions toward the emperor. In the title role, Stuart Burrows is in good form for "Ah, se fosse intorno al trono," a regal and thoughtful utterance, as is Frederica von Stade for "Tu fosse tradito" in the second trouser role of Annio. Janet Baker (Vitellia), who lacks incisiveness and lightness for the recitatives, works up steam for the Act I trio, though she ducks the high D that Mozart devilishly inserted in an otherwise dramatic-soprano or mezzo assignment. Lucia Popp repeats her bright Servilia from the Decca performance. String playing is less than elegant in certain attacks, notably the accompanied recitatives. In every other respect this is a Clemenza di Tito with clear destination and a tone of nobility appropriate to its classical subject. Except for an omitted exchange between Vitellia and Publio (Robert Lloyd), the recitative is presented without heavy abridgment.

1979 DEUTSCHE GRAMMOPHON (S) CD

Julia Varady (A), Edith Mathis (B), Teresa Berganza (C), Marga Schiml (D), Peter Schreier (E), Leipzig Radio Chorus, Dresden State Orchestra—Karl Böhm

Teresa Berganza, who recorded the role of Sesto for Decca, repeats it here. If anything, she is even more touching in such a tender moment as "Deh per questo istante solo," though the edge of brilliance is gone from her coloratura in the fast closing of the "Parto, parto" aria. Julia Varady offers a temperamental Vitellia, interesting and intense in timbre, solid on the low notes, soaring on the high. Her coloratura lacks natural ease but has the required impetus. Next to this high-powered pair, the cozy if not radiant Servilia of Edith Mathis sets a note of contrast, matched by Marga Schiml's Annio. As for the male voices, Theo Adam provides a Publio of substance and dignity, also sounding concerned and expressive. Peter Schreier in the title role is puzzling for his nasal tone in the recitatives, more appropriate to Don Curzio in Le Nozze di Figaro than to a Roman emperor; yet the tenor is impressive in the challenging fioritura of "Se all'impero." Böhm introduces the opera with an Overture of warm, intimate spirit, and while doing justice to the formal elements that make an opera seria he keeps us constantly aware that the music is by Mozart, with a full and subtle emotional range. Because the recitatives are not heavily cut, the plot is easy to follow, though pauses between the numbers are a bit pronounced.

1990 DEUTSCHE GRAMMOPHON ARCHIV (S) CD

Julia Varady (A), Sylvia McNair (B), Anne Sofie von Otter (C), Catherine Robbin (D), Anthony Rolfe Johnson (E), Monteverdi Choir, English Baroque Soloists—John Eliot Gardiner

Varady, repeating her Vitellia from the earlier DG album, presents the character's wide emotional as well as vocal range, projecting with ping and vibrancy. From her very first recitative, the soprano is dramatically involved. Anne Sofie von Otter plays a sincere, noble, conflicted Sesto, and the two singers maintain a taut emotional exchange. Sylvia McNair's modest, nicely sung Servilia complements Catherine Robbin's pleasant, slightly more assertive Annio, whose reedy top tones suggest the character's masculinity. Anthony Rolfe Johnson captures the compassion and dignity of the sorely tested emperor, with touching sweetness in his lyric lines, dignity in his public persona. The least effective soloist, Cornelius Hauptmann as Publio, seems to lack a solid core to his bass, though he shades his lines with variety of expression.

John Eliot Gardiner's conducting, even more than in his contemporaneous *Idomeneo* recording with some of the same singers, favors briskness. The prevailing *andante*, Mozart's mean tempo, is animated, and *allegro assai*, as in the conclusion of Sesto's "Parto" aria, surges forward, though von Otter is able to keep up with her difficult triplets. The recitatives are shortened by perhaps one-fourth, eliminating some interesting minor exchanges between characters, and the *continuo* is led by a fortepiano, which—thanks perhaps to adjustments by the engineers—blends more smoothly into the dialogue and ensembles than is the case with Gardiner's *Idomeneo*.

———

All four stereo recordings present the score admirably and are worth owning. Those partial to a more historically accurate interpretation will be happiest with Gardiner, whose period instrumentalists play with a smoothness that never grates on today's ears. Kertész, too, keeps the music flowing, with lively, expeditious tempos. Those with limited patience for recitative (in this case not Mozart's own) are likely to welcome the pared-down versions used by these two maestros. For a more romantic but still energetic view of Mozart's valedictory opera, Böhm provides a solid compromise between drive and sweep on the one hand, majesty on the other. Davis is more dignified: this is Mozart with hindsight from an age that knows Beethoven.

JOHN W. FREEMAN

SPEIGHT JENKINS
General Director, Seattle Opera

1. **Puccini,** *Tosca*: Callas, di Stefano, Gobbi—de Sabata. EMI / ANGEL
2. **Wagner,** *Die Walküre* (Act I): Lehmann, Melchior, List—Walter. EMI / ANGEL
3. **Wagner,** *Tristan und Isolde*: Nilsson, Ludwig, Windgassen, Wächter, Talvela—Böhm. DEUTSCHE GRAMMOPHON
4. **Wagner,** *Tristan und Isolde*: Flagstad, Thebom, Suthaus, Fischer-Dieskau, Greindl—Furtwängler. EMI / ANGEL
5. **Strauss,** *Salome*: Behrens, Baltsa, Böhm, van Dam—Karajan. EMI / ANGEL
6. **Beethoven,** *Fidelio*: Ludwig, Hallstein, Vickers, Unger, Berry, Frick, Crass—Klemperer. EMI / ANGEL
7. **Wagner,** *Tannhäuser*: Dernesch, Ludwig, Kollo, Braun, Sotin—Solti. DECCA / LONDON
8. **Strauss,** *Der Rosenkavalier*: Donath, Crespin, Minton, Wiener, Jungwirth—Solti. DECCA / LONDON
9. **Verdi,** *La Traviata*: Callas, Kraus, Sereni—Ghione. EMI / ANGEL
10. **Verdi,** *Il Trovatore*: Milanov, Barbieri, Bjoerling, Warren, Moscona—Cellini. RCA / BMG

WOLFGANG AMADEUS MOZART

DIE ZAUBERFLÖTE (1791)

A: Pamina (s); B: Queen (s); C: Papagena (s); D: Tamino (t);
E: Monostatos (t); F: Papageno (bar); G: Sarastro (bs)

*D*ie Zauberflöte, a crowd-pleaser from its opening night on, has never lost its popularity. After two centuries of productions, performers and audiences still love the work. The only change in perspective is that we now take the opera seriously—perhaps *too* seriously, for a survey of the recordings reveals how many conductors assume that slow tempos, weighty orchestral sonorities, and heavy accents automatically result in profundity. The best performances are led by conductors who remember that the opera is an eighteenth-century work, a product of the Age of Enlightenment, and that even the greatest philosophers can have a sense of humor.

A surprising number of the older recordings have already been transferred to compact discs—further proof of the opera's great popularity.

The only major textual problem in *The Magic Flute* concerns the spoken dialogue, which is an integral part of the work. Most of the older recordings eliminate the dialogue altogether, to the great detriment of the drama. The more recent recordings tend to include at least enough dialogue to provide continuity between the musical numbers; often, however, the dialogue is not only abridged but rewritten, usually in order to remove some of Emanuel Schikaneder's grosser buffooneries. Several of the complete recordings assign the dialogue to a separate cast of actors. This is rarely a satisfactory procedure—not only because of the inevitable discrepancies between sung and spoken timbres, but because German actors tend to adopt a

highly sophisticated, confidential, radio-play style of delivery, at odds with the mythic naiveté of the opera. It is worth pointing out that many of the international opera singers heard on these recordings handle the dialogue very convincingly.

In general, *The Magic Flute* has brought out the best in its interpreters on records. At least among the studio versions, disappointments are rare, and several of the complete sets are truly distinguished. Furthermore, even the performances that are less persuasive as totalities often contain individual contributions of merit.

1937–38 EMI / ANGEL (M) CD

Tiana Lemnitz (A), Erna Berger (B), Irma Beilke (C), Helge Rosvaenge (D), Heinrich Tessmer (E), Gerhard Hüsch (F), Wilhelm Strienz (G), Favres Singers' Association, Berlin Philharmonic Orchestra—Thomas Beecham

This classic set, the first "complete" studio recording of *The Magic Flute*, omits all of the dialogue. The performance is deservedly famous for Sir Thomas Beecham's conducting, which is swift, elegant, and spirited. His conception of the work is beautifully realized by the Berlin Philharmonic, heard at its prewar peak. The chorus—really a chamber choir—is a very small ensemble; as a result, it makes an unusually intimate impression.

The cast list contains many famous names, and these singers, like the instrumentalists, phrase with old-fashioned *portamento*, often to revelatory effect.

Tiana Lemnitz sings with tonal purity and complete technical control, but I must confess that her Pamina leaves me cold: Lemnitz seems emotionally remote throughout the opera, and her "Ach, ich fühl's" might as well be a concert aria from some long-forgotten *opera seria*. Erna Berger sings the Queen of the Night's arias with spectacular ease, but—to make a truly ungrateful criticism—her voice is too beautiful for the part: it has a youthful, even girlish, quality that would be more suitable for Pamina.

Rosvaenge is an uncommonly rich-toned Tamino, and sings with a great deal of dramatic imagination. The Papageno of Gerhard Hüsch, effortlessly vocalized and genuinely funny, sets a standard by which all subsequent recorded performances must be judged. Wilhelm Strienz is excellent as Sarastro, his firm, smooth bass voice full of human overtones.

The supporting roles are exceptionally well sung. The recorded sound inevitably shows its age in some respects: the solo voices are unnaturally forward, and the dynamic range is limited. The recording, fifty years old, is now in the public domain, which explains why several record companies, including Pearl and Melodram, have been able to reissue it on CD with impunity. I would urge collectors to buy either the "official" EMI transfer (which benefits from one of Keith Hardwick's brilliant remastering jobs) or the one by Nimbus (which is derived from a different set of 78s, and is less immediate—but also mellower—in sound than the EMI). The Nimbus package has the advantage of a really luxurious booklet, which contains the complete libretto (including the spoken dialogue), good background material on the opera, and biographical essays about each of the singers.

1950 EMI / ANGEL (M) CD

Irmgard Seefried (A), Wilma Lipp (B), Emmy Loose (C), Anton Dermota (D), Peter Klein (E), Erich Kunz (F), Ludwig Weber (G), Vienna Singers' Association, Vienna Philharmonic Orchestra—Herbert von Karajan

This recording, originally issued on 78s, once again amounts to a "concert performance" of the opera, omitting all of the spoken dialogue. For collectors with a specific historical interest, the CD reissue does have its attractions.

The mono sound holds up surprisingly well on CD. There is naturally not much richness or depth to the reproduction of the orchestra, and the solo voices are closely miked, although every so often they seem to recede and take on a halo of hall resonance.

Karajan's conducting is not at all what I anticipated. Much of the performance is quick, bouncy, even glib. The whole approach is vastly different from his 1980 digital remake for DG, which, if anything, takes the opera too seriously. On this mono set, there is some beautiful orchestral playing, but the chorus sounds undermanned and tentative at times. Even at this early date, though, Karajan encouraged his singers to adopt a suave, understated vocal manner.

Some of these singers are heard to better advantage on other recordings. Ludwig Weber wobbles a bit, and George London (the Speaker) also produces some spread, ill-focused tones. Irmgard Seefried makes some lovely sounds, but is emotionally reticent—the scene of her thwarted suicide attempt just slips by. Wilma Lipp was a famous Queen of the Night, but often sounds as though she would be happier singing Pamina: her voice is pretty and she dispatches the coloratura neatly enough, but there is no regal dignity or vindictiveness in her portrayal (Karajan's very fast tempos for her two arias are no help). Finally, Erich Kunz handles Papageno's music in a splendidly free, easy way, but—much to my surprise—is quite lacking in earthiness or humor; he could be mistaken for Tamino's brother. Kunz's portrayal probably suffers the most from the elimination of the dialogue. However, Anton Dermota is a fine Tamino.

1955 DEUTSCHE GRAMMOPHON (M) CD

Maria Stader (A), Rita Streich (B), Lisa Otto (C), Ernst Häfliger (D), Martin Vantin (E),

Dietrich Fischer-Dieskau (F), Josef Greindl (G), RIAS Chorus and Symphony Orchestra, Berlin—Ferenc Fricsay

This is the first studio recording to include the spoken dialogue: it is drastically abridged, however, and at least some of it is handled by a separate cast of actors (Dietrich Fischer-Dieskau seems to be speaking Papageno's lines himself, though).

The performance is on the conservative side. Ferenc Fricsay, a fine musician in other repertory, does not seem to be attuned to this particular score. Much of the reading is heavy and literal, with stiff phrasing; the orchestral playing tends to be monotonously loud and uninflected.

Once again we have an unconvincing mother/daughter pairing. Maria Stader, a thoughtful artist, sings Pamina with mature, even matronly, tones. Rita Streich, by contrast, is an uncommonly fresh and youthful-sounding Queen; she negotiates the coloratura with exhilarating ease. Lisa Otto is a delightful Papagena.

Ernst Häfliger's Tamino is competent rather than inspired. Fischer-Dieskau, in warm, easy voice, is a rather too sophisticated Papageno: he works so hard at scoring musical points, and conveying subtle verbal nuances, that the earthiness of the character escapes him.

Josef Greindl is a dull, unsteady Sarastro; Kim Borg, the Speaker, has the more impressive bass voice. Martin Vantin is a superior Monostatos, though, and there is excellent work in some of the supporting roles—Marianne Schech as the First Lady, for example (her partners, Liselotte Losch and Margarete Klose, are less impressive).

The mono sound is clean enough, but the solo voices are so closely miked that the more distantly recorded orchestra often seems to be playing in an adjacent room.

1955 DECCA / LONDON (S) CD

Hilde Gueden (A), Wilma Lipp (B), Emmy Loose (C), Léopold Simoneau (D), August Jaresch (E), Walter Berry (F), Kurt Böhme (G), Vienna State Opera Chorus, Vienna Philharmonic—Karl Böhm

This recording omits all of the dialogue. Karl Böhm shapes the music with a skilled and loving hand, on the whole; some of his tempos are hard-driven. The Vienna Philharmonic does not quite live up to its reputation: for a studio production, this one contains a surprising number of slips and shaky ensemble. The Boys are sung by women.

The cast is uneven. The trio of Ladies—Judith Hellwig, Christa Ludwig, and Hilde Rössl-Majdan—is superb. But, in major roles, Kurt Böhme's gruff, wobbly Sarastro is a serious liability; Lipp's Queen now has moments of shrillness and insecurity; and Paul Schöffler, the Speaker, is frankly beginning to show his age. Hilde Gueden shades the underside of the pitch and scoops up to high notes, in the approved Viennese fashion, and her Pamina is rather too pert—she would have been an ideal Papagena (which is not to imply that Emmy Loose is anything but charming in the latter role).

Léopold Simoneau makes Tamino a genuine aristocrat, despite a voice that is just a size too small to fill out some of the music, and some exotic German pronunciation. Walter Berry impersonates Papageno with great relish.

Like several Decca / London opera sets of this vintage, this one was recorded in both mono and stereo, but originally released in mono only. The Richmond LP reissue (which is the format I heard) is based on the stereo tapes, and is often quite vivid in sound. I have not heard the new CD transfer.

1963 EMI / ANGEL (S) CD

Gundula Janowitz (A), Lucia Popp (B), Ruth-Margret Pütz (C), Nicolai Gedda (D), Gerhard Unger (E), Walter Berry (F), Gottlob Frick (G), Philharmonia Chorus and Orchestra—Otto Klemperer

The omission of the dialogue is particularly unfortunate here, because Otto Klemperer's is the best-conducted *Magic Flute* on records. His tempos are by no means invariably slow, but the reading has tremendous weight and authority. All of the instrumental lines are firmly and clearly drawn; each number in the score is persuasively shaped. As a result, the musical structures acquire a true logic and sense of inevitability. What is remarkable is the wit and delicacy that Klemperer brings to the lighter episodes of the opera, without sacrificing the qualities just mentioned. The Philharmonia Chorus and Orchestra respond to his leadership with some of their finest recorded work.

Two members of the all-star cast are reliable, but do not quite live up to their reputations. Nicolai Gedda's singing is more efficient than beautiful. Gottlob Frick, caught a few years past his best vocal form, is somewhat of a compromise as Sarastro, sounding rusty and wobbly; as partial compensation, he inflects the words majestically.

Gundula Janowitz, with her pure, cool, absolutely even soprano, offers singing of truly instrumental accuracy—an exquisite piece of vocalism, although some listeners may find her Pamina too self-contained. Lucia Popp is a sensational Queen of the Night, combining a vibrant, sensuous sound with complete technical security.

Berry repeats his sturdy Papageno from the 1955 Decca set, and Elisabeth Schwarzkopf, Christa Ludwig, and Marga Höffgen are an incomparable trio of Ladies.

The solid stereo engineering sounds clear and impactive on the CD transfer.

1964 DEUTSCHE GRAMMOPHON (S) CD

Evelyn Lear (A), Roberta Peters (B), Lisa Otto (C), Fritz Wunderlich (D), Friedrich Lenz (E), Dietrich Fischer-Dieskau (F), Franz Crass (G), RIAS Chamber Choir, Berlin Philharmonic Orchestra—Karl Böhm

This recording preserves Karl Böhm's mature thoughts on the opera: his beautifully proportioned, unsentimental reading, mellower than before, is exceptionally well executed. It's also fascinating to hear the Berlin Philharmonic of the mid-1960s under the direction of a conductor other than Karajan: the ensemble sounds much less tonally rarefied, much more like just another good German orchestra. The choral work is expert.

On the male side, this cast could hardly be bettered. Franz Crass is as good a Sarastro as we

have ever had on a complete set; Hans Hotter is luxurious casting as the Speaker; James King and Martti Talvela are altogether extraordinary as the Two Armed Men; and Friedrich Lenz is an uncommonly musical Monostatos. Fritz Wunderlich sings beautifully if a bit impersonally as Tamino; Dietrich Fischer-Dieskau, on the other hand, sings beautifully *and* has personality to burn—his Papageno, a substantial improvement upon his work in the Fricsay set, is one of the very best things this unpredictable but undeniably great artist has ever committed to disc.

With the exception of Lisa Otto's Papagena, which is every bit as delightful as before, the women are less satisfying. Roberta Peters has a stronger lower register than most Queens of the Night, and as a result is unusually impressive in the slow section of her first aria; she also enunciates the text more clearly than many of her European rivals on records. The actual sound of her voice, however, is not particularly beautiful or exciting. Evelyn Lear makes a warm and sympathetic sound, but her upper register often sounds careful and lacking in tonal body.

The spoken dialogue is rather heavily abridged on this recording, which some listeners will count as an advantage. The sound is slightly conservative but holds up well in the CD transfer.

1968 EURODISC (S) CD

Helen Donath (A), Sylvia Geszty (B), Renate Hoff (C), Peter Schreier (D), Harald Neukirch (E), Günther Leib (F), Theo Adam (G), Leipzig Radio Chorus, Dresden State Orchestra—Otmar Suitner

This version is somewhat underrated: if not the most exciting *Flute* on records, it is a solid production overall, with some outstanding individual contributions. Suitner conducts firmly, maintaining tension throughout, despite some daringly slow tempos. His orchestra and chorus are excellent. The singers cast in the supporting roles do not always have the most glamorous voices imaginable, but they form a strong ensemble. The three anonymous boy sopranos are wonderfully vivid.

Helen Donath is a lovely Pamina, combining vocal control with warmth and intensity. Sylvia Geszty has a few wiry moments, but is a haughty, imperious Queen.

Günther Leib is an amusing, cynical Papageno. Instead of the traditional buffoon, Leib suggests a tough-minded, working-class man who is determined to survive the bizarre situations he finds himself in.

Peter Schreier, in the first of his several recorded Taminos, sings musically and displays a good grasp of the character; his liability is a dry vocal timbre that can turn "white" and unsupported when he sings softly and hardens under pressure. If only this intelligent and musical artist had been endowed with a voice like Wunderlich's! Sarastro's music really lies too low for Theo Adam, and the sustained writing exposes the fact that his voice, with its pronounced vibrato, is not ideally steady. Adam makes a fairly successful effort to darken and round his tone to meet the demands of the part, though: both arias are imposing, and the opening scene of Act II benefits from his dignified delivery.

The recording includes a generous amount of spoken dialogue, well handled by the singers. The recorded sound is powerful but very close—even claustrophobic—with the solo voices brought somewhat unnaturally forward, in the kind of "radio broadcast balance" favored by German engineers.

1969 DECCA / LONDON (S) CD

Pilar Lorengar (A), Cristina Deutekom (B), Renate Holm (C), Stuart Burrows (D), Gerhard Stolze (E), Hermann Prey (F), Martti Talvela (G), Vienna State Opera Chorus, Vienna Philharmonic—Georg Solti

Decca obviously worked hard to assemble an all-star cast for this version. The supporting roles are particularly well taken: Fischer-Dieskau (the Speaker), Yvonne Minton (Second Lady), Kurt Equiluz (First Priest), René Kollo and Hans Sotin (the Two Armed Men), etc. The three anonymous Vienna Choirboys make exquisite sounds. Gerhard Stolze is often harsh and penetrating as Monostatos, but certainly conveys the character's nastiness.

The best of the leads is Hermann Prey, whose warm baritone voice and hearty manner make him a natural Papageno. Pilar Lorengar, with her characteristic quick vibrato and warm, vulnerable delivery, is a touching Pamina. Stuart Burrows's Tamino, by contrast, is vocally efficient but a little lacking in individuality.

Some listeners may object to Cristina Deutekom's hard timbre and her peculiar way of articulating the coloratura, but for my taste she is one of the most dramatically convincing Queens on disc. She sounds mature, forceful, and wily.

Martti Talvela, of course, has a magnificent voice, but his nasal timbre and stiff, non-*legato* phrasing are not my idea of how Sarastro should sound.

These somewhat disparate elements are pulled together by Sir Georg Solti's firm conducting. An experienced man of the theater, he is intense and dramatic, without sacrificing warmth. The Vienna Philharmonic is in sumptuous form.

The polyglot cast results in some exotic accentuation of the dialogue. The engineers stage the opera for stereo quite vividly, with many sound effects.

1972 EMI / ANGEL (S) CD

Anneliese Rothenberger (A), Edda Moser (B), Olivera Miljakovic (C), Peter Schreier (D), Willi Brokmeier (E), Walter Berry (F), Kurt Moll (G), Bavarian State Opera Chorus and Orchestra, Munich—Wolfgang Sawallisch

This recording is unusual because it includes "Pamina, wo bist du?," a duet for Tamino and Papageno in Act II (inserted between the Two Priests' "Bewahret euch vor Weibertücken" and the quintet "Wie? Ihr an diesem Schreckensort?"). Tamino longs for Pamina; Papageno, for Papagena. The number was first performed in 1802, when Schikaneder revived *The Magic Flute* at the new Theater an der Wien. Schikaneder claimed that the duet had been composed by Mozart, but did not explain why it was not included in the original production of the opera. The duet is printed in some vocal scores, but most authorities dismiss it as spurious. If it is authentic, then it is exceedingly minor Mozart.

I suppose there is some value in having at least one recording of the opera that includes it, so that curious listeners can make up their own minds.

There is a distinguished cast. Schreier repeats his Tamino, to good effect. Berry's third recorded Papageno reveals some vocal wear and tear—his vibrato has loosened, and his upper register is careful—but is as lively as ever (and we are finally given a chance to hear him in the dialogue).

The newcomers include Anneliese Rothenberger, often typecast by record companies in soubrette and operetta roles, but a warm, womanly Pamina, despite a fluttery vibrato. Edda Moser is an exciting Queen, flying through the technical challenges of both arias with supernatural ease; her *staccatos* in "Der Hölle Rache" are particularly eerie. Kurt Moll is a magnificent Sarastro, from both the vocal and interpretive standpoints; his only real rival on the stereo recordings is Crass.

Wolfgang Sawallisch, an experienced opera conductor, takes an unusually objective approach to this score. His reading is fast, clear, rather hard-edged, and completely unsentimental. I'm not sure I like the concept, but it is brilliantly executed by the fine Munich orchestra and chorus.

1978 BARCLAY (S)

Kiri Te Kanawa (A), Edita Gruberova (B), Kathleen Battle (C), Peter Hofmann (D), Norbert Orth (E), Philippe Huttenlocher (F), Kurt Moll (G), Rhine Opera Chorus, Strasbourg Philharmonic Orchestra—Alain Lombard

Despite the presence of several famous names in the cast list, this recording dropped out of the catalogue fairly quickly. It is an interesting, if decidedly uneven, production. Alain Lombard favors extremes of tempo—some numbers are taken very slowly, others quite briskly—as well as abrupt changes of tempo within numbers.

Kiri Te Kanawa makes a lovely, sympathetic sound, but she is not very dramatic; in her very first line, "O welcher Marter, welcher Pein!," she seems no more than mildly piqued. Edita Gruberova, in the first of her several recorded

Queens, also is stronger on accuracy than characterization. Kathleen Battle, however, is a charming Papagena.

It is interesting to hear Peter Hofmann as an aspiring Mozart tenor, before he decided to specialize in Wagnerian roles: on this early outing, his vocalism is secure and attractive, his dramatic instincts right. Philippe Huttenlocher is a bland Papageno, often approximately pitched. Moll repeats his impressive Sarastro from the Sawallisch set.

The sound—at least on the Erato LP pressings—is blurry, with too much empty-hall resonance.

1980 DEUTSCHE GRAMMOPHON (S,D) (D

Edith Mathis (A), Karin Ott (B), Janet Perry (C), Francisco Araiza (D), Heinz Kruse (E), Gottfried Hornik (F), José van Dam (G), Chorus of the Deutsche Oper, Berlin Philharmonic Orchestra—Herbert von Karajan

It is hardly surprising that Karajan should have changed his conception of the opera thirty years after he recorded it for EMI. This performance has all the hallmarks of Karajan's mature operatic style: playing of superhuman tonal beauty, transparency, and refinement from the Berlin Philharmonic; a tendency, on the conductor's part, to smooth out accents and contrasts; a cast of attractive, rather lightweight voices.

Edith Mathis and Francisco Araiza are an appealing pair of lovers. Janet Perry displays a fresh soprano and a teasing, feminine charm as Papagena.

José van Dam temporarily abandons his usual role, the Speaker (well sung here by Claudio Nicolai), in order to try on Sarastro for size. The experiment is not a complete success. The problem is not the low tessitura, but the relative lack of weight and dark coloration in the voice. Although van Dam is often billed as a bass-baritone, he is definitely more of a baritone than a bass. It seems odd that he has never recorded Papageno, a role which would seem to suit his voice very well.

No doubt at Karajan's insistence, Gottfried

Hornik sings Pagageno fairly "straight," eschewing most of the traditional comic business; unfortunately, Hornik's basically attractive baritone thins out noticeably in the upper register, robbing his vocalism of the spontaneity it should have. Karin Ott is an accurate Queen of the Night, with a more substantial voice than most, but her temperament is decidedly placid.

Like so many of Karajan's opera recordings, this one has some decidedly odd sonic balances and perspectives, and is not a particularly good advertisement for digital recording techniques.

1980 RCA / BMG (S,D) CD

Ileana Cotrubas (A), Zdislawa Donat (B), Elizabeth Kales (C), Eric Tappy (D), Horst Hiestermann (E), Christian Boesch (F), Martti Talvela (G), Vienna State Opera Chorus, Vienna Philharmonic Orchestra—James Levine

This recording, based on a 1978 Salzburg Festival production, is the only one that includes virtually all of the original spoken dialogue. The dialogue is exceptionally well performed by the singers (only the Queen of the Night's few lines are given to an actress), but the inclusion of so much speech significantly alters the proportion of speech to song: the opera now seems more like a play with incidental music. Because James Levine favors deliberate tempos, this is also the longest *Magic Flute* on records: the total playing time is just six minutes under three hours.

Levine's conducting does not do full justice to the wit of the comic episodes, which tend to be a little sober, but he is magnificent in the "serious" parts of the score. The Vienna Philharmonic plays even better for him than it did for Solti—a warm, glowing sonority, with remarkable dynamic control.

Although it's always good to hear van Dam as the Speaker, the cast does not strike me as being of true festival quality. Zdislawa Donat, for example, is an inadequate Queen: she hits all the notes accurately, but could hardly be less interesting from an interpretive standpoint. (Gruberova sang the role for Levine at Salzburg, but contractual restrictions probably prevented her from recording the opera again so soon.) The Three Ladies and the Papagena are, frankly,

rather ordinary, even without reference to their many distinguished rivals on disc.

Ileana Cotrubas is a fine artist whose attractive soprano is handicapped by the veiled, husky sound of its middle register. Eric Tappy, another intelligent singer, makes the most of his good, but hardly outstanding, tenor voice.

Talvela sounds vocally less secure than he did on the Solti set, but his conception of Sarastro has deepened and gained in eloquence. The Papageno, Christian Boesch, indulges in some of the traditional buffoonery (he renders much of the dialogue in Viennese dialect), but sings sturdily enough.

The digital sound is splendid.

1981 EMI / ANGEL (S,D) CD

Lucia Popp (A), Edita Gruberova (B), Brigitte Lindner (C), Siegfried Jerusalem (D), Heinz Zednik (E), Wolfgang Brendel (F), Roland Bracht (G), Bavarian Radio Symphony Chorus and Orchestra—Bernard Haitink

Bernard Haitink's first recording of a complete opera is an impressive achievement. His shaping of this score reminds me of Klemperer's: there is the same sense of calm and order, the same stateliness and repose (both conductors' tempos create an unhurried impression, even when they are no slower than the norm). Haitink prefers a lighter, smoother orchestral sonority than Klemperer's, though. Like a lot of Haitink recordings, this one sounds dangerously understated and lacking in sharp interpretive profile at first hearing, but becomes more persuasive with subsequent listenings. The orchestra and chorus are outstanding.

The high voices take the honors here. Lucia Popp is no longer as steady or lush of timbre as she was when she sang the Queen of the Night for Klemperer, but her bright-toned, sensitive Pamina has the kind of individuality I miss in several more smoothly sung portrayals (e.g., Seefried's, Janowitz's, or Te Kanawa's). Gruberova is once again an above-average Queen of the Night: not ideally forceful or imperious, she certainly delivers the goods in the coloratura passages. There is a good trio of Ladies, and three rather chirpy boy sopranos—who, at least, blend beautifully with Popp in their Act II quartet.

I must admit that Roland Bracht, with his slightly rusty, cavernous tone, sounds more like a Fafner than a Sarastro to me. Wolfgang Brendel is hardly in Berry's or Kunz's class, let alone Fischer-Dieskau's, as Papageno; nor is Siegfried Jerusalem, for all his sensitivity and good taste, a true rival for Rosvaenge or Wunderlich.

The sound has a trace of that glassy, unreal quality that bothered a lot of people when the first digital recordings appeared (i.e., on LPs, even before the introduction of CDs)—it's difficult to tell exactly what sort of a space the performance is taking place in. On the positive side, the solo voices are not reproduced larger than life, and the studio acoustic, unnatural though it may be, is neither too dry nor too echoey. EMI includes more of the spoken dialogue than most other recordings, quite vivid stereo separation, and many elaborate staging effects (thunder, etc.), most of which are convincing.

1982 ERATO (S,D,P)

Marjanne Kweksilber (A), Isabelle Poulenard (B), Thea van der Putten (C), Guy de Mey (D), Henk Vels (E), Michel Verschaeve (F), Harry van der Kamp (G), Viva la musica Chamber Choir, Utrecht, Amsterdam Baroque Orchestra—Ton Koopman

This is the first recording of *The Magic Flute* to employ "original" instruments. Although I am an advocate, in principle, of such authenticity, this is simply not a very good performance of the opera.

It's a live recording, made during a concert performance in June of 1982. There is a surprising amount of extramusical noise (was the performance semi-staged?). Only a few scraps of dialogue are included. Inexplicably, the final stanza of Papageno's "Der Vogelfänger bin ich ja" is omitted.

The small orchestra (only twenty-eight players) sounds tonally undernourished and is often scrappy in ensemble. For once, though, we hear a truly magical-sounding flute: the soloist, playing a boxwood instrument with a conical bore, produces a soft, mellow tone of exquisite quality. Pitch, by the way, is a half tone lower than standard modern tuning.

Ton Koopman's conducting tends to be brisk and bouncy—a welcome corrective to the exaggeratedly slow and solemn tradition, perhaps, but the serious element in the opera eludes him completely; Sarastro and his priests seem downright flippant much of the time.

Despite the welcome presence of vocal embellishments, the singing is unimpressive, on the whole. The tiny chorus is simply unoperatic in sound and style—it might as well be singing Renaissance madrigals.

Most of the soloists have small, colorless voices. Many of them are Dutch, and pronounce the German with distinct accents. Worst of all, virtually all of these people have an infuriating habit of pecking away at individual notes, instead of sustaining the musical line. This kind of vocalism is surely inappropriate in Mozart's vocal writing, which calls for a sensuous, Italianate *cantabile* phrasing.

Guy de Mey is a pleasant if very light-voiced Tamino, but Michel Verschaeve (Papageno), Harry van der Kamp (Sarastro), and Henk Vels (Monostatos) are among the least effective exponents of their roles on disc.

The women are no more persuasive. Marjanne Kweksilber has a pure, fragile tone that makes her Pamina sound—literally—childlike (a full-bodied lyric soprano like Donath sounds like a potential Isolde by comparison). Isabelle Poulenard, operating with a pretty, light soprano no larger or fuller in timbre than Kweksilber's, makes a brave stab at the Queen of the Night (including an interpolated cadenza in the second aria), but just wasn't cut out for the part.

The digital sound is acceptable.

1984 PHILIPS (S,D) CD

Margaret Price (A), Luciana Serra (B), Maria Venuti (C), Peter Schreier (D), Robert Tear (E), Mikael Melbye (F), Kurt Moll (G), Leipzig Radio Chorus, Dresden State Orchestra—Colin Davis

This fine recording could be recommended without serious reservation, except for the producer's decision to assign the dialogue to a separate cast of actors. Some of the matching of spoken and sung timbres is fairly convincing, but at other times it is disastrous. The actors who impersonate Pamina and Monostatos do not resemble the voices of Margaret Price and Robert Tear at all, and it seems odd that Schreier and Moll, who do their dialogue so well on other recordings, are replaced by actors here.

Sir Colin Davis and the superb Dresden orchestra give a beautifully proportioned account of the score.

Price, with her cool yet sensuous soprano, is a lovely Pamina. Luciana Serra is another technically fluent but dramatically unexciting Queen. Schreier is even drier in timbre than before, but still an expert Tamino; Moll's Sarastro, on the other hand, is even more impressive than it was on his previous recordings. The Papageno, Mikael Melbye, is accurate and tasteful, but vocally small-scaled and bland.

The Philips engineers have captured the performance in superior digital sound.

1988 TELDEC (S,D) CD

Barbara Bonney (A), Edita Gruberova (B), Edith Schmid (C), Hans Peter Blochwitz (D), Peter Keller (E), Anton Scharinger (F), Matti Salminen (G), Chorus and Orchestra of the Zurich Opera House—Nikolaus Harnoncourt

Despite my admiration for Harnoncourt in other repertory (e.g., Monteverdi), I found this a frustrating release. The dialogue is replaced by a running narrative, often maddeningly arch in tone, spoken by an actress (a few lines are still handled by the singers). This device distances the listener emotionally and all but destroys the opera as a dramatic entity.

The Zurich Opera House orchestra uses modern instruments (although the string section employs gut strings on this recording), but Harnoncourt encourages them to play as though they were performing on period instruments. The strings conscientiously scale down their vibrato; the winds blare away heartily; the brasses tend to be raucous. The conductor favors violent accents, drastic tempo contrasts, and a strange sort of *rubato* in which all sorts of

melodic figurations are underlined by sudden ritards. As a result, the performance—though undeniably intense—is sadly lacking in continuity.

The cast is uneven. Matti Salminen, who certainly possesses a Sarastro voice, does not seem to be in his best vocal form—or perhaps he is uncomfortable with Harnoncourt's erratic beat and eccentric phrasing in the arias. Barbara Bonney is a musical singer with a pure, delicate lyric soprano: she might be a good Papagena, but her Pamina seems immature. Anton Scharinger indulges in some shameless mugging as Papageno, and actually doesn't sing the part all that well.

On the positive side, Gruberova continues to refine her conception of the Queen—she is the one singer here who seems to thrive on Harnoncourt's energetic, strongly accented approach. Hans Peter Blochwitz does not have the most beautiful tenor voice imaginable, but he is an unfailingly tasteful and resourceful artist, and shows considerable dramatic involvement. Thomas Hampson is an eloquent Speaker.

The digital engineering has sensational clarity and presence; for better or worse, every nuance of the performance can be heard. An oddity of the CD tracking is that each of the two finales is treated as a single band, with no internal access points.

1989 ERATO (S,D) CD

Luba Orgonasova (A), Sumi Jo (B), Martina Bovet (C), Gösta Winbergh (D), Volker Vogel (E), Håkan Hagegård (F), Franz-Joseph Selig (G), Romand Chamber Choir, Lausanne Pro Arte Choir, Paris Orchestral Ensemble—Armin Jordan

This set has quite a lot going for it, but it is not quite good enough as a totality to face down the recorded competition. One disappointment is that the dialogue is heavily abridged (presumably in order to fit the performance onto two CDs) and spoken by actors (perhaps inevitably, given this international cast).

Armin Jordan conducts in a relaxed yet disciplined fashion, allowing the beauties of the score to speak for themselves. The chorus does not have the sharpest German enunciation imaginable. The orchestral playing is expert, if occasionally rather plush and soft-focused in quality (an impression emphasized by some over-reverberant recorded sound).

Luba Orgonasova is another light-voiced Pamina, whose basically pretty sound can turn thin and brittle under pressure; nevertheless, she is a musical singer, and conveys an appealing vulnerability. Sumi Jo's voice remains round and attractive right up to the high Fs; though not very fiery of temperament, she handles the coloratura most impressively. Martina Bovet is an uncommonly vivacious Papagena.

The two Swedes—Gösta Winbergh and Håkan Hagegård—sing pleasantly enough, without giving particularly memorable characterizations. Franz-Joseph Selig, the Sarastro, and Alfred Muff, the Speaker, both sound underpowered.

This is the kind of well-prepared, enjoyable performance that one would be grateful to encounter in the opera house; on records, though, it is up against some quite tough competition.

1989 PHILIPS (S,D) CD

Kiri Te Kanawa (A), Cheryl Studer (B), Eva Lind (C), Francisco Araiza (D), Aldo Baldin (E), Olaf Bär (F), Samuel Ramey (G), Ambrosian Opera Chorus, Academy of St. Martin in the Fields—Neville Marriner

This recording, entering a crowded field, has many strengths. Although contained on two CDs, the performance includes extensive dialogue, persuasively handled by the singers.

Sir Neville Marriner's conducting combines elegance with solemnity, where appropriate. The reading suggests Beecham's—high praise, indeed. As early as the Overture, one can admire the conductor's crispness and attention to detail. His orchestra plays superlatively well for him.

Three of the singers have recorded their parts before. Te Kanawa, sounding a little cautious vocally compared to her work on the Lombard set, is much more animated. Araiza, also marginally less fresh of voice than he was for Karajan, partners her well. Van Dam is back as the Speaker, and is as eloquent as ever.

The newcomers include Cheryl Studer, an impressively accurate Queen who achieves force without sacrificing tonal quality, and Olaf Bär, a warmly lyrical Papageno who prefers geniality to silliness. Samuel Ramey sings Sarastro's music beautifully, but—perhaps because he is relatively new to the part—does not yet project the character as nobly as Crass and Moll do on their recordings. The record companies have tried hard to establish Eva Lind as a coloratura star, without much success; Papagena is a much more suitable assignment for her.

The engineering of this album is unobtrusively first-rate in quality, and indeed the entire production shows signs of unusual care.

1990 DECCA / LONDON (S,D) CD

Ruth Ziesak (A), Sumi Jo (B), Lotte Leitner (C), Uwe Heilmann (D), Heinz Zednik (E), Michael Kraus (F), Kurt Moll (G), Vienna State Opera Chorus, Vienna Philharmonic—Georg Solti

Billed by Decca as a "200th Anniversary recording," this set might also be thought of as a remake of Solti's 1969 version. There are some interesting differences between the two performances. Solti has mellowed noticeably—the new performance is more intimate in scale, without the emphatic dramatic accents of its predecessor. Once in a while, the conductor takes us by surprise: such interpretive choices as the near-*staccato* phrasing of "Bei Männern," or the dancelike lilt of the March of the Priests, are unexpected but effective.

The Vienna orchestra once again plays magnificently, and has no difficulty adjusting to the rather different demands Solti makes upon it this time.

Rather daringly, Decca has cast most of the roles with singers whose names are not likely to cut much ice on the international market. An obvious exception is Moll, whose vocal resources are undiminished and who continues to refine his portrayal of Sarastro. Like Solti, Moll has mellowed—this time around, he doesn't even allow himself the standard flash of anger and contempt when Sarastro refers to the Queen of the Night as "ein stolzes Weib" in the Act I finale.

Jo repeats her Queen from the Erato/Jordan set, but projects both the music and the character much more sharply here—probably as a result of Solti's influence. I doubt that real ferocity is part of her temperament, but her "Der Hölle Rache" is exceptionally well sung.

Virtually all of the other singers have light, lyrical voices. The Tamino of Uwe Heilmann is representative: a pleasant but small sound, like that of a very good operetta tenor. As a result, Heilmann seems underpowered in general, and cautious in the climaxes.

Michael Kraus possesses a beautiful lyric baritone, but he too sounds as though he might have difficulty projecting in a large auditorium. He avoids most of the traditional comic business, and nearly always finds something original and spontaneous-sounding to replace it.

Ruth Ziesak has a sweet, pure voice, with just enough vibrato to lend it some character. She is a touching Pamina; although one might legitimately prefer a soprano with more tonal body—i.e., with more warmth and roundness in her actual sound—Ziesak holds her own quite well against the intimidating recorded competition.

Decca has clothed this fine performance in superlative sound (the bass response, for example, is nothing short of phenomenal). The production indulges in fewer staging effects than the 1969 set—instead of "real" thunderclaps, for instance, we hear rolls from what sounds like a huge drum of indeterminate pitch. Finally, although this recording has been contained on only two CDs, it contains a surprising amount of the dialogue—well handled by this cast (which, of course, is made up primarily of native German speakers).

1990 EMI / ANGEL (S,D) CD

Dawn Upshaw (A), Beverly Hoch (B), Catherine Pierard (C), Anthony Rolfe Johnson (D), Guy de Mey (E), Andreas Schmidt (F), Cornelius Hauptmann (G), Schütz Choir of London, London Classical Players—Roger Norrington

Like the 1982 Erato/Koopman set, this one features an orchestra of period instruments, and instrumental tuning noticeably lower than standard modern concert pitch. Although I am very much in favor of such "authentic" performances in general, this is not an outstanding example of its type. Roger Norrington seems so determined to cleanse this score of the accumulated weight of tradition that he has gone to the opposite extreme: his *Magic Flute*, much like Koopman's, is fast, slick, and rather anemic in effect. There is not enough contrast between the "serious" and the "comic" episodes of the opera—everything is lighthearted and bouncy here.

The timbres of the period instruments—astringent and dulcet by turns—are fascinating to hear, but all too often the orchestral sonority is thin and ill balanced, with the winds, brasses, and timpani drowning out the comparatively weak and colorless strings. Norrington favors extremely rapid tempos, and there is a clipped, breathless quality to the articulation that is not ingratiating. Another problem is the choral sound, which is exceptionally light and clear, but also completely devoid of vibrato. We have grown accustomed to this kind of choral singing in Monteverdi and Bach, but it is not suited to the dramatic choruses in *The Magic Flute*—Sarastro's priests sound like a college glee club.

Anthony Rolfe Johnson is a most impressive Tamino. Although his voice is a light one, and certainly does not possess the warmth and roundness of a Wunderlich, he is a tasteful and unfailingly resourceful artist who creates a real character.

Dawn Upshaw has a beautiful voice, but she cannot vary its basically bright color very much, and some of her sustained tones acquire a brittle, glassy quality. At the risk of sounding sexist, I must say that I find her interpretation of Pamina altogether too aggressive. It's one thing for Pamina to come across as spunky, but quite another for her to seem more determined than the Queen.

Unfortunately, there are serious weaknesses elsewhere in the casting. Beverly Hoch sings all of the Queen of the Night's notes accurately, but her voice is small and colorless, and produces a decidedly chirpy effect in the high *staccatos*. Cornelius Hauptmann is miscast as Sarastro, and fades away to near inaudibility on the low notes. Andreas Schmidt sings well as Papageno, but is quite unfunny.

This international cast has not been carefully enough coached: some of the singers are unidiomatic in their German pronunciation. The recorded sound, although a little dry and analytical, maintains a high technical standard. This version also uses the two-CD format, which will presumably become standard.

1991 TELARC (S,D) CD

Barbara Hendricks (A), June Anderson (B), Ulrike Steinsky (C), Jerry Hadley (D), Helmut Wildhaber (E), Thomas Allen (F), Robert Lloyd (G), Scottish Chamber Chorus and Orchestra— Charles Mackerras

Unlike Norrington, Sir Charles Mackerras is an experienced opera conductor, and his elegant yet amply dramatic reading of the score is a persuasive one. A note in the accompanying booklet makes a point of the fast tempo choices (singling out "Ach, ich fühl's" for special mention), but after Norrington's performance Mackerras's does not seem at all radical in this regard. Like Norrington, Mackerras is scrupulous in his use of *appoggiaturas*, and even includes discreet vocal embellishments.

The small orchestra and chorus play and sing well, if without the richness of tone heard on the new Solti set; Mackerras no doubt prefers these leaner, more pointed timbres as more appropriate to the music, and so may many listeners.

This recording (another two-CD job) contains an unusually generous amount of the dialogue, and all of the singers handle it with confidence and poise.

Thomas Allen is a distinguished Papageno, singing strongly and combining sly sophistication and earthy humor in just the right proportions. Robert Lloyd's Sarastro is surprisingly good—dignified and firmly vocalized. He "plays

to the microphone" in a way that suggests his voice may not have the kind of weight and resonance that would enable him to project the role this convincingly in a large auditorium, but on this recording the relative lack of power is of minimal importance.

Barbara Hendricks is an expert, touching Pamina, although her lovely voice does seem almost fragile at times. June Anderson vocalizes brilliantly and makes an unusually seductive-sounding Queen; she also works herself into a fine frenzy in the dialogue before her second aria.

As Tamino, Jerry Hadley gives a thoughtful, incisive performance. If only his voice didn't sound just a bit tight and steely in the upper register, his performance could be enjoyed.

Like the 1972 EMI / Sawallisch set, this one includes the Tamino / Papageno duet "Pamina, wo bist du?"—as an appendix, after Act II. Oddly enough, the text of this number is not included in Telarc's otherwise comprehensive booklet.

Telarc's sound is clear but a little lacking in presence. The bass, in particular, could have more impact. For some reason, the "real" cracks of thunder heard here are less convincing than the various thunder effects on some of the other recordings.

———

To make a recommendation, when so many of the recordings are distinguished, is difficult. Choice depends to a large degree upon the listener's own taste in conductors and singers. The EMI sets conducted by Beecham and Klemperer surely belong in any comprehensive opera library, but they both lack the spoken dialogue. Of the stereo recordings with dialogue, the Böhm, the 1969 Solti, Haitink, and Levine versions all have substantial musical merits, and all four of these sets also "play" convincingly as drama.

If you have no recording of the opera in your collection, are not particularly sentimental about individual performers of the past, and simply can't decide which *Magic Flute* to buy, I would point out that the new Marriner set is as good as any of the digital versions: it's well conducted, played, sung, and recorded, and it has the advantage of being on only two CDs.

But most of these advantages are shared by Solti's new version—another strong entry, despite its lack of superstar singers. The Telarc/Mackerras is an impressive production, on the whole;

listeners who value conductorial nuance may well prefer it to either the Marriner or Solti sets.

ROLAND GRAEME

Unavailable for review:
1955 GUILDE INTERNATIONAL DU
    DISQUE
1974 CONCERT HALL

MARY, QUEEN OF SCOTS (1977)

A: Mary, Queen of Scots (s); B: Darnley (t); C: Bothwell (t);
D: James Stewart (bar); E: Riccio (bs-bar); F: Gordon (bs)

Thea Musgrave's work was premiered by the Scottish Opera in 1977 at the Edinburgh Festival and in America the next year by the fledgling Virginia Opera Association, whose highly praised production was recorded. One wishes it had also been videotaped, for the libretto presents complicated conflicts with striking dramatic economy and panache, and the staging is reported to have been both powerful and cogent. The work dramatizes the years of Mary's rule from her return from France in 1561 (she was nineteen) until her escape to England seven years later. Its focus is on the power struggle between her brother (James), her husband (Lord Darnley), and her protector (the Earl of Bothwell)—baritone, lyric tenor, and dramatic tenor. At its center is the youthful and adventurous but solitary figure of Mary herself, a Bellini-Donizetti heroine in her desperate need for protection but here demonstrating a Renaissance strength and motivation with her ambition, her sexual passion, and her need to protect her son. The conflicting forces are vigorously characterized in music of atmosphere and rhythmic force. If there is a dramatic difficulty it is in the matter of subsidiary characterization, for James (the central figure of the unpublished play upon which the opera is based) is striking but somewhat unresolved in motivation, while Darnley, musically at any rate, suggests instability but not much charm. The rough, impassioned figure of Bothwell, however, makes a unified impression, and all of the major roles provide singing actors with first-rate dramatic and musical challenges.

1978 MOSS MUSIC GROUP (S)

Ashley Putnam (A), Jon Garrison (B), Barry Busse (C), Jake Gardner (D), Kenneth Bell (E), Francesco Soriano (F), Virginia Opera Association Chorus and Orchestra—Peter Mark

This is one of the few major twentieth-century operas outside the central repertory to receive a musically adequate recording. Its central attraction is Ashley Putnam, fresh, steady, commanding, warm in sound, and outspoken theatrically. One can imagine a darker voice here, but her *legato* (of mood and tone) serves her well dramatically and she has the range of color for the romance, outrage, and disillusion of the role: a star performance less than two years after her debut. Jake Gardner's James is equally forceful. He sang the world premiere at Edinburgh as well, and has the vocal size and attack for the role's tyrannical aspects and the warmth for other elements. Barry Busse, who has a voice of dramatic color but lyric dimension, is an impassioned Bothwell, with a manner recalling Jon Vickers. Jon Garrison is unable to suggest much of the charm of Darnley, though he sings neatly enough. Kenneth Bell's Riccio (Mary's beloved minstrel and later her secretary) is a neutral presence (the role is oddly scored), as is Francesco Soriano's Lord Gordon—something of a Raimondo figure, who nevertheless needs to suggest conviction enough to stab James at the conclusion: ideally, the role calls for a Christoff or Rossi-Lemeni. Peter Mark conducts with vigor and precision, but in this live performance the chorus is sometimes vague in attack and diction. The recording has clarity and depth, though the voices are occasionally a trifle dis-tant. Diction is relentlessly American, which means that verbal bite is periodically relaxed. Altogether, this is a strong recording of one of the most striking and attractive of contemporary operas in English.

LONDON GREEN

MODEST MUSSORGSKY

BORIS GODUNOV (1874)

A: Marina (s or ms); B: Dmitri (t); C: Shuisky (t); D: Rangoni (bar or bs); E: Boris Godunov (bar or bs); F: Pimen (bs); G: Varlaam (bs)

*I*n a sense, *Boris Godunov* is not one opera, but many. This opera's textual options and problems, although unparalleled among standard-repertory works, are no longer a mystery to the general public. The relevant scores are available, and many discussions of the textual issues have appeared in print since the release of the 1976 EMI recording conducted by Jerzy Semkow, the first to use one of Mussorgsky's own scores, as opposed to the once-standard Rimsky-Korsakov rewrite. Therefore, a brief recap should suffice.

It is important to keep in mind that when we refer to Mussorgsky's original score, we are oversimplifying. The composer left not one version of the score, but three.

The first *Boris Godunov*, completed in 1869, was an extremely concise opera, in only seven scenes. The action was dominated by Boris himself and there was no prominent female role at all.

In 1871–72 Mussorgsky revised his opera extensively. Boris is no longer the exclusive focus of attention: Dmitri, the Pretender, is given musical and dramatic parity with the czar. The composer added the two scenes of the Polish act, thus creating the roles of Marina and Rangoni, and allowing Dmitri to assume—however briefly—the guise of a conventional romantic tenor. Mussorgsky eliminated an episode set in front of St. Basil's Cathedral, replacing it with the Kromy Forest tableau. But he retained two incidents from the deleted scene—

the Simpleton's taunting by the children, and his final lament—and transferred them to the new scene.

A vocal score prepared under the composer's supervision and published in 1874 is based on this version, but contains a number of cuts. Although it has been assumed that Mussorgsky authorized these cuts in order to avoid trouble with the imperial censorship, it is quite possible that the composer considered the cuts to be genuine improvements, from the standpoint of musical and dramatic pacing.

The opera had its admirers from the beginning, but it was also severely criticized, and even in its expanded form it enjoyed no more than a *succès d'estime*. Had Rimsky-Korsakov not turned his attention to the score, *Boris Godunov*'s acceptance within Russia, and its entrance into the international repertory, would surely have been much more gradual and problematic. Using the 1871–72 and 1874 material, Rimsky introduced further cuts. In addition to reorchestrating the opera from beginning to end, he "corrected" Mussorgsky's rhythms, harmonies, and modulations, and "improved" his vocal writing. In some places (e.g., the end of the Coronation Scene, the Polonaise and the final pages of the Polish act, the choruses of the Kromy Forest Scene) Rimsky-Korsakov for all practical purposes threw out the original and composed new music of his own.

Today, we prefer to hear the great musical works of the past as their creators envisioned them—to the extent that the composer's intention can be determined. Increasingly, opera houses have favored Mussorgsky's own score(s) over the Rimsky-Korsakov rewrite, and record companies are following suit.

All of the "complete" recordings of *Boris Godunov* made prior to 1976 use the Rimsky-Korsakov edition. Most contain cuts (i.e., they don't even include all of the music from Rimsky-Korsakov's 1908 score), which correspond to Soviet stage practice. A surprising number of these recordings try to save the St. Basil's Scene by inserting it immediately after the Polish act. Since Rimsky-Korsakov did not revise this scene, a 1929 reorchestration in his style, by Mikhail Ippolitov-Ivanov, is used. Including both the St. Basil's Scene and the Kromy Forest Scene in the same performance means duplicating the Simpleton's lament, which ends both of these tableaux; his persecution by the children—an episode comprising 65 bars—is generally cut from the Kromy Forest Scene, to avoid a further redundancy.

In five of the recordings discussed below, Mussorgsky's own score is used. All of these sets utilize the critical edition of the score prepared by David Lloyd-Jones and published in 1975; each conductor, however, makes his own textual choices—as a result, only two of the five maestros end up performing exactly the same music! Basically, the Lloyd-Jones score corresponds to Mussorgsky's rewrite of 1871–72—the cuts in the 1874 vocal score are restored, but so is some material unique to 1869. Thus, to a degree, this edition second-guesses the composer, who never put his opera together in precisely this way: in its broad outlines, however, this version is undeniably sound. At least, the options it offers performers are clearly labeled as such.

Ideally, a collector should own recordings of both the Mussorgsky and the Rimsky-Korsakov versions: hearing them in proximity is a fascinating experience in itself, and reveals at least as much about the textual problems as many pages of learned exegesis.

The opera's interpretive challenges begin with the choice of edition. Although the differences can be exaggerated, the Rimsky-Korsakov score is undeniably the more colorful and the more conventionally "operatic." Mussorgsky's more austerely orchestrated original is more intimate and conversational in style—the vocal lines (both solo and choral) are more exposed, and the words must carry a greater part of the expressive burden.

Note: In dealing with Russian and Slavic proper names, I have generally adopted the spelling used by the individual record company, except where an alternate form is likely to be more familiar to record collectors. Thus, I have ignored the fact that Erato, a French label, bills Galina Vishnevskaya as "Vichnievskaia" (even though the latter may well be the more accurate transliteration, from a phonetic point of view). When a performer appears on more than one recording but the name is spelled differently (a not uncommon occurrence), I have simply made an arbitrary choice and stuck to it, in the interests of consistency.

1948 MELODIYA (M)

Maria Maksakova (A), Georgi Nelepp (B), Nikander Khanayev (C), Alexander Pirogov (E), Maxim Mikhailov (F), Vassily Lubenchov (G), Bolshoi Theater Chorus and Orchestra—Nicolai Golovanov

This recording, originally on 78s, circulated on LP during the fifties not only as a Melodiya direct import but on the Period and Colosseum labels as well. Neither of these transfers does the performance justice: Period's sound is quite poor—the solo voices penetrate the sonic murk with reasonable clarity, but many of the subtleties in the instrumental writing are lost, and the loud choral passages verge on bedlam. The reproduction on Colosseum is noticeably cleaner, though hardly high fidelity. One is forced to conclude that—unless this performance can be resurrected in significantly improved sound—this version is strictly for the historically minded, specialist collector.

A further problem is the many cuts, which probably correspond to Soviet stage practice at the time, but may strike today's listeners as excessive.

A curiosity throughout the performance is the "improvement" of Rimsky-Korsakov's orchestration by some anonymous hand: in addition to some significant rewriting (i.e., thickening and coarsening) of the brass parts, many pages of the score contain extra gong strokes, bass-drum rolls and thuds, cymbal clashes, and harp and celesta doublings of other instrumental lines.

All of this is unfortunate, because the performance is a distinguished one, on the whole, and often quite exciting. Nicolai Golovanov gives a highly subjective, melodramatic account of the score, alternating violent attacks with a lush, expansive treatment of the lyrical episodes. There are some hair-raising tempo shifts; the music often speeds up and slows down again in the course of a single bar. Some of the accelerations can be attributed to the need to fit the music onto the 78s—at times, the crowds in the Coronation Scene and the Kromy Forest Scene sound not just excited, but agitated to the point of hysteria. But it is clear than many of the choices are Golovanov's own. I find them expressive; purists may be horrified.

There is a fine cast; in fact, virtually everyone is outstanding, and the high quality extends to the supporting roles.

Alexander Pirogov, with his huge, pulverizing bass, is a formidable Boris, unapologetically extroverted and larger than life. As Pimen, Maxim Mikhailov—another powerful bass—sounds authoritative yet warmly human. There is an appropriately blustery Varlaam, Vassily Lubenchov.

One of the cuts, the omission of the first scene of the Polish act, is particularly annoying, because Maria Maksakova is such a good Marina. She is rather more womanly and sympathetic than many of her recorded rivals, but her strong *spinto* soprano has just enough of an edge to suggest the character's determination. The Dmitri is Georgi Nelepp, a mainstay of these mono Melodiya complete-opera recordings: he sometimes sounds a little tense on loud high notes, but he has good dramatic instincts, his timbre is attractive, and he phrases with assurance and elegance. In what little is retained of the second Polish scene, he is soulful as only a Russian tenor can be, once again making one regret the cuts.

1948–50 MELODIYA (M)

Cast the same as above except: Mark Reizen (E)

Except for the title role, the cast of this recording is identical to that of the version discussed above. Most of the time, the performance is identical, too. But independent recordings of the czar's music, sung by Mark Reizen instead of Pirogov, have been inserted in order to get some extra mileage from the set. Most of these interpolated 78 sides are conducted by Golovanov, but some are not—this performance of the St. Basil's Scene with Reizen, for example, is a series of new takes from beginning to end, and the tempos of Vasily Nebolsin (another experienced and high-intensity maestro) are noticeably slower.

Reizen's voice is more beautiful than Pirogov's, and his manner is much more restrained—his verbal emphases, though effective, never break the musical line. His is a classic portrayal, capped by a touching account of the Death Scene; against very tough competition, Reizen is, in my opinion, the finest Boris on any of these complete sets.

This hybrid recording was reissued on LP in 1974 by Recital Records, a short-lived California-based label. The sound is even worse than on the Period set: the 78s, plagued by surface noise, wow, and flutter, are ineptly joined together.

1952 EMI / ANGEL (M)

Eugenia Zareska (A), Nicolai Gedda (B), Andre Bielecki (C), Kim Borg (D), Boris Christoff (E, F, G), Chernikovsky Choeurs Russes de Paris, Orchestre National de la Radiodiffusione Française—Issay Dobrowen

Seraphim's LP reissue, dating from 1974, is only fair in terms of sound quality (although much better than either of the two recordings discussed above).

EMI makes the standard cut in Pimen's Act I narration, but Feodor is allowed his song in Act II. The St. Basil's Scene is omitted, and as a result the Kromy Forest Scene is performed intact. The first Polish scene is included, but

Rangoni is eliminated from the second, and Dmitri isn't even allowed his bitter little monologue after the Polonaise—we move right on to Marina's entrance and the love duet.

Issay Dobrowen conducts firmly, but is flexible enough to allow his singers and instrumentalists to mold the more lyrical phrases with real eloquence. The orchestra is French, and sounds like it—saxophone-like horn tone, and pronounced vibrato from the flutes—but much of the playing is clear, well balanced, and beautiful. The chorus is fervent, if occasionally shaky.

One amusing aspect of the performance is the doubling and even tripling of roles. The most famous of these multiple assumptions is Boris Christoff's triple turn as Boris, Pimen, and Varlaam, possible only in a concert performance or on a recording. Christoff's voice, of course, is nothing if not individual in timbre, and some listeners may be bothered by the fact that he is instantly recognizable in all three roles. He coarsens his sound a bit for Varlaam, and belts out the song about the siege of Kazan with tremendous relish; for Pimen, Christoff pulls back on the volume and keeps everything soft, gentle, and rather otherworldly. These are both interesting portrayals, although they are really just warm-ups for the Boris. In this role, Christoff makes a gutsy bass like Pirogov seem almost bland by comparison; Christoff's singing is filled with color and emotion, his inflections are highly personal, and in the Clock Scene and the Death Scene he indulges in some good, old-fashioned scenery-chewing. This is one of those utterly individual operatic assumptions that must either be rejected outright or swallowed whole.

Eugenia Zareska, a vibrant, rich-toned mezzo, sings both Marina and Feodor, and differentiates between the two characters with remarkable success. Kim Borg is imposing as Shchelkalov and Rangoni (despite the fact that both parts lie rather high for his deep, dark bass), and Andre Bielecki nails down his triple assignment—Shuisky, Missail, and Khrushchov—with great skill.

This was Nicolai Gedda's first recording of a complete opera, and his is still, on balance, the most satisfactory Dmitri on any of the complete

sets. His singing, always firmly phrased and emotionally direct, is sweet yet manly in timbre.

1955 DECCA / LONDON (M)

Melanie Bugarinovich (A), Miro Brajnik (B), Stepan Andrashevich (C), Miro Changalovich (E), Branko Pivnichki (F), Zharko Tzveych (G), Chorus and Orchestra of the National Opera, Belgrade—Kreshimir Baranovich

Decca recorded several Russian operas in Belgrade during the fifties. The performances are variable in quality, but this *Boris Godunov* may well be the worst of the series. All of the standard cuts are made, and then some.

Ironically, Melanie Bugarinovich, who suffers the most from the cuts, is by far the best singer in the cast. Her soft-grained contralto makes a sumptuous sound in the love duet, and she also displays some temperament. The only one of her colleagues who approaches her level is Dushan Popovich, who possesses a warm, steady baritone and good dramatic instincts; unfortunately, he is cast as Shchelkalov, a relatively small part.

Miro Changalovich, whose vocal production sounds nasal and muffled throughout, is a subdued Boris. He is badly extended by the high notes. Zharko Tzveych makes a certain impact as Varlaam, but his singing is technically crude.

Some of the other singers are genuinely awful. Branko Pivnichki, the Pimen, sounds like a parody of a Slavic bass, wobbly and lugubriously overweighted of timbre; Miro Brajnik, the Dmitri, sounds like a parody of a Slavic tenor—a raw, steely instrument, used without inhibition. The Shuisky, Stepan Andrashevich, seems on the verge of hysteria much of the time.

Kreshimir Baranovich plods through the score. The chorus makes a good sound, but the orchestral work is substandard. The recorded sound (mono only, by the way, even on the Richmond reissue) is undistinguished.

1959 MELODIYA (S?)

Irina Arkhipova (A), Vladimir Ivanovsky (B), Georgi Shulpin (C), Yevgeny Kibkalo (D), Ivan Petrov (E), Mark Reshetin (F), Alexei Gueleva

(G), Bolshoi Theater Chorus and Orchestra—Alexander Melik-Pashayev

This version was once available as a direct import in its original Melodiya format. The complete set was reissued by the Musical Heritage Society. The recording is supposedly stereo, but the sound is so cramped and flat, and the separation effect is so minimal, that I suspect the engineering may be mono, with some artificial rechanneling applied after the fact. In the familiar Soviet tradition, the solo voices are once again crudely overmiked.

Most of the traditional cuts are observed. The St. Basil's Scene is included, and so is the first scene of the Polish act.

Alexander Melik-Pashayev, an experienced maestro, provides a firm, energetic reading of the score, with rhythms exceptionally well defined. His approach is sometimes not warm or relaxed enough for my personal taste, and the orchestral playing—good though it is in most respects—is hardly a model of tonal refinement. The chorus is impressive.

The cast is uneven, but only Georgi Shulpin—another piercing, querulous Shuisky—is really objectionable. The Dmitri, Vladimir Ivanovsky, seems to be driving his voice in the climaxes, and never sounds really unpressured, but his keen dramatic awareness offers partial compensation.

Ivan Petrov sings the title role with firm, smooth tone and has absolutely no difficulties with the range. But somehow the character escapes him: we hear a disembodied bass voice, but no guilt-ridden czar.

The Polish act goes well: Irina Arkhipova's rock-solid mezzo makes an exciting effect in Marina's music, although such an authoritative singer can't help sounding more like Catherine the Great at her most formidable than the seductive, yet insecure, young woman drawn by the libretto. She does lighten up enough to deliver an exceptionally beautiful performance of her share of the love duet. As Rangoni, Yevgeny Kibkalo displays a handsome baritone and an ideally insinuating manner.

Mark Reshetin brings the right kind of severe dignity to Pimen's music. Alexei Gueleva is a surprisingly subdued Varlaam, although his approach has the advantage of avoiding the traditional exaggerated comic business.

1959–63 COLUMBIA (S)

Cast the same as above except: George London (E)

In 1960 George London was invited to sing Boris at the Bolshoi. He returned in 1963 to record the role—his contribution being inserted into the 1959 Melodiya recording, the cast of which was reassembled where necessary (e.g., in Act II). These 1963 inserts are definitely in stereo sound, at least, but the splices are often quite audible. This reconfigured set was issued by Columbia in the United States.

Unfortunately, London was not in good vocal form at these sessions. His Russian seems idiomatic, and his phrasing is always artistic; in the Death Scene he pulls himself together and does some beautiful, expressive soft singing. But much of his vocalism is constricted and inaccurately pitched, and he is too aggressive in Act II—if you want this approach to the role, then Christoff brings it off much more convincingly. (London's 1955 recordings of the Act II monologue and the Clock Scene show him to better vocal advantage.)

1962 EMI / ANGEL (S) CD

Evelyn Lear (A), Dimitr Ouzounov (B), John Lanigan (C), Anton Diakov (D), Boris Christoff (E, F, G), Chorus of the National Opera of Sofia, Orchestre de la Société des Concerts du Conservatoire—André Cluytens

Essentially, this is a stereo remake of the 1952 EMI / Dobrowen set. The performance has one significant textual advantage over most of its competitors: it offers the 1908 Rimsky-Korsakov score absolutely uncut (as on the earlier EMI recording, the St. Basil's Scene is omitted—quite correctly, of course). The major restoration is the complete Dmitri / Rangoni conversation.

Once again, as on the EMI / Dobrowen set,

we hear a French orchestra—a good one, though with the characteristic horn and wind timbres. The chorus makes a most impressive sound.

André Cluytens's realization of the score is less dynamic, and therefore less dramatic, than Dobrowen's. One problem is a persistent softness of attack, which makes the music sound "beautiful" but deprives it of urgency. Individual passages are well executed, but somehow the opera does not build as it should. In fairness to Cluytens, he often creates a mood that is exactly right—the music to which Rangoni first tempts, then threatens, Marina acquires an otherworldly, *Parsifal*-like aura that is fascinating to hear in itself but is also dramatically appropriate. Cluytens's account of the Kromy Forest Scene is consistently taut and exciting—had the entire performance been on this level, this recording could be recommended without serious reservation.

Christoff repeats his triple turn, and is once again an imposing vocal and dramatic presence. His singing may be marginally less smooth and beautiful than before, but it has a compensatory bite and urgency. His Pimen is less meek and one-dimensional, which is all to the good; his Varlaam is once again uniquely vivid. Christoff's Boris is still a strong portrayal, although it's possible to prefer his earlier recording; if there was anything his interpretation didn't need, it was more violence in Act II, or more "realism" during the final death agonies.

Evelyn Lear's warm, soft-grained lyric soprano is an interesting change from the powerful mezzo or dramatic-soprano sound we usually hear in Marina's music; Lear makes the character convincingly youthful as well as willful.

As Dmitri, Ouzounov drives his voice awfully hard in the climaxes, is deficient in *legato* flow, and seems reluctant to sing softly, but he understands what the opera is about and conveys some of the aggressive, ambitious side of the character.

John Lanigan seems a strange choice for Shuisky: he brings more real singing tone to the role than do some of his recorded rivals, but he really doesn't do anything out of the ordinary from an interpretive standpoint, and his Russian sounds careful and correct rather than fluent.

1970 DECCA / LONDON (S) CD

Galina Vishnevskaya (A), Ludovic Spiess (B), Alexei Maslennikov (C), Zoltan Kélémen (D), Nicolai Ghiaurov (E), Martti Talvela (F), Anton Diakov (G), Vienna Boys' Choir, Sofia Radio Chorus, Vienna State Opera Chorus, Vienna Philharmonic Orchestra—Herbert von Karajan

Once again the performance text is Rimsky-Korsakov's, heard here complete except for the cut in the Kromy Forest needed to accommodate the St. Basil's Scene.

The recording, based on Herbert von Karajan's Salzburg Easter Festival production, is inevitably dominated by the conductor, who manages to place his unique stylistic imprint on virtually every page of the score. This is unquestionably the most sensuously beautiful reading of the opera on records; in fact, the set has been criticized for precisely this reason.

The instrumental playing is beautiful—but I find it expressive as well. The massed choruses also make a sumptuous sound, although here I would prefer a crisper and more intense delivery (as in all of the Bolshoi versions).

The very impressive cast doesn't hurt. Nicolai Ghiaurov is in easy, beautiful voice, and is especially good in the tender and melancholy moments, emphasizing the czar's paternal feelings and remorse rather than his frustration and final desperation. Martti Talvela, also tonally suave, is a very good Pimen, and Anton Diakov makes a vivid Varlaam. As Rangoni, Zoltan Kélémen's high, slightly nasal baritone provides an effective contrast to the three basses.

The two Russian stars imported for the recording sessions provide welcome authority. Alexei Maslennikov doubles Shuisky and the Simpleton very satisfactorily. Galina Vishnevskaya is an expressive and unusually specific Marina, despite the fact that her slightly edgy voice, with its backward placement and white, vibrato-less tonal qualities, is hardly what one expects to hear in the role. From the interpretive standpoint, Vishnevskaya leaves most of her competitors on records in the dust.

Ludovic Spiess displays a large, handsome voice, somewhat metallic and open on top, but still a pleasure to hear in Dmitri's music. He is a good musician, and a resourceful vocal actor.

The many smaller roles are all at least adequately filled, and it sounds as though a real effort was made to find singers with attractive voices who were also comfortable with the Russian language.

The sound is well up to this label's generally high standards: very rich and detailed, almost suspiciously "warm," and with the solo voices audible at all dynamic levels in a way that they could never be in a theater. The stereo spread, in particular, is quite spectacular. On the CD set, only the offstage perspectives (e.g., the chanting monks overheard in Pimen's cell) sound slightly unnatural—a characteristic of a number of Decca's analogue complete-opera recordings that have been transferred to CD. The CD booklet is handsome, although the essay skims over the facts of the opera's textual history and indulges in some special pleading for the Rimsky-Korsakov edition.

p.1975 HARMONIA MUNDI (S) CD

Alexandrina Milcheva-Nonova (A), Dimiter Damianov (B), Liubomir Bodurov (C), Peter Bakardjiev (D), Nicola Ghiuselev (E, F), Assen Tchavdarov (G), Bodra Smyana Children's Chorus, Sofia Opera Chorus and Orchestra—Assen Naidenov

This recording represents an opportunity missed. There are some good voices in the cast, and the orchestral and choral work is more than adequate; it's entirely possible that a different conductor might have inspired this ensemble to come up with something above the ordinary. But Assen Naidenov's lifeless conducting makes this the dullest account of the score on any of these complete sets. Naidenov's tempos are invariably too slow, and he is unable to sustain them with any conviction: the music constantly sags and loses impetus, and many scenes seem to be taking place in slow motion.

The text is identical to that on the Karajan set: Rimsky-Korsakov plus the St. Basil's Scene, complete except for the cut in the Kromy Forest Scene.

Nicola Ghiuselev sings Pimen in addition to the title role, providing strong, idiomatic vocalism but relatively little in the way of individuality or dramatic insight. The Varlaam, Assen Tchavdarov, does some rough singing, which the listener may or may not find acceptable as part of his characterization.

Alexandrina Milcheva-Nonova is a rather neutral Marina—her voice is a solid enough mezzo, but she seems to be feeling her way. The Dmitri (Dimiter Damianov) and Shuisky (Liubomir Bodurov) are accurate, if decidedly bleaty in timbre.

The other singers are never less than competent, if rarely distinguished; the recorded sound is acceptable.

The original Harmonia Mundi LP set included the libretto in French only; the CD reissue, on Fidelio, doesn't provide any libretto at all!

1976 EMI / ANGEL (S)

Bozena Kinasz (A), Nicolai Gedda (B), Bohdan Paprocki (C), Andrzej Hioski (D), Martti Talvela (E), Leonard Mroz (F), Aage Haugland (G), Boys' Chorus from Krakow, Polish Radio Chorus of Krakow, Polish Radio National Symphony Orchestra—Jerzy Semkow

As the first recording of one of the authentic Mussorgsky scores, this set will always have its place in the history books. And it is a solid production, if not quite the triumph one had hoped for.

There is one unfortunate textual decision. Mussorgsky's 1871–72 score is the basis, and all of the cuts sanctioned by the composer are restored. But the St. Basil's Scene, from the 1869 score, is once again included—not as an appendix, but in its usual place as the first scene of Act IV. As a result, the standard cut is made in the Kromy Forest episode, and the listener is denied the option of hearing an unabridged performance of the 1871–72 version.

At least the St. Basil's Scene is heard, for the first time on records, with the composer's own instrumentation, instead of Ippolitov-Ivanov's. Many other passages are also recorded for the first time. And, of course, many familiar parts of the opera will sound startlingly different to ears accustomed to the Rimsky-Korsakov edition.

Unfortunately, the performance is quite unexciting, and once again the conductor must take the blame. The Polish chorus and orchestra are obviously proficient and work hard. Jerzy Semkow's tempo choices are often simply too slow, however, and his beat is sluggish and ill defined. Dynamism of any kind is lacking. Semkow's range of colors is limited, and a dull haze settles over the music.

Gedda is, naturally, not nearly as sweet or pliant of voice as he was back in 1952, but he knows the character of Dmitri inside out and still makes a fine effect in the role. Talvela, abandoning Pimen for Boris, is impressive. He seems to have taken Ghiaurov, rather than Christoff, as his model: his is a rather gentle, understated czar, most persuasive in the moments of paternal tenderness. Aage Haugland is a gruff, dark-voiced Varlaam.

Most of the other soloists are Polish. Bozena Kinasz is an efficient Marina, not very glamorous in timbre. Andrzej Hioski doubles Shchelkalov and Rangoni to fine effect, though, and there is good work from Leonard Mroz (Pimen), Stefania Toczyska (the Hostess), and Wiera (or Vera) Baniewicz (Feodor).

1978–83 PHILIPS (S) CD

Irina Arkhipova (A), Vladislav Piavko (B), Andrei Sokolov (C), Yuri Masurok (D), Alexander Vedernikov (E), Vladimir Matorin (F), Artur Eisen (G), "Spring" Studio Children's Chorus, USSR TV and Radio Large Chorus and Symphony Orchestra—Vladimir Fedoseyev

A disappointing version, on the whole. Philips bills its recording as "based on the 'definitive' version (1872)." In practice, this translates into the 1871–72 score, without the St. Basil's Scene (as a result, the Kromy Forest Scene is heard complete, as it is not on the EMI / Semkow set). So far, so good. The performance has in its favor an undeniable rightness in linguistic and stylistic matters, and an appropriately epic largeness of scale, but much of the actual execution is flawed.

One problem is purely technical. The recording was made between 1978 and 1983 (the Soviets did not do this sort of thing in a hurry),

presumably in order to accommodate the schedules of some of the singers. The (analogue) sound is quite poor. The close miking gives the engineering a claustrophobic quality and a fatiguing harshness. The orchestra and chorus, as reproduced, nearly always sound too loud. Crude spotlighting of the solo voices emphasizes the singers' breathing (the entire cast appears to be suffering from asthma) and wreaks predictable havoc on loud high notes. Finally, the stereo is primitive—the sort of thing we heard from tasteless record producers in the late fifties.

The sonics have a direct bearing on our experience of the performance—the whole thing sounds bloated, heavy-handed, and unsubtle. I have the distinct impression that the performers would be happier doing the Rimsky-Korsakov score, and have not really come to terms with the Mussorgsky original, which calls for a more intimate, conversational treatment much of the time. Vladimir Fedoseyev's conducting is efficient, but some of his tempos drag, and he has not inspired his soloists to dig below the surface of their music.

The strongest singing comes in the Polish act. Arkhipova repeats her stern Marina from the Melik-Pashayev recording(s): her voice is now slightly tough in timbre, and never exactly seductive-sounding, but still commanding. She finds a worthy adversary in Yuri Mazurok, a powerful Rangoni. Vladislav Piavko, the Dmitri, is yet another Slavic tenor who seems to be squeezing out his high notes by means of sheer will power; elsewhere, however, he sings with tonal clarity, a good sense of line, and dramatic involvement.

Alexander Vedernikov is a competent but uninteresting Boris. If some bass voices are "black" in timbre, then Vedernikov's is a dull slate gray. His persistent softness of attack lends an appropriately gentle, paternal quality to the czar's scenes with his children, but is an irritating mannerism in the long run.

Artur Eisen, on the other hand, manages to bring something fresh to Varlaam. His second song is done straight, without comic effects, and is quite beautifully vocalized; Eisen is also quite touching in the episode in which Varlaam struggles to read the warrant.

1985 MELODIYA (S) CD

Elena Obraztsova (A), Vladimir Atlantov (B), Konstantin Lissovski (C), Yuri Mazurok (D), Yevgeny Nesterenko (E), Anatoli Babykin (F), Artur Eisen (G), Bolshoi Theater Chorus and Orchestra—Mark Ermler

This recording reverts to the Rimsky-Korsakov version, with Ippolitov-Ivanov's orchestration of the St. Basil's Scene included, and the corresponding cut made in the Kromy Forest episode.

Mark Ermler's conducting resembles Cluytens's in its broad outlines. Ermler's reading is warm and expansive, often rather relaxed in tempo, with all sorts of instrumental detail neatly dropped into place. At times, he summons an imposing weight. There is not much urgency or bite, however. The Bolshoi orchestra and chorus once again perform superbly well.

Ironically, at its best the performance has the kind of nuance and intimacy missing from the Philips set. There is a true sense of teamwork and dramatic interplay here—surely the result of the fact that some members of the cast sang their roles regularly at the Bolshoi for at least a decade prior to the recording.

Yevgeny Nesterenko's Boris is unconventional. His voice is definitely more baritone than bass. His upper register, however, is often curiously thin and colorless, and at times he seems to want to declaim the part rather than sing it. Both of these peculiarities are apparent in the Act II monologue. Nesterenko is an imaginative artist and comes up with some striking effects, but next to such richly endowed singers as Pirogov, Reizen, and Christoff he sounds a bit pallid.

Elena Obraztsova, though undeniably a strong vocal presence, is not a completely satisfactory Marina. Her security in the vicinity of middle C is an asset, but her timbre is harsh and she has a heavy vibrato. Furthermore, she is monotonously loud, and too aggressive in manner. The overall effect is rather matronly.

Vladimir Atlantov's Dmitri is impressive. The voice is a genuine dramatic tenor, solid and resonant throughout its range (the conversation with Rangoni in Act III, Scene 2, sounds like a scene for two baritones) and with an exciting ring at the top. He is also a good vocal actor—intense, but never obvious or exaggerated in his effects.

The Shuisky, Konstantin Lissovski, has an unusually beautiful voice, a bit nasal in timbre but free and lucid; he sounds as though he, too, could be a fine Dmitri.

Anatoli Babykin's Pimen is in the slightly lugubrious tradition that seems limiting, but his voice is a fine one. Eisen (Varlaam) and Mazurok (Rangoni) repeat their strong performances from the Philips set, and actually sound marginally more comfortable singing Rimsky-Korsakov's vocal lines.

The recorded sound, though slightly conservative, is superior to that on the Philips set. Only the rather backward placement of the chorus is cause for serious concern. There are some good stereo staging effects, but the various bells are disappointing—the tintinnabulation in the Coronation Scene is a feeble tinkle, and the Death Scene is punctuated by the shallow clang of tubular chimes.

The CD transfer, on Le Chante du Monde, includes the libretto in French only.

1986 KONTRAPUNKT (S,D,P) CD

Stig Fogh Andersen (B), Heinz Zednik (C), Aage Haugland (E, F, G), German Radio Choir and Symphony Orchestra—Dimitri Kitaenko

This set (recorded live at a February 27, 1986, German radio concert performance) is a classic example of false advertising. Billed as "based on the 1868 / 69 version," it is in fact no such thing. What we hear is the 1871–72 score, with a lot of cuts. Thus, in Act II, the 1871–72 additions (e.g., Feodor's song) are omitted, but such passages as the czar's monologue, his dialogue with Shuisky, and the Clock Scene are performed in their familiar 1871–72 versions, rather than in the 1869 Urtext. The Polish act, the St. Basil's Scene, and the Kromy Forest Scene are all eliminated, so that the Death Scene follows hard upon the czar's collapse at the end of Act II.

Dimitri Kitaenko conducts rather firmly, and in fact rushes a few passages. The orchestra is good. The chorus sings well, but its Russian enunciation is indistinct.

Aage Haugland, who sang Varlaam on the EMI / Semkow set, here imitates Christoff's stunt by singing Boris and Pimen as well. He is a good singer, with a big, dark, handsome voice, but rather monotonous—hardly the kind of specific, imaginative vocal actor who could bring off this tour de force. His inability to differentiate the three characters is emphasized by this abridged version of the opera, since the cuts ensure that he is never "offstage" for so much as ten minutes.

Stig Fogh Andersen is a dull Dmitri, but of course he has little to sing in this version. Heinz Zednik sounds tight-voiced and strained as Shuisky, and overinflects the text.

For a "live" recording, the sound is quite good, and the audience is admirably quiet and attentive. But the cuts disqualify this set from serious consideration: it is no substitute for a recording of the authentic 1869 score, and the omissions are likely to annoy any listener who has heard the full 1871–72 score.

1987 ERATO (S,D) CD

Galina Vishnevskaya (A), Vyacheslav Polozov (B), Kenneth Riegel (C), Nikita Strorojev (D), Ruggero Raimondi (E), Paul Plishka (F), Romuald Tesarowicz (G), Chevy Chase Elementary School Chorus, Oratorio Society of Washington, Choral Arts Society of Washington, National Symphony Orchestra—Mstislav Rostropovich

Of the four recordings offering Mussorgsky's own music issued to date, this one is by far the most successful. Mstislav Rostropovich performs the 1871–72 score complete, but then throws in the St. Basil's Scene anyway, inserting it in the usual place (i.e., immediately after the Polish act). This means that if one plays the recording straight through, the children torment the Simpleton twice! Clearly, though, the intention is to give the listener the option of playing either the St. Basil's Scene or the Kromy Forest Scene, but not necessarily both.

Rostropovich's is, above all, an unapologetic reading. He not only accepts Mussorgsky's stylistic quirks, he positively revels in them—finding an expressive purpose behind the composer's boldest experiments with harmony and instrumentation. Like many of his predecessors, Rostropovich indulges in some daringly slow tempos, but he maintains tension throughout.

The orchestra plays beautifully, and always seems to be giving the conductor that something extra that distinguishes an inspired performance from a merely well-prepared one. The choruses produce a clear, well-balanced sound; the children are especially good. The American choristers do not always enunciate the text with the bite and confidence of their Slavic counterparts, although they have obviously been carefully coached in the language.

Ruggero Raimondi's Boris strikes me as a great success: his voice is lighter in timbre and more baritonal in quality than what we usually hear in the role, and he does some beautiful lyrical singing. Predominantly gentle of temperament and intimate in scale, his czar is very different from the traditional interpretation but always dramatically persuasive.

Vyacheslav Polozov, as Dmitri, combines an attractive voice with fervent delivery. He is certainly one of the more persuasive exponents of the role since the young Nicolai Gedda. Gedda himself appears on this set, having abandoned Dmitri for the Simpleton; although the gesture of casting a major singer in the latter role is appreciated, Gedda betrays a wide wobble on his sustained tones in the lament.

Paul Plishka is a touching and authoritative Pimen, although his warm vibrato sometimes makes his intonation seem approximate.

Vishnevskaya repeats her Marina from the Decca / Karajan set, and doubles as the Hostess. In the latter role, she sounds young and seductive, and is delightful in the little song addressed to the duck. With Romuald Tesarowicz (Varlaam) and Misha Raitzin (Missail) making a vivid pair of renegade monks, the Inn Scene is an unqualified success.

Vishnevskaya's second recorded Marina is likely to start some arguments. The voice is steady and on pitch, but the timbre is harsh. She is, by quite some distance, the most grasping and bitchy Marina on any of these complete sets; no other singer seems quite so fiercely determined to make every word—indeed, every syllable—of the text count. It's all a bit much, perhaps, but Polozov and Nikita Strorojev (a ferocious Rangoni) give it right back to her, and the result is the most intensely dramatic account of the Polish act on records.

Kenneth Riegel is a wily, uncommonly musical Shuisky. Casting a boy soprano as Feodor could have been disastrous, but Mathew Adam Fish is altogether extraordinary in the part, singing securely and attractively, and projecting the text with confidence.

The digital sound of this set is outstandingly good.

1991 SONY (S,D) CD

Stefka Mineva (A), Michail Svetlev (B), Josef Frank (C), Boris Martinovich (D), Nicolai Ghiaurov (E), Nicola Ghiuselev (F), Dimiter Petkov (G), Sofia National Opera Chorus, Sofia Festival Orchestra—Emil Tchakarov

Recorded in 1986, this version, not released until December 1991, makes exactly the same textual decisions as the Erato / Rostropovich performance: we are given the full 1871–72 score, with the Kromy Forest Scene uncut, and the St. Basil's episode inserted in the appropriate place (the St. Basil's tableau is, however, clearly labeled as an alternative scene in the accompanying booklet).

Tchakarov was a fine opera conductor, and demonstrates a particular affinity for this work. To a greater extent than even Rostropovich, he focuses on the vocal lines and the text. The singers take a subdued, spontaneous, conversational approach to their parts, avoiding rhetoric or vocal display; there is a good deal of rhythmic flexibility. The orchestra, too, is restrained: Tchakarov keeps the dynamic levels low and the textures exceptionally clear.

The engineers have followed through: instead of utilizing the close miking heard on the Erato set, Sony's technical crew has backed away and allowed the performance to come at us from a slight distance, the way it might sound from a good seat in an opera house.

Sony has assembled a superior cast: no one is less than good, and the line-up of low-voiced male singers is particularly impressive. Ghiaurov is the first singer to record the title role in both the Rimsky-Korsakov and the Mussorgsky versions. When we compare his work here to that on the Decca / Karajan recording, his voice shows some of the inevitable signs of age—a loss of power, in general; some patches of rough tone; occasional unsteadiness on sustained notes. But he also displays the wisdom of age and experience—his portrayal of the czar is much more deeply felt and three-dimensional than before. He is magnificent in the Death Scene.

Ghiuselev repeats his Pimen from the Harmonia Mundi / Naidenov set, but to much better effect—the voice is in splendid condition, and the singer clearly benefits from true support from the podium. Dimiter Petkov contributes a rousing rendition of Varlaam's song. Boris Martinovich may be the slyest, most insinuating Rangoni on records: even when he seems to be barely whispering his lines, his voice retains its dark timbre and weighty resonance.

The Marina, Stefka Mineva, is not the kind of specific vocal actress that a Vishnevskaya is, but her medium-weight mezzo is an attractive, healthy instrument and her instincts are good. The Dmitri, Michail Svetlev, is a little deficient in *legato* and emits some tight high notes, but he, too, is dramatically effective.

Josef Frank continues the welcome trend of really *singing* Shuisky's music.

Before choosing a complete recording of the opera, a collector must first decide between the Mussorgsky and Rimsky-Korsakov versions. The Erato / Rostropovich set seems to me to be the best recording of Mussorgsky's 1871–72 score.

Most of the recordings of the Rimsky-Korsakov edition have their attractions; only the Decca / Baranovich set can be dismissed as a near-total failure.

The Decca / Karajan production is a beautiful all-around job, and can be safely recommended to those who enjoy the conductor's operatic work and are not bothered by his occasional idiosyncrasies of style. Perhaps inevitably, though, the Melodiya / Ermler recording is the more authentically Russian in style.

ROLAND GRAEME

DIE LUSTIGEN WEIBER VON WINDSOR (1849)

A: Frau Fluth (s); B: Anna Reich (s); C: Frau Reich (ms);
D: Fenton (t); E: Fluth (bar); F: Falstaff (bs); G: Reich (bs)

If Biedermeier art can have summits, this is certainly one of them—modest, tuneful, exquisitely made. Into the German *Singspiel* tradition the much traveled Nicolai blends, with apparent ease, the nature-poetry of Weber and the rhythmic sure-footedness of Donizetti, scoring the amalgam with a delicacy that again and again reminds one of Mendelssohn. Musically charming, *The Merry Wives* can also be genuinely amusing, given performers (including a conductor) who know how to put across its not very subtle humor. That's partly a matter of casting, partly a matter of balancing two kinds of authenticity: that of tradition and that of text. Of the four more or less complete recordings, the two earlier present a (once-)living tradition, cuts, embellishments, and all; the two newer ones take a more literal view of what Nicolai actually wrote.

There are also some special problems in committing a *Singspiel* to disc. Too much spoken dialogue has a rather chilling effect away from the stage, and is a particular trial to listeners who don't understand the language; leave it out, on the other hand, and the whole dramatic rhythm of the work is lost—it turns into a concert of operatic excerpts. Of the four recordings listed above, the wartime Berlin broadcast under Rother may originally have included dialogue, but only the musical items seem to have been preserved. Heger's recording was originally issued in Germany on three LP discs with fairly full dialogue, discreetly modernized, but for

English-speaking countries EMI omitted the dialogue and the first scene of Act III to get it on two records; the CD reissue is complete. Kubelik's recording for Decca / London has dialogue, but differently abbreviated, and with rather less respect for the original. For Klee's version, however, DG attempts a much more radical (and to my mind unsuccessful) solution: for details see below. As for cuts, Rother and Heger, as one might expect, take most of the traditional ones; Kubelik and Klee open them. For home listening, where musical considerations take precedence, completeness seems preferable.

1943 URANIA (M,P)

Irma Beilke (A), Lore Hoffmann (B), Marie-Luise Schilp (C), Walther Ludwig (D), Georg Hann (E), Wilhelm Strienz (F), Hans Florian (G), Chorus of the Berlin Civic [i.e., Municipal] Opera, Symphony Orchestra of Radio Berlin—Artur Rother

This stems from tapes of a wartime broadcast from Berlin, and inevitably sounds like it: hard and shallow, with some distortion and the voices too closely miked for comfort. As a document of a "traditional" performance it would be more valuable if it were not for Rother's rather coarse conducting, which reminds one how easily tradition can become routine. In its generation, however, the cast was a strong one, and in two instances superb. Alone among these Falstaffs, Strienz presents the old boy as a gentleman, however down at heel, even in the conventionally *buffo* situations that the plot puts him in. The voice is also in excellent shape: note the agility of his little song "Als Büblein klein" at the beginning of Act II (corresponding to Verdi's "Quand' ero paggio"). Lore Hoffmann's Anna is full of character too; her big aria in the last act is delivered with an authority that establishes her as the work's heroine—and a close relative of Weber's Agathe. The remainder of the cast, though not quite up to this level of imaginative intensity, would rejoice the heart of anyone who happened to hear them in the theater today— particularly Beilke and Hann as the *Ehepaar* Fluth and Walther Ludwig as Fenton. But the quality of the sound and Rother's briskly pedestrian conducting will probably put this version out of consideration for most listeners.

1963 EMI / ANGEL (S) CD

Ruth-Margret Pütz (A), Edith Mathis (B), Gisela Litz (C), Fritz Wunderlich (D), Ernst Gutstein (E), Gottlob Frick (F), Kieth Engen (G), Bavarian State Opera Chorus and Orchestra—Robert Heger

It is no disrespect to the fine singers in this version to say that its real star is the conductor, Robert Heger. He was nearly eighty when it was made, and this may show in tempos that are occasionally a shade more easygoing than necessary, but this is more than compensated by the ease, the loving care, with which those tempos are molded and modified. Throughout one has the sense that Heger knows the work inside out as a stage piece and is concerned above all with helping his singers project their roles in the action. Not that Frick's wonderfully ripe Falstaff needs much help—a bit broad, perhaps, in comparison with Strienz, but hugely enjoyable. Wunderlich, not surprisingly, is an ideal Fenton, ardently lyrical in the love music; his scene with Herr Reich (a finely authoritative Kieth Engen) has real dramatic bite. Mathis's Anna (one of her earliest appearances on records) makes a good partner for him; she may bring less fire to the role than Lore Hoffmann in the Urania version, but both voice and characterization have an appealing freshness. The merry wives themselves, it must be said, are

adequate rather than exciting; they know what the words mean and how the music goes, but somehow remain a bit generic. But the performance as a whole goes so well, its gaiety and poetry (the famous moonrise in Act III, for instance) so perfectly balanced, that it fully merits its reissue on CD.

1976 DEUTSCHE GRAMMOPHON (S)

Edith Mathis (A), Helen Donath (B), Hanna Schwarz (C), Peter Schreier (D), Bernd Weikl (E), Kurt Moll (F), Siegfried Vogel (G), Chorus and Orchestra of the Deutsche Oper, Berlin— Bernhard Klee

With this recording we reach the 1970s and the "new school" of conductors and record producers who, rather than being content to reproduce for home consumption what their listeners might expect to hear in the theater, grasp the opportunity that recording gives for a fresh look at the score—a needed revolution, no doubt, but one in whose name crimes have sometimes been committed. As far as the music of this opera goes, authenticity has meant little more than opening all the traditional cuts (mostly of longer or shorter repeats), and doing away with a few traditional embellishments. Those who know and love Lotte Lehmann's incomparable recording of Frau Fluth's tongue-in-cheek *scena* "Nun eilt herbei" will miss the interpolated high notes, and some may also regret the time-consecrated shtik in Falstaff's famous duet with Fluth, "In einem Waschkorb." But Nicolai's music is fresh and strong enough for the repeats to be sheer gain—particularly in the home, where we don't have to watch embarrassed singers trying to think up something new to do during them. Oddly, though, DG's regard for textual accuracy is confined in the present case to the musical numbers; the original spoken dialogue is almost entirely replaced by a narrator, in the guise of a waiter at the Garter Inn, who sets the scene and summarizes the stage action. This is not, as one might think, a concession to non-German-speakers incapable of following the dialogue, since the narration is in German too: its only effect, so far as I can see, is to chop up the action and distance us from the drama. Still, irritating as this is, the set's musical qualities do help one to overlook it. Perhaps none of the singers, not even Moll as Falstaff, gives a performance so completely realized that one would be tempted to call it definitive, but none of them, equally, is less than accomplished, and under Klee's direction they work together beautifully as a team. Donath, not a natural soubrette, is here much more convincing as Anna than she is as Frau Fluth in the Kubelik set. Schreier's artistry, as always, does much to compensate for his inescapably sandy tone quality. Moll brings a nice unctuousness to his portrayal of Falstaff, if not quite the gargantuan relish of a Frick. But it is, above all, the sparkling alertness of the orchestral playing (beautifully recorded, it must be said) that makes it possible to compare this version with Heger's for musical good humor.

1977 DECCA / LONDON (S)

Helen Donath (A), Lilian Sukis (B), Trudeliese Schmidt (C), Claes Haaken Ahnsjö (D), Wolfgang Brendel (E), Karl Ridderbusch (F), Alexander Malta (G), Chorus of the Bavarian Radio, Bavarian Symphony Orchestra—Rafael Kubelik

A Kubelik performance is never less than musical, but this one seems in several ways misguided. Credit first of all, though, to its virtues: it gives us the dialogue straight, if abbreviated, and it also contains, in the Swedish tenor Claes Haaken Ahnsjö, a Fenton worthy to rival Wunderlich himself—not quite so heroic, perhaps, but even more sensitive in his phrasing. All the more of a waste, then, that he should be saddled with Sukis's completely unacceptable Anna. The other two ladies are pleasant enough, but Donath seems at times to be relying on Schwarzkopf mannerisms to give character to her part, and Schmidt doesn't seem

to have given much thought to realizing hers at all. But that is a weakness that seems endemic to this performance: apart from Ahnsjö not one of the men, certainly not the sonorous bass of Karl Ridderbusch, sounds as if he has ever sung his role on the stage. For this I think Kubelik must really take some of the responsibility. Although his tempos are often quite plausibly judged in purely instrumental terms, they rarely seem to spring from physical gesture or comic action, and so fail to convey those implications to the armchair listener. There are exceptions: Kubelik takes the pinching chorus in the final scene ("Mücken, Wespen, Fliegenchor") a shade slower than the rest, and the result is both clearer and more malicious. But more often than not he rushes into a tempo that works well enough for the instruments but is simply too fast for effective projection of the words. And over and above this—and all around it—is an acoustic that is simply too spacious for the nature of a work that needs to sound as clear and dry as *Sekt*.

As far as recommendations go, the conclusion is pretty clear. For a loving, knowing presentation of the work as more than a century of German performances have shaped it, Heger's would be hard (nowadays probably impossible) to beat. If, on the other hand, one wants to hear Nicolai's *music* as nearly as possible in the form that he wrote it—and as a composer he deserves that respect—the DG version under Klee is a more than acceptable choice, in spite of that maddeningly intrusive waiter.

JEREMY NOBLE

Unavailable for review:
1950 OCEANIC

JACQUES OFFENBACH

LES CONTES D'HOFFMANN (1881)

A: Olympia (s); B: Giulietta (s); C: Antonia (s); D: Nicklausse (ms);
E: Hoffmann (t); F: Lindorf (bar); G: Coppélius (bar); H: Dappertutto (bar); I: Dr. Miracle (bar)

When death came to Jacques Offenbach in October of 1880, he was at work on the fourth act of the vocal score for a five-act opera that would have been his valedictory to the lyric stage. How he would have finished the opera we shall never know, for it was his habit to assess public reaction to his premieres, to rearrange and rewrite numbers, if necessary, before setting his seal on a work. The introduction of *Les Contes d'Hoffmann* at the Opéra-Comique on February 10, 1881, was far from what Offenbach had originally intended. He had planned a grand opera without spoken dialogue; the character of Hoffmann was to be a baritone. But when his producer, Vizentini, went bankrupt, Carvalho accepted the work for the Opéra-Comique and its contracted singers. This meant eliminating the accompanied recitative Offenbach had written, using dialogue between set numbers. It meant transposing Hoffmann's part into higher keys for Carvalho's star tenor Talazac and tailoring the music of the four heroines (including the Muse), to suit the lyric coloratura Adele Isaac. Offenbach died before he could give Giulietta a grand aria. This may explain why the Venetian act, which was to follow the one set in Munich, was not performed at the premiere and did not appear in the first published edition of the opera. When Choudens commissioned Ernest Guiraud to produce recitatives to replace the spoken dialogue, the publisher was only doing what the composer originally intended.

Hans Gregor restored the Venetian act, placing it before the Munich act in his famous 1905 Berlin production, which included the Diamond Aria (written not by Offenbach but by André Bloch) and the septet (probably composed by Guiraud), both taken from Raoul Gunsbourg's Monte Carlo staging of 1904. This version, largely orchestrated by Guiraud, was published by Choudens in 1907 and is the basis for six of the nine recordings *Les Contes d'Hoffmann* has received. Offenbach wrote his four heroines' roles for the same singer, but only three sopranos on records attempt what the composer planned for the clearly remarkable Mlle. Isaac. Most of the time one finds a coloratura Olympia, a mezzo Giulietta, and a lyric Antonia. Hoffmann's quartet of nemeses was intended for one singer, but here again one often encounters basses in the roles other than Dappertutto.

1948 CBS / SONY (M)

Renée Doria (A), Vina Bovy (B), Géori Boué (C), Fanely Revoil (D), Raoul Jobin (E), Louis Musy (F), André Pernet (G), Charles Soix (H), Roger Bourdin (I), Chorus and Orchestra of the Opéra-Comique—André Cluytens

This earliest of recorded *Hoffmanns*, easily the most effective of the six based on the standard Choudens score, is a relic of the by-now-vanished style that best illuminates Offenbach's "fantastic opera in five acts." Quick, light, intimate, almost at times conversational, it is altogether more human in scale than the grand opera style usually employed (more suitable to Meyerbeer than to Offenbach). The vigor and the spontaneity of the entire ensemble, so comfortable and natural in the swiftly flowing stream of Cluytens's tempos, is bracing. No other recorded *Hoffmann* has its narrative impact; no other so effortlessly suspends time. Whatever Jobin may lack in tenderness or vocal personality, he makes up for with his sharp, committed, unsentimental delivery, notable for unusual care in dynamics. The three heroines are unrivaled. Doria is a light, yet full-toned automaton, accurate, with a good trill and a perfect high E. Bovy, who in 1937 became the first singer to perform all three heroines at the Met, is heard here as an uncommonly spirited Giulietta. Géori Boué, the first lady of the Opéra just after the war, sings an exciting, impassioned Antonia, more desperate than vulnerable in her life-and-death struggle with Dr. Miracle. Revoil contributes an inimitably saucy Nicklausse. All four villains are capital, sinister without ham or bluster. Pernet is especially fine as a Coppélius whose rage and spite are conveyed with refreshing clarity and economy of address. Bourvil, a beloved comedian in the Paris of his day, creates unassailable standards in the four servant roles; for once, Frantz's song is not affected and tiresome but touching. Although big moments such as the septet are obviously monitored, the recording on LP—without completely concealing the surface noise of its 78-rpm origins—is at least serviceable and generally flattering to the voices.

1950 DECCA / LONDON (In English) (M)

Dorothy Bond (A), Margherita Grandi (B), Ann Ayars (C), Monica Sinclair (D), Robert Rounseville (E), Bruce Dargavel (F, G, H, I), Sadler's Wells Opera Chorus and Royal Philharmonic Orchestra—Thomas Beecham

This soundtrack of Michael Powell and Emeric Pressburger's film *Tales of Hoffmann* has little to recommend it other than the conducting of Sir Thomas Beecham; and even that is a mixed blessing. For all his elegant and graceful phrasing in numbers for which there are suitable tempos, his overdeliberate pacing of others, perhaps predicated by the exigencies of the film action, saps their vitality and weakens the continuity of the whole. The film permits shuffling of numbers and numerous cuts. There is no muse, only one verse of "J'ai des yeux" and "Elle a fui," and Lindorf's speech is gone. The sound is afflicted with a persistent hum and steep monitoring. The singers, probably chosen as much for appearance as for vocal endowment, are generally disappointing; although Robert Rounseville does have steady, appealing tone and a youthful manner, Bruce Dargavel a dark, rich baritone and immaculate English diction in all the villainous roles, and Monica Sinclair, the sweet and sour qualities appropriate to Nicklausse. The objects of Hoffmann's affection are either vocally pale (Olympia), uncomfortable (Giulietta), or unpolished (Antonia).

1955 MET (M,P)

Roberta Peters (A), Risë Stevens (B), Lucine Amara (C), Mildred Miller (D), Richard Tucker (E), Martial Singher (F, G, H, I), Metropolitan Opera Chorus and Orchestra—Pierre Monteux

This recording preserves the Met broadcast of December 3, 1955, in well-focused, close-up sound, quite good for its day. The performance of the Choudens score with standard cuts (no Muse) is memorable for the leadership of Pierre Monteux, musically and stylistically magisterial. Martial Singher's trenchant and waspish account of Hoffmann's adversaries is marred only by an effortful high note in his transposed Diamond Aria. Richard Tucker is aglow with vocal health, but misses much of the romantic poet's dreamy rapture and obsessed spirit. Mildred Miller, pleasing and secure of tone, is a deliciously mocking Nicklausse. Roberta Peters, the most effective of the three heroines, sings brightly with admirable flexibility and lustrous sound, except for the tight quality of her highest sustained notes. Giulietta has much the most unflattering and awkwardly written role in this opera. The role gives Risë Stevens, like most of those who have recorded it, problems in maintaining pitch and sustenation of line. Her characterization is steady, her rich mezzo attractive but not ideally supple in quick tempo. Lucine Amara is overly robust and wanting in pathetic grandeur. Mention is due Alessio de Paolis, characterful if a bit decrepit, as the four servants, and James McCracken, an unusually vivid Nathanael.

1958 GUILDE INTERNATIONAL DU DISQUE (also EPIC) (S)

Mattiwilda Dobbs (A,C), Uta Graf (B), Nata Tuescher (D), Léopold Simoneau (E), Heinz Rehfuss (F, G, H, I), Concerts de Paris Chorus and Orchestra—Pierre-Michel le Conte

For vocal, musical, and stylistic refinement, Léopold Simoneau is a Hoffmann without peer. If only his portrayal were half so impressive as his singing. One will search in vain for some suggestion of the poet's obsessive qualities or his masochism. The best all-round effort comes from Heinz Rehfuss, whose sable-dark bass colors four keenly observed impersonations of evil. The Diamond Aria, of course, is transposed, and there is no high note. As Olympia, Mattiwilda Dobbs, discloses an agreeable soprano uneven in scale and sometimes rhythmically flustered; as Antonia, she is wan, neither steady nor in tune in her aria. Uta Graf dispatches Giulietta's lines with welcome ease, but she is consistently plain. Nata Tuescher, her voice forward, her accents lively, is a satisfying Nicklausse. Pierre-Michel le Conte conducts a vigorous, straightforward, heavily cut performance. Again, no Muse. Sonics are a bit pale and obviously monitored.

1964–65 EMI / ANGEL (S) CD

Gianna d'Angelo (A), Elisabeth Schwarzkopf (B), Victoria de los Angeles (C), Jean-Christophe Benoit (D), Nicolai Gedda (E), Nicola Ghiuselev (F), George London (G, I), Ernest Blanc (H), René Duclos Chorus and Paris Conservatory Orchestra—André Cluytens

Some of opera's most lustrous stars of the sixties and a conductor who had presided over a distinguished recording of this opera augered well for the success of this entry. But that was not to be. Cluytens led with neither the energetic spring nor the conviction of his earlier effort, and was inadequately supported by an engineering team who magnified the looseness of his ensemble and blunted whatever intimacy of expression there was with a recording most unsuitably over-resonant. Nicolai Gedda, intelligent without spontaneity, the villains often coarse and overdrawn, a male Nicklausse to add to the confusion, are not all the liabilities. Gianna d'Angelo, a doll without charm or brilliance, Elisabeth Schwarzkopf woefully miscast, and Victoria de los Angeles, unsteady, ill at ease, fighting pitch, placed too close to the mike for her aria, complete a catalogue of misfortunes rare among recordings involving so many fine artists.

1971 DECCA / LONDON (S) CD

Joan Sutherland (A, B, C), Huguette Tourangeau (D), Plácido Domingo (E), Gabriel Bacquier (F, G, H, I), Swiss Radio, Lausanne Pro Arte, and Du Brassus Choruses, Orchestre de la Suisse Romande—Richard Bonynge

Richard Bonynge's use of spoken dialogue instead of accompanied recitative is unique among recorded *Hoffmanns*. In search of the swiftly moving drama Bonynge believes Offenbach intended, the conductor has opted for dialogue instead of recitative on the grounds that much of the latter—neither by Offenbach nor Guiraud—is heavy, boring, and dramatically destructive. It must be said that his version, over an hour shorter than the Oeser reconstruction heard in EMI's latest entry, fits on two compact discs, one less than EMI's. Bonynge's compromise between Choudens and historical research places the Venetian act before that set in Munich. Its dialogue, extracted from Barbier and Carré's play rather than from their libretto, has Hoffmann kill Schlémil in their duel around the middle of the act rather than at the end, where Giulietta now unwittingly takes poison intended by Dappertutto for Nicklausse. Bonynge retains the Diamond Aria but not the septet, the music for which he transfers to the last act on the assumption that it is the long-lost quartet (referred to by Offenbach in a letter) planned for the opera's denouement.

This is one of only three recordings in which one soprano sings all the heroines. For all her gifts, Joan Sutherland, brilliant and witty as the doll, faceless as Giulietta, too mature as Antonia, merely confirms the great difficulty of finding one singer who can successfully cope with all these parts. Gabriel Bacquier as the four villains is occasionally overemphatic in an intense performance scaled more for the theater than for the phonograph. Domingo has a field day with Hoffmann, one of the tenor's most congenial roles. Hugues Cuénod, equally impressive, draws distinct portraits as the four servants. Bonynge's direction is lively and straightforward. The wide-range recording, resonant and a bit grainy in the ensembles, offers some pre-echo in the LP edition.

1972 EMI / ANGEL (S)

Beverly Sills (A, B, C), Susanne Marsee (D), Stuart Burrows (E), Norman Treigle (F, G, H, I), John Alldis Choir and London Symphony Orchestra—Julius Rudel

This is an unsatisfactory souvenir of Beverly Sills and Norman Treigle, two artists beloved by the New York City Opera public, for their roles seem as uncongenial to them on records as in the theater. Sills, bright and precise as Olympia, is miscast as Giulietta and inexpressive as Antonia, odd in the light of her opera-house successes as Manon and Marguerite. Treigle, similarly, does not bring to the four demons the intensity and personal force he brought to Gounod's Méphistofélès onstage. Stuart Burrows, vocally pleasing, is as bland and unfocused in character as the conducting

of Julius Rudel. The over-resonant recording flatters nothing.

1988 EMI / ANGEL (S,D) CD

Luciana Serra (A), Jessye Norman (B), Rosalind Plowright (C), Ann Murray (D), Neil Shicoff (E), José van Dam (F, G, H, I), Chorus and Orchestra of Théâtre de la Monnaie, Brussels—Sylvain Cambreling

It was inevitable that someone should try to produce an edition of *Hoffmann* that reflects modern scholarly scrutiny of this troubled opera. The musicologist Fritz Oeser has produced a critical edition of *Hoffmann* based not only on long-available source material but on 1660 pages of manuscript discovered a few years ago by the conductor Antonio de Almeida. This edition places Hoffmann's tales in their conceived order and the unknown "trio des yeux" in its original position in the Olympia act, while giving back the music for the familiar "J'ai des yeux" to Dappertutto, as originally intended. The spurious septet is eliminated. Oeser uses passages from Offenbach's *Die Rheinnixen* to flesh out his edition. Most important, he restores—in its entirety—the second most important role, that of the Muse / Nicklausse, the good protector of Hoffmann, thereby changing the dramatic focus of the opera. The Muse now battles for Hoffmann's soul with the diva Stella, the incarnation of Hoffmann's distractions—the mindless Olympia, a voice with no soul; Antonia, a singer destroyed by obsessive ambition; Giulietta, the faithless courtesan.

Not everyone will appreciate Oeser's effort. He has made the opera longer, darker, more complex. Few are apt to prefer the more authentic Venetian scene to the corrupt one, well known and loved. And no one will deny that much of the recitative is dull and heavy, very likely neither by Offenbach nor Guiraud. Nevertheless, the drama of the opera is finally clear, and some of the additional music of excellent quality, particularly that for the Muse at the beginning and close of the opera.

EMI presents the Oeser edition for the first time and also includes the spurious Diamond Aria and septet as appendices, so the audience can have its cake and eat it too. The recording has the atmosphere of the theater and is mostly evocative, except for much of the Venetian scene which is neither well defined nor well balanced. Sylvain Cambreling leads a stylish performance with affection and ardor. The cast, excepting Robert Tear as the four servants and Jocelyne Taillon as Antonia's mother (both too bland), is musically strong and generous in portrayal. Neil Shicoff, in his finest outing on records to date, brings the tormented poet to life with expressive singing of zeal and tenderness, notwithstanding a few over-lacrymose touches and some struggles with French pronunciation. Ann Murray, not always steady of tone in the big role of the Muse / Nicklausse, satisfies by never missing a dramatic trick. José van Dam displays why he is one of the great singing actors of his day with superb singing and riveting verbal intensity; as Miracle, his "Pour conjurer le danger, il faut le reconnaître" is blood-chilling. For once, the heroines do not let us down. Luciana Serra's Olympia is well and accurately sung, even with a stingy trill. Rosalind Plowright does not achieve proper tonal poise in Antonia's opening air (almost as if she were not warmed up), but she is sympathetic and, thereafter, sings with an intensity equaled only by Géori Boué. Jessye Norman, not always recorded well and generalized in expression, is seductive whether in the gondola, in the gaming room, or persuading Hoffmann to part with his shadow.

1990 DEUTSCHE GRAMMOPHON (S,D) CD

Edita Gruberova (A, B, C), Claudia Eder (D), Plácido Domingo (E), Andreas Schmidt (F), Gabriel Bacquier (G), Justino Díaz (H), James Morris (I), Chorus and Orchestre National de l'ORTF—Seiji Ozawa

In the wake of the Oeser edition, it is no surprise to see a recording that conflates Choudens and some of the recently discovered music. DG's is the first, but I daresay it will not be the last. Over an hour shorter than the most recent EMI, it is less expensive—two CDs instead of three.

The version presents the scenes in their proper order, so that one may witness Hoffmann's love affairs as descending steps into degradation. The Venetian scene is essentially Choudens—a practical decision since Choudens works better than Oeser and both, in any event, are hypothetical completions of Offenbach's remnants. The Olympia act is mostly Oeser, as is the finale—another wise decision, since Choudens is skimpy and unsatisfactory. One, however, loses the connection between the Muse and Nicklausse, because DG unhappily omits the Muse's contribution to the opening scene.

This the best-sounding *Hoffmann* yet—clean and persuasively balanced. Domingo's second recorded Hoffmann leaves mixed feelings. His latest effort reveals less sheer vocal velvet (and none of the optional high notes heard in the London set) but altogether greater sophistication in prosody and in his projection of the text. As Offenbach desired, Gruberova, like Sutherland, sings all of Hoffmann's loves. Her voice is a shade brittle and colorless, but what a clever singer she is. She may not match Sutherland in vocal radiance and sparkle (particularly as Olympia), but she is superior in defining each of her three characters. Her Antonia has the proper pathetic accents and vocal thrust; her Giulietta is assured and passionate. Claudia Eder, a bright presence as Nicklausse, scores with sprightly singing of her alternative second act aria "Voyez-la sous son éventail."

Unfortunately, the villains are taken by different singers. The usual excuse for this policy is that Dappertutto's part lies high and one must be content with a baritone who can scale the upper reaches of the Diamond Aria rather than the bass who often sings the remaining roles. Here, unaccountably, we have Justino Díaz, poorly cast, a bass having the devil's own time with the aria. Hoffmann's other nemeses are well taken. Bacquier is long in the tooth but has plenty of flair as Coppélius. In the theater Morris has a tendency to overact Dr. Miracle, but here he shows enough restraint to produce a memorable characterization. The minor roles are well cast; the ever reliable Michel Sénéchal repeats his superior Frantz; Christa Ludwig copes with a cameo role as Antonia's mother. All the singers and the forces of the French radio are alert and on their best musical behavior, responding to Seiji Ozawa's lively, stylish, and sympathethic direction.

———————

The essential recordings of Hoffmann are the first, an affectionate reminder of a vanished style and a worthy advocate for the 1907 Choudens edition, and either of EMI's latest, where one finds presumably everything Offenbach wrote and then some, or the new, less expensive DG, on balance a bit less well sung than EMI's but probably the best compromise version of *Hoffmann* at this moment.

C. J. LUTEN

Unavailable for review:
1991 PHILIPS

GIOVANNI BATTISTA PERGOLESI

LA SERVA PADRONA (1733)

A: Serpina (s); B: Uberto (bs)

*I*s it possible that the time of *La Serva Padrona*, which came with the LP, has also gone with the LP? Its roughly forty-five-minute length, conveniently divided into two scenes, was a natural for LP, and of course it had the virtue of economy. If you've got a few string players, a keyboard instrument for the *continuo*, and a female and a male soloist who can sort of sing, why, you can have *Serva Padrona!*

Alas, for CD the opera is awfully meager, even with the modest strategies so far devised to add a bit of bulk (see 1986 Hungaroton and 1989 Omega). And there seems to be a feeling that *Serva Padrona* is insufficiently sophisticated for present-day tastes, which prefer to impose sophomoric witlessness on material of more substantive respectableness.

Which is too bad, because the piece can be a little gem if taken seriously. Both singers are given wonderful opportunities, and Uberto in particular has considerable vocal possibilities. Although the role can be faked, it really asks for a singing bass with a confident reach up to F and secure anchoring down to low F. (The Scene 2 aria "Son imbrogliato" in fact asks for low E-flats, but let's not get carried away.)

And the interplay between the two can be quite delightful. Not if it's viewed as the Entrapment into Marriage of a Befuddled Master by His Wily Maid. But if instead you work from the relationship of two people who know each other so well as to have most of the inconveniences of marriage without the amenities, then

you've got something—including permission for both of them to behave as outrageously toward each other as they do.

Properly speaking, *Serva Padrona* isn't an opera in two scenes, but a pair of intermezzos. It came into the world as between-acts entertainment for Pergolesi's *opera seria Il Prigionier Superbo*. It is of course the comic intermezzos that have endured: the start of a tradition that flowered in the great comic operas of Rossini and Donizetti—and a laboratory as well for the "comic" clichés that disfigure those masterpieces.

Despite the absence of an autograph manuscript, the only serious textual issue concerns the choice of duet-finale: the once-standard 4/4 "Per te io ho nel core" or the more recently favored 6/8 "Contento tu sarai." "Contento," long suspected of being a dubious Parisian addition, turns out to appear in at least one pre-Paris score. (*Serva* was first performed in Paris in 1752, sixteen years after Pergolesi's death. The Paris edition would substitute spoken dialogue for recitative and incorporate a number of clearly inauthentic interpolations. Three little soprano arias are performed as an appendix to 1986 Hungaroton.)

The two finales are sometimes performed sequentially, an obvious temptation aimed at bulking out this short opera. But given their length, and given the cloying comic-reconciliation mode in which they're customarily performed, the conflation can produce the aural equivalent of sugar shock.

p.1949 VOX (M)

Maria Erato (A), Aldo Bacci (B), Milan Philharmonic Orchestra—Arrigo Pedrollo

Serva Padrona's entrance into the record catalogue coincides with the dawn of the LP era, but the format isn't quite the expected one-scene-per-side. The second scene spills onto side 1 since, surprisingly, both finales are included (this won't happen again until 1962 RCA), and all of the recitatives are omitted except the one that goes into *accompagnato*, between Serpina's "A Serpina penserete" and Uberto's "Son imbrogliato" in Scene 2.

The performance, obviously a shoestring affair, has spunk and some endearing mannerisms: the frequent dotting of rhythms to avoid even-value sequences, as with the sixteenth notes of the opening theme; the *continuo* piano joining in at the cadences in the introduction; the string *portamento* in "A Serpina penserete." The scrappy little string ensemble plays with spirit, and no quarter is given: more professional singers might have insisted on some relief in the "Lo conosco" duet that ends Scene 1. These folks give it a shot.

Maria Erato's penetrating little soprano is applied with more alertness than we will hear from many Serpinas to come. Aldo Bacci, meanwhile, with a generally nondescript baritone, early on punches out some nice E-flats (he simply ducks the sustained Fs); later the voice falters, although he fights valiantly on.

Apart from the omission of the *da capo* repeat in "A Serpina penserete," the musical numbers are given in full, and then some—some repeats are added (Uberto's opening aria) or expanded (the original finale). Technical note: at least some copies were pressed on pretty, if not especially high-quality, red vinyl, qualifying this as the opera's most colorful recording.

p.1950 CETRA (M)

Angelica Tuccari (A), Sesto Bruscantini (B), Italian Radio Orchestra—Alfredo Simonetto

That this is a considerably more professional undertaking is established straightaway through the rhythmic drive of Alfredo Simonetto's conducting and the striking weight, presence, and color of the young Sesto Bruscantini's bass, with its easy upward reach to a limitless supply of vigorously pealed Fs and some equally impressive soft singing. Interpretively, this Uberto is a fairly standard comic-opera kind of performance (where exasperation is illustratively expressed as Exasperation), but executed at this level it remains a treat.

The Comic Opera Practitioner's Bag o' Tricks is less endearing practiced with a voice as pressed and limited as Angelica Tuccari's. This does allow for a marked contrast when she sings "A Serpina penserete" as straight as possible, but the basic vocal level limits the potential for an interesting confrontation between master and maid.

Since, in addition, the orchestral execution is more emphatic than polished (the *continuo* instrument is again a piano), this isn't a dream performance. But it's an entertaining one, with strengths not matched in subsequent efforts.

The finale used is "Per te io ho nel core."

1955 EMI / ANGEL (M)

Rosanna Carteri (A), Nicola Rossi-Lemeni (B), La Scala Orchestra—Carlo Maria Giulini

Considering the high-powered talent involved, the result is a bit disappointing. Neither singer is heard to best advantage, and the performance's tendency to heavy-footedness isn't helped by the somewhat muffled recording of the orchestra. (The problem is worse in the 1979 Seraphim LP reissue, which sounds as if a heavy quilt had been thrown over the proceedings.)

There are so many oddities in the production of Nicola Rossi-Lemeni's bass that they overtake the satisfaction of hearing Uberto performed by a major singer. Similarly, Serpina offers unfairly limited credit for Rosanna Carteri's vocal fluency and alertness and her believable response to the text, and constantly focuses instead on the voice's slightly sour edge.

The finale is "Per te io ho nel core."

1955 DEUTSCHE GRAMMOPHON ARCHIV (M)

Giuditta Mazzoleni (A), Marcello Cortis (B), Württemberg State Orchestra—Ferdinand Leitner

It's fun to recall that this wonderfully broad, weighty, curvaceous performance, which would drive a latter-day authenticist berserk, was presented under the "authentic" auspices of DG's Archive Production. (Authenticity note: This is the first *Serva* recording to reinforce the *continuo* harpsichord with a cello, though the reinforcement takes the form of sustained *legato* playing rather than single-note strokes.)

Marcello Cortis's reasonably attractive bass-baritone allows for one of the better-sung Ubertos, while Giuditta Mazzoleni makes up—to an extent—in bright and incisive attack what she lacks in tonal allure. Neither is riveting, but they're both all right, and help make this, all-around, perhaps the most musically satisfying recording of the opera.

The finale is "Per te io ho nel core."

1956 RCA / BMG (M)

Fanny Colorni (A), Teodor Rovetta (B), Pro Arte Instrumental Ensemble—G. Serra

A perfectly presentable performance, with one of the better Ubertos. Teodor Rovetta's bass-baritone, with a distinctive quick vibrato, is a gritty, forceful, and not at all unpleasant sound, and he gives a lively performance.

Fanny Colorni is another Serpina making the most, such as it is, of limited resources. She makes a pretty enough sound in the mid-range when not under pressure, and she avoids the more obvious clichés of the role.

The orchestra is on the dim side.

The recitative is trimmed somewhat, and so are the repeats of the musical numbers. In Uberto's "Sempre incontrasti" and the final duet, the little B section and the repeat of A are omitted entirely. In Serpina's "Stizzoso, mio stizzoso" and "A Serpina penserete," the repeat of A is shortened.

The *continuo* instrument is a piano. The finale is "Per te io ho nel core."

1959 MUSICA ET LITERA (S)

Virginia Zeani (A), Nicola Rossi-Lemeni (B), Musica et Litera Chamber Orchestra (Hamburg Radio Symphony Orchestra)—George Singer

Surprisingly, Nicola Rossi-Lemeni sounds a good deal better here than in 1955 EMI. No doubt in part because this recording is a whole lot peppier, but probably also because the voice is in better working order, the vocal production here is considerably cleaner and firmer.

Contrarily, it seems to me that Virginia Zeani's special personal quality might have been more fully exploited in a less revved-up performance, but what matters most is that she *can* function in this environment. No matter how quick the tempo, she sings with exceptional precision and tonal substance, and her sympathetic timbre and unfussy phrasing humanize her tough-as-nails Serpina in a way that doesn't happen, for example, with Renata Scotto (1960 Ricordi).

This isn't the only way I would want to hear the opera, but, despite the hectic edge, the performance generates a distinctive exhilaration, in excellent stereo sound.

The finale is "Per te io ho nel core."

p. 1960 RICORDI (S)

Renata Scotto (A), Sesto Bruscantini (B), I Virtuosi di Roma—Renato Fasano

This seems in many ways an updating of 1950 Cetra. Renato Fasano leads a similarly emphatic and full-bodied performance, with considerably more elegant playing by the Virtuosi di Roma and considerably superior sonics. The performance begins unhurriedly in Uberto's two arias but shows that it can move nimbly in Serpina's "Stizzoso, mio stizzoso" and the "Lo conosco" duet. The "Contento tu sarai" finale is performed with irresistible gusto.

Sesto Bruscantini's Uberto has by now ripened interpretively (his confusion in the *accompagnato* recitative and "Son imbrogliato" is touching as well as funny), and the voice remains highly serviceable, especially toward the top. But it's now a middling-attractive baritone, lacking the strikingly plush bass support of 1950.

Renata Scotto's Serpina is commandingly if a bit edgily vocalized. Nobody spits out with such unanswerable confidence the explanation "Serpina vuol così" in the first aria; she asserts dignity rather than abjectness in "A Serpina penserete"; "tempestuous" seems the appropriate description of her impromptu invention of the phantom fiancé, the fearsome Capitan Tempesta. But otherwise, I wonder about the literalness of her understanding of Serpina's manipulative control over Uberto, which is defensible but less interesting, it seems to me, than an assertiveness that evolves naturally out of their relationship.

Since the original Mercury issue, this recording has appeared on Everest and Musical Heritage Society LPs. It's certainly worthy of consideration.

1960 CLUB FRANÇAIS DU DISQUE (S)

Mariella Adani (A), Leonardo Monreale (B), Pomeriggi Musicali of the Teatro Nuovo of Milan—Ettore Gracis

Long a staple of the LP catalogue in its Nonesuch edition, this recording afforded collectors who knew Leonardo Monreale from his numerous *comprimario* bass roles the opportunity to hear him step out front, and he acquits himself tolerably well: a voice of presence if not distinction, a bass rather than baritone, handled with great sensibleness.

Mariella Adani is a take-charge Serpina with above-average equipment for the role. She can limn a clean, forceful line in "Stizzoso, mio stizzoso," then scale down appealingly, and even take in stride the low Ds and C-sharps on "Cheto . . . e non parlar." Quite nice.

Ettore Gracis leads a fleet, characteristically graceful and animated performance, in a somewhat resonant recording that features lots of stereo stage movement—if you enjoy that sort of thing. The finale is "Contento tu sarai."

1962 RCA / BMG (M)

Anna Moffo (A), Paolo Montarsolo (B), Rome Philharmonic Orchestra—Franco Ferrara

This performance, the soundtrack for a film, starts with mixed signals. On the one hand, there's an emphatic, weighty orchestral introduction announcing conductor Franco Ferrara's gradualist interpretive intentions.

On the other hand, there's Paolo Montarsolo. Although he's making a firmer sound than he would in later recordings, from syllable one he's deploying the Operatic Artist's Nauseating Palette of Comic Bass Colorations, supplemented in recitative by the Operatic Yukster's Deluxe Assortment of Boffo Buffo Funny Voices and Rhythmic Distensions. To be fair, it's not as awful as it might be, or as it probably would have been five or ten years later. But in the face of What Is, who wants to be fair?

Naturally, playing opposite him is one of the really good recorded Serpinas. Hearing the young Anna Moffo's authentically operatic-scale lyric soprano applied to the writing provides a reminder of the relatively undemanding range of that writing—Moffo scores her most distinctive vocal points at its "low" end. Since she can't significantly vary the very pretty mid-range coloration, she has to depend here primarily on sensible, assured phrasing. "A Serpina penserete" is thus given simply and gently—sensibly enough, without the *da capo* repeat—but what Moffo as a genuine operatic soprano can do is to reach up for full-bodied Fs and Gs.

Both finales are performed.

p.1969 HARMONIA MUNDI DEUTSCHE (S) CD

Maddalena Bonifaccio (A), Siegmund Nimsgern (B), Collegium aureum (Franzjosef Maier, concertmaster)

Here's another attempt at "authenticity" that actually yields vital musical results, somewhat smoother and more buoyant than those of 1955 DG Archiv (for what it's worth, Fritz Neumeyer is the harpsichordist in both), but no doubt equally contemptible to current whims.

Collegium aureum's period instruments allow the little band—which includes, in addition to concertmaster Franzjosef Maier, such illustrious soloists as violinist Sigiswald Kuijken and cellist Anner Bylsma—to attack the strings with full fervor and to sustain intensity of tone without overstepping into inappropriate lushness. The performance has an enormously appealing brightness and vigorous lyricism.

The Germanic quality of Siegmund Nimsgern's singing doesn't bother me as much as it originally did. Yes, the sound has a guttural tinge, the vowels are too dark, and the consonants often explode inappropriately. But all the same, the singing has a lovely, albeit baritonal ring, and Nimsgern unquestionably upholds the performance's powerful lyrical impulse.

And Maddalena Bonifaccio does her best to as well. The voice encounters patches of strain but is still a decidedly pretty instrument, and it's used with considerable spirit. Although this isn't a performance dominated by the personalities of the soloists, it does have a good deal of personality—the good kind, the kind that comes from the score.

The finale is "Per te io ho nel core."

1970 TELDEC (S)

Olivera Miljakovic (A), Reiner Süss (B), Berlin State Orchestra—Helmut Koch

The pace is moderate, the articulation on the blunt side without being exactly weighty. We should perhaps be grateful for the rocklike solidity of this performance, which comes to rest—in, note, the "Contento tu sarai" finale—in an unaccustomed but appropriate atmosphere of comfortable domesticity.

The only problem is that "rocklike" may not suggest an optimal tone, weight, or color for most of the piece. For example, while Uberto's Scene 2 confusion aria, "Son imbrogliato," often emerges as a precipitous muddle, it's slowed down here into something more like a boredom aria. And the absence of any Italianate brightness of tone in the singing contributes to the prevailingly gray coloration.

It's hard to tell whether Reiner Süss is deliberately attempting a vocal coloration of grouchiness or his voice just sounds this way—especially singing in Italian—but it really doesn't matter. This is a serviceable but rather dull Uberto. Olivera Miljakovic is also serviceable but rather dull: an accurate, vocally rather undernourished Serpina.

1973 ENSAYO (S) CD

Carmen Bustamante (A), Renato Capecchi (B), English Chamber Orchestra—Antoni Ros-Marbá

This recording, which has circulated on Philips and Musical Heritage Society LPs, didn't make that strong an initial impression. But returning to it after listening *en bloc* to fifteen recordings of *Serva Padrona*, I am more impressed.

In simple terms, this is a smooth, unpressured performance, which gives the impression of being conspicuously slower than the norm, although it actually isn't. This isn't a romantically lush performance, however. It's more that the usual balance between *legato* and *staccato* articulation in this normally chop-chopped opera has been reversed, with *legato* now the dominant mode and *staccato* the variant-for-effect.

More dazzling execution might have produced more immediately captivating results. The orchestra isn't completely polished, and the singers aren't attention-getting-outstanding. But they do, in fact, get into areas that the other *Serva Padrona* casts hardly touch.

Carmen Bustamante, vocally far from the best-endowed Serpina on records, is allowed, or even encouraged, to use her soprano to the fullest, without caricature. "A Serpina penserete" is for once directed so feelingly toward Uberto that for once he has to exert comparable effort to resist her—or at least to resist her as long as he does.

There is a feeling that Renato Capecchi is executing preset interpretive choices rather than playing off what he gets from Bustamante, and by this time his voice is no longer in prime condition, and is in any event a short-topped baritone rather than any kind of bass. All that said, he remains an engaging performer. An enjoyable if not inspired performer. An enjoyable if not inspired Uberto.

The finale is "Per te io ho nel core."

p.1974 QUADRIFOGLIO (S)

Annette Celine (A), Sesto Bruscantini (B), Rome Radio Symphony Orchestra—Alberto Zedda

This recording, which has circulated in the United States as an Everest LP, has a nice basic format: an unforcedly solid tone, with an unforced sense of animation.

Sesto Bruscantini's voice has by now sunk back into a more basslike sound, though of course not of the solidity of 1950 Cetra. There are still resonant E-flats and Fs, though they're now subject to some wobble interference. Unfortunately, the performance is now prone to a good deal more exaggeration, especially in recitative—where syllables are now more likely to be stretched out or otherwise overemphasized. This may be in part compensation for the generally moderate pacing, in which case quicker tempos might have been a more productive adjustment.

Annette Celine isn't insensitive, but is handicapped by the limitations of a light voice that can't muster much more than moderate prettiness in the mid-range at moderate dynamics—the attempt at *mezza voce* for "A Serpina penserete" produces pretty much constant tremulousness.

The finale is "Contento tu sarai."

1986 HUNGAROTON (S,D) CD

Katalin Farkas (A), József Gregor (B), Capella Savaria Pál Németh

The specter of authenticity looms over what might otherwise have been a more enjoyable performance. The "authentic" instruments played have the opposite effect of the galvanizing Collegium aureum strings in 1969 HMD: a muted, almost soporific quality. This isn't enhanced by an articulation mode that tends to a spongy sort of Baroque Bounce, or by sound that might have originated in an acoustically favorable subway tunnel.

Both soloists have virtues that are only partially exploited by the performance. Katalin Farkas's nice lyric soprano, despite a touch of acid, has a firmer core of tone than most of the voices heard as Serpina, and she seems to have nice instincts for the role. But she falls too easily into fake-comic overemphases in the recitative and even, occasionally, in musical numbers (e.g., the protracted "Non sono io bella . . ." in the "Lo conosco" duet).

József Gregor, who is primarily a legit bass, once recorded a recital of comic-bass scenes that made him seem the *basso buffo* of one's dreams, but the complete *Don Pasquale* that followed fell back on the interpretive clichés one was hoping to escape. His Uberto strikes

me as another only partially fulfilled promise. The tone is generally pleasing (it's certainly nice to hear an authentic singing bass in the second-scene confusion aria, "Son imbrogliato"), but it's not generally shaped with great creative authority. The narcotized atmosphere can't have been a great help.

Both finales are performed, and as an appendix there are three interpolated arias (of distinctly sub-Pergolesian inspiration) for "Zerbine," as Serpina is known in the French edition.

1989 OMEGA (S,D) CD

Julianne Baird (A), John Ostendorf (B), Philomel Baroque Chamber Orchestra—Rudolph Palmer

Here's another approach to *Serva* on CD: the two scenes are separated by a Vivaldi flute concerto. While this inverts the scenes' original function as *opera seria* entr'actes, it does have the virtue of converting them back into little free-standing units rather than continuous dramatic structures. It also pads the CD to a still hardly generous 54 minutes.

The performance is generally light-toned, but not insubstantial. The small string complement strikes a nice balance between sawing Baroque-style and maintaining textural appeal. In the recitative, the cello reinforcement is unaccustomedly well used, taking on a genuinely structural as opposed to ceremonial function—frequently leading phrases in a way that the harpsichord cannot because of its inability to sustain sound.

Julianne Baird perhaps goes too far in the same direction in the recitative: purring or spitting out consonants, "acting" in the style of a conservatory comic-opera workshop. However, in the musical numbers, for the most part there is a highly winning attention to characterization through the shape of the musical line. Although the tone is slight, there's a good deal of lovely singing, and some appropriate embellishment in the repeats—especially welcome here, given the length of the *da capos*.

John Ostendorf's bass-baritone isn't a particularly attractive instrument, and he has a tendency to distort vowels or push the tone into imaginedly comic configurations that circumvent rather than address vocal problems. There's no lack of energy, and the performance isn't objectionable, but it's not memorable either.

So where does all of this leave us? The logical approach would be to put together: 1955 DG Archiv or 1969 HMD, for robust, enlivening musical ambience; 1973 Ensayo, for general dramatic aptness and a touching Serpina; and 1959 Musica et Litera, for deft realization of its supercharged approach.

For a single recording, over the long haul 1973 Ensayo might make a durable choice. You could do worse than 1960 Ricordi, or even 1960 Club Français du Disque.

For the Uberto of Sesto Bruscantini, 1950 Cetra remains invaluable (with a nod to 1956 RCA's Teodor Rovetta), and 1962 RCA is of interest for Anna Moffo's Serpina. Although it's of little interest vocally, for something completely different there's the bourgeois hominess of 1970 Teldec.

KENNETH FURIE

Amilcare Ponchielli

La Gioconda (1876)

A: La Gioconda (s); B: Laura (ms); C: La Cieca (c);
D: Enzo Grimaldo (t); E: Barnaba (bar); F: Alvise (bs)

La Gioconda has hardly been neglected by the recording companies, and yet no one version can be singled out for its overall excellence. Most recordings have foundered on the basic necessity of assembling no fewer than six major singers, one in each vocal category. Increasingly, on records as in the theater, the opera has been treated not as an ensemble effort but as a vehicle for the leading soprano (or tenor). Virtually every recorded cast has at least one weak link. The role of La Cieca, whose music calls for a true contralto of the Louise Homer or Ernestine Schumann-Heink type, is particularly difficult to cast today. It is also worth noting that no fewer than three famous Enzos of the stereo era—Richard Tucker, Franco Corelli, and Plácido Domingo—have all failed to record the opera commercially.

There are only two standard cuts in *La Gioconda*—both rather baffling. The less objectionable excision is a tiny one—five and a half bars—in the coda of the Act IV trio. The omitted passage takes only a few seconds to perform and is not vocally difficult (the dynamic indication for all three vocal parts is *pp* throughout); if the number is to be abridged, this seems like an oddly ineffectual way to do it.

The second and much more destructive cut occurs in the Act II finale, at the point just after Gioconda's "Riguarda al mar!" and the choral exclamation "Le galee, le galee! Salvi chi può, salvi che può!" There is a cannon shot, followed by four bars of suspense-filled orchestral prepa-

ration. Then Gioconda launches into the finale with a solo statement of the "Tu sei tradito!" melody; Enzo replies with a variant—"Taci! E un insulto de'vili il consiglio"—of the tune, and this is followed by another choral outburst ("Fuggiam! Ah! Più speranza no, non v'ha!"). Then there is a concerted passage in which Gioconda, Enzo, and the chorus all sing simultaneously.

The usual procedure is to cut directly from the fourth bar after the cannon shot to the concerted passage. There seems to be no logical reason why this particular number, and none other, should be singled out for such mutilation. The cut saves little time; the eliminated music makes no extraordinary demands upon the performers, and observing the cut deprives the soprano and the tenor of some nice opportunities. Worst of all, the cut makes Ponchielli sound like a clumsy composer, since the "Tu sei tradito!" melody is not only abruptly introduced but is "developed" without ever having been heard in its original form.

All of the recordings issued prior to 1967 observe both of these cuts as a matter of course. The Decca / Gardelli set was the first to restore the traditionally omitted passages, and both of the studio recordings released subsequently have, commendably, followed Decca's example.

1931 EMI / ANGEL (M)

Giannina Arangi-Lombardi (A), Ebe Stignani (B), Camilla Rota (C), Alessandro Granda (D),

Gaetano Viviani (E), Corrado Zambelli (F), La Scala Chorus and Orchestra—Lorenzo Mola-joli

Despite dim sound and some precipitous tempos (dictated, no doubt, by the need to fit the music onto 78-rpm sides), this first complete recording of the opera contains enough good singing to maintain the listener's interest throughout. Lorenzo Molajoli's conducting is tidy, and sometimes he surprises the listener with some warm, sensuous phrasing. The orchestra and chorus are obviously proficient, however indistinctly reproduced.

At times, Giannina Arangi-Lombardi sounds like a throwback to the sopranos heard on excerpts from the opera recorded prior to World War I. There is passion in her singing, but she rarely allows it to disturb the evenness of her tonal emission or the calm *legato* flow of her phrasing.

Ebe Stignani sounds remarkably girlish and soprano-like, so that, for once, Barnaba's description of Laura as a maiden *(vergine)* does not seem sarcastic. Although Stignani's por-trayal probably gained in timbral richness and authority during the next decade, this is still an impressive performance.

Camilla Rota, the Cieca, has an impressively rich, deep mezzo; some sources, by the way, confuse her with Ana Maria Rota, a singer of a later generation.

The Enzo, Alessandro Granda, tends to maul the line with Gigli-like sobs, and is almost comically petulant in the confrontation with Gioconda in Act IV; the voice is a fine one, though, and has the appropriate *spinto* quality for the role.

Gaetano Viviani's Barnaba is conventionally nasty, with much use of a snarling attack but vividly enunciated. Corrado Zambelli, on the other hand, has a nice smooth bass voice, but is an incredibly unimaginative singer: the vicious reproaches and threats hurled at Laura in Act III, Scene 1, might as well be a recitation of the proverbial laundry list; and when, in the subse-quent scene, Alvise invites his guests to inspect his wife's (supposedly) dead body, Zambelli could be announcing that tea is served, for all the emotion he conveys.

In the smaller roles, Giuseppe Nessi (Isepo) and Aristide Baracchi (Zuane) are outstanding.

1946 MET (M,P) CD

Zinka Milanov (A), Risë Stevens (B), Margaret Harshaw (C), Richard Tucker (D), Leonard Warren (E), Giacomo Vaghi (F), Metropolitan Opera Chorus and Orchestra—Emil Cooper

Despite some harshness and constriction, the sound of this broadcast recording is good for the circumstances. The one potential obstacle to the listener's enjoyment of the performance is intermittent surface noise—there are isolated pops and clicks throughout, and the worst patch of crackle occurs right at the beginning of "Sui-cidio!"

Standard cuts are observed at the end of Act II and in the Act IV trio; 16 bars of the Act I Furlana are also dropped. The only other cut is an unusual one: in Act III, Scene 1, after Laura has swallowed the sleeping potion, Alvise doesn't come back to confirm that she has taken the "poison." (Was this cut made in order to give the bass time to change his costume for the next scene?)

Emil Cooper's conducting reveals an excel-lent grasp of the score. He is energetic, with plenty of rhythmic snap and drive where these qualities are appropriate. Elsewhere, though, the conductor is not afraid to ease up, to good effect: he sets some rather slow tempos for the lyrical numbers, but breathes with the singers and always maintains tension. The orchestra is in good form—there is some fine solo playing, notably in the Dance of the Hours—and the chorus sounds enthusiastic.

The cast is most impressive. It is easy to understand why many of those who were lucky enough to hear Zinka Milanov in the theater remember her as the greatest Gioconda of them all. Her portrayal is at once large in scale and filled with eloquent details. She digs into the violent outbursts with gutsy urgency, and yet manages to sound young and vulnerable most of the time. Milanov's Act IV, especially, is vocalized with great distinction throughout.

I am slightly disappointed by Risë Steven's Laura. In Act II, in particular, she seems preoccupied with purely technical matters. She is not the Barbieri kind of powerful dramatic mezzo, and is overextended by the demands of "L'amo come il fulgor del creato." Elsewhere, her singing is always secure, but never really imaginative or seductive-sounding.

Margaret Harshaw is an extraordinary Cieca: a vivid vocal actress, she produces a huge but well-focused sound and demonstrates a fine instinct for *legato* phrasing.

At this point in his career, Richard Tucker actually sounds a bit lightweight for Enzo. He is in good voice here, though (a lovely, lyrical "Cielo e mar"), and his forthright manner is most welcome. Leonard Warren, in splendidly fresh, free voice, is an unusually sympathetic Barnaba. He almost persuades us that Barnaba's feelings for Gioconda transcend the sordidly physical.

Despite its inevitable sonic limitations, this set is a valuable supplement to the studio recordings of the opera.

1952 CETRA (M) CD

Maria Callas (A), Fedora Barbieri (B), Maria Amadini (C), Gianni Poggi (D), Paolo Silveri (E), Giulio Neri (F), Italian Radio Chorus and Orchestra, Turin—Antonino Votto

This is one of Maria Callas's most exciting recordings of a complete role—which will be recommendation enough for many listeners. No other Gioconda on records has her verbal immediacy and wide range of vocal colors (although it must be admitted at once that several surpass her in terms of steadiness, tonal purity, and vocal evenness). Hers is a veristic approach to the part, at times almost frightening in its intensity (the hatred she feels for Barnaba, and her jealous resentment of Laura, fairly leap out of the grooves). As so often with Callas, she somehow achieves this intensity while shaping the music with instrumental accuracy and poise. She has some uncomfortable moments on loud high notes, but this is a revelatory performance.

Fedora Barbieri is a powerful and incisive Laura, who quite matches Callas in these respects. The only possible criticism, in fact, is that Barbieri's Laura sounds like such a formi-

dable lady that it's hard to believe she would be afraid of Alvise for a moment.

Unfortunately, Callas and Barbieri must carry the show virtually unaided by their colleagues. The only exception is Giulio Neri: his vocalism is not exactly beautiful or polished, but it is imposingly dark and firm.

Maria Amadini is a dull Cieca; Gianni Poggi, an irritatingly callow Enzo, who always seems to be whining. Paolo Silveri has some interesting ideas about Barnaba, but is vocally too rough-edged and unbalanced to realize all of them satisfactorily.

Antonino Votto's conducting is workmanlike: he obtains good playing and choral singing from the capable Turin ensemble, but rarely attempts anything exceptional in the way of shaping or nuance.

Everest's fake stereo is ghastly. I have not heard the Fonit-Cetra CD reissue.

1952 URANIA (M)

Anita Corridori (A), Miriam Pirazzini (B), Rina Cavallari (C), Giuseppe Campora (D), Anselmo Colzani (E), Fernando Corena (F), La Scala Chorus and Orchestra—Armando La Rosa Parodi

This mediocre performance has been out of print for many years, and I cannot in all honesty recommend its speedy restoration to the catalogue. La Scala's orchestra and chorus sound off-form here, as though the project's budget did not allow for either sufficient rehearsal or retakes. Armando La Rosa Parodi's conducting is reasonably idiomatic, but too fast and slick for my taste.

A better cast might have helped. The women are especially disappointing. Anita Corridori has neither the voice nor the temperament for Gioconda; she is sometimes shrill and clumsy, and often dull. Miriam Pirazzini has the gusty commitment that Corridori lacks, but her big, dark mezzo, with its heavy vibrato, makes her Laura sound rather matronly, and there is little seductiveness in her phrasing. The Cieca of Rina Cavallari is downright bad—a raw, wobbly sound, with harsh chest tones and pitch problems.

The men's vocalism is better, although never

truly distinguished. Giuseppe Campora phrases with sensitivity and takes the drama seriously, but his tenor is on the small side for Enzo's music, and the big moments extend him badly. Anselmo Colzani's Barnaba, crudely villainous, is acceptably but not excitingly sung.

The recorded sound is awful—shallow and afflicted with a booming echo.

1957 DECCA / LONDON (S) CD

Anita Cerquetti (A), Giulietta Simionato (B), Franca Sacchi (C), Mario del Monaco (D), Ettore Bastianini (E), Cesare Siepi (F), Chorus and Orchestra of the Maggio Musicale Fiorentino—Gianandrea Gavazzeni

Anita Cerquetti's career was brief, and she made only two commercial recordings—this one, and an aria recital. Her surviving broadcast performances are eagerly sought by collectors, and her Gioconda shows why. Her voice is the real thing: large, secure, attractive and youthful in timbre, with some interesting technical strengths (notably, the ability to maintain control at a variety of in-between dynamic levels throughout a wide range). Interpretively, Cerquetti is better at conveying tenderness, resignation, and hurt than the more violent emotions. Nevertheless, her restraint is a legitimate way of playing the role, and provides an interesting contrast to the more extroverted approaches of other sopranos.

This is one of Mario del Monaco's best recorded performances: he makes a predictably exciting effect at such places as Enzo's defiant call for help in Act I ("Su, fratelli del mar! Alla lotta!"). What is above and beyond the call of duty is the surprising control and restraint he brings to the more lyrical passages—while his singing does not exactly have the liquid ease of the best lyric or *spinto* tenors, it is not stiff or crude, either. Del Monaco is also, by quite some distance, the most sensual Enzo on any of these complete sets.

Giulietta Simionato is not in her very best voice, occasionally attacking notes gingerly when her vocal line takes her high and loud, but this resourceful artist makes Laura sound both aristocratic and sympathetic.

Ettore Bastianini and Cesare Siepi are both in representative form: their vocalism may not always be a model of subtlety, but it is always rich, bold, and impactive.

The weak link in this cast is the Cieca of Franca Sacchi: soft-grained of timbre and tentative of attack, she sounds particularly feeble next to her high-powered colleagues.

Gianandrea Gavazzeni's conducting is often lyrically pleasing but occasionally rhythmically limp and lacking in dramatic tension. The chorus is energetic, but the orchestral execution is uneven in quality, with some thin violin tone and edgy brasses. Decca's early-stereo sound, full-bodied and detailed, is still very satisfying to listen to.

1957 DECCA / LONDON (S)

Zinka Milanov (A), Rosalind Elias (B), Belen Amparan (C), Giuseppe di Stefano (D), Leonard Warren (E), Plinio Clabassi (F), Chorus and Orchestra of the Accademia di Santa Cecilia, Rome—Fernando Previtali

While this recording is hardly the ultimate in polish, at its best the performance has enough life in it to suggest a good, old-fashioned night at the opera. Fernando Previtali's conducting is rather lightweight: some of the lyrical portions of the score take on a pleasing chamber-music texture as a result. Previtali is always very considerate toward his soloists, but he is not greatly helped by the orchestra or chorus. As on the Decca / Gavazzeni set, the strings sound thin (especially the violins, when playing high) and the brass section is weak. Some of the choral singing is ragged.

Ironically, the best singing is done by the two least famous members of the cast. Belen Amparan comes closer than most of her recorded rivals to meeting the vocal demands of Cieca, and sings richly and firmly. Plinio Clabassi does not possess the most sumptuous bass voice imaginable, but his vocalism is secure and his interpretation of Alvise has the right kind of suave malevolence.

None of the other principals is heard at his or her best. Rosalind Elias, for example, ought to be well suited to Laura, and her performance here is good as far as it goes. But she seems to be pushing her handsome mezzo rather hard in the climaxes.

Giuseppe di Stefano displays just the right sort of extroverted passion for Enzo, but the tenor is in terrible vocal condition on this set. He pulls himself together for some reasonable vocalism in such passages as "Gia ti veggo immota e smorta" in the Act III ensemble, but most of his singing is raw and strained, with some desperate lunges at high notes, and dismaying to hear.

Both Milanov and Warren—perhaps inevitably—sound less good than they did back in 1946, when the Met performance was recorded. Milanov's Gioconda is caught here a few years past her peak. She has some effortful moments, and a critic must point out her quite regular habit of abandoning the text and vocalizing on "ah" whenever the words threaten to get in the way of a good, clean attack on a high note. Much of the time, though, the soprano displays the grandeur and command characteristic of her best recorded work, and she sings some passages more eloquently than any other soprano on these complete sets—the famous floated high B-flat at "Madre! Enzo adorato! Ah, come t'amo!" is one such instance (it's even better than it was on the 1946 broadcast, in fact).

Vocally, Warren now has some guttural moments. He has also completely rethought his approach to the character of Barnaba—but along conventional lines, and the resultant tough-guy inflections can sound mechanical rather than deeply felt. Warren's is still a major voice, though, and he outsings di Stefano in their Act I duet.

1959 EMI / ANGEL (S) CD

Maria Callas (A), Fiorenza Cossotto (B), Irene Companeez (C), Pier Miranda Ferraro (D), Piero Cappuccilli (E), Ivo Vinco (F), La Scala Chorus and Orchestra—Antonino Votto

On this stereo remake of her Gioconda, Callas gives a performance that is at once tremendously exciting and quite painful to listen to. The voice, to put it bluntly, is coming apart at the seams: harsh, almost baritonal chest tones alternate with oddly thin, colorless head tones; loud high notes are strident; and the wobble is omnipresent. The phrasing is even more eloquent than before, and the spontaneity of the declamation is startling—even when the voice is in its worst shape, the singing seems as natural a mode of expression as speech.

The supporting cast is not supportive enough. Irene Companeez is a vocally secure Cieca, but one quite lacking in urgency; it's difficult to picture this placid woman as the mother of Callas's Gioconda. As Barnaba, Piero Cappuccilli makes pleasant sounds and cannot be accused of not understanding the character, but next to Callas's intensity he sounds almost casual.

It is interesting to hear a real-life husband-and-wife team as Alvise and Laura, but in fact neither Ivo Vinco nor Fiorenza Cossotto does anything out of the ordinary. The bass is reliable but bland, with a slightly rusty edge to his timbre; the mezzo sounds young and attractive, but also lightweight and rather tentative much of the time—one wishes she could have recorded the part a few years later, when her voice had gained in richness and authority.

Pier Miranda Ferraro's thick, ungainly tenor lends Enzo a certain basic sturdiness, but he simply bruises most of the music: "Cielo e mar" and the duet with Laura form a particularly unpleasant sequence.

Votto's conducting is once again correct but tame, although he has a superior orchestra and chorus at his disposal.

1967 DECCA / LONDON (S) CD

Renata Tebaldi (A), Marilyn Horne (B), Oralia Dominguez (C), Carlo Bergonzi (D), Robert Merrill (E), Nicola Ghiuselev (F), Chorus and Orchestra of the Accademia di Santa Cecilia, Rome—Lamberto Gardelli

This, the first uncut recording of the opera, has held up well despite some peculiarities in the casting. Lamberto Gardelli's conducting is disciplined, but he manages to combine dramatic intensity with an expansiveness and warmth not heard on many other versions. The Santa Cecilia orchestra and chorus respond to his leadership with accurate, animated playing and singing—far superior to their uneven work on the Decca / Previtali set made a decade earlier. Decca has captured the performance in typically full, solid stereo sound.

Renata Tebaldi waited until fairly late in her career to add Gioconda to her repertory, but the role became a congenial vehicle for her. Not all of her singing here is comfortable: she carries her chest voice dangerously high, and her upper register turns tense and steely under pressure. Much of the time, though, one can admire her sympathetic timbre and her luxuriant way with the phrases. She is an uncommonly dignified, womanly Gioconda, and yet she brings a surprising ferocity to the violent moments.

Compared to Tebaldi's involvement, Carlo Bergonzi and Marilyn Horne don't always seem to be performing in the same opera. For all his intelligence and musicality, the tenor is light-voiced for Enzo: he sounds suave and velvety in "Cielo e mar" and the other purely lyrical sections of the score, but is hard-pressed in the climaxes. Horne sings magnificently as Laura, and always sounds aristocratic, but she too is phlegmatic—a casual adulteress, who seems oddly unperturbed by Gioconda's and Alvise's threats on her life. Bergonzi and Horne do unite for an exceptionally beautiful performance of the Act II duet—one of the best recorded versions of this problematic piece.

Robert Merrill is not exactly a model of impassioned delivery, either, but his Barnaba is as well sung as anybody's, and one must be grateful for his avoidance of superficial sneering. He is particularly good in the Act II barcarolle.

The Cieca, Oralia Dominguez, sings smoothly and attractively, but is another in the long line of mezzos who would probably be more suitably cast as Laura.

1980 DECCA / LONDON (S,D) CD

Montserrat Caballé (A), Agnes Baltsa (B), Alfreda Hodgson (C), Luciano Pavarotti (D), Sherrill Milnes (E), Nicolai Ghiaurov (F), London Opera Chorus, National Philharmonic Orchestra—Bruno Bartoletti

Among this version's strengths is the solidly idiomatic and affectionate conducting of Bruno Bartoletti. I do miss a certain elasticity of tempo that is surely stylistically appropriate in this music. But Bartoletti obtains beautiful playing from his fine orchestra: his Dance of the Hours, for example, is as good as any version on a complete set. The choral work is also quite lively throughout the performance.

Decca's digital sound is another advantage: clear, warm, full-bodied, but ungimmicky, this recording is a model of how such an operatic score should sound on CD.

Of the "name" singers in the cast, Sherrill Milnes makes the best impression. Curiously enough, he avoids all of the high options, but when he must sing out in his upper register his notes are splendidly firm, warm, and virile. He also manages to convey evil without resorting to superficial huffing and leering.

Luciano Pavarotti's Enzo is disappointing. His work in Acts III and IV is acceptable from an interpretive standpoint, and offers some good singing in the *pezzo concertato* ("Già ti veggo immota e smorta") and in the final trio with the two women. But throughout much of Acts I and II, he is in poor voice and seems to be operating on automatic pilot. In "Cielo e mar," the voice turns thin and unsupported on the cadenza.

Montserrat Caballé is a great, but exasperating, soprano. On this recording, in fact, she is *two* sopranos. One is the mature artist who brings both dignity and intensity to the role (for example, in the little monologue after "Suicidio!"). This Caballé phrases much of Gioconda's music with a revelatory instinct for *portamento*.

The other sounds like a young, technically insecure soprano who seems hell-bent upon finding out how much abuse her lovely voice can withstand. This Caballé shoves in head voice at the top, and slams in chest voice at the bottom, all in a reckless and undisciplined manner, so that there is really not enough on the middle ground between these two extremes.

Agnes Baltsa's is a lighter, more intimate Laura than the norm—a good match for Caballé's Gioconda in these respects. Baltsa is fine as long as one doesn't expect the power and coloristic variety of a true Italian dramatic mezzo.

Since real contraltos are all but nonexistent these days, it comes as no surprise that Alfreda Hodgson, like Baltsa, is lightweight for her role. She's an acceptable Cieca by current standards, but sounds much too youthful to be Caballé's mother.

Nicolai Ghiaurov is in rather rough voice, and Alvise's tessitura exposes the increasing shallowness of his bottom register. Still, the music and the character are not slighted: Ghiaurov, experienced artist that he is, understands the value of restraint and knows that certain things have to be thrown away.

1987 CBS / SONY (S,D) CD

Eva Marton (A), Livia Budai (B), Anne Gjevang (C), Giorgio Lamberti (D), Sherrill Milnes (E), Samuel Ramey (F), Hungaroton Opera Chorus, Hungarian State Orchestra—Giuseppe Patanè

Giuseppe Patanè gives a thoughtful, introspective reading of the score—often relaxed in tempo and expansive in phrasing; his Dance of the Hours, for example, has elegance rather than hard-edged brilliance. Some of the more dramatic episodes in the opera might benefit from a greater degree of tension, but this is an interesting performance.

There is a very uneven cast. Milnes repeats his strong Barnaba from the Decca / Bartoletti set: if the baritone now occasionally sounds a little careful, his is still a shrewd portrayal. Samuel Ramey sings Alvise with great distinction, despite a voice that is on the light, baritonal side for some of the music. He easily dominates Act III.

In the title role, Eva Marton has the advantage of a real Gioconda voice—big, lush, womanly. She sometimes presses a bit in her determination to be "dramatic," however; minor infelicities of balance and intonation prevent her work from reaching the highest level. Still, hers is an impressive performance. There is care in her phrasing, and eloquence in her projection of the heroine's shifting moods.

The Enzo, Giorgio Lamberti, brings a welcome urgency to the character, but his bright timbre is monochromatic, with little warmth or roundness. He has the advantage, of course, of being a native Italian: there is a clarity to his vowels and consonants, coupled with an almost instinctive way of weighting and steering the voice, that proclaims his nationality in his every scene.

Livia Budai is a nondescript Laura: her mezzo has a curiously unsettled quality, with a bleak, shallow timbre intruding at odd moments, and her temperament is bland.

Anne Gjevang has a fine voice, with more of a contralto quality than most latter-day Ciecas; although she makes all of the obvious points with the role, her delivery is not quite warm enough or Italianate enough to be ideal.

The Hungarian orchestra and chorus bring refinement as well as enthusiasm to their task. The record sound is a little too reverberant at times, but clear and detailed.

———————————

Callas is the primary attraction of both of her versions, although her Gioconda may be an acquired taste for many listeners.

The three uncut recordings—the Decca / Gardelli, Decca / Bartoletti, and CBS / Patanè—are all well recorded, well conducted, and unevenly sung, making a choice among them difficult. Gardelli and Bartoletti conduct the opera at least as well as any of their rivals on records. If pressed, I would recommend the Decca / Gardelli—if only because, despite individual weaknesses in the cast, the performance has a genuine dramatic sweep and a convincingly Italianate quality. The less idiomatically sung Decca / Bartoletti set, is, however, definitely the best-engineered recording of the opera; the CBS / Patanè version, nearly as impressive in terms of sound quality, has strong performances by Marton, Milnes, and Ramey.

ROLAND GRAEME

Francis Poulenc

Les Mamelles de Tirésias (1947)

A: Thérèse La Cartomancienne (s); B: Lacouf (t); C: Le Fils (t);
D: Le Journaliste (t); E: Le Mari (t or bar); F: Le Directeur (bar);
G: Presto (bar); H: Le Gendarme (bar)

It amused Poulenc to style himself as half-monk and half-guttersnipe. True or not, the irreverent side of the composer's persona was definitely responsible for *Les Mamelles de Tirésias*, written during the last year of World War II and first performed on June 3, 1947, at the Opéra-Comique in Paris. The work enraged many at the time—how could Poulenc pen such a frivolous piece in dubious taste just as France was emerging from a nightmare? Guillaume Apollinaire's libretto, actually written some forty years earlier, is a mad pre-surrealist romp in which the wife, Thérèse, tires of her lot as a woman, transforms herself into a man, and leaves her husband, who must make babies on his own—40,049 in one day, with the help of a magical incubator. Numerous music-hall routines and burlesque characters turn up before the sexes are straightened out, all accompanied by music of tremendous charm, wit, and compositional sophistication—and, as we can now plainly hear, an aura of nostalgia that gives this sometimes puzzling but always lively assemblage of words and images a truly touching poetic dimension. "If my music succeeds in producing laughter," Poulenc once wrote, "while still allowing some moments of tenderness and real lyricism, my aim will have been fully attained; thus I shall not have been false to Apollinaire's poem, in which the most violent buffoonery alternates with melancholy."

1953 EMI / ANGEL (M)

Denise Duval (A), Leprin (B), Jacques Hivert (C), Serge Rallier (D), Jean Giraudeau (E), Robert Jeantet (F), Julien Thirache (G), Emile Rousseau (H), Chorus and Orchestra of the Opéra-Comique—André Cluytens

This recording features several members of the original cast, including the creator of the title role, Denise Duval, one of Poulenc's favorite singers. Indeed, her distinctive soprano, with its cut-diamond sparkle and clarity coupled with an equally scintillating vocal personality, makes it difficult to imagine other interpreters of the composer's opera heroines, at least on disc. The other roles require voices of character rather than tonal glamour, although Jeantet's resonant Theater Director and Giraudeau's suave Husband (singing the higher options for tenor as noted in the score) supply both. Everyone catches the antic spirit of the piece as well as its haunting wistfulness—the definitive performance, neatly and affectionately shaped by Cluytens, and one that conveys a wonderfully vivid sense of theater.

Peter G. Davis

FRANCIS POULENC

DIALOGUES DES CARMÉLITES (1957)

A: Blanche de la Force (s); B: Mme. Lidoine, New Prioress (s);
C: Sister Constance (s); D: Mme. de Croissy, Old Prioress (ms);
E: Mother Marie (ms)

ust after World War II, Georges Bernanos was asked to write the dialogue for a French film based on a novel about the execution of a group of Carmelite nuns during the Reign of Terror. The project was later shelved for more than a decade, but the unfilmed script was published in 1949 after his death, and in the 1950s it was set operatically by Francis Poulenc, on commission by Ricordi. Like his later *La Voix Humaine*, the work is an extraordinarily responsive setting, with music designed to heighten both the prosody and the implications of the text. One of the most frequently played of contemporary operas, it is an exploration of faith as a response to terror. The major supporting characters (all women) provide us with differing reactions to the certainty of death: blind fear, instinctive belief strengthened into conscious conviction, and a growing sense of beatitude. Moving through the opera from chaotic terror to serene martyrdom is the young Sister Blanche of the Agony of Christ. The work is a series of relatively tranquil discussions of these responses against an offstage background of violence—the two exceptions are the gripping onstage death of the Old Prioress and the final guillotining of the nuns. Since the music is patterned to dramatize the emotional and philosophical implications of the dialogue without (in general) expressionistic devices, melodrama,

or satire, the major challenge of the singers is to vivify a sensitive and subtle score with all the arts of vocal characterization available to them.

1958 EMI / ANGEL (M) CD

Denise Duval (A), Régine Crespin (B), Liliane Berton (C), Denise Scharley (D), Rita Gorr (E), Paris Opéra Chorus and Orchestra—Pierre Dervaux

The cast here is that of the Paris premiere, and classic, including as it does Duval, Scharley, Crespin, Gorr, and Berton, all in their prime. The singers are all French, which means a unified vocal approach and a touching declamation of the words. Conceivably there could be greater variety among the voices; though Gorr was a superb mezzo and Crespin a star soprano, they had at this point a similar vocal richness and later both went on to sing the role taken here by Denise Scharley. Denise Duval is a sensitive heroine, even without the histrionic opportunities afforded her in *La Voix Humaine*. Scharley is a wonderfully vivid Old Prioress, and Liliane Berton genuinely charming as the young Sister Constance. Subsequent productions have often been more obviously theatrical, and perhaps more fully, if not more deeply, felt—one thinks of Maria Ewing, Betsy Norden, and Leontyne Price, and Gorr and Crespin in their later role. Nevertheless, this is a splendid recording, beautifully sung (one would never guess from it that the "French School" was in decline), well paced by Pierre Dervaux, and resonantly, although monophonically, recorded: one of the most satisfying productions of a postwar European opera.

LONDON GREEN

Unavailable for review:
1991 VIRGIN

FRANCIS POULENC

LA VOIX HUMAINE (1959)

A: Elle (s)

Among other projects, the theater artist Jean Cocteau occasionally wrote works for favorite performers, such as Edith Piaf, Edwige Feuillère, Arletty (of *Les Enfants du Paradis*), and the Comédie Française actress Berthe Bovy, who in 1930 created his *La Voix Humaine*, a touching telephone monologue for a fashionable young woman rejected by her lover, with whom she is speaking for the last time, following a suicide attempt. Though the play's social assumptions about women are dated, its psychology is not. As in Cocteau's films and the novels of Françoise Sagan, to have lost love is to have lost everything, even in the sophisticated milieu of Paris. Poulenc's operatic version opened to great success in 1958 with soprano Denise Duval, who then played it around the world. The role is a panorama of intimate evasions and emotions: "A killer," as Duval has said, "because the phrasing—sometimes long, sometimes short, always in a low key, half singing, half *parlando*—is a tour de force of no mean order. It lies better really for a darker voice . . . but that sort of instrument cannot quite produce the hysterical impression that is so essential."

1959 EMI / ANGEL (S) CD

Denise Duval (A), Opéra-Comique Orchestra—Georges Prêtre

Until recently, this has been the only generally available recording of Poulenc's most accessible work—but the performance happens to be superb. The closeted passion, desperate sophistication, dependence, spiritual desolation, and graveyard humor of "Elle" are all immediately reflected in the music, a fluent and masterly setting of Cocteau's text: melodic speaking. Denise Duval's voice is clear, forward, very French in tone, and completely at the service of the words. Her characterization is both invasive and defenseless, manipulative and apologetic and charming—at once appalling and moving—and she performs with an extraordinary illusion of spontaneity. The magnitude of her accomplishment becomes apparent when listening to other performances; neither Elisabeth Söderström nor Magda Olivero, two of the most distinguished singing actresses of this century, has quite the focus (in every sense) of Duval, and Ingrid Bergman, in a very fine recording of the Cocteau play, lacks the variety and the necessary element of asperity that Duval captures so well in Poulenc's intimate masterpiece. Five minutes into it, and Duval's singing seems more natural, more spontaneous than Bergman's speaking. Of course, one would like to hear others in this work (what would Sayão, de los Angeles, Ewing, Schwarzkopf, Crespin, Cotrubas, Sills, or Caballé—to say nothing of some of the greatest *verismo* sopranos—do with it?) But here we have a definitive reading, splendidly supported by Prêtre and his orchestra.

1991 ERATO (S,D) CD

Julia Migenes (A), National Orchestra of France—Georges Prêtre

Can there be two definitive performances of a score such as this? Migenes moves in forty-five minutes from hysteria to ecstatic memory and despair to a tremulous uncertainty, with an intimately expressive singing tone and an actress's use of the words. Her voice is a trifle heartier than Duval's, but she completely avoids the easy traps of *verismo* sentiment and frigid self-interest. The sound is fine and, as before, Prêtre and his orchestra are splendid. Of the soprano's work it can be said in summary that she completely reveals the emotional aims of Poulenc's extraordinary orchestration. There can be no greater praise.

Duval was the superb creator, and Migenes is at once original and equally moving. Each performance is magnificent, and for the enthusiast both are necessary.

LONDON GREEN

Unavailable for review:
1978 CHANT DU MONDE
1981 CHANDOS
1982 CHANT DU MONDE

SERGEI PROKOFIEV

THE LOVE FOR THREE ORANGES (1921)

A: Ninetta (s); B: Fata Morgana (s); C: Clarissa (c); D: Prince (t);
E: Truffaldino (t); F: Leandro (bar); G: King (bs)

ased upon a Carlo Gozzi parody of seventeenth-century Italian *commedia dell'arte*, written for an American audience during his 1919 stay in New York, and translated by the composer from Russian into French for its world premiere in Chicago, *The Love for Three Oranges* is the most international of Prokofiev's eight operas. And by far the most popular. Still, it has been surprisingly little recorded. That may be in part because *Oranges* remains primarily a Russian opera; its exaggeratedly ironic tone emulates Russian theatrical fashion of the time (and even Prokofiev's French is often sung with Russian accents). But it is also undoubtedly because a recording is not easy to pull off. Prokofiev's music, which so effectively and hilariously mimics the frenetic action onstage of *commedia dell'arte*, can sound overly nervous on its own, especially without singers and conductor able to gauge its constantly changeable moods just right. Nor is *Oranges*—with only the Prince, among the large cast of ludicrous characters, undergoing any kind of development throughout the opera—a star vehicle. As an opera without grand arias, choruses, or generic set numbers of any kind, it demands, instead, dazzling ensemble work, the kind not easily manufactured in a recording studio. The French version had to wait until 1989 for a recording (although a 1982 video version of the Glyndebourne production is sung in French). An opera of non-stop action, there are no possible cuts, and none is made in the three recordings.

1956 PHILIPS (M)

Unknown (A), Vanda Guerlovich (B), Bogdana Stritar (C), Yanaz Lipushchek (D), Drago Chuden (E), Danilo Merlak (F), Latko Koroshetz (G), Chorus and Orchestra of the Slovenian National Opera, Ljubljana—Vogo Leskovich

Coming from the Slovenian national opera in the 1950s, this first complete recording of *Oranges* was bound to be a provincial affair. And indeed the orchestra is less than brilliant, the cast decidedly uneven, the recorded sound constricted. Still, this proves a strongly characterful performance. Most of the credit for that goes to Leskovich. He brings a tremendous bite to the sardonic side of Prokofiev's score, but that doesn't prevent him from achieving a really joyful climax at the end. The set also boasts an impressive Prince. Lipushchek, an Italianate tenor, grandly conveys the Prince's transformation from sniveling hypochondriac wimp to rapt and heroic lover, all the more an accomplishment given the tremulous nature of his Ninetta. The only other singer who stands out is the electric, Electra-like Fata Morgana of Vanda Guerlovich. The cast otherwise is solid at best—Latko Koroshetz a firm king, Danilo Merlak a nicely nasty Leander, Bogdana Stritar a properly menacing Clarissa. Drago Chuden keeps Truffaldino from seeming too ridiculous.

p. 1962 EMI / ANGEL (S)

Tatiana Kallistratova (A), Nina Poliakova (B), Lyutsia Rashkovets (C), Vladimir Makhov (D),

Yuri Yelnikov (E), Boris Dobrin (F), Viktor Ribinsky (G), Moscow Radio Chorus and Orchestra—Dzhemal Dalgat

As the first recording of *Oranges* to gain wide, international release, and the only one readily accessible for practically two decades, this performance served to introduce a generation of listeners to Prokofiev's opera. But it may also have served to give a generation the wrong idea about the tone of the work. However Russian the opera may be, the Russian performance tradition of it by the 1960s had become something of a collection of bad habits, turning sophisticated farce into heavy-handed, one-dimensional slapstick, with every character becoming a grotesque buffoon. Worse, this burlesque exaggeration is pretty much all you get, this being primarily a singers' performance, thanks to flabby conducting and a flat recorded acoustic in which the orchestra is recessed. Makhov surely makes a farcical Prince, but his paroxysms of passion become laughable in the wrong sense. Often heavy vibrato shows up, sometimes effectively as in a truly absurd role as the Cook, for which Georgy Abramov's hoarse bass is just right. But Ribinsky plays the King as if he were a parody of Boris. Poliakova is a screechy Fata Morgana, Rashkovets a hectoring Clarissa, Yelnikov a tiresomely hysterical Truffaldino.

1989 VIRGIN (In French) (S,D) CD

Catherine Dubosc (A), Michèle Lagrange (B), Helene Perraguin (C), Jean-Luc Viala (D), Georges Gautier (E), Vincent Le Texier (F), Gabriel Bacquier (G) Lyons Opera Chorus and Orchestra—Kent Nagano

Oranges can seem practically a different opera when sung in French and presented by a French opera company. Gone, here, is all that bluster of the Angel / Melodiya version, replaced instead by refined playfulness. The opera could withstand, perhaps, a bit more slapstick, but it is not missed when in its place is a far more sophisticated sense of fantastical atmosphere. The hero of the set is Nagano, who leads a precise and musical account of the score, full of wit and color. He gets fleet and finely nuanced playing from his orchestra, and he integrates the constantly changeable score with considerable finesse and charm, rather than taking the easier approach of emphasizing contrast. There is far less clowning from the singers in this performance than in the Russian sets, as if the drama were more fanciful than farcical. Viala is a lyric tenor who turns slightly hoarse when he tries to push, but he is a believable Prince, whose coming out of his melancholic cocoon is touching rather than absurd. Dubosc's Ninetta is all sweetness and floated high notes. There is none of the bloated Boris to Bacquier's King, but rather a nobility that, in the circumstances, is actually funnier. The other singers are all honorable but Jules Bastin, the only Cook who actually sings the role as music, not sheer hysteria, alone stands out. That is the beauty of this performance, the seamless ensemble work of the Lyons company, which brings the polish of its stage performance to the recording studio. The CD sound is also suave and beautiful.

While the old Leskovich set serves the Russian version fairly well, and is the most dramatic performance, the opera itself benefits the most from the sophisticated French version on Virgin.

MARK SWED

SERGEI PROKOFIEV

WAR AND PEACE (1945)

A: Natasha (s); B: Sonya (ms); C: Hélène (ms); D: Pierre (t); E: Anatol (t);
F: Andrei (bar); G: Napoleon (bar); H: Kutuzov (bs)

*L*ike so many Russian operas, *War and Peace* has not come down to us in a definitive, composer-approved edition. Prokofiev began work on his sprawling operatic adaptation of Tolstoy's epic novel in 1941, and he was still tinkering with it when he died in 1953. The problem is not the state of the score, which is as complete as Prokofiev apparently intended it to be and contains over four hours of music, but how much of it to perform. The opera splits neatly down the middle, part 1 dealing with the unhappy love affair of Natasha Rostova and Andrei Bolkonsky, and part 2 with Napoleon's invasion of Russia. But the loosely connected sequence of scenes in both halves inevitably encourages conductors and directors to help themselves to as much, or as little, as seems appropriate to the occasion. Judging from the 1960 and 1982 Bolshoi recordings, both of which use an edition that trims around forty-five minutes' worth of music from the "war" section, the Soviets decided early on what worked for them. We in the West are still testing options, and the three non-Russian recordings differ radically in what is included and what is left out.

1958 M-G-M (S)

Radmilla Vasovic-Bakocevic (A), Biserka Cvejic (B), Milica Miladinovic (C), Alexander Marinkovich (D), Drago Starc (E), Dushan Popovich (F), Nikola Cvelic (G), Djordje Djurdejevic

(H), Vienna Chamber Chorus, Vienna Opera Orchestra—Werner Janssen

Recorded in Vienna with singers from the Belgrade National Opera, this performance might more accurately be described as highlights from *War and Peace*, since almost half the opera has been omitted. Two long scenes (Nos. 7 and 11) are dispensed with entirely, reducing the important character of Pierre to little more than a walk-on. Beyond that, so many cuts are made in the other eleven scenes that a listener scarcely has an inkling of the work's scope and Prokofiev's considerable accomplishment in translating Tolstoy's vision into operatic terms. Vasovic-Bakocevic's poignant Natasha provides a few moments of pleasure (she sang briefly at the Met in the late 1960s), but the other soloists are uniformly undistinguished, as is Janssen's faceless presentation of the colorful score. Unfortunately, this pioneering but sadly misrepresentative recording may have given many people a false first impression of *War and Peace*, turning them off the opera for good.

1960 MELODIYA (S)

Galina Vishnevskaya (A), Valentina Klepatskaya (B), Irina Arkhipova (C), Vladimir Petrov (D), Alexei Maslennikov (E), Yevgeny Kibkalo (F), Pavel Lisitsian (G), Alexei Krivchenya (H), Bolshoi Theater Chorus and Orchestra—Alexander Melik-Pashayev

This is essentially the cast of the Bolshoi's premiere production of the opera in 1959, a performance that still commands attention, despite the severe cuts in part 2. The singers' recent stage experience with the piece, and possibly memories of the late composer, could account for the energy and commitment, particularly from Vishnevskaya, a young, fragile, and passionately involved Natasha. With the exception of Arkhipova's glamorous Hélène and Lisitsian's *bel canto* Napoleon, the singers have the wide vibrato and cutting edge that have characterized so many Slavic-trained voices of the postwar generation, qualities that always seem to disturb Western ears. If one does not demand the last word in creamy vocalism, though, there is much to savor in Kibkalo's dreamily idealistic Andrei, Krivchenya's iron-willed Kutuzov, Maslennikov's oily Anatol, and a host of lively Bolshoi *comprimarios*. Melik-Pashayev may not have been the most spellbinding Russian conductor of his generation, but he was a crafty professional who effectively projected the important theatrical and musical features of each opera placed under his care. Mostly, though, this is a cohesive, alive ensemble effort by a real opera company responding to a mighty operatic challenge.

1982 MELODIYA (S)

Galina Kalinina (A), Nina Terentieva (B), Tamara Sinyavskaya (C), Yevgeny Raikov (D), Yevgeny Shapin (E), Yuri Mazurok (F), Alexander Voroshilo (G), Alexander Vedernikov (H), Bolshoi Theater Chorus and Orchestra—Mark Ermler

The Bolshoi's second recording of *War and Peace* is a disappointment. Using essentially the same version of the score as before, with even a few extra small cuts, the performance has none of the vitality and onstage spirit of its predecessor. Ermler hustles the proceedings along smartly, but his perfunctory direction only creates a depressing aura of routine, to which the cast all too obligingly contributes. Most of the singers have more conventionally "pretty" voices than their 1960 counterparts, no doubt a plus for sensitive ears, but the smoother sounds also mean blander interpretations. Mazurok's finely grained baritone largely goes to waste, and his

Prince Andrei is not much more than a cipher. Kalinina sings more sweetly than Vishnevskaya, although her Natasha is so neutral that one is scarcely aware of her. At least Vedernikov's gritty Kutuzov registers strongly (apparently this is one of those fail-safe Russian bass roles), but there are few memorable performances from the other principals. Even the sonics are inferior, although that may be partially the fault of the pressings I heard. The 1960 recording, on a British-mastered EMI set, has considerably more detail, impact, and atmospheric presence than the 1982 version that has been circulating in the West on foggy-sounding discs from France's Chant du Monde label.

1986 BALKANTON (S) CD

Roumyana Bareva (A), Veneta Radoeva (B), Stefka Mineva (C), Petko Marinov (D), Konstantin Yankov (E), Lyubomir Videnov (F), Stoil Geogiev (G), Stefan Elenkov (H), Chorus and Orchestra of the Sofia National Opera—Rouslan Raichev

This is an earnest, well-prepared, solidly sung provincial performance that one would be happy to encounter on an evening in Sofia, but not necessarily at home on the phonograph, given the recorded alternatives. The standard Bolshoi edition is used, with minor exceptions: Prokofiev's short Overture replaces the choral epitaph at the beginning of the opera, and there are a few tiny restorations in scene 11, which depicts the sacking of Moscow. Otherwise, the hardworking cast is not particularly distinctive apart from Elenkov, who brings more sonorous tone to Kutuzov's big aria than his recorded counterparts. Perhaps the most serious drawback is the orchestra, which sounds rather scrawny and in need of more rehearsal.

1986 ERATO (S,D) CD

Galina Vishnevskaya (A), Katherine Ciesinski (B), Stefania Toczyska (C), Wieslaw Ochman (D), Nicolai Gedda (E), Lajos Miller (F), Eduard Tumagian (G), Nicola Ghiuselev (H), Chorus of Radio France, National Orchestra of France—Mstislav Rostropovich

With this recording, Rostropovich set out to fulfill the mission that, he tells us, was assigned to him by the dying Prokofiev: to make *War and Peace*, in its fullest form, known throughout the world. More music may possibly be unearthed one day, but for now this edition must be regarded as note-complete and, for that reason alone, indispensable. The performance itself does not render the 1960 Bolshoi edition obsolete, but the dedicatory atmosphere is equally intense. Rostropovich is clearly an inspirational presence, and if he does not command ideally idiomatic choral and orchestral forces (ironically, in this of all operas, an army of French musicians), they respond enthusiastically and skillfully to his fiery direction. Vishnevskaya repeats her Natasha, and although most of what she achieves is now accomplished through clenched teeth and will power, her soprano still retains much of its characteristic quality, and her detailed impersonation is even more vivid. Miller is in the tradition of smoothly vocalized but dramatically blank Andreis, except in the death scene, where he paradoxically comes to life and sings in moving, hushed *mezza voce* tones.

In assembling the rest of his cast, Rostropovich ingeniously drew on the available pool of Russian-opera specialists active in the West. The seducer Anatol is entrusted to Nicolai Gedda, who proves he can still give a most convincing portrayal of a dashing rake. Pierre emerges as the true hero of the opera, now that we can hear the complete role at last, and Wieslaw Ochman's plangent tenor conveys all of this wonderful character's naiveté, questioning spirit, and deep concern for everything and everyone around him. As Kutuzov, Nicola Ghiuselev is appropriately crusty and cavernous, although an even richer, more rolling bass would be welcome in the General's much expanded apostrophe to Russia before ordering the evacuation of Moscow. Forty other soloists, some in multiple roles, contribute positively to this United Nations effort, clearly a labor of love on behalf of an opera that seems increasingly important as time passes.

The Bolshoi's second recording of the opera is perhaps the most idiomatic and consistently satisfying, vocally and orchestrally. That must remain first choice, but Rostropovich's dedicated performance of the complete score is a necessary adjunct for anyone with a special interest in Prokofiev's awesome effort.

PETER G. DAVIS

Unavailable for review:
1992 PHILIPS

JOAN RIVERS
Comedienne

1. **Puccini,** *Turandot*: Nilsson, Tebaldi, Bjoerling, de Paolis, Sereni, Tozzi—Leinsdorf. RCA / BMG

2. **Bellini,** *La Sonnambula*: Callas, Monti, Zaccaria—Votto. EMI / ANGEL

3. **Bellini,** *Norma*: Callas, Stignani, Filippeschi, Rossi-Lemeni—Serafin. EMI / ANGEL

4. **Puccini,** *Madama Butterfly*: Tebaldi, Cossotto, Bergonzi, Sordello—Serafin. DECCA / LONDON

5. **Bellini,** *I Puritani*: Sutherland, Pavarotti, Cappuccilli, Ghiaurov—Bonynge. DECCA / LONDON

6. **Strauss,** *Der Rosenkavalier*: Stich-Randall, Schwarzkopf, Ludwig, Wächter, Edelmann—Karajan. EMI / ANGEL

7. **Mussorgsky,** *Boris Godunov* (excerpts): Rossi-Lemeni—Stokowski. RCA / BMG

8. **Bizet,** *Carmen*: Resnik, Sutherland, del Monaco, Krause—Schippers. DECCA / LONDON

9. **Giordano,** *Andrea Chénier*: Stella, Corelli, Sereni—Santini. EMI / ANGEL

10. **Puccini,** *La Bohème*: Freni, Harwood, Pavarotti, Panerai, Maffeo, Ghiaurov—Karajan. DECCA / LONDON

GIACOMO PUCCINI

MANON LESCAUT (1893)

A: Manon (s); B: Chevalier des Grieux (t); C: Edmondo (t);
D: Lescaut (bar); E: Geronte (bs)

Manon Lescaut, written 1890–92, was Puccini's first international success. Manon may be the most difficult of all Puccini heroines to cast really well, for she must convey the impression of extreme youth in the first act, demonstrate considerable vocal flexibility in the second, and yet possess the vocal weight to balance a full ensemble in the third and to surmount the heavy orchestration in the highly charged drama of the fourth. Of course, these elements must be unified by a dramatic approach that sustains interest in the opera as a whole. Manon is seen against a somewhat broad range of events and milieux, from flirtation at Amiens to a *levée* at Geronte's house, to dishonor and then, in the wilds of America, an agonizing death. The soprano must demonstrate the capacity to express not only deep romantic feeling and extreme physical suffering, but also shallowness, vanity, and calculation—all of them qualities which must be made in some way bewitching. Too light a voice may be strained, and too heavy a voice, especially on records, destroys the illusion of Manon's fragility and indecisiveness. The role of des Grieux makes almost equally broad demands: he must be both the *gallant* and the passionate lover in the first two acts, with something of the heroic in his voice for the last two.

The history of complete recordings of *Manon Lescaut* has not been particularly happy. Until the 1950s, there was only one such set, so that we have none of the most memorable Puccini sopranos of the twenties and early thirties in complete renditions. With two or three brilliant exceptions, discussed below, the work of later participants has not been strikingly individual or persuasive.

1931 EMI / ANGEL (M)

Maria Zamboni (A), Francesco Merli (B), Giuseppe Nessi (C), Lorenzo Conati (D), Attilio Bordonali (E), La Scala Chorus and Orchestra—Lorenzo Molajoli

This earliest complete *Manon Lescaut* is interesting in that it preserves the routine practice of a time quite distinct from our own. The performance is rushed, impetuous, and open-hearted but rough—in contrast to our own time, when commonplace performances of such repertory are generally bland, wobbly, or eccentrically paced. Lorenzo Molajoli is, as usual, more successful at the vivacious than at the expansively romantic. That benefits Act I, when the crowd is allowed no time to languish over its spirited music. Elsewhere the playing can be metronomic and restless, and the singers often lack the time to build phrasing as they might. Of them, Francesco Merli is the most intriguing. He has a voice without much of the sweet softness of timbre essential to des Grieux, but he really does try for a certain noble intimacy, and, in his nonchalant opening aria, "Tra voi, belle," has an occasional smile in the voice. His tone is fresh throughout and, with its bright vibrato, thrilling on top. In Act IV, he sounds more like Otello than an exhausted youth, but it's a more thoughtful performance than one might expect.

Maria Zamboni, who was the first Liù, has a touching if uneven Puccini voice that cuts through the violins. It is also occasionally rough and colorless in the middle, and she can't shape the music nearly as artfully as more memorable sopranos of her time, but even so the perfume of another age clings to this rather perfunctory performance. Lorenzo Conati and Giuseppe Nessi, as Lescaut and Edmondo, are cynical when required, but neither suggests youth or much of a sense of fun. As a whole the set is notable mainly as a sample of the ordinary stylistic assumptions of a period close to Puccini's own.

1953 CETRA (M)

Clara Petrella (A), Vasco Campagnano (B), Tullio Pane (C), Saturno Meletti (D), Pier Luigi Latinucci (E), Italian Radio-Television Chorus and Orchestra, Turin—Federico del Cupolo

Puccini's lyric soprano heroines are delicate but dynamic. Within their limits they shift emotionally from moment to moment, and it is that changing pattern of delight, fervor, and despair that gives them their vitality. Manon is in turn playful, thoughtless, elegant, passionate, and exhausted, and the singer must suggest the constant play of these capacities within a vocal style that gives the character continuity. Clara Petrella has both fervency and a colorful voice. Her first act has a suggestion of the adventurous, her second considerable ardor, and Acts III and IV are full of industrious suffering, but she has not dug deeply enough into the music to make Manon more than a generically *verismo* heroine. Her lyric effects are sometimes smudged: the introduction to "In quelle trine morbide," for example, is not as pensive as she could make it, and in the aria the high notes are just a tad flat and the *legato* effortful. Without such delicate detail the characterization emerges as hearty rather than charming.

Vasco Campagnano is a knotty, rugged des Grieux with a beat in the middle of his voice. The mad lover is there, but not the poet or the aristocrat. The impassioned outcries of Act III go better than the rest, but the voice seems to be wearing out as we listen. Saturno Meletti is a grasping, practical, older Lescaut: more Geronte's crony, it would seem, than a young soldier on the make. Federico del Cupolo conducts a performance of spirit and more finish than Molajoli's, but he does not shape the big moments with the precision that can make this score overwhelming.

1954 DECCA / LONDON (S) CD

Renata Tebaldi (A), Mario del Monaco (B), Piero de Palma (C), Mario Boriello (D), Fernando Corena (E), Chorus and Orchestra of the Accademia di Santa Cecilia, Rome—Francesco Molinari-Pradelli

Renata Tebaldi is in sumptuous voice here—rich, firm, and flowing—a trifle shrill at the top but elsewhere inimitably full. The arias in Acts II and IV are handled with great care, and the *pianissimo* tone, when she uses it, is exemplary. But what has her characterization to do with *Manon Lescaut?* She sings with an admirably mature self-possession, and sometimes a cold command, that mocks any pretense that this is Puccini's flirtatious, irresolute, winsome heroine. In Act II she coerces rather than tantalizes her admirers, in Act III she sounds mildly inconvenienced and unpleasant about deportation, and in Act IV the tone is grandly outspoken, rather as if Puccini had written music for Cleopatra or Hippolyta.

As des Grieux, Mario del Monaco provides equally glorious tones in bronze but lacks Tebaldi's dynamic control. There is a promising moment of courtliness when he first meets Manon, but both "Tra voi, belle" and "Donna non vidi mai" sound inappropriately angry. The Act II love duet elicits striking sounds from both of them but no image of affection. "Ah, Manon, mi tradisce," filled with a self-righteous sense of betrayal, is his best moment. His outburst at the close of Act III is punctuated by crying that sounds like laughter, and in Act IV his splendid challenge to the heavens goes for almost nothing because we have heard similar effects so often from him previously.

As Lescaut, Mario Boriello gives us a few charming moments of compliance and good humor at the close of Act I, but elsewhere there is little evidence of the irony, self-satisfaction, or opportunism of the man, and his voice is sometimes covered by the orchestra. Fernando Corena plays Geronte effectively for polished brutality; he really plots with the innkeeper in Act I. Francesco Molinari-Pradelli conducts a spirited but impersonal performance. He's not destructive, like some conductors of this score, but his reading has speed without much animation. He is dealing with exceptionally headstrong lovers.

1954 RCA / BMG (M) CD

Licia Albanese (A), Jussi Bjoerling (B), Mario Carlin (C), Robert Merrill (D), Franco Calabrese (E), Rome Opera Chorus and Orchestra—Jonel Perlea

There are some recordings that forever redefine what one hears. A Patzak suddenly epitomizes the vision of Hoffmann, or a Patti, recording at an age when she can hardly clamber through the notes, illuminates in some immortal way the youthful intimacy of a Bellini aria. There is in Licia Albanese's portrayal of Manon Lescaut much of that effect. I know well the criticism of some of her vocalism in it, but the basic tone is yielding and inimitable: at once frail, charming, courageous, and despairing. That makes the portrayal attractive; what makes it unforgettable is the singer's attention to detail and evocation of so many layers of understanding. The voice at the start may not be precisely that of a girl of eighteen, but the opening is simply and modestly performed, as the libretto specifies, and the approach full of youthful wonder. Her recollection of home is filled with nostalgia (we see at once that Manon not only enjoys but fabricates romance) and her elopement with des Grieux seems here the essence of impulse. At the start of Act II, we see fully the pampered Manon, and yet she makes even that touching, and not the repellent thing of so many grander or rougher Manons. In later moments, the girlish delight, the longing, the

vanity, and the lassitude are both captivating and infuriating, as they should be, even when the vocalism is on occasion not entirely graceful. The meeting of lovers in Act III projects quite a different image: the longing is still vibrant, but exhausted. The deportation scene, one of Puccini's most striking passages, is beautifully structured, with gradations of intensity and a climax from Albanese that seem, once they are heard, inevitable. The final act is here an intensification of the qualities of Manon seen so vividly before. The aria is desperately visionary; the singer has the unique gift of expressing emotional strength and physical fragility at the same time. Altogether it is one of the most moving and complete characterizations on records.

As des Grieux, Jussi Bjoerling is in glowing voice and impassioned mood. He is the captivated *gallant* in Act I, and in Act II manages to suggest intimacy even as he is singing *forte*. In "Ah, Manon, mi tradisce," he rises through grief and frustration to a climax suffused with anguish but not strained by it. In Acts III and IV the idealism and heartbreak increase and yet the singer never loses tonal beauty and a certain grace of manner: a memorable achievement. The others are in healthy voice. Robert Merrill is an unsubtle but good-humored Lescaut; it is a pleasure to hear a first-class baritone in this role. Franco Calabrese as Geronte has a handsome voice with a vibrant core. He sounds mature, manipulative, and even, interestingly, attractive. The chorus is not always neat in Act I, but Jonel Perlea supports his soloists brilliantly, balancing languor with agitation and building exciting climaxes without distorting the music. It is a set that expands one's understanding of Puccini's achievement.

1957 EMI / ANGEL (M) CD

Maria Callas (A), Giuseppe di Stefano (B), Dino Formichini (C), Giulio Fioravanti (D), Franco Calabrese (E), La Scala Chorus and Orchestra—Tullio Serafin

Maria Callas gives us a Manon Lescaut entirely unlike anyone else's, and perhaps closer to Prévost's heroine than to Puccini's. She cannot, or does not wish to, offer warmth, openness, and vivacity: what she gives is a picture of magnetic self-interest and, at the same time, need. One of the paradoxes of Callas's performances is that her heroines (Medea and Norma, for example), who seem to direct the fate of all around them, can nevertheless suggest complete dependence on the men whose fate they determine. Something of that paradox lies at the center of this performance, too. In Act I she manages to suggest innocence and at the same time a conscious total surrender to the romance that des Grieux brings into her life. The opening of Act II is delicate and yet full of longing, but the love duet is not so much a declaration of passion as an opportunity for her exquisitely calculated extraction of a statement of love from des Grieux. Acts III and IV work less well. The vivid sense of what Manon can give is needed to make her fate touching: pathos is precisely what is lacking. Her death scene is well sculpted but has a certain chilly monumentality which seems to lack spontaneity. She is also in unreliable voice for this exceptionally demanding passage.

As des Grieux, Giuseppe di Stefano is likewise imaginative, though he forces in the later acts. "Tra voi, belle" is lightly dismissive of love, and in that context his first scene with Manon seems all the more charming and courtly and "Donna non vidi mai" the more passionately reflective. His voice in the early acts is just as one might expect: forward, and a little hard and nasal at moments of stress, but generally captivating. In Act III he is effortful and in Act IV strained; there his conception and method seem to call for the heroic resources of a Pertile. As for the others, Giulio Fioravanti's Lescaut is light-voiced and practical, and Franco Calabrese is less vividly recorded than in the Perlea set. Dino Formichini has a warm sound for the mercurial Edmondo. Tullio Serafin is authoritative but hasn't the special urgency and plasticity of Perlea, and in Act IV seems to demand more of his singers tonally than they can give. Nevertheless, the set is memorable for the interplay between Callas and di Stefano in Acts I and II.

1971 EMI / ANGEL (S) CD

Montserrat Caballé (A), Plácido Domingo (B), Robert Tear (C), Vicente Sardinero (D), Noel Mangin (E), Ambrosian Opera Chorus, New Philharmonia Orchestra—Bruno Bartoletti

Montserrat Caballé is in ravishing voice in nearly all of this recording. Her sound is fresh, rich, and fluent, the soft singing as lovely as any you will hear, and the phrasing and breath beautifully controlled. The entire role, though, is performed in her habitual tone of melancholy resignation, which is entirely applicable only in Act III. Act I, for example, betrays no sense of impetuous youth: she sounds as if she is being sent to that convent at the age of about thirty. There is a world of difference between this sedateness and the ingenuousness of Callas or the vivacity of Albanese, both of whom could be said to have an older sound than Caballé. Her tone is incomparably smooth in both "In quelle trine morbide" and "L'ora o Tirsi," but a single excerpt tells the whole story of her Manon.

Plácido Domingo is in rich voice and offers a passionate characterization, though he often seems to be playing into a dramatic void. In his opening scene the voice is a little thick: "Tra voi, belle" has not quite the radiance or gaiety implicit in the music. He is at his best in Act III, expressing the agony well. In Act IV there are some unconvincing tears, but otherwise he outdoes himself in frustrated conviction. Vicente Sardinero is a pleasant Lescaut. As Edmondo, Robert Tear is rushed by the orchestra. The voice is sizable but neither sensuous nor ironic in tone. Noel Mangin plays Geronte for repulsiveness. Bruno Bartoletti, as noted, is rather heartlessly fast at the start, but reasonably passionate in the rest. Much of the orchestral comment goes for relatively little, though, with such an unvaried heroine.

1983 DEUTSCHE GRAMMOPHON (S) CD

Mirella Freni (A), Plácido Domingo (B), Robert Gambill (C), Renato Bruson (D), Kurt Rydl (E), Chorus and Orchestra of the Royal Opera House, Covent Garden—Giuseppe Sinopoli

This performance manages to be both dull and infuriating. It is dominated by its conductor, who has an ear for orchestral color but who exploits the score for the obvious in a frenzy of extreme tempos. Continuity and subtlety are both destroyed. The love duet will do for an example; it is by turns thumpingly sentimental and inexpressively fast. The Intermezzo is interminable, and Act III begins in deepest Wagnerian gloom but speeds up alarmingly when the choristers enter. Manon herself is almost obliterated in the ensemble, which, in a sense, exists to dramatize her suffering. Sinopoli's Act IV vacillates between rambling and bombast. The orchestra and chorus perform these feats expertly, but the characters are largely reduced to anonymity, since the singers cannot develop natural vocal climaxes or color such distortions expressively. Mirella Freni vocalizes very well, with considerable grace and a suggestion of suffering in the finale. Her performance remains pretty but unconvincing. It is not that big theatrical gestures must be made to animate this music. Quite the contrary: in this performance an innumerable series of small but telling vocal effects has been scuttled.

Plácido Domingo sings with a generally rich and mature tone; his performance lacks intimacy and a certain youthful glow. His best moment is "Ah, Manon, mi tradisce," done with feeling but without exaggeration. Renato Bruson is a precise but humorless Lescaut, and Kurt Rydl plays Geronte so heavily that he loses interest as a character. Brigitte Fassbaender sounds a little unsteady in the Madrigal, which is, for once, played at a pleasant tempo. None of the others has much sense of character. Thus the performance emerges as bland, expert, and eccentric all at once.

198–(?) RCA ITALIANA (BULGARIA) (S)

Raina Kabaivanska (A), Giuseppe Giacomini (B), Lyubomir Dyakovski (C), Nelson Portella (D), Giancarlo Lucciardi (E), Bulgarian Television and Radio Mixed Chorus and Symphony Orchestra—Angelo Campori

This set promises to be more interesting than it is. Angelo Campori, Giuseppe Giacomini, and Raina Kabaivanska have all appeared at the Metropolitan and none of them has recorded very widely. Campori, though, conducts a listless performance, the orchestral commentary muted and often unshaped for dramatic revelation. Giuseppe Giacomini is the strongest of the cast members, full-voiced but prosaic in this role, with little romance in Act I or impetuous passion elsewhere. Like many tenors, he is more potent in Act IV than earlier, but the dramatic voltage around him is low. As Manon, Raina Kabaivanska has a fairly large, dark voice, reasonably steady, and some effective high notes. The portrayal lacks thoughtful dramatic detail and development. Nelson Portella is a light-voiced and bland Lescaut, and the others are generally ineffective.

1987 DECCA / LONDON (S,D) CD

Kiri Te Kanawa (A), José Carreras (B), William Matteuzzi (C), Paolo Coni (D), Italo Tajo (E), Chorus and Orchestra of the Teatro Communale, Bologna—Riccardo Chailly

This is another disappointing set, despite the réclame of some of its cast and a few interesting supporting characterizations. Riccardo Chailly's conducting is alternately skittish and casual, so that Act I sometimes lacks warmth and the rest continuity and drive. He is at his best at the start of Act II, where his quick tempos are a blessing for Kiri Te Kanawa, who seems to have little to say about Manon. She has a lovely voice and muses nicely in "In quelle trine morbide." "L'ora o Tirsi" is also sung lightly and well, but elsewhere much of Manon's passion simply remains unexpressed. In "Sola, perduta, abbandonata," her quick vibrato provides an element of excitement, but the performance remains cool and self-possessed. José Carreras projects a stronger sense of the progression from romance to desperation, though he is in rather poor voice. His rawness becomes a trifle more suitable as the opera continues, but it is particularly in Acts III and IV that the orchestra supporting him loses impetus.

Paolo Coni has the right voice for Lescaut and is one of the few to bring charm, irony, and a sense of practicality to the role. Italo Tajo offers a very detailed and ripely sung Geronte: the unpleasant amusement, the attempts at delicacy, the outrage, and the brutality are all there. William Matteuzzi, with a warm voice for Edmondo, suggests the part's wit and romance. Nevertheless, the neutrality of its soprano and conductor and the roughness of its leading tenor limit the set's appeal.

———————

One will find attractive vocalism per se in several of the albums (Tebaldi's, Caballé's, Freni's, Te Kanawa's) but hardly a hint among them of who this fascinating creature Manon may be. For that one must turn to Albanese, recording a little late in her career, but at once summing up a tradition and placing her own inimitable stamp of passion on the role. Luckily her des Grieux is Bjoerling and her conductor the impassioned Perlea. In other recordings, Callas, in uneven voice, offers an intriguing comment on the heroine, Domingo is in representative form for des Grieux, and di Stefano and Merli offer flawed but interesting characterizations.

LONDON GREEN

Unavailable for review:
1992 SONY

GIACOMO PUCCINI

LA BOHÈME (1896)

A: Mimì (s); B: Musetta (s); C: Rodolfo (t); D: Marcello (bar);
E: Schaunard (bar); F: Colline (bs)

The libretto of Puccini's opera took three times as long to put together as the score. From Henri Murger's ramshackle novel of Bohemian life in the Paris of the 1830s, Puccini wanted to extract a special essence: a greater mixture of warmth, intimacy, humor, extravagance, and passion than had been seen on the operatic stage before, even in his own work. Puccini had his own vision of *verismo* (realism), which was characterized by a crossing of genres often experienced in life but seldom on the stage. It marks much of his work from *Manon Lescaut* through the *Trittico* and *Turandot*, but in no other opera are those elements quite so thoroughly integrated as in *La Bohème*. It is largely the quality of that integration that caused Puccini to fight with his librettists. Even Benoit, the landlord, can be played in alternate ways, and basses and conductors are always haggling over the speed at which Colline's Coat Song is to be sung: is it sentimental or ironic, or both? The leading characters have even more of that rich potential, and the great singers of *Bohème* have been able to project both the joy and the sentiment. The Puccini singing style took a while to develop. In the formation of that tradition, the names of Rosina Storchio, Lucrezia Bori, Gilda dalla Rizza, Rosetta Pampanini, and Beniamino Gigli, among a dozen others, come to mind. Whatever their limitations may have been, they all had the capacity to suggest that complex response. They had a generation of distinguished followers, but what was once a central approach to

Puccini's music has become very rare indeed. One need only compare the recordings of, say, Pampanini in the 1920s with any of the latest Mimìs to see this. Increasingly, too, the concept of the conductor as the central figure has influenced performance, with further effect on the expressive capacities of singers and the orchestral-vocal relationship, as the sixty years of complete recordings of *Bohème* surveyed below demonstrate.

1928 EMI / ANGEL (M)

Rosina Torri (A), Marisa Vitulli (B), Aristodemo Giorgini (C), Ernesto Badini (D), Aristide Baracchi (E), Luigi Manfrini (F), La Scala Chorus and Orchestra—Carlo Sabajno

This set is memorable more for the spirit of the ensemble under Carlo Sabajno than for individual vocal contributions. The opening is full of wintry youthful energy, even if the voices are a little aged, and the duet at the end of Act I has charming flow. Act II is sparkling despite a harsh Musetta, and Acts III and IV are persuasively paced though sometimes a little fast for complete expressivity. As Rodolfo, Aristodemo Giorgini discloses a high, full tenor, rather thick and aging in the middle but freer at the top. The Act I aria is transposed downward, a rather jarring moment on the cassette reissue. He is energetic if not especially poetic or graceful, and is most at home in the outspoken moments of Act III.

Rosina Torri is a reasonably charming Mimì.

The voice has color and sting but is sometimes precarious at the top. There is no special grace in her phrasing, but the "Addio" is expansively done and in Act IV she is touching and direct. Ernesto Badini is an energetic Marcello. The voice lacks youth and sometimes warmth but has at moments a comically saturnine quality. Oddly, though, in Act III he seems bad-tempered rather than amusingly exasperated. Aristide Baracchi is, as always (he recorded the role four times), a delightful Schaunard. Every line has specific dramatic intention. Luigi Manfrini has a meaty voice and delivers an affectionate Colline; he kisses his coat noisily before his final "addio." Salvatore Baccaloni is a robust and, at this early point in his career, straightforward Benoit. The whole of the performance is better than its parts, and spontaneous in a way that some much better sung and more subtly acted sets are not: a pleasant reminder of an earlier age.

1928 EMI / ANGEL (M)

Rosetta Pampanini (A), Luba Mirella (B), Luigi Marini (C), Gino Vanelli (D), Aristide Baracchi (E), Tancredi Pasero (F), La Scala Chorus and Orchestra—Lorenzo Molajoli

I could obtain only excerpts from this recording, and they did not include "Che gelida manina," anything from Act II, or "Ah, Mimì, tu più." As Rodolfo, Luigi Marini has a bright, focused voice of the right weight. There is little poetry in his sound, but his work is lively and impassioned in Act III. Rosetta Pampanini's Mimì is the memorable thing in the set; she has a large, lovely tone with a romantic fragrance. Her voice, delicately used, is a little dark; it is not surprising that she later sang Leonora (La Forza del Destino) and Aida. The characterization is generously felt, if without quite the detail of others of her school such as Favero, Olivero, and Albanese. Act IV is touchingly phrased and full of feeling.

Gino Vanelli is a warm, vibrant Marcello. Luba Mirella as Musetta sounds a little coarse but also concerned in her Act IV prayer; in Act III she has some dreadful laughs, right on mike. Tancredi Pasero provides an outstandingly beautiful and vibrant voice for "Vecchia zimarra," which he sings without much imagination but at a bracing tempo. Lorenzo Molajoli, as usual, paces some of the opera well, but tends to rush the singers a little, as in Mimì's "Addio" and at the very end. The recording offers in Pampanini's performance a winning example of the Puccini vocal style in the years just after his death.

1938 EMI / ANGEL (M) CD

Licia Albanese (A), Tatiana Menotti (B), Beniamino Gigli (C), Afro Poli (D), Aristide Baracchi (E), Duilio Baronti (F), La Scala Chorus and Orchestra—Umberto Berrettoni

This famous set offers both a delightful ensemble and many memorable individual portrayals in a generously emotional yet subtle style which seems to have left us. It is the only recording in which all of the major singers evince a delightful sense of humor. Beniamino Gigli, for all his mannerisms, sings with unmatched golden tone and expansive lyricism. Here is a Rodolfo in love with extravagant emotionalism and yet with a marvelous enjoyment of his own prodigality. For beautiful tone and infectious sentimental verve, his "Questa è Mimì" has never been equaled. In Act III, he enters full of self-concern which under Marcello's comic attack then turns to anguish; the manner and the voice combine to make the moment overwhelming. Earlier, the climax of "Che gelida manina" is a trifle strained, but his performance of the closing scene of the opera remains unmatched for spontaneity.

At the start of her career, Licia Albanese was already a marvelous Mimì, full of fragile charm and fervency. She has an unique mixture of passion and simplicity; she does not become coy, nor does she sacrifice feeling to modesty. The climax of her first-act aria has both rapture and reserve. In Act III, the voice remains youthful but has become colored with illness, and in Act IV her realization of the death scene is masterful. Afro Poli gives us one of the liveliest and warmest Marcellos on records. In the scenes with Gigli he projects a genuine sense of musical conversation, and his moments with Musetta are endearing in their amusing overstatement. The others are equally engaging. Umberto Berrettoni provides fine continuity and tempos that are always right for the expressive capacities of his singers. Even with its rather dated sound, this is one of the great *Bohèmes*.

1946 RCA / BMG (M,P) CD

Licia Albanese (A), Ann McKnight (B), Jan Peerce (C), Francesco Valentino (D), George Cehanovsky (E), Nicola Moscona (F), Chorus and NBC Symphony Orchestra—Arturo Toscanini

This recording is taken from the NBC broadcasts of February 3 and 10, 1946, fifty years after the world premiere, also conducted by Arturo Toscanini. It is unforgettable for his contribution and those of two of his singers. The conductor leads a brisk performance, sparkling with continual accesses of energy. Some of the conversational passages between the Bohemians lack a little in elasticity and good humor, but they are always vigorous, and in Act II the chorus really sounds like a joyful Christmas throng. Despite the somewhat restricted sound, one hears more of the orchestral commentary, so flavorful in this opera, than in almost any other set. The great lyric moments have an urgency, an immediacy, unique to this conductor. In Act IV one feels the pulse of life and the chill of death at one and the same time.

Jan Peerce sings a manly, passionate Rodolfo, the voice splendidly even and forthright throughout its range. The portrayal is not particularly visionary or youthfully easy in the first act, but in Acts III and IV he is full of outspoken tragic commitment. His phrasing is very musical and the tone quality alone often gripping. Licia Albanese's Mimì is larger in voice than in her previous set; she was in her sixth season at the Metropolitan. This is a very loving Mimì, sung with great finish. One need only hear Torri and Pampanini in earlier complete sets to realize the detail she has worked out beyond their tradition. Her first-act aria, discovery in Act III, "Addio," and death scene are highlights of her performance; the youth, the passion, and the illness are completely realized, and yet the characterization and vocal tone could be none but hers.

The others are all less striking but given a great lift by their surroundings. Francesco Valentino and Nicola Moscona are sonorous enough, but Ann McKnight is a harsh Musetta; the redolence of the Waltz Song escapes her. George Cehanovsky, for all his fame as a character singer, emerges as a humorless Schaunard. It is Toscanini (who can sometimes be heard singing along) and his two leading singers who make this set an enduring musical treasure.

1947 CBS / SONY (M)

Bidú Sayão (A), Mimi Benzell (B), Richard Tucker (C), Francesco Valentino (D), George Cehanovsky (E), Nicola Moscona (F), Metropolitan Opera Chorus and Orchestra—Giuseppe Antonicelli

This is one of the Metropolitan Opera sets produced by Columbia in the late 1940s and early 1950s, but it is oddly undistinguished, considering some of its participants. Giuseppe Antonicelli is better in some of the spirited scenes than elsewhere: the opening of Act I, for example, goes nicely. At other times the tempos are pushed about, attacks are fuzzy, the orchestration becomes unclear, and the singers are allowed obstreperous and inappropriate mannerisms. Richard Tucker is in strong voice for his first recorded Rodolfo: the tone is warm and rich. His manner, though, is occasionally pompous, and tearful at the strangest moments. He seems to take the mock heroics of the garret seriously, and there are little awkwardnesses of phrasing which betray his relative inexperience with the role. The climax of his aria is typically rushed, "Questa è Mimì" is rather matter-of-fact, and the finale is played for melodrama. He is tonally at his best in Act III, though there he is not given the conducting support he needs.

Bidú Sayão is a charming and cultivated singer. Her Mimì, though, is disappointing. It lacks, of all things, intimacy; what worked well against such orchestration in the opera house is a little coarse and loud here. In the quartet, for example, she sounds almost shrewish, though the last act is more artful and expressive. The voice itself is not capable of much warmth or a great variety of color, but she is an artist. It is a misfortune that she does not work with a stronger conductor here, and could not take the time to perfect for close-up recording what was a touching achievement in live performance. As Musetta, Mimi Benzell sings one of the more charming Waltzes, but her fourth act is less convincing. The others are unremarkable. In general, they sang less broadly but a little more expressively in the Toscanini broadcast of the previous year.

1951 DECCA / LONDON (M)

Renata Tebaldi (A), Hilde Gueden, (B), Giacinto Prandelli (C), Giovanni Inghilleri (D), Fernando Corena (E), Raffaele Arié (F), Chorus and Orchestra of the Accademia di Santa Cecilia, Rome—Alberto Erede

This set is an interesting example of Renata Tebaldi's early work. Her voice is very beautiful here and of an appropriate weight for Mimì. She begins her Act I aria with great delicacy and spins out certain phrases movingly: one can imagine her breathing in the scent of the rose she mentions. There are delightful *pianissimos* in the later acts, too. On the big phrases, both the sound and the mood sometimes become steely. In some of the conversational passages she is either prosaic or rather commanding, despite the text, and in Act III she breaks into a roughened *parlando* tone. This is a Mimì of many lovely moments, though there is often the sense that Tosca is lurking beneath.

The rest of the cast is variable. Giacinto Prandelli is a poetic Rodolfo with a vision of ecstasy he can't quite transmit in vocal terms. His introduction of Mimì in Act II characterizes his accomplishment and problems well: he phrases it movingly, but with a rather dry sound and a strained top voice not quite capable of the required expansion. Giovanni Inghilleri sings well enough, though without any special flair for expressing Marcello's humor, self-knowledge, or ironic passion. Raffaele Arié is a lyrical Colline, observing all the markings in his tender aria, and Fernando Corena is a lively Schaunard, though the role lies high for him. His

comment on Mimì's death is a touching moment. Hilde Gueden, as Musetta, sings a lovely Waltz; she has a substantial middle voice here and a brilliant top. Elsewhere she lacks a little in warmth of tone, but the final prayer is touching. Alberto Erede conducts an efficient performance, with some persuasive lyrical moments. The high spirits are rather low here, though, and the orchestra somewhat distant. The major interest of the recording today is in the promise and some of the accomplishment of its two sopranos.

1952 CETRA (M)

Rosanna Carteri (A), Elvira Ramella (B), Ferruccio Tagliavini (C), Giuseppe Taddei (D), Pier Luigi Latinucci (E), Cesare Siepi (F), Italian Radio Chorus and Orchestra, Turin—Gabriele Santini

Ferruccio Tagliavini had one of the loveliest lyric voices of the last half-century. It was not large, but exceptionally smooth and caressing in quality. He could reduce it to a thread of tone which an entire opera house held its breath to hear. At other times he could push, break up phrases, and orate pompously, even in roles which were of the perfect weight for him. This was sometimes noticeable in his live performances, but it is particularly obvious in his recordings—especially the later ones. What makes it so exasperating is that the tone at its best is so magnetically charming, the impression of resonant intimacy so natural, that he has no need to inflate the voice. This recording reflects both aspects. There are several strikingly beautiful moments: the opening of the Act I aria is one and "Questa è Mimì" in Act II is another. But then he will begin commanding the troops, with an attempt at volume when he already has the capability for persuasion through tone color. At those moments his Rodolfo becomes smug and humorless. His Act III *scena* is like that: alternately effective and mannered. In Act IV he tends to coo or shout. "Ah, mia Mimì, sempre, sempre" is one of his moving moments, and at the close he provides a series of broken sobs which are quite convincing.

His fellow Bohemians are a healthy lot. Giuseppe Taddei is in splendid voice, scrupulously musical and a vital actor: warm, youthful, and touching in his concern. Cesare Siepi has a fine tone for Colline, though the role remains largely unacted. Pier Luigi Latinucci as Schaunard is full-voiced, and he has worked out his little scene about the parrot with careful detail.

Rosanna Carteri shows promise in this early recording and handles the role of Mimì with some delicacy, but the voice is actually rather hard and coarse for the effects she intends. Elvira Ramella is a brash Musetta, but touchingly simple and intense in her Act IV prayer. Gabriele Santini conducts warmly; one wishes his cast were a little more evenly matched in vocal displacement. The set is notable chiefly for Taddei's Marcello and as a souvenir of Tagliavini.

1952 REMINGTON (M)

Frances Schimenti (A), Mafalda Micheluzzi (B), Giacomo Lauri-Volpi (C), Giovanni Ciavola (D), Enzo Titta (E), Victor Tatozzi (F), Rome Opera Chorus and Orchestra—Alberto Paoletti

By any normal standard this is a perfectly awful performance. Frances Schimenti is shrill, unsteady, and uninteresting dramatically: lachrymose and coy without being convincing. Mafalda Micheluzzi is possibly the least reliable Musetta on records. The voice cuts like glass, the lower register is weak, and there is incipient unsteadiness. Giovanni Ciavola is a glum Marcello in every way. The set sounds as if it had been recorded in a refrigerator. The conducting is dreadful. The ensemble falls apart in Act II, and elsewhere the conductor follows the singers without supporting them; the thought occurs that the orchestra and perhaps the chorus were prerecorded and the soloists added later. And Giacomo Lauri-Volpi's voice is aged (he was sixty at the time), penetrating, thick, hoarse, and unreliably pitched.

But. Though Lauri-Volpi's quality of voice is manifestly inappropriate, his performance may in certain respects be regarded as a little master class in some of the devices of spontaneity. Throughout, he is playful; he seems to be hav-

ing as much fun as anyone. He uses the words. His performance of "Che gelida manina," with all its exaggerations and unfulfilled promises, can be considered either outrageously self-serving or a minor coaching gift from a singer of enormous and sometimes bizarre experience; he had a reputation for upstaging but also wrote several interesting books on singers and singing. The recording offers one or two other rewards, such as Victor Tatozzi's slow but nicely felt Coat Song. As Schaunard, Enzo Titta may not sing well, but he tells his Act I story convincingly and stages the dinner and dance in Act IV with conviction.

However, do not be deceived; these little moments must be searched out. Otherwise, this set is to be avoided.

p. 1952 REMINGTON (M)

Daniza Ilitsch (A), Ruthilde Boesch (B), Ratko Delorco (C), Theo Baylé (D), Georg Oeggl (E), Marjan Rus (F), Vienna State Opera Chorus, Austrian Symphony Orchestra—Wilhelm Loibner

I have been able to hear only a disc of excerpts from this set. They are largely disqualified by slow tempos. Although there is care in orchestral detail, the life is dragged out of the opera and the singers, too: music for a mausoleum. Beyond that, the set is notable for its Mimì, Daniza Ilitsch. Hers is basically a sizable and rather cold voice, with an element of lead in it. The interesting thing is the care with which she attempts to disguise this by forward placement and rounded phrasing. Ratko Delorco sings with delicacy of line, though the tone is occasionally unsteady and wiry at the top. There are stretches of intimacy and careful charm from both singers, sometimes elongated beyond endurance by the conductor. Of the others, Ruthilde Boesch is a bright Musetta. German accents abound. Such a performance reminds one how much more there is in Puccini's opera than mere romantic nostalgia.

1956 EMI / ANGEL (M) CD

Victoria de los Angeles (A), Lucine Amara (B), Jussi Bjoerling (C), Robert Merrill (D), John

Reardon (E), Giorgio Tozzi (F), RCA Victor Chorus and Orchestra—Thomas Beecham

Sir Thomas Beecham's recording of *La Bohème* is certainly wonderfully cast; it has some of the freshest and most beautiful voices of its day. Jussi Bjoerling is in a particularly prodigal vocal mood, with a soaring vibrance and tonal halo that set him apart from most of his competitors. Victoria de los Angeles shares that quality. Her sound and phrasing convey a modest sensuality and an inner generosity of feeling that are at the heart of this character, and she has virtually complete technical security. Both voices shimmer, and they complement one another. As Musetta, Lucine Amara is piquant and inviting, and she handles the music with rare beauty of tone. Robert Merrill is in the prime of vocal health; the good humor of his sound and approach suit this amiable character nicely. John Reardon is a strikingly spirited Schaunard and Giorgio Tozzi a pleasing Colline. Fernando Corena's Benoit has been admired; I find it exaggerated.

Presiding over this vocal feast is Sir Thomas Beecham. In clear sound, the orchestral finish and the play of instrumental harmonies are very lovely. He noted in a discussion published with the original issue that he was particularly aware of the challenge of musical continuity in a tightly written libretto such as this one, in which all the words are set to an interplay of musical themes highlighting their emotional significance. He certainly achieves such continuity. The elegant but not precious care for detail and a sense of musical proportion are hallmarks of Beecham's conducting style: the very qualities that distinguish his Delius recordings, for example. There are, however, some drawbacks to Beecham's reserved approach. Though Bjoerling, for instance, has a vibrance in his tone that is in itself moving, there is not much in his reading here that suggests the genuinely impetuous. Some of the first act is a little vacuous in dramatic intention, and his Act III lacks a degree of passionate impulsiveness, partly because of the restraint with which Beecham conducts it. The whole of Mimì's first scene is rather languid, so that the moments of greatest

lyric outpouring are relatively undifferentiated in approach and tone from the rest—and this mercuriality, this apparent spontaneity of feeling, is one of the work's chief attractions. The humor, the reproof, the contradictions remain somewhat unexplored. Nevertheless, for its balance, aural beauty, and gracious spirit, this remains among the most distinctive recordings of Puccini's score.

1956 EMI / ANGEL (M) CD

Maria Callas (A), Anna Moffo (B), Giuseppe di Stefano (C), Rolando Panerai (D), Manuel Spatafora (E), Nicola Zaccaria (F), La Scala Chorus and Orchestra—Antonino Votto

Here is another unforgettably touching view of Puccini's lovers. Giuseppe di Stefano is at his charming mid-career best in a role which suits him emotionally and musically. One might cavil now and then at his characteristic open tone, but the *brio* of his first two acts, the youthful heartbreak of his third, and his jubilance and despair in the last act together make up a movingly realized Rodolfo. He and Rolando Panerai as Marcello carry on musical conversations of shifting emotional response; they are, for example, genuinely cold at the start, it seems, and just as genuinely elated when Schaunard enters. Di Stefano's scenes with Maria Callas are truly intimate. They listen to one another. His Act I aria has a smile in the voice, and "Dammi il braccio," sung as the lovers begin to leave the garret, has just the right note of courtly sentiment.

Callas, as always, has the gift to suggest vocally the complex beneath the simple. "Rodolfo and Mimì are simple people," she cautioned singers, and her own kind of simplicity is what we are given here. What we hear at her first entrance is a shyly self-respecting young woman who draws us, and Rodolfo, in to focus on her. It is not until "Ma quando vien lo sgelo" in her aria that we see fully revealed what Rodolfo has already suspected: her capacity for poetic wonder. In Act II, her happiness is genuine, and yet tinged with a sense of reflection which never leaves her. Her Act III entrance is hushed and ill, although vibrant with feeling, and the "Addio" is quietly wrenching. In Act IV she compels emotional attention without distorting the scene. With great care for pronunciation and vocal color, she lends each syllable of "Sono andati" heightened emotional significance. Few if any other singers could use so dark a tone without destroying the fragility of the character, but Callas's darkness remains delicate and clear throughout. Her final moments are also quietly magnetic. There are, one should add, a few sour high notes, but the rest is inimitably expressive.

Whether warm or grumbling, Rolando Panerai is a Marcello of distinctive sound and clear emotional response. Anna Moffo's Musetta may overplay the sensuous—she slides about a good deal—but the voice is at least fresh and pretty. Under Antonino Votto's baton, the ensembles generally go with élan. He is both proportionate and accommodating to his two leading singers, who are thus given the opportunity to say wonderful things about this score.

1957 PHILIPS (M)

Antonietta Stella (A), Bruna Rizzoli (B), Gianni Poggi (C), Renato Capecchi (D), Guido Mazzini (E), Giuseppe Modesti (F), San Carlo Opera Chorus and Orchestra—Francesco Molinari-Pradelli

Well, there *is* Marcello. Renato Capecchi is possibly the most inventive of all of them: a delightful, sensitive character played by a singer with a good, medium-sized voice, sometimes artificially darkened and a little wooden at the top. He is notably compassionate in Act III: when he says to the distraught Mimì, "Don't make a scene," he is one of the few to sound more concerned for her well-being than for his own embarrassment. In Act IV, when anything touching happens, it's generally Capecchi who has done it. The rest of the performance is exceptionally dreary under the baton of Francesco Molinari-Pradelli: his orchestra maunders through the opera with neither rapture nor interest. Gianni Poggi is a graceless, whining Rodolfo, and Antonietta Stella is in poor voice; she pushes a tremulous sound carefully through the score. Giuseppe Modesti is pleasant enough

in the Coat Song. Bruna Rizzoli is a hard, relatively efficient Musetta, but under this conductor the "commedia" is anything but "stupenda."

1959 DECCA / LONDON (S) CD

Renata Tebaldi (A), Gianna d'Angelo (B), Carlo Bergonzi (C), Ettore Bastianini (D), Renato Cesari (E), Cesare Siepi (F), Chorus and Orchestra of the Accademia di Santa Cecilia, Rome—Tullio Serafin

This was the first *Bohème* set recorded in stereo, and it has considerable sonic depth. The orchestra, though, seems closer to us than the singers, which further distances the effect of an already rather impersonal performance. Instrumental timbres are lovely. Tullio Serafin conducts a lyrical reading with finished phrasing and proportion, but it all has a measured tread and at times a monumental quality, outsized and yet attractive—more like a nostalgic memory of *La Bohème* than the experience itself. Renata Tebaldi is in lovely voice and sings with fine control, but her sound and approach are even darker than in 1951. The melancholy is there but not much of the fragile ecstasy, especially at these tempos. Carlo Bergonzi sings an earnest, finely phrased Rodolfo, though the distance of the recording, the lightness of his voice, and his Mimì's dark command all tend to destroy the illusion of an impetuous and youthful romance between them. He has, however, many beautifully sustained stretches of singing, among them the Act I aria, "Questa è Mimì" and his touching scene in Act III. Ettore Bastianini has a rich Verdi baritone voice of great security and health but lacks some of the spontaneity, humor, and intimacy that individualize the role. Cesare Siepi is again a sonorous but uninteresting Colline. Gianna d'Angelo's Musetta is light and pungent, and in Act IV touching, though with the magisterial Tebaldi the two seem more like the lady-in-waiting and the queen than two young women who have become friends. Though there are many lovely passages in this performance, the intimate charm and improvisational elements of Puccinian romance are often lost.

1961 DEUTSCHE GRAMMOPHON (S) CD

Renata Scotto (A), Jolanda Meneguzzer (B), Gianni Poggi (C), Tito Gobbi (D), Giorgio Giorgetti (E), Giuseppe Modesti (F), Chorus and Orchestra of the Maggio Musicale Fiorentino—Antonino Votto

With Renata Scotto and Tito Gobbi present as Mimì and Marcello, it is unfortunate that a better additional cast and a more demanding conductor could not have been secured for this recording. Gianni Poggi is a mite improved here since his first Rodolfo, but the voice is still nasal and strained, the manner generally vulgar. Neither of Renata Scotto's recordings of Mimì catches her at her expressive peak. As it is, hers is the only voice of real beauty in this set, though even at this early point it has a cutting edge and some attenuation at the top. Otherwise it is fresh and distinctive, and her phrasing musical, though one gets only a suggestion of that remarkable vocal acting that was a feature of her Metropolitan career later. She sings the first two acts nicely. Act III is more interesting. Like the subtler Mimìs, she seems at first not to want to tell what she reveals to Marcello; desperation makes her do so. The "Addio" is touching and yet not melodramatic. Her fourth act is very moving: the voice has a silken cling and there is a charming delight in the fragile recollections and a memorable vocal pallor in her final phrases.

Tito Gobbi is, of course, dramatically alert as Marcello, but also dry-voiced and unromantic in tone. The words and phrases are pointed, as one would expect with such an accomplished singing actor, but they often seem short-tempered rather than ironic. Nevertheless, there are some traits of distinction: Gobbi's reading of the phrase "Ah, miseria" in Act IV is, for example, strikingly pained. Jolanda Meneguzzer is a light, acid-toned Musetta, although she sings neatly enough and in Act IV provides a terrified entrance and an anguished prayer. With these voices, the quartet at the close of Act III is not engaging. Giuseppe Modesti once again sings a pleasant "Vecchia zimarra" but is otherwise unremarkable as Colline. Antonino Votto's

conducting at the close of Act II is rousing, but elsewhere, without such an accomplished ensemble as in his Callas-di Stefano set, his performance often drags.

1961 RCA / BMG (S) CD

Anna Moffo (A), Mary Costa (B), Richard Tucker (C), Robert Merrill (D), Philip Maero (E), Giorgio Tozzi (F), Rome Opera Chorus and Orchestra—Erich Leinsdorf

This is a well-sung and firmly conducted performance. The major singers are all American and perform with full, steady tone and generally with commendable moderation. Erich Leinsdorf conducts a lucid and flowing performance of some delicacy; Act II is particularly notable for both its spirit and its restraint. Richard Tucker is in prime voice and at the start of "Che gelida manina" manages a pleasing conversational tone which serves the music well. There is something of Canio in his Act III scene and at the very end, but the voice is smooth throughout. The other men are in similar vocal health. Robert Merrill sings Marcello well, though without real wit, and Philip Maero is a full-voiced Schaunard. Giorgio Tozzi provides a pleasant "Vecchia zimarra." One misses imaginative characterization from all of them, but the vocalism is consistently first-class. Anna Moffo is a dark-voiced but delicate Mimì of finish, and Mary Costa is an elegantly soft Musetta. Their voices are surprisingly similar. The Waltz is quite intimately done and its ending charmingly offhand. Enthusiasts for these singers will find them all at their best in a performance generally admirable for discipline and polish.

1963 EMI / ANGEL (S) CD

Mirella Freni (A), Mariella Adani (B), Nicolai Gedda (C), Mario Sereni (D), Mario Basiola, Jr. (E), Ferruccio Mazzoli (F), Rome Opera Chorus and Orchestra—Thomas Schippers

Conductor Thomas Schippers is an inspiring presence here, rhythmically energetic all through but especially in Act II, where he balances the orchestral and stage voices brilliantly and shapes the joyous music for cumulative impact. The chorus is generally superb for both spirit and exactitude, and the moment of Marcello's capitulation to Musetta is a memorable one. Elsewhere in the opera there are many details revealed, but the energy and precision sometimes overwhelm the romance, though a differently endowed cast might have eliminated that problem. Nicolai Gedda is a stimulating and vital Rodolfo who observes most of Puccini's markings, performs with rhythmic vitality, and has a sense of humor. In a clear attempt to let the score speak for itself, he also avoids many traditional *portamentos*. The voice is strong and a little thick, and the performance, admirable as it is, lacks something in romance and plasticity, though there is much that is refreshing about it.

Mirella Freni offers beautiful and steady voice for Mimì. Her first aria is a very pleasurable stretch of singing, and the "Addio" and her final scene are arches of lovely sound. It is a fine performance, but there are few of those innumerable small shifts of color and emphasis that distinguish the great characterizations. Mario Sereni is resonant and knowledgeable, but there is more fun, insinuation, and sympathy in Marcello than he brings to it. Mariella Adani sings the Waltz intimately and is at times vivacious and touching, but the voice is frequently acid or unsteady. Every major opera company, incidentally, ought to offer a class in stage laughter, with attendance required for all prospective or practicing Musettas. Ferruccio Mazzoli sings the Coat Song with delicacy; ideally it wants a little more courtliness to give it a special character. Mario Basiola, Jr., plays a forthright Schaunard, but without much sense of fun. His distinctive sound, however, does clarify the ensembles. Schippers's reading as a whole is rousing, there is an interesting contribution from Gedda, and Freni sings one of her loveliest performances.

1972 DECCA / LONDON (S) CD

Mirella Freni (A), Elizabeth Harwood (B), Luciano Pavarotti (C), Rolando Panerai (D), Gianni Maffeo (E), Nicolai Ghiaurov (F), Deutsche Oper Chorus, Berlin Philharmonic Orchestra—Herbert von Karajan

Though it has an illustrious cast, this set is as completely dominated by its conductor as any on records. The sound is, of course, very full, and the performance in many respects a superb dissection of the score. Dynamics are calculated, instrumental timbres are exploited, and the orchestra has a wondrous beauty of tone. The voices, too, are among the most beautiful of the day. Karajan's is a provocative statement, fully thought out and full of his own conviction, however one may disagree with it. For all its loving care and the conductor's desire to give back everything that Puccini put into his opera, the effect is at times overblown, deficient in spontaneity, and even dull. For example, though the chill at the start of Act III is beautifully realized, much of Act II emerges as bulky and ponderous. Again, when the death scene is rendered so slowly and painstakingly, it loses the evanescence and the pulse which give it half of its appeal.

And certainly at such tempos the singers are given the task of not only managing breath sensibly but also maintaining musical continuity and dramatic variety. Luciano Pavarotti has, of course, a golden tone and ideal mobility for the role, a playfulness and yet a capacity for open-hearted but not lugubrious emotional response, and the technical capacity to handle all of the problems which Karajan sets him. There are wholly persuasive stretches of singing here. His first encounter with Mimì has animated intimacy, and his aria begins almost offhandedly, developing in rapture to a magnificently free and steady climax. In Act III, "Mimì è tanto malata" is a hushed and beautiful moment. But much of the rest of the scene— and the opera—drags, losing musical and dramatic impact. Puccini gets on with it (as Sir Thomas Beecham is reported to have said) but Karajan doesn't. He bullies the music often, refusing to allow it to flow and build its own climaxes.

Mirella Freni is again in lovely voice for Mimì, but there is little of the special animation that can make her scenes more than merely appealing. Karajan's tempo for "Mi chiamano Mimì" is very slow; it loses tension and emotional continuity, and "Ma quando vien lo sgelo" is sung with such scrupulous care that one's mind can wander. Other scenes are also robbed of their vitality: the "Addio," for example, meanders in a way that destroys what would seem an almost ineradicable impact. Rolando Panerai is in fine form but the deliberate tempos force him to overplay. Elizabeth Harwood's performance of Musetta's Waltz begins very slowly and with an obviously sensuous tone: the pace and approach distract interest from the character, though she accomplishes the ending with delicacy, point, and accuracy. Gianni Maffeo is a rather bleak-sounding Schaunard: fastidiousness robs him of spontaneity. Nicolai Ghiaurov is a vocally impressive but dramatically dull Colline. In all, this set is a fascinating if troublesome analysis of the opera, done with some extraordinary voices. The *Bohème* enthusiast will certainly want to have an example of what Pavarotti can do with one of his best roles, and will also want to hear Karajan's views on the subject, but there is more in the score than this brilliantly meticulous performance provides.

1973 RCA / BMG (S) CD

Montserrat Caballé (A), Judith Blegen (B), Plácido Domingo (C), Sherrill Milnes (D), Vicente Sardinero (E), Ruggero Raimondi (F), John Alldis Choir, London Philharmonic Orchestra—Georg Solti

Though their approaches are sometimes quite different, Georg Solti shares some of Herbert von Karajan's problems in this familiar, evergreen score: how to reveal its charm and its mercurial nature and at the same time make a personal statement with it. The work becomes a series of Ultimate Moments, expertly examined individual sequences. Some of them have their own highly persuasive logic and effect, but they have not been reintegrated into a whole, or lovingly explored with the singers to discover what endures in the context of a single performance. The result is in certain respects brilliant—no one will doubt that a first-rate musical mind is dealing with the score—but it is also, in the long run, alienating and fragmentary.

Such an approach may force the singers to extremes, too. The sound that Montserrat Caballé

produces in this performance is utterly gorgeous, but it is all in the same melancholy mode. In Acts I and II, she sings almost as if in a trance. Acts III and IV reinforce the points already made. Plácido Domingo's Rodolfo is very well sung, in a bright, resonant, and rich tone. A fine performance, but where are the half-lights of humor, the thrown-away moments of flirtation? Solti's slow tempo in his Act III scene does not deepen Rodolfo's youthful frustration, but it dulls the edge of the character by eliminating his impetuousness. We get this sort of exaggeration fairly often from the conductor, and the climactic moments become melodramatic or drawn out because they must increase the effect of what has rather heavily preceded them.

As Marcello, Sherrill Milnes is superbly resonant and gives a well-phrased performance, but the character's intimacy and humor (ironic or sentimental) are at most indicated rather than played. Judith Blegen gives a very musical reading of Musetta, though one wants more warmth in her middle voice to convince us of the character's true nature. Ruggero Raimondi is an uncommonly lively Colline, shivering at his first entrance and then warmed by the little fire. His "Vecchia zimarra" is genuinely intimate— slow and sentimental, but at the same time touching and courtly. Like several *Bohème*s of the last two decades, this one combines many elements of expertise. Fragmentary testing has been done but the work of art has not been completely reassembled.

1979 PHILIPS (S) CD

Katia Ricciarelli (A), Ashley Putnam (B), José Carreras (C), Ingvar Wixell (D), Håkan Hagegård (E), Robert Lloyd (F), Chorus and Orchestra of the Royal Opera House, Covent Garden— Colin Davis

Colin Davis's performance is as a whole one of the more satisfactory modern recordings. It avoids the extremes (and sometimes the illuminations) of other more eccentric performances and is in general nicely sung and pleasingly recorded, though the orchestra occasionally covers the singers. José Carreras is the best of them; he is in fine, flowing form here and sings his aria with both restraint and passion. Act III also goes well, though Davis sometimes impedes its flow with slow tempos. The Act IV duet "O Mimì, tu più non torni" is both lovely and lyrical. As Marcello, Ingvar Wixell is inventive throughout. His healthy, rather grainy voice makes every word count; sometimes the ideas seem to be occurring right at the moment of utterance. He lacks only a romantic tone for some moments in Acts II and IV, but he compensates there with finished phrasing.

Katia Ricciarelli as Mimì offers a pretty, warm, and fresh voice, occasionally a little unsteady under pressure. She phrases knowingly. She is at her best in Act III, with a striking note of panic at first, and a lovely, full tone in the "Addio." The characterization is not particularly distinctive, but it has a pleasing charm and continuity. Ashley Putnam is in general a fresh though not especially lighthearted or enticing Musetta. Her middle voice sometimes threatens unsteadiness. Håkan Hagegård is one of the liveliest Schaunards on records, full of rhythmic vitality and fun, and Robert Lloyd is satisfactory as Colline. Colin Davis paces it all rather soberly but neatly, with more mercurial charm than some of his competitors, although portions of Acts III and IV seem overstressed. A pleasant set.

1979 EMI / ANGEL (S)

Renata Scotto (A), Carol Neblett (B), Alfredo Kraus (C), Sherrill Milnes (D), Matteo Manuguerra (E), Paul Plishka (F), Ambrosian Opera Chorus, National Philharmonic Orchestra— James Levine

This set is interestingly cast, but the performance is more provocative than satisfactory. Under James Levine, one hears a gratifying amount of the orchestral comment, but individual scenes are often either humorlessly fast or portentously slow, demanding just the kind of expansive flow of steady tone that several of his singers cannot provide. Alfredo Kraus is a conscientious and knowing vocalist but he lacks the fullness and warmth of tone for this music, and a certain dry unsteadiness compromises the cli-

maxes, artful and imaginative as he may be. In a differently cast performance he might show to more advantage, but here he is battling a vibrant, expansive orchestra, Sherrill Milnes's large voice, and Renata Scotto's unsteady one. He handles the final moments of the opera affectingly.

Scotto's first entrance is lovely, filled with wonder. That smoky lower register of hers is, as always, fascinating, and her performance is full of imaginative innuendo and dramatic detail. At her re-entrance to light the candle, though, we first hear that unsteadiness under vocal pressure that afflicts much of her later work. Levine's slow tempos do not help, and the effect of rapture that she clearly wishes to provide is lessened. Sherrill Milnes is in excellent vocal health and sings with more nuance than previously, but he and the light-voiced Kraus do not make especially apt partners. As Musetta, Carol Neblett has a big, blooming middle range and a somewhat unreliable top voice. Oddly, she lacks flirtatious charm, and one is aware of her attempt to manipulate such a voice through the music. Again there is an ensemble problem. The conclusion of the Waltz, for example, is uncomfortable as Scotto's striated tones join with Neblett's overpowering and unstable ones. Matteo Manuguerra, who has sung imaginatively in other sets, is a rich-voiced but rather diffident Schaunard, and Paul Plishka is a sonorous but bland Colline. Italo Tajo voices Benoit lightly and is rather touching. In sum, there are some cherishable elements in this set, but its mismatched and variable cast and occasionally mannered conducting present problems.

1987 ERATO (S,D) CD

Barbara Hendricks (A), Angela Maria Blasi (B), José Carreras (C), Gino Quilico (D), Richard Cowan (E), Francesco Ellero d'Artegna (F), Chorus and Orchestre National de la RTF— James Conlon

This set derives from a film soundtrack. It is an admirably clean performance. James Conlon's interpretation has spirit and savor, though one would like more expressive *rubato* at times. It is cast with some attractive voices, but only

José Carreras gives much evidence of the vitality, subtlety, and variety of response that the score can really evoke. Of the four Bohemians, he is the liveliest—almost unprecedented in recordings, where the Marcello and Schaunard have such strong opportunities in the ensemble scenes. Carreras is in good if sometimes careful form, retaining much of the vocal freedom of former years. The Act I aria is unfortunately his least attractive moment, with a rather rough sound and a driven climax. The other cast members are neat, but some of them are limited in expressive warmth. The most interesting is Barbara Hendricks, with a light, poised tone which suggests fragile passion. Hers is a highly controlled performance, shorn of many of the shifting emotional overtones of an earlier tradition. She offers, for example, an "Addio" full of focused, delicate tone: the care bestowed on the singing is more arresting than the performance itself. The net result is admirable but a little calculated, and she often undercuts Carreras emotionally.

Gino Quilico's Marcello is intelligent and pleasant, but lacking in the volubility and warm humor that the score allows him. Angela Maria Blasi has a bright and sparkling tone for Musetta, and does her last act with commitment. The others are less effective. Richard Cowan is efficient, no more, as Schaunard, and Francesco Ellero d'Artegna is an anonymous Colline. Presumably because of recording levels associated with the film, a few of the intimate moments cannot be heard clearly, and some that can lose a little in resonance. Altogether, the album offers a trim and vital performance from Conlon, something rather more than that from Carreras, an artful Mimì in Hendricks, and a pleasing new voice in Blasi's Musetta, if nothing else particularly memorable.

1988 DEUTSCHE GRAMMOPHON (S,D) CD

Angelina Réaux (A), Barbara Daniels (B), Jerry Hadley (C), Thomas Hampson (D), James Busterud (E), Paul Plishka (F), Chorus and Orchestra of the Accademia di Santa Cecilia, Rome—Leonard Bernstein

As one might expect, Leonard Bernstein compels central attention in his recording of *La Bohème* with a beautifully articulated orchestral performance. The instrumental commentary is continually audible without overwhelming the singers, and whatever the pace and dramatic destination, there is always a sense of musical shape. Seldom have textures been so clear, the solo playing so lovely, and the chorus so accurate and unified in attack. Bernstein gives a remarkably slow, nostalgic performance, though: more like the memory of youth than the experience of youth itself—a somberly considered version of Puccini's "gay and terrible" romance, which can lose power if too much of it is made explicitly sentimental. As in several other of the newer *Bohèmes*, his tempos are sometimes beyond the capabilities of his cast: a youthful one but not always convincing in expressing the half-realized conflicts of feeling which make Puccini's score so continually suggestive.

Angelina Réaux has the voice for Mimì—pretty, rather fragile, and warm enough—but the characterization is still in the formative stages. The first act is pleasantly conventional and touching. By Act III she needs more vocal variety and subtle expressive devices if she is to fill out Bernstein's designs; she begins to repeat herself and to become blatant. Jerry Hadley has a more refulgent tone on records than elsewhere, and he finishes his phrases well. His work is conscientious, musicianly, and reasonably rich. What it wants is a degree of youthful impetuosity and a sense that he has made the role his own. The striking thing about the very last moments of the opera is that none of the characters is prepared for tragedy, but in this performance the scene sounds rehearsed and almost ritualistic, and is surprisingly unmoving.

Barbara Daniels is a rather hard Musetta, though she sings with reasonable grace. The laugh and the scream over the shoe are more distracting than amusing, though. Thomas Hampson has a well-schooled voice and plays Marcello sensibly but without much humor. Paul Plishka is a little more lively than the other Bohemians as Colline. None of them seems to have much fun, desperate or otherwise. It seems incredible to say it of a recording headed by

Bernstein and a cast of youthful singers, but what it lacks as a whole is spontaneity.

198–(?) OPUS (S) CD

Veronika Kincses (A), Sidónia Haljáková (B), Peter Dvorsky (C), Ivan Konsulov (D), Balázs Póka (E), Dariusz Niemirowicz (F), Bratislava National Theater Choir and Radio Symphony Orchestra—Ondrej Lenárd

This set from Czechoslovakia is memorable for the Rodolfo of Peter Dvorsky, whose tone is rich and golden throughout its range, with a buoyancy that suggests Bjoerling. His ideas about the role are not particularly striking, but he does phrase nicely most of the time and has a certain radiance of spirit and capacity for delicacy. The Act III quartet, for example, begins with a pleasing intimacy. Conductor Ondrej Lenárd sometimes rushes him. With such glorious tone and even resonance, one wants Dvorsky to expand a little at "Dal mio cervel" (Rudolfo's introduction of Mimì in Act II), for instance, since he has the wherewithal to make the most of its lyricism.

Dvorsky is backed up by a spirited production, reasonably paced for the most part by the conductor, who seems attuned to the capacities of his singers. Veronika Kincses sings Mimì attentively in a lyric voice of some warmth but occasional strain. She has absorbed the routine of the role well, though (as in her first-act aria) she sometimes seems more careful than enraptured. Ivan Konsulov is a resonant, rather throaty Marcello; his duet with Dvorsky in Act IV is a highlight of the performance. Sidónia Haljáková is the regulation Musetta, a little less shrill and insecure than some. As a whole the set is pleasant: not especially subtle but not eccentric either. It is Dvorsky who lends the performance special interest.

1990 EMI / ANGEL (S,D,P) CD

Daniela Dessì (A), Adelina Scarabelli (B), Giuseppe Sabbatini (C), Paolo Gavanelli (D), Alfonso Antoniozzi (E), Carlo Colombara (F), Chorus and Orchestra of the Teatro Communale, Bologna—Gianluigi Gelmetti

This album is marked "Ricordi, Edizione Critica" and reflects the new edition of *Bohème* published in 1988. From the listener's standpoint the changes are not great; they involve a few minor omissions and errors and the addition of several dozen dynamic marks found in the autograph score, together with other editorial work on text, tempo indications, and stage directions. What gives this release its central interest is that the conductor seems to have reconsidered deeply Puccini's remarkable orchestration and instrumental phrasing. He provides some extraordinary vitality in the first two acts and translucent playing throughout. The entrance of Mimì, the climax of Rodolfo's aria, and the orchestral blossoming at "Ma, quando vien lo sgelo" in Mimì's aria and at "O soave fanciulla" are all thrilling. The opening of Act II is uncommonly spirited and the children's chorus both deliciously brash and exact in execution. The last two acts present a few structural problems; tempos are sometimes slow, as if depending on complex characterizations his cast cannot always deliver, while the gavotte and Coat Song are *very* speedy. The intent is surely to dramatize Puccini's characteristic mixture of the "gay and terrible," but the dramatic effect is ambiguous. Rodolfo's final anguished response is here very quiet, and carefully pitched in line with autograph score: not the only way to perform it, of course, but touching as the tenor Sabbatini does it here. As a whole the performance has rhythmic élan, together with a few ragged moments and noises typical of a live event: nothing important. In other ways the recording is quite ordinary. Missing are many of the individual strokes of characterization that are such a feature of, for example, the Berrettoni (1938) and Votto (1956) performances. Of the singers, only two are of special interest in these roles: Sabbatini and Adelina Scarabelli. The tenor appears to have a small and rather tight voice with, however, a rich upper extension, thrilling at the climax of his aria. He is also a convincing vocal actor. Scarabelli has a warm lyric soprano. The conductor and she begin the Waltz with a wonderful sinuousness—in manner a little reminiscent of Supervia—and she sings it pleasantly. Carlo Colombara is a light, pleasing Colline, but Paolo Gavanelli is humorless as Marcello and Daniela Dessì a cold and rather grating Mimì. Not a landmark *Bohème*, then, but worth an aficionado's hearing sometime for its scattered moments of rapture.

———————

For the *Bohème* experience in which one is totally involved with the characters and living their passions and frustrations from moment to moment, three monophonic recordings seem to me to be still unmatched. The 1938 Berrettoni recording, with Albanese, Gigli, and Poli, gives us a wonderfully responsive cast creating a world of their own. Toscanini's 1946 broadcast is unmatched for emotional vibrancy, and shares Albanese's distinctive Mimì. And Callas and di Stefano are memorable in their 1956 recording. In addition, Beecham's 1956 set has a fine array of voices, if less dramatic commitment. None of the stereo sets, fine as they are in sound and sometimes distinctive in treatment, can match the three earlier ones for depth and involvement. The 1979 set conducted by Colin Davis is probably the best balanced and least eccentric, and it is nicely cast. On the other hand, the Karajan is mannered but has splendid voices in Pavarotti and Freni.

LONDON GREEN

Unavailable for review:
1917–18 EMI / ANGEL
1955 GUILDE INTERNATIONAL DU DISQUE

GIACOMO PUCCINI

TOSCA (1900)

A: Floria Tosca (s); B: Mario Cavaradossi (t); C: Scarpia (bar)

In contrast to many of the operas considered in this volume, *Tosca* has seen a reasonably happy overlapping of its prime performance years with its history of complete recordings. For while we can be certain that a number of its greatest performances occurred in the twenty-nine years preceding the first of these (an assumption supported by the quality of dozens of 78-rpm versions of individual excerpts), the sixty years covered here have been, for the most part, a time when singers and conductors capable of both understanding and executing the piece have been in reasonably plentiful supply. The fact that *Tosca* is relatively young has meant that its theatrical and musical language has only very recently shown signs of drifting away from us. The fact that the effects that produce its basic impact are simple for both performers and audiences has made it theater-tough. The fact that its major roles can be handled by only moderately accomplished singers of the sort that became dominant around the turn of the century (it calls for Verdian voices, but makes less than Verdian technical demands) has made it fairly easy to cast, and the fact that there need be only three of them affords the continuing possibility of an occasional adequate performance even now. This does not at all mean that *Tosca* is easy to perform really well. On the contrary, its melodramatic traps are so inviting that high artistic goals are seldom set for it, and truly distinguished renditions of *Tosca* are as rare as those of, say, *Parsifal*. But the rudiments of the piece are hard to miss at the professional level,

and very few of these recordings fail to inflict at least some damage. The 1950s and 1960s, when a good stock of healthy *Tosca* talents coincided with the high-water mark of operatic recording techniques, afforded particularly rich opportunities, even though—as we shall see—these were not always taken full advantage of.

1929–30 EMI / ANGEL (M)

Carmen Melis (A), Piero Pauli (B), Apollo Granforte (C), Milan chorus and orchestra—Carlo Sabajno

This set now serves historical curiosity, but not too much else. Melis was at the time of the recording very near the close of her career—a considerable one centered in Italy and South America. As heard here, her voice is bright and strong, somewhat metallic and occasionally fluttery. It has good body in the upper-middle area, and sometimes the top rings out impressively. But the parlous state of the lower range (weak and often sharp) and the less than ravishing timbre undercut much of her effort. Interpretively, she is alert without having any special insight to offer, though in the healthy stretches of her range her phrasing often has a definition and profile that can still be admired. Pauli sings a fairly forceful and, at moments, nicely shaded Cavaradossi. His tenor is clean and focused, but not really rich or beautiful. Granforte is a different case: he was one of the finest Italian baritones of the interwar period, and his voice's warmth and potency, the technique's solidity, are in evidence throughout his

411

Scarpia. Even he, though, is not heard to best advantage in this comparatively low and often declamatory music, and a surfeit of inserted vowels and pushed phrase-endings knock his style down a rank or two. The supporting casting is weak; the savvy Sabajno is too often in unseemly haste; and the orchestra sounds like only a tolerable aggregation whose string cohort needs reinforcements.

1929 EMI / ANGEL (M)

Bianca Scacciati (A), Alessandro Granda (B), Enrico Molinari (C), La Scala Chorus and Orchestra—Lorenzo Molajoli

In the United States this was Columbia's *Tosca* entry in its rivalry with the HMV / Victor series, represented by the version considered above. It is in every way a more thorough and satisfying rendition. The orchestral and choral elements sound fuller and better balanced, and perform with greater care and point. Molajoli gives the music more breathing room than does Sabajno. He creates some fine, theatrical *ruba-tos*, and projects a measure of atmosphere and color even at this sonic distance. The superiority extends to the engineering (though I should note that I was able to hear this set via the originals, as opposed to an LP transfer, and that usually helps) and to the supporting singers. Scacciati, who recorded a good deal of Verdi and some interesting duets with Merli, is tonally representative of Italian sopranos of her era: a penetrating, high-set sound that probably cut excitingly in the theater. On records, the insistent brightness, the absence of enrichening or softening elements in the texture, can rather wear the listener down. However, the voice is well controlled and balanced. She shows communicative specificity in sections like the "Non la sospiri," phrases the Act I duet in shapely manner, and is passionate—even a little wild— in Act II. The constricted patch in her lower-middle range somewhat compromises her nicely felt "Vissi d'arte." Granda's voice is at times beset by a bit of tremolo, and, like many of the Italian tenors of this period, he is a rather erratic singer. His voice is prettier than Pauli's, though. He phrases with a true line, aims for some

effects beyond the basic ones, and pops out convincing top notes. The Scarpia, Molinari, seems not to have had quite the reputation of Granforte, but at least in this instance, he does not suffer in the comparison. His baritone is dark but not overweighted; he sings with both force and suavity; and he is rhythmically attentive without losing his feel for theatrical timing. In the Act II scenes with Tosca, as well as in the questioning of Cavaradossi, he and his partners sustain some real tension.

1938 EMI / ANGEL (M) CD

Maria Caniglia (A), Beniamino Gigli (B), Armando Borgioli (C), Rome Opera Chorus and Orchestra—Oliviero de Fabritiis

This is the first version of *Tosca* to offer a portrayal by one of the vocal gods—the Cavaradossi of Gigli. Except for the 1934 *Pagliacci*, Gigli's complete opera recordings were made just as his voice began to lose the freshness and spin of his prime years. Of these, though, this is probably the best. His luxurious lyric tenor retains most of its liquid, springy timbre, his high notes their meaty, juicy resonance. No vocal quibble is possible except by comparison with the same voice a few years earlier, which for exuberant freedom and tonal refulgence has had not more than three or four rivals in our century. Don't look to Gigli for insight into character (he is alive and enthusiastic, but invariably simple and heart-on-sleeve) or for lessons in musical manners (plenty of sobs and aspirates, though the line is always basically there, the phrasing instinctively understood). Look for sumptuous, exciting singing, and be content. Caniglia's Tosca, too, has much to offer. An intermittent rattle in the tone and the thinning of a few upper notes, in combination with her all-out, go-for-it style, tell us why her prime was to be brief. But the voice is still together here, and it is a big, biting one. She is capable of lighter, softer effects, but her proclivity is for the strong proclamation, the chiseled profile. What we would call vulnerability is largely absent—Caniglia is authoritative and commanding, and her approach (like Gigli's) is a broad-stroke, overtly emotional one. These are big-house *veristi* at work, and they are not toning down or smoothing over for the microphone. Armando Borgioli knows his way around the role of Scarpia, and fulfills the basics of the music. His voice has ample thrust, but sounds like a naturally lighter baritone darkened to dramatic purposes—it's rather gruff and dry, not too long on either range or *legato*. The Rome orchestra plays well, and de Fabritiis offers a brisk, well-defined reading that does not sentimentalize. The sound, too, though still thirties mono, is noticeably advanced over that of the two previous efforts.

1951 WESTMINSTER (M)

Simone dall'Argine (A), Nino Scattolini (B), Scipio Colombo (C), Vienna Chamber Chorus, Vienna State Opera Orchestra—Argeo Quadri

This edition is fairly representative of the efforts of the independent labels in the days of LP's infancy to hit a standard-repertory market opening before the majors could strike decisive blows. Quadri gives the impression of a solid opera man doing his realistic best under unforgiving conditions—his orchestra (title notwithstanding) sounds only competent and rather undersized, and the production gives every indication of adherence to a schedule with no slack in it. The conductor presides over a generally slow, wary reading, but there are instances enough of a dramatically chosen accent, or an out-of-ordinary tempo that makes a point, to show that he is not just going through the motions. This is the first *Tosca* to resort to non-Italian supporting singers, and the results are truly doleful, with one exception: Hans Breitschopf, who sings the Shepherd, has the loveliest tone of any on these recordings. The best of the soloists is Colombo, and indeed he is as persuasive a Scarpia as one can be with a less-than-great voice. His baritone is a steady, dark middleweight, smoothly handled. He shirks nothing, has an ear for detail, and shows both intelligence and intensity throughout. Dall'-Argine and Scattolini together could well summarize the story of Italian singing since the war: marvelous material in both cases, technique in neither. Scattolini is the more consistent and

musical of the two, and his powerful, clear *spinto* has its moments in this music. But the voice is not in good balance—he is forced to stiffen it too much of the time, and is apt to follow an imposing few bars near the top with a frazzled few pages near the bottom. Dall'-Argine's booming and often beautiful soprano moves ponderously, one note at a time, almost as if a foreigner were trying to recite both the verbal and musical languages of the score. Things fall apart for her in Act III. Both these singers offer isolated thrills, usually on high notes.

p.1951 REMINGTON (M)

Vassilka Petrova (A), Eddy Ruhl (B), Piero Campolonghi (C), Chorus and Orchestra of the Maggio Musicale Fiorentino—Edidio Tieri

Interest in this set will be restricted to those with boundless curiosity about, or scholarly interest in, lesser performers of its era. The exception is Campolonghi, an entirely professional, burly-voiced Scarpia who could reasonably be preferred to several others who have recorded the part. New Yorkers of a certain age will recall Eddy Ruhl: he sang in the summer open-air performances on Randall's Island, popped up in places like Holland and Greece, and surfaced in the occasional concert-opera extravaganza. He shows a voice of decent quality, capable of some clearly ringing high notes, and pulls together a very presentable "E lucevan le stelle." In terms of musical expression, his Cavaradossi is at a basic minimum level. What makes this set The *Tosca* From Hell, however, is the Floria of Vassilka Petrova, which has long enjoyed some status as a camp artifact. It's astonishing. This was certainly something close to a cold-reading, no-retake recording job, and Tieri does well to hold most of the sections together, secure a bit of underlining (he and his orchestra do know the points), and circle around all but one or two major scrambles.

1952 CETRA (M)

Adriana Guerrini (A), Gianni Poggi (B), Paolo Silveri (C), Italian Radio Chorus and Orchestra, Turin—Francesco Molinari-Pradelli

This performance has the feel of a run-through by a bunch of pros who have the idiom well in hand and are determined to examine nothing for fear of making inconvenient discoveries. Molinari-Pradelli pushes his middle-level orchestral forces through the score as if it were over-familiar food he hopes will pass through his system without having to be tasted or digested. Guerrini has a strong voice of a type appropriate to the role, and is very secure with it from about the midpoint down. But she has to pressure her way through the part; she cannot really do much with her voice, and constriction gives her tone a hard, unbeautiful surface in much of the music. No question, Poggi owned an important instrument—a firm, clear, reasonably well-balanced tenor with a fine, focused top. It is heard in youthful estate here, and the whining overtone that soon became so annoying is incipient, not dominant. He sustains long lines on the breath and is nowhere insecure. But every note is literal and square, nothing is colored or pointed, and the dynamic level never flags; this is dogged, mechanical singing. Silveri at his best was an important baritone, and he is in steady voice here, without the wobbly, compressed quality that detracts from a number of his artistically admirable recordings. His musicality and taste make his Scarpia the best thing on this set, but it is only well-sung sketchwork, not the sort of study we might have expected. The supporting parts pass muster, no more.

1952 DECCA / LONDON (M)

Renata Tebaldi (A), Giuseppe Campora (B), Enzo Mascherini (C), Chorus and Orchestra of the Accademia di Santa Cecilia, Rome—Alberto Erede

There is still one excellent reason for turning to this recording: the sound of the young Tebaldi sailing through one of her signature roles. Good as her later versions are, this one shows the fluidity of action, the float and buoyancy of tone, that signify this great voice at its peak. The voluminousness she commanded so easily, and her ability to project a full-throated *pianissimo* so that even the largest theater seemed full of soft sound, are of course only suggested by any recording. But the depth and warmth, the

Mediterranean voluptuousness of the timbre, are decently conveyed, and to hear this gorgeous flood of tone pouring through the music is a unique *Tosca* experience. Her interpretation might be described as the most complete fulfillment of traditional expectations—nothing startling, but all of it musical and finished, and certainly not lacking for power and intensity. Giuseppe Campora possessed a tenor of basically lovely lyric quality. But he seems to have heard himself as a *tenore robusto*; instead of striving for the qualities that might have earned him a lengthy career as an outstanding lyric tenor, he adopted a clamped sort of cover rather low in the range and then drove into the top, and so passed by with some dispatch as a mediocre *spinto*. He gets through Cavaradossi without calamity, and at points secures some freshness and ring, but the phrasing is held to a crude level by the technique; the *passaggio* is contentious, and the low range is often husky. Mascherini, another singer of evanescent promise, is an adequate Scarpia, his baritone solid and right enough in weight and timbre—though at times slightly guttural and veiled—and his approach invested with generalizations. Erede and his orchestra shove through the score in slovenly, tensionless fashion.

This version is the first of some half-dozen (most of them more recent) to restore the one cut customarily made in this opera: the three and one-half bars that follow "Vissi d'arte," wherein Scarpia urges Tosca to choose her course of action, and she prostrates herself at his feet. This is a useful fragment, inasmuch as it brings the section to a tidy musical close, finishes the action of the aria, and sets up the impetus for what follows. It's cut in the theater because the applause for the aria covers it. But if its logic were followed back into the aria, the latter might be accorded its true dramatic function, which is that of an urgent, last-ditch effort to enlist Scarpia's sympathy and get his mind off sex, as opposed to that of arousing the pity and lust of the audience.

1953 EMI / ANGEL (M) ⓒⒹ

Maria Callas (A), Giuseppe di Stefano (B), Tito Gobbi (C), La Scala Chorus and Orchestra—Victor de Sabata

Rehearing this famous performance after a hiatus of several years, and in close juxtaposition with its rivals, has only confirmed the received wisdom: its reputation as one of the finest of all operatic recordings is warranted. It does not start off well. Melchiorre Luise is a thin-voiced and exaggerated Sacristan, and in his first aria di Stefano's blandishing lyric tenor already shows the marks of his heedless custodianship: the low notes are not grounded; the high ones are tight and dull. But even in these pages, de Sabata is laying groundwork, for the illustrative writing is played with swing and flavor, and each motif is given its color and profile. As the score unfolds, it becomes clearer how seriously he takes it—Racine, not Sardou; high drama, not melodrama. His view of the piece is dark and elevated. He arrives at balances and blends of sonorities that invariably reinforce an atmosphere of menace and oppression; it weighs in on the characters. In this he is much assisted by the splendid mono engineering, which, without cheating us of any detail that counts, secures a massed and compacted effect of great force. De Sabata shows the essential operatic understanding—that of how each accent, each rhythmic event, each melodic scrap or harmonic tint, can be used without distortion or undue highlighting to help impel the dramatic moment, to build the dramatic arch and maintain suspense. The power of this Te Deum is unequaled in my experience, and in the confrontations of Act II the conductor unleashes orchestral storms that are all the more vicious for being so disciplined and focused. De Sabata also succeeds more completely than any other conductor with Act III, mainly by allowing moments to be filled out without losing the urgency of the conditions. The Scala orchestra, in full complement and top form, plays magnificently throughout. This performance also displays both Callas and Gobbi in mint condition and in congenial parts. From her first entrance, Callas makes it clear that there will be a sculpting of musical line, a carrying-through of dramatic intent of an order that remains *sui generis* among the recorded interpretations. Her choices are consistent: Tosca is passionate and volatile, but never without a womanly dignity, strength, and intelligence. Consequently, her fate engages

us at a high level. The peculiarities of Callas's voice are mustered in their most positive form. The morbid color, the snap in the tone, the flashing quickness of articulation, the fine command of dynamic and timbral shading, are all on tap. As is true of Tebaldi's singing at this time, a couple of the Cs blink early warning signals—a trace of wobble and thinness for Callas, some shortfall of pitch for Tebaldi. Gobbi's theatrical presence and musico-dramatic intelligence were never in question, even in roles that were vocally problematic, and if his stylistic sensitivities sometimes seemed not overfine, this was in large part due to his technical limitations. In this role, the heavy weather he could encounter with high tessitura, *piano* dynamics, vocal mobility, or *legato* is much calmed by the nature of the writing, while his strengths go straight to the requirements. That tirelessly bull-like, domineering full voice sounds inexorable; the curiously gummy, hooded *mezza voce* is oily and insinuating; the aggressively covered and rather straight sound of the top is nasty and leonine; and his authority in the rhetorical declamation of his language keeps the text sharp and pregnant. And he's not afraid to be genuinely unsympathetic—a Dennis Hopper in sound.

Di Stefano's contribution is not on a level with the rest, but it's not chopped liver, either. As always, his singing has energy, emphasis, emotion. He's lively in most of the exchanges. The voice's native beauty is evident most of the time. He can still summon a connected *mezza voce* for "O dolci mani." At times (usually on a lyric line) the upper notes shine through; at others, they get stuck. The casual nature of his characterization is apparent alongside his colleagues, but actually he is doing more than most—our attention is called to how little the authors have given any Cavaradossi to work with.

1955 CETRA (M)

Gigliola Frazzoni (A), Ferruccio Tagliavini (B), Giangiacomo Guelfi (C), Italian Radio Chorus and Orchestra, Turin—Arturo Basile

We have here a solid, lively account. The RAI Turin troops, familiar from the previous

Cetra set, play with more care and color here for Basile, an old-fashioned theater conductor who knows how to make all the key points, keep the structure intact, and point up the descriptive detail without letting it get out of hand. Frazzoni's voice is round and rich in the lower and middle reaches and strong higher up, though without much breathing room—rather like Guerrini's, only more open-throated. She's an unabashed sort of singer who's not afraid to scream now and then, and while she does nothing all that individual, she sings with feeling and commitment. Tagliavini owned a beautiful tenor, lyric with a dash of *spinto*. It was the most like Gigli's of any of the latter's successors, but never quite as free or as flexibly integrated between high and low, loud and soft. He sometimes sings a true line, and sometimes an extremely clever imitation of one, and his way of doing this creates inimitable inflections: Stylings by Ferruccio, for your listening pleasure. He sings a good, likable Cavaradossi that rises close to the classic level in "O dolci mani" and "Amaro sol per te." Guelfi's huge, ponderous voice is heard to advantage as Scarpia. He is almost incessantly loud, but not without some dramatic sense, and within his rather crude framework he does make some singing points. The best of his work (as at the top of Act II) makes us regret that he shouts away the Te Deum.

1956 METROPOLITAN OPERA RECORD CLUB (M)

Dorothy Kirsten (A), Daniele Barioni (B), Frank Guarrera (C), Metropolitan Opera Chorus and Orchestra—Dimitri Mitropoulos

Most albums in this series are no more than extensive highlights versions, but this is substantially complete, though in this opera any cuts in a version that pretends to continuity are altogether weird. The important ones here: Act I, most of the Scarpia / Sacristan investigation; Act II, Tosca pleading with Mario through the door; Act III, the Shepherd and dawn. Two or three other little snips, and the same two discs used by the complete editions. You explain it. Kirsten's Tosca is well worth a listen, the most

successful I know in terms of adopting a purely lyric voice to the role. It has an ingenuously girlish, spitfire quality that is refreshing, and is very well sung throughout, with a pretty, blond coloration seldom heard in the part. At a few of the more violent spots, she is a shade careful, but never lazy or tentative. She was a smart, gifted singer. Barioni, another of the 1950s meteors, shows the handsome, bronzed tenor that created a stir right around the time of this recording, as well as some squeezing into the upper range. It is blunt, unsubtle vocalism, but the power and quality of the instrument are genuine. Guarrera—an intelligent, versatile, willing baritone with a fine voice—was worked to death in every conceivable assignment at a time when he should have been carefully brought along. Here, traces of wear are already showing up, and the voice is darkened to lend it a weight that was not natural. But he gives full value with a tough, dramatically aware performance that has some excellent moments. I shall reserve comment on Mitropoulos for the next entry, save to observe that his reading works less well here, and there is some sloppy orchestral work.

1956 MET (M, P)

Renata Tebaldi (A), Richard Tucker (B), Leonard Warren (C), Metropolitan Opera Chorus and Orchestra—Dimitri Mitropoulos

This is a hot live performance, not flawless, but exciting and gratifying. Mitropoulos is nothing if not idiosyncratic, sometimes to the point of willfulness. There are big *allargandos* followed by impetuous *stringendos*, and there are tiny stops and *accelerandos*. But there is also a fiery, galvanic thrust to the work, and the cooperation with the singers is something to hear—Mitropoulos knows what each soloist does best and helps each one do it. Each of these principals brings to the performance a full divo ego, mounting jealous guard over the right to shape the music, to showcase effects. Since all three are musical and shrewd, and the effects they seek are relevant, Mitropoulos (certainly no lesser light himself, and far from weak-willed) knows there is everything to gain by giving them well-rehearsed room. Listen to the juicy expansion at "e bruna Floria" in the first tenor aria, or the complete dramatic reading of "Non la sospiri," for a lesson in the vanished crafts of operatic collaboration. Tebaldi's voice does not handle quite as airily here as in her previous rendition, but it is still working well. The intonation at the top is actually better, and there is more bite, thrust, and passion—an electric performance. Tucker is in top form, and gives us one of our strongest Cavaradossis. The phrasing is broad and warm, the voice firm and brilliant, the temperament full-hearted. As always, he is prone to some exaggeration (when Tucker whacked an Italian double consonant, it stayed down for the count), but not more than a few other tenors fill out the music's line as satisfyingly. Warren is not heard at quite his best, partly because this sort of writing never fit his voice as well as Verdian *cantabile*, and partly because he clearly hasn't settled into the part—there are several telltale memory slips and false entrances. Nevertheless, this is an imposing Scarpia, and interesting in that it is constructed largely around the singer's propensity for ostentatious understatement: when Warren wants to be sure of a point, he stretches the tempo to the breaking point, drops his plump, chewy baritone down to its memorably beautiful and audible *mezza voce*, and makes an aria out of each syllable. In a sense, this is representative of the performance philosophy in effect here: all the participants (but most especially the Americans) tend to treat rather obvious insights as if they were discoveries of the gravest significance. Naive underlining, we might call it, by three tremendous voices and a splendid conductor, and the results are moving and powerful.

1957 RCA / BMG (S) CD

Zinka Milanov (A), Jussi Bjoerling (B), Leonard Warren (C), Rome Opera Chorus and Orchestra—Erich Leinsdorf

There's a great deal of quality performing on this set, but as a totality it does not quite jell. The very best of it is from Bjoerling, and most of all in the last act, where he sounds very close to his prime—than which there is no primer. Throughout, in fact, his voice's supple, clear line, silvery timbre, and precise poise are in evidence. It's just that—as with many of his records from around this time—the top of his voice does not always find its freest resonance, and he feels called upon to resort to little lifts and plosives, so that climactic spots like "La vita mi costasse" or "Vittoria!" or "Non ho amato" come out tightly muscled. Still one of the best-sung Cavaradossis, it could disappoint a listener acquainted with the earlier Bjoerling. Milanov came to this role late in her career, and the recording was accomplished a few seasons past her best years. Still, she brings much to the music: her creamy, full-bodied tone; her command of *portamento* and *legato*; her famous suspended *piano*, mysterious and soft, yet connected; her unaffected ease with the grand style. A few hard-sounding *acuti*, traces of labor or toughness in the tone, and in some of the more frantic passages a choice between being too careful or losing the center of the sound are periodically bothersome. But there's never doubt about the credentials, and as always, her singing is heartfelt. Warren's live-performance insecurities have vanished here. Except for a few tremulous spots in mid-range declamation, he rolls through the music, making his points with decisiveness and economy. In some of the silkier passages, he is incomparable. Leinsdorf presents the score in clarified layers and segments, angular of phrase and *sec* of texture. The early Victor stereo—bright, separate, highlighted—seems an extension of the conductor's view. I don't care for it, but we should take note of another maestro of stature who collaborates intelligently with great singers.

1957 PHILIPS (S)

Antonietta Stella (A), Gianni Poggi (B), Giuseppe Taddei (C), San Carlo Chorus and Orchestra—Tullio Serafin

This generally solid account, part of a series circulated in the United States by Columbia, has two outstanding elements: the leadership of Serafin and the Scarpia of Taddei. The conductor's work has no quirks, no real surprises. Serafin, one gathers, would not have considered it his role to make us hear the score in a new light. Rather, he satisfies us with the old one. Like Tebaldi in her traversal of the title role, he usually makes what sound like the obvious choices of a wise, experienced musician, then carries them out with the utmost conviction and care, and with no little drive and swing. (The slackness that invaded some of his readings at this stage of his life is not manifest.) The San Carlo forces sound like an absolutely first-rank operatic ensemble here; the smaller roles are well taken (a splendid Angelotti by Ferruccio Mazzoli); and the recording is superb. Stella, a tremendous favorite in Naples during these years, had a *lirico-spinto* soprano of a quality that should always be welcome (lovely in timbre, ample in size), if not quite the individuality and authority of voice and temperament to put her in the league with the most formidable competition of her time. In her generously felt Tosca, the sound is almost always attractive, the phrasing idiomatic. "Vissi d'arte" is quite beautifully sung, with some melting suspended soft notes, and she has engaging moments in the more conversational scenes. Still, there is something vague in much of her singing—a lack of core, as if she were trying to sing too lightly—and several of the Cs are raw-sounding. Taddei is a fine, traditional Scarpia. His large, velvety baritone—postwar Italy's nappiest in the middle, though erratic on top—is in excellent shape, and lies well on the role's range. The interpretation is forceful and alive, if somewhat on the broad side. Poggi's Cavaradossi is certainly an advance over his previous version. There is greater freedom with dynamics, more flexibility in the phrasing (even touches of elegance in "E lucevan le stelle"), and the voice is still in youthful estate. His way of conveying emotion remains blatant and lachrymose, but vocally he is by no means at the bottom of the heap.

1959 DECCA / LONDON (S) CD

Renata Tebaldi (A), Mario del Monaco (B), George London (C), Chorus and Orchestra of the Accademia di Santa Cecilia, Rome—Francesco Molinari-Pradelli

This is the heaviest of all the *Toscas*. Some of the weight derives from the vocal caliber of the principals, and has artistic legitimacy. And some, unhappily, is the dead weight of Molinari-Pradelli's leadership. The playing is better here than in his Cetra performance, and the excellent stereo sound and staging help, too. Purely as accompanist, he has his merits. The reading, though, has a limp and taken-for-granted feeling. Where singers assume command or the writing provides its own energy, things go well enough; everywhere else, they just sit there. This is late-prime Tebaldi, the voice still rich and puissant, consistently glamorous in the middle and at *piano*. A granitic quality to some of the high *fortes* and a little tug (or simply more loudness) on the flow of certain lighter passages are the chief differences from her earlier singing. Del Monaco, in a role that was in his repertory but was not entirely characteristic for him, is in the same late-summer condition. A big, awkward gong of a voice, unmistakable for its bedrock resonance, and a heroic attack on the music, as if engaged in a primitive combat that must be won. His normal tussles with *legato* and the modulation of dynamics—C-plus with A for effort. Suave he is not, or judicious. But thrilling and inspirational he is. London's voice is the deepest, the most *pesante*, of all the Scarpias, and one that is powerful and technically controlled, as well. By comparison with the best Italian singers of the role, he at first sounds somewhat literal and heavy-handed. But as the performance proceeds, the consistency of his approach, the intelligence of his interpretive decisions, and the sheer beauty and size of the voice add up to an interesting and authoritative Scarpia, one that fires its own salvos in this Big Bertha *Tosca*.

1962 DECCA / LONDON (S) CD

Leontyne Price (A), Giuseppe di Stefano (B), Giuseppe Taddei (C), Vienna State Opera Chorus, Vienna Philharmonic Orchestra—Herbert von Karajan

The conductor and producer dominate this recording, and while both do some very striking things, they should not be earning our attention so easily. Karajan presides over a superbly played orchestral performance whose beauty, color, and delicacy are constant sources of pleasure. His producer (John Culshaw) collaborates to secure some marvelously evocative and well-integrated sound effects and staging. They are particularly wonderful on bells: the little chiming one of the Sacristan's Angelus; the fatefully donging mid-range one of Tosca's "Tradirmi egli non può"; the fearsome, deep-throated tolling ones of the Te Deum; the variously pitched and distanced ones of Act III, calling across the Roman hills—all aptly chosen, magically rendered. And at points, Karajan's interpretive approach—basically slow, controlled, highly detailed, though hardly lacking in force when that is demanded—makes true dramatic statements. One instance is the questioning of Cavaradossi early in Act II—slow but inexorably steady, full of a quiet, matter-of-fact kind of menace, with the low string *pizzicatos* plucking along like the Chinese water torture. But where the actions of the characters should take over from the environment (most of the time, can we agree?), the singers have too little to offer. Price is in good voice, and sings the upper two-thirds of the part very prettily (the lower third requires a working chest register and coordination with same: Price is unable to oblige). Although she has a generalized musicality, a point of view is hard to detect; there is some feeling, but little insight. The line is seldom distinguished, and many of the effects sound learned rather than absorbed. One can enjoy the full lyric tone, but it's hard to get caught up in a moment. Di Stefano is for all practical purposes disabled, though he sings with his customary spirit. The bottom of his voice is a wisp, while most of the upward excursions are painfully thin and tight. He still does some things well (he is wonderful in the above-mentioned interrogation), but they're hard to appreciate when one is in recovery from the last calamity or in dread of the next one. Taddei's second Scarpia finds his voice still strong and well oiled, though hints of a loosening focus slip in, and the recording is less flattering to his

voice than Philips's. More disappointing, the characterization has gone over the top; it is filled with sneering and gloating, and announcements of evil intent that would blow the baron's cover in an instant.

1964–65 EMI / ANGEL (S) CD

Maria Callas (A), Carlo Bergonzi (B), Tito Gobbi (C), Chorus of the Paris Opéra, Orchestra of the Société des Concerts du Conservatoire— Georges Prêtre

This set is one of the more ill-advised early-sixties stereo remakes, but since it never displaced its predecessor (the de Sabata), this has not mattered much, and it can be looked at on its own merits. It has some. Bergonzi does not really rank with the greatest of our Marios—the singing lacks some of the tonal sheen and excitement for that—but he is thoroughly enjoyable: this Cavaradossi is smoothly sung, technically admirable, stylistically idiomatic. Giorgio Tadeo is an unusually fine Sacristan, with a beautiful light bass and lots of life, minus the bladder-over-the-head routines that generally pass for comic characterization. Prêtre is an interesting and intelligent musician who gives us a well-conducted *Tosca*, strong on the graphic detail. It's well played by a good orchestra that is not quite at the Scala or Vienna Philharmonic level, and whose brass and woodwind sections offer some French timbral variants that are at times quite pungent. Callas, though, has gone from a peak to a valley. The musical specificity and sense of character are still here, but the voice has thinned and whitened, and a serious and persistent wobble has taken over the upper range. A listening ordeal, and why bother, when her contribution can be heard without the obstacles on the de Sabata? A point of gloomy interest: whereas her restudy of this part with Zeffirelli around this time made her Tosca vastly more interesting in the theater (behaviorally more specific), the changes emerge on the recording as mere vulgarization and loss of subtlety. All this applies to Gobbi as well. His voice has suffered less—it is still loud and steady—but it has become more stiff and blarey, while his interpretation has slipped toward the obvious and forced.

1966 DECCA / LONDON (S)

Birgit Nilsson (A), Franco Corelli (B), Dietrich Fischer-Dieskau (C), Chorus and Orchestra of the Accademia di Santa Cecilia, Rome—Lorin Maazel

Two great singers give us the better part of a sensational *Tosca*. Nilsson is, from the vocal point of view, incomparable. It is true, of course, that the color of her soprano is cooler than that of the best Latin voices. But no other singer approaches her smooth, easy power, her balance and completeness of tone throughout the range, her floating delicacy and precision in the lighter phrases, her on-the-button intonation, her free brilliance at the top. Further, she phrases with taste and sensitivity, and presents the character with a grounded simplicity that, while it never blinds with flashes of insight, has a cumulative honesty that is quite moving. Callas has a complexity that is more fascinating from moment to moment, and Tebaldi a more lovable vocal warmth and temperamental gutsiness. But this is the best-sung Floria in recorded history. Corelli, too, brings superior vocal equipment to this music—the power of the *tenore di forza* with a good measure of the malleability and dynamic control of a fine lyric tenor, and a prevailingly beautiful timbre to boot. It's a voice that was always cheated in some degree by studio recording, and here he is not consistently into the meat of it, especially in Act I. But this is still rewarding singing, and in Act III he hits and maintains his stride. Fischer-Dieskau is, in a word, awful. Of all the Scarpias to record the role, his voice is the most inappropriate, his technique the least adapted to the music. He sounds scrawny and raw at *forte*, salon-pretty at *piano*. Beyond this, his acting is preposterous melodramatic ranting, and he treats the style with little respect. From an artist of such proven musicality and intelligence, it's a performance that leaves one shaking the head. Maazel raises the level of the Santa Cecilia's playing, but the reading is erratic and unpersuasive, going by fits and starts and sudden fades and swells, and making points that, upon inspection, turn out to be non-points.

1972 RCA / BMG (S) CD

Leontyne Price (A), Plácido Domingo (B), Sherrill Milnes (C), John Alldis Choir, Philharmonia Orchestra—Zubin Mehta

Mehta conducts a strong, clear interpretation that is somewhat matter-of-fact, but not without tension. He has a fine orchestra to work with. Domingo's Cavaradossi is also straightforward, without either eccentricities or imagination. The voice is burnished and firm, with traces of nasality and pinching. It's all certainly listenable but rather unformed—the sort of singing one calls promising. There is a splendidly sung Sacristan from Paul Plishka. Since her earlier recording of the part, Price's voice has grown bigger and more commanding in the middle, but has thinned at the top, while the lower range (never convincing) has turned hollow and breathy, like a club singer's. Her interpretive limitations remain as before, but are worsened by her pushy efforts to transcend them. Milnes is in uneven vocal condition: at times one hears the bright, fresh sound of his exciting early seasons in high baritone roles; at others, the duller, grayish timbre and roughness at the break of his later work in heavier repertory emerges. Scarpia is not a well-chosen assignment for him in any case, for it does not show the beauty and soaring upper range of his voice, and the character leads him into the sort of penny-dreadful villainy that, we must observe, is becoming something of a norm in the role. The acting-with-the-voice is elaborate, but never sounds genuine.

1973 MELODIYA (S)

Tamara Milashkina (A), Vladimir Atlantov (B), Yuri Mazurok (C), Bolshoi Theater Chorus and Orchestra—Mark Ermler

This is a strongly cast edition, and not uninterestingly conducted. The male principals do not tread gently, nor do their engineers soften their utterances. "I leave in the world a person dear to me," screams Atlantov, directly into our cochlear ducts. He does so, nevertheless, with one of the important tenor voices of recent times, a clangorously full-throated one reminiscent of del Monaco's in both its hairy-chested resonance and its ham-fisted, high-pressure technique. Actually, he's not totally clumsy—"E lucevan le stelle" is reasonably smooth, though *forte* throughout. This sort of voice is always penalized by recording: if it's close-to, as here, it's garishly incessant; if not, it loses some of the tingle. Mazurok offers a well-sung Scarpia. Like Milnes's, his instrument is basically a strong, sunny high baritone, not ideal for the role. But Mazurok's voice has better balance and unity, and much less audible gear-shifting, so there is no sense that he is imposing on his voice to sing the music. We must settle for the good vocalism, for while the general style is in the ball park, he has but one or two primary colors, and employs more or less the same tone of voice regardless of whom he is singing to, or about what, or under what conditions. Milashkina gives the most complete performance of these principals, and provided one can accept a Slavic tint to tone and language, she is really an excellent Tosca. Her voice is round and ripely attractive; she can sing powerfully or softly, and connect the two; and she finds many interesting things in the qualities of moments. "Vissi d'arte" is sung with deep, lovely tone and honest feeling, and only in Act III does the extra vibrato and timbral harshness typical of some Eastern sopranos become at all troublesome. Obviously, none of the principals has quite the native Italian way with style and language, but they do no worse than their American or Germanic counterparts. From the supporting cast, though, there are some hilarious moments. Ermler leads a well-shaped, big-boned reading that has a good deal of atmosphere, and he has a reasonable rapport with his singers. There are some odd accents of phrase, but they do not sound arbitrary.

1976 DEUTSCHE GRAMMOPHON (S)

Galina Vishnevskaya (A), Franco Bonisolli (B), Matteo Manuguerra (C), Chorus and Orchestra de la RTF—Mstislav Rostropovich

Apart from the solid Scarpia of Manuguerra, this set has little to offer. Rostropovich is certainly an outstanding musician, but except for the interesting pointing of some small moments, his strengths are not engaged here. His orchestra lacks pit experience, and the conductor is unable to sustain the tensions and shapes of theatrical scenes; the reading falls slack too much of the time. Vishnevskaya, such a cherishable Tatiana and Natasha on earlier operatic recordings, is as usual at it with a will here, but sounding worn and out of her element. Her voice, at its best a shiny lyric one, is thickened and hardened, and she gusts through the part with little line, dealing in fussy vibrato tricks, her Italian opaque. It simply does not work. Bonisolli is yet another "coulda been a contender." The set-up top notes are fit as a fiddle, and the fine native quality of the voice often audible. The balancing of the voice, however, is just patchwork, and there is no continuity between loud and soft. Though there are impressive notes, there is seldom any shape or finish to the line. Manuguerra's fine, open baritone has sap and hue, and while the technique embraces nothing fancy, the knit of the voice is good. If he does very little with the part beyond singing it well and roughing in the basic attitudes, at least there's no foolishness.

1976 PHILIPS (S) CD

Montserrat Caballé (A), José Carreras (B), Ingvar Wixell (C), Chorus and Orchestra of the Royal Opera House, Covent Garden—Colin Davis

The orchestra plays most beautifully for its (then) music director. Like many contemporary conductors, Davis seems to want transparency and exactitude above all, whether or not these qualities are the most important ones for the writing. Consequently, it is the exquisiteness of instrumental detail and the dainty lucidity of the more chamberish moments that one finds oneself listening to—with considerable pleasure, till one realizes that a scene has been going by. (Modern recording, too, almost automatically gives these aspects a disproportionate prominence.) Of course, *Tosca* still happens— one can go only so far. The priorities seem strangely ordered, though, at least to these ears. And here is Caballé, essentially placid of demeanor, lyrical of voice, and fluid of technique, a trifle past her prime, pretending to be a veristic singing-actress. She gives it a vigorous try, but it's a strain, and the results are mixed. There's pretty sound in the more *cantabile* sections, and by dint of forcing she nails some good high notes. But the parts of the role she sings well tend to expire from very slow tempos that haven't enough rhythmic underpinning (Davis aids and abets), while the heavier scenes are essentially beyond her scope, evoking the glottal attacks, the driving chest, the lumpy line that has invariably resulted when she puts her lovely but rather fragile voice to dramatic tasks. Carreras is at his best here. Already, there is some sense of a voice in overdrive—an insistently emphatic way of singing, along with occasional fibrous sounds and a faked *mezza voce*. But both the voice and the affinity for the idiom are the real thing, and this is a prevailingly pleasurable Cavaradossi. Wixell's soft-grained baritone, Nordic vowels, and studied way of dabbing in little color changes do not make him a natural for Scarpia, but there is intelligence and musicality in his work, and he puts together a respectable performance.

1977 ELECTRACORD (S)

Virginia Zeani (A), Corneliu Fânăţeanu (B), Nicolae Herlea (C), Chorus and Orchestra of the Romanian Opera, Bucharest—Cornel Trăilescu

This performance is rather like most of the Romanian cuisine we have access to in the United States—slow-cooked and heavy. The orchestra has some tonal warmth and a feeling for *cantabile* but not much spark, and Trăilescu's tempos tend to tramp. Like the Remington, this version extends to six sides. Zeani was a thoroughly capable *verista* in the fifties and sixties, but by 1977 the top of her voice was dry

and pinched. She is stylistically secure, often has something individual to offer interpretively, and her vocal street smarts enable her to hang in for an interesting "Vissi d'arte." Herlea, the other singer here of some international reputation, flashes impressive top Fs and G-flats, and sings an Act II that is effective in a thickly underlined way. In the first act, there is too much muddy tone and doubtful intonation. The middle range of Fânăţeanu's voice suggests a quality tenor of dark, hefty properties, but his labored and constricted *acuti* never free up, and the constant pressure in the singing makes it impossible to enjoy. The male voices further suffer from extremely close miking.

1978 DECCA/LONDON (S) (D

Mirella Freni (A), Luciano Pavarotti (B), Sherrill Milnes (C), London Opera Chorus, National Philharmonic Orchestra—Nicola Rescigno

Rescigno has the reputation of a complaisant singers' conductor, and while he does nothing much to contradict that here, he also reminds us that there are worse things in the world. True, we could use a stronger hand at points. Like most non-opera orchestras, this one tends to go dead during small conversations and the little stretches we call "transitional"—the players don't sense the underlying theatrical point, and thus have hold of nothing to give direction to the bars. But most of the reading flows quite naturally. It certainly is not direction-less, and is well enough played. Much of the instrumental commentary is nice, and the illustrative passages are rendered as if the conductor believed in their importance. Freni's voice, caught here in late mid-career, is of course a lyric one, albeit full-bodied. As we have heard with Kirsten, this need not disqualify a Tosca. But when Freni sings music of this nature, she loses some of her balance, and consequently some of the line. She is perfectly all right when she can stay away from *forte* singing in the lower half of the range; much of the rest is extremely pretty, and the aria is solid. She's emotionally sincere but not often specific—a nice kid in a tough jam. Pavarotti sings well in mid-range, his lyric tenor retaining most of its appealing quality and freedom there. The top is in-and-out—a satisfying note when he has adequate prep time and a congenial vowel, a thin or tight one otherwise. The Pavarotti Cavaradossi is absolutely the generic brand. Nothing is tasteless or out of style, and nothing will take you by surprise, even in a minor way, unless you're hearing *Tosca* for the first time. Vocally, Milnes's second Scarpia is marginally improved on his first— a bit more consistency, the weight of the part sitting more naturally, though the pieces of the *passaggio* puzzle have drifted farther apart. The interpretation remains an exercise in chewed-up words and exaggerated inflections.

1979 DEUTSCHE GRAMMOPHON (S) CD

Katia Ricciarelli (A), José Carreras (B), Ruggero Raimondi (C), Chorus of the Deutsche Oper, Berlin Philharmonic Orchestra—Herbert von Karajan

This has a dejected, half-hearted air that is most dispiriting. Karajan's tempos are not that different from those of his earlier recording, but they have lost their bone and tension; there is a heavy, enervated feel to whole stretches. The conductor's fussiness is still apparent, but its positive side—the insistence on some creepy, subterranean musico-dramatic point that must be made—has for the most part slipped aside. Although the Berlin Philharmonic executes with the best, there is seldom any suggestion of magic or of participation in the drama. Both the soprano and tenor are gifted with choice south-of-the-mountains voices that should have been at the full stretch of their powers at the time of this inscription. However, Carreras shows a shocking falling-off in the scant three years since his first Mario. The voice has lost most of its liquidness, has opened and loosened (in the negative senses of those words) in the middle, and thinned at the top. He pushes through, managing a convincing if strenuous "Vittoria!" and figuring out a presentable "E lucevan le stelle." But of true singing there is very little. Ricciarelli slips through most of Act I in a relaxed, pretty, pop-like half-voice, as if marking a rehearsal; Karajan's predilections do not

help. Later, she sings out more honestly, and though it's often clear that her technique is not set up to handle the pressure, at least this sounds like operatic vocalism, and the fine quality of the voice gets through at times. Her attention is infrequently intruded upon by thoughts of musical shapes or dramatic meanings. Once past the opening of Act II, Raimondi turns loose his potent bass-baritone, odd vowels and all, and sings the kind of Scarpia we could well use: mature, feline, and powerful. Till then, I've no idea what he is up to, mincing through even declamatory passages in a breathy croon. The supporting cast is exceptionally poor; all in all, Act I emerges a feebler unit than one would have supposed possible.

1980 EMI / ANGEL (S,D) CD

Renata Scotto (A), Plácido Domingo (B), Renato Bruson (C), Ambrosian Opera Chorus, Philharmonia Orchestra—James Levine

The notable element here is Domingo's Cavaradossi—a rare and gratifying instance of substantial improvement over an earlier effort. The voice is cleaner and better balanced, the resonance more focused and consistent. He phrases with greater definition and finish, and there is increased care and understanding in the shaping of episodes. There is still not much of what we could term personality or individuality, but there is presence to his work, and it's the best-sung Cavaradossi since Corelli's. In Scotto we have an aging light soprano who happens to be a mistress of the descriptive moment, and indeed of many aspects of veristic style that are not to be lightly set aside. Her performance can be appreciated for its understanding and connectedness, and for many special inflectional touches in the lyric sections of the score. Regrettably, the voice at this stage was shrill and wobbly when called upon to step up either pitch or volume, and so the larger share of her singing is hard to enjoy. Bruson has a voice of decent Scarpia weight and Italianate color, and is not about to be taken to task for scenery-chewing. His work is strong, stolid, and phlegmatic, and seemingly content to be so; considering the level of vocal competence, it's astonishingly boring.

Levine's reading is strong-limbed, the elements extremely clear, the tempos logical. He works with Scotto in a conciliatory fashion but is otherwise on the rigid side. The overall feel is crisp and explosive, and, combined with the digital engineering, this sometimes suggests a forced, high-tech imitation of life.

1983 BALKANTON (S,D) CD

Raina Kabaivanska (A), Nazzareno Antinori (B), Nelson Portella (C), Bulgarian National Choir, Sophia Philharmonic Orchestra—Gabriele Bellini

This recording (distributed in the United States on the Frequenz label) is a bit of a sleeper. Its only participant of international reputation is Kabaivanska, caught late in the day, at that. But her mid-caliber *spinto* soprano is still seaworthy, and she is a most interesting Tosca. True, her voice—never of outstanding beauty—has properties of toughness and edginess, and she is sometimes scrambling when the music covers a lot of ground quickly. But her Tosca is immensely alive; emotional commitment and musical intelligence are always present in her work. She rises to all the big moments, and the many theatrical effects are never just theatrical effects, but grow directly from the playing of situations. She has a worthy antagonist in the Scarpia of Portella. His well-seated baritone is at moments thick in quality, but it has color, dynamic range, and considerable command. He shows definite sense for the life of a line, and sees the point of many small things in the writing. Antinori is not at this level: his technique is stiff, and his only means of diddling with the volume and tone controls is to expunge vibrato. However, it's a big voice, with the ring of true coin, and in fresh, steady estate, so not all is lost here, either. He suffers more than the others when the blades of reverb and digitalization are drawn from their scabbards; otherwise, the engineering is good. Bellini's leadership is not exciting or very individual, but it is well controlled and proportioned. He pays some attention to his principals, and sets up moments knowledgeably. The orchestral and choral standard is quite high.

1984 DECCA / LONDON (S,D) CD

Kiri Te Kanawa (A), Giacomo Aragall (B), Leo Nucci (C), Welsh National Opera Chorus, National Philharmonic Orchestra—Georg Solti

This does not sound like a performance. It sounds like a job. The folks who work at the job show up punctually. They are experienced, top-of-the-line workers, accustomed to forming teams that fall easily into place and perform coolly, efficiently, under pressure. They do so here, whipping together a sort of prefab opera, which they assemble without difficulty from parts that are cut and stamped to fit. One has the impression they have done so quickly, without having to think or feel anything through on the spot. Then, relieved that everything has gone as planned, without a hitch, they have hurried off to a pint, or a flight, or some shopping, or just back home to look over their pension-fund statements. Among them, none are more satisfied than the technicians, who have gotten everything to be as they wished. They have arranged for a synthesization of *Tosca*, a *Tosca* machine, a *Tosca* floppy disk. The world in which it functions is windowless, soundproof, climate-controlled. In it, the light is white, strong, and utterly even, and each passing second is reported. Predictability is total, and this is the point. A world of dust-free beauty for machines, but a soulless void for humans and an impossible environment for art. As to the cogs of the machine: Te Kanawa's round, lovely tone is intact except at the bottom, where it never was. Her work is nice, detached, abstract, with a few imitation affects that sound sprayed on. Aragall's virile tenor has never sounded better, but his singing is even more uninflected than Te Kanawa's—relentless is the word. Most depressing is this: Solti is a master musician, whose career came out of real-world opera houses and has had its hours of glory. That he should preside over this sort of mechanical, impatient read-through, then approve the playbacks, is incomprehensible. The orchestra is of high, anonymous competence. It is to be doubted that a single member of it has read the libretto of *Tosca*. Three indications of life: 1) The Sciarrone tries to get it going on the line "No! Melas è in fuga!" 2) Piero de Palma, recording his seventh Spoletta over a period of thirty-three years, retains most of his slender but true voice, and continues to rally the tiny territories under his jurisdiction. 3) The protest of Leo Nucci: with a fine voice about three shades too light for Scarpia, and no means of locating an actor's connection to the role, he yells and barks his way disgracefully through it. And this is to his credit, for it is a sign he knows something is very, very wrong.

1988 SONY (S,D) CD

Eva Marton (A), José Carreras (B), Juan Pons (C), Hungarian State Radio and Television Chorus, Hungarian State Orchestra—Michael Tilson Thomas

This is a fundamentally limp performance into which the soloists inject occasional shots of life. The orchestra has a warm, comfortable sound. Thomas leads a slow, lyrical reading that lapses into dreamy-eyed lassitude whenever given the chance: all the music that is not explicitly confrontational has a pretty, meandering feel that betrays no hint of dramatic intent. The recording has a vagueness about it, too, for while the overall sound is good and such effects as shots and door-slams well handled, there's an aura of splice-and-mix and an undefined voice-orchestra relationship in it. Marton's is certainly a full-bodied Tosca voice, with the needed amplitude and reach. Some of her singing is quite beautiful and / or powerful, and some is overly tremulous or afflicted by impurities of

timbre and intonation. There's a general sincerity to her work, and she makes interestingly restrained choices at spots like "Voglio vederlo" or "E avanti a lui." Carreras sings with care for the music, with temperamental life, and with some of the poetic feel for word and phrase that first distinguished his singing. He manages everything with some shapeliness, and must be admired for fighting his way this far back. But wear and strain do show in the singing. Pons's mellow, monocolored, modest-sized voice and rather stolid stage personality do not suggest an outstanding Scarpia, but he sings the role with technical and musical security, and with some sense of expressive purpose even when his voice will not expand to fill the need. István Gati and József Gregor are very strong casting for Angelotti and the Jailer. As has been the case for over fifty years in roles large and small, Italo Tajo leaves no vaudevillian turn unturned as the Sacristan; it's truly shameless. Several notes in his voice are still quite lovely. The choir is superb in the offstage cantata.

As an all-round statement of the piece, no question: it's still the de Sabata. For the many individual performances that should not be missed, see above.

CONRAD L. OSBORNE

Unavailable for review:
1918 EMI / ANGEL
1919 EMI / ANGEL
1991 DEUTSCHE GRAMMOPHON

GIACOMO PUCCINI

MADAMA BUTTERFLY (1904)

A: Cio-Cio-San, Madama Butterfly (s); B: Suzuki (ms);
C: Pinkerton (t); D: Sharpless (bar)

One sometimes wonders how many voices have been broken on the wheel of *Madama Butterfly*. The role invites full commitment without vulgarity: a lyric soprano of youthful appeal and fresh middle voice who yet must give the impression of extending herself to the limit, both dramatically and physically, at the climaxes of "Un bel dì" and "Che tua madre," at the sighting of the "Abramo Lincoln," and in the death scene. The sort of containment that sopranos speak of when they discuss vocal longevity must be very cannily managed here; without its moments of extraordinary vocal intensity a *Butterfly* evening is at most merely pleasant. With them it can be unforgettable. A large voice, though, does not ensure success with it, either. A splendid Aida or Leonora may fail as Butterfly, for the idea of fragility tested to the utmost is central. Rosina Storchio, the first Butterfly, had a delicate voice and wholehearted approach; the comments made by others about her art, and the potential to express heartbreak implicit in her delightful record of an aria from Leoncavallo's version of *La Bohème*, make that clear. As with Puccini's *Bohème*, two generations of remarkable singing actresses gradually formed a tradition in singing Cio-Cio-San, each individual examining the words and the melodies for tiny revelations, layered meanings, a mixture of humor and pathos which can amount to the tragic in intensity of effect. A few of these singers have recorded the opera complete.

In recent years the center of performance control has moved further in the direction of the conductor, so that we often get performances of extraordinary orchestral clarity but emotional sluggishness and imbalance, with casts of vocal accomplishment but dramatic anonymity. A combination of the best vocal and orchestral approaches is of course ideal, and a look at the complete recordings over the last seven decades, representing an evolution of traditions, can help one to find just what is really available in the work.

1924 EMI / ANGEL (In English) (M)

Rosina Buckman (A), Nellie Walker / Gladys Peel (B), Tudor Davies (C), Frederick Ranalow (D), Chorus and orchestra—Eugene Goossens

This was the first complete recording of *Madama Butterfly* and is sung in English. Rosina Buckman sang Butterfly and additional roles for Beecham's company, among others. Her voice is, in its rather motherly way, charming and warm: one understands why she was used so much. There is little *portamento* and she is apt to sound both coy and sensible at once, but "Vogliatemi bene" is touching in its way and "Un bel dì" fully acted. She is at her best in the dramatic rather than the amorous scenes. There are no tears at the end, though "Va, gioca, gioca" is breathless and broken-hearted.

Tudor Davies as Pinkerton, on the other hand, sounds repressed and absolutely humorless in Act I but a little more convincing in an earnest Farewell. He has a darkish, rather throaty tenor, full at the top; he later sang heavier roles. Frederick Ranalow, the Sharpless, was Papageno and Hans Sachs with Beecham. One has difficulty squaring this with what is heard on the record. The voice seems light and the manner is almost comically spineless. The others are very proper indeed. Eugene Goossens's orchestra plays with great speed; sometimes the score sounds gabbled, but nothing lingers to the point of dullness. The recording certainly illustrates some aspects of a national style removed from Puccini's, but Buckman has a forward and occasionally glistening voice for the title role.

1929 EMI / ANGEL (M)

Rosetta Pampanini (A), Conchita Velasquez (B), Alessandro Granda (C), Gino Vanelli (D), La Scala Chorus and Orchestra—Lorenzo Molajoli

I have been able to hear only extensive excerpts from this, the first complete recording of *Madama Butterfly* in Italian. Rosetta Pampanini was the Butterfly when Arturo Toscanini reintroduced the opera to La Scala twenty-one years after its ill-fated premiere there, and sang the role more than a thousand times during her career. She offers a larger, darker sound and a more aggressively emotional approach than anticipated. It is very much a stage performance recorded up close: there are tears and exclamations and considerable use of the chest voice. What must have appeared subtler in the opera house is rather blatant here. Emotionally it is demonstrative, if vocally not so finished as other interpretations: certainly a persuasive theatrical characterization on which later sopranos could build refinements.

The Peruvian tenor Alessandro Granda is quite unpoetic in the love duet: gritty but steady and straightforward. At discovering Butterfly's death he bursts into tears. As Sharpless, Gino Vanelli has a strong lyric baritone, but he also gets a little tearful when he doesn't know what else to do. Lorenzo Molajoli conducts a very fast performance. Butterfly's duets with Pinkerton, Sharpless, and Suzuki all zip along, which deprives them at times of delicacy and a certain lyric repose. In listening to sixty years of Puccini performances, one remembers Saint-Saëns's remark to Sir Thomas Beecham about conductors. There are, he said, two kinds: one takes the music too fast, and the other too slow. There is no third!

1929–30 EMI / ANGEL (M)

Margaret Sheridan (A), Ida Mannarini (B), Lionel Cecil (C), Vittorio Weinberg (D), La Scala Chorus and Orchestra—Carlo Sabajno

Even with its early electric sound, this is a very touching performance of *Madama Butterfly*. Margaret Sheridan has a warm, forward, lyric voice: the urgency, radiance, and romantic melancholy are there naturally, it would seem. "Un bel dì" and the death scene are both well done; perhaps her best moments are the love duet, in which she captures all of the moods but particularly that of quiet contentment, and the scene with Sharpless in Act II. She becomes agitated without vulgarity or distortion: the edge and color of the voice sharpen, and she gets a peculiar urgency into the tone. Some of "Che tua madre," the scene in which she imagines taking up her geisha life again, is quite fast, as if she cannot get past these dreadful thoughts quickly enough, and her treatment of "Morta, morta, morta" at the end of it is very convincing. The little scene of anger at Goro is done savagely and has rare conviction; one is again struck by what a skilled dramatist Puccini was. The sighting of the ship is handled with riveting excitement, and she has a delicious impatience in the Flower Duet. After such a sequence, Butterfly's exhaustion seems completely believable. There is vibrant resignation in her third-act confrontation with Sharpless and Kate. Her farewell to the child sounds defenseless rather than heroic, and the crying afterward is as natural as I have heard. At other points one or two high notes are cut off rather abruptly, and the entrance, always a difficult moment for the soprano and here recorded right on mike, is a little rushed, but this is a memorable performance.

Lionel Cecil has a rather tight voice for Pinkerton, very forward and with a pronounced vibrato, but he becomes buoyant and develops some poetry in the love duet, though he sounds a little hard-pressed in the "Addio." Ida Mannarini is a vibrant light mezzo who blends well with Sheridan; the two really seem to carry on a conversation. Vittorio Weinberg is a sympathetic Sharpless, and Nello Palai is among the best Goros, bossy but not bizarre, and having fun with Cecil in the opening scene. Carlo Sabajno offers a speedy but graceful performance, very supportive of the singers. Occasionally he may be a little fast, as at the climax of "Che tua madre," but both the conviction and exhaustion of Act II are well realized, and the Intermezzo is sinuous and graceful. The set is notable for Sheridan's lovely voice and remarkably accomplished characterization.

1939 EMI / ANGEL (M) CD

Toti dal Monte (A), Vittoria Palombini (B), Beniamino Gigli (C), Mario Basiola (D), Rome Opera Chorus and Orchestra—Oliviero de Fabritiis

Toti dal Monte's Butterfly is at the same time the summing up of a style and quite unlike any previous complete recording of the role. She took on Butterfly relatively late in her career, which had been made in lighter repertory. Anyone who has heard her earlier recordings will know that her voice was remarkably lovely, warm, and mobile, with a peculiar carrying power that had nothing to do with tonal weight. The voice in *Butterfly* may be a shock at first; it seems at the start a little tremulous, juiceless, perhaps worn. Technique and characterization transform it and the role. The *legato* and phrasing are unique and exemplary. Precise weight and color are given to each word; everything expresses wonder and aspiration. It may be a childlike interpretation—and the child is what this Pinkerton sees in her—but to us she presents a far more complicated picture almost immediately: proud, ashamed, direct, fragile, unbendable, self-sustaining. The sensual mood deepens throughout the first act, without becoming heavy or overbearing. "Un bel dì" comes as the result of accumulating tensions and responses, and the scene with Yamadori,

with its ironically visionary theme, has just that element of tragic fun of which Puccini was such a master. Later, her "Che tua madre" is a study in deepening narrative intensity without exploitation of the music for a generalized "tragical" effect. With her shifting colors and use of the words, the many conversational moments become as memorable as the climaxes. "Con onor muore" is spoken in a vibrantly dead tone. The farewell to her child and the tears seem spontaneous and believable and could be no one's but dal Monte's, but the thing to remember is that her characterization is the accumulation of many creative details. Even though this may not be one's usual, or preferred, idea of a Puccini soprano voice, her imagination informs that voice with her own special vision of the character.

Complementing this is Beniamino Gigli's beautifully sung Pinkerton. He is one of the few tenors to realize the nature of the character and yet make him irresistible. Many others simply avoid the problem of the charming rake and sing the love duet with the humorless nobility of Manrico or the good-hearted charm of Ernesto in *Don Pasquale*. Gigli, of course, begins with a totally beguiling voice and a sense of humor. There is shallow but delightful camaraderie in his conversation with Sharpless, and it is sensual comfort that he offers to his child-bride: persuasive even while there is a repulsive element in it. His tearful *Addio* is really rather distasteful, and yet entirely in character and bewitchingly sung.

Mario Basiola as Sharpless is a little dry in voice but perfectly supportive in Act II, and Vittoria Palombini a responsive Suzuki. Oliviero de Fabritiis paces the performance with both energy and lyricism—looking back, a relatively rare accomplishment. The performance is one of the unforgettable ones.

1946 MET (M,P)

Licia Albanese (A), Lucielle Browning (B), James Melton (C), John Brownlee (D), Metropolitan Opera Chorus and Orchestra—Pietro Cimara

This remarkable recording is taken from the Metropolitan Opera broadcast of January 19,

1946: the first *Madama Butterfly* to be given at the Met since the start of World War II. It is unique as a complete onstage record of Licia Albanese's portrayal, captured at a prime moment in her career. It is also very much a live performance by a lyric soprano projected to a big house but recorded up close; there is little of the repose or engineered intimacy of the recording studio here. The portrayal is both impassioned and infinitely detailed. Yearning and aspiration never leave the voice in Act I, where she is mistress of the arching musical phrase and the text. The long love duet has seldom been built so carefully and yet so rapturously by a soprano to its climax. Her "Un bel dì" is striking; all its moods are reflected in a public performance remarkable for its finish. Act III is equally memorable; this is one of those performances in which artist and audience seem at one.

The other performers are less memorable. James Melton sounds at least young and steady, if stiff and underpowered at the top. Lucielle Browning has a properly light mezzo voice, a little tremulous. Her characterization is conventional, but she does not disfigure the score, destroy her duets with vocal weight or vibrato, or produce crocodile tears—common faults among Suzukis. As Sharpless, John Brownlee is in blunt voice and seems to have little notion of *legato*. Pietro Cimara is a rousing if unsubtle conductor, and the orchestra is enthused but rough. Each of the acts has firm dramatic shape, though sometimes the tempos are a little fast for complete vocal expressiveness. Albanese's Butterfly, though, is at once passionate, powerfully projected, and beautifully controlled: a great performance.

1949 CBS / SONY (M)

Eleanor Steber (A), Jean Madeira (B), Richard Tucker (C), Giuseppe Valdengo (D), Metropolitan Opera Chorus and Orchestra—Max Rudolf

This set is part of the series that Columbia recorded with the Metropolitan in the years after World War II. The fact that the majority of the Met's leading singers were under exclusive contract to RCA Victor led to some strange casting. Steber has an admirable voice and a substantial technique, but not for Butterfly: the tone lacks warmth and the manner vulnerability. The death scene, done here in a quasi-heroic style, comes closer to matching Steber's capacities than anything else in the score. For Suzuki, Jean Madeira has a huge sound; she and Steber make a particularly unlikely pair of Japanese victims of American insensitivity. As Pinkerton, Richard Tucker sings richly, but despite his efforts at lightness the character emerges as inappropriately sedate and responsible. With this sort of approach, the tears in his "Addio" seem beside the dramatic point. Giuseppe Valdengo has a beautiful lyric baritone voice, though he acts the role routinely. In moments of urgency and thrust Max Rudolf does well, but many of the lyric sections lack dramatic definition.

1951 REMINGTON (M)

Daniza Ilitsch (A), Hildegard Rössl-Majdan (B), Ratko Delorco (C), Jovan Gligor (D), Vienna State Opera Choir, Austrian Symphony Orchestra—Wilhelm Loibner

Though the opera is sung in Italian, the German accent (linguistic *and* musical) is heavy in this painstaking performance. Daniza Ilitsch weighs every effect, singing a thoughtful, careful, accurate Butterfly, restrained but not unfeeling and marked by some shimmering tone. In the death scene, things are, paradoxically, more vigorous, and she does some of her most convincing singing there. Ratko Delorco is a lyrical Pinkerton. August Jaresch has a full and forward tenor for Goro, though he slides over the words. Wilhelm Loibner offers a plodding performance, particularly in the later acts, to his Butterfly's cost. The Intermezzo is damp. The set is interesting mainly for the care in some of Ilitsch's performance and Delorco's warm tone.

1951 DECCA / LONDON (M)

Renata Tebaldi (A), Nell Rankin (B), Giuseppe Campora (C), Giovanni Inghilleri (D), Chorus and Orchestra of the Accademia di Santa Cecilia, Rome—Alberto Erede

Renata Tebaldi is certainly in lovely voice for this, the first of her two recorded Butterflies. The tones are full and round; the top, though it has something of an edge, is under control; and the soft singing is ravishing. Her kind of command, though, strains one's belief in the character. We don't get much of the innocence, the vulnerability, and the proud fragility that are essential. In the love duet, for example, she sounds essentially independent, assured, and occasionally cozily sentimental: certainly not the trembling fifteen-year-old. In Act II her anger with Suzuki is more terrifying than that of any Bonze, and in the big scenes she often becomes the invincible Dramatic Soprano. Perhaps her most convincing moment is at the start of the letter duet, where she is truly intimate and seems to be listening. It is perfectly possible to enjoy and admire this well-sung performance, but to do it one must largely set aside the character given us in the libretto and score.

Giuseppe Campora's Pinkerton sounds, in fact, more romantic, intimate, and vulnerable than she. This was the year of Campora's La Scala debut, and he sings warmly and plangently throughout. Though at first a little deficient in humor and brio, he is charmingly overcome by his Butterfly. In Act III he sings his "Addio" tearfully but well. Giovanni Inghilleri, who made his debut thirty years before, is a lyrical, slightly gruff Sharpless. He is conventionally bland in Act I but more sympathetic and specific in response in Acts II and III. Nell Rankin is a vivid if rather cold Suzuki. The Flower Duet goes well, but elsewhere her crying sounds like an old man's drunken laughter. Piero de Palma offers what may be the best of his several recorded Goros: well sung and full of character—a canny but rather graceful salesman. Alberto Erede is efficient and lyrical, but there is little compulsion in his work, much of which sounds like pleasant accompaniment. The set as least gives us Tebaldi in fine vocal form and Campora's pleasing Pinkerton.

1953 CETRA (M)

Clara Petrella (A), Mafalda Masini (B), Ferruccio Tagliavini (C), Giuseppe Taddei (D), Cetra Chorus, Radio-Television Italiana Orchestra, Turin—Angelo Questa

Clara Petrella offers an emotional performance, with a full *spinto* voice and many moments of conviction, some of delicacy, and generally persuasive phrasing. The vocal sound is a little dark and coarse, and the high notes are sometimes cut short, as at the end of the entrance music and "Un bel dì." She knows the tradition and has temperament, but much of the detail is approximate; at times in the second and third acts she might almost as easily be singing *Tosca* or *Fanciulla del West*.

Her performance receives a better setting than those of some more illustrious sopranos. Though his voice is too light for hers, Ferruccio Tagliavini is often charming as Pinkerton, using his honeyed *pianissimos* to express rapture, as in the delightful conversation following Butterfly's first entrance. Later there are some explosive top tones.

Giuseppe Taddei is a splendid Sharpless, full-voiced and three-dimensional in characterization: mobile, authoritative, and intimate, especially in Act II. Mafalda Masini's lyric mezzo blends well with Petrella's soprano, so that the Flower Duet is a success. Mariano Caruso is a brilliantly responsive Goro, lively and amusing in Act I and defensive and harsh in Act II. Angelo Questa's conducting is often energetic in the manner of earlier conductors, but some of the lyric sections lack the compulsion which gives them theatrical life, and the recording puts him in the background. Like so many Cetra sets, this is a spirited, likable performance with a few memorable moments, but careless enough to keep it from being consistently persuasive. It does have a first-class Sharpless.

1954 EMI / ANGEL (M)

Victoria de los Angeles (A), Anna Maria Canali (B), Giuseppe di Stefano (C), Tito Gobbi (D), Rome Opera Chorus and Orchestra—Gianandrea Gavazzeni

In both of her recorded Butterflies, Victoria de los Angeles provides a performance of outstanding lyric grace, with the fresh and clinging tone for which she is famous, generous phrasing, and a tingling *legato*. All these qualities serve her well in a truly lovely entrance scene. The voice is a shimmering lyric soprano with just a shadow of darkness in the lower reaches, so that she need not shift into a rough chest voice to be heard there, nor must she affect coyness to suggest youth: the glow in the tone already does that for her. "Ieri son salita," the passage in which Butterfly describes her visit to the American Mission, is very inward and sung with consummate beauty, and the love duet has charm and considerable passion. Acts II and III are equally lovely; they are sung with a sometimes bemused lyricism. With so much radiant singing, it seems churlish to be unsatisfied, but in certain respects one is. De los Angeles demonstrates a warm idealism in the role; perhaps what is missing is an inner agony. "Un bel dì" needs a visionary passion, "Che tua madre" a more immediate sense of degradation, and the death scene an arresting desolation; these are not quite manifest, despite the distinguished vocalism.

She has as her partner Giuseppe di Stefano, in fine voice here. His humor and anger seem quite spontaneous, and he shares her wonderful *legato* in the love duet. His "Addio," too, has a touching lyricism. As Sharpless, Tito Gobbi is oddly inconsistent: he is immediately a presence, properly breathless at first, cosmopolitan, and a little stern, though later his responses seem indifferent. Anna Maria Canali is a tender Suzuki who sings well with her Butterfly, although, like many, she hasn't quite the high note for "Piangerò tanto." Gianandrea Gavazzeni conducts with fitful energy but lingers in the lyric sections, which need greater vigor and definition.

1955 EMI / ANGEL (M) CD

Maria Callas (A), Lucia Danieli (B), Nicolai Gedda (C), Mario Borriello (D), La Scala Chorus and Orchestra—Herbert von Karajan

Maria Callas creates a Butterfly like no other. Many Butterflies attempt to conceal their feelings—and so emerge as bland. Callas manages to conceal hers so as to increase the impression of complexity and to draw us into a private, half-glimpsed world. Even with that voice, which

by the time of the recording had sung Brünnhilde, Kundry, and Turandot as well as Lucia, she is the only Butterfly to suggest even remotely that she might be ten years old, as Sharpless guesses in Act I. It's not the quality of voice so much as the sense of unformed emotional expression at a few key points. When asked about her father's fate, her "Morto" seems absolutely unfeeling; the orchestra at this point carries the subtext. The high notes may occasionally blare, but she suggests genuine innocence in her flirtation, and both reserve and blind faith in the love duet. She builds the musical climaxes with exquisite care. "Un bel dì" is a treasured private vision. After so much concealment, her outburst in "Ah, m'ha scordata" (He has forgotten me) is shockingly revealing: here, for a moment, is the whole woman underneath. Again, in this context her anger at Goro has a tremendous effect; it reveals so much more than a momentary response to humiliation. "Vedrai, piccolo amor" is not simply a soft little romance, but the expression of a desperate desire to escape. This is in striking contrast to her breathless, totally focused attention a moment later on the ship in the harbor. When in Act III she is faced with the truth, the voice becomes dead. She is beyond seeking for pity. Left virtually alone for the first time in the opera at the death scene, she lets the full voice out at last in a cathartic reading. There are no tears. "Gioca, gioca" is exhaustedly said directly to the child.

Not everyone will like this performance. One wonders what Puccini would have thought of it. It has little of the traditionally eloquent in it, but a depth of concealed feeling and an evocation of fundamental exoticism that are unique. She gets, for once, at something deeper, if not necessarily more moving, than tears; she makes a tragedy of the opera.

In all of this she is helped immeasurably by Herbert von Karajan and the La Scala orchestra. Karajan's thoughtful, very well-articulated work is mainly sensible in tempo. Occasional moments are ponderous: "Che tua madre" is one of these and Pinkerton's "Addio" another, but in general the Callas conception is given the support it deserves.

Nicolai Gedda is a lighthearted, conversational, and romantic Pinkerton. The concealed nature of his Butterfly makes this appealing characterization work; with a more obviously defenseless Butterfly it might seem callous. The love duet is among the most tender and intimate on records. He is, incidentally, one of the relatively few Pinkertons whom one can imagine uttering the endearments that she repeats in "Un bel dì." Mario Borriello's Sharpless, though occasionally thin at the bottom of his range and tremulous at the top, is exceptionally gentle with his Butterfly in the final act. Lucia Danieli at least has the high notes and sings gracefully in the Flower Duet. The recording as a whole is distinguished for its restrained and yet gripping performance of the title role, its charming Pinkerton, and its strong conducting.

1958 DECCA / LONDON (S) CD

Renata Tebaldi (A), Fiorenza Cossotto (B), Carlo Bergonzi (C), Enzo Sordello (D), Chorus and Orchestra of the Accademia di Santa Cecilia, Rome—Tullio Serafin

Renata Tebaldi's second recorded Butterfly, in stereo and with Tullio Serafin on the podium, is sung with much beauty of tone and cool delicacy, but they are often the beauty and delicacy of Turandot, not Butterfly. Her phrases in the love duet are firm and nostalgic rather than tremulously visionary. With Serafin taking a very leisurely stroll through the score, her Act II is accomplished in its mature way, but girlish intimacy, impulsiveness, terror, and youthful jubilance are all in short supply. Occasionally one gets some Anna Magnani laughter. The death scene is admirably sung but also iron-willed and not particularly touching.

Carlo Bergonzi sings Pinkerton like a gentleman. He has no humor, but once he gets to straightforward passion and long lyric lines, he is on home ground. The voice is a little light for the Tebaldi of 1958, and the high notes are not as luxurious as the rest of the voice, but he is neither patently insincere nor pompous in tone, and he handles the slow tempos very well. The "Addio" is lyrical, and he allows himself only one tear. As Sharpless, Enzo Sordello displays a fine Italian baritone of medium weight. Since he and Bergonzi are neutral dramatically,

their scene in Act I goes for little except in terms of pleasant sound, but in the later acts Sordello is touchingly gentle. Fiorenza Cossotto is a fresh, lyrical Suzuki. Although her voice is a little light in this context, she and Tebaldi are well matched in the Flower Duet. The recorded sound is lovely. Tullio Serafin is authoritative, but also reflective and quite slow, depriving the score of its youthful impulse. There is much taste and cultivated vocalism here, but the performance treads very heavily indeed.

1958 RCA / BMG (S) CD

Anna Moffo (A), Rosalind Elias (B), Cesare Valletti (C), Renato Cesari (D), Rome Opera Chorus and Orchestra—Erich Leinsdorf

It was RCA's intention with this album to cast the opera with smaller voices so as to maintain its fragile appeal as a lyric drama. Interestingly, though Anna Moffo's voice is light, the tone color is dark enough to give an impression of greater weight. Her treatment of the music is softer and sweeter than some, but she is still rather hearty in approach and coy rather than truly innocent. Suddenly, though, at "Ora a noi" (the letter scene with Sharpless), she takes on fire and spontaneity. From then on, the dramatic impulse of the role seems to eliminate most of her glossy mannerisms and give her the vulnerability of a real Butterfly in tone color and manner. The remainder of her performance is quite involving.

Cesare Valletti likewise has a small sound for Pinkerton, and a rather grainy one, too. Though Valletti's opening scene, surprisingly, lacks much insouciance, he has a mannerly passion, points the text quite nicely, and introduces energy and a sense of the adventurous moment into the love duet, despite some stodgy conducting. The "Addio" is sung with earnest remorse and considerable self-hatred. Renato Cesari as Sharpless has a throaty production and occasionally oratorical manner, but he provides some moments of gentleness in Act III. For Suzuki, Rosalind Elias has a warm, mobile, shaded voice but is sometimes unconvincing dramatically. Mario Carlin as Goro is smooth and lyrical; at the opening one can't always distinguish him from

Valletti. Basically he is believable but occasionally he lapses into caricature. Leinsdorf is efficient and forceful in the faster sections: Butterfly's lashing out at Goro, the sighting of the ship, the tumbling excitement of the ensuing Flower Duet, and the Intermezzo and introduction to Act III. Elsewhere he tends toward the prosaic. The set is of some interest for Moffo's commitment in the latter half of the opera and for Valletti's light charm of manner.

1959 EMI / ANGEL (S) CD

Victoria de los Angeles (A), Miriam Pirazzini (B), Jussi Bjoerling (C), Mario Sereni (D), Rome Opera Chorus and Orchestra—Gabriele Santini

In her second recording of *Madama Butterfly*, Victoria de los Angeles offers again a warm, silken, inimitable tone, exemplary finish, and a characterization that speaks more of affection and sadness than passion and despair. Jussi Bjoerling is in superb voice and phrases very well, though he brings neither much humor nor much intimacy to the first act. Miriam Pirazzini is in tough voice for Suzuki. Though she tries for tenderness, this is really Azucena hiding out in Japan. Mario Sereni is a conventional but resonant Sharpless, though his reading of the central question about Pinkerton's return in Act II is exceptionally gentle and quite moving. Gabriele Santini's conducting is listless, except in a few places of obvious activity. The romantic passages lose color and definition, and in Act III the languor seems cosmic. Bjoerling's pristine sound is an attraction, but for those who want a de los Angeles recording, the earlier set (monophonic) offers a livelier setting.

1962 RCA / BMG (S) CD

Leontyne Price (A), Rosalind Elias (B), Richard Tucker (C), Philip Maero (D), RCA Italiana Opera Chorus and Orchestra—Erich Leinsdorf

No one can deny the glory of the two leading voices here. Leontyne Price is in radiant form: brilliant above the staff and firm and focused elsewhere. In the love duet and "Un bel dì" her voice sails. She works diligently to lighten her sound for the work's conversational passages, but the long lines of Verdi are in general much more suitable for this treasurable singer than the layered conversations of Puccini's heroines. The broad outlines of the character are there, but little of the subtext—the small, effortless manifestations of pride, bravery, fear, and rejection that lend continuing interest to the character.

As Pinkerton, Richard Tucker is in fine, smooth form, with a liquid top voice. Though he, too, works hard to appear offhand, his manner remains grand, sententious, and a little tearful. What Sharpless needs is a voice of great focus and coloristic variety, since he is always reflecting on and responding to the passions of others. Philip Maero, however, has a dark, monochromatic sound, though he and Price do become more conversational than one might predict in Act II. Again Rosalind Elias brings an apt voice to Suzuki, if no special dramatic skills. Erich Leinsdorf is again businesslike and firm in the bustling sections but more prosaic in the romantic passages. Despite its shortcomings, the performance does offer long stretches of glorious, well-managed vocal tone.

1966 EMI / ANGEL (S) CD

Renata Scotto (A), Anna di Stasio (B), Carlo Bergonzi (C), Rolando Panerai (D), Rome Opera Chorus and Orchestra—John Barbirolli

The most memorable element in this *Madama Butterfly* is the performance of the title role by Renata Scotto. Hers is a splendid voice for Butterfly: lyric, full, mobile, and forward, with an inimitable flavor and an ability to penetrate the orchestra by means of color and focus. The lower voice is uniquely shadowed without being dark, the very top is a little wiry, and it all retains a distinctive quality which suggests the Oriental. All of this is only the beginning. She is an enchanting vocal actress, with colors for the personal and ecstatic and for the pure and yet sensual. One can sense these aspects in the love duet and in many smaller moments—for example, the one after she says she is fifteen: "Son vecchia diggià" (I'm already old). Somehow her delivery is ingenuous and quite seductive at the same time. She does not laugh; she lets the orchestra do it for her. The love duet is very tenderly phrased and its tensions built with accomplished art. "Un bel dì" tells a story and yet illustrates the storyteller more fully than the events imagined. On the entrance of the suitor Yamadori, Butterfly has a rising musical phrase often noted as one of the most beautiful in the opera and suggestive of aspiring passion. Scotto sings it tenderly and yet with a slight ironic edge, both acknowledging and quietly satirizing Yamadori's feelings—as close, despite their shallowness, as any in the opera to the intensity of her own feelings for Pinkerton: a remarkably complex moment. At the end of "Che tua madre" there are no tears and only an understated "Morta": not the only way to do that scene, but nevertheless a striking effect is made here because there is heartbreak in the tone itself. The final scene, too, is less outspoken emotionally than, for instance, dal Monte's or Albanese's. There is something, though, of the gravity of a tragic ritual in Scotto's performance of it. The sensuality, the innocence, the honesty, the self-deception: they are all there in her portrayal.

Carlo Bergonzi's Pinkerton is a little more playful than with Tebaldi, but not much. He plays the role as a romantic idealist and sings very well. As Sharpless, Rolando Panerai offers a friendly voice, never pompous and often tender. In Act II, he is just brutal enough with the question about Pinkerton's return to justify his apology later. Anna di Stasio sings lyrically as Suzuki, and Piero de Palma's fourth Goro is both well sung and convincing. Sir John Barbirolli's conducting is sensuous and articulates the score delicately, but it is also slow, though not so heavy as that of Serafin and some others. One wonders what Scotto might have done under the constraint and inspiration of someone with the theatrical vitality of Toscanini or Ettore Panizza, but at least Barbirolli's pacing allows her to give us all of the detail of a brilliant characterization.

1972 EURODISC (S) CD

Maria Chiara (A), Trudeliese Schmidt (B), James King (C), Hermann Prey (D), Munich Bavarian Broadcasting Chorus and Orchestra—Giuseppe Patanè

Maria Chiara presents the cool, doll-like exterior of the character, an approach which may be intended to simulate the element of Japanese reserve. What emerges is, though fitfully pretty, quite unmoving. With this music one always needs a strong sense of the reserves of passion, the hidden conflicts which drive Cio-Cio-San first to Pinkerton, and then to fantasy, hopeless illusion, and death. Here in the second and third acts Chiara remains strikingly uninvolved, despite passages of considerable vocal control and a pleasantly lyrical Flower Duet. Her voice is bright, a little hard, and not always fully supported in the more strenuous sections. Altogether it is a remarkably alienated portrayal. In this she is abetted by her conductor, Giuseppe Patanè, who leads a careful performance of emotional lassitude.

Of the others, James King offers a fairly ardent but leathery Pinkerton; his top notes are effortful and he tires during the love duet. Hermann Prey is a throaty Sharpless, sounding both oily and undercharged. In line with German practice, he calls his compatriot Linkerton, while Chiara calls him Pinkerton: don't these people listen to one another? As Suzuki, Trudeliese Schmidt is also throaty; her top notes blast a bit and the lower ones are sometimes covered by the orchestra. A tiresome performance.

1974 DECCA / LONDON (S) CD

Mirella Freni (A), Christa Ludwig (B), Luciano Pavarotti (C), Robert Kerns (D), Vienna State Opera Chorus, Vienna Philharmonic Orchestra—Herbert von Karajan

In his second recording, Karajan gives a superb exposition of the riches of the score, but often at the cost of spontaneity. Put the needle down at any given point, and the performance may seem as abstractly beautiful as anything you have ever heard. Section after section of the opera is laid out in unimaginable detail, but sometimes at debilitating length. A few passages, such as the introduction to Act III, have tremendous verve, and there are sections of paralyzing loveliness, among them parts of the Flower Duet, the Humming Chorus, and "Dormi amor mio." But the mercurial aspect of the score is gone, and the singers are sometimes dwarfed by the conception.

Mirella Freni sings with admirable control and warm tone. Her Butterfly is in some respects like a specimen pinned to Karajan's orchestra for examination. Under his magnifying glass, segments are revealed as lovely and interesting, but the whole of the performance is exhausting and lacking in the continuity of feeling that is so much a part of Puccini's perception. "Un bel dì," for example, begins in a studied hush; there is a musing quality that is quite memorable—ecstasy in slow motion—but there is also a sense that the orchestra is more expressive than the voice. The letter scene and "Che tua madre" are marked with delicacy, though too deliberate for any conception of Butterfly as a palpitating being. The death scene is very fully sung, with great tenderness.

Luciano Pavarotti is in magnificent voice as Pinkerton, and delivers some of his asides in a charmingly infatuated whisper. In the slow love duet he is extremely tender and in the "Addio" manages to combine beauty of tone with reasonable self-disgust; the moment is both beautiful and convincing. Robert Kerns sings a lyrical and dramatically obliging Sharpless, and Christa Ludwig is one of the best Suzukis on records, producing a lovely, firm sound of middle weight, with real delicacy and finish in the interpretation. Her despairing "Che giova?" in Act III, for example, is truly intimate. Though the recording as a whole seems more often like a beautifully realized reminiscence than the living experience itself, it is certainly worth hearing for its unique clarity.

1976 DECCA / LONDON (S)

Montserrat Caballé (A), Silvana Mazzieri (B), Bernabé Marti (C), Franco Bordoni (D), Gran Teatro del Liceo Chorus, Barcelona Symphony Orchestra—Armando Gatto

This set is disqualified by its slow, dull, and shapeless conducting. The lethargy does even

the best of the singers in; they simply cannot sustain the opera musically or make it dramatically interesting. The timings listed tell me that the set is slightly faster than the Serafin and Barbirolli performances, but it seems interminable. Montserrat Caballé characteristically provides lovely *pianissimos*, but also limited volume on high notes and a beat when the tone is *mezzo forte* or louder. The interpretation is melancholy and devoid of impulsive passion; when Pinkerton comments on Butterfly's childlike ways, we wonder what he means. Bernabé Marti provides a rather rough, grainy Pinkerton with considerable unsteadiness but a few good high notes at the start. The slow tempos are particularly problematic for him. Franco Bordoni is a dull Sharpless at this speed, and Silvana Mazzieri has a wide tremolo on high notes. During the endless Flower Duet she and Butterfly seem to be lugging around redwood trees. Juan Pons is an impressive Bonze. The performance does an injustice to everyone, including its remarkable leading soprano.

1978 CBS / SONY (S) CD

Renata Scotto (A), Gillian Knight (B), Plácido Domingo (C), Ingvar Wixell (D), Ambrosian Opera Chorus, Philharmonia Orchestra—Lorin Maazel

In her second recording of *Madama Butterfly*, done twelve years after the first, Renata Scotto offers a performance of even greater detail. If I prefer the first version, it is partly because her highest voice is a little more stable there, and partly because its conducting, cast, and the balance of its recorded sound are more helpful. Lorin Maazel is sensitive to orchestral timbres but his tempos are slow enough to eliminate some of the dramatic contrasts which Puccini has so carefully set up in each of the three acts and to make things a little uncomfortable for his soprano, particularly in Act II. Then, too, the orchestra is recorded clearly but a little distantly and does not cushion Scotto's voice as well as it might. Plácido Domingo is a full and rich Pinkerton, though not encouraged to enjoy himself in the early scenes of Act I. Likewise, his part in the love duet and the

"Addio" are well sung but somewhat laborious in effect. Gillian Knight is a dark, sometimes wobbly Suzuki. Ingvar Wixell, interestingly, is an embarrassed and gruff Sharpless who tries to be tender. That's provocative but one really wants a little more lyricism in the Act III trio, for example. Though Scotto again presents a distinguished interpretation, she finds a more congenial setting in her first recording.

1980 HUNGAROTON (S) CD

Veronika Kincses (A), Klara Takács (B), Peter Dvorsky (C), Lajos Miller (D), Hungarian State Opera Chamber Chorus, Hungarian State Opera Orchestra—Giuseppe Patanè

This performance is notable for the singing tone of its Pinkerton and Suzuki and a few special moments from its Butterfly. Unfortunately, Giuseppe Patanè's conducting is as unsatisfying as in the Eurodisc set with Maria Chiara. The orchestral sound is sensuous, but he ambles through much of the score, losing cumulative tension and then rushing ahead at climaxes. The Flower Duet, Humming Chorus, and Intermezzo, all of which are reflective, go nicely, but the letter scene and other key passages are slow. Veronika Kincses offers a careful, lyrically sung Butterfly with a restraint that often sounds a little like indifference. "Un bel dì" is well sung but distinctive only at "Chi sarà?," for which she has a breathless, intimate sound. Later, her anger at Goro is terrifying, and the Flower Duet is sung by both soprano and mezzo with great beauty. Other sections are smooth enough but conventional. Peter Dvorsky offers a rich and radiantly youthful voice as Pinkerton. There is no special humor in his scene at the start, but following Butterfly's entrance he seems utterly charmed. In the love duet there is reasonable ecstasy from both, though it must be said that his high C at the end drowns hers out. In the "Addio" the singing is again of remarkable richness. As Suzuki, Klara Takács has a very lovely mezzo, lyrical and silvery in this range. Her crying before "Un bel dì" is quite unconvincing, but in the Flower Duet she sings charmingly. Lajos Miller as Sharpless has a pleasant voice, deprived of much dramatic

impetus by the pace of the conductor. Altogether this is a rather conventional set with a fine Pinkerton and some other beauties in unexpected places.

198–(?) FREQUENZ (S) CD

Raina Kabaivanska (A), Alexandrina Milcheva-Nonova (B), Nazzareno Antinori (C), Nelson Portella (D), Bulgarian National Choir, Sofia Philharmonic Orchestra—Gabriele Bellini

This is another of those sets in which the efforts of what is, at best, a problematic cast are killed by the conductor. Act I is hopelessly sentimentalized and the rest deprived of dramatic impulse. The Humming Chorus and the trio in Act III, for once at a viable tempo, are two of the more satisfying passages. Otherwise there is little sense of the score's variety of mood and the theatrical acumen of the composer. Raina Kabaivanska is a dark-voiced Butterfly who nevertheless sings with considerable delicacy at moments in the love duet and elsewhere. With such a conductor, though, several of her best efforts are stillborn. When the most exciting scene in Act II is Butterfly's anger at Goro, it is obvious that something is wrong with the pacing. Nazzareno Antinori is too light a tenor for this Butterfly and is deprived of what animation he might have by the tempos. The "Addio" goes nicely, but one would think he were singing a simple love song; until the last syllable, there is little of desolation or self-hatred. Nelson Portella is a reasonable but dull Sharpless and Alexandrina Milcheva-Nonova has a closed, pushed sound for the lyric role of Suzuki; oddly she is sometimes covered by the orchestra in Act III. An exasperating performance.

1988 DEUTSCHE GRAMMOPHON (S,D) CD

Mirella Freni (A), Teresa Berganza (B), José Carreras (C), Juan Pons (D), Ambrosian Opera Chorus, Philharmonia Orchestra—Giuseppe Sinopoli

Like many conductors who hope to capture this score with a painstakingly unconventional approach, Sinopoli loses the essence of the opera. He has a fine eye for orchestral textures but not for dramatic structure. He conducts it as portentously as if it were *Tristan*, and with the usual Sinopoli discontinuities and exaggerations. The opening is at first rushed and lacking in charm, and then pretentious and glum as Pinkerton describes "lo Yankee vagabondo." The wedding party is manic-depressive rather than volatile, and the love duet more sorrowful and self-indulgent than impulsive. Acts II and III are alternately languishing and monumental. Mirella Freni is in healthy voice but reduced to the melancholy and monochromatic by these tempos: there is little leeway for the moments of flirtation, happiness, or impulse that are at the root of this character. Nor is the pacing of help to José Carreras, who is sometimes in rather gravelly voice and has in any event little opportunity in this performance for charm. Juan Pons is a resonant but lugubrious Sharpless. Teresa Berganza sings a lovely Suzuki; she might have even more individuality at faster tempos. On the other hand, Anthony Laciura as Goro sings efficiently but cannot characterize very effectively at the fast speed at which most of his scenes are taken. One asks seriously what a knowledgeable repertory conductor of the older school, like Pietro Cimara, would do with a cast like this.

Madama Butterfly is so rich in interpretive possibilities that no fewer than four sets contain great performances—and only one of these is stereophonic. Each of them is inimitable. The earliest is Toti dal Monte's, whose characteri-

zation is still after half a century unequaled for childlike delight and heartbreak and is partnered by Gigli's persuasive and beautifully sung Pinkerton. Then there is Licia Albanese's Metropolitan Opera broadcast of 1946, capturing that unforgettable singer before an audience and at a theatrical and vocal peak, with the conductor's vibrant pacing helping along her supporting cast. Maria Callas is outwardly reserved and yet infinitely suggestive, and she is joined by Gedda's charming Pinkerton and Karajan's exceptionally atmospheric conducting. Finally we have the enchanting Renata Scotto recording of 1966, exquisitely subtle and touching, and to my mind better supported (by Bergonzi, Panerai, and Barbirolli) than in her equally moving later version.

Of the others, Margaret Sheridan's of 1929 is a moving recording of a somewhat forgotten singer, and Pampanini, de los Angeles, and Tebaldi (first version) are all well represented. Karajan's second recording, with Freni, presents a challenging view of the score's orchestra possibilities. Other cherishable characterizations are the Pinkertons of Pavarotti, di Stefano, Bjoerling, and Peter Dvorsky; the Sharpless of Taddei; and the Suzukis of Ludwig and Berganza.

LONDON GREEN

Unavailable for review:
1953 ROYALE
1966 GUILDE INTERNATIONAL DU DISQUE
1969 ACANTA
1972 MELODIYA
1983 MELODIYA

GIACOMO PUCCINI

LA FANCIULLA DEL WEST (1910)

A: Minnie (s); B: Johnson (t); C: Rance (bar); D: Wallace (bar)

*L*a Fanciulla del West provided what was probably the most distinguished world premiere in the Metropolitan Opera's history when, on December 10, 1910, it was performed with Toscanini conducting and a cast headed by Caruso as Johnson, Emmy Destinn as Minnie, and Pasquale Amato as Jack Rance. Yet, despite its auspicious start, Puccini's seventh opera has had an uphill road finding its place in the repertory, especially in America—perhaps because Americans found a California gold-mining camp a bizarre venue for an Italian opera, with its risible cries of "Whiskey per tutti!" and "Dooda, dooda, dooda, day" and perhaps because in its plot and principal characters it has strong affinities with *Tosca* without the primary appeal of the earlier opera. Instead, Puccini produced a score whose dense orchestral mosaic links him to Strauss and whose harmonic daring shows that he knew his Debussy. The composer's melodic genius is still evident, but except for the tenor's "Ch'ella mi creda" in Act III, the arias are tightly integrated into the fabric of the score. It calls for three leading singers of the same caliber as needed for *Tosca*, it benefits from the casting of first-class *comprimarios*, and a strong conductor is essential. Perhaps for these reasons the opera has been well served on records. Although the score lists the role of the wandering minstrel Jake Wallace as a baritone part, all of these recordings cast it with a bass, and convincingly so. Only one of these sets is absolutely complete (DG), while the others make certain cuts in the first act.

1950 CETRA (M)

Carla Gavazzi (A), Vasco Campagnano (B), Ugo Savarese (C), Dario Caselli (D), Radio Italiana Chorus and Orchestra—Arturo Basile

Like many of the Cetra recordings of the early fifties, this was the first and for many years the only recording of *La Fanciulla del West*. Although it still makes for rewarding listening, it is surpassed by all the later recordings in the quality of the principal singers and of the recorded sound. Perhaps it is best described as a good, solid, idiomatic repertory performance for its time, carried along by the knowing musical direction of Arturo Basile. Carla Gavazzi compensates for slightly lightweight vocal equipment by bringing considerable nuance to her portrayal of Minnie, here more the innocent barmaid than the latent Valkyrie, making her rescue of Johnson in the final scene seem against character yet thus all the more heroic. Vasco Campagnano, her Johnson, does not seem worth the effort. He goes the route stalwartly enough, but with monochromatic voice and little in the way of dramatic subtlety. Ugo Savarese's rough and somewhat woolly baritone is not out of place for the sheriff, and he turns in a strong and idiomatic performance. Dario Caselli doubles adequately as Jake and as Ashby the Wells Fargo agent. Although this version dates from the Stone Age of full-length recorded opera, there is a decent effort to supply the atmospheric background effects indicated in the score (i.e., the wind howling outside Minnie's cabin). There is a minor cut in the first act.

1958 EMI / ANGEL (S) CD

Birgit Nilsson (A), João Gibin (B), Andrea Mongelli (C), Nicola Zaccaria (D), La Scala Chorus and Orchestra—Lovro von Matačic

The obvious attraction of this version is the presence of Birgit Nilsson as Minnie. While one might expect that this incomparable Wagnerian would naturally emphasize the heroic side of this virginal young woman holding her own among a rough gang of hard-drinking Gold Rush characters, the soprano uses her formidable vocal resources with considerable restraint and dramatic subtlety. She balances the different aspects of Minnie's character, yet easily dominates the scene whenever she is present—rather too easily when she is sharing the stage with João Gibin, who, while never less than competent, is never much more either. His narrowly focused tenor is not the instrument to make him a match for this Minnie. Andrea Mongelli, a baritone little known on records, is very much in the picture as Rance, with an ample, slightly rough-edged baritone and a dramatic vigor the part demands. His scenes with Minnie provide the most effective moments in this version. Nicola Zaccaria is a sonorous Jake, even if he does not wring the last ounce of melancholy out of his song, and a number of the minor roles are cast from strength, notably Enzo Sordello as the lovelorn Sonora and Renato Ercolani as Nick the waiter. Lovro von Matačic is the solid if hardly impetuous conductor. One blemish, and an incomprehensible one, is a cut (about ten pages in the piano-vocal score) that eliminates the scene in which Sid is caught cheating at cards and gets impromptu and surprisingly mild justice from Rance.

1958 DECCA / LONDON (S) CD

Renata Tebaldi (A), Mario del Monaco (B), Cornell MacNeil (C), Giorgio Tozzi (D), Chorus and Orchestra of the Accademia di Santa Cecilia, Rome—Franco Capuana

If the Metropolitan had done *Fanciulla* during the 1950s, this could have been the cast for the three principal roles. Whereas in the Cetra and EMI versions, it is the tenor who comes up short in the balance among the principals, that problem does not arise here. Mario del Monaco was the preeminent Otello of the decade, a true dramatic tenor with a thrilling trumpet of a voice used with declamatory power. He was frequently criticized for depending too much on these qualities and for rarely coming down much below a *mezzo forte*. But that charge does not stand here. Del Monaco is sensitive to the text, heroically tender as he sweeps past Minnie's emotional defenses, peremptory in playing the macho game with the menacing Rance, and cool enough to take his whiskey with water and brush off the incredulity of the neat-drinking regulars of the Polka Bar. Renata Tebaldi's Minnie hardly needs an endorsement, at least not at the time of this recording. Her radiant *lirico spinto* is at its peak, as is her seemingly spontaneous affinity for a fluid Puccinian line. Cornell MacNeil's Rance is not out of place in this company. His formidable baritone, impressively controlled, conveys menace without tonal gruffness and enough nobility to make credible his sporting acceptance of Minnie's outrageous winning poker hand. Giorgio Tozzi's mellow nostalgia in Jake Wallace's song is a bit of luxury cameo casting and Piero de Palma's Nick is first among a well-balanced group of camp regulars. Franco Capuana seems to be in relaxed, flexible control of familiar territory, and the spacious recorded sound for which London was known has stood up very well.

1977 DEUTSCHE GRAMMOPHON (S) CD

Carol Neblett (A), Plácido Domingo (B), Sherrill Milnes (C), Gwynne Howell (D), Chorus and Orchestra of the Royal Opera House, Covent Garden—Zubin Mehta

This version has some substantial overall virtues, aside from being by far the most recent of the recordings under consideration. It was made when the same musical forces were fresh from a production at Covent Garden, with a consequent unity of purpose and ensemble, as well as the unusually strong casting of the smaller roles drawn from the Royal Opera's deep roster. It is spaciously and spatially recorded, with excellent definition and rich orchestral presence. It is effectively "produced" in a theatrical sense, with everything from the zip of a deck of cards being shuffled to the wind howling through the trees—all atmospheric without being obtrusive. And it is complete. Carol Neblett is a highly satisfying Minnie, with a clear, strong, and forward lyricism that is not only equal to the musical task but conveys a kind of uncomplicated frontier openness that encourages the suspension of disbelief, whatever she might have to concede to the competition in sheer vocal glamour. Plácido Domingo had already begun to sing Otello by the time he made this recording, and it tells for the better, his intense lyricism being reinforced by the dramatic weight the part really demands. Sherrill Milnes, even when he is not entirely convincing as a heavy, brings dramatic vigor, a rich and even baritone, and a touch of Jack Rance's fastidiousness to his sheriff's duties. Still, there were moments with both men when a sacrifice of pure tone in favor of a more pointed projection of text would have been welcome. Gwynne Howell's warm bass almost manages to convey a real person in Jake Wallace's brief appearance, and of the miners and other peripheral characters, Jonathan Summers (Sonora), Francis Egerton (Nick), Malcolm King (Larkens), and Robert Lloyd (Ashby) are particularly successful at showing how much can be made of a secondary role. Zubin Mehta's brisk tempos and forward drive give the whole a sense of impetuosity and vigor and, aided by DG's sound and the Covent Garden orchestra, bring out much of the elaborate tapestry of Puccini's score.

With its excellent principals and strong secondary casting, its superior recorded sound and impressive musical and dramatic ensemble, DG is the inevitable choice among these recordings. Still, for anyone wishing a memento of Tebaldi and del Monaco in their prime, London offers that in the context of a very satisfying all-around recording for its time.

DAVID STEVENS

Unavailable for review:
1991 RCA / BMG
1991 CBS / SONY

GIACOMO PUCCINI

LA RONDINE (1917)

A: Magda (s); B: Lisette (s); C: Ruggero (t);
D: Prunier (t); E: Rambaldo (bar)

The 1917 premiere of *La Rondine* was preceded by an eventful gestation period, involving a Viennese commission, a libretto originally written in German, extensive revision by the Italian translator / librettist, and completion of the work while Austria and Italy were wartime adversaries. The opera attracted favorable attention at first, and has occasionally enjoyed local popularity in particular productions since, but in general it remains the least-often performed of Puccini's mature operas. Its libretto must bear some blame for this, for despite the often-remarked echoes of *La Traviata* and *Die Fledermaus*, remarkably little really happens in the story, and the characters have scant opportunity to make a memorable impact. What the opera does have in its favor is a unique atmosphere such as Puccini was always able to create—in this case a perfumed intimacy that finds time for lively dance measures, some lovely vocal solos, and one rousing ensemble for the full company.

For a 1920 Vienna production, Puccini revised the work extensively, altering some vocal ranges and adding new music. A subsequent revision essentially reverted to the first version, and this is the text heard on all three recordings.

p.1955 CBS / SONY (M)

Eva de Luca (A), Ornella Rovero (B), Giacinto Prandelli (C), Luciano della Pergola (D), Vladimiro Pagano (E), Antonio Guarnieri Chorus and Orchestra of Milan—Federico del Cupolo

If no other recording of *La Rondine* existed, this one would represent the opera respectably. Though not incandescent in any respect, it holds together decently and offers more appropriate casting (which is not quite the same as "better singing") for one or two of the leading roles than more recent versions do.

As Magda, Eva de Luca clearly knows what she's about, inflecting her lines intelligently with a voice that is firm but acidic in timbre; the resultant lack of magic in her big moments takes its toll on the performance's effectiveness. Giacinto Prandelli's medium-weight lyric tenor fits the character of Ruggero well, and he shapes his solo moments with a loving, caressing touch that even brings the usually inert Act III aria to life. His effectiveness is diminished by a loss of tonal solidity at unexpected moments.

The role of the poet Prunier is written on a scale that is rather too demanding for the usual "second" tenor, as Luciano della Pergola demonstrates with his dry, strained sound and his struggles with anything above an F. The Lisette, however fragile in tone, possesses the right youthful sound and enough liveliness to make a success of her role. The Rambaldo delivers his few but important lines in a firm baritone, and the supporting voices are flimsy but adequate.

Everyone tends toward carelessness about exact synchronization of voices and orchestra, though otherwise the conductor Federico del Cupolo has things well enough in hand. The recording quality, crude even for its time, really hurts the performance, giving no hint of numerous delicious orchestral details and keeping the chorus at such a distance that the whole opening ensemble of Act II is a total loss. On the other hand, the requested distance effects are not even attempted—offstage voices and instruments are right up front. This lack of atmosphere, combined with the shrewish-sounding Magda, pretty much negates the main attractions of *La Rondine*.

1966 RCA / BMG (S) CD

Anna Moffo (A), Graziella Sciutti (B), Daniele Barioni (C), Piero de Palma (D), Mario Sereni (E), RCA Italiana Chorus and Orchestra—Francesco Molinari-Pradelli

A *Rondine* recording of the same quality as would be expected for the standard Puccini operas did not materialize until the mid-1960s. Its centerpiece and strongest asset is the Magda of Anna Moffo, a touching and personal creation. The role's introspective wistfulness clearly suits Moffo's interpretive sympathies; she here succeeds admirably at building a character through the musical materials provided by Puccini, without histrionic superimposition. This recording found her in good vocal form, with only a relatively narrow dynamic range, a lack of power in reserve, to her marginal discredit.

Sensibly for this conversational opera, the cast is otherwise virtually all Italian. An adequate Ruggero was unfortunately not included, and Daniele Barioni must count as the recording's main deficiency. Nondescript but not overtly offensive in his early scenes, he eventually reveals a coarse vocal production that admits no feeling of romance or tenderness, cannot modulate to a suitable level for duets, and makes his aria and final duet sound like poorer music than they are.

The secondary couple is brought to life with canny professional skill and idiomatic delivery by Piero de Palma and Graziella Sciutti; as he is a character tenor (albeit an exceptional one), she an aging soubrette, both are also on the thin, precarious side for roles that ideally call for fuller vocal qualities. The other roles, aside

from a sonorous Rambaldo by Sereni, are handled suitably but not memorably.

Francesco Molinari-Pradelli, not always an asset in grander-scaled works, here shows his skillfulness at maintaining an easy flow through the many tricky tempo transitions, making them seem natural and inevitable. He supports his singers well and allows much of the orchestral detail to shine.

1982 CBS / SONY (S,D) CD

Kiri Te Kanawa (A), Mariana Nicolesco (B), Plácido Domingo (C), David Rendall (D), Leo Nucci (E), Ambrosian Opera Chorus, London Symphony Orchestra—Lorin Maazel

In the series of Puccini operas undertaken by CBS beginning in the 1970s, this ranks as one of the more valuable contributions. Unlike the other *Rondine* recordings, it has only minimal Italian connections (the Rambaldo), and it lacks the conversational fluency that formed a natural part of those productions. Yet it does wonderful justice to another side of *La Rondine*: its aural appeal. Puccini in this work is playing with instrumental and vocal colors, combining them in diverting and ravishing ways, and Lorin Maazel is enjoying them too, eliciting plenty of gorgeous playing and choral singing. Maazel's conducting is less satisfying in terms of the score's progression through time: though he carefully obeys the expression and tempo markings (and does not deny the soloists a bit of extra license), he rarely makes them sound truly flexible and spontaneous. There remains an unconvincing stiffness at points where an irresistible flow is needed.

The cast is well chosen for maximum mellifluousness, and all are in good representative form. Though Kiri Te Kanawa does not inhabit Magda and make her live as Moffo does, her general air of poised graciousness suits the overall lines of the part well enough, and she certainly sings it gloriously—at the time of the recording her soprano was one of the most beautiful sounds one could hope to hear. Plácido Domingo easily surpasses all other recorded Ruggeros: paying serious attention to the spirit of the role, singing gently and sweetly when he can, and never lacking in passion or golden tone. David Rendall, a lyric tenor who usually undertakes leading roles, represents a luxurious level of casting for Prunier; despite fleeting hints of unsteadiness and uncertain intonation his able vocalism turns the poet into a major character. Casting with a leading singer works out less well for Lisette, who after all fails in her attempt to become a chanteuse and change her social station. Mariana Nicolesco's rich, complex timbre tells us that she is herself a prima donna equal in grandeur to her mistress; in aural terms Nicolesco is simply miscast, her vibrant singing and interpretation welcome in themselves but too much for this role.

Leo Nucci contributes capably as Rambaldo,

and the rest of the cast maintains the polished vocal standard, with especially nice work from sopranos Lillian Watson (Yvette) and Elizabeth Gale (offstage voice).

For so brief a work with so little competition, a recommendation proves surprisingly difficult. Duty seems to demand a preference for the persuasively idiomatic command of Moffo, Molinari-Pradelli, and company for RCA; yet the aural seductions of the singing and playing offered by the 1982 CBS have their value for this opera too. The two performances complement each other, and only personal taste can decide which strengths matter more.

JON ALAN CONRAD

IL TRITTICO: IL TABARRO (1918)

A: Giorgetta (s); B: Luigi (t); C: Michele (bar)

Il Tabarro is the first opera in Puccini's *Il Trittico*, a trio of one-act operas that includes *Suor Angelica* and *Gianni Schicchi*. *Tabarro* is a melodramatic tale in which the lights of Paris flicker across the grimness of life aboard a tugboat on the river Seine. Capturing the chiaroscuro nature of the opera is one of the great challenges for performers, particularly for the conductor. Although the opera takes less than an hour to perform, it is a complete story with passionate characters who evolve during the course of it. Revealing the complexity of those characters and developing them within this brief time span is the task of the leading singers. All three major roles demand true singing-actors to impart the full impact of this masterly score. *Tabarro* has been recorded both as part of the triptych (Cetra, London, CBS, Eurodisc) and as a separate entity (EMI and RCA). Two of the recordings include, as a bonus, the aria Puccini originally wrote for the baritone, "Scorri fiume eterno." The composer replaced it with the more dramatic "Nulla! silenzio!" in 1921.

1949 CETRA (P)

Clara Petrella (A), Glauco Scarlini (B), Antenore Reali (C), Orchestra of Radio Italiana—Giuseppe Baroni

This recording was made at a commemorative concert marking the twenty-fifth anniversary of Puccini's death. Clara Petrella portrays a sunny Giorgetta, a woman of great passion and vitality. Her full, vibrant voice embodies the character she creates. Scarlini is the stock tenor hero. He communicates Luigi's feelings in some passages, particularly in his aria, but the role is not truly internalized. Although his singing improves during the course of this live performance, the voice is generally unfocused. Antenore Reali, a resonant baritone, provides some powerful moments vocally, but he tends to sing everything *mezzo forte* and makes a two-dimensional character of Michele. Two minor roles are exceptionally well cast in this recording. In a delightful performance, mezzo Ebe Ticozzi captures the earthy humor of Frugola, and Dario Caselli brings a rich bass voice to the role of Talpa. Baroni's tempos are often ponderous, with few of the subtle variations noted in the score.

1955 EMI / ANGEL (S) CD

Margaret Mas (A), Giacinto Prandelli (B), Tito Gobbi (C), Chorus and Orchestra of the Rome Opera—Vincenzo Bellezza

In this recording, *Il Tabarro* becomes Michele's tale of yearning and frustration as told in the very sound of Tito Gobbi's voice. During his duet with Giorgetta, he is truly loving in the lyrical passages, then devastated by the realization of their difference in age, furious when Giorgetta retires to their cabin, and, finally, driven to tears. When he breaks down, his sobbing is the inevitable conclusion to the emotions he has built with such care, and the pathos is deeply moving. His aria, "Nulla! silenzio!," is the highlight of this recording. The baritone mulls over the names of Giorgetta's potential lovers, turning each "sei tu" into a fierce accusation. Other than Gobbi's performance, this set tends to be bland. Both Mas and Prandelli have pitch problems, and neither is convincing dramatically. Mas's soprano is uneven and forced; her interpretation lacks style. Prandelli's lower voice is thin and his portrayal of Luigi rather bland. Bellezza's performance is well paced but pedestrian. Some sound effects in the opening, such as the automobile horn which is as much a part of Puccini's orchestral introduction as the instruments, are arbitrarily eliminated. The engineers for this recording favored the singers, and, as a result, many of the orchestral details are lost.

1961 DECCA / LONDON (S) CD

Renata Tebaldi (A), Mario del Monaco (B), Robert Merrill (C), Chorus and Orchestra of the Maggio Musicale Fiorentino—Lamberto Gardelli

Tebaldi's performance here is a gem. Her voice is golden, the character she creates is strong, and her musicianship is impeccable. Her Giorgetta is both shrew and lover. With Michele she is cold, demanding, and irritable. With Luigi, the sound of her soprano is mesmerizing as she recalls the joys of Paris life, seductive as she plots his return in their second duet. In del Monaco's interpretation, Luigi is a brusque, volatile character. His fury in the aria deploring working conditions is explosive. His huge voice is secure; high notes ring out with ease. His voice blends well with Tebaldi's, but his stentorian performance lacks the nuance and expressivity that make her performance enchanting. Merrill is a tender Michele. His baritone is lush, and he sings the lyrical passages with genuine feeling. His Michele is a man more hurt than wronged, however, and as a result his transformation from jealous husband to murderer is not wholly convincing. The minor roles are well sung, and all the singers get into the spirit of the piece, as in the delightful organ grinder's scene. Gardelli is the most satisfying of the conductors on these complete

recordings. The music flows, filled with subtle *rubatos* and tempo shifts, moving effortlessly from mood to mood. As a bonus, this recording includes the original baritone aria, "Scorri fiume eterno." It is more lyrical than "Nulla! silenzio!" and Merrill sings it well.

1970 RCA / BMG (S) CD

Leontyne Price (A), Plácido Domingo (B), Sherrill Milnes (C), John Alldis Choir, New Philharmonia Orchestra—Erich Leinsdorf

This recording captures Price, Domingo, and Milnes in the prime of youth, and the freshness of their voices is one of its pleasures. The sultry sound of the Price voice makes her an appealing Giorgetta. The sheen of her soprano as she describes the beauty of a Paris evening is one of many memorable moments of her performance, as is the ravishing sound of her voice when she calls Luigi's name at the beginning of their second duet. On the whole, however, her performance lacks commitment. Domingo's fresh tenor imbues the role of Luigi with energy and charm. His subtle shifts in dynamics serve to convey the restlessness of the character. Domingo's is a compelling performance, although he himself surpassed it seven years later on the CBS recording. Michele is one of Milnes's finest recorded roles, both vocally and dramatically. His voice is free and robust in this recording. Totally immersed in the text, he develops the role skillfully from his curt comments at the opening of the opera to his tender pleading in the duet with Giorgetta. His aria, "Nulla! silenzio!," builds steadily to its explosive climax. In the murder scene, when Michele commands that Luigi confess to the affair, each repetition of the word "confessa" takes on a different shade of meaning. Then, in a startling reversal of mood, he becomes aloof when Giorgetta enters. Puccini's original baritone aria is a bonus here, and Milnes sings it with appropriate lyricism. The Tinca in this recording, Piero de Palma, is exceptionally strong. Despite excellent performances by the singers, the overall performance lacks urgency, and Leinsdorf seems to rely on erratic shifts in tempo for dramatic effect.

1977 CBS / SONY (S) CD

Renata Scotto (A), Plácido Domingo (B), Ingvar Wixell (C), Ambrosian Opera Chorus, New Philharmonia Orchestra—Lorin Maazel

The opening moments of this recording promise a performance of extraordinary subtlety, intensity, and beauty. That promise is fulfilled. Renata Scotto is an ideal Giorgetta, creating moments that delight, that disturb, that move. She savors the text, giving each word its proper weight, almost as though it were spoken. She is capable of capturing an entire facet of Giorgetta's personality in a single phrase: in her opening line, for instance, in which the ice of her voice conveys her boredom with married life; in the silvery sound she spins out as she looks at the evening sky, revealing her romantic yearnings. Her scenes with Luigi are highly sensual. In their ecstatic love duet, Scotto and Domingo deliver performances of overwhelming passion. The tenor's Luigi is more virile and volatile in this recording than in his earlier one for RCA, and his voice is freer and more opulent. The aria in which he denounces the life of a bargeman rings with anger, the duets with Giorgetta exude desire and frustration.

Although Wixell's characterization is not as subtle or varied as those given by Scotto and Domingo, it is nonetheless a performance of unrelenting intensity. His firm baritone is vibrant, and he displays real tenderness toward Giorgetta in their duet within the context of the sinister character he has created. The yearning and restlessness that are at the heart of *Tabarro* are embodied in this recording. Maazel gives an urgent, well-paced reading, remarkable for its clarity and for the fluid shifts from melodrama to poetry.

1987 EURODISC (S,D) CD

Ilona Tokody (A), Giorgio Lamberti (B), Siegmund Nimsgern (C), Chorus of the Bavarian Radio, Munich Radio Orchestra—Giuseppe Patanè

Tokody is an expressive singer who portrays Giorgetta as neither the coquette nor the cold-hearted wife, but rather an intensely emotional woman trapped in an impossible situation. Although her voice tends to tighten on top, it is warm and full in the middle and lower registers. Unfortunately, Tokody's performance is the only convincing one in this recording. Lamberti lacks the warmth to make Luigi believable. His tenor is constricted and he tends to slide into notes. Nimsgern portrays a tender, vulnerable Michele. This approach works early in the opera, but as the tragedy unfolds, the character fails to develop and Nimsgern relies on lachrymose sounds for effect. He too tends to slide into notes, and his diction is poor. In fact, diction is generally a problem in this recording, and some of the minor characters sing without a feel for the pronunciation of Italian. Patanè conducts an energetic performance.

The CBS *Tabarro* is the most effective of these complete recordings. Both Scotto and Domingo give performances imbued with passion. Hers is a marvel of nuance, and his is notable for its expressivity and sheer beauty of sound. Although Wixell does not develop the character of Michele as fully as Gobbi and Milnes (on Angel and RCA respectively), he is convincing in the role. Maazel conducts an intense performance that captures the chiaroscuro nature of the opera.

BRIDGET PAOLUCCI

GIACOMO PUCCINI

SUOR ANGELICA (1918)

A: Suor Angelica (s); B: Principessa (c)

Suor Angelica, the second opera in Puccini's *Il Trittico*, is the tender work of the trio, coming between the melodramatic *Il Tabarro* and the comic *Gianni Schicchi*. Angelica, a young nun, is one of Puccini's typical *piccole donne*. In contrast, the stern Principessa (a forerunner of the composer's Turandot) is a radical departure from any character Puccini created before this. The confrontation between Angelica and the Principessa is the dramatic core of the opera. After that, the work is essentially an extended solo scene for the young nun; her aria, "Senza mamma," is one of the most sensitive ever written by Puccini. The title role is a showpiece that has drawn major sopranos to record it as a separate entity as well as part of the *Trittico*. The opera contains many eloquent orchestral interludes which not only offset the sound of the female cast but also serve a dramatic purpose.

1950 CETRA (M)

Rosanna Carteri (A), Miti Truccato Pace (B), Chorus and Orchestra of Radio Italiana—Fernando Previtali

The burnished sound of Carteri's soprano is well suited to the title role. Her performance is marked by beautiful *legatos* and a total commitment to the text. Her portrayal of Angelica is drenched with sadness, yet she knows when to pull back from that undercurrent of pain. In her aria, for instance, she is restrained at first: Angelica is stunned on hearing about the death of her son. Then, after an intensely emotional passage, Carteri's voice floats as she describes the baby fluttering ("aleggiare") around her. Miti Truccato Pace is not convincing as the Principessa. She relies on the darkness of her lower voice for effect, resorting to a kind of sung-speech to express the character's emotions. Under Previtali, the orchestra throbs with life. Interludes are eloquent and the entire performance is marked by subtle, fluid changes in tempo. The strings are exceptional (in the luminous interlude describing the nuns' recreation, for instance), and the long interlude following the confrontation scene is filled with pathos. In this *Angelica*, the scene with the nursing sister is cut. The sound of the recording is muffled, and the chorus seems to be placed too far from the microphone.

1957 EMI / ANGEL (S) CD

Victoria de los Angeles (A), Fedora Barbieri (B), Chorus and Orchestra of the Rome Opera—Tullio Serafin

Suor Angelica's background is embodied in the de los Angeles reading of the part. She is both noblewoman and nun, and the soprano's depiction of the character is consistently poised between these two facets of the young woman's personality. Her brief aria at the beginning, "I desideri," is devout and trusting. She is noble in the confrontation scene, even haughty when she reproaches the Principessa. There is a dignified reserve about this Angelica. There is never a total emotional release, even when she inquires about her son. Yet her profound yearning is palpable. Her aria, like the rest of her performance, is exquisite for its musicality and detail. Unfortunately, de los Angeles's top voice sounds thin, often strained in the more dramatic passages, but her interpretation is deeply sensitive. Barbieri is a dour, commanding Principessa. She is one of the few to bring a true contralto quality to the role. Her lower voice is full and rich, but the pitch is not always true. Minor characters are generally well sung, and the Suor Genovieffa in this recording, soprano Lydia Marimpietri, is exceptional. Hers is a luminous voice and she makes the Shepherdess Aria sparkle with joy and tenderness. The chorus frequently does not blend. The orchestra, under Serafin, gives a refined performance, creating an aura of intimacy.

1961 DECCA / LONDON (S) CD

Renata Tebaldi (A), Giulietta Simionato (B), Chorus and Orchestra of the Maggio Musicale Fiorentino—Lamberto Gardelli

Tebaldi's Angelica is a young woman matured by pain. The soprano's performance is deeply expressive, communicating Angelica's many emotions and moods in constantly shifting vocal colors. The silken sheen of her soprano captures the sadness in her arioso, "I desideri," yet in the nursing scene that follows she assumes a heroine's stature. "Non si lamenti," she advises. She has suffered, but is strong as a result. When she asks about her son during the confrontation scene, it is like a dam bursting; the sound is brilliant, the passion overwhelming. In her aria, Tebaldi truly mourns the child. As the Principessa, Simionato is the first, and one of the few on these recordings, to make a three-dimensional woman out of this character. Her confrontation with Tebaldi is chilling.

The minor roles in this recording, even occasional solo lines sung by members of the chorus, are consistently well sung. The chorus is truly involved in the action, whether gossiping about Angelica's past or greeting the two Alms sisters. Gardelli conducts a well-paced performance filled with subtle dynamic changes. The conductor is totally committed to the expressive markings in the score, all of which he observes meticu-

lously. The orchestral interludes are impassioned, from the gracious sweep of the recreation music to the ominous passage introducing the Principessa.

1972 RCA / BMG (S)

Katia Ricciarelli (A), Fiorenza Cossotto (B), Polyphonic Chorus of Rome, Orchestra of the Accademia di Santa Cecilia, Rome—Bruno Bartoletti

In the hands of Katia Ricciarelli, Angelica becomes a very specific character: an abandoned child who is fragile and depressed. Her spirits lift when she hears news of the visitor to the convent. Her thrilling response, trembling with hope, is like a shaft of sunlight in the life of this sad little girl. And when she asks the Abbess who the visitor is, she almost sobs—a logical reaction in this exquisitely thought-out portrayal. Emotions run high, yet Ricciarelli's portrait of Angelica is painted in pastels. Her "Senza mamma" is limpid and ethereal, as befits a girl of this temperament. She is mesmerized at the thought of seeing her son again, and her final "ah" is the epitome of delicacy. In this recording, Ricciarelli's voice lacks fullness, but she uses it skillfully to achieve her unique realization of the title role. Cossotto's Principessa is not one of the mezzo's better efforts. Her lower range is rich and unforced, but the voice overall sounds throaty and uneven. She tends to convey a somber mood rather than sing into the words; much of the text verges on the unintelligible. The choral singing is exceptionally cohesive, and minor roles are sung expressively. Bartoletti emphasizes the delicacy of the score, an approach that is both effective and appropriate, given Ricciarelli's interpretation of the title role.

1976 CBS / SONY (S) CD

Renata Scotto (A), Marilyn Horne (B), Ambrosian Opera Chorus, New Philharmonia Orchestra—Lorin Maazel

Flowers are a recurring image in the story of Suor Angelica. She delights in nurturing them, she heals the other nuns with them, and, finally, she kills herself with the very herbs she has tended with such care. Whenever Renata Scotto sings "fiori," she gently leans into the word as though there were a mystical link between the flowers and the character. It is this kind of sensitive attention to detail that makes Scotto's performance extraordinary. Those details, her sense of dramatic timing, her musicality, and, above all, the way in which she colors the voice make her Angelica live. There are unforgettable moments in her performance: the release of restraint as she describes the family coach; the tenderness she expresses for her sister; the gasp as she suspects the truth about her child. Her conversational lines take on the rhythms of natural speech and the aria is a model of nuance. At first, Scotto's voice is that of a woman haunted by the thought of her dead child, but the second part of the aria becomes an outpouring of maternal love, and when she says, "Sei qui" (You're here), she assumes the kind of intimate tone a mother uses when speaking to her little one. The passage is deeply moving. Her farewell to the other nuns is congenial, as her relationship with them has always been, and the plea for salvation is a wildly emotional moment made more effective by the restraint that has preceded it. Vocally, Scotto is at her most secure in this recording. As the Principessa, Marilyn Horne presents a traditional reading of the role: she is the severe aunt. The honeyed sound of her evenly produced mezzo is at its peak here, but Horne's voice is not always focused and she tends to flat in the sustained passages at her entrance. A welcome bonus in this cast is Ileana Cotrubas as Suor Genovieffa. In her vibrant soprano, she conveys a character full of the sparkle of youth. Other minor roles vary vocally. Their Italian pronunciation, and that of the chorus, is generally unacceptable. Tempos are generally well chosen, and the interlude following the confrontation scene brims over with pathos. Maazel does not hesitate to linger over telling moments, paralleling the sensitivity to detail that is at the heart of Scotto's performance.

1978 LONDON / DECCA (S)

Joan Sutherland (A), Christa Ludwig (B), London Opera Chorus, National Philharmonic Orchestra—Richard Bonynge

The outstanding performance in this recording is Christa Ludwig's Principessa. Ludwig portrays a woman who is long-suffering rather than cruel. In the confrontation scene, she communicates a variety of emotions: grief when talking about the death of Angelica's parents, affection for Angelica's little sister, resentment when she intones "di penitenza." She is a woman capable of volcanic fury, but that fury is just part of the complete emotional spectrum—a spectrum vividly depicted by Ludwig.

Sutherland's Angelica is most convincing in the fiery moments, such as her warning to the Principessa that the Virgin will judge her. There is a lovely simplicity about her performance, but the voice often sounds tired. She sings her aria, "Senza mamma," too carefully, without truly communicating the text. The chorus in this set sounds disinterested, frequently even cloying. Pronunciation by both chorus and minor characters is poor. Tempos are frequently slow, resulting in a rather languid performance.

p.1983 HUNGAROTON (D) CD

Ilona Tokody (A), Eszter Poka (B), Hungarian State Opera Chorus and Orchestra—Lamberto Gardelli

Tokody's Angelica is the tragic heroine from the very beginning of this opera. Her voice is anguished, drenched with emotion. She creates some beautiful moments, particularly in the big dramatic scenes, but her performance lacks nuance and some high notes are shrill. Eszter Poka makes the Principessa a caricature. Her voice is unsupported, and there is little, if any, variation in expression. The chorus is eloquent, and minor roles are sung energetically. The tempos selected by Gardelli are almost identical to those he used on the 1961 recording with Tebaldi. The overall mood in this later recording, however, is more uniform and somber.

1987 EURODISC (D) CD

Lucia Popp (A), Marjana Lipovšek (B), Chorus of the Bavarian Radio, Munich Choir Boys, Munich Radio Orchestra—Giuseppe Patanè

Patanè knows how to build a scene and, as a result, the orchestra in this set is remarkably eloquent. When the carriage arrives at the convent, for example, the repeated notes are both delicate and urgent; then the orchestra gently swells as Angelica begins to realize that the visitor is for her. During the interlude in which Angelica prepares the poison, the orchestra itself seems transported to another realm, entering her madness and her ecstasy. Unfortunately, Popp is not convincing as Angelica. She becomes more involved in the role in the confrontation scene, but on the whole her emotions tend to be generic. Vocally, Popp has the unsettling habit of sliding into notes for emphasis. Lipovšek is a highly original Principessa, totally committed to the text. At first her unusual voice sounds spectral, as though she is chanting the family history that Angelica knows only too well. The voice becomes brighter—more focused and more forbidding—as the Principessa gets to the purpose of her visit. In Lipovšek's reading, she is there not only to get Angelica's signature but to haunt her with the past, to crush her yet again. The chorus in this recording is exceptionally expressive, and minor roles are well sung.

Overall, the finest performances of *Suor Angelica* are on the CBS and London recordings. Scotto gives the more finely detailed performance of the title role, yet Tebaldi also provides a touching portrait of Angelica in brighter sounds and colors. Horne presents a traditional reading of the Principessa on CBS, whereas Simionato, teamed with Tebaldi, creates an unforgettable human being. CBS has Cotrubas as a bonus, but the language problem on that recording mars performances by many of the other minor characters. Both conductors give a fluid, well-balanced performance.

Although Gardelli is the more eloquent conductor, Maazel illuminates the details of the score with great sensitivity.

BRIDGET PAOLUCCI

CHRISTOPHER KEENE
General Director,
New York City Opera

1. **Barber,** *Vanessa*: Steber, Elias, Resnik, Gedda, Tozzi—Mitropoulos. RCA / BMG

2. **Britten,** *Peter Grimes*: C. Watson, Elms, J. Watson, Pears, Pease—Britten. DECCA / LONDON

3. **Menotti,** *The Saint of Bleeker Street*: Lane, Poleri—Schippers. RCA / BMG

4. **Mussorgsky,** *Boris Godunov*: Zareska, Gedda, Bielecki, Borg, Christoff—Dobrowen. EMI / ANGEL

5. **Poulenc,** *Dialogues des Carmélites*: Duval, Crespin, Berton, Scharley, Gorr—Dervaux. EMI / ANGEL

6. **Prokofiev,** *The Flaming Angel*: Rhodes, Depraz—Bruck. WESTMINSTER

7. **Puccini,** *La Fanciulla del West*: Tebaldi, del Monaco, MacNeil, Tozzi—Capuana. DECCA / LONDON

8. **Strauss,** *Salome* (Final Scene): Welitsch—Reiner. EMI / ANGEL

9. **Verdi,** *Otello*: Nelli, Merriman, Vinay, Assandri, Valdengo—Toscanini. RCA / BMG

10. **Wagner,** *Das Rheingold*: Flagstad, Madeira, Svanhold, Kuen, London, Neidlinger, Kreppel, Böhme—Solti. DECCA / LONDON

11. **Mozart,** *Don Giovanni*: Souez, Helletsgrüber, Mildmay, von Pataky, Brownlee, Henderson, Baccaloni, Franklin—Busch. EMI / ANGEL

GIANNI SCHICCHI (1918)

A: Lauretta (s); B: Rinuccio (t); C: Schicchi (bar)

The third opera in Puccini's *Il Trittico* is a comedy set in Florence in the year 1299. *Gianni Schicchi* is the story of a commoner who outwits the patrician Donati family. The opera consists of a rapid succession of scenes propelled by sudden shifts from fast to slow tempos and tempered by bursts of lyricism. It requires singers with a sure sense of style—singers who can bring wit without coarseness to their performances, who can make mercurial shifts in tempo and dynamics with ease. The title role is a challenge for baritones who must find a balance between Schicchi the schemer and Schicchi the loving father. Both the soprano and the tenor have major arias: Lauretta's familiar "O mio babbino caro" and Rinuccio's hymn to the city of Florence. The minor singers, who comprise the Donati family, act and react principally as a group. The opera demands carefully balanced ensemble singing.

1949 CETRA (M)

Grete Ripisardi (A), Giuseppe Savio (B), Giuseppe Taddei (C), Orchestra of Radio Italiana—Alfredo Simonetto

The cornerstone of this Cetra recording is Giuseppe Taddei. He brings precisely the right weight to every note, precisely the right emphasis to every word. In a myriad of vocal colors, he can be cunning, insinuating, furious, and disdainful with the Donatis, as well as tender with his daughter. Taddei's full-bodied voice is consistently beautiful. He is eminently musical,

producing exemplary *legatos* in the "Addio, Firenze," for instance. And his delight when he assumes the role of the deceased Buoso is transparent. Neither Ripisardi nor Savio match Taddei vocally or stylistically. The soprano's voice is thin, and the tenor's sounds swallowed. Although his aria is spirited, his performance lacks warmth. The minor characters are all specific individuals; their bickering is genuinely humorous, never overplayed, and their ensemble work is superb. The orchestra is both participant and commentator in Simonetto's lively reading of the score. The conductor highlights details with finesse, such as the delicacy of the orchestra when Rinuccio sends for Schicchi and the piquant interlude during the reading of the will. Simonetto's tempos are so well chosen as to seem inevitable, and he goes from one to the next with easy flexibility. Unfortunately, the technical quality of this delightful recording is poor.

1958 EMI / ANGEL (S)

Victoria de los Angeles (A), Carlo Del Monte (B), Tito Gobbi (C), Orchestra of the Rome Opera—Gabriele Santini

Gobbi's highly sophisticated portrayal of Schicchi brims over with imaginative details. The baritone uses an astonishing variety of vocal colors to elucidate the character he creates with such care. The deep-rooted class antagonism between this Schicchi and the patricians is revealed shortly after his entrance when he expresses his utter disdain for the Donatis in a single phrase, "C'è l'eredità." One of the most memorable moments in this recording is the passage in which the Donatis individually ask Schicchi for a special share of the inheritance. His answer to each of them is the same: "Sta bene" (That's fine). Gobbi's witty reading of these words is nothing short of ingenious: each "Sta bene" reflects both the character he is speaking to and the size of the bequest suggested by that character. As the deceased Buoso, he is unmatched, particularly when he pretends to be touched by the concern of the lawyer and his cronies. With Gobbi, there is always an undercurrent of getting back at the people he detests; he is conniving rather than cunning yet capable of true tenderness with his daughter. De los Angeles is the finest Lauretta on these complete recordings. She sings the role with highly polished musicality, creating a character of exceptional warmth and refinement. Her aria provides a moment of real poignancy that tempers the comedy. Del Monte portrays a passionate Rinuccio. He sings the conversational passages with admirable naturalness and his aria is spirited. Although his voice is warm, it tends to tighten on top. Minor characters are variable, both vocally and dramatically. Santini builds some scenes well, such as the reading of the will, yet the performance overall lacks piquancy. The performances by Gobbi and de los Angeles are such sterling examples of style, musicianship, and characterization, however, that they override the negative aspects of this recording. This Schicchi is part of a set that includes *Il Tabarro* and *Suor Angelica*, conducted by Bellezza and Serafin respectively.

1961 DECCA / LONDON (S) CD

Renata Tebaldi (A), Agostino Lazzari (B), Fernando Corena (C), Orchestra of the Maggio Musicale Fiorentino—Lamberto Gardelli

The sparkling opening of this recording provides a sense of buoyancy that carries through the whole of the opera. That buoyancy is at the heart of Corena's performance. His Schicchi is a charismatic character who is genuinely delighted by his own cunning, a man more amused than angered by the patrician Donatis.

Impersonating Buoso as a lovable old geezer, this Schicchi fairly gloats when he leaves himself the best of the spoils. Corena's voice is resonant and beautiful, and he savors the words, but Tebaldi's voice sounds too mature for Lauretta. The soprano sings "O mio babbino caro" artistically, but she does not seem to be in touch with the character, and her voice does not blend well with Lazzari's, whose tenor is well suited to the role of Rinuccio. Lazzari is totally immersed in the character, and his aria about the splendors of Florence is sung with verve and genuine commitment to the text. Minor roles are exceptionally well performed, with Lucia Danieli as a delectably bossy Zita, Dora Carral a lively Nella, and Paolo Washington a blustery Simone. The ensembles are superbly balanced and witty. Gardelli conducts a remarkably fluid performance, skillfully balancing the witty elements of the opera with the lyrical. Spoken words, sighs, and groans are occasionally interjected (as in a live performance), but all in good taste, adding to the vitality of this recording.

1976 CBS / SONY (S) CD

Ileana Cotrubas (A), Plácido Domingo (B), Tito Gobbi (C), London Symphony Orchestra—Lorin Maazel

As in the Angel recording, Gobbi's Schicchi is remarkable for its palette of vocal colors and its eloquent details. That was an ingenious interpretation, and Gobbi wisely let most of his earlier portrayal stand. There are subtle differences in his second recording of the role: this Schicchi is more autocratic than Gobbi's earlier effort, although every bit as disdainful, and the series of "Sta bene" lines is significantly less humorous. His warning about exile from Florence takes on a Scarpia-like tone in this recording with the tremulous sound that marked his sinister portrayal of that role. In the nineteen years between recordings, Gobbi's voice lost some of its luster, particularly in the upper register, but his Schicchi remains a marvel of vocal acting. Domingo is an ardent Rinuccio. He trims back his clarion tenor for the conversational parts of the role and sounds young, whether boasting that his uncle loved him in a delightfully giddy voice, or begging Schicchi to save the family in a tone of sweet desperation. His tenor rings out brightly in the aria, and his *legatos* are a pleasure to hear. Although Cotrubas's soprano has a pronounced beat, her warm voice is well suited to the role. Her charming reading of the "Babbino" aria is the plea of a forlorn child. Minor roles are competently sung, with all the singers wholly into their respective roles. Maazel's performance bursts with energy, but it tends to be a trifle heavy, particularly vis-à-vis the nuance and wit of Gobbi's characterization.

p.1984 HUNGAROTON (D) CD

Magda Kalmár (A), Denes Gulyas (B), Gyorgy Melis (C), Hungarian State Opera Orchestra—János Ferencsik

The Schicchi created by Melis is a stock comic character with little charm or wit. His voice wobbles, and when he sings wide intervals, he tends to approximate the pitch of the second note. The natural warmth of Magda Kalmár's soprano conveys a young woman deeply in love. The simplicity of her Lauretta is touching, the sound of her voice generally pleasing. Gulyas creates a strong Rinuccio; his aria to Florence bursts with vitality. The tenor makes excellent use of a variety of dynamics for expression, but his performance is marred by sibilance. The minor characters are problematic: some voices wobble while others tend to sharp, resulting in disconcerting ensemble singing. The performance lacks style. Tempos are often slow, with singers occasionally straining not to rush ahead of the conductor.

1988 EURODISC (D) CD

Helen Donath (A), Peter Seiffert (B), Rolando Panerai (C), Munich Radio Orchestra—Giuseppe Patanè

The dark sound of Panerai's voice is ideal for the commanding Schicchi he creates. This commoner can intimidate the entire Donati family in two words, "Zitti, obbedite" (Hush, obey), uttered in a voice they would not dare oppose. The baritone establishes a specific character, then lets the humor emanate from the situation. Panerai makes Schicchi's thought process shine through the music, as in the moment when he is confronted by the doctor's arrival and goes from panic to decisiveness in the space of two lines. Helen Donath portrays a gracious young woman who demurely cajoles her Daddy in the "Babbino" aria. There are many beautiful moments in her performance, but her voice is unevenly produced. Seiffert relishes Rinuccio's words and conveys the vitality of the character in the very sound of his bright tenor. Although his lower voice tends to be unsupported, the top is secure. Minor roles are all sung very much in character. Voices are above average and the ensemble work is exceptional, due in large part, of course, to Patanè. He conducts a translucent, colorful, well-paced performance, making the transitions from tempo to tempo with a suppleness that seems eminently natural. Each orchestral detail is given meaning as though the orchestra, too, had its own text to sing.

Giuseppe Taddei is the ideal Schicchi, but his extraordinary portrayal cannot compensate for mediocre performances by the leading soprano and tenor and for the poor quality of the recording. Tito Gobbi gives a highly sophisticated, imaginative portrayal of Schicchi in both of his recordings, yet neither is wholly satisfying in terms of the rest of the cast. The better of the two is the 1958 version on Angel. Gobbi is wittier and his voice is fresher on the earlier recording, and de los Angeles is enchanting as Lauretta. Overall, the London recording is the most successful, with Corena a vocal and comedic delight in the title role. Minor characters are exceptionally well played and Gardelli keeps scene after scene moving along with remarkable buoyancy.

BRIDGET PAOLUCCI

Unavailable for review:
1957 PHILIPS

GIACOMO PUCCINI

TURANDOT (1926)

A: Turandot (s); B: Liù (s); C: Calaf (t); D: Emperor Altoum (t);
E: Ping (bar); F: Timur (bs)

*P*uccini had no successors, and his last opera rings down the curtain on the great Italian opera tradition of Rossini, Donizetti, Bellini, and Verdi. After an initial burst of interest, *Turandot* was slow to make its way, although today the opera is an established repertory piece, much loved for its melodic richness, exotic instrumental coloring, and the opportunities it provides for lavish spectacle. The major problem at first was that the composer died in 1924 before completing the score. Working from Puccini's rough sketches for the final duet, Franco Alfano did his best, but the results have never sounded more than makeshift—even in its superior, long-suppressed unabridged form, which can be heard on a London disc featuring Josephine Barstow and Lando Bartolini. The second stumbling block has been the need for a soprano with the vocal brilliance, declamatory power, and physical stamina to encompass the title role. Fortunately, there has always seemed to be at least one of these paragons available, and no major world opera house can now do without *Turandot*.

miere at La Scala, was already a historic document by the time it reached a wider audience, on Cetra long-playing discs in the early 1950s. None of the principal singers participated in the first performance, although by 1937 they had all sung their roles onstage and they respond to the work as a living, contemporary music drama—no subsequent *Turandot* recording conveys quite the same sense of vitality or immediate contact with the work.

That said, later recordings offer improvements in other departments, especially reproduction. Cetra's boxed-in, prewar studio sonics hardly do justice to Puccini's glittering orchestral palette, even though Ghione's incisive yet expansively symphonic interpretation holds up splendidly. As for the singers, Merli's gloriously refulgent Calaf has been equaled but never surpassed—even by Bjoerling or Corelli—but Cigna's cutting, often unsteady tone and Olivero's delicately quivering soprano will probably always be acquired tastes. To these ears, though, Olivero is still the most idiomatic, heart-stopping Liù on disc.

1937 CETRA (M)

Gina Cigna (A), Magda Olivero (B), Francesco Merli (C), Armando Giannotti (D), Afro Poli (E), Luciano Neroni (F), Chorus and Orchestra of RAI, Turin—Franco Ghione

This recording, made in the studios of Radio Italiana only eleven years after the world pre-

1953 REMINGTON (M)

Gertrude Grob-Prandl (A), Renata Ferrari-Ongara (B), Antonio Spruzzola-Zola (C), Angelo Mercuriali (D), Marcello Rossi (E), Norman Scott (F), Chorus and Orchestra of La Fenice, Venice—Franco Capuana

This is little more than a blip in the *Turandot* discography, a recording that seemed interesting when new mainly because of its marginal sonic superiority over the old Cetra edition, an asset that is no longer relevant. The performance, featuring a provincial cast of no distinction whatever, was charitably and accurately summarized in *High Fidelity* magazine at the time of its first release as "a hodgepodge of the good, disappointing, and practically incompetent."

1955 DECCA / LONDON (S) CD

Inge Borkh (A), Renata Tebaldi (B), Mario del Monaco (C), Gaetano Fanelli (D), Fernando Corena (E), Nicola Zaccaria (F), Chorus and Orchestra of the Accademia di Santa Cecilia, Rome—Alberto Erede

One of the first opera recordings made in stereo, London's *Turandot* was a sonic revelation in 1955, even though the binaural version did not appear until several years after the initial monophonic release. Erede's sturdy but bland presentation of the score largely undercuts that advantage, however, and the Santa Cecilia orchestra can hardly be called a virtuoso ensemble. This writer treasures youthful memories of Borkh's frequent Turandots in Germany during the late 1950s, a few years after the soprano made this recording. Those performances were sung in German, of course, and Borkh seemed more comfortable in that language, posing her cruel riddles to exciting effect. Here, singing in Italian, she sounds less appropriate and her rather thick, guttural voice refuses to soar. The only abiding value of this recording is the young Tebaldi's ravishingly nuanced Liù, although del Monaco's ringing tenor, tirelessly trumpeting out Calaf's music, registers plenty of thrills if not much expressive variety.

1957 EMI / ANGEL (M) CD

Maria Callas (A), Elisabeth Schwarzkopf (B), Eugenio Fernandi (C), Giuseppe Nessi (D), Mario Borriello (E), Nicola Zaccaria (F), La Scala Chorus and Orchestra—Tullio Serafin

Nothing Callas recorded is entirely without interest, but Turandot was far from her most congenial role. She sang only a handful of performances onstage, and retired the part from her active repertory entirely eight years before making this recording. The most impressive aspect of her interpretation here is its declamatory imperiousness—especially in the all-important riddle scene—as she adopts an authoritative tone that somehow never quite masks the princess's underlying fear and insecurity as she confronts the man who will finally conquer her. No other soprano on disc suggests this subtle dichotomy in Turandot's character quite so tellingly. Otherwise, Callas is sorely tried by the high tessitura, and for all her remarkable refinements, musical as well as dramatic, one finally wants more vocal ease and power in this taxing music.

Badly miscast, Schwarzkopf sings with a slippery tone and phrases archly, an inappropriately sophisticated Liù who sounds as if she had strayed in from a Lehár operetta. Fernandi's brief career was probably shortened by singing such roles as Calaf, and his attractive light tenor is more often than not swamped by the music's heroic demands. Ensemble is rather loose under Serafin's typically benign direction, but this knowing conductor misses very little of the opera's gorgeous instrumental color or dramatic thrust. The artful way in which he shapes the hesitant orchestral phrases as Calaf ponders Turandot's riddles is itself a lesson in Puccinian tension and eloquence.

1959 RCA / BMG (S) CD

Birgit Nilsson (A), Renata Tebaldi (B), Jussi Bjoerling (C), Alessio De Paolis (D), Mario Sereni (E), Giorgio Tozzi (F), Chorus and Orchestra of the Rome Opera—Erich Leinsdorf

Throughout the 1960s, there was only one Turandot for most opera goers: Birgit Nilsson. This, she always insisted, was her "party role," a welcome vacation from the longer and more exacting Wagnerian parts that were her main province. Indeed, it's doubtful that any Turandot before or after Nilsson was able to sail so effortlessly through the music or to produce such clear, unobstructed tones without a hint of shrillness or forcing. True, she never suggested that very much was going on inside the icy princess's head other than making preparations for the next thrilling high C—a one-dimensional portrait perhaps, but that dimension was formidable. RCA's edition is the first of her three official recordings. They all sound pretty much the same, which is to say that each displays one of the century's vocal phenomena at her peak.

One suspects that Bjoerling's Calaf might have been somewhat overpowered onstage by this Turandot, but on disc his tenor sounds consistently appealing, plangent, and expressive. Tebaldi repeats her superb Liù, only slightly less fresh and vulnerable than it had been four years earlier for London. Leinsdorf hardly finds much poetry in the score, but at least his direction has plenty of energy and theatrical muscle.

1961 MET (M,P) CD

Birgit Nilsson (A), Anna Moffo (B), Franco Corelli (C), Alessio De Paolis (D), Frank Guarrera (E), Bonaldo Giaiotti (F), Metropolitan Opera Chorus and Orchestra—Leopold Stokowski

After a thirty-year hiatus, *Turandot* returned to the Metropolitan Opera in 1961, and this Saturday-afternoon broadcast of March 4th was the production's second performance. Here Nilsson found the worthy tenor partner for Puccini that she never had in the Wagnerian repertory: Franco Corelli, who matches her note for note in Act II, reveling in the glorious vocal freedom and ringing *spinto* style that sadly seems to have become extinct among Italian tenors. No doubt the live-performance circumstances further energized Nilsson—not to mention the competitive presence of such a redoubtable leading man—and of her three recordings this is the most dramatically involved without sacrificing a whit of vocal splendor.

The performance also offers a valuable memento of Anna Moffo in her prime years, when her lovely lyric soprano was fresh and her musical instincts disarmingly true and spontaneous. In her double aria before Liù's suicide, movingly phrased and tonally beguiling, Moffo very nearly steals the opera away from the two heroic protagonists. The supporting roles are all in reliable hands, although the chorus occasionally betrays its unfamiliarity with the opera and there are quite a number of spots where the orchestra threatens to come unglued. That may have something to do with Stokowski's indisposition (he had broken his hip two months earlier and conducted on crutches), his relative inexperience in leading staged opera, or his typically "creative" conducting style. Even if the Stokowski magic only arrives in fits and starts, the performance as a whole—in bright, cleanly defined FM sound—most decidedly generates the excitement of a genuine occasion.

1965 EMI / ANGEL (S) CD

Birgit Nilsson (A), Renata Scotto (B), Franco Corelli (C), Angelo Mercuriali (D), Guido Mazzini (E), Bonaldo Giaiotti (F), Chorus and Orchestra of the Rome Opera—Francesco Molinari-Pradelli

This recording-studio documentation of the Nilsson-Corelli team duplicates the vocal success of their 1961 Met broadcast, even if the live-performance frisson between two competing superstars is necessarily missing. Their scenes together are so businesslike, in fact, that one sometimes wonders if the two singers were even recorded in the same room. Nilsson in particular sounds more detached than usual, although she is in characteristically stupendous voice. So is Corelli, who turns in the most glamorously recorded Calaf since Merli. The sheer vitality of Corelli's singing is irresistible: the sustained arching lines, ringing climaxes, shining verbal clarity, and generous temperament—a fabulous performance from a tenor who, at the time, was perhaps not fully appreciated.

Scotto should not be overlooked either, singing one of her most affecting and exquisitely shaped recorded performances. Her Liù is delicate, fragile, and understated, but driven by an iron-willed interior motivation that leaves few facets of this perplexing character unexplored. Beyond the obvious three-star attractions, the recording offers nothing special beyond the solid, unexceptional merits of a provincial supporting cast, chorus, and orchestra under the direction of a well-schooled but routine conductor.

1972 DECCA / LONDON (S) CD

Joan Sutherland (A), Montserrat Caballé (B), Luciano Pavarotti (C), Peter Pears (D), Tom Krause (E), Nicolai Ghiaurov (F), John Alldis Choir, Wandsworth School Boys' Choir, London Philharmonic Orchestra—Zubin Mehta

Sutherland never attempted Turandot onstage, but her recording of the role is a grand success. This was exactly the right time for such an experiment: her soprano was in its mature shining glory, the drooping mannerisms of the past had largely been expunged, and her diction had taken on a new clarity. Perhaps no other recording Sutherland made lets us hear the sheer amplitude and volume of her voice when fully unleashed—and this is no trick of an engineer's dials. That alone is sufficient to make her Turandot a commanding presence, and her typically confident, direct, no-nonsense approach to every vocal challenge pays dividends in a flood of warmly rounded, gleaming tone—entirely different from Nilsson's clarion brilliance, but equally convincing and authoritative.

For all-round excellence, in fact, it would be hard to find a better *Turandot* on disc. Pavarotti's ardent, golden-toned Calaf is more lyric than heroic—closer to Bjoerling than Corelli—but none the worse for that. Caballé occasionally indulges in her habit of vocalizing vowel sounds rather than enunciating the words, but otherwise she is on best behavior as Liù, her soft-grained soprano spinning out one lovely phrase after another. The deluxe casting extends to the smaller roles: Krause, an unusually characterful Ping; Ghiaurov, a sonorous and mournfully Slavic-tinged Timur; and Pears, a properly ancient Emperor whose aristocratic breeding tells in every note. None of the Italian orchestras that had previously recorded *Turandot* can match the instrumental polish of the London Philharmonic, and Mehta successfully conveys the score's symphonic grandeur as well as its colorful textures. The recording still sounds magnificent—an exceptionally spacious, well-defined but never clinical acoustical environment, with sonic perspectives blended and balanced to perfection.

1977 EMI / ANGEL (S)

Montserrat Caballé (A), Mirella Freni (B), José Carreras (C), Michel Sénéchal (D), Vicente Sardinero (E), Paul Plishka (F), Maîtrise de la Cathédrale, Chorus of the Rhine Opera, Strasbourg Philharmonic Orchestra—Alain Lombard

Like its predecessor on London, EMI's third *Turandot* seems to have been assembled specially for the recording studio, although this time the results are not so fortuitous. The three principals each have something genuine to contribute, and perhaps they would have made more of an effect in less provincial musical surroundings—Lombard and his forces offer respectable support, no more, and the other roles, apart from Sénéchal's intriguingly mystical Emperor, are quite drearily sung. Caballé is inevitably a softer, more vulnerable Turandot than the norm. She occasionally makes good dramatic capital from the fact, and her voice is in fine shape, but one seldom feels that this plush-velvet soprano was designed for the part. In a role ideally suited for the leading Mimì of the day, Freni floats many lovely phrases but her overall interpretation seems strangely detached. Carreras belongs to the Bjoerling-Pavarotti school of lyric-tenor Calafs, although in terms of vocal glamour and musical imagination he clearly rates third in this distinguished company—a dull performance, but at least one can savor an important voice before overuse and an inappropriately heavy repertory wore off its natural beauty.

1981 DEUTSCHE GRAMMOPHON (S,D) CD

Katia Ricciarelli (A), Barbara Hendricks (B), Plácido Domingo (C), Piero de Palma (D), Gottfried Hornik (E), Ruggero Raimondi (F), Vienna Boys' Choir, Vienna State Opera Chorus, Vienna Philharmonic Orchestra—Herbert von Karajan

The dominant presence on this recording is plainly Karajan, who stretches and bends Puccini's score in every possible direction, frequently to the breaking point. Tempos are painfully slow, the dynamic extremes wildly exaggerated, instrumental details doted upon, orchestral textures almost indecently luxuriant—the conductor seems determined to prove that *Turandot*, as the final flowering of a great operatic tradition, is not only an exotic and luscious bloom but also an overripe and thoroughly decadent one. Some would agree and revel in the indulgent extravagances of this interpretation, particularly since the Vienna Philharmonic plays with such virtuosity and seductive tonal allure. Others will find it much too self-regarding, if not downright loathsome.

As he so often did in his late opera recordings, Karajan perversely chose predominantly light-voiced singers to fight a losing battle with the orchestral splendors he conjures up. A Liù by nature, Ricciarelli is here asked to struggle with the title role, which she does with considerable insecurity and vocal discomfort, never really suggesting the character's inner vulnerability—at least, one assumes that was the intention behind such bizarre casting. Hendricks's delicate Liù would be more effective had it not been crushed by the powerhouse orchestra, and even Domingo's Calaf sounds faceless and under strain. The most successful performance comes from Raimondi, whose Timur registers with appealing pathos and restraint. Otherwise, this is definitely a controversial recording, to be approached with caution.

1983 CBS / SONY (S,D,P) CD

Eva Marton (A), Katia Ricciarelli (B), José Carreras (C), Waldemar Kmentt (D), Robert Kerns (E), John Paul Bogart (F), Vienna Boys' Choir, Chorus and Orchestra of the Vienna State Opera—Lorin Maazel

Also from Vienna—recorded live at the State Opera in September 1983—Maazel's *Turandot* resembles Karajan's in its lush, symphonic opulence and tendency to linger. Maazel, however, is not nearly as excessive, once again showing himself to be a sensitive, perceptive, and urgent Puccini conductor while drawing superlative results from the Viennese musicians. The live-performance conditions no doubt contribute to the lively theatrical atmosphere, which is largely free of distracting stage noises and audience interruptions. That said, the principal roles—and minor ones, too, for that matter—have all been taken to better effect on other recordings.

Even though Ricciarelli has wisely renounced the title part for Liù, it is too late—by 1983 her once lovely soprano had become unpredictable, here sounding insecure and wobbly. Carreras sings with more ardor and abandon than when he last recorded Calaf, seven years previously, but the tone has turned raw and juiceless. Aside from Maazel, the main attraction is Marton, the first Turandot on disc since Nilsson to project the music with the accents of a truly heroic soprano. Marton is just as accurate and tireless as her predecessor, and even more dramatically involved, but her voice as recorded tends to be monochromatic and without Nilsson's brilliant edge.

———————

The most overall satisfying *Turandot* continues to be the 1972 London edition, although connoisseurs will surely want one version with Nilsson—the 1959 RCA recording is the recommended choice—as well as the 1957 EMI performance for Callas's insights into the title role and Serafin's idiomatic shaping of the score.

PETER G. DAVIS

HENRY PURCELL

DIDO AND AENEAS (1689)

A: Dido (s or ms); B: Belinda (s); C: Sorceress (ms); D: Aeneas (t or bar)

*P*urcell's perfect little jewel of an opera has been well served on records. The fact that the work fits neatly onto a single LP (or CD) no doubt accounts in great part for the number of recorded versions.

Dido and Aeneas is often thought of as a vehicle for the leading soprano (or mezzo). But I would argue that the opera is a true ensemble work and that it contains no unimportant roles. The best recorded performances are those in which a strong Dido is surrounded by equally vivid artists, each of whom makes the most of his or her brief moments before the microphone.

Listening to the recordings of Purcell's opera in chronological order reveals that from the beginning, performers recognized the intimate proportions of the score, and strove to achieve an appropriately light, lyrical style. In the early 1960s, vocal and instrumental embellishments began to appear, and the older performing editions of the score were discarded in favor of textual readings derived from the earliest surviving manuscripts. The last decade has seen an increased emphasis on "authenticity"; these more recent recordings generally employ original instruments, small orchestral and choral forces, and light-voiced singers, and are characterized by a faster range of tempos and sharper articulation.

Dido and Aeneas presents certain textual problems for its performers. From the original 1689 performance, only the libretto survives. It contains an elaborate allegorical Prologue and a brief spoken Epilogue. At two points in the action of the opera itself, enigmatic stage directions (e.g., "gittars ground a dance") seem to call for dances accompanied by guitar music. Act II ends, after Aeneas's recitative, with a gloating chorus for the Witches—"Then since our charms have sped"—followed by the Groves Dance, presumably performed by "the nymphs of Carthage," whom the Witches refer to.

The earliest extant score of the opera, c. 1760, seems to be a copy of performance material used in 1704—nine years after Purcell's death. It lacks the Prologue and the guitar dances; Act II ends with Aeneas's recitative. There are other discrepancies between this manuscript and later scores, but they are relatively minor.

Some conductors base their recorded performances on one of the standard published editions of the score—e.g., by Thurston Dart, Edward Dent, Neville Boyling, or Benjamin Britten—often incorporating their own ideas. Others create their own edition, realizing the *continuo* and adjusting the instrumentation to suit themselves. Several of the recordings insert music for the missing guitar dances; some restore the two numbers missing at the end of Act II by adapting other music by Purcell; at least one attempts to reconstruct the lost musical setting of the Prologue.

1951–52 EMI / ANGEL (M) ℗

Kirsten Flagstad (A), Elisabeth Schwarzkopf (B), Arda Mandikian (C), Thomas Hemsley (D), Mermaid Singers and Orchestra—Geraint Jones

Based on a famous stage revival (in which, however, Maggie Teyte rather than Elisabeth Schwarzkopf sang Belinda), this recording, like its predecessors, uses the Edward Dent edition, but it is the first one to provide music for the missing numbers at the end of Act II.

The performance now sounds old-fashioned in some respects: Geraint Jones adopts slow tempos and weighty accents, and the rich, vibrato-saturated string sound will startle the listener accustomed to more recent recordings. But there is nothing fundamentally impure about warm, full-bodied instrumental playing or passionate singing of true operatic caliber; at its best, the performance combines sensuality, drama, and poetry, setting a high standard for subsequent recordings to match.

Kirsten Flagstad was nearing the end of her career in 1952. I suppose her voice is a couple of sizes too large for Purcell's music, and there are some sustained tones in the upper-middle register that an honest critic would have to describe as flat. But, for me, there is no resisting the sheer sound of this voice, as it flows through the music with calm *legato* and ripely maternal tone. And Flagstad is often surprisingly specific from the interpretive standpoint (her English pronunciation, not so incidentally, is admirable). In a word, she is *majestic*, in a way that no other Dido on records has matched.

Schwarzkopf doubles Belinda with the Second Woman, at one point ("Fear no danger") singing a duet with herself by means of overdubbing. It was a mistake, though, for her to take on the part of the Spirit as well, for her voice is nothing if not recognizable. Her English is lightly accented, which bothers me less than her squeezed tonal production and occasionally fussy phrasing. Like many Schwarzkopf performances, this one is artful but self-conscious, and ultimately lacking in spontaneity.

Thomas Hemsley is a sturdy, stoic Aeneas; he often sounds as though he were singing Mendelssohn's *Elijah* instead of Purcell, but somehow his performance meshes convincingly with Flagstad's. Arda Mandikian, by contrast, is a mordant, malevolent Sorceress, who certainly can't be accused of placidity.

For a recording of this vintage, the engineer-ing is excellent, provided the listener can accept the forward placement of the solo voices. The CD reissue sounds especially clear and impactive.

p.1952 PERIOD (M)

Eleanor Houston (A), Adele Leigh (B), Evelyn Cuthill (C), Henry Cummings (D), Stuart Chorus and Chamber Orchestra—Jackson Gregory

Even though I have not heard every commercial recording of *Dido and Aeneas* ever released, I am prepared to assert that this version is the worst. The orchestra, chorus, and even the conductor are hiding behind pseudonyms; the engineers have wisely chosen anonymity. The sound is poor: shrill and shallow, with the solo voices grotesquely overmiked. There are audible tape splices in virtually every number. The singing might charitably be described as amateurish, and the orchestra is scrappy. The liner notes boast that the harpsichord *continuo* was improvised at the recording sessions, which probably explains why the *continuo* is consistently out of sync, often lagging behind the other instruments by several beats. (Some of the resultant harmonic clashes are worthy of Berlioz or Liszt at their most experimental.) This performance is an unmitigated disaster and ought to be decently interred.

1961 L'OISEAU-LYRE (S) ⓒ

Janet Baker (A), Patricia Clark (B), Monica Sinclair (C), Raimund Herincx (D), St. Anthony Singers, English Chamber Orchestra—Anthony Lewis

Despite incidental flaws, this is still, on balance, the most satisfactory *Dido and Aeneas* ever recorded. Sir Anthony Lewis and his fine orchestral and choral forces are accurate and lively, and the performance has unusual spontaneity: there is a playful, improvisatory quality to the playing and singing, as though the performers were creating the work as it goes along, rather than simply reading notes off the page.

Thurston Dart, whose edition of the score is performed here, also plays the harpsichord *con-

tinuo. There are vocal embellishments, but no interpolations to replace the lost music.

Janet Baker sings with her customary intensity. Her voice, heard here at its most beautiful and expressive, is noticeably darker in timbre, with more of a contralto quality, than it became later on in her career. Her rhythmic articulation of the music, and her vivid inflection of the text, are unmatched by any other Dido on records.

Patricia Clark and Raimund Herincx are good without quite reaching Baker's level. Monica Sinclair, the Sorceress, is a true contralto, though rather hooty in timbre. She and her fellow Witches (both solo and choral) indulge in a good deal of cackling, but certainly can't be accused of not entering into the spirit of the piece. It is interesting to hear a future Rienzi and Tristan, John Mitchinson, as the Sailor. There is a soprano Spirit, Dorothy Dorow.

The clear, spacious sound of the original LP holds up well on the new CD transfer.

1964 HARMONIA MUNDI (S)

Mary Thomas (A), Honor Sheppard (B), Helen Watts (C), Maurice Bevans (D), Oriana Chorus and Orchestra—Alfred Deller

Alfred Deller will be remembered as a pioneering countertenor whose vocalism is preserved on many worthy recordings. His contributions as a musicologist and conductor are, frankly, much more uneven in quality, and his *Dido and Aeneas* suffers from slack conducting, sloppy orchestra playing, and the impersonal, oratorio-style sound of a too-large chorus.

The cast is acceptable, although most of the singers are on the bland side; Helen Watts, the exception, distorts her magnificent contralto into a sort of nasal snarl in a misguided attempt to sound malevolent. Robert Tear is impressive as the Sailor and the Spirit.

1965 EMI / ANGEL (S)

Victoria de los Angeles (A), Heather Harper (B), Patricia Johnson (C), Peter Glossop (D), Ambrosian Singers, English Chamber Orchestra—John Barbirolli

Sir John Barbirolli, using the Neville Boyling edition of the score, gives us a full-bodied, richly colored reading, with sumptuous string tone. Some of the tempos are very slow, and sometimes the music sounds more like Beethoven than Purcell, but Barbirolli is too good a musician to do anything really unstylish, and he is superb in the serious episodes of the work.

Victoria de los Angeles does some lovely singing, and is particularly good at conveying vulnerability and pathos; it would be a hard-hearted listener indeed who was not moved by her rendition of "When I am laid in earth." But her English has just enough of a foreign accent to be distracting at times.

The supporting cast is uneven, with Heather Harper's edgy, uningratiating Belinda and Peter Glossop's sturdy but woolly-toned Aeneas balanced by Patricia Johnson's strongly voiced Sorceress. Tear is once again the Sailor.

Raymond Leppard plays the harpsichord. The sound of the LP is excessively reverberant. There is no extra music at the end of Act II, but this is one of the few recordings that respond to the stage direction "Thunder and lightning; horrid music," after the Echo Chorus, by providing appropriate sound effects.

1967 DEUTSCHE GRAMMOPHON ARCHIV (S) CD

Tatiana Troyanos (A), Sheila Armstrong (B), Patricia Johnson (C), Barry McDaniel (D), Hamburg Monteverdi Choir, Hamburg Radio Chamber Orchestra—Charles Mackerras

This recording attempts a greater level of "authenticity" than previous versions, but with uneven results. The edition is once again Neville Boyling's, modified by the conductor. The two guitar dances are inserted where the 1689 libretto calls for them; the guitars and a lute also alternate with the harpsichord as *continuo* instruments. Music for the end of Act II has been adapted from other Purcell scores: *Dioclesian*, *King Arthur*, *Timon of Athens*, and *The Tempest*.

Unfortunately, the performance is dull, on the whole. The recitatives drag, and the massive, impersonal choral sound weighs down virtually every choral number. Sir Charles Mackerras, though a fine musician, rather overdoes the double-dotting. Much of his phrasing seems fussy, and there are some erratic tempo changes.

Tatiana Troyanos has a fine voice, but her vocalism is monotonously dark in coloration and her delivery solemn throughout: her Dido sounds suicidally depressed from the beginning. Furthermore, her artificial darkening of vowels prevents clear enunciation of the text (no one would guess, from this recording, that she is an American).

Sheila Armstrong's bright soprano and Barry McDaniel's warm lyric baritone are enjoyable, though. Johnson repeats her powerful Sorceress from the Barbirolli recording, to good effect. Nigel Rogers is a fine Sailor, and countertenor Paul Esswood is the best Spirit on any of these recordings, combining eerie, sinister tone with a pointed delivery of the words.

The recorded sound is boomy and indistinct to begin with, and not helped by the use of an echo chamber in Act II, Scene 1. The original LP edition of this recording contains extensive, informative notes that are models of their kind.

1970 PHILIPS (S) CD

Josephine Veasey (A), Helen Donath (B), Elizabeth Bainbridge (C), John Shirley-Quirk (D), John Alldis Choir, Academy of St. Martin in the Fields—Colin Davis

This version ought to satisfy anyone who is not interested in an "original instrument" approach to Dido and Aeneas: Sir Colin Davis employs a substantial body of modern strings and a cast of singers with large, colorful voices, but everyone involved plays and sings so stylishly that the performance is authentically seventeenth century in spirit, if not in letter. The edition is once again Dart's, modified by the conductor; there are no interpolations. John Constable's harpsichord continuo is rather busy.

Josephine Veasey, the only singer who has recorded Berlioz's Dido as well as Purcell's, is regal yet passionate, giving us vocalism that is unapologetically "operatic" in scale. She has worthy opponents in Elizabeth Bainbridge's

strong-voiced, mercifully unexaggerated Sorceress and the subordinate Witches of Delia Wallis and Gillian Knight. Helen Donath's Belinda, by contrast, is all pure tone and delicate feminine charm.

John Shirley-Quirk is a sturdy Aeneas, despite a pronounced vibrato. Frank Patterson offers an Irish-accented Sailor, Thomas Allen a baritone Spirit (an unusually robust-sounding "trusty elf"). The CD reissue, offered at mid-price, is a genuine bargain.

1975 DECCA / LONDON (S)

Janet Baker (A), Norma Burrowes (B), Anna Reynolds (C), Peter Pears (D), London Opera Chorus, Aldeburgh Festival Strings—Steuart Bedford

It's hard to tell what went wrong here: all of the participants seem to carry the right basic credentials, but the result is one of the least persuasive recorded accounts of the opera. One problem is the Benjamin Britten / Imogen Holst performance edition, which fills out the string writing with extra parts, prescribes tempos, accents, and dynamics, and even writes out the continuo in detail—straitjacketing the performers, and providing little leeway for improvisation or spontaneity.

Steuart Bedford's conducting, rhythmically limp and often too slow, is just plain dull. He should have been locked in a room and forced to listen to the Lewis and Davis recordings before these sessions.

Janet Baker suffers from this lack of true musical support: weighed down by Bedford's tempos and the thick string accompaniments, her Dido now seems monotonously lugubrious, even morbid. Her voice is lighter in timbre than before, with some unsteadiness on sustained tones. Veteran tenor Peter Pears, miscast in the baritone role of Aeneas to begin with, sounds wobbly and strained throughout—an embarrassing performance. Casting a boy soprano as the Spirit is not a bad idea in principle, but Timothy Everett is excruciatingly off pitch.

There is some good work in the other roles (in addition to Norma Burrowes and Anna Reynolds, Felicity Lott as the Second Woman;

Felicity Palmer and Alfreda Hodgson as the Witches; Tear in his third recorded Sailor), but that is not enough to salvage the recording as a whole.

p. 1977 ERATO (S) CD

Tatiana Troyanos (A), Felicity Palmer (B), Patricia Kern (C), Richard Stilwell (D), English Chamber Choir and Orchestra—Raymond Leppard

The unspecified edition is probably Raymond Leppard's own, with no conclusion to Act II, but some vocal decoration and retouching of the string parts. Leppard's conducting dominates the performance: it's a brisk, colorful reading, filled with illuminating detail, and legitimately exciting.

Troyanos sounds like a different singer here: she brings more vocal light and shade to the music, and makes far more of the words. Felicity Palmer is an unusually mature-sounding, incisive Belinda—an interesting change from the standard soubrette approach to the role. Patricia Kern's Sorceress is mercifully restrained.

The sound of the LP is slightly dull, and benefits from a treble boost.

1978 HARMONIA MUNDI (S)

D'Anna Fortunato (A), Nancy Armstrong (B), Bruce Fithian (C), Mark Baker (D), Boston Camerata—Joel Cohen

This recording has its advocates, but I cannot work up much enthusiasm for the performance. Joel Cohen, who conducts, plays *continuo* lute, and sings the Sailor, has interesting ideas about the music, but often lacks the technical control to bring them off. He adds flute, oboe, and percussion parts to Purcell's scoring, to distracting effect. The orchestra and chorus both sound undermanned and under-rehearsed.

D'Anna Fortunato is an impassioned, interesting Dido, and Mark Baker makes an unusually positive Aeneas. Most of their colleagues, though, are inadequate. Nancy Armstrong has a pretty but pale soprano. Bruce Fithian, a tenor Sor-

ceress, is vocally insecure and hopelessly campy from the interpretive standpoint.

Cohen's singing, as the Sailor, is an embarrassment. Ken Fitch is a whiny countertenor Spirit who makes the listener long for Esswood. The recorded sound is unimpressive.

1981 CHANDOS (S,D) CD

Emma Kirkby (A), Judith Nelson (B), Jantina Noorman (E), David Thomas (D), Taverner Choir and Taverner Players—Andrew Parrott

This intimate, graceful performance treats *Dido and Aeneas* as a true chamber opera. Andrew Parrott and his small, nimble instrumental ensemble reproduce the score with the lightest of brushstrokes. In anything other than a very small theater, this approach might be almost too subtle—it is the kind of music making that draws the listener toward it, rather than reaching out to embrace the audience—but it is absorbing and convincing on a recording.

Emma Kirkby, the queen of the British early-music scene, is the Dido, and a greater contrast to Flagstad's classic interpretation, or the performances of Troyanos and Veasey, could scarcely be imagined. Even Baker sounds huge-voiced by comparison! Kirkby, with her pure, delicate, vibrato-less soprano, is a remarkably gentle, girlish-sounding Queen of Carthage, and yet her performance works, because she sings with a total identification with the character that illuminates every phrase.

Judith Nelson and David Thomas have often partnered Kirkby on records, and they once again give her fine support. The choral singing is exquisite.

Jantina Noorman, the possessor of a remarkably ugly voice, is unpleasant to listen to as the Sorceress (which may be the point). For many collectors, this is the finest recording of *Dido and Aeneas* currently available; while my personal preference is for something gutsier, I can see their point.

1982 TELDEC (S,D) CD

Ann Murray (A), Rachel Yakar (B), Trudeliese Schmidt (C), Anton Scharinger (D), Arnold

Schönberg Choir, Concentus Musicus, Vienna—Nikolaus Harnoncourt

This recording is a perfect antidote for anyone who thinks that all "authentic instruments" performances must be bland and anemic. Nikolaus Harnoncourt and his orchestra tear into the music with exaggerated tempo contrasts, violent accents, and sharply differentiated instrumental colors. It's all a bit extreme, perhaps, but the result is certainly never dull, and often rivetingly dramatic.

Ann Murray is a dignified Dido, her powerful mezzo capable of a melting tenderness when required. She sounds as though she has studied the Baker recordings; if so, she has certainly imitated the right things. Paul Esswood repeats his definitive Spirit from the DG Archiv recording. Rachel Yakar is a pleasant enough Belinda, though a little thin and brittle of tone.

Most of the other singers are German or Austrian. They have obviously worked hard to master the English text, and Trudeliese Schmidt's fierce, bitter Sorceress is particularly convincing. But Anton Scharinger's inflections give us a most peculiar aural image of Aeneas: he sounds smug and fatuous at every turn of the plot.

There are no insertions at the end of Act II. The digital engineering is vivid—a good match for the boldly idiosyncratic performance.

1985 PHILIPS (S,D) CD

Jessye Norman (A), Marie McLaughlin (B), Patricia Kern (C), Thomas Allen (D), Unidentified chorus, English Chamber Orchestra—Raymond Leppard

Essentially, this is a remake of the Erato recording, with the same conductor, orchestra, and Sorceress. Leppard has not radically altered his conception of the work. His reading is once again lively, colorful, and dramatic; his tempos tend to be faster than before, though, and he seems to be encouraging his modern strings to imitate the needlepoint articulation and narrow vibrato of period instruments. Once again, he inserts no music at the end of Act II. It was a

mistake, though, to have the sailors (both solo and chorus) affect cockney accents.

The performance is dominated by Jessye Norman's Dido. Inevitably, she invites comparisons with Flagstad: she displays the same weight and opulence of tone, the same majesty of delivery. Norman is decidedly more passionate than her great predecessor, though, unleashing real ferocity and despair in the Act III confrontation with Aeneas. In the more lyrical, introspective passages (e.g., "Ah, Belinda, I am pressed") she works hard to scale her heroic sound down to the intimate proportions required by the music.

Thomas Allen, Davis's Spirit, has graduated to the role of Aeneas, and is excellent. Kern, less firm of voice than she was on the Erato recording, is still effective. Derek Lee Ragin is a good countertenor Spirit. The Belinda of Marie McLaughlin, however, is a serious disappointment: her singing is small-scaled, shallow of timbre, and turns shrill under pressure, and next to Norman she sounds immature.

1985 HARMONIA MUNDI (S,D) CD

Guillemette Laurens (A), Jill Feldman (B), Dominique Visse (C), Philippe Cantor (D), Les Arts Florissants—William Christie

One minor reservation apart, this is an excellent version: it is beautifully played, sung, and recorded. William Christie conducts with a kind of controlled flexibility that carries the listener from beginning to end in one powerful sweep; the performance is all of a piece. The band of period instruments makes delicate or incisive sounds as required, and the *continuo* (with two harpsichords, viola da gamba, and violone) is lively. There is a great deal of vocal embellishment, most of which is effective; occasionally, a phrase is slowed down in order to incorporate a decoration in a way that seems somewhat mannered.

The only problem is linguistic: many of the singers are French. Guillemette Laurens, Philippe Cantor, and Dominique Visse all form some of their words too carefully to be completely idiomatic, and Michel Laplenie is a

Sailor who must hail from Marseilles. The small chorus, however, sings in excellent English; so does Agnes Mellon, who doubles the Second Woman with the First Witch.

Jill Feldman, with her reedy, tightly focused tone, is an atypical Belinda, but an effective one. Linguistic questions aside, Laurens and Cantor make a persuasive pair of lovers: she proud yet sensual, he suave and manly. Visse is a countertenor Sorceress, but a very good one, his piercing tonal production positively dripping venom.

There are no insertions of extra music. The digital sound is exceptionally clear and detailed.

1989 DEUTSCHE GRAMMOPHON ARCHIV (S,D) CD

Anne Sofie von Otter (A), Lynne Dawson (B), Nigel Rogers (C), Stephen Varcoe (D), English Concert and the Choir of the English Concert—Trevor Pinnock

This version has many virtues—and some serious defects. Its strengths include superb digital engineering, virtuoso string playing (discreetly reinforced by oboes and bassoons much of the time, by the way), and beautiful choral singing. Above all, Anne Sofie von Otter's Dido is as touching as any on records. Her warm, supple mezzo seems capable of an infinite variety of colors, and she enunciates the text like a native Englishwoman. Here, at last, is a portrayal that can be compared to Janet Baker's first recording, on L'Oiseau-Lyre.

Lynne Dawson is a nice Belinda, but the usually reliable Stephen Varcoe is a disappointment as Aeneas: Varcoe vocalizes so discreetly (relying almost exclusively on a heavily damped, crooning *mezza voce*, and hardly ever letting his voice out) and does so little with the words that the character is reduced to a complete nonentity.

Trevor Pinnock is not an experienced opera conductor, and the performance—for all its high level of moment-to-moment execution—is fatally lacking in atmosphere and dramatic sweep. The Witches' scenes sound polite, even

pretty, which cannot possibly be right. There is one major piece of miscasting: tenor Nigel Rogers sings the Sorceress absolutely straight, making nothing of the part; and doubling this role with that of the Sailor is particularly unfortunate.

There are no insertions at the end of Act II.

1989 GLOBE (S,D) CD

Rachel Ann Morgan (A), Camille van Lunen (B), Myra Kroese (C), David Barick (D), Academy of the Begynhof, Amsterdam—Roderick Shaw

This recording is unique in that it employs Edward Dent's reconstruction of the Prologue. The music is adapted from a bewildering number of other Purcell scores, and the sequence adds nearly twenty minutes to the playing time of the disc. The singers double up, as was presumably done at the first performance: thus, Rachel Ann Morgan sings Venus in the Prologue and Dido in the opera; David Barick sings first Phoebus and then Aeneas; and so on.

The ersatz Purcell is pleasant enough to hear, but personally I find that the Prologue adds little to my enjoyment of the opera. (Surprisingly, the producer did not take the logical next step of squeezing in the spoken Epilogue as well; but just wait—now that Globe has set a precedent, we'll no doubt be given a "really complete" *Dido and Aeneas* on records before long.)

The performance is small-scaled, with only ten strings, a tiny chorus, and generally lightweight vocalism. Morgan displays a rich mezzo timbre, but also some hootiness and tremulousness on sustained tones; she is clearly a singer with potential, but a recorded Dido from her is premature. Camille van Lunen and Barick are accurate but unimpressive; Myra Kroese, however, is a very good Sorceress, with a firm contralto voice.

Roderick Shaw brings a light touch to the lyrical episodes, but tends to underplay the more dramatic moments. The Dutch instrumentalists are good, but I wish there had been more of them—the ensemble sounds undernourished at times, an impression reinforced by the closely miked recorded sound.

While I cannot imagine being without either the Flagstad recording of the opera or Baker's first version, on L'Oiseau-Lyre, many listeners will prefer a performance in more up-to-date sound. For them, I would recommend the Sir Colin Davis version, on Philips, because of its consistently high quality.

Collectors who want an "original instruments" performance now have several fine recordings to choose from. The Parrott record-ing has many lovely moments in it, and is a safe recommendation; but I would like to put in a good word for the Christie, which is sometimes quirky but interestingly "different" and often quite stimulating.

Happily, *Dido and Aeneas* is a relatively inexpensive opera to acquire on records, so no one need feel guilty about owning more than one version.

ROLAND GRAEME

Unavailable for review:
1934 EMI / ANGEL
1935 DECCA / LONDON
1992 TELDEC

MAURICE RAVEL

L'HEURE ESPAGNOLE (1907–11)

A: Concepción (s); B: Gonzalve (t); C: Torquemada (t);
D: Ramiro (bar); E: Don Inigo Gomez (bs)

Each of Ravel's operas creates a special world that takes some effort to penetrate, but each rewards that effort immoderately—these are operas not to like but to love. And while *L'Heure Espagnole*, the earlier of these two one-acts, is generally judged less substantial than the easily sentimentalized *L'Enfant et les Sortilèges* (1925), I don't think I agree. The harmonious accommodation that this strange cast of characters reaches in the glorious quintet-finale, if truly earned in the performance, reaches a plane of joyous resonance worthy of Mozart.

It's sobering to remember that Franc-Nohain's play *was* a play before the presumptuous Ravel added music to it. Trying to think of the text without the music, it's hard to imagine summoning much tolerance for these distinctly unsavory people without the composer's mediation. As they play out their roles in Concepción's frustrated determination to cuckold her poor Totor, Ravel has found lurking inside them an unexpected and touching innocence that cries out for the audience's indulgence, or even protection.

The thorny question of vocal style bequeathed by the composer is discussed under 1929 EMI. All of the recordings are complete.

1929 EMI / ANGEL (M)

Jeanne Krieger (A), Louis Arnould (B), Raoul Gilles (C), J. Aubert (D), Hector Dufranne (E), Symphony Orchestra—Georges Truc

This recording, supervised by the composer, holds up well, at least in some respects. (It sounds remarkably present in the 1984 Conductart cassette transfer.) There's a good deal of fun to be derived from the orchestral part, which is reproduced with clarity, delicacy, and atmosphere. Really, I would hate to be without it.

Alas, however, there's not much fun to be had in the singing, notwithstanding the admirable verbal clarity. It may be that these were the best singers who could be found and afforded. More likely, though, we are hearing the result of the composer's score admonition, *"dire* plutôt que *chanter"*—"declaim rather than *sing.* . . . It is, almost all the time, the *quasi-parlando* of the Italian buffo recitative," with two official exceptions: the final quintet and ("for the most part") the role of Gonzalve ("the affectedly lyrical").

One suspects that what's really at work is Ravel's determination, held in common with an historic roster of operatic "reformers," to preserve his creation from the debased estate to which the form had sunk, and one sympathizes. One wouldn't wish to cause him distress by slathering his opera in mindless vocal refulgence, although one may perhaps be forgiven for furtively imagining *L'Heure* at least lightly slathered. It's an *opera*, for goodness' sake, and to my knowledge nobody has yet found a satisfactory operatic substitute for the expressive power of the singing voice.

And while one is listening through this

recording, with its essentially nonsinging cast, listening for example to the especially thread-voiced Ramiro, it's hard not to fantasize about Tibbett in the role at the Met in 1925. Pleasant as it is to hear in the recording such a flavorful orchestral evocation of Ramiro's uncle the toreador, surely the full effect depends on a baritone who can seize the opportunity of this *bravura arioso* (cf. Heinz Rehfuss or Gabriel Bacquier). Yes, the verbal sense is important, but surely not *in place of* the musical sense.

To be sure, Louis Arnould, the Gonzalve, does sing more and better than the others, and the comparison makes his light, quavery tenor appear pleasanter than it otherwise would. But this is only by comparison, which doesn't count for much in the grand scheme of pleasantness. A moment of truth comes in the quintet, where everyone has license to sing: how likely is it that we're suddenly going to hear singing of a satis-factoriness hitherto unhinted at? (No, we don't.)

1951 VOX (M)

Janine Linda (A), André Dran (B), Jean Mollien (C), Jean Hoffman (D), Lucien Mans (E), Radio France Symphony Orchestra, Paris—René Lei-bowitz

There are real strengths here, beginning with René Leibowitz's conducting, which has a strength of rhythmic profile otherwise approached only by Lorin Maazel (1965 DG), without sac-rificing subjective atmosphere as Maazel to an extent seems to. And the singers, who thank-fully are trying to sing, have achieved an impressive degree of ease with the tricky pitches and rhythms. They tend to be a bit casual about Ravel's dynamic markings, though, which is worrisome not because of inaccurate score-ren-dering but because of the loss of potentially valuable clues as to what in the needs of the characters creates the music.

In addition, the cast isn't vocally over-whelming, and is somewhat oddly matched. The striking vocal presence of Jean Mollien's Torquemada makes an immediate impact that isn't sustained by the rest of the cast. Through much of the performance, I find myself won-dering when that nice clockmaker is going to

return home, which certainly makes for an unusual perspective on the opera. At the very least, André Dran's entirely competent Gon-zalve is undercut—one is distracted into specu-lation as to whether the tenors shouldn't have been transposed. Both Jean Hoffman, the Ramiro, and Lucien Mans, the Don Inigo, are vocally less full and focused than I would like.

And somehow Janine Linda's quite pretty soprano doesn't seem to fit the surroundings. First off, although the score specifies a soprano for Concepción, the lie of the writing seems to argue for a mezzo. For example, her "aria" in Scene 17, "Oh! la pitoyable aventure," begins with a sweeping descent that implies some real lower-range presence, as indeed the character's general earthiness seems to. Linda sounds like an Adina-Norina sort of soprano: light, accu-rate, a bit edgy in timbre—not my idea of a Concepción, except perhaps in a specially tai-lored cast. The high B at the end of the quintet certainly has some ping, though.

1953 DECCA / LONDON (M)

Suzanne Danco (A), Paul Derenne (B), Michel Hamel (C), Heinz Rehfuss (D), André Vessières (E), Suisse Romande Orchestra—Ernest Anser-met

The two 1953 recordings give a vivid and wonderfully rounded picture of the opera, fall-ing short only in their sonic representation of the orchestral part.

Ernest Ansermet preceded Lorin Maazel (DG) and Armin Jordan (Erato) in recording both *L'Heure* and *L'Enfant et les Sortilèges*. (His *L'Enfant*, fortunately, is in good early stereo.) All three are fine musicians; all achieve lovely results. But in both operas Ansermet starts with the advantage of an inquisitive, fertile imagina-tion that, instead of being bound by the printed page, ranges widely to justify and animate what's on the page. His *L'Heure* Prelude doesn't just build to a powerful climax—it starts in a world of hushed mystery that seizes attention. He is less inclined than other conductors to push forward (this final quintet is an almost languor-ous habañera), and less apt to take details for granted, or contrarily to mistake them for self-contained phenomena. He grounds the dance forms that stud the opera so solidly that they take us inside the characters' consciousness.

And that consciousness is actually followed through by the singers—allowing for the arguable vocal superiority of some of the singers in 1965 DG, this strikes me as the strongest cast on records. To begin with, the bass-baritone presence and lovely nap of Heinz Rehfuss's Ramiro restore a dimension of the opera lost in the earlier recordings, despite occasional impulses to vocal mugging that seem to me to misunderstand the joke of the character, which is that there is none: the poor muleteer is always in deadly earnest.

Suzanne Danco's warm, mezzo-ish soprano is well suited to Concepción, and her sympathetic temperament makes for an unusually rounded portrait. André Vessières as Don Inigo doesn't have the vocal freedom and assurance of 1965 DG's José van Dam, but it's such a nice, resonant voice, so comfortably used, that I find the performance enormously appealing. One of Ravel's most remarkable achievements in *L'Heure* is making the rather odious financier sympathetic, and one of my favorite moments in the opera is the waltz that erupts ("Tant pis, ma foi, si je déroge!") when Don Inigo, acknowledging the ridiculousness of his continued pursuit of Concepción, decides he doesn't care. The tenors are perfectly satisfactory.

1953 EMI / ANGEL (M)

Denise Duval (A), Jean Giraudeau (B), René Hérent (C), Jean Vieuille (D), Charles Clavensy (E), Orchestra of the Opéra Comique, Paris—André Cluytens

Far from wilting under the comparison, André Cluytens's performance stands up resolutely to Ansermet's. It has a deliciously idiomatic, unabashedly Gallic tone that creates a strong and coherent, goofily exotic local flavor. Cluytens has a feeling for grounded detail as alert as, and interestingly unlike, Ansermet's—note the contented sigh in the strings when Torquemada responds to his dear wife's summoning "Totor!"

Denise Duval, although tonally less warm and distinctive than Danco, is a famously inge-

nious singer, and her Concepción is strong on the itchy restlessness that after all sets the opera's plot in motion. As a soprano, she is again at a disadvantage in "Oh! la pitoyable aventure." Opposite her, that fine character tenor Jean Giraudeau is a tenderly poetic Gonzalve—the full-bodied lyric line he attempts to maintain compensates for the uncertain handling in the upper part of the voice exposed in the process. René Hérent is an adequate Torquemada.

Jean Vieuille's Ramiro and Charles Clavensy's Don Inigo are less plush-toned than their Decca / London counterparts, but both give solid, idiomatic performances, and Clavensy in particular traces some admirably firm lines.

1965 DEUTSCHE GRAMMOPHON (S) CD

Jane Berbié (A), Michel Sénéchal (B), Jean Giraudeau (C), Gabriel Bacquier (D), José van Dam (E), Orchestre Nationale de la RTF—Lorin Maazel

DG has done a fine job with the CD reissues of its Maazel-conducted Ravel operas, with careful transfers and booklets containing complete texts and translations and sets of essays (different ones in French, German, and English) substantial enough to be worth quarreling with. The performances themselves continue to command considerable respect. They're executed with precision and exuberance, and they're attractively recorded.

And while the cast for *L'Enfant* is—inevitably—uneven, that for *L'Heure* is extremely strong. This Don Inigo introduced many of us to José van Dam, and the rich evenness and easy handling of his bass-baritone still distinguish him from the recorded competition. (Of course, there has been only one recording since!) Gabriel Bacquier's solid baritone is virtually ideal for Ramiro, and again, despite some smudging of the line for presumably comic intent, he gives a lovely performance.

Jean Giraudeau, the excellent Gonzalve of 1953 EMI, is now a fine Torquemada, and Michel Sénéchal is a worthy successor as Gonzalve. Again, it's a somewhat pinched sound, but applied to the role with unabashedly lyrical seriousness that's hard to resist. Jane Berbié, a full-fledged mezzo, is a generally strong and persuasive Concepción.

What then keeps me from recommending this recording unequivocally? At times it strikes me as so satisfactory that I wonder why at other times it leaves me so grumbly. But at those times, grumble I do. The best explanation I can offer is that, brilliantly conceived as the performance is, it remains at heart calculating and manipulative, rather than impulsive and subjectively involved.

1985 ERATO (S,D) CD

Elisabeth Laurence (A), Tibère Raffalli (B), Michel Sénéchal (C), Gino Quilico (D), François Loup (E), Nouvel Orchestre Philharmonique—Armin Jordan

Armin Jordan's special qualities as a conductor—the specificity and inclusiveness with which he breaks down and imagines a musical text—are made to order for the Ravel operas. These may be short pieces, but they aren't "small." They're both made up of fantastically concentrated little scenes, most of them no more than a few minutes long, which means that performers don't have the luxury of warming into the material. If you're not up to speed at the start of the scene, it will pass you by.

The cast is decent enough. While Ramiro seems to me to want a burlier baritone—you know, in order to tote those heavy clocks—Gino Quilico gives a quite distinctive high-baritone account. Elisabeth Laurence and Tibère Raffalli are a pleasant, lightweight, not especially memorable Concepción and Gonzalve. François Loup makes a nice, weighty sound as Don Inigo, although there's something a bit tricked-up about the performance. (You can see some of this quality in the video version of the Glyndebourne *L'Heure*.)

For both *L'Heure* and *L'Enfant*, Erato's CD packages, at least as originally issued, are less satisfactory than DG's. There are fewer track cues (DG tracks each scene), meager annotations, and texts in French only.

As a complete package, 1965 DG has so much going for it that I wish I could suspend my reservations. It would combine well—if you can manage more than one recording—with 1953 Decca / London, 1953 EMI, or 1985 Erato. For that matter, any pairing among the four would make an interesting combination.

And if I could have only one version? That would probably be 1953 Decca / London.

KENNETH FURIE

MAURICE RAVEL

L'ENFANT ET LES SORTILÈGES (1925)

A: Princess (s); B: Child (ms); C: Mother (c)

*I*t is a pity that Maurice Ravel, with his love for the stage and motion pictures, wrote only two short operas. In 1906, when he was thirty-one, he considered a full-length opera, but being a slow, painstaking worker, he never got to it. For a short work, he was capable of acting on impulse, and a little amoral farce called *L'Heure Espagnole* struck his fancy—partly because of its Spanish subject, partly because it involved a clock. Spain and its atmosphere fascinated Ravel; he also loved clocks and mechanical devices of all sorts. He set the play to music, and his version had its premiere at the Opéra-Comique in 1911.

More than a decade passed before Ravel wrote another opera, this quite a different undertaking, though it too involved a grandfather clock. It was a story of childhood that seized his imagination. His collaborator was the popular French writer Colette, who celebrated the natural world as Ravel did the imaginary. World War I, during which Ravel volunteered as an ambulance driver, slowed the work's progress, and it did not reach the stage until 1925 in Monte Carlo.

Sortilège means "witchcraft, charm, spell," making the title *L'Enfant et les Sortilèges* elusive to translate. *The Child and the Sorcerers* is a version sometimes given, but there are no sorcerers in the story—only the transformation of reality by the imagination of the Child, who is the central character. Furniture and toys come to life, animals talk, and only a desperate call for his Mother puts the Child back in touch with the real world. Stage performance is notoriously difficult: how to play a singing armchair, a pair of talking cats? On records, however, disembodied voices free the listener's imagination, so the mood of Ravel's delicate, amusing, and touching score can take over.

1948 EMI / ANGEL (M)

Martha Angelici (A), Nadine Sautereau (B), Denise Scharley (C), French Radio Chorus and National Orchestra—Ernest Bour

This classic version, despite its age (or perhaps because of it, since a certain misty atmosphere adds to the recorded ambience), captures the enchanted world of Ravel's characters. Sautereau's Child has a ping and vibrancy that ultimately make her portrayal poignant. Scharley's pointed diction and intimate projection also make the most of her brief appearance as the Mother. As the Princess from the Child's storybook, Angelici sounds sweet but not cloying. Solange Michel creates a character of the Shepherdess, though her coloratura is not notably accurate; André Vessières's Armchair, another plausible if imaginary entity, is enhanced by the most humorous contrabassoon grunts to be heard in any recorded *Enfant*. In general it is the lightness of the singing by this expert ensemble that creates a performance like a fairy tale or a dream—" . . . et les débris d'un rêve."

1954 DECCA / LONDON (S) CD

Suzanne Danco (A), Flore Wend (B), Marie Lise de Montmollin (C), Motet Choir of Geneva, Orchestre de la Suisse Romande—Ernest Ansermet

Though Ansermet rates second to none as a conductor of French music, in this case his clinical, clear, accurate reading takes away some of the magic of Ravel's score. Wend's characterization of the Child is somewhat repressed and pallid. Montmollin's Mother is unremarkable, but the Princess of Danco and the Shepherdess of Geneviève Touraine are distinctively styled, as is the triple characterization of Hugues Cuénod. In this opera, multiple casting is common; Cuénod's roles are the Wedgwood Teapot, the Little Old Man ("C'est l'Arithmétique!"), and the Frog. Ansermet's pacing and shaping show his natural affinity for Ravel's style, but the orchestra's presence—objectively captured by Decca's early, gimmick-free stereo—is too much with us, especially in such moments as the *glissando* for slide-flute, which sounds like an instrument, not a bird call in an enchanted garden.

1960 DEUTSCHE GRAMMOPHON (S) CD

Sylvaine Gilma (A), Françoise Ogéas (B), Jeannine Collard (C), French Radio Chorus and National Orchestra—Lorin Maazel

Ogéas really sounds like a child, while Collard, a sensibly mature Mother, is a bit matronly for the *bel canto* of the tea-dance foxtrot she gets to sing in her other persona as the Teacup. Maazel, a specialist in brilliantly scored showpieces, has chosen his cast with care; it also includes Camille Maurane (a distinguished Pelléas) as the Grandfather Clock and one of the Cats, Michel Sénéchal as the Teapot and Little Old Man, Heinz Rehfuss and Jane Berbié, all estimable cameo artists, with Gilma quite charming as the Princess.

Ravel, wanting an antique or exotic sound like that of a lute harpsichord (with gut strings) or cimbalom, calls for a *luthéal* or specially prepared piano. Since this is a unicorn among instruments, some sort of improvised solution appears in most performances. Here we have what sounds like a period fortepiano, but it has a weak voice and cannot be heard during the

pastoral chorus. Otherwise the recording is well balanced and pleasantly atmospheric.

1981 EMI / ANGEL (S,D) CD

Arleen Augér (A), Susan Davenny Wyner (B), Jocelyne Taillon (C), Ambrosian Singers, London Symphony—André Previn

This version, a digital first, features an iridescent orchestra with sharply etched nature sounds. Previn, a scrupulously faithful interpreter, brings out Ravel's sonic palette. His solution for the Armchair episode is a prepared piano somewhat like a harpsichord, suggesting the chair's *ancien régime* vintage. His singers are a lively crew, with Davenny Wyner wide-eyed and slightly husky as the Child, Taillon a sensible French Mother (she also does three other roles), and Augér a bright, light Princess, coloratura Fire, and Nightingale. Jules Bastin, Philippe Huttenlocher (a good falsettist), and Jane Berbié are among the others. Mood, ranging from echoes of *La Valse* to a finale redolent of *Ma Mère l'Oye*, is warmly spun throughout.

1986 ERATO (S,D) CD

Audrey Michael (A), Colette Alliot-Lugaz (B), Arlette Chedel (C), Chorus and Orchestre de la Suisse Romande—Armin Jordan

Alliot-Lugaz is outstanding as the Child, enthusiastically rebellious at first, gentle and touching in the "Toi, le coeur de la rose" episode. Chedel, light and with clear words, etches the Mother a little more finely than does Taillon in the Previn album. Michael's Princess benefits from Jordan's slightly more animated movement during her solo, a trait that also enlivens the opening of the work. As the high-reaching Fire, Elisabeth Vidal is flickery but less spectacular than Previn's Augér. Huttenlocher repeats his Grandfather Clock and Cat from the Previn, while Sénéchal, the Little Old Man and Teapot of the Maazel recording, reappears here, adding the Frog to his list of fabulous impersonations. The "papered" piano, which sounds too mechanical, disappears during the pastoral chorus, but otherwise the recording tends to favor the orchestra.

———————————

Because this opera demands to be prepared with maximum finesse, there is no "bad" version. The pioneering Bour recording remains unique, its sonic limitations actually an asset to the veiled mystery of the piece. Among modern digital editions, the Jordan has the edge, though competition is close: Previn's Augér, for example, outshines every other Princess.

JOHN W. FREEMAN

Nikolai Rimsky-Korsakov

The Golden Cockerel (1909)

A: Queen of Shemakha (s); B: Cockerel (s); C: Amelfa (c);
D: Astrologer (t); E: King Dodon (bs)

This is not Rimsky's richest operatic score—*Czar Saltan*, *Sadko*, and *Christmas Eve* would vie for that rank—but it is the one that has had some performance life in the West. The composer's final opera, it is also his most musically concise and dramatically focused. Vladimir Bielsky's libretto elaborates on its source (a short verse tale by Pushkin), but sticks close to the point, much influenced by the political climate of the time. The piece does not sprawl. Unlike most of the composer's operas, it does not presume any familiarity with old Russian historical or legendary themes, nor any receptivity to Pantheist doctrine. The creators' satirical eye, trained in earlier works on fairly harmless targets, is here fixed on essentials of the Russian political system, and the tone is bitter, not affectionate: for all the sensuousness of much of the writing, there is a keen modern edge on it. Finally, the fairy-tale framework provided by the character of the Astrologer gives *Cockerel* a shapeliness that is satisfying to audiences. Regrettably, this fine and pertinent opera seems to be losing its modest place in our repertory. It has been played for the wrong values by directors who think its exotic or cartoonish aspects will carry it, and by performers who want their characters to be liked by the audience. The trenchancy of the work has been lost, and we're left impatient at the doofus comedy, faintly entertained by the seductive Queen, and just a little puzzled.

1962 MELODIYA (S)

Klara Kadinskaya (A), Nina Poliakova (B), Antonina Kleshcheva (C), Gennady Pishchayev (D), Alexei Korolyov (E), Chorus and Opera-Symphony Orchestra of the All-Union Radio—Aleksei Kovalev

This performance has been available in the United States on the Ultraphone (mono only) and Westminster Gold labels; the attributed date above is educated guesswork. Fortunately, the sound is reasonably rich and spacious; the chorus and orchestra are full and sharp; and the casting is appropriate. The principal roles present big challenges. The Queen has most of the choice singing to do, and while she is supposed to possess a sustained high E and much melismatic fluency in the upper mid-range, her voice also needs body and warmth in the lower and middle areas. Kadinskaya's soprano has the range, strength, and evenness needed. But there is not really any sorcery in either her timbre or her shaping of the line, so she must be accounted an efficient, capable Queen, and no more. Similarly, one wants a great voice and personality for Dodon. But the part has scant singing rewards—it lies high, and is filled with the sort of declamation that most singers will solve with a *parlando* approach. Korolyov is a solid, strong character bass who registers the points without often making one sit up and take notice. Poliakova has a quick, penetrating sound that is right for the Cockerel; Kleshcheva's matronly contralto does justice to Amelfa's lullaby; and Pishchayev's high, white tenor, with its well-managed blend into falsetto, serves well in the Astrologer's abnormal tessitura. The smaller parts are strongly taken. Kovalev secures the score's tautness and bite without ever driving at it, and retains the Klingsor's-Garden languor of the second act while keeping its long seduction scene structurally together.

1988 MCA (S,P,D) CD

Elena Brileva (A), Irena Udalova (B), Nina Gaponova (C), Oleg Biktimirov (D), Artur Eizen (E), Bolshoi Theater Chorus and Orchestra—Yevgeny Svetlanov

This set was recorded during a live performance in May 1988. While its odd mating of CD ferocity with boomy Bolshoi acoustic does not bring forth a really satisfactory result, it reasonably conveys the color and impact of Rimsky's scoring. Svetlanov's leadership is commanding and sober, a trifle short on wit and snap at some points, but amply sensuous and weighty—it pays off as it goes along. The veteran Eizen's timbre hasn't much richness or depth, but he offers more genuine singing than one hears from most Dodons, and has the character in focus. Brileva's Queen gets off to a dreadful start with a stiff, badly tuned stab at the gorgeous entrance aria; then she settles down to disclose a strong, rangey high soprano with which she delineates the Queen's cheerfully sinister appetites. Gaponova is a competent Amelfa, but nothing else here reflects well on the recent state of this great company. Biktimirov's tenor is not only messily aligned, but is the wrong sort for the role; his is a dark sound with a pronounced break into the falsetto extension. Udalova's Cockerel is acidulous and sharp of pitch. Among the lesser roles, only the Guidon is acceptable. The choral and orchestral forces are in solid shape.

We have a veritable Hobson's choice. You may prefer poor eighties sound to poor fifties sound, but the earlier performance is at least marginally better.

CONRAD L. OSBORNE

GIOACHINO ROSSINI

L'ITALIANA IN ALGERI (1832)

A: Elvira (s); B: Isabella (ms); C: Lindoro (t);
D: Mustafà (bs); E: Taddeo (bs)

*L*aunched in 1813, *L'Italiana in Algeri* was Rossini's first internationally successful comic opera, and remains his most masterful reach for sheer manic absurdity, in the onomatopoetic *stretto* to the first-act finale and the nonsensical ritual of the mythical order of "Pappatacci." Both Isabella, the supremely self-confident Italian girl of the title, and Mustafà, the besotted Bey of Algiers, are memorably and wittily defined in music, and the plot offers ample occasion for the ensembles of stupefaction—action and music static but madly spinning in place—that were a Rossini specialty.

Working in a great hurry, to fill a sudden hole in the schedule of Venice's Teatro San Benedetto, Rossini employed an unknown collaborator, who composed the *secco* recitatives, Haly's "Le femmine d'Italia" (No. 11), and possibly also Lindoro's "Ah, come il cor di giubilo" (No. 9). These numbers, thus traditionally under a cloud, have often been omitted, and the recitatives treated very cavalierly, to the detriment of essential plot detail (for example, the drunkenness of the Bey's servants at the opera's end is explained only in the Ferro recording). The recent spate of Rossini scholarship has produced a critical edition by Azio Corghi, restoring the original orchestrations. It also includes several alternative arias, of which the most important is an authentic replacement for the questionable No. 9, which might well be—but apparently has not yet been—accepted into the standard performing text.

1954 EMI / ANGEL (M) CD

Graziella Sciutti (A), Giulietta Simionato (B), Cesare Valletti (C), Mario Petri (D), Marcello Cortis (E), La Scala Chorus and Orchestra—Carlo Maria Giulini

Aftermath of a 1953 La Scala production (Franco Zeffirelli's first work there as a designer), this recording evidences the virtues of ample rehearsal and stage experience. The first-act finale is wonderfully "orchestrated," each nonsense syllable given a distinctive vocal color and the whole balanced to a fare-thee-well, while the precise pitching in *staccato* ensembles is a continuing delight. We may regret that the practices of the time yielded such a shredded text; not only the dubious Nos. 9 and 11 are omitted but also Mustafà's "Già d'insolito ardore" (No. 6) and many other pieces, as well as the recitatives, are severely trimmed. (The Seraphim LP reissue edition restored a few passages left on the editing-room floor in the original publication, and these are retained in the CD mastering.)

What remains has, on average, hardly been done better. Simionato's Isabella is a masterpiece of energy and inflection: her "Perchè?" at the beginning of Act I, Scene 5, is the perfect aural equivalent of a raised eyebrow, and she understands how to make Rossini's rhythms bounce and crackle, as well as how to shape a lyrical line. To be sure, her voice and technique were not made for the vocal embroidery of the role, which can cause her to simplify or lose the pitch; still, she's always right there theatrically. Much the same may be said of Mario Petri's Bey: his sound may be slightly cavernous and gravelly, but he creates a genuine authoritarian, spoiled character and articulates the coloratura surprisingly well (though of course he is spared the arduous No. 6).

Valletti (also relieved of some challenges by the omission of No. 9) is the most musical and imaginative of Lindoros, with caressing *portamentos*, considerable fluency, and splendid rhythmic verve: hear him launch "Fra gli amori" in No. 14, the "Pappataci" trio. Cortis is a stylish if vocally ordinary Taddeo, and Sciutti, occasionally thin-toned, shows her worth in leading the *stretto* of the first-act finale with point and precision. The chorus is equally keen on the comic possibilities (their number preceding "Amici, in ogni evento," one of the Seraphim restorations, is neatly accented). Aside from a lumpy horn solo in "Languir per una bella," the orchestra is superior: if not quite a match for the coruscating brilliance of Abbado's Vienna Philharmonic in the eighties, it executes accompaniment figures with elegance and melodies with idiomatic phrasing. Giulini's deadpan approach yields admirably humorous results, and in the recognition scene of Isabella and Lindoro he finds a whiff of the sexual passion that Rossini notoriously failed to put there (or elsewhere in his operas). Best of all, the music always feels unselfconsciously at ease with itself, whether taking breath between phrases or pushing forward to a climax.

1963 DECCA / LONDON (S) CD

Giuliana Tavolaccini (A), Teresa Berganza (B), Luigi Alva (C), Fernando Corena (D), Rolando Panerai (E), Chorus and Orchestra of the Maggio Musicale Fiorentino—Silvio Varviso

London was a leader in the revaluation of Italian opera's "standard" cuts, and in this recording the main musical text is advertised as "virtually complete" (the qualification referring to two excisions from No. 6), though "the recitatives . . . have here been reduced to what is really relevant"—a characterization with which some would disagree. The gain is offset by a loss

of character vis-à-vis Giulini's performance. Berganza is certainly a neater, more fluent singer than Simionato, but there's little magnetic about her Isabella, a nice girl who has done her lessons well but makes little contact with her music's potential for tonal and rhythmic (and personal) flavor. Corena has the Bey's rhetoric in his armory, if no longer his coloratura. By contrast, Panerai is a substantial and enthusiastic Taddeo, skilled at articulation and accenting. Alva's Lindoro gets further than you might expect on slender resources ("Languir per una bella" comes down a semitone); Simionato's Isabella would overpower him completely, but he manages to stand next to Berganza's more pallid figure. The orchestra lacks the distinction and the ensemble of the Scala band, although some solos (not the horn or flute, alas) are well played. Varviso's articulated tempos, unexceptionable in themselves, are not with enough concentration and spirit to make the music dance. The recorded sound is nicely airy and focused.

1978 ACANTA (S) CD

Norma Palacios-Rossi (A), Lucia Valentini Terrani (B), Ugo Benelli (C), Sesto Bruscantini (D), Enzo Dara (E), Dresden State Opera Chorus and Orchestra—Gary Bertini

Although Corghi's edition was not published until 1981, this and subsequent sets apparently had access to its textual revisions. Bertini includes more recitative than either earlier recording, and shortens No. 6 differently from Varviso. He has a firm grip on Rossinian structure and rhythm, and in the ensembles obtains clear textures and controls the buildups well. The Dresden chorus and orchestra are excellent, though not quite idiomatic—note the winds' Eastern European vibrato.

His cast has no standouts, no utter disasters either. Valentini Terrani's gentle mezzo floats the coloratura, unaspirated, on its rapid tremolo with fluent but rarely truly snappy results; in slow music, she is occasionally under the note. It's a performance one can admire for musicality and smoothness, though hardly for verve and spontaneity. Like Corena, Bruscantini is beyond his coloratura days, and No. 6 is rather a slog; what's left of his stylistic resources can best be appreciated at the end of No. 14, where he finds innumerable ways to caress the word "Pappatacci." Benelli makes a Lindoro even lighter than Alva, with a sweet manner, conspicuous aspirates, and a gingerly approach to the top notes. Dara's Taddeo is well articulated and pitched, a skillful piece of comic singing (as it will remain in two subsequent recordings).

1979 CBS/SONY (S) CD

Jeanne Marie Bima (A), Lucia Valentini Terrani (B), Francisco Araiza (C), Wladimiro Ganzarolli (D), Enzo Dara (E), West German Radio Male Chorus, Capella Coloniensis—Gabriele Ferro

This is, to date, the only complete recording of the score, and is also unusual in its use of period instruments (noticeable mainly in the natural horn introducing "Languir per una bella" and a twangy fortepiano for the recitatives), which seems less important than idiomatic style, of which Bertini's Saxons produce a more convincing facsimile than Ferro's Rhinelanders. Valentini Terrani and Dara are here again, and much as before. If Araiza's technical skills matched his engaging presence, his musical feeling, and his rhythmic vitality, he'd be a fine Lindoro, and he remains the most interesting figure in this cast, which also boasts the worst of all Mustafàs, Wladimiro Ganzarolli. There's personality here, but the man hardly ever sings in tune, and his struggles with the florid writing (or even with his simplifications thereof) fatally impede Ferro's generally well-intentioned efforts to bring the opera to life. Thanks to the complete recitatives, Alessandro Corbelli has more to work with than anyone else in making Haly a character rather than a caricature, and does an effective job, though Paolo Montarsolo (London) and Alfredo Mariotti (Acanta) sing "Le femmine d'Italia" better.

1980 ERATO (S) CD

Kathleen Battle (A), Marilyn Horne (B), Ernesto Palacio (C), Samuel Ramey (D), Domenico Trimarchi (E), Chorus of Prague, I Solisti Veneti—Claudio Scimone

This recording promises to be more enjoyable than it proves to be, and I'm inclined to place the blame at the foot of the podium. At one level, Scimone rarely gives the singers firm backgrounds against which they can make their rhythmic points. At another, he hasn't figured out how to make the longer numbers (e.g., the first finale and "Pappatacci") work with a minimum of gear-shifting and ends up interrupting their flow too often and needlessly. Finally, how odd that a Baroque specialist should so conspicuously miss the pastoral character of the opening of the second finale! Had Horne and Ramey been working with the Giulini and Valletti of 1954, we would have had quite an *Italiana* recording—but such time-traveling configurations can only be imagined, not actually heard. Horne's amazingly fluent and virtuosic Isabella has a sense of humor—not always quite the same as Rossini's, but one that meshes rewardingly with his (if not with Scimone's sogginess). Ramey is vocally the most imposing Mustafà, and technically adept as well (best in straightforward scales, he tends to smear when corners have to be turned). But he, too, needs more help from the conductor than he's getting: the already rather mechanical writing of "Già d'insolito ardore" doesn't take fire here despite his presence and skill. Kathleen Battle, the firmest of Elviras, likewise makes less impression than she might have. Neither the bantamweight Lindoro of Ernesto Palacio nor the wobbly Taddeo of Trimarchi increases the recording's appeal.

The main musical text is complete, and the recitatives are somewhat trimmed. In its original LP form, though not in Erato's CD edition, this set was filled out with four of the alternate pieces from the Corghi edition.

1987 DEUTSCHE GRAMMOPHON (S,D) CD

Patrizia Pace (A), Agnes Baltsa (B), Frank Lopardo (C), Ruggero Raimondi (D), Enzo Dara (E), Vienna State Opera Chorus, Vienna Philharmonic Orchestra—Claudio Abbado

Back in the 1970s at La Scala and Edinburgh, Claudio Abbado conducted some memorable Rossini performances and recordings—the approach often more affectionate than boisterous, the orchestral textures perhaps more Mendelssohnian than Rossinian, the result nonetheless hard to resist for integrity and conviction as well as polish. Something has hardened in the arteries since then, if this recording, made in conjunction with Vienna State Opera performances, is representative. To be sure, everything is in place, and the Vienna Philharmonic yields to no other orchestra in virtuosity of execution and articulation: check out the accompaniment figures in the chorus before "Cruda sorte" and the *stretto* to the second-act quintet. The wind solos in the introduction even have some *rubato*—but that's the exception; most of this performance is propelled with an essentially mechanical rigidity that scuttles both entertainment and expressive values. The march opening the first finale lacks rhetoric; it might as well be a music box, and the subsequent "Confuso e stupido" ensemble sleepwalks through its modulatory jokes without the slightest bounce. Agogics as a resource appear to no longer interest Abbado, and his singers mostly follow suit.

They aren't a bad lot. Baltsa offers almost no charm or humor that might make us overlook the unevenness of her reasonably fluent technique: unequal registers, failure to really articulate the divisions and therefore the music's rhythmic life. She is most effective in spitfire mode, challenging the Bey, who at least is Somebody: Raimondi has a commanding voice and manner, acceptable command of the florid matter, and real gusto for the character and the nonsense—listen to him savoring "Pappatacci" at the start of No. 14. Lopardo is a substantial voice for Lindoro, surprisingly flexible, if constricted at the upper register break; he's most effective in the ensembles, for the solo singing is plain (even when ornamented, if you know what I mean). Dara is again a reasonable Taddeo, and Pace a plausible Elvira. At the end, alas, one feels one has heard a performance not of the opera but of the notes. (The recitatives are cut, but the main text is almost complete—the "almost" indicating the curious omission of just two bars in the coda of "Cruda sorte.")

The most of Rossini's notes are in CBS / SONY, the most of his spirit in EMI, the Acanta perhaps the most acceptable compromise between the two alternatives. If limited to one, I'd hang on to EMI.

DAVID HAMILTON

GIOACHINO ROSSINI

IL BARBIERE DI SIVIGLIA (1816)

A: Rosina (s or ms); B: Almaviva (t); C: Figaro (bar);
D: Basilio (bs); E: Bartolo (bs)

A couple of generations ago (i.e., at the beginning of the LP era), the general public took for granted that there was only one "right" way to perform an opera; therefore, what was heard in the theater and on records was "authentic."

Of course, it was well known that Rossini wrote the role of Rosina for a mezzo-soprano. Despite the splendid example set by mezzos like Conchita Supervia and Giulietta Simionato, the tradition of casting a high, agile soprano in the part died hard. The standard textual changes that enable a *soprano leggiero* to sing Rosina include not only transpositions and embellishments, but some switching of lines with Berta, and even with the men, in the ensembles. But a soprano Rosina was only one of the many departures from Rossini's intentions that needed to be addressed.

As early as the late 1950s, record companies began making tentative efforts to return to "what the composer wrote": opening cuts, restoring the original instrumentation, and correcting mistakes that had accumulated in printed scores and parts over the course of a hundred and fifty years.

Coincidentally, the public became aware that Rossini expected his tenors, baritones, and basses to possess the kind of agility traditionally associated with "coloratura sopranos." A new generation of male singers struggled to meet the challenge of the composer's florid vocal writing, instead of simplifying their parts as their predecessors had generally done.

As a result of these changes in awareness and taste, our *Barber of Seville* is not quite the same opera our grandparents knew and loved. We now take Rossini seriously as a composer, and sometimes our scrupulously accurate, well-intentioned performances kill his music with a surfeit of respect.

An uncut *Barbiere*, either in the theater or on records, is still a rarity. As comic operas go, it is lengthy, containing at least two and a half hours of music. The traditional cuts include drastic compression of the recitatives, and internal cuts (often extensive) in many of the musical numbers. Almaviva's aria in the final scene, "Cessa di più resistere," is often omitted *in toto*.

It is possible to make too much of textual questions. The recordings prove that an inspired group of performers can make almost any edition of the score sound convincing, and that the opposite is also true: no amount of textual "authenticity" can compensate for a lack of stylishness or vocal command.

1929 EMI/ANGEL (M) CD

Mercédès Capsir (A), Dino Borgioli (B), Riccardo Stracciari (C), Vincenzo Bettoni (D), Salvatore Baccaloni (E), La Scala Chorus and Orchestra—Lorenzo Molajoli

There seems to be no fence-sitting as far as this performance is concerned: it's either an abomination or a revelation, depending on the listener's point of view.

The shortcomings are obvious. Every conceivable cut is observed. To cite only a few examples: in "Dunque io son" the singers jump from the opening words right into the *a due* section; the ensemble "La testa vi gira" is shaved down to almost nothing; and the storm music comes immediately after Berta's aria. In this abridged form, the opera plays for just over two hours. The orchestration is thoroughly inauthentic, with trombones and cymbals added as early as the Overture. A piano clunks along in the recitatives.

Salvatore Baccaloni, the Bartolo, replaces Rossini's "A un dottor" with Pietro Romani's "Manca un foglio." The Rosina, Mercédès Capsir, takes all of the traditional high-soprano options and then some. In the Lesson Scene, Capsir scraps "Contro un cor" in favor of what she describes (in the preceding recitative) as "a simple folk song." The piece, beginning with the words "Un aria praticel," turns out to be variations (composer or arranger unspecified) on a French song.

On the positive side, the electrical recording is surprisingly good: the solo voices are placed well forward, of course, but a great deal of instrumental detail can be heard. Except for a few instances of rushed tempos (almost certainly dictated by the need to fit the music onto 78 sides), Lorenzo Molajoli's conducting is both lively and affectionate. The orchestral playing is expert, with much gracious application of old-fashioned string *portamento*. Despite the many cuts in the recitatives, they are remarkably spontaneous-sounding, and truly suggest musical speech (there are many ad libs).

I find Capsir an interesting and exciting performer. She has some wiry moments, but her florid technique is astonishing. In the recitatives, she suggests that Rosina is a bit of a handful: the willful kind of girl who wouldn't take any nonsense from Bartolo for a moment, and who will become a far-from-submissive Countess.

Dino Borgioli's timbre also takes some getting used to: it is very open and metallic. He, too, has an impressive florid technique, displayed to advantage in a splendidly free handling of "Ecco ridenti," for example.

Riccardo Stracciari, unquestionably a major

singer, seems uncomfortable in Figaro's music. He simplifies much of the *fioriture*, but still sounds effortful much of the time. It's as though Rigoletto had wandered into the wrong opera.

Baccaloni is a funny, unexaggerated Bartolo, his warm, rich bass filling out the music magnificently. Vincenzo Bettoni's saturnine Basilio is also first-rate.

The Arabesque LP reissue is a transfer from rather noisy originals. The Music Memoria CD edition seems to be derived from a different and much quieter set of 78s; it includes, as a bonus, ten songs and arias sung by Stracciari.

1950 CETRA (M,P)

Giulietta Simionato (A), Luigi Infantino (B), Giuseppe Taddei (C), Antonio Cassinelli (D), Carlo Badioli (E), Milan Radio Chorus and Orchestra—Fernando Previtali

This is a typical rough-and-ready Cetra production (a concert performance, prepared for broadcast by Italian Radio); the Everest LP edition is in ghastly artificial stereo. All of the standard cuts are observed. Fernando Previtali's conducting defines the words "provincial" and "routine," and the orchestral work is more enthusiastic than accurate or polished. Surprisingly, we once again hear a piano instead of a harpsichord in the recitatives.

Giulietta Simionato, a celebrated mezzo-soprano Rosina, is not a perfect vocalist: she sings with an uneven scale and heavily aspirated coloratura; her trill is suspect, and some of her low notes are a little hollow-sounding. But few artists have known how to put this kind of music across with her individuality. She sings rings around Luigi Infantino, a painful Count.

Giuseppe Taddei, in excellent vocal form, is a superlative Figaro. Antonio Cassinelli's well-sung Basilio is a little solemn and uninflected, but Carlo Badioli is a shrewd Bartolo.

1952 EMI / ANGEL (M)

Victoria de los Angeles (A), Nicola Monti (B), Gino Bechi (C), Nicola Rossi-Lemeni (D), Melchiorre Luise (E), Unidentified chorus, Milan Symphony Orchestra—Tullio Serafin

Once again, the score is heavily cut. *All* of the recitative between Berta's aria and the thunderstorm is eliminated; as a result, in the subsequent episode, when Rosina denounces "Lindoro," the listener has no idea what she is talking about.

Tullio Serafin prefers a moderate range of tempos; nearly all the music is taken more slowly than what we are accustomed to. The performance has an unusual weight and sense of importance as a result, but is by no means lacking in elegance.

Victoria de los Angeles, although a soprano, sings in the original mezzo-soprano keys, throwing in an occasional high note just to remind us that she can do it. She is wonderfully sweet, womanly, and mischievous, a classic portrayal.

Nicola Monti's light, rather pale tenor blends beautifully with de los Angeles's voice; if a little cautious in some of the florid passages, he sings stylishly, and is a resourceful comedian in the recitatives.

Gino Bechi, although only thirty-nine years old when this recording was made, already sounds well past his prime, struggling with the drastically simplified *fioriture* and straining at the high notes. Melchiorre Luise also sounds elderly, but is able to turn this to characterizational effect. Despite his typical wide vibrato, Nicola Rossi-Lemeni sings well as Basilio and threatens to steal the show with his sly portrayal.

1956 DECCA / LONDON (M)

Giulietta Simionato (A), Alvinio Misciano (B), Ettore Bastianini (C), Cesare Siepi (D), Fernando Corena (E), Chorus and Orchestra of the Maggio Musicale Fiorentino—Alberto Erede

Alberto Erede opens a few of the standard cuts, and insists on a harpsichord for the recitatives; his conducting is tidy and idiomatic rather than inspired. It's astonishing how crude and sloppy the ensemble's playing is.

Simionato repeats her strong Rosina from the Cetra set, to marginally better effect, in fact, if only because we can hear her more clearly in Decca's clean mono sound.

Ettore Bastianini is hardly a subtle performer,

and bulldozes his way heartily through much of his music. His voice is a magnificent instrument, though, and he's certainly never dull. Fernando Corena, in the first of his three studio recordings of Bartolo, is fairly restrained, and does some attractively smooth, dark-toned singing. Cesare Siepi's Basilio is first-rate in every respect.

Unfortunately, the tenor, Alvinio Misciano, sounds particularly uncomfortable next to his high-powered colleagues. Misciano has good intentions, but simply does not vocalize on an international level.

1957 EMI / ANGEL (S) CD

Maria Callas (A), Luigi Alva (B), Tito Gobbi (C), Nicola Zaccaria (D), Fritz Ollendorff (E), Philharmonia Chorus and Orchestra—Alceo Galliera

In this recording, most of the standard cuts are observed, which is unfortunate because Galliera conducts the opera well and has a marvelously responsive orchestra at his disposal. Despite some inauthentic textual readings and some thickening of the original instrumentation, this performance has a "rightness," a stylishness and conviction, approached by few of its competitors.

Maria Callas sometimes sticks to the original mezzo lines, sometimes takes the standard soprano options, and sometimes sings third alternatives of her own devising, including an elaborate harpsichord-accompanied cadenza at the end of "Contro un cor." Her Rosina is uniquely demure and insinuating. Can this really be the same voice that expressed the violent passions of Tosca, Norma, and Medea?

Tito Gobbi is one of the few Figaros on records who doesn't hesitate to suggest that the character's primary motivation is venality. Gobbi's voice, of course, is not a conventionally beautiful instrument, but in musical precision, agility, and imaginative verbal nuance, his performance leaves many a more richly sung Figaro in the dust.

Luigi Alva, in the first of his four studio recordings of Almaviva (in none of which, by the way, does he attempt "Cessa di più resistere"), is slightly nasal of timbre, but elegant, ardent, and witty.

Fritz Ollendorff is a surprisingly Italianate Bartolo, well partnered by the nicely understated Basilio of Nicola Zaccaria.

The stereo sound is remarkably vivid on EMI's CD reissue, making it difficult to believe that this recording is over thirty years old. The cuts have made it possible to fit the performance on only two CDs.

1958 RCA / BMG (S) CD

Roberta Peters (A), Cesare Valletti (B), Robert Merrill (C), Giorgio Tozzi (D), Fernando Corena (E), Metropolitan Opera Chorus and Orchestra—Erich Leinsdorf

This recording is practically complete, although thirty-two bars of "Contro un cor" and a couple of other snippets are omitted. The major restoration is "Cessa di più resistere," brilliantly sung by Cesare Valletti—on balance, the best Almaviva on any of the complete sets. His handling of words and music is so easy and natural, his vocalism so secure and tasteful, that his performance is almost beyond criticism.

Roberta Peters avails herself of all the traditional high-soprano transpositions and options, adding some startling embellishments of her own (high Es abound), and capping "Contro un cor" with a long cadenza filled with byplay with the harpsichord. She's efficient and musical, and her delivery of the text is often quite pointed. It must be admitted that the actual sound of her voice is somewhat of an acquired taste: she is predictably bright, girlish, and even chirpy in the upper register, but produces a surprisingly large, chesty sound in the bottom octave—the timbre we hear at the beginning of "Contro un cor" is almost indistinguishable from that of a dramatic soprano.

For better or worse, Robert Merrill, Fernando Corena, and Giorgio Tozzi form a team that is entirely consistent in sound, style, and interpretive approach: all three gentlemen have big, handsome voices, better suited to high-energy output than to filigree work; and all three indulge in some broad clowning, particularly in the recitatives.

Erich Leinsdorf's firm, finely detailed conception of the score is well executed by the Metropolitan Opera Orchestra. His tempos are often quite deliberate—at two hours and forty minutes, this is the longest of all these recordings—but the performance never drags, thanks to its basic rhythmic energy. The sound, at least on the BMG CD reissue, is very immediate; the overly bright treble can be tamed by adjusting one's playback equipment.

1960 DEUTSCHE GRAMMOPHON (S)

Gianna d'Angelo (A), Nicola Monti (B), Renato Capecchi (C), Carlo Cava (D), Giorgio Tadeo (E), Bavarian Radio Chorus and Orchestra—Bruno Bartoletti

So many of the Act I cuts are opened here—even Fiorello's recitative before the scene change—that the extensive cutting in Act II is all the more puzzling: "Contro un cor" is shortened even more than usual, with the exchanges leading to Almaviva's outburst of "Giubilera" simply omitted. Once again, the storm follows hard upon Berta's aria.

The small-scaled, intimate performance is excellent: Bartoletti eschews superficial excitement in favor of elegance, and his orchestra plays beautifully. (The chorus sings in German-accented Italian, but that is a minor distraction.)

Gianna d'Angelo, another high-soprano Rosina, has a very small, light voice; however, it never turns shrill, retaining its softness and body even above high C. Her embellishments are often non-standard, but suit her voice and temperament very well. In its intimate, understated way, her performance is charming.

She is well partnered by Monti, whose slender, "white" *tenorino* would be swamped by a heavy mezzo Rosina. Monti sounds just a bit careful here, compared to his work on the Serafin set a decade earlier, but his Almaviva is still fluent and witty. One regrets that, once again, he does not attempt "Cessa di più resistere."

Renato Capecchi's Figaro is peculiar. His light baritone voice turns narrow and colorless in the upper register, and, as though in an attempt to compensate for the uneasy vocalism, he is often downright manic from the interpretive standpoint. There are all sorts of fussy inflections in the recitatives, and the use of falsetto effects (not just in the traditional parts of "Largo al factotum," but in the subsequent duet with the Count, the shaving scene, and the trio in the final scene) quickly becomes tiresome.

Giorgio Tadeo sings Bartolo exceptionally well, scoring all sorts of subtle comic points without sacrificing vocal quality or compromising the musical line—a classy performance. Carlo Cava is a solid musician, but his monochromatic bass has a nasal, muffled timbre, as though he is suffering from a head cold.

1962 EMI / ANGEL (S) CD

Victoria de los Angeles (A), Luigi Alva (B), Sesto Bruscantini (C), Carlo Cava (D), Ian Wallace (E), Chorus of the Glyndebourne Festival, Royal Philharmonia Orchestra—Vittorio Gui

Vittorio Gui opens a few of the standard cuts, but is curiously reactionary from the instrumental standpoint: "Ecco ridente" is accompanied by a harp instead of a guitar, and trombones blare away in the Act I finale. (The string accompaniment to "A mezzanotte in punto" is played *staccato* rather than *legato*, for which there seems to be no precedent whatsoever.) The leisurely paced reading is warm and affectionate, but somewhat lacking in energy.

De los Angeles repeats her Rosina virtually unchanged from the 1952 EMI / Serafin set—a lovely performance. Alva, not surprisingly, also sounds much the same as he did before: he may be in marginally fresher voice for Gui, but Galliera elicited a livelier, more pointed portrayal from him. Sesto Bruscantini, much more restrained here than he usually is in his comic roles, is an uncommonly warm-voiced, musical Figaro.

Unfortunately, neither bass is on this level. Ian Wallace has excellent comic instincts, but is very dry of timbre and often seems to be scratching at the notes. Carlo Cava, in marginally less good voice than he was for Bartoletti, is

once again a dull, heavy Basilio, who makes no effect at all in the climax of his aria.

1964 DECCA / LONDON (S) CD

Teresa Berganza (A), Ugo Benelli (B), Manuel Ausensi (C), Nicolai Ghiaurov (D), Fernando Corena (E), Rossini Chorus and Orchestra of Naples—Silvio Varviso

This is the first recording in which a greater degree of textual authenticity is attempted by consulting the composer's manuscript. Many erroneous or corrupt readings are corrected, and the original instrumentation is restored. The recitatives are rather heavily abridged, but the only cut in a musical number is the standard compression of "A un dottor." This means that we hear not only "Cessa di più resistere" but also, for the first time on records, *all* of "Contro un cor."

The small orchestra, apparently a pickup group, is excellent. Silvio Varviso is not exactly a ball of fire on the podium; he prefers relaxed tempos and a comparatively restrained range of dynamics. The performance is appropriately *col canto*, though, always riding with the singers.

Here, as on her subsequent recording, Teresa Berganza gives us what is, on balance, the best-sung Rosina on disc. Her warm, clear mezzo moves effortlessly through the music; she phrases with distinction, is in complete command of the coloratura, and throws in a few interpolated high Bs and Cs. The only possible criticism is that her characterization is a little solemn and unsmiling, although this is a welcome corrective to the perky antics of some of her soprano rivals. On both of her recorded versions, she is partnered by the first-rate Berta of Stefania Malagu, whose voice is similar enough to Berganza's in timbre to create some momentary confusion in the ensembles.

Ugo Benelli, whose slender, bright voice has little warmth or sensuality of timbre, is nevertheless a highly accomplished Almaviva; of his recorded rivals, only Valetti is clearly preferable.

Manuel Ausensi is a vigorous Figaro, although his voice is too unwieldy to bring off all the fine detail. Corena still sings Bartolo well, and his interpretation is closer to his subtle work on the 1956 Decca / Erede set than to his exaggerations on the 1958 RCA / Leinsdorf version. The young Nicolai Ghiaurov impersonates Basilio with great relish, and sings "La calunnia" with ease in the original high key of D.

1968 DEUTSCHE GRAMMOPHON (S)

Maria Casula (A), Luigi Alva (B), Mario Stecchi (C), Paolo Washington (D), Alfredo Mariotti (E), Chorus and Orchestra of the Teatro Verdi, Trieste—Arturo Basile

This performance need not detain us long. All of the standard cuts are observed, and the recorded sound is crude, with the closely miked solo voices poorly balanced against the distant, weakly reproduced orchestra. Arturo Basile's conducting is unimaginative, the orchestral work mediocre.

This is the least interesting of Alva's four recorded Counts: clearly uninspired by his surroundings, he seems to be going through the motions. Nor is he in his best voice; he shows some strain in the upper register and sings some decidedly ragged roulades.

Next to his colleagues, however, Alva sounds like Fernando de Lucia reincarnated. Maria Casula has a powerful voice, but her strong singing is handicapped by a wide, uneven vibrato, rough coloratura, and pitch problems. She does almost nothing to draw a character for us. Mario Stecchi is a disastrous Figaro, bellowing his way through the music and leering in the recitatives like a provincial Baron Scarpia. Paolo Washington is an adequate Basilio, but no more. Alfredo Mariotti, a sturdy-voiced young bass, is quite miscast as Bartolo: Mariotti sings the entire role virtually "straight" (in itself, a considerable novelty), displaying no sense of humor whatsoever.

1971 DEUTSCHE GRAMMOPHON (S) CD

Teresa Berganza (A), Luigi Alva (B), Hermann Prey (C), Paolo Montarsolo (D), Enzo Dara (E), Ambrosian Opera Chorus, London Symphony Orchestra—Claudio Abbado

Claudio Abbado is the first conductor to base a recording on Alberto Zedda's critical edition, although he does not follow it slavishly. Once again, "Cessa di più resistere" is eliminated; there are cuts in the recitatives, and even in some of the ensembles; "A un dottor" and "Contro un cor" are both tightened by internal cuts. The original instrumentation, however, is used, and it is superlatively well played by the London Symphony Orchestra, heard at the peak of its form.

Abbado, as so often on his opera recordings, seems more interested in shaping the abstract musical structures than in projecting the drama; the reading has an undeniable logic, but lacks the ultimate in warmth and sparkle.

Berganza and Malagu are back, and both sing at least as well for Abbado as they did for Varviso. Alva is once again an expert and ingratiating Count, despite the fact that his voice is no longer as pliant as it was before.

Hermann Prey, an experienced Figaro, sings very smoothly, with an exceptionally easy command of the top; ideally, one might wish for more crispness—not only in his projection of the text (which is clear but lacks the "bite" of the native Italian baritones), but in his articulation of the rapid figurations.

Enzo Dara's Bartolo, well sung and ripely characterized, is one of the best on records. He is particularly good at conveying exasperation, doing an audible slow burn at several points. Paolo Montarsolo has some patches of rough tone, but, like Dara, is a resourceful performer.

The sound, whether on LP or CD, is beautifully transparent. The CD reissue manages to fit the opera onto two well-filled discs (most of the other CD sets require three).

1975 EMI / ANGEL (S)

Beverly Sills (A), Nicolai Gedda (B), Sherrill Milnes (C), Ruggero Raimondi (D), Renato Capecchi (E), John Alldis Choir, London Symphony Orchestra—James Levine

An opportunity missed. The first truly complete *Barbiere* on records, this version is, in fact, more than complete—Beverly Sills inserts an aria ("Ah, se è ver che in tal momento") before the thunderstorm. The aria is from Rossini's opera *Sigismondo* (1815) and was interpolated into *Barbiere* as early as 1819. A shallow display piece, it may well be a high point in *Sigismondo*, but it's a low point in *Barbiere*. However, Levine includes all of the recitative and makes no cuts in the musical numbers.

The conductor's rather slow, weighty, carefully articulated reading of the score is interesting, and it is beautifully executed by the London Symphony Orchestra, which produces a noticeably fuller, richer sound than it did for Abbado. Unfortunately, the cast seems to have been chosen on the basis of box-office appeal rather than suitability to the opera. An exception is Ruggero Raimondi, a firm-voiced, thoughtful Basilio, who sings his aria in D.

Sills, frequently sounding shrill and tremulous, takes all of the traditional upward transpositions and embellishments and then some, hammering away at the upper register with an insistence that is fatiguing to hear. Sometimes, as in "Dunque io son," she eases up and reveals the kind of soft, feminine quality that might have characterized her singing of the entire role, but the performance is, for the most part, both misconceived and poorly executed. Nicolai Gedda, sounding tired and strained, with heavily aspirated coloratura, simply waited too long to record Almaviva—he might have been superb opposite Callas in 1957, or de los Angeles in 1962.

Sherrill Milnes is a blustery Figaro, who smears a lot of the fine detail. Capecchi, who was an unsatisfactory Figaro on the Bartoletti set, is miscast as Bartolo, underpowered and frequently scratching at the notes.

The recording was originally issued in "compatible quad," and the sound of the Angel LPs seems oddly veiled and blurry. The cassette edition, made from digitally remastered tapes, has noticeably better sound.

1982 CBS / SONY (S,D) CD

Marilyn Horne (A), Paolo Barbacini (B), Leo Nucci (C), Samuel Ramey (D), Enzo Dara (E), La Scala Chorus and Orchestra—Riccardo Chailly

This performance is uncut and obviously well prepared. Chailly's conducting is relaxed but by no means slack; the orchestral and choral work are thoroughly idiomatic.

The cast is dominated by Marilyn Horne. Not content with the mezzo tessitura, she plunges down into contralto territory and avails herself of some of the high-soprano options; she also indulges in some wild embellishments, including chromatic runs. She inserts cadenzas even into the recitatives, and rewrites the fast concluding section of "Dunque io son" beyond recognition (carrying Leo Nucci along with her, by the way—I'm not sure just what he's singing here, but it bears no relation to any score or recorded performance known to me). I might be more impressed by Horne's vocal stunts if she did not betray a noticeable beat on many sustained tones; her voice is rarely ideally steady.

Samuel Ramey, on the other hand, turns in a thoughtful, self-effacing performance: Basilio has rarely been this well sung, or so subtly characterized. Nucci is a rather good Figaro: suave, easygoing, nimble. Dara is less secure than he was on the DG/Abbado set, but still very funny.

Paolo Barbacini's Almaviva is problematic. His voice is clear and attractive in quality, but very small; Horne sounds as though she could wipe him out with one deep breath. His coloratura technique is inadequate—effortful and heavily aspirated, suggesting heroic gargling at times; since this uncut performance includes all of the tenor's florid hurdles, Barbacini is at a distinct disadvantage. He has a nice sense of humor and scores some points in the recitatives, at least.

This is the first recording of the opera in digital sound—a good engineering job, on the whole.

p.1983 PHILIPS (S,D) CD

Agnes Baltsa (A), Francisco Araiza (B), Thomas Allen (C), Robert Lloyd (D), Domenico Trimarchi (E), Ambrosian Opera Chorus, Academy of St. Martin in the Fields—Neville Marriner

This set has many virtues: an uncut text, superb digital sound (it is easily the best-recorded *Barbiere* to date), a fine orchestra, and the pleasantly tangy sound of a fortepiano in the recitatives. But the overall effect is curiously studio-bound.

Sir Neville Marriner scrupulously observes the composer's markings; his reading is tidy and often elegant, but too polite and deficient in theatrical flair (in fairness to Marriner, it should be pointed out that this was his first recording of a complete opera).

The cast is variable. Agnes Baltsa's bright mezzo-soprano voice is rather vinegary in timbre on this release. She sings all the notes correctly, but without the kind of smoothness and abandon that can make the florid passages really memorable. Her Rosina is aggressive, in the Capsir tradition.

Francisco Araiza is a resourceful and likable performer whose Almaviva is attractive despite a husky, grainy vocal quality and aspirated coloratura. There is an amusing, musical Bartolo from Domenico Trimarchi: although he is more of a baritone than a bass, he seems to benefit from Marriner's disciplined framework. Sally Burgess is a first-rate Berta, singing her aria as well as any of her competitors.

Thomas Allen sings Figaro so well that it seems ungrateful to wish he would cut loose and have more fun, both with the character and the music. Much the same must be said of Robert Lloyd's Basilio, which is securely sung but neutral.

A peculiarity of this set is the virtual absence of vocal embellishments: the singers generally perform only what is written. This austerity will be perceived as either a virtue or a liability, depending upon the listener's personal taste.

1987 NUOVA ERA (S,D,P) CD

Luciana Serra (A), Rockwell Blake (B), Bruno Pola (C), Paolo Montarsolo (D), Enzo Dara (E), Chorus and Orchestra of the Teatro Regio, Turin—Bruno Campanella

This is a live performance, with relatively poor sound. The edition is a peculiar one and seems to have been chosen to highlight the talents of the two stars: many of the standard cuts are observed, but Rockwell Blake includes "Cessa di più resistere" and Luciana Serra fol-

lows Sills's example by inserting the *Sigismondo* aria before the storm.

The tenor, as on most of his other recordings, displays remarkable agility; the actual sound of his voice, to my taste, is hard and uningratiating. The recitatives reveal him to be a lively, resourceful vocal actor. The soprano's embellishments take her all the way up to high F; her performance is impressive enough as a succession of vocal feats, but there is no aural picture of Rosina—only a healthy young singer showing off.

Bruno Pola is a vocally crude, unfunny Figaro, while Dara and Montarsolo both sound decidedly past their good singing years. Campanella obtains decent playing from the orchestra and certainly knows how the opera ought to go, although he often drastically slows down the pulse of the music in order to let Blake and Serra do their thing. The chorus sounds undermanned and amateurish.

1988 DECCA / LONDON (S,D) CD

Cecilia Bartoli (A), William Matteuzzi (B), Leo Nucci (C), Paata Burchuladze (D), Enrico Fissore (E), Chorus and Orchestra of Teatro Comunale, Bologna—Giuseppe Patanè

This handsomely produced studio recording contains peculiar textual choices: virtually all of the traditional cuts are opened, but "Cessa di più resistere" is omitted. In a note printed in the booklet accompanying the set, the late Giuseppe Patanè announced his intention to restore certain "traditional" performance practices. In practice, these consist almost entirely of unwritten high notes, belted out by the soloists at the ends of their numbers in lieu of any real embellishment. Patanè's tempos are generally quite slow, and as a result the performance lacks animation in the long run. (Had the Count's last-act aria been included, this recording would have run longer than Leinsdorf's.) The orchestra produces a warm, rich sound that is most attractive; the playing is well reproduced by the engineers, although in a slightly too resonant acoustic.

The singing is pleasant but unmemorable, on

the whole. The very young mezzo Cecilia Bartoli—only twenty-two years old at the time of the sessions—has a beautiful, dusky-timbred voice and good instincts. Like Berganza, she takes Rosina rather seriously, but she is not yet in Berganza's class when it comes to sustaining a *cantabile* line or dispatching the coloratura with true ease. William Matteuzzi displays comic skill, reasonable agility, and an unpliant, metallic timbre. Nucci sounds much the same as he did on the CBS / Chailly set, except that the tendency of his tone to spread under pressure has become more pronounced.

Enrico Fissore is a restrained Bartolo who actually sings the music more securely than most. The most striking vocalist in the cast is Paata Burchuladze, whose huge, black bass is a magnificent instrument. He doesn't sound like an "Italian" bass (his vowels are distinctly impure, and his timbre is simply too dark and mournful), and he is not much of a comedian, but he provides a rock-solid foundation for the ensembles in which he participates. Gloria Banditelli is a fine, earthy Berta.

————————

Several of the "complete" recordings of the opera are excellent, making a recommendation difficult.

If you insist on an uncut text (and digital sound), then your choice is between the Philips / Marriner and CBS / Chailly sets—the former admirably executed, but decidedly bland;

the latter quirky and uneven in quality, but intermittently compelling.

If you are willing to accept some of the traditional cuts, and even some of the textual inauthenticities as well, then you have a number of fine performances to choose from. I cannot imagine being without the EMI / Galliera set, because of the Callas / Gobbi / Alva trio, the superb conducting, and the elegant production. But I also feel that a collector should own one of the Berganza recordings—either the Decca / Varviso, for the sake of Benelli, or the DG / Abbado, for the conducting (both sets have many other strong points, of course).

The Music Memoria / Molajoli set has undeniable historical interest. And many connoisseurs will want to be able to hear, at will, such distinguished individual performances as the Rosina of Simionato or de los Angeles, or Valletti's Count, or Taddei's Figaro. After all, no one ever promised us that record collecting would be inexpensive, or easy.

ROLAND GRAEME

Unavailable for review:
1918–19 PHONOTYPE
1919 EMI/ANGEL
1960 ELECTRECORD
1960 HUNGAROTON
1970 SUPRAPHON
1970 FESTIVAL
1982 FREQUENZ
1991 DEUTSCHE GRAMMOPHON

GIOACHINO ROSSINI

LA CENERENTOLA (1817)

A: Angelina (Cinderella) (ms); B: Ramiro (t);
C: Dandini (bar); D: Magnifico (bs)

The success of *La Cenerentola* following its premiere in 1817, one year after *Il Barbiere di Siviglia*, established the Cinderella story as a staple of Western musical theater. The effectiveness of this work on stage and records is dependent partly on a low voice with exceptional coloratura technique for the title role, but even more on a responsive sense of ensemble among all members of the cast. They are expected to be as versatile at acting with the voice as in negotiating Rossini's florid writing, and although Cinderella's final aria ("Naqui all'affanno") and rondo ("Non più mesta") brilliantly crown the work, it is the preceding sextet in Act II and the quintet in Act I that offer the most musical rewards.

Seven recordings span forty years; two of these are substantially abridged. Besides brief cuts in recitatives and *stretta* passages, most also omit the three numbers written for the premiere by Luca Agolini (Alidoro's "Vasto teatro" aria in Act I, and in Act II an opening chorus, "Ah, della bella incognita," and Clorinda's aria, "Sventurata! Me credea"). A new critical edition of the score by Alberto Zedda for the Rossini Foundation at Pesaro is the basis of most recordings since 1970. Zedda changed some details of dynamics and instrumentation, excluded everything not by Rossini, but allows Alidoro in Act I the alternative aria, "Là del ciel nell'arcano," which Rossini is known to have written for Gioacchino Moncada in 1820.

1949 CETRA (M)

Giulietta Simionato (A), Cesare Valletti (B), Saturno Meletti (C), Cristiano Dalamangas (D), Radio Italiana Chorus and Orchestra—Mario Rossi

One of the first Cetra operatic recordings, made during a studio season of Radio Italiana, the performance is so heavily cut as to be considered an abridged version. Besides omitting all recitatives and the three Agolini numbers, it loses most of the opening scene of the sisters and Alidoro; all the Act I quintet in which Magnifico repudiates Cinderella, and several passages of *stretta*; in Act II a large part of the sextet, "Siete voi?," and more passages in other numbers, including Cinderella's rondo finale. Crucial aspects of the story are simply discarded, including Alidoro's important interventions, and the stepsisters hardly get a look-in; consequently, too much is taken for granted to communicate any logical narrative.

What remains (four shortish sides) has a musically lively performance under Rossi, whose generally spirited conducting coaxes a decent lilt from sometimes rough orchestral playing. Simionato's voice is young and fresh, with a bloom on her tone and plenty of coloratura agility. Though she is hardly given time to introduce herself at the start she comes into her own in the first duet with Ramiro; the final aria is securely sung and decorated though, like most of the role, bluntly attacked. Valletti's Ramiro is suave, smoothly phrased, tending to explode in reaching for high notes up to B-flat, but flexible in runs and warm in *legato*. Meletti is a forthright Dandini of some vocal style but with labored technique in runs and patter-music, and the rough-toned Dalamangas is inclined to splutter as Magnifico, accenting the burlesque element in words and character.

1953 EMI / ANGEL (M) CD

Marina de Gabarain (A), Juan Oncina (B), Sesto Bruscantini (C), Ian Wallace (D), Glyndebourne Festival Chorus and Orchestra—Vittorio Gui

A performance always notable for the strength of ensemble singing in all concerted numbers, it demonstrates the advantage of taking an already well-rehearsed cast from stage into the studio. Here the 1953 Glyndebourne Festival cast came together under Gui, who was responsible for a memorable Rossini series at Glyndebourne which began with *La Cenerentola*. Many of Carl Ebert's staging details, involving vocal character and response, enliven the individual singing on the recording. These are shaped by Gui with sparkling spirit, taut rhythms, flexible and brightly articulated expression.

De Gabarain was a Spanish forerunner of Berganza in the florid mezzo repertory. She had the necessary ease and flexibility, as well as appealing warmth of vocal tone, but her coloratura lacked the diamond edge to scintillate, as in the final "Non più mesta." Otherwise her performance is affectingly lyric, and she contrasts well with the stepsisters of Alda Noni (Clorinda) and Fernanda Cadoni (Tisbe), who deserve noting for the absolute joy and merriment of their characterization from the outset, as does Hervey Alan for his benignly authoritative Alidoro.

Oncina, also Spanish, makes a personable Ramiro in elegance of vocal style and abundant feeling, except when he takes off into falsetto. Bruscantini is the most compelling focus. His beautiful baritone was in its prime and the sheer verve of Dandini's character is irresistible. Wallace became acclaimed in Italy and elsewhere for his genial humor and wealth of *buffo* char-

acter; Magnifico's second aria is regrettably omitted. There are numerous other small cuts besides the Agolini numbers; some make more sense than others in their context, but the performance remains enjoyable for its period.

1963 DECCA / LONDON (M,S) CD

Giulietta Simionato (A), Ugo Benelli (B), Sesto Bruscantini (C), Paolo Montarsolo (D), Chorus and Orchestra of the Fiorentino Maggio Musicale—Oliviero de Fabritiis

Simionato's second recording of the title role finds her sounding somewhat mature. She was approaching the end of her career and some florid singing is noticeably effortful when she takes extra breaths in mid-phrase. Against this must be set her feeling for Rossinian style, which lends her performance warmth of tone and touching pathos, satisfying in all but the final rondo. Bruscantini is a second-time Dandini, but the gap between recordings was shorter and he is still totally in command of the role's essential verbal technique and dapper insouciance.

Benelli sounds sturdier than Oncina as Ramiro, with a full, confident tone in florid writing as well as sustained line and warmth of feeling: very much a prince. Montarsolo has much fun with Magnifico; both his arias are sung with ripe vocal humor. The Agolini aria "Vasto teatro" is included and Giovanni Foiani sounds gravely impressive in it as he encourages Cinderella's hopes before she is taken to Ramiro's party. Dora Carral and Miti Truccato Pace make their presence known as a lively pair of stepsisters, and take an adequate part in concerted numbers.

Conducting is well paced: de Fabritiis whips along the faster passages with *brio*, and is concerned with shaping a line that will be comfortable for the singers. He omits the other two Agolini numbers and makes conventional small cuts in recitatives and *strettas*. The orchestral playing is buoyant and accurate, not specially polished but almost as much a sense of active performance as the Glyndebourne album, though without Gui's understanding.

1971 DEUTSCHE GRAMMOPHON (S) CD

Teresa Berganza (A), Luigi Alva (B), Renato Capecchi (C), Paolo Montarsolo (D), Scottish Opera Chorus, London Symphony Orchestra—Claudio Abbado

Another instance of a festival cast kept together for a recording, this one follows a production at the Edinburgh Festival. It is the first recording of Zedda's Rossini Foundation edition, in which anything not by Rossini is omitted; otherwise changes are limited to details of instrumentation and dynamics. These contribute to the nature of a performance derived from the theater but sounding "of the studio" in its precision and perspective.

Berganza is a winning Cinderella, young and pliant of voice, with masterly control of technique in florid music and a wonderfully even tone quality throughout her range. To fault her at all is only to acknowledge some lack of pathos and sentiment in her portrait: the sad little fireside song is graceful but somehow bereft of yearning. Alva's Ramiro has rather more feeling in his ardor, and manages most of the florid music accurately if dryly. Capecchi, late in his career, lacks Bruscantini's bounce, but his experience helps effective variation of tone in comedy projection. Montarsolo's second Magnifico is roundly sung and more disciplined than before.

Having discarded the Agolini-Alidoro aria, "Vasto teatro," Zedda's edition substitutes Rossini's authentic "Là del ciel nell'arcano," written for the 1820 Rome performances. It is doubly unfortunate that the aria sounds inappropriate, having a grand, dramatic style more suited to Rossini's tragic operas, and that Ugo Trama here has problems encompassing it. Margherita Guglielmi and Laura Zannini are correct and competent stepsisters. Abbado draws polished and spirited playing from the London Symphony Orchestra; orchestral detail and balance with voices are finely judged.

1977 ACANTA (S)

Bianca Maria Casoni (A), Ugo Benelli (B), Sesto Bruscantini (C), Alfredo Mariotti (D), Berlin State Opera Chorus and Radio Symphony Orchestra—Piero Bellugi

A studio recording made for the soundtrack of a West German television production and not issued until 1979, this has little more music than the early Cetra album and therefore also verges on being classified as abridged rather than complete. Missing are the three Agolini numbers, also all the wine-tasting scene with Magnifico and the chorus in Act I, as well as the scene with Dandini before that. As a result the quintet goes directly to the Act I finale. Magnifico's second aria is also omitted in Act II, and there are the usual recitative and *stretta* cuts throughout.

The singing is not especially distinguished except for Benelli's in his second Ramiro: his polished sense of style is again evident, with natural beauty of tone in excellently managed florid music and in *legato* and concerted passages. Bruscantini is on his third time round as Dandini and shows signs of wear in the voice, though his mastery of character is still keen. Casoni is adequate as Cinderella, better at expressing pathos than agility: the coloratura has little zest. What little there is of Mariotti makes the absence of both Magnifico's main numbers a matter for regret.

The stepsisters (Giovanna di Rocco, Teresa Rocchino) lack definition of character and Federico Davià has only token appearance as Alidoro. Bellugi's conducting amiably moves the performance along with adequate though not distinctive orchestral playing that seldom conveys the desirable Rossinian wit and charm.

1980 FONIT-CETRA / CBS (S,D) CD

Lucia Valentini Terrani (A), Francisco Araiza (B), Domenico Trimarchi (C), Enzo Dara (D), West German Radio Chorus, Cappella Coloniensis—Gabriele Ferro

This is the only recording to date featuring original instruments of the period, including a fortepiano for recitative (played by Georg Fischer). But the aural perspective puts the players so far back in relation to the singers that the point of their tone quality is almost completely lost. Nor does Ferro redeem this by enough poise or character in his conducting, which subdues the music's wit and sparkle to leave the work sounding pedestrian, even long-winded. He uses Zedda's Rossini Foundation edition with its added Act I aria for Alidoro, "Là del ciel," effectively sung here by Alessandro Corbelli.

Valentini Terrani is a musically sensitive, vocally pleasing Cinderella in the Berganza manner; a sense of expressive pathos contrasts with well-managed coloratura. Araiza sings with ardent warmth in his feeling for her, but is less fluent in the faster or more florid passages. Trimarchi is adequate for Dandini, but finds too little humor in the character. Dara makes more of Magnifico, however, giving presence to the main numbers as well as adding a ripe bass to the concerted passages. Emilia Ravaglia and Marilyn Schmiege are a chirpy pair of stepsisters, but the cast as a whole never becomes more than a series of individuals, failing to achieve that responsive ensemble on which so much of the work's overall effect depends.

1987 PHILIPS (S,D) CD

Agnes Baltsa (A), Francisco Araiza (B), Simone Alaimo (C), Ruggero Raimondi (D), Ambrosian Opera Chorus, Academy of St. Martin in the Fields—Neville Marriner

A performance for those who like comic Rossini to have substance of character beneath surface charm and frivolity. Marriner sweeps it along ebulliently, eliciting a polished style from the London-based orchestra and taking much care in balance and phrasing, like the exact placing of rhythmic emphasis in rapid passages and subtle dynamic shading. He uses the Rossini Foundation edition virtually complete.

There may be some difficulty in accepting that a woman of Baltsa's strong character would submit to being elbowed aside as a downtrodden servant. She nevertheless sings with the requisite pathos and feeling, following a tremulous excitement in her duet with Ramiro, gaining increased vocal stature as her fortunes change. The final scene is grandly imposing, the coloratura electrically charged yet in a certain way compassionate as well.

Araiza's second Ramiro holds his own very strongly and sustains a good line throughout. Alaimo makes less of Dandini than might be expected: he sings the notes effectively but does not have the same fun with the role that others do. Raimondi is a powerful Magnifico, hugely enjoying the comedy of his wine-tasting scene, in particular, but regrettably adding a sob and a blowing of the nose to his poignant denial of Cinderella. Alidoro comes over strongly from John del Carlo, including the "Là del ciel" aria; Carole Malone and Felicity Palmer are vigorous stepsisters.

———————

Only brief acquaintance with this latest recording makes it uncertain how enduring the undoubted enjoyment of first impression will be. An alternative choice would be DG / Abbado for its all-round character as well as Berganza's most musical Cinderella, but the EMI / Gui / Glyndebourne performance must still claim lasting affection for its overall spirit and style.

NOËL GOODWIN

GIOACHINO ROSSINI

SEMIRAMIDE (1823)

A: Semiramide (s); B: Azema (s); C: Arsace (ms);
D: Idreno (t); E: Assur (bar)

With a title role that requires a Lady Macbeth, Medea, and Jocasta all rolled into one, *Semiramide*, Rossini's thirty-fourth opera and the last of his Italian *opere serie*, presents one of the more extravagant coloratura soprano challenges in the repertory. Rossini's great accomplishment here, though, is to make a repentant Semiramide—the Babylonian queen who murders her husband and attempts to marry her son—one of his most affecting characters. Although an especially popular and influential opera following its premiere at Venice's La Fenice in 1823, *Semiramide*, with its innovative dramatic techniques of Rossini's Neapolitan operas here applied to the formal mold of more traditional *opera seria* while using the popular florid singing style of the day to rare psychological and expressive ends, was pretty much forgotten from the end of the nineteenth century until 1962, when Joan Sutherland revived it at La Scala. Since then the opera has returned to the international repertory, but usually with substantial cuts and using an inaccurate edition. The first performance of the Rossini Foundation edition, with newly found material and the composer's original scoring, was given by the Metropolitan Opera in 1990.

1965–66 DECCA / LONDON (S) CD

Joan Sutherland (A), Patricia Clark (B), Marilyn Horne (C), John Serge (D), Joseph Rouleau (E), Ambrosian Singers, London Symphony Orchestra—Richard Bonynge

This recording has come to attain something of a classic status, and deservedly. It documents Sutherland at her absolute prime, and in a role that was vocally ideal for her. It exposed Horne to a wide audience, presenting her in really exciting form. It contains, in "Assur, i cenni miei," the big Semiramide / Arsace duet of Act II, some of the most glorious *bel canto* singing of the era. And most important of all, the set introduced opera lovers not only to *Semiramide* but to Rossini's *opera seria* style, which was practically unknown at the time. That said, this is a flawed effort nonetheless. For all the breathtaking agility of Sutherland's performance, and the sheer silvery splendor of her sound, she is a blandly regal and maternal Semiramide, the soprano's cautious phrasing exploring little of the Babylonian queen's murderous side. Consequently Horne's robust, youthful, and spectacularly negotiated Arsace is the real highlight of the recording. Next to the ladies, Rouleau pales: a capable dark baritone but not nearly flamboyant enough Assur, especially underplaying the evil prince's mad scene. Cuts reduce Azema's role, which is uninterestingly sung by Clark, to hardly more than a walk-on, and also limit Idreno to a single aria; that is a hollow affair from Serge, who can negotiate the notes but whose raspy tenor turns particularly unpleasant in the loud high passages. A ringing Spiro Malas, the priest Oroe, properly lords over all the male voices, small as the part is. As for the cuts, they are too extensive to numerate, but for the most part they tend to be trims, both large and small, of recitative and choral sections, often making dramatic and musical transitions choppy. The most damaging, however, is the deletion of Semiramide's accidental murder by Arsace, thus turning his poignant Pyrrhic victory into an empty-headed happy ending. But this is a singers' performance more than a theatrical one, and Bonynge obliges, always more supportive of his cast than he is of the drama.

Clearly, as the only recording of *Semiramide*, the Decca effort is valuable, and the performances of Sutherland and Horne are likely to retain their appeal even when a more authentic version of the opera is finally available on disc. But as a representation of an important opera, and a great one, it is inadequate.

MARK SWED

CAMILLE SAINT-SAËNS

SAMSON ET DALILA
(concert 1877; stage premiere 1892)

A: Dalila (ms); B: Samson (t); C: High Priest (bar);
D: Abimélech (bs); E: Old Hebrew (bs)

In spite of a supercilious attitude taken by many critics and commentators, *Samson et Dalila* has continued to enjoy a degree of popularity with audiences which is not reflected in the relatively small number of recordings that exist. An obstacle to recording may be the fact that so few singers native to the French language have become internationally prominent; others who attempt to sing it, with varying degrees of success, inevitably impart some qualities alien to its character.

This is made the more evident by the survival of the earliest complete recording from 1946, made in Paris with a conductor and cast who had worked together at the Opéra. It was recorded in the year after World War II when a prewar "school" of French singing had not yet been overtaken by the later international exchanges. These have altered forever the way in which opera is performed and recorded, for the better in many ways, but with a certain loss of inherited distinction in others.

1946 EMI / ANGEL (M)

Hélène Bouvier (A), José Luccioni (B), Paul Cabanel (C), Charles Cambon (D), Henri Médus (E), Paris Opéra Chorus and Orchestra—Louis Fourestier

For a survivor from the days of 78s there is still much to be said for this performance, even though some of the choral and orchestral detail now depend on faith. It is nevertheless evident that Fourestier has a fine grasp of the work in his pacing and phrasing, neither indulging its sentiment too much nor content to tag along after the voices. He puts each scene firmly into context, with a surge of drama in the first and last acts and a more romantic feeling at the center of the work, as it should be up to the moment when Samson is at Dalila's mercy.

Bouvier belongs to a tradition of French singing older than that current nowadays, though she did not make her debut at the Paris Opéra until 1939, singing her first Dalila there. Her tone is notably smooth and warm, and she imparts a certain dignity of presence to the role as well as conveying Dalila's feelings with idiomatic expression. "Printemps qui commence" is sung with uncommon vitality and charm, "Mon coeur s'ouvre à ta voix" with unforced feeling. It is all part of a developing, consistent character, to which Luccioni responds ardently, his timbre often heroic but less effective in conveying "Vois ma misère" in Act III.

Cabanel is dark and menacing, a High Priest suitably devious in plotting with Dalila, authoritative in public pronouncements, taunting Samson viciously. His ability to point words keenly is a virtue shared by Cambon, and the rich, round bass of Médus makes the Old Hebrew scene worth its musical weight instead of passing almost unnoticed. The chorus is adequately sturdy, the Bacchanal vigorous but muted by the vintage recording. Worth hearing as representative of French operatic tradition at the time.

1962 EMI / ANGEL (M,S) CD

Rita Gorr (A), Jon Vickers (B), Ernest Blanc (C), Anton Diakov (D,E), René Duclos Chorus, Paris Opéra Orchestra—Georges Prêtre

Vickers is the key feature, imparting a blazing conviction to his role that comes across as a moral force, full of generous feeling and instinctive musicality. The tenor has said that moral integrity in operatic character was important to him; his performance illustrates that conviction by the passionate belief in divine mission he expresses in Act I, eventually undermined by Dalila's blandishments and turning to a Florestan-like depth of despair in "Vois ma misère" at the start of Act III. Samson's ultimate triumph is possible, he suggests, because it is divine retribution.

Against his sense of heroic purpose Gorr presents a feminine wiliness which is the more telling in its subtlety. She is outwardly a dignified Dalila, keeping seductive charms under wraps as far as the voice is concerned, but singing with breadth of feeling and warm tone in her main arias and the duet with Samson; plotting with the High Priest, she is appropriately more edgy. A similar quality from Blanc in this scene would have improved it; the baritone verges on blandness, though elsewhere he sings with proper command and self-importance. The doubling of Abimélech and the Old Hebrew is not successful in character or tone.

Chorus and orchestra are well balanced, and are conducted to often thrilling effect by Prêtre. His feeling for the work is evident everywhere, from the restless and quarrelsome first act and the dancelike "Printemps qui commence," through an atmospherically sultry Act II that rewards close attention to words, on to Samson's agony as he implores Heaven, "Prends ma vie en sacrifice," and an exhilarating bacchanal with attractive orchestral coloring. The performance consistently redeems Saint-Saëns from the charge of staged oratorio on one hand and vulgarity on the other.

1973 RCA / BMG (S) CD

Christa Ludwig (A), James King (B), Bernd Weikl (C), Alexander Malta (D), Richard Kogel (E), Bavarian Radio Chorus and Munich Radio Orchestra—Giuseppe Patanè

To what extent a non-French cast can carry such idiomatic vocal writing is demonstrated here by singers who respond to the demands with different degrees of success. Their French is acceptable enough for the most part, but they often give the impression of achieving it with some difficulty, not simply in stress and pronunciation, but in the way the words lie on the phrase. Ludwig favors a long, elegant line with a velvet tone quality, but not much shading to differentiate between, say, "Printemps qui commence" and "Amour, viens aider ma faiblesse"; however, it is always a lovely voice to hear. King sounds best the closer he comes to a Wagnerian phrase; he always demonstrates flexibility and flow, but the character stays in the middle range of emotions: honest but neither resolute nor anguished enough to carry conviction.

Weikl is least at home with the language, and he tends to counter this by a brusque, clipped manner of delivery: blunt rather than devious in his dealings with Dalila, and seldom more than two-dimensional in character. The other singers are competent but less than well marked. The overall effect is further weakened not so much by the conductor's variable tempos (though he certainly whips up the frenzy in Act III) as by a generally low level of recording in a rather narrow acoustic. An otherwise good standard of orchestral playing suffers accordingly, and is only heard to best effect in the softer passages like the dance in Act I or the sultry scene-setting in Act II.

1978 DEUTSCHE GRAMMOPHON (S) CD

Elena Obraztsova (A), Plácido Domingo (B), Renato Bruson (C), Pierre Thau (D), Robert Lloyd (E), Chorus and Orchestre de Paris—Daniel Barenboim

A festival production in the famous Roman amphitheater at Orange, France, conducted by Barenboim in July 1978, led to this recording almost immediately, though with two changes of cast in Bruson and Lloyd. The advantage of having worked with singers at festival performances, and with the Orchestre de Paris (it is not clear if the chorus is the same but it seems likely), is reflected in a tight overall ensemble. Barenboim conducts this in a familiar mannered style, indulging emotional sentiment in phrasing and accent, sometimes disregarding score markings like "sans presser," whipping up tempo at the least pretext, and generally looking to intensify all the music's most superficial characteristics.

The result is undeniably colorful in a Hollywood-like way, with Saint-Saëns given the glossy treatment that some might think is needed to cover the work's weaknesses, while others will find here an exaggeration or distortion of its lyrical qualities. The singing is of a similar quality, especially from Obraztsova, who sounds malevolent from the start and has a ready snarl at phrase-ends on words like "sein" and "gloire"; she lacks *legato* line for the slow tempos at which Barenboim takes her main arias, but earns merit for singing "Ah, réponds ma tendresse" without repeating the word "réponds" as other Dalilas do. Domingo has trouble with the French "u," sounding it more like "ee," but otherwise he is forceful and expressive, whereas Bruson is merely bland. The others are fine, the chorus is eagerly in character, and the recording has spacious perspective.

1989 PHILIPS (S,D) CD

Agnes Baltsa (A), José Carreras (B), Jonathan Summers (C), Simon Estes (D), Paata Burchuladze (E), Bavarian Radio Symphony Chorus and Orchestra—Colin Davis

Again a cast without a singer native to French, and therefore a variability in the style of vocal performances, nevertheless knitted together under Davis's committed conducting to make a largely enjoyable musical experience, both sensitive and sensuous. The Munich-based orchestra, of which Davis has been music director since 1983, plays expertly for him, so the often-overlooked subtlety and skill of instrumental coloring can be fully relished, whether in lyrical line or bacchanalian vitality; a bright, forward recording balance helps its impact.

Davis achieves a natural-sounding flow of pace and rhythm to set the voices in flight. Carreras has the most to benefit from this in his evidence of recovered strength and artistry. His notes become strained in the higher reaches, once or twice disturbingly so, and he does not approach the depth of heroic fortitude voiced by Vickers. But he expresses the warmth of his love and the agony of his guilt and remorse with well-judged inflection of vocal character. Baltsa gives Dalila compelling personality with an edge to verbal meaning even when the line is broken by technical awkwardness in the famous numbers.

Summers sings a fiercely fanatical High Priest with attack and candor, and it is regrettable that so much accomplishment in major aspects of performance is undermined by inadequacies in lesser roles. Estes is such a crude Abimélech and Burchuladze so insecure an Old Hebrew that it seems incomprehensible that their contributions were ever approved in this form.

The initial thrill of the DG / Barenboim version fades as its mannerisms grow irritating with repetition, whereas EMI / Prêtre steadily gains stature through its more cogent style and Vickers's magnificent central performance. For an idiomatic performance in the older French tradition, EMI / Fourestier still merits hearing.

NOËL GOODWIN

Unavailable for review:
1969 ELECTRECORD
1991 EMI / ANGEL

ARNOLD SCHOENBERG

MOSES UND ARON
(concert 1954; stage premiere 1957)

A: Aron (t); B: Moses (speaker)

choenberg drafted his libretto for *Moses und Aron* in 1928, and composed the first two acts in 1931/32. While the ensuing upheavals in the composer's life doubtless initially impeded setting the brief third act, his continuing failure to do so before his death in 1951 bespeaks some more fundamental problem, conceivably some dissatisfaction with the libretto's attempt at dramatic resolution. The subject Schoenberg imposed upon the biblical narrative is the irreconcilable conflict between transcendental Thought (Moses) and the all-too-concrete Word (Aron): the impossibility of accurately communicating profound and complex insights through the inadequate, even falsifying tools of words and images. Schoenberg's purpose was not, as some have said, to express the inexpressible, but rather to embody the conflict between the inexpressible and the crude tools of communication. Most listeners have felt that the two completed acts do this brilliantly and movingly, ending with Moses' despair at ever expressing his own conception of the Deity. (In line with a suggestion Schoenberg entertained late in his life, some performances end with his Act III spoken over music: for example, in the 1959 Berlin production, Hermann Scherchen used the choral and orchestral part of the opera's first scene as background.)

Schoenberg's realization of the central dichotomy entailed casting Moses as a speaking part, Aron as a glib and golden-tongued tenor.

The voice of God is embodied in six solo voices and a speaking chorus, while the large chorus of the Israelite people both speaks and sings. All of their music, and that of the orchestra, is demanding—wide in range, expressionistic in melodic character, flexible, even fussy, in rhythm. The *Sprechstimme* presents special problems, for Schoenberg's instructions about how precisely his notated pitches should be performed remain contradictory and confusing. As with Mahler's more massive works, the extreme contrasts between full forces and chamber-like scoring pose additional challenges for the recording engineers. As far as performance history is concerned, this opera is not yet four decades old, and its expressive possibilities are still being explored; in that sense, virtually every recording has important things to tell us.

1954 CBS / SONY (M,P)

Helmut Krebs (A), Hans Herbert Fiedler (B), North German Radio Chorus and Orchestra—Hans Rosbaud

Moses und Aron was not performed until after Schoenberg's death (the Dance around the Golden Calf had been heard at Darmstadt in July 1951), and this recording derives from the unstaged radio concert that was the official premiere. Rosbaud, a distinguished specialist in the music of the Schoenberg school who took over from an indisposed colleague just days before the event, has a firm grasp of the work's

498

expressive tone. Despite various incidental disasters such as missed entries and wrong notes, he moves the performance along well, though today, in the light of later performances, some of his tempos seem sluggish. He is aided by Fiedler's forcefully varied Moses, and especially by the almost Italianate timbre and fluency Krebs brings to Aron's music; among the smaller roles, the Ephraimite is dreadful, but Ilona Steingruber's Young Girl is uncannily accurate and musical (her bang-on delivery of the line "Er wird uns befreien!" effaces any other I've heard). The muddy, dynamically restricted mono sound doesn't help matters much. For nearly two decades, this set was the only way to hear *Moses*; today, it has mainly historic importance.

p.1974 PHILIPS (S)

Louis Devos (A), Günter Reich (B), Austrian Radio Chorus and Symphony Orchestra—Michael Gielen

Twenty years were to pass before *Moses und Aron* received a studio recording, whereupon two arrived in rapid succession, the first made by the Austrian Radio in conjunction with a film version, the second as part of CBS's continuing Schoenberg project under Pierre Boulez. Both reflect the substantial increase in familiarity with Schoenberg's idiom and greater fluency in dealing with its demands acquired over those two decades, and both share the same Moses.

For Gielen, Günter Reich gives a performance of considerable vehemence, perhaps modeled on Fiedler's in the 1954 recording; like the other exponents of this role, he utters real pitches, but they often vary considerably from Schoenberg's notation, even altering its contours. Louis Devos is a commendably accurate Aron, though less mellifluously persuasive than Krebs; his top notes (the role ascends frequently to B-flat) are not easeful. The otherwise unfamiliar singers of the secondary roles are capable enough. For all of its precision, textural clarity, and ensemble, the chorus remains the most disappointing aspect of this recording, for it is simply too small to convey the full impact of the climaxes. Nevertheless, both it and the orchestra elucidate the polyphony and dig into

the orgiastic passages with real gusto and into the marching choruses with swing and vigor. The sound is clear and reasonably balanced.

1974 CBS / SONY (S)

Richard Cassilly (A), Günter Reich (B), BBC Singers and Symphony Orchestra—Pierre Boulez

A different recording approach rules here: large forces in a large space make for a strong general impact, but also rather less specificity of detail. Interestingly, Reich's Moses is here more subdued, almost as if to signify his inability to communicate—but that's not necessary: that inarticulateness is automatically established by the fact that in a world where everyone else can sing, he cannot. Cassilly has more vocal heft than Devos or Krebs, but his upper register is neither secure nor attractive, and he is tangibly less accurate. The supporting singers do well, though their German accents are somewhat patchwork. Boulez's tempos sometimes seem merely efficient, even brusque (the dancing counterpoint of Act I, Scene 2 has little grace), nor does he infuse the whole with quite the dramatic intensity or rhythmic vigor that Gielen manages, while the textural clarification that is one of his greatest strengths is not always well served by the somewhat cavernous recording.

1976 ETERNA (S)

Reiner Goldberg (A), Werner Haseleu (B), Leipzig Radio Chorus and Orchestra—Herbert Kegel

Little known in the West, this recording is possibly the most remarkable to date. To begin with, the protagonists are at least equal to the best in any other recording. Haseleu's granite-like, black voice bears vivid witness to Moses' inarticulateness, and his anger retains a monumental quality, never sinking to vehemence or petulance. Goldberg's tenor was in prime form in 1976, and his variety of delivery and rhetorical resource capture more of the snake-oil-salesman side of Aron's character than anyone since Krebs. The Young Girl is inappropriately chirpy, the Priest weak in the lowest register but

500 · ARNOLD SCHOENBERG

otherwise vigorous. The chorus is large and effective, the not quite first-rate orchestra is so well rehearsed and fluent in the music that its modest deficiencies hardly matter. Kegel really moves the music along, and the Dance around the Golden Calf has never sounded more barbaric and exciting and coloristically vivid.

1984 DECCA / LONDON (S,D) CD

Philip Langridge (A), Franz Mazura (B), Chicago Symphony Chorus and Orchestra—Georg Solti

Georg Solti has been an advocate of Schoenberg's opera since 1965, when he conducted the British premiere at Covent Garden; he later led the Paris premiere, several concert performances, and this recording with the Chicago Symphony. That orchestra and its excellent chorus (directed by Margaret Hillis) are the greatest strengths of this recording: their work is precise in detail and ensemble, beautiful in tone, responsively expressive. The sturdy, vibrant Aage Haugland is the best recorded Priest, and his colleagues are generally adequate, barring a woolly Ephraimite.

The protagonists are less convincing. In the light of his excellent characterizations in Berg operas, Mazura is disappointing: fussy and fierce, wildly free with pitches and even melodic contours, and frequently disruptive of mood and texture—much less effective than the competition. Langridge is always musical—no mean achievement—but also penny-plain in tone and inflection; the more ecstatic statements, such as the promise of a "land where milk and honey flow," find his modest resources badly overextended.

All in all, Solti and his forces serve best the vigorous parts of the score. Here and there, he makes an effect with a detail previously overlooked. His reading is less linearly inclined than any of the others, and the orchestra seems less at ease with the springily flexible rhythms found, for example, in the neo-Bachian opening of the second scene. The recording has impressive dynamic range and a good deal of clarity in the lighter textures.

As of this writing, only the London set is available, and is a not unworthy presentation of the opera. Eterna best serves both musical and dramatic aspects, with Philips a reasonable second. Most of all, *Moses und Aron* needs to be performed, for its expressive possibilities are still being discovered.

DAVID HAMILTON

BEDŘICH SMETANA

THE BARTERED BRIDE
(1866; revised 1870)

H: A: Mařenka (s); B: Esmeralda (s); C: Ludmila (s);
D: Háta (ms); E: Jeník (t); F: Vašek (t); G: Circus Barker (t);
H: Krušina (bar); I: Kecal (bs); J: Mícha (bs); K: Indian (bs)

edřich Smetana's *The Bartered Bride* (*Prodaná Nevěsta*—literally "Sold Bride") is the most beloved of the composer's eight operas. Its tunefulness, rhythmic vitality, and tonal brilliance all contribute to the universality of its appeal. That a work so drenched in local color, idealized village country life, and unsophisticated sincerity has had such international success is a tribute to its freshness and spirit.

When first given in 1866 at the small Prague Provisional Theater, with the composer conducting, *The Bartered Bride* was quite different from the version performed today. Essentially a musical comedy, the opera had only two acts, no dances, no drinking chorus, no recitatives, and no third-act aria for Mařenka. The opera was revised three times and was produced in 1870 in the form we know today. All of the recordings of the work are of this final version.

The record companies have always been faced with a dilemma over language with *The Bartered Bride*. A Czech-speaking cast is obviously better suited to convey the distinctly national flavor of the music, while a cast singing in translation could better satisfy sales in the larger international marketplace. The irony of *The Bartered Bride*'s recorded history is that of the eleven complete recordings of the work, only five are in Czech (3 of which were available for review), while five are in German and one in Russian.

1952 SUPRAPHON (M)

Milada Musilová (A), Jarmila Pechová (B), Štěpánka Štěpánová (C), Marie Veselá-Kabeláčová (D), Ivo Žídek (E), Oldřich Kovář (F), Karel Hruška (G), Václav Bednář (H), Karel Kalaš (I), Zdeněk Otava (J), Ladislav Mráz (K), Chorus and Orchestra of the Prague National Theater—Jaroslav Vogel

This recording is chronologically the second to use the Czech language. The conductor, Jaroslav Vogel, leads his forces with verve and precision, most clearly evident in the orchestral sections of the opera. The Overture is taken at breakneck speed, but the orchestra nevertheless manages to observe the dynamic markings and preserve the rhythms. The polka which concludes the first act alternates between grand and intimate statements of the theme, and it too is played swiftly but precisely, as are the second-act furiant and the third-act Dance of the Comedians. Overall, Vogel's approach is propulsive and joyous, yet with a natural rightness to the phrasing.

The singing in this recording is on the whole quite fine. Milada Musilová, the Mařenka, possesses a warm, lyrical soprano with a rapid vibrato and a solid vibrant top. She is pleasantly free of what is often characterized as a "Slavic wobble," an affliction of many Eastern European sopranos involving a shrillness and wide, slow-moving vibrato which worsens as the voice grows louder or climbs higher. The soprano is also wonderfully responsive to words and phrasing, and her third-act aria combines yearning with gentle eloquence, the climax of a lovely portrayal.

Her Jeník is the young Ivo Žídek, an important Czech tenor who was still only in his mid-twenties at the time this recording was made. His voice is lyrical, if a bit effortful on top notes. He weighs phrases with expression and care, and his second-act aria is evocative and heart-warming.

The lovable, pompous marriage broker Kecal is portrayed by Karel Kalaš. This role is often victimized by a local casting tradition calling for a veteran *basso buffo* past his better days, but fortunately the tradition is ignored here. Kalaš can encompass the two octaves required for the role, with steadiness and some *legato*, and he can trill with relish. He approaches the role with a chuckle in the voice, and uses *portamento* for characterization at jollier moments. The famous second-act duet with Jeník finds both in optimal voice, energetic and high-spirited.

Oldřich Kovář as Vašek gives an endearing performance, immediately establishing his character as the shy village simpleton with his second-act solo. His duet with Mařenka is a highlight of the recording, beautifully acted and characterized, with a real connection and joy in the interchange between the two. His third-act aria is quite beautifully sung and his stuttering throughout is enchanting rather than annoying.

The chorus of the Prague National Theater is large—the men being particularly fine—and they follow Vogel's musical leadership by singing with clarity and precision.

1961 SUPRAPHON (S)

Drahomíra Tikalová (A), Jarmila Pechová (B), Jaroslava Dobrá (C), Štěpánka Štěpánová (D), Ivo Žídek (E), Oldřich Kovář (F), Rudolf Vonásek (G), Václav Bednář (H), Eduard Haken (I), Jaroslav Horáček (J), Jiří Joran (K), Chorus and Orchestra of the Prague National Theater—Zdeněk Chalabala

This is the first stereo recording of *The Bartered Bride*. Another product of the Prague National Theater, the recording has a number of cast members in common with the 1952 Supraphon, although the ensuing nine years have been less than kind to many of them.

The conductor this time is Zdeněk Chalabala, and his approach is markedly different from Vogel's. While the latter employed large forces with drive and precision, Chalabala draws a somewhat leaner, drier sound from what appears to be a smaller group of musicians. His approach is energetic, but lacks elegance and atmosphere. The polka is loud, raucous, and muscular, while the furiant is brassy with craggy rhythms. The Dance of the Comedians captures Chalabala's approach best: vibrant string playing, vivacious rhythms, but without Vogel's joy and precision. The chorus is likewise medium-sized, rustic-sounding, and a bit ragtag, but again without the scope and verve of Vogel's group.

Drahomíra Tikalová is the Mařenka, and she is a more typical representative of the "Slavic soprano." Her voice is edgy and metallic, with some warmth in the lower register, but afflicted with a pronounced vibrato that slows and widens at the top of her range. She can, however, float a *pianissimo* when called for, and her third-act aria is elegiac and atmospheric, although Chalabala's stop-and-go approach works against its cumulative effect.

The Jeník is again Ivo Žídek, now drier of voice and even more effortful and unsteady on top than he was in 1952. He still manages to bring a good deal of dynamic control to his singing, and his youthful exuberance has mellowed into even greater tenderness, but the voice is no longer fresh and is decidedly strained in his second-act aria.

Kecal is portrayed by Eduard Haken, who has a rangy bass-baritone with a steady, even vibrato, some *legato*, and good patter. He has a tendency to bellow, but his characterization of the cynical marriage broker is complete. However, there is little playfulness in his approach and as a result he inspires less affection.

As in 1952, Vašek is again Oldřich Kovář, by this time nearing the end of his career, having sung the part in Prague for more than twenty years. Every detail of his endearing characterization has been perfected, and his duet with Mařenka has lots of spirit and charm, although the *allegro* section is a bit wild. He again uses the stuttering to good effect, fitting the speech defect into the music with spontaneity and verve.

The smaller roles in this recording are something of a trial to hear, with plenty of worn, woolly, and woofy singing.

1980–81 SUPRAPHON (D) CD

Gabriela Beňačková (A), Jana Jonášová (B), Marie Veselá-Kabeláčová (C), Marie Mrázová (D), Peter Dvorsky (E), Miroslav Kopp (F), Alfred Hampel (G), Jindřich Jindrák (H), Richard Novák (I), Jaroslav Horáček (J), Karel Hanuš (K), Czech Philharmonic Chorus and Orchestra—Zdeněk Košler

This most recent recording was produced in 1980–81 as the soundtrack for a television film, which is now also available on home video release. Although the early digital process has some glariness and provides an aggressive immediacy to the voices which verges on the strident, this is overall the finest performance of the opera in the Czech language, and is also the only one currently available on compact disc in the original language.

The distinguished Czech Philharmonic Orchestra is led by Zdeněk Košler, and at times the overlush orchestral splendor almost threatens to overwhelm the opera's rustic charms. The Overture is grand and performed with energy, crispness, and clarity, but also with a good deal of atmosphere and affection. The polka is vibrant and the furiant and Dance of the Comedians are virtuosic. The work of the Czech Philharmonic Chorus is large-scaled but youthful-sounding, with clear diction, rich blend, and beautiful phrasing, albeit in a "symphonic" style employing less vibrato, which is more reminiscent of the concert hall than of the opera house.

Gabriela Beňačková brings to Mařenka a gleaming, clear, focused *spinto* soprano, with beautifully round tone and only a hint of a Slavic edge. Her vibrato is always even, and she has a free, soaring top with plenty of *pianissimos* as well. The vibrato and *portamento* are used for expressive purposes, especially in her third-act aria, and each phrase is weighted with meaning. Her individual, plaintive timbre, stylistic insights, and tonal allure easily make her the finest complete Mařenka on records in any language.

The Italian-trained tenor Peter Dvorsky is the Jeník. He has been one of the brighter lights of the post-Pavarotti generation on the international operatic scene, and here he is ardent, youthful-sounding, and fresh-voiced, with a firm lyricism and gorgeous *legato*. Top notes pose no problem for him at all, and his excellent singing is a pleasure to hear.

Richard Novák's Kecal unfortunately upholds the casting tradition of the wobbly veteran past his prime. Although he has a good sense of the character, he produces hoarse, dry, and unfocused sounds. His low notes are firm, but he is the only major drawback in this recording.

As if to compensate, the Vašek of Miroslav Kopp provides another stellar performance. He possesses a lyric tenor with beautiful *legato*, and sings characterfully and with a lot of heart. His two arias have many felicities, and his duet with Mařenka is delightful. This is no *comprimario* approach, but that of a singer with charm and imagination and plenty of voice.

The most recent recording, the 1980–81 Supraphon, is the clear standout. The combination of Gabriela Beňačková, Peter Dvorsky, and Miroslav Kopp, together with the tonal brilliance of the Czech Philharmonic, combine to make the recording an instant classic. These qualities more than compensate for the dry *buffo* of Richard Novák and the somewhat overly grand approach.

STEWART PEARCE

Unavailable for review:
1933 EMI / ANGEL
1956 PHILIPS

JOHANN STRAUSS, JR.

DIE FLEDERMAUS (1874)

A: Rosalinde (s); B: Adele (s); C: Prince Orlofsky (ms); D: Gabriel
von Eisenstein (t); E: Alfred (t); F: Dr. Falke (bar); G: Frank (bar)

*D*ie Fledermaus, a mere operetta, hobnobbing in this fancy operatic company? Probably no one would have been more surprised than the composer, who thought several other of his operettas likelier candidates for the operatic stage. Of course he was wrong, which just goes to show how unreliable an authority the mere composer can be.

Strauss responded to these endearingly eccentric characters' attempt to escape their everyday realities, Cinderella-style, at Prince Orlofsky's ball with an imaginative outpouring that has no real counterpart in the operatic repertory. And there is surely no question that operatic resources are required. Does anyone want to hear "operetta voices," or an operetta orchestra, negotiate music that challenges top-quality operatic professionals?

Ironically, opera companies, instead of rising to the challenge, have generally smothered the piece in fake-comic mugging. The problem is compounded, at least in the English-speaking world, by translations that essentially substitute a new set of characters with the same names: a gaggle of musical-comedy geese. Fortunately, *Fledermaus* on records is a more civilized experience. Performers are allowed to respond to the rich store of wit and seriousness that brought forth such memorable music. And the casting is stronger and deeper: lots of nice Adeles and Alfreds, a surprising number of decent Orlofskys, and some real singers for Falke and Frank. (The Rosalindes, surprisingly, aren't all that remarkable. And the Eisensteins aren't at all remarkable.)

Setting aside minor variants, the principal textual issue concerns the ballet at Prince Orlofsky's, plus any optionally interpolated entertainments. Although a number or two from the ballet music that Strauss wrote for *Fledermaus* can be heard in other recordings, only 1960 Decca / London and 1987 Teldec present the complete five-number suite: "Spanisch," "Scottisch," "Russisch," "Böhmisch" (a choral polka), and "Ungarisch." The refrain of the "Ungarisch," none other than the Friska of Rosalinde's Csárdás, is sometimes tacked on as a coda to other ballet options.

Since we're dealing with the all-time greatest composer of dance music, it's not hard to understand the impulse to substitute something snazzier. But the original ballet music shouldn't be denigrated. What Strauss chose to write is well suited to Prince Orlofsky's gathering, which is *not* an imperial New Year's ball. It offers delicious opportunities for legitimately broad characterization; these are, after all, national styles as interpreted by the prince's musicians. (A sample of what's possible: Robert Stoltz's heavily accented "Böhmisch" in 1964 Eurodisc.)

As for interpolated entertainments, 1960 Decca / London contains the famous guest-artist gala, while 1986 EMI has an operetta gala performed by the *Fledermaus* principals, and 1963 RCA has a charming mini-gala.

1907 EMI / ANGEL (M)

Emilie Herzog (A), Marie Dietrich (B), Ida von Scheele-Müller (C), Robert Philipp (D), Julius Lieban (E), Max Begemann (F), Alfred Arnold (G), Chorus of the Berlin Royal Court Opera, Orchestra—Bruno Seidler-Winkler

Isn't it interesting that this much of *Fledermaus* found its way onto records as early as 1907? The little orchestra is scrappy; the cuts are extensive, especially in Act I; and the generally quick tempos are presumably also concessions to recording exigencies. But the spoken-dialogue selection is at points more extensive than any subsequent recording, and the performers sound more comfortable with the speech-song mix, albeit in a rather stagey mode, than most of their successors.

The 1907 technology, as reproduced in the Court Opera Classics LP transfer, isn't kind to the sopranos. Emilie Herzog's all but vibrato-less Rosalinde is even further bleached out by the loss of overtones, while Marie Dietrich's otherwise distinctly promising-sounding Adele loses presence in the upper range. You would expect a mezzo to be less affected, and Ida von Scheele-Müller as Orlofsky, although somewhat pressed by the tempos, is a presence.

Robert Philipp's voice, an odd match for Eisenstein, recalls one of those light G&S tenors whose quaver is considered part of the charm. There are hints of real tenor quality in Julius Lieban's Alfred, but again the recording hardly flatters the tone. (Lieban, the oldest of four singing brothers, is joined here by youngest brother Adalbert as Blind.) The Falke and Frank are functional.

The ballet is the choral "Böhmisch."

1950 DECCA / LONDON (M) CD

Hilde Gueden (A), Wilma Lipp (B), Sieglinde Wagner (C), Julius Patzak (D), Anton Dermota (E), Alfred Poell (F), Kurt Preger (G), Vienna State Opera Chorus, Vienna Philharmonic Orchestra—Clemens Krauss

This first big-time *Fledermaus* is in one respect less complete than its distant predecessor. It includes no spoken dialogue. Its priorities are musical, and its unforced musicality still yields considerable listening pleasure.

It's fascinating to observe, when following the score, how Clemens Krauss makes musical sense of such fine distinctions as contrasting articulation markings: slurs present or absent, *staccato* markings, etc. The point isn't his "fidelity" to the score but the way he draws inspiration from it. The Vienna Philharmonic responds with zest—I love the string *portamentos* in the Overture at the climax of Rosalinde's "So muss allein ich bleibe" leading into "O je, o je, wie rührt mich dies." I have only two reservations. First, all those wonderful discoveries remain a bit anchored to the page instead of sailing irresistibly off it. And second, the absence of the spoken dialogue deprives the listener, and perhaps the performers as well, of a context for the music.

Hilde Gueden is a lively, silvery-toned Rosalinde. It's not her fault that the lightness of her voice creates a problem that recurs in several other recordings: when the Rosalinde's voice is of a light weight and texture naturally associated with Adele, even if both performers are quite good, as they are here, the performance suffers a certain aural meagerness at the soprano end. That said, Wilma Lipp really is a quite good Adele: the coloratura not only highly accurate but shaped with a winning lyric impulse. Since she's deprived of her spoken-dialogue opportunities here, it's fortunate that she turns up again in 1959 EMI.

The same is true of Anton Dermota, who does some of his most beautiful singing as Alfred. This performance in particular is just lovely, the tone pouring forth with seeming effortlessness. Julius Patzak, even allowing for the built-in problems of Eisenstein, is at best adequate and at worst fairly awful. Sieglinde Wagner's ample mezzo unfortunately isn't mobile enough to cope well with the sharp angles and tight curves of Orlofsky's writing. Although Alfred Poell's baritone isn't especially attractive, he commands a comforting authority as Falke. Kurt Preger is an unassuming Frank.

The ballet is "Voices of Spring."

1950–51 CBS / SONY (In English) (M)

Ljuba Welitsch (A), Lily Pons (B), Martha Lipton (C), Charles Kullmann (D), Richard Tucker (E), John Brownlee (F), Clifford Harvuot (G), Metropolitan Opera Chorus and Orchestra—Eugene Ormandy

To the extent that this performance's being in English is thought of as an attraction, caution is indicated.

To begin with, the language creates problems for both sopranos. For Ljuba Welitsch, English just doesn't seem to be a good language. Her accent, while light, is peculiar enough to be disturbing, but more important, unless she's just not in good voice, it appears that the sounds of the language impart a muffled quality to the voice, except when it shakes free in the upper range. For example, in the eight-bar transition to the Friska of the Csárdás ("Und bin ich auch von dir weit" in the original), where she can cut loose on those Gs, As, and Bs, the voice at once warms up and regains its slashing freedom.

Meanwhile Lily Pons, in brittle vocal estate to begin with, is articulating up a storm and yet is pretty much incomprehensible. Which brings us to the larger language problem. To the extent that the singers embrace Howard Dietz's high-profile lyrics, they are grossly misrepresenting the tone and content of the piece.

Consider what happens when Richard Tucker, an ardent, juicy-toned Alfred who throws himself into the text with gusto, finally sweeps Rosalinde off her feet. His giddily elegant and provocative "Glücklich ist, wer vergisst, was doch nicht zu ändern ist," which inspired from Strauss such an urgent and irresistible waltz tune, is replaced with the insipid "You alone, you alone, here we are, we two alone." Then, of course, new lyrics have to be devised when Alfred startles Frank with the same philosophy of life.

The rest of the cast is ordinary. In his Berlin years almost twenty years earlier, Charles Kullmann made some quite decent operetta recordings. What the voice now retains is mostly scar-tissue toughness, which up to a point is useful for Eisenstein, but only up to a point. Martha Lipton is a tonally plain Orlofsky, John Brown-

lee a dry-voiced but tolerable Falke, and Clifford Harvuot an adequate Frank.

In making this recording, Columbia of course couldn't use Met cast members who were under contract to RCA Victor, notably Patrice Munsel and Risë Stevens. Victor recorded its own excerpts disc, outstandingly conducted by Fritz Reiner, with a markedly superior Rosalinde (Regina Resnik), Adele (Munsel), and Orlofsky (Stevens), another fine Alfred (Jan Peerce), a sweet-sounding Eisenstein (James Melton), and a partly outstanding Falke (Robert Merrill—the duet with Eisenstein is rushed, but "Brüderlein" can't be sung much better). It's too bad the whole opera wasn't recorded. Even the Ruth and Thomas Martin translation is less egregious.

The CBS recording omits the spoken dialogue. The ballet is again "Voices of Spring."

1955 EMI / ANGEL (M) CD

Elisabeth Schwarzkopf (A), Rita Streich (B), Rudolf Christ (C), Nicolai Gedda (D), Helmut Krebs (E), Erich Kunz (F), Karl Dönch (G), Philharmonia Chorus and Orchestra—Herbert von Karajan

The competitive attractions of this recording are limited by several factors: (1) The sound is dull, especially in the upper range, and the lack of sparkle is especially regrettable with *Fledermaus*; (2) pretty much everything that's done well here is done better, and often a good bit better, elsewhere; (3) even allowing for varying interpretive preferences, not everything is done all that well here.

The casting, although reasonably successful at recreating Vienna in London, isn't strong in the supporting roles and is positively perverse in the cases of the Alfred and Orlofsky. Is the idea of an Alfred who can't sing (Helmut Krebs's tenor is cramped, essentially topless, and aggressively unattractive) supposed to be an interpretive innovation? And a tenor Orlofsky is a bad enough idea to begin with; what's the idea of having one who can't sing?

Elisabeth Schwarzkopf displays a charming "Hungarian" accent in the spoken dialogue of Act II. In general she spins reasonably attractive vocal threads, but the threads are generally arranged in her self-consciously precious way. If only she attempted more choices that don't allow such careful placement. The transition to the Friska of the Csárdás, for example, while it doesn't challenge Welitsch's clarion brilliance, is sent with a ringing directness that grabs the attention even as it offers sensory pleasure.

Rita Streich's Adele is accomplished, but also frustrating, because she ought to blow us away and doesn't quite. She sings with considerable beauty of tone and with noteworthy accuracy and freedom (the Act III aria is capped with a lovely high D), and she has a strong, sympathetic feeling for the character's frustrations and fantasies—she and Karajan really get the stakes of the letter reading. But this *Fledermaus* as a whole has a tendency to fall back on cuteness, and Streich could never entirely resist such temptations.

Nicolai Gedda does some pleasant singing but can't do much with the special difficulties of Eisenstein. The straight singing requirements of Falke also overextend Erich Kunz; in Act I he can't muster enough tone for the sensible approach he seems to have in mind for the duet with Eisenstein, and in Act II he settles for a rather croony "Brüderlein." Karl Dönch's thinish baritone unfortunately sounds rather similar, and in Act III we get consecutive badly clichéd drunk scenes from the Frosch (Franz Böheim) and the Frank. Not that this performance ever shies from cliché. Granted, it's cliché executed at a high level of professionalism (a weird combination), and even I enjoy the generalized high spirits of Karajan's reading. But his 1960 remake seems to me better in every way.

There's no ballet, creating an odd segue that occurs in several recordings: Orlofsky's admonition "Genug damit, genug," which as written refers to the just completed ballet, instead refers to the "Brüderlein / Duidu" ensemble.

1959 EMI / ANGEL (S) CD

Gerda Scheyrer (A), Wilma Lipp (B), Christa Ludwig (C), Karl Terkal (D), Anton Dermota (E), Eberhard Wächter (F), Walter Berry (G), Philharmonia Chorus and Orchestra—Otto Ackermann

Otto Ackermann's collaborations with producer Walter Legge have qualities rarely encountered in the latter's legendarily "perfectionist" productions: flexibility, poise, relaxation. This *Fledermaus* has an expansiveness and a fullness of sound otherwise pursued on commercial records only by Karl Böhm. The woozy sentimentality of the "Brüderlein / Duidu" ensemble has a mellowness and charm that spring naturally from possibilities already established in the characters.

The cast isn't glamorous, but it's nicely balanced. First off, our old friends Wilma Lipp and Anton Dermota are back as Adele and Alfred. Both are somewhat more constrained vocally, but both still sing with considerable flair and now get to speak as well. Dermota also gets to indulge in Alfred's traditional bits of operatic exhibitionism in his spoken scenes.

Karl Terkal, who *doesn't* speak (his dialogue is done by an actor), also sings rather well, if not notably assertively. In straight singing terms, though, he probably realizes the music more successfully than any of the other Eisensteins. Gerda Scheyrer's soprano has some presence and color, and she's not unpleasant or unintelligent—there's just nothing memorable about her Rosalinde. Which also gets us into the problem of duel-soprano insubstantiality.

Virtually ideal singers were chosen for Orlofsky, Falke, and Frank, with good if not quite ideal results. The puffed-up and hooty "Chacun à son goût" must be somebody's idea of clever "interpretation"; thereafter, Christa Ludwig sings a fleet and spirited Orlofsky. Eberhard Wächter just about delivers the Falke promised by his full, beautiful high baritone; a relentlessly over-dreamy approach to the first part of the duet with Eisenstein results in some loss of profile. Walter Berry's bass-baritone is fine for Frank in Acts I and II, but mindless "comic" hamming mars the Act III drunk scenes of both Frosch and especially Frank. Erich Kunz isn't terrible as Frosch, but compare his more believable work in 1960 Decca. The clichés that pop up in this performance are all the more jarring in the context of Ackermann's prevailingly anti-stereotypical approach.

The ballet consists of the "Russisch" and the complete "Ungarisch."

1960 DECCA / LONDON (S) CD

Hilde Gueden (A), Erika Köth (B), Regina Resnik (C), Waldemar Kmentt (D), Giuseppe Zampieri (E), Walter Berry (F), Eberhard Wächter (G), Vienna State Opera Chorus and Orchestra—Herbert von Karajan

This is a sweetheart of a performance. It's not an innovative one, but what it does, it does so well and with such seeming effortlessness that it's easy to undervalue.

The performance dates from probably the most vital period in Karajan's career. There's never any sense of routine here, and the attention to detail can be breathtaking, in a way that furthers rather than disrupts the continuity of the performance. Listen to the pulsing color in those little three-chord sequences that introduce the stanzas of "Chacun à son goût." It should be added, because it's so easy to take for granted, that the Vienna Philharmonic plays brilliantly.

The cast is solid rather than dazzling. Hilde Gueden repeats her lovely, winning Rosalinde, now fleshed out with spoken dialogue. Again, however, the two sopranos are collectively on the insubstantial side, even though, again, the Adele is individually just fine. Although Erika Köth is in unusually fluttery vocal shape, her distinctively penetrating timbre, not usually an asset, lends an immediate off-kilter fascination to her Adele.

Similarly, the vocal toughness that's often a problem for Waldemar Kmentt is an asset here. He's actually in pretty decent voice, which may not constitute great singing but for Eisenstein is well above average. Giuseppe Zampieri is also a well-above-average Alfred. His sweet light tenor squeezes under pressure, but he has the commitment and ardor for the role.

Walter Berry and Eberhard Wächter, heard in 1959 EMI in the roles one would naturally assign them, are reversed here, with moderately interesting results. Regina Resnik is a strong-

voiced Orlofsky, and Erich Kunz an amusing Frosch.

As noted, this set includes the complete original ballet music. This is followed by the star-studded gala, which includes charming offerings from Birgit Nilsson ("I could have danced all night"), Giulietta Simionato and Ettore Bastianini ("Anything you can do"), and a knockout "Dein ist mein ganzes Herz" from Jussi Bjoerling.

1963 RCA / BMG (S)

Adele Leigh (A), Anneliese Rothenberger (B), Risë Stevens (C), Eberhard Wächter (D), Sándor Kónya (E), George London (F), Erich Kunz (G), Vienna State Opera Chorus and Orchestra—Oscar Danon

If I could keep only one *Fledermaus*, this might be it. The performance has an unfailing freshness, the sense that the music is being recreated for the first time. The performance defies typing. Sometimes it's quickish and pointedly articulated: the Overture is even more than usually exhilarating; the Entr'acte to Act III has an airy breathlessness. More often, though, the freshness shows in an inner animation of the musical line that requires no external mechanical manipulation. You won't hear *Fledermaus*'s profusion of great tunes more infectiously brought to life.

The freshness also shows in unostentatious appreciation of details. In the Act I Rosalinde-Adele-Eisenstein trio, after the second round of "O je, o je, wie rührt mich dies," note the quiet expectation in the usually thrown-away little dotted figure for the first horn, which will blossom into the brass fanfare that announces Adele's "Es gibt ein Wiedersehen." The exceptionally full-bodied and vibrant recording complements the impact and delicacy of the conducting.

Adele Leigh is quite a good Rosalinde. Her soprano has a Schwarzkopf-like edge but is produced with a considerably more connected line, and there's a winning sense of character. This Csárdás is as good as there is in a complete recording. Anneliese Rothenberger also numbers among the most successful Adeles. Risë Stevens, although vocally thicker and less malleable than in the 1950 RCA excerpts, is still a lively, robust Orlofsky.

Eberhard Wächter has his moments as Eisenstein, but the role really doesn't take much advantage of his good baritone. Although Sándor Kónya as Alfred is sometimes not quite on pitch, the sound is so distinctive, bold, and forward-moving that he's hard to resist. The weight of George London's bass-baritone provides a nice contrast in the Eisenstein-Falke duet, and in general lends Falke an interesting gravity. To accommodate him, "Brüderlein" is transposed down a step. But then, as Falke is coming in for a solo landing in E-flat, Orlofsky launches the ensemble repetition in the original F, a hair-raising effect. Erich Kunz is a lightweight Frank.

Instead of a ballet, there's a mini-gala in Act II: Rothenberger as "Fräulein Olga" singing "Voices of Spring" (as successful a vocal rendering of a Strauss waltz as I've heard), Kunz and Herbert Prikopa singing an old Viennese song, rounded out by the Friska of the "Ungarisch."

Note: At the same time, RCA recorded an English-language excerpts disc, with comparably fine orchestra and choral work, though with a mostly different cast.

1964 EURODISC (S) CD

Wilma Lipp (A), Renate Holm (B), Elisabeth Steiner (C), Rudolf Schock (D), Cesare Curzi (E), Claudio Nicolai (F), Walter Berry (G), Vienna State Opera Chorus, Vienna Symphony Orchestra—Robert Stolz

Robert Stolz's expressive contouring, the product of unmatched insight and experience, isn't meant to be confused with prescriptions from the composer, or to be imitated. It's meant to incorporate the singers in making particular sense of the score, and this is in its way the most thoroughly considered, and yet intuitive-sounding, performance on records.

Wilma Lipp's transition from Adele to Rosalinde is surprisingly successful, even though the sound isn't wildly attractive—sometimes a problem where sustained singing tone is important (e.g., "So muss allein ich bleiben"). Nor is Rudolf Schock exactly a mellifluous Eisenstein,

but his ability to make himself heard counts for a good deal in this role.

Renate Holm's somewhat under-virtuosic Adele will wear thin once we've heard it twice more, but at this point, with Stolz's assistance, it's still fresh and charming, though the Act III aria exposes the meagerness of the tone. Against some real competition, Cesare Curzi may be the best Alfred on records, especially in Act I, where the voice has a remarkable sweetness coupled with an almost manic intensity that seems to me quite correct: the character's behavior only makes sense if he's a little nuts, or at any rate lives in a world of his own.

Elisabeth Steiner, without the vocal endowment of a Fassbaender or Baltsa, is an outstanding Orlofsky, her fine mezzo moving confidently through the writing. Claudio Nicolai is a solid Falke, and Walter Berry again a pretty good Frank—he still does a sillier drunk scene than the circumstances seem to me to warrant, but it fits this performance better than 1959 EMI.

Otto Schenk is an amusing Frosch; I wish more of his scene was included. In general the spoken dialogue is quite well done (with some genuinely appropriate sound effects), and very much of a piece with the musical performance.

The formal ballet is the choral "Böhmisch" plus "Unter Donner und Blitz," but the "Spanisch" is used earlier as background music under dialogue. Subsequently, the Friska of the "Ungarisch," similarly used, gives Rosalinde the idea for her Csárdás.

1971 EMI / ANGEL (S) CD

Anneliese Rothenberger (A), Renate Holm (B), Brigitte Fassbaender (C), Nicolai Gedda (D), Adolf Dallapozza (E), Dietrich Fischer-Dieskau (F), Walter Berry (G), Vienna Volksoper Chorus, Vienna Symphony Orchestra—Willi Boskovsky

This recording has one indispensable ingredient: the Orlofsky of Brigitte Fassbaender. Her full, blooming mezzo is in prime condition, and she pounces on every opportunity. She actually *sings* instead of hiccuping those Gs and A-flats in "Chacun à son goût," and in the champagne trio she's able not just to articulate every syllable but to give each full vocal weight.

As with her Adele, Anneliese Rothenberger sings very nicely as Rosalinde. If we were to speculate about a lack of "personality," we might seem to be asking for the sort of thing that Schwarzkopf does, which isn't it at all. Whatever is missing is clearly connected to the perhaps overly sensible course the conductor is steering. Nicolai Gedda is no dynamo either, but his Eisenstein is a significant improvement over 1955 EMI. While the voice is now less lyrical in sound, its increased projective quality is useful for this role.

Renate Holm's Adele is, as before, rather pretty, as long as the vocal demands don't overwhelm her. The Act III aria goes somewhat better here than in her other recordings. Adolf Dallapozza's Alfred offers a light, attractive tenor with the right sort of spirit. Walter Berry is again a solid Frank, but I don't care for Dietrich Fischer-Dieskau's Falke. In "Brüderlein" he at least maintains a line of sorts, albeit a light, strained sort. Elsewhere, the leering and lurching delivery, in speech and song, has a vaguely "Twilight Zone"-ish aura. The moderately paced duet with Eisenstein leaves him altogether too much space for maneuvers.

The performance as a whole is fairly well sung and unforcedly flowing, if somewhat over-deliberate. For the most part, the spoken dialogue is well done, and highly stereophonic. Otto Schenk does a nice Frosch scene, with appropriate collaboration from Dallapozza. Although the "Spanisch" is heard earlier under dialogue, there's no formal ballet. (Orlofsky's "Genug damit" has been sensibly edited, however.) By way of compensatory bonus (?), Fischer-Dieskau sings "Die ganze Nacht verschwärmt" from Strauss's *Waldmeister* after the Csárdás, ostensibly under the guise of Falke telling the "Fledermaus" story. Maybe if it were better sung its pertinence would seem less suspect.

1971 DECCA / LONDON (S)

Gundula Janowitz (A), Renate Holm (B), Wolfgang Windgassen (C), Eberhard Wächter (D), Waldemar Kmentt (E), Heinz Holecek (F), Erich Kunz (G), Vienna State Opera Chorus, Vienna Philharmonic Orchestra—Karl Böhm

This performance has qualities not duplicated elsewhere, starting with the swinging robustness of the orchestral playing. Listen to the earthy vitality Karl Böhm finds in what's usually "just" a transitional section: the 6/8 runup from the champagne trio to the "Brüderlein" ensemble in Act II. Böhm moves *Fledermaus* into a heavier weight class, and the added life the music takes on proves that he's on to something.

What he doesn't seem to have is the right cast for this approach. Gundula Janowitz and Renate Holm are tonally lightweight for their roles, a problem in any *Fledermaus*, which becomes more serious in Böhm's framework. Janowitz sings reasonably well but isn't very distinctive, while Holm sounds a bit more overmatched here than in her other Adeles. Heinz Holecek and Erich Kunz are similarly light-voiced for Falke and Frank.

There is audible slippage in Eberhard Wächter's baritone since his last Eisenstein, but more important, the role mostly reduces him to aggressiveness. Waldemar Kmentt makes the transition from Eisenstein to Alfred fairly well; the voice isn't lustrously beautiful, of course, but it has presence, which for once *does* suit Böhm's approach. The Viennese tradition of a tenor Orlofsky is carried to grisly lengths in the casting of Wolfgang Windgassen, who sounds wheezy and ancient.

The absence of spoken dialogue doesn't help create a musical or dramatic context. The ballet is "Unter Donner und Blitz."

1975–76 DEUTSCHE GRAMMOPHON (S) CD

Julia Varady (A), Lucia Popp (B), Ivan Rebroff (C), Hermann Prey (D), René Kollo (E), Bernd Weikl (F), Benno Kusche (G), Bavarian State Opera Chorus, Bavarian State Orchestra—Carlos Kleiber

Many listeners apparently enjoy this performance for Carlos Kleiber's iconoclastic freshness, and I enjoy it in spots too. In the Overture, for example, there's wonderful momentum at the waltz, and when clarinet and cellos take over the theme of Rosalinde's "So muss allein ich bleiben"—but some of the things Kleiber has to do to get there!

It's an admirable impulse to insist on hearing a score untainted by preconception, and I have no problem with an attempt to find a style for *Fledermaus* outside the Viennese tradition, in this case more straight-ahead than curved. However, Kleiber's reluctance to trust accepted musical relationships leaves him constantly reinventing the score, which means that even a respectable success rate results in a dangerously high percentage of failures.

For example, the rapier-like sharpness with which Kleiber etches Frank's entrance *Melodram* in Act III is delectable, but bizarrely at odds with the clichéd slobbering-drunk scene the veteran Benno Kusche is doing. Or consider the erratic support given Julia Varady, so well suited to Rosalinde vocally and temperamentally. One wonders what the conductor is thinking in the Csárdás, which begins well, with an intense, evocative Lassan, and is then destroyed by a preposterously zippy tempo for the Friska. When the singer can't do anything with the tempo, it's automatically a bad idea, and it's the conductor's job to know the difference.

Lucia Popp's impulse to phraseological finickiness proves a rather good match for Kleiber, and if you don't mind the air of fussiness, this is an interesting Adele. René Kollo as Alfred sounds better offstage than on; mightn't Eisenstein be his role? Hermann Prey, who isn't as schmaltzy as one might fear, is still more disposed to croon than to sing. And with Bernd Weikl, the Falke, also disposed to croon, and with the conductor lobbing ideas like grenades, the two-baritone Eisenstein-Falke duet is no treat.

Somebody must have thought it would be an amusing idea to cast the stunt bass Ivan Rebroff as Orlofsky, singing in falsetto. A different idea would have been to examine the text for ideas: for indications of who the character is, how he functions in the opera, what makes him potentially interesting. But then, the collective intent of the performance seems less to perform *Fledermaus* than to make an amusing diversion of it.

There's a fairly extensive dialogue selection, moderately well performed under Otto Schenk's direction. The ballet is "Unter Donner und Blitz."

1982 DENON (S,D,P) CD

Mirjana Irosch (A), Melanie Holliday (B), Dagmar Koller (C), Waldemar Kmentt (D), Ryszard Karczykowski (E), Robert Granzer (F), Hans Kraemmer (G), Vienna Volksoper Chorus and Orchestra—Erich Binder

There's a case to be made for this Volksoper-on-tour *Fledermaus* (recorded in Japan), mostly having to do with its upbeat spirit. The orchestral work isn't razor-sharp, nor is the vocal standard pristine, yet the whole thing *plays*. The strings may scramble a bit, but the orchestral sound conveys warmth and affection.

The Alfred and Adele have the makings of significant voices, though Ryszard Karczykowski's tenor doesn't hold up to heavy use and Melanie Holliday's soprano isn't well controlled. Then we have some utilitarian voices: Mirjana Irosch has enough for a plausible Rosalinde; Waldemar Kmentt, now reduced to a determined croak, knows the ropes as Eisenstein; and Dagmar Koller holds her own as Orlofsky. Robert Granzer's baritone isn't up to sustaining Falke's lines. Hans Kraemmer is a satisfactory Frank.

The ballet is "Unter Donner und Blitz," inserted after the opening chorus of Act II. With no ballet in the proper ballet position, Orlofsky's "Genug damit, genug"—here reassigned to Falke, who sings it excruciatingly—once again refers to the "Duidu" ensemble. Speaking of reassignment, in the Act I Rosalinde-Eisenstein-Adele trio, Eisenstein rather than Adele introduces the idea that "Es gibt ein Wiedersehen!"

The CDs have no track cues except for the act beginnings.

1982 DECCA / LONDON (In English) (S,P)

Joan Sutherland (A), Monique Brynnel (B), Heather Begg (C), Robert Gard (D), Anson Austin (E), Michael Lewis (F), Gregory Yurisch (G), Australian Opera Chorus, Elizabethan Sydney Orchestra—Richard Bonynge

This generally inoffensive live performance has a certain interest as the only complete-with-dialogue English-language *Fledermaus*.

The one individual effort of interest is the Orlofsky of Heather Begg: a nice, deep mezzo that's a bit ponderous in "Chacun à son goût" but thereafter makes a moderately good effect. Monique Brynnel is a perky Adele, though the voice falters where real brilliance is called for, and the accent is conspicuous. (A French maid, perhaps? But sister Ida has no such accent.) Adele might have been an interesting role for Joan Sutherland if taken on seriously. Even Rosalinde might have been plausible for her if she hadn't tackled it as adorable operetta kitsch, and if the voice were in fuller shape.

Robert Gard is a lightweight, fairly inconspicuous Eisenstein; Anson Austin, a lightweight but pleasant enough Alfred—in the jail scene, he's the only Alfred I've heard offer a scrap of Count Almaviva's "Ecco ridente."

The translation is less overbearingly irritating than the Met version, and the extensive spoken dialogue is intoned in opera-house comedy-speech style. There's no ballet, and, again, Orlofsky's "Enough, my friends, enough" refers to the "Duidu" ensemble.

1986 EMI / ANGEL (S,D) CD

Lucia Popp (A), Eva Lind (B), Agnes Baltsa (C), Peter Seiffert (D), Plácido Domingo (E), Wolfgang Brendel (F), Kurt Rydl (G), Bavarian Radio Chorus, Munich Radio Orchestra—Plácido Domingo

On the whole, this is a fluid, pleasant enough performance, though not an especially ingratiating or illuminating one, and the recorded sound doesn't help. There's not much body in the sound if you keep the volume low enough to tame the echo that appears in ensembles, where in addition voices pop out eerily.

The performance shares with the other Munich *Fledermaus* a tendency to build musical structures by piling on layers of sound rather than by shaping phrases. And sometimes, especially in Act I, I just don't get what the performers are going for. There are, for example, lots of ways of justifying Adele's letter reading, to make

it something she does for herself rather than for the audience. What I don't understand is an inflectionless reading that isn't pursuing anything—not even cheap audience gratification.

Eva Lind is a pale Adele, which also doesn't make for a good match with the pinched tone of Lucia Popp's Rosalinde—she has trouble filling out conductor Domingo's rather ambling phrases. Singer Domingo vocalizes handsomely (and how often do we hear a *Lohengrin* snippet sung by an Alfred who actually is a Lohengrin?), if without the urgency that marks the best Alfreds. Peter Seiffert also sings Eisenstein rather well but without much animation. Wolfgang Brendel sings pretty well but also has trouble filling out the large spaces of the lead-in to "Brüderlein" and the solo itself. Kurt Rydl is a forgettable Frank, and in Act III a partly forgotten one—his entrance *Melodram* is omitted.

The one standout performance is the Orlofsky of Agnes Baltsa, not as strikingly full in sound as Brigitte Fassbaender's (1971 EMI), but remarkably even, lithe, and zestful.

A sensible spoken-dialogue selection is performed in a manner that has many appropriate qualities of conversation but unfortunately not including the aspect of people conversing *with* one another. A lackluster operetta gala is inserted after the Csárdás. Then, in the normal ballet position, we get "Unter Donner und Blitz."

1987 TELDEC (S,D) CD

Edita Gruberova (A), Barbara Bonney (B), Marjana Lipovšek (C), Werner Hollweg (D), Josef Protschka (E), Anton Scharinger (F), Christian Boesch (G), Netherlands Opera Chorus, Concertgebouw Orchestra—Nikolaus Harnoncourt

The playing of the Concertgebouw is an attraction: so richly textured, so wholesomely full-bodied. Phrasing is generally linear, with no attempt to mimic either the sound or the style of the Vienna Philharmonic, which is fine, because even without any great interpretive vision this respectfully unhurried performance provides a functional alternative. It works, and demonstrates how little *Fledermaus* depends on provincial mannerism.

As Rosalinde, Edita Gruberova has a problem: the actual sound not being terribly agreeable, she's sometimes less effective when the music demands sustained tone. Barbara Bonney is a superior Adele: a pleasing lyric soprano handled with good measures of accuracy and liveliness. Marjana Lipovšek's ample, attractive mezzo is welcome for Orlofsky, though she doesn't attempt the razor-sharp articulation that Fassbaender and Baltsa do.

Werner Hollweg's mousy tenor is oddly cast as Eisenstein, but he occasionally manages some lyric quality in passages where weightier-voiced singers can't. Josef Protschka is an agreeable but frequently thin- and uncertain-toned Alfred; pair him with a similarly straining Gruberova and "Glücklich ist, wer vergisst" doesn't exactly soar. Anton Scharinger, with a serviceable rather than beautiful baritone, is a perfectly competent Falke, and Christian Boesch a competent Frank.

The dialogue is replaced with bits of arch narration by (of all people) Frosch. The original ballet music is performed complete.

1990 PHILIPS (S,D) CD

Kiri Te Kanawa (A), Edita Gruberova (B), Brigitte Fassbaender (C), Wolfgang Brendel (D), Richard Leech (E), Olaf Bär (F), Tom Krause (G), Vienna State Opera Chorus, Vienna Philharmonic Orchestra—André Previn

André Previn, encouraging the Vienna Philharmonic to do what it still does so well, summons a fizzy ebullience reminiscent of Karajan's 1960 Decca but from a generally mellower perspective. The performance isn't always entirely persuasive when it broadens; interesting as the extra breadth and weight of the waltz in the Overture is, does it quite dance? But the more introspective slant often pays off. For example, the boozy festivities at Prince Orlofsky's seem to have a thickening effect. The champagne trio itself is slowed down a bit, so that the characters seem to be overarticulating in compensation; then the "Brüderlein" develops unsentimental breadth, and the quickish "Unter Donner und Blitz" (introduced with thunder and lightning) seems *intended* to pick up the proceedings.

Wolfgang Brendel is easily the best of the baritone Eisensteins. He truly tries to *sing* the role, with results that are sometimes pleasing and sometimes peculiar (e.g., the high-lying phrases of the Act II scene with Rosalinde). His baritone is used to good effect in Act III.

It's also peculiar to have a Falke—Olaf Bär, singing very nicely—who sounds higher and leaner than the Eisenstein; one has the momentary impulse to transpose the singers. By voice type, Tom Krause would be yet a third Falke; as Frank, he earns credit for his determination to *sing* the role, and his Act III drunk scene is more than usually believable.

Kiri Te Kanawa has a good outing as Rosalinde, to which her one vocal color and weight is well suited. After a whoopy entrance, Edita Gruberova settles in for a fairly satisfying Adele. Nineteen years after her spectacular Orlofsky in 1971 EMI, Brigitte Fassbaender is still awfully good, if not as fearlessly flamboyant and tonally rock-solid. And Richard Leech is a first-rate Alfred, the tone generously produced, the spirit eager.

The ballet is "Unter Donner und Blitz," topped off by the Friska of the "Ungarisch."

For a traditional *Fledermaus*, the obvious candidates would be 1960 Decca / London and 1990 Philips—the former more brilliantly executed (and containing the gala sequence), the latter more mellow and perhaps more interestingly, or at least more diversely, sung. Worth some consideration, especially if individual elements have particular appeal, are 1971 EMI and 1986 EMI.

In the category of performances that explore beneath the surface, along with the subversively "traditionalist" 1959 EMI, the prime contenders are Robert Stolz's sophisticated and wise 1964 Eurodisc and Oscar Danon's masterfully considered 1963 RCA. Don't overlook the wholesome buoyancy of 1987 Teldec and the weightier emphasis of 1971 Decca.

For *Die Fledermaus* in English, the best bet is to watch for RCA's 1950 or 1963 excerpts disc (see 1950–51 CBS and 1963 RCA).

KENNETH FURIE

RICHARD STRAUSS

SALOME (1905)

A: Salome (s); B: Herodias (ms); C: Herodes (t); D: Jochanaan (bar)

ermany has always had an appetite for the plays of Oscar Wilde. To this day, they are more often performed there than in the United Kingdom. *Salome,* if not the best, surely the most daring of Wilde's plays, could be seen in Germany in a translation by Hedwig Lachmann as early as 1902, many years before it was mounted in London. In fact, Strauss was already thinking about it as the subject for his third opera when he saw it early in 1903 at Max Reinhardt's Kleines Theater in Berlin. He found two-thirds of the play to be suitable as a libretto— just about the way it was written. It is amusing that as Strauss began composing his incendiary *Salome* later that year he was also finishing up his *Domestic Symphony,* a paean to the joys of everyday family life. During the nearly two years it took him to complete the opera, he made a tour of America and updated Berlioz's treatise on orchestration as well.

The premiere of *Salome* took place in Dresden on December 9, 1905, and was a sensation even though it had been preceded by only a month of stormy rehearsals. First Marie Wittich, a Bayreuth Isolde with a Junoesque figure who was the first Salome, went on strike. ("I won't do it, I'm a decent woman.") Then the orchestra became rattled. Strauss told his battalion of musicians that it would be easier and to his taste if they played everything but the few grand climaxes lightly, as if it were fairy music by Mendelssohn. "Gentlemen," he said, "there are no difficulties or problems. This opera is a

scherzo with a fatal conclusion!" Although Strauss did not have his ideal Salome ("a sixteen-year-old princess with the voice of an Isolde"; a dancer was employed for the Seven Veils episode) and later admitted that the opera "succeeded in spite of Auntie Wittich," the audience demanded thirty-eight curtain calls and the opera was off and running. In only two years *Salome* was heard in fifty opera houses.

No doubt, *Salome* makes its deepest impression in the theater. But hearing it on records saves one the risk of viewing a corpulent Salome and trying to imagine her as a sixteen-year-old princess. The most successful recordings of this opera have two things in common—a soprano with a girlish timbre and enough metal to pierce the highest rises in the orchestral brocade and a conductor who can create an ongoing, doom-haunted atmosphere with Mendelssohnian texture and clarity.

1950 OCEANIC (M)

Christel Goltz (A), Inger Karen (B), Bernd Aldenhoff (C), Josef Herrmann (D), Saxon State Orchestra—Joseph Keilberth

Salome, never the opera to withstand 78-rpm's four-minute breaks, had to wait until LP to make its recording debut. When Christel Goltz stunned audiences at the 1950 Munich Festival with her singing and impersonation of the Princess of Judea, a recording was inevitable. Accordingly, the Mitteldeutsche Rundfunk arranged to broadcast a performance at Dresden's Saxon State Opera, where she had sung leading roles for eight years. The dominant Salome in Europe for a dozen years, Goltz, heard in three of the opera's nine recordings, was in her mid-thirties and at the peak of her powers when Oceanic transferred the broadcast source onto LP and made her famous all over the world.

Only in this recording can one hear what the shouting was all about. Goltz is in her freshest, most girlish voice and her perverseness, sensuality, and spontaneity go a long way toward overcoming one's resistance to the set's gritty, poorly focused sound and its recessed climaxes. Joseph Keilberth knew how *Salome* should go; the shape and flow of the performance is convincing and the orchestral playing warmly expressive. There is, however, some sloppy ensemble, characteristic of Keilberth, and little of the feline quality the score possesses. Bernd Aldenhoff, a *Heldentenor*, is vocally secure, his years of distressing, ever-widening vibrato still ahead of him. He is a blunt, unimaginative Herod despite his good enunciation. Josef Herrmann makes a better impression as an impassioned prophet, but his voice is a bit thick and he lurches at high notes. Inger Karen is the usual termagant Herodias. Rudolf Dittrich has a sweeter tenor than most Narraboths. Kurt Böhme has an off-day as an unsteady, insufficiently tender First Nazarene.

1952 PHILIPS (M)

Walburga Wegner (A), Georgine von Milinkovic (B), Laszlo Szemere (C), Josef Metternich (D), Vienna Symphony Orchestra—Rudolf Moralt

This is a decent performance that would go down well enough in the theater, but it does not compete with the better recordings of *Salome*. Walburga Wegner, more often Chrysothemis in *Elektra* than Salome, sings with sweet, steady tone and is careful about correct pitch. What she cannot provide is the heat of Salome's manic obsession. The Herod couple are stagewise and appropriately disagreeable. Josef Metternich's ample baritone does not achieve Messianic fervor. Rudolf Moralt, a stalwart captain in the regiments of the Vienna Opera, is a capable leader.

1952 MET (M,P)

Ljuba Welitsch (A), Elisabeth Höngen (B), Set Svanholm (C), Hans Hotter (D), Metropolitan Opera Orchestra—Fritz Reiner

For those who saw her in the forties, Ljuba Welitsch was the Salome of a lifetime. For those who attended *Salome*s in February and March of 1949, or heard the radio broadcast, Welitsch and Fritz Reiner are forever identified with Strauss's opera and are the artists by whom all others are measured. They resumed their partnership at the Met three years later; one of those performances, that of January 19, 1952, was broadcast and later issued by the Met. Although it has a better supporting cast (unmatched by any published recording), it does not efface memories of the earlier broadcast. *Salome* is, above all, about Salome. By 1952, Welitsch's phenomenal voice was less compact, the high range in particular, loosened in texture under pressure. It continues, nonetheless, to create a genuine presence; her conversational passages have color and bite, and the variety of her inflections in her many requests for the head of Jochanaan are uniquely telling.

Among Herods, only Set Svanholm (and Julius Patzak in the 1954 London recording) convinces the listener that Herod is a ruler. He really sings the part, almost without strain; no one betters him in his attempts to deflect Salome's intentions. Elisabeth Höngen is a matchless Herodias, using every one of her opportunities to make a useful comment on this ungrateful role. Magisterial in voice and portraiture, Hans Hotter transforms Strauss's cigar-store Indian of a prophet into a wild-eyed but somehow dignified evangelist. No one equals his shuddering "Niemals, Tochter Babylons." Reiner achieves unfailing ensemble clarity, supple phrasing, and finely graded dynamic shading with a light hand

and disinterested passion. Abetted by remarkably clear 1952 sonics, reasonably wide in range except for the "Dein Haar ist grässlich" episode and some of the finale, one can hear how Reiner, above all other conductors, has satisfied Strauss's request for Mendelssohnian grace and buoyancy.

1954 DECCA / LONDON (M)

Christel Goltz (A), Margarita Kenney (B), Julius Patzak (C), Hans Braun (D), Vienna Philharmonic Orchestra—Clemens Krauss

This was the first *Salome* by a major label to be taken seriously as a recording. Its rich, resonant sound has color and amplitude, except in the grandest orchestral climaxes. The presence of Clemens Krauss—a Strauss specialist, a friend of the composer's and the librettist of his last opera, *Capriccio*, in the last sessions over which he presided—and an experienced cast promised and delivered a performance of style and authority which is wanting only that little extra sizzle and sting that would make it indispensable. This is Christel Goltz's second recorded Salome; the four intervening years have erased some of the all-important youthful shine from her voice and some of the high notes are attained with greater effort; it sounds more mature, less seductive, its middle looser, tending to wobble. Hans Braun has a good upper voice but is an unimaginative Jochanaan, neither exalted nor biting. Margarita Kenney does little to enhance our image of Herodias. Some of the smaller contributions are choice: Anton Dermota, on top of the role of Narraboth; Else Schürhoff, a page who makes an impression; ditto Walter Berry as the First Soldier; and Ludwig Weber, aging, but tender and noble as the First Nazarene. The star of this performance is its Herod, Julius Patzak. Like Svanholm, he is regal, not a raving roughneck. He also has perfect diction, coloring the words as no other, catching the many moods of Herod. As one listens to this very great singing actor, one sees him smiling, frowning, commanding, shuddering, terrified, beseeching, losing his temper.

1961 DECCA / LONDON (S) CD

Birgit Nilsson (A), Grace Hoffman (B), Gerhard Stolze (C), Eberhard Wächter (D), Vienna Philharmonic Orchestra—Georg Solti

This recording, produced by John Culshaw, the first to employ the "Sonicstage" technique, created quite a stir in its day for its theatrical realism. A new high in orchestral detail and impact was disclosed, and stage movement was suggested in ways never before attempted. Like most pioneering efforts, "Sonicstage" had a drawback. In his zeal to duplicate what one hears in the theater, Culshaw gave the orchestra a priority over the singers that after a while leaves one weary trying to hear the voices in something less than full cry. This set-up can be heard in the London's next major opera recording in Vienna, the Solti *Siegfried*; thereafter, balances were adjusted so that voices had parity with the instrumental ensemble.

For all of that, the tingle of Georg Solti's nerve's-end *Salome* is not easily forgotten. Neither is Birgit Nilsson's confident, almost impudently effortless singing of the title role. Nevertheless, Nilsson's timbre and manner evoke more the Valkyrie than the sixteen-year-old princess. The remainder of the cast is effective, if one is tolerant of Gerhard Stolze's predilection for *Sprechstimme* to emphasize a dramatic point. Eberhard Wächter is a forceful prophet, Grace Hoffman offers a well-considered Herodias, and Waldemar Kmentt shows what a talented singing actor he is even in the brief role of Narraboth.

1963 EMI / ANGEL (S)

Christel Goltz (A), Siw Ericsdotter (B), Helmut Melchert (C), Ernst Gutstein (D), Dresden State Orchestra—Otmar Suitner

Christel Goltz's third recording of *Salome* is a case of going to the well too often. Now unpleasant to hear, her voice worn and loosened in all registers, effortful in tough passages and distressingly flat during her wheedling of Herod, Goltz has little left but her savvy and intense concentration. A lovely recording, a good pair of Herods, Theo Adam as the First Nazarene, and some fine playing by the Dresden Staatskapelle are just about all there is on the credit side. The conducting of Otmar Suitner is not recommendable; it is bland, without personality or sustained impetus.

1968 RCA / BMG (S) CD

Montserrat Caballé (A), Regina Resnik (B), Richard Lewis (C), Sherrill Milnes (D), London Symphony Orchestra—Erich Leinsdorf

RCA's is another version to avoid. Montserrat Caballé is interesting only in the way a good singer, wildly miscast, can be. Salome's difficulties don't faze her and her soft singing of certain high-lying passages is its own reward. What is missing is any edge to her interpretation, any sense of willfulness, obsession. Even her femininity and sensuality are the wrong kind—overripe, drowsy, matronly. Sherrill Milnes's baritone is fresh but often unfocused; his impersonation is prosaic, without appropriate mystical fervor. The Herods are flat, with little theatrical flavor, and James King, in fine vocal fettle, is a wooden Narraboth. Perhaps the quality of this performance stems from the unatmospheric, featureless conducting of Erich Leinsdorf. The engineering provides pleasant sound but not a lot of presence until the last two scenes.

1970 DEUTSCHE GRAMMOPHON (S,P)

Gwyneth Jones (A), Mignon Dunn (B), Richard Cassilly (C), Dietrich Fischer-Dieskau (D), Hamburg State Opera Orchestra—Karl Böhm

DG's Salome, cobbled from live takes and rehearsals in November of 1970 at the Hamburg Opera, is another failure. Gwyneth Jones, unlike Caballé, is not even interesting, because her squally, unsteady voice can't cope with the part. Dietrich Fischer-Dieskau, often at sea in straightforward parts, is an unacceptable Jochanaan. Richard Cassilly and Mignon Dunn, effective enough, are just as unpleasant in voice as in characterization. The one memorable act in this lamentable set is the grand and fine-tuned conducting of Karl Böhm, but even it is vitiated by awkward mike placement.

1977–78 EMI / ANGEL (S) CD

Hildegard Behrens (A), Agnes Baltsa (B), Karl-Walter Böhm (C), José van Dam (D), Vienna Philharmonic Orchestra—Herbert von Karajan

We come to one of the best Salomes, EMI's souvenir of the 1977 Salzburg Festival, recorded in Vienna's Sofiensaal. The recording is no world beater, the first twenty minutes or so coarse-grained with metallic "highs," pianissimo passages not quite in focus, the page too far off mike and Jochanaan's voice too diffused, when first heard from the cistern. Happily, the sound improves after that rocky beginning. One hears the recording at its best on CD. Apart from Jules Bastin, too unsteady vocally to suggest the nobility of the First Nazarene, EMI fields an admirable cast. Hildegard Behrens comes about as close as anyone to Strauss's "sixteen-year-old princess with the voice of Isolde." Her sweetness of tone and air of innocence heighten the depravity of her desires. She is also unsparing in lines such as "Lass mich deinen Mund küssen." Equally impressive is José van Dam, an expressive prophet, infinitely tender in "Er ist in einem Nachen" and biting in his rejection of Salome. Karl-Walter Böhm and Agnes Baltsa are appropriately repellent and careful to color their words. Only Herbert von Karajan achieves a tonal texture comparable in lightness to Fritz Reiner. Furthermore, his cool detachment and deliberate tempos create a remote and sensual atmosphere, doom-laden from start to finish, without any sacrifice to orchestral heat (hear the Vienna Philharmonic sizzle in the long passage after Jochanaan's curse).

1990 SONY (S,D) CD

Eva Marton (A), Brigitte Fassbaender (B), Heinz Zednik (C), Bernd Weikl (D), Berlin Philharmonic Orchestra—Zubin Mehta

The twelve years that separate this recording and its predecessor indicate the very real shortage of able Salomes. Eva Marton's soprano has the right heft for the part but little else. Her overly mature sound, her often intrusive vibrato which mitigates against steadiness of tone, her unsubtle dramatics, all undermine any suggestion of a charming teenager without a conscience or any control of her emotions. Bernd Weikl is a believable prophet but his baritone shows signs of hard use—an eroded command of *legato* and strained high notes. Although there is little song in Heinz Zednik's Herod (hear Patzak), he makes his words tell without screaming. Brigitte Fassbaender is a convincing termagant. The remainder of the cast is quite adequate, Keith Lewis, portraying an unusually youthful Narraboth, rather more than that. This cast, indeed the entire production, has clearly been well prepared. Even the least convincing singers are musically alert and at least suggest they have looked deeply into their roles.

The Berlin Philharmonic plays up a storm for Zubin Mehta. Too much of one. The sheer volume of sound, faithfully captured by the Sony engineering team, will be exciting on its own terms for some, but others will long for more of the Mendelssohnian quality Strauss said suited the vast majority of the music best.

1990 DEUTSCHE GRAMMOPHON
(S,D) CD

Cheryl Studer (A), Leonie Rysanek (B), Horst Hiestermann (C), Bryn Terfel (D), Berlin Opera Orchestra—Giuseppe Sinopoli

Hard on the heels of Sony's *Salome* comes a superior entry from DG. Cheryl Studer triumphs in the leading role, her most arduous vocal test to date, confirming the unusual range of her versatile soprano. No Salome on disc has been so vocally appropriate in timbre, so assured, youthful, willful, seductive, wild since Ljuba Welitsch. Her *pianissimos* are as admirable as her sustained cascades of sound.

Also impressive is the recording debut of young Welsh baritone Bryn Terfel, notable for his warm, ample sound and vigorous address, as Jochanaan. On the other hand, the Herod—and, for that matter, the rest of the cast—is not altogether satisfactory. By force of personality and theatrical instinct, Leonie Rysanek, despite declining vocal resources, makes something of Herodias, but Horst Hiestermann as her consort has an unattractive voice, a distressingly wide vibrato, and speaks more than he sings.

DG's engineering, not quite so crystalline as Sony's, is warmer, recorded at a higher level and flattering to Giuseppe Sinopoli's lush sonic palette. For once, the Italian conductor avoids those ponderous tempos which disfigure many of his operatic efforts, and generally achieves an agreeable sense of continuity.

Although Sinopoli's cast is uneven, he leads an honorable, effective *Salome* that just misses equaling those of Karajan and Reiner, each of the latter without serious major flaw.

C. J. LUTEN

RICHARD STRAUSS

ELEKTRA (1909)

A: Elektra (s); B: Chrysothemis (s); C: Klytämnestra (ms);
D: Aegisth (t); E: Orest (bar)

*D*espite its status as a repertory opera, *Elektra* has not been recorded often. The reason, of course, is the obvious difficulty of the title role. The vocal compromises and adjustments that might enable a soprano to make an effect with the part in the opera house—to "get away with it," after a fashion—are likely to be quite mercilessly exposed by the close scrutiny of a microphone. An Elektra must possess a true dramatic-soprano voice capable of filling out the music with a secure, unforced tone. She must have stamina, but raw power (however desirable) is not enough: much of her music calls for delicacy and intimate delivery as well. She must be a resourceful vocal actress, with verbal incisiveness and a temperament that can encompass just about every emotional stop between stoic dignity and unrestrained frenzy. Finally, an ideal Elektra should have a warm, beautiful, womanly timbre, and sound like a young girl: when she laments to Orest in the Recognition Scene that she has sacrificed her femininity to avenge their father, the listener should feel that she had a great deal to lose.

This is not to imply that the other roles in the opera are easy. Chrysothemis is almost as difficult as Elektra from the purely vocal standpoint, and the interpreter's problem is how to convey desperation and barely suppressed hysteria without sacrificing vocal beauty or control. Although Klytämnestra has been sung by a distinguished line of mezzo-sopranos, her music

ideally calls for a true contralto—a vocal type that has become all but extinct. Her extended conversational passages in the vicinity of middle C inevitably show up any deficiency in the singer's technique.

As a one-act opera that makes severe demands upon its heroine, *Elektra* is invariably cut in the opera house. These cuts were, admittedly, sanctioned by the composer and practiced by him when he conducted his own work in the theater. It is surprising, though, that even the studio recordings have tended to observe the stage cuts as a matter of course. Of the eight recordings discussed below, only two—the 1966–67 Decca / Solti and the 1990 EMI / Sawallisch versions—are complete. All of the others make the standard abridgments. These cuts obviously ease the vocal burden on the opera's heroine. I suspect that they were originally made, however, because somebody found the language and imagery of Hugo von Hofmannsthal's libretto offensive.

There's absolutely nothing wrong with the music, as the two uncut recordings prove, and there is no reason why a studio recording should be abridged at all.

1943 ACANTA (M) CD

Erna Schlüter (A), Annelies Kupper (B), Gusta Hammer (C), Peter Markwort (D), Robert Hager (E), Hamburg State Opera Chorus and Orchestra—Eugen Jochum (?) or Hans Schmidt-Isserstedt

There is some doubt about who conducts this performance: Acanta states that it is Hans Schmidt-Isserstedt, but other sources claim that this attribution is a mistake and that the maestro is actually Eugen Jochum. In either event, this is a solid, straightforward, and rather unexciting reading, quite well executed by the Hamburg orchestra.

Erna Schlüter displays some of the basic qualifications for Elektra: a big, steely sound, belted out with abandon, complete with some exciting (if hard-edged) high notes. There is not much subtlety or variety to her portrayal, though, and her timbre isn't really beautiful enough to make the proper effect in the Recognition Scene.

Annelies Kupper doesn't phrase with ideal *legato*, but her large, bright tone and energetic delivery create an interesting aural image of Chrysothemis.

The Klytämnestra, Gusta Hammer, has some raw and uncontrolled moments, but brings a biting intensity to the role.

Peter Markwort is a querulous-sounding Aegisth, but perhaps not inappropriately so. Robert Hager is an impressively dark-toned Orest, and the young Gustav Neidlinger contributes a vivid cameo as his Tutor.

Despite the backward placement of the orchestra, the sound is quite good for its date.

1950 CETRA (M,P)

Anny Konetzni (A), Daniza Ilitsch (B), Martha Mödl (C), Franz Klarwein (D), Hans Braun (E), Chorus and Orchestra of the Maggio Musicale Fiorentino—Dimitri Mitropoulos

For several years, this Cetra set was the only commercially available recording of *Elektra*. Both the performance and the recording, however, are so poor that this version was barely acceptable even as a stopgap.

Dimitri Mitropoulos was a great operatic conductor, and paces the music well, but everything is against him here. The Florentine orchestra is simply not up to the demands of this score: the splayed attacks, uncertain ensemble, wrong notes, and patches of unattractive tone may be forgivable on an individual basis, but are cumulative in their annoyance value.

With a single exception, the cast is inadequate. The opening scene is shocking, all right, but only because it is sung by an assortment of screeching, wobbly sopranos and mezzos.

Anny Konetzni had no business singing Elektra: her sound is raw and white, and undermined by a pronounced tremolo and uncertain pitch. Most of the time, she is just flinging her voice at the music, and one can scarcely speak of characterization. Daniza Ilitsch is every bit as shrill and tremulous as Konetzni, so her Chrysothemis emerges as an hysterical shrew.

The only singer who emerges from this debacle with her dignity intact is Martha Mödl, as the doomed queen. Her voice, somewhat strenuously produced and hooty in quality, can hardly be described as conventionally beautiful, but it is large and steady, she employs it with confidence, and she makes a great deal of the words.

Hans Braun is a dull, stiff Orest. Franz Klarwein, a competent enough tenor, is extended by the demands of Aegisth's music and sounds strained in the climaxes.

Everest's fake stereo is strident, shallow, and echoey—and if there's anything these particular soprano voices don't need, it's more edge and resonance!

1952 MET (M,P)

Astrid Varnay (A), Walburga Wegner (B), Elisabeth Höngen (C), Set Svanholm (D), Paul Schöffler (E), Metropolitan Opera Chorus and Orchestra—Fritz Reiner

It is a shame that Fritz Reiner did not conduct a studio recording of *Elektra*; this February 23, 1952, Metropolitan Opera broadcast, though an imperfect document, is good enough to suggest how extraordinary a Straussian Reiner was. His tempos are often surprisingly slow, and he emphasizes warmth and lyricism rather than hysteria; and yet the reading has great intensity and forward momentum. The orchestra—dimly reproduced much of the time, unfortunately—seems to be playing well.

Astrid Varnay is a stern Elektra, with no vulnerability or tenderness audible in her portrayal. She sings indefatigably, although her highly individual voice (huge and steady, but often harsh and acidulous in timbre) is some-what of an acquired taste.

Walburga Wegner is an accurate but unexcit-ing Chrysothemis; next to Varnay, her vocalism seems small-scaled and her temperament too passive and emotionally reticent.

Elisabeth Höngen, the Klytämnestra, is a shrewd artist, but her vocal equipment is by no stretch of the imagination first-class: her mezzo sounds lightweight for this role, is unvaried in color, and takes on an edge and an incipient wobble under pressure. (In addition, Höngen *sounds* much younger than Varnay—even gir-lish at times—which creates a definite dramatic imbalance.)

Paul Schöffler may not be in his best voice, sounding both dry of timbre and cautious in his approach to the top, but his Orest has the right kind of uneasiness masked by a display of calm dignity, and he declaims the words vividly. Set Svanholm, on the other hand, sings Aegisth as well as anybody on records, and shows a real grasp of the character.

The recording is a transfer from acetate discs, and the sound is, frankly, nothing special. The voices come through with reasonable clarity, but most of the instrumental detail has to be taken on faith.

1960 DEUTSCHE GRAMMOPHON (S) CD

Inge Borkh (A), Marianne Schech (B), Jean Madeira (C), Fritz Uhl (D), Dietrich Fischer-Dieskau (E), Dresden State Opera Chorus, Dresden State Orchestra—Karl Böhm

Karl Böhm led some even more exciting performances of *Elektra* in the theater, but his studio recording is a solid achievement. Here, the reading is notable for its restraint: it's as though Böhm deliberately set out to prove that the violence and craziness of the drama are carefully written into the music, and do not need to be emphasized by the conductor. Although Böhm secures a weighty, imposing orchestral sonority much of the time, he also maintains transparency; the instrumental tex-tures never become thick or congested. The Dresden orchestra plays magnificently for him,

with a rather lean, pointed sound that seems ideal for the conductor's conception.

Böhm has one of the best casts ever assembled for a recording of the work. Although she sang a wide range of dramatic-soprano roles, Inge Borkh was somewhat of a Strauss specialist, and Elektra was the role for which she was probably best known. Her voice is powerful and accurate, but unvaried in color; although she makes all of the obvious dramatic points, and has moments of stinging intensity, there is something curi-ously impersonal about her portrayal as a whole.

Marianne Schech, by contrast, is warm and direct as Chrysothemis; the listener feels that this woman would indeed make a loving wife and mother. Her lush, creamy voice tends to spread under pressure, but it's an attractive, healthy instrument, and a good match for the role.

Jean Madeira's dark-timbred mezzo has more of a true contralto quality to it than most Kly-tämnestras' voices, and she gives a powerful yet subtle account of the role.

For all his intelligence and application to the task, Dietrich Fischer-Dieskau does not have the right kind of vocal heft for Orest. He is in good voice on this set, though, and—as one might expect—he does a great deal with subtle inflections (e.g., the conscious irony of "Ich war so alt wie er, und sein Gefährte bei Tag und Nacht").

Fritz Uhl is a fine Aegisth, who sings the part more securely than most, and manages to sug-gest the unpleasant side of the character without lapsing into caricature.

Like so many of DG's early-stereo opera sets, this one places the solo voices too far forward, the orchestra too far in the background, for the balances and perspectives to be altogether natu-ral.

1966–67 DECCA / LONDON (S) CD

Birgit Nilsson (A), Marie Collier (B), Regina Resnik (C), Gerhard Stolze (D), Tom Krause (E), Vienna State Opera Chorus, Vienna Phil-harmonic Orchestra—Georg Solti

The first uncut recording of the opera, this set would be a welcome addition to the catalogue for that reason alone, but the performance has not worn very well. Individual episodes are extremely well executed by conductor and orchestra alike, but for some reason they fail to cohere—there is little sense of the action building toward a climax, of one scene flowing inevitably and seamlessly into the next. Perhaps this is simply one of the dangers of assembling an operatic recording from many isolated "takes," taped over a period of time.

The recording preserves two of the great operatic impersonations of our time: Birgit Nilsson's Elektra and Regina Resnik's Klytämnestra. Nilsson's cool, steady, even soprano negotiates the heroine's music with complete security and ease. She is the only Elektra, in fact, who sings the role with room to spare—she sounds as though she would be delighted if the music took her even higher or lower, or required even more volume from her. But it would be unjust to imply that Nilsson brings nothing more than a big, exciting dramatic-soprano sound to the role. She does some beautiful soft singing (particularly in the Recognition Scene). And, while she is not quite the kind of intense, specific vocal actress that Varnay and Borkh can be at their best, Nilsson is good at projecting Elektra's resentment, bitter irony, and tenderness.

Resnik's Klytämnestra was probably recorded a few years past its absolute best: here, her sound is not always as full or steady as it could be. But it is still a major voice, used with great skill, and as an interpreter Resnik is in a class by herself: hers is a uniquely three-dimensional portrayal, with all of the seemingly contradictory elements of the queen's character in perfect balance.

Marie Collier made few recordings, so it's too bad that this one shows her to such poor advantage. She obviously has good ideas about the character of Chrysothemis, but her singing is small-scaled, shrill, and tremulous—and of course these deficiencies are all the more apparent when set beside Nilsson's security.

Tom Krause is a rather neutral Orest—a good voice, and a careful artist, but he seems to be feeling his way through the part. Even if we concede, for the purposes of argument, that

Aegisth is basically a character part (and I disagree), Gerhard Stolze's wildly exaggerated, camped-up portrayal is an embarrassment. I'm sure Strauss wanted, at a minimum, accurate rhythms and recognizable pitches from the singer, and Stolze's ugly, out-of-tune vocalism simply wrecks the music.

I have reservations about Decca's relentlessly hi-fi sound, in which what is supposed to be a quiet woodwind solo can seem as loud as Nilsson in full cry. Some of the "staging" effects are ludicrous. Klytämnestra's offstage laughter, after her exit, is bounced off the walls of an echo chamber, and sounds comical rather than sinister as a result. But this is nothing compared to the producer's literal-minded response to the stage direction, a moment later, "Chrysothemis enters, running, through the gate of the courtyard, howling loudly like a wounded beast." Here Ms. Collier's voice is turned inside out with electronic distortion, so that the sounds she emits resemble the bleating of a demented sheep. It is, hands down, the silliest special effect I have ever heard in thirty years of listening to recorded opera.

1984 RODOLPHE (S,D,P) CD

Ute Vinzing (A), Leonie Rysanek (B), Maureen Forrester (C), Horst Hiestermann (D), Bent Norup (E), Radio France Chorus, National Orchestra of France—Christof Perick

This broadcast recording of a January 14, 1984, concert performance is uneven in quality, but often quite exciting. Christof Perick has the score well in hand: although his tempos are not rushed, he keeps the adrenalin flowing and builds the climaxes surely. There are thoughtful touches in his reading, such as the *portamento* phrasing in Elektra's dance (which takes on a surreal Viennese waltz quality as a result). Despite a few misfires from the brass section—forgivable, considering the "live" circumstances—the orchestra plays well, with particularly strong wind and percussion work.

Ute Vinzing sings the title role accurately and without audible strain—in itself, no mean accomplishment. She also has a good basic grasp of the character, conveying stoic determination, if not much else—there is little real tenderness in her Recognition Scene, for example. But her rather steely voice is dull and gray in timbre, and turns oddly colorless at low volume levels. She is an impressive Elektra, but not an overwhelming one.

The Rodolphe recording was made about a decade too late to catch Rysanek at her best. She sings with her unique impulsiveness and generosity, but the creamy timbre has thickened and the voice responds sluggishly, as though not properly warmed up. There are some effortful moments, and some exaggerated emphases. Interestingly, Rysanek does her best singing in the final scene—some sort of overdrive seems to have kicked in, the years fall away, and she partners Vinzing excitingly in their duet.

Maureen Forrester sings strongly as Klytämnestra, with a more attractive tonal quality than most interpreters of the part. Some of her German vowels are strange, though, with an exaggeratedly dark, covered coloration.

Bent Norup is another dull Orest, who doesn't sing *legato* but emits one distinct note at a time; Horst Hiestermann, however, is a bright-toned, incisive Aegisth.

The digital engineering is good. The orchestra comes dangerously close to drowning out the singers in some of the climaxes, but that is no doubt an accurate reflection of the way this opera sounds in actual performance. Annoyingly, these CDs contain no direct-access points whatsoever—each disc is a single, uninterrupted track.

1988 PHILIPS (S,D,P) CD

Hildegard Behrens (A), Nadine Secunde (B), Christa Ludwig (C), Ragnar Ulfung (D), Jorma Hynninen (E), Tanglewood Festival Chorus, Boston Symphony Orchestra—Seiji Ozawa

This recording is a composite, drawn from rehearsals and two Boston Symphony concert performances in November 1988, plus subsequent patch-up sessions. The real star of the performance is the Boston Symphony: the orchestral playing is on the highest level, actually more focused and dynamically varied than the Vienna Philharmonic's under Solti, for example.

Seiji Ozawa takes full advantage of the superb ensemble he has at his disposal. This is a broad, expansive, surprisingly lyrical reading of the opera, more emotional than Böhm's, but much less hard-driven and revved-up than Solti's; it resembles Reiner's. Ozawa and the Bostonians remind us that long stretches of this score are actually quite delicately instrumented.

Hildegard Behrens's Elektra amounts to a shrewd vocal compromise. Her voice is a couple of sizes too small for the part to begin with, and her sustained tones can turn tight or wobbly under pressure. The lack of true vocal freedom actually hurts her interpretation—the timbre, however sensitively manipulated, is monochromatic, and there are patches of indistinct enunciation.

On the positive side, she is an uncommonly youthful, vulnerable-sounding Elektra—the listener really gets a sense of a gentle young girl driven to desperation. And Behrens is a genuinely imaginative recreative artist, who never does anything routine.

I wish that Christa Ludwig could have recorded Klytämnestra ten or fifteen years earlier, when her voice was still both powerful and tonally sumptuous. The instrument is simply less "alive" than it once was: she sounds hard-pressed at the beginning and the end of her scene, and does her best singing during the insinuating, conversational exchanges in the middle. Interpretively, she is very strong—creating a believable (indeed a sympathetic) woman, not a monster.

As Chrysothemis, Nadine Secunde displays a warm, round tone and plenty of power; she's a musical singer, and pays attention to textual values. It's just that, compared to Behrens and Ludwig, she doesn't always project her character as vividly as one would like.

Jorma Hynninen, on the other hand, interacts perfectly with Behrens in the Recognition Scene. And it's good to have some commercial documentation of one of Ragnar Ulfung's roles: his mercifully unexaggerated Aegisth is well above the recorded average.

As "live" recordings go, this set is a superior

example of the genre from the engineering standpoint. The sound is full, clear, and well balanced.

1990 EMI / ANGEL (S,D) CD

Eva Marton (A), Cheryl Studer (B), Marjana Lipovšek (C), Hermann Winkler (D), Bernd Weikl (E), Bavarian Radio Chorus and Symphony Orchestra—Wolfgang Sawallisch

Despite the presence of an impressive cast, this fine performance is dominated by Wolfgang Sawallisch's conducting. Even though some of his tempo choices are on the fast side for my taste, his is the most distinguished account of the score on records. Every instrumental detail seems to fall effortlessly into place, and the music builds logically and inexorably toward its true climax, Elektra's collapse at the end of her dance. This kind of control and shaping is difficult enough to achieve in the theater; it is altogether extraordinary on a recording made under studio conditions. Sawallisch reproduces the composer's dynamic markings more faithfully than any other conductor (with the possible exception of Ozawa); there is a lot of beautiful quiet playing (and singing) on this set. As a result of this general restraint, the violent outbursts make an even greater impact than usual. Sawallisch also makes an even better case than does Solti for the opening of the stage cuts.

Eva Marton gives an intelligent, musical account of the title role. Vocally, her performance is somewhat of a compromise: she has to work hard for some of the loud high notes, and sustained tones can develop a hint of a beat. Marton doesn't possess Nilsson's power or Behrens's subtlety, but her big, voluptuous soprano is a more attractive instrument than Varnay's or Borkh's. Interpretively, she is strong—fierce and angry, but good at suggesting that Elektra has

gentler emotions that she is forcing herself to suppress.

Cheryl Studer's bright, well-focused soprano is not quite the kind of lush, womanly sound one longs to hear in Chrysothemis's music, but she is a remarkably accurate singer (her intonation is virtually flawless), and the intensity of her portrayal never threatens to spill over into hysteria.

Marjana Lipovšek, another resourceful artist, follows Resnik's and Ludwig's example by making Klytämnestra a believable woman rather than a monster, and she actually vocalizes the part more firmly and smoothly than either of her distinguished predecessors.

Bernd Weikl, an uneven singer, gives one of his best recorded performances here: his Orest sounds grave but not excessively lugubrious, and his inflections rival Fischer-Dieskau's in their subtlety. Hermann Winkler is an excellent Aegisth, singing with a bright, attractive tone and conveying just the right combination of smugness and exasperation in his exchanges with Elektra.

The digital engineering is superb, with a realistic dynamic range and great clarity.

———————

The Decca / Solti set has Nilsson and Resnik, and good orchestral work, but not much else. This is one of the rare instances in which the most recent, sonically up-to-date recording of an opera can be recommended without serious reservations: the EMI / Sawallisch set is a distinguished production in every respect. It is definitely the *Elektra* to begin with, or to add to an existing collection as a supplemental version.

If one can accept dated (but hardly inadequate) analogue sound, the DG / Böhm version holds up extremely well as a performance.

ROLAND GRAEME

Richard Strauss

Der Rosenkavalier (1911)

A: Sophie (s); B: The Marschallin (s); C: Octavian (s or ms);
D: Faninal (bar); E: Baron Ochs (bs)

With its large orchestra and cast, *Der Rosenkavalier* is an expensive opera to record. There have been twelve "complete" commercial versions—not exactly a shortage, of course, but not quite as many rival sets as one might expect, given the work's great popularity.

On records, this opera depends so much upon great orchestral playing if it is to make its effect that the monophonic sets are at a serious disadvantage: they simply cannot reproduce the instrumental writing as satisfactorily as a good stereo recording can.

The score also makes such obvious technical demands on the conductor that it is no surprise that most of the recordings have been led by established maestros. Before taking up the challenge, a conductor must first decide what *kind* of an opera this is. Is *Der Rosenkavalier* a boisterous farce? A sentimental comedy of manners, with serious undertones? A glittering, three-part symphonic poem with vocal lines superimposed on the elaborate orchestral textures? The best recorded versions acknowledge all three of these elements and attempt to strike a balance amongst them. There are also certain passages in the opera (particularly in Acts II and III) that sound manufactured rather than truly inspired, and it is the conductor's job to persuade us that they are every bit as effective as the famous highlights.

Der Rosenkavalier is a long opera, and Strauss authorized cuts in the score; in fact, uncut performances are a rarity in the theater. Of the twelve recordings, only five are truly complete: the 1954 Decca / Kleiber, the 1958 DG / Böhm, the 1968–69 Decca / Solti, the 1976 Philips / De Waart, and the 1990 EMI / Haitink. The standard cuts are made on the other recordings.

Some *Rosenkavalier* performance traditions are so deeply ingrained that they might as well be notated in the score. For example, most Octavians distort their voices with nasality, or sing flat, or both, as part of their impersonation of "Mariandel." All four of the recordings of the opera made with the Vienna Philharmonic respect a curious Viennese tradition in Act III: when Annina, pretending to be the Baron's wife, sings "Die Kaiserin muss ihn mir wiedergeben!," with an extravagant unaccompanied cadenza up and down the scale on the word "Kaiserin," the orchestral players sing or hum along with her. I have never heard, or seen in print, an explanation of how this tradition came about—i.e., why this particular passage, and none other, is singled out for such treatment. The effect can be heard very clearly on the CBS / Bernstein set (in all formats), and is faintly audible on the CD transfers of the Decca / Kleiber, Decca / Solti, and DG / Karajan sets—in each case, a good test of one's playback equipment.

1939 MET (M,P)

Marita Farell (A), Lotte Lehmann (B), Risë Stevens (C), Friedrich Schorr (D), Emanuel

List (E), Metropolitan Opera Chorus and Orchestra—Artur Bodanzky

This January 7, 1939, Metropolitan Opera broadcast was preserved on acetate discs: the sound is dim (and occasionally distorted), but will not deter any listener who is interested in hearing the famous singers. All of the standard cuts are observed, as well as many decidedly non-standard ones. Particularly jolting is the omission, in Act III, of twelve pages of full score. Artur Bodanzky has an interesting way of underlining some of the instrumental motifs, but on the whole his conducting is too quick and nervous for my taste: the music is rarely given a chance to settle down and sink in. Some of the orchestral work is scrappy, even after allowance is made for the live-performance circumstances.

Of the principals, the real standout is Friedrich Schorr, an uncommonly rich-voiced Faninal, but also a well-characterized one. Risë Stevens sounds young and ardent as Octavian, although the actual vocal quality is not as plush as one might wish. In Act III, her nasal whining as the drunken Mariandel elicits delighted laughter from the audience.

Lotte Lehmann was probably not in her best vocal form on this afternoon. She brings her customary verbal acuity to the Marschallin, but her big, warm voice seems to be moving rather sluggishly much of the time, and there are some uneasy ascents into the upper register. She does her best work here in the monologue, which is both pointed *and* beautifully sung.

Emanuel List undeniably gives the Met audience its money's worth, but is a rather crude Ochs. He is very free with the musical notation, often lapsing into *parlando* effects and embellishing his big scenes (especially in Act III) with many spoken ad libs. The end of Act II is more acted than sung by him.

Marita Farell is a disappointing Sophie. She makes an attractive sound in the middle register, so long as the music moves slowly enough to allow her to form her notes—thus the two duets with Octavian are effective. In rapid conversational passages, her sound turns hectic. Worst

of all, her high notes are effortful, which quite spoils the scene of the Presentation of the Rose.

There is an excellent supporting cast.

1944 VOX (M,P)

Adele Kern (A), Viorica Ursuleac (B), Georgine von Milinkovic (C), Georg Hann (D), Ludwig Weber (E), Bavarian State Opera Chorus and Orchestra—Clemens Krauss

This broadcast recording of an April 1944 concert performance of the opera is not very good from the technical standpoint—the sound on Vox's LP pressings is murky throughout, and occasionally suffers from distortion in the climaxes. As a result, it is impossible to judge fairly the orchestra's contribution—too much of the instrumental detail is simply inaudible. One can hear tempos, however, and it is obvious that Clemens Krauss is taking a brisk, unsentimental approach to the score, with razor-sharp definition of some of the accompanimental figurations. Interestingly, Krauss performs Act I complete (i.e., Ochs sings all of his narration), and opens two of the usual cuts in Act III; he makes the standard cuts in Act II.

Two members of the cast are outstanding. Ludwig Weber, as Ochs, is in firm, resonant voice, and strikes just the right balance between haughtiness and vulgarity. With his rock-solid baritone, Georg Hann is an enormously impressive Faninal, threatening to steal the show at his every appearance.

Viorica Ursuleac, Krauss's wife, was a great favorite with Strauss and with German audiences. She must have possessed a personal magnetism that does not come through on her many records, most of which are dull. Her Marschallin is no exception. Ursuleac's voice is a good-sized soprano, but decidedly tough in timbre; she belts out the high notes, and there is enough hootiness and strain in her tonal production even in the middle register to compromise many of the composer's carefully calculated effects.

As Octavian, Georgine von Milinkovic displays a solid mezzo, a little heavy and monotonously dark in color to be ideal for the role.

The Sophie, Adele Kern, sings prettily with a small, relatively colorless voice.

Except for Franz Klarwein's Italian Tenor, the other singers are a surprisingly mediocre lot.

1950 ACANTA (M)

Ursula Richter (A), Margarete Bäumer (B), Tiana Lemnitz (C), Hans Löbel (D), Kurt Böhme (E), Dresden State Opera Chorus, Saxon State Orchestra—Rudolf Kempe

Rudolf Kempe was a fine Strauss conductor, and we must regret that he recorded so few of the composer's operas. His conducting is the major strength of this disappointing version: tempos are relaxed enough to allow clear articulation, and the Dresden orchestra (though wretchedly reproduced) seems to be supplying a warm, idiomatic sound. In Act I, the second of the two standard cuts in the Baron's narration is opened. Kempe observes the usual cuts in Act II, and abridges the Act III interrogation scene somewhat differently than do most other conductors, opening one cut but making two others of his own.

The singing is, for the most part, quite terrible. Margarete Bäumer has a big, steely soprano under imperfect control; no doubt miscast as the Marschallin to begin with, she also sounds past her prime here. Her high notes are hit or miss and her intonation unreliable. Tiana Lemnitz, who might have been a fine Octavian a decade earlier, also shows her age—her silvery timbre has tarnished badly and her voice is often pinched and effortful. The Act I scenes between the two lovers are decidedly short of ardor, with this pair of senior citizens struggling through the music.

The Sophie, Ursula Richter, has a hard, narrow timbre and is utterly charmless.

The Ochs of the young Kurt Böhme is not without interest: his big, black bass moves easily through the music, although he tends to be monotonously loud and his characterization does not seem fully formed. He is much better on his later recording (see below).

The sound is poor, with a dim, distant orchestra and overmiked singers.

1954 DECCA / LONDON (M) CD

Hilde Gueden (A), Maria Reining (B), Sena Jurinac (C), Alfred Poell (D), Ludwig Weber (E), Vienna State Opera Chorus, Vienna Philharmonic Orchestra—Erich Kleiber

Ever since its initial release, this recording has been considered something special. The performance is uncut, which is a true advantage. Strauss may have been a Bavarian, and Der Rosenkavalier may have had its premiere in Dresden, but the Austrians consider the opera to be their personal property, and on this recording the Vienna Philharmonic stakes its claim to the score with playing of virtuosity, warmth, and refinement.

Beginning with a brilliant but never hard-driven or harsh-sounding account of the Act I Prelude, Erich Kleiber makes just about every interpretive point that could be made with this score, and does so with unobtrusive mastery. He seems to have taken to heart the composer's own prescription for a successful performance of the opera: "Light, flowing tempos, but not so rapid that the singers must gabble their words." Under Kleiber's baton, the music unfolds with a true sense of inevitability.

There is a good cast, led by the Octavian of Sena Jurinac—a touching and vocally skilled assumption. Her Viennese accent is more authentic than any other Octavian's, and she always sounds like an aristocrat; her Mariandel is funny without being exaggerated. Hilde Gueden has a more substantial voice than most of the Sophies on records, and this is one of her most direct and unaffected performances.

Maria Reining, the Marschallin, is usually described by critics as being past her prime on this set, and certainly her tone thins out in the upper register at times. But her voice—a lyric soprano, without the lushness of timbre we often hear in the part—still has an attractive gleam, and moves easily and confidently through the conversational passages. Her approach to the character is interestingly humorous and ironic, with a minimum of sentimentality.

Weber, caught late in his career, has some uncomfortable moments but is a resourceful enough artist to disguise them fairly successfully. His Ochs is wonderfully human—a classic portrayal.

The sound holds up well, particularly on the CD reissue. The engineering is on the conservative side, even for its date—there are other monophonic recordings of complete operas from this period that manage to do more with perspectives and thus create the illusion of movement about a stage.

1956 EMI / ANGEL (S) CD

Teresa Stich-Randall (A), Elisabeth Schwarzkopf (B), Christa Ludwig (C), Eberhard Wächter (D), Otto Edelmann (E), Philharmonia Chorus and Orchestra—Herbert von Karajan

There is undoubtedly something synthetic about this recording, but many of the component parts are extraordinary. Herbert von Karajan makes only the first of the two cuts in the Baron's Act I narration, and opens one of the standard cuts in Act II; Act III, though, is tightened up in the usual manner. Karajan seems to approach the score as pure music, in the sense that he downplays both the boisterousness and the sentimentality. He is even more scrupulous than Kleiber in observing the composer's dynamic markings, especially where quiet playing is called for. The reading is beautifully executed by the Philharmonia Orchestra of London, which need not take a back seat to any orchestra—including the Vienna Philharmonic—in this music.

The singers are an oddly assorted group, and it is a tribute to Karajan that he is able to pull them into a cohesive ensemble. The Marschallin was Elisabeth Schwarzkopf's most famous operatic role, and she left her mark on it—many younger sopranos have clearly been influenced by her interpretation. She can be accused of overinflecting the text (although Hofmannsthal, who had a healthy ego, probably would have insisted that this isn't possible; and Strauss himself, in a note in the score, advises the conductor to reduce the number of strings in any passage where the audibility of the words requires it). Whatever reservations one may

harbor about her approach, she is in good voice here, and the recording does the purely aural aspects of her performance justice.

Christa Ludwig is a strong Octavian, although I wish that she could have recorded the part a few years later, when her voice had developed a uniquely soft, velvety quality not always in evidence here—some of her high notes have a hard edge to them on this set.

Teresa Stich-Randall, though American by birth, sounds like an archetypical Viennese soprano as Sophie—a cold, white, vibrato-less tone; a tendency to attack notes just a shade flat for expressive effect; and oddly mannered enunciation, with heavily covered vowel sounds. In its idiosyncratic way, hers is a beautiful performance, but at times she almost seems to be doing a Schwarzkopf imitation.

Otto Edelmann sings Ochs richly and with a wealth of interpretive detail, although he indulges in too much of the traditional coarse bluster for my taste.

The recording was originally issued in mono, but was also taped in experimental stereo, and soon reissued on LP in the two-channel format. The CD transfer is a digital remastering of the stereo tapes, and is a fine technical job in every respect.

1958 DEUTSCHE GRAMMOPHON (S)

Rita Streich (A), Marianne Schech (B), Irmgard Seefried (C), Dietrich Fischer-Dieskau (D), Kurt Böhme (E), Dresden State Opera Chorus, Saxon State Orchestra—Karl Böhm

Karl Böhm, like Kleiber, performs the score absolutely complete. In some other respects, Böhm's performance is quite different. An experienced Straussian, he is less warm and outgoing than Kleiber, and consistently refuses to serve up the glut of emotion that some other conductors consider *de rigueur* in this music; Böhm also prefers a drier, more astringent palette of instrumental colors. In Act I, in fact, Böhm is frankly a little too restrained for my taste. His Act II is noteworthy for a really ravishing Presentation of the Rose; later on in the act, Strauss's sly exercise in self-parody—when the orchestra explodes into the *Elektra* idiom after Ochs's wounding—is amusing, but always sounds like music, rather than noise, thanks to the conductor's control. In Act III, Böhm is just about perfect.

He has a fine orchestra to work with. The opera, of course, had its premiere in Dresden, and the members of the Staatskapelle Dresden (which, at the time this recording was made, was still billing itself as the "Saxon State Orchestra") seem determined to prove that they can play the score as accurately and beautifully as their Vienna and London rivals.

All three sopranos are good, and their voices are well contrasted to one another. Marianne Schech, though animated, doesn't attempt to "act with her voice" in the detailed Schwarzkopf manner. In Act I she is lively, with a hint of motherliness toward Octavian; in Act III she is comparatively straightforward and unsentimental. Her singing is always warm, full, and attractive in quality.

By this date, Irmgard Seefried's silvery timbre had darkened a bit, and the highest notes of the part are not quite ideally free or clear. She also has a habit of singing just under the pitch for "expressive" effect that may bother some listeners. But she is an appealing Octavian, and her impersonation of Mariandel is amusing and unexaggerated.

Rita Streich is a superlative Sophie—a bright, sweet high soprano that never turns thin or shrill, with plenty of body even in the bottom register, and a sure, touching projection of character.

Böhme improves upon his earlier recording of Ochs. The singing is not perfect—the voice is nasal in timbre, some of the high notes seem pushed, and the phrasing can be short on *legato*—but it is always big and dark and imposing in quality, and his impersonation now has just the right touch of rustic coarseness and lechery.

As might be expected, Dietrich Fischer-Dieskau is an uncommonly specific Faninal—whether fawning over Ochs in Act II or sputtering away in frustration and indignation in Act III.

DG's clean, ungimmicked sound has held up well on LP.

1968–69 DECCA / LONDON (S) CD

Helen Donath (A), Régine Crespin (B), Yvonne Minton (C), Otto Wiener (D), Manfred Jungwirth (E), Vienna State Opera Chorus, Vienna Philharmonic Orchestra—Georg Solti

In some ways, this recording is an even more impressive overall achievement than the earlier Decca set. Sir Georg Solti, like Kleiber and Böhm, opens all the stage cuts. Solti's interpretation is warmer and more expansive than Böhm's, more intense than Kleiber's—a distinguished account of the score. The Vienna Philharmonic plays well even by its own high standards.

Best of all, Solti was given a superb cast to work with. Régine Crespin's soft, voluptuous voice, which takes on a hint of an edge only on some of the loud high notes, fills out the Marschallin's music beautifully. Her portrayal is, in its way, as richly conceived and carefully executed as Schwarzkopf's, but seems much more spontaneous.

With her rich mezzo, easy command of German, and lively response to the various dramatic situations, Yvonne Minton is one of the most satisfying Octavians on records. She is ideally paired with Helen Donath, a Sophie pure and radiant of voice, who nevertheless always sounds like a warm, believable human being.

Manfred Jungwirth brings an overpowering Viennese accent to Ochs, along with many inflections, some of them subtle, others not. He sounds, at times, like the bass register's answer to Schwarzkopf. The voice is a fine one, though—lighter in timbre and more baritonal in quality than that of most other Ochses, and supple enough to avoid ponderousness.

Decca has cast the other roles with its customary care. Luciano Pavarotti perhaps makes too much of a star turn out of the Italian Tenor's aria, but is in fine voice.

This is still one of the best-engineered recordings of the complete opera: sumptuous sound, with many subtle "stereo staging" effects. There are instrumental details which can be heard more clearly than on any other version. If anything, the orchestra *as recorded* is too loud at times, but most listeners will not find this objectionable.

The original LP set is noteworthy for containing one of the thickest and most luxurious booklets ever provided with an operatic recording—a true collector's item. The booklet supplied with the CD reissue is Spartan by comparison, although it contains the essentials.

1971 CBS / SONY (S) CD

Lucia Popp (A), Christa Ludwig (B), Gwyneth Jones (C), Ernst Gutstein (D), Walter Berry (E), Vienna State Opera Chorus, Vienna Philharmonic Orchestra—Leonard Bernstein

Because this recording was based on a Vienna State Opera production, it observes all of the standard cuts, and in fact makes two further brief excisions during the Police Commissioner's inquiry in Act III.

Leonard Bernstein takes a rather slow, luxuriant, overtly emotional approach to the score—an effective reading, although very different from Böhm's crispness; the Vienna Philharmonic responds to Bernstein's leadership as wholeheartedly as it did to Kleiber's and Solti's.

Of the principals, only Gwyneth Jones's Octavian is disappointing. Despite her obvious good intentions, the soprano's singing is often hooty and effortful, and her enunciation can be indistinct; as Mariandel, furthermore, she indulges in too much off-pitch whining for my taste.

Christa Ludwig has switched from Octavian to the Marschallin, and does some extraordinary things with the role. Except for some edginess at the very top, her mezzo-soprano fills out the music with warm, sumptuous tone, and the dark coloration automatically gives her Marschallin maturity and dignity. A fine artist, Ludwig knows the value of understatement, and scores one subtle point after another.

Walter Berry's Ochs manages to be funny while avoiding most of the traditional exaggerations.

Lucia Popp is one of the most satisfying Sophies on records, combining a bright, sweet, but full-bodied sound with a strong projection of the girl's willful character. Ernst Gutstein is a good Faninal, although the actual quality of his voice is more penetrating than beautiful.

Plácido Domingo, who was brought in just for the recording, cannot be accused of singing badly; but in fact his voice is too large and dark to make the right effect in the aria.

The sound is good, but not as impressively full or detailed as that of the stereo Decca set.

1976 PHILIPS (S)

Ruth Welting (A), Evelyn Lear (B), Frederica von Stade (C), Derek Hammond-Stroud (D), Jules Bastin (E), Helmond Concert Choir, Netherlands Opera Chorus, Rotterdam Philharmonic Orchestra—Edo de Waart

Made in conjunction with a 1976 Holland Festival production, this studio recording shows every sign of careful preparation, and preserves some individual performances of distinction, but somehow the totality is less persuasive than the best of the competitive versions. Edo de Waart, like Kleiber, Böhm, and Solti, performs the score absolutely complete, and his reading recalls Böhm's in its clarity and logic. The Rotterdam Philharmonic Orchestra is obviously not the Concertgebouw of Amsterdam, let alone the Vienna Philharmonic, but it is a good enough ensemble to realize de Waart's conception with some force. The recorded sound is excellent.

So what's wrong? For one thing, the supporting cast is made up almost entirely of Dutch singers. There are some good voices among them, but most of these people sing German with pronounced Dutch accents. As a result, the listener is transported, in his imagination, from Vienna to Rotterdam often enough to be distracted.

Although the principals work well together as a team, often conveying a real sense of dramatic interaction, the vocalism is uneven in quality. The best by far is Frederica von Stade—who may, in fact, be the best Octavian on any of the complete sets. Her voice is close to ideal in weight and timbre for the role, and she immerses herself in the character with a combination of aristocratic poise and vulnerability that makes her Octavian extraordinarily sympathetic.

Evelyn Lear's Marschallin resembles Schwarzkopf's in its arch inflections and sophistication; unfortunately, she has intonational problems, and her upper register is always very careful. Ruth Welting, a specialist in the high coloratura repertory, sounds a little brittle and monochromatic in Sophie's music.

The Ochs of Jules Bastin is barely adequate: Bastin is a shrewd artist who does a great deal with the words, but his voice is short in range for this part, being deficient both at the bottom and the top; in addition, too much of his singing is rough-edged, unsteady, and noticeably off-pitch. José Carreras, in resplendent voice, gives an above-average account of the Italian Tenor's aria.

1982 DEUTSCHE GRAMMOPHON (S,D) CD

Janet Perry (A), Anna Tomowa-Sintow (B), Agnes Baltsa (C), Gottfried Hornik (D), Kurt Moll (E), Vienna State Opera Chorus, Vienna Philharmonic Orchestra—Herbert von Karajan

Based on a Salzburg Festival production, this recording is very beautifully executed, but Karajan fails to match the achievement of the EMI set. The conductor goes even farther than before in his search for euphony and transparency; the Vienna Philharmonic, once again in fine form, produces a light, silvery sound, with homogenized woodwind timbres and airy strings—very different from the plush sonority heard on the Kleiber, Solti, and Bernstein sets. Karajan's tempos are often slower than before, and he brings off many memorable effects. Act III, for example, begins and ends magnificently: the prelude has a quicksilver playfulness, while the trio and duet are as hushed and magical as one could wish. But too many of the edges have been smoothed away; there is no rhythmic spine, no bite, no variety to the attacks or the phrasing.

There is a *good* cast, in the sense that everybody sings attractively and accurately, but few of these people project much individuality. Anna Tomowa-Sintow, for example, sings really

beautifully as the Marschallin, but her personality seems subdued. From a purely vocal point of view, Kurt Moll is the best Ochs on records—the vocalism is astonishingly secure, controlled, and dead-accurate in intonation; he also does far more with subtle dynamic shadings than most interpreters of the part. But his Ochs is, quite simply, too much of a gentleman: while a certain degree of restraint is welcome, there is no bawdiness or crudity in Moll's portrayal at all, and as a result the opera's plot ceases to be plausible.

Agnes Baltsa is a surprisingly unsuccessful Octavian: her voice sounds hard and narrow in timbre, her singing is too aggressive in the climaxes, and her German is unidiomatic. Janet Perry is a pleasant Sophie, but a subdued one, lacking vocal allure and animation of delivery. Vinson Cole's high, sweet lyric tenor meets the requirements of the Italian Tenor's aria almost perfectly, and he makes a better effect in the piece than do most of his superstar competitors.

Karajan now observes all of the standard stage cuts, so this version is marginally less complete than even the EMI set. The digital sound is clear, but has some odd balances and perspectives—there is an uncomfortably claustrophobic acoustic in the scene of the Presentation of the Rose, for example, with no sense of air or space around the closely miked voices and instruments.

1985 DENON (S,D,P) CD

Margot Stejskal (A), Ana Pusar-Joric (B), Ute Walther (C), Rolf Haunstein (D), Theo Adam (E), Dresden State Opera Chorus and Orchestra—Hans Vonk

Der Rosenkavalier had its premiere in the Semper Opera House in Dresden on January 26, 1911. The theater was gutted by Allied bombs during World War II and took forty years to rebuild. It reopened with a performance of Weber's *Der Freischütz* in 1985, and appropriately, *Der Rosenkavalier* was the next work to be performed. Denon is a little evasive about what is actually heard on the finished sets; the recordings apparently were made during the dress rehearsals of the operas "between January

7 and February 14," although there may be some inserts from the actual inaugural performances.

For a "live" recording, the digital sound on the *Rosenkavalier* set is good—almost too good, for it picks up the prompter's voice with annoying clarity, and there is an inordinate amount of stage noise.

Unfortunately, the performance isn't very good. The orchestra plays well, but Hans Vonk's conducting is shockingly insensitive and, at times, even inept. He manages to be hasty and rhythmically limp at one and the same time, and even the simplest tempo changes seem to defeat him. All of the standard cuts are made, by the way.

Nor is the cast, made primarily of local artists, particularly distinguished. Theo Adam, a native of Dresden and a great local favorite, brings intelligence and wit to Ochs, but his voice is very dry in timbre, often marginally unsteady, and relatively weak at the bottom. In addition, he has pitch problems. Even with his voice in such bad shape, Adam manages to "bring off" the role after a fashion—and I'm afraid he is the cream of the cast.

Ana Pusar-Joric has a pretty voice, a little flutey and unfocused; she is an appealing Marschallin, but has not yet begun to plumb the depths of the part. Neither the Octavian nor the Sophie is a match for the recorded competition. Ute Walther's mezzo is rough in quality and sounds strained on the high notes. Margot Stejskal is a tight-voiced, charmless Sophie. Their duets in Acts II and III are somewhat of a trial to listen to.

1990 EMI / ANGEL (S,D) CD

Barbara Hendricks (A), Kiri Te Kanawa (B), Anne Sofie von Otter (C), Franz Grundheber (D), Kurt Rydl (E), Dresden Kreuzchor, Dresden State Opera Chorus, Dresden State Orchestra—Bernard Haitink

We will have to live with this new *Rosenkavalier* for a while before deciding whether it is really as good as it seems at first hearing. It is uncut and exceptionally well recorded.

The Dresden orchestra has never sounded better on records; Bernard Haitink's approach to the opera resembles Karajan's in its seamless *legato* flow and translucent instrumental balances. Each act seems to consist of a single, enormously long, musical paragraph, effortlessly sustained and pointed toward its climax. Like Karajan, Haitink tends to underplay the more boisterous comic episodes in Acts II and III. In general, though, Haitink is quicker in tempo and more energetic in phrasing. This is operatic conducting on a very high level.

Kiri Te Kanawa has several advantages over some of her recorded rivals: her voice, almost ideal in weight and timbre for the Marschallin's music to begin with, is still very much in its prime. The upper register, in particular, is always easy, full, and floating. Furthermore, her extensive stage experience in the role shows; this is among her most carefully thought-out and imaginatively executed recorded portrayals. She is especially good in the light, teasing, seductive moments. There is emotion in her final renunciation of Octavian, but it is always contained.

Barbara Hendricks's pure, delicate, but never thin sound is consistently lovely to hear in Sophie's music. Sometimes her enunciation of the German seems a little careful, but it is always very clear. She makes the young girl sound not passive but determined and resourceful.

I hope it will not seem insulting if I suggest that Anne Sofie von Otter is the most masculine-sounding Octavian on any complete recording of the opera to date. By means of tasteful vocal colorations and a consistently energetic delivery of the words, she conveys aristocratic arrogance, sexual desire, and macho self-absorption. There is less vulnerability and introspection than usual in her portrayal. It is effortlessly well sung.

These three beautiful voices, individually excellent, unite in an uncommonly satisfying rendition of the Act III trio.

Kurt Rydl is a genuine bass—not an extended baritone—and fills out Ochs's music richly and securely. The close scrutiny of the microphone exaggerates his vibrato, but also reveals a convincingly fluent Viennese accent. His concept of the character is subtler than most, with many touches of sly humor.

What really distinguishes this production, though, is that all of the participants seem to have gone back to the libretto and score, and studied the opera from scratch, without preconceptions. The performers are respectful of tradition, but have not followed it slavishly.

EMI's abridged *Rosenkavalier* of 1933 is one of the few "legendary" operatic recordings that fully deserves its reputation. The excerpts add up to approximately half the score. Lehmann's Marschallin (definitely superior to her performance on the 1939 Met / Bodanzky set), Elisabeth Schumann's Sophie, and Richard Mayr's Ochs are all justly famous assumptions. Maria Olszewska's Octavian has always seemed to me to be a little heavy and unsmiling, but she too was a great singer. The orchestral work, by the Vienna Philharmonic, falls short of the standard set by the same ensemble on its LP-era sets, but Robert Heger (who lived long enough to make some fine stereo recordings of complete operas) conducts firmly and with obvious affection for the score.

There are six truly distinguished complete recordings. My personal favorites are the EMI / Karajan and CBS / Bernstein performances. Both of these recordings, it is true, are cut, and both are well, but not spectacularly, recorded.

But if there is room for only one *Rosenkavalier* in an opera collection, then it should probably be either the Decca / Solti set or the new EMI / Haitink version. Solti has a great orchestra and an impressive cast. The Decca production is a beautiful job in every respect and still sounds as fresh and exciting as it did when it was first released, twenty years ago.

The new EMI recording promises to wear just as well. Haitink is emotionally cooler than Solti, and this quality of restraint is shared by his Marschallin and Octavian (and even by the Ochs, though to a lesser extent). The orchestral work and the supporting cast could scarcely be improved upon.

ROLAND GRAEME

JEREMY ISAACS
General Director, Royal Opera House

1. **Puccini,** *La Bohème*: De los Angeles, Amara, Bjoerling, Merrill, Reardon, Tozzi—Beecham. EMI / ANGEL

2. **Mozart,** *Così Fan Tutte*: Schwarzkopf, Otto, Merriman, Simoneau, Panerai, Bruscantini—Karajan. EMI / ANGEL

3. **Mozart,** *Don Giovanni*: Souez, Helletsgrüber, Mildmay, von Pataky, Brownlee, Henderson, Baccaloni, Franklin—Busch. EMI / ANGEL

4. **Strauss,** *Ariadne auf Naxos*: Schwarzkopf, Streich, Seefried, Schock, Prey, Dönch—Karajan. EMI / ANGEL

5. **Rossini,** *Le Comte Ory*: Oncima, Barabas—Gui. EMI / ANGEL

6. **Beethoven,** *Fidelio*: Ludwig, Hallstein, Vickers, Unger, Berry, Frick, Crass—Klemperer. EMI / ANGEL

7. **Donizetti:** *Lucia di Lammermoor*: Callas, Tagliavini, Cappuccilli, Ladysz—Serafin. EMI / ANGEL

8. **Donizetti,** *Lucia di Lammermoor*: Sutherland, Pavarotti, Milnes, Ghiaurov—Bonynge. DECCA / LONDON

9. **Rossini,** *Il Barbiere di Siviglia*: Berganza, Alva, Prey, Montarsolo, Dara—Abbado. DEUTSCHE GRAMMOPHON

10. **Wagner,** *The Ring of the Nibelung*: Hunter, Curphey, Remedios, Bailey, Hammond-Stroud, Haugland—Goodall. EMI / ANGEL

Richard Strauss

Ariadne auf Naxos
(1912; revised 1916)

A: Prima Donna / Ariadne (s); B: Zerbinetta (s); C: Composer (s);
D: Tenor / Bacchus (t); E: Harlekin (bar); F: Music Master (bar)

*I*nseparable from its original context and therefore rarely played, the original *Ariadne* of 1912 served as the grand entertainment concluding Hofmannsthal's Teutonicization of Molière's *Le bourgeois gentilhomme*; to date it has received no commercial recording. (Beecham's 1950 Edinburgh performance, which has circulated on disc, is incomplete and uses a composite of the two versions of Zerbinetta's aria.) The free-standing 1916 revision, in which the opera is preceded by a Prologue that sets up the necessary confrontation of *opera seria* and *commedia dell'arte*, has become the modern version of choice. Above and beyond the extreme difficulty of the music (the range and laciness of Zerbinetta's aria, even in its simplified and abbreviated 1916 form; the strenuous tessitura of Bacchus's part; the intricate ensembles for the comedians; and the virtuoso chamber orchestra writing), performers of *Ariadne* face the challenge of unifying the considerable stylistic contrasts: conversational / lyrical, *buffo* / *seria*, Wagnerian / neoclassic pastiche. Nevertheless, the ensemble standards of recordings have proved to be remarkably high, perhaps because most of them originate in the longstanding Strauss centers of Vienna, Dresden, and Munich. All except the first recording below are note-complete.

1935 ACANTA (M,P) *(Opera only, without Prologue)*

Viorica Ursuleac (A), Erna Berger (B), Helge Rosvaenge (D), Karl Hammes (E), Stuttgart Radio Symphony Orchestra—Clemens Krauss

The earliest recordings feature some performers who worked with the composer himself. The Ariadne of 1935 Acanta (a radio performance that apparently omitted the Prologue), Viorica Ursuleac (Frau Clemens Krauss), created several Strauss roles, but her mealy-voiced, uncertainly tuned singing completely offsets a certain dramatic boldness of attack, and fails to explain her eminence; perhaps her stage presence did. A unique attraction of this set is Helge Rosvaenge's ringing Bacchus: he's the only tenor in the lot who completely commands the fundamentally unrealistic writing. Also treasurable are Erna Berger's enchanting, fastidiously embroidered Zerbinetta and Karl Hammes's highflying Harlekin. The other comedians are excellent musicians and lively singers, though the tenors are on the dry side; the nymphs (including a pre-Hollywood Miliza Korjus) are a soggy lot. (Both groups suffer from the tendency of the generally tolerable AM-quality broadcast sound to congest in ensembles and under pressure from high soprano notes.) Krauss guides the performance with an easy security, making less of the stylistic distinctions than more recent (and inevitably more style-conscious) conductors.

1944 DEUTSCHE GRAMMOPHON (M,P)

Maria Reining (A), Alda Noni (B), Irmgard Seefried (C), Max Lorenz (D), Erich Kunz (E), Paul Schöffler (F), Vienna Philharmonic Orchestra—Karl Böhm

Another chunk of history, this time a Viennese concert performance in the composer's presence, celebrating his eightieth birthday. Karl Böhm moves the music along in a theatrical way, and his cast is distinguished. Alda Noni's Zerbinetta has a more brilliant edge than Berger's, a little less charm; Maria Reining is a blandly creamy Ariadne—nothing wrong with the sound, but others have conveyed her plight more vividly. Though less polished technically than Rosvaenge, Max Lorenz is also an authentic *Heldentenor* Bacchus. In the Prologue, Irmgard Seefried, then only twenty-four and in her first Vienna season, is an intensely spontaneous and engaged Composer, the voice shining and vibrant; opposite her, Paul Schöffler's Music Master offers an endearing combination of paternal sternness and warmth. The occasionally murky and fuzzy sound transmits few subtleties of orchestral detail but quite enough to still project the sense of an event fashioned by experienced and committed hands.

1954 EMI / ANGEL (M) CD

Elisabeth Schwarzkopf (A), Rita Streich (B), Irmgard Seefried (C), Rudolf Schock (D), Hermann Prey (E), Karl Dönch (F), Philharmonic Orchestra—Herbert von Karajan

For many older listeners, this recording provided the first encounter with *Ariadne* (DG 1944 was not published until the 1960s), and it still seems a worthy representation, suffering not at all from the fact that it was put together from scratch in a London studio; the Philharmonic Orchestra plays gloriously, the solo horn lines nobly uttered by Dennis Brain. A decade later, Seefried's Composer remains compelling—if only the Music Master were again Schöffler, instead of Karl Dönch's caricature! Though she favors some curious vowel sounds, Elisabeth Schwarzkopf phrases generously and rises to Ariadne's climaxes fervently if now and then effortfully; this is less self-consciously fussy than her later Strauss recordings. Without matching Berger's detail of character or Noni's panache, Rita Streich is a fluent Zerbinetta. The *buffo* ensembles, led by the young Hermann Prey, are elegantly (perhaps too elegantly?) finished, the nymphs sweetly tuned; Hugues Cuénod contributes a refined cameo as the Dancing Master. Rudolf Schock, a faceless singer whose tenor has little ring, gets through the role of Bacchus, no more. Herbert von Karajan's preference for surface polish over rhythmic vitality exacts a toll on the work's contrasts. The sound of the CD edition has more dimension and a firmer bass than did the original Angel LPs.

1959 DECCA / LONDON (S)

Leonie Rysanek (A), Roberta Peters (B), Sena Jurinac (C), Jan Peerce (D), Walter Berry (E, F), Vienna Philharmonic Orchestra—Erich Leinsdorf

This first stereo version is less evenly cast than EMI's set. Its special adornment is Sena Jurinac's deeply felt Composer, not quite as secure vocally as Seefried's but comparably impetuous and vulnerable. With somewhat unkempt enthusiasm, Leonie Rysanek alternates glorious high phrases with hollow low and middle ones. Zerbinetta is limned accurately and with spirit by Roberta Peters, and musicianship and technical security get Jan Peerce through the role of Bacchus with reasonable success (if perhaps with more microphonic assistance than his competitors). Walter Berry doubles Harlekin and the Music Master, a little heavy at both. The Viennese ensemble teams are excellent, and Leinsdorf controls tempos and builds the climaxes of the final duet with a sure hand.

1968 EMI / ANGEL (S) CD

Gundula Janowitz (A), Sylvia Geszty (B), Teresa Zylis-Gara (C), James King (D), Hermann Prey (E), Theo Adam (F), Dresden State Orchestra—Rudolf Kempe

In the transparent, spacious ambience of this set, the orchestra really sounds like a chamber ensemble; the voices stand out, yet also participate in the chamber feeling. Thanks to the vertical clarity and the superb playing of the Dresden band, the harmonies always register truly and progress logically. Rudolf Kempe tends carefully to details: when the Dancing Master predicts the post-prandial stupor of the opera's audience, the *diminuendo* and the concomitant dampening of instrumental and rhythmic color amusingly and tellingly reinforce him. The pacing has ample line to sustain some very slow tempos, and musters pointed energy when needed. The Prologue plays theatrically and the Zerbinetta-Composer duet is ravishingly lucid. In the opera itself, orchestra and singers sustain a strong forward-moving line in the *seria* music, a polished but not over-suave verve in the *buffo* sections. Gundula Janowitz's silvery, verbally bland, ever-so-musical Ariadne, more instrumental than characterful, is nonetheless beguiling. Sylvia Geszty is less precise than her predecessors as Zerbinetta, James King makes a sturdy if unglamorous Bacchus, and Prey repeats his easy dealings with Harlekin's high tessitura. The last soprano among recorded Composers for two decades, Teresa Zylis-Gara makes less of the text than Seefried or Jurinac but sings fervently, and enjoys the collaboration of Theo Adam's dry, carefully characterized Music Master.

1969 DEUTSCHE GRAMMOPHON (S)

Hildegard Hillebrecht (A), Reri Grist (B), Tatiana Troyanos (C), Jess Thomas (D), Barry McDaniel (E), Dietrich Fischer-Dieskau (F), Bavarian Radio Symphony Orchestra—Karl Böhm

Böhm's studio recording is less successful than his 1944 concert version. The playing (abetted, perhaps, by the close recording) lacks refinement, and is often over-vigorous and clattery. Hildegard Hillebrecht is a pallid, mushy Ariadne who phrases squarely and sings flat much of the time, and Jess Thomas is a leathery Bacchus. On the plus side is Reri Grist's fluent Zerbinetta, and the Prologue comes to life between Fischer-Dieskau's amusingly fussy Music Master and the passionate Composer of Tatiana

Troyanos (a soprano would open up more easily into the ascending phrases, but Troyanos has always found this role exceptionally congenial). The *buffo* ensemble led by Barry McDaniel is vigorous but hardly subtle—characteristics of the entire performance, alas.

1977 DECCA / LONDON (S) CD

Leontyne Price (A), Edita Gruberova (B), Tatiana Troyanos (C), René Kollo (D), Barry McDaniel (E), Walter Berry (F), London Philharmonic Orchestra—Georg Solti

Georg Solti's rather monotonous leadership yields results no more satisfying than Böhm's remake—indeed, unlike 1954 EMI, this whole affair reeks of the studio. In the title role, Leontyne Price offers her accustomed intensity, neutralized by an unidiomatic stiffness as well as a voice that time has rendered dry and wooden of tone. René Kollo has to work hard at Bacchus; his saving grace is some awareness of the text's detail and meaning. Edita Gruberova's brittle Zerbinetta is accurate but charmless (on an Orfeo aria collection, she has also recorded the longer, higher-pitched, even more difficult 1912 version of "Großmächtige Prinzessin"). Repeaters in the cast are Troyanos, McDaniel, and Berry (this time as only the Music Master); except for the last mentioned, all are heard to better advantage in their earlier essays.

1986 DEUTSCHE GRAMMOPHON (S,D) CD

Anna Tomowa-Sintow (A), Kathleen Battle (B), Agnes Baltsa (C), Gary Lakes (D), Urban Malmberg (E), Hermann Prey (F), Vienna Philharmonic Orchestra—James Levine

Vienna is once again the site of an *Ariadne* recording, and under James Levine the orchestral playing is again sumptuous, the ensemble superior, though the individual voices of the comedians do not match the standards of earlier decades. Because the recorded sound is somewhat contrived in character and balance (different singers seem to come at us from different ambiences), the totality fails to satisfy despite many excellences, notably a degree of nuance in orchestral detail comparable to Kempe's. Anna Tomowa-Sintow's hefty soprano moves clumsily from note to note, and her high tones only reach full quality some time after they begin; the effortful and squealy singing coarsens the character. Opposite her, Gary Lakes sounds—not inappropriately for the dramatic situation—exceptionally fresh and naive; more comprehension of the text would be welcome, but the health and vigor of the singing are promising. Kathleen Battle's Zerbinetta ought to have been better; somehow the fine-grained filigree of the aria is too cautious, and in the *commedia dell'arte* ensembles she is occasionally swamped. Battle is best in the Prologue, opposite Agnes Baltsa's intelligent if inordinately chesty Composer. More than three decades after his first Harlekin, Prey is a fine Music Master, in splendid voice right up to top G-flat.

1988 PHILIPS (S,D) CD

Jessye Norman (A), Edita Gruberova (B), Julia Varady (C), Paul Frey (D), Olaf Bär (E), Dietrich Fischer-Dieskau (F), Leipzig Gewandhaus Orchestra—Kurt Masur

The Prologue's opening is encouraging, both orchestrally and sonically: fluent playing, a spacious but transparent acoustic (the piano's role in the textures is especially well registered). When voices enter, the instruments can still be heard around them, but the balance turns out to be excessively cautious, and eventually a good deal of orchestral tracery is simply masked. However, Masur keeps the varied materials of the Prologue flowing well, making smooth transitions in and out of the Major-Domo's spoken interjections (where Rudolf Asmus suggests amusement rather than the standard Viennese cynicism). Julia Varady's bright-toned, slightly accented Composer is prone to vehemence in the climaxes but is more appealing than Gruberova's Zerbinetta, harder of voice and even less endearing than in 1977 London. Alas, Fischer-Dieskau is now past conveying the warmer side of the Music Master. A certain metrical stiffness evident in the Prologue (particularly in cadenza-like instrumental solos and in the music of the Dancing Master, well sung by Martin Finke)

doesn't bode well for the extended *buffo* material later on. In fact, Masur and company are much more effective in the *seria* music, especially the final duet, where the conductor refuses to wallow—or let his singers wallow—in the lush tunes and harmonies. Singing with variety and spontaneity, Jessye Norman and Paul Frey bring their sometimes abstruse lines to life, and Masur's pacing clearly differentiates the levels of successive climaxes. Frey's voice, reasonably attractive in softer singing, sprouts an unattractive, obviously artificial resonance in the climaxes. Most of Norman's singing is rewardingly straightforward, if not always technically flawless in its *legato*; the monologue has energy and line, but also some gentleness. The nymphs sing cleanly and blend well. When Masur allows the mellifluous Olaf Bär such nice *rubato* in Harlekin's initial "Lieben, Hassen," our hopes are raised for the comedians, but thereafter their music, though neatly enough sung, is metrically stiff and mechanical, lacking the desired bounce. What's bracing for the mythological material is counter-productive in the *commedia dell'arte*.

(The CD editions of 1954 EMI and 1986 DG place the single sidebreak before Ariadne's "Es gibt ein Reich," 1988 Philips puts it afterward—neither ideal, but then, until CDs play for eighty minutes or more, the opera will have to be split at some inconvenient place. A more legitimate complaint: all three sets are stingy with indexes, leaving stretches well over ten minutes innocent of access points.)

In the complete sets, no Ariadne gets both words and lines of the monologue to soar quite as compellingly as the 78-rpm versions by Lotte Lehmann (on her EMI CD recital) and Maria Cebotari, though Schwarzkopf and Norman, in their different ways, both convince in the role as a whole. The most memorable individual performances are Berger's Zerbinetta, Seefried's and Jurinac's Composers, Rosvaenge's Bacchus, Prey's Harlekin, and Schöffler's Music Master. Krauss and Kempe realize more of the opera's range than any of the other conductors, but of course the former is incomplete and an antique.

Of the sets already on CD, no obvious champion can be discerned: the best sung is the mono 1954 EMI, the best played is the vocally uneven 1986 DG, while the real strengths of 1988 Philips are offset by the rigid treatment of the comedians. Not superior in any single element (except perhaps the sonic balance and perspective), Kempe's 1968 EMI probably represents the most rewarding combination of good qualities.

DAVID HAMILTON

RICHARD STRAUSS

DIE FRAU OHNE SCHATTEN (1919)

A: Empress (s); B: Dyer's Wife (s); C: Nurse (ms); D: Emperor (t); E: Barak (bar)

ichard Strauss liked to describe *Die Frau ohne Schatten (The Woman without a Shadow)* as his favorite among his operas—the sort of preference often felt by creative artists for works on which they lavished enormous care without commensurate public acclamation. This is undeniably one of Strauss's richest scores, one that encompasses delicate impressionistic orchestration, grand romantic spaciousness, and further steps along the harsh road explored by *Elektra*. Any questions about the opera's stature will likely focus on aspects of Hugo von Hofmannsthal's libretto; its mixture of mythic elements and use of symbols (even symbols of symbols) may not always sustain the weight he assigns them. Yet Hofmannsthal created a compelling tale of self-examination and integrity, perhaps all the more fascinating for its abundance of detail, and he inspired Strauss to write marvelous music for it. Its mysterious power can even draw doubters back again and again.

Given its enormous musical complexity, its strenuous vocal demands, and its unfamiliarity to audiences, it is not surprising, however regrettable, that *Die Frau ohne Schatten* has usually been abbreviated in performance. In his first recording Karl Böhm took half a dozen cuts; both DG live recordings—like most later productions—make sweeping curtailments, to damaging effect. Only the EMI and 1989 London recordings are complete.

1955 DECCA / LONDON (S) CD

Leonie Rysanek (A), Christel Goltz (B), Elisabeth Höngen (C), Hans Hopf (D), Paul Schöffler (E), Vienna State Opera Chorus, Vienna Philharmonic Orchestra—Karl Böhm

This studio recording (in genuine stereo, though not initially released as such), the result of a production for the reopening season of the Vienna State Opera, made *Die Frau ohne Schatten* available at a time when it was little known internationally. The recording's most consistent asset is the resplendent playing of the Vienna Philharmonic, with vibrant presence for each textural strand, a uniquely sumptuous brass sound, and magnificent solo work (as in the Act II cello mini-concerto). Supporting roles include such eminences as Emmy Loose (Guardian of the Threshold) and Kurt Böhme (Spirit Messenger).

Of the principal singers, the Empress and Barak afford greatest satisfaction. Leonie Rysanek, at the start of a lengthy reign as Empress of choice in the world's opera houses, binds the high-soaring phrases into an intense, committed personal statement. Her voice, always a difficult one to record, here lacks sensuousness and variety, as well as the clarion impact it made in the opera house, but this is clearly a rendition of stature. Paul Schöffler's Barak is even better, with the sort of darkly voluminous bass-baritone that maintains a sense of spaciousness even in his quietest utterances.

539

The other three leading singers each balance drawbacks against strengths. While Hans Hopf's voice never quite flows freely and his musical ideas remain squarely literal, his secure tenor encompasses the punishing role without strain. Christel Goltz's soprano may seem harsh; it is always used with understanding and involvement. Elisabeth Höngen sounds aged and worn as the Nurse (a norm for the role), but when the music isn't too fast or disjunct she displays impressive dramatic subtlety.

For getting good work from all these performers, maintaining continuity and balance, and making a fine case for the then-unfamiliar opera, Karl Böhm deserves praise. His greatest successes come at what one might call the obvious points: the great vocal and instrumental solos and the pictorial orchestral effects. Some of the intervening scenes come off as filler that has to be endured, and thus some of the score's potential remains unrealized. But what Böhm did achieve, in company with his able executants, remains admirable.

1963 DEUTSCHE GRAMMOPHON (S,P)

Ingrid Bjoner (A), Inge Borkh (B), Martha Mödl (C), Jess Thomas (D), Dietrich Fischer-Dieskau (E), Munich Opera Chorus and Orchestra— Joseph Keilberth

For another reopening of a theater (the Munich State Opera), *Die Frau ohne Schatten* was again the choice, and DG recorded it live. This works less well than its predecessor. For one thing, the sound is problematic enough to mar one's pleasure, with voices occasionally coming from two places at once, and a very vocal prompter. Second, the need to get this opera onto the stage with minimal chance of disaster led to a seriously truncated edition, with almost more cut from Act III than is retained, and several off-stage effects simply omitted. In addition, Keilberth for the most part fails to inspire his orchestra; however proficiently they play, they provide little sense of direction except in the half-dozen best-known passages. Whether because of Keilberth or the recording, the interludes sound unusually muddy and ill balanced. The singers of the small roles leave little positive impression.

There is something to be said for four of the principal singers (Martha Mödl, under strain from the start and increasingly desperate as the performance progresses, will be charitably bypassed). Ingrid Bjoner and especially Jess Thomas handle their altitudinous roles with finesse and dramatic engagement, as long as one doesn't demand actual beauty of tone. Inge Borkh puts a tense-sounding but substantial dramatic soprano and a sophisticated dramatic imagination to good use as Barak's wife, with a thrilling outburst at the end of Act II and a gripping solo early in Act III. And Dietrich Fischer-Dieskau, when not tempted into explosive attacks, has some extraordinary scenes in which he makes Barak's loving generosity personal and real. Someone studying either of these two roles might well wish to sample this recording, but others are unlikely to find sustained pleasure in it.

1977 DEUTSCHE GRAMMOPHON (S,P) CD

Leonie Rysanek (A), Birgit Nilsson (B), Ruth Hesse (C), James King (D), Walter Berry (E), Vienna State Opera Chorus and Orchestra— Karl Böhm

In the 1960s and 1970s a quartet of *Frau* principals began to appear in major opera houses (opening season at the new Metropolitan Opera, for one), giving the opera's popularity an enormous boost. The quality of Rysanek, Christa Ludwig, James King, and Walter Berry is best preserved in Rysanek's London recording and in excerpts recorded by the others. This Austrian Radio tape, first issued in 1985, though better than nothing as a memento of three of these singers (Ludwig having relinquished her role), seriously disappoints as a representation of the opera. By this time Karl Böhm was snipping bits from almost everything in Acts II and III except the big solo scenes, unbalancing dramatic proportions and undermining character development.

Further, on this occasion the distinguished principals were all approximating the musical requirements rather loosely, despite some good performances. Birgit Nilsson, in the last new role she undertook, retains her unique dead-on tone and fearless projection, conveying the spite and hurt of the Dyer's Wife especially well. King sings out unstintingly too, and though the voice's range of choice has narrowed, so that he sounds desperately heroic rather than confidently so, this is still an important voice well cast. Berry remains as ever a genial presence with many successful moments, the vocalism now a bit casual and given to shouting. Rysanek gives the occasion its greatest distinction by her fervor and concentration.

Ruth Hesse, tonally steadier than previously recorded Nurses, proves no more successful than they at getting beyond the purely musical requirements. The orchestra plays beautifully, though moments that call for repose do not get it. Böhm probably must take the blame for that. Too bad he did not make a complete studio recording in the late 1960s.

1987 EMI / ANGEL (S, D) CD

Cheryl Studer (A), Ute Vinzing (B), Hanna Schwarz (C), René Kollo (D), Alfred Muff (E), Tölz Boys' Choir, Bavarian Radio Chorus and Orchestra—Wolfgang Sawallisch

The second studio recording of *Frau* turned out, somewhat unexpectedly, to be one of the most successfully realized operatic recordings of the 1980s. A great deal of the credit must go to Wolfgang Sawallisch, who really understands the opera's expressive possibilities and realizes them masterfully with the aid of the Bavarian Radio Orchestra in top form. His tempos, often swifter than Böhm's or Keilberth's, match Strauss's markings closely and enhance continuity (only the interlude called "Barak's goodness" misfires in this respect). Especially gratifying is his successful projection of material slighted or omitted in other recordings, especially in Act III, and his gradation of climaxes in that act so that it concludes with the needed sense of elation and resolution. In Sawallisch's hands, the opera makes so much sense that it seems surprisingly short.

He has chosen a cast of correspondingly expert calibre. They all project their roles with conviction and maintain an exceptional level of accuracy that justifies itself in increased expressivity— a significant step forward in *Frau* interpretation. Not that all are ideal vocalists; three of them lack the means fully to realize their good intentions. Ute Vinzing would have seemed acceptable on a first *Frau* recording, where her musicality and reliability would have counted for much, but in this role we have learned to hope for more tonal focus and beauty, more personality than Vinzing commands. René Kollo sings most of the Emperor impressively, but then his sour, squeezed high notes compromise his climactic moments; his musical assurance and dignity remain valuable assets. Alfred Muff has a perfectly pleasant bass-baritone which encompasses the full range of his part; he simply lacks the musical imagination, the vocal presence, that his predecessors on records have commanded, and for once Barak relinquishes the spotlight.

Cheryl Studer makes a worthy successor to Rysanek as Empress, and in terms of subtlety and vocal beauty even surpasses her; Studer's effortless command of high tessitura and her warmly personal inflections give enormous pleasure throughout her scenes. In Hanna Schwarz we finally have a Nurse with a compact, quick-speaking tone that can render the vocal line accurately, and a clarity of intention that brings this enigmatic individual into focus. For the glass-harmonica solos in the final scenes (vibraphone is generally substituted), EMI even engaged the eminent Bruno Hoffmann—one of the most remarkable examples of the care taken with this superb production.

1989–91 DECCA / LONDON (S,D) CD

Julia Varady (A), Hildegard Behrens (B), Reinhild Runkel (C), Plácido Domingo (D), José van Dam (E), Vienna Boys' Choir, Vienna State Opera Concert Chorus, Vienna Philharmonic Orchestra—Georg Solti

The greatest asset of Georg Solti's long-planned recording is that its four principal singers are intelligent artists with attractive and expressive voices; the beauty and subtlety of the vocal writing are more consistently realized than in most previous recordings. Strongest of all is

Hildegard Behrens, in a role whose writing suits her voice extremely well; she sounds splendid, and gives repeated evidence of her musical and histrionic insight. José van Dam proves a worthy partner for her, his gentle bass-baritone handled with fine musical sensitivity, and the scenes featuring the two of them are all highlights of the recording.

Plácido Domingo floods the Emperor's music with golden tone, and his avoidance of the stiffness and strain characteristic of other Emperors encourages one to minimize his odd treatment of German as only a minor drawback. By contrast, Julia Varady's mezzo-tinted soprano may not be a natural fit for the Empress, but she makes the role her own nonetheless, with warm spontaneity and only an occasional suspicion of shrillness.

Completing the quintet of principals is Reinhild Runkel, a Nurse scarcely less precise than Hanna Schwarz, and closer to the hefty dramatic mezzo suggested by the writing; a brief patch of misalignment with the orchestra in Scene 1 fortunately proves atypical. All the principals, in fact, have their moments of vagueness—not crucial individually (though some obliterate thematic phrases) but indicative taken together of too-brief acquaintance with the roles, and uncertainty about where the lines and scenes are heading. In this respect, they compare unfavorably with Sawallisch's cast.

Georg Solti's experience with the opera and his love for it show in his assured handling of the orchestra and its lustrous playing, but he does not always balance the textures for optimum meaningfulness, nor does he always handle tempo modifications convincingly. He, like his cast, is stronger on moment-by-moment sound than on a long-term sense of direction.

The supporting singers include a brilliant Falcon (Sumi Jo), a properly magnetic Young Man (Robert Gambill), and very capable singers for all the other roles except the Guardian, which needs a more focused line than Eva Lind can supply. Overall, the effect is complementary to the Sawallisch—more sumptuous-sounding, nearly as revelatory (in a different way) about the opera's stature, less gripping as a musical-dramatic experience.

With the two DG recordings of interest only for some individual contributions, the choice lies between Böhm's 1955 recording, Sawallisch, and Solti. Despite some excellent singing on the first and third of these, preference must go to EMI, for its completeness, for Sawallisch's prodigiously insightful conducting, and for the all-around competence and comprehension of its cast.

JON ALAN CONRAD

RICHARD STRAUSS

ARABELLA (1933)

A: Arabella (s); B: Zdenka (s); C: Adelaide (ms); D: Matteo (t);
E: Mandryka (bar); F: Waldner (bs)

*L*ong misperceived as an inferior sequel to *Der Rosenkavalier*, *Arabella* has gradually won a place in the repertory and is now appreciated for its own special qualities—a moving love story of Vienna in the 1860s, with a more intimate and delicately colored score than its exuberant predecessor. Certainly the most direct and down-to-earth collaboration between Strauss and Hugo von Hofmannsthal, *Arabella* is also their most immediately lovable and glowingly human creation, a fitting conclusion to this fruitful operatic partnership. True, the latter half of the work may not sustain the sheer perfection of Act I. Hofmannsthal unfortunately died before working out all the knots in his text, but a bit of judicious pruning in live performances helps to solve the problem, preparing us for the glorious scene of reconciliation between Arabella and Mandryka—surely one of opera's most heart-tugging boy-gets-girl finales.

1957 DECCA / LONDON (S) CD

Lisa della Casa (A), Hilde Gueden (B), Ira Malaniuk (C), Anton Dermota (D), George London (E), Otto Edelmann (F), Vienna State Opera Chorus, Vienna Philharmonic Orchestra—Georg Solti

Enshrined here is the postwar Vienna cast that perhaps more than any other helped bring *Arabella* the attention, respect, and love it deserved. Visually and vocally, della Casa was the ideal heroine, combining great physical beauty, a magnetic stage presence, a creamy soprano, and an intriguing aura of mystery—everything that makes Arabella such a fascinatingly ambiguous character. Of course, only the lovely sound is captured here, but in the mid-1950s della Casa was at the very peak of her vocal powers, and her singing on this set is consistently ravishing. Gueden's lighter but equally pure and silvery timbre both contrasts and blends with della Casa to perfection in the crucial Arabella / Zdenka scenes, and the two sopranos relish every dramatic nuance of Hofmannsthal's words.

In most important respects, London was also a superb Mandryka. Onstage, he presented the very picture of a virile, impulsive, open-hearted man of incorruptible virtue and incapable of guile. He is not always completely at ease with the music—the role makes difficult demands, both in the highest and lowest parts of the baritone's register, and London occasionally adjusts the tessitura—but he more than compensates with a richly satisfying vocal characterization. (The only Mandryka on disc who sounds completely comfortable in the part is Josef Metternich, who recorded the opera's major scenes in 1954 for EMI opposite Elisabeth Schwarzkopf.) Malaniuk and Edelmann make an amusing pair as the low-living Waldners, and Dermota's ardent lyric tenor is a definite luxury in the thankless role of Matteo. The only serious drawback here is Solti's rather tense and hard-driven account of the score, although the Vienna

543

Philharmonic plays with its customary polish and sheen.

1963 DEUTSCHE GRAMMOPHON (S,P) CD

Lisa della Casa (A), Anneliese Rothenberger (B), Ira Malaniuk (C), Georg Paskuda (D), Dietrich Fischer-Dieskau (E), Karl Christian Kohn (F), Bavarian State Opera Chorus and Orchestra—Joseph Keilberth

A live recording from Munich's newly rebuilt National Theater, this *Arabella* offers memorable moments, and they are bound to be cherished by those who were lucky enough to be in the house. For others the performance may remain just a collection of moments. Although still a lovely instrument capable of much expressive warmth, della Casa's voice no longer soared with quite the easy freedom and ripe bloom that one hears on the Decca/London recording of six years earlier. Mandryka was one of Fischer-Dieskau's most celebrated operatic roles, and he was a mesmerizing presence in it as well as a wizard at shaping many of the part's most telling phrases. For some of us that was enough to compensate for the fact that his light baritone did not have sufficient tonal substance to fill out all the musical implications of the notes. Rothenberger is a radiant and urgent Zdenka, the elder Waldners are in the most reliable hands, but Paskuda whines irritatingly as Matteo. While Solti for Decca was excessively brisk and businesslike, Keilberth tends to be rather too slack and *gemütlich*, although he obligingly accommodates the singers, giving them plenty of time to make their own expressive points.

1981 ORFEO (S,D) CD

Julia Varady (A), Helen Donath (B), Helga Schmidt (C), Adolf Dallapozza (D), Dietrich Fischer-Dieskau (E), Walter Berry (F), Bavarian State Opera Chorus and Orchestra—Wolfgang Sawallisch

After they were married in 1978, Varady and Fischer-Dieskau sang frequently together, and *Arabella* inevitably became one of their joint vehicles—and, on the face of it, an ideal one. Unfortunately, the chemistry fails to work. Varady gives a winningly forthright and spirited portrayal of the heroine, but her soprano, with its rough edge and dash of vinegar, hardly seems suited to a character so romantic and exuding such allure. Fischer-Dieskau is even more disappointing. By 1981 Mandryka was even further out of his reach than it had been in 1963, and an occasional elegant turn of phrase cannot compensate for so much bluster and barking. The rest of the cast is adequate, although each role has more appropriate and effective interpreters on other recordings. Sawallisch generates the most musical interest here. His treatment of the score may be a trifle too brisk and objective for some tastes, but no other conductor on disc lets us hear so much relevant compositional detail in this miraculously crafted score.

1986 DECCA / LONDON (S,D) CD

Kiri Te Kanawa (A), Gabriele Fontana (B), Helga Dernesch (C), Peter Seiffert (D), Franz Grundheber (E), Ernst Gutstein (F), Chorus and Orchestra of the Royal Opera House, Covent Garden—Jeffrey Tate

Delightful to look at and lovely to hear, Kiri Te Kanawa would seem to be the ideal Arabella. She rejoices in a lusciously smooth-textured voice that somehow manages to sound cool and hot at the same time, and her provocative physical presence hints at an intriguingly enigmatic personality lurking behind the glamorous exterior. Alas, the appearances are deceiving. In all surface respects Te Kanawa is della Casa's natural successor to the role, but something is missing, at least on this recording. Her performance has a curiously blank, faceless quality, an automatic by-rote response that suggests a tiresome duty being duly dispatched. True, the sound of the voice is often very beautiful, but the full character of the words and music never registers.

Even the most fabulous supporting cast could never save an *Arabella* with a cipher in the title role. As it turns out, Te Kanawa's colleagues are a variable lot with Seiffert as the principal standout, an ardent and secure Matteo—possibly the best on disc. Grundheber manages the extreme highs and lows of Mandryka's music with commendable assurance, but as an interpreter he is almost as dull as his partner. Fontana's hooty, acid-toned Zdenka is a total disaster, although Dernesch's charmingly befuddled Adelaide and Gutstein's ripe Waldner are both definite assets. Tate gives an affectionate but rather lax reading of the score, at times losing the symphonic thread and muddying the instrumental textures.

The *Arabella* recording of choice continues to be the first one. No other to date offers such vocal consistency or a cast able to identify so closely with the appealing characters that inhabit this touching love story.

PETER G. DAVIS

RICHARD STRAUSS

CAPRICCIO (1942)

A: Countess (s); B: Clairon (ms); C: Flamand (t); D: Count (bar);
E: Olivier (bar); F: La Roche (bs-bar)

A humorous text by the Abbé Giovanni Battista Casti entitled *Prima la Musica e Poi le Parole* (First the Music, Then the Words), made into a short opera by Antonio Salieri in 1786, appears to have sparked the origins of *Capriccio*. It was natural for Richard Strauss, who had devoted his career largely to lieder and opera, to be concerned about the effect that words and music have on each other, as well as their relative importance. As his valedictory to the opera stage in 1942, *Capriccio* finds the seventy-eight-year-old composer artfully dodging the question: poetry and music have their individual persuasion, but in combination they form a new work of art, different from either. In *Capriccio*, the Countess Madeleine, standing for the friendly conflict between head and heart, finally cannot choose between two suitors, the poet Olivier and the composer Flamand: the song they have created *together* is what sticks in her mind and pleases her fancy.

Strauss's collaborator, the conductor Clemens Krauss, revealed unsuspected talents as a librettist. His text is long but consistently witty, literate, and stimulating. The resulting work he dubbed a "conversation piece for music." Much of Strauss's score, like that of his *Intermezzo*, is conversationally written, and its ensembles obscure many of Krauss's lines, making it imperative that the audience have prior familiarity with the libretto. Because every line and nuance needs to be grasped, *Capriccio* is made to order for home listening.

Few are the operas (or plays or films, for that matter) that deal truthfully with the artistic process. Berlioz's *Benvenuto Cellini* and Hindemith's *Mathis der Maler* spring to mind as exceptional examples. *Capriccio*, written by and for connoisseurs, has its abstruse stretches. It also reaches stirring moments, touched by the cool radiance of Strauss's final, "autumnal" style. Above all, it is entertaining, in the best sense of the word, as most art in one way or another aims to be.

1957 EMI / ANGEL (M) CD

Elisabeth Schwarzkopf (A), Christa Ludwig (B), Nicolai Gedda (C), Dietrich Fischer-Dieskau (D), Eberhard Wächter (E), Hans Hotter (F), Philharmonia Orchestra—Wolfgang Sawallisch

Recorded in London during the heyday of the Philharmonia Orchestra, this recording has stood as a classic, thanks to a blend of meticulous casting, lively ensemble, and unobtrusively clear recording. Schwarzkopf studied and weighed every line; if the result is a less than spontaneous characterization of the pivotal Madeleine, the woman's breeding and civilized phraseology are illustrated with polish and a pale warmth appropriate to Strauss's score. Ludwig offers a richly clever, worldly-wise actress Clairon. Gedda, an outstanding Flamand in every respect, sings with exquisite musical correctness, as one would expect a composer to do, but also gives a sense of contained ardor that fills out his lines. Wächter, smooth and assured as his friendly rival, sings naturally and genially, voluble with words as one expects from a poet. Fischer-Dieskau's only vice as the Count is to stress syllables too forcibly, denting the shape of his cantilena in long-breathed lines. Hotter—the first Olivier, in 1942—here sings his more famous role of La Roche, the self-important, practical theater impresario, encompassing its full bass-baritone range with ready command. His big monologue, in which he admonishes all artists to come down to earth and collaborate sensibly, is the dramatic linchpin of an opera that may be just conversation, but in which the conversation grows heated.

Sawallisch, thoroughly fluent in Strauss style of all periods, knows when to play the accompanist and when to play the symphonist. His pacing is so natural that one scarcely notices it, but as the pace gradually livens, he keeps the excitement discreetly going. The Philharmonia sounds transparent and chamberlike, highlighted by the solos of its various star players, notably Dennis Brain on the French horn.

1971 DEUTSCHE GRAMMOPHON (S) CD

Gundula Janowitz (A), Tatiana Troyanos (B), Peter Schreier (C), Dietrich Fischer-Dieskau (D), Hermann Prey (E), Karl Ridderbusch (F), Bavarian Radio Orchestra—Karl Böhm

Under Böhm's energetic but fine-lined leadership, there is a maximum of animation (in both the character and movement sense) without pushing. The orchestra always has just the right weight, clarity, and elasticity, while the frequent short flights of melody have warmth without stickiness. Janowitz, a more forthcoming, less subtly shaded Countess than Schwarzkopf, sings with tireless grace, firm focus, and floating tone. Troyanos captures both humor and underlying voluptuousness in Clairon, while her would-be lover, the Count (brother of the Countess), is played with a mixture of class, intelligence, and drive by Fischer-Dieskau, a repeater from the EMI cast. Schreier's poised, pointed tenor contrasts Flamand against the well-intentioned, emotionally wider-ranging Olivier of Prey. Ridderbusch, resisting the temptation toward vocal overkill in La Roche's big monologue, creates a certain charisma by adhering, as all his colleagues do, to equal attention toward both words and music—a balance which, after all, is the very subject of *Capriccio*.

Since there are only two complete recordings of this opera, and those two of equal quality, one cannot go wrong with either. For devotees of Schwarzkopf and her school of meticulously calculated interpretation, EMI is a foregone conclusion. Its mono sound, while state of the art for its period, takes second spot, however, to DG's stereo, which gives us even more lucidity and dimension for Strauss's orchestra and somewhat more perspective on the voices, not recorded quite so close up. Sawallisch and Böhm are equally accredited Strauss stylists, leading with the necessary equipoise between delicacy and dash. If every opera were as fortunate in its recorded history as *Capriccio*, there would be no need for books such as this.

JOHN W. FREEMAN

IGOR STRAVINSKY

THE RAKE'S PROGRESS (1951)

A: Anne Trulove (s); B: Baba the Turk (ms);
C: Tom Rakewell (t); D: Nick Shadow (bar)

Stravinsky's only full-length theater work crowned and concluded his three-decade-long exploration of a neoclassical musical language. Into the eighteenth-century milieu suggested by Hogarth's celebrated cycle of paintings, the libretto by W. H. Auden and Chester Kallman injects the Faust theme. Using the framework of a "number opera," Stravinsky took much specific inspiration from Mozart (especially *Così fan tutte*), and also from Monteverdi, Donizetti, and Verdi, yet time has shown the end product to be very much his own. The vocal writing is also modeled on eighteenth-century practices and types, but Stravinskian metrical displacements and angular intervals give it a special flavor—and provide a special challenge to performers.

A recording of the Venice world premiere, conducted rather uncertainly by the composer, was briefly available from Fonit-Cetra. Besides preserving a historic event, it allowed us to hear Elisabeth Schwarzkopf's powerful, committed Anne and Hugues Cuénod's witty Sellem: Anne's big aria and the auction scene were clearly the evening's highlights. Any new—and novel—opera needs time and performances to reveal its potential, and the *Rake* was no exception; this and three subsequent commercial recordings document stages in this progress, as musicians learned to play it and singers and directors and conductors learned to define the distinctiveness (and particularly the touching, lambent lyricism) rather than the background conventionality of the music and the characters.

1953 CBS / SONY (M)

Hilde Gueden (A), Blanche Thebom (B), Eugene Conley (C), Mack Harrell (D), Metropolitan Opera Chorus and Orchestra—Igor Stravinsky

This first studio recording stemmed from the American premiere, at the Metropolitan Opera. The performances, meticulously prepared and conducted by Fritz Reiner, were significantly superior to the Venice opening night, but Reiner was contracted to RCA and the Met to Columbia, which was then building up a "Stravinsky conducts Stravinsky" series. So the composer took the podium for the recording, and under his vaguer baton the ensemble suffers (as confirmed by a hearing of the 1953 broadcast). Worse, Columbia's engineers contrived an opaque, voice-heavy registration that smothers most of the intricate, delicious orchestral detail.

Nevertheless, the set retains interest for the vocal performances: Mack Harrell's elegantly sung Shadow is subtler in irony and menace than any since, and Blanche Thebom's Baba is crisply spoken, smoothly sung, and dead-pan funny. Eugene Conley's *spinto* tenor, more vibrant than the writing requires, is surprisingly fluent, but he misses the pensive, dreamy aspect of Tom's rakedom. His diction is admirable, in contrast to Hilde Gueden's markedly accented English, for which her spirit, musicality, and sound compensate somewhat; now and then, the skips in the writing discover inequalities of register. (Auden and Kallman gave Stravinsky an album of 78s to illustrate the vocal types they had in mind for the characters; their idea of Anne was Eleanor Steber, and we may regret that her energy, communication, and voice were never harnessed to the role.) In its best moments—Nick's entrance, Baba's aria, the finale of Act II, Scene 1, the Epilogue—this recording catches the work's spirit, but even in these places detail is sadly lacking, and such crucial passages as the string prelude to the graveyard scene emerge as merely shapeless and incoherent.

1964 CBS / SONY (S) CD

Judith Raskin (A), Regina Sarfaty (B), Alexander Young (C), John Reardon (D), Sadler's Wells Opera Chorus, Royal Philharmonic Orchestra—Igor Stravinsky

Following the advent of stereo in 1956, Columbia recapitulated and expanded its Stravinsky project for the new technique, but a new *Rake* remained out of reach (the first one had not sold well) until 1964, when producer John McClure managed to match up the principals of a recent New York concert version, other singers and chorus from a Sadler's Wells production, and the Royal Philharmonic, which had played the score at Glyndebourne the previous summer. The result is superior to CBS 1953 on most counts, notably the balance and clarity of the textures. Stravinsky's hand on the baton is firmer, despite a few soggy spots (the end of the exposition of Anne's aria, for example, and the Bedlam scene after Anne leaves), and orchestra and singers often capture his distinctive vitality and specificity of accenting, so that the brio of the comic scenes is infectious.

Conceived for a Handelian tenor, Tom Rakewell is in the hands of England's finest such singer at the time, Alexander Young, whose meaty tone, adept technique, varied color and articulation, and beautifully formed words make for a rounded, individual impersonation. John Reardon's accomplished Nick, almost too genial, succeeds in mustering some needed menace in the graveyard. While just lacking the tonal clout and virtuosity to carry off Anne's cabaletta with the ultimate élan, Judith Raskin is in every other respect a superior, affectingly lyrical Anne.

Regina Sarfaty's Baba appears to be modeled—successfully—on Thebom's, if with a little less voice. The smaller roles are well taken. A curiosity: in 1953, the cuckoo clock in Mother Goose's establishment is fitted to the music iambically, in 1964 trochaically.

1983 DECCA / LONDON (S,D) CD

Cathryn Pope (A), Sarah Walker (B), Philip Langridge (C), Samuel Ramey (D), London Sinfonietta Chorus, London Sinfonietta—Riccardo Chailly

Another generation further along, this recording, like its predecessors, reflects experience in the theater. The score is now at everyone's fingertips, and matters of harmony, texture, and phrasing that in the composer's performances often took second place to articulation and rhythmic character are now given more justice. Chailly and the Sinfonietta bring clearly to our ears details previously only implicit, such as the harmony of the dissonant epilogue to Tom's aria at the beginning of the second act, or the 3/4 vs. 6/8 cross-meters of the trio in the subsequent scene. The singers share the precision—note how Sarah Walker finds wit in the dotted rhythms of Baba's "Come, sweet, come."

Yet this admirable concinnity involves some sacrifice, in the form of a certain metrical rigidity, notably in the reading of the recitatives. To be sure, in Stravinsky's hands these are often distant from the even-valued patter of the eighteenth century; he displaces and syncopates, sometimes in intricate ensemble with the harpsichord, in ways that will not be meaningful if singers and listeners do not sense an underlying rhythmic spine. But in the more straightforward passages the composer's recordings suggest that he expected a modicum of freedom, of inflection derived from the words and their own meters as much as from the note values. The *allegro* finales of several scenes also suffer from this stiffness, emerging with less sheer buoyancy and fun than in Stravinsky's second recording.

The vocal star here is Samuel Ramey, whose firm, focused bass gives Shadow's music a darker color than can baritones, yet he is not strained by the heights and was then capable of remarkably light articulation; his reading is not strong on irony, however, and his introductory aria is too hurried. Sarah Walker is an original and witty Baba, quite independent of the Thebom precedent. Philip Langridge's earnest Tom, slender of voice, is occasionally overwhelmed by Ramey in their duets, and Cathryn Pope's Anne is working with still slimmer resources, but their musicality and spirit keep them in the picture. John Dobson's Sellem is a particularly vivid vignette, but unfortunately the Mother Goose of Astrid Varnay is an ill-advised undertaking: her ravaged tone might have been ignored in a stage performance on behalf of an original characterization, but on disc we have only the voice. The pauses between the scenes are often too long—especially when the dominant that ends the first scene is left hanging for ten seconds of silence, instead of being resolved immediately, as clearly indicated in the score, by the first chord of the bordello scene.

The Venice and Met recordings are now of mainly historical interest. Because of its strong and consistent casting, coupled with the composer's authority and style, 1964 CBS seems the choice, although connoisseurs of the opera will find much that enlightens, if less that delights, in 1983 London.

DAVID HAMILTON

PIOTR ILYICH TCHAIKOVSKY

EUGENE ONEGIN (1881)

A: Tatyana (s); B: Olga (ms); C: Lensky (t); D: Onegin (bar); E: Gremin (bs)

Tchaikovsky did not designate *Eugene Onegin*—his fifth opera and the first of his ten to achieve popular success—an opera at all, but "lyrical scenes in three Acts and seven Tableaux." Based upon Pushkin's novel in verse, which was so beloved it had been absorbed into the Russian national consciousness, *Eugene Onegin* serves more to explore emotional states of familiar characters than to give a narrative explication of a story everyone already knew. Written during 1877, the year the homosexual Tchaikovsky entered into a disastrous sham marriage and attempted suicide, *Onegin* is infused with the composer's despondent obsession with fate and suffused with his sympathy for Tatyana, into whom he put so many of his own emotions. Far more important than the opera's title character, Tatyana—whose profound attraction to Onegin can be seen as sexual awakening, spiritual conversion, or both—provides one of the literature's great soprano challenges. No one else in the opera is so sympathetically portrayed or fully developed, but each—Onegin, the bored aristocrat; Lensky, an ardor-drunk poet; Olga, Tatyana's harebrained, fun-loving sister; Gremin, the deluded old prince looking for his lost youth in the young Tatyana—is an interesting and peculiarly Russian type. Tchaikovsky reveals each in few but subtle strokes, but the real character of the opera lies in the orchestra and the skillful alternation between grand operatic scenes and intimate ones. Although Tchaikovsky entrusted the first performance to students, feeling the music too personal to be ruined by silly prima donnas, the opera quickly became a mainstay of the Bolshoi. It has remained so ever since, and five complete recordings of it have been made by the Moscow company. Still, the opera, for all its challenges to non-Russian-speaking singers, suits an Italianate lyric voice. It has fared well outside Russia, although it was not recorded in the West until Covent Garden's ground-breaking version in 1974. All performances are complete.

1936 MELODIYA (M)

Glacier Zhukovskaya (A), Bronislava Zlatogorova (B), Sergei Lemeshev (C), Panteleimon Nortzov (D), Alexander Pirogov (E), Bolshoi Theater Chorus and Orchestra—Vassily Nebolsin

The first complete recording of *Eugene Onegin*, made about a half century after the opera was written, is a sometimes wacky, dramatically irreverent, yet fully engaging affair typical of the Bolshoi in the 1930s. Nebolsin's often reckless tempos are hair-raising, especially when he accelerates through choruses and dances at almost risible speeds, with orchestra and singers in a mad and rarely synchronized dash to the end. The Polonaise and Ecossaise of the third act are riots of breakneck excitement and verve. But there are authentic excitement and drama, as well, in this performance. At his best, Nebolsin makes a striking dramatic occasion of the Act II ball, building steady momentum from a carelessly raucous Waltz to an explosive finale. Likewise, the duel is full of many terrific dramatic touches, a haunting stillness precedes the climax, followed by a denouement of profound understatement. At its worst, though, Nebolsin's approach encourages overdramatization from his singers. And he gets it from Lemeshev, a Lensky extravagant in his fervor, shamelessly indulgent with his held high notes. Zlatogorova is nearly as bad; her Olga is downright silly as she sings of her unperturbed nature. Not so the principal couple, Tatyana and Onegin, who are the performance's major disappointment. A prim soprano, Zhukovskaya exudes little of Tatyana's warmth or spiritual abandon, and her Letter Scene is distinguished primarily by Nebolsin's direction; it is the orchestra, not Tatyana, that suggests flip casualness at the start and builds to an overwhelming climax at the end. Nortzov requires just the opposite from Nebolsin, who must be on continual watch over the baritone to prevent his Onegin from descending to sheer tastelessness. Pirogov, another scene stealer, begins the tradition for booming basses to use Gremin's poignant aria as a star turn, as if they were trying out for Boris. The sound, on an undated Melodiya LP transfer, tends to get quite rough in patches; most big climaxes come with considerable distortion and there are also many dim-sounding passages.

c.1936 MELODIYA (M)

Elena Kruglikova (A), Elizaveta Antonova (B), Ivan Kozlovsky (C), Panteleimon Nortzov (D), Maxim Mikhailov (E), Bolshoi Theater Chorus and Orchestra—Alexander Melik-Pashayev / Alexander Orlov

Although this and the Bolshoi performance above were recorded around the same time and both feature Panteleimon Nortzov as Onegin, they are surprisingly dissimilar. Whereas Nebolsin's feverish conducting gives the other performance its arresting sense of inevitability (something unequaled in any other recording of the opera), here it is a certain choppiness that is inevitable, what with the duties shared by two conductors. Melik-Pashayev leads most of the performance, but three key episodes—Tatyana's Letter Scene, the Act II Prelude and Waltz, and the final duet of Tatyana and Onegin—are

entrusted to Orlov. The difference between the conductors is fairly evident. Melik-Pashayev always emphasizes the lyrical nature of the score, even when he builds up a feverish pitch for, say, the first approach of Onegin. Orlov, on the other hand, is a more dramatically expressive conductor, although that is a not unwelcome contrast for his scenes. But what mainly separates this from its contemporary Bolshoi account is Kruglikova's transfixing Tatyana. Few sopranos are able to convey such a complete transformation of character as does Kruglikova, from demure girl to, in this case, practically a saint. In her Letter Scene—which is among the most beautifully sung and deeply felt on records—Tatyana's impulsiveness, doubt, growing resolve, and profound, rapturous realization of her love, have all the qualities of a religious conversion. And that is both the beauty and problem of Kruglikova's idealized, slightly bloodless Tatyana: her every utterance seems to fit perfectly on a linear graph of evolving spirituality. Still, Kruglikova glows, and that glow is reflected and complemented in a wonderfully sung performance throughout. Kozlovsky, a suave and honey-toned tenor, is an unusually seductive Lensky, his smoothness enhanced by Melik-Pashayev's light, creamy lyricism. Nortzov is no more impressive here than in the competing recording, but he is considerably less indulgent and his lack of depth only serves to underscore the profundity of Tatyana's character. All the other voices are never less than pleasant although their characters, too, fade into insignificance next to St. Tatyana. The sound on the Colosseum pressing, more distorted than the other Melodiya effort, adds to the impression that this recording is an ancient relic.

1955 DECCA / LONDON (S)

Valeria Heybalova (A), Biserka Cvejic (B), Drago Starc (C), Dushan Popovich (D), Miro Changalovich (E), Chorus and Orchestra of the National Opera, Belgrade—Oscar Danon

Everything about this, the first recording of *Eugene Onegin* made outside of the Soviet Union, bespeaks a diligent provincial effort. Danon oversees a dryly straightforward, unsentimental performance. His phrasing is firm, even Spartan, suggesting, perhaps, the romantic outbursts so characteristic of the Russian style are just a bit self-indulgent. He manages to maintain perfectly acceptable ensemble, keeping an undistinguished cast and chorus well in line, although only so much discipline can be enforced upon an orchestra as tinny and ill-tuned as this: the oboe sounds like a toy. And in the end, the lack of dramatic spontaneity allied with competent but rarely personable singers substantially weakens the opera's spirit. The most impressive singer of the cast, Drago Starc, for instance, could be a luminous and heroic Lensky if Danon allowed him a small amount of leeway, but the tenor compensates by accentuating every downbeat. However, not much could help the mismatched principal couple. Heybalova is a businesslike Tatyana whose letter writing comes off as more secretarial than heartfelt; Popovich's messy Onegin, an aristocrat overly imperious and tortured from the start, simply sounds out of place in the otherwise staid proceedings. The resonant Changalovich is so undersupported in Gremin's aria that the lugubrious *basso* sounds almost as if he is falling asleep during it, but Cvejic's light and pretty Olga could be just right if Danon permitted her some buoyancy.

c. 1956 MELODIYA (M) CD

Galina Vishnevskaya (A), Larisa Avdeyeva (B), Sergei Lemeshev (C), Yevgeny Belov (D), Ivan Petrov (E), Bolshoi Theater Chorus and Orchestra—Boris Khaikin

If there is an ideal performance of *Eugene Onegin*, this is it. It is the first recorded *Onegin* that asks a listener to appreciate the opera on its many levels, the first to play Tchaikovksy's exquisite sentimentality against Pushkin's more cynical poem, the first to fully address the characters' sexuality. Boris Khaikin's conducting is at once faithful to the tiniest nuances in the score yet is analytical enough to indulge none of them. By getting every syncopation just right, by obtaining a transparency of texture that brings out instrumental colors with great subtlety and vibrancy, by remaining sensitive to

every gradation of tempo change, Khaikin is, like Pushkin, the observer, ideally setting the stage for his characters. Of all Tatyanas on records, the young Vishnevskaya, in splendidly strong and vital voice, is the most sensual. She does a remarkable job of capturing Tatyana just at the point of sexual awakening, where she can be girlish one moment, surprisingly mature the next, until that edginess reaches its explosion in the most erotic Letter Scene on disc, with Khaikin's pointed restraint making the climax all the more astonishing when it happens. And the growth continues from there, until Vishnevskaya attains genuine dignity in the final duet, again thanks in great part to Khaikin's refusal to milk its sentimentality. So overpowering is this growth of Tatyana that the whole opera is seen as if through her eyes. Belov is a manly Onegin, suitably reserved at the beginning, awed by the animal force of Tatyana in the end. Lemeshev's shameless Lenksy of twenty years earlier now, under a more refined and sophisticated circumstance but with voice in tatters, sounds like a small-town crooner who saves it all for his big moments. Slightly uncharacteristically, perhaps, Khaikin indulges the resounding Ivan Petrov in his star-turn performance of Gremin's aria, and he underplays Onegin's and Lensky's duel. But he knows for whom he is saving his interpretation. The Bolshoi orchestra plays for Khaikin with much greater precision and color than they do for any other conductor in this survey, and the mono sound captures it better than might be expected from Melodiya.

1970 EMI / ANGEL (S)

Galina Vishnevskaya (A), Tamara Sinyavskaya (B), Vladimir Atlantov (C), Yuri Mazurok (D), Alexander Ognivtsev (E), Bolshoi Theater Chorus and Orchestra—Mstislav Rostropovich

The atmosphere, along with everything else about this white-hot account of *Eugene Onegin*, is radically different from the Khaikin Bolshoi recording of fourteen years earlier. Recorded in Paris during the company's 1970 tour, the performance is undoubtedly affected by its rapturous French reception. It is, of course, the product of a conductor hyper-expressive under any circumstance. But the fever-pitch emotions must surely have been further exacerbated by what, at that time, was the profound dissatisfaction felt by Rostropovich and his wife Vishnevskaya, with Soviet life—they defected four years later. How else to explain—except perhaps the fact that the cellist was a less experienced conductor in 1970 than he was to become after becoming music director of the National Symphony in 1975—Rostropovich's ferocious attack on the fate motive every time it occurs. Indeed, this performance revolves around the gripping province of fate just as singlemindedly as Khaikin's 1956 performance focuses on Tatyana's sexual awakening. One hears it from the heaving Prelude, in which every note is made heavy with significance and emotion, and such heady extremes are remarkably sustained throughout the entire performance. The peasant choruses are massive, heroic; the arrival of Onegin and Lensky in Act I is accompanied by a tremendous sense of foreboding; the ensuing quintet (so floating under Melik-Pashayev) is here always serious and ominous. A manic Polonaise is driven, drunken, hardly danceable. All the characters fit into Rostropovich's vision. No longer the young girl awakening to sexuality, a more mature and less vocally secure Vishnevskaya is now a force of change rather than a victim of it; her Letter Scene is one of unbendable resignation, pain, and ultimately a Brünnhilde-like resolution. It is hard not to read into it the soprano's upcoming defection. Mazurok's Onegin is a hugely forceful performance; the baritone sings with such desperation to Tatyana in the third act that he practically scares her away. And desperation seems to overcome nearly all the other characters, as well. The usually carefree Olga is melodramatically sung by Sinyavskaya; Lensky becomes a granitic, humorless, almost oafishly exaggerated, romantic figure, but Atlantov's robust Italianate passion is always impressive. Keeping in the nature of the performance, Ognivtsev is the most sepulchral of Gremins; Vitali Vlassov, the most mannered (and amusing) of Triquets. The sound is gritty, the Bolshoi playing far less spectacular than in the previous company effort and the chorus less disciplined. But refinement has nothing to do with this searing performance.

1974 DECCA / LONDON (S) CD

Teresa Kubiak (A), Julia Hamari (B), Stuart Burrows (C), Bernd Weikl (D), Nicolai Ghiaurov (E), John Alldis Choir, Orchestra of the Royal Opera House, Covent Garden—Georg Solti

This performance, based upon an acclaimed Covent Garden production, is the first *Eugene Onegin* to be recorded in the West, a fact it proclaims loudly under Solti's baton. It is Solti the Wagnerian, adding coarse punctuation marks to every brass accent, who pilots the proceedings throughout. Subtle syncopations get rushed in the process; orchestral colors are painted in thick swatches; rude, phrase-breaking *sforzandi* seem to come out of nowhere. The conductor, in just one of many clumsy instances, cares nothing about the girlish triplets and trills in the orchestral introduction to Tatyana's scene with her nurse, and they are stiff and literal; the Letter Scene is worse, a series of brutish, unsupported climaxes between blank passages. Throughout, the singers are left to find their own characterizations. With the dramatically passive Teresa Kubiak the result is a not very engaging Tatyana. Julia Hamari, one of the fullest, most lush-sounding of Olgas, fights to get some cheerfulness out of the dull accompaniment. Burrows—a light, lyric, appealing Lensky—generally sounds too refined for the surroundings, while Weikl is constantly encouraged toward making Onegin the opera's hero. Only Triquet's slow and sensually sung couplets by Michel Sénéchal force anything approaching elegance from the conductor. Otherwise, for Solti, the important musical occasions are the dances, the choruses, the fight music, and any other spots where the brass can blare. Covent Garden's orchestra is dynamic enough, but not really the showcase ensemble that seems the point of this gross performance.

1979 MELODIYA (S)

Tamara Milashkina (A), Tamara Sinyavskaya (B), Vladimir Atlantov (C), Yuri Mazurok (D),

Yevgeny Nesterenko (E), Bolshoi Theater Chorus and Orchestra—Mark Ermler

Nine years after Rostropovich's *Eugene Onegin* recording with the Bolshoi, and five after the conductor and Vishnevskaya left the Soviet Union, the company had apparently lost much of its luster. Here are three of the same principals—Sinyavskaya, Atlantov, and Mazurok—but without a charismatic, chance-taking conductor they all seem tired, bland. Each has gotten vocally heavier, and each sounds complacent and pompous. Ermler's is traffic-cop conducting, not allowing any too great indulgences from the cast but also not expecting anything outside of a well-rehearsed, clockwork result. Mainly, though, in a recording in which the orchestra is recessed, allowing the voices unnatural prominence, Ermler simply seems to disappear. Arias—including an unmemorable Letter Scene—are never more than pretty set pieces. The Duel is an exercise in sleepwalking. The dances are for the concert hall, not the ballroom or opera stage. Where Rostropovich's performance felt like a last attempt to capture the Russian soul, this seems no more than the product of a comfortable, don't-rock-the-boat bureaucratic, committee-approved Soviet Union. The recorded sound and the playing also seem lazy.

1987 DEUTSCHE GRAMMOPHON (S,D) CD

Mirella Freni (A), Anne Sofie von Otter (B), Neil Shicoff (C), Thomas Allen (D), Paata Burchuladze (E), Leipzig Radio Chorus and Dresden State Orchestra—James Levine

At first this seems like an almost preposterously overblown performance. Levine makes everything slower, bolder, louder, bigger than anyone before him, Rostropovich included. But if such a scope is out of proportion with Tchaikovsky's "lyrical scenes" and with the subtle nature of the characters, it is not out of proportion with Tchaikovsky. The fascinating prospect of this performance, the only recorded interpretation made from a late twentieth-century perspective, is that it characterizes not so much

Tatyana and her emerging sexuality or spirituality, or Onegin and the pathos of his belated self-knowledge, but rather the composer himself. Levine underscores every emotional utterance, as if he is more compelled by why Tchaikovsky might have written a particular motif than why Tatyana sings it. And so one hears *Onegin* as the representation of the societal terrors, the sexual fears, the inner torment the suicidal composer suffered while composing the opera. In no other recording does the tragedy seem so profound, the suffering so monstrous, the fate motif so weighty. Tatyana, in a radiantly sympathetic portrayal from Freni, is a completely tragic heroine here, her desires to find romantic satisfaction doomed from the start. Allen's carefully sung Onegin is the most cruel on disc, but his cruelness is felt to come from his own self-torture. Shicoff provides a high-strung but electric Lensky, a too sensitive and hence unstable poet; Otter is a gorgeous but exceedingly dark Olga; and the somberness includes Burchuladze's Gremin and Michel Sénéchal's Triquet, each haunting in its own way. While Levine can push beyond the music's boundaries—even the dances are tortured and massive—he also can keep a listener glued to every note. The precise, focused playing of the Dresdeners captures the color of the score better than anywhere else on disc, heard in beautifully recorded sound. The result is a luminous quality to Tchaikovsky's scoring that keeps the whole thing from seeming too suffocating.

1990 SONY (S,D) CD

Anna Tomowa-Sintow (A), Rossitza Troeva-Mircheva (B), Nicolai Gedda (C), Yuri Mazurok (D), Nicola Ghiuselev (E), Sofia National Opera Chorus and Festival Orchestra—Emil Tchakarov

The latest *Eugene Onegin* demonstrates just how limp the opera can seem when it lacks a firm point of view. It features three veteran and well-characterized singers left pretty much to their own dramatic devices by Tchakarov's flabby conducting. The performance's primary virtue is a sweet-toned Tatyana from Tomowa-Sintow, whose demure Dresden-china *pianissimos* early on made her monumental singing of the Letter Scene seem an astonishing spiritual conversion. Gedda, too, is a massively radiant presence, but by this point his voice is beyond mature, and one senses the strain throughout, however much he makes of every utterance. Mazurok, in his third Onegin on disc, sounds weary not of the world but of the role. Troeva-Mircheva's Olga is as wobbly as Gedda—they seem like a middle-aged couple at best. But mainly the disappointment lies in the dullish accompanimental role Tchakarov assumes, bringing with him little splendor to the choruses and dances, and minimal dramatic emphasis throughout. Orchestra, chorus, recorded sound, and secondary characters never rise above adequate.

For all its glitter, *Onegin* is a psychological opera, and the most interesting recordings are the ones that offer insight into both the charac-ter of Tatyana, one of Tchaikovsky's most personal creations, and into the emotionally complex composer himself. The two best Tatyanas, Elena Kruglikova (in a 1936 Bolshoi account) and a young Galina Vishnevskaya (in the 1956 Bolshoi version under Boris Khaikin), present the extremes of Tatyana's development, the first as a purely spiritual one, the latter as a sexual awakening. Though a fragile opera, perhaps best served by the objective conducting in Khaikin's 1956 Bolshoi performance, it proves to be not *that* fragile, since the two most compelling readings overall are extreme ones. Rostropovich (in his 1970 Bolshoi reading) wrings emotion from its every bar, a dissident's representation of the suffering of the Russian people; Levine presents the opera as a reflection of the composer's own complex emotional conflicts.

MARK SWED

Unavailable for review:
1952 MELODIYA

PIOTR ILYICH TCHAIKOVSKY

PIQUE DAME (1890)

A: Lisa (s); B: Countess (ms); C: Pauline (c); D: Gherman (t);
E: Yeletsky (bar); F: Tomsky (bar)

Tchaikovsky composed *Pique Dame*, the ninth of his ten operas, in forty-four days between January and March 1890, shortly after completing his Fifth Symphony. It is a late work—three years later the composer was dead—and, like the last three symphonies, haunted by notions of inexorable fate and human vulnerability. Based on Pushkin's short story *The Queen of Spades*, and with a libretto by the composer's brother, Modest, the opera's principal character, Gherman, is transformed from Pushkin's cynical, opportunistic protagonist into a self-destructive Tchaikovskian obsessive, first with his love for Lisa, then with possession of a gambling secret. But what makes Gherman—a basically unsympathetic neurotic who becomes increasingly demented with his every overwrought utterance—a compelling character is the way Tchaikovsky creates wonderfully atmospheric surroundings that either mirror Gherman's romantic dementia or contrast it with the courtly world of eighteenth-century St. Petersburg. It is an opera that fuses lyric Russian song with Gherman's ravings. And the effectiveness of *Pique Dame* often lies in achieving the tricky balance between Gherman's mania and the evocation of his colorful surroundings. Although the opera is included in many international repertories, each of its recordings but one is a Russian or Slavic effort. Moreover, although this is the quintessential St. Petersburg opera, both in its brilliant evocation of the eighteenth-century city (which is as much a protagonist as Gherman)

and in the fact that it had its premiere there, all the Russian recordings come from Moscow's Bolshoi, which presented a new account on disc each decade from the 1940s through the 1970s. And even the one non-Slavic rendition is very much a reaction to the Bolshoi style by the Soviet Union's most famous musical émigrés at the time, Mstislav Rostropovich and his wife, the soprano Galina Vishnevskaya.

1946 MELODIYA (M)

K. G. Djerzhinskaya (A), Bronislava Y. Zlatogorova (B), Maria P. Maksakova (C), N. S. Hanaiev (D), P. M. Nordzov (E), A. I. Baturin (F), Bolshoi Theater Chorus and Orchestra—Samuil Samosud

This first complete recorded *Pique Dame* is a generally sympathetic one, undone mainly by quite poor Soviet sound and a sometimes careless Bolshoi ensemble. Samosud sets the tone in a grandly symphonic manner; he emphasizes clarity of articulation which makes the more animated sections delightful, the stormy ones characterful. He is not a subtle conductor, and his insistent tone, however effectively it hammers at the incessant fatefulness of the music, can also be wearying, leading to inevitable climactic letdowns. Moreover, the combination of a weak-toned orchestra, an obstinate conductor, and recorded sound with severely constricted dynamic range can hamper any attempt to achieve an authentically terrifying atmosphere, which is what Samusod should be the best at.

The singing is confident all around, Tchaikovsky's style sounding effortlessly natural, but it is also without great charisma. Hanaiev's ringing tenor serves Gherman's great passion and evolving nuttiness equally well, if unremarkably. Djerzhinskaya's Lisa is very beautifully sung, with nuance and feeling, although an occasional tremulousness or dramatic vagueness creeps in. Maksakova contributes a hearty Pauline, Zlatogorova a dark, mysterious Countess, able to sustain a spooky slow line; both baritones supply just the kind of robust, suave songfulness called for in the score. The Intermezzo is a treat, far more Tchaikovskian technicolor than Mozartian, but probably just the way the composer himself heard Mozart and French Age-of-Enlightenment music.

p. 1952 MELODIYA (M)

Evgenia Smolenskaya (A), Elena Verbitskaya (B), Vera Borisenko (C), Georgi Nelepp (D), Pavel Lisitsian (E), Andrei Ivanov (F), Bolshoi Theater Chorus and Orchestra—Alexander Melik-Pashayev

Melik-Pashayev, the principal conductor of the Bolshoi from 1953 to 1962, was an old-school Russian conductor whose performances can seem archaically melodramatic today. And here he may not convey the full symphonic scope of *Pique Dame*, but he is incomparable among recorded conductors in evoking the opera's macabre side, in generating and building tension in each scene, in inspiring the singers to convey at all times a sense of gripping theater in their performances. But what is most striking about this performance is the dramatic sweep that Melik-Pashayev and the healthy-voiced Nelepp together employ to transform Gherman's initial hysteria into a positively heroic resolve. Whereas previous tenors (and most who follow) portray Gherman as increasingly neurotic throughout the opera, Nelepp seems to transcend Gherman's obsessiveness into a powerful determination to follow his destiny nobly, his great final questioning of life becomes poignant, even stirring, instead of pathetic. Smolenskaya's lavishly dramatic soprano is perhaps too mature a sound for Lisa, but she never loses

her lyricism while managing to hold her own against Nelepp's power and heroic attitudes, making for a thrilling interaction. Borisenko, a dark, amber mezzo, takes Pauline's Romance very slowly, luxuriating in its gorgeously long lines. Verbitskaya's Countess is an old squawky character who fits in well with the more ghoulish qualities of Melik-Pashayev's conducting. Both baritones—Lisitsian's sincere Prince and Ivanov's carefully inflected Tomsky—are noteworthy. If there is any complaint, it might concern the unseemly drive of the Mozartian Intermezzo. The one major drawback is the Soviets' technologically backward sonics, which served to make Melik-Pasheyev seem even more old-fashioned than he already was.

1955 DECCA / LONDON (S)

Valeria Heybalova (A), Mira Verchevich (B), Biserka Cvejic (C), Drago Petrovich (D), Alexander Marinkovich (E), Alexander Veselinovich (F), Chorus of the Yugoslav Army, Orchestra of the National Opera, Belgrade—Kreshimir Baranovich

The Belgrade National Opera series of Russian opera recordings made in the mid-1950s featured predictably stolid performances, their primary advantage being that they were usually the first readily distributed recordings of the works outside of the Soviet Union, and their first recordings in stereo. This first non-Russian and first stereo *Pique Dame* is, however, an exception. It begins full of promise, with its strongly rendered and expressive orchestral Introduction, followed by an especially buoyant opening scene in the Summer Garden. Gherman enters with all the uncontrollable ardor he is supposed to have. But it only takes a few opening lines to expose Marinkovich's wobbly baritone and woefully overindulgent mannerisms, and the messy quintet that follows, to undo any dramatic tensions that had been created. And so the performance goes, swinging wildly from one extreme to another. Veselinovich is the baritonal opposite of Marinkovich, a singer with rounded tone, long-breathed phrases, and taste. Petrovich, a soulful Pauline, contrasts with Heybalova, a generic Lisa who tries to make every emotion sound important. Meanwhile, Verchevich, a deep-voiced Countess, is simply grandstanding, extravagantly pompous. Baranovich seems to get taut, expressive playing from his uneven orchestra one minute and then to lose all the tension in the ensemble's poor string intonation, squeaky winds, and anemic percussion. In general, things tend to go more wrong than right as the opera progresses: Petrovich's outbursts become regularly strident; Heybalova and Verchevich grow noticeably tired; the orchestra exchanges whatever fervor it had early on for unrelieved sloppiness. The recorded sound, like the performance, does little for the atmosphere.

p.1967 EMI / ANGEL (S)

Tamara Milashkina (A), Valentina Levko (B), Irina Arkhipova (C), Zurab Andezhaparidzye (D), Mikhail Kiselev (E), Yuri Mazurok (F), Bolshoi Theater Chorus and Orchestra—Boris Khaikin

Given Khaikin's sensitive and sensual Bolshoi recording of *Eugene Onegin* from the 1950s, one might expect more of the same here. The urgent orchestral Introduction promises it, but the bubble bursts immediately in a lumbering, soft-edged, seemingly endless performance that presents a plushly smug company at its conventional worst. Every phrase after the Overture sounds like the overblown preservation of a masterpiece embalmed for museum admiration, not as living drama. Such is the attitude of the singers as well. Andezhaparidzye's is a vocally coarse, dramatically blustery Gherman, Milashkina a soul-weary Lisa; they sing their love duet like a parody of Tristan and Isolde. All else is bloated as well, and the eighteenth-century Intermezzo becomes a travesty. There is some beautiful singing from Arkhipova and Mazurok, but both are, necessarily, dramatically detached. The others are just as detached without singing beautifully.

1974 PHILIPS (S) CD

Tamara Milashkina (A), Valentina Levko (B), Galina Borisova (C), Vladimir Atlantov (D),

Andrei Fedoseyev (E), Vladimir Valaitis (F), Bolshoi Theater Chorus and Orchestra—Mark Ermler

Ten years later and the Bolshoi offers another official-sounding version of *Pique Dame*, but not all, at least, is business as usual. The orchestra has been cleaned up; the sonics are more than acceptable, particularly on the Philips CD version; and Ermler supplies a decently work-a-day reading, effective enough when a broadly symphonic style is required, although prosaic in the balmier or spookier moments. But mainly it boasts Atlantov's Gherman. Atlantov's is less a *portrayal* of Gherman than an exercise in superb vocalizing, in the perfectly placed tone, the show-stopping ringing high note, the always tastefully shaped phrase. And although it is probably just what Tchaikovsky didn't want, since the composer cared more about dramatic involvement (and Atlantov seems exactly the same at the end of the opera as he does at the beginning) than beauty of tone, still Atlantov is a model for making an often thankless and tasteless role sound attractive. The performance also boasts another fresh voice, Makvala Kasrahvili, who sings Chloë in the Intermezzo like the star she was soon to become. Change, of course, never came quickly or easily to the Bolshoi, and the performance does also include some unfortunate holdovers from the flat recording of a decade earlier. Milashkina's soprano, ten years older, is now in shambles, more suitable for a soprano version of the Countess than the young heroine; Levko's Countess has become downright geriatric. Valaitis is a polished Tomsky, Fedoseyev a pompous Yeletsky—neither memorable. For Ermler profundity is equated with slow tempos.

1977 DEUTSCHE GRAMMOPHON (S)

Galina Vishnevskaya (A), Regina Resnik (B), Hanna Schwarz (C), Peter Gougalov (D), Bernd Weikl (E), Dan Iordachescu (F), Tchaikovsky Chorus, French Radio Women's Chorus, National Orchestra of France—Mstislav Rostropovich

As if to show Soviets just how much they had lost, Rostropovich and Vishnevskaya, having recently emigrated to the West and been erased from the official history of the Bolshoi, answer the stodgy Bolshoi routine with the most characterful, soulful, and searching performance of *Pique Dame* on disc, and, ironically, the only one to have been produced in the West. Not everyone is likely to agree with Rostropovich's need to make every bar so richly expressive, leading as it does to massive distortions—even the children playing soldier at the opening sound like a punishing Soviet regiment driving tanks into Prague. But the results are never less than arresting and often downright spectacular. This is entirely Rostropovich's performance. He brings every scene vividly to life. It is the conductor, not his piteous tenor, who makes Gherman's melancholy so exquisite, something to savor like a fine brandy. No other conductor expels such fury on the storms, comes close to capturing the profound mysteriousness of the Countess's world, brings more rapture to the love music or more spirituality to the demented Gherman than does Rostropovich, who also integrates the Intermezzo into the drama far more effectively than it is done on any other recording. The French orchestra plays for him as if Russian—this is, by far, the finest played of the *Pique Dame* recordings. Unfortunately, it is anything but the best sung. About the only reason to imagine why an obscure tenor, so out of his league here, would be brought into this project is that he draws attention away from Vishnevskaya's vocal decline. Gougalov produces a well-defined tone when the dynamics remain at *mezzo forte* and the pitch remains comfortably below middle range. But that isn't often, and under Rostropovich's gregarious urgings, he seems mostly to be flailing about out of control dramatically and vocally. Vishnevskaya is never out of control dramatically or musically, and hers would be an exciting portrayal of a big-hearted Lisa, as it once surely was, were her soprano still serviceable. And then there is Iordachescu, a pinched, nasal, mannered Tomsky. In peculiar (and maybe symbolic for Rostropovich and Vishnevskaya) contrast, the Western singers are wonderful. Schwarz and Weikl both offer rich and gorgeous accounts of their arias, while Lucia Popp is the most silvery of Chloës in the Intermezzo. Res-

nik contributes the most formidably mysterious and memorable of all Countesses on disc.

1990 SONY (S,D) CD

Stefka Evstatieva (A), Penka Dilova (B), Stefania Toczyska (C), Wieslaw Ochman (D), Yuri Mazurok (E), Ivan Konsulov (F), Svetoslav Obretenov Bulgarian National Chorus, Sofia Festival Orchestra—Emil Tchakarov

Sony's Bulgarian series of Russian opera recordings, all conducted by Tchakarov and featuring a mix of local and stellar singers, has generally been the present-day equivalent of the uninspired provincial Russian operas from Belgrade recorded by Decca in the mid-1950s. This one is a little better. Tchakarov here leads a comfortable account of the score, more lightweight than Rostropovich and less atmospheric than Melik-Pashayev, but capably presenting the opera's striking contrasts between sunshine and storm, between eighteenth-century pastiche and nineteenth-century passion. Ochman, a light-voiced Gherman, brings an usual and not-unwelcome eloquence to the character—this Gherman certainly follows his fate with more class than any other tenor on disc—although he can sound effortful for the necessary dramatic outbursts. A lighter Lisa than Evstatieva, a broad-sounding soprano, would have made a more suitable partner for Ochman, but she, at least, is a grounded singer always in control. All the other singers make a bit much of their roles. Mazurok is ostentatiously grand with the Prince's aria; Konsulov is gruffly threatening in Tomsky's Ballad; Dilova seeks earthy profundity in Pauline's simple Romance, Toczyska's Countess is a witchy caricature. But Tchakarov keeps the performance moving agreeably, so that no singer's indulgences are dwelt upon.

Pique Dame has proven a more difficult opera to capture on disc than might be expected. Only two versions, Melik-Pashayev's 1952 Bolshoi account and Rostropovich's Parisian project two decades later, fully document the score's rich atmosphere or the depth of Gherman's pathos.

The Bolshoi performance is particularly fine for Nelepp's unconventionally noble Gherman, the only notable Gherman on disc, although Ochman's lyric elegant portrayal on Sony does have its appeal. Rostropovich, arresting as his conducting is, is undercut by an inadequate Gherman and Lisa, but his set does preserve Resnik's unforgettably spooky Countess.

MARK SWED

Unavailable for review:
1991 RCA / BMG

Ambroise Thomas

Mignon (1866)

A: Philine (s); B: Mignon (ms); C: Frédéric (t or ms);
D: Wilhelm Meister (t); E: Lothario (bs)

Charles Louis Ambroise Thomas wrote twenty operas. Only two have survived (*Mignon* and *Hamlet*, composed back to back in 1866 and 1868), and they are breathing faintly these days. The Metropolitan Opera has not presented *Mignon* since 1945. That is understandable. As drama, the opera is ridiculous. Far from easy to sing, it requires top-flight singers.

On the other hand, there are reasons why it had a hundred performances to its credit in the first year of its life and an average of fifty performances annually for the next twenty years in Paris.

Mignon is meant to please its bourgeois audiences; it is full of charm but with few surprises and not much personality, except that of its period. Written with grace and deftly orchestrated, it has more than a fair share of pleasant, even memorable, melodies. Thomas also knew how to flatter the voice. As numerous recordings of its arias and duets made on 78-rpm discs prove, earlier singers and audiences loved this opera.

Mignon was written for the Opéra-Comique and had spoken dialogue. The original finale was a notable combination of Philine's fiery forlana, her reconciliation with Mignon, and her marriage to Frédéric. That finale was replaced in short order by the familiar, sober trio and the omission of Philine altogether. The opera found its enduring form at its London premiere in 1870. The dialogue was dropped, the role of Frédéric changed from *buffo* tenor to mezzo

soprano, and the new finale put in place. Thomas composed additional music: a second verse for Lothario's "Fugitif et tremblant," a second, altogether vapid, aria for Philine, and, much the best, a sparkling rondo-gavotte for Frédéric.

Having lost a good part of its hold on the public before the advent of LP, it will come as no surprise that *Mignon* has achieved only two complete recordings.

1953 DECCA / LONDON (M)

Janine Micheau (A), Genevieve Moizan (B), F. L. Deschamps (C), Libéro De Luca (D), René Bianco (E), Brussels Monnaie Theater Chorus, Belgian National Orchestra—Georges Sebastian

The first recording of *Mignon* remains a disappointment. Like other London sets of the day, its sound, afflicted with hum, is not easy to take. The voices are too close, the orchestra too distant. Congestion in *tuttis* robs the ensembles of their effect. The conducting, consistently wanting in lightness and animation, is no help to a cast far from ideal. Although Moizan understands the style, her attractive mezzo is overly ripe for this youthful role. Micheau's lyric soprano has neither the quickness nor lightness for Philine's brilliant passages, some of which have been simplified for the occasion. De Luca offers some admirable soft singing, but his voice turns hard under pressure. Bianco has a grainy baritone rather than the preferred rich bass. Frédéric may be more credible when taken by a tenor (as here), but the role, minus the Gavotte, intended only for a mezzo, borders on insignificance.

1977 CBS / SONY (S)

Ruth Welting (A), Marilyn Horne (B), Frederica von Stade (C), Alain Vanzo (D), Nicola Zaccaria (E), Ambrosian Opera Chorus, New Philharmonia Orchestra—Antonio de Almeida

In contrast with its predecessor, this set offers a fetching performance with few weaknesses, augmented by an appendix which includes Philine's second aria and the entire original finale. The engineering produces clean, impressively warm sonics in a suitable acoustic frame. Antonio de Almeida's winning leadership is informed, affectionate, sensibly paced, with never a moment of heaviness. The role of the reticent, mostly melancholy Mignon is a change of pace for Marilyn Horne. Although her beautiful voice no longer suggests the bloom of youth, she scores a triumph for her sensitivity, eloquence, and splendid vocal finesses. Welting is a refresh-ing Philine, generous and merry—no standard coquette but a real person. Her lightness of address, agility, and admirably clean articulation are everywhere praiseworthy, especially in her scintillating account of the forlana in the original finale. Vanzo, an admirable artist in romantic French roles, has a tenor with both sweetness and metal. He is heard at his best in Wilhelm Meister's vagabond song, to less advantage in "Adieu, Mignon," which is a bit deficient in tenderness and marred by a couple of sobs. Frederica von Stade, singing like a Golden Age great, is such a gay and vivid Frédéric that she makes the role seem larger than it is. Surely there has never been another recording of the Gavotte to equal hers. Zaccaria has the right feeling for Lothario and provides some artful phrasing even though his bass often seems worn and lusterless. His compassionate Berceuse earns respect. All told, this recording of *Mignon* is not likely to be equaled for a very long time.

C. J. LUTEN

VIRGIL THOMSON

THE MOTHER OF US ALL (1947)

A: Susan B. Anthony (s); B: Angel More (s); C: Constance Fletcher (ms);
D: Jo the Loiterer (t); E: John Adams (t); F: Daniel Webster (bs)

Here is one of the most touching and stimulating of American operas, its appeal direct and its music spirited, sometimes flippant, and nostalgic but free from sentimentality. It is based, in a way which seems artless but is not, on the rhythms of American speech. Though its central character is Susan B. Anthony, the suffragette, the work is really intended to present a broad landscape of American ideals, with a cast including Daniel Webster, John Adams, Lillian Russell, and Ulysses S. Grant carrying on historically impossible conversations and relationships: "a memory book of Victorian playgames and passions . . . with its gospel hymns and cocky marches, its sentimental ballads, waltzes, darned-fool ditties and intoned sermons," as Thomson decribed it. He and Gertrude Stein had been friends for more than twenty years when she wrote the libretto for him just before her death in 1946. The following year the opera was presented at Columbia University and since then has been performed across the country more than a thousand times. Sir Thomas Beecham admired the score and proposed to broadcast it for his seventieth birthday celebration, but the BBC turned it down. The opera's stylized conversations call for grace, a sense of humor, and an easy, unforced projection of character, as Thomson and Stein evoke a picture of the assumptions of a century and a half of American life. The opera is something of a romance, not without bitterness, of rising expectations. It ends with the passing of the Nineteenth Amendment; there is a strand of sadness even in celebration.

1976 NEW WORLD (S) CD

Mignon Dunn (A), Ashley Putnam (B), Helen Vanni (C), James Atherton (D), William Lewis (E), Philip Booth (F), Santa Fe Opera Chorus and Orchestra—Raymond Leppard

This recording stems from the 1976 Santa Fe Opera production, spiritedly played and at least respectably sung. The mood is often one of tender or comic banter between highly theatricalized characters, allusive and homiletic in a way that reminds one of Ionesco without the violence. Cogent and amusing parallels are drawn between marriage, slavery, and the realities of political life. Each of the characters stands for an attitude: Webster is the windy, practical politician, Grant simply demands not to be bothered, Adams is the sentimental idealist, and others attract, repel, or mediate between such figures in a series of dreams and confrontations. Raymond Leppard offers a performance of charm, fluent and well integrated. On average, the singers are pleasant, but a number of them lack dramatic cogency. Ashley Putnam, at the very beginning of her career, has a gleaming sound as the aptly named Angel More, James Atherton is sympathetically lax as Jo the Loiterer, and William Lewis provides the pompous sentimentality of John Adams, if not much tonal beauty. On the other hand, Philip Booth cannot *act* the compulsive Daniel Webster; as with some of the others, the text is a clearer guide to the character than the singer. At the center is that fine singer Mignon Dunn (I remember her as the most hair-raising Ortrud I have ever seen), with a beautiful mezzo voice smoothly managed—and seldom recorded. She has the mood of reminiscence and the magnetic power of the character well in hand, though the flintiness and the frustration largely escape her. Her diction is indistinct here, but the major problem is that the role, written for dramatic soprano, lies high, so that some of the lyric passages have an element of desperation about them. Altogether, though, this is a very attractive and intriguing opera, quite unlike anything else in the repertory, and neatly performed in this recording.

LONDON GREEN

MICHAEL TIPPETT

THE MIDSUMMER MARRIAGE (1955)

A: Jenifer (s); B: Bella (s); C: Sosostris (c); D: Mark (t);
E: Jack (t); F: King Fisher (bar)

The first of Tippett's five operas, *The Midsummer Marriage* was greeted with incomprehension, suspicion, and even derision when first performed at Covent Garden in 1955. Since then, audiences have become more comfortable with Tippett's libretto, which describes the mystical journey toward self-awareness of two couples, one high-mindedly spiritual and intellectual, the other more down to earth. It's a familiar operatic theme (see *The Magic Flute* and *Die Frau ohne Schatten*), but one presented here in multilayered scenes that explore the subconscious in a text brimming with complex literary images, influences that range from T. S. Eliot's verse plays to Jungian philosophy. The profusely melodic and eminently singable music has never been a problem, however—an astonishing burst of creative energy with few parallels in operatic writing at that time. Today, it is rightly considered a major work (in England, at least), if not one of the richest, most prodigiously inventive scores in the entire twentieth-century repertory.

1970 PHILIPS (S)

Joan Carlyle (A), Elizabeth Harwood (B), Helen Watts (C), Alberto Remedios (D), Stuart Burrows (E), Raimund Herincx (F), Chorus and Orchestra of the Royal Opera House, Covent Garden—Colin Davis

Colin Davis's long association with Tippett's music pays off in every measure of this radiant performance, based on the 1968 Covent Garden revival. The conductor projects all the vibrancy and lyrical intensity of the score without getting carried away or losing track of the musical discourse's sometimes intricately woven threads. Even the densest contrapuntal textures emerge with exactly the sort of the shimmering clarity and sonorous pungency that must have been in the composer's ear. The two sets of soprano-tenor lovers are nicely contrasted: Remedios's sturdy heroic tones and Burrows's lighter lyrical timbre, Carlyle's silvery purity and Harwood's earthier appeal. Herincx is a forceful presence as the grasping and bullying King Fisher, and Watts uses her luscious contralto to excellent advantage in Sosostris's great visionary monologue in Act III. Everyone involved in this recording—especially the chorus, which has a virtuoso role—seems totally absorbed by the work and properly convinced that they are performing a contemporary masterpiece.

PETER G. DAVIS

GIUSEPPE VERDI

NABUCCO (1842)

A: Abigaille (s); B: Fenena (ms); C: Ismaele (t);
D: Nabucco (bar); E: Zaccaria (bs)

*I*t is a wonder *Nabucco* was ever composed. Even though he had a contract from La Scala, Verdi, who had recently lost his wife and remaining child to a mysterious disease, had no appetite for work. The *Nabucco* libretto languished in a corner of Verdi's room for five months while the depressed composer read cheap novels. One day he picked it up, set the last scene, and in three months he had completed the opera. Numerous complications delayed its premiere until the following spring; it might not have been staged without the intervention of Giuseppina Strepponi (who became Verdi's wife years later) and Giorgio Ronconi, both leading singers of the day, who created the roles of Abigaille and Zaccaria.

The importance of the chorus in *Nabucco* makes it unique in the Verdi canon. As Julian Budden has written: "*Nabucco* is a drama not of people but of *a* people." Each of the principal characters has a strong profile, but none is developed. The opera, divided not into acts but into parts, is static, "such action as occurs being telescoped into a moment's scuffle. *Nabucco*, more than any other of Verdi's operas, resembles a series of vast tableaux, rather than a drama relentlessly moving towards its denouement."

Even with a weak last act, the crude marches and chorus of the Levites, mostly commonplace recitatives, a few conventional arias, and some unnecessarily noisy orchestration, *Nabucco* remains the most consistently expressive opera

Verdi composed before *Rigoletto*. With all its flaws, it is virtually irresistible.

After its initial popularity at La Scala, *Nabucco* unexpectedly disappeared from the big house's repertory until 1912 and then was unheard until it opened the 1933–34 season. With its political overtones, it was the perfect opera for La Scala to resume postwar operation. After all, "Va pensiero," the great third-act chorus of the Hebrew slaves, had been Italy's unofficial national hymn for over a century.

1951 CETRA (M,P)

Caterina Mancini (A), Gabriella Gatti (B), Mario Binci (C), Paolo Silveri (D), Antonio Cassinelli (E), Chorus and Orchestra of the RAI, Rome—Fernando Previtali

The first complete recording of *Nabucco* was issued by Cetra from a tape of one of the 1951 Radio Italiana broadcasts celebrating the fiftieth anniversary of Verdi's death. Although welcome at the time, even with its crude engineering—overloaded, with high-frequency distortion in loud passages—it can have little interest today. Caterina Mancini is undaunted by the role of Abigaille, a voice killer that puts one in awe of the sopranos who Verdi might have thought were equipped to sing it. Mancini challenges it with gusto, but the wild swings of her unwieldy, unreliable soprano are too often inadequate. Paolo Silveri, in the title role, is more sympathetic than commanding and, therefore, only marginally effective until his third-act duet with Abigaille. The Zaccaria (Antonio Cassinelli) is provincial in every way. The secondary singers, Mario Binci (Ismaele) and Gabriella Gatti (Fenena), are the most effective. The Radio Italiana chorus gives the performance a lift time and again. Fernando Previtali's conducting is unrefined, although spirited and committed.

1965 DECCA / LONDON (S) ℗

Elena Suliotis (A), Dora Carral (B), Bruno Prevedi (C), Tito Gobbi (D), Carlo Cava (E), Vienna State Opera Chorus, Vienna Philharmonic Orchestra—Lamberto Gardelli

The first satisfactory *Nabucco* on disc appeared in 1965 and it continues to give pleasure. The impassioned Abigaille of Elena Suliotis, here in her early twenties, is easily the brightest impression we have of that soprano's brief candle of a career. Her voice, insufficiently trained, with some unsupported, hollow tones, nevertheless has body in all three registers, is rounder and steadier at the top and bottom than those of her competitors, and generously, boldly, excitingly disposed. And along with all her flashes of lightning there is a moving and unmatched "Su me morente" in her death scene.

The years had rubbed away the gleam from the top of Tito Gobbi's baritone (Nabucco's hectoring no longer comes easily); and in this clearly made-on-the-quick recording, such things as his forte reading of "Tremin gl'insani del mio," rather than Verdi's *sotto voce* marking, are tolerated. But Gobbi makes the character live. No other baritone gives such a complex account of the wanderings of Nabucco's mind, his rage and grief. No other is so touching in either "Deh perdona ad un padre" (heard in the confrontation with Abigaille) or in the prayer, "Dio di Giuda." Carlo Cava is a willing Zaccaria without the fiery authority the role demands. Bruno Prevedi does about as well as one can with Ismaele's conventional lines. Dora Carral is a mostly inadequate Fenena, her lovely aria in the last act going for little. Lamberto Gardelli guides the mellow Vienna Philharmonic and State Opera Chorus, trained by the La Scala chorus master, Roberto Benaglio, with convic-

tion and authority. One suspects minimum rehearsal time is the cause of occasional ensemble blemish. The sound is warm, the voices have convincing presence, but the biggest numbers are not so sharply focused as in later recordings.

1977–78 EMI / ANGEL (S) ℗

Renata Scotto (A), Elena Obraztsova (B), Veriano Luchetti (C), Matteo Manuguerra (D), Nicolai Ghiaurov (E), Ambrosian Opera Chorus, Philharmonia Orchestra—Riccardo Muti

Among recordings of *Nabucco*, Angel's entry stands out for festival atmosphere and polish, thanks to Riccardo Muti. The Italian conductor's operatic offerings on disc are uneven, but this is one of his most impressive achievements—as always, scrupulously prepared, not only energetic but spontaneous as well, and effectively paced. Especially notable is his maintenance of continuity in numbers with contrasting tempo indications. London's Philharmonia Orchestra, in top form, and an unimposing English chorus perform for Muti with zest and unwavering attention to detail. The recording has real presence but is a trifle overlit here and there. Renata Scotto was an admired lyric soprano when she was tempted by her own intellectual curiosity and ambition—with the encouragement of conductors and impresarios, who admired the amplitude of her theatrical gifts—to tackle vocally unsuitable *spinto* roles. As it happens, Scotto is in her best voice throughout this set and is becomingly recorded. Most of her top notes have loosened, but only a couple flap like a banner in the wind, unhappy auguries of the future. Her characterization, like her singing, is differentiated and fiery. Nicolai Ghiaurov more than adequately suggests the nobility of Zaccaria, even though he is clearly past his prime, as a comparison with his earlier London recording of two of his arias reveals. Matteo Manuguerra, an admirable Nabucco in word and tone, follows Muti's lead in making the most of dynamic contrast. His *pianissimo* singing—following his roaring announcement that he, Nabucco, is God—is breathtaking. The ever musical Veriano Luchetti is a satisfying

Ismaele, but Elena Obraztsova, with her heavy, ripe mezzo, is unsuitable as the maidenly Fenena.

1982 DEUTSCHE GRAMMOPHON (S,D) CD

Ghena Dimitrova (A), Lucia Valentini Terrani (B), Plácido Domingo (C), Piero Cappuccilli (D), Yevgeny Nesterenko, Chorus and Orchestra of the Deutsche Oper, Berlin—Giuseppe Sinopoli

The most recent *Nabucco*, the first to be recorded digitally, was produced by DG with the forces of the Deutsche Oper Berlin and an international cast of singers that looks good on paper. The project is undermined from the very beginning by the wayward and excessively mannered conducting of Giuseppe Sinopoli. The Overture warns the listener of what to expect. Sinopoli has an annoying habit of beginning a phrase with a force that is not sustained to its end. He is in love with over-elaborate inflection for its own sake and the contrast of a strong phrase followed by a prissy one. These mannerisms destroy any sense of spontaneity or musical continuity. Is it any wonder the singers make only fitfully positive impressions? Abigaille has been Ghena Dimitrova's success role since her debut in Sofia in 1965, her 1981 triumph in the Verona Arena well documented on a Pioneer Artists video laserdisc. In an interview in *Opera News* she reported that she was under par the year of this recording. Even under par, she contributes some exciting moments when her sizable, somewhat steely dramatic soprano rings out. From time to time her lyric gifts are in evidence, as in a gracefully sung "Anch'io dischiuso un giorno," counterbalancing some awkward phrasing and some driven notes above the staff.

The Russian bass Yevgeny Nesterenko is not at his most forceful, ocassionally so ill at ease with Sinopoli's conducting that he sounds as if he is sight-reading. He suggests his real capabilities in the cabaletta to his first aria. Piero Cappuccilli's style and impersonation of the demented Babylonian king have authority, but his voice sounds strained in the high tessitura of such a lyrical passage as "Oh, di qual' onta aggravasi." Lucia Valentini Terrani's mezzo does not sound as youthful as is appropriate to Fenena, but it is sensitively employed. Plácido Domingo is luxury casting as Ismaele. The recording has a crisp clarity, but the sound is rather juiceless, despite an adequate frame of resonance; the string sonority is dry and undernourished, even by opera pit-orchestra standards.

Listeners desiring a single recording of *Nabucco* are directed to either the London or the Angel set. Both serve Verdi's early masterwork well. Decision is likely to depend on whether one thinks Scotto's art is compensation for her vocal frailties.

C. J. LUTEN

GIUSEPPE VERDI

ERNANI (1844)

A: Elvira (s); B: Ernani (t); C: Don Carlo (bar); D: Silva (bs)

George Bernard Shaw was a tireless advocate of *Ernani*, of the "fierce noonday sun" of its music and of "the superb distinction and heroic force of the male characters, and the tragic beauty of the women" in Verdi's operas generally. After two predominantly choral works (*Nabucco* and *I Lombardi*), Verdi turned to Hugo's *Hernani*—a romantic manifesto if ever there was one—and composed an opera that put the characters in the foreground. Elemental passions and Spanish pride and honor provide the dramatic propulsion, while a wealth of melodic expression, rhythmic vigor, and the careful building of the ensembles and finales are the musical engine. It is true that the characters are archetypes rather than well-defined individuals, but this is no more a drawback here than in the later *Il Trovatore*. Although Verdi relied on the musical conventions of the time, *Ernani* also looks forward in that after its expansive first act, it becomes progressively terse and dramatically compact. The fifth of his operas, it was the first to make him known outside Italy, reaching London in 1845 and New York two years later. It is a kind of model for *Il Trovatore*, and in matters of casting, except for the absence of a leading mezzo, makes the same stringent vocal-dramatic demands in the principal roles. Of the present recordings, two are complete (RCA, Hungaroton), one (EMI) drops a familiar number, of which more below, and the fourth (Cetra) cuts no numbers but omits the repeats, considerably abridging the first act.

1950 CETRA (M)

Caterina Mancini (A), Gino Penno (B), Giuseppe Taddei (C), Giacomo Vaghi (D), Italian Radio-Television Chorus and Orchestra, Rome—Fernando Previtali

Under the experienced and energetic hand of Fernando Previtali, this was one of the glories of Cetra's early LP catalogue. Behind the dated sound and some occasional sonic overloading there is an exciting performance that can still give much pleasure. Gino Penno had a relatively brief career, but during the few years he was at his best he was a thrilling *tenore robusto*, with penetrating tones, a somewhat metallic timbre, an easy top, and remarkable clarity of diction. (When he made his Metropolitan debut in the 1950s one critic remarked that Penno sounded louder facing the back of the stage than most tenors do facing the front.) Caterina Mancini is the type of Italian dramatic soprano that now seems to have largely disappeared from the scene (Cigna and Caniglia were others). Despite her voice's size and power, she uses it with considerable flexibility and dramatic purpose, and negotiates her high Cs with only slight evidence of strain. Giuseppe Taddei was thirty-four years old when this recording was made, but he had already reached the distinguished level of vocal and dramatic power that he would sustain for decades to come. He uses his supple and distinctive baritone with the expansiveness and nobility worthy of the emperor he plays. As Silva, Giacomo Vaghi delivers a forceful account of the elderly, stiff-necked noble who presumes

570

to compete with younger rivals for Elvira's favor. All the principals make an earnest effort to observe the trills, turns, and expressive markings, although some of the actual results are approximate.

1967 RCA / BMG (S) CD

Leontyne Price (A), Carlo Bergonzi (B), Mario Sereni (C), Ezio Flagello (D), RCA Italiana Opera Chorus and Orchestra—Thomas Schippers

The considerable merits of this recording are the radiant lyricism and impressive technical security of Leontyne Price's Elvira, the surpassing warmth and elegance of Carlo Bergonzi's Ernani, and the propulsion and clarity of Thomas Schippers's conducting. Price is at her memorable best here. The darkly glowing tone, the precision and dramatic purpose with which she handles the vocal embellishments, the ease of ascent to the top Cs, and above all the rare flexibility of her phrasing—all conspire to flesh out what can easily be a two-dimensional character. Although Bergonzi does not really have the vocal weight for an Ernani, he once again comes through dangerous territory not just unscathed but triumphant, overcoming his limitations with mellow, unforced tone, restrained passion, impeccable phrasing, and general stylishness. The other two male roles are less well served. Mario Sereni is an agreeable lyric baritone and he sings "Vieni meco" caressingly, but he simply does not have the vocal or temperamental equipment to convey a notion of regal authority, while Ezio Flagello's solid bass sounds rather too young to be convincing as the aged grandee.

1982 EMI / ANGEL (S,D,P) CD

Mirella Freni (A), Plácido Domingo (B), Renato Bruson (C), Nicolai Ghiaurov (D), La Scala Chorus and Orchestra—Riccardo Muti

This is a "live recording made in cooperation" with La Scala of the opening production of the 1982–83 season. It is a highly convincing document of an important occasion: a great theater put its best foot forward with the company's music director and a first-rank cast in the service of a composer this house claims as its own. Live recording in a theater has its pros and cons, and in this case there are many more of the former than the latter. One suspects that the tenor and soprano might have paid more attention to the score's expressive indications in a studio atmosphere than before an audience, but given the prodigal expenditure of vocal riches one can only envy the audience. The clatter of mass troop movements onstage is kept to a minimum and recorded applause is confined to the ends of acts. The recorded sound is very live and well balanced between stage and orchestra, and this is a performance of an exciting, highly alert *Ernani*, with Riccardo Muti's hand at the controls every step of the way. Plácido Domingo gives both dramatic weight and rich lyricism in the title part, even if at times more variety of tone would be welcome. Since graduating to heavier parts, Mirella Freni's *spinto* voice has lost some of its bloom and she sometimes gives the impression of operating close to the edge, but this is still an ardent performance of ample musical-dramatic range. Renato Bruson's dark-hued baritone has all the vocal color to encompass Don Carlo's emotional variables, whether he is being seductive, enraged, authoritarian, or nobly forgiving. Nicolai Ghiaurov is an imposing Silva, although he is deprived of the saber-rattling first-act cabaletta, "Infin che un brando vindice." This is presumably attributable to Muti's rectitude in the matter of original texts; since this piece was written not for the Venice premiere but for another bass in a later production, out it goes, even if it is in the published score. The Verdi scholar Julian Budden argues for its exclusion in his liner notes on the grounds that it is an "exit" aria without an exit, Silva still being needed onstage, and that in any case the vigor of the music is out of character for the aged Silva. The Scala orchestra is on its best behavior and the chorus, under Romano Gandolfi, sings with electrifying élan.

1982 HUNGAROTON (S,D) CD

Sylvia Sass (A), Giorgio Lamberti (B), Lajos Miller (C), Kolos Kováts (D), Hungarian People's Army Men's Chorus, Chorus and Orchestra of the Hungarian State Opera, Budapest— Lamberto Gardelli

Presumably the Hungarian state recording company (in the days of its state monopoly) wanted to give some of its homebred singers exposure on the world market, for it is hard to imagine any other reason for this recording. It is perfectly acceptable as a good night in the Budapest State Opera, but not anywhere near interesting enough to be competitive in the record market, despite up-to-date sound. Sylvia Sass has the kind of *lirico spinto* that permits her to venture into the dramatic repertory, and she is intermittently impressive here when she is not trying to imitate some of Callas's vocal

tactics. Lajos Miller is too dry of voice and wooden of temperament to impose himself as Don Carlo, while the bass Kolos Kováts is a rather rough-and-ready Silva. The ringer in this Magyar lineup is the Italian tenor Giorgio Lamberti, who has an agreeable voice, but too light for this employment and used without any sense of the necessary style. There is a distinctly unidiomatic feel to this version, and Lamberto Gardelli's conducting does nothing to disperse this impression.

———

The 1982 EMI recording is the best available version.

DAVID STEVENS

GIUSEPPE VERDI

MACBETH
(1847; revised 1865)

A: Lady Macbeth (s); B: Macduff (t); C: Malcolm (t);
D: Macbeth (bar); E: Banquo (bs)

lthough I yield to no one in my admiration for such works as *Nabucco, Ernani,* and *Luisa Miller,* in my opinion *Macbeth* is the best of Verdi's pre-*Rigoletto* operas. The composer evidently agreed, for *Macbeth* was the first of his works that he thought good enough to dedicate to his father-in-law, Antonio Barezzi.

The opera had its premiere in Florence in 1847, and was extensively revised for an 1865 Paris production. (This does not mean that the 1865 *Macbeth* is "really a French opera," in the sense that *Don Carlos* is. Verdi worked with the original librettist, Francesco Maria Piave. The musical revisions were thus made to an Italian text, which was then translated into French by Charles Nuttier; all of the recordings of the opera, needless to say, are sung in Italian. Today, *Macbeth* is sung in Italian even at the Paris Opéra!) The differences between the two versions are discussed in detail by Julian Budden in Volume I of his *The Operas of Verdi,* to which interested readers are referred.

All of the recordings of *Macbeth* are based upon the 1865 score, although some make cuts, and some even interpolate music unique to the 1847 score.

Macbeth has generally been thought of as a "conductor's opera," rather than a "singer's opera." The work contains some of Verdi's most imaginative instrumental writing—many passages seem almost experimental, and must have struck nineteenth-century listeners as terribly avant-garde. For the conductor, the great challenge is to do justice to the shifting chiaroscuro of the score—its continual alternation between introspective gloom and brash vigor.

Macbeth did not really become a repertory work until well after World War II; as a result, we cannot speak of standard cuts. The opera's commercial recorded history did not begin until the stereo era; the absence of mono versions is unfortunate. Still, the standard is high. Each of the eight complete sets has at least one element of distinction not duplicated elsewhere.

1959 RCA/BMG (S) CD

Leonie Rysanek (A), Carlo Bergonzi (B), William Olvis (C), Leonard Warren (D), Jerome Hines (E), Metropolitan Opera Chorus and Orchestra—Erich Leinsdorf

This recording is based on the 1958 Metropolitan Opera production. Cuts are minimal until the third act: there, the ballet is omitted, and so is the song-and-dance sequence. Although these cuts create holes in the musical continuity, they are defensible from the dramatic standpoint. In Act IV, however, the climactic sequence is mutilated by the inexplicable omission of both its beginning and its end; only half of the number is performed, and it is brought to a close with a few bars composed by somebody other than Verdi. Macbeth's death scene ("Mal per me") from the 1847 score is then inserted, before the 1865 finale.

Erich Leinsdorf, a fine musician, does not seem to be at his best here. The reading has a good deal of intensity and forward momentum, with all musical lines clearly and firmly drawn, and it is well executed by the Metropolitan Opera Orchestra. At times, though, Leinsdorf seems impatient with the music, and rushes it in a way that makes the composer's effects sound perfunctory—the introduction to "Vieni! t'affretta!" is a good example: it sounds almost flippant here, like something from a Rossini comic opera.

Leonard Warren is impressive in the title role, combining vocal stamina and variety with a well-thought-out portrayal. This is not perfect vocalism—as early as the duet with Banquo in the opening scene, Warren switches back and forth abruptly between a raw, open sound at *forte* and a heavily damped *mezza voce*, with not enough on the middle ground between these two extremes. But the baritone seems to get better as the opera goes along, and is tremendous in Acts III and IV.

Leonie Rysanek makes an exciting sound in Lady Macbeth's music: even her characteristically hollow, unsupported lower register is exploited to dramatic effect, and her soaring, impulsive top makes a thrilling impact in the climaxes and the ensembles. She works hard in the florid passages, although the sheer size and lushness of her voice seem to make needlepoint articulation impossible. Her lack of a trill is a serious handicap in the Act II Brindisi.

Carlo Bergonzi is a fine Macduff, phrasing "Ah, la paterna mano" with liquid ease and somber beauty of tone. Jerome Hines makes an imposing Banquo, although the actual sound of the voice is a little rusty.

The recorded sound is strange. A cavernous acoustic comes and goes, clearly betraying the fact that the performance was assembled from different "takes." Some of the stereo staging is downright bizarre.

BMG's reissue fits the opera onto two CDs (most of the other CD versions require three discs).

1964 DECCA / LONDON (S) ©

Birgit Nilsson (A), Bruno Prevedi (B), Piero de Palma (C), Giuseppe Taddei (D), Giovanni Foiani (E), Chorus and Orchestra of the Accademia di Santa Cecilia, Rome—Thomas Schippers

This is a disappointing performance, on the whole. For one thing, although this recording dates from a period when Decca was making a point of opening many of the traditional cuts in standard-repertory operas, this *Macbeth* is heavily cut—more so than the RCA set, in fact.

Thomas Schippers drives some of the music too hard for my taste—I miss a sense of suspenseful repose, of brooding mystery, in such episodes as Lady Macbeth's "Regna il sonno su tutti" or Banquo's "Oh, qual orrenda notte!" (both in Act I, Scene 2, before the finale). The conducting is legitimately exciting in the more extroverted parts of the score, and the orchestral execution is superior.

The recording preserves one truly great performance: Giuseppe Taddei's Macbeth. Taddei has the perfect voice for the role—large, warm, and dark, but never unwieldy. It seems incredible that the same instrument can fill out the climaxes with such rich, steady tone and still be capable of true *mezza voce* and *piano* effects. And Taddei is a superb vocal actor, who makes all of Macbeth's responses sound spontaneous and inward. His handling of the many declamatory passages is operatic artistry of the highest order.

Birgit Nilsson's Lady Macbeth is incomparable whenever steely power and security are required, and the soprano brings a surprisingly beautiful soft, round vocal quality to the more introverted passages. But she just doesn't sound like an Italian dramatic soprano: it is not a question of her enunciation of the text (which is very good indeed), but of actual vocal color, and to some extent of style. Nilsson is also defeated by the florid music: she simplifies much of the coloratura, and treads cautiously through what remains (like Rysanek, she does not attempt the trills at all). Still, we are not badly off when we can find a soprano of Nilsson's stature wanting in this music.

Bruno Prevedi is a burly-sounding, slightly dull Macduff; Giovanni Foiani makes a comparatively lightweight Banquo, monotonously lugubrious in manner. The smaller roles, however, are exceptionally well sung.

I have heard the recording only on open-reel tape; the sound seems excessively reverberant, with a really intrusive echo blanketing loud orchestral outbursts, and some artificial balances: the solo voices tend to be either unnaturally close or very distant.

1970 DECCA / LONDON (S)

Elena Souliotis (A), Luciano Pavarotti (B), Ricardo Cassinelli (C), Dietrich Fischer-Dieskau (D), Nicolai Ghiaurov (E), Ambrosian Opera Chorus, London Philharmonic Orchestra— Lamberto Gardelli

Decca here gives us, for the first time on records, the integral Paris score, without either cuts or interpolations from the 1847 version. Lamberto Gardelli is, of course, an experienced opera conductor, whose reading fairly crackles with theatrical excitement. Not once does the listener feel uncomfortable with a tempo choice, and the moods of the various episodes are caught with exceptional precision.

The London Philharmonic Orchestra plays the score quite brilliantly. The brass section deserves special praise: its work in such episodes as the ballet, the Apparitions Scene, and the Battle Fugue is nothing short of stupendous. All of this is reproduced in typically rich, wide-ranging Decca sound.

The cast splits right down the middle. Luciano Pavarotti and Nicolai Ghiaurov have rarely been equaled in their respective roles. The tenor is in exceptionally suave, plangent voice and phrases with exemplary line. If he does not capture the mournfulness of "Ah, la paterna mano" as memorably as some of his recorded rivals, this is still a great performance. The bass has almost the perfect voice for Banquo, and his magnificent sound is always at the service of the music and the drama.

Dietrich Fischer-Dieskau has a double handicap: his is not the right kind of voice for this role, and moreover, he is not in his best vocal

form here. Fischer-Dieskau's instrument is too light (in both weight and color) for the music, and the dry, open sound of his upper register spoils the climaxes. In addition—perhaps because he is trying to make his voice sound bigger and more imposing than it really is—he has some guttural, shaky moments. In fairness to Fischer-Dieskau, he does some eloquent things with the recitatives, and some of the more restrained lyrical sections (e.g., the last-act aria, "Pietà, rispetto, amore") are effective. But the performance as a whole is a compromise, and does not add up to a satisfying portrayal of Macbeth.

Elena Souliotis is frustrating for different reasons. She has power, reasonable agility, and all the temperament and dramatic imagination a listener could ask for; the only thing that's wrong is the actual sound of the voice—which is frequently excruciating. If some sopranos have register "breaks," then Souliotis has what can only be described as chasms—the gaps between her baritonal chest register, unsupported middle, and raw, squealy top are negotiated with a sort of heroic yodeling. Although she was only twenty-seven years old when this recording was made, her timbre sounds old and worn, like that of a fading dramatic soprano in her late fifties.

1976 DEUTSCHE GRAMMOPHON (S) CD

Shirley Verrett (A), Plácido Domingo (B), Antonio Savastano (C), Piero Cappuccilli (D), Nicolai Ghiaurov (E), La Scala Chorus and Orchestra—Claudio Abbado

This performance is uncut—indeed, it is more than complete, since it follows RCA's example by inserting "Mal per me" before the Paris finale.

Claudio Abbado gives us a beautifully proportioned, somewhat understated reading of the score, extremely well executed by the La Scala forces; the performance tends to be relaxed in tempo and soft in attack. Verdi's frequent requests for exaggeratedly quiet dynamics—*pppp* and the like—are respected throughout.

The Macbeth of Piero Cappuccilli is cleanly and tastefully vocalized, and intelligently projected—without quite possessing the tormented, larger-than-life quality that one longs to hear in the role. Cappuccilli's reflectiveness is preferable to carelessness and vulgarity, of course. No doubt Abbado is a restraining influence.

Shirley Verrett, though a mezzo, sings Lady Macbeth's music with a security and abandon that many of her soprano colleagues must envy, and her smoky, sensual timbre and strong upper register enable her to create many striking effects in the role. Her portrayal has both intensity and dignity—here, one feels, is a woman who was born to be a queen.

Plácido Domingo sings Macduff's aria well, and his large, warm, handsome sound makes an impressive contribution to the ensembles. Ghiaurov does not sound as vocally secure as he did on his earlier recording—his bass is lighter in timbre and marginally unsteady on some sustained tones—but he is still an imposing Banquo.

The engineering is unobtrusively excellent, and as a result this recording still sounds well after fifteen years.

1976 EMI / ANGEL (S) CD

Fiorenza Cossotto (A), José Carreras (B), Giuliano Bernardi (C), Sherrill Milnes (D), Ruggero Raimondi (E), Ambrosian Opera Chorus, New Philharmonia Orchestra—Riccardo Muti

Riccardo Muti performs the 1865 text complete, and then gives us, in a series of appendices (on the LP version only), three numbers from the 1847 score. These are: (1) Lady Macbeth's Act II cabaletta "Trionfai! securi alfine" (replaced, in 1865, by "La luce langue"); (2) Macbeth's Act III cabaletta "Vada in fiamme" (replaced by the duet "Ora di morte"); (3) the original end of the opera—Macbeth's "Mal per me," followed by a brief choral outburst to bring down the curtain. Although these excerpts are no substitute for a complete commercial recording of the 1847 score, they have an obvious value.

Muti's conducting is as taut and exciting as one could wish, and he has a superb orchestra to work with. My only reservation is that Muti takes some of the fast numbers very rapidly indeed. In Act I, Scene 1, for example, the

Witches' chorus "Le sorelle vagabonde" is whipped into such a frenzy that my reaction is simple amazement that voices and instruments can execute the notes accurately at such a pace. However, the words being sung are indistinguishable; and the whole approach seems suspiciously exhibitionistic—the listener is being invited to admire a performance feat instead of concentrating on the action of an opera. Whenever Muti does calm down and allow the music to breathe, though, he is most impressive.

Sherrill Milnes, as Macbeth, turns in one of his best recorded performances: the vocalism is firm, and more varied in color and dynamics than usual; the interpretation thoughtful, but direct and unfussy.

Fiorenza Cossotto, another mezzo Lady Macbeth, has some tense, edgy moments in the upper register, but otherwise sings with a combination of technical control and temperamental abandon.

José Carreras sounds a bit casual at times, as though he is doing a good job of sight-reading (he has not sung Macduff on stage), but his voice is heard at its most beautiful. In direct contrast, Ruggero Raimondi is in less than his best voice as Banquo—his tone is more nasal and muffled than usual—but is most expressive in his delivery of the text. Once again, there is an excellent supporting cast.

Aside from the fact that the engineers—like the conductor—indulge in some exaggerated dynamic contrasts, the recorded sound is stunning.

1983 PHILIPS (S,D) CD

Mara Zampieri (A), Neil Shicoff (B), Claes H. Ahnsjö (C), Renato Bruson (D), Robert Lloyd (E), Chorus and Orchestra of the Deutsche Oper, Berlin—Giuseppe Sinopoli

Giuseppe Sinopoli is an enormously talented conductor, but he often seems to have a compulsion to make his performances "different." This *Macbeth* is a typical example. On virtually every page of the score, the conductor can be heard fussing with tempo, phrasing, and dynamics; his balancing of the instrumental voices is often unorthodox, and he inserts all sorts of unwritten pauses and accents. His Berlin orchestra, it must be conceded, is with him all the way, producing a bright, tightly focused sonority that is convincingly Italianate in quality. The results are often fascinating, but they are anything but spontaneous; the listener catches himself paying attention to the conductor's interpretive decisions instead of experiencing the opera.

Sinopoli deserves praise for going to the trouble to consult the composer's manuscript and correcting some textual errors and corruptions that have crept into printed scores (and previous recorded performances). A curiosity, though, is the use of repeated gong bashes to represent the "knocking at the gate" in Act I—is this simply an aberration, or has Sinopoli dug up the original Paris performance materials?

The cast is good. Renato Bruson does not possess the world's most opulent baritone voice, but he sings with unfailing taste, subtlety, and imagination. This is a thoughtful, introspective Macbeth—almost too much so: it's hard to picture this intellectual cutting a swath through a battlefield, or committing any crime except after endless deliberation. Mara Zampieri's is a highly idiosyncratic Lady Macbeth. She sings virtually without vibrato, producing a cold, "white" sound devoid of color or sensuality. Technically, Zampieri is most impressive, tearing into the music with reckless abandon—high notes, low notes, runs, trills; you name it, she's ready to tackle it. She is also very much "with" Sinopoli's sophisticated approach to the music, manipulating her lines with infinite dynamic adjustments. The result is a performance that manages to be both tremendously exciting and quite mannered.

Neil Shicoff sings Macduff efficiently, and at times even excitingly, but his sound is consistently bright and shallow, and (like Zampieri's) lacks warmth and color. Robert Lloyd is an above-average Banquo, and there is excellent work in some of the other roles.

The sound is superb in every respect, making this the best-recorded version of the opera to date.

1986 HUNGAROTON (S,D) CD

Sylvia Sass (A), Peter Kelen (B), János Bándí (C), Piero Cappuccilli (D), Kolos Kováts (E), Hungarian Radio and Television Chorus, Budapest Symphony Orchestra—Lamberto Gardelli

Gardelli's conducting is marginally less good than it was on his previous recording—many of the tempos are noticeably slower, to no evident expressive purpose. The orchestral work is acceptable, but not particularly precise or idiomatic; one often has the impression that the players are feeling their way. The final section of the ballet music, for example, is slow and heavy, where it should have exactly the opposite qualities. The large chorus sings well, but its Italian is poor. (Several of the Hungarian *comprimario* singers also have pronounced accents.)

Cappuccilli now has some rough moments in the upper register, but by way of partial compensation he brings greater intensity to many of his declamatory passages. On balance, though, his earlier recording is preferable—it is more smoothly sung and benefits from Abbado's more supportive conducting. (The text is Paris, uncut, and this time Cappuccilli does not interpolate "Mal per me.")

Sylvia Sass is an interesting Lady Macbeth. This is a singer with many faults: her sound is oddly congested in the lower-middle register; her intonation is not always accurate; and her Italian enunciation is extraordinarily opaque. On the other hand, she has a basically attractive timbre and a strong top; she possesses both agility and temperament; she confronts the technical challenges unflinchingly. Her Sleepwalking Scene is particularly eerie.

The Macduff, Peter Kelen, is tight-voiced and phrases stiffly—adequate, but no more. Kolos Kováts, who sings Banquo and the First Apparition, sounds both woolly and unsteady.

The recorded sound is frequently cramped and shallow in quality.

1986 DECCA / LONDON (S,D) CD

Shirley Verrett (A), Veriano Luchetti (B), Antonio Barasorda (C), Leo Nucci (D), Samuel

Ramey (E), Chorus and Orchestra of the Teatro Communale, Bologna—Riccardo Chailly

This studio recording was made as the soundtrack for a film version of the opera directed by Claude d'Anna. The opera appears to have been recorded complete (in the Paris version, without "Mal per me"), but in order to fit the CD edition comfortably onto two discs, the ballet is eliminated.

The performance is a fine one, on the whole. Chailly's straightforward, unfussy leadership resembles Gardelli's (on the 1970 Decca set), and Chailly handles the more lyrical passages of the score in an even warmer, more appropriately *cantabile* way. The orchestra produces a rich, full sound. The chorus is occasionally guilty of that exaggeratedly *cupo* tonal quality beloved of Italian choral directors, but the sound is not inappropriate to this opera.

Leo Nucci has a good voice and is an intelligent, musical singer, but his Macbeth simply isn't as persuasive as Taddei's or (even if we limit the discussion to the Italian baritones) as individual as Cappuccilli's or Bruson's. Nucci's vibrato is intrusive at times, and his voice often sounds artificially puffed up, especially in the upper register (as on most of his recordings for Decca, he is very closely miked, which makes it difficult to judge the size of the voice, but the instrument seems relatively small and narrow).

Verrett is even more exciting than on her earlier recording of the opera, bringing a feverish intensity to bear on many episodes. But her voice sounds worn—hollow and unsupported at the bottom, often tight, and with an incipient wobble in the upper register.

The Macduff, Veriano Luchetti, has a relatively slender voice, metallic in timbre, but he is a conscientious, hard-working artist, and it's good to hear an Italian tenor in the part. Samuel Ramey sings Banquo very smoothly and richly, but I would have to say that Ghiaurov, for all his shortcomings, brings more grandeur to the role.

The recording was made in a church, and a recording-session photo in the booklet shows a structure with stone walls and a high, narrow nave. The acoustic is very reverberant, and with a good pair of headphones you can hear anything louder than *mezzo forte* quite literally bouncing off the walls of the church. As a result, the opera really does seem to be taking place in a succession of dank, claustrophobic castle corridors (and, in Act III, in a cavern!), but it would be idle to pretend that this is state-of-the-art engineering.

––––––––––

As a first version, I would recommend either the DG / Abbado or EMI / Muti recording. Both are uncut; both are well conducted, played, sung, and recorded; both are available on CD. More adventurous listeners may want to investigate the Philips / Sinopoli set—an impressive production, on the whole, despite (or because of) the highly idiosyncratic contributions of its conductor and soprano.

ROLAND GRAEME

GIUSEPPE VERDI

LUISA MILLER (1849)

A: Luisa (s); B: Federica (m); C: Rodolfo (t);
D: Miller (bar); E: Walter (bs); F: Wurm (bs)

Although the plot and setting of *Luisa Miller* are vintage romanticism, this transitional opera is more intimate and subtle than Verdi's earlier works. It foreshadows *La Traviata*, which was composed almost four years later. The major characters seem like stock roles on the surface, but all of them are multifaceted individuals depicted on a human scale. The character of Luisa develops from a young ingenue in the first act to a mature tragic figure in the last. Her father is a commoner of great personal dignity. Rodolfo, a young man of extraordinary candor, is both tender and heroic. The two bass roles, Walter and Wurm, are less complex, but they too are not stock characters. Walter is a ruthless autocrat, even a murderer, yet he is also a caring father. As for Wurm, he is a villain with a difference: Verdi wanted him portrayed with "a certain comic touch." The challenge to the soloists in this opera is to convey the psychological truth of these characters while singing music that ranges from the grandiosity of early Verdi to his more intimate mature style. The score is filled with eloquent orchestral details, and the Sinfonia that opens the opera is one of Verdi's finest overtures.

1951 CETRA (M,P)

Lucy Kelston (A), Miti Truccato Pace (B), Giacomo Lauri-Volpi (C), Scipione Colombo (D), Giacomo Vaghi (E), Duilio Baronti (F), Italian Radio Chorus and Orchestra—Mario Rossi

This set was recorded live before a radio studio audience. The sound is muffled; moreover, soloists are frequently heard clearing their throats, and individual soprano voices in the chorus stand out. Performances are tentative at first, but the singing improves noticeably as the opera progresses. Kelston's bright soprano easily cuts through the ensembles, but the sound has a bleating quality and her performance is disturbingly uneven. In her second-act aria, for instance, she approximates what is written and scoops wildly. Yet the recitative that follows is highly expressive and well sung. Kelston becomes the tragic heroine too soon, losing some of Luisa's youthful charm. She is more in character in the third act and also superior vocally, spinning out the soft passages with finesse. Although past his prime, Giacomo Lauri-Volpi gives a vigorous performance. His Rodolfo is the traditional hero, stentorian in sound, reveling in his bright, secure top voice. Yet this legendary tenor can also sing an exquisite *piano*, such as that in the third-act duet with Luisa. Scipione Colombo has a light baritone, evenly produced but rather throaty. A superb interpreter, he is totally involved in the text, communicating the dignity and tenderness of Miller. His subtle use of dynamics and his impeccable sense of phrasing bring the text to life. Giacomo Vaghi is an imposing Walter, but, more often than not, he is barely in control of the pitch. Duilio Baronti conveys a somber rather than a sinister Wurm. His bass voice is dry and his performance bland, with no hint of the comic touch stipulated by Verdi. Mario Rossi conducts a remarkably fluid, well-paced performance. The orchestra is eloquent throughout, beginning with an exceptionally expressive reading of the Sinfonia. Numerous cuts have been made in this recording: part of the ensemble in the first scene; Rodolfo's scenes with Walter and Federica; the second verse of most arias; and even the *a capella* quartet.

1965 RCA / BMG (S) CD

Anna Moffo (A), Shirley Verrett (B), Carlo Bergonzi (C), Cornell MacNeil (D), Giorgio Tozzi (E), Ezio Flagello (F), RCA Italiana Chorus and Orchestra—Fausto Cleva

Verdi once wrote that *Luisa Miller* should have two prima donnas: Luisa and Federica. This recording has both. Verrett's Federica is riveting; she is totally immersed in the text, capturing the many layers of the proud young noblewoman's emotional state with intensity and psychological truth. The mezzo's voice is vibrant and full-bodied. As Luisa, Moffo excels in the tragic scenes, conveying the heroine's anxiety and vulnerability to fine effect at the end of Act I and in the Letter Scene. Her warm soprano has a secure top, but the lower register sometimes sounds unsupported. Both Moffo and Bergonzi come into their own in the last act. Here both sing into the text, imbuing the words with meaning. The sweet sound of Bergonzi's voice embodies the tender aspect of Rodolfo's character. The tenor spins out beautiful *pianissimo* passages, such as the recitative before Federica's entrance, and sings his aria, "Quando le sere al placido," with exemplary *legato*. MacNeil gives the most fully realized portrait of Miller on these complete recordings. He is restrained at first, giving the character room to develop. His first-act cabaletta is sung more lyrically and with greater sensitivity than that of other baritones and as the opera progresses, MacNeil captures the depth of Miller's feelings, such as his profound anguish when he realizes that Luisa is planning suicide. Tozzi is an elegant Walter, but his voice is throaty and the pitch not always precise. Flagello sings with greater nuance than Tozzi even though his role

is more two-dimensional. He is superb in the Letter Scene. Throughout the opera, he savors the words and combines successfully the sinister and the humorous aspects of Wurm. Cleva brings great warmth to the score. His tempos are generally sprightly and the orchestral details are exceptionally clear. The chorus is outstanding; it participates fully in the drama.

1975 DECCA / LONDON (S) CD

Montserrat Caballé (A), Anna Reynolds (B), Luciano Pavarotti (C), Sherrill Milnes (D), Bonaldo Giaiotti (E), Richard Van Allan (F), London Opera Chorus, National Philharmonic Orchestra—Peter Maag

All three leads in this set are strong performers. Caballé communicates Luisa's emotions in the very sound of her voice. At her entrance, for instance, the purity and delicacy of that voice convey the joy and innocence of the character. Early in Act III, Caballé projects the near-madness of the young girl in the silvery sheen of her soprano, and later, in the duet with Rodolfo, her ethereal high notes make Luisa's compassion for her lover palpable. Pavarotti embodies the gentleness and candor of Rodolfo, yet his character can also be forceful, particularly in confrontations with Walter. Throughout the opera, the tenor colors his seamless voice with sensitivity to the text, using telling, imaginative details that bring his performance to life. He can convey the complexity of Rodolfo's emotions even in a single word, as, for instance, when he tells Luisa that the cup of poisoned wine is bitter. In a vividly etched performance, Milnes captures both the proud commoner and the caring father in Miller; the anguish he brings to the closing scene is deeply moving. Although Milnes tends to flat slightly on loud climactic notes, his voice is warm and full-bodied, yet capable of a fine *pianissimo* such as that at the end of the third-act duet with Luisa. As for the rest of the cast, Giaiotti's Walter is rather two-dimensional, yet he is excellent in the duet with Wurm, portraying an imperious count whose pride is shattered by overwhelming guilt as he relives the murder of his precedessor. Van Allan, whose rich bass is darker than Giaiotti's, provides a good contrast in their duet. Van Allan knows how to snarl and sneer musically, particularly when recalling details of the murder. Reynolds's Federica is a seductive character; her cadenza when she meets Rodolfo has a caressing quality. Maag conducts a sensitive, well-proportioned performance, emphasizing the intimate and the lyrical rather than the grandiose. He captures the idyllic charm of the opening and builds steadily to the tragic finale.

1979 DEUTSCHE GRAMMOPHON (S) CD

Katia Ricciarelli (A), Elena Obraztsova (B), Plácido Domingo (C), Renato Bruson (D), Gwynne Howell (E), Wladimiro Ganzarolli (F), Chorus and Orchestra of the Royal Opera House, Covent Garden—Lorin Maazel

Every musical detail is infused with meaning and dramatic purpose in Katia Ricciarelli's touching portrayal of Luisa. The delicate trills and *staccato*s of her opening cavatina become a natural expression of joy, and the way in which she lingers over the cadenza in her second-act aria turns that cadenza into a poignant musical sigh. Ricciarelli's sensitivity and musicality more than compensate for occasional raspiness in her voice. Domingo portrays an intense and vulnerable Rodolfo. He too uses musical detail to full dramatic advantage, such as the descending vocal line when he thinks he has been betrayed—a line in which the character seems to sink into despair. Domingo covers a wide emotional spectrum, yet his portrayal is remarkably cohesive because it all emanates from that core of vulnerability established early in the opera. Although Domingo's voice occasionally tightens in the upper register, his singing is heartfelt and his phrasing highly musical. Renato Bruson provides some dramatically viable moments, but on the whole his performance verges on the aloof. His baritone sounds dry, he is often not in the center of the pitch, and he cuts off the last notes of phrases prematurely. One of the joys of this recording is Gwynne Howell's firm, vibrant bass; his is the most fully developed Walter on these complete sets. He is in touch with the whole of the character, finding a full

range of emotions, for instance, in just the first few lines of his opening recitative. Ganzarolli gloats over Wurm's evil deeds, his voice slithering downward when he dictates the infamous letter to Luisa. In his confrontation with Rodolfo and in the duet with Walter, he introduces an element that rounds out the character: he reveals that Wurm is basically a coward. Obraztsova's Federica is regal, but she is more imposing than passionate, and her emotions seem generic. Her voice is velvety, particularly in the lower register, yet the sound tends to be unfocused. Maazel conducts a vigorous performance propelled by a sense of urgency. Though the conductor knows how to linger effectively over delicate passages, his reading is largely grandiose, marked by unnecessarily heavy accents and huge climaxes. Technically, the chorus is not sufficiently present, and a splice made to correct pitch problems at the end of the *a capella* quartet is all too obvious.

1991 SONY

Aprile Millo (A), Florence Quivar (B), Plácido Domingo (C), Vladimir Chernov (D), Jan-Hendrik Rootering (E), Paul Plishka (F), Metropolitan Opera Chorus and Orchestra—James Levine

Domingo's voice soars freely in this recording, without the strain evident in the 1979 Deutsche Grammophon set. This time around, his Rodolfo is more the nobleman, ever tender and gentle, but less vulnerable than his earlier portrayal. This is particularly evident in his aria, "Quando le sere al placido," which Domingo sings with unrelenting intensity, peaking with a true sense of the *disperazione* noted by Verdi in the score. Although Millo's opening scene is marred by tight high notes, the soprano comes into her own in the first-act finale with exquisite *pianissimos* and vibrant, arching lines in the ensemble. The burnished sound of her voice serves Millo well in her impassioned reading of Luisa's second-act aria, "Tu puniscimi," and her touching performance in the final duet and trio of Act III. Vladimir Chernov brings a bright, hefty, penetrating baritone to the Miller role. He successfully conveys the dignity of Luisa's father, but the role calls for more nuance and dynamic shading to flesh out the character. The sheer sound of the formidable Chernov voice, however, is thrilling. Jan-Hendrick Rootering communicates both the aristocratic demeanor and paternal concern inherent in the character of Walter. Vocally, his performance is less satisfying: his bass is resonant and pleasing, but unevenly produced. The other bass in this set, Paul Plishka, finds endless variety in the nefarious character of Wurm and seems to relish every word. In the letter scene, for instance, Plishka commands, insinuates, mocks, and gloats with his sonorous voice—all in the space of a few lines. Florence Quivar, who is also totally immersed in the words, uses her rich mezzo to create a truly passionate, fully developed Federica. The chorus sings with understanding of mood and text, and James Levine elicits incisive, highly eloquent playing from his orchestra. Levine carefully shapes each scene, driving it to its inexorable climax without rushing, and highlighting musical details without sacrificing the flow and balance of the piece.

Although many of the performances on other labels are outstanding, the evenly matched trio of leading singers on the London recording gives it a slight edge over the other sets. The sheer purity of Caballé's voice makes her Luisa luminous; Pavarotti's finely detailed performance is exquisitely sung; and Milnes's portrayal of Miller is stirring.

BRIDGET PAOLUCCI

GIUSEPPE VERDI

RIGOLETTO (1851)

A: Gilda (s); B: Maddalena (ms); C: Duke (t);
D: Rigoletto (bar); E: Sparafucile (bs)

Verdi's *Rigoletto* is an opera of paradox: Gilda is pure but capable of the deepest romantic passion; the Duke is charming but also shallow and cruel; and, of course, Rigoletto is bitterly angry but also full of the tenderest feelings. The tragedy turns on these elements, and three such complex roles have been savored from the beginning by the greatest singers; few operas have had such an illustrious casting history and yet have stood so firmly on their own. The earliest complete recordings contain "standard" cuts: some second verses and transitional passages, and the Duke's cabaletta "Possente amor," in which he prepares to meet the captured Gilda. As noted below, several of the later complete sets restore all the cuts, though they are not necessarily better performances because of that.

1916–17 EMI / ANGEL (M)

Ayres Borghi Zerni / Olga Simzis (A), Renata Pezzati (B), Carlo Broccardi (C), Giuseppe Danise / Ernesto Badini (D), Vincenzo Bettoni (E), Unidentified chorus and orchestra—Carlo Sabajno

In 1916–17 HMV recorded *Rigoletto* complete, using three Rigolettos and three Gildas. Several years ago Bongiovanni reissued on a single LP the selections made for that recording by the baritone Giuseppe Danise and a few others. His performance is cherishable. At the time of recording Danise was thirty-four and had sung two seasons at La Scala. He later sang

at the Met from 1920 until 1932, and in 1947, incidentally, married Bidú Sayão. His voice seems to be of medium size, and though not perhaps as warm as Giuseppe de Luca's, it is fresh and the top is plausible for the role. Where other Rigolettos are ferocious, he often convinces with a measured tenderness and exemplary phrasing. One can see why he was more a singer's singer than a great star—the voice is not of that sort, but his artistry and care are very much in evidence. Even in his duet with Sparafucile and "Pari siamo," he maintains a certain nobility of tone. At the moment when Rigoletto changes from bitter buffoon to gentle father, Danise takes the time to do so. His "Cortigiani" is outstanding for touching lyricism and finish. "Piangi, fanciulla" is taken more slowly than usual, and he shapes it beautifully at that speed; this may be the most artful version, from the baritone, at least, on records.

Of the others in these excerpts, Carlo Broccardi is a workmanlike Duke, with a few *appoggiaturas* in "Questa o quella" but a rushed "La donna è mobile" without cadenza. Of the two Gildas, one is a bit brassy and the other seems to have a clearer voice and warmer top range. Vincenzo Bettoni, who later recorded some Rossini with Conchita Supervia, is a vibrant, threatening Sparafucile, and, also playing Monterone, does a brilliant curse.

1927–28 EMI / ANGEL (M)

Lina Pagliughi (A), Vera de Christoff (B), Tino Folgar (C), Luigi Piazza (D), Salvatore Baccaloni (E), La Scala Chorus and Orchestra—Carlo Sabajno

In this first electrical recording of *Rigoletto*, Carlo Sabajno leads a spirited and relatively graceful performance, neither frenetic nor languishing, though the ensemble is at points untidy. In the title role, Luigi Piazza has a generally firm and vibrant baritone of great color. He rather storms through the tender moments but finds himself in his element in a rattling "Cortigiani": a sturdy, forthright portrayal, not notable for subtlety or finish but healthy and theatrical enough. Lina Pagliughi was just twenty when she recorded Gilda. There are a few raw, or rawly recorded, notes and some labored passagework, but "Caro nome" has some beautiful tone and a tenderness and yearning beyond several subsequent sopranos. From "Tutte le feste" onward she is consistently fragile and warm, with a sweetness complementing both Piazza's vehemence and Tino Folgar's charm. As the Duke, Folgar uses his light tenor with a certain courtly grace if not ultimate polish. He is dexterous in Act I, if perhaps too light for complete satisfaction in Acts II and III, where he must not only persuade but also manipulate and betray characters about whom we care. Then at the beginning of his career, Salvatore Baccaloni as Sparafucile shows a beautiful bass voice, and a slightly lugubrious delivery that even here suggests the comic. Aristide Baracchi (a baritone who incidentally sings Schaunard in four early recordings of *Bohème*) is surprisingly effective in the bass role of Monterone. Altogether the recording is nicely paced and gives us a view of Lina Pagliughi in her first recording and also of Luigi Piazza and Tino Folgar, intriguing singers hardly known except for this set.

1930 EMI / ANGEL (M)

Mercédès Capsir (A), Anna Masetti Bassi (B), Dino Borgioli (C), Riccardo Stracciari (D), Ernesto Dominici (E), La Scala Chorus and Orchestra—Lorenzo Molajoli

Though there are other contributions of some merit, this performance is dominated by its Rigoletto, Riccardo Stracciari, who at fifty-six had a magnificently full, focused, and mobile voice and considerable rhythmic energy. He may avoid full expression of all the dramatic elements called for by the text (envy, love, ironic misery, idealism, bitter wit), and some of the tender passages may sound a little casual, but he does have vocal grandeur and also something of the earth in his tone. The "Cortigiani," for example, reveals a nobility of sound which gives his breakdown stature. The voice and an element of savage heartbreak make this portrait memorable.

In general, Mercédès Capsir, who sang Gilda under Toscanini at La Scala in 1924, is steady and respectable, but hardly enlightening. When asking to see the city, she is sulky rather than wide-eyed with expectation, and her lyric, musing "Caro nome" has no real flowering of joy at the end. Under Molajoli, her death scene is a little rushed and lacks a measure of poetry and tragic repose. She is at her best in "Tutte le feste," where there are a piercing youthful passion in the singing and both power and control at the conclusion: a fine version. Dino Borgioli, rich in voice, is an earnest and sentimental Duke; he vocalizes pleasantly, if often without the requisite buoyancy and fury. The recorded sound is restricted, as one might expect, but listenable. The major interest here is in Stracciari, who provides a splendidly free and commanding tone and plenty of dramatic energy.

1950 RCA / BMG (M)

Erna Berger (A), Nan Merriman (B), Jan Peerce (C), Leonard Warren (D), Italo Tajo (E), Robert Shaw Chorale, RCA Victor Orchestra—Renato Cellini

This is a strongly sung and straightforwardly acted version of Verdi's opera which certainly recalls a style typical of the Metropolitan Opera in the period just after World War II. The cast is mostly American, the conducting is energetic if without ultimate tragic sweep, and everyone is in healthy voice. Leonard Warren is at his best here—and a voice of rolling grandeur it certainly is—with few of the fussy mannerisms of his later performances. The sound is fresh, weighty, and clarion at the top, and the musicianship earnest. With all his vocal amplitude, he does not employ a wide spectrum of vocal colors; one need only compare him with Giuseppe de Luca or Tito Gobbi to see that. Throughout the role, his two dramatic alternatives are simple tenderness and simple outrage. He has no real humor, bitter or otherwise: the jokes in Act I are delivered mirthlessly indeed. In the duet with Italo Tajo it is clear who is the consummate vocal actor. "Pari siamo" is full of general concern, but the specific dramatic possibilities are no more than sketched. "Cortigiani" is overwhelmingly earnest, and a little hamfisted. But what Warren did well, he did superlatively: there are stretches of inimitably smooth singing—"Deh non parlare," in a luscious *pianissimo*, is one of them. The phrasing here and elsewhere is expansive and thoughtful, and the upper register is in splendid shape. One is sometimes touched by specific moments of this performance, but one is continually moved, in quite a different way, by the glory of the sound he could produce.

Similarly, the tone and manner that Jan Peerce as the Duke provides are so full, impassioned, and direct that one's response is simply to sit back, listen, and ignore the unpleasant elements in the figure he is required to portray. What the tenor gives us is not in the least the decadent Duke of the libretto. There is little suggestive humor in Peerce's first act, and in "Parmi veder" he seems to be seriously moralizing, as Alvaro might in *La Forza del Destino*. It is all very fully and, in its way, compellingly sung. Erna Berger as Gilda is sweet, light, and musicianly. The scenes of innocence are neatly done, but the scenes of humiliation are prosaic: one wants in her sound more heft, warmth, and suggestion of tragedy. Italo Tajo is a superlative Sparafucile, with the knell of death in his voice: the totally cynical, fatally unimaginative man. It is an engrossing performance, with a lovely *pianissimo* on the pronunciation of his name. Nan Merriman is fresh-voiced but quite unconvincing as the temptress Maddalena. The conducting is energetic and the cuts standard for the period: they include the first verse of "Veglia o donna" and all of "Possente amor." That is

unfortunate, since Warren and Berger do the rest of the duet well and Peerce had just the sort of decisive delivery needed for the Duke's cabaletta. This set is often engaging, and gives first-class evidence of what people found so satisfying in the work of Peerce and Warren.

p.1951 REMINGTON (M)

Orlandina Orlandini (A), Lidia Melani (B), Gino Sarri (C), Ivan Petrov (D), Mario Frosini (E), Chorus and Orchestra of the Maggio Musicale Fiorentino—Erasmo Ghiglia

I have heard only extensive excerpts from this recording, which is interesting for some of its rarely heard singers. Gino Sarri has recorded heavier things, such as *Andrea Chenier* and *Otello*, but he demonstrates qualifications better suited to the Duke: a warm, steady voice of middle weight, if not the technique to avoid strain in the high range or any dramatic imagination. In "Questa o quella" there are no ornaments and little fun; the duet "È il sol dell'anima" is somewhat careless in rhythm; and in "Parmi veder" the top notes begin to develop a beat. As Gilda, Orlandina Orlandini has a hard voice of some size in the middle range. At the end of an efficient "Caro nome," she ascends to a not-quite-perfect E-flat in alt. Her best work is in "Tutte le feste," of which she makes a dramatic experience. Ivan Petrov as Rigoletto shows first-class potential; the interpretation is conventional but lively, though the voice is occasionally strained. His duet with Sparafucile (the vibrant Mario Frosini) is one of the better recordings of that scene. Altogether the excerpts suggest a strong but routine performance, more durable than some with more famous participants.

p.1954 CETRA (M)

Lina Pagliughi (A), Irma Colasanti (B), Ferruccio Tagliavini (C), Giuseppe Taddei (D), Giulio Neri (E), Cetra Chorus, Orchestra of Radio-Television Italiana, Turin—Angelo Questa

This performance has some absorbing elements but is done in by the distant and reverberant sound on the Everest pressing available to me. The mature Lina Pagliughi is a luminescent Gilda, full of warmth and specific response, and anything but somnambulistic or hard. Tetrazzini proclaimed Pagliughi as her successor, but I have always felt that Pagliughi recalls more fully Galli-Curci's warmth and pliability of tone, which she uses here to create a vibrant character within the limits of a "coloratura" voice. "Caro nome" is exquisitely modest and charming, save for one minor scramble. She handles "Tutte le feste" expertly, passion welling up halfway through it, and there is conviction in the succeeding duets with Taddei. In the final scene she has a lovely dying tone.

As Rigoletto, Giuseppe Taddei begins excitingly, with a chillingly offhand manner and a droll imitation of Monterone. "Pari siamo" sounds spontaneous and "Deh non parlare" is a beautiful stretch of unconstricted *piano* singing. The close of the act and "Cortigiani" are not so imaginative, though the later duets with Gilda are alternately tender and full of conviction. Altogether it is a provocative performance; perhaps he needed an authoritative conductor to shape it more carefully.

After some of the Dukes one has heard, Ferruccio Tagliavini seems a miracle of grace. Much of it is charming, some precious, and some needlessly breathy and awkward. The seductive phrasing in "Parmi veder" is typical, and he offers one verse of "Possente amor," tasteful in tone but a little sloppy in execution. The quartet shows him variable: the basic tone is light and fine, but there are the occasional mannerisms of forcing and nasality. Giulio Neri finds in Sparafucile a good role for his huge, dead voice: an Italian Hagen. Antonio Zerbini is a strong Monterone. With this cast a great conductor might have fashioned an unforgettable *Rigoletto*; Angelo Questa's performance sometimes lacks cumulative tension.

1954 DECCA / LONDON (M)

Hilde Gueden (A), Giulietta Simionato (B), Mario del Monaco (C), Aldo Protti (D), Cesare Siepi (E), Chorus and Orchestra of the Accademia di Santa Cecilia, Rome—Alberto Erede

This performance is a very mixed grill indeed; there are major problems with all of the leading roles *and* the conducting. The difficulties are obvious from the first curtain, for Mario del Monaco as the Duke is at once golden-toned and completely charmless. Alberto Erede begins "Questa o quella" at one speed and the tenor at another; del Monaco wins and then fails to keep the tempo he has set. His little scene with the Countess Ceprano is as flirtatious as a siege, and the garden duet with Gilda noisy and abrasive. "Ella mi fu rapita" can absorb some of his continual anger, but the one verse of the cabaletta included is disgracefully inaccurate. Even "La donna è mobile" is brash and uncertain in rhythm, and the quartet is begun *forte* and soon becomes a shouting match: a magnificently awful performance.

Hilde Gueden's Gilda shows some dramatic concern, but there is a Viennese sophistication in this characterization that contradicts everything we know about Gilda and accords particularly ill with del Monaco's brutish Duke. However, she does a touching "Tutte le feste," in which the natural warmth and fullness of her middle voice are useful, and also sounds attractive in the final duet, which is taken too quickly.

The real victim here may be Aldo Protti. He begins promisingly, making his murderous suggestions in the first scene as if thinking them up on the spot. In the second scene the voice is healthy and there are moments of distinctive acting in the monologue. In the duet with Gilda, though, the wonderfully evocative line is broken up with obvious breaths. The "Cortigiani" has variety but is roughly handled; again it is the *cantabile* sections that are dispiriting. He seems to have the equipment for a better performance: what circumstances might have coaxed it from him? Giulietta Simionato sings a lively but tremulous Maddalena and Cesare Siepi is a foggy, ill-defined Sparafucile. As Monterone, Fernando Corena offers a strong curse, although there is a slight beat in some of his tone. Conductor Alberto Erede is sometimes lyrical and supportive, but del Monaco rushes him, he rushes Protti, and little of the performance has dramatic shape.

1955 EMI / ANGEL (M) CD

Maria Callas (A), Adriana Lazzarini (B), Giiseppe di Stefano (C), Tito Gobbi (D), Nicola Zaccaria (E), La Scala Chorus and Orchestra—Tullio Serafin

Despite its shortcomings, this is in many ways the most revealing of all recorded *Rigolettos*: the performance in which the complexity of Verdi's vision is most fully realized. Here the Duke is self-obsessed yet charming; Gilda is innocent yet passionate; and Rigoletto's bitterness and tenderness are seen to arise from a common cause—his virtues, in effect, produce his tragic fate. Though elsewhere the roles may be sung more sweetly, the opera's paradoxes have never been made so clear.

The whole of Tito Gobbi's art can be seen in the little scene in which Rigoletto imitates Monterone: the buffoon becomes oracular, aged, and prissy, and finds a different and galling color for each insult. There is similar precision in "Pari siamo." Each of the words he uses to describe the hated Duke has a different and apposite hue, and yet Gobbi provides the character with psychological continuity. His scenes with his Gilda are at once tender and authoritarian. At the completion of "Tutte le feste," this baritone does not rush ahead with a practiced expression of vengeance; his indignation grows as he sings the words, and, finally, his "Piangi, fanciulla" exceeds anything previous in fatherly concern. This Gilda and Rigoletto, in addition, take on each other's tonal shading, revealing uniquely the personal element in their relationship. With such attention to detail, it is not surprising that the greatest challenges, such as "Cortigiani," go as successfully as they do.

As Gilda, Maria Callas is at the start all tender concern; this is a heroine of worth beyond her innocence. In "Tutte le feste," she does not broadcast her shame; she hides it at first, and the horror of her perception seems to grow with the music. In the final scene she suggests with the voice not merely frailty but death itself. As usual, neither of them does particularly well with sustained forte high notes; his tend to sound wooden and hers predatory. What these singers do is to reveal Verdi's characters.

In dramatic intent, at least, Giuseppe di Stefano is especially accomplished, though the challenges are different. He begins with a smile in the voice and continues with a shallow yet enticing tenderness. There is more amazement than anger in "Ella mi fu rapita" and the quartet for once begins intimately. It is all (quite rightly and uniquely) both attractive and alienating. Technically though, the singer has some serious problems: the tone thickens, the pitch is sometimes unsure, and frequently he cannot project the grace he envisions.

The supporting cast is equal to its tasks, and Tullio Serafin in general shapes things well, allowing time for his remarkable cast to explore the score but not for self-indulgence. There are occasional vocal difficulties here—and some vocal glory, too—but this is as searching an examination of the tragedy as we have.

1956 RCA / BMG (M) CD

Roberta Peters (A), Anna Maria Rota (B), Jussi Bjoerling (C), Robert Merrill (D), Giorgio Tozzi (E), Rome Opera Chorus and Orchestra—Jonel Perlea

This largely Metropolitan Opera cast, recorded in Rome, features very healthy and beautiful voices in most of the leading roles—with hardly a characterization among them. As if trying to combat this blandness, conductor Jonel Perlea consistently rushes, robbing the singers of some of the grace they might have had and providing more agitation than excitement. Jussi Bjoerling, in resplendent voice, is nevertheless a nervous, charmless Duke; neither "Questa o quella" nor "La donna è mobile" has any sense of amusement, and the duet with Gilda is sung without intimacy. "Ella mi fu rapita" has at least a genuine romantic indignation, which may be beside the point but is lovely to listen to. Bjoerling smiles for the first time in the quartet, where his tone is, as always, uniquely rich.

Robert Merrill is likewise in plangent voice, but there is little wit in first scene and he is rushed through most of the rest. "Pari siamo" and "Cortigiani" are at least resonant, but the tender duets with Gilda emerge only as fast and efficient. One would have scant idea from the vocalization that love, betrayal, and death were being discussed. As Sparafucile, Giorgio Tozzi is also in peak condition, but his sinister duet with Merrill sounds positively sunny here. Roberta Peters is a bright and rather hard-voiced Gilda. Like many sopranos, she is most persuasive in "Tutte le feste," in which the spectrum of attitudes is so vividly dramatized in the music. Elsewhere she is, like the others, a singer in search of a character.

1959 PHILIPS (S)

Gianna d'Angelo (A), Miriam Pirazzini (B), Richard Tucker (C), Renato Capecchi (D), Ivan Sardi (E), Chorus and Orchestra of the San Carlo Opera—Francesco Molinari-Pradelli

This is a set of some vocal and dramatic interest despite its failings. That fine singing actor Renato Capecchi is a very responsive Rigoletto, quick and witty in the first scene, desperate but dramatically varied in "Pari siamo." There are tears in the duets with Gilda, but "Cortigiani" has subtler elements of irony and grief. The voice, though, is occasionally constricted and unsteady. Gianna d'Angelo is warm-toned but generally a blank dramatically, while Richard Tucker is fervent, though he cannot convince as a charming wastrel. The Duke's cabaletta is cut. Miriam Pirazzini is a plausible Maddalena and Ivan Sardi resonant as Sparafucile. The conducting has its elements of grace but is generally routine.

1959 BIS (M, P)

Margareta Hallin (A), Kerstin Meyer (B), Nicolai Gedda (C), Hugo Hasslo (D), Arne Tyren (E), Chorus and Orchestra of the Royal Opera, Stockholm—Sixten Ehrling

This live performance will be no one's idea of the perfect *Rigoletto*: the sound is merely serviceable, the ensemble ragged, the singers variable, and some of the pacing eccentrically fast and rigid. And yet it is a fascinating set, and for collectors possibly an essential one. For one thing, it provides a view of several half-known singers (Hugo Hasslo and Margareta Hallin among them) and a record of some of Erling's

work in opera. Then there are in smaller roles singers who later became Swedish stars, such as Ingvar Wixell (Ceprano), Barbro Ericson (Giovanna), and Birgit Norton (Page). Most important, it is a rousing, if flawed performance.

. Hugo Hasslo has a moderate-size baritone, somewhat blunt in quality, thin at the bottom and thick on top. His conception of the role, though, is brilliant, and he is not afraid to distort his voice for dramatic effect. His "Qual vecchio maledivami" sounds for once, genuinely lost and frightened, and he colors and phrases "Pari siamo" fully for envy, fascination, and self-pity.

Margareta Hallin is a dramatic coloratura with a dark voice but dramatic intelligence. "Caro nome" reveals spine underneath that youthful purity, and she often phrases touchingly. The performance has some of Callas's grit, and some of her fragility, too. Nicolai Gedda is, very surprisingly, a muscular and purposely crude Duke. "Questa o quella" lacks grace entirely, and in Scene 2 he seems to want to take Gilda almost by force. "Ella mi fu rapita" is quite angry and the aria is sung in full voice with terrific rhythmic verve and extended high notes. The cabaletta is cut. Later he clatters through "La donna è mobile"; it is very high-spirited, with a long final note that gets enormous applause. He seems a restless singer here, trying all kinds of effects to suggest the ruthlessness of the character. The excess, the experimentation, and the wildness are interesting from a singer with his reputation for grace and exactitude. Kerstin Meyer is a smooth Maddalena: one of the few who is not singing around an obvious and ugly break in the voice. With his thin orchestra, sometimes ragged ensemble, and a charmless first scene, Sixten Ehrling nevertheless leads a performance of some excitement. Full of obvious faults, the set is nevertheless invigorating.

1960 RICORDI (S)

Renata Scotto (A), Fiorenza Cossotto (B), Alfredo Kraus (C), Ettore Bastianini (D), Ivo Vinco (E), Chorus and Orchestra of the Maggio Musicale Fiorentino—Gianandrea Gavazzeni

This cast looks very promising. Ettore Bastianini had one of the most beautiful baritone voices in the world, Renata Scotto had facility and dramatic capacity, Alfredo Kraus is still noted for his elegance of style, and Gianandrea Gavazzeni has done some lyrical work in other recordings. Their performance here, however, is generally harsh, with first-rate voices driven to provincial shouting. Bastianini begins with plenty of spirit; he laughs at his own jokes and suggestions. Later, "Pari siamo" has a bitter, ironic edge. The volume level, though, is *mezzo forte* and remains so: soon, Renata Scotto and he are shouting at one another and at the end of "Veglia, o donna" he drowns her out. "Cortigiani," "Piangi, fanciulla," and "Si, vendetta" are rough and monochrome, and in Act III, he evinces not the slightest sense of wonder or astonishment at the events disclosed: ultimately, a tiresome performance.

Nor is Scotto well represented. She has a fine voice for the role: lyric with a touch of the dramatic when she needs it. However, the shouting produces rawness of voice and characterization. Alfredo Kraus is vocally fine as the Duke: a little dry perhaps, but flexible and powerful enough. "Questa o quella," though, is robbed of delight by its speed. Act II, however, displays the singer's capacity for both anger and grace, and one verse of "Possente amor" is reinstated. Fiorenza Cossotto is an excellent Maddalena, with a telling upper register, rhythmic exactitude, and steady tone. Conductor Gianandrea Gavazzeni begins with an exceptionally dramatic Prelude—and a rushed, humorless first act. Thereafter he takes many of the *cantabile* sections too fast for full dramatic elaboration.

1961 DECCA / LONDON (S) CD

Joan Sutherland (A), Stefania Malagù (B), Renato Cioni (C), Cornell MacNeil (D), Cesare Siepi (E), Chorus and Orchestra of the Accademia di Santa Cecilia, Rome—Nino Sanzogno

This was the first recording of the opera for both Joan Sutherland and Cornell MacNeil and represents their best work in it. It is also uncut. MacNeil sings particularly well here—the voice

is full, free and fresh—but much of his dramatic work is in the same generalized elegiac mood. "Piangi, fanciulla," for example, is a lovely moment, but by the time it comes its attitude has so often been expressed that the piece seems, of all things, dull. Joan Sutherland is likewise in healthy voice and, as one might expect, does the *fioriture* beautifully and provides many moments of exquisitely poised singing. From the start, though, she languishes, neutralizing the emotional contrasts Verdi has set up. To take one example, her "Caro nome" is a marvel of tone, but also a sort of mad scene, complete with opaque vowels and a melancholy rather than musing mood. Sutherland sounds like a willing victim from the first, and the important tragic point about Gilda is that she really wishes to succeed, to live, to be happy.

Renato Cioni has a more pointed sound than Gedda or Domingo, a welcome flexibility, and both mettle and delicacy in his approach. There is something of a bleat in the voice, but he sings his second-act aria cleanly, if a little tearfully, and does "Possente amor" complete. "La donna è mobile" is pleasant. Cesare Siepi is again a benevolent Sparafucile; the duet with Rigoletto here sounds rather innocuous. Conductor Nino Sanzogno is lively at the start, but once Sutherland is on the scene, things lapse into somnolence. In sum, there is little characterization but much attractive vocalism in this set, and for those who want Sutherland or MacNeil, this is the version to hear.

1963 ELECTRECORD (S)

Magda Ianculescu (A), Dorothea Palade (B), Ion Buzea (C), Nicolae Herlea (D), Nicolae Rafael (E), Bucharest National Opera Chorus and Orchestra—Jean Bobescu

The makings of an exciting performance are here, but it's hobbled by shapeless conducting and some insufficient vocal technique. The dominant figure is Nicolae Herlea, who has splendid tone and a vivid if entirely conventional dramatic conception. Here he is occasionally sharp, though the *cantabile* singing and the high notes are often brilliant. Ion Buzea has a richer, steadier voice than many more famous

Dukes, but he and the conductor lumber through the music without much charm or compulsion. Magda Ianculescu is a better musician than she is a vocalist: the phrasing is often touching though the tone can be grating and the pitch suspect. She is frequently recorded at greater distance than the others. The sound is occasionally both boxed in and reverberant. The set is interesting for documenting Herlea's remarkable voice and Buzea's raw promise.

1963 RCA / BMG (S) CD

Anna Moffo (A), Rosalind Elias (B), Alfredo Kraus (C), Robert Merrill (D), Ezio Flagello (E), RCA Italiana Opera Chorus and Orchestra—Georg Solti

Robert Merrill again vocalizes quite beautifully in a role meant for his voice, but again can't extract much of the vengefulness or the heartbreak implicit in the score. Some scenes are more broadly but no more deeply enacted than before, but much of the performance, especially at Georg Solti's rapid tempos, seems casual. Alfredo Kraus plays a humorless but fluent Duke, and in Act II is in a blind fury. Both verses of "Possente amor" are included, the second sung more compulsively than the first. It is a laudable attempt to project the evil aspects of the character, but the charm *is* sacrificed. As Gilda, Anna Moffo has a warmer voice and a greater range of colors than some others, but Solti rushes so many of the reflective passages that she has little time to develop them. Though she sometimes croons and slides up to a note, there are several lovely passages: the end of "Caro nome" is one of them. Ezio Flagello is an interestingly circumspect Sparafucile and Rosalind Elias an apt Maddalena. As noted, Solti rushes along brashly, lacking repose in the tender passages and humanity in the faster ones. This may be an effort to instill excitement into the proceedings, but the effect is generally both nervous and bland.

1963 DEUTSCHE GRAMMOPHON (S) CD

Renata Scotto (A), Fiorenza Cossotto (B), Carlo Bergonzi (C), Dietrich Fischer-Dieskau (D), Ivo Vinco (E), La Scala Chorus and Orchestra—Rafael Kubelik

Here we have one of the most intriguing of all *Rigoletto* sets. Dietrich Fischer-Dieskau may have too light and friendly a tone for the ideal Rigoletto, but he brings to the role imagination, intelligence, and conviction—some of it a little self-conscious, but valid still. For example, at his first entrance he gives some evidence of actually being a buffoon: he talks—he does not orate. His caricature of Monterone is light and dismissive, and he uses a broken-down trill to suggest old age. In "Pari siamo" he is splendid when imitating the Duke, but, of course, cannot do everything he wants with "O dannazione" because the voice has not the edge and power of a Stracciari or Ruffo. He may broadcast a little obviously the ironies of the scene with courtiers in Act II, but when the Page arrives he is suddenly all command. What he cannot supply in power he does with phrasing and a suggestion of gruffness. His lyric scenes may be pathetic rather than tragic, but they are fascinating for his range of colors and beautiful soft singing.

Renata Scotto responds to Fischer-Dieskau, completing an exceptionally tender relationship. Her Gilda here is passionate in nature and yet innocent. She may be in love, but she also has a conviction about the joy she can bring her father. "Tutte le feste" may be, like some of Fischer-Dieskau's work, a little self-consciously dramatic—Kubelik's slow tempo encourages that—but her work is often enchanting. Carlo Bergonzi is a gentlemanly Duke. He is rhythmically exact and enlivening, though without much humor or guile, but "È il sol dell'anima" is charming and the "Addio" for once delightful: youthful and pointed rather than merely a scramble. In Act II, like so many tenors, Bergonzi projects gentility and concern rather than self-interest. "Possente amor" is included. All that his "La donna è mobile" lacks is a smile. Rafael Kubelik conducts warmly and persuasively, though his tempos are slow for the Rigoletto-Gilda duets; there and elsewhere one wants more thrust. Nevertheless, this is one of the most challenging of recorded *Rigoletto*s.

1967 EMI / ANGEL (S)

Reri Grist (A), Anna di Stasio (B), Nicolai Gedda (C), Cornell MacNeil (D), Agostino Ferrin (E), Rome Opera Chorus and Orchestra—Francesco Molinari-Pradelli

In his second recording, Cornell MacNeil is in variable voice, with strong work in "Pari siamo" but patches of unsteadiness, wear, and flatness elsewhere. The characterization is conventional. Nicolai Gedda's Duke is a refinement of what he attempted in the Hasslo set: an admirable effort, but much of his singing here is a little leathery. One verse of "Possente amor" is included. Reri Grist sings "Caro nome" with charm. The rest is also neat and accurate but light and occasionally colorless. Agostino Ferrin is a suitable Sparafucile, though Anna di Stasio is tough as Maddalena. Ruggero Raimondi provides a commanding Monterone. Francesco Molinari-Pradelli conducts a rather sleepy performance.

1971 DECCA / LONDON (S) CD

Joan Sutherland (A), Huguette Tourangeau (B), Luciano Pavarotti (C), Sherrill Milnes (D), Martti Talvela (E), Ambrosian Opera Chorus, London Symphony Orchestra—Richard Bonynge

Sherrill Milnes is in spectacularly good voice for this, his first complete Rigoletto. He has worked it all out in admirable detail. One listens with fascination, for example, to the four "va"s at the end of the duet with Sparafucile: each one is more horrified and the last is a sort of hoarse cough. The *cantabile* sections he sometimes overloads with effects. "Veglia, o donna" is not so affecting as it could be if sung more simply and slowly, with absolute attention to line and purity of tone. "Cortigiani" is resonant and "Si, vendetta" is done with the appearance of ease: a strong performance.

As Gilda, Joan Sutherland provides a few fabulous cadenzas and some lovely top notes, but the rest is throaty, a trifle unsteady, and quite unbelievable as a characterization of this passionate, innocent, victimized young woman. In general, Luciano Pavarotti sings magnificently as the Duke, though the whole first scene

is, surprisingly, humorless and rather nervous-sounding. In Act II he has exactly the right voice and sense of line for the aria. There are little elisions in the cabaletta, but this remains one of the best versions that I know. "La donna è mobile" is delightful, endless high note and all. Altogether, he is the finest of recorded Dukes.

Martti Talvela has a wonderfully closed sound for Sparafucile, while Huguette Tourangeau's Maddalena is so thick-voiced and dark as to lack allure. She and Talvela have a vivid and surprisingly intimate fight over their prospective victim: she takes a couple of notes lower than the score indicates and succeeds in sounding like her brother for a moment or two! Richard Bonynge conducts an uncut performance with most of the usual high notes retained. It is an occasionally ponderous but in general considerately led recording.

1977 ACANTA (S) CD

Margherita Rinaldi (A), Viorica Cortez (B), Franco Bonisolli (C), Rolando Panerai (D), Bengt Rundgren (E), Dresden State Opera Chorus and Orchestra—Francesco Molinari-Pradelli

Vocally this is among the most satisfying of all the *Rigoletto* sets. Margherita Rinaldi, who has not been widely recorded, is something of a revelation. She has warmth, power, and reasonable facility, together with the range of color to express a doomed appetite for life. Of how many Gildas can that be said? Rolando Panerai has power, technique, and that inimitably warm timbre, and Franco Bonisolli, in rich voice, is tenderer and more tasteful than one might imagine. Despite a few muscular moments, his vocalism is remarkably easy and accurate, and he presents a vibrant character with a sense of humor. Viorica Cortez is at least youthful in sound and steady, and Bengt Rundgren resonant. The *comprimarios*, it is true, are generally shallow-voiced and dramatically anonymous, but the real problems of the set lie elsewhere. Molinari-Pradelli is as sleepy here as in his two previous *Rigoletto* sets, though he does better with moments of tenderness than those of fury or terror. Panerai, too, handles affection nicely. "Deh non parlare" and "Miei signori" are touching, if not the overwhelming moments they might be with a compelling conductor. Where he is lacking is in the passages of irony. That big, friendly, immediately identifiable voice seems unsuited to anything underhanded, so that much of what distinguishes Rigoletto from some other great Verdi baritone roles is lost. Nonetheless, despite this limitations, the dull conducting, and the *comprimarios*, this is a very pleasant set to hear.

1978 EMI / ANGEL (S)

Beverly Sills (A), Mignon Dunn (B), Alfredo Kraus (C), Sherrill Milnes (D), Samuel Ramey (E), Ambrosian Opera Chorus, Philharmonia Orchestra—Julius Rudel

Once again we have Milnes's skillful and well sung Rigoletto and Alfredo Kraus's elegant, self-centered Duke, this time a little more alive to the character's charm than previously. Since this is an uncut performance, he sings "Possente amor," and with spirit. Something of Beverly Sills's charm and histrionic authority in the opera house is consistently lost on records. Here she is a thoughtful and warm Gilda of some spirit, without quite the resources of color to project her view of the role. The voice is tremulous but forward. Despite vocal problems she and Kraus course rather delightfully through most of the "Addio." Elsewhere she is appealing, but one must get used to the sound in order to experience her rounded, sympathetic vision of the part. Julius Rudel is the competent conductor, a little fast in some of the lyric passages. Altogether it is not a brilliant set, but it has its worthy elements.

1979 DEUTSCHE GRAMMOPHON (S) CD

Ileana Cotrubas (A), Elena Obraztsova (B), Plácido Domingo (C), Piero Cappuccilli (D), Nicolai Ghiaurov (E), Vienna State Opera Chorus, Vienna Philharmonic Orchestra—Carlo Maria Giulini

One of the charms of this set is the conducting of Carlo Maria Giulini. His work is lively, proportionate, and moving: better than the conducting in any other *Rigoletto* since Serafin's. Best of all, he has a view of the piece as a whole and supports the efforts of his singers, working to their strengths and not asking them to do what is impossible or awkward. The edition used is complete.

Piero Cappuccilli is one of the more satisfactory modern Rigolettos. The voice is modest in size and rather blunt, but he scales his performance to his means and makes his dramatic points with vigorous accents and color. "Pari siamo" is notable for its variety: intimacy, disgust, amazement, and fear are all present. The *cantabile* passages in the opera are sometimes rough but nearly always touching, though he has not quite the tonal resources for the moments of command or outrage. As Gilda, Ileana Cotrubas has her usual freshness and glow. She has that now-rare ability (common to lyric sopranos of a previous generation) to suggest interesting innocence and vulnerability. "Caro nome" is filled with yearning and yet not distorted. "Tutte le feste" is equally convincing and the death scene movingly fragile. Both she and Cappuccilli have a sense of *legato*, and Giulini stresses that admirably, so that the duets generally go well. There is a tremulous element in her voice, but somehow it suggests not unsteadiness but generosity of feeling.

Plácido Domingo's voice and style may be a little bulky for the Duke, but he sings intimately and at times affectionately. The "Addio" bubbles along, and he does "Ella mi fu rapita" and "Parmi veder" with command and careful grace, and "La donna è mobile" with good humor. Nicolai Ghiaurov as Sparafucile has a splendid voice, but its warmth does not really illuminate the character, while Elena Obraztsova, with that enormous contralto, is an exotic but not particularly convincing Maddalena. Though there is little in this set of spectacular interest save for Cotrubas's Gilda and Giulini's conducting, this is one of the more satisfactory stereophonic *Rigolettos*.

1983 EMI / ANGEL (In English) (S,D) CD

Helen Field (A), Jean Rigby (B), Arthur Davies (C), John Rawnsley (D), John Tomlinson (E),

English National Opera Chorus and Orchestra—Mark Elder

This recording, in English, comes from the Jonathan Miller production set in the 1950s in New York, with the Mafia doing duty for the Mantuan court. Such a production certainly emphasizes the ruthlessness in the original libretto. The *raison d'être* of the production was how it looked; if the recording is to have more than souvenir status, the judgment must be on how it sounds. There is an additional problem for Americans. The idiom of the performance is decidedly English, not American, so that we are, in a sense, removed from the new setting as well as the old. Aside from that, the translation is clear and more or less straightforward, though (perhaps necessarily) it has clichés from time to time which are either melodramatic ("Oh, horror!") or vaguely comic ("I'm no fool!"). As for diction, John Rawnsley's is the clearest. It is helpful that a libretto is enclosed with the album.

Rawnsley, an interesting actor, has a steady but light voice for the title role. The duets with Gilda go along nicely, save that the voice sometimes loses vibrance when he sings softly. He phrases "Cortigiani" intelligently, though he occasionally lacks the edge and variety of tone to do what he has in mind. Helen Field is a polished Gilda but provides little but gentle melancholy. As the Duke, Arthur Davies sings richly enough, if now and then rather nasally. His duet with Gilda and "La donna è mobile" go well, but he can't suggest strongly enough the character's self-interest. Under Mark Elder, the performance is generally neat, though without the harsh subtext and compulsion implicit in the score. The album is provocative, but it is something of a paradox that though the production's setting emphasizes the opera's brutality and immediacy, the vocal performance is less engaged than some conventional Italian ones.

1984 PHILIPS (S,D) CD

Edita Gruberova (A), Brigitte Fassbaender (B), Neil Shicoff (C), Renato Bruson (D), Robert Lloyd (E), Chorus and Orchestra of the Accademia di Santa Cecilia, Rome—Giuseppe Sinopoli

This recording has superb sound and an excellent orchestra. The score is uncut, with no added high notes. The only difficulty is with the performance itself. Giuseppe Sinopoli's tempos are either ludicrously slow or too fast for expressivity. Continuity is destroyed, the singers are cruelly exposed, and the subtlety of the score is largely lost. Renato Bruson is a lyric baritone pushed to the limit not only by the role but by the tempos. The voice is thus sometimes tired, constrained, and unsteady. Edita Gruberova is a throaty and metallic Gilda, forced to laboriousness by the conductor. Neil Shicoff has the right sort of voice for the Duke, but much of the first scene, for example, is taken so fast and loudly that there is little time for humor and charm. Elsewhere he is resonant but muscular and a little graceless. Brigitte Fassbaender is a vivid Maddalena, and Robert Lloyd a large-voiced and implacable Sparafucile. There is much talent in this cast, but most of it is seen in a bad light.

1988 EMI / ANGEL (S,D) CD

Daniela Dessì (A), Martha Senn (B), Vincenzo la Scola (C), Giorgio Zancanaro (D), Paata Burchuladze (E), La Scala Chorus and Orchestra—Riccardo Muti

Let's hope that Riccardo Muti is going through a phase. Recently he has been rushing through Verdi with no allowance for the specific gifts of his singers and little recognition that a free-flowing *rubato* and other minute and mutable devices can transform a score like that of *Rigoletto* into a living theater work. Here we have a strongly played performance in which brisk and unyielding tempos rob the opera of tragic potential and the singers of anything beyond surface identification with their characters. Generally they just sing the score (*all* of it) with reasonable accuracy.

Giorgio Zancanaro appears to be the best Verdi baritone of the moment, with technical control, burnished and vibrant tone throughout his range, and a strong sense of the words: he magnetizes attention with every entrance. However, at Muti's speed his duets with Gilda often seem more angry than concerned, and their drama is telescoped. He rushes into the sublime "Veglia, o donna," for example, without a moment for thought, and as a result loses completely the profound progression of feelings that Verdi has built so carefully into the music. Rigoletto's Act II *scena* before the courtiers is effectively vocalized, but a conductor genuinely sympathetic to all the momentary shifts of feeling in this piece could have helped Zancanaro to shape a masterwork. In the final act the baritone is in tighter voice and the conducting full of exaggerated tempos, facts which further diminish the emotional range and effect of the character.

The others do even less well. Vincenzo la Scola has a fresh and meaty lyric voice, the top of which opens out promisingly, but rigid tempos deprive him of charm and good humor at court and tenderness elsewhere. "Addio, addio" sounds like mouse music. "Parmi veder le lagrime" is poised, but the cadenza is awkward, and at the end he prepares for a trill which never materializes and then drops all the high notes. What effect is intended here? Daniela Dessì has a grainy lyric soprano with some potential for tragic coloring, but most of her performance is like her cadenza at the close of "Caro nome": an uncertain mixture of the fluent, the careful, and the strained. Paata Burchuladze has the black voice for Sparafucile, but the sound alone will have to do for the villainy, since he phrases awkwardly and never varies the vocal color to suit the text. Giorgio Surian is one of the few strong Monterones. So we have, then, a *Rigoletto* notable mainly for the fine voice of its protagonist and the promising sounds of a young tenor, but cursed with a deficiency in tragic vision.

1989 DECCA / LONDON (S,D) CD

June Anderson (A), Shirley Verrett (B), Luciano Pavarotti (C), Leo Nucci (D), Nicolai Ghiaurov (E), Chorus and Orchestra of the Teatro Communale, Bologna—Riccardo Chailly

Nearly everything about what promised to be a notable issue is a grave disappointment. After an impressive Prelude, Chailly, who has done persuasive work elsewhere, gives a rushed and graceless account of the score. The opening scene is more nervous than high-spirited and much of the rest lacks basic plasticity and warmth. Whether this tension was planned to compensate for cast shortcomings or in fact drives the singers to inexpressivity, none of them is at all well represented. Pavarotti, generally in strong voice, is deprived of *all* of his charm (is such a thing imaginable?) in a role in which he has proven peerless in two previous recordings. Here he is distraught, without a smile from beginning to end—especially bizarre in Act II, where he sounds rather more like a crazed Rumpelstiltskin than a lustful young duke. "Possente amor," given uncut, is driven and a little careless, and it ends with what must be the ugliest high note he has ever committed to records. The final scene is marginally better, but for the real joy of earlier performances he has substituted in "La donna è mobile" a *staccato* stress which will convince no one. June Anderson has, of course, first-rate potential, but she is dramatically neutral throughout and a little unsteady, revealing an amiable and rather dark tone, unvarying in color, and some marginally sharp top notes. Her few moments of passagework are dazzling, but even in "Tutte le feste," where ordinary sopranos evoke sympathy, she makes small emotional impression. Leo Nucci is elsewhere an effective actor with a pleasant lyric baritone voice not quite commanding enough for some of the roles he undertakes. Caught here between the neutral and the nervous, and driven by a conductor without faith in the music, he overstresses and exaggerates more than usual. Even the lyric sections, in which he might be expected to take things more easily, lack smoothness and color. Shirley Verrett hasn't quite the low voice for Maddalena, but what she has is focused and bright, and she makes the conversation with her brother interesting by performing it rather quietly and suggestively. Ghiaurov is a drab Sparafucile. As a happy footnote to this sad report, a baritone named Roberto Scaltriti makes a strikingly rich-voiced Marullo.

Among all these sets, the 1955 Serafin is the most probing, though it has the standard cuts of its period. If one must have stereo, the 1963 Kubelik set with Fischer-Dieskau is quite interesting, and the 1979 Giulini set is well conducted and in general nicely sung. The 1971 Bonynge set has attractions in Milnes and Pavarotti. Among older sets the 1950 Cellini with Warren and Peerce is still potent for their contributions and the Sparafucile of Italo Tajo.

Several other sets have notable individual performances by such artists as Stracciari, Danise, Taddei, Pagliughi, Hasslo, Herlea, Rinaldi, and Zancanaro.

LONDON GREEN

Unavailable for review:
1915–18 PHONOTYPE
1918 EMI / ANGEL
1962 FABBRI
1964 ORPHEUS

GIUSEPPE VERDI

IL TROVATORE (1853)

A: Leonora (s); B: Azucena (ms); C: Manrico (t);
D: Count di Luna (bar); E: Ferrando (bs)

Il Trovatore has hardly been neglected by the phonograph. Still, a survey of the available recordings leaves one with certain regrets. Many of the great singers of the past—Rosa Ponselle and Beniamino Gigli, for example—can be heard in this opera only in tantalizing excerpts. There is an inexplicable two-decade gap (1930–50) between complete commercial recordings of the opera: as a result, such interpretations as Giovanni Martinelli's Manrico and Ezio Pinza's Ferrando are not documented in full. Finally, we must regret that Arturo Toscanini, who conducted *Il Trovatore* often in the theater, did not give us a broadcast recording of the opera to set beside his intriguing versions of *La Traviata, Un Ballo in Maschera, Aida, Otello,* and *Falstaff.*

We had to wait until 1969 for a truly complete recording of *Il Trovatore.* The traditional stage cuts in this opera are fairly standard. Two numbers are often omitted altogether: the Act III *duettino* "L'onda de'suoni mistici" and, in Act IV after the Miserere, Leonora's cabaletta "Tu vedrai che amore in terra."

Three of the other cabalettas—Leonora's "Di tale amor," Luna's "Per me, ora fatale," and Manrico's "Di quella pira"—are often abridged by the suppression of the middle section and repeat.

At least four other passages—the *stretta* of the Act I trio, the fast final sections of the Act II Azucena / Manrico and Act IV Leonora / di Luna duets, and the Act III ensemble launched by Azucena's "Deh! rallentate, o barbari"—

often suffer from nibbling little cuts that seem to me to have no justification whatsoever.

While we are on the subject of the cabalettas, it is a curiosity that none of the recordings offers us anything in the way of true vocal embellishments in the repeats. When both stanzas of a cabaletta are performed, the repeat is usually sung exactly the same way as the initial statement, barring the odd interpolated high note.

1930 EMI / ANGEL (M)

Bianca Scacciati (A), Giuseppina Zinetti (B), Francesco Merli (C), Enrico Molinari (D), Corrado Zambelli (E), La Scala Chorus and Orchestra—Lorenzo Molajoli

Recorded in September 1930, this version makes all the standard cuts. Lorenzo Molajoli's conducting is admirably taut and responsive to the drama, and the La Scala orchestra and chorus live up to their reputations with precise, idiomatic playing and singing.

The cast contains none of the era's superstars, but the men are more impressive than the women. The best of the singers is Francesco Merli, whose bright, well-focused tenor is well suited to the requirements of the title role. (His "Di quella pira" is transposed down a semitone, to B-flat—a common enough procedure in the theater, but rather surprising on a studio recording.) Merli also scores some dramatic points that elude many of his more famous rivals on disc—in Act II, Scene 1, for example, he really does suggest a man talking intimately with his mother.

Enrico Molinari has a fine voice and uses it well, but he is entirely too pleasant of temperament—this is a gentlemanly di Luna, who sounds downright apologetic much of the time. Corrado Zambelli is an acceptable Ferrando.

Bianca Scacciati, the Leonora, has a big voice which turns raw and edgy under pressure; the soprano also possesses reasonable agility and plenty of temperament. There's nothing subtle about her performance, but she's never dull or clumsy. Giuseppina Zinetti's Azucena is rather matronly-sounding.

1930 EMI / ANGEL (M)

Maria Carena (A), Irene Minghini-Cattaneo (B), Aureliano Pertile (C), Apollo Granforte (D), Bruno Carmassi (E), La Scala Chorus and Orchestra—Gino Nastrucci

Having completed one recording of the opera, the La Scala forces began another almost at once, in October and November of 1930. Even in contemporaneous record catalogues and reviews, Carlo Sabajno is credited as the conductor of this performance; it now turns out that he led only two of the 78 sides (those beginning with "Tace la notte" and "Vedi! le fosche notturne"). Since Gino Nastrucci actually conducted most of the opera, he is now given posthumous credit. His pacing—more relaxed than Molajoli's—is admirably flexible, and as on the earlier recording there does not seem to have been any undue pressure to rush the music in order to fit onto the 78s. The orchestra and chorus, though dimly reproduced at times, are once again good. The choral *portamentos*, in "Squilli, echeggi," are revelatory.

Maria Carena, the Leonora, has a light lyric soprano, reedy in timbre and with a bright, thin top. Her technique has one peculiarity: she sings virtually without vibrato, except on loud high notes, which she gives an extra push, resulting in a wide vibrato that often borders on a tremolo. The effect seems quite deliberate, but it isn't a vocal school or style; it's just a strange way of singing. In addition, Carena cannot trill at all—a serious liability in this music.

Irene Minghini-Cattaneo, by contrast, is a secure, exciting Azucena—really more of a dramatic soprano than a mezzo, but fully in command of the role both vocally and interpretively.

Aureliano Pertile sings cleanly and fervently, despite a cautious approach to anything above G (like Merli, he takes "Di quella pira" down a semitone).

Apollo Granforte is a magnificent di Luna, who really does sound like an aristocrat in love. His "Il balen" is a model of *rubato* phrasing (and it is precisely accompanied by Nastrucci, despite its departures from the score): it makes one impatient with more literal renditions.

1951 CETRA (M)

Caterina Mancini (A), Miriam Pirazzini (B), Giacomo Lauri-Volpi (C), Carlo Tagliabue (D), Alfredo Colella (E), Chorus and Orchestra of Radio Italiana, Turin—Fernando Previtali

This recording has a certain honesty and documentary value. The performance is not very good, but it is the kind of performance one might have encountered in an Italian opera house at the time.

The *duettino* is included, but most of the other theater cuts are observed. Fernando Previtali goes about his business efficiently enough, but is far too lenient toward his singers: his tendency to slow down every time a solo vocal line starts to go high and loud becomes almost comically predictable after the first couple of LP sides.

Both women are good. Caterina Mancini has a big, handsome voice, under imperfect control but always vital and imposing. Miriam Pirazzini has a powerful mezzo, not ideally smooth or beautiful, but always dramatically alive. Previtali, perversely enough, rushes her in "Stride la vampa" and "Condotta ell'era in ceppi"; with a more sympathetic conductor, Pirazzini might have been more eloquent in the part.

Giacomo Lauri-Volpi was fifty-nine years old when he made this recording—not quite ready for the Casa di Riposo, surely, but decidedly past his prime. Occasionally, he surprises us with a suave phrase or an interesting inflection, but most of the singing is crude and pushy, and there is a serious problem with breath control—it is distressing to hear him breaking up phrases with extra breaths and cutting note values short with a sort of punctuating gasp. "Di quella pira" (one stanza only) is capped with a blood-curdling scream (on the final "All'armi!") sustained through the end of the orchestral postlude. Surely this set does not give a fair picture of Lauri-Volpi's Manrico: for that, the listener must turn to the tenor's earlier recordings of excerpts.

Carlo Tagliabue, another veteran, is wildly inconsistent here: many of the lyrical passages, like "Il balen," are controlled and expressive, but whenever the emotional temperature rises the baritone resorts to shouting and snarling.

The Everest and Turnabout reissues are both in fake stereo, plagued by added echo and a strident treble.

1952 RCA / BMG (M) CD

Zinka Milanov (A), Fedora Barbieri (B), Jussi Bjoerling (C), Leonard Warren (D), Nicola Moscona (E), Robert Shaw Chorale, RCA Orchestra—Renato Cellini

For many collectors, this classic set remains the finest version of *Il Trovatore* recorded. It has three fairly serious deficiencies, however. First, the performance includes the *duettino*, but observes virtually all of the other standard cuts. Secondly, the mono sound is no more than adequate in quality even for its date (although BMG's CD reissue is superior to the Victrola LP pressing). Finally, Renato Cellini's conducting is surprisingly lightweight, emphasizing the lyrical element in the score—this is not necessarily a fault, so far as it goes, but the gutsier side of the music simply isn't served. The orchestra is a good one, but Cellini does not demand anything extraordinary from it in the way of nuance. The chorus sounds small—again, not necessarily a disadvantage: most of the choral episodes make a more intimate impression than usual, and the text is projected with exceptional clarity and point.

Jussi Bjoerling is the most satisfactory Man-

rico on any of the complete sets—and this despite the fact that his tone is a bit slim and careful at the extreme top. The unique beauty of his timbre and the seemingly instinctive musicality of his phrasing make him a plausible troubador. He sounds like a young man—and, if we take the libretto literally, Manrico is still a teenager. More to the point, Bjoerling possesses the kind of dramatic imagination that turns "Mal reggendo," for example, into a mini-drama, progressing from boastfulness to—at the reference to the "voice from heaven"—awe and self-examination.

Zinka Milanov is very much the diva, dignified and larger than life. There is passion in her singing, but it is of a generalized sort. She has two bad habits. She abandons the text and vocalizes on "ah!" in many of the difficult (i.e., high-lying or florid) passages—"Vivra! Contende il giubilio" is a particularly blatant example. Cellini also allows Milanov to distend certain phrases in a way that impedes the flow of both the music and the drama: "M'odi!," just before the Act I trio, is the first of many examples. On the other hand, the soprano has moments of unforgettable beauty and grandeur: "Tacea la notte," its arcing melody floated on a seemingly endless supply of breath, is only the most extraordinary of them.

Fedora Barbieri is a true Italian dramatic mezzo-soprano, the voice rock-solid and penetrative even at low volume levels, and quite thrilling when its owner lets it out in the climaxes. A trace of coarseness in her chest register is not incompatible with Azucena's character.

Leonard Warren, one of the few baritones who could make a satisfactory di Luna on vocal endowment alone, sings in a thoughtful, understated way that is altogether exceptional.

1956 EMI / ANGEL (M) CD

Maria Callas (A), Fedora Barbieri (B), Giuseppe di Stefano (C), Rolando Panerai (D), Nicola Zaccaria (E), La Scala Chorus and Orchestra—Herbert von Karajan

This is the first recording to make a serious attempt to open most of the cuts. Some episodes—e.g., the Act I trio; the end of the Act II

Azucena / Manrico duet—are still tightened up by the omission of a few bars; and only one stanza of "Di tale amor" is performed. But all of "Di quella pira" is included, for the first time on records; so is one stanza of "Tu vedrai che amore in terra," etc.

Herbert von Karajan's is the best-conducted *Trovatore* on records. Some other versions are just as exciting; a few are just as beautifully executed. The difference is that Karajan's is a beautiful, exciting *performance*—it is all of a piece. The reading combines musical logic with Italianate fire: it is disciplined *and* impulsive, elegiac *and* intensely dramatic. The La Scala orchestra plays as though it knows exactly how good Karajan is making it sound.

It will come as a surprise to no one that Maria Callas is a highly individual Leonora. Her voice is in unusually secure condition on this recording, although as early as the cadenza to "Tacea la notte" there are some tense, wiry high notes. (On the other hand, Callas takes the leap of a tenth to a top D-flat in "D'amor sull'ali rosee," which most sopranos avoid.) The soprano's supple phrasing, and her seemingly instinctive application of dark and light vocal colorations, yield many fascinating dividends. Interpretively, too, her performance is filled with illuminating details. Two typical examples occur in the final scene of Act II. Leonora's line in the ensemble, somewhat surprisingly marked by the composer to be sung *leggierissimo e brilliantissimo*, for once has both of those qualities in abundance; a moment later, Callas really does sound out of her mind with terror when she cries out (twice) "M'atterrisce!" in response to the Count's ravings.

Barbieri is not quite as smooth and secure vocally as on her earlier recording, but Karajan coaxs an even more musical and multi-dimensional performance out of her.

Giuseppe di Stefano sounds as though he is going to explode every time he attacks a loud high note. This reservation aside, his singing is warm and beautiful, his manner irresistibly impulsive and ardent. Rolando Panerai's incisive way with the music is not always a paragon of *bel canto* style, but results in an uncommonly vivid aural portrait of the Count.

The mono sound is still perfectly acceptable, particularly on the CD reissue.

1956 DECCA / LONDON (S) CD

Renata Tebaldi (A), Giulietta Simionato (B), Mario del Monaco (C), Ugo Savarese (D), Giorgio Tozzi (E), Chorus of the Maggio Musicale Fiorentino, Orchestra of the Grand Theater of Geneva—Alberto Erede

This recording follows the trend toward greater completeness begun by EMI: Decca also includes all of "Di quella pira" and half of "Tu vedrai," but goes even further by letting us hear—for the first time on records—the B section and repeat of "Di tale amor."

Alberto Erede slows down drastically whenever he wants to underline a passage he likes, particularly when the soprano is singing. Still, one cannot really describe the performance as slack or self-indulgent—the musical line is maintained even at very slow speeds, and passages like the cabalettas, the Anvil Chorus, and the opening of Act III have plenty of rhythmic precision and snap. The Swiss orchestra and Florentine chorus turn in solidly professional work.

It is interesting to compare Giulietta Simionato's Azucena to Barbieri's: Barbieri has the bigger, richer, better-equalized voice. Simionato, however, uses her less imposing instrument with such skill that she almost persuades the listener that she is the superior vocalist. And she is a wonderful artist, more restrained than Barbieri but every bit as vividly communicative.

I am afraid that neither of the two "stars" is completely satisfactory. Renata Tebaldi never sang Leonora on stage. The actual sound of her voice is close to ideal for the role, and she does some beautiful things in lyrical passages and scores many points in the recitatives. But she is uneasy in the florid music; she simplifies and smears the runs, and ignores the trills altogether. In addition, on too many loud, high-lying phrases, she tends to tense up and belt out the notes—the climax of "Tacea la notte," and its cadenza, are the first of several instances.

Mario del Monaco's Manrico is, predictably, the most macho on records. His intentions are admirable: he understands the character, takes the action seriously, and in fact does some interesting things with inflection and vocal coloration. But the voice simply does not function efficiently at low volume levels, and the phrasing is stiff and non-*legato*.

Ugo Savarese is a conscientious, well-trained singer with an uninteresting voice. As a result, his is the kind of performance that is difficult to assess fairly: the baritone can hardly be preferred to Granforte, Warren, Panerai, et al., in this music, but heard in isolation he is persuasive enough.

The early stereo sound of this set is excellent even on my old LP pressing. The CD reissue is even better: the remastered sound has a presence, a dynamic range, and a solidity in the bass register that put many more recent opera recordings to shame.

1959 RCA / BMG (S) CD

Leontyne Price (A), Rosalind Elias (B), Richard Tucker (C), Leonard Warren (D), Giorgio Tozzi (E), Chorus and Orchestra of the Rome Opera House—Arturo Basile

This version can probably be left on the shelf, for the only element of distinction not duplicated elsewhere is Richard Tucker's Manrico—a sturdy, unsubtle performance, convincingly Italianate in manner. Arturo Basile observes most of the cuts (with "Tu vedrai" omitted altogether) and plods through the score as though he wishes it were shorter still. This is lifeless conducting, indifferent to the singers' needs and a disservice to the music. The orchestra is monotonously loud and uninflected, although one can forgive the players for not being inspired; the chorus at least summons some rough energy.

Warren is less good than he was on the 1952 set, often sounding either muffled or overemphatic.

Leontyne Price displays a sumptuous tone and a rather stately approach to the music, full of little glides. The soprano also brings a new element to Leonora: a smoldering sensuality. When she breathes out "Un'altra notte ancora senza vederlo!" it's obvious that the lady has

more than just looking in mind, and when she offers the Count "Me stessa!" the listener understands why he jumps at the chance. But Basile drags Price down at every turn, and one can only be grateful that she recorded the opera again ten years later, to infinitely better effect.

Rosalind Elias actually sings Azucena quite well, with a ripe tone and careful attention to the text, but for some reason—perhaps Basile again—the result is distinctly unexciting.

1962 DEUTSCHE GRAMMOPHON (S) CD

Antonietta Stella (A), Fiorenza Cossotto (B), Carlo Bergonzi (C), Ettore Bastianini (D), Ivo Vinco (E), La Scala Chorus and Orchestra—Tullio Serafin

In this performance, most of the cuts are opened (once again, a single stanza of "Tu vedrai" is reinstated). Tullio Serafin's conducting represents the best of Italian tradition. Under his baton, the music flows with complete naturalness: nothing seems either skimped or exaggerated. The excellent La Scala orchestra plays at least as well for Serafin as it did for Karajan, and cushions the singers with true *col canto* playing.

Antonietta Stella's Leonora resembles Mancini's: well-schooled vocalism, not exceptionally beautiful or individual but direct and emotionally honest. Fiorenza Cossotto sings Azucena's music very beautifully, with clear, firm tones; compared to Barbieri or Simionato, though, her interpretation is cool and restrained.

Carlo Bergonzi, on the other hand, not only vocalizes exceptionally smoothly, but shows more animation and passion than usual. The only blot on his performance is his insistence on capping "Di quella pira" (of which he sings one stanza only) with the traditional sustained bellow—in strange contrast to his poised, aristocratic singing of the rest of the role.

Not even Serafin can curb Ettore Bastianini's tendency to skate through the short, incidental phrases in his hurry to arrive at—and hold onto—the loud, high, impressive ones. In "Il balen" we hear a baritone showing off his voice rather than a Spanish nobleman in love; still, the voice is the genuine article, always big and secure.

1964 EMI / ANGEL (S) CD

Gabriella Tucci (A), Giulietta Simionato (B), Franco Corelli (C), Robert Merrill (D), Ferruccio Mazzoli (E), Rome Opera Chorus and Orchestra—Thomas Schippers

The death of Thomas Schippers at a relatively young age deprived us of a first-rate operatic conductor; nevertheless, this *Trovatore* is not one of his most persuasive recordings. The conductor seems to be going after drama at all costs: fast tempos, incisive rhythms, and sharp accents dominate, and there is a breathless, hard-driven quality to the proceedings. The Roman orchestra and chorus respond with more enthusiasm than polish. The performance is anything but dull, but *Trovatore* needs elegance as well as excitement. Schippers performs the B section and reprise of "Di tale amor," but "Di quella pira" is reduced to AC form, and "Tu vedrai" is missing altogether.

Simionato sings Azucena at least as well for Schippers as she did for Erede, and has no difficulty adapting to Schippers's more energetic approach.

Gabriella Tucci's soprano is on the light side for Leonora, and it has a fluttery vibrato on sustained tones that may bother some listeners. She sings the role extremely well, though—the trills are in place, as well as the top D-flat in "D'amor sull'ali rosee"—and is always dramatically convincing.

Franco Corelli slurs and scoops, and his pronunciation of his native language verges on the bizarre. "Ah! si, ben mio" is blared out at full volume, with a maddening indifference to the dramatic situation or the sense of the words. Still, the voice is a genuine *tenore di forza*, more malleable than most, and the performance undeniably has its exciting moments ("Di quella pira," with the *staccatos* rapped out as though by a hammer striking a chisel, is—predictably—one of them).

Robert Merrill's di Luna is as well vocalized as any on the stereo sets, and the role does not require anything from him dramatically that is not well within his competence.

1969 RCA / BMG (S) CD

Leontyne Price (A), Fiorenza Cossotto (B), Plácido Domingo (C), Sherrill Milnes (D), Bonaldo Giaiotti (E), Ambrosian Opera Chorus, New Philharmonia Orchestra—Zubin Mehta

This is the first truly complete recording of the opera. The major novelty, of course, is the inclusion of *all* of "Tu vedrai." It is worth pointing out, though, that the singers usually perform their cadenzas as written, proving, I think, that Verdi's suggestions are generally preferable to the options heard on other recordings.

Price clearly shows the benefit of having sung innumerable stage performances in the decade since her earlier RCA recording. The voice is even richer and more sensuous in timbre than before, and the phrasing has even more subtlety and poise. In complete command of the role's technical difficulties, Price also conveys Leonora's emotions with greater immediacy.

Cossotto also improves upon her good work on her previous recording. The vocalism is at once bolder and more refined than before, the interpretation imposing. This is an Azucena worthy of comparison to the classic Barbieri and Simionato performances.

This was Plácido Domingo's first complete opera recording. On it, we hear the voice that quickly conquered the world: definitely a lyric tenor, but intriguingly dark and nasal in coloration, produced with liquid ease, and wedded to wholly musical instincts. The vocalism rivals Bjoerling's and Bergonzi's in beauty, and is more extroverted in temperament. Sherrill Milnes, also heard in exceptionally smooth form, proves himself to be a worthy successor to Warren and Merrill, although Milnes is operating with a voice lighter (in both color and weight) than theirs.

Zubin Mehta doesn't get in the way of the performance; he sets sensible tempos, and obtains good orchestral and choral work. The reading tends to be relatively literal and uninflected, though; given this fine cast, it's a shame that the conductor is unwilling to take risks.

Unfortunately, the recording is a rather artificial studio affair, with the solo voices unnaturally balanced against the orchestra.

1975 EURODISC (S) CD

Raina Kabaivanska (A), Viorica Cortez (B), Franco Bonisolli (C), Giorgio Zancanaro (D), Giancarlo Lucciardi (E), Chorus of the German State Opera, Berlin State Orchestra—Bruno Bartoletti

Bruno Bartoletti knows how this music ought to go, and his German orchestra and chorus are thoroughly professional. Both stanzas of "Di quella pira" are included, but "Tu vedrai" is once again missing.

The cast is wildly uneven. Franco Bonisolli, heaven help him, seems to have taken del Monaco and Corelli as his models, imitating their mannerisms rather than their strengths: a tasteless, self-indulgent performance. Viorica Cortez is a crude Azucena, her powerful mezzo sabotaged by a fierce vibrato, insecure intonation, and pronounced register breaks.

In contrast to the excesses of their colleagues, Raina Kabaivanska and Giorgio Zancanaro almost seem to be performing in a different opera. The soprano sounds vocally undernourished for Leonora, but her delicate, silvery instrument traces the music accurately enough, and she has many touching moments. The baritone displays a healthy young voice but little musical or dramatic imagination.

The engineering is mediocre, with the voices too closely miked for comfort.

1976 DECCA / LONDON (S) CD

Joan Sutherland (A), Marilyn Horne (B), Luciano Pavarotti (C), Ingvar Wixell (D), Nicolai Ghiaurov (E), London Opera Chorus, National Philharmonic Orchestra—Richard Bonynge

There are some odd textual choices on this recording. Richard Bonynge makes the standard cut of a few bars in the *stretta* of the Act I trio. Other episodes are in fact "more than complete," for—although the performance is sung in Italian—it incorporates a couple of readings from the 1857 Paris version of the opera, *Le Trouvère*. In Act I "Di tale amor," for example, is two bars longer each time, because Joan Sutherland inserts some flourishes (with orchestral accompaniment) unique to the Paris vocal score.

The ballet sequence from Act III was included on the LP version, but deleted from the CD.

Bonynge's conducting shows a real sensitivity to his singers' needs, and he obtains a rich, warm sound from the orchestra. At times, though, his pacing is both too slow in tempo and sluggish in rhythm. *Il Trovatore* has its graceful moments, but it should not sound like nineteenth-century salon music.

The casting presents us with four superstars, all heard at less than their best. Luciano Pavarotti has the right kind of voice for Manrico, and in many passages his clear tone and direct, idiomatic delivery are most enjoyable. But the tenor seems to be pushing his essentially lyric instrument hard, in an attempt to make it sound bigger and more imposing; as a result the vocalism lacks smoothness and ease, and cannot be compared with what Bjoerling, Bergonzi, and Domingo accomplish in the role.

Sutherland handles the trills, scales, and *staccato*s as securely as any Leonora on records. She sings with an animation and rhythmic crispness unusual for her, and some phrases are as beautifully realized as they are by Milanov or Price. But the voice is often tremulous on sustained tones in the upper-middle register, and the unsteadiness is exaggerated by Decca's typical close miking.

Like Sutherland, Marilyn Horne demonstrates a revelatory agility: the long trills in "Stride la vampa" are sensational, and so is the big cadenza on the words "Tu la spremi dal mio cor" in the subsequent duet with Manrico. Elsewhere, the voice simply isn't functioning as efficiently as it once did—the register breaks are more pronounced than before, and the timbre is drier and stiffer. Dramatically, she is strong, suggesting stoic resignation instead of the phony hysteria that some Azucenas are guilty of.

Ingvar Wixell, a lightweight di Luna, sings tastefully but with far too much vibrato: the fluctuations in pitch blur the line in lyrical passages (e.g., "Il balen") that need firmer definition.

The recorded sound is Decca's usual reliable product.

1977 EMI / ANGEL (S) CD

Leontyne Price (A), Elena Obraztsova (B), Franco Bonisolli (C), Piero Cappuccilli (D), Ruggero Raimondi (E), Chorus of the Deutsche Oper, Berlin, Berlin Philharmonic Orchestra—Herbert von Karajan

Like many of Herbert von Karajan's opera recordings, this one was made in conjunction with a Salzburg Festival production, with the same cast. The uncut performance is dominated by the Berlin Philharmonic, which provides playing of almost supernatural tonal beauty and refinement throughout; the listener may find it necessary to block out some rather unimpressive singing in order to concentrate on this or that instrumental detail. Much of what the conductor chooses to emphasize is very beautiful, but there are several eccentric moments.

Karajan takes much of the music—especially the cabalettas—more slowly than he did in 1956; the result is lethargic at times.

The cast is variable. Price still makes a beautiful sound in the middle of her voice, but her low notes are hollow and her upper register often pinched and narrow in quality. Despite her mature artistry and the sympathetic support given to her by Karajan, this performance cannot compare to that on the 1969 RCA set.

Elena Obraztsova and Franco Bonisolli, however, clearly benefit from the disciplined framework Karajan provides. They scrupulously observe the *staccatos* indicated in the vocal parts in "Ai nostri monti," for example, as many singers on records do not. Elsewhere, the mezzo

displays plenty of extroverted temperament, and if her singing cannot always be described as beautiful—the voice turns tough and metallic under pressure—it is always vital and authoritative. Bonisolli, obviously on his best behavior for Karajan, sings sturdily and with considerable dramatic involvement.

Piero Cappuccilli and Ruggero Raimondi are both disappointing. The baritone is in less than his best voice, often sounding hollow and unsupported; his broad *cantabile* phrasing is exemplary, though, and he always sounds involved in the drama. The bass—no doubt with Karajan's encouragement—seems to be working so hard on cultivating a velvety *mezza voce*, and on "interpreting" his lines with little verbal nuances, that in a sense he almost forgets to sing.

The recording has a huge dynamic range, and at times the soloists (instrumental as well as vocal) seem to be a mile away from the microphones. The original LP set was in "compatible quad," and is particularly murky in sound. An LP reissue on the Angel Voices label, and the EMI CD set, are both derived from the same digitally remastered tape, and are preferable.

1980 PHILIPS (S,D) CD

Katia Ricciarelli (A), Stefania Toczyska (B), José Carreras (C), Yuri Mazurok (D), Robert Lloyd (E), Chorus and Orchestra of the Royal Opera House, Covent Garden—Colin Davis

This is a baffling release. The uncut score is exceptionally well executed by the Covent Garden orchestra and chorus, who have the obvious advantage of having performed the opera often in repertory. The recorded sound (early digital), clear and detailed, is also excellent.

Sir Colin Davis's conducting is disciplined—this must be one of the most accurate readings of the score on records—but surely too polite: an essential element of earthiness (of vulgarity, if you will) is lacking.

The cast is very uneven, not so much in vocal quality, but in their divergent approaches to the piece: in a way that has become all too common in recorded opera, these people don't seem to be listening to each other.

Katia Ricciarelli is a frustrating performer. Her voice is basically a beautiful instrument—soft, round, flutey in timbre—but it often turns glassy or congested. Leonora's writing exposes the fact that the top and bottom of the voice are both much weaker than the middle. In addition, Ricciarelli negotiates the *fioriture* cautiously, and is so gentle and restrained of temperament that her Leonora seems timid.

Stefania Toczyska has an attractive mezzo-soprano, although there is not much trace of depth or darkness in the timbre, and the vibrato is pronounced enough to be troublesome at times. Like Ricciarelli, she is guilty of excessive restraint; her Azucena has dignity, but the big moments are underplayed.

José Carreras's singing is monotonously loud, with tight high notes, and the tenor seems to have been introduced to Manrico only under the briefest and most formal of circumstances: one can scarcely speak of characterization at all.

Yuri Mazurok sings with energy and passion. His powerful baritone sometimes rides rough-shod over the fine detail—"Il balen" is haughty and defiant rather than amorous—but Mazurok is easily the most committed of the soloists.

1983 DEUTSCHE GRAMMOPHON (S,D) CD

Rosalind Plowright (A), Brigitte Fassbaender (B), Plácido Domingo (C), Giorgio Zancanaro (D), Yevgeny Nesterenko (E), Chorus and Orchestra of the Accademia di Santa Cecilia, Rome—Carlo Maria Giulini

It is a tribute to Carlo Maria Giulini that he is able to pull together an extraordinarily cohesive performance from such disparate elements.

Giulini claims to have based his interpretation, and his tempo choices in particular, upon a study of the composer's manuscript. Nearly everything is slower than we are accustomed to hearing it in the theater. The deliberate pacing of the cabalettas and the *strettas* takes some getting used to, but the performance is by no means static or undramatic—it builds in

momentum and sustains the listener's interest throughout.

The orchestra playing is not only phenomenally precise and well balanced; it is tonally beautiful and filled with passion as well. Against very stiff competition, this is the most distinguished account of the opera's orchestral score on records.

Two members of the cast have recorded their parts before. Domingo's singing is heavier and less spontaneous-sounding than it was in 1969, but he is still a major-league Manrico. (He actually sings "Di quella pira" exactly as written the first time around, saving the high C for the repeat.) Zancanaro, on the other hand, has improved almost beyond recognition as the Count—an intense, scrupulously musical performance.

Giulini probably deserves a great deal of the credit for the superb performances of his soprano and mezzo. Rosalind Plowright's Leonora must be ranked beside the Callas interpretation as the most interesting on records. The voice is a true dramatic soprano *d'agilità*, bright and well focused, yet even in quality throughout its range. Plowright creates the impression that, having mastered all of the role's technical difficulties, she is free to concentrate entirely upon expression.

Brigitte Fassbaender, with her very dark, plummy timbre, just doesn't sound like an Italian dramatic mezzo: she throws herself into the part, however, giving a performance that is exciting but not at the expense of musical precision.

The performance is absolutely uncut, and the digital sound is excellent. The recording, originally released on three CDs, has now been reissued on two.

If one is looking for the best-conducted *Trovatore*, then the choice is an impossible three-way split among the mono Karajan, the DG / Serafin, and the DG / Giulini. All three of these performances, not so incidentally, feature superb instrumental playing by Italian orchestras.

Otherwise, choice obviously depends upon a collector's personal taste in singers. The true enthusiast will want to own certain individual performances—Simionato's Azucena, for example.

If pressed for a recommendation, though, I would have to point out that *Il Trovatore* is one of the rare instances in which a fairly recent, uncut, well-engineered version—the DG / Giulini—is, on balance, as good as any of the older sets. The RCA / Mehta recording is also a strong overall production: it has worn well for over twenty years, and should continue to provide satisfaction. Both of these sets have the advantage, of course, of being uncut and in stereo.

ROLAND GRAEME

Unavailable for review:
1950 EMI / ANGEL
1953 ACE
1962 ELECTRECORD
1965 GUILDE INTERNATIONAL DU DISQUE
1969 SUPRAPHON

GIUSEPPE VERDI

LA TRAVIATA (1853)

A: Violetta (s); B: Alfredo (t); C: Germont (bar)

For all its popularity, *La Traviata* has not had a particularly happy history on complete recordings. Prior to World War II there were only two such albums generally available, and neither of them was remarkable. After the war there was nothing of distinction until RCA released the 1946 Toscanini-Albanese broadcast performance several years following the event. Not until 1959 was there anything approaching a first-class studio recording. Since that time there have been some touching individual performances, but little to compare with the Giulini *Don Giovanni*, the De Sabata *Tosca*, or the Furtwängler *Tristan*, for example.

Violetta is in every way a test of the soprano's voice, style, and dramatic range. She needs technical brilliance in Act I, lyric beauty in Act II, and the powers of a tragedian in the final scene—and, of course, a thread of vocal and dramatic continuity to unite all of these elements. Alfredo is also a challenge: a romantic hero who is full of solicitous care, but in effect actually does little on the stage but denounce the heroine on the basis of a misunderstanding which she has perpetrated. What is the key to showing him as attractive and sensitive despite his actions? Germont is a simpler task, but even with him there is the problem of making his stance viable and sympathetic in our time.

Until the 1960s, all *Traviata* recordings, like virtually all live performances, were rather heavily cut: the second verses of "Ah, fors'è lui" and "Addio del passato," repetitions in the duets, and cabalettas for Alfredo and Germont were the usual major deletions. The reintroduction of Alfredo's cabaletta is a clear benefit. Although there have been several note-complete recordings, a popular compromise has been to keep the old cuts and insert one verse each from the two cabalettas. Completeness in this case is interesting, but the eloquence of a great performance, whether cut or not, is unforgettable.

1928 EMI / (M)

Mercédès Capsir (A), Lionel Cecil (B), Carlo Galeffi (C), La Scala Chorus, Milan Symphony—Lorenzo Molajoli

This was the first electrical recording of *La Traviata*. It observes all the cuts then standard. Though the Preludes droop, Lorenzo Molajoli leads a quick performance, sometimes too fast for full vocal characterization, as in the second-act scene for Violetta and Germont and the letter-writing scene. Mercédès Capsir has a bright, rather coarse voice and some coloratura ability, and sings with reasonable efficiency. Her best work is in the Act II duet with Germont and in "Addio del passato," which is nicely phrased. In the rest she is neither playful nor sickly: just routine. Lionel Cecil has a forward, vibrating voice—something of a bleat, in fact—without much grace or glamour, though the sound is healthy enough. Carlo Galeffi's baritone is strong, but he is no actor. He sings out sonorously, observing all the standard dramatic practices, of which the tear is the major one. Of the others, Aristide Baracchi as the Baron and Salvatore Baccaloni as Dr. Grenvil are both full-voiced. If the set is memorable for anything, it is Galeffi's sound.

1930 EMI / ANGEL (M)

Anna Rosza (A), Alessandro Ziliani (B), Luigi Borgonovo (C), La Scala Chorus and Orchestra—Carlo Sabajno

This set is interesting for its Violetta, Anna Rosza, whose voice is a bright lyric soprano with an occasionally shimmering quality. Much of the performance goes too fast for full dramatic projection, but her work reveals a delicate and subtle temperament. The last act particularly is robbed of tragic weight by speed, but she has nevertheless a frail and lovely tone here. Alessandro Ziliani is efficient and alert as Alfredo, though he does bleat a bit, and his role, too, is robbed of romance by tempo. Luigi Borgonovo is a gentle Germont. The voice is a lyric baritone, gritty at the bottom. Only one verse of "Di Provenza" is left him, but he sings it smoothly. As noted, Carlo Sabajno conducts a nervous performance which often prevents the leading singers from expressing themselves as fully as they might.

1946 RCA / BMG (M,P) CD

Licia Albanese (A), Jan Peerce (B), Robert Merrill (C), Chorus, NBC Symphony Orchestra—Arturo Toscanini

This performance adds up to one of the great recorded statements of Verdi's score. There is, even in its most problematic moments, a sense of the evanescence of life, of joy that can be snatched only for a moment. That urgency is shared by the conductor and the two leading singers. Arturo Toscanini, Licia Albanese, and Jan Peerce work together to capture these hectic nuances: the performance, taken from two 1946 radio broadcasts, is fevered and passionate, but sometimes delicate, too. One senses almost immediately something demonic in the depiction of Violetta's social life. Verdi's Act I, though, is a pattern of gaiety and repose; if there is a problem with the recording it is that the moments of repose in Act I are too rushed to savor. In the four remaining scenes, however, the pacing is superb, and it is there that Albanese does her most memorable work. Hers is a heartfelt Violetta who in the first scene of Act II does not distort the music with effects but acts through it, using the text and vocal colors brilliantly to build tension through the long duet with Germont to the scene's climax a few moments afterward with "Amami, Alfredo." All the moods of Act III, from despair to ecstasy, are fully dramatized by this singer and her conductor. No one will deny that there are other ways of doing Violetta, but this performance not only gives a picture of the singer's art but sums up and refines an important approach to nineteenth-century opera.

As in everything he sang, Jan Peerce performs with commitment. His voice and manner may be a little mature for Alfredo, but his scrupulousness and fullness of sound are in themselves exciting, and particularly effective in the gambling scene. Robert Merrill's voice is beautiful and his management of it laudable, though his vocal acting is rudimentary. The quick tempos lend his work an urgency it might not otherwise have. Toscanini shapes a cohesive dramatic experience. Even without its moments of relaxed charm, the opening party scene has irresistible brio, the offstage band in Act I providing just the counterpoint of excitement needed for the duet of Violetta and Alfredo. At Flora's the Gypsy music has a spacious lightness. The Prelude to Act III has the stamp of sickness on it, and the distant carnival chorus sounds like a street crowd. The sound is boxy but clear, and the conductor can occasionally be heard singing along. Whatever its faults, this is one of the revelatory performances of *La Traviata*.

1946 EMI / ANGEL (M)

Adriana Guerrini (A), Luigi Infantino (B), Paolo Silveri (C), Rome Opera Chorus and Orchestra—Vincenzo Bellezza

This was, I believe, the first new Italian opera album to be released in the United States following World War II. Adriana Guerrini, Luigi Infantino, and Paolo Silveri had been singing for only three years when it was made. Guerrini's is one of those voices that cuts and is particularly difficult to record well. She sounds joyful in the Brindisi, but the rest of Act I is neither sickly nor especially elegant, though there are some pleasant passages in "Ah, fors'è lui." In "Sempre libera" the bright, metallic edge in her voice becomes a little fearsome.

The rest of her performance has its moments of delicacy ("Alfredo, Alfredo" and "Addio del passato" are two of them) but otherwise she sings rather coarsely and seldom surprises.

Luigi Infantino is an exceptional Alfredo. He has a light but rich voice, handles the Brindisi well, and shapes and colors "Un dì felice" with great attention to the words. Both his anger and his care are convincing; it is obvious that this Alfredo has centered his life on Violetta. Paolo Silveri is reasonably touching in his scene with Guerrini, though he hasn't quite the authority later for "Di sprezzo degno." Vincenzo Bellezza conducts a lively performance, neither particularly revealing nor pretentious. The chief attraction is Infantino's personable Alfredo.

p.1952 REMINGTON (M)

Rosetta Noli (A), Giuseppe Campora (B), Carlo Tagliabue (C), Unidentified chorus and orchestra—Umberto Berrettoni

The recorded sound here is boxy and shrill, and the orchestra is the poorest of any on complete recordings. The performance is also oddly cut. Nearly all the standard omissions are observed, but there are additional oddities: one "E strano" is dropped from the start of Violetta's Act I scene; and the revelers' chorus, a few lines for Germont, and all of the lines following Violetta's death are cut from the last act.

The cast is of some interest. Rosetta Noli is a porcelain Violetta, youthful and vulnerable, more melancholy than tragic. The voice is brittle, delicate, and slightly nasal, and the characterization graceful though incomplete. Giuseppe Campora is a young and believable Alfredo, accurate and charming in the Brindisi, warm in "Un dì felice," and full of quiet, radiant joy at the start of Act II. In later scenes, he is both passionate and sensitive, and, though the orchestra drowns him out at one point in "Ah si, che feci," he remains one of the best Alfredos on records. Carlo Tagliabue is an unimaginative but acceptable Germont. Umberto Berrettoni leads a comfortable performance despite the orchestra. It is a misfortune that Campora's Alfredo cannot be heard under better conditions.

1953 CETRA (M)

Maria Callas (A), Francesco Albanese (B), Ugo Savarese (C), Cetra Chorus, Orchestra of Radio-Televisione Italiana, Turin—Gabriele Santini

Maria Callas is working virtually alone in this studio recording. The orchestra under Gabriele Santini often lacks both delicacy and cumulative drive: Flora's party is slumbrous, and in Act III he provides little sense of the conflict between Violetta's desire for life and her fate. Francesco Albanese has a nice voice but gives a sluggish performance: "De' miei bollenti spiriti" hardly strikes the note of rapture desired. As Germont, Ugo Savarese sounds healthy enough but produces the same empty baritonal resonance for every situation. In the midst of all of this depressing respectability, Callas tries to create a character: publicly charming and confident, inwardly tormented by a loneliness intensified by her frailty. Near the end of Act I, "Ah, quell'amor" reflects not so much a grand passion as a private need for peace. In Act II the top tones, as elsewhere, are harsh or attenuated, but the rest is done in a lovely tone of considerable intimacy. In the final scene, Callas colors every word, but with such lackluster support from her colleagues that her enactment seems more like a demonstration for a master class than a performance. The finale is beautifully enacted.

1954 DECCA / LONDON (M) CD

Renata Tebaldi (A), Gianni Poggi (B), Aldo Protti (C), Chorus and Orchestra of the Accademia di Santa Cecilia, Rome—Francesco Molinari-Pradelli

Few albums offer the range of abilities and disabilities shown in this one. First we have in Renata Tebaldi a Violetta who varies between warlike command and lyrical sorrow. In some passages the voice is round, glittering, and under easy control: "Ah, quell'amor," "Dite alla giovine," "Alfredo, Alfredo," and particularly Violetta's great outcry in the final act, "Gran Dio! morir sì giovine," in which she begins with a thread of tone, swelling it with complete control and mesmerizing effect. There are, however, other passages which emerge as loud and coarse rather than spirited or anguished, and some high notes which sound more like angry attacks than expressions of hectic joy.

As Germont, Aldo Protti provides a pungent voice capable of vigorous attacks and some tenderness: nothing subtle, but nothing embarrassing, either. Quite unequivocal, though, is the effect of Gianni Poggi, a whining, carping Alfredo who shouts much of his conversation and gets through "De' miei bollenti spiriti" ignoring most of the score's expressive markings. One verse (smeared) of "O mio rimorso" is provided. Of the others, only Piero de Palma as Gastone is persuasive. Conductor Francesco Molinari-Pradelli is sometimes graceful, but mostly vapid where he needs to be commanding. Aside from some passages of delicacy from Tebaldi and a passable Germont from Protti, there is little of appeal in this set.

1955 EMI / ANGEL (M)

Antonietta Stella (A), Giuseppe di Stefano (B), Tito Gobbi (C), La Scala Chorus and Orchestra—Tullio Serafin

Tullio Serafin conducts an affectionate and rather stately orchestral performance: a suitable framework for a great singing actress's assumption of the title role. The Preludes to Acts I and III are touching, but the party scenes and others lack the compulsion that can make them riveting. Antonietta Stella is punctilious and pleasant in Act I, but lacking the technique and abandon to make its closing memorable. For the rest she provides a pretty but sometimes unstable sound and a restricted emotional palette. Among her most persuasive moments is a touching "Addio del passato." Giuseppe di Stefano has here a rather hard voice, but his characterization is sympathetic and youthful: he seems delighted to be in love. In the opening of Act II one hears a quiet joy in his phrasing and vocal coloring. In the confrontation at Flora's he sounds not only brutal but deeply hurt. Later his "Parigi, o cara" is very tender.

The completeness and care in Tito Gobbi's characterization of Germont are evident from the first. His voice on this occasion is a little dry

and tends to run sharp at odd points, but it is steady. He often sings intimately and provides "Di Provenza" with quiet dignity and warmth. Of the others, Silvio Maionica is a touching Dr. Grenvil. The interesting elements of this performance are the characterizations of di Stefano and Gobbi, for no one is in exceptional voice.

1955 EMI / ANGEL (M,P) CD

Maria Callas (A), Giuseppe di Stefano (B), Ettore Bastianini (C), La Scala Chorus and Orchestra—Carlo Maria Giulini

Onstage Maria Callas had an unrivaled capacity for public intimacy: the gift to draw an audience to her character rather than flinging it out to them. It is that magnetic quality which is demonstrated in this live recording of the renowned 1955 Visconti production at La Scala. One is drawn into her private conversations, her private rejections, the intimacies of death. The voice is at first glittering and cold—flinty, perhaps—but possessed of some secret allure. In "Un dì felice" she mocks Alfredo lightly and quietly and in "E strano!" she muses, and yet there is an indefinable passion behind these moments. The aria and its cabaletta are delicately colored, full of subtle variety. "Sempre libera," with riveting passagework, is in fact relaxed in speed, but one is listening so hard that it seems faster than it is. The great duet with Germont is imbued first with pride, and then with shock, sorrow, and helplessness. Each of these qualities has its own vocal color. In the final scene, she projects a sickly vibrance as few have before her. The "Addio del passato" is a mere wisp of bright tone—with, however, no diminution of emotional vitality. Throughout, the singer is in secure voice, although there is that one now-famous moment of sharp pitch at "Dite alla giovine."

For once in *Traviata* she finds herself in more or less worthy surroundings. Giuseppe di Stefano is in healthy mid-career voice—gritty but in tune—and his singing is, barring an ensemble problem or two, both eager and accomplished. His denunciation of Violetta is particularly successful—so committed that it gains an eruption of applause. In the last scene he is both comforting and distraught: a positive force to an extent matched by few other Alfredos. Ettore Bastianini hammers away like Siegfried with that superb voice of his, dramatically innocent but at least not destructive. In supporting roles Giuseppe Zampieri (sounding oddly like an Otello in the making), Arturo la Porta, Antonio Zerbini, and Silvio Maionica are all vital, and Carlo Maria Giulini, as is his habit, everywhere shapes the score with sensitivity to his singers and a consistent dramatic vision. The orchestral tone—indeed, the sound in general—is glum, and in fact inferior to that of the EMI 1958 Lisbon performance. Nevertheless, technical deficiencies and all, this seems to me to be the superior recording: one of the great performances.

1956 RCA / BMG (M)

Rosanna Carteri (A), Cesare Valletti (B), Leonard Warren (C), Rome Opera Chorus and Orchestra—Pierre Monteux

It must have seemed like a very good idea: a French conductor noted for the geniality and warmth of his interpretations leading an opera which, though it is Italian, deals with Parisian society. The result is curious, though. This *Traviata* must be the slowest and the dullest on records. The tempos are debilitating in both the party and the intimate scenes, where the singers are hard put to maintain convincing characterizations. The effect is to turn this private drama into something resembling a dull tragedy of state, with the accusatory chorus at Flora's party sounding like a selection from *Aida*. Rosanna Carteri, a charming figure onstage, has the right instincts about playing Violetta, but her voice is in perilous condition: both steely and insecure. Act I is almost joyless and "Sempre libera" particularly effortful. In the second act, she confronts Leonard Warren's Germont with what sounds like heavy authority rather than delicate feeling. At that, she has a few striking passages: "Alfredo, Alfredo" is nicely handled at the close of the gambling scene, and her reading of Germont's letter is dark-voiced but tender.

Even such an artist as Cesare Valletti is partly defeated by the tempos. There is little buoyancy in his Brindisi, and though he sounds like a young man in love, his tone in Act I is often unbeguiling. In Act II he is more like himself; his rendition of the opening aria is manly, delicate, and flushed with affection and care. At the slow pace he still manages to suggest those tamed "boiling spirits" by means of alert rhythmic punctuation and the use of consonants, and by phrasing as if he can hardly keep the sentiments within. He does equally well in the gambling scene, phrasing both the denunciation and the passage of remorse in a heroic manner even if the voice itself is lyric. As Germont, Leonard Warren is at both his worst and his best. He enters blustering, overpronouncing, and torturing his basic tone with all sorts of mannerisms, though in the succeeding duet he occasionally provides some memorable tones. He then marches at a funereal pace into "Di Provenza," which, surprisingly, goes at a comfortable speed. There is still a slight shudder in his tone, but the aria is phrased with exemplary smoothness and has ravishing *pianissimos*: an arresting performance. Other than that and Valletti's solution to his problems, there is little to savor here.

1958 EMI / ANGEL (M,P) CD

Maria Callas (A), Alfredo Kraus (B), Mario Sereni (C), Chorus and Orchestra of the San Carlos Opera, Lisbon—Franco Ghione

In this live performance from Portugal, Maria Callas offers nearly all the qualities of her La Scala performance of three years earlier, if in less secure voice. The singing here is beautifully thought out, if not always beautiful: the tone is sometimes edged and ugly high notes are occasionally prominent. Few portrayals with such obvious drawbacks, though, remain so hypnotic. Alfredo Kraus is a young and graceful Alfredo with a full, agile voice. He is persuasive in Act I, elated and convincingly furious in Act II, and gentle in the final scene. As Germont, Mario Sereni sounds the intended note of stern kindness and sings "Di Provenza" with some eloquence. Franco Ghione accompanies; sometimes the ensemble is ragged and the tempos are a little slow. The *comprimarios* are drab. The prompter can be heard from time to time, but the sound is somewhat fuller than that of the 1955 Callas recording. However, in that set the conductor is much more effective, the cast in general more accomplished, and Callas in stronger voice and inspired to even greater heights. Either is superior to the 1953 Cetra studio performance as a record of her aural impact in the role.

1959 EMI / ANGEL (S) CD

Victoria de los Angeles (A), Carlo del Monte (B), Mario Sereni (C), Rome Opera Chorus and Orchestra—Tullio Serafin

For sheer beauty of tone Victoria de los Angeles is almost peerless. There are in her middle register a mesmerizing shimmer and warmth, as if the distinctive qualities of Ljuba Welitsch and Lucrezia Bori had somehow been brought together. The voice is clear and glittering, and has the suggestion of a smile or of darkness when she wishes to use it. This makes her particularly beguiling in the conversational passages of *La Traviata* and in the recitatives. "È strano" reveals almost everything of the singer's excellence: warmth of tone, sensitive phrasing, inherent dignity and charm. Act II further discloses this Violetta's nobility of spirit and melancholy gravity, capped by an "Alfredo, Alfredo" filled with sorrow and moving grace: regretful, already lonely and alone. Her reading of Germont's letter is all tears submerged in the voice, and "Addio del passato" is more reflective than desperate. Her final moments have an arresting shudder in the voice; one feels in the presence of death. Why, then, is she a touching but not an overwhelming Violetta? I suspect it is because her assumption lacks a little in impulsiveness: the madness that leads Violetta through life and marks all her decisions, and for a moment joins us to her.

Carlo del Monte is one of the better Alfredos, with a manly, flexible sound, light in weight though rather dark in color. He lacks something occasionally in tenderness and finish, but the voice is never ugly. In the gambling scene he manages to be furious and yet touchingly

defenseless at the same time, and in Act III the depth of his concern is moving. Mario Sereni is again a warm and sympathetic Germont. Tullio Serafin leads an expansive and touching performance.

1960 RCA / BMG (S) CD

Anna Moffo (A), Richard Tucker (B), Robert Merrill (C), Rome Opera Chorus and Orchestra—Fernando Previtali

This is such a nicely recorded, pleasantly sung, and traditionally acted performance that it seems ungrateful not to be more enthusiastic about it. All of the leads sing well and their style, if conventional, is generally tasteful. Anna Moffo has a rather dark but healthy sound and considerable dexterity. Aside from her habit of sliding into notes occasionally, she sings the role with delicacy and neatness. "È strano" is comfortably thoughtful and "Sempre libera" charming; what is missing is a real conflict of feelings in the former and a fever in the latter. She sings the Act II duet with Germont with tender intimacy, but she appears at times to be reflecting nostagically on events rather than experiencing the pain directly. Act III is also well sung: an informed, competent, and sometimes touching portrayal.

For all his vocal health and steadiness, Richard Tucker is unsuited to Alfredo. The singing is smooth, but despite his intimate moments, his passion is the passion of a general, not a romantic young man of the bourgeoisie. The anger is convincing, and the desire to protect, but not the youthful vulnerability. As Germont, Robert Merrill is in sumptuous voice, though the character is only sketched. He occasionally rushes the tempo of "Di Provenza" a little, but in general the voice and its use are exemplary. Of the others, Piero de Palma is an excellent Gastone. Fernando Previtali conducts a proficient and respectable performance, except at the start of the scene at Flora's, where things suddenly go with military speed and the vocal delivery of the *comprimarios* is mostly devoid of characterization. All in all, a neat and healthy performance, but . . .

1962 DEUTSCHE GRAMMOPHON (S) CD

Renata Scotto (A), Gianni Raimondi (B), Ettore Bastianini (C), La Scala Chorus and Orchestra—Antonino Votto

Here is an interesting recording featuring the young Renata Scotto, her voice quite distinctive in timbre, with that penetrating and yet shadowed quality that in itself suggests a complex of feelings. Vocally this is one of her most attractive recordings, the upper register particularly free and effective. She and baritone Ettore Bastianini miss a special note of intimacy, but they sing healthily together. In the third act her reading of Germont's letter is exhausted and "È tardi!" an outcry, and in the "Addio" she employs her *pianissimo* well. The rest is more outspoken emotionally than many other performances, and full of a measured and touching sadness.

Gianni Raimondi, as Alfredo, has a pleasant tone and sings nicely enough, though without special joy or intimacy. His opening aria in Act II is genial and the rest respectable if unsubtle. Ettore Bastianini is in magnificent voice and has a considerate if unsubtle way with the music. "Di Provenza" is, typically, beautifully voiced and reasonably tender. Antonino Votto conducts sensibly for the singers, though with no special charm or tragic compulsion in the later acts. The set is a valuable reminder of the special pleasures of the early Scotto and the tragically short-lived Bastianini, with a representative sample of Raimondi's work.

1962 DECCA / LONDON (S) CD

Joan Sutherland (A), Carlo Bergonzi (B), Robert Merrill (C), Chorus and Orchestra of the Maggio Musicale Fiorentino—John Pritchard

This was the first entirely uncut version of *Traviata* to be recorded. It includes second verses to some of the arias, cabalettas for Alfredo and Germont, and some transitional material. As Violetta it features Joan Sutherland, then in the early years of her international career. The voice is generally firm and fresh, the dynamic range complete, and the passagework superb: technically an astonishing performance. For characterization she provides a kind of retrospective tenderness, and for warmth she thick-

ens the voice and loses the consonants. So we get an expert traversal of the score, but little more than indications of Violetta's willful charm, weariness, grand passion, and desperation. The insistence on performing the score complete is here a disadvantage. When, for example, the second verse of "Ah fors'è lui" is to be sung, it must intensify the vision, the longing expressed in the first verse, if it is not to seem merely a repetition. Sutherland is not the singer to provide that kind of subtlety. She is not always helped by the conducting of John Pritchard, which, though impressive, is in the party scenes occasionally too fast for the characters to express themselves with conviction, and elsewhere slow enough to demand really expert character work from the singers so as to prevent ponderousness.

Carlo Bergonzi's Alfredo is fresh, tender, and pliant, with a fine sense of *rubato*. He sings Alfredo's cabaletta "O mio rimorso" complete, with both grace and conviction. The free rhythmic treatment of "Ah si, che feci," the passage in which Alfredo expresses remorse for having flung his winnings at Violetta, is so overdone as to be blatantly melodramatic, but his singing in the final act is a model of loving care. Robert Merrill is once again a rich-voiced Germont of conventional character. This time he sings the cabaletta, which, as usual, is an anticlimax and, with its jogging rhythm, seems to express a repellent self-satisfaction. As a whole, the set is more accomplished technically than moving, though it represents the best work of its three leading singers.

1967 RCA / BMG (S) CD

Montserrat Caballé (A), Carlo Bergonzi (B), Sherrill Milnes (C), RCA Italiana Opera Chorus and Orchestra—Georges Prêtre

Again the score is performed uncut. Though Verdi's original plan is of prime interest, I must say that the cut version is generally more effective. The one striking restoration is Alfredo's "O mio rimorso," following his discovery of Violetta's indebtedness. It illuminates Alfredo's conception of honor, throws a revealing light on his later responses in the gambling scene, and provides an exhilarating emotional contrast to the Germont-Violetta duet which immediately follows. On the other hand, Germont's cabaletta of forgiveness following "Di Provenza" always seems musically trivial and dramatically unnecessary as the closing to a scene of extraordinary emotional tension. One can see Verdi's point in wanting to expand on Germont's relationship with his son, but much of that is implied in the preceding aria. The second verses of other arias and duets generally prolong the opera and attenuate its emotional effect. Act III in particular has in the cut version a psychological and musical economy of devastating power.

Montserrat Caballé, in silken voice, projects a mood of radiant melancholy throughout. That suits the longing of "Ah, fors'è lui" and the pain of Violetta's meeting with Germont well. It illuminates less clearly the drinking song and flirtation in Act I, the fevered intensity of the gambling scene, and the visionary doom of the final act. With Caballé a portion of the character is thus exquisitely realized, and that must stand for the whole. Carlo Bergonzi as Alfredo is as gracious as before, and he differentiates nicely between the two verses of "O mio rimorso," the second more spirited than the first. His denunciation of Violetta is powerful and the final scene full of affection. Sherrill Milnes is a Germont both splendidly resonant and intimate when the score and his Violetta require it. The characterization is well coached if not yet definitive, and he sings the restored cabaletta well enough so that it seems no more than lightheaded and inappropriate. The lyric scenes go well in general, but Georges Prêtre sometimes whips the party scenes into a frenzy, destroying continuity and charm. Much of the vocalism in this set is very lovely, though the characterization of its Violetta, enchantingly sung as it is, remains monochromatic.

1968 DECCA / LONDON (S)

Pilar Lorengar (A), Giacomo Aragall (B), Dietrich Fischer-Dieskau (C), Chorus and Orchestra of the Deutsche Oper, Berlin—Lorin Maazel

This recording arose from a Berlin production utilizing these leading singers and conductor. It includes one verse each of the cabalettas for Alfredo and Germont but observes all the other standard cuts. As elsewhere, Lorin Maazel

has provocative ideas but often drives them to such extremes that the result is mannered rather than convincing. Here he tends to speed through the party scenes at such a rate that his soloists and chorus have little time to characterize. Though these parties may occasionally be uproarious, the characters still seek charm and grace in one another, but this performance sometimes prevents expansion along those lines. Pilar Lorengar is a bright-voiced Violetta. Her distinctive vibrato provides an initial impression of dramatic commitment, but that effect soon wears thin and her performance as a whole emerges as responsible but monochromatic.

Giacomo Aragall has a handsome voice for Alfredo, barring a couple of strained high notes, but he provides only sporadic grace. His best moment is "De' miei bollenti spiriti," where he sings with an easy joy. Dietrich Fischer-Dieskau's Germont is lyrical and sensitive, but with an odd result: no one as acute as the character he has created could honestly say the things which Germont says, so that the thought occurs that Alfredo's father is crassly manipulative and connivingly self-interested. Fischer-Dieskau also provides a delightful "Di Provenza," intimate and comforting. The cabaletta is handled nicely; it accords rather well with this lighter realization of the character. "Di sprezzo degno" he handles with convincing gravity: a real accomplishment, considering the problems many heavier baritones have with this music. Altogether the performance is neatly sung though sometimes eccentrically conducted. The production may have had more dramatic impact in the theater, but on records it seems rather alienated. Fischer-Dieskau's conception of Germont, however, is provocative.

1971 EMI / ANGEL (S) CD

Beverly Sills (A), Nicolai Gedda (B), Rolando Panerai (C), John Alldis Choir, Royal Philharmonic Orchestra—Aldo Ceccato

This recording is interesting as much for the dramatic ideas of Beverly Sills and Nicolai Gedda as for their performance. As so often with Sills, one must search beyond the voice (which is light for the role though here steady and well disciplined) to her intent. In this case, she is also hobbled at times by the conductor's lingering tempos, which on occasion demand a fuller and more varied sound than hers. She offers a charmingly fragile Violetta in the first act: the passagework is dazzling, but she has not quite the heft for the recklessness suggested in "Sempre libera." The voice lacks ideal body and warmth for the first scene in Act II, but she enacts it eloquently. "Dite alla giovine" is a measure of her art: she phrases it touchingly, with dignity and sorrow. "Amami, Alfredo" is sung very expansively but is perfectly proportioned. The final act also has elegance, though here the careful tempos and the restored cuts contribute to a ponderous effect.

Nicolai Gedda is on a quest to find a living character in Alfredo. He gains strength and passion through rhythmic articulation, and scales his performance to the delicacy of his Violetta. At times he sounds thick-voiced and a little precious, but he is one of the few tenors to express in "De' miei bollenti spiriti" an intimate ecstasy of spirit and in "O mio rimorso" self-disgust rather than anger. In the confrontation at Flora's, he emerges as hateful rather than as an emotionally generous young man hurt to the quick; but Gedda's imagination, subtlety, and technical control are nevertheless of special interest. Rolando Panerai offers his distinctively warm tone, some intimacy, and the outline of a character. Much of "Di Provenza" is quite intimate, though the cabaletta sounds, as usual, distractingly trivial. Aldo Ceccato's conducting is quite expansive, lacking the nervous energy that would really benefit his light-voiced heroine, particularly in the final act. This is a recording notable in that two of the leading singers offer interesting conceptions of character which are not always fully realized in their performance.

1973 ACANTA (S) CD

Mirella Freni (A), Franco Bonisolli (B), Sesto Bruscantini (C), Berlin State Opera Chorus, Berlin State Orchestra—Lamberto Gardelli

Here is an interestingly cast performance which, however, adds up to little more than the sum of its attractive moments, since Lamberto Gardelli is in this instance a somnolent conductor unable to galvanize his varied personnel into a single cogent statement of the work. Mirella Freni is in her loveliest voice here—full, fresh, and mobile—and phrases gracefully throughout. Her mood is mostly pensive, though: the pretense of reckless joy and the moments of desperate commitment are somewhat beyond her range. Her sound, however, like Caballé's, may be reward enough. The Alfredo of Franco Bonisolli is certainly one of "boiling spirits." He has a splendid time at the first-act party, and it's only when sentimentality intrudes on "Un dì felice" that star tenor mannerisms threaten to take over. His work in Act II is very vivid, if sometimes strained, among the sleepy surroundings, and he has at least a modicum of grace elsewhere: a likable performance. Sesto Bruscantini makes a character role of Germont. The anger and the stringency are there, and even some of the sorrow, but the part is quite roughly sung, with strain on top and insufficient *legato*: Freni and he are not well matched. The supporting roles are all done ineffectively by members of the Berlin State Opera. There are substantial attractions here, but the performance as a whole does not quite coalesce.

1976–77 DEUTSCHE GRAMMOPHON (S) CD

Ileana Cotrubas (A), Plácido Domingo (B), Sherrill Milnes (C), Bavarian State Opera Chorus and Orchestra—Carlos Kleiber

Ileana Cotrubas is one of the few artists able to maintain the illusion of theatrical spontaneity in the recording studio. Frailty and passion for life are at the center of her characterization. From the start, she suggests all the attributes of a Violetta: sensuous grace, humor, illness, restless enjoyment. "Ah, fors'è lui" is vibrant and touching, and "Sempre libera" feverishly glittering. With Germont she has both fragility and conviction, and in "Dite alla giovine" she suggests sorrow so great that she can hardly contain it. It is strange that, here and in live performances, her "Amami, Alfredo" is rather prosaic in comparison with her superb emotional buildup to it. The confrontation with Alfredo at Flora's is strikingly immediate, and when she sings "Alfredo, Alfredo" at the conclusion of the act, she sounds, quite properly, as if she has just awakened from a faint. In Act III, she remains full of submerged feeling. Though "Gran Dio!" is rushed, the rest is riveting in its evocation of hope and death.

As Alfredo, Plácido Domingo is rich-voiced—indeed, a little muscular for his frail Violetta—and sings his second-act aria with youthful passion and wonder. After receiving Violetta's letter, he is white-hot with conviction, which carries over to the scene at Flora's. Sherrill Milnes as Germont is in wonderful voice and sings with considerable intimacy. He gives us one verse of the cabaletta, sung lightly and yet with great energy. In the work of Carlos Kleiber there is much that is moving and some that seems arbitrary. He never drags; the most lyrical moments move forward and possess life, pulse, and pattern. The party scenes are sometimes rushed and thus lose continuity and charm. The end of the Brindisi, for example, is suddenly fast, and the opening of the scene at Flora's is so quick that the *comprimarios* don't have a chance to make a conversation of their words. There are one or two other distracting passages, but these do not really hide the great gifts of his Violetta, who, remarkably, can keep all her grace, as in Act I, when the conductor is rushing in a way that would drive almost anyone else to rigidity or blank vocalization. Most of the standard cuts are observed, but, as mentioned, we do get one verse each of the cabalettas of Alfredo and Germont. This is one of the performances to which one wants to return, for there are subtleties in the work of Cotrubas that can be tasted again and again.

1979 DECCA / LONDON (S,D) CD

Joan Sutherland (A), Luciano Pavarotti (B), Matteo Manuguerra (C), London Opera Chorus, National Philharmonic Orchestra—Richard Bonynge

In her second recorded *Traviata*, done seventeen years after the first, Joan Sutherland struggles to maintain the vocal clarity so readily available to her in that early recording. The top notes and the quick passages remain as impressive as before, but the middle voice, so important in this opera, is now opaque and unsteady. Despite her attention to details of rhythm and accent, the diction remains unclear, the coloring of the words is insufficiently varied, and the lines often emerge without specific dramatic intent. In Alfredo one should sense the devotion and outrage of a young romantic, and Luciano Pavarotti projects this as well as anyone on records. Offering a bright, sunny sound and clear articulation, he sings with ease and intimacy and carries on the conversational exchanges deftly. "O mio rimorso" is precise as well as passionate, and in Acts I and III he is all concern and charm.

At his first entrance, Matteo Manuguerra demonstrates the qualities necessary to a fine Germont: a beautiful, focused voice of middle weight, a strong vocal technique, and convincing bourgeois anger. "Pura siccome un angelo" and "Di Provenza" have a simple and touching intimacy; in the phrase "Dio me guido," for example, he is not just shouting at the heavens, but making a little prayer. He does what he can with the cabaletta, singing it with warmth and dignity. Richard Bonynge's conducting is supportive but becomes more ponderous as the opera proceeds: a disadvantage to his soprano, who is not able to fill out the expanses with detailed characterization. The score is performed complete. The set's distinction rests on its exceptional Alfredo and Germont.

1980 EMI / ANGEL (In English) (S) CD

Valerie Masterson (A), John Brecknock (B), Christian du Plessis (C), English National Opera Chorus and Orchestra—Charles Mackerras

Singing a foreign masterpiece in English offers challenges beyond the matter of good translation and clear diction. A singer must learn to project the words not only with clarity but with dramatic distinction—and that goes for the minor roles as well as the major: the dramatic illusion can be broken in an instant. Then there is the issue of national styles of singing and how they affect the work undertaken. English or American singers can absorb a foreign style when singing in a foreign tongue, but how much of that can they use for a foreign work in their own language? The problem for English singers of *Traviata* is to maintain enough of the Italian singing style to illuminate the music being sung, and yet project the English with clarity and sufficient conviction to keep us centered on the important emotional aspects of the work of art.

On the issue of clarity, Valerie Masterson and John Brecknock do rather well, the others less so. On the matter of musical and dramatic style, judgment is more complex. Masterson is a fragile but cool Violetta, the music more forthright emotionally than the singer who voices it. In Act I her singing is intimate, fleet, and accurate. In the second act, certainly, there is need for a voice of more warmth and coloristic variety, though she provides thoughtful and touching moments. Throughout, the vocalism per se is accomplished, though in characterization she never gets beyond the melancholy; the overtones and subtext of romantic tragedy are missing. John Brecknock handles the language clearly but lacks the tonal heft to project Alfredo's passion, despite his care and flexibility. Christian du Plessis, as Germont, has a richness of tone that the others lack but uses the language with less conviction and much less clarity. Sir Charles Mackerras leads a performance more effective in the party scenes than in the intimate ones which, though neatly handled, sometimes lack dramatic spine. Like his singers, he evokes an image of fragility but not always the passion that drives these characters to their fate.

1980 EMI / ANGEL (S,D) ⓒ

Renata Scotto (A), Alfredo Kraus (B), Renato Bruson (C), Ambrosian Opera Chorus, Philharmonia Orchestra, Band of the Royal Marines—Riccardo Muti

This is another uncut *Traviata*, and beset with problems. Riccardo Muti gives us a performance filled with individual "effective" moments but with little sense of emotional continuity. Violetta's party, for example, is speedy but graceless. The buildup to the Brindisi would be excessive for a salute to the United Nations, but

the piece itself is paced without charm or *rubato*. He tends to rush the conversational passages so that the singers have little time to act them out. Elsewhere he often either speeds ahead or languishes; there is little sense of cumulative impact in a given scene. Renata Scotto is one of the great singing actresses of recent times, but here one must often take the will for the deed, for she is unsteady enough even in the middle range to compromise her dramatic and musical aims. At the end of Act I, for example, every line is full of color and motivational intention and there is much adroit phrasing, but the constant need to keep the voice in line results not in the delicacy and spontaneity she wants, but in a rather precious attenuation of tone. Later on the vocal harshness lessens the effect of vulnerability she seeks. "Addio del passato" goes rather smoothly, except at the climaxes. The fact that she is singing the score uncut only emphasizes these problems.

Alfredo Kraus is a musicianly singer, rather dry here and with a hint of unsteadiness. In Act I the effect is somewhat charmless, but in Act II he presents the aria with a welcome tenderness—a certain wonder that Violetta could love him. Against Muti's orchestra he simply hasn't the heft for the angry scene at Flora's. Renato Bruson is an uninteresting Germont: his many changes of attitude are not really dramatized, "Di Provenza" is rather sleepy, and the cabaletta is even more soporific than usual. So here we have the spectacle of a distinguished cast, some of whom are having vocal problems, with a conductor who apparently does not trust the score or understand the ways in which he can accommodate vocal limitations.

1981 ELEKTRA (S)

Teresa Stratas (A), Plácido Domingo (B), Cornell MacNeil (C), Metropolitan Opera Chorus and Orchestra—James Levine

It is difficult to know for whom this album is intended. It is the soundtrack for Zeffirelli's astonishing film. As a souvenir of that experience it is inadequate, since the striking element there was visual, and as a recording it is not only heavily cut but does serious injustice to some of the singers who participate in it. Not only are all the standard old cuts observed but there are some new ones: part of "Un dì felice," part of the second-act Violetta-Germont duet, the second verse of "Di Provenza," everything in Act III up to the reading of the letter, and the section from Alfredo's entrance to "Parigi, o cara." The film was a beautiful and moving thing, as was Teresa Stratas's performance as Violetta. For records she has a fresh and frail tone, and an imaginative and committed way with the music. "Sempre libera" is, though, frankly awkward, rushed, and inaccurate, but much of the rest is deeply felt and interesting. Act III is particularly persuasive, despite the conductor's rushing and the cuts. Plácido Domingo sings with conviction and some grace, though his voice is, as before, a bit thick for the role. His denunciation of Violetta and his remorse are both strongly sung, and in Act III he does "Parigi, o cara" sympathetically.

Cornell MacNeil's performance as Germont is inexplicable. Vocally he is worn, but aside from that the portrayal is quite the most insensitive on records: it sounds either calculating or offhand, and seldom sympathetic. James Levine is alternately eloquent and rushed. As a performance this has its moments, but no one escapes undamaged except Domingo, and he is better represented on the Ileana Cotrubas set with Carlos Kleiber.

1989 CAPRICCIO (M,P,D) CD

Lucia Aliberti (A), Peter Dvorsky (B), Renato Bruson (C), Fujiwara Opera Chorus, Tokyo Philharmonic Orchestra—Roberto Paternostro

A thoroughly depressing concert reading, badly sung and shapelessly conducted. All of the major participants show ability, but most of them cannot get beyond a struggle with the music. Lucia Aliberti has a full, dark voice of promise but pressured and insecure everywhere except in the simplest lyric moments and certain fleet-

ing passagework. The joy, exhaustion, and sorrow of the work remain beyond her. Peter Dvorsky is now reasonably comfortable only at *mezzo forte* but lacks support and security at any other level. Renato Bruson's Germont is at least pleasantly reflective but strained at the climaxes. The *comprimarios* are all distractingly inadequate. Roberto Paternostro provides lush, painless Preludes but with him the opera itself wants emotional continuity and structural tension. The cuts are as usual, though Alfredo and Germont are given one verse each of their cabalettas.

Unlike several Verdi operas, *La Traviata* has not been led on records by a long roster of distinguished conductors. Arturo Toscanini, Pierre Monteux, Tullio Serafin, Carlo Maria Giulini, Carlos Kleiber, and James Levine are among the few who qualify that way, and Monteux's and Levine's are very disappointing performances. There are three recordings that seem to me unforgettable, two of them live and monophonic: the Toscanini broadcast of 1946 with Licia Albanese, memorable for its yearning and dramatic imagination; the 1955 La Scala performance with Maria Callas, full of subtle insight; and the 1976–77 Kleiber set with Ileana Cotrubas, profoundly poignant and beautifully vocalized. There are, of course, some memorable individual portrayals, noted earlier, among the other sets discussed. The opera and its characters have become legendary, and like any legend they invite new and striking interpretations.

LONDON GREEN

Unavailable for review:
1915 EMI/ANGEL
1952 REMINGTON
1962 CONCERT HALL
1966 FABBRI
1968 ELECTRECORD
1991 DEUTSCHE GRAMMOPHON
1991 TELDEC

GIUSEPPI VERDI

I VESPRI SICILIANI (1855)

A: Elena (s); B: Arrigo (t); C: Monforte (bar); D: Procida (bs)

*L*es Vêpres Siciliennes was Verdi's first original commission from the Paris Opéra. He took his task seriously and produced one of his most unconventional and fascinating scores (the Act IV finale, for instance, is a far from predictable ensemble). If the work nevertheless remains on the fringe of operatic repertory, part of the problem is surely the inept translation (as I Vespri Siciliani) nearly universally performed; this adaptation includes circumlocutions and misaccentuations inconceivable in a libretto directly set by Verdi, and the consequent mismatch between word and tone muffles the opera's impact.

For a Paris revival, Verdi wrote an alternative tenor aria which has found almost no subsequent use. The extended ballet, one of Verdi's best, is generally omitted in performance; it is included in both recordings, complete renditions of the Italian score.

1973 RCA / BMG (In Italian) (S) CD

Martina Arroyo (A), Plácido Domingo (B), Sherrill Milnes (C), Ruggero Raimondi (D), John Alldis Choir, New Philharmonia Orchestra—James Levine

The overall character of this performance has clearly been determined by its conductor. James Levine exacts a rhythmic snap from his orchestra that provides a distinctive framework for the action; the Overture may emerge a bit noisy, but the lengthy ballet is quite arresting, and the ensemble scenes have a convincing purposeful-

ness. The precision is perhaps less helpful to the soloists; more inclined toward gentle curves than hard edges, they sometimes seem to be fitting in with their accompaniment, rather than buoyantly supported by it.

RCA's principals are all major Verdi voices, not all equally suited to these particular roles. Some lapses of accuracy and intonation betray an unfamiliarity with this music, but the spirit and intention are usually right. Least impressive is Ruggero Raimondi, effective with the simple high-lying declamatory phrases called for in massed scenes, but weakening as he descends, and without real attention to the shaping of his music. Martina Arroyo by contrast displays exactly that kind of attention, demonstrating her artistic and vocal distinction in the poise of her opening scene and Act IV solo. Ideally, the role calls for a voice with a cutting clarity all the way to the bottom, and with a dazzling (rather than merely respectable) florid technique for the Sicilienne; but Arroyo's contribution is of high quality, and very beautiful to hear.

As Arrigo, Plácido Domingo sings with thrilling consistency and tonal splendor, and with reliable musicianship too, but without much thought for the details of character and nuance that bring such music to life. He evidently worked hardest on his big scene in Act IV, and projects it successfully despite inattention to the softer dynamics. Strongest of the principals on this occasion is Sherrill Milnes, who has clearly observed and absorbed the score's detailed suggestions, and translated them into a wealth of inflection and color. Of the principals, he alone

618

avoids the impression that a year or two of experience with this opera would not come amiss before recording the results for posterity. The smaller roles are cast with familiar British and American names; among them Leo Goeke (as Daniele, who must act as principal tenor in ensembles that exclude Arrigo) stands out.

1989–90 EMI / ANGEL (In Italian)
(S,D,P) ⑩

Cheryl Studer (A), Chris Merritt (B), Giorgio Zancanaro (C), Ferruccio Furlanetto (D), La Scala Chorus and Orchestra—Riccardo Muti

The second commercial recording unfortunately fails to provide a real alternative to the RCA, for in many respects the two are similar in their strengths and weaknesses. In particular, Riccardo Muti's conductorial priorities as heard here resemble James Levine's, with a preference for strict tempo and straightforward phrasing. Direct comparison at almost any point, however, shows Muti as less imaginative and atmospheric, less ready to use Verdi's markings as a springboard for thrilling or beautiful effects, and seemingly less encouraging of initiative from his cast. Despite being recorded during live performance, the Angel set has little feeling of the theater about it; undoubtedly perception of the performance is colored by the unattractively dry, remote sonic quality.

The most satisfying vocal presence is that of Giorgio Zancanaro: though not long on finesse (he offers aspirate "h"s in place of a true *legato*),

he makes an attractive sound with some depth and bite in it, and sings real phrases with intention behind them. Cheryl Studer's exceptional vocal poise also makes a memorable effect; her soprano has both clarity and thrust, she can meet most of the role's florid demands with relative ease, and the reserved dignity which she projects suits the role of Elena. Her only problematic moments come when she tries to mimic a different kind of voice—the conventional image of a Verdi soprano—which causes her momentarily to lose control and sound unpleasant.

Ferruccio Furlanetto's lovely bass voice is a size or two small for Procida under these conditions; the need to make himself heard and keep producing tone removes most of his chances for variety and leaves him sounding merely light and monochrome, however sensitive. As heard here, Chris Merritt fails to satisfy; though he manages all the notes, no small task, his vocal production apparently allows him neither tonal variety nor linguistic clarity, and whatever musical imagination he may have remains uncommunicated. The singers of the small roles leave little impression one way or another, which might also be said of this performance in general.

Neither performance is of a quality to sweep all reservations aside, but the RCA is decidedly the more convincing and impressive of the two.

JON ALAN CONRAD

GIUSEPPE VERDI

SIMON BOCCANEGRA
(1857; revised 1881)

A: Amelia (s); B: Gabriele (t); C: Simon (bar); D: Fiesco (bs); E: Paolo (bs)

The structure of a narrative is said to be "broken backed" when it embodies a violent separation in time. *Simon Boccanegra* qualifies, not only for its libretto but for its strange history as well. Francesco Maria Piave, Verdi's original collaborator, fashioned the scenario on a play by the same Spaniard whose work had inspired *Il Trovatore*, Antonio Garcia Gutierrez, an author with a penchant for overplotting and confused identities.

Simon, which followed the made-for-Paris *Vespri Siciliani*, was the first of Verdi's operas written for an Italian audience to abandon the formulas of his early operas. Its dark subject, its weird plot, the way Verdi had turned his back on hit tunes and cabalettas in his search for larger dramatic truths were repellent to the original Venetian audiences of 1857. Even Verdi found it "sad and depressing." It is said that he could not resist tinkering with *Simon* because he loved it so much. That may be true, but equally true was Verdi's abhorrence of wasting the work that went into a failed opera. His career is marked by efforts at salvaging and reshaping: *Macbeth, I Lombardi, Stiffelio, La Forza del Destino,* and *Don Carlo,* not to mention *Simon,* all exist in two versions.

Verdi's revision of *Simon* began around 1880 after he had composed *Aida* and the Manzoni Requiem. It was his first collaboration with Arrigo Boito, who accepted the decidedly unpromising assignment of making Piave's libretto coherent. Boito clarified some of the text's key incidents—Simon's death, for instance—by adding a scene in which Paolo puts poison in the Doge's goblet of water. Most significantly, Boito wrote a new finale for the first act, set in the Doge's council chamber. Verdi responded to these efforts with some of his most inspired writing, which is the heart of the 1881 revision, the principal reason for its success and for the eclipse of the 1857 original.

Although *Boccanegra*'s composition and revision are separated by twenty-five years, there is not the collision of styles one might expect. Under the circumstances, the opera is remarkably unified and continuous in texture.

1939 MET (M,P)

Elisabeth Rethberg (A), Giovanni Martinelli (B), Lawrence Tibbett (C), Ezio Pinza (D), Leonard Warren (E), Metropolitan Opera Chorus and Orchestra—Ettore Panizza

This issue was recorded at the Met over a half century ago. It documents what was probably the most significant between-the-wars revival of the opera anywhere in the world. Warts and all, the recording is decent enough for its day. The sound is well balanced and clear, except for congestion in some of the *fortes;* volume levels do, however, sometimes change from the end of one of the original acetate sides to the louder beginning of the next. There are three unfortunate cuts: the cabaletta of the Amelia-Gabriele duet in the first act and the Paolo-Pietro dialogue which ends the scene, plus four measures from the final cadence of the second act.

Although it took place six seasons after its Met premiere, the musical performance has held its edge, thanks to the authoritative supervision and stylish conducting of Ettore Panizza—the right-hand man of Arturo Toscanini at La Scala during the twenties—and an illustrious and dedicated cast. Boccanegra was a favorite role of the American baritone Lawrence Tibbett, and his affection for it is continually felt. The sweetest *pianissimo* "Figlia," the nobility of his "Plebe, patrizi, popolo," the tenderness of "Piangio su voi" in the same ensemble, the denunciation of Paolo with its many hues of scorn, all are unique, indelible impressions. Ezio Pinza brings fire and ice to his unsurpassed portrayal of Fiesco, his magnificent dark bass like a lash in his first encounter with Simon and in "Delle faci festanti al barlume," as he gloats over the Doge's impending death, followed by a "Piango, perchè mi parla" sung with infinitely touching *cantabile*. Some driven high notes and vocal strain betray time's erosion of Elisabeth Rethberg's voice. But it has not affected its size, exquisite, silvery quality, or velvety softness of attack. Her breath control insures a command of *legato* and *portamento* that, guided by innate musicality, permits a rare amplitude of phrasing. Toscanini adored her. Giovanni Martinelli was not in his best vocal estate the day of this broadcast. He is strained by his aria and in some of the high notes with which the role of Gabriele abounds, but he still gives pleasure, with his heroic style and his unmatched verbal and musical intensity. The nobility of his *sostenuto* singing with Pinza in the duet "Vieni a me, ti benedico" is unforgettable. Leonard Warren is heard here in his first Saturday matinee broadcast. His big baritone foretells stardom; but he is often careless about dynamics, much too loud for Verdi's *sotto voce* markings for "L'atra magion vedete" in the Prologue and in "Qui ti stillo una lenta."

1951 CETRA (M)

Antonietta Stella (A), Carlo Bergonzi (B), Paolo Silveri (C), Mario Petri (D), Walter Monachesi (E), RAI Chorus and Orchestra, Rome—Francesco Molinari-Pradelli

Like many Italian operas on the fringes of standard repertory, *Simon Boccanegra* was recorded complete for the first time via RAI radio tapes, transferred to discs, and issued by Cetra. The original release, long out of print, reasonably clear despite its constricted sound, is far superior to its reissue by Everest, electronically enhanced for stereo effect and trailing clouds of phony echo-chamber resonance. The performance is lively but provincial in character, with little refinement of sonority or inflection of phrase. Paolo Silveri in the title role lacks nobility but not commitment. Mario Petri has a strong, attractive bass, a trifle weak in the lowest notes, and struggles with pitch here and there. He is more careful about dynamic indications than his colleagues, thereby enriching the texture of his portrayal. Antonietta Stella is coarse in line and tone as Amelia. At the time of this recording, most likely his first, Carlo Bergonzi was an unformed artist, his pliable phrases jostled by adjacent gaucheries. In fairness to the singers, little good can come about in the orchestral context provided by Francesco Molinari-Pradelli, sometimes fiery but largely insensitive, lumpy in texture, and bumpy in continuity.

1957 EMI / ANGEL (M) CD

Victoria de los Angeles (A), Giuseppe Campora (B), Tito Gobbi (C), Boris Christoff (D), Walter Monachesi (E), Rome Opera Chorus and Orchestra—Gabriele Santini

The next recording of *Boccanegra* appeared in mono under major-label auspices in 1957 at the stereo watershed. Like its predecessor, it is lamed by mediocre engineering. The overall sound is insufficiently rich, voices predominate, and there is some peaking caused by overrecording. Worse still is the conducting, the opera poorly paced and shaped. Despite these liabilities, the set commands attention for the contributions of Tito Gobbi, the Simon, and Boris Christoff, the Fiesco, both in best vocal estate, displaying psychological insight into their demanding roles. Together they throw off a shower of dramatic sparks in their two confrontations. Victoria de los Angeles, also heard in prime vocal time, sings exquisitely, especially in her aria, and offers an unforgettable trill at the close of the great ensemble in the Council Chamber Scene. Her temperament, however, is at odds with the dramatic amplitude required of most Verdi heroines. Gabriele Adorno, too often sung by a lyric tenor, is written for a heavier instrument (Tamagno, Verdi's Otello, first sang the part in 1881) and is too much for Giuseppe Campora, however hard he tries. Walter Monachesi is a routine Paolo, whose voice has lost some of the luster it had in the Cetra recording.

1973 RCA / BMG (S)

Katia Ricciarelli (A), Plácido Domingo (B), Piero Cappuccilli (C), Ruggero Raimondi (D), Gian Piero Mastromei (E), RCA Italiana Chorus and Orchestra—Gianandrea Gavazzeni

It was sixteen years later before the first stereo *Boccanegra* turned up. RCA made it with a pick-up orchestra and chorus in its Roman studios led with sympathetic flair by Gianandrea Gavazzeni and judiciously paced. More than a few patches of imperfect ensemble betray insufficient rehearsal. Fullness of sound and effects of theatrical staging set it apart from those it succeeded. Not so crisply detailed in the Prologue and first act, the recording, like the performance itself, improves as it goes along, reaching its peak in the last act. Piero Cappuccilli sings the title role honorably, even memorably, in the last half of the scene with Amelia, in the reconciliation duet with Fiesco, and in the wonderful quartet beginning "Gran Dio, li benedici" near the end of the opera. He brings greater control, more light and shade to the Council Chamber Scene in the DG recording four years later. A more compact, flintier bass

than that of Ruggero Raimondi is needed for the obdurate Fiesco. No surprise, then, that he is most satisfying in the religious duet with Gabriele and in the aforementioned scene with Boccanegra. Katia Ricciarelli's gentle and appealing soprano could be a model for Amelia, but it continually betrays its inadequate schooling and is often ungainly in *portamento*. In the tenor role, Plácido Domingo proves himself worthy of comparison with the dominant Gabriele of the thirties, Giovanni Martinelli. He is a veritable firebrand in his aria, although he does not shade at "s'ei mille vite avesse" as the score advises. Gian Piero Mastromei is convincing as the villainous Paolo.

1977 DEUTSCHE GRAMMOPHON (S) CD

Mirella Freni (A), José Carreras (B), Piero Cappuccilli (C), Nicolai Ghiaurov (D), José van Dam (E), La Scala Chorus and Orchestra—Claudio Abbado

With the 1977 DG *Boccanegra*, one inhabits another world, one of unfaltering care, sensitivity, and achievement unique to commercial recordings of this opera. It is already a classic and the finest hour yet in Claudio Abbado's recording career. One could write a lengthy review and not run out of examples of the responsiveness of a very fine ensemble to his inspiring leadership and his dramatic imagination in faithful service to Verdi's instructions. Here are only a few instances of the latter: the postlude to "Il lacerato spirito," hushed, moving, magical; the atmospheric playing of the opening pages in the first act depicting the stillness at dawn and the cry of the sea gulls, the seven energetic bars that introduce the Gabriele-Fiesco scene with the religious duet played with such perfect chording it takes one's breath away.

Most of the singers are veterans of the celebrated Giorgio Stehler production at La Scala. Normally a blunt artist too seldom concerned with musical or dramatic differentiation, Piero Cappuccilli gives the recorded performance of his life under Abbado's baton, one with consistent sensitivity, elegance in long phrases, and without rant. After Ricciarelli, it is a pleasure to encounter Mirella Freni, an Amelia with the vocal technique to do it justice. Her professionalism, the warmth and vulnerability of her impersonation, make up for the lyric voice she has so cunningly trained to approximate the *spinto* quality appropriate to most of the Verdi heroines she sings. Nicolai Ghiaurov gives a performance representative of his standing as the leading Fiesco of his day, one that is vocally firm and even in scale, musically attentive, and well characterized. This set's great surprise is José Carreras, giving a convincing exhibition of mind over matter. His lyrical tenor, still sweet and true at this stage of his career, somehow satisfies the heavier-weight demands of Gabriele Adorno. One of the great stretches in this performance is the opening of the Prologue, thanks to José van Dam. His vivid presence in each of his appearances in the opera proclaims that vocally, musically, and dramatically he is the Paolo by which all others must be judged. Happily, DG has provided first-class engineering, a pleasing frame of resonance, and splendid theatrical effects to preserve this extraordinary rendition of Verdi's somber masterpiece.

p. 1983 HUNGAROTON (S,D) CD

Veronika Kincses (A), Janos B. Nagy (B), Lajos Miller (C), József Gregor (D), István Gáti (E), Hungarian State Opera Orchestra and Chorus—Giuseppe Patanè

The first digital recording comes from Hungary, which numbers, among its many releases over the past decade, quite a few notable for an ensemble polish that is the result of singers and conductors accustomed to working together. Although it is quite respectably recorded (but well shy of state-of-the-art presence), the entry is not, alas, up to the company's best standards. Here is a stolid performance led by the usually vital Giuseppe Patanè of an opera whose gloom must be countered by animation to survive and which is diminished by cuts, however small. A worthy Carlo in the Hungaroton *Ernani*, Lajos Miller led one to expect a more filled-out portrait of the Doge than the sketchy public figure

offered. If Miller has looked deeply into Simon's soul, he has not found the means to communicate his vision to the listener. Veronika Kincses is yet another underpowered Amelia, competent in quiet passages except for her apparent inability to trill, unfazed by her high-lying aria, but stretched too far in outspoken ensemble. József Gregor has a grainy bass and is a boring Fiesco, unable to differentiate the dark shades of the character. Janos B. Nagy goes at Gabriele in a rough-and-ready manner with as many vocal misses as hits. István Gáti is a poor Paolo, carelessly singing *mezzo forte* or louder at all times. Pass this *Boccanegra* by.

1989 DECCA / LONDON (S,D) CD

Kiri Te Kanawa (A), Giacomo Aragall (B), Leo Nucci (C), Paata Burchuladze (D), Paolo Coni (E), La Scala Chorus and Orchestra—Georg Solti

The pleasure of hearing this work in a digital recording that is first-rate (except for its attempts at suggesting distance) is mitigated by a performance that never leaves the ground, in spite of polished, idiomatic execution by the forces of La Scala.

Solti's vigorous address and care for dynamics insures a certain dramatic vitality, but the older maestro does not have the younger Abbado's unfaltering ability to find tempos that honor Verdi's instructions and convince the listener of their rightness. Nor does Solti achieve maximum expression with no sacrifice to continuity. His work is in need of finer rhythmic pointing and a higher level of musical and dramatic sensitivity.

The vocal team is even more disappointing. Te Kanawa's lovely tone, for much the time a blessing, shows strain in some outspoken passages and, in any event, is insufficient compensation for an expressively pallid characterization. With Aragall, it's the other way around. Even with the nap worn from his attractive tenor and his struggles with some of his role's high notes, he is a believable Gabriele. Only Paolo Coni's intense Paolo achieves his level of verisimilitude. Despite the attractive timbre of his voice, Leo Nucci proves once again he is not the latest in the line of stylish Verdi baritones. Time and again, he forces his voice in Simon's powerful episodes (e.g., the scenes with Fiesco and the great ensemble "Plebi, patrizi, popolo") and loses any sense of nobility. His prosody is minimal and in long phrases his tone is insufficiently poised to draw a firm musical line. Less acceptable is Burchuladze. Now poorly knit together, his once impressive bass is victimized by slovenly vocal production and is frequently out of tune. He conveys neither Fiesco's dignity nor the passion of his vengeful obsession.

A selective collection of recordings of complete operas by Verdi must include two *Simon Boccanegras*, one representing the best of the past—the Met set—and one representative of the more recent best—the DG set. Each honors the dignified solemnity of this strange and affecting product of Verdi's genius.

C. J. LUTEN

GIUSEPPE VERDI

UN BALLO IN MASCHERA (1859)

A: Amelia (s); B: Oscar (s); C: Ulrica (ms); D: Riccardo (t); E: Renato (bar)

By about 1900, *Un Ballo in Maschera* had come to be thought of as old-fashioned, even vulgar, but the wheel of understanding has turned and the opera is now firmly reestablished, with sixteen commercial recordings—not surprising since it is arguably the most completely achieved opera of Verdi's later middle period: less diffuse than *Forza*, higher spirited and more consistent than *Simon Boccanegra*, more economical and fuller of primary Italianate qualities than the even greater *Don Carlo*.

The opera has as starting point the assassination in 1792 of Gustavus III of Sweden, who presided over a liberal court and whose reforms initiated what became known as the Swedish Enlightenment. Since by 1858–59, one of Verdi's strengths was to produce by mainly musical means a unique atmosphere for each opera—an individual *tinta* or color—the Neapolitan censor's veto on the stage depiction of a king's murder, following an attempt on the life of Napoleon III and after the opera was complete, had a devastating effect. The court of the Swedish King was not musically to be confused with the Duke's in *Rigoletto* or the King of Spain's in *Don Carlo,* and had nothing to do with the substituted venue of Boston. It had been in *Rigoletto* that Verdi first introduced stylistic elements from operetta—effectively, the manner of light music—and *Ballo*'s Gustavus responds to stimulus with even more wit and exuberance than the Duke. So it is a precise atmosphere stimulated by historical events and personalities

which recordings of *Ballo* are attempting to bring to listeners.

The role of Amelia, with great arias in Acts II and III, the love duet, and the sweeping, high-lying line of the ensembles, seems to epitomize the characteristics essential to the Verdian soprano: an even compass, firm in the middle register, a secure top, a certain penetration (or power), and a sensitivity to musical nuance. It sounds no more than you are entitled to expect, but the qualities are fully present in fewer than half a dozen of these recordings. Ulrica lies low, but few mezzos who cannot make an effect as Azucena or Amneris make much of its single scene. The role of Renato is shorter than most of Verdi's for baritone, but it contains in "Eri tu" what may be his single most impressive baritone aria. *Ballo* is rare among Verdi's operas in being dominated by the tenor and the success of a performance is governed by the degree to which the Riccardo rises to the demands of the central role. His elegant, witty reaction to the challenge of events not only suggests the enlightened Swedish king of the story Verdi thought he had set but also places in high relief the lyrical romanticism of "La rivedrà," with which he announces himself to the public, and in the penultimate scene, in which he resolves to renounce his love for Amelia.

Complete recordings of Italian opera tend to be most successful when they reflect either a public performance or a period and style within which the work has been successfully performed. Four of the first five I have managed to hear fit that description: Panizza's because it was of the opening production of a Metropolitan season; Serafin's because he and his cast, albeit separately, had successfully revived the opera in Rome and Milan; Toscanini's because it was prepared for live broadcast; Votto's because the cast was associated with one of La Scala's most esteemed revivals of the opera. For the record, according to Italian tradition, short internal cuts were usually made in Act II's trio, and in the quintet and ballroom chorus of Act III. The sets conducted by Panizza (1940), Serafin (1943), Questa (1954), Votto (1956), Gavazzeni (1960) and, surprisingly, Karajan (1989) all observe these cuts.

1940 MET (M,P)

Zinka Milanov (A), Stella Andreva (B), Bruna Castagna (C), Jussi Bjoerling (D), Alexander Sved (E), Metropolitan Opera Chorus and Orchestra—Ettore Panizza

The earliest complete recording remains one of the most wholly enjoyable, partly because of the conviction carried by painstakingly prepared performances, partly because Panizza, after years at La Scala and the Met, shows a master hand—albeit an idiosyncratic one. Milanov was never the most meticulous of singers, but with her rare beauty of voice she could be one of the most communicative. Here she demonstrates the virtues of a Verdi soprano: a healthy middle octave and a glorious top underpinned by the breath control of an Olympic runner. Only some indecisive and placid musicianship stands between her and the ideal. Castagna sings very well, Andreva is accurate and sprightly, Sved—unfortunately coarse and heavy but presumably also big-voiced and reliable—is, for recording, the only weak link in the strong cast. The glory of the performance is Bjoerling's Riccardo, with his impeccable *legato*, brilliance of timbre, impetuous musicality, the embodiment of youthful ardor which, it seems to me, the music absolutely demands. The recording is excellent for the period, and if there were no other reason to recommend the set—and there are many—

Bjoerling's elegant, stylish, radiant singing would be quite sufficient.

1943 EMI / ANGEL (M) CD

Maria Caniglia (A), Elda Ribetti (B), Fedora Barbieri (C), Beniamino Gigli (D), Gino Bechi (E), Rome Opera Chorus and Orchestra—Tullio Serafin

Representative of opera performance standards in Italy in the late 1930s and early 1940s, Serafin's set included three principals—Gigli, Caniglia, and Bechi—who had sung the opera at La Scala in 1941. To describe it as polished would be to misuse the word, but there is a refreshing atmosphere of confidence about the way everyone approaches the music, even when they don't sing it very well—like Ribetti, of whom one can say little except that her top is secure. Caniglia, under forty but shrill and flat above the staff (the top C bursts in the gallows scene), squally and explosive elsewhere, nonetheless has the measure of the role, which she was still singing at La Scala with Bjoerling in 1951, and additionally the Italian faculty of taking over an aria as if it belonged to her by right. Gigli at fifty-three is no classical stylist—a natural singer of arias and songs, not a "conscious" artist—but there is glory in the voice, a genuine ring on A-natural and B-flat. He has the essential high spirits, the *strettas* to the first two scenes go along at a spanking pace, and the last-act aria, after a less than ideally firm recitative, is fine. What is curious about Serafin's study of the opera is that, contrary to his later studio practice, he seems to have made little attempt to reconcile the "old" style of Gigli and Caniglia with the "new" of Barbieri and Bechi. Barbieri, at twenty-three only three years into her career, is admirably cast, and the latter delivers a sizable "Eri tu," long-phrased and grandiose, lacking only the grace and buoyancy the greatest singers bring to it. The magnificent punch of his high Gs cannot disguise a certain unfamiliarity with the use of *portamento*, for instance, about which Gigli from example and Serafin with precept might have taught him much.

This Roman recording at its best sweeps away

all doubts, incidentally illuminating a period of Italian opera (no mention of "Inghilterra" in the text) when Rome had won ground from La Scala.

1954 RCA / BMG (M,P) CD

Herva Nelli (A), Virginia Haskins (B), Claramae Turner (C), Jan Peerce (D), Robert Merrill (E), Shaw Chorale, NBC Orchestra—Arturo Toscanini

Toscanini conducted *Ballo* during both his first and last periods at La Scala and was responsible for the start of the opera's American rehabilitation when he revived it at the Met in 1913–14 with Caruso and Destinn, so it is logical that he should have chosen it in 1954 for his last complete opera for NBC—last, and in certain ways most satisfactory as, whatever the shortcomings of his cast, there are few where the doyen of Italian maestros is concerned. Starting with the Prelude, Toscanini's rhythmic strength and passionate attack inform the score at all points: Amelia's entry, the wonderfully *squillante* brass in her Act II aria, the ferocious timpani as she picks a name out of the urn, the tension in the final scene; and he conducts in primary colors, winds (as in Act II's Prelude) standing away from strings, demonstrating much more than clarity, more a positive, perhaps beneficial, idiosyncrasy. The love duet may be hard-driven, but who could resist the (exaggerated ?) urgency of the *staccato* string underpinning of "O qual soave brivido?" With Toscanini, the pressure is on all the time, but to what effect!

There is not much to be said for Herva Nelli, with her raw top notes (a dreadful C in the gallows aria) and rather mild response to the music. This is her fifth major recorded collaboration with Toscanini but she sounds overparted and blowsy except perhaps in "Morrò, ma prima in grazia." Merrill, with one of the most beautiful of modern recorded baritones, reacts well to the conductor's urging, Claramae Turner is no more than adequate as Ulrica, but Haskins is very positive as Oscar, brilliant in "Volta la terrea," which Toscanini shapes with the reprise (marked *brillante leggero*) much faster

each time than the verse. Peerce sings with musicality, unremitting fervor, and a highly serviceable if slightly unvarying sound. He has not the vocal beauty of a Bjoerling, but his artistic standing is unquestioned.

1954 CETRA (M)

Mary Curtis-Verna (A), Maria Erato (B), Pia Tassinari (C), Ferruccio Tagliavini (D), Giuseppe Valdengo (E), Turin Radio Chorus and Orchestra—Angelo Questa

An unsatisfactory issue from Cetra demonstrates Italian performance of the period with good singers in theaters at a level just below that of Milan, Naples, or Venice. Tagliavini, whose singing always gives some pleasure, and his wife Tassinari have roles that fit them only occasionally well, but Curtis-Verna and Valdengo have the vocal qualities if not the imagination for Amelia and Renato. Erato makes a good Oscar.

1956 EMI / ANGEL (S) CD

Maria Callas (A), Eugenia Ratti (B), Fedora Barbieri (C), Giuseppe di Stefano (D), Tito Gobbi (E), La Scala Chorus and Orchestra—Antonino Votto

Callas sang only five performances of the opera (at La Scala in 1957) some eighteen months after this recording, but the cast, Gobbi apart, is typical of that great theater when Callas was its leading singer. Votto secures a performance that is well balanced and what the Italians would call correct, but he seldom achieved more than that and the live performance with this cast from La Scala under Gavazzeni in 1957 brought out more of the score. Di Stefano was at the top of his career in 1956 and the voice rings out bravely in what was then for him rather a hefty undertaking. He brings clear, clean articulation to text and music, and the voice is intrinsically beautiful, but he sounds unaware of the music's call for elegance. Barbieri is less good than thirteen years before, but Ratti has the measure of her role, though she finds top C a long way up. Gobbi makes up in imagination what he lacks in vocal bloom—some bleak sounds, particularly at the top of the voice—and produces an admirably shaped though not vocally beguiling "Eri tu."

There remains Callas, who brings her familiar intensity to this music even though she had not yet sung the role on stage. The great phrase of the trio in Act I is grandly enunciated and it is followed by a perfectly executed turn, all part of the same impulse; and in Act II's aria she suggests Amelia hovering on the brink of hysteria better than anyone else. As always, she pushes the voice to extremes: after a C in the gallows aria, which is not her best effort, she moves persuasively away from the climax, caressing the following phrases and the cadenza so that the aria emerges as a triumph. She could give anyone lessons in musical style, but the sad truth is that the remainder of the cast is not sufficiently on her level to recommend the set.

1960 DEUTSCHE GRAMMOPHON (M) CD

Antonietta Stella (A), Giuliana Tavolaccini (B), Adriana Lazzarini (C), Gianni Poggi (D), Ettore Bastianini (E), La Scala Chorus and Orchestra—Gianandrea Gavazzeni

Gavazzeni paces the performance with sanity and balance, but his conducting has none of the precision and brilliance brought post-Toscanini to this score by today's young Turks. Stella sang Amelia with him at La Scala in 1956 and 1960 and the voice is fine, though not backed by a technique sufficiently disciplined for Verdi. Poggi makes golden sounds, but his phrasing is square and wooden, and the shorter female roles are frankly inadequately taken. The set is worthwhile only for Bastianini, whose burnished golden tone makes him for my money the best Renato on disc; his aristocratic phrasing is that of a man who gave perhaps half his performances at La Scala. Otherwise, an earthbound performance.

1960–61 DECCA / LONDON (S) CD

Birgit Nilsson (A), Sylvia Stahlman (B), Giulietta Simionato (C), Carlo Bergonzi (D), Cornell MacNeil (E), Chorus and Orchestra of the Accademia di Santa Cecilia, Rome—Georg Solti

This is the first set based not so much on a performance, or utilizing the ingredients of related performances, but rather an assemblage of international stars (Americans, Italians, a Swede), a procedure entailing a reconciliation of diverse styles. The great Birgit Nilsson may sound a little Nordic and indeed there are some hard top notes, approached without benefit of Italianate *portamento*, but the voice is glorious and in her singing she regularly contradicts the calumny that she was a cold performer (Amelia was one of her Stockholm roles). Simionato achieves her effects as much by intensity as by purely vocal means, and she negotiates the climax of the second part of her scene as well as anyone on record. Stahlman is alert and charming and MacNeil, at the top of his career, suave and impressive.

The great performance nonetheless comes from Bergonzi, whose voice caresses the phrases, who meets climaxes with the confidence of the complete vocalist, who demonstrates the music's grace with every phrase he sings. Only a certain elegiac quality replaces the score's sheer high spirits, but there is energy in plenty as well as meticulous respect of all Verdi's expression markings. If the dance sounds a little portentous in the last scene, the conversational exchange which follows it is light and high-spirited, and Solti has the Italian orchestra playing very well throughout. His energetic style suits the music and the set represents a considerable achievement.

1966 RCA / BMG (S) CD

Leontyne Price (A), Reri Grist (B), Shirley Verrett (C), Carlo Bergonzi (D), Robert Merrill (E), Chorus and Orchestra of RCA Italiana—Erich Leinsdorf

Another Italian-made set with its cast oriented to the American market, again with the splendid Bergonzi in comparable form to that of five years before. Merrill is excellent in his second recording of Renato, "Eri tu" demonstrating a great voice in prime condition. Grist makes a youthful-sounding, brilliant Oscar, a true coloratura prima donna in a role which requires nothing less. I only regret that someone so well qualified was denied the trills and cadenzas with which Selma Kurz and Tetrazzini and many others used to adorn the music as I am convinced Verdi assumed they would and as none does in any complete recording. Assured decoration of Oscar's music is more appropriate than the little cascade of laughter between notes (the so-called *risata*) which the great Alessandro Bonci brought to "È scherzo"—an ornament where none truly is needed but sung in these recordings, sometimes unattractively, by every tenor except Bjoerling, Domingo, and Carreras.

Verrett sings an imperious Ulrica, with the easy top without which the role is liable to collapse. There remains Leontyne Price, a preeminent Verdian at the time but here afflicted by a slight huskiness in the middle and lower part of the voice which was never to me apparent in the theater. Like the other leading singers except Verrett, she sang her role at the Met around the time of this recording, and the great phrase of the first-act trio soars magnificently, as does the second-act's aria. Leinsdorf paces it all very well and with the control of a highly experienced operatic conductor.

1970 DECCA / LONDON (S)

Renata Tebaldi (A), Helen Donath (B), Regina Resnik (C), Luciano Pavarotti (D), Sherrill Milnes (E), Chorus and Orchestra of the Accademia di Santa Cecilia, Rome—Bruno Bartoletti

I doubt if this cast sprang direct from any theatrical performance, but it is spirited and generates some fine singing. The set was made in Italy but is, like some others, firmly aimed at the American market (they even smooth out the rude reference to black blood in the first scene!). Sherrill Milnes's career was then at its zenith and his singing is grand in scale. Donath is a neat, lyrical Oscar, sweet-voiced rather than brilliant. At this stage of their splendid careers, neither Regina Resnik nor Renata Tebaldi was in a vocal state to record their roles, and the former often sounds upset at what she has to sing but valiant in pursuit of truth. I don't believe Tebaldi ever sang Amelia in the theater and here she is too often short of breath with

little evidence of the magical beauty of voice which distinguished her for so long. Nevertheless, she warms up, much of Act II is acceptable, but only in the third-act aria is her sovereign lyrical quality truly audible. Pavarotti, on the other hand, is nothing short of magnificent—in great voice, everything brilliantly articulated and high-spirited, and his singing of Riccardo seems to me the best on records since Bjoerling. It is hard to imagine finer, more delicately poised and yet robust singing in this role. Bartoletti gets warm if by no means precise sound from the orchestra, and his is a red-blooded reading. The efforts of the engineers are rather less successful, with some added resonance for the conspirators in the first scene and an even more peculiar echo effect at the end of Ulrica's incantation. For Pavarotti's performance alone the set is almost essential for lovers of this opera.

1975 EMI / ANGEL (S) CD

Martina Arroyo (A), Reri Grist (B), Fiorenza Cossotto (C), Plácido Domingo (D), Piero Cappuccilli (E), Chorus of the Royal Opera, Covent Garden, New Philharmonia Orchestra—Riccardo Muti

Muti conducts a strong, vivid performance, very brilliant in both preparation and execution, with such things as the play-out after the *stretta* of the first scene nothing short of tremendous. The impetus is maintained throughout, with sharp attack, super-incisive *staccato*, the strings biting like Toscanini's into the music, the inner parts always clear. The recording characteristic is clear and my only reservation would be that there is less suggestion of a smile than in the performances of the older generation, like Panizza and Serafin.

The cast is very strong, with Domingo powerful, buoyant but perhaps not naturally exuberant. Nonetheless, everything is expressive, and the long-breathed phrasing and control in, for instance, the love duet something to savor. Arroyo is the best Amelia in any of these sets, the voice wholly apt to the role, with a wide, easy vocal span and tone that is bright as well as solid. If she has not the vocal purity of Milanov in her early days, you have the feeling that nothing could go wrong. Grist remains the best Oscar in any complete recording, and Cossotto has magnificent vocal means to her purpose, heft which does not preclude light and shade. Cappuccilli is a serious, powerful singer, and he is a reliable element in an overall performance of total conviction.

1978 PHILIPS (S) CD

Montserrat Caballé (A), Sona Ghazarian (B), Patricia Payne (C), José Carreras (D), Ingvar Wixell (E), Chorus and Orchestra of the Royal Opera House, Covent Garden—Colin Davis

This is a low-powered performance of an essentially spirited work. Colin Davis's response to the score's challenges is workmanlike rather than inspired, and nobody sings as if the situations or the music mattered crucially to them. Carreras is the best, in fine voice and singing smoothly. Caballé constantly gives lessons in delicate use of *portamento* and has individual moments of great beauty, but the role does not truly suit her, and she sounds out of sorts for too much of the time. Ghazarian is often lively, Ingvar Wixell in contrast rather ponderous, but Patricia Payne's acquaintance with Italian style or language strikes this listener as no more than coincidental.

1980 DEUTSCHE GRAMMOPHON (S) CD

Katia Ricciarelli (A), Edita Gruberova (B), Elena Obraztsova (C), Plácido Domingo (D), Renato Bruson (E), La Scala Chorus and Orchestra—Claudio Abbado

It would be easy to assume beforehand that the performance of so noted a Verdi specialist as Abbado would be definitive, but, in spite of urgency in the Prelude and a fine impact in the early part of Act II, it is not so. The exaggerated slowing down at the declaration of love in the duet stems in style from Vienna rather than Milan, and there are performance details (such as a lack of unanimity in pitch and timbre between Amelia and Oscar in Act III's finale) which are not the hallmark of the finest recordings. Ricciarelli enunciates the text poorly, is

almost inaudible in the lower range, and the voice sounds bottled up at moments of stress. There is also, as one would expect from her, some beautifully sensitive singing—not a word which springs to mind to describe the massive vocal equipment and sometimes grotesque manner of Obraztsova. Like the Russian, Gruberova sings with accented Italian and is clumsy and heavy of foot, at her best surprisingly in her lead of Act III's quintet. Bruson, on the other hand, is an artist in the grand tradition, with constantly expressive musical line, an inclination to sing softly when asked, but capable of a weighty recitative before "Eri tu" and a line to rejoice over in the aria itself. Domingo's commanding manner and heroic timbre is impossible to resist in the role's heavier moments, but there is not as much light and shade as one could have hoped for. Was his voice too heavy for the role by 1980?

1982–83 DECCA / LONDON (S,D) CD

Margaret Price (A), Kathleen Battle (B), Christa Ludwig (C), Luciano Pavarotti (D), Renato Bruson (E), National Philharmonic Chorus and Orchestra—Georg Solti

It is odd that Solti recorded *Ballo* twice but never conducted it while he was at Covent Garden, odder still that the second set is less good than the first. He has an obvious affinity with the score, but I began to wonder if this one wasn't a little self-conscious, with more detail than dash. The cast is a strong one, even if made up of disparate units rather than people used to working together. Bruson is impressive from the start, Kathleen Battle has charm and a lovely top C, and, difficult as I find it to think of Margaret Price as an Italian soprano, she has innate beauty of sound, the music is deeply felt, and only her lack of acquaintance with role and style seems to stand between her and success. Solti extracts a moment of extraordinary (if exaggerated) tenderness from Price and Pavarotti as Riccardo tries to persuade Amelia to admit she loves him, but Pavarotti's contribution is the query point in the set. Even his entry involves a hectoring tone, and as I listened I became convinced that most of his role was spliced in later, with some not quite believable resonance and moments of irrelevant explosiveness—in the second scene, his "Arrivo il primo" comes over like a stentorian station announcement. Of course, there is a fine ring to much of his singing, but most of his role sounds as if recorded at a higher level than anyone else's. To my mind, this ruins the set and the plain fact is that he sounds much softer of tone, fuller of detail, more ingratiating in the earlier recording.

1989 DEUTSCHE GRAMMOPHON (S,D) CD

Josephine Barstow (A), Sumi Jo (B), Florence Quivar (C), Plácido Domingo (D), Leo Nucci (E), Vienna Philharmonic Orchestra—Herbert von Karajan

Karajan's last opera recording was made in January-February 1989, but he did not live to conduct the new production at the Salzburg Festival seven months later. From the measured opening of the Prelude to the slow death scene it is a reflective performance, orchestrally very clear and full of atmosphere (e.g., the taut suspense in the trio after the love duet). Only exuberance is lacking, so that the overall effect is a little old-fashioned.

The newcomer Sumi Jo is allowed no ornamentation but is bright and youthful as Oscar, with a nicely poised top line in Act II's quintet. Quivar offers a beautiful if not conventionally Italianate voice, and Nucci, who has both attributes, reverses normal experience by sounding lighter on disc than on stage (I heard the performance in Salzburg). He observes semiquavers and dotted notes meticulously and only his habit of attacking higher notes from below intrudes between him and the listener. The casting of Josephine Barstow was Karajan's "wild card" in this otherwise conventionally international cast and she admirably suggests the tension under which Amelia operates, full of nerves at the foot of the gibbet and appropriately frenzied at the confrontation which starts the love duet. This is no conventional Verdian soprano, even over a two-octave span, nor has she the blandness which sometimes accompanies that sort of endowment. Starting a little tentatively, she draws out the long phrase at the trio's center (marked dolcissimo) to rare and admirable effect. Act II's aria has an impressive climax and the tender moments in which the role abounds produce some beautiful soft singing; "Ah, deh soccorri tu, cielo" has about it some of the mixture of resignation and ecstasy found there by Callas.

There remains Domingo, fiery rather than youthful but with the grandest legato amongst international tenors today. Moments when he seems marginally out of balance (as in his opening solo) suggest some of his part was "tracked" in later than the rest of the recording, but if that impression is true, the engineers have done their part with startling skill, and he dominates the whole set, as he should.

In the end, you may want to decide whether you will get most pleasure from Price and Bergonzi backed up by Leinsdorf, or Ricciarelli and Domingo with Abbado; Callas with di Stefano, or Solti urging on Nilsson and Bergonzi; or you may go for the young Pavarotti with the not so young Tebaldi. For my money, to hear Ballo at its best, you should choose between Toscanini with a cast that is not so extraordinary; Panizza with a pedigree cast but a recording which shows its age; or—the best all-round bet—Muti with as lively an approach as you could want and a cast which is without weak link.

LORD HAREWOOD

Unavailable for review:
1951 PERIOD
1954 PLYMOUTH

GIUSEPPE VERDI

LA FORZA DEL DESTINO
(1862; revision 1869)

A: Leonora (s); B: Preziosilla (ms); C: Alvaro (t); D: Carlo (bar);
E: Brother Melitone (bar); F: Padre Guardiano (bs)

*L*a Forza del Destino is a profoundly probing opera about allegiances: to parents, to lover, to family, to country, to God, to oneself. Destiny drives its characters apart from those to whom they feel most closely bound. Preparing to escape her beloved home with her lover Alvaro, Leonora describes herself as an orphan, and very soon she is one. Alvaro is an orphaned Peruvian of Incan ancestry, living incognito in Spain and Italy. Carlo is forever trying to regain through vengeance that family honor lost to him when his father is killed and his sister, as he prefers to believe, dishonored. It is no accident that in this opera of doomed allegiances the lovers meet only twice—at the beginning and at the end—and that three of the greatest passages in the work are monologues in which the characters reveal, directly or by inference, their lonely defenselessness. Beyond all this there is allegiance to God, but that can be consummated only in death, as the final moments make clear.

To mount this opera is a gigantic task; there are no less than six principal roles, all of them demanding first-rate vocal material, together with a conductor of brilliant coordinative abilities. *Traviata* may succeed with a star soprano and a *routinier* in the pit, but not *Forza*, with its Shakespearean diversity of character, genre, and milieu. Although many single excerpts were recorded in the early days of the phonograph,

the first relatively complete recording was made in 1941, in Italy. Subsequent issues have been comparatively few. The earlier sets have one or two major scenes cut, but since 1955 the recordings have all been substantially complete. *La Forza del Destino* is so diverse a work that it can easily collapse of its own weight. It demands unanimity of style and, if not subtlety, at least attractive forcefulness. In a sense it is more difficult to bring off than *Aida*, which may also have monumental elements but in addition has a terseness of construction that relentlessly drives its audience toward its unifying themes. *Forza* demands a cast and conductor of extraordinary skill and power to make those clear; with them it is revealed as a work of the greatest profundity.

1941 CETRA (M)

Maria Caniglia (A), Ebe Stignani (B), Galliano Masini (C), Carlo Tagliabue (D), Saturno Meletti (E), Tancredi Pasero (F), EIAR Chorus and Symphony Orchestra—Gino Marinuzzi

The first complete *La Forza del Destino* on records, this performance is a brilliantly effective one. The only important cut is the vengeance duet of Carlo and Alvaro in Act III. Marinuzzi's Overture, like the rest of the performance, is commanding, visionary, and passionate. The tempos and dynamics throughout the set strike a fine balance between vibrance and introspection, and the genre scenes are full of rhythmical vitality and lyricism. Marinuzzi has a first-rate cast of Italian star singers to work with. Maria Caniglia is in fine form here, with a vigorous, earthy voice and committed manner shared by virtually all of her colleagues. Though there is little that is ethereal in her performance, her long scene with Guardiano is reverently sung and informed by deep spiritual yearning. Caniglia once remarked that she thought "La Vergine degli angeli" the most inspired music Verdi had ever written, and she sings it with that sort of commitment. Her "Pace, pace" is equally vivid.

Galliano Masini plays an Alvaro of action and aspiration, the voice a mixture of brass and gold. The style is outspoken and sometimes tearful, though he can sing with intimacy. There is something open and appealing about his tone and manner which quite eludes Richard Tucker and Mario del Monaco in later sets, fine as their voices are. Carlo Tagliabue is a resonant Carlo. This is a difficult role to characterize: obsessed with vengeance, he is an honor-bound young aristocrat who can tell a story well and adapt to circumstances when they further his vengeful plans. Tagliabue is not all of that, but he sings healthily and is splendidly implacable in the Act IV duet with Alvaro, one of the strongest moments in the set. As Padre Guardiano, Tancredi Pasero is not an especially imaginative actor: just a fine singer with a superb bass voice, noble and vibrant throughout its range. Saturno Meletti is the best of all Melitones. His rather grainy baritone is full and focused. Rhythmically alert, he sings with immense zest; the humor comes not from vocal tricks but from his quite convincing grumbling and portrayal of zealotry. Likewise, Ebe Stignani is a brilliant Preziosilla with a magnificently clear and centered tone, her articulation of the passagework breathtakingly confident. Ernesto Dominici is a resonant Marquis and all of the *comprimario* singers are excellent. Aside from the talents of its cast and conductor, the strong thing about the set is its unanimity of style. Though the performance has its occasional faults and excesses, it also has a driving passion which informs even the lyric moments, and a rare combination of

earthy vitality and committed faith that are central to Verdi's setting of this sweeping tale.

p.1952 URANIA (M)

Adriana Guerrini (A), Miriam Pirazzini (B), Giuseppe Campora (C), Anselmo Colzani (D), Fernando Corena (E), Giuseppe Modesti (F), La Scala Chorus and Orchestra—Armando La Rosa Parodi

Armando La Rosa Parodi leads a rough and rhythmically unstable performance filled with La Scala regulars from the early 1950s: the ensemble is sometimes ragged and the arias in general taken rather ploddingly. Despite a few delicate moments, Adriana Guerrini is tough in tone and inelegant in manner—she lacks a capacity for operatic intimacy and nobility. For the heroic Alvaro, Giuseppe Campora has coarsened his lyric voice and style; his best moments are the pensive ones in Act III. Anselmo Colzani is turgid, Miriam Pirazzini lively but technically erratic, Giuseppe Modesti woolly, and Fernando Corena sometimes strained in a surprisingly ordinary characterization of Melitone. They create a burly, knockabout tragedy, likable at times but lacking the precision needed to capture the vibrant nobility of this score.

1954 EMI / ANGEL (M) CD

Maria Callas (A), Elena Nicolai (B), Richard Tucker (C), Carlo Tagliabue (D), Renato Capecchi (E), Nicola Rossi-Lemeni (F), La Scala Chorus and Orchestra—Tullio Serafin

Tullio Serafin conducts a vigorous and well-proportioned performance. As Leonora, Maria Callas sets before us in the first five minutes a figure of tragic dimensions. Her initial utterance, "Oh, angoscia!" is half weariness, and "Ah, padre mio!" reveals in a phrase her love for her father. At the end of her first aria, we have a complete outline of the character: lost, intrepid, addicted to a dream of love. In addition to this, she reveals, upon arrival at the monastery, an element of desperate spiritual solitude and a radiant simplicity of faith in "La Vergine degli angeli." In Act IV, "Pace, pace" sounds once again the note of unanswerable longing, and finally she dramatizes acceptance of the peace of death at the end. Of course, this is what Verdi put into his score, but how often do we hear it laid out so vividly, in all its mysterious complexity, in performance? There are, it should be said, a few wobbly top notes, but generally the voice is rich, steady, and infinitely expressive.

Richard Tucker sings powerfully and smoothly throughout, the loud *legato* much in evidence. His third-act monologue begins quietly and nobly, but soon there are tears and self-righteousness, which increase throughout the rest of the opera. Carlo Tagliabue, here fifty-six, is the Carlo, as he is in the 1941 Cetra set. The voice is more burly, though the top is still firm; the characterization is conventional. Nicola Rossi-Lemeni plays a Guardiano of dimension: magisterial, kindly, shocked, protective. It is a rare and thrilling sensation to find two singers of the subtlety of Callas and Rossi-Lemeni conversing in a Verdi performance. Rossi-Lemeni does this despite severe limitations in technique: a throaty tone, some suspicious pitches, and none of the open Italian glory of a voice like Pasero's. With all of these problems, he is still more interesting than anyone else in the role. Renato Capecchi is a resourceful Melitone; it is unfortunate that his scene with the beggars and the succeeding duet with Guardiano are cut. Elena Nicolai is a spirited Preziosilla, not completely accurate but with a wonderful laugh. The genre scenes are rousing and the *comprimario* roles well done. The cuts here are a little different from those in the 1941 Cetra set. Gone are one verse of Preziosilla's "Al suon del tamburo," part of Carlo's cabaletta in Act III, and, as noted, the entire begging scene and the duet for Guardiano and Melitone which follows it. The recording is essential for the work of Callas, and especially worth while for the contributions of Serafin and Rossi-Lemeni.

1955 DECCA / LONDON (M) CD

Renata Tebaldi (A), Giulietta Simionato (B), Mario del Monaco (C), Ettore Bastianini (D), Fernando Corena (E), Cesare Siepi (F), Chorus and Orchestra of the Accademia di Santa Cecilia, Rome—Francesco Molinari-Pradelli

With such an ensemble, one might expect a recorded masterpiece, for each of the singers is tonally resplendent and dramatically forceful. What we get, though, is merely a strikingly sung traversal of the score, for Francesco Molinari-Pradelli is not the conductor to rouse his cast to a brilliantly theatrical exposition of the tragedy and the illusions that lie behind it. The recording is substantially complete. Though impressively vocalized, the performance is often melancholy when it should be profoundly disturbing and playful when it should be ironic and earthy. Renata Tebaldi, as Leonora, is in prime voice, singing with both power and delicacy, but her tragic concern is sometimes generalized and her delicacy can verge on passivity. The long scene in which she first meets with Padre Guardiano while seeking refuge from the world is an example. The scene really mirrors all the aspects of Leonora's spiritual turbulence: despair, yearning, fear, grace, and the need for prayer. Tebaldi sounds lovely and concerned but lacks the wrenching conviction and the arsenal of vocal colors to project these difficult distinctions. Likewise, she sings "La Vergine degli angeli" and "Pace, pace" nobly, but both lack that ultimate urgency that defines tragedy. If such a criticism seems unfair, it is made only because these singers as a group are so gifted that they suggest the tragic possibility even if they have not accomplished it here.

Mario del Monaco enters like a warrior rather than an impetuous lover. He yells at Curra, bullies Leonora, and then babies her at "Pronti destrieri"; it is all quite unappealing, despite the glorious tone. There is a delightful surprise in Act III, though: in "La vita è inferno" he gets a modicum of yearning and introspection into his voice and "O tu che in seno" is done without tears and much of it rather softly. Elsewhere the warrior takes over; in fact, Bastianini's Carlo at times seems more sympathetic than del Monaco's Alvaro. Still, del Monaco has done nothing better on records. Bastianini is also in fine voice, particularly in "Solenne in quest'ora" and "Urna fatale." Cesare Siepi is a resonant but lugubrious Guardiano, and Fernando Corena, a lively Melitone, is sometimes strained in this baritone role. Giulietta Simionato is a vivacious and confident Preziosilla. All told, this recording catches most of the principals at their tonal best in a performance of considerable beauty, though dramatically it is sometimes fragmented, slack, and simplistic.

1958 DECCA / LONDON (S)

Zinka Milanov (A), Rosalind Elias (B), Giuseppe di Stefano (C), Leonard Warren (D), Dino Mantovani (E), Giorgio Tozzi (F), Chorus and Orchestra of the Accademia di Santa Cecilia, Rome—Fernando Previtali

This recording memorializes Zinka Milanov in one of the roles for which she was renowned. At her best she could wrap that incomparable voice around the music like a great velvet cloak. She also had her mannerisms and faults, more intrusive than those of other major singers, perhaps: sliding into notes, overshooting the pitch, and occasional unsteadiness. There is considerable evidence of both the grandeur and the mannerisms in this recording, made twenty years after her Metropolitan Opera debut. At one time she could sing "La Vergine degli angeli" more beautifully than anyone, I suspect, in history. Here it has much of that grandeur still, but it is a little unsteady, a trifle sharp at times: a potent reminder of a great moment rather than the great moment itself. Let that example stand for the whole performance, which has many evocations of glory.

Giuseppe di Stefano has no business singing this heavy role, but, having taken the plunge, he plays the most interesting and subtle Alvaro on records. From the first he sings with his accustomed rhythmic verve and phrases like a man in love. Almost alone among the tenors of his time he can suggest tragic melancholy without losing energy and without sentimentalizing. There is a world of sadness in his third-act monologue. The aria itself is a quiet reflection, taken rather slowly, with musical tension and *legato* maintained throughout. The effect is of a young man fighting for peace and love but dogged by tragic misfortune—not a warmongering bully, as is so often the case. The voice is light and the top congested at times: precisely the problems which shortened his career. In other words, the performance is better than the voice in which he sings it. Despite all that, it is reassuring to have these operatic heroes played like grown-ups now and then.

Leonard Warren had magnificent tonal equipment, though like Milanov he had his mannerisms, which seemed to increase in the final years of his career: laborious overpronunciation, stolidity, and misplaced energy that broke up the *legato* line. Here we have examples of all of that. "Urna fatale," for instance, is pompous and its cabaletta pressured and awkward—through capped by a superb high note that only Warren could have produced. Giorgio Tozzi is a resonant Padre Guardiano, Dino Mantovani a vital Melitone, and Rosalind Elias a hardworking Preziosilla. The conducting of Fernando Previtali is efficient but unexciting. The album is a reminder of some major figures not at their best, and yet another example of the gifts and shortcomings of Giuseppe di Stefano.

1964 RCA / BMG (S) (D

Leontyne Price (A), Shirley Verrett (B), Richard Tucker (C), Robert Merrill (D), Ezio Flagello (E), Giorgio Tozzi (F), RCA Italiana Opera Chorus and Orchestra—Thomas Schippers

This set presents a cast of Americans in all the major roles under Thomas Schippers, who heads an energetic and reverent performance of the complete score. As Leonora, Leontyne Price is in radiant voice: large, glittering, and dark at once, with a special brilliance at the top. It is a voice unlike anyone else's and she has remarkable control over its special capabilities. In her gentlest moments she never loses tonal vitality, and in the most demanding she never sacrifices quality to volume. She is especially vibrant in the long and difficult scene with Guardiano preceding "La Vergine degli angeli," which demonstrates an earthly lambency of tone quite different from the angelic qualities of some other sopranos. Perhaps "Pace, pace" does not quite catch the element of profound weariness and yearning that one expects as the climax of such a fully considered performance, but it is a beautiful stretch of singing nonetheless.

Richard Tucker, rather husky in tone and

characterization, sings well in a chastened but still sometimes melodramatic style. As Carlo, Robert Merrill produces strong tone and finished phrasing. Giorgio Tozzi is a mellow Guardiano, but the balance with the Melitone of Ezio Flagello is odd. Flagello has the fuller voice and the greater authority of manner, so that the extremes of temperament and understanding basic to their scenes together are not clearly dramatized. Shirley Verrett as Preziosilla drives her beautiful lyric mezzo hard in a vivacious and brilliantly articulated "Rataplan." Altogether it is a genial and sincere performance, richly sung, with especially memorable contributions from Price and Schippers.

1969 EMI / ANGEL (S) CD

Martina Arroyo (A), Bianca Maria Casoni (B), Carlo Bergonzi (C), Piero Cappuccilli (D), Geraint Evans (E), Ruggero Raimondi (F), Ambrosian Opera Chorus, Royal Philharmonic Orchestra—Lamberto Gardelli

After a sensationalized Overture, Lamberto Gardelli settles down to lead a performance of reasonable vitality. As Leonora, Martina Arroyo has a voice of lovely quality, admirably trained and certainly equal to the music. Beyond her notes, however, one has little sense of the anguish, passion, and spiritual frustration of this heroine. Carlo Bergonzi's tone, sweet and full though it is, may lack visceral excitement, but he phrases with grace throughout and sings his third-act monologue with fine ease and melancholy feeling. Piero Cappuccilli is an efficient if not rousing Carlo, without special edge or thrust. Ruggero Raimondi is a light but admirably steady and focused Guardiano, with Geraint Evans a commanding Melitone, which upsets the dramatic balance between them. In this rather bland cast, Bianca Maria Casoni stands out as a vibrant Preziosilla. As a whole, this is a healthily vocalized *Forza del Destino*. All it lacks is a sense of the force of destiny.

1976 RCA / BMG (S) CD

Leontyne Price (A), Fiorenza Cossotto (B), Plácido Domingo (C), Sherrill Milnes (D), Gabriel Bacquier (E), Bonaldo Giaiotti (F), John Alldis Choir, London Symphony Orchestra—James Levine

James Levine has a marvelous grasp of the dynamics and pacing needed to unify this extraordinarily complex work. The spiritual, carnal, earthy, and idealized elements are all bracingly presented, and balanced so that one has the impression of seeing the whole world of eighteenth-century Spain from a single point of view, and not as a group of inexpertly assembled fragments. The conductor has a wonderfully gifted and intelligent cast to work with. Again Leontyne Price offers a radiantly vocalized Leonora, this time with a duskier lower voice and even stronger commitment. Once more, I find that her "Pace, pace" lacks a little in depth of feeling, beautifully sung though it is. Plácido Domingo is exceptionally well cast as Don Alvaro: the voice has both size and sweetness, the phrasing is accomplished, and he knows how to express despair by tone color alone. "O tu che in seno" is glowing in sound and the duets with Sherrill Milnes are exciting. The end of the Act III confrontation between the two has not quite the desolation one hopes for, but in general the performance is superb in its depiction of love, anguish, and the claims of honor.

Sherrill Milnes offers a Carlo unexcelled on complete recordings in detailed characterization and striking vocalism. In the inn scene, he makes a clear distinction between his public and private utterances (obvious but not often done) and sings "Son Pereda" as a good story, at a jaunty tempo. "Solenne in quest'ora" is nobly done by both tenor and baritone, and Carlo's "Morir, tremenda cosa!" is given a performance worthy of the music: the elements of comradeship, suspicion, honor, outrage, and malevolent joy are all present, and in primary colors. He handles the cabaletta with exceptional rhythmic vitality, stressing its cruelly celebratory nature.

Bonaldo Giaiotti is a responsive Guardiano. Ideally the role needs the warmth of a Pinza—one singer who has never been replaced. Gabriel Bacquier is a vivid Melitone, full of officious vitality, though the top notes are something of a shout. Fiorenza Cossotto's Preziosilla has tremendous panache and security, and the Marquis of Kurt Moll splendid vocal authority. Little in this set is marked with striking originality of concept per se, but the singers have honed the best of the classic responses to a point of excellence and are working with a conductor who sees the opera as a temporal yet spiritual whole: a brilliant performance.

1985 DEUTSCHE GRAMMOPHON (S,D) CD

Rosalind Plowright (A), Agnes Baltsa (B), José Carreras (C), Renato Bruson (D), Juan Pons (E), Paata Burchuladze (F), Ambrosian Opera Chorus, Philharmonia Orchestra—Giuseppe Sinopoli

I suppose this recording will be known as Sinopoli's *Forza*: as conductor, he continually distorts the rhythms and dynamics of the work to stress what is already obvious. He almost never seems to sense the most expressive rhythm of a scene: that which gives it life and yet reveals its subtleties and relates it to the surrounding material. The results of his approach are heard immediately in the Overture, sections of which are either senselessly fast or lugubriously slow. Once the curtain is up, the contemplative and military scenes are often leaden and the others unstable. The opera becomes a series of discontinuous moments without cumulative dramatic or musical impact.

Unfortunately, he does not have the sort of imaginative cast who might use these bizarre opportunities to create diverting variations on character. As Leonora, Rosalind Plowright displays a large voice, unremarkable in the middle but coldly powerful on top. With Leonora we must always sense what the wonderful possibilities for her life could have been—otherwise there is no tragedy. Plowright does little but sing the notes: a generally vacuous performance. Nor is José Carreras well cast here. The voice in this recording is rather blunt and without radiance. In "O tu che in seno" he is tearful, sharp in pitch at times, and strained. All of these difficulties are stressed by the slow tempo. Later he develops a beat on the high tones.

Renato Bruson is a dull Carlo, "Urna fatale" dragged on beyond his ability to sustain it dramatically. Paata Burchuladze's Guardiano is cavernous but uninteresting, and Juan Pons, at the mercy of Sinopoli's beat, is alternately bland and effortful as Melitone. The best of the principals is Agnes Baltsa as Preziosilla. Her voice is a little light in timbre, but despite some unsteady rhythms from Sinopoli she hangs on and produces a brilliant cadenza at the end of the "Rataplan." The *comprimario* roles are by and large not effectively taken. The Ambrosian Opera Chorus sings neatly and the Philharmonia Orchestra plays superbly. A depressing release.

1986 EMI / ANGEL (S,D) CD

Mirella Freni (A), Dolora Zajick (B), Plácido Domingo (C), Giorgio Zancanaro (D), Sesto Bruscantini (E), Paul Plishka (F), La Scala Chorus and Orchestra—Riccardo Muti

Riccardo Muti conducts a performance of extraordinary speed, which is proportionate and bracing but also trivializes some of this score. "O tu che in seno," Alvaro's third-act aria, is one example of many moments which simply need a little more time to breathe the air of tragedy. Mirella Freni gives us a remarkably detailed if conventional characterization of Leonora, but she remains a lyric soprano performing a *spinto* or dramatic-soprano role. Technically she handles it admirably: she does not force at the climaxes, although the voice does coarsen at times. There are touching intimate moments, but the power, the range of colors, and the command are not there to transform a pathetic Leonora into a tragic one. Giorgio Zancanaro is a splendid Carlo: with Sherrill Milnes, the best on any of the complete recordings. The voice is beautiful, the technique secure, the characterization detailed, and the delivery energetic. "Urna fatale" is sung very well, if a little quickly for fullest effect, and the Alvaro-Carlo duets are highlights of the performance.

Paul Plishka sounds marvelous as Guardiano; in sheer vocal presence and easy authority he exceeds all of his rivals but Tancredi Pasero.

Sesto Bruscantini, well past sixty when this recording was made, is in fine voice with fresh top tones: an accomplished Melitone. As Preziosilla, Dolora Zajick has a big, vibrant, and colorful voice and a secure technique. Although the "Rataplan" is just too fast for comfort, she makes a brilliant impression. The drawbacks to this set (the speed of many sections and the thoughtful if miscast Leonora) are central, but some of the excellences (the vibrance of Plishka and the fine voices of Domingo, Zajick, and Zancanaro) are heartening.

More than many repertory operas, Verdi's sprawling masterpiece needs a commanding conductor to unite its rambunctious elements into a single overwhelming experience. Luckily three sets of the greatest vocal brilliance are led by conductors of this stature. The 1941 Cetra set is a performance of extraordinary energy and vivid style, with inimitable contributions from Maria Caniglia and Galliano Masini; classic performances by Ebe Stignani, Tancredi Pasero, and Saturno Meletti; unequaled *comprimario* work; and fervent conducting by a master almost forgotten, at least in the United States, Gino Marinuzzi. The 1954 EMI set has in the performance of Maria Callas the most profoundly tragic of all Leonoras. She is supported by a generally strong cast under the authoritative Tullio Serafin. The 1976 RCA set is truly complete and brilliantly conducted by James Levine, with sensitive and very beautifully sung performances by Leontyne Price, Plácido Domingo, Sherrill Milnes, and others. Each of these recordings commemorates not only the opera but its own era and style, and none is replaceable.

LONDON GREEN

Unavailable for review:
1970 SUPRAPHON

ALBERT INNAURATO
Writer

1. All Callas recordings of all provenances; if forced to choose:
   Rossini, *Il Barbiere di Siviglia*: Callas, Alva, Gobbi, Zaccaria, Ollendorff—Galliera. EMI /ANGEL
   Verdi, *Rigoletto*: Callas, Lazzarini, di Stefano, Gobbi, Zaccaria—Serafin. EMI / ANGEL

2. **Strauss,** *Ariadne auf Naxos*: Schwarzkopf, Streich, Seefried, Schock, Prey, Dönch—Karajan. EMI / ANGEL

3. **Strauss,** *Die Frau ohne Schatten*: Rysanek, Goltz, Höngen, Hopf, Schöffler—Böhm. DECCA / LONDON

4. **Mozart,** *Così Fan Tutte*: Schwarzkopf, Otto, Merriman, Simoneau, Panerai, Bruscantini—Karajan. EMI / ANGEL

5. **Rameau,** *Platée*: Micheau, Sautereau, Castelli, Linval, Sénéchal, Gedda, Jansen, Benoit, Santana—Rosbaud. EMI / ANGEL

6. **Wagner,** *Der Ring des Nibelungen*: Mödl, Konetzni, Jurinac, Grümmer, Cavelti, Malaniuk, Klose, Suthaus, Windgassen, Patzak, Frantz, Frick, Neidlinger—Fürtwangler. EMI / ANGEL

7. **Massenet,** *Manon*: Féraldy, Vayon, Rambert and Ravery, Bernadet / Fenoyer, Rogatchewsky, de Creus, Villier, Gaudin / Vieuille, Guénot—Cohen. EMI / ANGEL

8. **Tippett,** *The Knot Garden*: Barstow, Gomez, Minton, Tear, Hemsley, Herincx, Carey—Davis. PHILIPS

9. **Puccini,** *La Fanciulla del West*: Tebaldi, del Monaco, MacNeil, Tozzi—Capuana. DECCA / LONDON

10. **Ponchielli,** *La Gioconda*: Arangi-Lombardi, Stignani, Rota, Granda, Viviani, Zambelli—Molajoli. EMI / ANGEL

Giuseppe Verdi

Don Carlo
(1867; revised 1884)

A: Elisabetta / Elisabeth (s); B: Eboli (ms); C: Carlo / Carlos (t);
D: Rodrigo / Rodrigue (bar); E: Filippo / Philippe (bs); F: Inquisitor (bs)

The textual problems of *Don Carlo* are formidable, and it would take a lengthy treatise to detail their intricacies. Until recently, live performances and recordings have followed Verdi's final revision of his longest, most ambitious, and possibly greatest opera, often with abridgments. After deciding that the original five-act work, composed to a French text in 1867 for the Paris Opéra, was more than most companies could accommodate, the composer devised a reduced edition in 1882–83 and had it translated into Italian. That version omitted much music—the entire first act was the most drastic cut—as well as incorporating numerous major revisions. Lately it has become fashionable to pick and choose from Verdi's earlier thoughts, reinstating Act I and, occasionally, other key sections. Some productions have even reverted to the original French *(Don Carlos* rather than *Don Carlo)*. The following chronological survey of *Don Carlo* recordings reflects this progress as well as a growing realization of the opera's stature and crucial importance in the Verdi canon.

1951 CETRA (In Italian) (M)

Maria Caniglia (A), Ebe Stignani (B), Mirto Picchi (C), Paolo Silveri (D), Nicola Rossi-Lemeni (E), Giulio Neri (F), Italian Radio Chorus and Orchestra, Rome—Fernando Previtali

Like so many Cetra sets from the early 1950s, this first-ever recording of *Don Carlo* has at least one special feature that would be difficult, if not impossible, to duplicate now: an all-Italian cast closely in touch with the text and musical idiom, singing with a naturalness and conviction that seem to elude today's international assemblages. That welcome quality is counterbalanced, perhaps fatally, by the overall rough-and-ready execution also typical of these RAI performances. The orchestra, no doubt underrehearsed, plays coarsely for Previtali, whose vigorous direction and keen understanding of the score deserved better documentation. Rossi-Lemeni gives a magnificent portrait of Filippo, both as troubled monarch and defeated husband; his expressive *basso* is far more secure here than on his later and better-known recordings with Callas. Both Caniglia and Stignani were authoritative singers nearing the ends of their careers, and they often sound hard-pressed, although Stignani's magisterial Eboli remains an imposing vocal creation. Picchi, Silveri, and Neri may not be in the same class, but they are never less than reliable. In addition to Act I, there are numerous other cuts, more or less traditional at the time, the largest and most regrettable being the insurrection scene after Rodrigo's death.

1954 EMI / ANGEL (In Italian) (M) CD

Antonietta Stella (A), Elena Nicolai (B), Mario Filippeschi (C), Tito Gobbi (D), Boris Christoff (E), Giulio Neri (F), Chorus and Orchestra of the Rome Opera—Gabriele Santini

Despite a few choice nuggets to savor, this performance is even less satisfactory than its predecessor. The prize is Gobbi, who gradually transforms Rodrigo from a dreamy idealist into a fanatic martyr who dies in a state of grace, mission accomplished—an extraordinary tour de force by a great singing actor. Christoff's Filippo is also a deservedly famous interpretation, vividly contrasting the king's public and private personae. Once heard, the penetrating Slavic timbre of this distinctive voice is not easily forgotten, either at full force as the cruelly unscrupulous ruler or modulated to a delicate *pianissimo* as the bitter introvert. Otherwise there is little to recommend: Stella's plain Elisabetta, Nicolai's blustery Eboli, Filippeschi's leathery Carlo, Neri's vocally diminished Inquisitor, and Santini's prosaic conducting— all distinctly second-rate. The insurrection scene is restored, but Act I is still missing, and the rest of the score is trimmed even more insensitively than on the Cetra set.

1961 DEUTSCHE GRAMMOPHON (In Italian) (S) CD

Antonietta Stella (A), Fiorenza Cossotto (B), Flaviano Labo (C), Ettore Bastianini (D), Boris Christoff (E), Ivo Vinco (F), La Scala Chorus and Orchestra—Gabriele Santini

As the first edition to include the long-unheard Act I, this recording created a considerable amount of interest when new. Otherwise most of the traditional egregious cuts are observed, and the performance itself is hardly noteworthy. As in the EMI edition, Santini gives a dull account of the score, although at least he has a superior chorus and orchestra at his disposal. The passage of seven years has not improved Stella's Elisabetta, which sounds even more pallid and worn than in 1954. Christoff, however, offers a carbon copy of his classic Filippo, an amazing set-in-stone interpretation that

scarcely changed throughout his long career. Bastianini's blunt but resplendently sung Rodrigo is more enjoyable in retrospect, considering his less generously endowed successors in the role. The same might be said of the young Cossotto, who eagerly hurls her fresh, secure mezzo-soprano at Eboli's music with awesome self-confidence if not much nuance. Labo's raw Carlo and Vinco's undersung Inquisitor are both depressingly provincial.

1965 DECCA / LONDON (In Italian) (S) CD

Renata Tebaldi (A), Grace Bumbry (B), Carlo Bergonzi (C), Dietrich Fischer-Dieskau (D), Nicolai Ghiaurov (E), Martti Talvela (F), Chorus and Orchestra of the Royal Opera House, Covent Garden—Georg Solti

Another textual milestone, this set was the first to record Act I together with Verdi's 1882– 83 revision unabridged. Decca's spacious soundstage engineering is also a major plus. Unfortunately, the performance is a spotty one, despite the high-powered musical forces. Solti presides over an excellent orchestra which plays magnificently, but the conductor's reading is dispiritingly uneventful and inexpressive: clarity without grace, weight without gravity, and excitement without passion.

The singers are also a mixed lot, but at least there is finally a worthy tenor in the title role— Bergonzi in best voice and completely engaged, singing with his customary musicianship and easy command of style. Fischer-Dieskau's controversial Rodrigo may be an acquired taste, but it is one worth cultivating; few other baritones suggest the character's ardent fanaticism while singing the music with such suave elegance. Heard here in its velvet prime, Ghiaurov's commanding voice suits Filippo to perfection, but a potentially fine performance is ruined by a barrage of explosive and unconvincing dramatic emphases that only succeed in transforming this tragic monarch into a petulant, petty tyrant. Talvela sings the Inquisitor in a monotonous drone—one wonders if he even knows what the words mean. Even at this late stage in her career, Tebaldi could still produce gorgeous sounds until sorely tested above the staff—clearly the work of a major singer, even if the overall effect is bland and generalized. Bumbry's Eboli is not very specific either, but it's good to be reminded of how exciting this mezzo could be in her early days, generous of spirit and singing with apparently limitless vocal resources.

1971 EMI / ANGEL (In Italian) (S) CD

Montserrat Caballé (A), Shirley Verrett (B), Plácido Domingo (C), Sherrill Milnes (D), Ruggero Raimondi (E), Giovanni Foiani (F), Ambrosian Opera Chorus, Orchestra of the Royal Opera House, Covent Garden—Carlo Maria Giulini

The famous 1958 Covent Garden production of *Don Carlo* did much to establish the opera in the international repertory, and the musical hero of that occasion was Giulini. He is also very much at the center of this recording, which presents the full five-act version in Verdi's final revision. Giulini conducts a noble interpretation that possesses an overall grandeur, dramatic coherence, and an eloquence of expression that his predecessors barely suggested. It's difficult to believe that this is the same orchestra staffed by essentially the same musicians who responded so plainly to Solti's leadership six years earlier on the Decca recording. The playing is again on the highest level, but this time instrumental details are ravishingly nuanced and judiciously blended. As remastered for compact discs, the spaciousness and wide dynamic range of the recording will also be a revelation to those who first encountered this performance on the shoddy domestic vinyl pressings that circulated during the 1970s.

There are no weak links in the cast, but neither are there are any strikingly individual performances, with the exception of Verrett's vibrantly characterized and excitingly sung Eboli. Everything else sounds perfectly lovely if a trifle bland, beginning with Caballé's stately Elisabetta, scrumptiously vocalized but only intermittently in touch with the queen's character and dilemma. The fresh, young voices of Domingo and Milnes sound glorious as well, even if they only skate over the surface of the

music. Raimondi's mild Filippo also sounds smooth as silk despite a weak lower register, not really a convincing foil for Foiani's dangerous Inquisitor.

1978 EMI / ANGEL (In Italian) (S) CD

Mirella Freni (A), Agnes Baltsa (B), José Carreras (C), Piero Cappuccilli (D), Nicolai Ghiaurov (E), Ruggero Raimondi (F), Chorus of the Deutsche Oper, Berlin, Berlin Philharmonic Orchestra—Herbert von Karajan

Like Giulini, Karajan also conducted a notable production of *Don Carlo* in 1958, at the Salzburg Festival, but waited even longer to bring his interpretation into the recording studio. Unlike Giulini, however, Karajan chose to omit Act I, giving us a complete performance of the opera in Verdi's final revision. There is certainly no question who dominates here: Karajan conducts the most ponderous, most symphonic *Don Carlo* on disc. Tempos are slow, orchestral textures dark and massive, the overall atmosphere is unrelievedly somber and oppressive— a powerful performance and spectacularly well played by the Berlin Philharmonic, but lacking color, contrast, and human warmth.

Given Karajan's weighty approach, the conductor's choice of a cast with predominantly lightweight voices seems positively perverse. Thanks to adroit engineering, we have no trouble in actually hearing Freni, Carreras, or Baltsa, and all three singers were to sing these roles the world over during the following decade. Here, however, although generally alert and in fresh voice, they tend to sound small-scale and ineffective. Not only has much of the velvet worn off Ghiaurov's voice since he recorded Filippo in 1965, but he also has even less to tell us about this complex character. It was also late in the day for Cappuccilli, whose fatigued and prematurely aged Rodrigo has little to offer. Raimondi, on the other hand, seems several decades too young for the implacable ninety-year-old Inquisitor. The conductor's name attracted stellar singers for the smaller roles— José van Dam (Friar), Edita Gruberova (Tebaldo), and Barbara Hendricks (Heavenly Voice)—but the gains are marginal. This recording will mainly appeal to Karajan admirers.

1983–84 DEUTSCHE GRAMMOPHON (In French) (S,D) CD

Katia Ricciarelli (A), Lucia Valentini Terrani (B), Plácido Domingo (C), Leo Nucci (D), Ruggero Raimondi (E), Nicolai Ghiaurov (F), La Scala Chorus and Orchestra—Claudio Abbado

DG's second recording is a very special affair indeed. The basic text is the complete 1882–83 edition, including the first act, but the performance is sung in the original French. There is also a generous appendix consisting of earlier material that had been either dropped from the first performance in 1867, eliminated in the four-act revision of 1882–83, or recomposed in that revision: 1) the ten-minute Prelude and choral introduction to Act I; 2) the offstage chorus and exchange of cloaks between Elisabeth and Eboli in Act III, Scene 1; 3) the ballet music; 4) a duet for Elisabeth and Eboli in Act IV, Scene 1; 5) the original finale to Act IV, including a lengthy scene between Carlo and Philippe; and 6) the extended Act V finale as it was performed in 1867.

For anyone with a special interest in *Don Carlo*, this recording is self-recommending. After hearing how smoothly and naturally the opera flows in French, thanks to Verdi's careful prosody and subtle inflection of the vocal lines, the awkward Italian translation customarily sung seems more insupportable than ever. Under the circumstances it's a pity that DG was not able to hire a more idiomatic-sounding cast, but qualified French-born Verdi singers are scarce indeed. Domingo is easily the best of the soloists and the one most at ease with the language. He is also in fine voice, and his Carlo emerges as a more interesting dramatic figure than in the 1971 recording. Valentini Terrani is a dependable Eboli, but Ricciarelli's Elisabeth lacks strong focus, Nucci is a four-square Rodrigue, Raimondi an even duller and less vocally secure Philippe than he had been for Giulini, while Ghiaurov's rusty Inquisitor is almost a total loss. Abbado gives an uncharacteristically detached, even chilly, account of the score, but the La Scala orchestra plays splendidly, supplying the necessary sweep and grandeur wherever possible.

The ideal recording of *Don Carlo* is yet to be made, but the best all-round choice continues to be the EMI / Giulini edition: superbly conducted and with a fine cast, although one perhaps stronger on vocal glamour than artistic perception. DG's French-language version, with its useful appendices, is an indispensable supplement, despite the disappointing performance.

PETER G. DAVIS

Unavailable for review:
1992 SONY

GIUSEPPE VERDI

AIDA (1871)

A: Aida (s); B: Amneris (ms); C: Radames (t); D: Amonasro (bar);
E: Ramfis (bs); F: King of Egypt (bs)

*A*ida, rivaled for most of our century only by *Carmen* and *La Bohème* in operatic popularity, has been in the doldrums these past two decades, for reasons related mostly to our glut of production sophistication and our dearth of heavy-caliber vocal resources. Nevertheless, it remains the most musically consistent and dramatically concise of all grand operas, the one that shows the form to its greatest advantage by reducing it to its essence. Verdi the editor is here in tight control over Verdi the composer. He explored nothing that is not part of his central drama, his story of characters who are defined entirely through their relationship to one another at a turning point in their lives, and through their position at one corner of the state-church-individual triangle. The drama proceeds directly from one essential event to the next. No number has a less than thoroughly justified function in the structure, and the writing is of such surpassing inspiration and finish that none fails in its effect.

With respect to cuts: a few of the earliest *Aida* sets omit a section of the opening Triumphal Scene ensemble and / or sections of the ballet, and the Molajoli leaves out Aida's solo statement of the *allegro* to the Nile Scene duet with Radames, at least in the Entre transfer. Otherwise, the recordings present the work in its entirety.

1928 EMI / ANGEL (M)

Dusolina Giannini (A), Irene Minghini-Cattaneo (B), Aureliano Pertile (C), Giovanni Ing-hilleri (D), Luigi Manfrini (E), Guglielmo Masini (F), La Scala Chorus and Orchestra—Carlo Sabajno

This was the first electrically recorded *Aida*. If there has ever been a good transfer of it from good originals, I have not heard it, and there is certainly enough of value about the performance to warrant the effort. The best singing is from Minghini-Cattaneo, a superb Amneris. Her voice was a true Italian dramatic mezzo of top quality: round, beautiful sound in the middle octave, well equalized downward into a convincing chest register, and upward to a brilliant top capped by stunning B-flats in the Act IV duet with Radames. She's stylistically authoritative and emotionally full, and altogether satisfying. Also of considerable interest is the Radames of Pertile, an erratic but often exciting singer. There is too much tone of a mealy, sprayed sort, too many forced phrase endings, for his vocalism to meet purist standards. But there is also a true *grandezza* to his phrasing and an impetuosity to his attack that are compelling; he is an imaginative artist who shades and colors with the suspense of a situation. When the voice gathers itself for some of the climaxes; a bit of a tingle cuts across the intervening decades. Inghilleri is an excellent Amonasro—a full, colorful baritone riding a broad *legato* in the big phrases of the Nile Scene. Giannini starts well, her strong soprano firm and focused, her dramatic senses alive. She's persuasive in the first aria and the scene with Amneris. Later, though, her inability to free the top makes for a bumpy ride through the *pianissimos* of the Nile Scene and final duet. Manfrini is a competent, run-of-the-house sort of Ramfis, Masini barely that as the King. After a slow, quite poetic Prelude, Sabajno's leadership is of an incisive, no-nonsense variety, but the orchestral and choral performances are not well enough conveyed by the recording for us to say much more than that.

1928 EMI / ANGEL (M)

Giannina Arangi-Lombardi (A), Maria Capuana (B), Aroldo Lindi (C), Armando Borgioli (D), Tancredi Pasero (E), Salvatore Baccaloni (F), Chorus of La Scala, Milan Symphony Orchestra—Lorenzo Molajoli

As with many of the albums from the Victor / Columbia, Sabajno / Molajoli wars of 78-rpm days, one wishes some elements had been swapped: put Minghini-Cattaneo and Pertile into this cast, and you have a great *Aida*. After more than sixty years, Arangi-Lombardi remains unsurpassed in the title role. A large voice that floats, with both warmth and brilliance in the timbre; splendid equalization and line; an open-throated *fil di voce* that yields heart-stopping moments in the Nile and Tomb Scene duets; a blooming *messa 'di voce*; ample temperament under a classical discipline; unerring instinct for the shapes of phrases—it would be hard to ask for more. And though even the greatest Ramfis will not make or break an *Aida*, we have the greatest here in Pasero, whose dark *basso cantante* roams the role's range on an oily *legato*. Also on the plus side are Borgioli and Baccaloni. The former is a somewhat sloppy but very lively Amonasro, his voice far brighter and firmer than it was for his Scarpia on the more widely circulated Gigli *Tosca*. The latter shows the light, fruity bass of his pre-*buffo* days, and sings a good King with it. Capuana is a gutsy, insinuating Amneris, and indeed her performance is, stylistically and musically, a strong one. But her voice is harsh and unappealing most of the time—to the extent that the medium is the message, her singing can't actually be enjoyed. Lindi is even more problematic: a hefty tenor with some ring, but scant control.

He has a few moments that are impressive, a few that are calamitous; most of the time, it's just rather messy. Molajoli's leadership is always well considered when accompanying the singers. In the purely orchestral and choral sections it inclines to be rushed; one always suspects 78 side restrictions in such instances. The sound, as heard via the Columbia Entre transfer, is quite tolerable for the era.

1946 EMI / ANGEL (M) ⓒ

Maria Caniglia (A), Ebe Stignani (B), Beniamino Gigli (C), Gino Bechi (D), Tancredi Pasero (E), Italo Tajo (F), Chorus and Orchestra of the Rome Opera—Tullio Serafin

Despite its impressive credentials, this is one of the sorrier versions of the opera. Rome in 1946 probably afforded tough conditions for pulling together a recording: the choral and orchestral performance is scrappy and sloppy, Serafin sounds bemused, and the engineering is dim and congested, even for the date. This was Gigli's last complete recording, and none too soon. The once-ravishing voice has come unraveled, its tone now dry, and the approach to the role is too often petulant and self-pitying, so that a rather unseemly second-childhood image is transmitted. Only in the Nile Scene are there a few glimpses of the Gigli we care to remember. Caniglia is not as far gone, but is past being able to handle the upper range, which tends to go thin and flat, or sing a true *legato*, which she replaces with insistent accenting. There is still her flair for dramatic declamation, and some solid sound in the middle and lower ranges. Most of Stignani's Amneris is well enough sung, but in truth there's a fairly persistent mouthiness to the lower head tones, some unevenness at the top, and only the standard interpretive gestures. As recorded here, the voice doesn't really have much impact. That leaves the lower-voiced males, among whom Bechi can certainly wake you with the snarl of his wide-open baritone, but who solves all of Amonasro's problems through emphasis; Pasero is in only marginally less superb voice than for Molajoli, though he's less well recorded here; and Tajo's lovely lyrical bass sounds splendid near the top of the King's short range, but insecure toward its bottom.

1949 RCA / BMG (M,P) CD

Herva Nelli (A), Eva Gustavson (B), Richard Tucker (C), Giuseppe Valdengo (D), Norman Scott (E), Dennis Harbour (F), Robert Shaw Chorale, NBC Symphony Orchestra—Arturo Toscanini

This is the earliest example we have of the sort of Aida that has more recently become standard—that is, one that is dominated by its conductor and orchestra. Of course, the complicity of the modern recording studio is missing; this Studio 8H broadcast undercuts the soloists handily enough, but does little to flatter the orchestra and chorus. Toscanini's conducting is dramatic in one sense: a tunnel-vision through-line is maintained from start to finish, and along the way his marvelous players blow and saw for their lives. The accented string chords that follow Aida's "e dal mio labbro uscì l'empia parola!" are savage and wrenching—the parts of the lady's insides that can be conveyed by the orchestra are spilling right there on the platform. The tremolando just before Ramfis's "Mortal diletto ai numi" bristles with tension and mystery. The marches and dances, so perfectly tuned, are sharp, clean, keen—though fierce, not joyful. And so on—much of the score yields to the approach. Yet in another way, the sort of conducting heard here is not dramatic, or operatic at all. The lives of the characters are being imposed from without, rather than from the bodies, souls, and throats of those who must embody them. This anti-dramatic philosophy is the governing fault of modern performance in both its musical and dramatic aspects. Here is its infancy, disguised as musical integrity.

In this Aida, the singers have an especially hard time getting through the first two acts, where the big ensemble scenes push them off-mike. Nelli actually sings quite well, though at times as if shot from a cannon. Her voice is always pretty, the acuti right on the button, and she is one of the few Aidas who don't finesse the C in "O patria mia." She sounds extremely light for the part, though, and not very colorful. One could not guess from this that her voice was actually a fairly full-bodied instrument capable of some expansion. The Norwegian mezzo Gustavson was one of the maestro's famous casting puzzlements: a perfectly nice, if somewhat muffled voice, in no way set up to deal with Italian dramatic-mezzo utterances. She's simply out of it in the first two acts, then makes a plucky stab at the Judgment Scene. Tucker contributes the set's best singing, and is quite exciting in the Nile and Judgment Scene duets, his voice fresh and elastic and squillante, his musical manners on red alert. Valdengo, who generally did his finest work with Toscanini, is not quite allowed to do so here: the scene with Aida is too hard-driven and matter-of-fact to allow him to register, and his voice, while warm and attractive, is on the lyrical side for this. Scott is a capable Ramfis in a bland, dullish way; Harbour actually makes the stronger impression, bringing some core and intent to the King's lines. Shaw's chorus is crack of its sort. It sounds neither Italian nor operatic, but sings with superb intonation and balance, and with fresh, open, ingenuous American sound—the best darn glee club ever.

1951 CETRA (M)

Caterina Mancini (A), Giulietta Simionato (B), Mario Filippeschi (C), Rolando Panerai (D), Giulio Neri (E), Antonio Massaria (F), Chorus and Orchestra of RAI, Rome—Vittorio Gui

Back to singer's opera with this set. Gui leads a weighty, "important" sort of account with some interesting marcato choices and no dead spots, despite the often deliberate tempos. The orchestra and chorus, while not of the very highest international caliber, are well above mere decency and give lively, committed performances. Mancini is the sort of singer you have to love: a true Italian dramatic voice—bold, colorful, and full—and a passionate, put-it-out-there temperament. She hasn't the ultimate technical control (the top occasionally flies wild at forte, and more than occasionally turns sticky at piano—the Tomb Duet is not good), nor does she have any unprecedented insight to offer, but she takes the full measure of your basic scrappy, rousing Aida. Simionato is marvelous—imperious and propulsive, the voice solid and full, with a bell-ringing top and a commanding, deep-seated chest register. The men are all forceful, if sometimes little else. Filippeschi, with his rigid tone and sour timbre, his dipping and gliding attempts at *legato*, his alternately squealy and imposing top, tends to win you by sheer persistence: either his performances improve as they go along, or the listener just gets used to the sound and grudgingly concedes that he's hanging in pretty well. Panerai was a fine artist with a good, thrusting baritone that often sounded rough when he tried to put it through the paces of the big singing roles—he could do it, but without much margin. That is exactly the case here. Neri was a weirdly un-Italianate *basso*. He had a buzzy voice with plenty of size and reach, but sang with prevailing straight tone, absolutely no *portamento*, and precious little *legato*. This makes a certain primitive impression, especially in the trial scene. Massaria shows a dark resonant bass that starts to rattle around middle C.

1952 DECCA / LONDON (M)

Renata Tebaldi (A), Ebe Stignani (B), Mario del Monaco (C), Aldo Protti (D), Dario Caselli (E), Fernando Corena (F), Chorus and Orchestra of the Accademia di Santa Cecilia, Rome—Alberto Erede

This is the first *Aida* in truly full-range sound. Decca's recording philosophy, soon to change so markedly, is at this time very singer-oriented—in the case of their two leads, here caught in youthful plenitude, rather too much so. It's like being trapped in the tower when Big Ben goes off. Nevertheless, Tebaldi is something to hear. There are a couple of flat Cs (including the one in "O patria mia," which is also devoid of vibrato). But otherwise, the voice is round, huge, gorgeous, deep, and floating, her reading alive and intense. "Ritorna vincitor!" could hardly be improved upon, nor could the rest of the second aria except for the C: "O verdi colli, o profumate rive" is especially mag-

ical, as is all of "Là tra le foreste." Del Monaco's voice is also at its roof-raising best, with its goose-bump *acuti* and its unique deep-throated set (has any other tenor, depending on the vowel, covered at D-natural and gotten away with it?). However, the uneasiness with lower dynamics, the lack of relaxed *legato*, and his tendency to press impatiently on the tempos (not always without reason, one must grant) conspire to let many of the role's moments slip through the cracks. Apart from these two, the performance is thoroughly ordinary. Stignani is much better recorded than in the Serafin performance, and the voice comes across with more character, resulting in a musical, idiomatic Amneris, with no shortfall at either range extreme. Yet it was late in the day for her, and the middle octave is too often either constricted or merely pale and lacking in punch. Protti is a respectable, house-brand Amonasro, Caselli a Ramfis with the right sort of timbre who tends to get tied up in an almost Greek-sounding, back-of-throat type of emission, and Corena a meaty-sounding King who doesn't always control either the line or the vibrato completely. Chorally and orchestrally, this performance is better than some of the Erede / Santa Cecilia sets—fairly well executed, at least—but still does not always avoid a plodding, slack feel, and seldom strikes any sparks.

1955 RCA / BMG (M) (D

Zinka Milanov (A), Fedora Barbieri (B), Jussi Bjoerling (C), Leonard Warren (D), Boris Christoff (E), Plinio Clabassi (F), Rome Opera Chorus and Orchestra—Jonel Perlea

Though some of its individual contributions are equaled or surpassed elsewhere, this version is matchless for all-round vocal strength. It happens to have other virtues as well. The RCA engineering—bright and clear, as usual—is at its best, and succeeds in keeping the soloists prominent without cheating the ensemble or hyper-highlighting. Perlea produces a sharp, peppy, theatrically on-the-toes reading, considerate of the singers without becoming indulgent, that shows why this Romanian conductor was attracting attention before illness restricted his career to the studio. Among the singers, Bjoerling, in his best post-*Trovatore* recording, is *hors concours*. He is no *tenore di forza*, but his ringing lyrical tone is so complete, so springily launched, that it is never unsatisfying. And his mastery of line, his command of the classical effects (try the *mezza voce* B-flat at "il ciel dei nostri amori") is of a sort that makes even very fine singers seem faintly amateurish. Also in peak condition is Barbieri, whose rangey mezzo—deep, roomy, and gutsy—gives us a compelling Amneris. She had no reputation for subtlety, but may surprise you with her musico-dramatic alertness. Milanov has a whoopy phrase, a leathery note, here or there, but rises to all the important tests with beautiful, soaring singing, her vaunted *piano* guided with exquisite control. Warren, too, has a genuine, resonant *mezza voce* at his fingertips, though without ever stinting on fat, full-throated tone where it's needed. He sings a fine Amonasro. The Slavic burr of Christoff's timbre is more or less bothersome, according to taste in Italian music; his voice is fresh and powerful here, and he sings a strong line. Clabassi is an exceptional King, with a lovely, round bass of good color that is right on the money musically.

1955 EMI / ANGEL (M) CD

Maria Callas (A), Fedora Barbieri (B), Richard Tucker (C), Tito Gobbi (D), Giuseppe Modesti (E), Nicola Zaccaria (F), La Scala Chorus and Orchestra—Tullio Serafin

This edition offers some important rewards, but as a totality it has a curiously dead feeling. The recording, made in the Scala theater, is rather muffled and cramped, more studio-like than other mono versions. Serafin has everything in good order here, but doesn't truly animate much of the score: a comfortable, tensionless lilt pervades the reading, and most of the ensembles and dances just sit around politely, waiting their turn. The best of it is the Nile Scene, where the singers can take charge and Serafin can exercise his considerable accompanimental skills. Callas, a rung or two below her best form, does some wonderful things. The shaping and coloring of phrase, a sense of being

in the situation, are in evidence, as one would expect. There is authority in the voice, and the mournful, desolate sound of her soft singing is very telling at moments like "Sventurata, che dissi?" In the big Nile duet with Radames, she finds uniquely interesting ways of cajoling, probing, suggesting. However, her singing also shows enough of the thinned tone and slow waver near the top, enough of the tug on the voice, to detract from important moments and to make it hard to relax with her. Tucker sounds just a mite thicker and stiffer than he had on the Toscanini set, but is still in excellent shape, and better recorded in the early scenes. Barbieri, though, is definitely below the form of her RCA Amneris, her voice in cruder condition and her interpretation unproductively fussed over. The hooty lock on Gobbi's upper range gives us some bad moments in "Ma tu, Re," but his characteristic timbre—sort of like a singing wild boar—is at home in the role, and both he and Callas engage the drama on a high level in their confrontation. Modesti and Zaccaria have similar basses of fine, typically Italianate quality, Modesti's marginally softer-textured and more smoothly modulated, Zaccaria's more solid and thrusting. They both do justice to their parts.

1956 CETRA (M)

Mary Curtis-Verna (A), Miriam Pirazzini (B), Franco Corelli (C), Giangiacomo Guelfi (D), Giulio Neri (E), Antonio Zerbini (F), Chorus and Orchestra of the RAI, Turin—Angelo Questa

This is a perfectly acceptable Italian performance—Upper Provincial, we might say—that packs some thrills in the Radames of the young Corelli. While his singing hasn't quite the technical finish of Bjoerling's, his voice is as close as we come to the ideal for the role. And he's no technical slouch—he sings a good *legato*, and his control of dynamics can include some beautiful high *diminuendos*. There is occasional awkwardness in the *passaggio*, but among all these tenors only del Monaco matches Corelli for focused, resonant power, and only Bjoerling surpasses him for tonal beauty and freedom. This is a formidable combination of attributes, and anyone preferring this Radames to any other will not get much argument here. Curtis-Verna and Pirazzini are of about the same rank: voices that are attractive and full without being of outstanding beauty, technical and musical gifts that are well schooled without embracing total command of the highest notes (the soprano's tend to spread and lose definition, the mezzo's to tighten and muscle at the pitch). These are honorable repertory performances, not quite competitive with the best to be heard on records. Guelfi's mammoth, labored baritone fulfills the basic requirements of Amonasro as leader of the tribe through trial by combat—not interesting, but not boring. Neri is a slightly faded version of his previous Cetra self. Zerbini's bass is strong and dark, but the cover clamps on at C-sharp, compromising some of the King's better moments. Questa leads a solid, unsurprising performance that is thoroughly professional without being in any way special. His forces are B-grade, and can sound loose and fuzzy at exposed moments.

1959 DECCA / LONDON (S) CD

Renata Tebaldi (A), Giulietta Simionato (B), Carlo Bergonzi (C), Cornell MacNeil (D), Arnold van Mill (E), Fernando Corena (F), Singverein der Gesellschaft der Musikfreunde, Vienna Philharmonic Orchestra—Herbert von Karajan

This recording announces a new era as far as *Aida* is concerned, not merely because it is the first one in stereo (elaborately staged stereo, in "realistic" perspective, as with most of John Culshaw's efforts) but also because from this point on, except in the heavily extenuated cases of the Marinov and Schippers versions, the glories of virtuoso orchestras and the interpretive perceptions of virtuoso conductors become the dominant—at times preemptive—occupants of the listening space. Some miraculous sounds result. The Vienna Philharmonic is an astonishing group, and Karajan and Culshaw know how to convey the full spectrum of its colors and weights, the full beauty and impact of choral and orchestral sound in a thoughtfully arranged acoustic. What they do not choose to do is to keep the singing voices in consistently audible perspective. At no point does any voice come as close to the listener's ear as the solo trumpet of the Triumphal Scene. In some group scenes (the terzetto of Scene 1 is an example), the voices wander disconsolately at such remote distances that it is literally hard to follow the course of the drama. The environment overwhelms the enactors of the story. Karajan's reading can be characterized as basically stately and deliberate (though most of the purely instrumental numbers are more up-tempo), at times in a way that projects a splendid weight, or an exciting opening out and elucidation of the writing, at others in a fashion that merely makes it hard for the principals to animate their scenes. Tebaldi is in rather tired, bumpy voice here—managing, rather than cutting loose, and with much of the luminous float gone. She's still a legitimate Aida, but one is much better off with the earlier version. Simionato, on the other hand, remains in excellent form. But recording perspective makes her first recording preferable, too—when one has difficulty hearing this voice on the A-flat at "A morte! A morte!" something's out of whack. Bergonzi sings a smooth, intelligent Radames, doing well by the aria and, especially, the Tomb Scene. But his fine-grained voice retreats just when one wants it to bloom on the cresting high phrases, and his colleagues on the production side are content to watch him slide from view. MacNeil's round, roomy baritone sounds lovely and expansive in this music; beautiful as it is, though, his Amonasro hasn't much dramatic bite. And certainly Ramfis has never been as nice-sounding a fellow as he is in van Mill's pleasant, lightish tones—there is no punch or annunciatory core. Corena's King does have these last qualities, and is much the same as before. The chorus sings powerfully, though at points its closed, heady Germanic timbre is as far from the native one as that of Shaw's Americans.

1961 DECCA / LONDON (S) CD

Leontyne Price (A), Rita Gorr (B), Jon Vickers (C), Robert Merrill (D), Giorgio Tozzi (E), Plinio Clabassi (F), Rome Opera Chorus and Orchestra—Georg Solti

This is, on the whole, a strong performance of international flavor. The engineering is again not helpful to the soloists, tending to distance them and / or surround them with a vague reverberance. Still, the sound is a bit more sensible, if less ambitious, than that of the Decca / Karajan. Solti leads a gradually paced, tightly controlled reading in which phrasings always point somewhere; it musters a fair degree of suspense, despite a tendency to lumber in the early scenes. In both scenes of Act II, however, the dances, played rapidly and savagely (and well—Solti secures the best from his Rome forces) are treated as the work's great stereo showcase opportunities, throwing the aural picture far out of proportion. Price is the first of a number of more recent Aidas whose voice is not of truly dramatic properties. For recording purposes, this would matter little if she had any convincing way of projecting her chest register, whose husky, hollow sound is a serious drawback more than once. But she is still a successful Aida, for the remainder of her voice is in fresh, soaring estate, and she is emotionally alive to this character's predicaments. In the Nile Scene, she rises to true eloquence, singing with supple line, a poised *messa di voce*, and ravishing tone. During its brief prime, Gorr's was the greatest mezzo-soprano instrument since World War II, and the one most like the contraltos of an earlier era—a settled, columnar voice, very smoothly blended into the bottom. Unlike the old contraltos, she also possessed a brightly ringing top, and at her best she sang with expert control of dynamics and line. She is in top form here, and sweeps through Amneris's music with tremendous command and vitality. Vickers's timbre, his treatment of line and language, are not apt to be taken for Italian. Yet his broad, cushioned, young-heroic tenor is here at its best, and on his own terms he is an impressive Radames, singing with dignity and feeling and without the mannered fussiness of much of his later work. Merrill's rich, major-caliber baritone lines out a fine Amonasro, though one could do without his habit of woofily shouting the most obvious points of emphasis. Tozzi's beautiful *basso cantante*, fractionally off its best condition, does well by Ramfis, and Clabassi is

again a first-rate King, if not quite the presence he'd been on the Perlea mono set.

1967 EMI / ANGEL (S) CD

Birgit Nilsson (A), Grace Bumbry (B), Franco Corelli (C), Mario Sereni (D), Bonaldo Giaiotti (E), Ferruccio Mazzoli (F), Rome Opera Chorus and Orchestra—Zubin Mehta

This recording dates from the days when Mehta was building a reputation as a hot, "galvanic" young maestro, and the whole thing sounds rather that way—brisk and pushed, seldom a moment's repose. Beyond this rather strained kind of excitement, the reading does not convey much to me, though it is executed on a high level. In some passages, Nilsson is unequaled. Her purity of tone and her easy command of the full dynamic range in the upper octave are as startling on hundredth hearing as on first. Yet this role does not quite work for her. She is sincere and committed, but not entirely comfortable with this kind of emotionalism; she sings a *legato*, but not often a true Verdian line; the sound of the lower range has not much depth or color. This Aida is like a stunning dress that cannot be made to really fit. Corelli, a bit more finished of phrase than for Cetra and opening the tone more around the break, is in excellent form. One might wish for a less lachrymose choice here and there, but the voice is like no other, and cannot be gainsaid. Bumbry, in the first of her three recordings of Amneris, has a bright mezzo of good quality, but lacking in depth and authority (particularly in the crucial lower-middle area) by comparison with the best of her predecessors. Here she sings with energy, but with the sort of explanatory underlining of one not quite inside the style. Sereni's warm, Latin baritone always recorded exceptionally well; he sings Amonasro with good line and considerable forcefulness. Giaiotti's beautiful, wide-ranging true bass, with its easy resonance, is always a pleasure to hear, but his singing is perplexingly square and affectless. Mazzoli also has a strong, warm bass, but disappoints us with some hooted upper notes.

1970 RCA / BMG (S) CD

Leontyne Price (A), Grace Bumbry (B), Plácido Domingo (C), Sherrill Milnes (D), Ruggero Raimondi (E), Hans Sotin (F), John Alldis Choir, London Symphony Orchestra—Erich Leinsdorf

This is an altogether peculiar performance, in which some classy talent seems to be worrying over how to play *Aida*. Leinsdorf begins with the sort of clean, balanced, comfortable approach we would expect from him, toning down such "vulgarities" as the frequent cymbal strokes or the blatancies of the brass. Then he begins to do some awfully strange things with tempo and *rubato*, pushing along here, suddenly broadening out there, extending little *tenutos* and *allargandos* for a bar or two either side of the accustomed spots, et cetera. Sometimes I see what he's shooting for, sometimes not—odd, though, to get rhythmic eccentricity from Leinsdorf. Price is in representative mid-career form: a darker, huskier sound, bigger in the middle, thinning toward the top. At some points (e.g., "Ritorna vincitor") this, plus some added interpretive sophistication, makes for an improvement on her first recording—it now sounds like a genuine Aida voice with trouble at both ends of her range. But in general the vocal freedom and dash of the first attempt are to be preferred. Domingo's first Radames isn't quite there yet—the singing is smooth and attractive, but has little bite or tension. Bumbry, interpretively unchanged since the Mehta recording, is either in somewhat better voice or better recorded (and in general, this is among the more successful stereo versions in offering some space and depth while keeping track of the principals), though her instrument's basic characteristics are, of course, unchanged. Milnes is in quite good voice here. Like Domingo, however, he seems intent on relaxing his way through—he scoops up for a crooned F at "Ma doman voi potria" that sounds like early Mel Tormé. Raimondi's voice is on the high side for Ramfis, but he sings reasonably well, the line smooth and the tone of some richness. Sotin, with more than enough voice for the King, sings the part in a flat, dull manner, and in a shameless German accent. The English chorus is a good group, but its men betray a King's College Chapel sound at moments, and the Italian is not always of the best—these citizens humbly render their "grotzee alley day."

p. 1971 BALKANTON (S)

Yuliya Viner-Chenisheva (A), Alexandrina Milcheva-Nonova (B), Nikola Nikolov (C), Nikolay Smochevski (D), Nicola Ghiuselev (E), Stefan Tsiganchev (F), Chorus and Orchestra of the National Opera, Sofia—Ivan Marinov

Such virtues as this version can boast are put in the shade by the vocalism of its protagonists, both of whom are hard to endure. Viner-Chenisheva's soprano is a harsh, wiry Slavic *spinto* with a vigorous oscillatory action, while Nikolov's tenor is beefy and dry—massive muscles fighting to a temporary standoff. Ghiuselev is a healthy, booming Ramfis, and Milcheva-Nonova a doughty Amneris—there is some discrepancy between the fruity, *cupo* sound of her lower range and the lighter adjustment of her upper notes, but she makes it hang together, and she knows her way around the part. These singers, plus the good Sofia chorus, make the Judgment Scene the recording's only extended passage of any interest. Smochevski brings a large, stiff sound to Amonasro, while Tsiganchev discloses a buzzy enough timbre for the King, but gives the Italian language a run for its money. The orchestral standard is quite good, and Marinov leads a sober, rather slow-paced reading that might carry weight in the theater. The engineering has the soloists ill-advisedly far foreword and the orchestra back; it is also heavy on the bass and light on the treble. So its faults are, at least, distinctly different from those of other modern recordings.

1974 EMI / ANGEL (S) CD

Montserrat Caballé (A), Fiorenza Cossotto (B), Plácido Domingo (C), Piero Cappuccilli (D), Nicolai Ghiaurov (E), Luigi Roni (F), Chorus of the Royal Opera, Covent Garden, New Philharmonia Orchestra—Riccardo Muti

This is the very model of a modern major recording: briskly and steadily conducted; nicely and cleanly executed by a group of good, smooth, low-calorie voices; and of generic quality most of the time. In the early scenes, Muti's reading is promising. The Prelude is beautifully shaped and balanced. There is rhythmic backbone to the ensembles, good atmosphere in the Temple Scene, and a feathery, gently *rubato*ed rendering of the dances that makes them sound like the nineteenth-century ballet *divertissements* they surely are. But then the Triumph is breathlessly whipped along and does not sink in, and after a lovingly accompanied "O patria mia," the Nile Scene chugs forward uneventfully, and the direction of the drama seems lost. The soloists do not seize hold when they must. Domingo again coasts on a velvety sound and lots of pretty *legato*. Cappuccilli, with that all-purpose tone that is always okay and never anything else, shouts the opening of the Nile Scene and then subsides into an obedient routine that becomes downright casual. Ghiaurov, a little past his best, sounds rich in the middle, but is being very careful. Fortunately, the women afford more interest. Caballé, indeed, does much gorgeous singing, and sounds more plugged in than is sometimes the case. At places she shows a convincingly full top, but as usual, her choices are nearly always toward the floated *pianissimo*. It's very lovely, and guided with excellent line, but is not *always* the appropriate solution. "O patria mia" and the Tomb Scene contain singing of an especially high order. Since the days of Simionato and Barbieri, Cossotto has been our closest approach to a true Italian dramatic mezzo. She is not quite that—her voice does not have the same size and depth, or the tonal roundness. But she is a good, projective singer, stylistically secure, and is in solid shape here. In this cast, she is the most authentic element. Roni uses a large, open-throated tone, not always completely steady, for the King. The recording is not successful, giving everything a synthesized overtone that is particularly unmusical in the *tutti*s.

1976 LÈVON (S, P)

Gilda Cruz-Romo (A), Grace Bumbry (B), Peter Gougalov (C), Ingvar Wixell (D), Agostino Fer-rin (E), Luigi Roni (F), Chorus and Orchestra of the Teatro Lirico, Turin—Thomas Schippers

This is taken from an outdoor performance during the summer festival at Orange, and has serious drawbacks associated with recording under such conditions. Principals are often in odd aural perspective, and the sound in concerted passages is not of the clearest. There are one or two ensemble mishaps, and some tuning troubles. Schippers, conducting an orchestra that's not top-line, gives a lively account of the score that has some suspense, but that's all that can be said of it. Cruz-Romo, a seldom-recorded singer, starts off poorly, and we seem headed for a wild, trouper-style Aida. But she gradually gains control, and by the Nile Scene is giving a distinguished performance, passionate and interestingly phrased, imaginative and insinuating, the soft singing exquisitely sustained. Bumbry one more time, and this is really her most persuasive Amneris, the live situation heating things up for her. She is extremely naughty with chest, kicking it right up to A for "empia razza!"—but there *is* a charge in the singing. Gougalov, stylistically and linguistically well below the waterline, is vocally a step up from Nikolov (1971 Balkaton) only by virtue of the occasional clarion noise on top. Wixell's fair-sized, warm baritone never sounds timbrally or technically quite right to me in Verdi; he sings a lively and musical Amonasro, though. Ferrin has a slightly woolly bass, but is a solid Ramfis, and Roni, by no means elegant, blows away the acoustical problem rather scarily as the King.

1979 EMI / ANGEL (S) CD

Mirella Freni (A), Agnes Baltsa (B), José Carreras (C), Piero Cappuccilli (D), Ruggero Raimondi (E), José van Dam (F), Vienna State Opera Chorus, Vienna Philharmonic Orchestra—Herbert von Karajan

It's the old half-full or half-empty question. Half full: the orchestral score is so magnificently played as to beggar description, and, on the whole, this nice *Bohème* cast stays afloat longer than we'd thought when we cut the boat loose. Half empty: only a conducting student can actually want the orchestra to hog all the attention even when it is the Vienna Philharmonic; further, it's still just a nice *Bohème* cast, and this is *Aida*. Unusual among latterday Karajan remakes, this reading is actually tighter and less portentous than its Decca predecessor. The tempos are in some cases a shade quicker and fizzier; there is a bit more backbone and drive. The sensational playing and the Oracle of Delphi engineering conspire with Karajan to lend the Triumph an exhilarating expansiveness, the Judgment a frightening weight. From the midst of this, like Mahler Eighth soloists given their very own desks and mikes just this side of the back row, the principals hold forth. Among them, van Dam is practically perfect as the King, though perhaps the most cultivated Pharaoh we've encountered. And Baltsa is, at least, very together. Her voice—lean, concentrated, cool, with its stretch of "baby chest" at the bottom—is no big-house Amneris for cataclysms like these. Raimondi, though back to the radio-crooner *piano* he always seems to fall into with Karajan and trying too hard to sound nasty, is still a presentable Ramfis. Cappuccilli sings a more specific, dramatically alert (and, in spots, picked-over) Amonasro than he did for Muti, and is better recorded. But the voice has grown even grayer, and is quavery at points. This leaves our two leads. Carreras does fairly well. He enlivens the recitatives, phrases poetically in the lyrical passages, and still has some juice and ring in the sound. No reason, in fact, why his voice should not record as efficiently as Bjoerling's in the part, except that he does not have the same technical control and judgment. He drives the tone into an open, white adjustment on many G's and A-flats, and must substitute a falsetto for a blended *mezza-voce*. Freni never fails to produce some nice sound, but this role makes no sense for her. The *fortes* often pick up some harshness or impurity, and we are always aware of the cruel choice between sounding feeble in the lower-middle range, or borrowing strength by stretching the chest, then riding the bumps. And though her phrasing is musical, it can't be said that there is the sort of special insight or imagination that would compensate for the vocal shortfall.

1981 DEUTSCHE GRAMMOPHON (S,D) CD

Katia Ricciarelli (A), Elena Obraztsova (B), Plácido Domingo (C), Leo Nucci (D), Nicolai Ghiaurov (E), Ruggero Raimondi (F), La Scala Chorus and Orchestra—Claudio Abbado

On his third go-round, recorded in the late-prime period that produced his best *spinto* tenorizing, Domingo is a satisfying Radames. The tone has more ring and metal, the line is firmer, and the phrasing more decisive, and there is more risk and heat in the singing. Raimondi is here the King, and a solid one in a baritonal fashion. Ghiaurov treads most cautiously and shrewdly, patching together a listenable but improbably gentle Ramfis. Nucci is a Valdengo-ish Amonasro, with an ingratiating lyric baritone that narrows into the top notes of this role; he sounds awake. Both the women display lavish gifts gone to pot. Ricciarelli has a beautiful middle range and some of that unpremeditated Latin emotionalism that puts us on her side. But the top is hard and wobbly on many of the *fortes*, thin and pinched on most of the *pianos*. Obraztsova's fine mezzo—the most authentic Amneris voice since Gorr's—is all over the place. Her imposing moments (there are some) don't balance out with the messy intonation, the inability to modulate dynamics, the frequently distorted tone and word. I am stumped as to whether or not Abbado has any point of view on the music, and incline to the negative. It's well enough played, but beyond the scoring of some really tiny rhythmic points and a fairly thoroughgoing tidiness, there is no profile at all to this reading.

1986 DECCA / LONDON (S,D) CD

Maria Chiara (A), Ghena Dimitrova (B), Luciano Pavarotti (C), Leo Nucci (D), Paata Burchuladze (E), Luigi Roni (F), La Scala Chorus and Orchestra—Lorin Maazel

Chiara offers an idiomatic, honorable Aida in a slightly gripped middleweight soprano of attractive Mediterranean hue. Nothing mind-boggling, but a live, capable performance. Pavarotti, too, gives most of the basic effects in an appropriate timbre. In one of the better-sung versions of the aria and, particularly, the more lyrical pages of the Nile Scene duet, he shows care for the music and some imagination. In the grander scenes (where the engineering balance is also less favorable to him), the voice seems thin for the role, and in the last act he is disappointingly sloppy with the line. Nucci is still on his toes as Amonasro, though the timbre is a bit muddier than before, and he does not sound comfortable trying to render the *sortita* softly, as indicated. These three are all on the light side for their roles, but are at least warm bodies. For the rest, we have an Amneris cast in the wrong vocal category (a heavy soprano with a weak, opaque patch in the lower-middle range is hardly the same as a dramatic mezzo, and Dimitrova's phrasing is square, the upper range alternately imposing and squally); a Ramfis with fine native vocal material but mealy Italian, a clumsily covered top, and a vibrato that emerges only on sustained notes; and a King (Roni, for the third time) whose range is clearly contracting and tone loosening. Presiding is a conductor who generally selects the most ponderous imaginable tempo and then hangs on for dear life. Since Maazel accompanies the arias rather well and concedes a more normal flow to Chiara and Pavarotti, it seems at first that he may be contrasting the private urgencies of the characters with the repressive, rigid structures of the public sphere—a potentially playable notion. But this does not pan out, and except for a few moments of thoughtful instrumental detail, by side 3 or so the reading has died.

1990 SONY (S,D) CD

Aprile Millo (A), Dolora Zajick (B), Plácido Domingo (C), James Morris (D), Samuel Ramey (E), Terry Cook (F), Metropolitan Opera Chorus and Orchestra—James Levine

Nothing calamitous happens here, but this performance has few moments of life, and no points of artistic interest, large or small, to set it apart from a thousand other high-level profes-

sional runthroughs. The recording's acoustic is tight and dry, with a dynamic range that few sound systems, living rooms, or next-door neighbors will be able to accommodate. The Met orchestra plays well, but Levine's slow, predictable reading is polished in the wrong sense—it has that slick, manufactured sheen. Ramey's Ramfis is the only truly satisfactory solo assumption. Millo starts poorly in the Scene 1 trio and the "Ritorna," with some curdled top notes and pressed phrase endings. Beginning with the Amneris interview, she improves, contributing a fine "O patria mia" and "Là tra le foreste." She must manage so carefully, though, that there is little spontaneity in the singing. Zajick's Amneris has some life in the Judgment Scene, and there are fine notes and phrases along the way. But her voice has neither the tonal richness nor the technical set and solidity of the Italian dramatic mezzo, and there is nothing musically or interpretively special to compensate. Domingo's Radames hangs in well enough. He's hard pressed, however, in the role's climactic moments—this is Plácido IV, and you want Plácido III, if you want Plácido at all. Though Morris's tone is dry and un-Italianate, he dives in with welcome energy, and Amonasro sounds like his proper *Aida* role until he encounters the crucial high arcs of the Nile Scene, which he is unable to fill out. Cook's King is not very stable vocally.

For all-round listening, I have no hesitation nominating the 1955 RCA / Perlea: fine cast down the line, vigorous conducting, clear recording. If you must have stereo, then Solti (1961 Decca), with Muti (1974 EMI) or Mehta (1967 EMI) a rather distant pair of second choices.

CONRAD L. OSBORNE

Unavailable for review:
1919 EMI / ANGEL
1950 EMI / ANGEL
1954 REMINGTON
1958 GUILDE INTERNATIONAL DU DISQUE

GIUSEPPE VERDI

OTELLO (1887)

A: Desdemona (s); B: Emilia (ms); C: Otello (t); D: Cassio (t); E: Iago (bar)

ry to give a plot summary of *Otello*, and you end up with a narrative of nonsense. The events are trivial beyond belief: the theft of a handkerchief, a misunderstood conversation, and then death. Yet it is the very triviality of the events in contrast to the depth of what they reveal that is the central irony of the tragedy. Verdi's greatness lay in the clarity with which he saw the tragedy of these simple actions and the complex characters behind them. Iago's drinking song could belong to no one but him, its rough-and-tumble intervals expressive of just the muscular good humor needed to entice the gentlemanly but politic Captain Cassio to drink. The mature passion of Verdi's love duet is exactly reflective of Otello's contentment and Desdemona's idealism, and the breathless desolation of the introduction to "Dio! mi potevi" (with its monotone A-flat then beating in the brain like fate) bespeaks a profound damnation. And then there is Otello's death scene, its noble simplicity reaching out beyond the theatrical to some bare plain of tragedy too stark to view all at once, and at the same time bringing the viewer and the protagonist to rest: what Aristotle called catharsis. The great Otellos have seen beyond the heroics to the impassioned fulfillment and the quiet despair of the role, just as the great Desdemonas have found variety and infinite yearning behind the placid exterior, and the great Iagos have created perverse vocal beauty in the obscene "Era la notte."

In the first half of the twentieth century only one complete *Otello* was recorded commercially: the 1931–32 set with Nicola Fusati. When Giovanni Martinelli took the role on in 1937 the opera had not been given at the Metropolitan for a quarter-century. A second studio recording, undistinguished, did not appear until 1951. Luckily, in the last forty years some remarkable performances, early and late, have found their way onto records.

1931–32 EMI / ANGEL (M)

Maria Carbone (A), Tamara Beltacchi (B), Nicola Fusati (C), Pietro Girardi (D), Apollo Granforte (E), La Scala Chorus and Orchestra—Carlo Sabajno

Carlo Sabajno conducts this first complete recording of *Otello* with vigor and discipline. Some sections, indeed, are taken too quickly for full dramatic revelation: "Ora e per sempre addio," "Dio! mi potevi," and Desdemona's Act IV arias are among them. The chorus at the start is excellent: an accurate and yet impetuous crowd of Cypriots in a storm. Aside from this, the most memorable thing about the set is the work of Apollo Granforte. His Iago, performed as librettist Arrigo Boito suggested, is in public a figure of guileless candor, but in private one of fundamental duplicity. Granforte has complete dynamic control of a beautiful and focused lyric-baritone voice, with fine command of the recitative passages and the vocal line. Much of it is chillingly conversational: he has a superb sense of the words. The Credo has a cold lyricism, its effect accomplished through detail and vocal color. He is not merchandising evil: he *is* evil. It is all done with an ease that suggests the instinctual. This may be the most complex Iago ever recorded.

Maria Carbone, only twenty in 1932, is a dramatic and sometimes touching Desdemona, though she lacks the long line and *pianissimo* to give the Willow Song, Ave Maria, and other passages real distinction. She herself has said that she did not have the smoothness for Verdi; she made her career largely in Puccini and contemporary works. By the time of recording, Nicola Fusati had been singing throughout Italy for a quarter-century. He has the range, stamina, and power for Otello, but his singing is nasal, tearful, and lacking in *legato* throughout: fatal to the nobility of character that Verdi was so careful to dramatize. Without it, Otello becomes simply a nagging, whimpering, and unpleasant husband, which is what happens here. Many of Fusati's climactic moments are rushed; given his technique and conception of the role, perhaps that is just as well. The set is valuable for its sense of ensemble but particularly for Granforte's incomparable Iago.

1940 MET (M,P)

Elisabeth Rethberg (A), Thelma Votipka (B), Giovanni Martinelli (C), Alessio de Paolis (D), Lawrence Tibbett (E), Metropolitan Opera Chorus and Orchestra—Ettore Panizza

Here we have three extraordinary singers under a fiery conductor in the live Metropolitan Opera performance of February 24, 1940. Ettore Panizza leads with impassioned thrust and lyricism, acutely responsive to the dramatic rhythms and gifts of his legendary cast.

Giovanni Martinelli's voice is unseductive, but also steady, accurate in pitch, and, most important, expressive of the most profoundly complex emotional response. His climactic first entrance is fearlessly phrased, although strained and some distance from the microphone. By the time of the love duet, however, he is demonstrating a subtlety and variety of feeling reserved only for the great. There is no pomposity, but a tender *legato* neither exaggerated nor sentimen-

talized. He expresses his ardor without breaking the vocal line or vulgarizing it, and there is real wonder in the final lines. This is an Otello capable of more than self-obsession: something noble and valuable is at stake. The tender majesty of his death scene is unforgettable.

From the start, there is in Lawrence Tibbett's sound a dulcet cruelty and darkness which suit Iago—and the Credo—admirably. Has "Era la notte" ever been more beautifully vocalized? The lines he attributes to Cassio have a tremulous vulnerability unsurpassed in any other performance. Elisabeth Rethberg was approaching the end of her career when she played Desdemona, but the voice is fresh, delicate, and full, though the top is a little jagged at times. Her enactment has the purity for which she was famous, and a depth of involvement seldom experienced in her studio recordings. Panizza brings them all together in a performance marked by tragic power, tenderness, and conviction.

1947 RCA / BMG (M,P) ⓒⒹ

Herva Nelli (A), Nan Merriman (B), Ramón Vinay (C), Virginio Assandri (D), Giuseppe Valdengo (E), NBC Symphony Chorus and Orchestra—Arturo Toscanini

This performance originates in two live NBC broadcasts in 1947. Under Toscanini, it has unparalleled excitement, rhythmic drive, and instrumental clarity, though some intimate moments, such as the love duet at the close of Act I, do not possess the full measure of tenderness. In such a setting, Ramón Vinay, a subtle artist, is strikingly forthright. The voice is an inimitable one: dark, blunt, and warm at the same time, with an immensely appealing timbre, though without the cutting edge of some Otellos. His performance is noble, affectionate, and anguished, and superbly proportioned by both conductor and singer. As Desdemona, Herva Nelli has a warm middle register and produces many casually beautiful phrases but lacks the compelling conviction and profile that would tell us just who Desdemona is. Interestingly, her Ave Maria, usually the most placid of arias, has moments that suggest what a full dramatic commitment from this singer might produce.

Playing Iago, Giuseppe Valdengo has a genuine lyric Verdi baritone voice with an interesting timbre; he can suggest harshness without actually making his voice ugly. His Iago is dangerously attractive and yet uncaring, and very well sung, though in the opera house it lacked power in the lower register. Though there are distinguished contributions from Vinay and Valdengo, and some passages of eloquence from Nelli, perhaps it says something about the nature of the enterprise that the monumental third-act ensemble, which almost always has its moments of discontinuity under even the most distinguished conductors, is here built magnificently under Toscanini and is perhaps the greatest moment in the performance.

1951 URANIA (M)

Anna la Pollo (A), Landi (B), Gino Sarri (C), Athos Cesarini (D), Antonio Manca Serra (E), Rome Opera Chorus and Orchestra—Alberto Paoletti

Among blazing live performances and polished studio recordings, this sometimes promising but routine effort is lost. The sound is unresonant and the orchestra far too often swamped by the singers, so that much instrumental detail is obscured. Though Alberto Paoletti's conducting has energy at the obvious points, most of the scenes lack structural clarity and rhythmic detail. There are two choral cuts: one in the serenade to Desdemona in Act II and the other in the great ensemble of Act III. As Otello, Gino Sarri has some of the basic vocal equipment necessary and a general idea of the role, but he tires. In any event he lacks poetry and true command, though he achieves a sympathetic sound in "Dio ti giocondi" and phrases "Dio! mi potevi" nicely. Though she has moments of delicacy, Anna la Pollo's harsh, shallow tone and prosaic manner are unsuitable to Desdemona. Antonio Manca Serra has a dark baritone and an interesting if unfinished conception of Iago. His top tones are often strained, but he remains the most interesting member of the cast.

1954 DECCA / LONDON (M)

Renata Tebaldi (A), Luisa Ribacchi (B), Mario del Monaco (C), Piero de Palma (D), Aldo Protti (E), Chorus and Orchestra of the Accademia di Santa Cecilia, Rome—Alberto Erede

This recording utilizes such superb voices that one feels a Shavian aesthetic anger that it is not better as a performance. Alberto Erede conducts with energy but in his rush often misses the ironic and tragic elements in the score. Gifted with a magnificent tone for Otello, Mario del Monaco has little conception of the emotional variety to be found in the role. The angry and public moments—"Esultate," the climax of "Dio! mi potevi," and the vengeance duet, for example—are thrilling but not the sum of the part. The singer, in fact, sounds angry rather than victorious at the start and remains so throughout the opera. That is alienating in the love duet, where his Desdemona seems to be placating him. Neither he nor Renata Tebaldi projects the impulsiveness of love; beautiful as their voices are, they seem instead like two public monuments. In Act II, del Monaco is in a whirlwind of fury from the first. There is little sense of what is central to the work: the image of a noble character gradually *reduced* to instinct. Verdi presents more than outrage here; longing, anguish, and loss are to be explored. Del Monaco's contribution to "Dio ti giocondi" is likewise golden yelling from the start. His death scene, though, is surprisingly restrained and noble, and gives a suggestion of just what he might have accomplished in the role.

Renata Tebaldi is likewise in beautiful voice, but has much more dynamic control than her colleague. It is not her fault that Desdemona seems a dolt to love such an Otello as del Monaco's. However, she generally seems cool and uninvolved rather than passionate and pure: there is a world of difference. The sheer sound—the delicate vibrance of that tone—is often touching, and the Ave Maria, for example, emerges as deeply felt. Aldo Protti as Iago is the career army man: hearty, gruff, and overbearingly chummy. The problem is that he remains that way in the Credo. With all its faults, this recording does present two major voices in roles for which they were renowned, and all that gold is still tempting.

1955 CETRA (M)

Cesy Broggini (A), Rina Corsi (B), Carlos M. Guichandut (C), Angelo Mercuriali (D), Giuseppe Taddei (E), Chorus and Orchestra of the RAI, Turin—Franco Capuana

I have heard only a record of excerpts from the complete set, which is interesting for its cast, some of whom have not recorded widely. Franco Capuana conducts a hurried performance, effective in some of the climaxes but lacking poetic expansion in the quieter scenes. Carlos Guichandut, as Otello, has the breath control and the mettle for such moments as his first entrance and the finale of Act II; the higher and louder he is, the happier. He lacks, though, the *legato* and poetic imagination for such a scene as the love duet. The final confrontation with Desdemona is exciting, but afterward he fails to use tone color to create a sense of moral desolation, and resorts easily to tears. Cesy Broggini has a lovely, fresh voice, with a suggestion of vulnerability in the tone. Though she lacks true intimacy, and simplicity in the Ave Maria, this is a performance of charm. Giuseppe Taddei is certainly one of the best Iagos on records, with a full, fresh, and steady voice which can be colored for ugly feeling without itself becoming dry. He has enormous energy and, though rushed by Capuana, conveys the compulsion of the Credo text and its rhythms brilliantly. As a performance, this set is superior to at least the Paoletti recording and has in Taddei a major interpreter of Iago.

1960 RCA / BMG (S) (D)

Leonie Rysanek (A), Miriam Pirazzini (B), Jon Vickers (C), Florindo Andreolli (D), Tito Gobbi (E), Rome Opera Chorus and Orchestra—Tullio Serafin

Tullio Serafin conducts an energetic but spacious performance which takes into account the special gifts of his remarkable cast of singing actors. Jon Vickers, I believe, had not yet sung Otello onstage when he recorded this performance, but nevertheless his conception of the role is profound, dominated by spiritual nobility and love. That can be seen as early as his interruption of the fight between Roderigo and Cassio, when he is as concerned as he is angry. Just as Verdi did in the music, Vickers in the love duet combines intimacy and wonder without losing his soldierly bearing. The martial sorrow of his "Ora e per sempre addio" and the monolithic grandeur of his "Sì, pel ciel" (difficult vocally for both Vickers and Gobbi) are very much to the dramatic point. "Dio! mi potevi," exact in tempo and pitch, is a moment of moral pain such as only this singer can summon. His entry in the final act is not really in the role of the angry husband but as the instrument of tragic fate which will destroy them both. Otello's own death scene has in his performance the calm of finality; he passes from life because he must.

Leonie Rysanek's Desdemona is a battleground of will and means. That dark, unsettled low register, the unsteadiness, and those gleaming high tones may be of dramatic use as Senta or the Empress in *Die Frau ohne Schatten* but they do not qualify her in *Otello*. No one could claim that she solves these problems, but the energetic creativity she uses in accommodating the role is almost as interesting as her conception of Desdemona as a woman whose passion for Otello will inevitably lead to her own death. Tito Gobbi's Iago is a rich portrait. We see the element of deceit even in his public acts, though the other characters do not. The Credo is sung with a fine sense of its architecture and musical line, and "Era la notte" with a sensuality attractive even as it repels. The LPs include the ballet music composed for the Paris premiere, but it has been deleted from the CD issue. With all its imperfections, this is one of a handful of opera recordings which suggest not only the passionate but the profound.

1961 DECCA / LONDON (S) (D)

Renata Tebaldi (A), Ana Raquel Satre (B), Mario del Monaco (C), Nello Romanto (D), Aldo Protti (E), Vienna State Opera Chorus, Vienna Philharmonic Orchestra—Herbert von Karajan

Such a wealth of talent and proficiency went into the making of this recording that one hates to dismiss it. The sound is fine and the chorus and orchestra superb. Karajan's performance is one of extremes, as if exaggeration were the path to the profound. The opening and other climaxes of tension are performed with outsize grandeur, but other passages, for all their beauty and clarity, are slow and lacking in tragic tension. We get the dramatic point long before Karajan is willing to relinquish it. The love duet, for example, is sensuous to the point of dullness, and several other scenes are weighted for a philosophical significance which then sinks the drama. As in the Erede set, Mario del Monaco flings out his voice impressively, but this time as if he wished it were a size larger than it is. The cleanliness of his singing and his brightly focused tone are welcome, but again anger and self-pity mask most of the other feelings of which an Otello ought to be capable: tenderness, warmth, wonder, respect. If Otello is primed for jealousy and vengeance from the first, we cannot be interested in him; he's just a crank. Unsuspected depths of feeling—surprising to him and everyone else but Iago—must be mined if the performance is to have significance.

Renata Tebaldi is again in sumptuous voice, and again phlegmatic, but this time at Karajan's slower speed. The major example is in Act IV, in which she sings beautifully but produces an effect of matronly placidity rather than passionate purity. Aldo Protti has worked out some villainous detail in the Credo; otherwise his performance is as workaday as before. The set included the ballet music in Act III on the original issue, but it has not been retained on the CDs. The surprising verdict must be that this performance is at once grander and duller than the Erede recording with the same principals.

Sir John Barbirolli's performance begins with crushing force and a wind machine, but thereafter it is a slow, affectionately detailed reading which often fails to cohere and leaves the singers fiddling around with effects to fill in the spaces. One result is that those singers seem to be listening to themselves more than to each other. James McCracken, always a passionate artist, has an element of madness in his voice and method from the start. Though he works at a plausible *legato* in a very leisurely love duet, the effect is careful rather than wondrous or serene. None of his subsequent outbursts comes as a surprise because we know he's unstable already. By the time of "Dio! mi potevi" he has reached the point of insanity and lost us. At the end, though, there are moments of touching simplicity that indicate another path that McCracken might have taken.

Gwyneth Jones, an adventurous singer, gives us a Desdemona of careful beauty and a bodiless, ethereal quality which is, frankly, dull after the first five minutes and beside the dramatic point. Purity need not compromise passion. Desdemona is a fervent and vibrant woman, and not an anesthetized or dead one—and not primarily a symbol for something. Dietrich Fischer-Dieskau is a brilliant if ultimately unconvincing Iago. Here is a singer sending out so many messages that the character is obscured. Scorn, coarseness, intelligence, wit, and deception are all given constant representation. The result is a comprehensive clinical demonstration rather than a smoothly integrated performance, particularly at the slow tempos that Barbirolli favors. It seems a peculiar thing to say about one of the great lieder singers of our era, but the performance lacks subtlety. As a whole, this stylistically mixed presentation exudes analytical intelligence but not dramatic conviction. In the world of recorded opera, how often can *that* be said?

1968 EMI / ANGEL (S)

Gwyneth Jones (A), Anna di Stasio (B), James McCracken (C), Piero de Palma (D), Dietrich Fischer-Dieskau (E), Ambrosian Opera Chorus, New Philharmonia Orchestra—John Barbirolli

1973 EMI / ANGEL (S) CD

Mirella Freni (A), Stefania Malagù (B), Jon Vickers (C), Aldo Bottion (D), Peter Glossop (E), Deutsche Oper Berlin Chorus, Berlin Philharmonic Orchestra—Herbert von Karajan

Again Herbert von Karajan provides a tumultuous opening and a performance so slow and detailed as to border on the inert. There are problems of orchestral balance, too. The opening of the love duet is wonderfully spacious, but toward the end of it the singers are distanced: a disappointment because one can't hear precisely what they are doing. Thirteen years after his first recording of the role, Jon Vickers gives us a somewhat more demonstrative but not necessarily more profound Otello. His voice and manner are more driven than before; some of the sorrow of the earlier version of "Ora e per sempre addio" is now gone. At the end of "Dio ti giocondi" Vickers does not bother to be ironic; his profound dejection leads into an extraordinarily moving performance of "Dio! mi potevi." In Act IV, he is a little rougher than with Serafin, where his sorrow is piercing. The death scene is again full of ritual gravity: at the end, only tenderness and pain are left. This performance is still magnificent.

Even at these slow speeds, Mirella Freni provides a touching and beautifully sung Desdemona. Peter Glossop's Iago is vivid: more practical and vulgar than Gobbi's philosophic blackguard. The coarseness of his voice makes for a coarse character, though he lacks a measure of the rocklike steadiness needed for "Sì, pel ciel." He is also, and more often than the others, a victim of slow tempos and faulty balance with the orchestra. The drinking song emerges as heavy, and Cassio appears to be handling his liquor better than Iago: a confusing effect. Glossop's Credo is interesting, with detailed vocal coloring, but the orchestra covers him occasionally, and some of the *pianissimos* are so extreme that one can hardly hear them. The set commands respect for the dramatic and musical vision of its participants, but Karajan's loving attention to detail finally diminishes the vitality of these characters and thus their tragic potential.

1977 DECCA / LONDON (S)

Margaret Price (A), Jane Berbié (B), Carlo Cossutta (C), Peter Dvorsky (D), Gabriel Bacquier (E), Vienna State Opera Chorus, Vienna Philharmonic Orchestra—Georg Solti

As might be expected, Sir Georg Solti conducts a compulsive and exciting performance. Though the storm scene is sometimes too fast for characterization and "Dio! mi potevi" rushes past its tragic implications, the tempos are generally equitable. His three leading singers, however, do not complement each other well in vocal style or dramatic approach. Carlo Cossutta has a strong, blunt voice which lacks the range of color to suggest profundity of feeling. The love duet needs greater *legato* and "Dio! mi potevi" more than tears to achieve Verdi's dramatic aims, while "Ora e per sempre addio" sounds, as so often, more like a greeting to battle than a sorrowful farewell. Cossutta concludes with a tasteful but entirely conventional death scene.

As Desdemona, Margaret Price sings beautifully but lacks the warmth and impulsiveness that explain her actions, though in her third-act confrontation with Otello there are tears at "Guarda le prime lagrime." One admires the exquisite vocal technique rather than the exquisite sensibility of the character. Gabriel Bacquier is imaginative and rhythmically alert in a broad characterization of Iago. In the Credo his top notes are there but blustery, and the rest is vocally unmemorable. He does, however, point up the words superbly, even if virtually every Iago on complete recordings outsings him. With Otello he is alternately obsequious and oily, and his "Era la notte" is one of the dirtiest on records. With an incisive conductor and a conventional Otello, a cool Desdemona, and a clever actor as Iago, all with different vocal approaches, this is an eminently respectable but not, in general, a revelatory *Otello*.

1978 RCA / BMG (S) CD

Renata Scotto (A), Jean Kraft (B), Plácido Domingo (C), Frank Little (D), Sherrill Milnes (E), Ambrosian Opera Chorus, National Philharmonic Orchestra—James Levine

James Levine conducts a brilliant and moving performance, better proportioned than Karajan's, more vital than Serafin's, warmer than Solti's, and more clearly structured than any but Toscanini's and Panizza's. And he has an excellent cast. Plácido Domingo is in full possession of a glorious and warm voice. His characterization of Otello is noble, if not yet truly individualized or, on the very highest level, consistently tragic. The stakes are, indeed, higher for Otello than for any other tenor role in the Italian repertory. To say that one wants more authentic intimacy in the love duet, more pain in the voice for "Ora e per sempre addio," a deeper sense of degradation in "Dio! mi potevi," and greater desolation in the final act is, in this case, not so much to criticize the singer as to note just how revealing a tragedy this is. Domingo's performance is one of the best on records, and his death scene, monolithic at first and touchingly intimate at "E tu, come sei pallida," is particularly moving.

Renata Scotto's Desdemona is a profound creation, full of an inner radiance and vitality that other sopranos have not quite found in the role. Almost any of them has healthier *forte* top notes than Scotto, but she has a voice of many colors and the genius to project more in the music than can be verbalized in even the most searching analysis. "Dio ti giocondi" is especially touching, and her response to Otello's public humiliation of her in Act III is given with heartbreaking intimacy. The Willow Song, with most other sopranos a tender but rather dull sequence with one verse too many, has here a fascinating variety of moods, all illuminating the text and yet possessing ideal continuity. The Ave Maria is almost spoken: a true prayer moving into music at "Prega." Her dying phrases are seraphic, quiet and pure.

As Iago, Sherrill Milnes uses his splendid voice well, though the characterization and vocalism are a little labored. The Credo is intelligently worked out, "Era la notte" accomplished, and "Sì, pel ciel" sung as well as on any of the sets. Whether or not this is the "best" recording is matter for debate, but it has special qualities not duplicated in any of the other performances.

1983 EMI / ANGEL (In English) (S,D,P) (D

Rosalind Plowright (A), Shelagh Squires (B), Charles Craig (C), Bonaventura Bottone (D),

Neil Howlett (E), English National Opera Chorus and Orchestra—Mark Elder

This recording derives from four live performances at the London Coliseum in January 1983. It includes for the first time on records the Paris revision of the Act III *concertato* ensemble, giving greater prominence to Iago's responses; otherwise it uses a critical edition based on Verdi's autograph score rather than the first published edition. Andrew Porter's English translation is so adroit and admirable as to validate the greatness of the opera. A libretto is included so that even if one can't get much of the translation on first listening, the words become clearer with repetition and study. Mark Elder's conducting has spirit and some elasticity, though the chorus hasn't quite as much snap as the orchestra. In the matter of diction, Charles Craig as Otello is clear fairly often and uses the words well. Neil Howlett as Iago is understandable less of the time, and Rosalind Plowright hardly at all. It is revealing to see how closely their dramatic vitality is linked to the clarity of their words.

When this recording was made, Charles Craig had been singing for more than thirty years, and much of that time in the most strenuous roles. He has a voice of middling size with some heroic mettle and also some gristle in it. It may lack a measure of the mystery and nobility of tone for a great Otello, but he has acquired the style and technique for a fine one. The top sometimes wobbles in Act I, but he has a strong *legato* in the love duet. The Act II scene with Iago is typical in its dramatic vibrancy. "Dio! mi potevi" the final test of a tenor's ability in the tragic mode, may lack the ultimate dejection, but the death scene is handled with great and moving dignity.

Rosalind Plowright has a lovely voice, rather dark at the bottom, bright at the top, and rich and fresh throughout her range. Technically she handles the role well, but emotionally she is indifferent: at most, gently melancholy. Neil Howlett, as Iago, also has a beautiful, fresh voice, with fine control at any volume level. He projects the character along conventional lines: friendly in the public scenes, with savage thrust in the Credo. His *piano* singing is of exceptional beauty and smoothness in both the Credo and "Era la notte." Altogether the performance is a fine accomplishment, with a committed Otello, a well-sung if dull Desdemona, a responsive Iago with fine tone and technique, and reliable, powerful conducting.

1985 EMI / ANGEL (S,D) CD

Katia Ricciarelli (A), Petra Malakova (B), Plácido Domingo (C), Ezio di Cesare (D), Justino Díaz (E), La Scala Chorus and Orchestra—Lorin Maazel

This recording is taken from the Zeffirelli film soundtrack, though it is complete, whereas the film has some major cuts. Technically the set is annoying, for the singers are so variously miked that one has little sense of a dependable aural relationship with the orchestra. There is also considerable post-echo in my copy. Dramatically it lacks cumulative impact and plays like something cobbled together in a studio. Lorin Maazel conducts a lively performance, though the lyric sections suffer from a lack of expressive *rubato* and the climaxes are often exaggerated. Plácido Domingo is in fine, rich voice, more outspoken dramatically though not necessarily more convincing than in his performance with James Levine. His singing in the love duet is very tender and the death scene is again handled with distinction, emotionally full and yet restrained to a remarkable degree.

As Desdemona, Katia Ricciarelli produces some pretty tones but is otherwise very tentative, with incipient unsteadiness, little *legato*, and pallid characterization. Playing Iago, Justino Díaz has a blunt voice, a little dry at the bottom and sometimes strained at the top, but he is an imaginative singer with rhythmic verve. He is, however, unreliably recorded: sometimes distant, sometimes unnaturally close, so that the balance with other singers and the orchestra is uncertain. This is a disappointing issue.

1991 DECCA / LONDON (S,D,P) CD

Kiri Te Kanawa (A), Elzbieta Ardam (B), Luciano Pavarotti (C), Anthony Rolfe Johnson (D), Leo Nucci (E), Chicago Symphony Chorus and Orchestra—Georg Solti

This recording was assembled from tapes of four 1991 concert performances held in Chicago and New York: Solti's last as music director of the Chicago Symphony Orchestra and Pavarotti's first of the title role. For all the burnished vocalism and orchestral panache, the set is a disappointment. Solti is, of course, powerful and his orchestra miraculously neat in tone and attack, but the performance is oddly impersonal; it lacks atmosphere, variety, conviction: love and pain. One need not check only the Toscanini or Levine performances to sense this. The savage energy of Panizza and the thrust of Sabajno, despite very constricted sound, ragged orchestras, and problematic vocalists, make the point clearly.

Luciano Pavarotti is here in fine voice, but that voice is limited in color and volume for the role, despite the tenor's welcome *squillo*. Dramatically he is tasteful but conventional; he has some of the sentiment and the anger but not the grandeur. "Dio! mi potevi," for example, is full of feeling but quite lacking in the sense of moral exhaustion differentiating this moment from virtually anything else in Italian opera. The love duet goes best, but even that is casual. In the final scene one has, at last, a sense that the singer's own responses are illuminating the presentation. This is a well-sung performance but, as Pavarotti must know, Otello demands different qualifications. Kiri Te Kanawa's Desdemona is well vocalized: the Willow Song and Ave Maria are full of gleaming purple tone and effortless intimacy, and the fearful interruption in the former is surprisingly convincing, but dramatically there is little else of real interest. Leo Nucci's lively intelligence is constantly compromised by a dark, knotty voice strained by the music. Given its mixed talents, who would have thought the assembled company capable of a dull *Otello*?

Otello performances are usually (or should be) major events, so that the percentage of memorable performances on records is remarkably high. Of the now historical recordings, both the 1940 Panizza set with Martinelli, Rethberg, and Tibbett and the 1947 Toscanini set with Vinay are indispensable. Of the newer recordings, the 1960 Serafin set with Vickers and Gobbi and the 1978 Levine set with Domingo and Renata Scotto are the unforgettable ones. Forced to select one performance from all of these, I would probably choose the Martinelli: for all the 1940 radio sound and live-performance imperfections, his portrayal seems to me to contain the essence of tragedy.

LONDON GREEN

GIUSEPPE VERDI

FALSTAFF (1893)

A: Alice (s); B: Nannetta (s); C: Meg (ms); D: Mistress Quickly (ms);
E: Fenton (t); F: Falstaff (bar); G: Ford (bar)

alstaff is one hundred years old. Few Verdi operas have enjoyed so distinguished a phonographic history. Eight complete commercial recordings may not seem like a lot, compared to the multiple versions of *Aida* or *La Traviata* on the market, but each of these *Falstaff* sets in some sense does justice to the work—none seems to have been planned primarily as a vehicle for a star singer, or to fulfill a record company contract. The obvious difficulties of the score, and the fact that it is not a vehicle for conventional vocal display, are no doubt factors: there is just no point in recording *Falstaff* without a group of exceptionally talented and dedicated performers.

One of a handful of operas that contain not a single superfluous note, *Falstaff* is never cut. Nor does the work present any real textual problems. Verdi made numerous tiny changes to the score during the rehearsals for the premiere, and he altered two passages after the opening night: he shortened the climactic ensemble in Act II, Scene 2, and rewrote the end of Act III, Scene 1. Some recent staged productions and concert performances of the opera have experimented with restoring the original, longer version of the Act II, Scene 2 *concertato*, but all of the recordings to date respect the composer's final thoughts on his opera.

Finally, some comments about the opera's vocal requirements. Mistress Quickly, though nominally a mezzo-soprano role, ideally should be sung by a true contralto—a vocal type that has become increasingly rare. It is possible for a mezzo to be a good Eboli or Amneris, and still run into difficulties with Quickly's lower tessitura. In my opinion, the roles of Nannetta and Fenton are often cast much too lightly, on records as well as in the theater. In each case, what is needed is a voice of exceptional warmth and beauty, capable of rising to the challenge of the soaring phrases ("Bella! Ridente!," etc.) in the Act II, Scene 2 ensemble.

1932 EMI / ANGEL (M)

Pia Tassinari (A), Ines Alfani-Tellini (B), Rita Monticone (C), Aurora Buades (D), Roberto D'Alessio (E), Giacomo Rimini (F), Emilio Ghirardini (G), La Scala Chorus and Orchestra—Lorenzo Molajoli

Lorenzo Molajoli's conducting might be described as old-fashioned—his approach to the music is warm and affectionate, and he is always considerate of the singers' needs—but this is not to imply that standards are allowed to drop: on the contrary, the playing and singing are admirably precise. Molajoli's tempos tend to be slower than most other conductors'. His relaxed handling of the final pages of Act I, Scene 1, which are usually whipped into a frenzy, is a good example.

There is a good cast, although only two of its members are really outstanding. Pia Tassinari is a lively, seductive-sounding Alice. Salvatore

Baccaloni does just about everything one could reasonably ask from a Pistola in purely vocal terms, and comes close to stealing the show whenever he appears.

The Falstaff, Giacomo Rimini, has an attractive baritone voice, very dark in timbre; he sings many passages virtually "straight," applying an occasional interpretive touch almost as an afterthought. For some reason, Rimini is much livelier and more specific in the third act than in the previous two, beginning with a fine account of "Mondo ladro!" and building from there.

The Quickly, Aurora Buades, and the Fenton, Roberto D'Alessio, were a husband-and-wife team who made many duet recordings together. Buades, with her bright timbre and aggressive temperament, might be described as the poor man's Conchita Supervia. D'Alessio phrases with great elegance and does some interesting things from the interpretive standpoint—he is one of the few Fentons on the complete sets who saturates the Act III aria with a sense of erotic longing—although he has a strong vibrato that some listeners may dislike.

Ines Alfani-Tellini's soprano sounds on the thin, fragile side even for Nannetta's music, although the recording may do her an injustice in this regard. Emilio Ghirardini also sings well, but his Ford is an amiable buffoon, whose jealousy has no sinister undertones.

The sound of this version is, of course, primitive. The solo voices come through with reasonable clarity, but the orchestra is pushed into the background much of the time—a serious disadvantage in this opera, which is replete with subtle instrumental details. There is a high-pitched whine which must be the piccolo, a low-pitched rumble which must be the timpani, etc. In Act III, the English horn solos sound as though they are being played on a kazoo.

1949 CETRA (M,P)

Rosanna Carteri (A), Lina Pagliughi (B), Anna Maria Canali (C), Amalia Pini (D), Emilio Renzi (E), Giuseppe Taddei (F), Saturno Meletti (G), Radio Italiana Chorus and Orchestra, Turin—Mario Rossi

This *Falstaff* is one of the stronger entries in the Cetra series of broadcast operas. It is refreshing to hear *Falstaff* treated like "just another opera"—this is very much a *col canto* approach, with the singers setting the pace and the tempos kept relaxed enough to accommodate them; the instrumental playing aims for warmth and *cantabile* expressivity rather than hard-edged brilliance. The Turin radio orchestra is a competent ensemble, but obviously cannot bear comparison to the NBC Symphony, or some of the other prestigious orchestras that have subsequently recorded the work.

There is one truly great performance: Giuseppe Taddei is the best Falstaff on any of the complete recordings of the opera. He was only thirty-five years old at the time, but sings with complete maturity and insight. His voice, rich and beautiful in timbre, is a magnificent instrument; his technical security enables him to cope effortlessly with the considerable challenges of the role. As though all this weren't enough, Taddei's Falstaff is genuinely funny in a sly, subtle way.

Only two of the other cast members approach this level. Rosanna Carteri's soprano is on the light side even for Alice, but she sings with accuracy and charm. Lina Pagliughi is an extraordinary Nannetta: her high lyric-coloratura voice has more body in its lower and middle registers than most, and yet she can lighten her tone to produce a truly ethereal effect in the intimate scenes with Fenton and the Act III fairy song.

The others, frankly, are no more than adequate, and rather less than that in the case of Amalia Pini's coarse, vibrato-ridden Quickly and Saturno Meletti's dull Ford.

Once again, Everest's fake stereo reprocessing—with its destructive echo, shallow bass, and strident treble—wreaks havoc on what was probably a decent enough monophonic recording.

1950 RCA / BMG (M,P) CD

Herva Nelli (A), Teresa Stich-Randall (B), Nan Merriman (C), Cloe Elmo (D), Antonio Madasi (E), Giuseppe Valdengo (F), Frank Guarrera

(G), Robert Shaw Chorale, NBC Symphony Orchestra—Arturo Toscanini

To devise further words of praise for this recording, which preserves broadcast performances of April 1 and 8, 1950, would be an exercise in futility. "One of the greatest of all recorded opera performances," Harvey Sachs proclaims in his notes accompanying both the RCA and BMG editions, and for once that is no idle boast.

This *Falstaff* is also one of the most influential opera recordings ever made: most conductors who have recorded the work subsequently studied the Toscanini performance carefully, and do not hesitate to imitate some of the older conductor's effects. A good example occurs near the end of Act II, Scene 1: after Ford's monologue, the violent orchestral *crescendo* suddenly gives way to an enchanting violin melody, as Falstaff reenters the room dressed in his finery. Toscanini has his strings phrase this passage rather expansively, with a hint of *glissando* on the rising fifths in the third and fourth bars of the tune, to wonderfully sly, graceful effect. Most of the other conductors follow his example.

In short, if ever a conductor could be said to own an operatic score, lock, stock, and barrel, then Toscanini owned *Falstaff*, and we are lucky to have the 1950 NBC broadcast recording as proof of his mastery.

The cast is uneven in terms of vocal endowment, but the whole is decidedly greater than the sum of its parts. In general, the women are better than the men. Alice is probably the most successful of the several Verdi roles that Herva Nelli recorded with Toscanini. Her voice, although attractive, is not a particularly colorful or sensuous instrument; in *Falstaff*, however, her accuracy is most welcome, and her light feminine charm has full play. The young Teresa Stich-Randall does some lovely things with her pure, delicate soprano in Nannetta's music. With her powerful, almost baritonal mezzo, Cloe Elmo makes an imposing Quickly, although some of her comic effects are a little broad.

Unfortunately, neither Giuseppe Valdengo nor Frank Guarrera is more than adequate from the vocal standpoint. Valdengo is an intelligent artist who knows what effects he is after, but his vocalism is more efficient than beautiful. Guarrera's voice turns harsh under pressure, and this is a serious handicap in Ford's music, which is quite strenuously written.

The Fenton, Antonio Madasi, with his thinnish *tenorino* and occasionally bleaty timbre, is a poor match for Stich-Randall's lovely voice in their scenes together. But there is a certain passion and manliness in his delivery that I like. The recorded acoustic, a typical product of NBC's infamous Studio 8H, is dry and hard, and there are some odd balances. I did spotchecks to compare a (worn) pressing of the RCA LP set to the new BMG CD reissue, and I feel confident in stating that the latter is the preferable format. Obviously, BMG has worked hard to improve the sound: the reproduction is more tightly focused in general; the dynamic range is wider, and the tape hiss has been reduced.

1956 EMI / ANGEL (S) CD

Elisabeth Schwarzkopf (A), Anna Moffo (B), Nan Merriman (C), Fedora Barbieri (D), Luigi Alva (E), Tito Gobbi (F), Rolando Panerai (G), Philharmonia Orchestra and Chorus—Herbert von Karajan

In this scrupulously prepared recording, a typical Walter Legge production, Herbert von Karajan's tempos tend to be just a shade slower than Toscanini's, and he encourages the Philharmonia Orchestra to produce a softer, rounder, more blended sound than the NBC Symphony's. As a result, a number like the final fugue is graceful rather than boisterous.

One could draw up a long list of beautiful effects. To cite only one example: in the final scene, during the mock-exorcism ritual, Falstaff sings the phrase "Ma salvagli l'addomine" four times. Each time, his voice is doubled by two flutes and two oboes; Karajan balances the passage in such a way as to emphasize the oboes, and Tito Gobbi precisely matches his timbre and rate of vibrato to their playing. The performance is filled with such moments of insight.

Despite my admiration for Taddei's classic portrayal, Gobbi is, for me, the most interesting Falstaff on any of the complete sets. Gobbi does not sing the role nearly as well (or even as comfortably) as Taddei, and indeed there are many things about Gobbi's vocalism that one would hesitate to recommend to a young student baritone—the squeezed production of the upper register, for example, or the shallow, colorless quality at low dynamic levels. But everything that Gobbi does with his voice has the kind of inner life and conviction that, at times, one fears has all but vanished from the operatic stage.

Rolando Panerai, with no fewer than three studio versions to his credit, virtually owns the role of Ford on records, and for good reason. Panerai's baritone, although a little tough in timbre under pressure even in 1956 (when he was thirty-two years old), is a magnificent instrument, capable of many shades of color. He is also a brilliantly resourceful vocal actor. He is particularly funny in Ford's moments of sputtering rage—the rapid patter ("Chiudete le porte!," etc.) in Act II, Scene 2, for example, is enough to make the listener breathless with empathy.

All four women are excellent, and their voices are so well differentiated that there is never any problem telling them apart in the ensembles. Alice is just the sort of role in which one would expect Elisabeth Schwarzkopf to excel: she is wonderfully sly and seductive, and, although she hardly sounds like an "Italian" soprano, this is one of her most spontaneous-sounding performances.

Anna Moffo has a warmer, more Italianate sound than Stich-Randall, although it must be admitted that her soft singing does not always seem ideally focused or supported. Fedora Barbieri has almost the perfect voice and personality for Quickly.

Luigi Alva seems just a bit too laid back and gentlemanly as Fenton, but sings well. The CD transfer, a digital remastering of the stereo tape, is an outstanding technical job.

1963 DECCA / LONDON (S) CD

Ilva Ligabue (A), Mirella Freni (B), Rosalind Elias (C), Giulietta Simionato (D), Alfredo Kraus (E), Geraint Evans (F), Robert Merrill (G), RCA Italiana Opera Orchestra and Chorus—Georg Solti

With two real-life knights in attendance (Evans and Solti), this is the most socially acceptable recording of the opera; it is also one of the best. Solti gives us perhaps the most accurate facsimile of the Toscanini performance on records—not only in tempo but in terms of the bright, polished orchestral sonority (with outstanding work by the trumpets).

If this is not necessarily the best cast on records, it is certainly the most euphonious. Both baritones are excellent. Geraint Evans actually vocalizes the title role more smoothly and beautifully than Gobbi, and displays impeccable musicianship and a lively dramatic response. Robert Merrill's Ford is warmly and richly sung, and genuinely funny without ever becoming blustery or exaggerated.

As Alice, Ilva Ligabue reveals a lovely voice, exactly right in weight and timbre for the role, and is at least as resourceful a vocal actress as Schwarzkopf—no mean accomplishment. Giulietta Simionato, a famous Quickly, is heard here in something close to her best vocal form: firm and clear. Although there is nothing exaggerated about her portrayal (rather the opposite, in fact—her inflections are usually quite subtle) she dominates the action whenever she appears.

Mirella Freni is surely the best Nannetta on any of the complete sets—a ravishingly warm, pure sound, with the many high As floated weightlessly, combined with great personal charm. If Alfredo Kraus's Fenton seems a bit phlegmatic by comparison, his actual singing cannot be faulted.

1966 CBS / SONY (S) CD

Ilva Ligabue (A), Graziella Sciutti (B), Hilde Rössl-Majdan (C), Regina Resnik (D), Juan Oncina (E), Dietrich Fischer-Dieskau (F), Rolando Panerai (G), Vienna State Opera Chorus, Vienna Philharmonic Orchestra—Leonard Bernstein

Like all the truly great opera recordings, this *Falstaff* (based on an acclaimed Vienna State Opera production) combines the precision and polish possible only under studio conditions with the kind of excitement and spontaneity we associate with a memorable night in the theater. Leonard Bernstein's colorful, affectionate shaping of the score is every bit as sharply executed as Toscanini's or Solti's: of Bernstein's too few opera recordings, this is probably the best. Although this is the tightest and most rhythmically alive reading of the score on records (surpassing even Toscanini in this respect), Bernstein does not hesitate to make unwritten tempo modifications at many points—a typical example is the expansive treatment of Alice's reading of the letter's climactic phrase ("Come una stella sull'immensità"), which takes on an almost Wagnerian grandeur and ecstasy as a result. The Vienna Philharmonic, in brilliant form (surely these horns have no rivals anywhere in the world), sounds inspired by the conductor.

The one controversial element is the Falstaff of Dietrich Fischer-Dieskau. To begin with, he does not possess the kind of fat, round, dark baritone the part ideally demands. The real problem with Fischer-Dieskau's performance is that he overloads every phrase (and, in some passages, every word) with fussy little vocal colorations and verbal inflections. In some of the rapid conversational exchanges, he resorts to a *parlando* approach that amounts to scratching away at the notes, in lieu of real singing. The result is going to strike a listener as either a brilliant piece of vocal acting or an intolerably mannered, self-conscious display; I find myself tending toward the latter.

Otherwise, the cast contains no weak link. Graziella Sciutti, the Nannetta, and Juan Oncina, the Fenton, both have small, even delicate-sounding, voices, but both are accomplished performers, and it seems appropriate that the young lovers should sound a little ethereal, in contrast to the adult passions of their elders.

Ligabue makes an even better impression here than she does on the Solti set, perhaps because the engineers seem to have reproduced her voice more flatteringly. Panerai also manages to improve upon his fine work on the EMI / Karajan recording: it's good to hear him experimenting with different inflections and colora-

tions (without going overboard in the Fischer-Dieskau manner), instead of simply giving a carbon copy of his earlier performance. Regina Resnik is a vivid Quickly, worthy of comparison to the classic Barbieri and Simionato performances.

This is another first-rate engineering job. The production is noteworthy for its bold use of sonic perspectives.

1980 PHILIPS (S,D) CD

Raina Kabaivanska (A), Janet Perry (B), Trudeliese Schmidt (C), Christa Ludwig (D), Francisco Araiza (E), Giuseppe Taddei (F), Rolando Panerai (G), Vienna State Opera Chorus, Vienna Philharmonic Orchestra—Herbert von Karajan

The Vienna Philharmonic plays the score at least as well for Karajan as it did for Bernstein; Karajan, however, encourages the orchestra to produce a softer, rounder, more mellow sound that is not, perhaps, ideal for this music. In general, the conductor's tempos are broader than they were in 1956. Although the overall effect is less spontaneous and theatrical, this is still a distinguished reading of the score.

Unlike most of the opera recordings Karajan led during the last two decades of his life, this *Falstaff* was not made in conjunction with a staged production. The cast, presumably handpicked by the conductor, is good, with reservations.

Taddei, sixty-four years old when this recording was made, still has plenty of voice left, but the actual tonal quality is often attenuated, and he is very careful in the upper register (the engineers are clearly cooperating by making it possible for him to sing almost everything at less than full voice). Unfortunately, the interpretation has become too broad and mechanical in many places—the corny falsetto squeals at "Te lo cornifico *netto*, netto!" are a typical example. I am grateful to have this flawed yet fascinating performance available, but I regret that it could not have been recorded ten or fifteen years earlier.

Panerai, at age fifty-six, now has more of a rough edge to his tone, and he must work hard for the top notes, but he still has few recorded rivals as Ford.

It's good to hear Raina Kabaivanska, a soprano neglected by the recording companies, as Alice, a role that suits her well: she resembles Ligabue in vocal type and in her approach to the part.

Christa Ludwig's Quickly looks like luxurious casting on paper, but she is less of a natural for the role than such mezzos as Elmo, Barbieri, Simionato, or Resnik—Ludwig's voice (at least, at this stage in her career) is really too light in timbre, and its very plushness seems to inhibit the production of bright, open Italian vowels.

Janet Perry sings prettily and accurately as Nannetta, but the overall effect is rather thin and monochromatic. Francisco Araiza, on the other hand, is an uncommonly warm-voiced, passionate Fenton.

This set was one of the first digitally recorded operas: a decade later, it still sounds impressive, despite some artificial balances.

1982 DEUTSCHE GRAMMOPHON (S,D,P) CD

Katia Ricciarelli (A), Barbara Hendricks (B), Brenda Boozer (C), Lucia Valentini Terrani (D), Dalmacio Gonzalez (E), Renato Bruson (F), Leo Nucci (G), Los Angeles Master Chorale, Los Angeles Philharmonic Orchestra—Carlo Maria Giulini

The 1982 Los Angeles production of *Falstaff* was the first time Carlo Maria Giulini conducted an opera in a theater since 1968. Such an event deserves to be recorded, and the DG set is a compilation, drawn from several performances during the run. Most of the time, one would never guess that this is not a studio recording; only a few stage noises and changes in perspective betray the fact, and it is delightful to hear faint ripples of laughter from the audience in a couple of scenes.

In some remarks quoted in the accompanying booklet, Giulini states his conviction that *Falstaff* is an essentially serious opera, and that Falstaff himself is a dignified, even potentially tragic, figure. It is possible to read these qualities

into the performance, which resembles the Philips / Karajan recording in its relaxed range of tempos and understated handling of the lyric episodes. The Los Angeles Philharmonic is a good ensemble, and works hard for Giulini, but numerous minor blemishes (not all of which can be blamed on the circumstances of live recording) prevent it from matching the achievement of most of the other orchestras that have recorded this music. At its best, though, the Californians' playing has a warm, autumnal glow about it that is most attractive.

Renato Bruson has a beautiful voice, capable of a velvety *mezza voce*. No doubt at Giulini's insistence, he eschews much of the traditional comic business. But, if anything, Bruson goes too far in the other direction—his Sir John is so serious and introspective that some of his behavior in the opera now seems implausible.

Leo Nucci is an acceptable Ford, although this live recording provides graphic evidence that his voice is much smaller than Panerai's or Merrill's. Oddly enough, Nucci seems to have taken Fischer-Dieskau as his interpretive model, rather than any of the Italian baritones—the monologue, for instance, is compromised by some grunted *parlando* effects (e.g., at "Prima li accoppio," etc.) that are neither good singing nor effective as a revelation of the character. Nannetta, Barbara Hendricks, sings with astonishing purity and control, although there is not much sensuousness in her bright, narrow, low-vibrato timbre. Katia Ricciarelli portrays Alice with great charm and subtlety, but one can't help speculating that her voice would be better suited to Nannetta.

While there is no reason why Quickly should look or sound like an old hag, Verdi and Boito surely intended her to have a certain maturity; Lucia Valentini Terrani simply sounds too youthful and vibrantly attractive for the role. In addition, the music often lies too low for her—her low Gs are breathy and unsupported.

Dalmacio Gonzalez is a pleasing Fenton.

There are four truly distinguished recordings. The RCA / Toscanini can still serve as one's only version of the opera, provided some allowance is made for the cramped mono sound and the uneven cast.

Of the three stereo sets, my personal favorite is the EMI / Karajan: some listeners may find the conducting lacking in spontaneity, but the orchestra is superb and Gobbi's vivid Falstaff heads a fine cast.

Those who do not share my antipathy to Fischer-Dieskau's Falstaff may find the CBS / Bernstein recording the most satisfying of all. Although it is a studio recording, it comes closer than any other version (including the live DG / Giulini set) to matching the Toscanini recording's sense of theatrical spontaneity.

The Decca / Solti—exceptionally well conducted, played, sung, *and* engineered—is a beautiful all-round job, free from eccentricity, the kind of recording that stands up well to the test of repeated hearings. It is probably the safest choice for those who are new to the opera, and want only one recording to start with.

ROLAND GRAEME

Unavailable for review:
1991 RCA / BMG

RICHARD WAGNER

DER FLIEGENDE HOLLÄNDER (1843)

A: Senta (s); B: Erik (t); C: Dutchman (bs-bar); D: Daland (bs)

The dramatic burden of *Der Flie-gende Holländer* is carried essentially by the central character, and the primary criterion for a recording must be the ability of the lead singer to convey the torment of the accursed sea-captain condemned to sail the oceans until eternity, as well as his demonic quality. Since Wagner originally conceived the work in a single act, but subsequently divided it into three, both versions have some claim to authenticity. The single-act version is preferred at Bayreuth and elsewhere too these days, and of the eleven recordings discussed, only Krauss, Fricsay, Sawallisch, and Klemperer adopt the three-act version. (For convenience's sake, reference will be made consistently to Act I, Act II, and Act III.) In 1860 Wagner revised the ending of the Overture and of the whole work, introducing a motif of redemption in the style of *Tristan*. Only Sawallisch, Nelsson, and Klemperer adhere to the original endings—the last in a slightly modified form. Most performances are complete: a couple of minor exceptions are noted.

1944 ACANTA (M) CD

Viorica Ursuleac (A), Karl Ostertag (B), Hans Hotter (C), Georg Hann (D), Chorus and Orchestra of the Bavarian State Opera, Munich—Clemens Krauss

The obvious technical imperfections of this early recording by Clemens Krauss should not be allowed to obscure its two salient virtues: the fine conducting and the performance of Hans Hotter in the title role. Indeed, the somewhat primitive sound quality even contributes to the raw, elemental character of Krauss's reading. The ferocity of the storm depicted in the Overture, the vigorous opening of Act I, and the ominous appearance of the Dutchman's ship are all superbly done. Hotter displays an astonishing authority for a singer of thirty-five. His extremely powerful rendering of the part harnesses a voice of enormous strength to an interpretation of uncompromising severity: his "Nirgends ein Grab! Niemals der Tod!" in the opening Monologue ("Die Frist ist um") is truly shattering in its force. There is, however, room for maturing: there's not much bloom to be heard on the voice—in fact, its edge begins to grate—and frequently considerations of line are sacrificed to forcefulness of utterance. But Hotter has no rival in terms of his darkly demonic timbre and commanding presence—which is not to say that I find this the most satisfactory performance, to the exclusion of all others. As Senta, Viorica Ursuleac is rather matronly; she sings with more conviction than beauty of tone, applying a remarkable amount of vibrato on even the shortest eighth note. The "sudden inspiration" that forms a postlude to her Ballad is squally in the extreme.

Georg Hann's Daland is grimmer, more robust than is customary nowadays, and his opening lines are chopped up excruciatingly. Karl Ostertag punches out the notes in Erik's duet with Senta in a most unmusical manner; when he reaches those with accents, they are fired like pistol shots. Franz Klarwein's Steersman is heavier and more full-blooded than is usual, with long rhetorical pauses in his opening song that elevate it beyond its real importance (though it's an approach that might recommend itself in a production seen through the eyes of the Steersman). Krauss directs the Act III chorus work with great brio, brilliantly catching both the swing of the hilarity and the menacing mood behind it. The ghostly crew's shouts of "Hui!" sound endearingly like children playing ghosts, but underpinning the whole act is the strength and intensity of Krauss's reading, which have scarcely been surpassed.

1952 DEUTSCHE GRAMMOPHON (M)

Annelies Kupper (A), Wolfgang Windgassen (B), Josef Metternich (C), Josef Greindl (D), RIAS Chamber Chorus and RIAS Symphony Orchestra, Berlin—Ferenc Fricsay

Fricsay's performance is an undistinguished one with few, if any, redeeming features. Josef Metternich, who two years previously had sung a superb Telramund for Schüchter, is here disappointing as the Dutchman: his plain account even tends toward the bland, and certainly in the Monologue he doesn't match Fricsay's intensity (unfortunately, as the performance progresses, Fricsay's interpretation also becomes less satisfying). Annelies Kupper's Senta is no more than acceptable, and altogether it is Josef Greindl as Daland who has the greatest presence. Wolfgang Windgassen gives an unsubtle account of Erik's Cavatina, and Sieglinde Wagner, despite her promising name, is lacking weight and character as Mary. The male chorus work is weak, and the challenge and response of the Act III antiphony pathetically inadequate. Although there is no unanswerable objection to the three-act version—at least when given in the opera house, with intervals—Fricsay's recording, like Krauss's and Klemperer's (Sawallisch has a novel solution), has an unsatisfactory feature: each act follows the last on the same side of the record, thus juxtaposing material never intended to be heard together.

1955 DECCA / LONDON (S,P)

Astrid Varnay (A), Rudolf Lustig (B), Hermann Uhde (C), Ludwig Weber (D), Chorus and Orchestra of the Bayreuth Festival—Joseph Keilberth

By contrast, this recording has much to recommend it, chiefly the performances of Hermann Uhde as the Dutchman, Astrid Varnay as Senta, and the finely controlled conducting of Joseph Keilberth. Uhde is one of the few interpreters of the title role who can rank alongside Hotter: his darkly colored tone, allied to a convincing characterization, yields a potent realization of the part. Even if he is not always rock-steady in the Act II duet—or perhaps because of this—he is movingly human. Varnay is not one hundred percent reliable here either, especially in the upper reaches, but if one is prepared to take the rough with the smooth, it is an intensely committed account by both singers, and well conducted. In her Ballad, Varnay is terrific, singing through the diphthong "Hui!" with eerie coloring, to chilling effect. A black mark to the producer for separating the first and second stanzas with a side-break, though he redeems himself by avoiding the highly undesirable break—a flaw in many of the recordings—in the Act III choral confrontation, a sure way to lose momentum. Keilberth maintains the tension splendidly at that point and right through to the end (the men of the Bayreuth chorus are firm and virile, the women somewhat wobbly). He also shows his skill as an accompanist in Senta's Ballad, where the rhythmic spring reinforces the propulsion of the vocal line, notwithstanding a slowish tempo. Ludwig Weber's Daland is thick-toned and hearty, but quite within character; Rudolf Lustig sings with a passion that at least makes Erik's part sound interesting. The recording quality is not wonderful by today's standards, but on the 1978 transfer reasonably acceptable.

1960 EMI / ANGEL (M)

Marianne Schech (A), Rudolf Schock (B), Dietrich Fischer-Dieskau (C), Gottlob Frick (D),

Chorus and Orchestra of the Deutsche Staatsoper, Berlin—Franz Konwitschny

Another fine interpretation of the title role is here offered by Dietrich Fischer-Dieskau. As always, his reading is informed by the art of the lieder singer: with his clarity of articulation and tonal coloring, he has an unparalleled ability to use the words themselves to convey emotions. It is a magisterial account, powerfully projected, and yet one is not absolutely persuaded that this is the tormented seafarer rather than just a great artist depicting him. Fischer-Dieskau's effortless command of even the high tessitura almost counts against him in this respect. Would that one could say the same for Marianne Schech as Senta! In her Ballad, she blasts each anacrucial top G to most unmusical effect, destroying the shape of the line; she lacks the rapt quality that one looks for in this part, and her "Ich sei's" postlude is scarcely an outburst of ecstasy. Erik's dream as recounted by Rudolf Schock is too rushed to be convincing, and Senta's interjections do not make her sound remotely interested. Her Act II duet with Fischer-Dieskau, however, is beautifully sung by both; it is also well paced by the conductor, rising to a heartwarming climax. The conducting of the Overture is more deliberate, less atmospheric than some, but both here and at the opening of Act I, rhythms are incisively pointed. Konwitschny's accompaniment of Daland's Act II aria ("Mögst du, mein Kind") is similarly neat and trim, playing up the superficiality of the character. Gottlob Frick is an admirable Daland and his exchanges with the Dutchman in Act I are delightfully done.

p. 1961 DECCA / LONDON (S) CD

Leonie Rysanek (A), Karl Liebl (B), George London (C), Giorgio Tozzi (D), Chorus and Orchestra of the Royal Opera House, Covent Garden—Antal Dorati

By the time of its next *Fliegende Holländer*, Decca had established itself as world leader in the field of recorded opera, with the first studio *Ring* well under way. The technical advances in its 1961 Dorati recording are immediately apparent and do much to enhance the dramatic tension generated by the performers. In the Act III choral confrontation, for instance, the differentiation of opposing crews, Norwegian and Dutch, is strikingly effected by means of the stereo separation. When the Dutchman impresses Daland with his wealth, you can actually hear the tinkling of treasure in his chest, while the whirring of wheels in the Spinning Chorus nicely complements the lighthearted chatter of the girls. The latter (from the Covent Garden chorus), with their bright, steady tone, for once really could be taken for young(ish) spinning girls.

George London's Dutchman is impressive in vocal stature and tone, but doesn't convey the character's intense anguish. Leonie Rysanek's Senta, though a shade mature, is involving in her Ballad. Especially effective is the third stanza, where her control of the high *piano* notes is put to telling use; the *poco riten.* and *più rit.* here result in a massive slowing up, but it works well. Giorgio Tozzi's bluff Daland is unobjectionable, even if it is Dorati who does most of the characterization for him, with pointedly jaunty rhythms. Karl Liebl's Erik is one of the best: he has a grateful tone and an earnestness, not least in his exchanges with Senta, that projects an exciting sense of drama. His dream is very well done, and again Dorati's contribution is considerable: the string tremolos and *pizzicato* basses are used to create a genuine air of suspense. Both here and elsewhere, the orchestral detail is well brought out. The Overture, however, is unpromising: though beautifully played by the Royal Opera House Orchestra, it sounds, alongside the likes of Krauss, simply too civilized.

1961 PHILIPS (S,P)

Anja Silja (A), Fritz Uhl (B), Franz Crass (C), Josef Greindl, (D), Chorus and Orchestra of the Bayreuth Festival—Wolfgang Sawallisch

Perhaps surprisingly, this live Bayreuth performance adopts the three-act version, though amended in such a way that the duplicated material at the end of one act and the beginning of the next is cut (a duplication that is undesirable on records, though less so in the theater, where the acts are separated by intervals). Sawallisch somewhat abruptly begins Act II with the Spinning Chorus, and Act III with the Sailors' Chorus; he also makes a cut (not uncommon in the theater) in the final trio. As a result there is no side-break in the Act III choral confrontation of Norwegian and Dutch crews (a big bonus), and considerable intensity is generated there (the Bayreuth chorus excellent as ever), driving to a climax with the approach of the ghostly crew. Sawallisch's performance throughout has much to recommend it, with a fine sense of drama that just occasionally sacrifices subtlety or beauty of tone. His Dutchman, Franz Crass, is also excellent: he has not only the requisite firm, dark-hued tone but also a quality of pleading in his voice which makes the middle section of his Monologue, "Dich frage ich," especially effective. When he retells the events of his life in an edited version for Daland, his exceptionally *legato* line brings out the weariness so much better than the usual forceful declamation. It is thoughtful touches like this that make Crass's a consistently searching interpretation. Anja Silja's bright-toned Senta is impetuous and outgoing rather than introverted and secretive. Her Ballad is sung with enormous vigor, the anacrucial eighth note hit each time (as by Schech) with excessive force, as though it were an accented beat. Too often her enthusiasm leads to looseness of delivery (in pitch and line) and roughness of tone, particularly in her duet with the Dutchman. Josef Greindl's nicely characterized Daland comes complete with an evil little laugh, though his tone is frequently unpleasant as he eases his way into the high notes. Fritz Uhl's Erik is impassioned but fortunately not as ludicrously inflated as Georg Paskuda's Steersman, which treats the song like a grand operatic aria.

1968 EMI / ANGEL (S) CD

Anja Silja (A), Ernst Kozub (B), Theo Adam (C), Martti Talvela (D), BBC Chorus, New Philharmonia Orchestra—Otto Klemperer

Klemperer's classic recording broadly adopts the original Dresden edition, the exclusion of

the redemption tailpiece to the Overture and end of opera according naturally with the bleak austerity of his conception. But that original ending is uniquely adapted, apparently by Klemperer himself: toward the end the harps break in (as for the revised 1860 version), but no redemption follows, and both Overture and opera end with a series of five severe tonic chords. The uncompromising intensity of Klemperer's vision is gripping. In the Act III choral antiphony, for example, the tension is impressively sustained and the confrontation with the supernatural crew takes on an apocalyptic quality. The New Philharmonia and BBC Chorus perform splendidly for Klemperer and the sound effects are excellent. Theo Adam's Dutchman is powerful in tone, but has a tendency to pass off sheer force for agony and inner turmoil. Klemperer is formidable in the Monologue and in spite of his seriousness he yields to no one in his characterization of Daland: his jaunty *staccato* horn accompaniment in the Act I duet for Daland and the Dutchman has an apt touch of ponderousness. Martti Talvela takes his cue with an appropriate reading of the part. Anja Silja's eccentric approach to the upbeats of the Ballad is again in evidence, but otherwise it is one of the most satisfactory renderings on offer: cleanly sung, at once resolute and visionary. In the latter stages of her Act II duet with the Dutchman, Silja's singing is incisive and very exciting (Adam's less so); at the end of the opera she is one of the few sopranos not to be defeated by the taxing tessitura.

1971 DEUTSCHE GRAMMOPHON (S,P) CD

Gwyneth Jones (A), Hermin Esser (B), Thomas Stewart (C), Karl Ridderbusch (D), Chorus and Orchestra of the Bayreuth Festival—Karl Böhm

Karl Böhm's conducting of the Overture, in a performance at the 1971 Bayreuth Festival, is brittle and atmospheric without quite grabbing the listener by the throat. However, his handling of the Act III choral confrontation is breathcatching, with firm rhythms punched out, and it falls foul only of the usual unsatisfactory side change. It is with Böhm's support that the Dutchman's Monologue eventually comes alive.

Initially, Thomas Stewart is hardly awe-inspiring, but in the last section, "Nur eine Hoffnung," aided by Böhm's savage, stabbing brass punctuation and fearsome timpani strokes, he at last finds not only the right demonic tone but also a sense of existential desperation. If Gwyneth Jones is a trifle squally in Senta's Ballad, that is not inappropriate in this tale of a storm-tossed mariner, and in the quiet middle section she sings beautifully and touchingly of his promised redemption. Provided one can accept Jones's vocal mannerisms, this is an account that gets right inside the character and it does so with an intensity and variety of tonal coloring comparable with that of Varnay. In the Act II duet, Stewart is superior in vocal allure, but comes nowhere near Jones in her ability to convey a mysterious sense of destiny. As the duet progresses to its climax, it is essentially Jones, abetted purposefully by Böhm, who raises the emotional pitch to its thrillingly high level. Hermin Esser sings Erik's "Mein Herz voll Treue" with an uninhibited passion and naiveté that are all that are required in this role, though his dream is recounted without an ounce of suspense: he could be telling Senta a nursery story. Fortunately, Jones's interjections, breathless with excitement, save the scene. Just as it is Erik's fate to be rejected in this work, so it is Daland's to be regarded as an ingratiating and thoroughly irritating boor. Karl Ridderbusch jovially does what is required to perfection.

1976 DECCA / LONDON (S) CD

Janis Martin (A), René Kollo (B), Norman Bailey (C), Martti Talvela (D), Chicago Symphony Chorus and Orchestra—Georg Solti

The Overture in this recording has the usual Solti landmarks of speed and superficial excitement, but no real tension or genuine dramatic feeling. The Act III choral confrontation, which should have found Solti in his element, is also disappointing. The tempo is a notch too slow, and the Chicago singers rather tame, so that the Norwegian chorus sounds measured and untheatrical. Nor is there any audible distinction between the Norwegian and Dutch crews (not that the score directs it, it is true). The final

stages of the confrontation do at last strike some sparks and the final moments of the work are effectively done. Norman Bailey's soft-grained, humane voice is not immediately obvious as that of a Dutchman, and indeed it does lack something of the essential dark, demonic element. Nevertheless, this is a profoundly thoughtful and penetrating interpretation. From the opening "Die Frist ist um," one is drawn into the inner world of this wanderer's torment. It is not a demonstrative, melodramatic display, but a deeply felt plea from the heart. Under Solti's direction, Janis Martin takes Senta's Ballad faster than usual: the two-in-a-bar goes with quite a swing and works well, as the extra momentum adds atmosphere to the account of the wretched mariner. It also relieves the strain on the voice which is sensed in the slower performances, making it less of an ordeal for both singer and audience. But alas, Martin fails to capture the imagination with this reading: it could be just another everyday bit of gossip—hardly a visionary experience of identification. She is at her best in the Act II duet with Bailey, where as she sings of the Dutchman's "leidenvollen Zügen" (sorrowful features) and the pain in her heart, she is very moving. In the slow opening of the duet, each singer draws out the long lines with real feeling, and the rest of the number is on a similarly high level.

Solti's treatment of the Act I duet for the Dutchman and Daland as a fast waltz rather nicely points up the latter's venality, as does the jocular dotted accompaniment of the ensuing exchange and the pert, neatly pointed introduction to "Mögst du, mein Kind" (Act II). Unfortunately, in spite of his attractive voice, Martti Talvela doesn't have the requisite lightness of touch and flexibility of line for Daland, and is unable to repeat the success of his account for Klemperer. With René Kollo we have one of the most distinguished Eriks on record—certainly a performance of great style, as one would expect from a notable Siegfried and Parsifal. But Kollo predictably turns his cavatina into a showpiece, which does little for his dramatic credibility. And his dream simply doesn't work at all: Kollo is far too matter-of-fact—no one would listen to his narration with bated breath and, hardly surprisingly, Janis Martin, when she joins in, sounds equally uninvolved.

1981–83 EMI / ANGEL (S,D) ⓒ

Dunja Vejzovic (A), Peter Hofmann (B), José van Dam (C), Kurt Moll (D), Vienna State Opera Chorus, Berlin Philharmonic Orchestra—Herbert von Karajan

This set also boasts a distinguished Erik, and Peter Hofmann's account of the role is one of the recording's greatest assets. However, it is the conductor who lets down the singer, for Karajan's accompaniment to Erik's dream is pretty, but lacking any suspense or mystery. There are other miscalculations from the podium too, such as the overblown symphonic peroration to the Dutchman / Daland number in Act I—quite out of place for this comic duet. Elsewhere Karajan's accompaniment is highly colored and frequently full of telling detail. Perhaps the most successful part of the recording is the Overture, which is searing in its intensity, even if the dynamic range—as throughout the set—is unnaturally and uncomfortably wide. José van Dam's Monologue has at once exceptional power and introspection: one has the sense here not of an operatic declamation projected over the footlights but of a personal soliloquy. Later on, this restraint becomes less convincing, suggesting that van Dam's ability to impersonate the hell-driven voyager is limited.

Daland is the sort of character Kurt Moll relishes, and Karajan gives him every opportunity to exploit the humor of the music. That leaves only the very disappointing Senta from Dunja Vejzovic. One has little confidence that this young woman would be capable of the visionary inspiration or spiritual conviction needed to motivate Senta's ultimate act of self-sacrifice. Her Act II duet with the Dutchman opens at an absurdly slow tempo: rapt self-absorption may be the name of the game, but this is pure narcissism, and the supreme control of line such breadth calls for is quite beyond Vejzovic (as is embarrassingly revealed at the first climax). Dunja Vejzovic's woeful inadequacies prevent any serious consideration of the duet; this was not her finest hour.

1985 PHILIPS (S,D,P) ⓒ

Lisbeth Balslev (A), Robert Schunk (B), Simon Estes (C), Matti Salminen (D), Chorus, Supplementary Chorus, and Orchestra of the Bayreuth Festival—Woldemar Nelsson

This set is the musical component of the electrifying production directed by Harry Kupfer at Bayreuth (1978–85). The recording was made in the last year of the production, by which time Woldemar Nelsson had conducted it for four seasons. The staging makes its impact on the recording in a negative sense in that there is quite a lot of clattering and banging, most distractingly in the silences punctuating the final chords of the work. But the positive side is that the performance is as gripping as in the theater. The Overture is one of the finest on records in its combination of atmosphere (though not as somber as Klemperer) and excellence of execution. Nelsson shapes the swirling of the waves extremely well, and the clarity of the digital recording enhances the sharpness of impact. The Act III choral confrontation, with its steadily increasing momentum, is tremendously exciting, making the traditional side-break on LP more infuriating than ever. However, after the appearance of the ghostly crew, things build up very dramatically again. The Bayreuth chorus is at its dependable best, not least in the Spinning Chorus, where the laughing and chattering of the women is so often risibly unsatisfactory.

Simon Estes's Dutchman is magnificently burnished in tone and forcefully projected. The Monologue is strongly accompanied by Nelsson and the orchestral playing and sound quality unsurpassed. But for all that, Estes never really gets under the skin of the character; the sound is glorious, but the anguish unreal. Lisbeth Balslev's reliable, steady-toned Senta is, on the other hand, totally involving (as, indeed, was demanded by the stage production, which revolved around her). Thanks in no small measure to Nelsson's pacing, taut control, and expressivity of orchestral detail, the Act II duet for Senta and the Dutchman is very successful, indeed quite riveting. The reservation about Estes remains, but it is a less crucial shortcoming here than in the Monologue. There is more than a hint of (unintentional) parody in Anny Schlemm's scolding as Mary, but Matti Salminen's Daland is a marvelous realization of the character by vocal means alone, and Robert Schunk's Erik is delivered with both ardor and plasticity of phrasing. In the sharpness and immediacy of the recording, and the high standard of the conducting and much of the singing, this modern set will be difficult to better. Only the vacuum where the agony of the suffering Dutchman should be—and it's a pretty significant vacuum—stands in the way of an unconditional recommendation.

————————

In terms of sonic and musical values, and for the excellence of its conducting, the modern Nelsson recording is consistently outstanding. But the Dutchman's tormented and demonic qualities are better conveyed by Hotter (for Krauss), Uhde (for Keilberth), Crass (for Sawallisch), and Bailey (for Solti).

BARRY MILLINGTON

RICHARD WAGNER

TANNHÄUSER (1845)

A: Elisabeth (s); B: Venus (s); C: Tannhäuser (t);
D: Wolfram (bar); E: Landgrave Hermann (bs)

The Wagner *Werk-Verzeichnis* identifies four "stages" of the development of *Tannhäuser*, of which the second and fourth correspond respectively to the versions traditionally known as "Dresden" and "Paris." Since these versions are actually the editions of 1860 and 1875, the labels are a trifle misleading, but will doubtless continue to be used—as here—on account of their familiarity and convenience. Of the recordings under consideration, Schröder, Heger, Konwitschny, Gerdes, and Haitink use Dresden; Elmendorff, Leinsdorf (both with cuts), Solti, and Sinopoli Paris; and Sawallisch Dresden with a Paris opening. The cuts often made in Act II (notably in the duet and the final ensemble) are not made by Heger, Konwitschny, Gerdes, Solti, Haitink, or Sinopoli.

1930 EMI / ANGEL (M,P)

Maria Müller (A), Ruth Jost-Arden (B), Sigismund Pilinsky (C), Herbert Janssen (D), Ivar Andrésen (E), Chorus and Orchestra of the Bayreuth Festival—Karl Elmendorff

Siegfried Wagner's new production of *Tannhäuser* at the Bayreuth Festival in 1930 was conducted by Arturo Toscanini—a historic occasion since Toscanini was the first non-German to appear on the rostrum there. It was actually Karl Elmendorff, the conductor of that year's *Ring*, who took over the forces for this recording, but Toscanini's spirit is not far away. Even on the original 78s, the clarity of sound is remarkable, and the instrumental detail exploited to project the drama powerfully forward (except for the Act I Pilgrims' Chorus, which sounds like a dirge). Although the Paris version is used, it is unfortunately only with savage cuts in the second and third acts. Nor can it be said that Ruth Jost-Arden brings to the extended form of the role of Venus anything like the sophistication of Christa Ludwig for Solti; her voice is pleasant enough, but scarcely voluptuous. Sigismund Pilinsky's short-breathed song to her in Act I conveys little passion or conviction, and his Rome Narration hardly wrings the heart either. Maria Müller's account of Elisabeth's Prayer is shapeless and uninteresting, Ivar Andrésen's Landgrave dour and inflexible. Only Herbert Janssen's artistry as Wolfram stands out on this recording as something special, though personally I find that several of the more modern Wolframs give me more pleasure in terms of tonal production.

1941 MET (M,P)

Kirsten Flagstad (A), Kerstin Thorborg (B), Lauritz Melchior (C), Herbert Janssen (D), Emanuel List (E), Metropolitan Opera Chorus and Orchestra—Erich Leinsdorf

Erich Leinsdorf's performance, also of the Paris version, is similarly disfigured by cuts: in Act I as well as the usual ones in Act II. Leinsdorf's interpretation is far from sensitive: too often things are rushed, with disastrous consequences for the ensemble; the big tune of the Overture is phrased almost one note at a time; and the accompaniment of the Act I duet is stabbed out in dry, *staccato* chords. For some, the presence of Melchior in the title role may prove a sufficient enticement, though not to those of us who find the vocal production, with its intrusive vibrato, unattractive, and the musicality questionable. His Rome Narration is highly characterized—its agonized defiance strongly projected—but with more theatricality than subtlety. It too frequently degenerates into a display of virility, and for my money Melchior is outsung both in beauty of tone and in musical sense by Kerstin Thorborg, who exploits the enhanced sensuality of her Paris-version blandishments to excellent effect. Regrettably her final climactic "Weh! Mir verloren!" is quite inaudible. In Elisabeth's Hall of Song aria (and later her intercession on behalf of Tannhäuser), Kirsten Flagstad displays all her familiar merits (fervency, warmth, humanity) and mannerisms (imprecision of attack). Her reading of the aria tends toward the fierce and her top B is wild; the Act II duet (which is abridged) is an unholy scramble. Herbert Janssen, again the Wolfram, spins an elegant line in "Als du in kühnem Sange," but it is spoiled by insensitive accompaniment and by the inability of singer and conductor to coordinate their downbeats.

1950 DEUTSCHE GRAMMOPHON (M)

Trude Eipperle (A), Aga Joesten (B), Günther Treptow (C), Heinrich Schlusnus (D), Otto von Rohr (E), Chorus and Symphony Orchestra of Hessian Radio—Kurt Schröder

Once again the Wolfram steals the show. On this recording conducted by Kurt Schröder, the part is taken by Heinrich Schlusnus, who immediately brings a sense of calm and dignity to the troubled proceedings. His "Als du in kühnem Sange" is admirable, sung with real beauty of tone, and if the phrasing leaves something to be desired here, he *can* produce an unparalleled *legato* when he chooses. Schlusnus's fine performance is all the more welcome for temporarily blotting out the memory of Günther Treptow in the title role. The tessitura is simply too high for this baritone voice, and

it is constantly under strain. The result, compounded by excessive aspiration, is exceedingly unpleasant: it's a mystery to me why he was given the part. Aga Joesten and Trude Eipperle are both acceptable rather than outstanding; the performance is conducted energetically and with a good sense of style by Schröder.

1951 ACANTA (M,P)

Marianne Schech (A), Margarete Bäumer (B), August Seider (C), Karl Paul (D), Otto von Rohr (E), Chorus and Orchestra of the Bavarian State Opera—Robert Heger

Robert Heger belonged to the old Kapellmeister tradition, which may help to explain why his conducting, on this record at least, is so stolid and uninspired. His direction of the Overture is certainly very different from the steady, unswerving three-in-a-bar of today's performances, but in trying to achieve its effect— and it is not clear precisely what effect is intended—it sounds merely effortful and labored. When Heger tries to make a decisive statement, it often sounds merely misjudged, if not grotesque. His inflated Dresden "Amens" in the Act III Prelude are one example. Another is in the Tannhäuser / Venus scene of Act I, which is very deliberate but to plodding effect: the accents are not used to generate dramatic tension. It doesn't much help that the Bavarian strings are so scrawny and ill-tuned, or that the chorus sounds superannuated. The sirens conjure up an impression less of nymphs than of wobbly old crones, while the later chant of Elder Pilgrims sounds like that of a band of geriatrics.

The Tannhäuser, August Seider, was from Dresden, as were many singers at Munich in the early fifties; Marianne Schech (Elisabeth) and Karl Paul (Wolfram) had similarly distinguished themselves in prewar Dresden. Seider is at his best in the Rome Narration, where his singing has considerable emotional force without undue sacrifice in terms of tonal beauty. Elsewhere he can sound harsh, and his repeated pleas to Venus (Act I)—"O Königin! Göttin! Lass mich ziehn!"—rate high on the decibel count, yet lack true intensity or urgency. His

Venus, Margaret Bäumer, has a degree more warmth and is competent if uninvolving; in the final moments of the work she is squally. Marianne Schech (Elisabeth) sings with some energy, though not a great deal of variety in tonal color. Her voice is straight, with no irritating mannerisms, but her climactic top B in the Hall of Song aria is ugly and unfocused, and her Act III Prayer fails to make much impact. Things look up briefly in the Act II duet with Seider: a few sparks fly and for a while it sounds like a real performance. One virtue of the recording is that Munich was able to cast its minstrels from strength: Karl Paul was also from prewar Dresden, and Franz Klarwein (Walther) and Karl Ostertag (Heinrich) were experienced tenors from the Krauss era. All acquit themselves admirably.

1960 EMI / ANGEL (S) CD

Elisabeth Grümmer (A), Marianne Schech (B), Hans Hopf (C), Dietrich Fischer-Dieskau (D), Gottlob Frick (E), Chorus and Orchestra of the Deutsche Staatsoper, Berlin—Franz Konwitschny

Hans Hopf's performance in the title role for Konwitschny—like that of Günther Treptow for Schröder—is effortful and rife with unattractive aspirates. Indeed, he fails to be convincing in a single bar from beginning to end: this is simply not a suitable role for his voice (again like Treptow, his baritone-colored timbre is not an asset here). The Act I duet with Venus never takes fire: Hopf is dull, labored, and clumsy in his articulation; Marianne Schech is plain and unseductive. The second act begins with a splendid orchestral opening to the Hall of Song aria, and Elisabeth Grümmer's rendering has an affecting virginal quality which is continued into the duet with Tannhäuser—though even Grümmer cannot quite redeem the performance from Hopf's dismal inadequacies.

Fortunately the recording does have some saving graces. These begin to be evident at the arrival of the Landgrave and the minstrels (Act I, Scene 4). Gottlob Frick as the former is in opulent voice and his authority and feeling for musical expression are never in doubt. Even

more outstanding is the Wolfram of a youthful-sounding Dietrich Fischer-Dieskau (he was then aged thirty-six). The inimitable artistry with which the lieder singer molds his lines makes for an account of exquisite subtlety. Fritz Wunderlich's Walther is also quite stylishly done and Rudolf Gonszar's Biterolf deserves a mention, but it is Fischer-Dieskau and Frick who carry the day.

Konwitschny's interpretation is an interesting one. His idea of Venusberg is not as red-blooded as some, the venereal delights being portrayed as sweet and delicate rather than unremittingly orgiastic. The dramatic climax to Act II—when the knights and minstrels round on Tannhäuser—is lacking in bite, and in general this is a somewhat restrained performance. In an opera about extremes of feeling, it is doubtful whether restraint is an entirely appropriate quality.

1962 PHILIPS (S,P) CD

Anja Silja (A), Grace Bumbry (B), Wolfgang Windgassen (C), Eberhard Wächter (D), Josef Greindl (E), Chorus and Orchestra of the Bayreuth Festival—Wolfgang Sawallisch

In his productions of *Tannhäuser* at Bayreuth in 1954 and 1961, Wieland Wagner attempted to solve the problem of stylistic inconsistency between the Dresden and Paris versions by experimenting with a hybrid edition. Opening with the Overture linked to extended Venusberg music (as per Paris), he returned to the Dresden version in Scene 2. This practice is not objectionable, but hardly solves the problem of stylistic inconsistency: it simply brings the shift forward to the beginning of Scene 2. In other words, the post-*Tristan* Venus music of Scene 2 is sacrificed, but not that of the ballet in Scene 1. There are a few other minor tinkerings with the score, to unclear purpose.

Given her limited role in what is basically the Dresden version, Grace Bumbry makes a brilliant impression, singing with style and distinction. Her victim, Wolfgang Windgassen, cannot match such artistry. He has very little sense of line and his pleas to her are chopped up into little snatches of phrase, breathless and ragged. Windgassen is much better in the Rome

Narration, where he dramatizes the situation by means of a vast range of tone color and expression. He makes us feel the harshness of the road ("sucht' ich Dorn und Stein") and spits out his disgust; his recollection of Rome and its pieties even brings forth a snarl, but he also manages more even-toned singing here than anywhere else on the recording. Nevertheless, one feels he could have been given a lesson or two in how to produce a beautiful line by his friend Wolfram, Eberhard Wächter; indeed, the latter runs Fischer-Dieskau a close second in this role. Gerhard Stolze's Walther penetrates the vocal ensembles with his characteristic pinched tone, sounding as if Mime has wandered in from another opera—which in a sense he has. Josef Greindl's Landgrave is no more than acceptable, but he does introduce some variety, even mystery, into his announcement in Act II. An interesting feature of the Act II ensemble is that all the voices accompany Tannhäuser at "Zum Heil den Sündigen zu führen" (as originally intended by Wagner) and to some considerable climactic effect. Tannhäuser's outburst of remorse, "Weh! Weh mir Unglücksel'gem!," is also affecting.

It is unfortunate that even when Windgassen is at his best—notably in the Rome Narration—Sawallisch doesn't rise to the occasion with him. His conducting of that passage—and, regrettably, this applies to most of the performance—is uninspired. While less prosaic and less rushed than, say, Gerdes (see below), Sawallisch rarely shows anything in a new light or offers any unexpected touches of beauty. This is a particular disappointment in view of his fine contemporaneous *Holländer* and *Lohengrin* recordings, and indeed his magnificent interpretation of the *Ring* in Munich more recently.

1968–69 DEUTSCHE GRAMMOPHON (S)

Birgit Nilsson (A, B), Wolfgang Windgassen (C), Dietrich Fischer-Dieskau (D), Theo Adam (E), Chorus and Orchestra of the Deutsche Oper, Berlin—Otto Gerdes

Windgassen is heard again in the Gerdes performance—now even nearer the end of his career and even less comfortable in the role

than before. His singing is coarse and imprecise almost throughout: at its worst when displaying a raw, ragged edge at the repeated cries of "Erbarm' dich mein!," once again at its best in the Rome Narration, where initial restraint gives way to rising bitterness. Birgit Nilsson, as both Venus and Elisabeth, is as always commanding. Her sterling Nordic qualities may not be ideal for the latter role: there is little hint of vulnerability and I hear no tingle of expectation in her Hall of Song aria. Even so, her very stylishness in drawing out a line in the following scene with Tannhäuser is winning, though the duet itself is ruined by Windgassen's unbelievably vulgar singing.

Dietrich Fischer-Dieskau returns as Wolfram and sings Windgassen—and indeed everyone else—right off the stage, with a warm and beautifully modulated line in all his solos. There is a magical moment of rapt contemplation of the stars in "Blick' ich umher," at the words "Da blick' ich auf zu einem nur der Sterne," which forms a wonderful contrast with the sincerity and fervor of the peroration. With touches like this, Fischer-Dieskau transforms the character out of his usual blandness. Theo Adam is a forceful but reliable Landgrave. Otto Gerdes's interpretation is on the whole uninvolving, to the point of being perfunctory; too much detail is glossed over. His accompaniment of the Act II duet, however, is vibrant, even if the ensuing Wartburg processional chorus is rather businesslike. The Berlin orchestra and choral forces are generally dependable.

1970 DECCA / LONDON (S) CD

Helga Dernesch (A), Christa Ludwig (B), René Kollo (C), Victor Braun (D), Hans Sotin (E), Vienna State Opera Chorus, Vienna Boys' Choir, and Vienna Philharmonic Orchestra—Georg Solti

So superior is the music of the Paris version—with its sophisticated orchestral fabric masking the four-square periods, and its deepening of the characterization of Venus—that it is astonishing that nobody until Solti in 1971 had committed it to disc (in its entirety), even though it was familiar in many houses. Decca's excellent recording, with Solti and his Vienna forces in top form, set new standards for this work, which were not to be challenged until EMI's version (Dresden) under Haitink fourteen years later.

Admittedly the competition has not been great, but René Kollo's Tannhäuser is quite simply the best on records to date. Onstage in this role Kollo has sometimes sounded stretched and inclined to rant. But here the testing tessitura of the Hymn to Venus generates an intensity which for once suggests the anguish of the dramatic situation rather than that of a tenor in acute discomfort. Despite a tendency to aspirate, Kollo is again trenchantly dramatic in the Rome Narration, spitting out his loathing with tremendous force. Christa Ludwig seizes her chance in the developed version of the role of Venus, with as alluring and sensual an account as one could ever hope for. "Tristanesque" is the usual description of the Parisian music, but time and again, especially with this fine interpreter of that role, it is the blandishments of Kundry that hang seductively in the air. Helga Dernesch's Elisabeth is somewhat effortful in her Hall of Song aria: vigorous rather than virginal. Some may find the beat in her voice intrusive, the tone unattractive; others will admire the intelligence and sincerity of her singing. Her somewhat plangent voice is more suited to her Act III Prayer, which is projected with conviction if not surpassing beauty. Hans Sotin, at his peak in the 1970s, is in good shape as the Landgrave, though his line is not as finely molded as such a glorious voice deserves. As Wolfram, Victor Braun's sensitivity to the words is spoiled by an unpleasant beat in the voice, which may account for the impression that he is constantly sharp.

The conducting bears the characteristic Solti hallmarks: raw vigor, breathlessness, and a certain superficiality—the last, however, not so serious a deficiency in a relatively immature work like *Tannhäuser*. The Viennese chorus and orchestra are superb throughout, and contribute in large measure to the success of the recording. Many passages are unequaled on any rival set: the exuberance of the knights welcoming back Tannhäuser (end of Act I) with whooping hunting horns; the fervor of the Act II duet for Tannhäuser and Elisabeth, preceded by a palpable veil of oblivion as Tannhäuser wrestles with his recollection of the past, "Fern von hier, in weiten, weiten Landen"; and, at the end of the opera, a gripping struggle over Tannhäuser's soul between Wolfram and Venus.

The evocative atmosphere of the recording is also first-rate. All in all, this is a highly commendable achievement.

1985 EMI / ANGEL (S,D) CD

Lucia Popp (A), Waltraud Meier (B), Klaus König (C), Bernd Weikl (D), Kurt Moll (E), Chorus and Symphony Orchestra of Bavarian Radio—Bernard Haitink

The rival EMI version under Haitink did not appear until 1985, but it was worth waiting for: the recording quality is of the highest order, the orchestral playing and choral singing of the Bavarian Radio forces first-rate, and the technical control and interpretive perception of Haitink superior to that of Solti. Haitink is as impressive in the massed-rank public scenes as in the intimate character confrontations. He keeps the action moving along—one is never conscious of its dragging—yet he is able to provide his soloists with the perfect backdrop for their more reflective passages. The rhythms of the Act II March (arrival of the guests) are well pointed, the triplets being given in a sprightly *staccato*, which makes a fine contrast with the ample phrasing of the broad *legato* melody.

Unfortunately, Haitink's Tannhäuser and Venus are inferior to Solti's. Line and phrasing are not Klaus König's strong suit, nor, in his Hymn to Venus, does he sound as passionately concerned about his subject as his words suggest. He is at his best in the Rome Narration, which has a dramatic urgency but with the contrasting emotions well modulated as the story of the journey unfolds. The climax of the Pope's pronouncement is disappointing, however, as König rushes instead of savoring the rhetorical moment. Waltraud Meier makes a much better impression in the theater than on records; here her tone is uningratiating and unalluring—a fatal flaw in a Venus. Lucia Popp's Elisabeth, on the other hand, is magnificent, sung with immense intelligence and touching sensitivity. In the lead-up to the Act II duet, her "O helfet mir" expresses the awakening of new emotions, while "die Freude zog aus meinem Herzen" a little later conveys a world of departed joy. Her intercession for Tannhäuser as the crowd rounds on him is utterly convincing: enough to win over the heart of the crustiest knight. Her Act III Prayer is also beautifully done: quietly intense and imbued with spiritual fervor. Bernd Weikl injects more passion than usual into Wolfram's "War's Zauber, war es reine Macht" (not inappropriately: he *is* urging Tannhäuser to return, after all). His "Blick' ich umher" is sung with artistry and feeling, while his anguished sympathy for Elisabeth's suffering (beginning of Act III, Scene 1) is superbly conveyed.

A recording, then, of mixed soloistic virtues, but with splendid conducting and choral singing: the Pilgrims' Chant rings in the ears for a long time after.

1989 DEUTSCHE GRAMMOPHON (S,D) CD

Cheryl Studer (A), Agnes Baltsa (B), Plácido Domingo (C), Andreas Schmidt (D), Matti Salminen (E), Chorus of the Royal Opera House, Covent Garden, Philharmonia Orchestra—Giuseppe Sinopoli

The packaging of this set says it all: in the cover photograph, Plácido Domingo, furrowed of brow and dressed in pseudo-medieval minstrel's outfit, clutches a harp while striking an unconvincing dramatic attitude. Domingo, of course, has never sung the part onstage, and the recording is as artificial in inspiration as the minstrel's gear. The thinking behind the casting of Domingo as Tannhäuser, as of Baltsa as Venus, has nothing to do with artistic considerations, everything to do with commercial ones. In the circumstances it is surprising that the set is as successful as it is, but it scarcely sweeps the board as the finest modern recording of the Paris version in the way it should.

Domingo never sings less than beautifully, and in this cruelly demanding role it is remarkable that he can manage the entire part without any sense of strain. Unfortunately, this is also his weakness: where is the agony, the suffering of this tormented character? He does succeed in roughening his voice for Act III, Scene 3—the introduction to the Rome Narration—and the Narration itself is infinitely better: almost for the first time one is conscious of the singer being inside the part. However, he misses the sequence of dramatic dualisms in this section: both König and Kollo spit out their defiance more convincingly. Domingo's cries of "Erbarm dich mein!" at the climax of Act II are similarly impeccably vocalized but with little sense of anguish.

Baltsa *does* have a streak of iron in her voice, and even if the occasional syllable is lashed rather unpleasantly, it all adds up to a more involving interpretation than Domingo's. Cheryl Studer's Elisabeth is, on the other hand, an unmitigated success. In the Hall of Song aria and the Act II duet she is both responsive to the text and in full technical command. She conveys a deep sense of melancholy as she tells Tannhäuser of her loneliness in his absence, and later in the act her intercession is beautifully controlled and most moving. Her Prayer is taken a shade faster than usual, but singer and conductor use the extra pace to suggest fervency, and the pleading in Studer's molding of phrases melts the heart.

As Wolfram, Andreas Schmidt's lovely voice is used with great sensitivity in each of his solos; by any normal standards a fine performance, though not quite on the elevated level of Fischer-Dieskau's or Wächter's.

Sinopoli's reading came under heavy fire from some quarters for the supposed willfulness of his approach, particularly as expressed in constant changes of tempo. But his approach does not seem to me to be out of character with the work in question: *Tannhäuser* is, after all, an exploration of the extremes of human experience. Certainly the touch of hysteria in the Bacchanale does not seem at all inappropriate. If anything, the tension at high points needs to be screwed up a notch or two: the final struggle over Tannhäuser's soul doesn't bear the whole weight of the drama as it needs to. The singing of the Royal Opera House Chorus is reliable. The recorded sound is good, but the dynamic range uncomfortably wide.

In sum, this is a frequently enjoyable set, but one which falls short of "definitive" status.

Solti's recording of the Paris version boasts the best Tannhäuser and Venus in Kollo and Ludwig. Haitink's is more perceptively conducted and more skillfully paced, with Popp an outstanding Elisabeth.

BARRY MILLINGTON

RICHARD WAGNER

LOHENGRIN (1850)

A: Elsa (s); B: Ortrud (ms); C: Lohengrin (t);
D: Telramund (bar); E: Heinrich (bs)

*L*ohengrin poses specific problems in performance. The title role calls not only for a *Heldentenor* with staying power, and the ability to dominate large public scenes, but also a singer of sensitivity for the intimate bridal-chamber scene. The conductor must similarly be able to integrate the public and private spheres, while much of the success of the former also depends on clean, firm chorus work. Unlike *Der Fliegende Holländer* and *Tannhäuser* there are no alternative editions, but there is the matter of cuts. In the theater, it is still regrettably common for part of the double male-voice chorus in "Früh'n versammelt uns der Ruf" (Act II) to be chopped, in spite of its imaginative antiphony; on records, only Sawallisch makes this cut. However, the other, more serious, traditional cut, after Lohengrin's Narration in Act II (from Elsa's swoon to "Der Schwan!"), is taken by Heger, Kempe (1952), Schüchter, Swarowsky, and Nelsson (at Bayreuth!), as well as Sawallisch. This cut—which in any case saves but a few minutes—is particularly damaging since it gives Elsa no chance to express remorse.

1942 PREISER (M,P)

Maria Müller (A), Margarete Klose (B), Franz Völker (C), Jaro Prohaska (D), Ludwig Hofmann (E), German State Opera Chorus, Berlin, Berlin State Orchestra—Robert Heger

Heger shapes the opening Prelude rather nicely (a vast improvement on his *Tannhäuser*), but alas the appearance of the cast is an unpleasant shock. Walther Grossmann's Herald and Ludwig Hofmann's Heinrich are both distinctly rough, and the latter's Prayer is painfully ill-tuned and undisciplined. No one could accuse Franz Völker of turning in a routine performance in the title role here, but to modern ears the vocal gesturing may well sound overemphatic. Jaro Prohaska's self-pity is similarly over the top in Telramund's Act II solo. Margarete Klose alone is convincing—as formidable an Ortrud as in the two subsequent recordings she made. The tuning and ensemble of the chorus are so embarrassingly approximate, the onstage trumpets so barbaric, and the whole sound so full of tonal distortions that the set can only be listened to as a historical document.

1952 ACANTA (M)

Marianne Schech (A), Margarete Klose (B), George Vincent (C), Andreas Boehm (D), Kurt Böhme (E), Chorus and Orchestra of the Bavarian State Opera—Rudolf Kempe

This is the first, and less satisfactory, of Kempe's two recordings. Largely owing to the primitive recorded sound, the Prelude is not the only passage to lack atmosphere, while nearly all the cast suffer from terminal wobble syndrome. For all that Richard Strauss considered him "the best Baron Ochs in the world," Kurt Böhme, with his plodding assertiveness in the rallying of his troops, sounds like a pantomime king. This lack of subtlety (combined with a bad vibrato) makes his Prayer an excruciating experience. George Vincent was, in fact, a stand-in for August Seider, the tenor originally intended for the title role when the recording was initiated in the late 1940s. Vincent never enjoyed the status of an international star, but he is sometimes capable of conveying more than those who did: he has some very good moments, notably in his Act III bridal-chamber duet with Elsa. Marianne Schech in the latter role suffers not only from acute wobble but also from a habit of hitting the note from below. However, her two interjections into Ortrud's hypocritically "friendly" warning ("Wie meinst du?" and "Welch' Unheil?") are superbly done: the first artless, the second bearing a dim intimation of dread. The duet shortly after this ("Ha! Dieser Stolz") is difficult to characterize because the music for Elsa and Ortrud is so similar. But these two manage it—Schech with her simple, trusting piety, Klose baleful and menacing—better than any rivals except those on Kempe's later recording. Klose is frequently mannered but undeniably powerful, both in this scene with Elsa and in that with Telramund; she and Andreas Boehm are the most effective singers in the set.

1953 DEUTSCHE GRAMMOPHON (M)

Annelies Kupper (A), Helena Braun (B), Lorenz Fehenberger (C), Ferdinand Frantz (D), Otto von Rohr (E), Chorus and Orchestra of Bavarian Radio—Eugen Jochum

Eugen Jochum keeps the music on the move, imparting an urgency to the proceedings, and showing much in a new light. His Lohengrin, Lorenz Fehenberger, has a pleasant tone and uses his voice with sensitivity, especially in the bridal-chamber duet, where he proves capable of eloquent expression. His fervent outburst in Act I, "Elsa! Ich liebe dich!," for once sounds as if it is really meant: the top A is given a long *crescendo,* and the following phrase (marked in the score with a pause) arrestingly drawn out. It is a marvelously still moment in the midst of the hurly-burly of the drama. The object of his adoration, Annelies Kupper, has many fine assets, not least her sense of line and steadiness of tone;

there is also an unaffected quality that makes her portrayal credible. Lohengrin's arrival in Act I fails to make much impact, largely due to the inadequacy of the chorus and recording quality. Ferdinand Frantz's Telramund is animated but hardly seems motivated by the progress of the drama or by the darkness of the character he is portraying. Helena Braun's Ortrud, on the other hand, does have a degree of dramatic presence, and although she has to distort her tone somewhat to produce the requisite pagan scorn, it is by no means a negligible portrayal. Otto von Rohr as Heinrich has an avuncular quality that serves him well in his exchanges with Elsa.

1953 EMI / ANGEL (M)

Maud Cunitz (A), Margarete Klose (B), Rudolf Schock (C), Josef Metternich (D), Gottlob Frick (E), Male Chorus of Northwest German Radio, Cologne, and Chorus and Symphony Orchestra of Northwest German Radio, Hamburg—Wilhelm Schüchter

This set, the second of three from the same year, is a very fine one indeed, from the point of view of both conductor and principals. Schüchter is constantly alive to the drama of the situation and in Act II, Scene 1, for example, he matches Telramund's outburst of bitter anger note for note, cutting deep into the sixteenth notes. But he is capable of tenderness too, and makes the brief lyrical efflorescence—as the King blesses Lohengrin and Elsa after their wedding—exceptionally moving. Gottlob Frick, who plays Heinrich, is more secure on top than he is in the later Kempe recording, and he puts the stamp of unmistakable authority on the proceedings, particularly with his Prayer. If in the public scenes one is tempted to suggest that Rudolf Schock delivers his lines with more passion than subtlety, he is always more than adequate, and in the bridal-chamber duet his warmth colors a well-molded line. Maud Cunitz, whose power in the higher register never tempts her to sacrifice tonal beauty, partners him well enough in that scene. For Schüchter, Margarete Klose produces the finest of her three interpretations of Ortrud. She is no longer mannered (as for Kempe) and again pulls no punches: it is a terrifyingly intense performance, not least in her big scene with Telramund (Act II, Scene 1), where, in conjunction with her vocal partner and the conductor, she evokes a chilling atmosphere of conspiracy. Josef Metternich's Telramund is one of the strongest on records: the character's murderous ruthlessness is projected with quite formidable power.

1953 DECCA / LONDON (M,P)

Eleanor Steber (A), Astrid Varnay (B), Wolfgang Windgassen (C), Hermann Uhde (D), Josef Greindl (E), Chorus and Orchestra of the Bayreuth Festival—Joseph Keilberth

The Telramund / Ortrud scene is also one of the highlights of the performance under Keilberth recorded at the Bayreuth Festival that same year. Astrid Varnay (previously an Elsa) is frightening in her vehemence, while Hermann Uhde convincingly charts his character's progression from doubt, through horror, to merciless determination. Wolfgang Windgassen and Eleanor Steber in the leading roles are more variable. Steber, to her credit, conveys a sense of being entirely withdrawn into her own world and fantasies. Pledging herself to Lohengrin in Act I, she produces a beautiful *piano* top A on "Mein Erlöser" (there's not too much of this sort of thing from Windgassen), and time and again shows imagination in the molding of her line and in the varying of dynamics—a refinement spurned by too many Wagner singers. Right from the start, in his farewell to the swan, Windgassen plays havoc with the notated rhythms (contrary to Wagner's explicit instruction that singers should follow the notated meters precisely). Keilberth's drawn-out phrasing in the bridal-chamber duet is ineffably tender, and Windgassen devotees may find a corresponding subtlety in his delivery—indeed, there is more flexibility here than in his public utterances—but I find Steber far more musical and moving. Windgassen comes into his own in the latter stages, however. His Narration is very thoughtful and actually sounds like an account of otherworldly affairs and destiny-filled events—not just a star tenor proving his virility. As Heinrich,

Josef Greindl sings with authority, but he's rather too solid and unyielding, and some notes are hit more securely than others. His singing of the Prayer is not very agreeable, though it is vitiated by the recorded sound, whose dynamic level lurches up and down. Toward the end of the opera his voice is so remote that his repeated interjections of "Weh!" are virtually inaudible. Keilberth's conducting of the Act I Prelude has a gravity and a radiance that shine through the scrawny string playing and thin sound quality. A crass side change (2 / 3) pulls up the music mid-phrase, indeed mid-note; 8 / 9 is scarcely any better.

1962–63 EMI / ANGEL (S) CD

Elisabeth Grümmer (A), Christa Ludwig (B), Jess Thomas (C), Dietrich Fischer-Dieskau (D), Gottlob Frick (E), Chorus of the Vienna State Opera, Vienna Philharmonic Orchestra—Rudolf Kempe

Kempe's second recording of *Lohengrin* remains, in several respects, unsurpassed to the present day. With the aid of the Vienna Philharmonic and an infinitely superior recording quality in the later set, Kempe gets the work under way with a glorious Prelude. The standard of playing and the sound are still, admittedly, inferior to those of the modern Solti recording (with the same orchestra), but I find the touch of ruggedness more appropriate to the barbaric medieval setting than the smoothness of Solti or Karajan. Kempe's strong rhythmic articulation of the chorus work in Act I gives it an admirable sense of propulsion, while the tension of the big Ortrud / Telramund scene in Act II is superbly transmitted. Jess Thomas's portrayal of the title role is a sensitive one: no extravagant heroics, but confident in its own inner strength. The Act III duet begins with a wonderful sense of calmness and bliss, the whispered intimacies of the couple sharing their brief moment of happiness almost unbearably poignant. No other recording captures this fragile moment so perfectly. As Elsa's doubts obtrude, Kempe steers the duet through, with tight control of the accumulating drama, to its painful conclusion. Lohengrin's Farewell is genuinely touching. Elisabeth Grümmer's line may not have the smoothness of Tomowa-Sintow (Karajan) or the sophistication of Norman (Solti), but her reading glows with conviction and pulsates with virginal passion. Like Steber, she produces a marvelously floated *piano* top A at "Mein Erlöser"; this whole passage encapsulates Grümmer's interpretation, which is of a devotion at once intense and delicate.

The pair of villains are in no way inferior. Indeed, Fischer-Dieskau's Telramund has scarcely been bettered. The lieder-singer's precision of detail is used to project the character's vehemence with maximum force, and his indignation—real or hypocritically feigned—is depicted with blazing conviction. Christa Ludwig's Ortrud is likewise in a class of its own: for its combination of characterization with sheer musicality it has, to my mind, no rival on disc. She presents a formidable enemy, twisting and turning mid-phrase as she seizes her advantage. Her delivery of the line "Ha, wie tödlich du mich kränkst!" (marked "with suppressed rage") in her scene with Telramund is just one example of a remarkable reading: no one matches the scorn with which she is able to invest this short, pregnant phrase.

The cast is completed by Otto Wiener, who is by no means the strongest Herald on disc but perfectly acceptable, and Gottlob Frick as Heinrich. The latter's opening address is more compelling than usual, if not very securely sung; indeed, Frick's high notes are a frequent cause for concern and he makes a meal of the Prayer.

1962 PHILIPS (S,P)

Anja Silja (A), Astrid Varnay (B), Jess Thomas (C), Ramón Vinay (D), Franz Crass (E), Chorus and Orchestra of the Bayreuth Festival—Wolfgang Sawallisch

This performance, recorded at the 1962 Bayreuth Festival, allows us to hear Jess Thomas's sympathetic interpretation again, but in a live performance. For once, in the bridal-chamber duet, we get a real impression of an intimate love scene; the singing here is characterized by languorous beauty rather than ardor—a wel-

come change from the all-too-common *Heldentenor* rant into an auditorium or studio. As the scene develops and Elsa's questioning becomes more urgent, the drama and tension are well handled, the sense of live performance potent. Thomas's Narration truly sounds as though he were conjuring up a vision of far-off places and events. As he tells of the descent of the dove, the atmosphere is rapt, but two phrases later his pride in the announcement of the Grail elicits a ringing tone. It is this variety of tone and shifting of pace that make his story-telling so compelling. Anja Silja is equally impressive from the moment of her abstracted entry, her voice glowing with expectation as the combat is proposed. Her open, ingenuous delivery has none of the asperities and inelegancies of her Senta for the same conductor the previous year. Ramón Vinay began his career as a baritone, and after a run of tenor roles including Tannhäuser, Tristan, Siegmund, and Parsifal, returned to baritone roles with this Telramund. His acceptance of Ortrud's suggestion that he has been duped (Act II, Scene 1) brings forth a ferocious intensity and bitterness, in which he is strongly supported by Sawallisch. Ortrud is admirably sung by Astrid Varnay; her tone and address are perfect, and she is entirely convincing in the role. Franz Crass and Tom Krause are both firm and true as Heinrich and the Herald.

The Act I Prelude is marred by audience participation, but Sawallisch's is a sublime account. One is continually aware of his sensitivity to the vocal lines, as in his accompaniment to Telramund's opening accusation, and he draws out solo woodwind lines very beautifully—for example, at Elsa's approach on the balcony. Wilhelm Pitz's chorus, absolutely secure and very exciting, is used most effectively by Sawallisch in the Act I finale, where the polyphony unfolds powerfully. In addition to the regrettably common cuts mentioned above, and doubtless in keeping with postwar German sensibilities, eighteen bars are snipped from Heinrich's jingoistic address to the Brabantines (Act III, Scene 3) and the reference at the end to Gottfried as "Führer" is changed to "Schützer" (protector).

1965 RCA / BMG (S)

Lucine Amara (A), Rita Gorr (B), Sándor Kónya (C), William Dooley (D), Jerome Hines (E), Boston Chorus Pro Musica, Boston Symphony Orchestra—Erich Leinsdorf

The most notable feature about Leinsdorf's recording is that it restores the second part of Lohengrin's Narration, a cut suggested, indeed insisted upon, by Wagner himself when the work was first performed in Weimar by Liszt. Lohengrin in the original version had gone on to explain that the knights in Monsalvat had heard Elsa's plea and taken the swan (the spellbound Gottfried) into service: one year's service for the Grail frees a victim from a magic curse. Thus the deleted passage explains Lohengrin's reference shortly after to "one year by your side," after which Elsa would have had Gottfried restored to her. There is also some new music which is worth hearing, but on balance I do not feel inclined to dispute Wagner's subsequent judgment that the extra section has an anticlimactic effect. Leinsdorf's performance of the work has been criticized for its insensitive briskness, but although some of the martial and other ensemble passages are fairly fast, the key solos and duets are if anything leisurely. He lingers lovingly, for example, over the accompaniment to Elsa's music (Act I), occasionally sacrificing momentum, but bringing out much beauty in the score. The Act I Prelude is one of the most deeply felt of all those on offer, though it is perhaps an expression of sensuality rather than spirituality.

The Hungarian tenor Sándor Kónya, well experienced in the role of Lohengrin, which he sang in many performances at Bayreuth, the Met, and Covent Garden, gives a fine account. His tone is gratifying, and in the public scenes he commands without hectoring, while fully exploiting Leinsdorf's sympathetic conducting in the intimate bridal-chamber duet. Lucine Amara sounds rather less happy as Elsa, an acceptable but hardly memorable interpretation. Nor is Rita Gorr fully inside the part of Ortrud, a fact which makes her frequent stridency even less tolerable; the demonic aspect of

this character is no excuse for ugly tone. William Dooley's Telramund is forthright, if without great refinement of style; his Act II, Scene 1, outburst is partly submerged by the undue prominence of the orchestra (a frequent failing in this set). Jerome Hines as Heinrich is similarly too recessed at the beginning, which doesn't improve his already threatened stature. His reading is undistinguished, and his Prayer lumpy, with no sense of line.

1968 WESTMINSTER (S)

Leonore Kirschstein (A), Ruth Hesse (B), Herbert Schachschneider (C), Heinz Imdahl (D), Walter Kreppel (E), Chorus of the Vienna State Opera, South German Philharmonic Orchestra—Hans Swarowsky

This undistinguished performance would be unlikely to win many new admirers for the work. As is well known, *Lohengrin* suffers from a surfeit of 4 / 4 time, but it is not necessary to draw attention to the fact with such a stolid four-in-a-bar: the Act I finale ensemble trudges despondently to its conclusion (though the male choruses of Act II go with more of a swing). Herbert Schachschneider, in the title role, is far too direct—not to say obvious—in his delivery. "Can you not smell the sweet scents?" he gently inquires of Elsa in their intimate duet, but it doesn't sound as if his heart is in it, so prosaic is his line and so inflexible his timbre and rhythm. His Narration could stand as a textbook example of how not to do it: it's poorly paced, uninvolving, the top notes unpleasantly strained and the dotted rhythms unsprung. Leonore Kirschstein as Elsa knows how to sing through a phrase and brings a welcome tonal variety and expression to her singing. Her contribution to the Act III duet demonstrates the resilience of the character that is to effect the couple's tragic downfall; unfortunately even her warmth fails to coax any real intimacy from what sounds like a physically distant as well as emotionally remote bridegroom. Heinz Imdahl's Telramund is strongly sung, while Ruth Hesse's Ortrud, though musically declaimed, lacks the compulsive menace, explicit or disguised, behind every note, that informs the performances of her greatest rivals.

1971 DEUTSCHE GRAMMOPHON (S)

Gundula Janowitz (A), Gwyneth Jones (B), James King (C), Thomas Stewart (D), Karl Ridderbusch (E), Chorus and Symphony Orchestra of Bavarian Radio—Rafael Kubelik

The cast for Kubelik, on the other hand, is strong all round. James King has all the address needed for the swan knight but also the musical intelligence to convey, at his first appearance, the impression that he is from some other plane. In the bridal-chamber duet he finds an ideal blend of ardor and tenderness; his resigned lines following the catastrophe are delivered with real sorrow. The Narration and aftermath are a shade disappointing, though overall King has a good command of the heroic style without any sacrifice in subtlety. His Elsa, Gundula Janowitz, brings a touching quality of naiveté and vulnerability to her Act I ordeal. She sounds as though she were truly reliving her vision, while the similarly rapt male-chorus interspersions, and the dramatic contrast of Heinrich's stern injunctions and Telramund's fierce accusations, together create a convincingly realized scene. Toward the end of Act I, as Elsa acclaims her deliverer, Janowitz sounds just occasionally under pressure; in Act II an impression grows that her continuing remoteness signifies a certain lack of involvement. The bridal-chamber duet, despite the great promise of both voices, cannot be described as the last word on the subject. As for the other couple, Thomas Stewart's Telramund is aptly vehement and threatening, while the biting scorn with which Gwyneth Jones inveighs against her husband and the world finds its mark, provided the listener is not repelled by the inimitable Jones vocal production. Her calls of "Elsa!" in Act II are a weird, rather unpleasantly eerie sound: no wonder Elsa remarks, "How horribly my name resounds through the night!" Karl Ridderbusch's Heinrich is firm in tone and true in intonation. The Bavarian Radio Symphony Orchestra under Kubelik plays

extremely well; if the score's warmest passages haven't quite the succulence of a Karajan, they are nevertheless relished and skillfully paced—the wedding procession likewise. The Act I Prelude is reasonably well done, but its radiance is not quite celestial enough; the less than perfect grading of its climax is partly the fault of the recording, as is the excessively abrupt brass at the appearance of Lohengrin.

1975–81 EMI / ANGEL (S,D) ⊕

Anna Tomowa-Sintow (A), Dunja Vejzovic (B), René Kollo (C), Siegmund Nimsgern (D), Karl Ridderbusch (E), Chorus of the Deutsche Oper, Berlin, Berlin Philharmonic Orchestra—Herbert von Karajan

Karajan's recording is characteristically problematic and paradoxical, with some of the finest orchestral playing and sound quality being put to destructively willful use. Initiated in 1975–76 but, for various reasons, suspended until 1981, the recording is full of technical tricks, giving rise to unnaturally extreme dynamics that demand a corresponding manual dexterity with the volume control from the listener. Even more serious are the problems with the musical interpretation. The opening Prelude is sublimely beautiful. There is a real sense of the mystic descent of the Grail, and the climax is built with an evenness and inevitability that are not found on many rival recordings. Throughout the set, Karajan brings out the subtlety and variety of the orchestration, with the wind choruses perfectly blended and the Berlin strings, of course, impeccable. But the choral interspersions that were so effective in Kubelik's recording here tend to revel in the beauty of sound for its own sake, and one momentarily loses touch with the dramatic situation. Similarly, the Act II acclamations of Lohengrin go with great gusto, though they barely suggest an army saluting its leader. Toward the end of that act, the choral and orchestral sound is ravishing, but the sense entirely lost. The orchestra is used to best advantage in Telramund's outburst in Act II, Scene 1, where Karajan succeeds in making the music sound as dramatically cogent as something out of *Die Walküre*. Siegmund Nimsgern as Telramund is a little rough here, but not inappropriately so, and he certainly has the requisite urgency in the subsequent exchanges with his baleful consort. In fact, this whole scene is gripping—surprising in view of Karajan's elevation of beauty over dramatic truth, and because the Ortrud, Dunja Vejzovic, is by no means the strongest on records (she is overstretched in her cry of vengeance at the end of the work). Regrettably, Karajan's grip begins to slacken after Elsa's balcony appearance, and Ortrud's hypocritical appeal to her, "In ferner Einsamkeit," is absurdly easygoing, with no urgency in the importuning. Much as one can appreciate the desire to avoid the monotonous tread of 4 / 4 in the wedding music later in the act, Karajan's solution is unacceptable. His procession has absolutely no sense of forward momentum: it could be a depiction of a glowing sunset.

Thanks to the ill-prepared entry for the hero in Act I—where Karajan creates a synthetic clamor rather than genuinely theatrical excitement—René Kollo in the title role doesn't get off to a very encouraging start. He then delivers his farewell to the swan in a sickly sentimental half-tone that is all too faithful to the overall style of the set. In the Act III duet he hits enough clean top notes to make one wish he was consistently as good, but here particularly one is conscious of his poor breath support, which results in a pinched tone and weak projection of high-lying phrases. Anna Tomowa-Sintow's Elsa, though a shade too mature for my taste, is, by contrast, one of the most evenly sung. She negotiates the vocal lines far more successfully than Kollo, but perhaps under the Karajan influence, the full sense of the drama is missing: one never really appreciates her predicament. Karl Ridderbusch, as secure a Heinrich as for Kubelik, is by turns kindly and stern to Elsa. In sum, then, this is a set whose positive virtues and potentialities are seriously undermined by Karajan's waywardness.

1982 CBS / SONY (S,P,D) CD

Karan Armstrong (A), Elizabeth Connell (B), Peter Hofmann (C), Leif Roar (D), Siegfried

Vogel (E), Chorus and Orchestra of the Bayreuth Festival—Woldemar Nelsson

This recording, made live at the Bayreuth Festival, offers orchestral and choral work of scarcely inferior standard, but without the handicap of Karajan's perversities. The big choral ensembles are superbly done, Nelsson building up the climaxes powerfully. If the jollifications of the Act I finale perhaps lack a little weight, those of Act II, under firmer rhythmic control, are rousing, and the ceremonial music of the last act is similarly excellent. The Prelude to Act I, though not exactly rushed, hasn't quite the spaciousness and luminosity of the finest recordings; however, when the music returns in Elsa's vision, it is refreshingly vital, conveying the excitement of her mystical experience. Karan Armstrong has many of the qualities needed for Elsa, not least a kind of shining innocence in her tone. Sadly, she is not always ideally secure in the upper reaches; in fact, her tuning is frequently suspect and sometimes saved only by her vibrato. Without the visual appeal of his handsome stage appearance, Peter Hofmann in the title role gives a somewhat harsh impression at first, and is inclined to hector; in the Act III duet, however, he finds more warmth and tenderness, and his expressive, well-sustained line finally makes this a praiseworthy performance. Elizabeth Connell, who has subsequently made the transition into the soprano repertory, offers a brighter, lighter tone than is usual for Ortrud. Yet if her command of the high-lying passages is total, she lacks the demonic cutting edge that must convey the sheer nastiness of the character. Leif Roar's Telramund is a bit blustery, but that is not inappropriate. Bernd Weikl's admirable Herald deserves a mention, and if Siegfried Vogel's tone as Heinrich is not quite so well focused, it is nevertheless perfectly acceptable.

1986 DECCA / LONDON (S,D) CD

Jessye Norman (A), Eva Randová (B), Plácido Domingo (C), Siegmund Nimsgern (D), Hans Sotin (E), Chorus of the Vienna State Opera, Vienna Philharmonic Orchestra—Georg Solti

And so to the most recent recording, which bids fair to sweep the board, though, in spite of many solid virtues, ultimately falls just short of the requirements for an unqualified recommendation. The finely controlled ebb and flow of the Act I Prelude promise well and the arrival of Lohengrin is excitingly portrayed. This kind of dynamism is, of course, a hallmark of Solti's conducting, but there is also much poetry in his reading, a quality reinforced by the opulence of the recorded sound. Indeed, in purely sonic terms, this is probably the most beautiful recording of all; it is also, all round, the best sung, with a truly splendid team of soloists and superb orchestral and choral work. For my taste, the Viennese sound, in the most euphonious passages, is just a shade too saccharine, too rich. Certainly Wagner would have expected to hear a much leaner sound, with considerably less vibrato. This must, however, remain a matter of personal preference. What disturbs me more in Solti's interpretation is a suspicion of artificiality that, once noticed, seems to pervade significant stretches of the work. It sometimes takes the form of affectation—self-conscious and unnatural dynamic contrasts or rhythmic accentuation, for instance—and sometimes of a quality that I can only call slickness, when passages that should carry a high charge of emotion emerge as brash but vacuous.

Plácido Domingo's account of the title role seems to me to capture that ideal but elusive blend of heroism and sensitivity. His handling of the line gives continual pleasure and this is a performance that I cannot, and have no wish to, fault. Jessye Norman's Elsa is a more complex matter. As always, this singer's artistry leaves one speechless with awe; the glowing self-confidence she radiates, for example, as she anticipates the arrival of her champion, is matchless. However, it is possible to feel that perhaps there is just too much artistry and sophistication here for a character whose primary trait is innocent naiveté. At first, I was inclined toward this view, but I have been won over by the sheer musicality of the reading and by the skill of Norman's delineation of mood. Occasionally it is healthy to have to reexamine one's prejudices as to what a character should sound like, and this performance makes us more aware than usual of the dignity of Elsa's bearing: this is not some flighty, capriciously inquisitive woman, but a noble heroine whose tragedy lies in her utter devotion.

Ortrud is the sort of role in which Eva Randová excels on stage, and although she paints a memorable picture of a schemer, one must record a slight sense of disappointment that the intensity of her portrayal is not fully registered here. But if the menace is consequently less pronounced, there is always a consciousness of it lying just beneath the surface. At her invocation of the gods, "Entweihte Götter!," in the middle of her scene with Elsa (Act II), she is truly formidable. Telramund's Act II solos are sung by Siegmund Nimsgern with great intelligence, and he makes the most of the role's potential throughout. Hans Sotin is more secure as Heinrich than he has sometimes been of late, though for sheer style and distinction he is outshone by his Herald—Dietrich Fischer-Dieskau in hearty, extrovert mood. It is characteristic of the vocal glories of this set that the role of the Herald, which hasn't traditionally attracted singers of the first rank, is taken here so brilliantly.

For opulence of sound and all-round vocal excellence, the Solti recording is unbeatable. But Kempe's 1962–63 version, though undeniably inferior in technical quality, has an honesty, an authenticity, that gives it the edge. His quartet of soloists is also a magnificent one.

BARRY MILLINGTON

Unavailable for review:
1991 PHILIPS

RICHARD WAGNER

TRISTAN UND ISOLDE (1865)

A: Isolde (s); B: Brangäne (ms); C: Tristan (t);
D: Kurwenal (bar); E: King Marke (bs)

*A*rguably the most influential opera of the nineteenth century, *Tristan und Isolde* changed the course of art, literature, and philosophy as well as music. Its challenges to performers were enormous, but the novel dissonances and melodic shapes of the musical language were eventually assimilated, while its popularity brought forth voices that could ride over the unprecedentedly large orchestra. There were never enough of these voices to go around, but, especially between 1920 and 1950, a number of remarkable interpreters appeared, some of whom endured into the age of complete recordings.

For the most part, the problem of endurance raised by the length of the work and its leading roles was dealt with by cutting, as documented in many performance recordings, among which those discussed below and a pair from Munich in the early fifties under Knappertsbusch and Erich Kleiber are particularly noteworthy. The usual "big cut" removed a major swath of Act II (from Tristan's "Dem Tage! dem Tage!" to Isolde's "Doch es rächte sich der verscheuchte Tag"), badly warping the act's dramatic and musical balance, while substantial tucks were often taken on the tenor's behalf in Act III (Act I was rarely if ever touched). Studio recordings minimize the strain, of course, and since 1952 all of these have offered the opera complete.

1928 EMI / ANGEL (M)

Nanny Larsén-Todsen (A), Anny Helm (B), Gunnar Graarud (C), Rudolf Bockelmann (D), Ivar Andrésen (E), Bayreuth Festival Chorus and Orchestra—Karl Elmendorff

This earliest attempt to record a Wagner opera in one piece (rather than by assembling independently recorded sides) began bravely, then apparently ran out of either confidence or budget. Act I loses two significant episodes, but Act II lacks only four relatively brief passages, surprisingly escaping the "big cut." However, Act III isn't even a reasonable torso, reduced to less than a half hour (leaving poor Tristan to die between record sides!). The recorded sound may be better than it seemed in a congested 1970s Electrola reissue, based on noisy sources.

If hardly a representation of the opera, the Bayreuth set remains a fascinating document of Wagnerian performance at that time. Some characteristics require acclimatization for modern ears: heavy *portamento* from the strings and the singers, less than precise ensemble and intonation. Elmendorff's tempos, far from slow, ebb and flow in a remarkably natural way. The Tristan / Isolde dialogues are delivered in a lyrical-conversational mode, less monumental and stylized than Flagstad and Melchior. (The Bayreuth coaching system placed a strong emphasis on delivery of the words.) The love duet seethes and surges with a remarkably erotic impact.

Two singers are notable: Bockelmann as Kurwenal (though the cuts leave him little to sing), a noble bass-baritone, and Andrésen, a gently rueful Marke. Though Larsén-Todsen and Graarud are not supervoices (he sounds spent by the end of the love duet, she has more reserves), both are expressive when not under stress, and more inclined than most modern singers to color with diction rather than timbre. Helm is a rare soprano Brangäne, with a good line in narrative (e.g., her description of Melot in Act II, Scene 1), though her song of comfort to Isolde in Act I is rushed and choppy. Hardly a recording for the ages, this is, at least, one that vividly preserves the style of its own age.

1936–37 EMI / ANGEL (M,P) CD

Kirsten Flagstad (A), Sabine Kalter / Margarete Klose (B), Lauritz Melchior (C), Herbert Janssen (D), Emanuel List / Sven Nilsson (E), Chorus of the Royal Opera House, Covent Garden, London Philharmonic Orchestra—Fritz Reiner / Thomas Beecham

Promising to be a major historical publication, this release was badly compromised by sloppy research and inattention to detail. Initially billed as a "live" 1937 Covent Garden *Tristan* under Sir Thomas Beecham with Flagstad, Melchior, Klose, Janssen, and Nilsson, it emerged as a composite of that event and a 1936 performance at the same theater under Fritz Reiner, with the alternate singers named above: Act II and the beginning of Act III (up to Tristan's first lines, by my reckoning, though the inserted errata sheet claims more) is Beecham, the rest Reiner. The original recordings were made by EMI, but not published at the time for technical and / or musical reasons.

Thus Kalter, the somewhat mushy Brangäne of Act I, is transmuted into the darker-toned, firmer-voiced, and vastly more decisive Klose in Act II, reverting to her earlier self in Act III, while the sturdy if insensitive Marke of the long monologue grows distinctly tubbier and wobblier after his channel crossing. Nor are the conductors much alike. Reiner's performance is measured, even staid; after a rather listless beginning, things pick up at Kurwenal's entrance, but never really pull together; the result is competent but not illuminating. Beecham's Act II is more distinctive and energetic, following Wagner's tempo indications very carefully, and his brief share of Act III is notable for the

Mendelssohnian lightness of Kurwenal's "Wo du bist? In Frieden, sicher und frei!" However, at least in this edition, his orchestra doesn't sound as good as does Reiner's, with the strings often scrawny and wiry. Only two cuts are taken: the "big cut" and the first of three standard excisions in Act III: from Tristan's "Isolde noch im Reich der Sonne!" to his "Ach, Isolde, süsse Holde!" (Nobody bothered to delete these passages, or to indicate their omission, in EMI's German-only libretto.)

Particularly in Act III, Melchior's proclivity for conserving his resources is exceptionally conspicuous in his frequent resort to *Sprechstimme*, and he is persistently lazy about rhythmic matters. He does better in Act II, with Flagstad to keep him up to snuff (they really do sing the dissonant intervals in the two climaxes before Brangäne's Watch in perfect tuning, and it's wonderful to hear), but he's rarely comparable to her in musicianship and accuracy; for all the tonal amplitude, the thrust and energy he musters for the climaxes, Melchior's Tristan is rough around the edges. Flagstad is more spontaneous than in 1941 MET or 1952 EMI; the clarity, ring, and evenness of her tone are amazing, though in the *allegro* near the end of Act I her usually impeccable intonation is under stress, and the tone grows edgy in the coda of the love duet. There's a gentleness and vulnerability in the singing ("Nicht Hörnerschall" in Act II, "Ich bin's, ich bin's" after Tristan's death, the start of the Verklärung) that was rarely heard after the war, while the anger of the early phases of Act I is regal, never shrewish. Not even she is perfectly coordinated with the pit—that's characteristic of Covent Garden live performances at the time (Met performances probably didn't have much more rehearsal, but those involved—singers and orchestra—worked together for rather longer seasons). Janssen, stretched by Kurwenal's first-act ballad, is warm and sympathetic in Act III.

The frequent failures of ensemble and the scrappy orchestral playing can be distracting, as are the by-products of the live-recording circumstances: frequent stage noise and, in the Beecham segments, an audible prompter. Particularly in 1936, singers often go off-mike for longer or shorter periods, distorting dynamics or rendering the vocal line inaudible. And the sound itself is often gritty; EMI gets more bass out of the 1936 tests than did earlier pirates, but its upper register is sandy and unpleasant, quite aside from the grinding of the occasional surface; the result would be good enough for documentary purposes, if EMI had not scrambled the documents. (After EMI published this set, a CD edition of the complete Reiner performance appeared in comparable sound, from Video Arts International.)

1941 MET (M,P)

Kirsten Flagstad (A), Kerstin Thorborg (B), Lauritz Melchior (C), Julius Huehn (D), Alexander Kipnis (E), Metropolitan Opera Chorus and Orchestra—Erich Leinsdorf

For sheer vocal prowess, this is hard to beat, with four principals—Flagstad, Thorborg, Melchior, and Kipnis—unsurpassed in vocal and technical suitability to their roles. On this occasion, near the end of a strenuous season, Flagstad is below her best—high notes sometimes strained and edgy, intonation occasionally drooping—but still fresher of sound, more youthful in manner than in her later studio recording; the ease of production, the clarity and firmness of tone, the accuracy of everything she sings are all amazing. Less spontaneous, verbal, and sensuous than Frida Leider in her recorded excerpts, she doesn't lack for *intenzione* and energy.

Another marvel of tonal evenness, stamina, and verbal force, Melchior is not always a musical plus, given his tendency to jump beats, race the tempo, or resort to *parlando*. In fast, tricky music, chaos sometimes results (e.g., at the ship's arrival in Act III), and the elegiac "Wie sie selig" passage is altogether without repose (his 1930 EMI studio recording is far superior), but, as in 1936–37 EMI, the even matching of the Flagstad-Melchior team has its own impact. Kerstin Thorborg is a Brangäne of Flagstadian amplitude and security, though also tiring and occasionally flatting as the performance goes on. Kipnis brings eloquent pronun-

ciation, nuance, and varied color to Marke; a bit strained at top, his soft singing is still solid and gentle, and he shapes his monologue to a powerful climax. Huehn's rough, unfocused Kurwenal is below the level of the others.

Leinsdorf favors a lighter, leaner orchestral tone than Elmendorff (or the conductors of the Covent Garden performances—or those of the next two recordings, for that matter), though the strings (and singers) still pursue an appreciable *portamento*. In broad outline, this is a more "systematic" performance, with less tempo indulgence for gestural purposes—despite which Leinsdorf is forced to follow when Melchior lunges ahead; he deserves much credit for keeping things together under such circumstances. While the tenor doubtless impedes maintenance of a truly slow tempo, Leinsdorf appears to have few significant urges in that direction: this is a fast, energetic, often exciting performance that plumbs few depths of erotic passion or Schopenhauerian pessimism; it's certainly less unkempt than the Covent Garden affairs.

In Act II, the "big cut" is taken, and three substantial chunks are absent in Act III. The broadcast sound is generally clear, with a few patches of surface noise from the source material; the first beat of the third act seems to have gotten lost somewhere along the way.

1950 URANIA (M)

Margarete Bäumer (A), Erna Westenberger (B), Ludwig Suthaus (C), Karl Wolfram (D), Gottlob Frick (E), Leipzig Radio Chorus, Leipzig Gewandhaus Orchestra—Franz Konwitschny

Made in long takes with minimal (if any) remakes, an act a day, this recording served as a stopgap in the early LP catalogue despite manifest flaws, including observance of the "big cut." The most palpable problem is the Isolde of Bäumer, a once-capable Wagnerian who at age fifty-two has little left on her side but experience. Top notes are still there, if effortfully, but the whole voice is beset by a tremolo that persistently undermines her convincing line readings: with such a quaver, her commands to Kurwenal lack authority. The similarity between her timbre and that of Westenberger, a light-weight mezzo, doesn't help.

Suthaus is a Tristan of substance, sensitivity, and energy, though less consistent in intonation, less musically accurate than in the studio (EMI 1952); he occasionally lapses into shouting in the Act III climaxes. Wolfram makes a good bluff effect in Act I, but softer music discloses an unsteady tone. This is Gottlob Frick's only commercial recording of Marke, sung with fine *legato* and intonation, a sure harmonic sense, and broad phrasing; very closely miked, he comes across as less gentle than Kipnis. Remarkable, too, is the Shepherd of Gert Lutze, a regular Bach soloist with Günther Ramin's Leipzig Thomanerchor.

The recorded sound is cautious and haphazard: uneven levels and textural congestion in the orchestra whenever the voices enter and cover it. The Leipzig band basically plays well, but the horn section includes one weak member whose trials and errors are made conspicuous by the sonic balance. Urania's economical mode of recording leaves a trail of fluffs and wrong entries that increase in frequency from act to act. The spontaneity and conviction of Konwitschny's conception is nevertheless clear; in the tension of the Act I Tristan-Isolde dialogue and more often in Act III, we can hear what this recording might have been.

1952 EMI / ANGEL (M) CD

Kirsten Flagstad (A), Blanche Thebom (B), Ludwig Suthaus (C), Dietrich Fischer-Dieskau (D), Josef Greindl (E), Chorus of the Royal Opera House, Covent Garden, Philharmonia Orchestra—Wilhelm Furtwängler

This studio project, produced by Walter Legge, is deservedly a recorded classic. Furtwängler's highly personal way with the score, slower and weightier than what American listeners were used to at the time, is instilled with strong forward motion and darkly colored by lower strings and brass. The elasticity of tempo is smooth and unforced, the melodic lines are warmly inflected, the expressivity is always specific. Others may make certain passages more physically exciting, but few match the broad

arches in which Furtwängler builds to his climaxes: the first scene of Act II reaches the extinction of the torch through several waves of tension and relaxation, achieving crushing force when the trombones enter at Isolde's "und hell sie dorten leuchte!" (Acts II and III of a 1947 Berlin stage performance under Furtwängler, issued by Fonit-Cetra, show a more volatile approach to the music, equally convincing.)

Flagstad's voice is heavier than in 1940, and the top range consistently edgy. (As is well known, Elisabeth Schwarzkopf stood by to fill in the high Cs—and, I believe, also the Bs; this was before the days of *ex post facto* "tracking.") Her characterization is also more matronly, yet her vocal authority is still pretty overwhelming, and the sheer strength of her tone helps clinch Furtwängler's orchestral climaxes. Her middle and lower registers have grown even more sumptuous, and Furtwängler's tempos certainly give her more time to make verbal and expressive points than did Leinsdorf's.

Suthaus lacks the brilliance of Melchior's upper voice, but his thicker tone is an apt vehicle for this more pessimistic approach to the work. The tempos help him, too, for he isn't as flexible as Melchior; however, when energy is called for—the sighting of the ship and the subsequent delirium—he is there in force. No other performance of Tristan's vision in Act III ("Wie sie selig") compares with this for its sense of repose and respite from unfulfilled longing.

According to the EMI contract files, Brangäne was originally to have been sung by Margarete Klose, but she was replaced by Thebom, whose warm, smooth mezzo, with its attractively husky coloration, contrasts effectively with Flagstad. Fischer-Dieskau, at age twenty-seven, is a youthful and touching Kurwenal, Greindl a well-routined but gravel-toned Marke whose scene remains moving because it is so beautifully shaped and accompanied by the orchestra.

Regrettably, EMI's CD edition, like the previous digitally remastered LPs, sacrifices much of the warmth and richness of the original analogue sound. The best edition is the mid-seventies Electrola LP pressings with the same cover design now found on the CDs.

1960 DECCA / LONDON (S) CD

Birgit Nilsson (A), Regina Resnik (B), Fritz Uhl (C), Tom Krause (D), Arnold van Mill (E), Singverein der Gesellschaft der Musikfreunde, Vienna Philharmonic Orchestra—Georg Solti

Made in the wake of Nilsson's successful 1959 Met debut as Isolde, the first stereo *Tristan* earned limited acclaim. Initial reservations centered on the journeyman Tristan, whose previous recorded achievements were in Bach cantatas and who at Bayreuth had not ascended beyond Loge and Erik. Even with assistance from the recording staff, Uhl is clearly beyond his vocal depth; a tone without a firm core, uncertain pitching in the upper register, extensive reliance on aspirates for emphasis. "Interpretation" is not an applicable term; Uhl's hands, throat, and mind are full merely dealing with the notes.

However, not much else is very satisfactory either. Though in gleaming voice, Nilsson sings with less *legato* than Flagstad, and also less force in the lower register (e.g., "Mir erkoren . . ." in Act I). Even when Isolde takes an imperious line in the first act, the effect is more glacial than regal; her orders to Kurwenal ("Herrn Tristan bringe meinen Gruss") lack the magisterial contempt shown by Flagstad—nor does Solti help here, with a tempo that favors speed over thrust. Perhaps for lack of effective foils, neither Isolde's anger nor her erotic passion is fully evoked. Resnik, an intelligent artist then moving into character roles, is simply not a functional Brangäne; the role wants precisely the warm and finished *legato* tone she no longer commanded.

As suggested, Solti isn't helpful: from the Vienna Philharmonic he elicits fine solo playing, but also an uncharacteristically sleek melodic progression, stiffly symmetrical rhythm, strikingly coarse and unblended climaxes (notably at the end of Act I and at Tristan's entrance in Act II)—and too many of the latter, undifferentiated and contra-cumulative. Much of the performance alternates between punchy hot spots and static torpor. (The punchiness invades the singing of both Krause and van Mill, easily the most percussive of Markes.) On top of that, the engi-

neers are in the early stages of Decca / London's sonic-steambath phase, allowing the orchestral tumult to swallow the voices. Since Nilsson went on to record a much better representation of her Isolde, this one can easily be forgone.

1966 DEUTSCHE GRAMMOPHON (also PHILIPS) (S,P) CD

Birgit Nilsson (A), Christa Ludwig (B), Wolfgang Windgassen (C), Eberhard Wächter (D), Martti Talvela (E), Bayreuth Festival Chorus and Orchestra—Karl Böhm

An amalgam of Bayreuth performances and rehearsals, this represents the most satisfactory recorded epitome of the fast, intense *Tristan*. So fast, in fact, that it's the only complete set to fit every act comfortably on a single CD, with great advantage to the persistent forward pressure of Böhm's reading. Though similar in pacing to Leinsdorf, Böhm achieves a different expressive *Gestalt*: darker and richer orchestral tone, more forceful and intense playing, more telling interplay between vocal and orchestral lines (e.g., Nilsson and the winds at "Isolde's Kunst ward ihm bekannt," in the Narration). And the entire cast delivers the words with much intensity—doubtless a consequence of Wieland Wagner's direction.

Isolde's Medea-like aspects are to the fore in Act I, but Nilsson's anger is much hotter here than under Solti. The contrast between her sound and Ludwig's is dramatically telling, and they play together superbly: in Ludwig's quotation of Isolde's command in Act I, Scene 2, the mistress's belligerence is finely shaded with the maid's timidity. The opening of Act II seethes in the orchestra, with a tingling edge on the string tone. Though the transition from stage horns to clarinets and strings at "Nicht Hörnerschall tönt so hold" is beautifully handled, the achieved tonal effect is more like bees buzzing than water flowing—the intensity never lets up. Between Nilsson's hairpin-shaped tones that impede the *legato* and Windgassen's effortful moments, the love duet is more muscular than erotic.

The tenor achieves an apter mood at the act's end ("Wohin nun Tristan scheidet"), and in Act

III his voice seems more plangent, less throaty; his accuracy and rhythmic thrust count powerfully in the jubilant music. Windgassen's interpretive choices, if almost always obvious and extroverted, are well shaped and executed with ample conviction. Generally, that's true of the entire performance, which is more assured when dealing with "day" than with "night," in terms of the opera's principal symbolic axis. The supporting cast is quite remarkably consistent: not only Ludwig's vibrant Brangäne but Wächter's sturdy Kurwenal and Talvela's solid Marke—a bit detached at first, gradually gaining in eloquence.

A general criticism, perhaps in part attributable to dynamic compression: very little in the performance seems truly soft. Onstage recording yields some stage noises, occasionally obtrusive in Act I's pregnant silences, but on the whole the sonic picture effectively conveys a performance impressively coherent if not ideally varied emotionally.

1971–72 EMI / ANGEL (S) CD

Helga Dernesch (A), Christa Ludwig (B), Jon Vickers (C), Walter Berry (D), Karl Ridderbusch (E), Chorus of the Deutsche Oper, Berlin, Berlin Philharmonic Orchestra—Herbert von Karajan

In this ponderous, self-conscious performance, the conductor's self-absorption effectively neutralizes some distinctive singers. One factor is sonic: in a basically spacious acoustic, the voices are not merely assisted but palpably manipulated: sometimes close, sometimes farther away, often swallowed up by the orchestral tone in climaxes—a token of hierarchy and artificiality that skews the drama. Though many tempos are slower than Böhm's, the problem is rather the somnambulistic suppression of pulse; the objective may be weight, but the result is ponderousness, and the blatant climaxes with braying horns yield the opposite of Furtwängler's accumulated force.

Dernesch, a lifted mezzo, is a primary victim of the turgidity: her Narrative is labored, her repetition of Brangäne's "Kennst du die Mutter Künste nicht" mournful rather than ironic. Her origins show in her squally delivery near the end of Act I (the high Cs in Act II sound "tracked in"—by the singer herself, to be sure), while the color remains dark. In passages such as "Schon goss sie ihr Schweigen" (Act II, Scene 1), we could mistake her for Brangäne. She delivers words with less force and color than Flagstad or Nilsson—or, closer to home, than either Ludwig or Vickers.

In fact, these lovers' voices aren't well matched; they don't blend in the love duet's quiet music, where she withholds expression to maintain dynamic control while he croons. Their dialogues are one-sided, Vickers pitching strong (if idiosyncratically pronounced) verbal gestures into a virtual vacuum. His last act is all at extremes of vocal expressivity—either crooned or frenzied—but, since Karajan declines to follow him to either edge, the outcome approaches absurdity. Berry is a strong, plain Kurwenal, Ridderbusch a smooth, effective Marke; Bernd Weikl, a baritone Melot, sounds whiny and effortful, suggesting if not clarifying some novel complexity of character.

1980–81 DECCA / LONDON (S,D)

Linda Esther Gray (A), Anne Wilkens (B), John Mitchinson (C), Phillip Joll (D), Gwynne Howell (E), Welsh National Opera Chorus and Orchestra—Reginald Goodall

Though sung in the original language, this recording was based on the reputation Goodall had built as a conductor of Wagner in English. Alas, the combination of an experienced, sophisticated conductor with essentially provincial forces fails to jell. Sometimes Goodall gets what he wants: after Brangäne's first intervention in the love duet, voice-leading and harmonic purport are exceptionally delineated; the orchestral run-up to "O ew'ge Nacht" is remarkable for shape and clarity, and the final stretch of the duet is remarkably sensuous in its ductus—though hardly "Very lively and fast" as Wagner requested.

Equally often, admirably conceived passages are smudged in detail, for the playing simply fails to reach acceptable standards for repeated hearing on a recording: the cello melody in the

Act II Prelude is infirm, the instrumental soloists (bass clarinet, English horn) lack distinction. To compound such problems, Goodall's
tempos in Act I sound sluggish, to the disadvantage of his singers, though the other acts have
ample energy despite comparable breadth.

Except for Gwynne Howell's smoothly sung
Marke, the cast can also be described as provincial, and remains so despite much informed
coaching. An effortful production makes Gray's
plummy Isolde sound shrewish and scolding,
without much variety of color; at climaxes, she
tends to scream. A lighter-than-usual Brangäne,
Wilkens focuses a squeezed, somewhat viscous
top better than Gray does. The baritonal Mitchinson is a utility Tristan who under pressure
develops a beat and pitch problems; in Act III
the strain on his upper range leads to shouting.
Joll sings Kurwenal's first-act song roughly, and
is not much better later. Though worth the
attention of *Tristan* mavens for its conception
and its attention to textural detail, this set is
otherwise dispensable.

1981 PHILIPS (S,D,P) ⟐

Hildegard Behrens (A), Yvonne Minton (B),
Peter Hofmann (C), Bernd Weikl (D), Hans
Sotin (E), Bavarian Radio Chorus and Sym-
phony Orchestra—Leonard Bernstein

The fruit of live performances and patch
sessions (an act at a time in January, May, and
November 1981), Bernstein's *Tristan* is another
in which the conductor is both the dominant
and the most successful element. The orchestra,
not quite world class, is several cuts above
Goodall's, and very responsive to Bernstein's
flexibility and highly personal touches. The
latter begin with the Prelude, one of the most
sustained and rhetorically distended performances on records, yet brought off by Bernstein's sense of harmonic line and continuity.

Indeed, a composer's eye and ear are evident
in many aspects of the performance. The initial
sailor's song makes the most of Wagner's highly
specific *fermatas* and dynamics, at once extending the steaminess of the Prelude and setting up
the more vigorous impulse about to emerge;
when part of this song returns at the beginning

of Scene 2, Bernstein observes the absence of
fermatas, confirming that the sensual stasis at
the end of the Prelude is finally dissipated. He
can be counted on to rethink the textural balance of Wagner's most contrapuntally complex
climaxes, to underline harmonic movement, to
attend to the larger rhythm (Brangäne's Watch
Song, breathing in two-bar periods, becomes a
slow, spacy nocturne). This is almost always
absorbing listening, even when the orchestra
isn't perfectly tuned or together, even when the
music's flow seems overly studied—as in Act II,
in the run-ups to Tristan's entry and to the final
allegro of the love duet (as with Goodall, anything but fast).

The slow tempos often strain these singers:
this magnificently textured but very broad interpretation of the Verklärung stretches Behrens's
resources of breath and exposes the tremor in
her voice. As always, she is an intelligent and
stimulating singer, though the inequalities of
her middle and lower registers compromise her
effectiveness in Act I. Both she and Hofmann
need electronic assistance in the climaxes, and
fail to match the orchestra's surge and richness
in Act II. Hofmann, with minimal tone in the
lower register and little variety above, barely
gets through Act III, where the orchestra provides all the expressivity.

Early in this act, Bernstein layers and contrasts the music of Kurwenal and the awakened
Tristan with an almost Stravinskian effect, assisted
by a strong performance from Weikl, who also
details his Act I ballad more than most. The
solidity of Minton's rich tone quite overwhelms
Hofmann's coreless sound in their Act I dialogue, and contrasts well with Behrens, though
she occasionally tends to go flat. Sotin's musically sung Marke lacks warmth and "face." As
suggested, voice / orchestra balances are sometimes quite unrealistic, though the ambience
and clarity are generally commendable.

1980–82 DEUTSCHE GRAMMOPHON (S,D) ⟐

Margaret Price (A), Brigitte Fassbaender (B),
René Kollo (C), Dietrich Fischer-Dieskau (D),
Kurt Moll (E), Leipzig Radio Chorus, Dresden
State Orchestra—Carlos Kleiber

The number and span of recording dates required to complete this set suggests either troubled sessions or extreme perfectionism—or both. It is, indeed, a recording in which everything in the score has been scrutinized and rethought—even the musical text, where Kleiber sometimes reverts to readings from Wagner's autograph rather than the standard ones of the first edition. Though leaning toward the fast track of Leinsdorf, Solti, and Böhm, the result is quite distinctive in character.

Even more than Bernstein, Kleiber brings to the score a modern, post-Stravinskian ear, favoring lean, linear textures, eschewing conventional richness and a low center of tonal gravity. As a result, a passage such as the coda of the love duet ("O ew'ge Nacht") acquires a light, dreamy eroticism heard nowhere else. Throughout, whether in the precise rhetoric of orchestral interjections in Act I's recitative dialogues, the flexibility of the cello melody in the Act II Prelude, or the bounding energy of Tristan's final hysteria, the orchestral contribution is always expressively specific: not only are the score's directions observed, their purposes have been clearly determined and vividly reenacted. The Dresden orchestra, its horns bearing an "Eastern" tinge, is close to magnificent.

Price's Isolde, untried on the stage, is remarkably good, with real *legato*, excellent intonation, surprising fire in her first-act anger and a feeling for the curve of the lines in the duet; the high notes come, though not easily, and here and there she can become abstracted, tonally and expressively. Though always used musically, Kollo's attractive voice develops a beat under stress, his "hairpinning" of notes ("So stürben wir") impedes *legato*, and soft passages are apt to emerge whiny and insecure.

Fassbaender is taxed by both the music and the tempos: at this speed, the breath problems of the long phrases in the first-act song "Welcher Wahn" are eased, its intonational challenges heightened. Ill-advised to return to the scene of his first complete opera recording, Fischer-Dieskau seems a caricature of his earlier Kurwenal, despite some affecting moments in Act III. Moll's monologue begins in a microphonic near-whisper but builds superbly, and is enacted with great sensitivity to words and tonal colors. Among these principals, he alone commands vocal ammunition and authority comparable to Furtwängler's or Böhm's casts. In his eighth decade, Anton Dermota still possesses a sweet timbre, and his Shepherd is touching.

All too clearly, both protagonists are assisted electronically in the competition with the orchestra. The overall perspective is more distant, the effect less warm than in the Goodall or Bernstein recordings, and the string tone manifests a certain amount of "early digital" steeliness. The LP edition was noteworthy for the use of cross-fades at some side-changes, a practice abandoned in the CD edition in favor of conventional clean breaks.

———

The most "central" interpretation to command great singing is EMI 1952, to which DG 1966 is an impressive complement. Of the more modern sets, DG 1980–82 is the best-realized—and different enough from the other two to make a good foil. Beyond that, the underground may prove more rewarding for those in search of first-class Wagnerian singing.

DAVID HAMILTON

RICHARD WAGNER

DIE MEISTERSINGER VON NÜRNBERG (1868)

A: Eva (s); B: Magdalene (ms); C: Walther von Stolzing (t);
D: David (t); E: Hans Sachs (bar); F: Sixtus Beckmesser (bar);
G: Fritz Kothner (bs-bar); H: Veit Pogner (bs)

So this, at least by the standard of *The Ring*, was Wagner's idea of a "practical" opera? And in a sense, it is. Any company that can muster the physical resources and stamina needed to put *Meistersinger* on is almost guaranteed the effect of its sheer energetic sweep.

But the opera's resonance and depth lie in its detailing, and when we get down to specifics, the hapless impresario may wish he had taken on *The Ring* after all. For *Meistersinger* we still need an authentic *Heldenbariton*, and he really ought to be a great one. There are singers we might willingly accept as Wotan whose voices simply aren't warm or beautiful enough to make a sympathetic Hans Sachs. This is, after all, arguably the greatest and most humane character in all opera, and in approaching the recordings of the opera we have to stipulate from the outset that any complete version(s) recommended will have to be supplemented by the assembled Sachs excerpts of Friedrich Schorr.

Beyond Sachs, our hapless impresario is supposed to get a break. Eva is the one Wagner heroine encompassable by a soprano of lyric weight, but singing the role really well and finding the real inner life is a murderously challenging assignment. Walther von Stolzing is also theoretically a lyric-tenor role, but the recordings that make the most sense of his music—and by a good margin—are Lauritz Melchior's, even though Melchior decided against singing the part publicly.

Once we have a Walther, we still need another robust lyric tenor for David, to realize the wonderful opportunities of the Act I crash course in Mastersinging and the Act III scene with Sachs. And, as we'll see, the "other" principal Masters—Pogner, Beckmesser, and Kothner—are ferociously difficult to cast. Solve all of these problems and we still need a conductor who has depth of spirit and the ability to inspire his cast, chorus, and orchestra.

All of the recordings are complete, except for the lacunae in 1943 EMI.

1943 EMI / ANGEL (M,P)

Maria Müller (A), Camilla Kallab (B), Max Lorenz (C), Erich Zimmermann (D), Jaro Prohaska (E), Eugen Fuchs (F), Fritz Krenn (G), Josef Greindl (H), Bayreuth Festival Chorus and Orchestra—Wilhelm Furtwängler

Despite the tantalizing rumors of a complete 1944 Bayreuth *Meistersinger*—in stereo!—it appears that we may have to make do with this 1943 one, which itself apparently still hasn't turned up in its entirety. The version issued by EMI in 1976 is missing two chunks: in the opening scene, from after the chorale up to David's "Nun sollt ihr singen"; and the end of the Act III workshop scene, from Sachs's "Ein Kind ward hier geboren."

It says something about Furtwängler's way with Wagner that every time I listen to this recording, as the gaps approach I find myself hoping that this time the music will somehow continue on. Furtwängler's known predilection for slow tempos can conceal his unmatched sense of dynamic movement: how the music gets from point A to point B inevitably and irresistibly. When his performance is on, it never sounds slow—the music is going as fast as it can. And the *Meistersinger* is prime Furtwängler, combining wonderful attention to detail with irresistible forward drive.

When a singer can really work with Furtwängler, the results are special, as with the already fifty-year-old Erich Zimmermann as David: not as full a sound as one would like to begin with, now decidedly breathy in timbre and short on top, but a genuine delight. There's also an agreeable Eva from Maria Müller, and a fairly effective Walther from Max Lorenz, hard in sound but productively concerned with lyric shapes. The Sachs, Beckmesser, Pogner, and Kothner are all representatives of baritone and bass voice types for which Germanic audiences apparently have high tolerance: a dry timbre that isn't sustained by vibrato and in compensation takes on a certain unvarying temperamental aggressiveness.

Nevertheless *Meistersinger*, the most Mozartian of Wagner's operas, thrives on the breadth of vision of a Furtwängler or Toscanini or Knappertsbusch. Even in this imperfect form, this recording presents a vivid image of the opera.

1950–51 DECCA / LONDON (M)

Hilde Gueden (A), Else Schürhoff (B), Günther Treptow (C), Anton Dermota (D), Paul Schöffler (E), Karl Dönch (F), Alfred Poell (G), Otto Edelmann (H), Vienna State Opera Chorus, Vienna Philharmonic Orchestra—Hans Knappertsbusch

This first studio *Meistersinger* is probably still, all things considered, the best. Although some of those things that have to be considered preclude a simple, unequivocal recommendation, the strengths are considerable, beginning with Knappertsbusch's generously proportioned, deeply considered reading and the vibrant, virtuosic playing of the Vienna Philharmonic.

Perhaps surprisingly for this conductor, the performance isn't unusually slow, especially in Act I—the Prelude gets off at a good clip. More space is allowed in the later acts, and the opening of Act III—one of Wagner's greatest scenes—is particularly memorable: a luminous Prelude and then, for David's scene, Anton Dermota's fine, full-bodied lyric tenor, the most suitable on commercial records.

It would also be hard to improve on Hilde Gueden's silvery-toned, dramatically winning Eva, except perhaps by being just as winning dramatically with a more substantial voice—viz., Elisabeth Grümmer in 1956 EMI. From this point, however, we get into trouble.

Otto Edelmann is, in his low-keyed way, a decent Pogner, as he is a Sachs (1951 EMI)—the roles are remarkably similar in range. Karl Dönch is, within the customary cartoon framework, a moderately amusing Beckmesser. Paul Schöffler, admirable artist though he is, simply can't, at this stage of his career, consistently produce a steady or beautiful enough sound for a wholly sympathetic Sachs, and Günther Treptow's sizable and potentially imposing tenor is produced with enough strain, especially toward the top, to keep the listener on edge.

1951 EMI / ANGEL (M,P) CD

Elisabeth Schwarzkopf (A), Ira Malaniuk (B), Hans Hopf (C), Gerhard Unger (D), Otto Edelmann (E), Erich Kunz (F), Heinrich Pflanzl (G), Friedrich Dalberg (H), Bayreuth Festival Chorus and Orchestra (1951)—Herbert von Karajan

Unless you count the singing in the lower voice ranges, there's not much actively objectionable in this well-disciplined, uneccentric performance. But there's nothing much that draws me back either, including the plain recorded sound, which has none of the atmosphere of the *Parsifal* that Decca / London recorded at this same Bayreuth Festival.

There's just nothing especially festive or poetical in this performance. Elisabeth Schwarzkopf, in her only Bayreuth season, does some attractive singing and some irritatingly "cute" singing. Otto Edelmann is an unforced, bearable Sachs; Hans Hopf a pressed-sounding but unhorrible if also unmemorable Walther; Gerhard Unger a pleasant but vocally insufficient David; and Ira Malaniuk a solid Magdalene.

1951 URANIA (M)

Tiana Lemnitz (A), Emilie Walther-Sacks (B), Bernd Aldenhoff (C), Gerhard Unger (D), Ferdinand Frantz (E), Heinrich Pflanzl (F), Karl Paul (G), Kurt Böhme (H), Dresden State Opera Chorus, Dresden State Orchestra—Rudolf Kempe

Although the Eva, Magdalene, Walther, and David hardly rank high among the competition, they actually play the opening scene as a scene, and with Rudolf Kempe's boisterous support, the performance starts agreeably: sort of an Apprentices' eye-view of *Meistersinger*.

And then Pogner and Beckmesser make their entrance, followed in due course by Sachs and Kothner: four of those minimally distinguishable, raucous-toned German baritones and basses. (Well, yes, of course you can distinguish Kurt Böhme's bass roar from the others. The question is, does the distinction matter?) If these are the Mastersingers, you may begin to wonder what the opera is about. If, nevertheless, you want to continue listening to the performance for the sake of Kempe's zestful approach, as you may well since no other conductor on records (including Kempe himself) has drawn this much sheer joy from the score, you will have to filter out the singing as best you can.

To be fair, Ferdinand Frantz's bass-baritone isn't quite as dried out as it is in 1956 EMI, but then neither does it have the genuinely attractive color of some of his live recordings.

There's more color in Böhme's voice than his later work would lead us to expect, along with a painful slow vibrato. Tiana Lemnitz, a once-lovely artist, no longer commands either tonal color or steadiness, while Bernd Aldenhoff, who might have had the fixings for an important voice, contributes mostly a beefy, trembly bellow.

On a brighter note, Emilie Walther-Sacks, although vocally ordinary, sustains the strong conversational impression from the opening scene, and Gerhard Unger, while no closer to the necessary vocal weight than in his other recorded attempts at David, sounds like a Golden Age vocalist in this company.

1956 EMI / ANGEL (M) CD

Elisabeth Grümmer (A), Marga Höffgen (B), Rudolf Schock (C), Gerhard Unger (D), Ferdinand Frantz (E), Benno Kusche (F), Gustav Neidlinger (G), Gottlob Frick (H), St. Hedwig's Cathedral Choir, Choruses of the Berlin Municipal Opera and Deutsche Oper, Berlin Philharmonic Orchestra—Rudolf Kempe

This is a very grown-up performance, with a grown-up cast, a grown-up orchestra, and a conductor who has, for better and worse, outgrown the mischievousness and spontaneity of 1951 Urania.

Of course, grown-upness isn't necessarily a bad thing. And so, while we may regret a loss of playfulness in this Prelude, it is set forth with muscular confidence and builds to a peroration for which all the stops seem to have been pulled out—until the St. Catherine's parishioners, with their thunderous organ accompaniment, erupt in song. Indeed, if you listen carefully to this recording, you begin to sense that a grandly scaled performance is trying to be heard through sonics that are mediocre even by comparison with 1950–51 Decca / London.

For all his grown-upness, Kempe hasn't lost his feel for the conversational structure of the score. The opening scene, for example, although it now has a more sober tone, still plays nicely. And of course it's all to the good that the arrival of the Masters this time doesn't bring a precipitous drop-off in vocal level. Gottlob Frick, in fact, while not as tonally plush as Karl Ridderbusch or Kurt Moll, is the most incisive Pogner on records; Benno Kusche brings a voice of substance to Beckmesser, even if he subscribes to the ungrounded but nearly universal notion that the character should peck at rather than sing notes; Gustav Neidlinger, although hardly a model of vocal refinement, again at least brings some real voice to Kothner.

The Pogner family is well represented here. Elisabeth Grümmer's full-bodied soprano is of uncommonly generous size for Eva (she could, after all, handle lighter dramatic-weight roles, like Wagner's Elisabeth and Elsa), and she was always a warm and captivating singer. She and Frick make much of the crucial but easily glossed-over scene that opens Act II; unfortunately, her other scene partners aren't on this level. On some occasions Rudolf Schock managed to get some lyrical quality into his squeezed-out tenor, but his Walther is at best workmanlike. Which isn't a bad description for Ferdinand Frantz's Sachs: now pretty much completely dried out vocally, but broader and more dignified than his performance in 1951 Urania.

Hermann Prey is a lovely high-baritone Nightwatchman. He's arguably too refined (he and Kempe get so carried away with praising God as to suggest a fugitive from the *Tannhäuser* pilgrimage), but then, you could think of this as part of the joke of the role.

1963 EURODISC (S,P) CD

Claire Watson (A), Lilian Benningsen (B), Jess Thomas (C), Friedrich Lenz (D), Otto Wiener (E), Benno Kusche (F), Josef Metternich (G), Hans Hotter (H), Bavarian State Opera Chorus, Bavarian State Orchestra—Joseph Keilberth

Let's first dispose of the Sachs: the best that can be said of Otto Wiener, with his colorless, slow-wobble-afflicted, cranky baritone, is that he doesn't completely stop the show when he sings. Perhaps some reservation should also be noted concerning Hans Hotter's Pogner. Sure, it's the work of a respected artist, intelligent, even authoritative, but my goodness, the sound! It's mashed, and shuddery, and all in all not easy to listen to.

That said, I love this performance, recorded at the November 1963 reopening of Munich's National Theater. There is, of course, a dark side to the association of *Meistersinger* and Munich, but it's obviously also a deeply felt bond, and for this special occasion the State Opera roused itself to a stirring and dynamic ensemble effort: richly and beautifully played and recorded, with wonderfully exciting choral work.

The 1963 performance was consciously designed to recall another gala *Meistersinger*: the first postwar performance of the opera permitted in Munich, in the Prinzregenten Theater in December 1949—another outstanding ensemble performance, conducted by Eugen Jochum, which happily survives in remarkably good sound. Four of the 1963 Masters, including two principals, had been in the 1949 cast. Hotter had been a generally first-rate Sachs; Benno Kusche was still singing Beckmesser, and the 1963 performance seems to me the most committedly sung and most successful of his recordings of the role. (The other repeaters: Max Proebstl, who had been an outstanding Pogner in 1949, now sang Foltz; Carl Hoppe was Nachtigall in both productions.)

The 1963 romantic leads are both American, and both fine. Claire Watson's lyric soprano isn't especially beautiful, but it's handled with considerable flair. Jess Thomas's big tenor does sometimes lock into an unlyrical blast, but on the whole this is attractive, forceful singing. There's also a rousing Kothner from the veteran baritone Josef Metternich.

1970 EMI / ANGEL (S) CD

Helen Donath (A), Ruth Hesse (B), René Kollo (C), Peter Schreier (D), Theo Adam (E), Geraint Evans (F), Zoltán Kélémen (G), Karl Ridderbusch (H), Leipzig Radio Chorus, Dresden State Opera Chorus, Dresden State Orchestra—Herbert von Karajan

This is a hard one to pin down. Karajan seems to have entered into genuine collaboration with the Dresden musicians, and the performance is built on a lyrical grace that may suggest autumn more than the opera's midsummer but that brings out all sorts of colors and resonances clearly integral to the score which no one else on records has looked for. The problem is that the job is only partially done. A real discovery process of this sort probably can't be whipped up from scratch in the amazingly few days in which this recording was made.

About two performances I have no complaint whatever. First, Karl Ridderbusch's Pogner is simply a gorgeous piece of work—a textbook demonstration of how extraordinary vocalism can be used to make a Wagnerian scene happen. The address to the Masters builds to a whopping high F, but he can be just as impressive singing gently in the Act II scene with Eva. And the Eva, Helen Donath, is altogether winning. Her lyric soprano sounds fine, and she creates a lively character free of the standard clichés.

The tenors are better than many. René Kollo's voice never was and never will be a beautiful one, but on occasion, as here, he has shown himself capable of relaxing the edge of his sound to allow for some real lyricism. Peter Schreier actually seemed like an inspired choice for David, but in the event he seems to be pushing out a lot of air that hasn't been converted into singing tone, and so the sound isn't much more substantial than that of most of the competition.

Theo Adam is an intelligent singer, and therefore a sensible Sachs, but the sound is too dry to invite much empathy. Geraint Evans had more voice at his command than the stock Beckmesser; I wish he had used more of it here. Zoltán Kélémen falters a bit in Kothner's intricate writing but is on the whole quite good. Kurt Moll sings the Nightwatchman's songs as well as I expect ever to hear them.

1974 PHILIPS (S,P) CD

Hannelore Bode (A), Anna Reynolds (B), Jean Cox (C), Frieder Stricker (D), Karl Ridderbusch (E), Klaus Hirte (F), Gerd Nienstedt (G), Hans Sotin (H), Bayreuth Festival Chorus and Orchestra—Silvio Varviso

A likable performance that doesn't cut very deep but does recall the playful flow of 1951 Urania, though Varviso doesn't have anything like Kempe's life force, the sense that the orchestra is phrasing in breaths. In turn, the vocal standard of 1974 Philips is considerably higher, and even includes some big-league singing.

Hans Sotin's solid-core, plush-toned bass is excellent equipment for Pogner, and his singing is generally quite lovely but less incisively directed than that of Ridderbusch (1970 EMI). The latter's transition from Pogner to Sachs is only partially successful. The Sachs is a decent, sympathetic piece of singing; unfortunately, at just this time—perhaps coincidentally, perhaps not—the voice underwent a major change, in which a fair measure of the color and bite was lost. It's saddening to compare the earlier, ravishing Eurodisc recital recording of Sach's monologues.

Otherwise, the cast offers a highly serviceable Magdalene, David, and Kothner; a fussily uninteresting, but at least not seriously objectionable, Beckmesser; a tonally plain but rather lively Eva; and a sometimes satisfactory, sometimes merely strenuous, Walther. An unequivocal success is the Nightwatchman of Bernd Weikl, whose no-fooling legit singing goes beyond the obvious joke to contribute a pair of vocally action-arresting events.

1975 DEUTSCHE GRAMMOPHON (S) CD

Catarina Ligendza (A), Christa Ludwig (B), Plácido Domingo (C), Horst R. Laubenthal (D), Dietrich Fischer-Dieskau (E), Roland Hermann (F), Gerd Feldhoff (G), Peter Lagger (H), Chorus and Orchestra of the Deutsche Oper, Berlin—Eugen Jochum

It might be misleading to say that something "went wrong" with this recording, which in fact is fluid and generally pleasing, with several strong individual contributions. The performance somehow doesn't hang together well, or build momentum.

To start on the plus side, the recording is pretty much indispensable for the Walther of Plácido Domingo. There are listeners who hear this gorgeous stream of sound and pronounce it un-Wagnerian; it seems to me, on the contrary, the sound that the music cries out for—for once, it's possible to understand the profound impact made on Sachs by what he hears in Act I. It's also a lively, intelligent performance: one of the classiest pieces of Wagner singing on records.

The two supporting baritones are also quite good. Gerd Feldhoff's fullness and agility of tone and warmth of personality enable him to really sing Kothner's roll call and "Tabulatur" reading, and enable us to take the baker seriously. Roland Hermann is, along with Bernd Weikl, the nearest thing we've had to an honestly sung Beckmesser—not a brilliant piece of interpretation, but at least free of that awful cartoon tradition. Hermann does make a less striking sound than Weikl in the mid-range, but the top is more comfortably integrated.

Either Feldhoff or Hermann might have managed Sachs more successfully than Fischer-Dieskau, whose whiny sound in the upper half of the voice seems better suited to Beckmesser—though probably not a Beckmesser I would much enjoy. The lower half of the voice lacks the weight the writing demands, and the singer's traditional fake-insightful overemphases aren't much compensation.

Catarina Ligendza is perversely cast as Eva. Why would you ask a voice that was blowsy and out of control in its own heavier-weight repertory to scale down to negotiate this finely detailed writing? By contrast, Pogner should have been a good role for Peter Lagger, and some of it sounds just fine, but you can hear the voice starting to spread all over the place—notably, and unsurprisingly, on top. Horst R. Laubenthal is another of those nice-sounding but too light Davids, and Christa Ludwig is a mature-sounding but satisfactory Magdalene.

1976 DECCA / LONDON (S) CD

Hannelore Bode (A), Julia Hamari (B), René Kollo (C), Adolf Dallapozza (D), Norman Bailey (E), Bernd Weikl (F), Gerd Nienstedt (G), Kurt Moll (H), Gumpoldskircher Spatzen, Vienna State Opera Chorus, Vienna Philharmonic Orchestra—Georg Solti

"The pacing is broad, the orchestral playing rich and beautifully textured, the phrasing almost wholly uninflected—a reference-shelf edition." This is how I once described Solti's Meistersinger, and the description still seems apt.

Curious Phenomenon Department: Hannelore Bode as Eva is just enough more tremulous than in 1974 Philips as to be now rather unpleasant to listen to; René Kollo as Walther has tightened up the lyrical component of 1970

EMI to produce an all-edge sound; Gerd Nienstedt as Kothner is vocally less confident than in 1974 Philips. Call it coincidence; call it a pattern (is there anyone at the helm?)—either way, it's not good news.

There is some good news on the lower-male front. Kurt Moll, while not as dramatically interesting a Pogner as Frick or Ridderbusch, sings with remarkable fullness and beauty of tone. Norman Bailey's Sachs, by the humble standards of the complete recordings, is a success, though the draggy pacing sometimes makes it difficult for him to sustain shudder-free tone (to nowhere near the extent, however, of his disastrous Dutchman). And Weikl, while he doesn't seem to have given Beckmesser much thought, and while he deploys that same confounded crooning top, brings to the role's mid-range an unaccustomedly luxurious sound.

Adolf Dallapozza is another pleasant lyric tenor too light-voiced for David. Julia Hamari, a good mezzo, is also light-voiced for Magdalene—a hard enough role in which to make an impression under the best circumstances.

You undoubtedly saw this coming: we can put together two or three complete recordings and, even with the Schorr excerpts added, still not have a really satisfactory representation of Meistersinger.

The two or three recordings would be 1950–51 Decca / London or 1963 Eurodisc, or both, plus 1975 DG. Then there are the contrasting special qualities of 1970 EMI and 1951 Urania, and some interesting casting options in 1956 EMI and 1976 Decca / London, and the congenial spirit of 1974 Philips. And of course there's the rich insight of 1943 EMI and the distinctive qualities of a number of other live performances. If I could have only one complete Meistersinger, it would probably be the 1949 Bavarian State Opera performance conducted by Jochum (see 1963 Eurodisc).

KENNETH FURIE

RICHARD WAGNER

DER RING DES NIBELUNGEN: DAS RHEINGOLD (1869)

A: Fricka (ms); B: Erda (c); C: Loge (t); D: Mime (t); E: Wotan (bs-bar);
F: Alberich (bs-bar); G: Fasolt (bs); H: Fafner (bs)

The first part of Richard Wagner's epic tetralogy *Der Ring des Nibelungen*—more precisely, the fore-evening preceding a trilogy—was not recorded commercially until Georg Solti's reading appeared in 1959. (The 1953 EMI set was not released until later.) Previously, excerpts had displayed some of the great Wagnerians of the earlier part of the century. As with the other segments of the *Ring* cycle, the best of these earlier recordings offer a vocal mastery and resultant interpretive magnetism superior to most of what can be heard on the complete recordings. Essential among the *Rheingold* excerpts are Wagner's greeting to Valhalla in the final scene ("Abendlich strahlt die Sonne"), grandly uttered by Friedrich Schorr, and magisterial renditions of Erda's warning ("Weiche, Wotan") by such contraltos as Ernestine Schumann-Heink, Sigrid Onegin, Karin Branzell, and Kerstin Thorborg.

All of the recordings discussed are complete.

1953 EMI / ANGEL (M,P) CD

Ira Malaniuk (A), Ruth Siewert (B), Wolfgang Windgassen (C), Julius Patzak (D), Ferdinand Frantz (E), Gustav Neidlinger (F), Josef Greindl (G), Gottlob Frick (H), Orchestra of the RAI, Rome—Wilhelm Furtwängler

Wilhelm Furtwängler conducted concert performances of the *Ring* cycle in the Rome Radio studios in 1953, before a specially invited audience, one act every three days. With Furtwängler's planned studio recording of the tetralogy incomplete at his death, EMI undertook the complex task of acquiring the Rome tapes and securing permission from all participants for an official release, which finally came to pass in 1972.

The cast—German-speaking rather than international—includes some noteworthy artists who audibly share a stylistic attitude and performance tradition, one that the conductor could rely upon while he tended to the orchestra. Several scenes achieve exceptional continuity and point through Furtwängler's molding of the orchestral commentary (despite common stereotypes, his tempos are by no means prevailingly slow). Unfortunately, the orchestra, however hard-working, betrays a debilitating unfamiliarity with the music and sometimes even with the instruments themselves (a few of which are virtually unique to the *Ring*). Rarely does the brass section meet acceptable modern standards, and some moments, such as the dragon's appearance, are downright comical. The rather dim mono sound, however inevitable given the circumstances, limits the impact of the performance as well.

Gustav Neidlinger easily meets the grueling

vocal requirements of Alberich in this, the first of his three recordings of it; though his interpretation was to become more detailed and complete in later years, he already creates an imposing figure. More so, certainly, than the rulers of the gods, with Ferdinand Frantz a wooden Wotan and Ira Malaniuk a well-intentioned but feeble Fricka. Elisabeth Grümmer makes an exquisite Freia (a rare exception to the unimpressive norm for this role), but her brothers Froh and Donner are in nondescript hands. The giants include a rough Fasolt and a strikingly beautiful Fafner.

The entrance of the fire god, Loge, brightens the vocal outlook considerably, for unlike many Loges Wolfgang Windgassen treats his role as a true singing opportunity and combines solid tenor tone with firm musical intent. This set is well off for tenors, in fact, for Julius Patzak is the best Mime on records. Erda's incursion into the last scene adds an additional note of distinction, as Ruth Siewert has both the voice and the imagination to command the aural stage. By this point the orchestra has become more secure, so the performance ends better than it began.

1958 DECCA / LONDON (S) CD

Kirsten Flagstad (A), Jean Madeira (B), Set Svanholm (C), Paul Kuen (D), George London (E), Gustav Neidlinger (F), Walter Kreppel (G), Kurt Böhme (H), Vienna Philharmonic Orchestra—Georg Solti

This *Rheingold* attracted enormous and well-deserved attention when it first appeared—not only as the work's first complete recording but also as a pioneering operatic stereo spectacular, and for Kirsten Flagstad's assumption of the role of Fricka for the first time. The sound, capturing such attractions as an antiphonal ensemble of eighteen real anvils, remains wondrously impressive even alongside more recent editions. No other *Rheingold* stages the action with such audible clarity—sometimes distractingly, but usually helpfully. Flagstad's Fricka, goddesslike in its authority and altogether remarkable under the human circumstances (she had retired from public performance and was soon to succumb

to the illness that ended her life), has perhaps been overpraised; the actual sound is sometimes faded and unattractive, much as one wants not to notice it.

The cast as a whole has no serious weaknesses, with a good Rhinemaiden trio, a capable pair of giants, and vital portrayals of the lesser gods (the latter including Claire Watson, a vivacious if frail Freia, and Eberhard Wächter, most sonorous of Donners). Paul Kuen sings and acts Mime with tactful skill, and Jean Madeira turns in an adequate Erda—adequacy in this role being a rarer commodity than one might expect.

The three principal male roles are all in able hands. If George London's voice does not always pour forth as voluminously as one expects, and his interpretation remains sensible rather than illuminating, his Wotan still ranks as an asset to the performance. Set Svanholm's Loge, free of caricature and consistently musical in its vocal attitude, benefits from the remains of the vocal heft that had made him a leading Wagnerian tenor. Gustav Neidlinger contributes the finest of his three recorded Alberichs, with an absolutely mesmerizing Curse that flashes by in an instant, so unswervingly is its intent maintained. He benefits from Solti's dramatically alive conducting, which makes the most of every moment and helps the singers to their effects with professional skill.

1966 PHILIPS (S,P) CD

Annelies Burmeister (A), Věra Soukupová (B), Wolfgang Windgassen (C), Erwin Wohlfahrt (D), Theo Adam (E), Gustav Neidlinger (F), Martti Talvela (G), Kurt Böhme (H), Bayreuth Festival Orchestra—Karl Böhm

The Philips *Ring* (the second Wieland Wagner Bayreuth production, recorded in 1966 and 1967) shares several of its leading singers with the roughly contemporary Solti and Karajan studio recordings. The release of a recording with so much overlap with its competitors presumably is justified by the extra vividness of live performance, but in this case the problems of recording this work from the stage seem to have outweighed the advantages. Atmosphere is minimal, and small inaccuracies inevitably become more annoying on repetition. More harmfully, in this production Karl Böhm tends to hurry the work along in a helter-skelter way, emphasizing forward motion (not always steadily maintained)—always on the way to something else, rather than fully realizing each scene as it happens. This approach accords well with the scenes structured as gradual buildups (like the amassing of the treasure), but too much of the music comes across with no specific character, despite mostly good orchestral playing.

As for the portrayals available elsewhere: Gustav Neidlinger remains an exemplary Alberich, perhaps a bit more generalized than for Solti, and Wolfgang Windgassen has improved his Loge in terms of dramatic detail since his excellent performance for Furtwängler.

As Wotan, Theo Adam is a thoughtful artist with an attractive but unheroic voice. His evident good ideas about his role are impeded by vocal limitations at key points—he sounds dry and sometimes unsteady—and by Böhm's unhelpful haste. As Fricka, Annelies Burmeister inflects with great point, almost compensating for a basically uninteresting voice. Gerd Nienstedt comes across very powerfully in Donner's call to the heavens, while Anja Silja destroys Freia's youthful image with shrill, unfocused singing. Věra Soukupová makes an impressive Erda, with traces of edginess but a fine deep mezzo (audibly prompted, alas); she's hurt by the lack of orchestral magic in her scene, but that is typical of this recording.

1967 DEUTSCHE GRAMMOPHON (S) CD

Josephine Veasey (A), Oralia Dominguez (B), Gerhard Stolze (C), Erwin Wohlfahrt (D), Dietrich Fischer-Dieskau (E), Zoltán Kélémen (F), Martti Talvela (G), Karl Ridderbusch (H), Berlin Philharmonic Orchestra—Herbert von Karajan

The second *Ring* recording created in the recording studio begins with a *Rheingold* that represents the Karajan approach at its most characteristic and most persuasive. The exquisitely balanced and played orchestral contribution, a prevailing vocal attractiveness and

conversational fluency—these constitute a valuable statement about the opera.

With the most mellifluous and characterful Rhinemaiden trio on records (Helen Donath, Edda Moser, and Anna Reynolds), a believable—even touching—Alberich, and Karajan's effervescent orchestral realization, the first scene receives its finest recorded rendering. Zoltán Kélémen deals strongly with all his opportunities throughout the work, in fact, and his scene opposite his brother Mime, the equally personable Erwin Wohlfahrt, features far more actual singing and characterization than usual.

The major drawback in the cast is the Wotan, Dietrich Fischer-Dieskau. Great artist that he is, he is still not well matched to the depth and breadth of a Wagnerian bass-baritone role; he deals fluently with the important conversational exchanges, but the climactic moments find him struggling and forcing to approximate the right kind of sound. Josephine Veasey outclasses him with every resonant, subtly shaded phrase she utters—a distinguished Fricka. Their relatives include an exceptional Froh (Donald Grobe), an appealing Donner (Robert Kerns), and a painful Freia (Simone Mangelssdorf). Talvela and Ridderbusch bring the giants to life with exceptional tonal beauty and distinct characterizations.

The casting of the screechingly assertive character tenor Gerhard Stolze as Loge would be questionable under any circumstances; in this refined performance, it seems contrary to the whole spirit of the occasion. Yet Stolze tells his tales and mocks his companions more forcefully than any other Loge; if he fails some of the basic vocal tests of the role, he at least offers something in compensation. Erda is also unconventionally but more successfully cast, with the mezzo-soprano Oralia Dominguez; her singing is firmly uttered and shaped, fulfilling the potential mystery and wonder of her important scene.

1968 WESTMINSTER (S)

Ruth Hesse (A), Ursula Böse (B), Fritz Uhl (C), Herold Kraus (D), Rolf Polke (E), Rolf Kühne

(F), Otto von Rohr (G), Takao Okamura (H), South German Philharmonic—Hans Swarowsky

For reasons that remain somewhat mysterious, Hans Swarowsky and the South German Philharmonic undertook a complete *Ring* recording for Interrecord Anstalt in 1968, and Westminster released the cycle in 1972. Few names in the cast are well known, and the conductor himself enjoys more fame as a teacher than an executant. Swarowsky is, in fact, the biggest liability of the *Rheingold*, failing to generate tension at such key points as Alberich's summoning of the Nibelungs and his loss of the ring. The orchestra has its own problems, with vibrato-laden brass and clarinets, and an undersize string section. As the strings still overpower the brass, one may reasonably deduce electronic manipulation.

With Wotan and Alberich the strongest singers in the Westminster *Ring*, this *Rheingold* accidentally focuses more keenly than most on the crucial conflict between the two. Rolf Polke, without a great deal of nuance and with a tendency to jump ahead of the beat, still brings a sturdy, attactive bass-baritone and good musical line to the role; comparison unexpectedly reveals him as one of the most satisfactory Wotans on complete recordings. Rolf Kühne, Alberich, runs into a limitation at the top at key moments (including the Curse), but otherwise offers characterful imagination and vocal strength; especially original and valid is his hurt—rather than snarling—reaction to being robbed of the ring. He certainly is the only sign of life in the first scene, as he contends with a very studio-bound and slovenly Rhinedaughter trio.

Fritz Uhl makes an effectively insinuating Loge. Herold Kraus as Mime has a substantial voice, albeit of a thick and ungainly kind, and some vitality. Of the others, Fricka, Erda, and Donner (Rudolf Knoll) fulfill the minimum requirements of their roles vocally and interpretively, the giants make little impact, and Freia and Froh are simply inadequate. All in all, a weak production, of interest mainly to students of the two principal bass-baritone roles.

1975 EMI / ANGEL (In English) (S,P) CD

Katherine Pring (A), Anne Collins (B), Emile Belcourt (C), Gregory Dempsey (D), Norman Bailey (E), Derek Hammond-Stroud (F), Robert Lloyd (G), Clifford Grant (H), English National Opera Orchestra—Reginald Goodall

This *Rheingold* forms part of a complete *Ring* in English, using Andrew Porter's translation as performed by the English National Opera. The live recording shows what a well-prepared production this was; Reginald Goodall's conception is evident in all elements, and most fruitfully so in his ability (by extended individual coaching) to coax a genuine *legato* and feeling for expressive possibilities from his cast. His musical preferences are evident from the start, in a slow range of tempos that can cause problems: the first scene gives no feeling of wave motion, the final minutes leave the Rhinemaidens gasping for breath, and the overall variety of the work is undercut by the avoidance of really fast speeds. Yet Goodall also displays such care for balance and phrasing that all the melodic strands shine, and his loving realization of the work is aided by the high quality of the translation and of the best of his cast.

At the head of that cast is Norman Bailey, one of the more successful Wotans in commercial *Ring* recordings. Sometimes the vibration of his likable bass-baritone loosens beyond desirable limits; other times it loses resonance momentarily. But he encompasses the great moments nobly, and molds the words and phrases with great sensitivity (he is also the only Wotan who sounds asleep for his first lines). His opponent Alberich is vividly embodied by Derek Hammond-Stroud in an interpretation that might not meet classic tests of vocalism (he hasn't a real half-voice, and some inflections recall the Gilbert and Sullivan roles he does so well) but has exceptional immediacy and menace.

Loge's first lines startle: Emile Belcourt's voice resembles that of a cabaret artist, one who puts a role over by force of personality and clever indication of pitches. Odd as it is to hear this in Wagner, Belcourt makes his bag of tricks work, and his different vocal identity from the rest of the cast comes to seem analogous to Loge's stance as the outsider among the gods.

Fricka, Erda, and the giants, all imaginative artists, sound lightweight and somewhat ineffectual for their assignments (since Anne Collins sounds better in the more extended *Siegfried* role, perhaps she was poorly recorded here); they surpass the negligible Freia-Froh-Donner trio, however. Gregory Dempsey has more voice than most Mimes, an advantage to which he adds biting enunciation; his work may not be pretty, but it's always vivid and intelligent. The Rhinemaidens make a nice trio, with Valerie Masterson an especially pleasing Woglinde.

1980 PHILIPS (S,D) CD

Hanna Schwarz (A), Ortrun Wenkel (B), Heinz Zednik (C), Helmut Pampuch (D), Donald McIntyre (E), Hermann Becht (F), Matti Salminen (G), Fritz Hübner (H), Bayreuth Festival Orchestra—Pierre Boulez

The cycle conducted by Boulez derives from a Bayreuth production presented from 1976 to 1981 and recorded at special private run-throughs in 1979 (*Götterdämmerung*) and 1980 (the others). Boulez here offers a new Wagner performing style, removing traditional accretions to the score and with a less weighty conception of orchestral color. No objection to such an innovation can be made in principle; periodic new "traditions" are essential to the continuing life of any music—the Furtwängler-style approach itself was one such. As it turns out, the Bayreuth Festival Orchestra realizes Boulez's intentions sufficiently well to demonstrate the drawbacks of this abstract attitude: if no accent is marked, as in Alberich's chase of the Rhinemaidens, no accent is made, with a consequent flatfooted effect; the descent-to-Nibelheim interlude, the storm, the entry of the gods into Valhalla all lack weight and impact. And a dragon with no roar from the tuba is a tame beast indeed. Sometimes the new look does make a legitimate point: Valhalla gets a face-lift with a light, un-Germanic brass sound, and eventually one grows to accept it.

Boulez's stylistic revolution is taking place only in the orchestra. Most of the singers can't match the clean instrumental execution, and some clearly need help from their conductor and aren't getting it. Stage director Patrice Chereau deserves credit for the fine feeling for character and intention shown by all the singers, despite vocal limitations. Still, something is out of order in a *Rheingold* when the most beautiful singing comes from Fasolt—in this case the admirable Matti Salminen. Wotan and Fricka, light-toned and unmemorable, fade into insignificance by comparison; Donald McIntyre remains aurally anonymous throughout, and delivers his final address to Valhalla dully. As Loge, Heinz Zednik is musical and highly characterful, but lacks real vocal juice. Nor does Hermann Becht quite measure up to Alberich; he's short-breathed in the Curse, with no power or *legato* at his disposal. Ortrun Wenkel, the Erda, is accurate and musicianly but tonally unimpressive. The others (including Siegfried Jerusalem, surprisingly only an adequate Froh) merit no individual mention.

1980 EURODISC (S,D) CD

Yvonne Minton (A), Ortrun Wenkel (B), Peter Schreier (C), Christian Vogel (D), Theo Adam (E), Siegmund Nimsgern (F), Roland Bracht (G), Matti Salminen (H), Dresden State Orchestra—Marek Janowski

The first studio *Ring* since Westminster's was undoubtedly timed and planned to take advantage of the advent of digital sound, and the probable market for a complete CD *Ring*. Indeed, this was the first cycle to appear on silver discs. Strong points throughout the cycle are the fabulous playing of the Dresden State Orchestra and the knowledgeable leadership of Janowski, who (like Boulez) takes a fresh look at the score's demands without (unlike Boulez) forgoing unwritten modifications or the input of solo singers. *Rheingold* is not Janowski's most persuasive segment, as the sound falls short of the near-ideal balance heard in later installments, and his ideas about the relative proportion of the big moments produce some odd results—a tame thunderstorm, for instance.

Also, the cast has its weak spots. Adam is no more authoritative than he was for Böhm in

1966 (no less, either, to be fair); he understands the role and works insightfully, but his thin, unimposing voice limits one's response. Peter Schreier contributes an alert, musically conceived Loge of the character-tenor type. Outstanding by any standard are the voluptuous, highly personal Fricka of Minton, the straightforward, vibrant Alberich of Nimsgern, and the distinctively suave Fafner of Salminen (his brother giant is disappointingly ill-defined). Lucia Popp makes a lovely Woglinde, and her sister nymphs (Uta Priew and Hanna Schwarz) match her level reasonably well, though the three do not blend well as a trio. Marita Napier comes through as a tolerable Freia, Christian Vogel an engaging Mime; Donner and Froh are undercast.

1988 DEUTSCHE GRAMMOPHON (S,D) CD

Christa Ludwig (A), Birgitta Svendén (B), Siegfried Jerusalem (C), Heinz Zednik (D), James Morris (E), Ekkehard Wlaschiha (F), Kurt Moll (G), Jan-Hendrik Rootering (H), Metropolitan Opera Orchestra—James Levine

James Levine's ideas about Wagnerian interpretation produce a very broadly paced *Rheingold* indeed, with plenty of time for each new action to register and develop, and maximum emphasis for each episode. The Met orchestra executes Levine's conception magnificently; the tempos rarely seem slow, for articulation and momentum remain buoyant. Levine's cast mostly can fill out his broad expanses, and the result is a highly absorbing *Rheingold*.

Among the cast, highest honors go to James Morris, and Levine surely deserves some credit for eliciting from him a Wotan that scarcely misses a musical possibility from start to finish. Morris's sonorous bass sounds especially ample and resplendent here, with a perfectly arched salute to Valhalla in Scene 2 unmatched on any of the other complete recordings (including his own second try). Despite some shrillness on top, Christa Ludwig radiates the authority and glamour to be a fit consort for this Wotan.

Ekkehard Wlaschiha has exactly the right penetrating bass-baritone for Alberich, and plenty of imagination and dramatic presence; if only

he insisted on singing every note beautifully as well as characterfully, he would equal the best Alberichs on records. Siegfried Jerusalem, not the most prodigious vocalist or most riveting interpreter of Loge, nevertheless has the two elements in equal balance; he shapes his solos beguilingly, and tells his tales and makes his unsettling comments with assured showmanship.

There is a new central role in this recording: Kurt Moll's riveting Fasolt is an object lesson in how beautiful vocalism and thoughtful interpretation can go hand in hand to revitalize any role. Jan-Hendrik Rootering's Fafner is not far behind in dramatic and vocal impact. Mari-Anne Häggender provides a fresh, healthy soprano as Freia, who must have such qualities if the drama is to make sense. Her brothers are less distinctive. Birgitta Svendén's alto, suitably dark in color and goddesslike in address, has a youthfulness that sits oddly on earth mother Erda, but the fault is an easy one to forgive.

Hei-Kyung Hong, Diane Kesling, and Meredith Parsons make a euphonious trio of Rhinemaidens, their well-matched voices shimmering in harmony; unfortunately, their un-German, coached-sounding delivery renders their scenes dramatically ineffective. Nevertheless, the general level of vocal-dramatic spark on this recording is high enough to make it an unexpectedly strong contender.

1988 EMI / ANGEL (S,D) CD

Marjana Lipovšek (A), Jadwiga Rappé (B), Heinz Zednik (C), Peter Haage (D), James Morris (E), Theo Adam (F), Hans Tschammer (G), Kurt Rydl (H), Bavarian Radio Symphony—Bernard Haitink

In the second portion of his *Ring* cycle to be released, Bernard Haitink's conducting is unexceptionable—carefully balanced, sensibly paced (with some welcome flexibility of tempo that only occasionally seems lax), reasonably though not remarkably well played. His is the sort of leadership that does not draw attention to itself, but instead seeks mainly to serve the musical and dramatic needs of the cast. It suffers at points where the conductor must dominate; the transitions within and after Scene 1 pass by tamely, for instance. But the biggest problem is that not all of Haitink's cast live up to the responsibility he allows them.

At least the gods are all in good hands here, with the three lesser deities perhaps the strongest such trio on records: Eva Johannsen, Andreas Schmidt, and Peter Seiffert. Marjana Lipovšek provides a rich-toned, not very individual Fricka; she might have been more of an asset to the cast as Erda, for which Jadwiga Rappé has the right manner but too bright a timbre. Finally, James Morris again provides the only completely adequate Wotan on complete recordings. He is just a shade less impressive here than in the DG *Rheingold*; he pushes a bit at points where easy sustainment would be preferable, and allows some potentially eloquent moments to pass by neutrally. But he remains a potent presence.

Theo Adam, a famous Wotan, is an interesting piece of casting as the Nibelung counterpart to Wotan. Alas, despite his imaginative absorption of his role, Adam can no longer consistently produce singing of the required quality:

his upper notes wobble, and some are little more than squawks. Peter Haage, with a voice of modest format for Mime, is satisfactory when singing quietly but hasn't the vocal control for loud outbursts or niceties like grace notes. Heinz Zednik, getting by with less voice than in his Loge for Boulez, remains a vivid and incisive exponent of the role in the character-tenor tradition. Both giants are highly musical, but light in tone and nondescript in their dramatic intentions. Similar comments apply to the Rhinemaidens, who sing well without making much impact. The final impression of the set is one of bits and pieces—some marvelous, others ordinary.

No one set excels the others at all points. Goodall and Furtwängler have important strengths, Solti and Levine still more, but in this case Karajan, with his songful approach and likeminded cast (a couple of jarring exceptions aside) comes off the best of any.

JON ALAN CONRAD

RICHARD WAGNER

DIE WALKÜRE (1870)

A: Brünnhilde (s); B: Sieglinde (s); C: Fricka (ms); D: Siegmund (t);
E: Wotan (bs-bar); F: Hunding (bs)

ie Walküre has always been the most popular opera in the *Ring* cycle—testimony to its musical appeal, as its story ends most inconclusively of the four. Before the era of complete recordings, many excerpts and individual acts appeared on records. Most noteworthy of these, in many ways more essential for appreciating the profound beauty of the work than any of the complete sets, is the Act I recorded in 1935 with Bruno Walter conducting the Vienna Philharmonic; Lotte Lehmann's Sieglinde and Lauritz Melchior's Siegmund still set the standard for their roles. The slightly cut Act II incorporating the same pair approaches the same level. A 1945 recording of Act III, with Helen Traubel and Herbert Janssen, made this the first *Ring* opera recorded essentially complete. Other recordings of single acts include two made by Decca / London as tests for a complete *Ring*, now interesting mostly as souvenirs of late-period Kirsten Flagstad: Sieglinde in Act I, Knappertsbusch conducting; Brünnhilde in the Annunciation of Death (Todesverkündigung) and Act III, Solti conducting. Essential earlier excerpts document the Brünnhilde of Frida Leider and the Wotan of Friedrich Schorr, irreplaceable artists and voices.

Die Walküre is sometimes slightly cut in live performance, but all recordings at hand are complete.

1953 EMI / ANGEL (M,P) CD

Martha Mödl (A), Hilde Konetzni (B), Elsa Cavelti (C), Wolfgang Windgassen (D), Ferdinand Frantz (E), Gottlob Frick (F), Orchestra of the RAI, Rome—Wilhelm Furtwängler

With its more continuously active orchestral role, *Die Walküre* allows the distinctive character of Furtwängler's conception to assert itself more successfully than it did in *Das Rheingold*: molded to a strong bass line, always moving forward however moderate the speed, never neutral in intent. From that last point originates the long line through whole acts and operas so often remarked upon in this conductor's work; a listener's attention is constantly maintained because nothing is treated as merely transitional. The shallow-toned, tentative Rome brass still hurts some important moments, but this time there's something gripping going on for them to spoil (in fairness, the orchestra also rises to some impressive climaxes).

The cast, not of incandescent level (including a merely decent Valkyrie octet), brings a shared stylistic background to its task. Wolfgang Windgassen provides a clean, strong vocalism for Siegmund, not magnetic or rich, but convincing in combination with his sincerity and good musicianship. Hilde Konetzni applies a lively temperament and impressive voice to Sieglinde, her success limited by a cautiousness in the face of the climactic moments (most damagingly in her final outbursts in Act III). Gottlob Frick offers some beautiful singing, expressing Hunding's viewpoint well in purely musical terms.

Elsa Cavelti clearly knows what to do with Fricka's music, but her blank, unfocused voice allows little beauty or expressiveness to come through. Wotan, luckily, finds Frantz more comfortable with his role than in *Rheingold*. Never quite imposing in sound, and limited at the range extremes, he nevertheless earns considerable respect by the time his well-conceived Farewell ends.

With the many passages of this youngest Brünnhilde that lie low in the soprano voice, apparently Martha Mödl's home territory, she makes a beautiful, imposing effect. She emits many a heave and gulp to launch herself into higher regions, and her interpretation is sometimes thus inadvertent—the anguish conveyed being her own—but when the line is congenial she can do some personal, touching things, as in her exchanges with Siegmund and Wotan. Because of such successful realizations, and a well-shaped Fire Music, the performance leaves one with a positive impression.

1954 EMI / ANGEL (M) CD

Martha Mödl (A), Leonie Rysanek (B), Margarete Klose (C), Ludwig Suthaus (D), Ferdinand Frantz (E), Gottlob Frick (F), Vienna Philharmonic Orchestra—Wilhelm Furtwängler

This, Wilhelm Furtwängler's last recording, was to have inaugurated a complete *Ring* for records. It provides the most complete idea available of his conception of the work—thanks in no small part to the Vienna Philharmonic, familiar with the opera in a way that the Italian orchestras involved in his available *Ring* tapings could not have been. The rich orchestral balance, the varying blends among the instruments, the achievement of a strong forward pulse that does not depend on haste—all of these are striking, as is the impression that all the performers share a familiarity with the opera that allows them to work easily together. Such developments as Wotan's growing pain and frustration during his narration are expertly controlled, and almost unbearably moving.

Ludwig Suthaus makes a striking first impres-

sion and on the whole lives up to it, with a nearly ideal feeling for line; what he lacks is true vocal beauty, as opposed to beauty of musical conception. Leonie Rysanek makes a neutral contribution in her first scene, a negative one as she begins "Der Männer Sippe" with unsteady, poorly tuned tone; her great moments come each time she can soar thrillingly aloft. Since both extremes matter for Sieglinde, Rysanek's performance can be accounted only a partial success.

Ferdinand Frantz's Wotan finds him straining for high notes even more than he had in 1953. His appealing vocal quality when not under duress (as in the Farewell) is compromised by a more limited musical outlook than before, content with sensible rather than meaningful delivery. Mödl's Brünnhilde remains much as in Rome, occasionally better sustained because of studio circumstances, but still tough- and effortful-sounding, happiest in low-lying scenes.

Margarete Klose's telling ideas about Fricka reach only partial fulfillment, for her voice had at this late point in her career become too dry and unmalleable for true expressiveness. Gottlob Frick improves on his already impressive performance for Furtwängler, with an easy size and menace. The Valkyries make a pretty strong group, enhanced by the bright and flexible Helmwige of Erika Köth.

1961 DECCA / LONDON (S) CD

Birgit Nilsson (A), Gré Brouwenstijn (B), Rita Gorr (C), Jon Vickers (D), George London (E), David Ward (F), London Symphony Orchestra—Erich Leinsdorf

The first stereo *Walküre*, and the only one not planned as part of a complete recorded cycle, Leinsdorf's recording was first issued as part of the deluxe RCA Soria series, then reissued on London. It is a straightforward performance, recorded with an orchestral emphasis that partially submerges some powerful voices. Erich Leinsdorf's direction appears to best advantage when simple execution of the score's indications will do the job, most notably the Ride of the Valkyries. At other points, it lacks detailed pointing and shaping of the musical-dramatic continuity, but it forms a highly adequate accompaniment to those singers who are willing to take charge on their own: Jon Vickers and Rita Gorr. Vickers sounds his youthful best, his gutsy tenor flowing freely and his imagination discovering and making vivid the point of every phrase. Perhaps his greatest gift here is his ability to invest a passage with a simplicity that makes it unforgettable, as in his explanation of his assumed name ("Nun weisst du") and in the Todesverkündigung. Gorr, with one of the great dramatic mezzo voices, presents her arguments against Wotan to magnificently unanswerable effect.

The other principals sing strongly but don't quite match their own best standards. Birgit Nilsson on this occasion interprets Brünnhilde in almost purely musical terms, shaping such passages as the Todesverkündigung and her pleading with Wotan sensitively and, of course, offering thrilling high notes, but allowing too many lines to pass uneventfully. George London's Wotan carries conviction in most of Act III; before that, his solid singing sounds uninvolved and sometimes ill-defined as to pitch. Gré Browenstijn's Sieglinde, too, comes to life only intermittently, despite a most sympathetic presence and attractive voice. David Ward's lovely bass-baritone is simply wrong for Hunding—he sounds a thoroughly amiable man. The Covent Garden-based Valkyries are as good as any on records; standouts for incisive delivery of solo lines are Waltraute and Rossweise (Margreta Elkins and Josephine Veasey).

1965 DECCA / LONDON (S) CD

Birgit Nilsson (A), Régine Crespin (B), Christa Ludwig (C), James King (D), Hans Hotter (E), Gottlob Frick (F), Vienna Philharmonic Orchestra—Georg Solti

This *Walküre* completed the first integral *Ring* made for records, and has a great deal to recommend it. In particular, it has Birgit Nilsson, in glowing form and more thoroughly involved than for Leinsdorf. Régine Crespin contributes a youthfully touching Sieglinde. Her

seductive vocal color and quite unique personal quality—simultaneously large-scale and intimate—count as strong assets for this role. James King has the bright, secure voice and the good intentions to make a memorable Siegmund; if he is not quite that (somehow his conscientious inflections miss real eloquence), he is never less than a very good one.

Wotan is Hans Hotter, an important singer near the end of his stage career and a master of the role; no Wotan narrates more fascinatingly, rages more humanly, or mourns more heartbreakingly. Honesty and the maintaining of standards demand that his vocal limitations, a yawn in the tone compounded by a wobble at full voice, be mentioned, and indeed these faults do impede enjoyment of his work. But some more recent recorded Wotans fall as short of vocal perfection without being remotely as communicative; Hotter emerges as a giant in direct comparison.

In his third recording of the role, Gottlob Frick stands as an epitome of the larger-than-life, pure-villain sort of Hunding, bitingly sung and compellingly enacted. Christa Ludwig brings vocal gold and her always alive temperament to Fricka, though others have pointed the argumentative line of her scene more sharply. The Valkyries are top quality all the way, with two future Brünnhildes leading the ensemble (Helga Dernesch and Berit Lindholm) and several impressive mezzos (Helen Watts, Vera Little, Brigitte Fassbaender).

Solti's direction is not the sort to attract attention for its differentness; he does what one expects of a conductor of this opera, and so is apt to be underrated. But the drama with which he builds the big scenes, and the yearning flexibility he brings to the romantic moments, ought not to be underestimated; one may ultimately come to want more than this, but certainly not less. Because Solti runs to no extremes, but simply serves the musical-dramatic needs, his interpretion remains most satisfying.

1966 DEUTSCHE GRAMMOPHON (S) CD

Régine Crespin (A), Gundula Janowitz (B), Josephine Veasey (C), Jon Vickers (D), Thomas

Stewart (E), Martti Talvela (F), Berlin Philharmonic Orchestra—Herbert von Karajan

Die Walküre began Karajan's *Ring* as it ended Solti's (the releases separated by mere months). It forms one of the strongest segments of the Karajan cycle, with his care for orchestral beauty and balance complemented by an interestingly chosen and surprisingly successful cast. Only half of the six principals seemed likely casting at the time, and indeed the two sopranos did not keep these roles in their repertory for long. But they all have something valid to offer, and (as would not always be the case in the later operas) Karajan was willing to let them contribute on their own terms, even if it meant subduing the orchestra to accommodate weak vocal registers. This was probably the origin of this cycle's inaccurate reputation as a chamber-music *Ring*.

Régine Crespin follows her Sieglinde for Solti with a provocative Brünnhilde, dark-toned and shimmering, more personal than most. Only her seeming restriction to extremes of loud or quiet singing detracts from her work. It's a liability she shares with Jon Vickers, already a fine Siegmund for Leinsdorf and even more inside the role here; but one can hear the loss in the way his soft singing, lovely as it is, can no longer build gradually when the music demands that it do so. It remains a major performance, by the only dramatic tenor to truly command the Wagnerian repertory in recent decades.

One might legimately find Gundula Janowitz far too light for Sieglinde, except that Karajan gives her the gentlest of accompanimental cushions, allowing her peerless ability to float and shape a phrase all the room it needs. In the end, she gets more out of the part than many other sopranos better endowed for it by nature. Of Thomas Stewart's Wotan, the only real complaint can be his obvious lack of a true bass-baritone's tonal strength and depth; but he brings fine line to his part as well as attractive tone, and stays in memory as a satisfying Wotan. With Veasey and Talvela well cast and in top form, we have an exceptional enough group of principals to make the squally Valkyrie ensemble relatively bearable. And with Karajan and the Berlin Philharmonic roaring through the storms and singing along with Wotan's Farewell as if on one inexhaustible breath, one may well find something special and irreplaceable about this set.

1967 PHILIPS (S,P) CD

Birgit Nilsson (A), Leonie Rysanek (B), Annelies Burmeister (C), James King (D), Theo Adam (E), Gerd Nienstedt (F), Bayreuth Festival Orchestra—Karl Böhm

Böhm's *Ring* gains in stature in its second installment, as any production would by the addition of Birgit Nilsson in her prime. (She can, however, be heard in equally fine form under Solti, and in more favorable surroundings.) The most pervasive problem is again the conductor, who fulfills only the most obvious requirements of the score: the tempos are plausible (on the fast side) and the notes get played. No real differentiation underlies the constant motion, which lets one musical event after another go by unmarked (listen to Siegmund's narration of his history as an example; the playing retains the same indifferent character throughout).

Despite Leonie Rysanek's intensity as Sieglinde, the role remains unsuited to her voice; all its low-lying conversational lines sound forced, and the recording does not capture the way her high notes can soar through a theater. She favors unscripted screams, most notoriously when Siegfried pulls the sword from the tree (a foolish idea, much imitated since). James King surpasses his Siegmund for Solti with a more involved, sympathetic performance, very solidly sung, lacking only the evocative magic that can transform the role's big moments.

Theo Adam's Wotan has impressive stretches when singing out strongly (as in the despairing opening of his Narrative), but his fine conception of the role can be only partially realized through his tonal limitations. He suffers considerably from Böhm's lack of repose, as does Annelies Burmeister's forcefully declaimed Fricka. More baritone than bass, Gerd Nienstedt unwisely tries to make up the difference by snarling like a provincial Alberich. The Valkyries constitute a solid group (Danica Mastilovic and Helga Dernesch on the top parts).

1968 WESTMINSTER (S)

Nadezda Kniplová (A), Ditha Sommer (B), Ruth Hesse (C), Gerald McKee (D), Rolf Polke (E), Otto von Rohr (F), South German Philharmonic—Hans Swarowsky

Rolf Polke's Wotan is the main asset of this segment of the Swarowsky *Ring*, and his Narrative and Farewell its most successful scenes. He may lack the poetic eloquence of a Schorr, but in basic vocal competence he holds his own among complete recorded Wotans, and surpasses several more famous names.

Ruth Hesse is a capable Fricka of less than top grade (gray and unfocused when she must sing high), and the duet between the godly couple goes relatively well. But Wotan's three children fail to satisfy. A brief sampling might disclose little wrong with Siegmund and Brünnhilde; the main problem in both cases is their lack of variety for such a long, dramatically complex work. Gerald McKee's tenor is unremittingly bright and sharp-edged (except when he shifts into a completely different voice for soft passages), Nadezda Kniplová's soprano is tough and sour, and neither displays much enlivening dramatic force; before long one simply tires of listening to them. As for Ditha Sommer's Sieglinde, her limitations show up instantly in an inability to control pitch accurately or sustain a note reliably. Hunding has more solidity, but bleats out of control on top. The Valkyries are a weak army, not always in tune.

In familiar material like the Preludes, Swarowsky understands what is needed and can get it from his orchestra. Elsewhere he lets tension drain away; the Wotan-Fricka scene is a good example, with its dramatic pauses merely dead air.

1975 EMI / ANGEL (In English) (S,P) CD

Rita Hunter (A), Margaret Curphey (B), Ann Howard (C), Alberto Remedios (D), Norman Bailey (E), Clifford Grant (F), English National Opera Orchestra—Reginald Goodall

Reginald Goodall's *Walküre* makes an even more convincing case than his *Rheingold* for his stature as a Wagnerian, with his realization of the music's long-term motion enhanced by the way he exposes the sensuous beauty of the instrumental writing. Even more impressive is his skill at talent-scouting and coaching: in addition to Norman Bailey, Goodall saw and developed the Wagnerian potential in Rita Hunter and Alberto Remedios. The work of these three, in combination with Goodall's effective direction, turns this set into a *Walküre* well worth hearing.

Remedios has his difficulties here, Siegmund staying at the bottom of the tenor voice more than he can gracefully manage. But he never lets it unsettle his vocal equilibrium, and he has some touching moments. Hunter encounters no problems, from her free-soaring "Hojotoho" onward. Perhaps her very best work comes in the final scene with Wotan, where Bailey is working on the same level. This is one of his best recordings; those who are usually bored by Wotan's Narrative should listen to his rendition in English to learn how gripping it can be.

With Clifford Grant a firm Hunding and Ann Howard a Fricka full of tellingly directed fire, the shorter roles are in good hands. The house team of Valkyries is also exceptionally strong (special commendations for poise and projection to Anne Evans, Elizabeth Connell, and Sarah Walker). If only Margaret Curphey were on the same level, but in fact her mushy, ill-defined soprano does let things down. Not enough, though, to spoil the overall quality of the set.

1980 PHILIPS (S,D) CD

Gwyneth Jones (A), Jeannine Altmeyer (B), Hanna Schwarz (C), Peter Hofmann (D), Donald McIntyre (E), Matti Salminen (F), Bayreuth Festival Orchestra—Pierre Boulez

The Boulez approach works better in *Walküre* than in *Rheingold*, his "pure music" emphasis reflecting something valid in the score's musical continuity (if not the whole truth about it). The clarity of timbre and texture in the orchestra, however, is not matched by the singing.

Peter Hofmann's voice sounds precarious on his first entrance, nor does it ever impress as a heroic tenor for the ages, but he shows his better qualities as the work proceeds: a dramatically live temperament, and a voice with some capacity for depth and shading. Not at home with the clear phrasing needed for "Winterstürme," he shows his worth in the strong, simple declamation of the second act.

Jeannine Altmeyer's colorful soprano makes a sympathetic impression as Sieglinde; her portrayal is kept from achieving more than just the basics by clumsy, unidiomatic German and a lack of real continuity, whether musical or dramatic.

Donald McIntyre does not emerge with credit in a vocal comparison with other recorded Wotans, for he is apparently not even trying to compete; bypassing most opportunities for musical expression, lapsing into breathiness when singing softly, he sounds involved solely with the acting challenge. In this he often succeeds, but most listeners will find the trade-off less than gratifying.

Gwyneth Jones's Brünnhilde probably ought to be experienced only in conjunction with her visual performance, preferably in person. An artist of exceptional imagination and presence, she was functioning by the time of this recording with a voice that simply would not respond consistently. When the writing is low or high, she can produce some stunning effects; when it stays in the middle (as it does most of the time), she attacks notes imprecisely in terms of both pitch and time, and often as not widens into a wobble. On records, this overpowers whatever else she might bring to the role.

Hanna Schwarz betrays her light weight for Fricka with some tremulous high notes and empty low ones. She also shows a clear, direct idea of the drama of her scene, and makes her points so decisively that her victory seems unusually chilling. Hunding and the Valkyries fulfill their assignments without leaving any personal imprint.

1981 EURODISC (S,D) CD

Jeannine Altmeyer (A), Jessye Norman (B), Yvonne Minton (C), Siegfried Jerusalem (D), Theo Adam (E), Kurt Moll (F), Dresden State Orchestra—Marek Janowski

Janowski's *Ring* improves in *Walküre*, partly due to interesting casting of the Wälsung twins. Siegfried Jerusalem, light-voiced by the standard of most earlier Siegmunds, makes his own imprint by means of his appealingly shaded timbre, his command of meaningful and personal phrasing, and his exceptional musicality. Short of a Vickers or Melchior, he's as memorable a Siegmund as there is on records. In comparison, there is something impersonal about Jessye Norman's Sieglinde, and hints of squareness or awkwardness in her vocal delivery. Yet it seems absurd to complain of such a voluminous, carefully molded outpouring of beautiful tone. Theo Adam has everything a Wotan needs except a really steady, ample voice.

At the time of the recording, Jeannine Altmeyer was just undertaking her first stage Brünnhildes, and the inexperience shows in her desperate lunges at high notes and attempts to push vocal weight into recalcitrant parts of the range; such manipulation prevents her voice from working as well as one hopes. Though the voice is probably no lighter than Rita Hunter's, her way of meeting the role's requirements is far less persuasive (and the problem of her mechanical German remains).

Kurt Moll sings a compelling Hunding: convincingly tough, but also an individual with justification for his behavior rather than a menacing stock figure. Yvonne Minton's Fricka is even better, conceived and sustained in the grand manner, gorgeously uttered from start to finish. The strong Valkyries feature an especially sparkling Helmwige-Ortlinde pair, complete with their seldom-heard trills (Ruth Falcon and Cheryl Studer).

As for Janowski, his opening storm, hasty and with weak Wagner tubas for the Donner theme, does not promise well, but he improves substantially later, with careful attention to the events of each scene within a straightforward tempo scheme. The transparency of the orchestral sound is wonderfully convincing, and some details work here as nowhere else: try the harp mini-*glissandos* in the loudest statements of the Ride of the Valkyries.

1987 DEUTSCHE GRAMMOPHON (S,D) CD

Hildegard Behrens (A), Jessye Norman (B), Christa Ludwig (C), Gary Lakes (D), James Morris (E), Kurt Moll (F), Metropolitan Opera Orchestra—James Levine

This performance adds a fourth great orchestra to the Vienna, Berlin, and Dresden ensembles already on records in the cycle. Benefiting from an unusually flattering balance, the Metropolitan Opera Orchestra displays a security and personality, a tonal glamour and technical aplomb, that maintains interest throughout the work and makes every note, even of Wagner's conventional "agitation" figuration, audible. Since there are no embarrassments among the six principals, and the Valkyrie ensemble is perhaps the most imposing on records, this set should have provided near-total satisfaction.

That it does not do so may be ascribed to some of the soloists' relative weak points, but still more to conductor James Levine. Levine apparently is after some kind of ultimate rendition, making each moment the broadest, biggest, most exciting that it has ever been. In this he succeeds, but the continuity of the piece suffers, as does the sense that the personages of the drama are human beings pursuing urgent needs. (The engineering also betrays its artificiality, audibly and needlessly altering orchestral balance at times.) A stately monumental quality alternates with restless energy, and some unusual gearshifts within scenes suggest the difficulty of reconciling all the conductor's goals. Certainly the reading remains on a high level, but it carries less conviction than several others.

Outstanding among a strong group of principals is the Hunding of Kurt Moll: standard-setting in terms of vocal and dramatic imagination, exceptional in combining menace and dignity. Jessye Norman does many admirable things (including some long phrasing in "Der Männer Sippe" that Wagner clearly wanted but

was impractical to expect), yet her stateliness misses the human, vulnerable quality of the best Sieglindes. Christa Ludwig, miraculously similar vocally to her twenty-year-old rendition for Solti, now seems even more concerned to supercharge each phrase with maximum passion, and thus misses the shaping and point that other Frickas give this marvelous scene.

Of the three newcomers, Gary Lakes has vocal fiber and some musical understanding; his only moderate effectiveness seems to stem mostly from a limited dynamic range, with little available of ringingly loud or meltingly soft singing. (The recording fails to convey the sheer size of his voice.) Hildegard Behrens has dramatic imagination to spare, and sings most affectingly when the demands are straightforward. When she must sing both high and fast, or other taxing combinations, an unattractively pressurized quality takes over. Finally, the greatest asset of this performance is its Wotan, James Morris. His attention to the shaping of his musical line means that not every passing detail is etched with the precision of more declamatory Wotans; but the combination of a sturdy, beautiful bass-baritone and thoughtful interpretation surpasses all Wotans on previous complete recordings.

1988 EMI/ANGEL (S,D) CD

Eva Marton (A), Cheryl Studer (B), Waltraud Meier (C), Reiner Goldberg (D), James Morris (E), Matti Salminen (F), Bavarian Radio Orchestra—Bernard Haitink

Simultaneously with the DG cycle, EMI launched its own, also with James Morris as Wotan—sounding even more involved and imposing here, partly due to Haitink's more human-scale framework. While perhaps not a truly subtle or thought-provoking Wotan, Morris supplies the vocal and musical essentials more completely than any other *Walküre* Wotan on records—listen to his forceful yet poised haranguing of the Valkyries in Act III for a remarkable example.

Another decided asset is the youthful, soaring Sieglinde of Cheryl Studer. Though she's really a bright high soprano and hence not ideally matched to this low-lying role, her tone remains round and lovely through the entire range required, and her interpretation is always alive and individual—sometimes startlingly so, as in her responses to Siegmund's first-act narrative. At the climactic points that do call for the soprano top, Studer delivers gloriously.

Nearly as good are the dark, smooth Hunding of Salminen (with hints of a conventionally slithery villain in his approach) and the moving, personal Fricka of Waltraud Meier; her singing has its thin and tight moments, but her verbal and musical articulation are those of an exceptionally imaginative artist.

In quieter moments Eva Marton shows fine sensitivity and vocal command. And there is the pleasure of hearing a big strong soprano who is not overtaxed by the role's requirements. But the quality is often strained when Marton must sing out, and she can be careless over details; an important scene like the Todesverkündigung sounds merely clipped and efficient. Still, hers is an interesting and sometimes exciting contribution, whereas the Siegmund of Reiner Goldberg ultimately frustrates more than it satisfies. At many moments one can hear the exceptional vocal quality that qualifies him for important assignments like this, as in his command of a resonant half-voice. But his singing is constantly compromised by inconsistencies that have almost an amateurish effect, with a change of vowel or pitch suddenly unsettling the basic quality.

Haitink seems to be pursuing quite a different goal from Levine's; much of the time he is content to set the scene and then support the singers in their creation of effects rather than try to supply everything himself. This approach can fall flat when soloists don't deliver the requisite vividness, but it allows for some striking individual successes as well. Like Solti, Haitink excels with storms and similar passages that benefit from sharp observance of rhythm. The scene of the gathering of the Valkyries (a quite strong group) is more clearly than usual a break from the prevailing tension, a Wagnerian *divertissement*. The orchestra is not as tonally homogeneous as some of the great ones to have recorded the work, but that is sometimes an advantage in terms of timbral variety, and it is certainly a good responsive group.

———

Recommendation of a single *Walküre* recording is difficult, as all have weaknesses. In the first rank of choices belong Solti, Karajan, and Goodall; for individual elements Furtwängler (in Vienna), Leinsdorf, Janowski, Levine, and Haitink also merit attention.

JON ALAN CONRAD

JOSEPH VOLPE
General Manager, Metropolitan Opera

1. **Beethoven,** *Fidelio*: Ludwig, Hallstein, Vickers, Unger, Berry, Frick, Crass—Klemperer. EMI / ANGEL

2. **Donizetti,** *Lucia di Lammermoor*: Sutherland, Pavarotti, Milnes, Ghiaurov—Bonynge. DECCA / LONDON

3. **Bizet,** *Carmen*: Troyanos, Te Kanawa, Domingo, van Dam—Solti. DECCA / LONDON

4. **Verdi,** *Otello*: Scotto, Kraft, Domingo, Little, Milnes—Levine. RCA / BMG

5. **Verdi,** *Simon Boccanegra*: Rethberg, Martinelli, Tibbett, Pinza, Warren—Panizza. MET

6. **Puccini,** *La Bohème* Freni, Harwood, Pavarotti, Panerai, Maffeo, Ghiaurov—Karajan. DECCA / LONDON

7. **Puccini,** *Tosca*: Callas, di Stefano, Gobbi—de Sabata. EMI / ANGEL

8. **Mascagni,** *Cavalleria Rusticana*: Milanov, Bjoerling, Merrill—Cellini. RCA / BMG and
   Leoncavallo, *Pagliacci*: De los Angeles, Bjoerling, Warren, Merrill—Cellini. EMI / ANGEL

9. **Wagner,** *Der Ring des Nibelungen*: Behrens, Norman, Ludwig, Lakes, Goldberg, Morris—Levine. DEUTSCHE GRAMMOPHON

10. **Wagner,** *Tristan und Isolde*: Flagstad, Thorborg, Melchior, Huehn, Kipnis—Leinsdorf. MET

RICHARD WAGNER

SIEGFRIED (1876)

A: Brünnhilde (s); B: Erda (c); C: Siegfried (t);
D: Mime (t); E: Wanderer (bs-bar); F: Alberich (bs-bar)

*S*iegfried owes its status as the most rarely performed of the *Ring* dramas not only to musical and dramatic factors but also to the difficulty of casting its title role, which needs a heroic tenor capable of sustaining enormous color and variety over hours of nearly continuous singing. In view of this problem (reflected in all the complete recordings), familiarity with the abridged *Siegfried* with Lauritz Melchior in the title role, assembled from various 78-rpm sets (transferred in the Danacord "Melchior Anthology"), is absolutely essential in order to hear the confident beauty—and the musical-theatrical mastery thereby released—lacking in other Siegfrieds. No cuts are made in any of the following recordings.

1953 EMI / ANGEL (M,P) CD

Martha Mödl (A), Margarete Klose (B), Ludwig Suthaus (C), Julius Patzak (D), Ferdinand Frantz (E), Alois Pernerstorfer (F), Orchestra of the RAI, Rome—Wilhelm Furtwängler

This *Siegfried* is distinguished by one of the finest individual performances on any of the *Ring* recordings: the Mime of Julius Patzak. While Mime is admittedly not the most arduous vocal challenge in the cycle, Patzak stands virtually alone in assuming that the dwarf is entitled to the most scrupulous musical treatment, and that his characterization should be rendered by the most scrupulous vocal subtlety, rather than by ugly singing. Patzak thus confers a

certain classic status on this recording, and it has other things to recommend it as well. The improvement of sound and orchestra in the course of the Rome cycle allows Furtwängler to make his points relatively unimpeded. He finds a distinctive yet natural shaping for every moment, and makes each lead logically to the next, in a way that adds to one's experience of and pleasure in the work. The Wanderer's first scene is a high point, with the brass section finally distinguishing itself.

Ludwig Suthaus's excellent ideas about Siegfried can be discerned and appreciated, but not, in the end, truly enjoyed. For this demanding role his voice is too audibly under strain; bright, clear phrases at the start of each scene yield to toneless, labored ones. His best work comes in the forest meditation, where he is not under pressure and can employ his feeling for lyricism and precise rhythmic articulation.

Ferdinand Frantz is a strong Wanderer, providing some extremely eloquent singing in the riddle scene. He faces an Alberich, Alois Pernerstorfer, whose concentration on singing rather than acting emphasizes the parallels between Wotan and Alberich made explicit in *Siegfried*. Margarete Klose's authoritative manner almost (but not quite) makes up for the weakened condition of her voice. Josef Greindl makes little of the dragon, but Rita Streich sings sweetly as one of the few outstanding Forest Birds. The awakening of Brünnhilde adds Mödl to the cast, never without some strain when she has to sustain the many high-lying lines, but also never holding back from a full-scale assault on the role, often to genuinely expressive effect.

1962 DECCA / LONDON (S) CD

Birgit Nilsson (A), Marga Höffgen (B), Wolfgang Windgassen (C), Gerhard Stolze (D), Hans Hotter (E), Gustav Neidlinger (F), Vienna Philharmonic Orchestra—Georg Solti

This first complete recording of *Siegfried* probably made its biggest impression when it was new. Its shortfall from the demands of the score has now become more apparent (all other recordings compromise one way or another too, of course). In Wolfgang Windgassen the set had the best available Siegfried at that time, and one who still stands up well. It's perfectly clear that he lacks the body and ring to dominate the orchestra convincingly when necessary. But his strong lyric qualities and tonal poise stand him in good stead, and his honest, unmagnetic performance wears well.

Other helpful elements are the suitably coarse, characterful Fafner of Kurt Böhme, the affecting Erda of Marga Höffgen, and Joan Sutherland's uniquely full-bodied high soprano as the Forest Bird. Strongest of all: the classic Alberich of Neidlinger and the truly goddesslike Brünnhilde of Nilsson. Others may have brought more richness to some of the Valkyrie's more introspective moments, but when the voice must soar out freely over the orchestra, no one else can touch her.

More problematic but still on the whole an asset is the experienced and expressive, but also unsteady, Wanderer of Hans Hotter. Even more questionable, and *not* an asset in the end, is the performance that Gerhard Stolze gives as Mime: bold and detailed, certainly, but almost entirely in nonmusical terms, as if singing were an irrelevant discipline. His squawks really have no place in Wagner.

Georg Solti's conducting makes the most of each scene's character—meditative, sadistic, cheerful, urgent by turns, none overemphasized at the expense of any other. The Vienna Philharmonic Orchestra carries out his interpretation brilliantly.

1966 PHILIPS (S,P) CD

Birgit Nilsson (A), Věra Soukupová (B), Wolfgang Windgassen (C), Erwin Wohlfahrt (D), Theo Adam (E), Gustav Neidlinger (F), Bayreuth Festival Orchestra—Karl Böhm

In this live performance, Wolfgang Windgassen shows how impressively he could conserve his vocal resources for such a taxing role as Siegfried, with lyric freshness available for the many long conversations and monologues and some power for the forging scene and final duet. Still, the effort shows, and in this respect, as well as musical care and a more advantageous aural presence, his studio performance for Solti remains preferable. Birgit Nilsson's arrival in the final scene does not immediately show her at her best, being marginally uncertain of pitch and rhythm, but this rights itself in about two minutes and from then on she's as overwhelming as ever. Though he's careful to sing all the notes, Erwin Wohlfahrt's Mime does not quite live up to the promise of his *Rheingold* portrayal; perhaps at the director's behest, he indulges in considerable cackling hysteria.

Gustav Neidlinger proves just as musically scrupulous as in the studio (conversely, in the studio he had been just as dramatically alive as in live performance); impossible to choose between his performances, or to imagine a substantially better one. Certainly in the exchange with Wotan, he makes a greater impact than Adam's earnest but uncharismatic Wanderer (best when singing full-out, as in his final scene): on the basis of their verbal duel, Alberich deserves to take over Valhalla! Böhme again makes a fierce Fafner, frighteningly cavernous thanks to suitable amplification, and true to pitch. Věra Soukupová, while missing the roomy low notes of some Erdas, brings a moving urgency to the personal distress of the goddess in her crucial scene; since Adam responds to her alertly, their scene adds up as the most distinctive (i.e., unduplicated elsewhere) achievement of this *Siegfried*. Erika Köth is only a decent Forest Bird, fluttery in a way one would rather not hear.

Böhm seems to concern himself little with the specific quality and balance of orchestral color—as such very different conductors as Solti, Karajan, and Furtwängler do—instead leaving such matters to the players' initiative. Perhaps the live-performance engineering has contributed (it certainly captured an inordinate volume of hammering, and plenty of prompter's interventions), but the Wanderer's portentous chords go for almost nothing, and in general Böhm passes uninvolved through crucial passages of arrival and repose (Siegfried's forest monologue, the beginning of the final scene). Where energy and momentum matter most, as in the excited end of Act II, Böhm delivers thrillingly, but in the long run this is not enough.

1968–69 DEUTSCHE GRAMMOPHON (S) CD

Helga Dernesch (A), Oralia Dominguez (B), Jess Thomas (C), Gerhard Stolze (D), Thomas Stewart (E), Zoltán Kélémen (F), Berlin Philharmonic Orchestra—Herbert von Karajan

In *Siegfried* the Karajan *Ring* encounters its weakest link. The quality of the Berlin orchestra and its conductor remain as high as ever, but some important casting problems remain unsolved, and the result makes for uncomfortable listening.

In particular, Jess Thomas as Siegfried gives little pleasure to the ears. He brings some of the smaller conversational moments to life with intelligent inflections, and occasionally makes an impressive effect when singing full-out, but most of the time his tone is gray and his interpretation unremarkable. The Mime, Gerhard Stolze, does not take up the slack, for he indulges in unpitched ranting nearly as often as he did for Solti. With such a pair to carry most of Act I, the appearance of Thomas Stewart as the Wanderer affords great relief; he seems more lightweight here than in *Die Walküre*, and the orchestra covers him at times, but his steady, handsome singing is balm to the ears.

Ridderbusch and Kélémen continue their lighter-than-usual but excellent Fafner and Alberich from *Rheingold*; likewise Dominguez as Erda, although the longer role finds her wanting tonally at a few points and also exposes her accent more noticeably. Catherine Gayer

makes a pleasant, slightly tremulous Forest Bird. As for Helga Dernesch: at the risk of indulging in the comfortable certainty of hindsight (she has since become an important mezzo-soprano), one cannot help hearing in her Brünnhilde a basically low-lying voice stretched to its limits to fill out the demands of the role. When a passage falls in a suitable tessitura (like "Ewig war ich"), she shows her sensitivity and the fine quality of her instrument. But at other times she is struggling, and her union with Thomas makes for a less than uplifting final duet. The undeniable orchestral beauties—the most diaphanous of forest murmurs, the most frightening of storms—provide only limited enjoyment in the face of such problematic singing, and this set cannot on the whole be considered a success.

1968 WESTMINSTER (S)

Nadezda Kniplová (A), Ursula Böse (B), Gerald McKee (C), Herold Kraus (D), Rolf Polke (E), Rolf Kühne (F), South German Philharmonic—Hans Swarowsky

With less time alloted to Wotan or Alberich than in the previous two operas, the Swarowsky *Siegfried* adds up as a correspondingly less attractive proposition. Rolf Polke completes his portrayal with a Wanderer who (a handful of top notes aside) speaks with dignity and power—to especially splendid effect in his meeting with Alberich, where he has Rolf Kühne's canny portrayal to react to.

Gerald McKee presents an initially plausible voice for Siegfried; the problem is that it is all so unmodulated and glaring. He quickly grows tiresome, and unintentionally sounds just as hysterical as Mime by the end of Act I. McKee shows his underlying good intentions when he croons into the microphone for a very subdued, slow-motion forest scene; it has little to do with the rest of his performance, but it works.

As Mime, Herold Kraus starts well enough, and has enough voice to be accorded a big hold for his high B; then he goes berserk in his later scenes, far more even than other Mimes, and beyond the limits of acceptability. Ursula Böse has an appropriate voice for Erda, and presents an intimate interpretation of a bewildered mother—an interesting idea, well carried out.

When Kniplová awakes as Brünnhilde, she brings no new note of tenderness or beauty into the performance, efficient as she is in her way. "Ewig war ich" emerges labored, and the final duet is downright ugly: she sounds furious with McKee, he sounds terrified, and Swarowsky rushes things to the point where both are reduced to yapping. The conductor does his best work when the singers are most in control: the Wotan-Alberich scene, for instance. But such crucial sequences as the forging scene have no backbone; the bottom keeps dropping out. Orchestral and engineering problems continue as before.

1973 EMI / ANGEL (In English) (S,P) CD

Rita Hunter (A), Anne Collins (B), Alberto Remedios (C), Gregory Dempsey (D), Norman Bailey (E), Derek Hammond-Stroud (F), English National Opera Orchestra—Reginald Goodall

The first installment of the Goodall *Ring* to be recorded allows all three of its strongest principals to show their quality. Alberto Remedios must compromise with Siegfried's requirements just as much as anyone else recorded in the role—more than most in terms of volume (the lowest notes of the forging song simply vanish). But he reveals musical and dramatic understanding, and a tenor of appealing quality (if insufficient heft) which he sustains through the long lines admirably. He also never lets the role's heavier demands throw him off balance into plain bad singing, as some others have done; he renders what he can, and that's that. The Brünnhilde of Rita Hunter sails easily through her scene, with a trill where needed and fine feeling for phrase shapes, including some well-judged *portamento*. Norman Bailey sounds wonderful as the Wanderer, seeming positively to luxuriate in Goodall's spacious conception of his music; the vocal layout of this particular Wotan suits him especially well.

Hammond-Stroud remains a highly effective if rather broad Alberich, and Dempsey claims his share of the limelight with a well-characterized Mime that does not stint on real singing. With Clifford Grant a sonorous dragon and Anne Collins a deep-toned Erda, the indifferent Forest Bird is easy to forgive.

Central to the overall feeling of the performance is Goodall's conception, for he must undoubtedly claim a share in the personal success of his principals. Yet even for one sympathetic to his cause, his pacing raises questions. However primeval a conductor's ideas about the work, several scenes want to move energetically and lightly, and Siegfried's forging songs need more perceptible metric drive than they are given. But such lacks are placed in perspective by the assets of these confident and imaginative principals making the most of an excellent translation. This *Siegfried* deserves to be considered even by those who might ordinarily bypass a version in English.

1980 PHILIPS (S,D) CD

Gwyneth Jones (A), Ortrun Wenkel (B), Manfred Jung (C), Heinz Zednik (D), Donald McIntyre (E), Hermann Becht, Bayreuth Festival Orchestra—Pierre Boulez

This *Siegfried* gets off to a distinctive start with a brisk, buoyantly articulated Prelude (most conductors only end it that way, building from near-motionlessness). Boulez's favored clarity and rhythmic precision benefit this score, and he makes good sense of most of its orchestral portion.

Heinz Zednik shows why he has become famous as Mime, with a detailed piece of characterization and a rhythmic energy to match Boulez. He is at his best for his final confrontations with Alberich and Siegfried, and with his death the most fully realized character departs this recording.

The first notes of Siegfried from offstage promise a youthful, likable hero who unfortunately never arrives. Manfred Jung sounds young, certainly, but also lightweight for this assignment, and the initially pleasant quality of his voice vanishes all too soon, the first act becoming a duet for two Mimes. The spirit with which he flouts his elders doesn't suffice for the final scene, which is simply not successfully negotiated, and often not up to pitch.

The entry of the Wanderer brings magic and mystery with it in the superb (and superbly balanced and blended) orchestral playing, but none in the lackluster singing of Donald McIntyre. For all his intelligent application to his task, he offers neither the vocal endowment of a great Wotan nor the care for musical shape which can offer partial compensation. Still, certain scenes do come to life (like the riddle scene, with its sense of a shared joke near the end—until the final question springs the trap), even without the vocal means to realize them. Erda is plausibly enacted by Ortrun Wenkel, her hurt and bewilderment sharply present; the vocal color changes disconcertingly from alto to soprano between phrases.

Gwyneth Jones alternates clean, penetrating tones and imprecise, ill-tuned ones in almost equal proportion. One might be willing to endure it in the context of a theater performance, but not at home. Too bad, for one can hear the care that conductor and singer have put into such details as her sighting of her horse. If this *Siegfried* is nearly a total write-off vocally, the quality of the dramatic interaction is noteworthy; all the characters are really listening and responding to the others, surely a result of several years' experience in the Chéreau production and a tribute to his direction. Unfortunately, that alone cannot make this recording competitive.

1982 EURODISC (S,D) CD

Jeannine Altmeyer (A), Ortrun Wenkel (B), René Kollo (C), Peter Schreier (D), Theo Adam (E), Siegmund Nimsgern (F), Dresden State Orchestra—Marek Janowski

Here the Janowski cycle reaches its peak. The casting of Peter Schreier as Mime promises a performance to match Patzak's in musical subtlety and resourcefulness; and if Schreier fails to live up to expectation completely, too often relying on clichéd colorations and inflections, he does make a great success of Acts I and II in partnership with René Kollo. Kollo delivers some of his best-ever work in Siegfried's early scenes, youthful and varied in timbre, alive to verbal nuance, with ringing climaxes where needed. Janowski's clear-sighted direction and textural clarification, not to mention the

orchestra's virtuosic execution, don't hurt either.

Adam remains a reliable, careful presence as before, perhaps somewhat better suited to the quiet reflectiveness of the Wanderer's role, and Nimsgern and Matti Salminen give strong support as Alberich and Fafner. Norma Sharp and Ortrun Wenkel repeat the roles they did for Boulez: Sharp still makes a good Forest Bird, not the usual chirper and all the better for it, but Wenkel has lost the concentration she had under Boulez, leaving only her inappropriate vocal color to command the attention. Finally, Altmeyer is still finding ways around the challenges rather than fearlessly encompassing them. Even so, her basically fresh and attractive tone, coupled with Kollo's musical understanding and reliability, make for one of the more listenable final duets among the complete recordings.

1988 DEUTSCHE GRAMMOPHON (S,D) CD

Hildegard Behrens (A), Birgitta Svendén (B), Reiner Goldberg (C), Heinz Zednik (D), James Morris (E), Ekkehard Wlaschiha (F), Metropolitan Opera Orchestra—James Levine

The Metropolitan Opera Orchestra's virtuosity provides enormous pleasure throughout this recording. James Levine obviously deserves credit for this, and for the care he takes with details often slighted. Yet the point of all this splendid execution seems sometimes to have been forgotten: the evocation of character, of action, of atmosphere, of urgent pictorial or dramatic impulses. The very slow pacing would not be problematic if the performance seemed more purposeful, less abstract.

In basic vocal endowment, Reiner Goldberg hints at the makings of a true Siegfried; when he sings out uninhibitedly, his tenor has solidity and ring, even some depth and color, though all these qualities can vanish a moment later. In this exposed role, however, nothing can disguise Goldberg's lack of imagination. He sings the notes, but without the slightest spark or magnetism, and although German is his native language his inflections are those of someone who has learned everything by rote. He is, in the end, boring.

His shortcomings are shown up all the more

by contrast with his able colleagues in Act I: on the one hand, the canny Mime of Heinz Zednik, fully characterized without exceeding musical limits; on the other, the masterfully voiced Wanderer of James Morris (more fully shaped than with Haitink). Two even more praiseworthy gentlemen make striking contributions to Act II, Ekkehard Wlaschiha, an Alberich who makes an equal antagonist for Wotan, and Kurt Moll, a uniquely beautiful and moving dragon.

Birgitta Svendén sings Erda sensitively, with lovely tone that for all its dark color remains too lightweight to conjure up a convincing Mother Earth. Kathleen Battle has the clear high soprano for her role, but her scoop-filled delivery makes the Forest Bird a "personality" rather than a voice of nature.

This Brünnhilde, predominantly lyrical and personal, fits Hildegard Behrens better than the earlier and later ones. She renders the more meditative sections expressively, but extroverted moments force her to stretch the voice until the tone becomes hollow and unsteady. The lack of a really convincing hero and, to a lesser extent, heroine makes this set hard to recommend, for all its other attractions.

1991 EMI / ANGEL (S,D) CD

Eva Marton (A), Jadwiga Rappé (B), Siegfried Jerusalem (C), Peter Haage (D), James Morris (E), Theo Adam (F), Bavarian Radio Symphony Orchestra—Bernard Haitink

Bernard Haitink's conducting of *Siegfried* has many admirable features: control of balance and pace for dramatic as well as musical ends, careful grading of the weights of different scenes, fine playing from the orchestra. Haitink also knows that a conductor cannot make an opera happen by himself, and he leaves room for the singers to contribute their share to the continuity of the performance. This, unfortunately, they mostly fail to do.

Siegfried Jerusalem sounds less satisfying than one might have hoped from some of his live performances of the role. His keen rhythmic sense is a great and rare asset, his tone remains attractive when not under stress, and he projects the text intelligently. He lacks tonal expansion and unforced ring at the climactic moments, real lyric shaping of the quieter sections, and the kind of personal magnetism to compel attention throughout the long role. This is a likable Siegfried, easier to take than many, but not superior to Windgassen or Kollo (except in the pipe-playing episode, where Jerusalem's experience as a bassoonist pays off hilariously).

James Morris's rich, smooth vocalizing is valuable for the Wanderer, but as in Haitink's *Rheingold* his work sounds unfinished; he leaves phrases unshaped, too often he scoops into them, and he sometimes pushes the tone rather than letting it flow. In passages that are not too loud or too high, Eva Marton reminds us what a substantial voice she has and what a sensitive artist she can be. But whenever pitch or volume climbs, her sound turns pressurized and uncontrolled, often downright fierce, and in the end her Brünnhilde is hard to enjoy.

Peter Haage offers a decent Mime in the hyperintense, semi-sung tradition. Theo Adam should not have been asked to sing Alberich, as he wobbles constantly and cannot project this short but important role with the needed authority. More satisfying are Kurt Rydl's sonorous dragon and Jadwige Rappé's well-sustained though light-toned Erda. Kiri Te Kanawa's cameo as Forest Bird is inexplicable save as a sales gimmick: however brief, the role needs precise enunciation, tonal clarity, and rhythmic alacrity, none of which she provides. With its solid conducting offset by an only intermittently effective cast, this set fails to make much of a competitive case for itself.

The great importance of the tenor protagonist means that no complete recording satisfies completely. Best strategy is to acquire the extensive Melchior excerpts to learn how Siegfried can sound, then choose a complete recording to experience the whole work. Furtwängler, Goodall, and Janowski all excel in this opera, with Solti nearly their equal.

JON ALAN CONRAD

RICHARD WAGNER

GÖTTERDÄMMERUNG (1876)

A: Brünnhilde (s); B: Gutrune (s); C: Waltraute (c); D: Siegfried (t);
E: Gunther (bar); F: Alberich (bs-bar); G: Hagen (bs)

*W*hen this very long opera was new, desperate measures were sometimes taken to shorten it: the Metropolitan Opera premiere, for instance, omitted the Norn and Waltraute scenes. The first of these, at least, used to be a fairly frequent casualty in performance, but all the sets discussed are complete, with the exception of the Fjeldstad.

1953 EMI / ANGEL (M,P) CD

Martha Mödl (A), Sena Jurinac (B), Margarete Klose (C), Ludwig Suthaus (D), Alfred Poell (E), Alois Pernerstorfer (F), Josef Greindl (G), Chorus and Orchestra of the RAI, Rome—Wilhelm Furtwängler

The rich textural tapestry of this final *Ring* opera gives Furtwängler his best opportunities, and he takes full advantage of them (with the usual caveats as to orchestra and sound): note the urgency of the ever-varied orchestral commentary in the first Gibichung scene, for instance. The long lines of the work emerge with exceptional clarity, aided by singers who, whatever their faults, have a reliable feeling for the phrases and their destinations. The undeniably sloppy chorus does provide a rousing contingent of Italian tenors who love their high notes.

The performance gets off to a splendid vocal start with three highly individual and authoritative Norns: Margarete Klose (audibly aging but still wonderfully expressive, both qualities

also evident in her slightly less convincing Waltraute), Hilde Rössl-Majdan, and Sena Jurinac. Jurinac's Gutrune merits a special prize, musically and dramatically polished and gloriously sung—incomparable in this role, outstanding among all individual *Ring* portrayals.

In each of her scenes Mödl makes a beautiful first impression, but effortfulness soon takes over and imparts a sour tone. Even so, she makes Act II work in her own way, clarifying the changing passions of this great scene to an exceptional degree and even driving convincingly through the climactic phrases; too bad she can't encompass the Immolation to equal effect. Suthaus remains very musical, effective in general terms, but lacking in real presence and bite. His considerable eloquence in his final scene lingers in the memory.

Both Hagen and Gunther are dramatically alive, vocally just adequate (Greindl is really remarkably effective, considering that he can only approximate the singing demands). The Rhinemaidens have gained in vocal solidity since *Rheingold*, but are undone by some of the few genuinely slow tempos in Furtwängler's cycle: they have to gasp extra breaths to keep going. Still, a worthy finale to an always interesting *Ring*.

1956 DECCA / LONDON (M, P)

Kirsten Flagstad (A), Ingrid Bjoner (B), Eva Gustavson (C), Set Svanholm (D), Waldemar Johnsen (E), Per Grönneberg (F), Egil Nordsjø

(G), Norwegian State Opera Chorus, Oslo Philharmonic and Norwegian State Radio Orchestras—Øivin Fjeldstad

This performance for Norwegian Radio, with a native cast, contained Kirsten Flagstad's last performance of Brünnhilde (she was officially in retirement at the time). When Decca / London offered her a recording contract, she proposed that the company first buy and release this tape. With extra recording sessions to repair some of the performance's omissions (though not the interlude in Act I) and mishaps, Götterdämmerung was released on records for the first time. (The 1953 EMI was not released until later.)

Flagstad constitutes, as expected, the chief distinction of the occasion. It is easy to underrate her performance here, especially with her earlier commercial excerpts and her 1950 La Scala *Ring* available for comparison. Signs of aging include discomfort with persistent high tessitura and a tonal loosening. Yet hers is still a voluminous, warm voice, guided by a generous temperament, and she rises to awesome heights in moments like the confrontations of the second act. Set Svanholm does not disgrace himself by her side, either. Had Decca / London scheduled a studio Götterdämmerung at this time, he might well have been their Siegfried: not really heroic, but always musical and lively.

And there the virtues of the cast largely end. Eva Gustavson had had an international career (Amneris with Toscanini), and Ingrid Bjoner would do so later, but the former contributes a dull, unfocused Waltraute and the latter a pretty but blank Gutrune. (At the retake sessions they contributed First and Third Norns, to similar effect—outclassing the tremulously girlish middle sister.) Hagen and Alberich (the latter's scene supplied in the retakes) prove unequal to the full demands of their roles. Gunther, Rhinemaidens, and the chorus are frankly inadequate.

Fjeldstad and the orchestra drag the performance further down, with so much approximation that the performance takes on a swimming feeling. Because of its evidence about the lasting health of the Flagstad voice, this recording

retains interest for scholars. But as a way of experiencing *Götterdämmerung*, it may safely be forgotten.

1964 DECCA / LONDON (S) ℗

Birgit Nilsson (A), Claire Watson (B), Christa Ludwig (C), Wolfgang Windgassen (D), Dietrich Fischer-Dieskau (E), Gustav Neidlinger (F), Gottlob Frick (G), Vienna State Opera Chorus, Vienna Philharmonic Orchestra—Georg Solti

Solti's cycle reaches its peak with a *Götterdämmerung* in which superlative orchestral playing and Decca / London's finest sound support an ideally chosen cast. Nilsson's brilliance is expectable and well captured; less predictable is the outstanding work of Windgassen, who never did anything finer for records than this Siegfried. He earns cheers for the concentrated fervor of his heroic singing, the moving restraint of his death scene.

The Gibichung family is in exceptionally able hands. The excellence of Watson and Frick is hard to miss, but one will sometimes encounter objections that the Fischer-Dieskau Gunther is "too intelligent." This misses the point about the king, which is not that he is stupid, but that he is sophisticated enough to be aware of his limitations and consequently insecure, in a quite modern way—and this the great baritone captures perfectly.

Christa Ludwig, not as deep of voice as some classic Waltrautes, shows herself their equal by virtue of her sumptuous mezzo-soprano and her unification of musical and dramatic expressiveness. And Neidlinger completes a flawless roster of principals by modulating his biting voice to the dreamlike insinuation needed for his one appearance here.

Rhinemaidens: Lucia Popp, Gwyneth Jones, Maureen Guy. Norns: Helen Watts, Grace Hoffman, Anita Välkki. Both trios make outstanding contributions, with no weak spots. The picture is completed by Solti's conducting, so satisfying because it does justice to all sides of this work. On any short list of superior opera recordings, this one is sure to find a place.

1967 PHILIPS (S,P) CD

Birgit Nilsson (A), Ludmila Dvořáková (B), Martha Mödl (C), Wolfgang Windgassen (D), Thomas Stewart (E), Gustav Neidlinger (F), Josef Greindl (G), Bayreuth Festival Chorus and Orchestra—Karl Böhm

The opening of the Prologue in this performance typifies the Böhm approach: though it may not be faster than other renditions, it sounds fast because it is so matter-of-fact, so devoid of mood. (It isn't helped by three dull Norns.) Some of Böhm's ideas, like the brisk Rhine Journey, work well; he also succeeds with active scenes like the fight at the end of Act I and the confrontations in Act II. But the balance and repose so necessary at other moments are sorely lacking, most notably in the orchestral conclusion—approximately balanced, unsteady in tempo, loud and angry in tone. The Bayreuth chorus, as always, is magnificent.

Brünnhilde and Siegfried are portrayed by the same superior artists who so distinguished the Solti set. For Böhm, Nilsson may manage a more personal note at some points, and Windgassen seems just perceptibly tired by the end, but the differences are small. Special credit to Windgassen for the most convincing of all Gunther disguises (for Solti he'd had electronic assistance, but he manages nearly as well here).

Thomas Stewart gives great pleasure as Gunther, sustaining a strong line and character, always musically scrupulous. Dvořáková's Gutrune is dark, matronly, and prone to slide into notes—not at all a helpful aural image. Josef Greindl, thirteen years after his Furtwängler performance, gets character and dramatic intent across gamely as Hagen, but the voice has largely crossed the line into unacceptability.

As Waltraute, Martha Mödl provides an unfortunate parodistic echo of her former Brünnhilde—bottom-heavy, lurching from one note to the next—despite undeniable presence and power. Neidlinger's ever-noteworthy Alberich is done less than justice by his very close and unatmospheric placement for his scene. No such excuse can be found for the sadly out-of-sorts Rhinemaidens.

1968 WESTMINSTER (S)

Nadezda Kniplova (A), Ditha Sommer (B), Ruth Hesse (C), Gerald McKee (D), Rudolf Knoll (E), Rolf Kühne (F), Otto von Rohr (G), Chorus of the Vienna State Opera, South German Philharmonic—Hans Swarowsky

A reasonably accurate foretaste of this performance is given by its opening chords, nasty-sounding and out of tune. Throughout, Swarowsky goes for the obvious, making even subsidiary brass themes loud and punchy (the Rhine Journey is especially noisy), usually allowing the momentum of a scene to run down. The orchestra is often hard-pressed, with the tremulous clarinet section transporting the Act I interlude into the world of swing bands.

As earlier in the cycle, the Brünnhilde-Siegfried pairing can sustain the roles, but in so unmodulated a way as to prove eventually unbearable. In the turmoil of Act II, Kniplová remains extremely accurate and often characterful, but sounds remarkably ugly. McKee conveys no expression, even in his death scene.

Hagen is tough and coarse, not quite in control of his high notes, effective in a no-nonsense way. Gutrune, the erstwhile Sieglinde, is again hopelessly uncontrolled. Gunther and Waltraute turn in respectable performances on a modest scale: both show some imagination, without the vocal resources to accomplish all their intentions.

Act II brings a final, welcome appearance as Alberich from the excellent Kühne, an untidy but spirited chorus, and the surprise of real steerhorns (or a convincing substitute). The Norns include a quite good Second (Margit Kobeck) sandwiched between mediocre sisters; their scene doesn't come to life at all. The Rhinedaughters are, as before, a trial, with a thick-sounding Flosshilde and a new Woglinde who tends to the sharp side.

1969–70 DEUTSCHE GRAMMOPHON (S) CD

Helga Dernesch (A), Gundula Janowitz (B), Christa Ludwig (C), Helge Brilioth (D), Thomas Stewart (E), Zoltán Kélémen (F), Karl Ridderbusch (G), Berlin Opera Chorus, Berlin Philharmonic Orchestra—Herbert von Karajan

The final portion of the Karajan *Ring* fulfills all that one might hope for orchestrally after the earlier installments; the Norns and Rhinemaidens float on delicate webs of tone, the many dramatic outbursts in Act II erupt with fiery precision, the Funeral March combines a steady tread with full characterization of each episode. All wonderful and unique.

But Karajan's cast, though usually euphonious, is only slightly better matched for their task than his *Siegfried* team was for theirs. The exception is Christa Ludwig, again an incomparable Waltraute and this time also an outstanding Second Norn. Also to the good: Kélémen's lovely Alberich; a First Norn from Lili Chookasian with some impressively deep notes; and a good Rhinemaiden trio, less distinctive than in *Rheingold* due to the substitution of Liselotte Rebmann for Helen Donath.

The real leading roles, however, are mostly in the hands of likable vocal personalities and fine musicians whose strengths are not the ones needed for the job at hand. At his first entrance, Brilioth sounds like the Siegfried of one's dreams—clear, accurate, attractive, and intelligent. Over the course of the opera, his voice reveals that it hasn't the tonal reserves (especially when singing softly) to meet all the role's demands. Dernesch, as in *Siegfried*, is persuasive in mid-range singing, but taxed when she must venture higher. Thus most of her Immolation Scene is moving, but its final minutes elicit mostly concern for her survival.

Ridderbusch shines whenever his music is high and loud, but lacks presence in lower-pitched conversational passages; his Watch Scene is almost totally uneventful. As for Janowitz and Stewart, they seem to have equated character and execution in a naive way, as if the passive Gutrune ought not to be interpreted and the primitive Gunther should bark roughly. Stewart at least comes through with some dramatic life and the right kind of voice; Janowitz is a cipher, puzzlingly so after her arrestingly original Sieglinde.

The chorus, a strong one when it can be heard, is covered up surprisingly often. That this performance does repay attention and rehearing is almost solely due to Karajan.

1977 EMI / ANGEL (In English) (S,P) CD

Rita Hunter (A), Margaret Curphey (B), Katherine Pring (C), Alberto Remedios (D), Norman Welsby (E), Derek Hammond-Stroud (F), Aage Haugland, English National Opera Chorus and Orchestra—Reginald Goodall

The final installment of the Goodall *Ring* adds up as the weakest. This can be partly ascribed to inadequate casting of the Gibichung family; with Gunther a baritone of negligible imagination and tonal appeal, Gutrune a soprano whose interpretive ideas cannot survive her inability to vary her stodgy tone, and Hagen a proponent of the vibrato-less roar, one comes to realize just how much of this work depends on this trio.

Further, the luxuriant texture and motivic interweaving of this work leads Goodall to draw out each individual episode for maximum lyricism—a choice with local rewards, but with damaging impact on the continuity of the drama as a whole. In the last act, Goodall does gather a certain massive momentum for Siegfried's and Brünnhilde's final scenes, capping the tetralogy in a way that must have been overwhelming in the theater—all the more so, perhaps, because so tantalizingly delayed.

In those final scenes Goodall is also working with the two most satisfying of his singers. Hunter and Remedios once again provide noteworthy examples of legitimate renderings of these roles on less than superhuman scale. Remedios never overweights his tone, stays clean and lyrical in style, and even turns Goodall's stately pacing to advantage; his opening duet is far more eventful than most, his narration of his life enthralling, his death extremely moving. Similar virtues can be catalogued for Hunter, who maintains secure, shining form to the end.

The rest of the cast has its strong points: the distinctive Alberich of Hammond-Stroud (albeit on this occasion more spoken than sung), a lightweight but intense Waltraute from Pring, and strong First and Third Norns (Anne Collins and Anne Evans; Gillian Knight is unfortunately stretched beyond her means as their partner). Rhinemaidens and chorus are no more than decent, orchestra impressive in its ability to follow through on Goodall's ideas but short on tonal glamour.

1979 PHILIPS (S) CD

Gwyneth Jones (A), Jeannine Altmeyer (B), Gwendolyn Killebrew (C), Manfred Jung (D), Franz Mazura (E), Hermann Becht (F), Fritz Hübner (G), Bayreuth Festival Chorus and Orchestra—Pierre Boulez

The Norn scene serves as a good example of the pleasures and frustrations of this performance: right from the first chords, heavenly in balance and color, the orchestral contribution flows with unfailing luminous beauty. One could almost listen to it without the voices, and one would be well advised to do so, for the accompaniment surpasses the singers.

As the work progresses, Boulez's limitations become more obvious, particularly his refusal to allow any hint of expansion (for instance, on the first appearance of the *Götterdämmerung* theme) unless score markings specifically sanction it. When the musical argument is reasonably self-sufficient, Boulez can be tremendous, as in the buoyant Rhine Journey, the detailed texture of Hagen's Watch, and the wonderfully bubbly realization of the Rhinemaidens' music. When something more is needed, it doesn't happen. His tendency to treat a gradual musical build-up blankly, without any sense of growth or development, hurts the Immolation Scene particularly, though he redeems himself somewhat at the end with his scrupulous balancing of the several themes in counterpoint.

Gwyneth Jones's troubles remain as earlier in the cycle: volume varies for reasons unrelated to choice, and she tries constantly to slow the tempo to give herself more maneuvering room. Her expedients for expression, including draining the voice of vibrato, call attention to themselves and so defeat their purpose. Manfred Jung is not so obviously objectionable, but sufficiently uneventful tonally as to vanish from memory almost immediately, except when his lack of variation makes him sound angry or hysterical, or when he becomes careless as to pitch.

Though tonally unprepossessing, both Franz Mazura and Fritz Hübner as the Gibichungs show the benefit of their stage experience in this production; they mean what they are saying and bring their scenes to life. Altmeyer, if not so specific, has exceptional presence and color for Gutrune, with the result that the Gibichungs' first scene receives one of its more absorbing performances, and their final scene works too.

In the context of this cast, the Waltraute of Gwendolyn Killebrew comes as a welcome contrast, with her healthy tone, firmly marked rhythms, and well-realized expressive goals. Hermann Becht is mostly a loud Alberich here, rather than an insinuating one. As always at Bayreuth, the chorus is first-class; the Rhinemaidens (Norma Sharp, Ilse Gramatzki, Marga Schiml, as in *Rheingold*) are good too.

1983 EURODISC (S,D) CD

Jeannine Altmeyer (A), Norma Sharp (B), Ortrun Wenkel (C), René Kollo (D), Hans Günter Nöcker (E), Siegmund Nimsgern (F), Matti Salminen (G), Dresden State Opera Chorus, Dresden State Orchestra—Marek Janowski

Janowski's *Götterdämmerung* finds conductor, orchestra, and engineering all at their peak. Not even Karajan or Boulez weaves the undulations of the Norn scene more magically, or balances the Funeral March so masterfully. The totality falls short of the team's *Siegfried* for several reasons. First, *Götterdämmerung* exposes vocal problems for the leading couple more clearly than the previous opera did. Kollo is much more his usual self here: intelligent, musical, but unvaried and forced. Though his timbre is not unappealing in itself, his inability to alter it (no half-voice for the death scene) and his lunging attacks eventually make it so. Altmeyer is too preoccupied with managing her role safely to do anything to bring Brünnhilde to life; the character remains a series of phrases, some emerging in good shape, some not.

Some of the new casting fails to maintain a sufficient standard, too. Nöcker is a dull, rough

Gunther, and Wenkel proves even less satisfactory as Waltraute than as Erda. Salminen fails to live up to his own standards as Hagen; convincing in his intimate moments, he resorts to a straight-toned blare at the big moments. Ideally speaking, Norma Sharp is too light a soprano for Gutrune, but her tone is so steady, her musical ideas so direct, and her character so specifically drawn, that she stands out in this cast. Norns: adequate without being memorable (Anne Gjevang, Daphne Evangelatos, Ruth Falcon); Rhinemaidens: more impressive than in *Rheingold* (the same singers, but somehow better attuned and blended here).

1989 DEUTSCHE GRAMMOPHON (S,D) CD

Hildegard Behrens (A), Cheryl Studer (B), Hanna Schwarz (C), Reiner Goldberg (D), Bernd Weikl (E), Ekkehard Wlaschiha (F), Matti Salminen (G), Metropolitan Opera Chorus and Orchestra—James Levine

The star here is undoubtedly the Metropolitan Opera Orchestra: every instrument brilliantly played, the whole group sumptuously recorded. Praise for James Levine's development of the orchestra to this superlative standard must be tempered by reservations about his conducting, which neglects the softer dynamics, gives too little attention to balance, and interrupts momentum with unmotivated changes of speed.

The orchestral spotlight leaves little room for singers to make memorable impressions, but some manage to do so anyway. Hildegard Behrens for one, even though her voice lacks the grandeur usually considered necessary for Brünnhilde and takes on an effortful edge when under pressure to emulate a bigger sound; in more congenial passages, she soars free and clear, and her delineation of character is persuasive, her musical ideas personal and convincing. Fully convincing both dramatically and vocally is Matti Salminen's immense Hagen. Cheryl Studer's urgent, personal, and vocally radiant Gutrune is one of the best. Ekkehard Wlaschiha and the three Rhinemaidens surpass their work in *Das Rheingold*: he sings with

hypnotic insinuation, and they bloom in the more ensemble-oriented, less individualized writing here. And the Norns get the opera off to an evocative start with three major voices: Helga Dernesch, Tatiana Troyanos, and Andrea Gruber.

Of the others, Hanna Schwarz is a musical and insightful artist with a fine voice, which is nevertheless too lightweight to bring out the full potential of Waltraute's enthralling scene. Bernd Weikl brings a real vocal presence to Gunther, but little character. Reiner Goldberg is an interesting puzzle. When he can simply sing out straightforwardly, as in the dawn duet, he sounds like that rare commodity, a real Siegfried voice: varied, ringing, and secure. At other times, like the drinking of the potion and the oath duet, his tonal security deserts him and he sounds more ordinary.

A fairly strong set, then, hampered by a lack of dramatic impact, both in its parts and as a whole. The very studio-like production, avoiding even obvious distance and directional effects, contributes to this result. Fortunately, Levine creates a compelling continuity for the last scene (aided by Behrens's firmly built Immolation), so that the final impression is a positive one.

1991 EMI / ANGEL (S,D) CD

Eva Marton (A), Eva-Maria Bundschuh (B), Marjana Lipovšek (C), Siegfried Jerusalem (D), Thomas Hampson (E), Theo Adam (F), John Tomlinson (G), Bavarian Radio Chorus and Orchestra—Bernard Haitink

In *Götterdämmerung*, the *Ring* opera which most benefits from an eloquently realized orchestral continuity, Bernard Haitink makes his strongest impression. Balances are precisely calculated, climaxes thoughtfully graded in strength, atmosphere and color vividly conveyed. The orchestra may not offer the tonal magic of the very greatest to have recorded this work, but its playing is so musical and purposeful that it must be accorded comparable respect.

Otherwise, this is an uneven recording, with a variously problematic cast. From this generalization must be exempted Marjana Lipovšek, a rich-voiced Waltraute who makes her scene newly riveting, and also a pleasant trio of Rhinemaidens. Many of the others are good artists who need all their resources to summon enough weight for their assignments. The Norns (Jard van Nes, Anne Sofie von Otter, Jane Eaglen) afford the first example of this, Thomas Hampson's Gunther (patrician in tone, insightfully interpreted) another, the well-prepared but undersized chorus still another. And Siegfried Jerusalem most of all: his lively rhythmic and dramatic response, his avoidance of bluster and wobble, his attractive tone in quieter moments all merit admiration, but Wagnerian-scale fullness and unforced ring are not his to command. His gifts work to best advantage, and make a touching effect, in the subdued requirements of his death scene.

Others in the cast, with voices of sufficient size, have different problems. John Tomlinson enlivens every phrase of Hagen's music with his dramatic imagination, but his tone—gritty in quiet moments, blaring in loud ones—affords limited pleasure. Much the same might be said of Theo Adam, though he makes a reasonably strong effect in this briefest and least proclamatory of the three Alberich roles. Eva-Maria Bundschuh's thick, matronly soprano conveys the wrong aural image for Gutrune.

There remains Eva Marton. In quiet phrases she reveals her sensitive intentions, but most of her performance is monotonously stentorian, effortful, and sometimes ill-defined as to pitch and rhythm. With Brünnhilde playing such a pivotal climactic role in this opera, Marton's performance makes the set hard to recommend competitively.

A clear recommendation is easier for this opera than the rest of the *Ring*. The strengths of the Solti set place it on a level of its own, though one might well turn to Furtwängler, Karajan, Goodall, Janowski, and Levine for individual elements (including other conductorial concepts), and to historical excerpts for great singing.

JON ALAN CONRAD

RICHARD WAGNER

PARSIFAL (1882)

A: Kundry (s); B: Parsifal (t); C: Amfortas (bar); D: Klingsor (bs-bar);
E: Gurnemanz (bs); F: Titurel (bs)

*S*trange but true: although hardly any opera is assaulted with more phony religiosity, murky mysticism, and psychobabble, hardly any opera has been more successfully recorded. In fact, it's hard to go seriously wrong.

And "seriousness" is clearly to the point. However off the wall the approach, *Parsifal* requires an unusual degree of commitment from its performers and its audiences, which tends to screen out the faint of heart. But the wrong kind of seriousness can be dangerous, leading to the imposition of images and attitudes rather than the discovery of the human drama that drives what Conrad L. Osborne has described as "bar for bar, Wagner's singingest score." At greatest risk is the two-hour expanse of Act I, which tends to fall apart except in the hands of such master *Parsifal* conductors as Hans Knappertsbusch (1951 Decca / London and 1962 Philips), Armin Jordan (1981 Erato), and János Ferencsik (see the conclusion).

All of the recordings are complete.

1951 TELDEC (M,P) CD

Martha Mödl (A), Wolfgang Windgassen (B), George London (C), Hermann Uhde (D), Ludwig Weber (E), Arnold van Mill (F), Bayreuth Festival Chorus and Orchestra—Hans Knappertsbusch

Appropriately, we start with a Knappertsbusch-Bayreuth *Parsifal*—as potent an identification as there is in the operatic repertory, even though Knappertsbusch was already sixty-three when he made his Bayreuth debut, at the first postwar festival, during which this recording was made. (In addition to the two commercial recordings, broadcast performances from 1956, 1958, 1960, and 1964 have been issued.)

It should come as no surprise that Knappertsbusch's *Parsifal* is slow, and never slower than in 1951. But there's no ritualistic reverence in his approach. He simply has to allow the opera this much space because there's so much going on in it. His Act I, instead of dissolving into episodic fragments like so many conductors', has a consistent animation that springs from sensitivity to the intricate web of relationships fanning out from Gurnemanz—with the Esquires, with Amfortas and the present administration of Monsalvat, with Titurel and the founding generation, with the outsiders Kundry and Klingsor. Everything is sustained by a singing quality that reaches into the depths of the orchestra and propels the line without artificial stimulation.

To fill out this grand-scale performance, the 1951 cast is long on combat-ready voices. It's especially strong in the lower regions, beginning with the Gurnemanz of Ludwig Weber. His full, rich bass has never been heard to better advantage, in a performance of remarkable urgency and compassion. The young George London brings to Amfortas's agonies a just-about-ideal combination of bass-baritone weight and liquid ease of tone. Hermann Uhde as Klingsor sometimes succumbs to quaver under the pressure of this treacherous writing, but the pressure comes from his attempt actually to *sing* it, full-out, with generally exciting results.

Parsifal and Kundry are more problematic. Wolfgang Windgassen sings intelligently and with as much lyric quality as the strained format of his tenor allows, but it's not a terribly sympathetic sound. Martha Mödl is vocally even less sympathetic, and the sympathetic qualities of Kundry are important. But she does make a big, even pulverizing sound in the bottom and mid-range—her Kundry is certainly a presence.

The large and important supporting cast is arguably the best on records.

1962 PHILIPS (S,P) CD

Irene Dalis (A), Jess Thomas (B), George London (C), Gustav Neidlinger (D), Hans Hotter (E), Martti Talvela (F), Bayreuth Festival Chorus and Orchestra—Hans Knappertsbusch

There are points of interest in all the Knappertsbusch *Parsifals* that have been made available, but for once the two commercial recordings represent the pick of the crop. Perhaps because the musicians knew they were being recorded, the playing in 1951 and 1962 achieves the highest level of intensity and finish, and the Decca / London and Philips engineering teams' recording pick-up conveys more of the famous "Bayreuth sound" than the standard broadcast pick-up of the other performances. The 1962 *Parsifal*, with its combination of sonic immediacy, clarity, blend, and richness, is surely the most beautiful recording to come from the Festspielhaus.

And this sound beautifully complements a performance that, while still rich and broad, is more lithe and more intimate than the more monumental 1951 one. The cast is again strong, and this time strongest in the protagonists. Jess Thomas is at this point showing only the early signs of the wobble that would shortly render his singing less than pleasurable—giving us a full-fledged *Heldentenor* Parsifal, with a sizable, often quite beautiful sound that scales down fairly persuasively and is used with considerable sensibleness if not great specific dramatic insight. Irene Dalis also gives us a strong representation

of the mezzo-soprano Kundry option. Her genuine dramatic mezzo has the fullness and steadiness in the bottom and mid-range to sustain a strong singing line.

Hans Hotter isn't a bass, and his *Heldenbariton* is in the shuddery condition familiar from his earlier Bayreuth broadcasts, only more so, and yet in collaboration with Knappertsbusch he sings an unfailingly alive, struggling Gurnemanz. The physically deteriorated Amfortas is paradoxically represented more successfully by the youthfully healthy George London of 1951 than by the throatier 1962 version. The voice remains a commanding and appropriate one, though, and the performance is fine.

Gustav Neidlinger puts those years of *Rheingold* Alberichs to good use in his Klingsor. Although he still can't bind the vocal line when it jabs upward, he can make powerful vocal actions of those venomous outpourings. The young Martti Talvela makes an imposing sound as Titurel, and the supporting cast is again strong. With the acid-voiced tenors Gerhard Stolze and Georg Paskuda cast as the two male-voice Esquires, we get a graphic image of the bigoted ignorance Gurnemanz has to cope with.

1970 DEUTSCHE GRAMMOPHON (S,P) CD

Gwyneth Jones (A), James King (B), Thomas Stewart (C), Donald McIntyre (D), Franz Crass (E), Karl Ridderbusch (F), Bayreuth Festival Chorus and Orchestra—Pierre Boulez

Because nearly every element of this performance comes with a "yes, but" qualifier, it's easy to underrate. The score sheet would look something like this:

• Despite the imbalance that drives Gwyneth Jones's big soprano out of balance from the middle up, this is a powerful voice and an uncommonly intelligent performance, with some notably beautiful singing when the music stays low.

• Notwithstanding the squeezed quality in James King's upper range, this is a major dramatic tenor, generously produced—next to Thomas's (in 1962 Philips) the most suitable instrument for the title role we've had in a commercial *Parsifal*.

• Although Thomas Stewart's voice isn't in its best shape, it has—like London's—the natural weight to make the necessary impact in the Grail scenes, where the vocal center of gravity is simply too low for most "regular" baritones.

• While Franz Crass's Gurnemanz isn't distinguished by any special intensity of tone or phrasing, there remains his full and beautiful bass, with its solid upper extension.

• You can hear in Donald McIntyre's Klingsor, just as you could subsequently hear in his sojourn in the big-time *Heldenbariton* repertory, the ingredients for a major voice, unfortunately not assembled in proper working order. Phrases that generate real force alternate with others that seem swallowed.

• Except for Karl Ridderbusch's Titurel, the best I've heard, the supporting cast and the orchestra, while still pretty good, represent an unmistakable fall-off in quality from the earlier Bayreuth recordings. (The sound is also less impressive.)

• And Pierre Boulez's conducting itself represents a marked drop-off in intensity level from Knappertsbusch's. Of course there's something to be said for a more easygoing approach (although the singers, as usual in a Boulez operatic performance, might have benefited from a bit of input), and the performance "plays" more naturally and more buoyantly than most of the later recordings. Like most of them, it hasn't solved Act I, but even here the interesting cast and the Bayreuth forces provide continuing points of interest.

1971–72 DECCA / LONDON (S) CD

Christa Ludwig (A), René Kollo (B), Dietrich Fischer-Dieskau (C), Zoltán Kélémen (D), Gottlob Frick (E), Hans Hotter (F), Vienna Boys' Choir, Vienna State Opera Chorus, Vienna Philharmonic Orchestra—Georg Solti

My description of Solti's *Meistersinger* as "a reference-shelf edition"—broadly paced, beautifully played, virtually uninflected—applies to the *Parsifal* as well. One difference is that the

Parsifal contains some performances worth returning to.

The 64-year-old Gottlob Frick, although he predictably gets little help from Solti in the sprawling Act I, gives Gurnemanz everything he has—it would be hard not to be stirred by this wonderfully humane performance. Even more surprisingly, Dietrich Fischer-Dieskau, whose voice by now should be much too flimsy, especially on top, somehow concocts a believable Amfortas—more believable, in fact, than his 1956 Bayreuth performance. And Christa Ludwig, although light-voiced for Kundry and unhelped by her conductor, certainly sings well. A more venturesome conductor might also have encouraged Zoltán Kélémen to dare a more cutting Klingsor than this nice but safe one.

René Kollo has some success with the pure-fool Parsifal of Act I but retreats behind his steel-edged vocal front for the balance. If you want to hear a truly decrepit-sounding Titurel, Hans Hotter's your man. The supporting cast is vocally adequate but again on the prissy side.

1975 ETERNA (S,P)

Gisela Schröter (A), René Kollo (B), Theo Adam (C), Reid Bunger (D), Ulrik Cold (E), Fred Tischler (F), Leipzig St. Thomas Choir, Berlin Radio Chorus, Leipzig Radio Chorus and Symphony Orchestra—Herbert Kegel

This concert-performance recording hasn't circulated much, but, judging from an excerpts disc that Eterna has issued, the loss isn't great.

The basic sound is pleasant enough, with a prevailingly reverent, Bayreuth-like blended quality. You notice, though, that the winds sometimes scramble when the music becomes quicker and / or more complex, and that the dynamic range tends to run from p through maybe *mf*. Except where it's unavoidable, the singers seem as reluctant as the orchestra to engage in full-voiced communication, creating a peaceful-pageant atmosphere. (Of course, moderation cuts both ways: the jaunty gait of the first Grail scene suggests a homecoming rally at Monsalvat U.)

Theo Adam as Amfortas does open out his voice as required, and in so doing firms up the sound to reasonably good effect; otherwise, we're stuck with his dry timbre and attendant narrow wobble, which is well matched to the wobbles of the Gurnemanz and Titurel. Neither Ulrik Cold nor Fred Tischler is abundantly represented on the excerpts disc—there's hardly anything of Gurnemanz from Act I. But we do get the impression of a gentle, avuncular, rather droning fellow, which isn't encouraging.

René Kollo as Parsifal doesn't sound quite as steel-edged as in 1971–72 Decca / London, which may have something to do with the voice's increased tendency to curdle under stress. The Kundry, Gisela Schröter, makes a nice soft sound at the bottom of the voice but is swamped when the music gets higher or louder.

1979–80 DEUTSCHE GRAMMOPHON (S,D) ⓒ

Dunja Vejzovic (A), Peter Hofmann (B), José van Dam (C), Siegmund Nimsgern (D), Kurt Moll (E), Victor von Halem (F), Chorus of the Deutsche Oper, Berlin, Berlin Philharmonic Orchestra—Herbert von Karajan

A seemingly minor point, perhaps, but Karajan has chosen to cast the role of the First Knight—whose most visible function is to report, in a remarkable five-bar solo, Amfortas's view of the shooting of the swan—with a pretty but tiny-voiced tenor, Claes H. Ahnsjö. The result, instead of giving us any sense of the event's significance to the king, and to those attending him, is to give us a little pageant presentation. There is throughout this performance a sense that *Parsifal* is being displayed rather than performed.

This is, however, in many ways a most impressive display. This is one studio recording that takes advantage of its venue, with huge orchestral climaxes that aren't available in the live performances. Significantly, the recording is conspicuously broader than Karajan's 1961 Vienna State Opera performance (released on CD by Hunt Productions), which had a bit more theatrical flavor but already inclined to the presentational mode.

Consequently, this is another cast that doesn't get much help from its conductor. Kurt Moll is

superbly equipped for Gurnemanz, and rouses himself in Act III—listen to the outpouring of "O Gnade! Höchstes Heil!" But most of Act I is presented rather than lived. It's often quite beautiful, but frustrating measured against what Moll is capable of.

Similarly, Dunja Vejzovic's mobile, pointed mezzo carries interesting Kundry possibilities, but Karajan seems actively to discourage her from pursuing them. José van Dam sings Amfortas attractively but smooths out all the obstacles built into the music—obstacles that Wagner built in to create the character's desperate reality. Peter Hofmann's dry, inelastic tenor isn't well adapted to this pageant approach, and Siegmund Nimsgern is a blustery Klingsor.

1981 ERATO (S,D) ⓒ

Yvonne Minton (A), Reiner Goldberg (B), Wolfgang Schöne (C), Aage Haugland (D), Robert Lloyd (E), Hans Tschammer (F), Prague Philharmonic Chorus, Philharmonic Orchestra of Monte Carlo—Armin Jordan

Here's a genuine alternative to the Knappertsbusch approach. *Parsifal* doesn't have to be slow, but a performance does have to account for the tremendous level of activity within, which Jordan does beautifully. He takes nothing for granted, encouraging both cast and orchestra to look for immediate dramatic needs, and the performance bursts with color and life.

Somehow Yvonne Minton finds for Kundry an intensity that shouldn't be available to such a lightweight mezzo, giving a searing and seductive performance. Reiner Goldberg, whose upper range isn't taxed by Parsifal, offers a pleasing measure of vocal heft and ring. Among recorded Gurnemanzes, Robert Lloyd may present the most satisfying combination of vocal solidity and dramatic attentiveness. Why, he sounds as if he's actually singing his opening lines *to the Esquires!*

Wolfgang Schöne has a medium-size, rather nondescript baritone but uses it to good effect: a highly competent Amfortas. Aage Haugland's bass is an interestingly weighty sound for Klingsor, but the voice's clumsy handling leaves it tied up on top. Hans Tschammer is a solid Titurel, and the supporting cast is capable.

1984 EMI / ANGEL (S,D) CD

Waltraud Meier (A), Warren Ellsworth (B), Phillip Joll (C), Nicholas Folwell (D), Donald McIntyre (E), David Gwynne (F), Welsh National Opera Chorus and Orchestra—Reginald Goodall

Goodall's *Parsifal* comes into its own in a broad, majestic Act III, but even earlier on, where the images of seriousness he's working for take a toll in dramatic immediacy, the performance retains interest thanks to some worthy individual efforts.

Heading the list is the moving Gurnemanz of Donald McIntyre, who sounds like a different singer relieved of the higher center of gravity of his normal *Heldenbariton* roles. Then, Warren Ellsworth comes close to a first-rate Parsifal, with a distinctive, buzzy timbre and a good deal of vocal presence. All I miss here is the willingness or ability to cut loose, most noticeable on sustained high notes. In some ways most exciting is Nicholas Folwell, who has barely begun to explore Klingsor but is the first recorded interpreter to *sing* the whole role, with weight and presence down below and some freedom on top.

Waltraud Meier scores points as Kundry too, but she simply sings through the functional glitches in her good-size mezzo, making it difficult to create a coherent impression. Phillip Joll's insufficiency is more conspicuous here than in his Kurwenal in Goodall's *Tristan*, and more damaging—Amfortas's scenes are so exposed that a weak performance can simply demolish them.

The orchestra isn't asked to produce crisp attacks, which can become fatiguing but may also be a trade-off Goodall has made to achieve the intensity of its playing, captured in recorded sound remarkable for its delicate textures.

1985 PHILIPS (S,D,P) CD

Waltraud Meier (A), Peter Hofmann (B), Simon Estes (C), Franz Mazura (D), Hans Sotin (E),

Matti Salminen (F), Bayreuth Festival Chorus and Orchestra—James Levine

You wouldn't mistake this recording for 1962 Philips, but in terms of orchestral playing and engineering, it's surely the best thing to have come out of Bayreuth since. There's none of the tonal radiance of 1962 Philips, or of Knappertsbusch's depth of purpose. But Levine and his Bayreuth cohorts are able to sustain a performance of fully Knappertsbuschian breadth—in objectively describable terms so similar to Levine's Met *Parsifals*, of which I have never been able to believe a note. Instead of being machine-tooled, the music is allowed to take living shape as it is being performed.

It helps that a strong Gurnemanz is on hand. As so often is the case, Hans Sotin's mind doesn't seem fully trained on the task at hand, but that plangent bass is in good shape and is generally pointed in the right direction—the Act I narrations aren't at all badly sustained. Amfortas and Titurel are also given vigorous voice by Simon Estes and Matti Salminen.

In conversational mode, Waltraud Meier's voice sounds better-knit than in 1984 EMI, but when stretched it turns tremulous. Peter Hofmann also gets off some nice conversational phrases, but whenever he has to sing a bit higher or louder the voice splatters. Nor is there much singing quality left in Franz Mazura's bass-baritone, so that no matter how high he turns up the energy level, he's not my kind of Klingsor. The supporting cast is generally adequate.

1989–90 TELDEC (S,D) CD

Waltraud Meier (A), Siegfried Jerusalem (B), José van Dam (C), Günter von Kannen (D), Matthias Hölle (E), John Tomlinson (F), Chorus of the German State Opera, Berlin, Berlin Philharmonic Orchestra—Daniel Barenboim

There are beautiful things here. The Act I and III scene transformations have impressive momentum, which carries over into the Grail choruses. In the Good Friday music there's some compelling lyricism. In the final Grail scene there's a powerful climax when Amfortas has his father's coffin opened, and then another strong moment when the lovely resolving motto is repeated at Amfortas's "Dir gab ich den Tod"—Barenboim responds to *something* here.

And the rest? Well, it's sensibly conceived and attractively executed—the full, blended sound of the Berlin Philharmonic inevitably suggests a Karajan performance, though *not* the latter's *Parsifal* (1979–80 DG). Barenboim's reading, in its generally measured tread, suggests a somewhat more mobile, less weighty variant of Solti's (1971–72 Decca / London). It's not that the thing doesn't move, or that it doesn't know where it's going, but that where it's going often doesn't seem terribly important.

And the cast proves uniformly unable or unwilling to take action on its own. Even in the unlively Solti recording there is *some* singing—from Frick as Gurnemanz, from Fischer-Dieskau as Amfortas—that to an extent finds its own urgency. Not so here. Those above-noted moments in the Act III Grail scene, for example, happen entirely in the orchestra. As in Amfortas's two earlier scenes, José van Dam is singing firmly, evenly, indeed quite handsomely (more so, perhaps, than in 1979–80 DG), but without any evidence of the king's consuming physical and mental agony—one of the opera's central given circumstances.

And while we have heard far worse Gurnemanzes than the honest, pleasant-sounding Matthias Hölle, the latter hardly possesses either the force of personality or the intensity of sound (the voice doesn't have much body in the midrange or bottom) to command attention on his own. Meanwhile John Tomlinson, with a voice of notably greater fullness and textural interest, is assigned to the decrepit Titurel. His Titurel is probably the strongest vocal performance here, which isn't an encouraging sign.

Parsifal might seem a good role for Siegfried Jerusalem, since most of it doesn't lie terribly high, and he makes a reasonably mellifluous sound. But there's an element of insolidity in the sound, which prevents him from singing with much authority, and consequently from committing to strong vocal actions. Waltraud Meier's third recorded Kundry (why?) is similarly short on vocal authority, especially when the writing becomes high and / or strenuous. Perhaps needless to say, the Act II Kundry-Parsifal scene doesn't build well.

And while Günter von Kannen as Klingsor gets Act II off to a good start, he too runs into trouble when—very shortly—*his* writing becomes high and / or strenuous. The supporting cast is professionally competent but, again, unable to capitalize on the small but rich opportunities Wagner has provided them.

For once, a simple recommendation is possible: 1962 Philips is one of the great opera recordings. There's even a simple supplementary (or, if you wish, alternative) recommendation: 1981 Erato. There's even a performance that combines the former's breadth of vision and the latter's dramatic immediacy: a 1983 Hungarian State Opera live performance (issued on LP by Hungaroton), in Hungarian, conducted by János Ferencsik—with an impressive Gurnemanz, László Polgár, and the powerful and seductive Kundry of Katalin Kasza, matched on records only by Rita Gorr, in a lovely 1960 La Scala performance (issued on LP by Melodram) conducted by André Cluytens.

The other recordings shouldn't be overlooked, however. Individual priorities will suggest which are most worth investigating.

KENNETH FURIE

DER FREISCHÜTZ (1821)

A: Agathe (s); B: Ännchen (s); C: Max (t); D: Ottokar (bar);
E: Caspar (bs); F: Hermit (bs)

*D*er Freischütz, Weber's sixth attempt at opera and his first success, struck its audiences in 1821 like a thunderbolt and laid the foundation for German romantic opera. The essentials of romantic opera—the fantastic, the national, the comic, and the realistic—had been present, if not all in the same work, in various operas for thirty years following Mozart's *Die Zauberflöte*. It was Weber who fused the four elements, treating his subject seriously and not as mere amusement. The mystical fervor and pantheism of *Der Freischütz* perfectly suited the religious sentiment of Weber's day.

A *Singspiel*, the opera combines musical numbers and spoken dialogue. Few of its recordings present a great deal of the dialogue; some offer only a smattering, some none at all. Of the former, some are marred by the assignment of actors to replace the singers in speaking parts. This dubious practice almost never yields the desired result, because the voices of the actors so seldom match those of the singers.

1951 ACANTA (M,P)

Elfriede Trötschel (A), Irma Beilke (B), Bernd Aldenhoff (C), Karl Paul (D), Kurt Böhme (E), Heinz Kramer (F), Chorus and Orchestra of the Dresden State Opera—Rudolf Kempe

The *Freischütz* experience is woefully incomplete without a fair measure of its spoken dialogue. The original issue of this recording is derived from a concert broadcast and presents the musical numbers intact but little of the dialogue (in some subsequent issues, none at all). It has other liabilities as well: the voices are too close miked to balance with the orchestra, which is always overly recessive, except in quiet passages; *fortissimos* are severely monitored. Except for Böhme, whose large, dusky, insinuating voice brings the villainous Caspar to life, the cast is substandard. Trötschel has little spontaneity as Agathe, is rhythmically slack, and has an annoying habit of attacking notes with a white sound. The loosened vibrato of Beilke's mature soprano undermines her characterization of the youthful Ännchen. Aldenhoff has the vocal size and metal for Max along with decent diction and rhythm; his tone, however, is usually distressingly unsteady and frequently off-pitch. Apart from Böhme, the only reason for hearing this antique is the poetic conducting of Rudolf Kempe. Even poor recording and some rough ensemble cannot dim his atmospheric and fiery direction of the Wolf Glen scene, heard, by the way, with all the sound effects referred to in the text.

1951 DECCA / LONDON (M)

Maud Cunitz (A), Emmy Loose (B), Hans Hopf (C), Alfred Poell (D), Marjan Rus (E), Otto Edelmann (F), Vienna State Opera Chorus and Vienna Philharmonic Orchestra—Otto Ackermann

Who would have guessed in the wake of this dismal recording that its conductor, before the

1950s were history, would go on to win the undying affection of collectors for his leadership of many now-classic recordings of Viennese operettas? Again, there is little dialogue, the chorus and orchestra sound tired, and the Agathe is inept. Hopf, tonally a little steadier than Aldenhoff, is seldom illuminating, more often heavy-handed. Rus merely scratches the surface of Caspar's demonic character. Loose's spirited Ännchen, Poell's dignified Ottokar, and Edelmann's vocal health are insufficient attractions to tempt a listener to trudge through this only passably recorded, hum-ridden issue.

1959 EMI / ANGEL (S)

Elisabeth Grümmer (A), Lisa Otto (B), Rudolf Schock (C), Hermann Prey (D), Karl Kohn (E), Gottlob Frick (F), Chorus of the Deutsche Oper, Berlin Philharmonic Orchestra—Joseph Keilberth

This first stereo registration of *Der Freischütz* is unevenly engineered, testifying to varying microphone placements over multiple sessions. The original issue is much the best; in the Seraphim reissue, the Overture and many of the choruses are deficient in bass, almost tinny. On the other hand, transfer of solos and duets is generally full and spacious. The original issue has dialogue, the reissue almost none. These debits cannot devalue the worth of this estimable rendition, four of its six leading roles performed as well or better than in competing sets. Grümmer is a model Agathe—responsive, urgent, with her youthful tone floated on the breath and shaped into apt, musical phrases, colored by diction sensitive to any change in emotional temperature. Otto, her faithful Ännchen and very nearly her equal, is a perfect partner—lively, charming, musical, precise. Schock's *Jugendheldentenor*, his ardor and concern, make him a superior Max, his tendency to aspirate notwithstanding. Kohn has a voice without personality but with the right size, color, and cutting edge for Caspar. Inconsistent dramatic concentration is another problem; for example, the expression of demonic intensity and focus on purely vocal matters vie for Kohn's attention during his aria which closes the first

act, but he seldom honors both at the same time. There is superb singing in two of the smaller roles—by Prey, the youthful aristocrat to the life, and Frick, a noble and humane Hermit, unmatched on disc. Careless about dynamics and rhythm, Keilberth permits a good deal of sloppy ensemble work. Nevertheless, with such an outstanding cast, he gets by on idiomatic security and high theatrical energy level.

1959 DEUTSCHE GRAMMOPHON (S)

Irmgard Seefried (A), Rita Streich (B), Richard Holm (C), Eberhard Wächter (D), Kurt Böhme (E), Walter Kreppel (F), Bavarian Radio Chorus and Orchestra—Eugen Jochum

With this recording, Jochum raised new standards for recorded performances of this opera. The German conductor's affectionate command, fastidious observance of Weber's directions, his preparation and support of a strong cast of singers, are telling in the context of a natural-sounding, analytical recording with good imaging. Surely no other orchestra and chorus has a stronger grip on the traditions of this opera and how it breathes than the musicians of Munich. To accommodate the work on two discs, DG cut the entr'acte between the second and third acts and about a third of the dialogue, most notably the ensuing scene. Seefried and Streich are adorable. The former, though not quite so full-toned or rapt in the prayer as Grümmer, has an appealing silvery timbre, warm expression and prosody, and unmatched enunciation (singing or speaking). An eager and vulnerable Agathe, her joyous "Er ist's" and "neu belebter Muth!" linger in the memory. If Streich does not quite equal Otto in consistent personal projection (her narration about the ghost that turns out to be the family dog falls a little flat), her voice is rounder and even more enchanting. Holm's tenor is somewhat light for Max, but his tender and anxious impersonation and musicianship outweigh moments of vocal strain. In his second recording of the part, Böhme, the peerless Caspar, displays even greater musical accuracy that intensifies his villainous portrayal. Wächter is superb, an authoritative

Ottokar. The rock-solid tones required for the Hermit's Sarastro-like statements are not supplied by Kreppel.

1967 EURODISC (S) CD

Claire Watson (A), Lotte Schädle (B), Rudolf Schock (C), Claudio Nicolai (D), Gottlob Frick (E), Kurt Böhme (F), Chorus and Orchestra of the Deutsche Oper, Berlin—Lovro von Matačic

This virtually complete presentation with dialogue spoken by the singers is well engineered, except for the choruses, which seem to have been recorded with a different microphone placement. In such an over-resonant ambience, they lack focus and bite. In any event, the sluggish performance has little vitality in direction and vocal polish. Watson, an American soprano whose musicality and dramatic intelligence suggest why she was a favorite in Munich for so many years, does not have the seamless line essential to either the first part of her aria or her prayer. Schädle is a bit drab in a role that should sparkle. Schock, his second recorded Max as expressive as before, now betrays vocal effort in patches of poor intonation and some unsupported tone in his lower register. Frick's jet-black bass and dramatic intensity endow Caspar with suitably desperate malevolence; however, at this stage in his career the role's high tessitura exacts its toll. Nicolai is an acceptable Ottokar, but Böhme, with a slow beat on sustained tones, is an ineffective Hermit.

1969 EMI / ANGEL (S)

Birgit Nilsson (A), Erika Köth (B), Nicolai Gedda (C), Wolfgang Anheisser (D), Walter Berry (E), Jürgen Förster (F), Bavarian State Opera Chorus and Orchestra—Robert Heger

This project looks better on paper than it sounds. To begin, the clean but bass-heavy recording militates against the veteran Heger's musically sensitive but somewhat untheatrical direction, always more effective in the domestic scenes than in the dramatic. Dialogue is abbreviated; the first scene of Act III is cut. Nilsson, rough and graceless, is miscast. Köth has the right spirit but not the tonal security Ännchen demands. Surprisingly, Max does not suit Gedda; the tenor fights the part with unsuitable overemphasis. Caspar is temperamentally alien to the conscientious Berry. The smaller roles are well taken.

1973 DEUTSCHE GRAMMOPHON (S) CD

Gundula Janowitz (A), Edith Mathis (B), Peter Schreier (C), Bernd Weikl (D), Theo Adam (E), Franz Crass (F), Leipzig Radio Chorus and Dresden State Orchestra—Carlos Kleiber

Love of *Freischütz* must run in the Kleiber family. First there was Erich, whose peerless conducting of Weber's masterpiece over three decades became legend. Now his son, Carlos, chooses it for his first opera recording and dominates the proceedings. Kleiber's preparation of his thoroughbred Dresden ensemble and the precision of its execution is impressive. Here and there one encounters some fussiness and a loss of spontaneity, some eccentric tempos—too fast for the opening chorus and Caspar's drinking song—but the greater portion of the score responds to his meticulous care, enthusiasm, and musicality. DG's production has its drawbacks. Its multi-mike production permits copious detail, but the mix-down produces sound that seems a trifle unnatural without much bloom. Actors, rather than the singers, speak the dialogue. Janowitz, smooth and poised in tone and delivery, is a cool, uninvolved Agathe, chaste as a silver moon. Mathis is her overly severe and sober companion. In his zeal to do justice to Max's desperation, Schreier, ever alert to all rhythmic and dynamic demands, lunges at some phrases. His low register is not always firm. Adam is fierce without achieving malevolence. The other bass roles are in good hands.

1979 DECCA / LONDON (S)

Hildegard Behrens (A), Helen Donath (B), René Kollo (C), Wolfgang Brendel (D), Peter Meven

(E), Kurt Moll (F), Bavarian Radio Chorus and Orchestra—Rafael Kubelik

The outstanding feature of this set is its sound, clear and strikingly full-bodied. Kubelik, like Heger, does not seize enough opportunities for dramatic contrast—e.g., the impact of the Overture is blunted when the opening *adagio* is followed by an overly low tempo nowhere near Weber's prescribed *molto vivace*. The performance is sometimes a bit lazy rhythmically; the peasant dance has little bounce, the opening of the second act is heavy and charmless, the Wolf Glen scene has insufficient impact until the casting of the bullets. The conscientious cast is largely disappointing—Behrens, sensitive to emotional content but without the steadiness and purity of tone essential to Agathe; Kollo, also dramatically convincing but strained by stressful passages; and Meven, gratefully less hammy than some Caspars but without sufficient vocal personality to convey the sharp edge of danger. Donath, often lively but tonally unpoised above the staff, is little better than a routine Ännchen. Brendel's Ottokar is wanting in authority. Moll is an outstanding Hermit, sympathetic and dignified.

1985 DENON (S,D,P) CD

Jana Smitkova (A), Andrea Ihle (B), Reiner Goldberg (C), Hans-Joachim Ketelsen (D), Ekkehard Wlaschiha (E), Theo Adam (F), Dresden State Opera Chorus and Orchestra— Wolf-Dieter Hauschild

This performance, which took place on February 13, 1985, and reopened the acoustically superb Semper Opera House, was preserved by Denon. The issue is an engineering triumph, if little else, probably the most effective recording of an operatic event I have yet encountered, with natural, convincingly balanced sound and imaging. The opera is absolutely complete, with a few lines of dialogue that are not even in my score. The Dresden ensemble is persuasive; its conductor, however, although musically neat, is deficient in dramatic spirit. In spite of attrac-

tive vocal quality and dramatic sensitivity, Smitkova is too often unable to trace a firm line; some of her long phrases are labored and the high notes are troublesome. Ihle also discloses some vocal unsteadiness as well as a weak low register. Goldberg's tenor has sufficient size, flexibility, and ping for Max, but he is careless about pitch and inclined to force. Wlaschiha is thorough but with a vocal personality easy to forget. The Ottokar is poor. Adam is a liability as the Hermit, his voice now a remnant of its past, his vibrato gratingly loose.

1990 PHILIPS (S,D) CD

Karita Mattila (A), Eva Lind (B), Francisco Araiza (C), Siegfried Lorenz (D, Ekkehard Wlaschiha (E), Kurt Moll (F), Leipzig Radio Chorus and Dresden State Orchestra—Colin Davis

Davis takes a double-dark view of this opera, clouding over even its sunniest moments, robbing them of spontaneity, losing the contrasts that are essential to *Freischütz*. He maintains that view with honorable consistency, but it is wrongheaded.

He has, however, presented all of the opera's music and insisted on his singers speaking the considerably abridged dialogue. Like most of Davis's projects, this one is ably prepared and executed; his chorus and orchestra attain a lustrous ensemble finish. No other version reveals greater adherence to Weber's rhythmic and dynamic instructions. His account of the Wolf Glen Scene (complete with the sound of owls, thunder, fire, boiling lead, lightning, horses, whips, and dogs) is a real chiller, and Philips's estimable engineering gives it a presence previously unmatched on disc.

Davis's selection of tempos is another matter. Some numbers are so deliberately paced, even finely pointed rhythms can't make them airborne—e.g., the *allegro molto* section of the Overture (*moderato* at best), the March and Waltz (clunky and utterly charmless).

Apart from Wlaschiha's forceful, baleful Caspar and Kurt Moll's nobly orotund Hermit, the singers are disappointing. Araiza, a flexible but vocally lightweight Max, is not the wanted hero under stress. Neither Mattila nor Lind has the purity and consistent firmness of tone to draw a smooth line when the tessitura is treacherous. The unsteady Ottokar is more plebeian than prince; the minor parts are routinely taken.

A CD reissue of EMI's first *Freischütz* has been released by Allegro, and it is the one to acquire.

C. J. LUTEN

Unavailable for review:
1950 REMINGTON

KURT WEILL

DIE DREIGROSCHENOPER (1928)

A: Polly Peachum (s); B: Lucy Brown (s); C: Spelunkenjenny (s);
D: Frau Peachum (ms); E: Macheath (t); F: Jonathan Jeremiah
Peachum (bar); G: Tiger Brown (bar); H: Street Singer (bar)

The Beggar's Opera of 1728 played the seamy side of London life against the pastoral / mythological conventions of *opera seria*. When adapted for the Berlin stage two centuries later by Bertolt Brecht and his secretary Elisabeth Hauptmann as *Die Dreigroschenoper*, it acquired further layers of irony; Kurt Weill's fresh, distinctive combination of seductive melodies, contemporary popular idioms, and neoclassic spareness became the foil for a Berlin of brown shirts and black markets. (Of the original 1728 music, Weill retained only Peachum's "Morning Chorale.") Though effectively banned from the stage after the Nazis' ascendancy in 1933, *Die Dreigroschenoper* again became an international success in the 1950s, sparking a continuing quarrel between apostles of Brecht and Weill about which deserves the greater credit—a quarrel reflected in a dichotomy of performing approaches favoring either text or music. With one exception, the recordings present only the musical score, a format possibly unflattering to theatrical characterizations developed primarily in the spoken text.

The original production and the 1928 published score omitted Frau Peachum's "Ballad of Sexual Dependency" (No. 12), restored in more recent editions; an opera-parodistic "jealousy" aria for Lucy (No. 14a), dropped still earlier, was never even orchestrated by Weill. Other numbers omitted from one or another recording are the "Melodrama" (No. 11), "Polly's Song"

(No. 11a), and the "Call from the Grave" (No. 19). But the list of *Dreigroschenoper* textual complications merely begins there: many recordings are cavalier with Weill's meticulous orchestrations, manhandling the score as if it were pop music. That applies even to the famous, severely abridged 1930 recording (available on a Teldec CD), featuring some members of the original 1928 cast (Erich Ponto as Peachum, Kurt Gerron as Brown, and Weill's wife Lotte Lenya as Jenny) under Theo Mackeben, who led the first production. This was recorded for release in connection with G. W. Pabst's film version (available on laser disc), from which it adopts certain practices, notably the assignment of Polly's "Pirate Jenny" to Jenny (in the recording, Lenya also sings the "Barbara Song") and the addition of three new verses of the "Moritat" at the work's end (also given to Lenya). Despite its liberties, this recording remains fascinating for flavor and ambience, for its testimony that the work's original performance tradition was based in true singing—and for the earliest recorded traces of Lenya's Jenny, then projected in soprano register instead of the whiskey contralto of her postwar career.

1954 VANGUARD (M)

Liane (A), Anny Felbermayer (B), Hedy Fassler (C), Rosette Anday (D), Kurt Preger (E), Alfred Jerger (F), Frederick Guthrie (G), Helge Rosvaenge (H), Vienna State Opera Chorus and Chamber Orchestra—F. Charles Adler

745

This first attempt to record the then-available score (omitting Nos. 11a, 12, and 14a) was a near-total disaster. Adler sets many tempos grotesquely slower than Weill's indications, and even the correct ones are vitiated by limp playing, poor ensemble, and soggy rhythm. Despite minor anomalies (e.g., the trombone with its slides is missing in Peachum's second entry in the Act I finale), the orchestrations are basically Weill's, and original keys are retained throughout—sometimes to the great disadvantage of the singers, many of them opera stars past their primes and at sea in the style. The "Moritat" lands in Rosvaenge's shaky lower-middle register, Anday wobbles badly, and Jerger misses the irony in Peachum's songs. The French cabaret artist Liane sings Polly's "Barbara Song" an octave lower than written, disassociating it from the high-register character of her preceding number, and cedes her part in the "Jealousy Duet" to Hedy Fassler, the Jenny, whose feeble *parlando* annihilates the line of the "Solomon Song." Macheath is an operetta tenor whose vocal *Gestalt* is built on comic rather than satirical caricature and whose musical habits, notably *portamento* and expressive *ritards*, are deeply inimical to the aggressive energy of Weill's music and Brecht's verses. But then everybody's instincts are of the same Viennese ilk, grotesquely fragmenting and denaturing the score. (Possibly some in the cast, working from scratch in the studio, had no idea of the story around the songs.)

1955 POLYDOR (In English) (M) CD

Jo Sullivan (A), Beatrice Arthur (B), Lotte Lenya (C), Charlotte Rae (D), Scott Merrill (E), Martin Wolfson (F), George Tyne (G), Gerald Price (H), Chorus and orchestra—Samuel Matlowsky

Marc Blitzstein's English version, first staged at New York's Theater de Lys on March 10, 1954, launched the *Dreigroschenoper*'s triumphant conquest of the Anglo-Saxon stage, and it remains, in David Drew's words, "unmatched in its musicality—its instinctive response to the gist, the gait, and the timbre of Weill's music." Blitzstein's treatment is not without willfulness; he smooths out some of Brecht's raspier edges,

alters the vocal lines to fit his words, combines Nos. 11 and 11a, abridges the first finale, skips a stanza here and adds another there. (All pieces except No. 14a are present, and so is the final "Moritat"; some of the theater lyrics were bowdlerized for the recording.) The jacket proclaims "Original orchestrations by Kurt Weill," but since the eight players aren't as versatile as Weill's original scoring assumes, occasional modifications are made, and the "Ballad of Sexual Dependency" is accompanied only by piano. The cast has much personality. Merrill's Macheath, aptly "cool" in both senses of the term, sings musically, even when tested by the finale's suddenly operatic tessitura. Jo Sullivan's sweet Polly loses not only "Pirate Jenny" to Jenny but also the "Barbara Song" to Lucy (another "tradition" from early Berlin days); Beatrice Arthur's octave-lower reading of the latter, though flavorsome, exudes an inappropriate maturity. Taking "Pirate Jenny" and the "Tango Ballad" down a minor third, the "Solomon Song" a major third, Lenya sings more broadly and dramatically than in 1930; her accent does not impede vivid projection of Blitzstein's words. The Peachums are both excellent, and the theatrical vitality of the whole attests to its origins in a well-integrated production.

1958 CBS / SONY (S) CD

Johanna von Koczián (A), Inge Wolffberg (B), Lotte Lenya (C), Trude Hesterburg (D), Erich Schellow (E), Willy Trenk-Trebitsch (F), Wolfgang Grunert (G), Wolfgang Neuss (H), Unidentified chorus, Orchestra of Radio Free Berlin—Wilhelm Brückner-Rüggeberg

Recorded under Lenya's supervision, this set presents the complete musical score (including No. 14a, scored by the conductor), along with Brecht's "captions" and a few other spoken bits. Lenya's auspices don't in fact guarantee utter fidelity to the score, for she takes her music down still further than in 1955 Polydor, and necessitates another transposition when (following an alteration made by Brecht but not by Weill) she appropriates Frau Peachum's stanza of the second finale. Polly does repossess the

"Barbara Song" and, while the closing verses of the "Moritat" from the film are still here, they are voiced, more aptly, by the Street Singer. A few adjustments are made to accommodate other performers, and Weill's orchestrations are occasionally altered.

In a cast of German theater and cabaret artists, Lenya, as potent as ever, is joined by two other survivors from the pre-Nazi era: as Peachum, Trenk-Trebitsch (Macheath of the 1930 recording), and as his wife, Hesterburg (Begbick of the 1931 Berlin *Mahagonny*). Hesterburg is a monumental presence, singing with immense relish and authority—an octave lower than written, which is not troublesome because Frau Peachum belongs to the senior generation (some believe this register shift goes back to the premiere). Trenk-Trebitsch, with less voice remaining, has slyness but little of Peachum's malice. Schellow's vivid, dashing Macheath, a tad raw in tone, is very accurate and musical; he reaches all the notes in the finale, with a strain that appropriately underlines the artificiality of this operatic convention suddenly imposed on an otherwise "real" drama. Von Koczián's sweet voice is less secure; her "Barbara Song" (a tone down) is blander than Arthur's or Lenya's—but not inaptly so (Polly's transformation, after Mack's imprisonment, into a gangster of high finance is another *ex post facto* Brechtian revision). The only real disappointment in the cast is Wolffberg, whose throaty, untrained mezzo can't encompass either her part in the "Jealousy Duet" or the solo aria (taken down a tone). Brückner-Rüggeberg is a pillar of strength; his tempos are considerate of Weill's metronome markings, and even the slow ones never lose vitality. The CD issue abandons the superior annotations of the original CBS LP edition in favor of an ill-informed essay, not improved by sloppy English translation.

1965 PHILIPS (S) CD

Karin Huebner (A), Ursula Dirichs (B), Edith Teichmann (C), Anita Mey (D), Hans Korte (E), Franz Kutschera (F), Albert Hoermann (G), Dieter Brammer (H), Members of the Frankfurt Opera Orchestra—Wolfgang Rennert

Probably all too typical of Brecht-oriented German productions of the sixties, this recording, based on a Frankfurt staging by Harry Buckwitz, gets just about everything wrong. The performers shout, bark, growl, bellow, rasp, belt, scream, bray, and squeak, but (except for the chorus in the finale) hardly ever really sing. Words are altered to incorporate changes Brecht made years later, without Weill's consent. Vocal pitches and rhythms are broadly ignored. The scoring is doctored and "improved" with added "jazzy" rhythm parts. The Overture is trimmed down to its final *ritornello*, which serves as background for the Street Singer's first speech (he later snarls the title of each number, but not Brecht's "slates"); Nos. 11 and 14a are omitted, along with occasional stanzas. Polly gets to keep all her songs, but Frau Peachum—who apparently can't even pretend to sing pitches—cedes to Jenny the "Ballad of Sexual Dependency" and her stanza of the second finale. In short, the performance makes little contact with Weill's work, transforming all the characters into howling caricatures rather than people for whom music is an essential and multifarious means of expression. According to the original LP liner note: "The commercialization of [the work's] most popular songs, in innumerable arrangements of the cheapest sort, has demonstrated that bourgeois society can live with Brecht's potentially revolutionary work without feeling in the least threatened by it." This performance demonstrates another, equally effective way to avoid *Die Dreigroschenoper*'s import: by making it a freak show.

1967/68 POLYDOR (S)

Karin Baal (A), Sylvia Anders (B), Hanne Wieder (C), Berta Drews (D), Hannes Messemer (E), Helmut Qualtinger (F), Martin Held (G), Franz Josef Degenhardt (H), Chorus and orchestra—James Last

To date the only recorded *Dreigroschenoper* to include the spoken text as well as the musical score, this set unfortunately belongs to the same performing tradition as 1965 Philips. These are actors, not singers; the women all take their music down an octave (permissible for Frau

Peachum, compromising to the aural image of Macheath's three lady friends), and everyone prefers shouting the words to singing the notes. Once again, Weill's orchestrations have been radically revised, and the singing and playing frequently eschew any dynamic nuance whatsoever. There is value in hearing the work as a whole, of course, and the spoken drama is well treated, especially by Qualtinger and Drews, who savor the satirical edge in the Peachums' scenes; sonic effects and perspectives are tellingly used. But the maltreatment of the music grows increasingly wearisome, reaching a climax when the second-act finale is turned over entirely to the Street Singer, accompanied only by a guitar, so that a clarion cry against social injustice is reduced to a tacky ballad. (Surprisingly, this is the only number transposed from Weill's original keys—though most of the women would have been more comfortable with a moderate downward shift than with the lower-octave compromise.) For the record, Nos. 14a and 19 are omitted. In both spoken and sung material, Brecht's subsequent revisions of the text are used, rather than the 1928 playing script; the dialogue is occasionally but not seriously abridged. A single disc containing all the recorded vocal numbers (but skipping the Overture, included in the complete set) was issued on the Heliodor label—but those are the least desirable parts of this set.

1976 CBS / SONY (In English) (S)

Caroline Kava (A), Blair Brown (B), Ellen Greene (C), Elisabeth Wilson (D), Raul Julia (E), C. K. Alexander (F), David Sabin (G), Roy Brocksmith (H), Chorus and orchestra—Stanley Silverman

Joseph Papp's New York Shakespeare Festival production at Lincoln Center used the translation made by Ralph Manheim and John Willett for the English-language edition of Brecht's collected plays—not a patch on Blitzstein's for style, and frequently at war with the rhythms of the music. Given Stanley Silverman's understanding of the score and the availability of a complement of instruments that, in his words, "enables us to play every note that Weill wrote

on the proper instruments," it's a mystery why so many details of the original orchestrations are altered, not to mention the extensive elaboration of the "Moritat." (Only one number is actually transposed—"Pirate Jenny," down a tone—and the opening of the third-act finale is omitted, as well as occasional stanzas elsewhere. Once again, Jenny lays claim to "Pirate Jenny" and Frau Peachum's verse of the second finale.) The decision to go for lower-class London accents is disastrous: Polly, Lucy, and Jenny all sound as if they're auditioning for the role of Eliza Doolittle, and the effort they expend on diction distracts them from characterization. Kava has some musical sense, but Greene's voice is weak, unable to shape the climactic line of the "Solomon Song." Julia's Macheath is a capable singer of pitches, but he's rhythmically inert and often trails the orchestra. As before, the message is clear: while this music may not need full-fledged operatic voices, the performers do have to be able to sing Weill's pitches and rhythms.

1988 DECCA / LONDON (S,D) CD

Ute Lemper (A), Susanne Tremper (B), Milva (C), Helga Dernesch (D), René Kollo (E), Mario Adorf (F), Wolfgang Reichmann (G), Rolf Boysen (H), RIAS Chamber Choir and Berlin Sinfonietta—John Mauceri

The latest recordings represent a reaction against performance traditions emphasizing Brecht's words at the expense of Weill's notes, and the published orchestrations are also adhered to. The Mauceri recording includes a modicum of dialogue, enough to separate the pieces if not enough fully to carry the plot. But these good intentions are compromised by what one assumes were box-office decisions. For the German cabaret star Ute Lemper, Polly's numbers (including "Pirate Jenny") have to be transposed down. The Italian cabaret star Milva, doubtless unwilling to portray Jenny unless she could sing "Pirate Jenny," gets to do an encore (transposed down still further) in Act II—but at least gives a real performance of it, showing Lemper to be still an amateur. Milva sings her other numbers an octave down, which isn't too disastrous; her "Solomon Song" is finely shaped, opening out well for the climax, and she achieves a touching effect at the end of last stanza by humming the harmonium's closing phrase in a dying fall.

At the other end of the vocal spectrum are two Wagnerians, René Kollo and Helga Dernesch. The producer points to the virtues of having the second finale sung by two such instruments, but neglects to note that the rest of the time they are paired with rather smaller organs: the mix-down engineer clearly had a job toning Kollo down to match Lemper in the "Liebeslied," and Tiger Brown tends to vanish under Siegfried in the "Kanonen Song." Kollo can't sustain notes for long without flapping in the breeze, and he doesn't sound comfortable with the ever-present patter, which really cannot be sung in *Heldentenor* fashion. He's also careless with the rhythm, but not in a purposeful, stylish way—it just sounds sloppy. Dernesch, too, is disappointing, singing the "Ballad of Sexual Dependency" richly but without much variety or sparkle; however, in the second finale, she manages to make the dotted rhythms sound easy and natural, as Kollo does not. The Lucy is adequate for her aria, which is played in an orchestration by the conductor. Mauceri's tempos are well conceived and the orchestra plays well, in a somewhat dry acoustic; his attention to detail can result in fussiness (e.g., the "Anstatt-daß Song") but generally yields good balances and textures.

1989 KOCH (S,D) CD

Stephanie Myszak (A), Natalia Afeyan (B), Anelia Shoumanova (C), Anita Hermann (D), Manfred Jung (E), Hermann Becht (F), Eugene Demerdjiev (G), Waldemar Kmentt (H), Bulgarian Radio and Television Mixed Chorus, Symphony Orchestra, and Big Band—Victor C. Symonette

Another "reformist" essay, this recording proposes to furnish a "really sung recording" of the music such as Weill wished for in a letter of 1928. The published score is followed pretty faithfully, without transpositions; traditional extra verses are added to "Pirate Jenny," "Tango Ballad," and the "Jealousy Duet" (but not to Mrs. Peachum's solo), and Lucy's aria is performed as Weill left it, with only piano accompaniment. One oddity: for a few bars of recitative in the third-act finale, a harpsichord materializes, marking a new high-water mark of misplaced "authenticity"—evidently someone forgot that Brecht's libretto is set in the nineteenth century.

Like 1954 Vanguard, this is a cast of operatic singers. Macheath is another *Heldentenor*, less glamorous in sound than Kollo but no better equipped for the music's technical demands. Peachum is an Alberich who overdoes tonal variety and dynamics and is rhythmically unsettled by the little patter notes in the "Lied von der Unzulänglichkeit." The "Moritat" actually suits Waldemar Kmentt fairly well, but he lets down the side by shouting the "Feuer in Soho" stanza. The American Polly, not ungifted at the narration that is central to her big solos, is as yet unpolished, and her dramatic credibility is reduced by a verbal slip in the last stanza of the "Barbara Song" that completely contradicts the sense. The other ladies, some of whom sport strong Slavic accents, are reasonably endowed but not very interesting. What really does this recording in, however, is the clumsy, unstylish, ill-balanced orchestra and the often labored, soggy tempos: for example, the "Jealousy Duet" has no rhythmic spine, possibly because the conductor seems to be following the singers instead of running with them. The recording is full of curious perspectives, and the balance of speech-over-song varies drastically. The booklet is an editorial shambles.

CBS 1958, though slightly compromised to accommodate Lenya, will not easily be displaced (nor, for that matter, will the 1930 Teldec excerpts) when it comes to communicating the work's essence, while 1955 Polydor conveys much of the impact of Blitzstein's adaptation. The others offer little of enduring interest, though some of them document astonishing misconstructions of the work's nature and power.

DAVID HAMILTON

AUFSTIEG UND FALL DER STADT MAHAGONNY
(1930)

A: Jenny Hill / Smith (s); B: Leokadja Begbick (ms); C: Jim Mahoney / Johann Ackermann (t); D: Fatty / Willy (t); E: Jack O'Brien / Jakob Schmidt (t); F: Trinity Moses / Dreieinigkeitsmoses (bar)

The social concerns underlying *Dreigroschenoper* are also fundamental to *Aufstieg und Fall der Stadt Mahagonny*, which was actually conceived earlier (some of the music first went into a cantata, the *Mahagonny Songspiel*). With its chorale-prelude textures and large *ritornello* forms enfolding the trademark "tunes," Weill's music is more expressively various and more elaborately structured than in *Dreigroschenoper*—also harder to pace and to sing (notably the difficult-to-tune harmonies in the ensembles). *Dreigroschenoper* was written for "singing actors"; *Mahagonny* is definitely for operatic voices, despite the 1931 Berlin production, which reached for the *Dreigroschenoper* audience by casting some leads with non-operatic performers, notably Lotte Lenya as Jenny. (Recordings of the time prove that she then sang the role in soprano register, to quite different effect from her more familiar later versions.)

Even before the first performance, the "suggestive" Act II bordello episode had to be bowdlerized, and other revisions followed, but Weill was never given an opportunity to revise the 1929 printed score and explicitly distinguish improvements from expedients. When all performance materials vanished after 1938, most of the evidence about the changes disappeared as well, and all traces of what Theodor W. Adorno described as an "extraordinary orchestral interlude," added to the Berlin production

before the "Gott in Mahagonny" episode. David Drew's 1969 edition incorporates "every verifiable revision undertaken by Weill himself, with or without Brecht's collaboration," giving both settings of Jenny's "Havanna-Lied" (only the second, written for Lenya in 1931, has ever been recorded), restoring the original form of the bordello sequence, and adopting some alterations at the end of Act II and the beginning of Act III. A sparely contrapuntal love duet for Jenny and Jimmy (the "Cranes Duet"), originally written for the sanitized bordello scene, Drew arbitrarily but not unreasonably moved to Act III, as a "farewell" duet (he has since proposed more radical reorderings). In short, *Mahagonny* never achieved a definitive form from its creators, and no acceptable modern intervention can make it wholly satisfactory—a circumstance we may regard as part of its provocativeness.

1956 CBS / SONY (M) CD

Lotte Lenya (A), Gisela Litz (B), Heinz Sauerbaum (C), Peter Markwort (D), Fritz Göllnitz (E), Horst Günter (F), North German Radio Chorus, Unidentified orchestra—Wilhelm Brückner-Rüggeberg

Imperfect but imperishable, this recording comes at us with the intensity of overwhelming discovery. Except for Lenya, the cast is from the opera house: almost all have substantial and well-focused if not particularly beautiful voices, and can both shape lines and sing words. Heinz Sauerbaum is a Jimmy of galvanic force: the character's appetites and passions are convincingly larger than life, the singing is true and vivacious (though the top notes give the microphones some difficulty). Gisela Litz realizes Begbick's moments of sensuality as powerfully as her grittiness. And Brückner-Rüggeberg conducts the Hamburg forces with energy, clarity, and flavor; perhaps the choice of Germany's raunchiest city as recording site enhanced the barrelhouse stride of the songs, the sweaty beerhall brassiness of the marches—but there's also a sexy *rubato* in Jakob Schmidt's satiation waltz and the bordello music. It's a bold and somewhat unsubtle performance, rather dryly recorded: a black-and-white rendering, if you will—but of stunning clarity. (I haven't heard the CD edition, but recall that the digitized LP version was harder-toned than the original analogue issue.)

Lenya's return to Jenny required compromises, but only a churl could regret the preservation of her "inauthentic" yet indelibly truthful performance. Her solos are all transposed down (a fourth or a fifth), she switches parts with Begbick in the "Benares Song," and elsewhere simply drops an octave—particularly compromising in the delicate "Cranes Duet," where she often ends up below the tenor. Still, nobody else ever gave these melodies such bite and individuality, her strophic variation is endlessly resourceful, and even from a vocal sub-basement she can project childlike character. Some pop practices are adopted in her solos, and she's probably the reason for the one cut from the 1929 score: the big ensemble following the "Havanna-Lied," which should introduce the "Jimmys aus Alaska" tune; without it, that tune's surprise "return" in a subsequent ensemble loses its rationale.

1985 CAPRICCIO (S,D) CD

Anja Silja (A), Anny Schlemm (B), Wolfgang Neumann (C), Thomas Lehrburger (D), Frederic Mayer (E), Klaus Hirte (F), Pro Musica Vocal Ensemble, Cologne Radio Orchestra— Jan Lathem-König

We needed a performance with more chiaroscuro than 1956 CBS, but this one is simply paler. Strike one: the engineers have created so cautious a balance that accompanying harmonies and rhythms are often masked by the voices, sapping the music's variety and validity. Strike two: Lathem-König, commendably faithful to Weill's tempo markings, rarely makes metrically repetitive accompaniment figures come to life and build, nor can he elicit vitality except in the most vigorous passages—which is perhaps why Act II comes closest to working. Strike three: the two ladies have big tremolo-ridden voices that curdle easily. It's good in principle to have Jenny's music in the original keys, but Silja's burly energy completely misses the point. Neumann is capable but has little of Sauerbaum's commitment and energy. The other roles are sung on a much smaller scale than in the 1956 CBS. Only the chorus, from the Cologne Hochschule für Musik, distinguishes itself.

In general, Drew's text is followed (with the Lenya version of the "Havanna-Lied"), yielding some unfamiliar music: the CBS cut in Act I is restored; though the chorale "Lasst euch nicht verführen" is omitted in Act III, Scene 3, a later Weill setting is included, as placed by Drew at the end of Act II; and the shorter, revised version of the ensemble that opens Act II, Scene 5 is used. The "Cranes Duet" is dropped—an omission we might have regretted more with a more disciplined Jenny.

In short, no contest: 1956 CBS is a genuine, intense performance, thrown slightly off kilter— yet unforgettably so—by Lenya's participation. The alternative will interest only *Mahagonny* textual mavens.

DAVID HAMILTON

RICCARDO ZANDONAI

FRANCESCA DA RIMINI (1914)

A: Francesca (s); B: Paolo (t); C: Malatestino (t); D: Gianciotto (bar)

Zandonai's most successful opera hangs on the periphery of the repertory by a delicate thread. Composed in 1914, its survival in recent years has depended on a handful of singers still in touch with *verismo* style and a few enthusiasts who don't mind being sneered at for relishing such unfashionable, slightly overripe *fin de siècle* fare. The leading roles ideally require singers with a solid *bel canto* technique, searing declamatory eloquence, a ferocious belief in the material, and a willingness to risk everything to bring the dramatic moment to life—all the traditional Italian vocal virtues, in short. When the right cast can be assembled, along with a conductor willing and able to draw out all the instrumental color and fragrance of this evocative score, *Francesca da Rimini* can still weave a potent spell. It happened at La Scala in 1959, a famous production starring Magda Olivero and Mario del Monaco, and a souvenir of their performances was recorded by Decca / London a decade later—unfortunately only a single disc of highlights, now available on CD, coupled with a complete performance of Giordano's *Fedora*, also with Olivero and del Monaco.

1950 CETRA (M)

Maria Caniglia (A), Giacinto Prandelli (B), Mario Carlin (C), Carlo Tagliabue (D), Chorus and Orchestra of RAI Rome—Antonio Guarnieri

For many years, this was the only *Francesca da Rimini* available for those who cared, but it proved to be a more than serviceable introduction—even today, the performance has still much to offer. True, Caniglia was well past her prime in 1951, and passages that take her above the staff tend to be something of an adventure. Even at that, she knows exactly what the opera is about, and her hot-blooded but tragically poised Francesca smolders with pent-up sensual energy. The young Prandelli is rather light of voice as Paolo, but his lyrical ardor contrasts effectively with Tagliabue's snarling Gianciotto and Carlin's malevolent Malatestino. What makes this recording special, though, is the conductor. A contemporary and erstwhile rival of Toscanini—and, some still swear, an even greater musician—Antonio Guarnieri leads a white-hot performance that responds to the opera's poetic sensibility, instrumental refinement, and theatrical excitement on every page. Since Guarnieri made so few recordings, this *Francesca*, despite its sonic limitations, remains an important document of his work.

1987 BALKANTON (S,D) CD

Raina Kabaivanska (A), William Matteuzzi (B), Piero de Palma (C), Matteo Manuguerra (D), Chorus and Orchestra of the Bulgarian Television and Radio—Maurizio Arena

Although not exclusively identified with the *verismo* repertory, Kabaivanska is one of the few singers of her generation with the voice and temperament to excel in it. True, her basic sound is not conventionally beautiful—rather glaring and definitely seasoned with a dash of vinegar—but it is a secure instrument that responds reliably to every demand put upon it. An intelligent and expressive singer, Kabaivanska delineates the dreamy side of Francesca's nature as well as her more passionate obsessions—a fully rounded, subtly nuanced interpretation. Matteuzzi is a light-voiced, colorless Paolo of small distinction, although Manuguerra gives a forceful portrait of the betrayed Gianciotto, and the indestructible Piero de Palma is properly chilling as Malatestino. After Guarnieri's aristocratic presentation of the score, Arena's perfunctory runthrough is a sore disappointment, but at least the sound is more than satisfactory and lets us savor many felicitous details of the orchestration.

For all of its sonic drawbacks, the first recording gives a better sense of the spirit of this opera.

PETER G. DAVIS

Contributors

JON ALAN CONRAD is an assistant professor of music at the University of Delaware. He writes frequently for *The Opera Quarterly* and *The New York Times*.

PETER G. DAVIS was on the music staff of *The New York Times*, and since 1981 has been the music critic for *New York* magazine.

MARK DEVOTO, composer, conductor, and pianist, is professor of music at Tufts University.

JOHN W. FREEMAN has been an associate editor of *Opera News* since 1960, and serves as its principal record reviewer. He is the co-author of *The Golden Horseshoe* and *Toscanini*, and the author of *The Metropolitan Opera Stories of the Great Operas*.

KENNETH FURIE is the former music editor of *High Fidelity* magazine. He has written for *Keynote*, *Opus*, and *The New York Times*.

ROLAND GRAEME has contributed reviews to *CD Review* and *The Opera Quarterly*.

NOËL GOODWIN has been the principal music and dance critic for the London *Daily Express*, the European music correspondent of the *New York Herald Tribune*, the executive editor of *Music and Musicians*, and associate editor of *Dance and Dancers*. He has written extensively for *Opera News*.

LONDON GREEN is a professor of drama at Bishop's University and a stage director. He writes for *The Opera Quarterly*.

DAVID HAMILTON, former music critic of *The Nation*, writes often for *Opera News*, *The New York Times*, and *The Opera Quarterly*. Co-producer of the Metropolitan Opera Historical Broadcast recordings, he is also the programmer and annotator of many Metropolitan Opera Guild recordings.

LORD HAREWOOD, the former managing director of the English National Opera and artistic director of the Leeds and Edinburgh Festivals, is now artistic director of the Adelaide Festival. He was the founder and editor of *Opera* magazine, and has edited several editions of *Kobbé's Complete Opera Book*.

MAX LOPPERT was chief music critic for the London *Financial Times*, and is now associate editor and a frequent contributor to *Opera*.

C. J. LUTEN reviews music and dance for the *Sarasota Herald Tribune*, and writes about recordings for *Opera News*.

BARRY MILLINGTON is the author of *Wagner* and the co-translator and co-editor of *Selected Letters of Richard Wagner*. For the Metropolitan Opera Guild he has written the "Talking

About Opera" tapes for *Parsifal* and *Die Meistersinger*.

JEREMY NOBLE was a music critic in London until 1963. Since 1966 he has been a professor of music at the State University of New York at Buffalo.

CONRAD L. OSBORNE has written for many publications, including *The New York Times*, *High Fidelity/Musical America*, *Opus*, *Opera News*, and *The London Financial Times*. He has published a novel, *O Paradiso*, performs as an actor and singer, and teaches voice.

BRIDGET PAOLUCCI lectures extensively for the Metropolitan Opera Guild, and has written and narrated several of the Guild's "Talking About Opera" cassettes. A Fulbright Scholar, she is a visiting lecturer at Manhattanville College and a music correspondent for National Public Radio.

STEWART PEARCE has worked at the Metropolitan Opera since 1976, and now serves as the company's planning and operations administrator. He has written music criticism for a variety of publications.

PATRICK J. SMITH is the author of *The Tenth Muse*, and the editor of *Opera News*.

DAVID STEVENS is chief music critic and associate editor of *The International Herald Tribune*.

MARK SWED has been a contributing editor of *Connoisseur* magazine, a regular contributor to *The Wall Street Journal*, and writes for many other publications, including *Opera News* and *The New York Times*. He is currently writing a biography of John Cage.

Index